[redacted]OUGHTON MIFFLIN SOCIAL STUDIES

A More Perfect Union

TEACHER'S EDITION

Beverly J. Armento
Jacqueline M. Córdova
J. Jorge Klor de Alva
Gary B. Nash
Franklin Ng
Christopher L. Salter
Louis E. Wilson
Karen K. Wixson

Houghton Mifflin Company • Boston
Atlanta • Dallas • Geneva, Illinois • Princeton, New Jersey • Palo Alto

Houghton Mifflin Social Studies

Consultants and Reviewers

Sandra Alfonsi
Academic Advisory Board
Hadassah
Queens, NY

Charmarie Blaisdell
Department of History
Northeastern University
Boston, MA

Alison S. Brooks
Department of Anthropology
George Washington University
Washington, DC

Edward Castillo
Department of Native American Studies
Sonoma State University
Rohnert Park, CA

Richard Griswold del Castillo
Department of Mexican American Studies
San Diego State University
San Diego, CA

Elliot N. Dorff
Rector
University of Judaism
Los Angeles, CA
Affiliate: The Skirball Institute

Ross Dunn
Department of History
San Diego State University
San Diego, CA

Robert Ellwood
School of Religion
University of Southern California
Los Angeles, CA
Affiliate: The Skirball Institute

Benjamin Elman
Department of History
University of California, Los Angeles
Los Angeles, CA

Thelma Foote
Department of History
University of California, Irvine
Irvine, CA

Stephen Fugita
Department of Psychology
Santa Clara University
Santa Clara, CA

Erich Gruen
Department of Classics and History
University of California, Berkeley
Berkeley, CA

Charles Haynes
Senior Scholar for Religious Freedom
Freedom Forum First Amendment Center
Arlington, VA

Lidwein Kapteijns
Department of History
Wellesley College
Wellesley, MA

Robert Hyung-chan Kim
Woodring College of Education
Western Washington University
Bellingham, WA

Judith Osborn Kraft
Department of Elementary and Bilingual Education
California State University, Fullerton
Fullerton, CA

Gary Kroesh
Co-Director
UCSD History-Social Science Project
University of Southern California Extension
Los Angeles, CA

Shabbir Mansuri
Director
Council on Islamic Education
Fountain Valley, CA

Michelle Maskiell
Department of History
University of Montana
Missoula, MT

Jacob Meskin
Department of Religion
Princeton University
Princeton, NJ

Doug Monroy
Department of Southwest Studies
The Colorado College
Colorado Springs, CO

B. Srinivasa Murthy
Department of Religious Studies (retired)
California State University, Long Beach
Long Beach, CA
Affiliate: The Skirball Institute

Ven. Dr. Havanpola Ratanasara
Buddhist Sangha Council of Southern California
Los Angeles, CA
Affiliate: The Skirball Institute

Rev. Thomas P. Rausch, S.J.
Rector, Jesuit Community
Loyola Marymount University
Los Angeles, CA
Affiliate: The Skirball Institute

Rita Roberts
Department of History
Scripps College for Women
Claremont, CA

Cliff Trafzer
Department of History and Ethnic Studies
Director of Native American Studies
University of California-Riverside
Riverside, CA

Forrest Turpen
Christian Educators Association International
Pasadena, CA

Rabbi Alfred Wolf
Founding Director
Skirball Institute
Los Angeles, CA

Acknowledgments: p. 181 Excerpts from *Democracy in America* by Alexis De Tocqueville, translated by Henry Reeve, revised by Francis Bowen and edited by Phillips Bradley, New York: Alfred A. Knopf, Inc. 1947, 1973. **p. 198** Excerpt from *Old-Time Schools and School Books* by Clifton Johnson. Copyright ©1963 by Dover Publications. Reprinted by permission of Dover Publications, Inc.

Photo Credits: T3 (t) © John Henley/The Stock Market; (m) © Mugshots/The Stock Market; (b) © Jose L. Pelaez/The Stock Market; **T10** © Gabe Palmer/The Stock Market; **T17** Ira Garber; **T19** © Gary Landsman/The Stock Market; **T26** (t) E. Curtis, University of Washington Libraries (detail): (b) J.G. Heron/ Stock Boston; **T27** (l) Museum of American Political Life, University of Hartford, photo by Sally Andersen-Bruce: (m) Henry Moore. *Family Group.* 1948-49. Bronze (cast 1950). 59 1/4 x 461/2", at base 45 x 29 7/8". Museum of Modern Art, New York. A. Conger Goodyear Fund: (r) Scala/Art Resource, NY

Printed in U.S.A.

ISBN: 0-395-93072-3

123456789-VH-04 03 02 01 00 99 98

Welcome to *A More Perfect Union*

The goal of Houghton Mifflin Social Studies is the development of literate citizens—individuals with the knowledge, skills, and civic values they need to become active and reflective participants in the world of the twenty-first century. Our program weaves together knowledge, skills, and citizenship to form an integrated program. And because we focus on depth rather than breadth, our program helps you take the time to truly captivate, develop, question, and stretch your students. Take a moment and discover some of the ideas and people that make this program a powerful classroom tool.

HOUGHTON MIFFLIN SOCIAL STUDIES

Table of Contents

Professional Handbook

Student Text

Meet Your Authors

Dr. Beverly Armento

"The overall goal of a sound social studies program is the development of an informed, active, caring decision maker who draws on meaningful knowledge, who has well-developed skills, who has a sense of what's important and what's not, and who is then able to take all of that and apply it to social issues."

Beverly J. Armento

Professor of Social Studies Education Department of Middle/Secondary Education and Instructional Technology Georgia State University, Atlanta, GA

Dr. J. Jorge Klor de Alva

"First all boys and girls need to see people like themselves in their textbooks. Then students will be ready to respect others who are different from themselves."

J. Jorge Klor de Alva

President University of Phoenix, Phoenix, AZ

Dr. Jacqueline M. K. Córdova

"LEP students may be able to share with classmates related cultural or historical information based on their prior life experiences and academic exposure. Inviting their participation is one of the most significant ways to build self-esteem, to actively engage them in the lesson, and to stimulate prior knowledge of the topic."

Jacqueline M. Córdova

Professor of Spanish and TESOL Department of Foreign Languages and Literatures California State University, Fullerton

Dr. Gary B. Nash

"Instruction in social studies should be based on the belief that an accurate portrayal of historical figures will inspire more admiration of them among students, not less. It may also help young people to recognize more of the hero in themselves, instead of viewing heroism as a trait reserved for superhuman men and women."

Gary B. Nash

Professor of History University of California, Los Angeles

Dr. Franklin Ng

"History opens up new vistas and panoramas. Explored with creativity and imagination, it socializes us into the human community. We learn about diverse lifeways and the many paths to the contemporary world in which we live."

Professor of Anthropology
California State University, Fresno

Dr. Christopher L. Salter

"An understanding of the needs and costs of land transformation is of vital concern in the study of geography and of growing importance in our finite world."

Professor and Chair
Department of Geography
University of Missouri, Columbia, MO

Dr. Louis Wilson

"A mature understanding of history and culture is empathetic as well as intellectual. As students learn to identify with the feelings and aspirations of those around them, you can extend this identification to people in other times and places."

Associate Professor/Chair
African American Studies Department
Smith College, Northampton, MA

Dr. Karen K. Wixson

"No matter how full the narrative or engaging the biography, if the instructional design doesn't facilitate the learning process, and if students aren't challenged to extend their knowledge by applying the information, the lessons and insights of a social studies education will be lost."

Professor of Education
University of Michigan, Ann Arbor, MI

A More Perfect Union

Program Components

Geography Kit

The **Geography Kit** engages students with basic concepts of geography. The portfolio-sized kit includes:

- Desk maps
- Map Masters
- Overhead Transparencies
- Wall map

Student Book

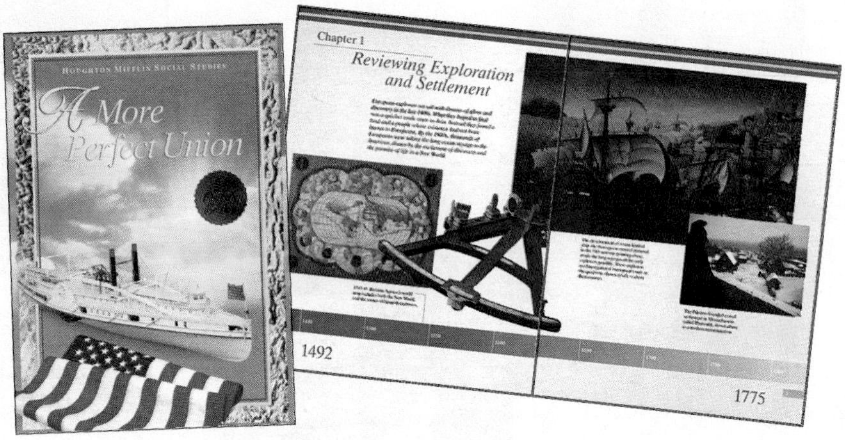

Each chapter in the **Student Text** opens with strong visuals and captions that help students focus. In addition to lesson pages and special features, the text includes an array of appendices:

- Minipedia
- Atlas
- Geographic Glossary
- Gazetteer
- Biographical Dictionary
- Glossary

Technology

www.eduplace.com

Houghton Mifflin Education Place provides a free on-line site for **The Social Studies Center,** which continually updates information and activities that support Houghton Mifflin Social Studies.

Teacher's Edition

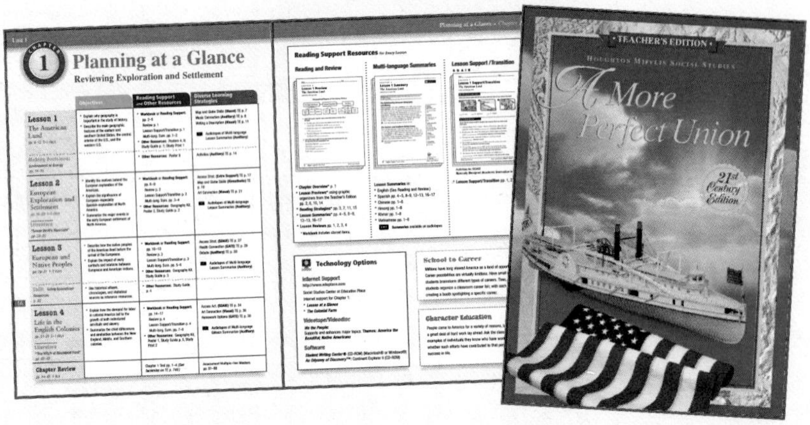

The Teacher's Edition provides instructional strategies and activities in the form of interleaf pages and point-of-use notes, with these additional features:

- A Professional Handbook
- An extensive bibliography including technical resources for each chapter
- A unit- appropriate Geography Project and notes on a unit-appropriate literary selection in Bookshelf II

Reading Support

Reading Support Resources

The **Workbook** and resource package are designed to support and develop the skills needed by all students for reading content.

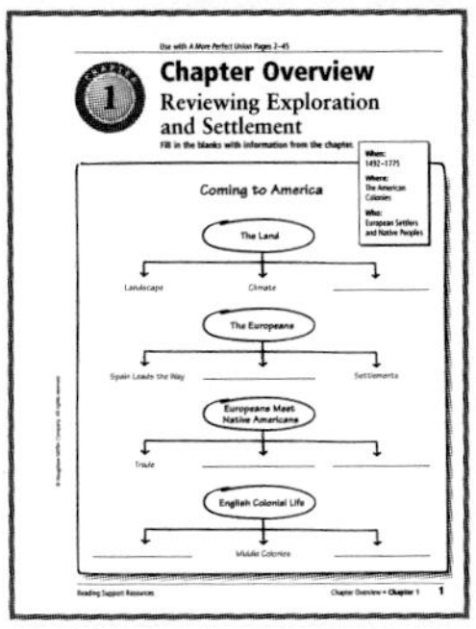

Chapter Overview

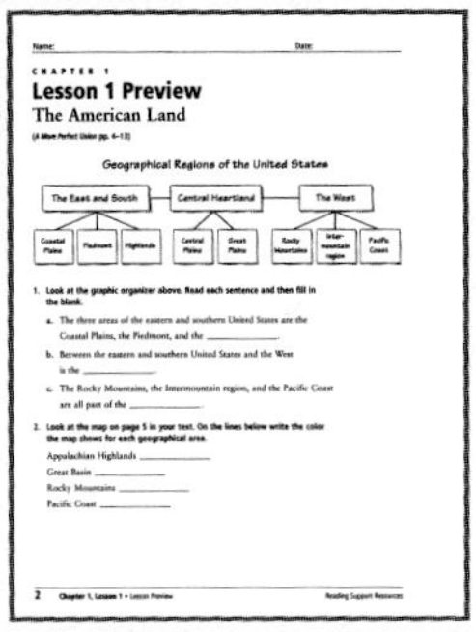

Lesson Preview

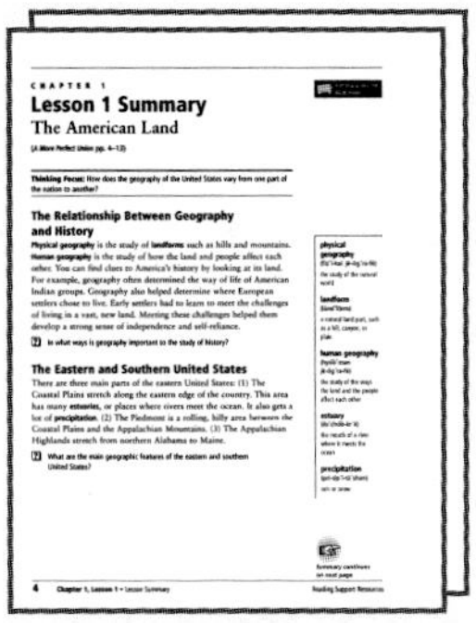

Lesson Summary
available in:
- English
- Spanish
- Chinese
- Hmong
- Khmer
- Vietnamese

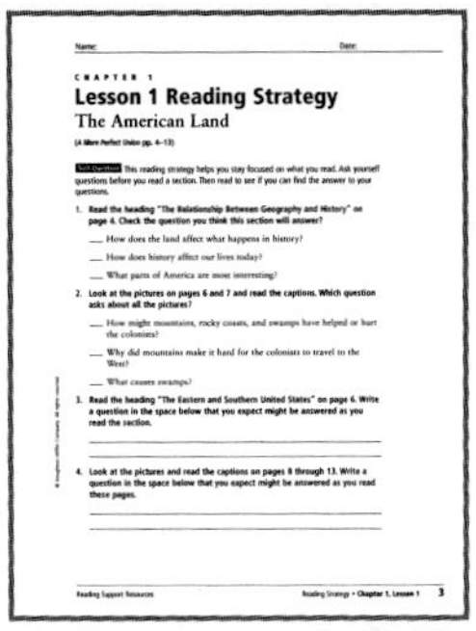

Reading Strategy

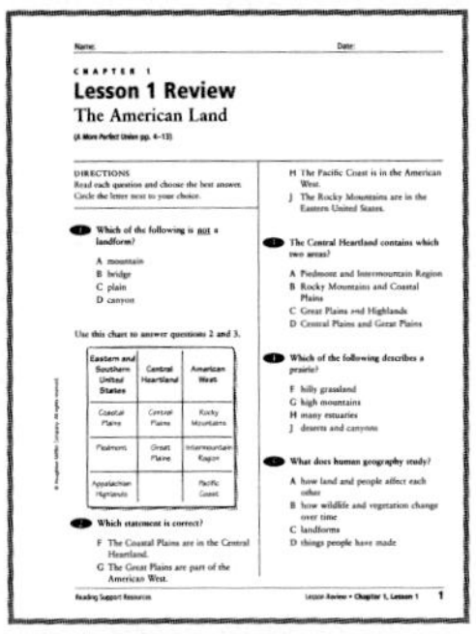

Lesson Review

Lesson Summaries available on audiotapes.

Lesson Support/Transition

Activities for SDAIE: **S**pecially **D**esigned **A**cademic **I**nstruction in **E**nglish

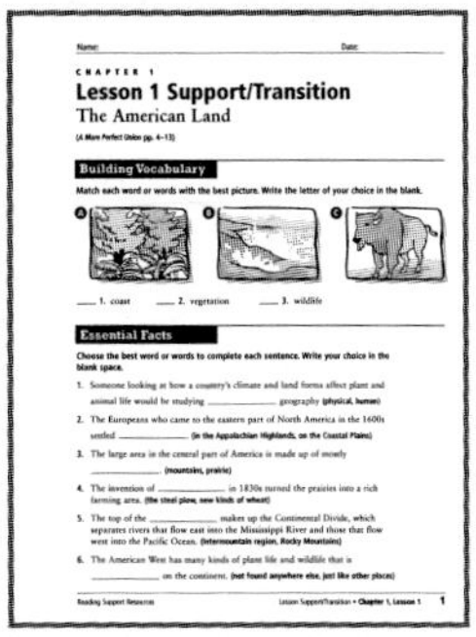

Ultimate Reader

This CD-ROM provides students complete access to the pupil text by enabling them to hear the text read aloud by computer-generated voicing.

Ancillaries

These ancillaries will help you assess and enrich your students, social studies experience:

- **Citizenship Simulations**
- **Research Handbook**
- **Lesson Planner**
- **Assessment Options**
- **Study Guides**
- **Study Prints**
- **Posters**
- **Home and Community Involvement** with letters to parents in English, Spanish, Chinese, Hmong, Khmer, and Vietnamese

Bookshelf II

The Bookshelf II offers seven or eight fiction and nonfiction paperbacks that entertain as well as raise student awareness of how people behaved during some of the major moments in history. The Bookshelf II Teacher's Resources help to connect titles with the unit contents.

Reading Support for Social Studies Content

Helping students develop and perfect their reading skills is one of the most important goals of elementary and middle school education. Much class time is spent teaching strategies for decoding and comprehending literature, and teachers who instill a love of reading in their students can rightly consider themselves successful.

Nonfiction is an important part of reading instruction, but students often do not get enough opportunity to apply language arts strategies and skills to informational text, particularly textbooks. As they move through the intermediate elementary and middle school grades, students must comprehend content and concepts from increasingly complex textbooks. All too often, teachers and students are frustrated by the difficulty in accessing this content, not realizing that there are particular strategies and skills that can be applied to make this possible.

The reading support provided by Houghton Mifflin Social Studies not only allows comprehension of the rich content of the program, but has as its goal the development of the student's ability to access informational text whatever it may be. Such ability is not only essential to students' success as they advance in their formal education, but is a vital life skill as well.

Building Background

Students' lack of prior knowledge is one of the main reasons they have difficulties understanding informational text. Researchers have found that the brain learns by sifting through new information looking for data that connects to ideas with which it is already familiar. These connections build knowledge; totally foreign information, on the other hand, is easily lost. Since the subject of history is often particularly foreign to the young student, it is unlikely he or she can retain the content without considerable assistance. Thus it is essential for teachers to build background and activate prior knowledge before the student begins to read.

Previewing the Chapter

Houghton Mifflin Social Studies provides a variety of prereading support toward this end.

- In the pupil edition, each chapter begins with a timeline preview of information, and a collage of visuals with captions that announce the content covered in the chapter.
- The Teacher's Edition presents a strong "Preview" strategy.
- *Reading Support Resources* uses a similar prereading approach. With the one-page Chapter Overview, students will become familiar with the key ideas and the organizational framework of the chapter before beginning to read. When appropriate to the lesson content, *When Where* and *Who* labels assist students' grasp of key concepts. Most important for students struggling for language proficiency, each Chapter Overview provides a graphic organizer that clearly depicts the key information presented in the chapter. Students must complete the graphic organizer as they preview the chapter.

Previewing the Lesson

Lesson previewing is another strong prereading strategy.

- In the pupil edition, the opening page of each lesson lists the Key Terms covered in the lesson.
- In the Teacher's Edition, an "Introduce" strategy at the start of each lesson includes preteaching these Key Terms, while a "Develop" strategy suggests how best to present an accompanying graphic organizer to students.

- The identical graphic organizer followed by two questions appears in the Lesson Preview in *Reading Support Resources.* Here, the focus of both questions is to engage students in previewing the lesson and thinking about what they will learn.

Graphic Organizers

Graphic organizers have proven especially effective for those students with diverse languages, reading abilities, and learning styles, as well as for others who may lack the skills necessary for success in content-area classes. The graphic organizer can help you use an interactive approach to show your students connections among the key ideas in each chapter and lesson. Teachers have found that students become more actively engaged in the previewing strategy as they work with this visual tool.

In each lesson, *Reading Support Resources* employs a graphic organizer best suited to the lesson content and to the instructional objectives. Among the types students will work with are:

- **hierarchical organizers** that present main ideas and supporting details,
- **comparative organizers** that show similarities and differences within key concepts,
- **cluster organizers** that emphasize relationships among sets of ideas,
- **sequential organizers** that illustrate a series of steps or events showing chronological order or emphasizing cause and effect.

Reading Support Resources presents, furthermore, carefully designed graphic overviews with similar supporting facts side-by-side in similarly shaped cells and, whenever appropriate, with similar wording. This format makes it easier for students to remember key facts and concepts.

Applying Reading Strategies

Many students who have already spent years learning reading strategies and skills may be unsure how they relate to their textbooks. Students who are still struggling with these strategies are truly at a loss. Houghton Mifflin Social Studies provides students with ample opportunties to apply the following strategies to their reading of informational text:

- Predict/Infer
- Self-question
- Find the Main idea
- Summarize
- Evaluate
- Think About Words
- Use the Visuals
- Cause and Effect
- Compare and Contrast
- Sequence

In the pupil edition, the "Thinking Focus" question at the start of each lesson should guide students' reading, directing them to look for the most essential information in the lesson. The red square question at the end of each section of the lesson is support for comprehension. If students can answer that question, they can identify the important concepts.

The Reading Strategy page in *Reading Support Resources* provides additional practice. Students can use the Reading Strategy page to guide their reading of the pupil edition page. The Reading Strategy page sequences questions from easy to more difficult, frequently with an activity modeling the strategy first, then a question requiring more critical thinking and, finally, asking for a student response.

Lesson Summaries

For some students, particularly non-native speakers of English and very poor readers, facing a textbook can feel overwhelming. They need even more background and alternative avenues to the content. Visuals, such as those provided in the Posters and Study Prints are powerful aids. In *Reading*

Continued on next page

HOUGHTON MIFFLIN SOCIAL STUDIES

Reading Support

Many students in today's diverse classrooms need material that is easier to read than the pupil edition for their grade level. Houghton Mifflin Social Studies provides the *Reading Support Resources* for non-native speakers of English and for other students you think need extra support. The materials will accommodate students with:

- diverse languages,
- diverse reading skills,
- and diverse learning styles.

Reading Support Resources:
You will find a Chapter Overview and six pages of support materials for each lesson in the pupil edition.

- Lesson Preview (1 page)
- Reading Strategy (1 page)
- Lesson Summary (2 pages)
- Lesson Review (1 page)
- Lesson Support/ Transition (1 page)

Reading Support for Social Studies Content *(continued)*

Support Resources, two-page Lesson Summaries written with simplified vocabulary to assist comprehension include a graphic that also helps to deliver the content. Furthermore, these Lesson Summaries have been translated into five languages besides English and are available on audiotape: Spanish, Chinese, Hmong, Khmer, and Vietnamese.

Each Lesson Summary presents the Thinking Focus question from the pupil edition. The Key Terms are used in context as well as defined in the margins. The Summary clearly and succinctly develops all of the main ideas included under each major lesson head, and the red square questions are repeated, ensuring that students comprehend those same key concepts covered in the pupil edition. Since these are translated, the teacher has a way of assessing student mastery of the content in all six languages.

Post Reading Activities

Building background, applying reading strategies, and using graphic organizers and lesson summaries are all methods that will enable students to develop their ability to access content from informational text. Post reading activities, however, are critical to helping them incorporate that content into their knowledge base. Individual, group, and whole class activities such as those found in the pupil edition's Chapter Review and in the Teacher's Edition offer many opportunities for students to take ownership of the concepts and information. Encourage students to raise their own questions while reading, and later in discussions with the whole class or small groups.

You may wish to check for understanding before or after these discussions. In *Reading Support Resources,* the Lesson Review page uses the Stanford 9 Test format to provide a check that permits you to assess students' understanding of the lesson. This review page is based on the

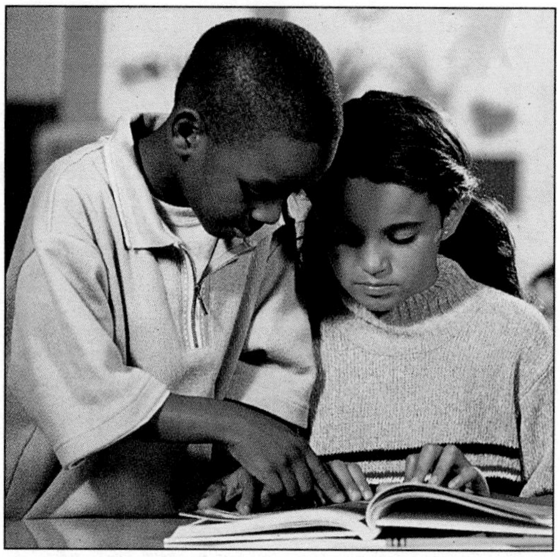

Lesson Summary, not on the pupil edition; consequently, students who have read only the Lesson Summary should be able to answer all Lesson Review questions. ■

For Further Reading

Feathers, Karen M. Infotext *Reading and Learning.* Ontario: Pippen, 1993.

Moore, David W. *Prereading Activities for Content Area Reading and Learning.* No. 233-961, International Reading Association.

Simpson, Anne. "Critical Questions: Whose Questions." *The Reading Teacher.* Vol. 50, No. 2, October, 1996.

Thomas, Ellen Lamar and H. Alan Robinson. *Improving Reading in Every Class, A Sourcebook for Teachers.* (3rd ed.), Boston: Allyn and Bacon, 1982.

Reading Support

Chapter Overview

(1 page)

Purpose

To familiarize students with the organization and the key ideas in the chapter before they begin to read the pupil edition

- *When Where* and *Who* labels assist students' grasp of key concepts.
- A graphic organizer depicts key facts, concepts and relationships in the chapter.

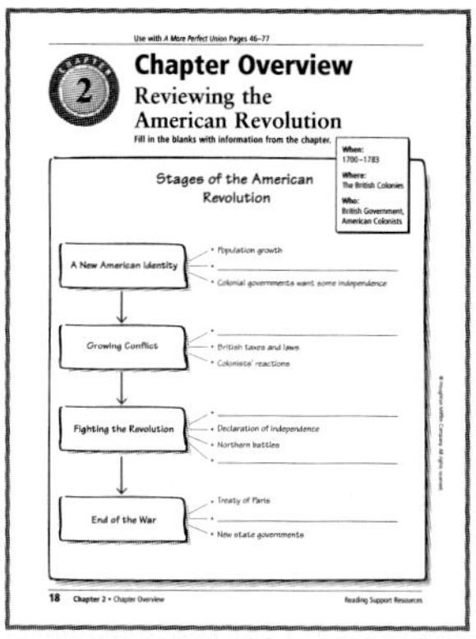

Lesson Preview

(1 page)

Purpose

To help students become familiar with the organization and key ideas in the lesson before they begin to read

- A graphic organizer from the Teacher's Edition presents key facts, concepts and relationships in the lesson.
- Questions direct students to study the graphic organizer and look at heads, maps and other visuals in the pupil edition.

Reading Strategy

(1 page)

Purpose

To help students apply ten reading strategies

- Concise directions define the strategy.
- Questions sequenced by level of difficulty reinforce the reading strategy.
- A variety of formats require simple responses easy to grade.

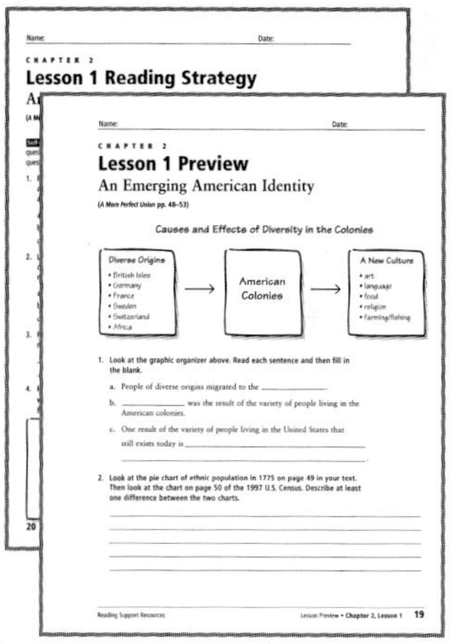

Lesson Summary

(2 pages)

Purpose

To provide reading support for non-native speakers and those needing extra support

- Summaries of key facts and ideas under each B head in the pupil edition use Key Terms introduced in the lesson.
- A variety of visuals, such as maps, timelines or other illustrations serve as memory enhancers.
- Simplified vocabulary assists comprehension.
- Translations in 5 languages: Chinese, Hmong, Khmer, Spanish, Vietnamese

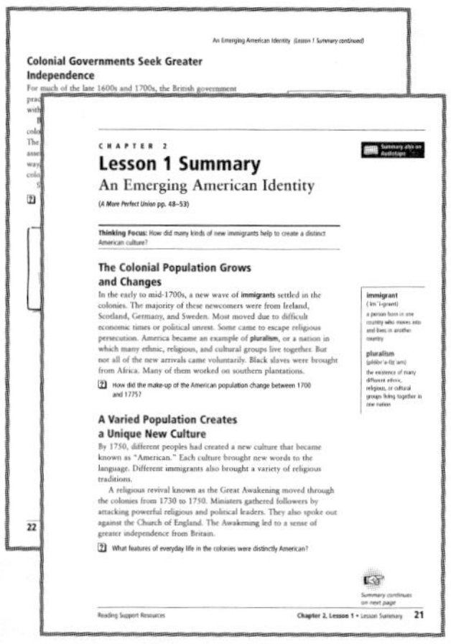

Summaries also available on audiotape.

Lesson Review

(1 page)

Purpose

To assess students' understanding of the lesson

- Students can answer the Lesson Review's sequenced questions by reading the Lesson Summary only.
- This page uses the Stanford 9 Test format.

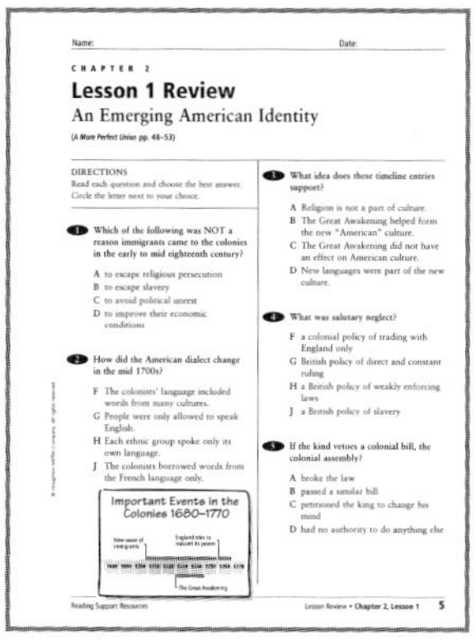

Access to Social Studies for Limited English Proficient Students

Because of rapid demographic changes nationwide, many school districts now enroll a significant number of students whose first language is not English. Language diversity in a social studies classroom poses new challenges to students and teachers alike. Not the least among these challenges is helping students acquire a new language at the same time that they are learning new subject content.

Social studies presents special challenges to learners. Because the content has many abstract and difficult concepts, social studies is very heavily language dependent. Finally, there is the demanding challenge of building self-esteem so that students can feel successful even in the most frustrating of circumstances.

In most cases, the Limited English Proficient (LEP) students in a school have widely different educational backgrounds and function at a broad range of achievement levels, depending on their prior academic experiences and level of proficiency in their own language(s). Almost invariably, well-prepared LEP students make the transition to studying completely in English more rapidly and efficiently than do those who, for whatever reason, have poor native language ability and less developed academic skills.

Students who are completely non-English speaking may need to access social studies through their first language while acquiring English. Or, students may be placed in classrooms where sheltered methodologies that employ English as a Second Language (ESL) techniques and strategies are used to teach social studies and other subject content areas. As students reach intermediate-level fluency in English, they usually can take in basic content taught in the new language when teachers make effective use of context clues such as visuals, realia (relief maps, models, real objects), interactive study guides, and role plays. Nevertheless, the complex and demanding language of social studies may necessitate further help for LEP students. For that reason, they also benefit greatly from those activities that highlight the significant vocabulary of each lesson and those that enable them to focus on the most relevant factual matter and the most important ideas.

Access Features of Houghton Mifflin Social Studies

Houghton Mifflin Social Studies has been designed to facilitate maximum access to social studies concepts for students from a wide variety of cultural and linguistic backgrounds. The unique Visual Learning strand and prominent instructional visuals throughout the program provide a channel of access for LEP students. Additional LEP-appropriate activities clearly identified for you in the Planning at a Glance chart preceding each chapter are:

- Reading Support and Review Pages
- SDAIE Lesson Support/Transition Pages
- Access Strategies and Activities
- Diverse Learning Strategies

Strategies for Accessible Instruction

Teachers can implement a number of techniques and strategies in order to enable LEP students to be more successful in the social studies. The following suggestions outline the most helpful.

Use language-sensitive techniques. Some techniques that lower the language barrier for LEP students of intermediate fluency are:

- **Modifying speech.** Effective strategies include articulating clearly, pausing frequently so that information can be absorbed, using shorter phrases and sentences, avoiding idiomatic speech, defining new vocabulary through words students already know and use, and clarifying contracted forms such as *won't, shouldn't,* and *I'll.*

- **Using TPR (Total Physical Response).** This strategy allows students to demonstrate comprehension through actions such as pantomime, pointing, and drawing, even when they are not yet fluent in the language or feel uncomfortable producing oral language in the classroom.
- **Using gestures and facial expressions.** Bear in mind that these may not be universal, and can, on occasion, cause miscommunication. It is frequently beneficial, when students seem not to understand gestures and other kinesthetic language, to clarify your meaning in order to prevent confusion.
- **Modeling the desired performance, whether in oral or written language.** Students from other backgrounds particularly benefit from such modeling since they may have little experience with making oral presentations, questioning the teacher, or applying information in creative ways.
- **Using visuals and realia.** While visuals are helpful, research shows that students who have never seen a certain object or scene profit more from seeing the real thing, whenever possible.
- **Showing a sample of the finished product.** Some LEP students will at first tend to produce replicas of what you show them. Nevertheless, this first step will provide them with some of the skills necessary to create their own products later.
- **Breaking down complicated tasks into subtasks.** This technique allows students to proceed sequentially and to focus on each step.
- **Checking frequently for understanding.** Asking students to repeat or paraphrase what you have just said or to share what they understand with classmates enables their fluency and builds confidence.

Build background knowledge.

You can help students unlock key concepts in the lesson by using the TE Access Strategy and by discussing the Study Prints, Posters, and Overhead Transparencies. Students who are from other backgrounds may have a great deal of knowledge about their countries of origin, but may not have the specific information required to fully comprehend lessons in Houghton Mifflin Social Studies.

Tap prior knowledge.

Have students brainstorm what they already know about the topic, do quick-writes, and use Venn diagrams to show similarities and differences among ideas or events. *(See page T36.)* LEP students may be able to share with classmates related cultural or historical information based on their prior life experiences or academic exposure. Inviting their participation is one of the most significant ways to build self-esteem, to actively engage them in the lesson, and to stimulate their prior knowledge of the topic.

Preteach essential vocabulary.

Remember, however, that for English language learners a seemingly innocuous word may be confusing and may delay access to the targeted concept, especially since when reading or listening to a new language, it is difficult to know which are the key words. Where possible, introduce families of words in context with interactive activities. *(See pages T36–T37.)* Encourage students from European language backgrounds to seek similarities in such cognate words as *history, historical, geography, geographical, circumnavigate, immigrate,* and so on. If possible, show pictorial representations of new vocabulary as well as the written or oral forms of the new concepts. Use Bingo and/or Flash Card games of the most

Continued on next page

Access to Social Studies for Limited English Proficient Students *(continued)*

important concepts in a unit to provide needed practice, repetition, and visualization of the new vocabulary needed for successful comprehension of the major ideas of the unit.

Use lesson summaries.
Introducing a lesson with a summary serves LEP students well, especially those who are most limited in English language proficiency. The summaries, found in *Reading Support Resources* provide an excellent synthesis of the lesson content using simplified vocabulary, and enable students to focus on the most important points prior to reading the dense material of each lesson.

Utilize collaborative learning.
These activities enable pairs and small groups of students to read selected sections of text together. *(See T34–T35.)* Research indicates that peer tutoring in which students with more proficient English skills are paired with less proficient speakers produces outstanding results. These strategies are also productive with written assignments and with the preparation of oral presentations.

Use oral and visual language.
Talk through the Graphic Overview and Thinking Focus for each new lesson to help LEP students focus on key concepts.

Assign the specially designed activities for LEP students.
The Lesson Support/Transition pages in *Reading Support Resources* are best used at appropriate times during the lesson or chapter. These activities focus on essential vocabulary and/or concepts. Since language, and especially vocabulary, is the key mode of access to the content of social studies, these activities will greatly facilitate student success.

Social Studies and the Overall LEP Program

There is no simple way to eliminate completely the language barrier to social studies for LEP students. Recent research indicates that it may take as long as seven years before the average second language learner is able to perform at the median on standardized tests! There are exceptions in both directions: those who are well prepared in language and concept development can make the transition more rapidly than those who require additional time and modification of instruction. However, there are many avenues that can be used to help students make a more rapid and successful transition to mainstream instruction.

In the majority of cases, LEP youngsters are most successful when they have a program that enables them to achieve functional fluency in both oral and written English quickly. Such a program begins with intensive ESL lessons designed to teach the basics of English. Introductory ESL may be followed by an advanced program known as ELD (English Language Development), in which students learn social studies and other content area vocabulary and build conceptual development. In some schools, students receive instruction called SDAIE (Specially Designed Academic Instruction in English), which is a compendium of techniques and strategies to modify instruction—without lowering expectations for comprehension and production of difficult subject content area. In all cases, these programs enable students to derive maximum benefit from the Houghton Mifflin Social Studies.

In addition to a sequential English language development program, students who are in the initial phases of acquiring English may need primary language support to comprehend fully the key concepts in the program. This may be provided by a bilingual classroom setting, the help of a bilingual aide (when possible), or by the use of peer tutors who speak the same language. To benefit all students, Houghton Mifflin Social Studies has been designed to facilitate access to grade-level social studies through instructional strategies that are grounded in language and learning theory as well as in good teaching. ■

For Further Reading

Brinton, D., M.A. Snow, and M.B. Wesche. *Content-Based Second Language Instruction.* New York: Newbury House Publishers, 1989.

Córdova, J. M. and B. Segal. *Linking the ESL and the "At Risk" Student to the Mainstream: A Resource Handbook.* Brea, CA: Berty Segal, Inc., 1994.

Cantoni-Harvey, G. *Content-Area Language Instruction: Approaches and Strategies.* Reading, MA: Addison-Wesley, 1987.

Crandall, I. A., D. Christian, and D.J. Short. *How to Integrate Language and Content Instruction: A Training Manual.* Berkeley, CA: Center for Language, Education and Research, University of California, 1989.

Diamond, B.J. and M.A. Moore. *Multicultural Literacy: Mirroring the Reality of the Classroom.* White Plains, NY: Longman, 1995.

Peitzman, F. and G. Gadda. *With Different Eyes: Insights into Teaching Language Minority Students Across the Disciplines.* Reading, MA: Addison Wesley Publishing Company, 1994.

Richard-Amato, P.A. *Making it Happen: Instruction in the Second Language Classroom, from Theory to Practice.* New York: Longman, 1988.

HOUGHTON MIFFLIN SOCIAL STUDIES

Access Features

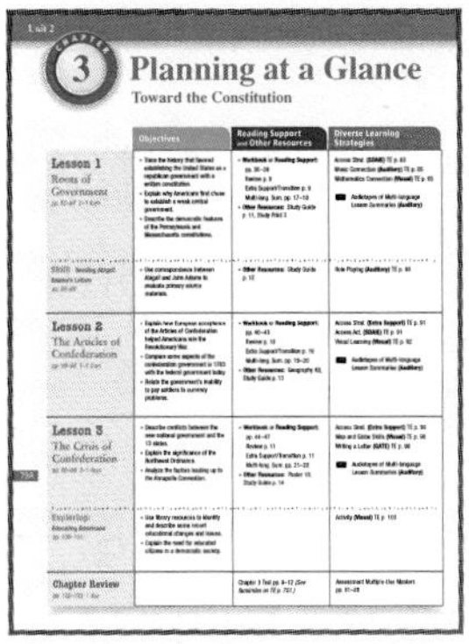
Planning at a Glance
Toward the Constitution

Diverse Learning Strategies

listed in the Planning at a Glance chart in the Teacher's Edition before each chapter facilitate maximum access to social studies content for students from a variety of cultural and linguistic backgrounds.

Teacher's Edition Features

Both the Access Strategy and Access Activity at the beginning of each lesson in the Teacher's Edition tap students' prior knowledge and emphasize essential vocabulary and, thus, promote access to unlocking key concepts.

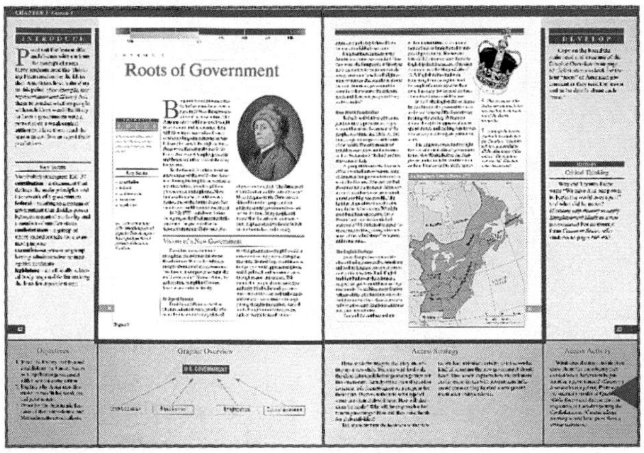
Roots of Government

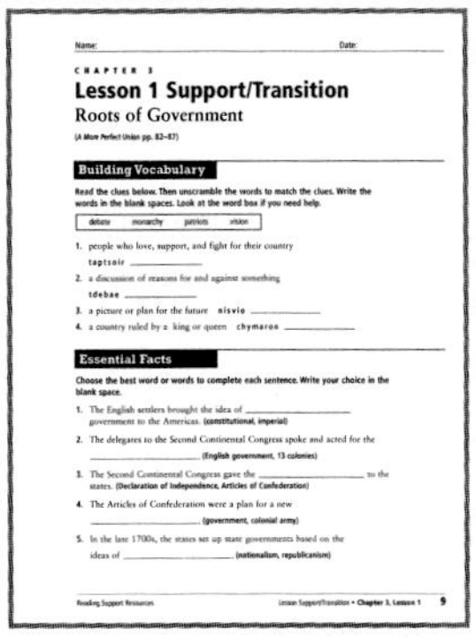
Name: Date:

CHAPTER 3

Lesson 1 Support/Transition

Roots of Government

(A More Perfect Union pp. 82–87)

Building Vocabulary

Read the clues below. Then unscramble the words to match the clues. Write the words in the blank spaces. Look at the word box if you need help.

debate monarchy patriots vision

1. people who love, support, and fight for their country taptsoir ________
2. a discussion of reasons for and against something tdebae ________
3. a picture or plan for the future nisvio ________
4. a country ruled by a king or queen chymaron ________

Essential Facts

Choose the best word or words to complete each sentence. Write your choice in the blank space.

1. The English settlers brought the idea of ________ government to the Americas. (constitutional, imperial)
2. The delegates to the Second Continental Congress spoke and acted for the ________ (English government, 13 colonies)
3. The Second Continental Congress gave the ________ to the states. (Declaration of Independence, Articles of Confederation)
4. The Articles of Confederation were a plan for a new ________ (government, colonial army)
5. In the late 1700s, the states set up state governments based on the ideas of ________ (nationalism, republicanism)

Reading Support Resources Lesson Support/Transition • Chapter 3, Lesson 1 9

Lesson Support/Transition

pages for students receiving SDAIE instruction are featured in *Reading Support Resources* and focus on essential vocabulary and/or concepts.

Individualizing Instruction in the Social Studies

Houghton Mifflin Social Studies has built into its program many opportunities for individualizing instruction, opportunities designed to help meet the needs of a widely diverse student population. These opportunities are contained in editorial features in the student text, suggested where applicable throughout the Teacher's Edition, and embodied in additional ancillary features in the program.

In the Teacher's Edition at the beginning of each chapter in the Planning at a Glance chart, labels for the various approaches are provided as a means of tracking the variety of teaching strategies in any lesson.

Diverse Learning Strategies

The listing in this article outlines the types of strategies to be found and the labels that identify these. The first three labels *(visual, kinesthetic,* and *auditory)* describe various types of intelligence, or learning styles; the last four categories *(GATE, extra support, SDAIE, and multi-age)* refer to academic, social, and/or behavioral differences.

Boundaries between and among these categories are exceedingly fluid. In actual classroom practice, one category seldom, if ever, stands in isolation. Usually more than one strategy can be used to reach a particular student, and a particular approach may be very effective with students of various types. For example, instruction appealing to the visual domain is effective not only with students identified as visual learners but also with most SDAIE students, given the universal language of images. A learner who thrives on instruction that focuses on the kinesthetic domain may also respond very well to visual stimulus. Further, those learners who don't immediately show themselves to be strong in, for example, the logic/mathematical domain can nonetheless be guided through these types of activities in order to foster or strengthen that area.

In like manner, no appealing activity should be reserved for only those students who immediately show a facility for it. While GATE students as a group tend to excel in drama, if given the chance, so too do many of those learners who need extra support. These labels provide easy reference during advance planning for the most appropriate individual and group instruction for the students in your class.

Visual

These activities use illustrations and other images to appeal to those students whose learning process is strongly visual. Of course, activities so labeled are also essential in strengthening visual awareness in all learners. Photographs, reproductions of paintings, facsimiles of historical documents, maps, and other artifacts are provided so that all students might construct meaning from what they observe. In addition, and where appropriate throughout the text, are activities that allow teachers to guide students in the creation and use of their own visuals such as graphic organizers, illustrations of various events or ideas, original maps, and posters.

Kinesthetic

Activities in this realm are specifically designed for students who learn best through physical action and hands-on experience. In addition, they serve all students well because they get members of the class out of their seats and moving about in a purposeful manner. Pantomimes, constructing models to scale or actual size, rearranging classroom furniture to create a particular environment, and making three-dimensional maps are only some of the activities found in the lessons.

Auditory
Activities with this label are designed to reach those students who respond better to the spoken word than to written text. However, they also hold universal appeal of the sort that has throughout history lent the bard, or storyteller, a fabled role in society. (Current educational research attests to the beneficial effect of reading aloud up to and throughout high school.) Activities suggested include this reading aloud, sharing information with a small group or a partner, role-playing, interviewing and reporting back, and presenting oral reports.

Gifted and Talented (GATE)
These activities work well with students classified as gifted and talented who require additional stimulation and challenge. Such suggestions include writing projects, in-depth research, and sharing results with classmates. Since lack of skill in English does not equate with lack of ability, teachers would do well to remember that there are gifted Limited English Proficient (LEP) students who would also enjoy the challenge of these activities.

Extra Support
Activities bearing this label are designed to help students having difficulty reading, comprehending, and making meaning from the written word. Tapping prior knowledge and connecting new ideas to students' lives, previewing, questioning, and predicting are only some of the strategies included that have proven helpful.

Specially Designed Academic Instruction in English (SDAIE)
Ever-increasing numbers of students whose first language is not English are being taught in English-only classrooms. These SDAIE activities focus on vocabulary development and help the teacher move these students through the stages of developing English proficiency. Since most of these activities rely on few words, they may be similar to visual and kinesthetic activities. Other activities facilitate learning for LEP students through the use of modified speech, choice of less demanding vocabulary, and help in identifying key words and concepts. They also draw on abilities found in the mixed class by suggesting pairing or grouping these students with others with greater English proficiency.

Multi-Age
Activities with this label contain suggestions for approaches to students in the classroom that contains several grade levels or in the ungraded, multi-age setting. These activities can be easily modified and individualized or used with less mature as well as more mature learners.

Ancillary support for even more effective individualizing is provided in the Reading Support and Review pages and the Lesson Support/Transition pages for SDAIE students found in *Reading Support Resources*, as well as through the multi-language lesson summaries in Spanish, Chinese, Hmong, Khmer, and Vietnamese with accompanying audiotapes. Taken together, these tools in Houghton Mifflin Social Studies provide a kaleidoscope of access strategies that will help practitioners reach all students in today's diverse classrooms. ■

For Further Reading

Armstrong, T. *Multiple Intelligences in the Classroom.* Association for Supervision and Curriculum Development (Alexandria, VA), 1994.

Gardner, Howard. *Frames of Mind: The Theory of Multiple Intelligences.* Basic Books, 1985.

Joyce, B., et al. *Models of Teaching.* Allyn and Bacon, 1994.

HOUGHTON MIFFLIN SOCIAL STUDIES

Diverse Learning

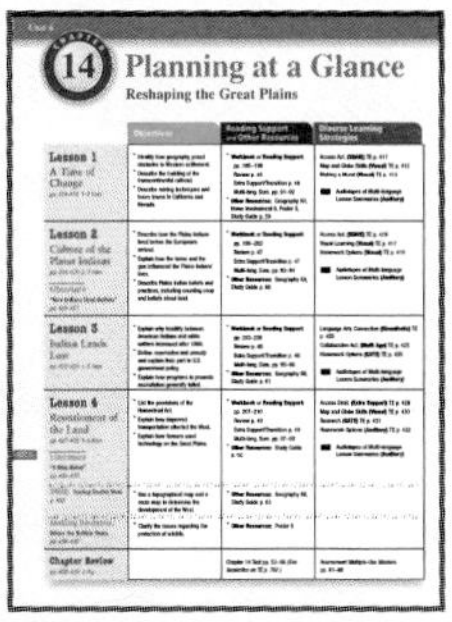

Planning at a Glance
Planning at a Glance charts in the Teacher's Edition before each chapter list the variety of teaching strategies in each lesson.

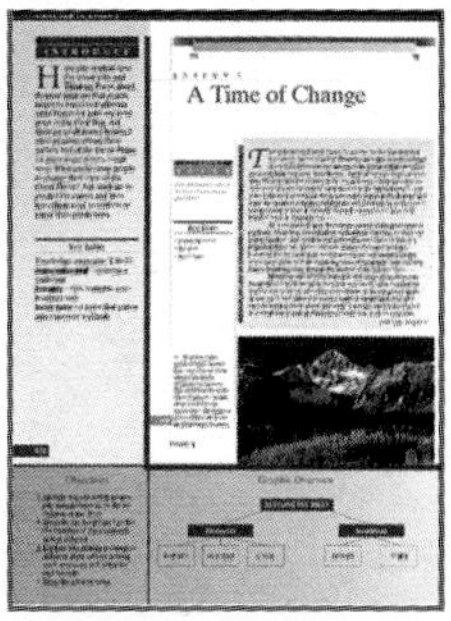

Graphic Organizers
Highly visual graphic organizers that show connections among key concepts in chapters and lessons appear in every lesson in the Teacher's Edition, and in every Chapter Overview and Lesson Preview in *Reading Support Resources.*

Using Technology in the Social Studies Classroom

The power of technology has transformed the classroom. New tools help teachers enrich and extend major topics while providing effective support to students with diverse learning styles. Through multimedia such as sound, video, music, or simulations, students can experience another culture, or a particular historical period. With widespread Internet access, students can reach beyond the classroom to a variety of additional content sources and educational experiences.

When teams of students and teachers utilize new technology tools, learners become interactive with ideas, information and with other learners in a new way. Technology challenges students to assume greater responsibility for their own learning as they seek information from a variety of sources to build knowledge. Major trends include a shift from whole-class to small group instruction, from a competitive to cooperative classroom structure, and from the primacy of verbal thinking to the integration of visual and verbal thinking.

Teachers' roles are also changing. Beyond instructing, teachers have become mentors and facilitators in a collaborative learning environment, as well as coaches as they circulate among students to encourage and give direction and assistance to those working on computers.

Technology has also allowed teachers to present material in a variety of formats. Utilizing CD-ROMs, video, and Internet access, social studies instructors can

- build background information, primary sources, and other data on a social studies topic or concept.
- enhance and enrich major topics by finding new data.
- provide a venue for learning and applying real-life information literacy and research skills.
- offer opportunities for collaborative and cooperative learning as students conduct research.
- assess and foster critical thinking and problem-solving skills.
- provide access to content for diverse learning styles.

Educational Value

Current learning theories focus on the process of knowledge construction. Many educators feel that learning goals can be achieved if students become active, self-directed learners. Utilizing authentic learning experiences and real-world problem-solving tasks, students gather information from many sources and many perspectives, formulate tentative conclusions, and then test those conclusions in relevant situations. This process of knowledge building mirrors the way children actually develop. One of the favorite aphorisms of famed child psychologist Jean Piaget was: "To understand is to invent."

Since multimedia programs invite interaction, students become active seekers of knowledge, rather than passive recipients of information. Multimedia packages can offer inquiry-based learning, where students construct and demonstrate solutions in a variety of simulated environments. Multimedia can also provide individualized learning paths so students can progress at their own pace—a critical issue for students of all abilities. Because children are so fond of computers and video, they are generally more highly motivated to use these tools.

Types of Technology

Technology offers learning opportunities through simulations, educational games,

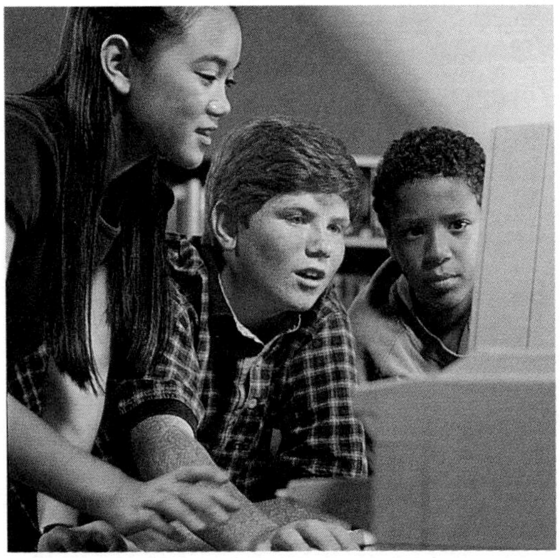

research and data collection, and direct video viewing. Primary classroom technologies include CD-ROMs, video, and the Internet.

CD-ROM

CD-ROMs can store enormous amounts of graphics, images, and sounds. They support an open-ended, discovery approach to learning and allow students to direct their own learning based on their individual abilities and interests. Unlike traditional materials, a CD-ROM can give immediate feedback at point of use, and is self-paced. Most CD-ROMs allow teachers to monitor student progress through printouts, on-screen journals, or built-in management systems.

Computer-based simulation programs place students into lifelike situations in which they must solve problems and make real-world decisions. Simulations can also build in primary resources and research materials, so that students can further their investigations.

Video

Videotapes and videodiscs effectively provide background information for major topics, enrich major topics and concepts, and reinforce prior learning. Videodiscs offer high-quality sound and picture, and quick access to information. With a remote control or barcode reader, a teacher or student using a videodisc can instantly go to any frame or video segment. Videodiscs can contain more than two hours of film clips, still images, maps, music, and narration, and often provide a separate audio channel for a second language.

Internet

The Internet can provide almost infinite resources and learning opportunities to teachers and students. By effectively utilizing the Internet, students first learn how to find useful information quickly and judge its accuracy, and then improve their research skills by learning how to seek reliable content and verify sources. Such information literacy helps students deal with the excessive amount of information encountered in daily life. Online cross-curricular projects offer students indispensable opportunities to build knowledge, connect and utilize ideas, and integrate multiple disciplines. Virtual field trips can take students all over the globe. Internet access can also provide teachers with useful classroom resources, like printable lesson plans, blackline masters, and theme extensions.

Houghton Mifflin Education Place™ (www.eduplace.com) provides integrated program support for Houghton Mifflin Social Studies. Online support aligned to the student textbook and Teacher's Edition provides an integrated, purposeful program with thematic coherence. *Education Place* Discussion Forums give teachers the opportunity to share ideas and discuss important topics in social studies instruction. *Education Place* also provides access to professional resources to help teachers apply technology effectively in the classroom and to extend the curriculum. ■

For Further Reading

Grabe, Mark and Cindy. *Integrating Technology for Meaningful Learning.* Boston, Massacusetts: Houghton Mifflin Company, 1996.

Braun, Joseph A. *Technology Tools in the Social Studies Classroom.* Wilsonville, Oregon: Franklin, Beedle & Associates, 1998.

HOUGHTON MIFFLIN SOCIAL STUDIES
Technology

Social Studies Center at Education Place (www.eduplace.com/ss/hmss/index.html) provides online overviews and outlines of every textbook lesson, student activities, monthly current events features, and teacher's discussion forums.

Rescue Geo 1 ®
is an interactive CD-ROM with 600 questions and over 1,400 maps that reinforce major geography concepts.

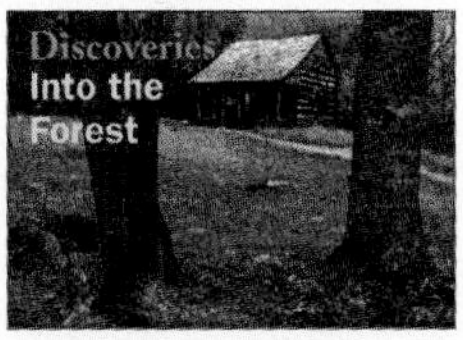

Discoveries™
offers students a video and animation-filled exploration of information hot spots, a reference library, and an online journal.

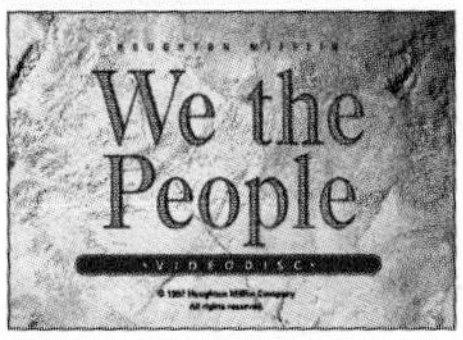

We the People
videotapes provide students with a compelling visual experience of history, geography, and culture, through photography, art, and maps.

Assessment in Social Studies

Assessment is the process of gathering information to aid in the evaluation of students' academic progress. That evaluation can be useful for both individual and collective decision-making.

Assessment today usually means balanced assessment, which includes and *values* a teacher's informal, day-to-day appraisal as well as more formal documentation of student performance. Thus it allows students to demonstrate their progress in a variety of ways. In social studies, this means measuring not just a student's ability to recall particular facts, but also their understanding of concepts, repertoire of skills, and insight into civic values and responsibilities.

Balanced assessment, then, becomes both a learning and teaching opportunity. It allows you to tailor your instruction to individual needs. It also involves students in the process, encouraging them to set goals and make decisions about their own learning and, ultimately, to become more reflective, critical learners.

Informal Assessment

Informal assessment utilizes the ongoing observations you make on a daily basis and focuses on the processes that students use as well as the products they create.

Any of the following may become elements in your informal assessment process: anecdotal notes, checklists and forms, oral presentations, performances assessment, conferences, interviews, conversations, journal entries, learning logs. The Assessment Multiple-Use Masters in the Test booklet will also provide opportunities for informal assessment. Keep in mind that not all assessment activities need to be done for all students at all times.

Informal assessment also involves students in the evaluation of their own learning process. While teachers are informally assessing students, students are assessing themselves as learners and can contribute insights that may help shape your instructional plans.

Formal Assessment

Formal assessment provides a "snapshot" of each student at a given time and often includes pencil-and-paper assessment instruments such as chapter tests. In a balanced assessment program, formal test results are one important component of the total assessment picture. Indeed, you may want to "test" the test results of your students against what you see in your observations and in their portfolios, presentations, and group work. While pencil-and-paper tests continue to be a traditional format for formal assessment, current formal assessment instruments are including more assessment *activities* that reflect instructional activities—for example, real-world writing activities such as letters, newspaper editorials, and speeches.

In today's education setting, formal assessment—especially standardized tests—play an increasingly prominent role. For that reason, a balanced assessment program will include exercises that familiarize students with the format and content of common standardized tests. Such assessment options provide one means to sharpen classroom focus on core content and key issues in social studies.

Self-Assessment

Involving students in the assessment and evaluation process is an essential part of balanced assessment. When students become partners in the learning process, they gain a better sense of themselves as learners and thinkers. As students reflect on what they have learned and how they learn it, they develop the tools to become more effective learners. As they examine their work, they can think about what they do well and in which areas they still need help. If you provide students with criteria or target behaviors, they will have the framework they may need for successful self-examination.

Portfolio Assessment

Portfolio assessment is a long-term approach to ongoing assessment that offers opportunities to monitor students' changing progress throughout the year. The collection of student products in a portfolio provide an overview of students' intellectual capabilities and academic experiences. Portfolios can help you focus on the growth of the individual over time rather than on how the student's performance compares to that of his or her peers.

Portfolios can be highly personalized, such as when an artist creates his or her own portfolio and makes all the decisions about content and presentation. On the other hand, they can be quite standardized, if a standard format is required by an individual teacher, school, district, or state. The intended purpose of the portfolio will determine its contents and the kind of assessment tool it will become. You may want to work with other teachers to develop evaluation criteria of portfolios.

As you revisit portfolio entries with your students, you may want to encourage them to continue a work-in-progress, revise or improve a draft, expand or extend a brief assignment, or look at a product as a basis of comparison for a similar piece of work. Portfolios also give you an opportunity to share an overview of a student's work with families, with other teachers, or with school administrators.

In all, a balanced assessment program with a variety of approaches best evaluates students' ability to relate ideas and concepts, to apply skills, and to think critically. ■

For Further Reading

Grant Wiggins, *Educative Assessment: Designing Assessments to Inform and Improve Students' Performance.* Jossey-Bass, San Francisco, 1998.

HOUGHTON MIFFLIN SOCIAL STUDIES

Assessment Components

Student Text Features

Houghton Mifflin Social Studies has built into its Student Text many instructional features that can also serve an assessment function. These features are found within lessons, special feature pages, and the Chapter Review.

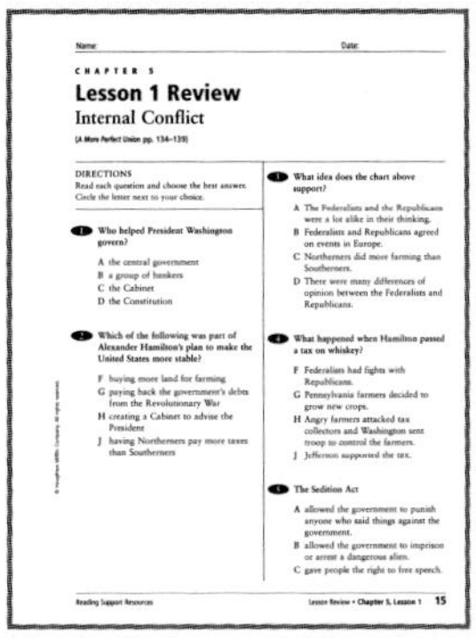

Lesson Reviews in *Reading Support Resources*

These one-page reviews follow the Stanford 9 test in both form and content. They can be used by students to review the lesson's text or by you to test students' understanding of each lesson.

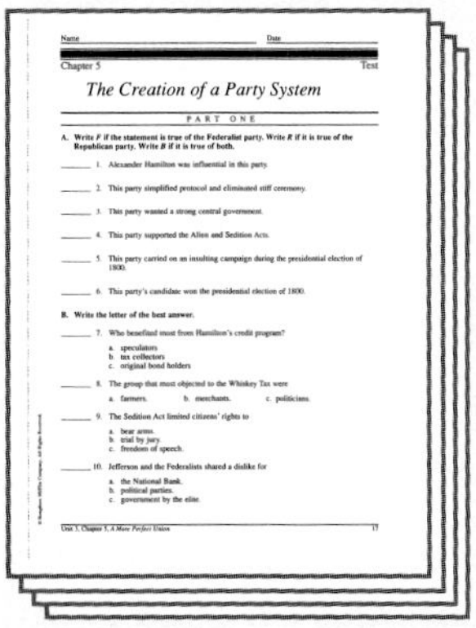

Chapter Tests

A four-page test in blackline master form is provided for each chapter. These tests assess each of the three strands and are structured as follows:

- Part I consists of a variety of short-answer formats.
- Part II consists of free-response questions, including at least one longer "essay" question.

Multiple-Use Masters

In the test booklet you will find a series of black-line master pages that offer options for self-assessment, open-ended questioning, and performance assessment.

Teacher's Edition Features

You may also use for assessment purposes many of the activities and strategies provided in the Planning at a Glance pages and lesson notes in the Teacher's Edition.

Integrating the Social Studies Strands

Social studies is the study of people in their social world. When you study people, you have to look at how they live, work, worship, and play together. You have to consider how they govern themselves, how they make a living, and how they make important decisions.

Developing Meaningful Knowledge

Knowledge of the social world should be holistic and interrelated; it should be representative of all the elements of life. Thus, the content of a social studies program should maintain an interdisciplinary balance that draws from history, geography, economics, culture, ethics and belief systems, and social and political systems. The Houghton Mifflin Social Studies program draws on the vast knowledge of the world, of United States history, and of the various social sciences to build a curriculum that is integrated and interesting, thematic yet thorough, and chronologically conceptual. How is this achieved?

History, geography, and culture form the major threads of this curriculum, with content and conceptual ideas from these and the other social science disciplines woven carefully through these major areas of study. History, geography, and culture are selected as the center of the curriculum, in part because of their inherently interdisciplinary nature. Historians study the lives of people at a particular time and in a particular place; they investigate the beliefs and social systems of the people, the ways they organize to govern themselves, and the ways they earn a living and produce goods and services. In addition, historians focus on the causes of events, and the ways different groups see and understand events and phenomena; they look at the lives of the people and see how events are influenced by different groups, and how the events affect different individuals and groups.

History

The study of history forms the center of this curriculum; yet, all the other areas of the social sciences are easily integrated into the study of the past and the present. The social studies curriculum has been compared to a symphony: sometimes all the instruments play together to form an integrated whole (resembling an interdisciplinary approach), and sometimes individual elements of the symphony are highlighted for a deeper look at one aspect. In such cases, for example, students may focus on learning particular geographic knowledge and skills so that later they can apply these to the content knowledge in the next unit of study. Both solo and integrated approaches to curriculum are used in Houghton Mifflin Social Studies, for both are needed to build a sound curriculum for young learners.

It is critical that history is made more accessible and relevant to students. Lively, honest accounts of the lives of historical characters can stimulate a student's interest in and empathy with that time in history and can provide an entry point for understanding the factual material. In addition, students should appreciate that the most important historical movements were the result of particular decisions and actions made by men and women of all classes, colors, and conditions. This emphasis in the study of history provides a strong basis for democratic citizenship.

Geography

Geography helps us see the links between the landscape of life and the unfolding of human development and history. The pupil editions in Houghton Mifflin Social Studies begin with a fifteen-page Map and Globe Handbook, each section reviewing a specific geographic skill. While the focus of the geography instruction throughout the program centers around the five themes of location, place, human/environment interaction, movement, and region, the Geography Projects located in the Teacher's Edition at the beginning of each unit also address the more comprehensive instructional Six Essential Elements and the Eighteen Geography Standards published in *Geography for Life: National Geography Standards 1994.* The Geography Education Standards Project resulted from the Goals 2000: Educate America Act, which mandated the inclusion of geography as a core subject in curricula nationwide. In Houghton Mifflin Social Studies, the instructional approaches that work with both themes and standards provide an ample framework for student inquiry into the role that geography plays in human history. They also help students realize a critical understanding of the world around them, both now and in the past. Such knowledge is fundamental to sound social studies instruction and will lead to informed judgment and better citizenship not only in matters of resources and the environment, but in life overall.

Economics

How people use the resources of the environment and of their abilities forms the basis of the study of economics. In the elementary and middle grades, it is important for students to recognize the choices people make and how these economic choices form patterns of different economic and ideological systems across the world. With trade and rapid communications, most countries of the world today are highly interdependent, and this economic reality brings benefits as well as introduces new issues.

Culture

Culture, or the total way of life of a people, including their beliefs and traditions, is a central concept in any sound social studies curriculum. In Houghton Mifflin Social Studies, students learn about the cultural similiarities and differences that exist among societies of different times and places. People often express their beliefs and heritage in their arts, literature, architecture, and legends; these human creations play a major role in helping students learn about the inner life of a people and their struggles and joys.

Through a culture's literature, art, and other documents and artifacts, students will recognize that all societies have ideals and standards of behavior. In addition, students will see the role and importance of religion in human society and will reflect on how people in different societies over time have struggled with ethical and moral issues.

An interdisciplinary balance in the social studies curriculum brings a new vitality and relevance to the study of people. By promoting the "big picture" and bringing all elements of life together, an integrated social studies instills in students a greater appreciation for their own culture. Furthermore, an integrated social studies provides students with a three-dimensional view of the world and a practical understanding of the ideas and issues that will influence their daily lives.

Civic Understanding and Values

In a democratic society, it is vital that all citizens are active, informed participants and that they understand and appreciate the kind of behavior necessary for the smooth functioning and maintenance of a democracy. In part, this means that students should understand the essence of democratic ideas and should realize that people create a national identity to reflect the essential beliefs of the nation. In addition, civic understanding implies developing a respect for human rights and for the rational settlement of disputes.

Continued on next page

HOUGHTON MIFFLIN SOCIAL STUDIES

Integrating the Strands

Both themes and standards provide an ample instructional framework for geography as a core subject.

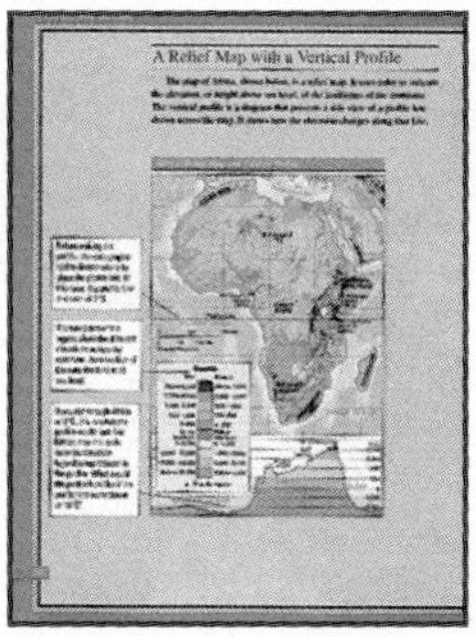

Each section of the 15-page Map and Globe Handbook covers a specific geographic skill.

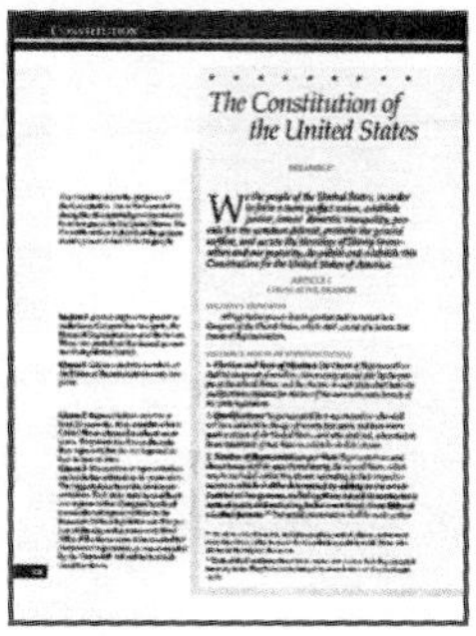

Students see how historical documents often reflect a society's ideals and standards of behavior.

Integrating the Social Studies Strands *(continued)*

Civic understanding and the development of values are goals of education; however, the social studies curriculum plays an important role in this area. Since social studies essentially is the study of people and their societies, it also is the study that undergirds one's perspective on one's own life. That is, social studies should enable students to better comprehend their own ways of life, the values that guide their nation and other cultures, and the issues that face their nation and community.

Skills

Study skills, visual learning skills, map and globe skills, critical thinking skills, and social participation skills are essential components of any effective social studies program. These skills play a major role in Houghton Mifflin Social Studies, for without these, knowledge cannot be meaningful, and civic understanding cannot become action. *Skills are best learned in the context of content knowledge, and are best applied to closely related content.* This principle of learning is maintained throughout the Houghton Mifflin Social Studies program. The Understanding Skills and Making Decision features are integrally related with knowledge developed in the unit of study, and the skill development within a grade level and across the program closely parallels our knowledge of child development and learning.

Since the study of the social world implies gathering a wide range of data, portrayed in a variety of forms (charts, tables, graphs, diagrams, maps, primary source documents, photographs, symbols, artifacts, and more), it is important that students learn how to "read" these data sources accurately and with a sense of purpose. These skills should be purposefully taught to students, for they are complex and critical to meaningful learning. Throughout the Houghton Mifflin Social Studies program, students are engaged in direct instruction in the necessary skills; in subsequent lessons, these skills are then actively applied.

In the same way that history and the social sciences provide a basis for an integrated and interdisciplinary knowledge base for the curriculum, the three major aspects of the Houghton Mifflin Social Studies program provide the foundation for a holistic approach to the study of the social world. Knowledge, civic understanding and values, and skills are all essential parts of a sound, powerful social studies program. Such a program should enable students to truly understand the "facts" as well as the issues. It should engage students in true inquiry and active involvement in the social world; it should help students see the complex interrelationships among beliefs and human choices; and it should enable the student to be a powerful citizen in the contemporary social world. ■

For Further Reading

Braun, Joseph A. *Technology Tools in the Social Studies Classroom.* Wilsonville, Oregon: Franklin, Beedle & Associates, 1998.

Carretero, Mario and James F. Voss, Editors. *Cognitive and Instructional Processes in History and the Social Sciences.* Hillsdale, NJ: Lawrence Erlbaum Associates, 1994.

Darling-Hammond, Linda, Jacqueline Ancess, and Beverly Falk. *Authentic Assessment in Action: Studies of Schools and Students at Work.* New York: Columbia University Press, 1995.

Leinhardt, Gaea, Isabel L. Beck, and Catherine Stainton, Editors. *Teaching and Learning in History.* Hillsdale, NJ: Lawrence Erlbaum Associates, 1994.

Houghton Mifflin Social Studies

Scope and Sequence

This Scope and Sequence has been designed to provide students with the comprehensive knowledge, civic values, and intellectual skill they will need to meet the challenge of citizenship in the 21st Century. The three strands of the program have been tightly integrated at all levels, so that skills are always taught in the context of the lesson content, and knowledge is enhanced by the application of sound values.

The three integrated strands are:

- ● **Knowledge and Understanding**
- ▲ **Civic Understanding and Values**
- ■ **Skills**

HOUGHTON MIFFLIN SOCIAL STUDIES

The Integrated Strands

The goals of each strand are listed on the following two pages. References in the Teacher's Edition key all learning objectives to these goals. Typically the student is introduced to a subject or skill at an early level, taught to actively use it at an intermediate level, and encouraged to analyze and critique it at an advanced level.

● Knowledge and Understanding	▲ Civic Understanding and Values	■ Skills
History	National Identity	Study Skills
Geography	Constitutional Heritage	Visual Learning
Economics	Citizenship	Map and Globe Skills
Culture		Critical Thinking
Ethics and Belief Systems		Social Participation
Social and Political Systems		

● KNOWLEDGE AND UNDERSTANDING

HISTORY

1. Develop an understanding of the reasons for studying history and of the relationships between the past and the present
2. Develop an awareness of the ways in which we learn about the past and the methods and tools of the historian
3. Create a sense of empathy for the past
4. Understand the meaning of time and chronology
5. Analyze the sometimes complex cause-and-effect relationships of ideas and events, recognizing also the effects of the accidental and irrational on history
6. Understand the reasons for both continuity and change
7. Recognize the interrelatedness of geography, economics, culture, belief systems, and political systems within history
8. Comprehend the history of women, minorities, and the full range of social classes, not just the history of the elite or the notable individual

GEOGRAPHY

1. Develop locational skills and understanding
2. Develop an awareness of place
3. Understand human and environmental interaction
4. Understand movement of people, goods, and ideas
5. Understand world regions and their historical, cultural, economic, and political characteristics

ECONOMICS

1. Identify and apply basic concepts of economics (basic wants and needs, scarcity, choices, decision making, opportunity costs, resources, production, distribution, consumption, markets, labor, capital)
2. Develop an awareness of past and present exchange systems
3. Recognize and analyze the economic systems of various societies, including the United States, and their responses to the three basic economic questions: what to produce (value), how and how much to produce (allocation), and how to distribute (distribution)
4. Recognize the economic global interdependence of societies
5. Recognize the impact of technology on economics

▲ CIVIC UNDERSTANDING AND VALUES

NATIONAL IDENTITY

1. Develop an appreciation for the multicultural, pluralistic nature of U.S. society
2. Understand the basic principles of democracy
3. Understand and appreciate American ideals, as expressed in historical documents, speeches, songs, art, and symbolic representations and activities
4. Recognize that the American patriotic ideals are not yet fully realized and that to be protected they must constantly be reaffirmed

CONSTITUTIONAL HERITAGE

1. Develop an appreciation for the balance of power established by the Constitution between majority and minority, the individual and the state, and government by and for the people
2. Understand the historical origins of the Constitution and how it has been amended and changed over time
3. Recognize the Constitution as an expression of democratic ideals that is reinterpreted from time to time

CITIZENSHIP

1. Recognize the reciprocal relationship between the individual and the state in a democracy
2. Understand and appreciate the kind of behavior necessary for the functioning and maintenance of our democratic society
3. Learn the duties and method of selection of our leaders
4. Develop a respect for human rights, including those of individuals and of minorities
5. Develop an understanding and appreciation for the rational settlement of disputes and for compromise
6. Recognize the special strategies required to allow the different elements within our pluralistic society to live together amicably
7. Develop an understanding of the processes that have led to the fall of democracies

■ SKILLS

STUDY SKILLS

1. Locate, select, and collect information by interviewing or by using appropriate reference materials
2. Organize information from reference sources to address issues or problems
3. Present information convincingly in spoken or written forms

VISUAL LEARNING

1. Develop careful and directed observation of images, objects, and the environment
2. Understand, use, and create graphic information (timelines, charts, tables, other graphic organizers, graphs, diagrams)
3. Interpret and respond to photographs, paintings, cartoons, and other illustrative materials
4. Understand and use symbols
5. Express meaning through sensory forms of representation

MAP & GLOBE SKILLS

1. Identify and use map and globe symbols; identify and use different map projections
2. Understand and use locational terms; locate places and positions on a map or globe
3. Interpret and use directional terms and symbols on a map or globe
4. Understand and use terms to describe relative size and distance; identify and use map scales
5. Construct and use maps and geographic models

CULTURE

1. Understand the concept of culture and how it is transmitted
2. Develop an appreciation for the rich complexity of a society's culture and an understanding of how the parts of a culture interrelate
3. Recognize and appreciate the multicultural and multiethnic dimensions of our society and the contributions made by various groups
4. Appreciate the cultural similarities and differences that exist among societies of different times and places
5. Recognize the special role literature and the arts play in reflecting the inner life of a people and in projecting a people's image of themselves to the world
6. Learn about the mythology, legends, myths of origin, and heroes and heroines of societies of different times and places

ETHICS & BELIEF SYSTEMS

1. Recognize that all societies have ideals and standards of behavior
2. Understand that the ideas people profess affect their actions
3. Recognize the importance of religion in human society and its influence on history
4. Become familiar with the basic ideas of major religions and ethical traditions of other times and places
5. Develop an understanding of how different societies have tried to resolve ethical issues when conflicts occur between individuals, groups, and societies

SOCIAL & POLITICAL SYSTEMS

1. Develop an awareness of the reciprocal relationship between the individual and various social and political groups: family, community, and nation
2. Understand the role of law and its relationship to social and political systems
3. Develop an appreciation for the tension between opposing ideals in human affairs
4. Develop an awareness of the structure of social classes and the changes in status of women and racial and ethnic minorities in U.S. society and other societies
5. Understand comparative political systems, past and present
6. Understand the complex relationship and interdependence that exists among the world's nations

CRITICAL THINKING

1. Define and clarify problems, issues, and ideas
2. Evaluate and judge information related to a problem, an issue, or an idea
3. Solve problems and draw conclusions related to an issue or idea*

*Critical thinking is taught both in a problem-solving and in a decision-making context.

SOCIAL PARTICIPATION

1. Develop interpersonal skills
2. Work successfully in groups

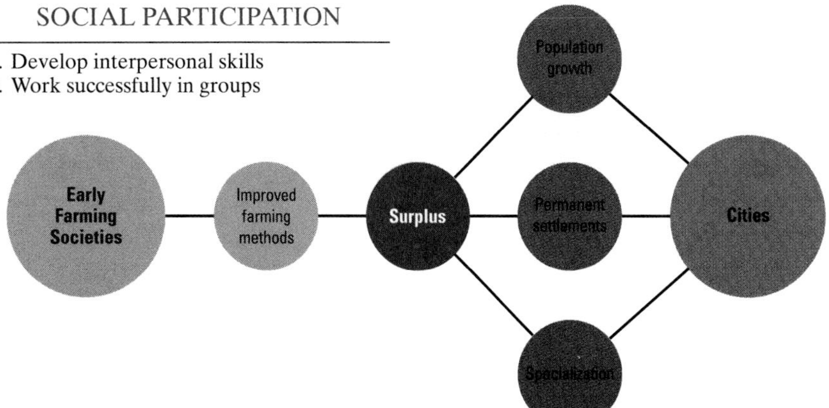

Teaching About Religion in Public Schools

Charles C. Haynes

Growing numbers of educators throughout the United States recognize that study about religion in social studies, literature, art, and music is an essential part of a complete public school education. States and school districts are issuing new mandates and guidelines for the inclusion of teaching about religion in the curriculum. As a result, textbooks are expanding discussions of religion's role in history and culture, and many new supplementary materials concerning religion in history are being developed.

In light of this national trend to include more about religion in the curriculum, the question for teachers is no longer "Should I teach about religion?" but rather, "What should I teach, and how should I do it?" This publication is designed to provide the civic and academic framework for answering the questions of "what" and "how." The aim of the guidelines and suggestions that follow is to help classroom teachers meet the challenges of teaching about religion in ways that are constitutionally permissible, educationally sound, and sensitive to the beliefs of students and parents.

Why Study about Religion is Important

Teaching about religion is important and necessary if public schools are to provide students with a complete education. Much of history, art, music, literature, and contemporary life is unintelligible without an understanding of the major religious ideas and influences that have shaped history and culture throughout the world. Even teaching religious liberty, the civic foundation that sustains the United States as one nation of many faiths, requires teaching about the role of religion in history and culture. A recent report by the Association for Supervision and Curriculum Development described the place of religion in the curriculum:

> The proper role of religion in the school is the study of religion for its educational value. The task is to teach about religions and their impact in history, literature, art, music, and morality. It seems natural that the art curriculum, for example, must pay attention to the impact of Christianity on the work of Michelangelo, just as a history class focusing on the colonization of America must pay attention to the religious upheaval in sixteenth-century Europe that fueled that colonization. [1]

Understanding the role religion plays in history and culture is of special importance in our increasingly diverse society. Expanding religious pluralism in the United States confronts our schools and our nation with unprecedented challenges. The United States has shifted from the largely Protestant pluralism of the eighteenth century to a pluralism that now includes people of all faiths and a growing number of people who indicate no religious preference. New populations of Muslims, Buddhists, and many other religious and ethnic groups are entering schools throughout the nation.

If we are to live with our differences, we must attempt through education to replace stereotypes and prejudices with understanding and respect. Students need to recognize that religious and philosophical beliefs and practices are of deep significance to much of our citizenry. Omission of discussion about the religious and philosophical roots of developments in history can give students

[1] An excerpt from *Religion in the Curriculum,* Alexandria, Virginia: Association for Supervision and Curriculum Development, 1987.

the false impression that the religious and ethical traditions of humankind are insignificant or unimportant.

A Civic Framework for Teaching about Religion

> Congress shall make no law respecting an establishment of religion, or prohibiting the free exercise thereof. . . .

The Religious Liberty clauses of the First Amendment to the Constitution provide the civic framework for teaching about religion in the public schools. The United States Supreme Court has interpreted the First Amendment to mean that public schools may neither promote nor inhibit religious belief or non-belief. The public school curriculum may not, therefore, include religious indoctrination in any form (including hostility to religions or religion in general). Such teaching would constitute state sponsorship of religion and would violate the freedom of conscience protected by the First Amendment.

Religious indoctrination, however, is not the same as teaching about religion. In the 1960s school prayer cases (which ruled against state-sponsored school prayer and devotional Bible-reading), the Supreme Court indicated that public school education may include teaching about religion. In *Abington v. Schempp* (1963), the court stated:

> [I]t might well be said that one's education is not complete without a study of comparative religion or the history of religion and its relationship to the advancement of civilization. It certainly may be said that the Bible is worthy of study for its literary and historic qualities. Nothing we have said here indicates that such study of the Bible or of religion, when presented objectively as part of a secular program of education, may not be effected consistently with the First Amendment.

All public school teachers must have a clear understanding of the crucial difference between the teaching of religion (religious education) and teaching about religion. In 1988, a broad coalition of seventeen religious and educational organizations published guidelines that distinguish between teaching about religion and religious indoctrination. The guidelines state, in part:

- The school's approach to religion is *academic*, not devotional.
- The school strives for student *awareness* of religions, but does not press for student *acceptance* of any one religion.
- The school sponsors *study* about religion, not the *practice* of religion.
- The school *exposes* students to a diversity of religious views; it does not *impose* any particular view.
- The school *educates* about all religions; it does not *promote* or *denigrate* any religion.
- The school *informs* students about various beliefs; it does not seek to conform students to any particular belief.

In addition to these baseline distinctions, the Religious Liberty clauses provide guiding principles for how teaching about religion may best be carried out in the classroom. These principles are the civic values at the heart of American citizenship. They are so fundamental and enduring that they may be called the three Rs of religious liberty:

- **Rights:** Religious liberty, or freedom of conscience, is a basic and inalienable right founded on the inviolable dignity of the person. In a society as religiously diverse as the United States, it is essential that schools emphasize that the rights guaranteed by the Constitution are for citizens of all faiths and none.
- **Responsibilities:** Religious liberty is not only a universal right, but it also depends upon a universal responsibility to respect that right for others, treating others as we ourselves desire to be treated. Students must recognize the inseparable link between the preservation of

Continued on next page

Charles C. Haynes

Charles C. Haynes is Senior Scholar for Religious Freedom at the Freedom Forum First Amendment Center in Arlington, Virginia. He presently serves on the Board of Directors of the Character Education Partnership. Dr. Haynes was one of the principal organizers and drafters of "Religious Liberty, Public Education, and the Future of American Democracy: A Statement of Principles," sponsored by more than twenty major educational and religious organizations. He also co-chaired the coalitions that produced a series of consensus guidelines on "Religion in the Public School Curriculum," and "Religious Holidays in the Public Schools." Dr. Haynes holds a master's degree in religion and education from Harvard Divinity School and a Ph.D. in theological studies from Emory University. He formerly taught world religions at Randolph-Macon College and social studies in both public and private secondary schools.

Teaching About Religion in Public Schools *(continued)*

their own constitutional rights and their responsibility as citizens to defend those rights for all others. This is what may be called the golden rule for civic life.

- **Respect:** Debate and disagreement are vital to classroom discussion and a key element of preparation for citizenship in a democracy. Yet, if we are to live with our differences, particularly our religious differences, how we debate, and not only what we debate, is critical. At the heart of good citizenship is a strong commitment to the civic values that enable people with diverse religious and philosophical perspectives to treat one another with respect and civility.

Rights, responsibilities, and respect, then, are the civic ground rules for teaching about religion in the public schools just as they are the ground rules of American citizenship. When we teach about the many cultures and religions of our nation and the world, we must simultaneously teach our common ground—the civic values and responsibilities that we share as American citizens. If this is done, teaching about religion becomes an excellent opportunity to teach respect for the universal rights and mutual responsibilities, within which the deep differences of belief can be negotiated.

Approaches to Teaching about Religion

Teachers need to make clear to students (and their parents) that teaching about religion is an important part of the curriculum in such subjects as social studies, literature, music, and art. Make them aware that all study about religion will be within the civic framework provided by the Constitution and will serve the educational goals of the academic program.

Natural Inclusion

Study about religion should take place within a historical and cultural context. Courses in history, literature, art, and music on the elementary and secondary levels as well as discussions of community and instruction about religious festivals and cultures offer natural opportunities to include discussion about religious influences and themes.

Keep in mind, however, that these discussions are not courses in religion or theology. What is taught about the religion or religions of a particular historical period or present-day culture should be only what is essential to understanding the events or peoples under consideration. Decisions concerning how much to discuss religion and which religions to include in the discussion should be determined by the academic requirements of the course being taught.

Students should be told that their study of religious traditions as a part of their study of history and culture is necessarily limited. Make clear why certain religious influences and themes have been selected for study. Remind students that there is much more to learn about the complexity and richness of each faith. Alert them to the fact that there is a wide diversity of opinion about religious events and ideas not only among the various religions, but also within the traditions themselves.

Fairness and Balance

Classroom discussions concerning religious traditions in history, literature, or other courses must be conducted in an environment that is free of advocacy on the part of the teacher. While various perspectives should be presented, no religious or anti-religious point of view should be advocated by the teacher. When discussing religious beliefs, teachers can avoid injecting personal religious beliefs by teaching through attribution (e.g., by reporting that "most Buddhists believe . . .").

Fair and balanced study about religion includes critical thinking about historical events involving religious traditions. Religious beliefs have had a part in some of the best and some of the worst developments in history. The full historical record (and various interpretations of it) must be available for analysis and discussion.

Teachers should use primary sources where possible so that students can work directly with the historical record.

Please note, however, that consideration of destructive or oppressive acts carried out in the name of a religious belief is not an opportunity to attack the integrity of the religion itself. All religious traditions can point to tragic chapters in their story and historical incidents where the ideals of the faith were not fully lived. This part of the record can be taught without condemning a particular religion or religion in general. Teaching that includes attacks on religion or on the theology or practice of any faith does not belong in a public school classroom.

Avoid asking qualitative comparisons between religions (e.g. religion A supercedes or is superior to religion B). Structural parallels, on the other hand, such as pointing out that most religious traditions have scriptures and community worship, may be a helpful way to organize the class discussion. It is also appropriate to compare and contrast the different perspectives religious groups might have on historical or current events.

Respect for Differences

When teaching about the major faiths of humankind in history, teachers must take great care not to present religious truth claims as relative or to reduce all religions to a common denominator.

Sometimes, in an effort to sound "tolerant" or "neutral," people speak of all religions as "all the same" underneath their differences. A Peanuts poster of some years ago parodied this approach by saying: "It doesn't matter what you believe as long as you are sincere." For many religious people, however, such "toleration" from others distorts their faith and is anything but neutral. It matters very much to a Christian or to a Jew or to a Muslim, for example, what one takes to be ultimately true. These faith communities, and many others, subscribe to absolute truths derived from the sources of revelation and authority in their traditions. The view that all faiths are ultimately the same may be compatible with some world views, but this is itself a philosophical position. For a teacher to advocate this view is a form of indoctrination.

Equally problematic are attempts by a teacher to "explain away" religious faith as merely social or psychological phenomena. Such teaching often leaves the impression that truth is relative and that there are no absolutes. It is permissible to present various theories of religion and to introduce students to the social, economic, and cultural context in which religions have formed and changed. However, it is first and foremost essential to report how people of faith interpret their own practices and beliefs, and how these beliefs have affected their lives historically as well as how they affect people's lives today.

Remember, public school teachers are required to teach about the various approaches to religious truth without advocating one religious or philosophical position over another. Teaching respect for differences is a key part of understanding the beliefs of the world's religious traditions. By taking care not to portray as relative or to reduce the truth claims of religions, the teacher allows the student to learn how each faith understands itself.

Use of Religious Scriptures

Study of history or literature would be incomplete without exposure to the scriptures of the world's major religious traditions. Some knowledge of biblical literature, for example, is necessary to comprehend much in the history, law, art, and literature of Western civilization, just as exposure to the Qur'an is important for understanding Islamic civilization. In this sense, the classical religious texts are part of our study of history and culture.

At the same time, students need to recognize that while scriptures tell us much about the history and cultures of humankind, they are considered sacred accounts

Continued on next page

Students need to recognize that religious and philosophical beliefs and practices are of deep significance to much of our citizenry.

Teaching About Religion in Public Schools *(continued)*

Understood properly, and carried out with sensitivity, the challenge of teaching about religion in public schools is an exciting opportunity for enriching the curriculum. Teaching about religion within the civic framework of religious liberty can do much to prepare citizens for living and working together in a pluralistic society.

by adherents to their respective traditions. Religious documents give students of history the opportunity to examine directly how religious traditions understand divine revelation and human values.

In a history class, selections from these accounts should always be treated with respect and used only in the appropriate historical and cultural context. Alert students to the fact that there are a variety of interpretations of scripture within each religious tradition.

Role Playing

Recreating religious practices or ceremonies through role playing activities should not take place in a public school classroom. Such activities, no matter how carefully planned or well-intentioned, risk undermining the integrity of the faith involved. Religious ceremonies are sacred to those who practice them. Recreations may unwittingly mock or, at the very least, oversimplify the religious meaning or intent of the ritual.

Role playing religious practices may also violate the conscience of students who are asked to participate. Use audio-visual resources and primary-source documents to introduce students to ceremonies and rituals of the world's religions.

Guest Speakers

When teaching about religion in history, it may be helpful to invite a guest speaker for a more comprehensive presentation of the religious tradition under study. Care should be taken to invite someone with the academic background necessary for an objective and scholarly discussion of the historical period and the religion being considered.

Faculty from local colleges and universities often make excellent guest speakers, or can make recommendations of others who might be appropriate for working with students in a public school setting. Religious leaders or clergy in the community can also be a valuable resource. Remember, however, that they have commitments to their own faith. Be certain that any guest speaker understands the First Amendment guidelines for teaching about religion in public education, and is clear about the nature of their assignment. When the goals of the course are clearly communicated and the task specific, religious leaders can be helpful.

The Beliefs of Teachers and Students

Teachers

We have already seen that teaching about religion in public schools must never be used by teachers as an opportunity to proselytize or to impose religious or anti-religious views on the students.

What should the response be, however, when students ask the teacher to reveal his or her own religious beliefs? Some teachers prefer not to answer the question, stating that it is inappropriate for a teacher to inject personal beliefs into the discussion. Teachers of very young children, in particular, sometimes find this to be the most satisfactory response.

Many other teachers, however, do not wish to leave students guessing about their personal views. In the interest of establishing an open and honest classroom environment, these teachers answer the question straightforwardly and succinctly.

The teacher who decides to answer the question by telling the students his or her religious background should probably not do so at the beginning of the course. Such questions are best answered once the teacher has had an opportunity to demonstrate how various religious and non-religious perspectives may be taught about with sensitivity and objectivity.

When answering the question, teachers may take the opportunity to say something like: "These are my personal beliefs, but my role here is to present with fairness and sensitivity a variety of beliefs as we study the history of the world's great cultures." Answering the question briefly, with little elaboration or discussion, can be a good lesson in civic values. Students learn that people with deep convictions can teach and learn about the convictions of others in ways that are fair and balanced.

Students

Teachers should not solicit information about the religious affiliations or beliefs of students. Nor should students be requested to explain their faith or religious practices to the class. Such requests put undue pressure on students who may not wish to act as spokespersons for their tradition. Keep in mind also that students may not be qualified or prepared to represent their tradition accurately.

Students may choose on their own to express their religious views during a class discussion or as part of a writing project or art activity. This is appropriate as long as it is relevant to the subject under consideration and meets the requirements of the assignment.

At the beginning of the course, especially in the social studies, students should consider the civic values that will be the ground rules for class discussion. Teachers may wish to introduce the first principles of rights, responsibilities, and respect that flow from the First Amendment. By teaching within this framework, they help students learn to respect religious distinctiveness while affirming our constitutional guarantees.

When civic values and responsibilities are in place, the classroom environment is conducive to exploring a broad range of beliefs and practices, of ideas and views, in a way that is non-judgmental and non-threatening. Students learn that differences, even our deepest differences, can be discussed with civility and respect, and that ridicule and prejudice have no place in our society.

Meeting the Challenge

The United States is fortunate to have many talented and dedicated teachers. Given proper educational and administrative support, and working with sound materials, teachers will meet the challenge of study about religion in the core curriculum of the public schools. As schools go forward with teaching about religion, it is important that teachers:

- Take advantage of educational opportunities offered by national institutes and local continuing education courses to learn more about the world's great religious traditions and about the role of religion and religious liberty in United States and world history.
- Encourage school districts to offer pre-service and in-service education for all teachers faced with the responsibility of teaching about religion. Such programs should focus on how to teach about religion in ways that are constitutionally permissible, educationally sound, and culturally sensitive.
- Be familiar with state and local guidelines for teaching about religion in the curriculum.
- Have clear educational objectives for the inclusion of study about religion in courses where such study may be appropriate.
- Make certain that administrators, students, and parents understand how and when study about religion will take place in the classroom (have guidelines available to help answer questions).
- Use textbooks and supplementary materials that discuss the role of religion in history and culture, and do so in a way that is fair and balanced.

Understood properly, and carried out with sensitivity, the challenge of teaching about religion in public schools is an exciting opportunity for enriching the curriculum. Teaching about religion within the civic framework of religious liberty can do much to prepare citizens for living and working together in a pluralistic society. Through education and commitment to civic values, public schools can and must ensure that our diversity remains a source of national strength. ■

For More Information

The Freedom Forum First Amendment Center is a non-profit, educational foundation that provides legal and educational guidelines on the constitutional role of religion in public education. The Center also offers seminars for teachers and suggests supplementary resources for teaching about religions in the classroom. For more information contact:

Charles C. Haynes, Ph.D.
The Freedom Forum First Amendment Center
1101 Wilson Blvd.
Arlington, VA 22209
(703) 528-0800

or

Marcia Beauchamp
First Amendment Center
Pacific Coast Center
1 Market St.
Steuart Tower, 21st Floor
San Francisco, CA 94105
(415) 281-0900

Web site
www.freedomforum.org

Using Collaborative Learning in Social Studies

Collaborative learning is a strategy or structure for learning that can be adapted to many lessons and activities. There are many models or approaches to collaborative learning (or cooperative learning), but all of these models share certain basic characteristics:

- Students work together to achieve a common goal.
- Students work face-to-face in heterogeneous groups.
- Each member of the group has a clearly defined role and is individually accountable for tasks.
- Each member makes an important contribution to the success of the group's effort ("positive interdependence").

Working together in collaborative groups is an excellent way to develop students' skills of social participation, always a key goal of the social studies curriculum. Furthermore, since interdependence is a hallmark of many cultures, collaborative learning techniques are especially useful with limited English proficient students (LEP). However, these students, and many fluent English speakers as well, do need special help with procedures when they have specifically assigned tasks they must carry out. Since they are not as likely to be able to divide up tasks, teachers need to demonstrate and have students practice grouping strategies, assigning individual responsibilities, and other group techniques such as reaching consensus.

Your Role as Teacher

It is important to bear in mind that collaborative learning supplements direct instruction—it does not replace it. As always, the teacher provides the solid instruction that is the basis for learning. Simply putting students in groups and giving them an interesting assignment does not lead to successful collaborative learning. Instead, you as teacher play the key role of providing structure, guidance, and feedback. In a very real sense, your role becomes that of coach or facilitator.

An important ingredient in the success of collaborative groups is effective use of interpersonal skills. As facilitator, you can help groups identify ahead of time the kinds of interpersonal skills that will be important to the task they are undertaking. These skills may range from something as simple as speaking quietly to a more complex skill such as giving constructive criticism. Modeling these skills for students and helping students practice them are important parts of your role.

Another area in which student groups need support is in learning to manage the process of group interaction. It is usually easier for students to divide up tasks such as research and writing than it is for them to make sure that someone keeps the group on target and monitors their progress. Supporting and guiding students in these process tasks can help assure the success of the group's efforts.

Practical Tips

1. It takes time for group members to become comfortable with one another and work together effectively. You may want to begin by having groups engage in some simple brainstorming activities just to become acquainted and begin to develop trust. For the same reason, it is usually best to keep groups together for at least several weeks before regrouping.
2. Try to build in time for groups to evaluate their performance after completing an activity. How well did they do not only with the academic task but with their interpersonal and group processes? What lessons can they apply to future collaborative efforts? The Multiple Use Master in the Assessment Options booklet that comes with the program can be used to assess groupwork.

Strategies

The following strategies can be adapted to many lessons and activities in Houghton Mifflin Social Studies.

Three-Step Interview

Procedures: Students work in pairs to interview each other about an assigned topic.

1. One student interviews the other about the topic.
2. The students switch roles as interviewer and interviewee.
3. Each student shares with the group what he or she learned during the interview.

Uses: The Three-Step Interview can be used effectively to build background knowledge in conjunction with the Introduce part of the Teacher's Edition lesson. You can use the notes under Introduce to formulate a question for the interview such as, "What do you know about [topic of lesson]?" As an option for the Close part of the lesson, occasionally you might also have students do a Three-Step Interview on a question such as, "What's the most important thing you learned about [topic of lesson]?" or "What else would you like know about [topic]?"

Benefits: Promotes participation, listening skills, divergent thinking

Jigsaw

Procedures: In the Jigsaw strategy, each member of the team becomes "expert" about a particular topic related to a larger team project. Team members then share information to prepare a presentation or solve a problem. Following are the main steps:

1. Identify several manageable topics related to a larger topic or concept.
2. Set up an "expert" group for each topic made up of one member from each team.
3. Have expert groups work together to research their topic.
4. Experts return to their original teams and share what they have learned.
5. You as teacher may assign or let teams select a particular format for presenting their findings.

Uses: The Jigsaw approach can be used with many of the Collaborative Learning activities in the Chapter Reviews. It is particularly effective in helping students prepare for informed debate or to acquire and present new information.

Benefits: Promotes interdependence, helps students discover connections among concepts and bodies of information

Group Investigation

Procedures: Students work in teams to prepare a presentation or project to share with the class. Students form teams and divide the work so that each student on a team has a definite task to perform.

Uses: This strategy helps students to synthesize information from several sources. Many Chapter Review activities lend themselves to this approach.

Benefits: Promotes organizational and presentation skills; helps students direct their own learning.

Pair Debate

Procedures: Students debate an issue in pairs. First, each student defends one side of the issue; then pairs switch partners, and each student must defend the other side of the same issue.

Uses: Pair Debate can be used as an effective Close, especially for lessons that deal with conflict or controversy in history.

Benefits: Promotes role-playing, knowing, and respecting different points of view. ■

For Further Reading

Slavin, R.E. *Cooperative Learning: Theory, Research and Practice.* Englewood Cliffs, NJ: Prentice Hall, 1990.

Stahl, Robert J. *Cooperative Learning in Social Studies: A Handbook for Teachers.* Menlo Park, CA: Addison-Wesley, 1994.

HOUGHTON MIFFLIN SOCIAL STUDIES
Collaborative Learning

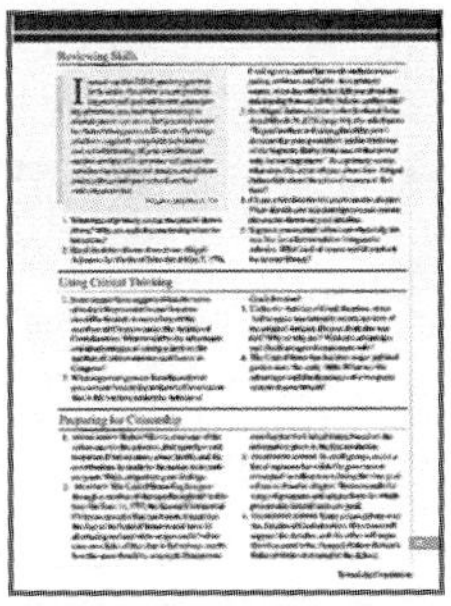

Chapter Review
In each Chapter Review, the Preparing for Citizenship feature has a Collaborative Learning activity.

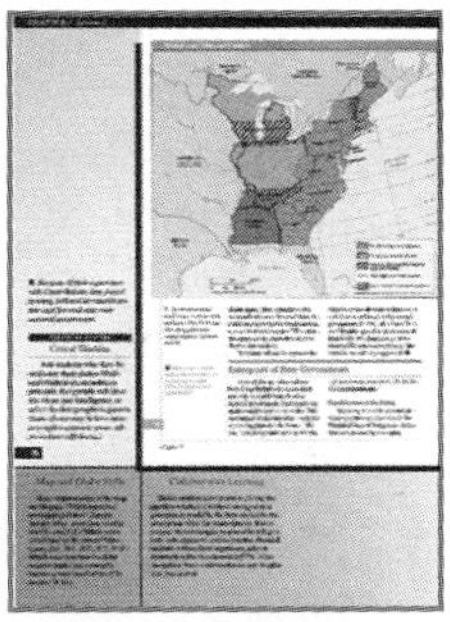

Teacher's Edition
Frequent stimulating Collaborative Learning and Social Participation activities at point of use provide practice in interpersonal skills.

Developing Concepts and Vocabulary

Vocabulary instruction plays an important role in social studies, as it does in all content area reading. But teaching students a social studies term usually does not mean teaching them a new label for a concept they already have. In most cases, it means teaching students an unfamiliar concept.

Houghton Mifflin Social Studies integrates vocabulary instruction with the teaching of other concepts and knowledge. Always the emphasis is on starting with what students already know and linking that prior knowledge to new concepts and information or by building background before they start reading. This approach is solidly grounded in research that shows that knowledge is not just unrelated facts but sets of relationships. We learn new information by relating it to what we already know.

Many features of this program will assist you in helping your students activate their prior knowledge and link new concepts. In the Teacher's Edition, the Unit Previews, the Chapter Overviews, and the Introduce portion of each lesson provide useful strategies. The Graphic Overviews—which are also presented to the student in the Lesson Preview pages in *Reading Support Resources*—can help you show your students connections among the key ideas in each lesson. The Lesson Support/Transition pages in the SDAIE portion of *Reading Support Resources* reinforce student understanding of essential vocabulary. In the students' own books, the Connect question in each lesson review helps students link what they have learned in that lesson to previous learning. The Key Terms taught in the lesson relate to important ideas in that lesson and, furthermore, are terms that students will encounter frequently in their social studies reading.

Vocabulary Strategies

The strategies that follow present useful options for preteaching and reviewing vocabulary for any lesson.

Semantic Feature Analysis

This stragegy is particularly effective in helping students identify connections among related concepts. For this reason, it works best with terms that are closely related in meaning. A Venn diagram can be used effectively for semantic feature analysis. Borrowed from the field of mathematics, a Venn diagram is a pictorial representation that uses intersecting circles to show features shared by two or more concepts and features peculiar to each concept.

Example:

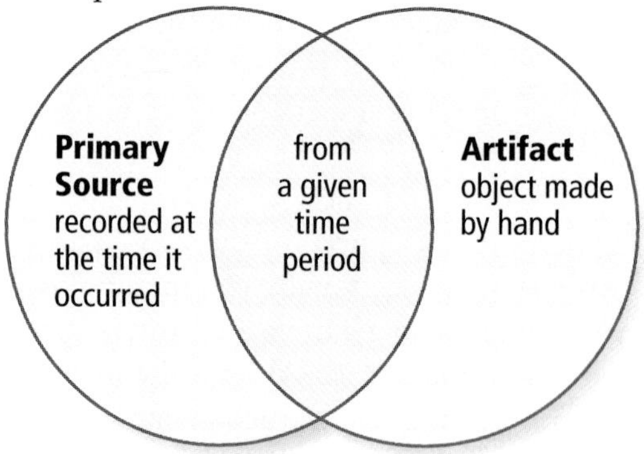

Contextual Redefinition

The strategy called contextual redefinition explicitly teaches students to use context as a clue to meaning. Because all Key Terms in Houghton Mifflin Social Studies are clearly defined in context, this strategy can be easily used with any lesson.

1. Present the words in isolation. Write each Key Term on the board or an overhead, and ask students to supply a meaning for each word. Students should defend their suggestions and come to consensus on the best definition.
2. Have students read the sentence from the lesson in which the term appears in boldface (dark type). Then ask students again to suggest definitions and defend

their suggestions. In this way, more skilled readers model for other students the thinking processes involved in formulating a definition from context.

3. Have students consult the Glossary, if appropriate, to confirm the definition.

Games

Research shows that students not only have fun, but are highly motivated by playing games. Games provide opportunities for learner-centered instruction, and can be used as cooperative learning activities. The games described below can be used to review Key Terms from a lesson or chapter.

Social Studies Bingo

Organization: Individual players

Length: 10-15 minutes

Preparation: Have students create a bingo board of five rows and five columns, writing a different Key Term in each empty space on the grid. Have students cut up paper into nine small pieces that can cover the spaces on the grid.

Rules of Play:

1. At random, read aloud a definition of a Key Term (definitions appear in the Teacher's Edition at the start of each lesson).
2. If students find the correct Key Term on their board, they should cover the space.
3. Continue reading aloud definitions. The first student to fill in a row or column (or the entire grid, if that is the goal) should shout "social studies," and wins if he or she identified the Key Terms correctly.

Olympic Password

Organization: Teams of two students.

Length: 10-15 minutes.

Preparation: Draw a tree like the one shown to keep track of how teams are doing, and have students fill it in as the game progresses.

Game Design for Olympic Password

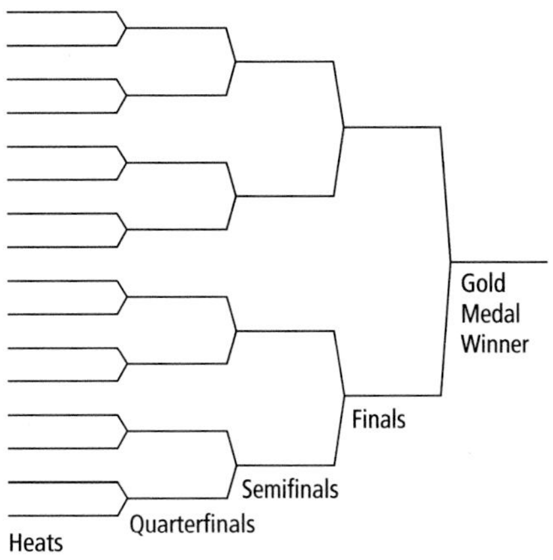

Rules of Play:

1. Have two competing teams sit with teammates facing each other. Give one player on each team a paper with the same Key Term on it, making sure that their teammates cannot see the term.
2. The player on the first team holding the term gives a one-word clue to his or her teammate, who has a chance to guess the term. If he or she guesses correctly, the team gets the point. If not, the person on the other team with the term gives a one-word clue. Teams take turns giving clues until the term is guessed.
3. Give the next term to the two players who guessed during the first round, and repeat the rules of play from above. Have the players take turns giving clues until all the Key Terms have been guessed.
4. The team with the most points wins the heat and continues to the quarterfinals. Teams can progress up the "tree" until the class has gold, silver, and bronze medalists. ■

For Further Reading

Bromley, Karen, Linda Irwin-De Vitis, and Marcia Modlo. *Graphic Organizers, Visual Strategies for Active Learning.* New York: Scholastic Professional Books, 1995.

Nagy, William E. *Teaching Vocabulary to Improve Reading Comprehension.* Urbana, IL: ERIC Clearninghouse on Reading and Communication Skills, 1988.

HOUGHTON MIFFLIN SOCIAL STUDIES

Vocabulary

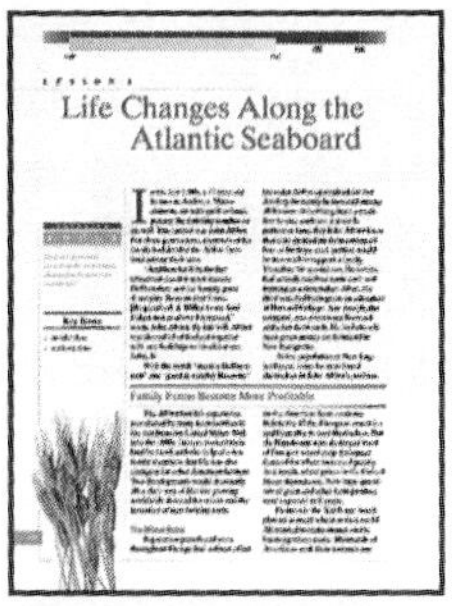

Student Edition

The opening page of the lesson lists the Key Terms covered in the lesson.

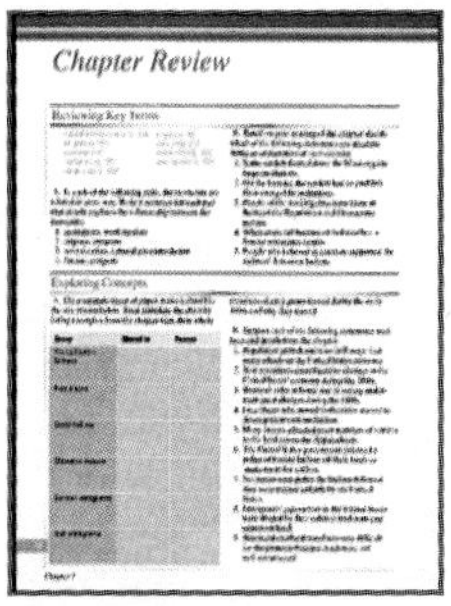

Chapter Review

Activities in Reviewing Key Terms in each Chapter Review enable students to use key terms in context.

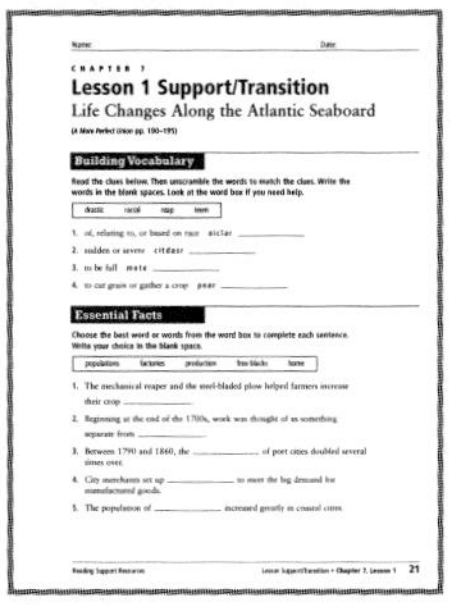

Reading Support Resources

The Lesson Support/ Transition pages reinforce students' understanding of essential vocabulary.

Character Education and Social Studies

Good citizenship in a democratic society such as ours implies active participation in the community, respecting and working together with other citizens to address common problems, and finding better ways to live in the community and in the world. Such activity suggests attitudes of respect for individuals and for the diversity amongst individuals and cultures, attitudes of caring for others and the environment, and attitudes of respect for human dignity.

In addition, young citizens must have a sense of responsibility, a belief that they themselves are responsible for the improvement of the society and the community, and that they must bring information and thoughtfulness to local, national, and international problems.

In Houghton Mifflin Social Studies, students examine historical time periods for evidence of civic behavior and civic values. They analyze the choices that individuals have made in certain circumstances, and assess the consequences of these actions. Students examine the personal and social qualities that contribute to a moral society within the context of the historical and cultural examples under investigation.

Proponents of character education urge that learners evaluate people from all of human history in light of those qualities that we consider admirable. They encourage educators to help students recognize and appreciate positive character traits and attitudes like those listed above. Qualities like these when taken together form the backbone of good citizenship. When most citizens aspire to these behaviors, the resulting society is the better for it. If students examine these qualities within their various historical contexts and determine whether and why such qualities are desirable, they will have taken the first step toward becoming civic-minded citizens. Houghton Mifflin Social Studies builds opportunity for this sort of examination.

Note how students first look closely at the period they are studying for evidence of civic virtue. From such concrete examples, they move to apply their knowledge to a larger context. Then they may be urged to actually take part in some civic project in their own community.

Because suggestions for character education are presented as natural outgrowths of the material under consideration, students won't feel they are being lectured or preached to. As with other elements of Houghton Mifflin Social Studies, character education is woven seamlessly into the general context. ■

For Further Reading

Boyer, Ernest L. "The Commitment to Character: A Basic Priority for Every School," *Update on Law Related Education* (vol. 20, no. 4) 1996

Character Education (Journal of the California Council for the Social Studies), vol. 37, no. 1, California Council for the Social Studies, 1997.

Haynes C.C. and L. James. *Fostering Civic Virtue: Character Education in the Social Studies,* National Council for the Social Studies, 1996.

Quigley, C.N., et al., *National Standards for Civics and Government,* Center for Civic Education (Calabasas, CA), 1994.

School-to-Career and Social Studies

In the closing years of the twentieth century, national attention becomes increasingly focused on the need for an alliance between the schools and the business world in order to prepare students for life outside the classroom.

With this attention comes the realization that the social studies already lends itself to and assumes responsibility for a large share of this preparation even as it seeks to find suitable channels to do more.

What Is

To speak of rapidly changing technology has become a cliché even as technology speeds ever faster toward the millennium. Employers in a world of work that moves so rapidly will seek applicants not with a particular field of technical expertise but rather with the skills necessary to approach and acquire new knowledge, and to adjust to an ever-changing workplace.

Ability to do this has been and is being fostered in the social studies classroom. Through methods that require formation and use of higher level thinking skills, of teamwork and cooperation, of respect for diversity and what can be learned from one's peers, the social studies classroom is indeed creating an atmosphere that provides learners the kind of liberal education necessary for the workplace of the future. In this workplace, the independent thinkers possessing effective social approaches to problem solving will reap the rewards.

What Is to Come

In addition to developing skills needed in the workplace, Houghton Mifflin Social Studies also offers means for students to deepen understanding of the human heritage connected with work. Note the School-to-Career feature, which appears on the Planning at a Glance pages before every chapter. In the feature, the discussion and suggested activities point out the world of work in a specific time and place and its continued importance in modern life. When appropriate, students trace the evolution of particular jobs up to the present day and may even get a chance to do some field work.

Too often today, with images of multi-million-dollar pro sports contracts and lives of the super models foremost in their minds, young people fail to appreciate—or at times even notice—those who perform and produce essential but less glamorous goods and services. Consistent reference to this School-to-Career feature in the course of instruction can lay realistic foundations and foster growth of respect for honest labor and for the full range of jobs available in the modern society.

Through their inquiry, students can begin to build a work ethic. All of us owe respect and a show of decency to those who perform less glamorous but completely essential jobs. Furthermore, those who prosper in any field will do a better day's work if they have a sense and sympathy for those forebears who dug coal, built roads, or sold trinkets from a pushcart to make a better life for those who followed them.

As stronger links between the schools and the workplace are forged, we can expect these to find reflections in the social studies. Even as this happens, students in today's social studies classroom continue to build strong foundations for the future as they make ready for the one thing they can be sure of—the inevitability of change. ■

For Further Reading

Bonstingl, John J., *Learning for the Future: Building Core Competencies for the 21st Century Through Quality Principles and Practices,* Association for Supervision and Curriculum Development, 1998.

Service Learning, (Social Studies Review vol. 32, no. 2), California Council for the Social Studies, 1997.

HOUGHTON MIFFLIN SOCIAL STUDIES

School-to-Career

The School-to-Career activity in Planning at a Glance before each chapter emphasizes the importance of the work ethic in the development of civilization.

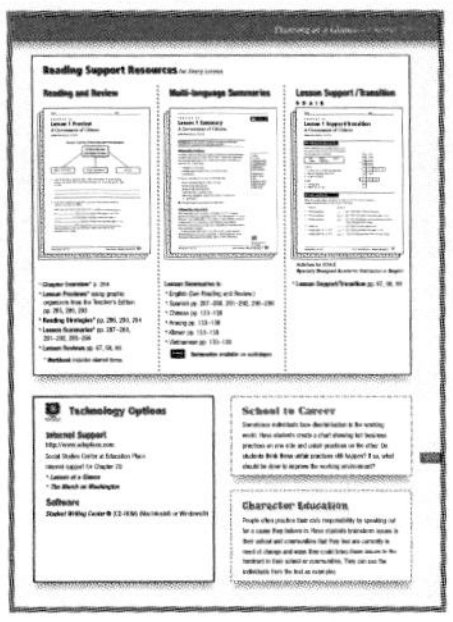

Teaching Multicultural Perspectives

Three important changes in the United States during the last 30 years have profoundly affected the content and methods of social studies education.

First, Asians and Latin Americans are now the largest immigrant groups. Newcomers from these and other parts of the world have dramatically altered the demographic composition of most classrooms.

Second, more than ever before, scholars have focused on the historical and social reality of gender, ethnic and racial groups. This research has resulted in the reevaluation of the roles these groups have played in the making of the United States.

Third, the momentous social and political changes resulting from the civil rights movement and the more recent affirmation of cultural distinctions have led to widespread concern with ethnic and racial identity. Expressions of this concern have ranged from celebration to censure.

Instructional Goals

With today's heightened awareness of cultural diversity, we must address our differences with respect and common sense. Houghton Mifflin Social Studies assists you in fulfilling that task. The multicultural perspectives employed throughout the series promote three important goals.

1. Facilitating readiness to learn in the classroom: Students who find people like themselves in their textbooks will be more at ease in the school setting and will gain the sense of belonging that prepares them to learn. The variety of foreign-born students in today's classroom makes inclusive representation more difficult. Houghton Mifflin Social Studies achieves inclusiveness through empathetic descriptions of the aspirations and achievements of all groups.

2. Providing a more accurate representation of historical events and the world today: To achieve the second goal, the program incorporates the most recent applicable scholarship in history, geography, anthropology, and the other social sciences. The aim is to represent factually the relevant groups and individuals—mainstream or minority—that have contributed to the making of the United States and other nations, while avoiding the suggestion that all cultures have been equally prominent in all times and places. Instructional materials make use of primary sources and quotations to present the positions of the affected actors in their own words. And multiple perspectives provide a stage for students to explore, debate, and make informed judgments regarding contrasting interpretations of human events.

3. Encouraging respect for ethnic, cultural, and social differences: The third goal requires balanced descriptions of ethnic, racial, and religious groups. Group or individual descriptions are scrutinized to avoid language that might appear patronizing, stereotypical, or demeaning. This commitment to accuracy allows exploration of the barriers that have restricted choices for racial and ethnic groups and for women.

Houghton Mifflin Social Studies includes a discussion of religious and ethical beliefs in contexts where such beliefs strongly influence the culture or history of a group. Care is taken that no belief system is ridiculed, trivialized, or portrayed as inferior.

What students read about people from other historical periods and other cultural backgrounds profoundly affects the students' attitudes. The goal of Houghton Mifflin Social Studies is to help students understand and respect all peoples as equals. ■

For Further Reading

Banks, James. *Teaching Strategies for Ethnic Studies.* Boston: Allyn and Bacon, 1991.

Nash Gary. *A Teacher's Guide to Multicultural Perspectives in Social Studies.* Boston: Houghton Mifflin Company, 1991.

Teaching Controversial Issues

In Jesse Stuart's classic American short story, "Split Cherry Tree," a father, angry about the way his son is treated by a teacher and even more so by a curriculum he does not understand, confronts that teacher, demanding some answers.

During the visit—and because the teacher is especially sensitive—the father appreciates what his son is learning and stops fearing the changes that have occurred in the classroom since his own youth.

Would that all problems like this were so beautifully resolved.

Today, with increasing frequency and vehemence, various segments of the public take to task schools and teachers for a variety of issues concerning both what is taught and how this knowledge is imparted. Educators often feel tugged in several directions at once as groups and individuals with varying beliefs insist that theirs is the one true way.

The controversial issue might be one of pedagogy. For example, a parent may demand to know why his or her child should be expected to help the less capable in a cooperative learning situation.

More often, the trigger for such conflict grows directly from course content. A student reacts strongly and emotionally to learning about the Nazi death camps; another is morally outraged to learn that white settlers in the Americas were less than tolerant of the native population. And both talk about their feelings at the dinner table.

The uproar that can result in situations like those just described might be said to be based on a "sin of commission" viewpoint that teachers have opened doors most often left closed and "put ideas in my child's head." At the same time, the profession is vulnerable to accusations of "sins of omission" from another wrathful camp that thinks the instruction is shying away from the upsetting details of human existence that form a less-than-rosy picture.

Addressing the Issues

Although there is no way to guarantee that a social studies program will not evoke some controversy, Houghton Mifflin Social Studies has taken a thoughtful and consistent approach to the problem. While the program does treat potentially controversial issues in a direct manner, it does so within the historical context in which these occur.

Furthermore, during the writing of the textbooks, every effort has been made to examine all issues of content and pedagogy—controversial and otherwise—from differing points of view, thus encouraging learners to develop an awareness of complexity and allowing them to exercise their own judgments once they have the data and experience to do so. Teachers have the comfort of knowing that a wide range of specialists have contributed to the makeup of the text and, in effect, stand with them if they are called upon to defend course content.

Teachers themselves play a role equal in its importance to that of the text. Knowledge of the local community, its political, sociological, racial, national, and ethnic makeup, can go a long way to stop problems before they start.

Whether teachers view controversy as a learning tool or wish to keep distracting controversy at a minimum, Houghton Mifflin Social Studies and the teachers' own good judgment and knowledge of their communities can work together at the task at hand, the education of our young. ■

For Further Reading

Nash, Gary, Charlotte Crabtree, and Ross E. Dunn, *History on Trial: Culture Wars and the Teaching of the Past,* Knopf, 1997.

The Role of Primary Sources and Literature

Primary source material and authentic literature represent the voices of the people of a particular time and place. What better way to study a culture or an event or historical issue than to read about it from the perspective of those living then and there!

In a well-designed social studies curriculum, students come face to face with a full range of human experience in many times and places. To convey the richness of this experience, a textbook must employ a variety of modes of presentation: exposition, narration, description, and visual presentation. The inclusion of literature and primary sources can enhance the effectiveness of all these modes of presentation.

Houghton Mifflin Social Studies integrates literature and primary sources throughout the program. Every unit includes at least one full-length literature selection. In addition, many lessons include shorter excerpts from literature. Most chapters make extensive use of primary sources, such as letters, speeches, diaries, and newspaper accounts as well as official documents. In most grades, the Time/Space Databank also includes a collection of important primary sources. The inclusion of these materials provides students the opportunity to learn how to synthesize information across various sources.

The major function of the literature in Houghton Mifflin Social Studies is to help students develop empathy for the experiences of people in other times and places. Through reading stories, legends, and poems, students can gain insight into the thoughts, feelings, and experiences of people who lived the history they are studying.

Using Literature

The major literature selections in Houghton Mifflin Social Studies are found before or after lessons at their most appropriate point of use. Sometimes literature provides an engaging point of entry for students into a new topic or period. Other times it expands on or exemplifies ideas of events that students have studied in a previous lesson. In either case, the goal is not to have students analyze the literature but rather to have them respond to it in ways that help them

- enrich their understanding of other times and places,
- promote their development of historical empathy,
- broaden their perspectives on historical events, and
- deepen their appreciation of the ways in which events and ideas affect people's daily lives.

The Teacher's Edition notes with each literature selection provide suggested activities and strategies for student response.

In addition, each unit opener spread in the Teacher's Edition lists the titles from the Houghton Mifflin Social Studies Bookshelf II that relate to that unit. Furthermore, on Teacher's Edition pages 43–49, you will find an extensive bibliography that includes other literature appropriate for use with the unit.

Using Primary Sources

Diaries, letters, newspaper accounts, photographs, and other primary documents also let people of the past speak directly to students. Reading these sources exposes students to opposing opinions, alternative points of view, and accounts of how events affected people in various walks of life. In this way, students also begin to develop familiarity with many of the kinds of evidence that historians use and interpret. ■

For More Information

A valuable source of information on recently published literature is the annual bibliography of outstanding children's trade books in the field of social studies that appears in the April/May issue of *Social Education,* published by the National Council for the Social Studies.

Bibliography for Teachers and Students

Bibliography Updates

Each year, new titles are correlated with *A More Perfect Union* and posted on the HMSS web site on Houghton Mifflin's Education Place: **www.eduplace.com.**

UNIT 1
A Land of Promise

Independent Reading

Easy Books

N. C. Wyeth's Pilgrims
by Robert San Souci
Chronicle, 1991 (40p)

Reproductions of Wyeth's murals of Plymouth Colony are accompanied by San Souci's text that clears up some misconceptions. Available in Spanish as *Peregrinos de N. C. Wyeth.*

Tapenum's Day: A Wampanoag Indian Boy in Pilgrim Times
by Kate Waters
Scholastic, 1996 (40p)

Photographed at Plimoth Plantation, this photo-essay reenacts the life of Tapenum, who is training to become a *pniese*, a special warrior prince.

African-Americans in the Thirteen Colonies
by Deborah Kent
Childrens, 1996 (32p)

The author presents an overview of pre-Revolutionary War social conditions and achievements of both free and enslaved African Americans.

Patrick Henry: Voice of the American Revolution
by Louis Sabin
Troll, 1982 (64p) also paper

The book explores the life of this Virginia orator, who was one of the strongest voices for independence.

Average Books

Morning Girl
by Michael Dorris
Hyperion, 1992 (80p) paper

In this portrait of a Native American family, a young Taino girl meets Columbus's landing party off her Bahamian island. Available in Spanish as *Tainos.*

Guests
by Michael Dorris
Hyperion, 1994 (128p) paper

In this coming-of-age story, Moss, a Native American boy, fears that the annual harvest—possibly the first Thanksgiving—will be ruined by guests.

Those Remarkable Women of the American Revolution
by Karen Zeinert
Millbrook, 1996 (96p)

During the Revolution, women made their presence felt in print, on the home front, and on the battlefield.

Challenging Books

Discovering Christopher Columbus: How History Is Invented
by Kathy Pelta
Lerner, 1991 (96p)

The author explains how many now see Columbus's accomplishments in both a positive and a negative light.

Abigail Adams: Witness to a Revolution
by Natalie Bober
Atheneum, 1995 (272p)

In her award-winning biography, Bober tells how Abigail Adams kept her husband John informed of events in Boston while he served in the Continental Congress.

My Brother Sam Is Dead
by James Lincoln Collier and Christopher Collier
Simon & Schuster, 1974 (224p) also paper

In this award-winning classic, the Revolutionary War has a wrenching effect on one nonpartisan family from Redding, Connecticut.

Samuel Adams: The Father of American Independence
by Dennis Brindell Fradin
Clarion, 1998 (192p)

Adams, thought by many to be an unlikely revolutionary, worked tirelessly behind the scenes to achieve American independence.

Books to Read Aloud

The Arrow Over the Door
by Joseph Bruchac
Dial, 1998 (96p)

Based on a true incident, this story tells of the meeting of an Abenaki boy who thinks all Americans are enemies and a young American who is scorned for his Quaker beliefs.

The Winter of Red Snow: The Revolutionary War Diary of Abigail Jane Stewart
by Kristiana Gregory
Scholastic, 1996 (174p)

In her diary, a young girl recounts how she and her family helped George Washington at Valley Forge.

Books for Teachers

Struggle for a Continent: The French and Indian Wars: 1690–1760
by Albert Marrin
Atheneum, 1987 (232p)

The author-historian explains the four wars that led to English supremacy in the colonies.

Who Was Who in the American Revolution
by L. Edward Purcell
Facts on File, 1993 (560p)

With 1500 entries, this reference covers everyone from major military leaders to infamous spies and traitors.

Bibliography for Teachers and Students

Multimedia Resources

Videocassettes

Beginnings of Exploration: Why did Europe "Discover" America in 1492? 18 min.
Age of Exploration Series
Encyclopaedia Britannica, 1990

American Indians: A Brief History 22 min.
National Geographic, 1985

Colonizing North America: Early Settlements 18 min.
Colonial and Founding Period Series
Encyclopaedia Britannica, 1990

Count Down to Independence: Causes of the American Revolution 22 min.
Rainbow Educational Media, 1990

American Revolution: Rebellion and Preparing to Fight 16 min.
AIMS Multimedia, 1993

Software

Paths to Freedom: The American Revolution (CD-ROM)
Encyclopaedia Britannica, 1995

Geography Search (Floppy Disk)
Tom Snyder Productions, 1993

World Geo Graph II (Floppy Disk)
The Learning Company, 1993

Real Picture World Atlas (CD-ROM)
Now What Software, 1995

UNIT 2
The Constitution of the United States

Independent Reading

Easy Books

A More Perfect Union: The Story of Our Consitituion
by Betsy Maestro
Lothrop, 1990 (48p) paper

This easy-to-read book explains simply how and why the Constitition was written. Available in Spanish as *Union mas perfecta.*

Shh! We're Writing the Constitution
by Jean Fritz
Putnam, 1987 (64p) also paper

The author focuses on the events in 1787 when delegates gathered to write the United State Constitution.

John Adams: Brave Patriot
by Laurence Santrey
Troll, 1986 (48p)

This biography of the outspoken and decisive Adams shows how he served his country in many ways.

Average Books

The Great Little Madison
by Jean Fritz
Putnam, 1989 (160p)

The author's exceptional book on Madison focuses on his personal and political lives and his determination to make the Constitution work.

Ben Franklin of Old Philadelphia
by Margaret Cousins
Random, 1981 (160p) also paper

This lively biography reveals the American statesman who was also an inventor, an author, and a printer.

Constitutional Amendments
by Barbara S. Feinberg
Twenty-First Century, 1996 (64p)

The author looks at the twenty-seven amendments that have been ratified since the Constitution was framed over two hundred years ago.

Challenging Books

Who Were the Founding Fathers? Two Hundred Years of Inventing American History
by Steven H. Jaffe
Holt, 1996 (227p)

Jaffe examines the on-going debate about who should really be considered founders of our country.

Books to Read Aloud

Ben and Me
by Robert Lawson
Little, 1939 (139p) also paper

In this well-known classic, Amos, the mouse, tells the story of Benjamin Franklin and his career, including his role in framing the Constitution.

Books for Teachers

Our Changing Constitution: How and Why We Have Changed It
by Isobel V. Morin
Millbrook, 1998 (176p)

This helpful reference book explains how and why the twenty-six amendments were made to the United States Constitution.

Multimedia Resources

Videocassettes

Against the Tide: Debating the Constitution 16 min.
New Dimension Media, 1992

Bibliography for Teachers and Students

UNIT 3
Establishing the New Nation

Independent Reading

Easy Books

The White House
by Leonard Everett Fisher
Holiday, 1989 (96p)

The author details the abandonment of the White House by the Madisons during the War of 1812, the looting and burning of the White House, and its subsequent rebuilding.

Old Ironsides: America Builds a Fighting Ship
by David Weitzman
Houghton Mifflin, 1997 (32p)

Using historical facts, black-and-white drawings, and a fictional eyewitness, Weitzman tells the story of the first frigate in the American Navy, the *U. S. S. Constitution*, later nicknamed "Old Ironsides."

The Amazing Impossible Erie Canal
by Cheryl Harness
Simon & Schuster, 1995 (32p)

Harness tells the history of the building of the Canal, from its groundbreaking in 1817, through the years it was known as "Clinton's Ditch," to its completion in 1825.

Only the Name Remains: The Cherokees and the Trail of Tears
by Alex W. Bealer
Little, 1996 (79p)

From 1837 to 1839, the Cherokees were forced to march from Georgia to Arkansas, when approximately a quarter of them died.

Average Books

The War of 1812
by Kathlyn and Martin Gay
Twenty-First Century, 1996 (64p)

Maps and reproductions, as well as quotations from primary sources, help detail the causes and outcomes of this war.

A Gathering of Days: A New England Girl's Journal 1830–32
by Joan W. Blos
Scribner, 1979 (144p) also paper

In this Newbery-winning novel, a thirteen-year-old girl records the events in her life on a New Hampshire farm, including aiding a runaway slave.

These Lands Are Ours: Tecumseh's Fight for the Old Northwest
by Kate Connell
Steck-Vaughn, 1993 (96p)

The Shawnee chief travels to other tribes in an effort to unite them against the encroaching white settlers.

Challenging Books

1812: The War Nobody Won
by Albert Marrin
Atheneum, 1985 (190p)

Marrin's lively book includes interesting details and anecdotes about the British, the Americans, and the Native Americans involved in the War of 1812.

Andrew Jackson and His America
by Milton Meltzer
Watts, 1993 (207p)

This biography of America's first Western president explores not only Jackson's life but also the history of that period and the ongoing significance of events during his presidency.

Sequoya's Gift: A Portrait of the Cherokee Leader
by Janet Klausner
Harper, 1993 (240p)

After teaching himself to write, Sequoya introduced written language to his people, making almost all of them literate within months.

Books to Read Aloud

The Last of the Mohicans
by James Fenimore Cooper
Dutton, 1962 (432p)

Cooper's classic tells the story of a man who faces a overwhelming moral dilemma. Other editions available.

Books for Teachers

After the Trail of Tears: The Cherokees' Struggle for Sovereignty, 1830–1880
by William G. McLoughlin
U. of North Carolina, 1993

The author traces the history of the Cherokee Nation during the forty years after its members were resettled in what is now Oklahoma.

Multimedia Resources

Videocassettes

Remaking Society in the New Nation 21 min.
Colonial and Founding Period Series
Encyclopaedia Britannica, 1991

American Indians: A Brief History 22 min.
National Geographic, 1985

Northeast 60 min.
Native American Series
Ambrose Video,, 1994

Southeast 60 min.
Native American Series
Ambrose Video, 1994

Southwest 60 min.
Native American Series
Ambrose Video, 1994

Island of Hope, Island of Tears 28 min.
New Dimension Media, 1990

Language of Editorial Cartoons 18 min.
Knowledge Unlimited, 1992

Bibliography for Teachers and Students

UNIT 4
The Development of America's Regions

Independent Reading

Easy Books

My Name Is York
by Elizabeth Van Steenwyck
Rising Moon, 1997 (32p)

York, the slave who traveled freely with Lewis and Clark on their expedition, was again enslaved when the journey was completed.

Reflections of a Black Cowboy Series
by Robert Miller
Silver, 1991 (104p) paper

This series about African Americans in the West consists of *Reflections of a a Black Cowboy, Buffalo Soldiers, Cowboys,* and *Mountain Men.*

Brigham Young: Mormon and Pioneer Leader
by William R. Sanford and Carl R. Green
Enslow, 1996 (48p)

The author recounts the life of the leader of the Mormons, who led them into what is now Utah.

Average Books

Black Frontiers: A History of African American Heroes in the Old West
by Lillian Schlissel
Simon & Schuster, 1995 (78p)

The author focuses on the African Americans who went west as soldiers, homesteaders, and mountain men, with biographical sketches of Jim Beckwourth, Stagecoach Mary, Bill Pickett, Biddy Mason, and others.

On to Oregon!
by Honoré Morrow
Morrow, 1991 (240p) paper

This enduring classic tells the story of the six brave Sager children who traveled alone to Oregon in 1848 after their parents died along the way.

Daily Life on a Southern Plantation
by Paul Erickson
Lodestar, 1998 (48p)

Life on a plantation in 1853 is seen through the eyes of slaves Daddy Major, Rosena, Scipio, and Cicero and their owners, the Henderson family.

Challenging Books

The Ballad of Lucy Whipple
by Karen Cushman
Clarion, 1996 (208p)

When her mother moves the family to a California mining town, a miserable Lucy finds comfort in books and letters while planning how to get back home to Massachusetts.

Lyddie
by Katherine Paterson
Lodestar, 1991 (192p) also paper

This historical novel focuses on three years in the life of Lyddie Worthen, who worked in the factories of Lowell, Massachusetts.

The Middle Passage White Ships/Black Cargo
by Tom Feelings
Dial, 1995 (80p)

Author-illustrator Tom Feelings uses pen-and-ink drawings to convey the horror of the Middle Passage.

Books to Read Aloud

A Line in the Sand: The Alamo Diary of Lucinda Lawrence, Gonzales, Texas, 1835
by Sherry Garland
Scholastic, 1998 (148p)

In her diary, young Lucinda records one of the most important events in her life and in the history of Texas.

Frederick Douglass: In His Own Words
by Milton Meltzer
Harcourt, 1995 (240p)

Meltzer has selected speeches and editorials written by the abolitionist ex-slave.

Books for Teachers

Undaunted Courage: Meriwether Lewis, Thomas Jefferson, and the Opening of the American West
by Stephen E. Ambrose
Simon & Schuster, 1996

This highly acclaimed biography of Lewis discusses not only his life but also details his trip with William Clark and the importance of their journey.

Gold Rush Women
by Claire Murphy and Jane Haigh
Alaska Northwest, 1997 (126p)

The authors draw on primary sources to tell the usually-ignored stories of women who joined the gold rushes in the Yukon and Alaska.

Far From Home: Families of the Westward Journey
by Lillian Schlissel, Byrd Gibbons, and Elizabeth Hampsten
Schocken, 1990

Letters and diaries reveal the stories of three families traveling west.

Multimedia Resources

Videocassettes

Industrial Revolution 30 min.
United Learning, 1994

Erie Canal 21 min.
Phoenix/BFA, 1990

South Central Region 20 min
U. S. Geography: From Sea to Shining Sea Series
Journal Films, 1995

Lewis and Clark 15 min.
Landmarks of Western Expansion Series
Agency for Instructional Technology, 1991

Heritage of the Black West 25 min.
National Geographic, 1995

Rancho Life 23 min.
American History Series
Barr Films, 1992

Bibliography for Teachers and Students

UNIT 5
The Nation Divides and Reunites

Independent Reading

Easy Books

The Day Fort Sumter Was Fired On: A Photo History of the Civil War
by Jim Haskins
Scholastic, 1995 (96p) paper

Photos capture life on the front lines and show the war's effects on people on the homefront.

Pink and Say
by Patricia Polacco
Putnam, 1994 (48p) also paper

Based on actual events, this story recounts the story of an African American Union soldier who saves the life of a white fellow soldier but is later hanged at Andersonville. Available in Spanish as *Pink y Say.*

Charley Skedaddle
by Patricia Beatty
Morrow, 1987 (192p) also paper

In this story based on documented material, a New York boy who deserts after a battle in Virginia fears he will forever be branded a coward.

Average Books

Undying Glory: The Story of the Massachusetts 54th Regiment
by Clinton Cox
Scholastic, 1993 (176) also paper

Archival photos accompany this story of the African American regiment who fought in the Union Army.

A Separate Battle: Women and the Civil War
by Ina Chang
Lodestar, 1991 (112p) also paper

During the Civl War, women fought in battles and assumed other unfamiliar and surprising new roles.

The Long Road to Gettysburg
by Jim Murphy
Clarion, 1992 (128p)

The Battle of Gettysburg is seen through the eyes of a sixteen-year-old Confederate lieutenant and and an eighteen-year-old Union soldier.

Challenging Books

Fiery Vision: The Life and Death of John Brown
by Clinton Cox
Scholastic, 1997(230p)

The author recounts the life of the controversial abolitionist who led the raid on Harpers Ferry.

Unconditional Surrender: U. S. Grant and the Civil War
by Albert Marrin
Atheneum, 1994 (208p)

In this award-winning biography, Marrin discusses Grant's pivotal role in the Civil War and points out many of the ironies of his life.

Virginia's General: Robert E. Lee and the Civil War
by Albert Marrin
Atheneum, 1995 (192p)

This biography that begins with Lee's refusal to lead the U. S. Army also contains many personal details about his life.

Books to Read Aloud

Across Five Aprils
by Irene Hunt
Berkeley, 1986 (100p) paper; other editions

In this classic story, Jethro, the youngest son of an Illinois farm family, is the only surviving son after the Civil War ends.

Bull Run
by Paul Fleischman
Harper, 1993 (112p) also paper

The drama of the Civil War is told through the lives and thoughts of sixteen people who were all involved in the Battle of Bull Run.

Voices from the Civil War: A Documentary History of the Great American Conflict
by Milton Meltzer
Harper, 1992 (224p) paper

Life during the Civil War is reflected through letters, newspaper articles, diaries, interviews, and speeches.

Books for Teachers

The Civil War
by Geoffrey C. Ward, Ric Burns, and Ken Burns
Vintage, 1994

The book, based on the PBS television series, features narratives from men and women who lived through the war, and essays by current historians.

Chickamauga and Other Civil War Stories
edited by Shelby Foote
Delta, 1993 (241p) paper

This re-issued collection contains Civil War stories by William Faulkner, Thomas Wolfe, F. Scott Fitzgerald, Stephen Crane, Ambrose Bierce, Eudora Welty, and Mark Twain.

Multimedia Resources

Videocassettes

With Malice Towards None: Lincoln's Second Inaugural Address 27 min.
American Documents Series
Learning Corporation, 1991

The Civil War Journal Series
48 min. each
A & E Home Video, 1991

The Massachusetts 54th Colored Infantry 58 min.
PBS Video, 1991

Steal Away: The Harriet Tubman Story 58 min.
PBS Video, 1991

Software

House Divided: The Lincoln-Douglas Debates (CD-ROM)
Grafica Multimedia, 1995

Bibliography for Teachers and Students

UNIT 6
A Time of Transformation

Independent Reading

Easy Books

The Nez Percé
by Virginia Driving Hawk Sneve
Holiday, 1994

Sneve writes about the history, culture, and legends of the Nez Percé. By the same author, see also *The Apaches* and *The Sioux.*

Going Home to Nicodemus
by Daniel Chu and Bill Shaw
Silver, 1995 (64p)

After the Civil War, a group of freed slaves headed west and founded what is now the oldest all-black town west of the Mississippi: Nicodemus, Kansas.

The Triangle Factory Fire
by Victoria Sherrow
Millbrook, 1995 (64p)

The catastrophic fire in the Triangle Shirtwaist Factory in New York in 1911 that killed over a hundred people, mostly young women, led to strict safety reforms.

Average Books

The Life and Death of Crazy Horse
by Russell Freedman
Holiday, 1996 (144p)

Called the greatest of the Teton Sioux warriors, Crazy Horse, who grew from a shy youth to a warrior desperately trying to save his people, defeated Custer in the Battle of Little Bighorn.

Full Steam Ahead: The Race to Build a Transcontinental Railroad
by Rhoda Blumberg
National Geographic, 1996 (160p)

Beatty looks at the politics around the signing of the Pacific Railroad Act in 1862 and its consequences for American history.

Bound for the Promised Land: The Great Black Migration
by Michael L. Cooper
Lodestar, 1995 (96p)

In the early 1900s, there was an exodus of African Americans from the South to northern cities in search of better opportunities.

Challenging Books

Prairie Songs
by Pam Conrad
Harper, 1993 (176p) paper

Louisa views pioneer life differently after the arrival of a doctor and his frail wife, who cannot endure the hardships and loneliness of the prairie.

We Shall Not Be Moved: The Women's Factory Strike of 1909
by Joan Dash
Scholastic, 1996 (166p)

The author describes the inhumane conditions in Manhattan's shirtwaist factories that caused immigrant women workers to strike.

Getting the Real Story: Nelly Bly and Ida B. Wells
by Sue Davidson
Seal Press, 1992 (160p) paper

The author looks at the similitaries in the careers of two pioneer women in the field of journalism.

Books to Read Aloud

Tales from Gold Mountain: Stories of the Chinese in the New World
by Paul Yee
Macmillan, 1990 (80p)

Eight original stories tell the experiences of Chinese immigrants in the United States.

Dreams in the Golden Country: The Diary of Zipporah Feldman, a Jewish Immigrant Girl
by Kathryn Lasky
Scholastic, 1998 (144p)

Zipporah keeps a diary when she and her family emigrate from Russia to New York in 1903.

Books for Teachers

Bury My Heart at Wounded Knee: An Indian History of the American West
by Dee Brown
Holt, 1981

A Native American looks at the systematic decimation of the Native American population in the second half of the nineteenth century.

Cowboys, Indians, and Gunfighters: The Story of the Cattle Kingdom
by Albert Marrin
Atheneum, 1993 (208p)

Beginning with the arrival of the first cattle from Spain in 1521, Marrin gives a realistic look at the people and events that shaped the development of the West.

Multimedia Resources

Videocassettes

Iron Road: The Story of America's First Transcontinental Railroad
60 min.
Zenger Productions, 1990

Americans Build the Panama Canal 1901–1914 20 min.
Agency for Instructional Technology, 1991

Plains II 60 min.
Native American Series
Ambrose Video, 1994

Software

The Genius of Edison (CD-ROM)
Compton's NewMedia, 1996

Bibliography for Teachers and Students

UNIT 7
The Promise Continues

Independent Reading

Easy Books

Cesar Chavez: Leader for Migrant Farm Workers
by Doreen Gonzales
Enslow, 1996 (128p)

The author records the life and accomplishments of Chavez.

One Nation, Many Tribes: How Kids Live in Milwaukee's Indian Community
by Kathleen Krull
Dutton, 1995 (48p)

This photo essay captures the everyday lives of Indian youngsters living in Milwaukee today.

The Lotus Seed
by Sherry Garland
Harcourt, 1993 (32p)

The lotus is the symbol that keeps a young immigrant girl and her grandmother in touch with their Vietnamese heritage.

Average Books

Samurai of Gold Hill
by Yoshiko Uchida
Creative Arts, 1985 (128p)

Koichi and his samurai father come to America in the days following the gold rush to establish a tea and silk farm.

Beyond the Western Sea: Book One—Escape from Home
by Avi
Orchard, 1996 (295p) also paper

After their landlord destroys their home, Maura and Patrick leave Ireland and sail for America and, during their voyage, encounter their landlord's son, who has run away from his unhappy home. See also *Beyond the Western Sea: Book Two—Lord Kirkle's Money.*

Letters from Rifka
by Karen Hesse
Holt, 1992 (160p) Puffin paper

Migrating to America from Russia, twelve-year-old Rifka, in sight of the Statue of Liberty, fears she will not be allowed to enter the country because of an ailment that caused her to lose her hair.

The Watsons Go to Birmingham—1963
by Christopher Paul Curtis
Delacorte, 1995 (210p)

In this award-winning novel, an African American family visiting Birmingham, Alabama, is profoundly affected when a bomb kills three little girls in an African American church.

Challenging Books

Fitting In
by Anilu Bernardo
Piñata Books, 1996 (200p)

In these stories, five Cuban immigrant girls living in Florida tell of the difficulties of adjusting to a bicultural life.

American Dragons: Twenty-Five Asian American Voices
collected by Laurence Yep
Harper, 1993 (256p) also paper

Americans of Tibetan, Korean, Thai, Chinese, and Japanese descent use poetry and stories to tell about growing up, fitting in, and relating to previous generations.

Books to Read Aloud

I Was Dreaming to Come to America: Memories from the Ellis Island Oral History Project
selected by Veronica Lawlor
Viking, 1995 (40p)

Presented here are recollections of fifteen immigrants, including eight children, who came through Ellis Island in the 1920s.

Now Is Your Time: The African American Struggle for Freedom
by Walter Dean Myers
Harper, 1991 (292p) also paper

In his history of African Americans in this country, Myers also tells the stories of many outstanding people and encourages the reader to continue the quest for justice.

Books for Teachers

Aiiieeeee! An Anthology of Asian American Writers
edited by Frank Chin
New American Library, 1991

This collection contains Asian American literature from the 1870s to the present.

Latinos in the Making of the United States
by James D. Cockcroft
Watts, 1995 (176p)

Cockcroft discusses the vital roles still being played in America's history by Mexican Americans, South Americans, Cubans, Puerto Ricans, Dominicans, and Central Americans.

Multimedia Resources

Videocassettes

Martin Luther King: Letters from a Birmingham Jail 26 min.
American Documents Series
Learning Corporation, 1988

Brown vs Board of Education 19 min.
American Documents Series
Learning Corporation, 1988

Pride and Prejudice: A History of Black Culture in America 20 min.
Knowledge Unlimited, 1993

African American Artists: Affirmation Today 28 min.
Crystal Productions, 1995

Our World, Many Worlds: Hispanic Diversity in the US 22 min.
Rainbow Educational Media, 1993

Software

Decisions, Decisions: Immigration (Floppy Disk)
Tom Snyder Productions, 1996

Decisions, Decisions: Prejudice (Floppy Disk)
Tom Snyder Productions, 1996

GTV: American People: Fabric of a Nation (Computer-interactive Videodisc)
National Geographic, 1993

We the people of the United States,
in order to form ***a more perfect union,***
establish justice, insure domestic tranquility,
provide for the common defense,
promote the general welfare,
and secure the blessings of liberty to
ourselves and our posterity,
do ordain and establish this Constitution for
the United States of America.

Preamble to the U.S. Constitution

Beverly J. Armento
Jacqueline M. Córdova
J. Jorge Klor de Alva
Gary B. Nash
Franklin Ng
Christopher L. Salter
Louis E. Wilson
Karen K. Wixson

A More Perfect Union

Houghton Mifflin Company • Boston
Atlanta • Dallas • Geneva, Illinois • Princeton, New Jersey • Palo Alto

Consultants

Program Consultants

Edward Castillo
Department of Native American Studies
Sonoma State University
Rohnert Park, CA

Thelma Foote
Department of History
University of California, Irvine
Irvine, CA

Stephen Fugita
Department of Psychology
Santa Clara University
Santa Clara, CA

Charles Haynes
Senior Scholar for Religious Freedom
Freedom Forum First Amendment Center
Arlington, VA

Shabbir Mansuri
Director
Council on Islamic Education
Fountain Valley, CA

Doug Monroy
Department of Southwest Studies
The Colorado College
Colorado Springs, CO

Cliff Trafzer
Department of History and Ethnic Studies
Director of Native American Studies
University of California, Riverside
Riverside, CA

Teacher Reviewers

David E. Beer (Grade 5)
Weisser Park Elementary
Fort Wayne, Indiana

Jan Coleman (Grades 6–7)
Thornton Junior High
Fremont, California

Shawn Edwards (Grades 1–3)
Jackson Park Elementary
University City, Missouri

Barbara J. Fech (Grade 6)
Martha Ruggles School
Chicago, Illinois

Deborah M. Finkel (Grade 4)
Los Angeles Unified School District, Region G
South Pasadena, California

Jim Fletcher (Grade 5)
La Loma Junior High
Modesto, California

Susan M. Gilliam (Grade 1)
Roscoe Elementary
Los Angeles, California

Vicki Stroud Gonterman (Grade 2)
Gibbs International Studies Magnet School
Little Rock, Arkansas

Lorraine Hood (Grade 2)
Fresno Unified School District
Fresno, California

Jean Jamgochian (Grade 5)
Haycock Gifted and Talented Center
Fairfax County, Virginia

Michael Kerwin (Grade 8)
Nativity School
Orchard Park, New York

Susan Kirk-Davalt (Grade 5)
Crowfoot Elementary
Lebanon, Oregon

Mary Molyneaux-Leahy (Grade 3)
Bridgeport Elementary
Bridgeport, Pennsylvania

Sharon Oviatt (Grades 1–3)
Keysor Elementary
Kirkwood, Missouri

Jayne B. Perala (Grade 1)
Cave Spring Elementary
Roanoke, Virginia

Carol Siefkin (K)
Garfield Elementary
Sacramento, California

Norman N. Tanaka (Grade 3)
Martin Luther King Jr. Elementary
Sacramento, California

John Tyler (Grade 5)
Groton School
Groton, Massachusetts

Portia W. Vaughn (Grades 1–3)
School District 11
Colorado Springs, Colorado

Acknowledgments

Grateful acknowledgment is made for the use of the material listed below.

The material in the Minipedia is reprinted from *The World Book Encyclopedia* with the expressed permission of the publisher. © 1998 by World Book, Inc.

–Continued on page 733.

Printed in the U.S.A.

ISBN: 0-395-93067-7
123456789-VH-04 03 02 01 00 99 98

Development by Ligature, Inc.

From Your Authors

James Madison of Virginia was always early. A short man with a serious expression, he was the first delegate to ride into Philadelphia in May 1787. Deeply concerned about the politics of the new nation, Madison had been reading and reflecting on the subject of constitutional government day and night.

So begins an account of the writing of the Constitution of the United States. Twelve of the original 13 states sent delegates to the convention. In Chapter 4 of this book, you will read more about the debates and the compromises that resulted in the signing of this important document. The Constitution continues to this day to direct the running of our nation.

Most of the people you will meet in this book lived long ago in places that may seem very far away from home. But they all had feelings just like yours and faced many of the same challenges you will face in your life. And whether they were great leaders or ordinary people, their decisions and actions helped shape the world you live in.

As you read about these people, places, and events, we hope you will ask many questions. Some questions may be about history: "What caused these people to make the decisions they did?" or "How do we know about these events?" Other questions may be about geography: "What are the land and weather like in that place?" or "Why did people choose to settle there?" Still other questions may be about economics: "How did people meet their needs for food and shelter?" or "How did people work out ways for using scarce resources?"

Most of all, we hope you catch the excitement of thinking, questioning, and discovering answers about your world—now and in the twenty-first century.

Beverly J. Armento
Professor of Social Studies Education
Department of Middle/Secondary Education and Instructional Technology
Georgia State University

Jacqueline M.K. Córdova
Professor of Spanish and TESOL
Department of Foreign Languages and Literatures
California State University, Fullerton

J. Jorge Klor de Alva
President
University of Phoenix

Gary B. Nash
Professor of History
University of California, Los Angeles

Franklin Ng
Professor of Anthropology
California State University, Fresno

Christopher L. Salter
Professor and Chair
Department of Geography
University of Missouri

Louis E. Wilson
Associate Professor and Chair
Department of African American Studies
Smith College

Karen K. Wixson
Professor of Education
University of Michigan

Contents

OUR
CHAMPIONS
1888
HOME

Understanding Skills

Each "Understanding Skills" feature gives you the opportunity to learn and practice a skill related to the topic you are studying.

Understanding Concepts

Each "Understanding Concepts" feature gives you more information about a concept that is important to the lesson you are reading.

Making Decisions

Much of history is made of people's decisions. These pages take you step-by-step through fascinating problems from history and today. What will you decide?

Exploring

The story of the past is hidden all around you in the world of the present. "Exploring" pages tell you the secrets of how to find it.

Literature

Throughout history people have expressed their deepest feelings and beliefs through literature. Reading these stories, legends, poems, and shorter passages that appear in the lessons will help you experience what life was like for people of other times and places.

Primary Sources

Reading the exact words of the people who made and lived history is the best way to get a sense of how they saw themselves and the times in which they lived. You will find more than 50 primary sources throughout this book including the following:

A Closer Look

Take a closer look at the objects and pictures spread out on these special pages. With the clues you see, you'll become a historical detective.

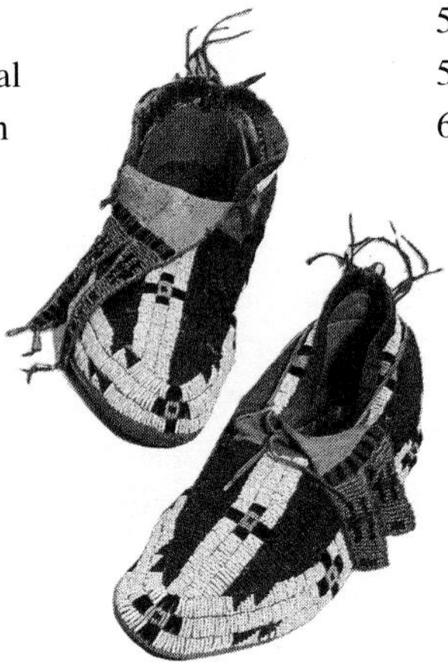

A Moment in Time

A person from the past is frozen at an exciting moment. You'll get to know these people by reading about where they are, what they're wearing, and the objects around them.

Charts, Diagrams, and Timelines

These visual presentations of information help give you a clearer picture of the people, places, and events you are studying.

Maps

The events of history have been shaped by the places in which they occurred. Each map in this book tells its own story about these events and places.

Starting Out

What makes this textbook so much more interesting than others you've used before? In this book, the people of the past speak directly to you, through their actual words and the objects they used. You'll walk inside their houses and look inside their cooking pots. You'll follow them as they go to school, build cities, fight wars, work out settlements for peace.

From unit to chapter to lesson—each step lets you see history in closer detail. The photos show you where events happened. The art introduces you to the people. The lower timeline on the chapter opener names the U.S. presidents of this period.

When and what? The timeline at the beginning of each lesson tells you when these events took place. The lesson title tells you what the lesson is about.

1790 1839 1850 1860

LESSON 3

The Changing World of American Indians

The only way to check and stop this evil is for all the red men to unite in claiming a common and equal right in the land . . . for it never was divided, but belongs to all, for the use of each.... No part has a right to sell, even to each other, much less to strangers.

So spoke Shawnee chief Tecumseh (*ti KUM se*) as he condemned and canceled the sale of Indian land to the U.S. government in 1809. Tecumseh had enlisted southern and northern warriors along the Mississippi Valley for a major united effort to recover lands lost to the white people. He was determined to hold the Ohio River as the boundary dividing the United States and Indian country.

As governor of the Indiana Territory, William Henry Harrison was also determined to defend white pioneers who invaded and settled in Indian territories. In 1810, Harrison met the Shawnee leader face to face at Vincennes, Indiana. As their talks began, Harrison's interpreter told Tecumseh, "Your father requests you to take a chair." Angrily Tecumseh replied, "My father! The sun is my father, and the earth is my mother..." Tecumseh spoke forcefully to Harrison of the position of the Indians.

He argued that the U.S. government had no real right to lands ceded, or transferred, to whites without the consent of all American Indians. Tecumseh shouted, "Sell a country! Why not sell the air, the clouds, and the great sea?"

The Great Spirit gave this great island to his red children. He placed the whites on the other side of the big water. They were not contented with their own, but came to take ours from us. They have driven us from the sea to the lakes—we can go no farther."

THINKING FOCUS

What were the different responses of the various American Indian peoples when their ancestral lands were threatened?

Key Terms

- revitalization
- cultural accommodation

Tecumseh is shown here saving American prisoners during the War of 1812.

201

People of the New Nation

Right from the beginning the lesson opener pulls you into the sights, the sounds, the smells of what life was like at that time, in that place.

Every age has its great storytellers. Each chapter includes short examples of fine writing from or about the period. Here Tecumseh's words are part of the oral tradition, but are literature nevertheless. The literature is always printed on a tan background with a blue initial letter and a multicolored bar.

Like a road sign, the question that always appears here tells you what to think about while you read the lesson.

Look for these terms. They are listed here so that you can watch out for them. The first time they appear in the lesson they are shown in heavy black print and defined. Key terms are also defined in the Glossary.

The titles outline the lesson. The red titles tell you the main topics discussed in the lesson on "The Changing World of American Indians." The blue titles tell you the subtopics.

Every map tells a story. The maps in this book tell the story of where people like the relocated Indian tribes came from, where they went, and what the land was like.

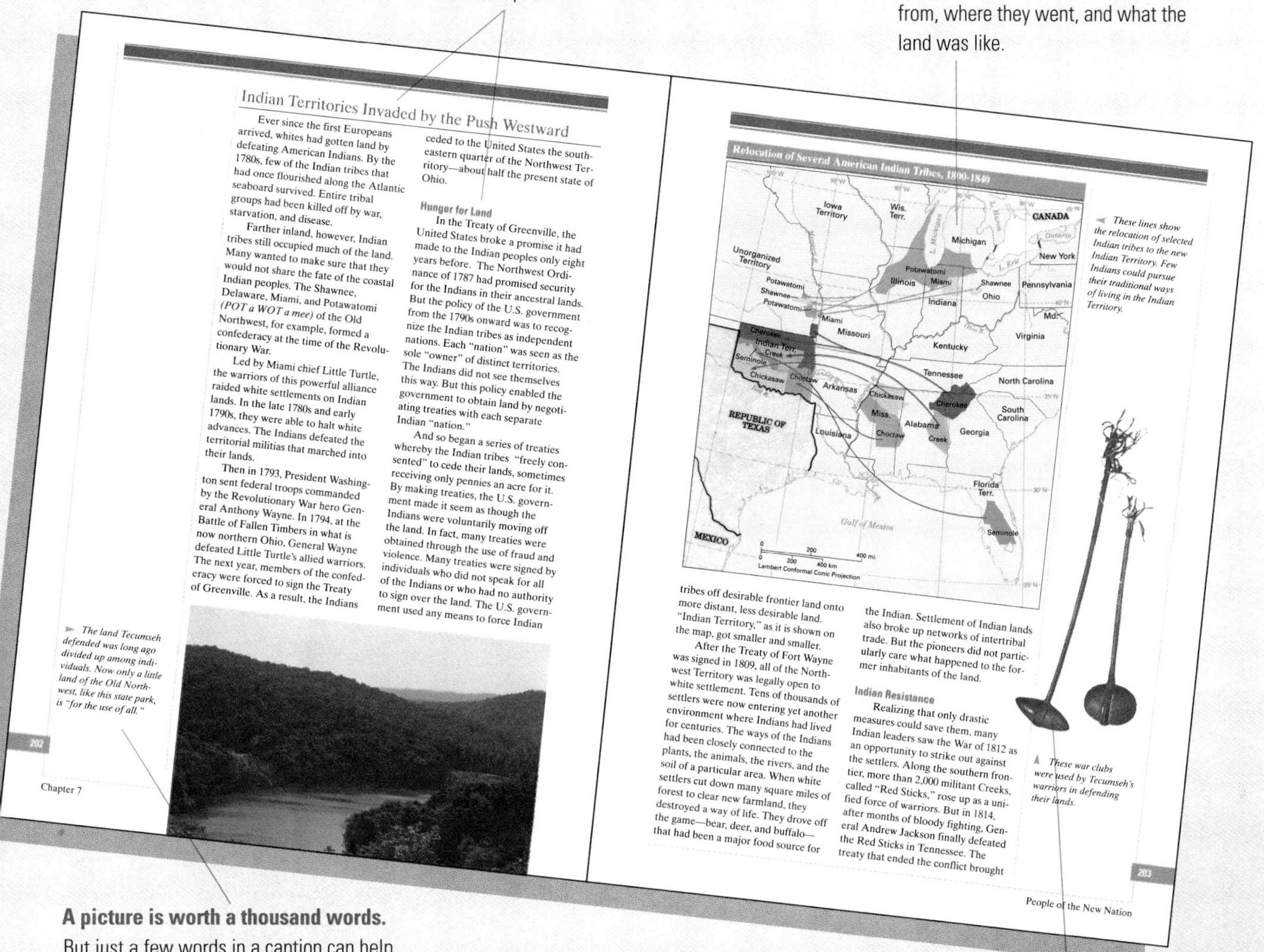

Indian Territories Invaded by the Push Westward

Ever since the first Europeans arrived, whites had gotten land by defeating American Indians. By the 1780s, few of the Indian tribes that had once flourished along the Atlantic seaboard survived. Entire tribal groups had been killed off by war, starvation, and disease.

Farther inland, however, Indian tribes still occupied much of the land. Many wanted to make sure that they would not share the fate of the coastal Indian peoples. The Shawnee, Delaware, Miami, and Potawatomi *(POT a WOT a mee)* of the Old Northwest, for example, formed a confederacy at the time of the Revolutionary War.

Led by Miami chief Little Turtle, the warriors of this powerful alliance raided white settlements on Indian lands. In the late 1780s and early 1790s, they were able to halt white advances. The Indians defeated the territorial militias that marched into their lands.

Then in 1793, President Washington sent federal troops commanded by the Revolutionary War hero General Anthony Wayne. In 1794, at the Battle of Fallen Timbers in what is now northern Ohio, General Wayne defeated Little Turtle's allied warriors. The next year, members of the confederacy were forced to sign the Treaty of Greenville. As a result, the Indians ceded to the United States the southeastern quarter of the Northwest Territory—about half the present state of Ohio.

Hunger for Land

In the Treaty of Greenville, the United States broke a promise it had made to the Indian peoples only eight years before. The Northwest Ordinance of 1787 had promised security for the Indians in their ancestral lands. But the policy of the U.S. government from the 1790s onward was to recognize the Indian tribes as independent nations. Each "nation" was seen as the sole "owner" of distinct territories. The Indians did not see themselves this way. But this policy enabled the government to obtain land by negotiating treaties with each separate Indian "nation."

And so began a series of treaties whereby the Indian tribes "freely consented" to cede their lands, sometimes receiving only pennies an acre for it. By making treaties, the U.S. government made it seem as though the Indians were voluntarily moving off the land. In fact, many treaties were obtained through the use of fraud and violence. Many treaties were signed by individuals who did not speak for all of the Indians or who had no authority to sign over the land. The U.S. government used any means to force Indian tribes off desirable frontier land onto more distant, less desirable land. "Indian Territory," as it is shown on the map, got smaller and smaller.

After the Treaty of Fort Wayne was signed in 1809, all of the Northwest Territory was legally open to white settlement. Tens of thousands of settlers were now entering yet another environment where Indians had lived for centuries. The ways of the Indians had been closely connected to the plants, the animals, the rivers, and the soil of a particular area. When white settlers cut down many square miles of forest to clear new farmland, they destroyed a way of life. They drove off the game—bear, deer, and buffalo—that had been a major food source for the Indian. Settlement of Indian lands also broke up networks of intertribal trade. But the pioneers did not particularly care what happened to the former inhabitants of the land.

Indian Resistance

Realizing that only drastic measures could save them, many Indian leaders saw the War of 1812 as an opportunity to strike out against the settlers. Along the southern frontier, more than 2,000 militant Creeks, called "Red Sticks," rose up as a unified force of warriors. But in 1814, after months of bloody fighting, General Andrew Jackson finally defeated the Red Sticks in Tennessee. The treaty that ended the conflict brought

▶ *The land Tecumseh defended was long ago divided up among individuals. Now only a little land of the Old Northwest, like this state park, is "for the use of all."*

Relocation of Several American Indian Tribes, 1800–1840

◀ *These lines show the relocation of selected Indian tribes to the new Indian Territory. Few Indians could pursue their traditional ways of living in the Indian Territory.*

▲ *These war clubs were used by Tecumseh's warriors in defending their lands.*

202 Chapter 7

203 People of the New Nation

A picture is worth a thousand words. But just a few words in a caption can help you understand a picture, an illustration, a map, or in this case, a photograph of the land Tecumseh defended.

The things people make and use tell a great deal about them. In this book you'll find lots of photographs of the paintings and statues people made and the tools, jewelry, and weapons they used.

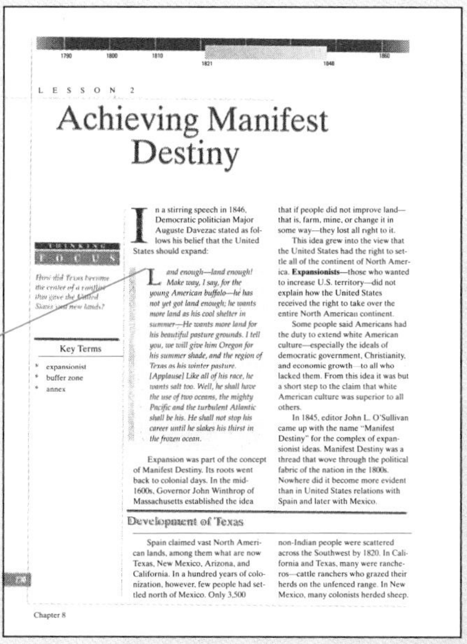

LESSON 2

Achieving Manifest Destiny

THINKING FOCUS

How did Texas become the center of a conflict that gave the United States vast new lands?

Key Terms

- expansionist
- buffer zone
- annex

In a stirring speech in 1846, Democratic politician Major Auguste Davezac stated as follows his belief that the United States should expand:

> *Land enough—land enough! Make way, I say, for the young American buffalo—he has not yet got land enough; he wants more land as his cool shelter in summer—He wants more land for his beautiful pasture grounds. I tell you, we will give him Oregon for his summer shade, and the region of Texas as his winter pasture. [Applause] Like all of his race, he wants salt too. Well, he shall have the use of two oceans, the mighty Pacific and the turbulent Atlantic shall be his. He shall not stop his career until he slakes his thirst in the frozen ocean.*

Expansion was part of the concept of Manifest Destiny. Its roots went back to colonial days. In the mid-1600s, Governor John Winthrop of Massachusetts established the idea that if people did not improve land—that is, farm, mine, or change it in some way—they lost all right to it.

This idea grew into the view that the United States had the right to settle all of the continent of North America. **Expansionists**—those who wanted to increase U.S. territory—did not explain how the United States received the right to take over the entire North American continent.

Some people said Americans had the duty to extend white American culture—especially the ideals of democratic government, Christianity, and economic growth—to all who lacked them. From this idea it was but a short step to the claim that white American culture was superior to all others.

In 1845, editor John L. O'Sullivan came up with the name "Manifest Destiny" for the complex of expansionist ideas. Manifest Destiny was a thread that wove through the political fabric of the nation in the 1800s. Nowhere did it become more evident than in United States relations with Spain and later with Mexico.

Development of Texas

Spain claimed vast North American lands, among them what are now Texas, New Mexico, Arizona, and California. In a hundred years of colonization, however, few people had settled north of Mexico. Only 3,500 non-Indian people were scattered across the Southwest by 1820. In California and Texas, many were rancheros—cattle ranchers who grazed their herds on the unfenced range. In New Mexico, many colonists herded sheep.

Chapter 8

Letters, diaries, books—short passages from these primary sources let people from the past speak to you. When you see a tan background, a red initial letter, and a gray bar, you know that the quotation is a primary source.

Continuing On

As you get to know the people of the past, you'll want ways of understanding and remembering them better. This book gives you some tools to use in learning about people and places and remembering what you've learned.

You're in charge of your reading. See the red square at the end of the text? Now find the red square over in the margin. If you can answer the question there, then you probably understood what you just read. If you can't, perhaps you'd better go back and read that part of the lesson again.

two-thirds of the Creek lands into the United States. The remaining Creeks withdrew to southern and western Alabama.

In the Old Northwest, the alliance led by Shawnee chief Tecumseh and his brother Tenskwatawa (*ten skwa TA wa*), known as "the Prophet," also tried to push back white settlement. Tecumseh believed that if different Indian nations united, they could stop white settlers from taking their lands. In 1811, William Henry Harrison fought a large force of the Prophet's warriors at Prophetstown, a group of Indian villages on the Tippecanoe

(*tip ee ka NOO*) River, while Tecumseh was away. White losses were higher than those of the Indians. But Harrison's army managed to burn most of Prophetstown, so he claimed a victory.

Tecumseh sided with the British in the War of 1812. Together their forces scored several dramatic victories. But Tecumseh died in 1813, at the Battle of the Thames (*temz*) in Ontario, Canada. This loss, along with the 1832 defeat of Black Hawk and the Fox and Sauk Indians in Wisconsin ended most Indian resistance in the Old Northwest. ■

■ *Find evidence to support this statement: The U. S. government did not deal fairly when signing land cession treaties with American Indians.*

Various Indian Responses

By the early 1800s, more was at stake for the Indians than land ownership. Constant pressure from white settlers and the U.S. government threatened their traditional culture and their livelihood. The Indians stood in danger of losing their entire way of life.

Cultural Revival

In his youth, the Prophet had fallen "victim," as he saw it, to the evils of white culture. He had become an alcoholic and had abandoned his people's customs. As a result of wars and invasions from whites, many Indians had given up their traditions. But the Prophet, possibly influenced by religious revivals that occurred among white settlers, recovered from alcoholism and changed his ways.

The Prophet began a new religious movement, and told his followers to give up alcohol and other behaviors. At first these behaviors included some white and some traditional Indian activities. Over time, however, the Prophet began focusing on the importance of traditional Indian ways. He preached that Indians could regain their power if they rejected all white cultural habits and

white trading goods. This effort to renew a people's culture is called **revitalization.**

The Prophet converted many Shawnee, Potawatomi, and other Indians of the Old Northwest, who were bitter over losing their land. They trusted his religious movement to provide a solution. Other warriors, however, looked to Tecumseh, who offered political unity as a way to protect their homelands. Tecumseh's political movement dissolved after his death in battle in 1813. Escaping the same battle, the Prophet fled to Canada, where his influence diminished over time.

Cultural Compromises

Other Indians believed that violent opposition to whites was no solution. The Cherokee, for example, recognized that the white presence in America was permanent. The Cherokee favored **cultural accommodation,** or peaceful compromises, with white society. They tried to combine the best features of both European and Cherokee culture.

Cultural accommodation brought about a remarkable period in Cherokee history. During the early 1800s,

▼ *This drawing of the Prophet shows him in the traditional dress of the Shawnee warrior. The Prophet shunned white culture.*

204

many Cherokee gave up hunting to become farmers. Some even became rich plantation owners with dozens of black slaves. Other Cherokee turned to commerce—managing stores, mills, and other businesses.

At this time, boarding schools run by Christian missionaries taught Cherokee children everything from geography to arithmetic. But the Cherokee educational system took even greater steps forward because of the achievements of Sequoya (*si KWOI a*), a Cherokee silversmith.

Sequoya saw the advantages whites enjoyed because of their ability to read and write. He set out to make an alphabet for writing the Cherokee language. After years of work, he made an alphabet of 85 symbols that stood for the different syllables of the Cherokee language.

Sequoya's system was easy to learn. In fact, most Cherokee were ... wrote effectively in ... leadership was very ... and cen-

Cherokee and English, side by side.

▲ *Sequoya is shown here with his alphabet. Note that his clothes are like those of the white settlers*

A MOMENT IN TIME

A Cherokee Mother and Son

1:37 PM. December 15, 1838
Along the Trail of Tears, on a frozen dirt path outside Greenville, Missouri

Leg Rattles
At the Green Corn Dance, she created loud rhythms by dancing while wearing these. She carries them in an oak basket to remind her of happier times.

Blowgun
This morning, the boy shot a pheasant with this simple gun. Georgia wild turkey is his favorite target.

Basket
An expert basket-maker, the boy's mother has taught many young girls to weave. In this basket, he now carries a few tools and dried fruit.

Hymnal
Methodist missionaries gave her this book of hymns. It is printed in Cherokee, so she can use it to teach her son to read after they reach Oklahoma.

Copper Pan
She had many fine pieces of copper cookware at home, but she can only carry one as she walks.

Red Clay
By carrying a handful of clay from Georgia and mixing it with the soil of his new home, the boy will keep part of his past alive.

204

Frozen at a moment in time, the Cherokee woman and her son give you a glimpse of a powerful moment in American history. You learn all about them, through the clothes they wear, the things they carry, and the trail they walk.

Some tools you'll always use. The Understanding pages walk you through skills that you will use again and again, as a student and later on in life.

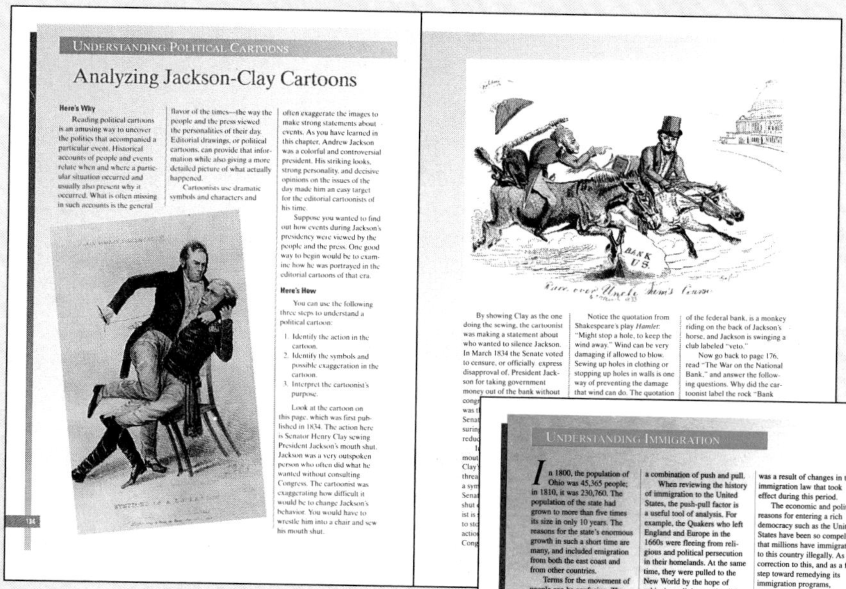

Giving you the inside story is the purpose of two special paragraphs. Across Time & Space connects what you're reading to things that happened centuries ago or continents away. Its companion, How Do We Know?, tells you where information about the past comes from. (See page 199 for an example.)

A special kind of Understanding page looks at concepts—the big ideas that help put all the pieces together. This section helps you understand ideas like Pluralism, Leadership, and in this case, Immigration.

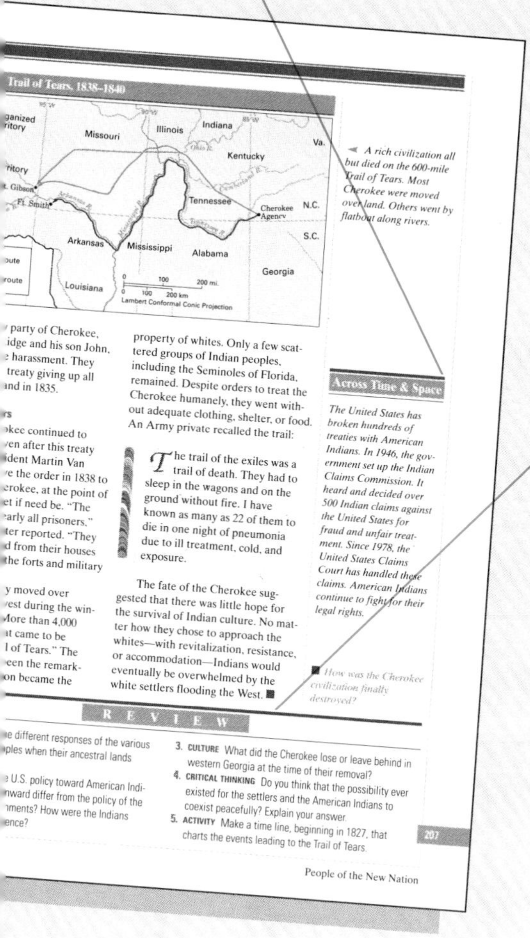
Trail of Tears, 1838–1840
Missouri
Illinois
Indiana
Kentucky
Va.
Tennessee
Cherokee Agency
N.C.
S.C.
Arkansas
Mississippi
Alabama
Georgia
Louisiana
Lambert Conformal Conic Projection
A rich civilization all but died on the 600-mile Trail of Tears. Most Cherokee were moved overland. Others went by flatboat along rivers.
Across Time & Space
The United States has broken hundreds of treaties with American Indians. In 1946, the government set up the Indian Claims Commission. It heard and decided over 500 Indian claims against the United States for fraud and unfair treatment. Since 1978, the United States Claims Court has handled these claims. American Indians continue to fight for their legal rights.
The trail of the exiles was a trail of death. They had to sleep in the wagons and on the ground without fire. I have known as many as 22 of them to die in one night of pneumonia due to ill treatment, cold, and exposure.
REVIEW
207
People of the New Nation

Take a closer look, in this case at the cities that were taking the place of Indian settlements. Look at the shopkeepers' signs; compare American cities to those in Europe.

After you read the lesson, stop and review what you've read. The first question is the same one you started out with. The second question connects the lesson to what you've studied earlier. Other questions and an activity help you think about the lesson you've read. Chapter Review questions help you tie the lessons together. (See pages 216 and 217 for an example.)

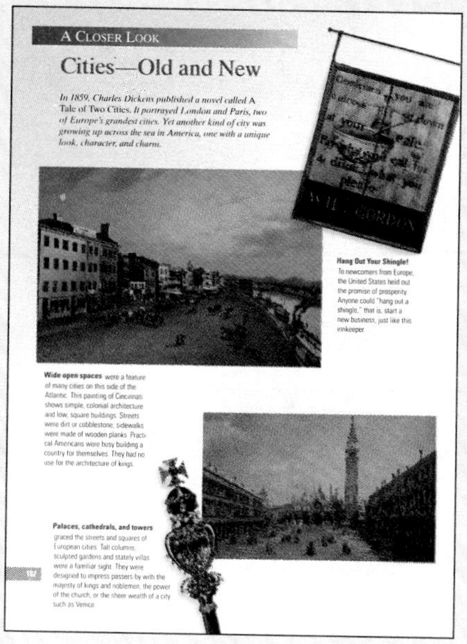

Also Featuring

Some special pages show up only once in every unit, not in every lesson in the book. These features continue the story by letting you explore an idea or activity, or read a story about another time and place. The Time/Space Databank in the back of the book brings together resources you will use again and again.

School isn't the only place where you can learn social studies. This feature gives you a chance to explore history and geography outside the classroom—at home or in your own neighborhood.

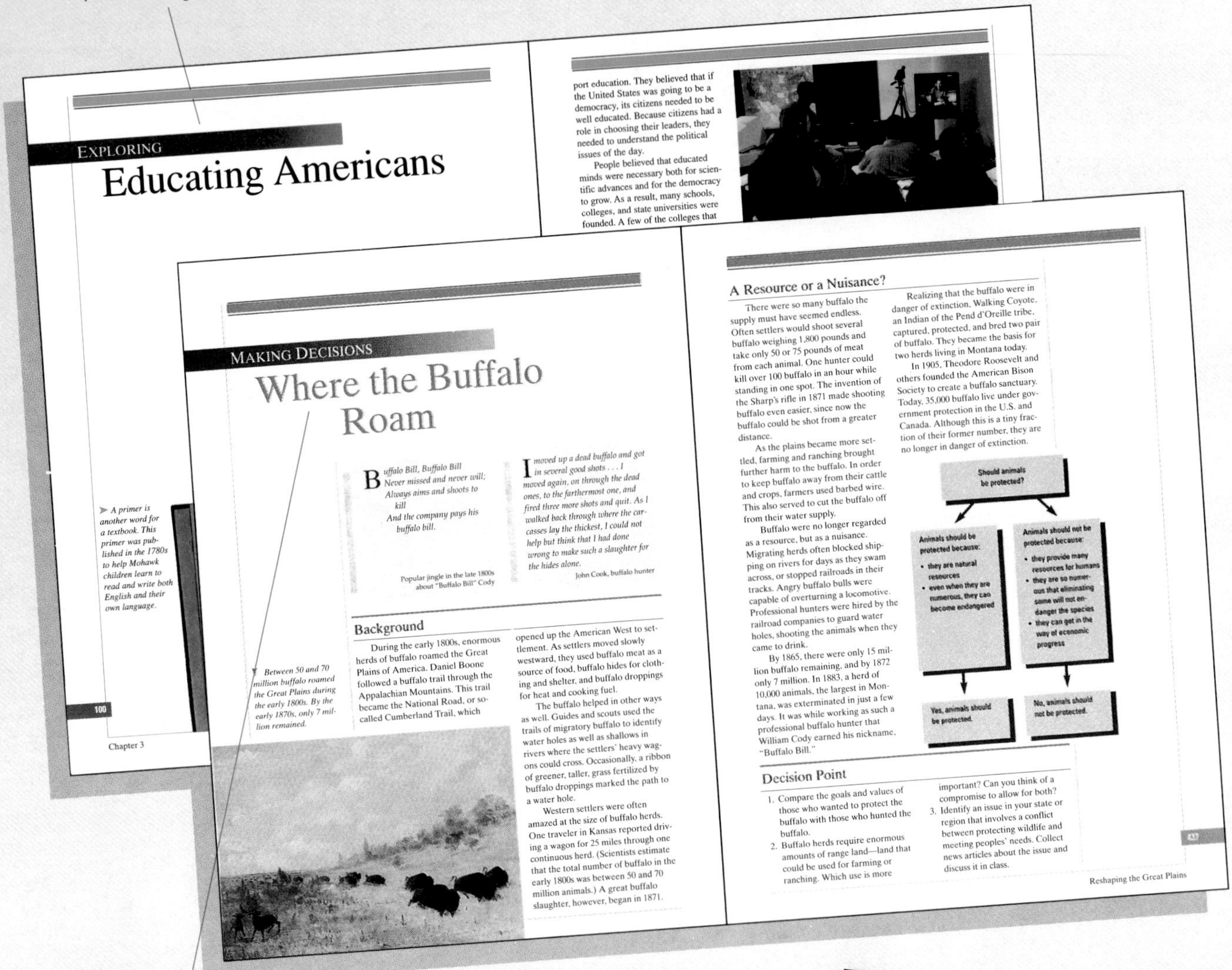
EXPLORING

Educating Americans

port education. They believed that if the United States was going to be a democracy, its citizens needed to be well educated. Because citizens had a role in choosing their leaders, they needed to understand the political issues of the day.

People believed that educated minds were necessary both for scientific advances and for the democracy to grow. As a result, many schools, colleges, and state universities were founded. A few of the colleges that

A primer is another word for a textbook. This primer was published in the 1780s to help Mohawk children learn to read and write both English and their own language.

100 Chapter 3

MAKING DECISIONS

Where the Buffalo Roam

Buffalo Bill, Buffalo Bill
Never missed and never will;
Always aims and shoots to kill
And the company pays his buffalo bill.

Popular jingle in the late 1800s about "Buffalo Bill" Cody

I moved up a dead buffalo and got in several good shots . . . I moved again, on through the dead ones, to the farthermost one, and fired three more shots and quit. As I walked back through where the carcasses lay the thickest, I could not help but think that I had done wrong to make such a slaughter for the hides alone.

John Cook, buffalo hunter

Background

During the early 1800s, enormous herds of buffalo roamed the Great Plains of America. Daniel Boone followed a buffalo trail through the Appalachian Mountains. This trail became the National Road, or so-called Cumberland Trail, which opened up the American West to settlement. As settlers moved slowly westward, they used buffalo meat as a source of food, buffalo hides for clothing and shelter, and buffalo droppings for heat and cooking fuel.

The buffalo helped in other ways as well. Guides and scouts used the trails of migratory buffalo to identify water holes as well as shallows in rivers where the settlers' heavy wagons could cross. Occasionally, a ribbon of greener, taller, grass fertilized by buffalo droppings marked the path to a water hole.

Western settlers were often amazed at the size of buffalo herds. One traveler in Kansas reported driving a wagon for 25 miles through one continuous herd. (Scientists estimate that the total number of buffalo in the early 1800s was between 50 and 70 million animals.) A great buffalo slaughter, however, began in 1871.

Between 50 and 70 million buffalo roamed the Great Plains during the early 1800s. By the early 1870s, only 7 million remained.

A Resource or a Nuisance?

There were so many buffalo the supply must have seemed endless. Often settlers would shoot several buffalo weighing 1,800 pounds and take only 50 or 75 pounds of meat from each animal. One hunter could kill over 100 buffalo in an hour while standing in one spot. The invention of the Sharp's rifle in 1871 made shooting buffalo even easier, since now the buffalo could be shot from a greater distance.

As the plains became more settled, farming and ranching brought further harm to the buffalo. In order to keep buffalo away from their cattle and crops, farmers used barbed wire. This also served to cut the buffalo off from their water supply.

Buffalo were no longer regarded as a resource, but as a nuisance. Migrating herds often blocked shipping on rivers for days as they swam across, or stopped railroads in their tracks. Angry buffalo bulls were capable of overturning a locomotive. Professional hunters were hired by the railroad companies to guard water holes, shooting the animals when they came to drink.

By 1865, there were only 15 million buffalo remaining, and by 1872 only 7 million. In 1883, a herd of 10,000 animals, the largest in Montana, was exterminated in just a few days. It was while working as such a professional buffalo hunter that William Cody earned his nickname, "Buffalo Bill."

Realizing that the buffalo were in danger of extinction, Walking Coyote, an Indian of the Pend d'Oreille tribe, captured, protected, and bred two pair of buffalo. They became the basis for two herds living in Montana today.

In 1905, Theodore Roosevelt and others founded the American Bison Society to create a buffalo sanctuary. Today, 35,000 buffalo live under government protection in the U.S. and Canada. Although this is a tiny fraction of their former number, they are no longer in danger of extinction.

Should animals be protected?

Animals should be protected because:
- they are natural resources
- even when they are numerous, they can become endangered

Animals should not be protected because:
- they provide many resources for humans
- they are so numerous that eliminating some will not endanger the species
- they can get in the way of economic progress

Yes, animals should be protected.

No, animals should not be protected.

Decision Point

1. Compare the goals and values of those who wanted to protect the buffalo with those who hunted the buffalo.
2. Buffalo herds require enormous amounts of range land—land that could be used for farming or ranching. Which use is more important? Can you think of a compromise to allow for both?
3. Identify an issue in your state or region that involves a conflict between protecting wildlife and meeting peoples' needs. Collect news articles about the issue and discuss it in class.

Reshaping the Great Plains

What would you do? The Making Decisions pages show you an important decision from the past. Then you practice the steps that will help you to make a good choice.

Stories have always been important parts of people's lives. Each unit in the book has at least one story about the time and place you're studying. In this case, it's a retelling of an American Indian creation story. Some Indian boys and girls probably listened to this story too.

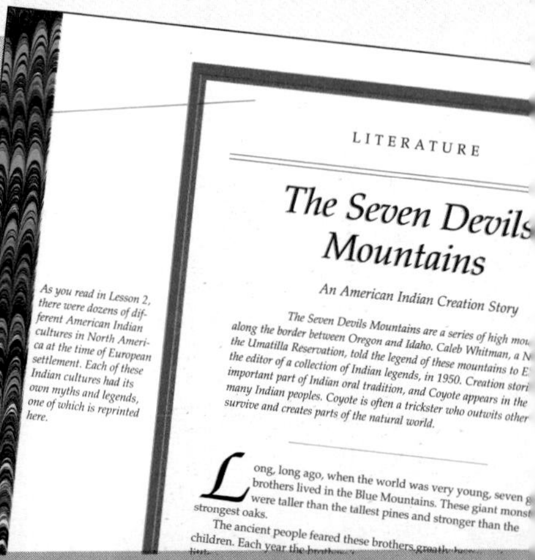
LITERATURE

The Seven Devils Mountains

An American Indian Creation Story

As you read in Lesson 2, there were dozens of different American Indian cultures in North America at the time of European settlement. Each of these Indian cultures had its own myths and legends, one of which is reprinted here.

The Seven Devils Mountains are a series of high mou... along the border between Oregon and Idaho. Caleb Whitman, a N... the Umatilla Reservation, told the legend of these mountains to E... the editor of a collection of Indian legends, in 1950. Creation stori... important part of Indian oral tradition, and Coyote appears in the... many Indian peoples. Coyote is often a trickster who outwits other... survive and creates parts of the natural world.

Long, long ago, when the world was very young, seven g... brothers lived in the Blue Mountains. These giant monst... were taller than the tallest pines and stronger than the strongest oaks.

The ancient people feared these brothers greatly...

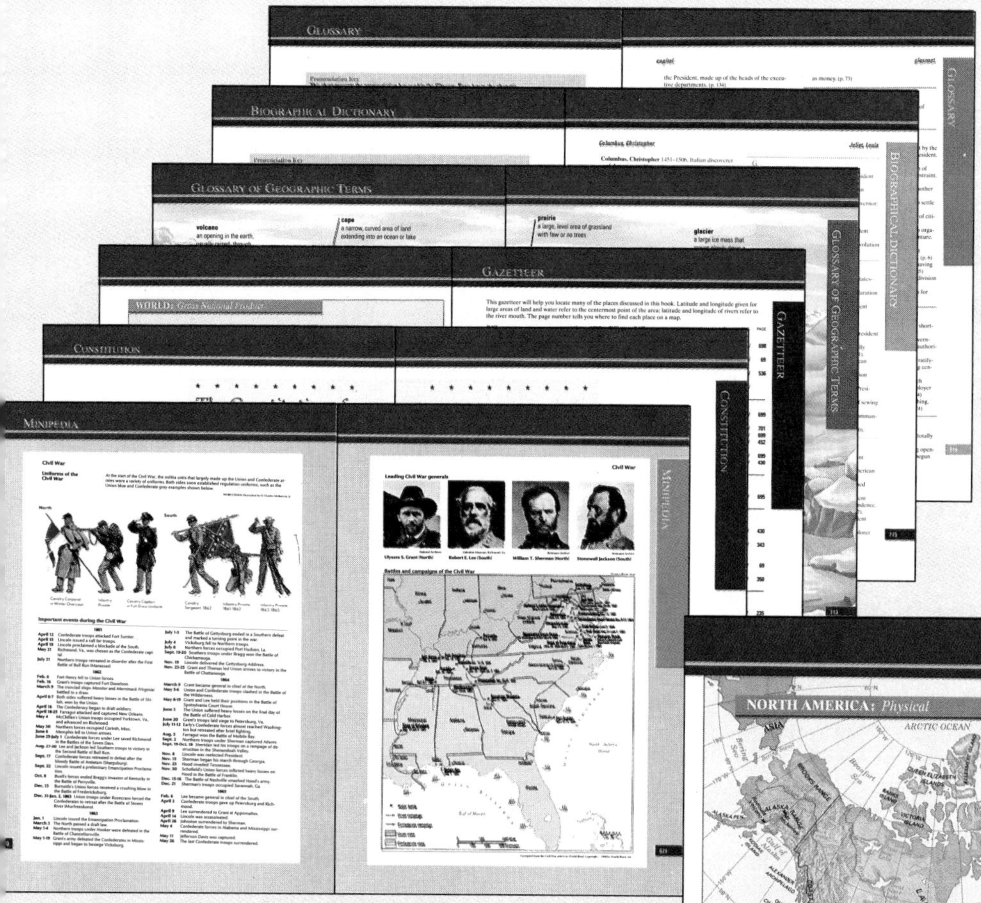

The Time/Space Databank is like a reference section of a library at your fingertips. It's the place to go for more information about the places, people, and key terms you meet in this book. Some of your country's most prized documents are reproduced here too.

What's a minipedia? It's a small version of an encyclopedia, one that you don't have to go to your library to use. It's bound right into the back of your book so you can quickly look up its articles, charts, and graphs.

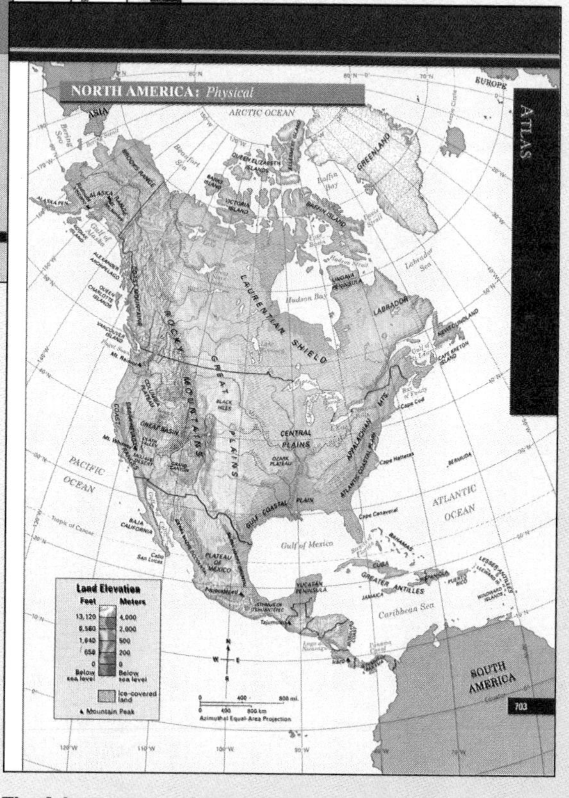

The Atlas maps out the world. Special maps tell you about the climate, vegetation, precipitation, and resources of the United States. Historical maps let you compare the nation's population at different times in its history.

CLASS ACTIVITY

Overview

Ask students where in the world they would like most to visit. Then pose this question: *Suppose you could travel back in time, which time period would you choose and why?* Inform students that the Map and Globe Handbook contains the means for them to travel to different places in the world and to different time periods. The maps in this Handbook will take them high above San Francisco, to Europe in the fourteenth century, to North America in the eighteenth and nineteenth centuries, and to Central America at the height of the Aztec Empire in the fifteenth and sixteenth centuries.

Looking Forward

As you can see from the Table of Contents, each section focuses on a specific geographic skill. The Handbook can be used as a review tool at the beginning of the year, or incorporated throughout the year. For additional support, students will encounter references in some map captions within the chapters to specific sections of this Handbook. Emphasize that the Handbook is a reference tool they can return to as often as they like.

Map and Globe Handbook

You're about to travel through an America—and a world—that you've never before seen. You'll learn how the plague, also known as the Black Death, spread from Asia to Europe. You'll find out what was happening in Mexico and Central America at the same time. You'll even travel to the highest elevation in Africa.

You'll use different kinds of maps to guide you through this journey. Your adventure is about to begin, so turn to page G1, and hold on!

Contents

BIBLIOGRAPHY

Books for Students

Henwood, Doug. *The State of the U.S.A.: The Changing Face of American Life in Maps and Graphics.* New York: Simon and Schuster, 1994. Maps and graphics present a diverse array of information about American life.

Historical Atlas of the United States. Washington, D.C.: National Geographic Society, 1996. This atlas will give students a new perspective on the past.

Books for Teachers

Ferrell, Robert H. *Atlas of American History.* New York: Facts on File, 1991. This historical atlas will unlock the past for teachers and students alike.

Hardwick, Susan Wiley and Donald G. Holtgrieve. *Geography for Educators: Standards, Themes, and Concepts.* Englewood Cliffs, NJ: Prentice Hall, 1996. This book emphasizes the natural connection between social studies and geography.

Understanding Our Planet

Without maps, our lives would be very different. Maps show us what our world looks like. By graphically representing a portion of the earth, we can see where we have been, where we are now, and where we might like to go.

The satellite image below, taken miles above the earth, shows one view of San Francisco. Images like these show different features of the earth's surface. They are only one of many sources that cartographers (mapmakers) use when they create maps. What similar features can you see on the satellite image and the map of San Francisco below?

Satellite images usually show the major landforms of a region. In this image, land with higher elevation is yellow. Where do you see the highest elevations near San Francisco?

The red areas on the image have lots of vegetation, like forests or parks. Compare the map to the satellite image. Which parks can you see clearly on both?

San Francisco

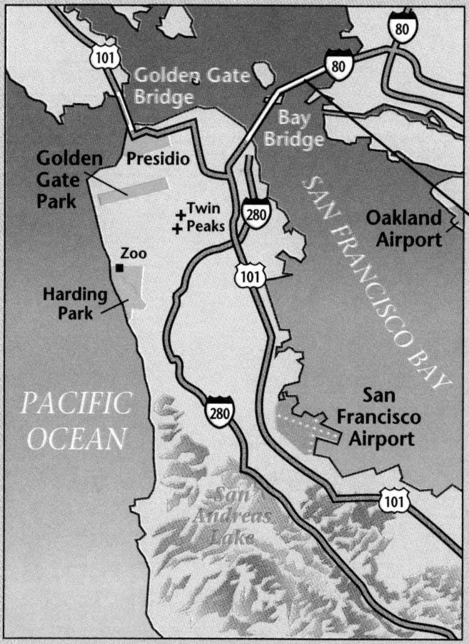

The satellite image also reflects some human-made features, like bridges, that you see on the map. While the image gives part of the picture, maps can show many details—whatever the mapmaker chooses to include—that do not show on satellite images.

CLASS ACTIVITY

Encourage students to talk about some of their favorite vacation spots. Ask them how maps helped them locate places they wanted to visit. Suggest the following scenario: *Suppose you visit a place that is unfamiliar to you and there are no maps available. What would you do? How would you find your way around?* Students may suggest alternatives such as asking residents of the place for information or mapping the place themselves, for example, the route from the hotel to a restaurant or the closest bus stop.

GEOGRAPHY

Visual Learning

Review the colors used in the satellite images—red indicates vegetation, yellow indicates elevation, and so on. Challenge students to tell which colors would predominate in a satellite image of their community and its surroundings. What human-made features would be evident?

Answer to Captions

Top caption: The highest elevations are near the center (north/south) of the peninsula and at the southern end of the peninsula.

Middle caption: Harding Park, Golden Gate Park, and the Presidio

Research

Have students learn more about the use of satellite imagery in mapping. For instance, they may concentrate on the history or the technical aspects. Their presentations should include several satellite images of places.

Objectives

1. Compare a satellite image of a place with a map rendering of it. (Geography 2/Map and Globe Skills 2/Visual Learning 1)
2. Compare images, maps, and globes to understand that maps are visual representations of real places. (Geography 2/Map and Globe Skills 2/Visual Learning 1)

CLASS ACTIVITY

Ask students to take a look at each map in this Handbook. What elements do all the maps have in common? Discover the steps students use in deciphering maps. Pose a series of questions about maps such as the following: *You want to know the distance between two places. What do you use?* (map scale) *You want to know whether one place is east or west of another place. What do you use?* (compass rose) *You want to find the exact location of a place. What do you use?* (grid formed by latitude and longitude) *You want to find out how much precipitation Florida receives. What do you use?* (legend)

GEOGRAPHY

Map and Globe Skills

Which states show the most extremes in precipitation? *(Texas and Oklahoma)* Describe how much rain falls in the different parts of one of those states.

Understanding a Map

As you'll see in this handbook, there are many different kinds of maps. Some maps show the whole world. Others focus on one or more countries. The land's physical features may or may not be represented. All maps, however, share several characteristics. Knowing these characteristics will help you to read any kind of map. The map below shows the precipitation in the southern region of the United States.

Precipitation in the South

An **inset** map is a smaller map that is related to the larger map. This **locator inset**, for instance, shows the location of the southern region in the United States.

Mapmakers use symbols to represent different things such as natural resources, goods, cities, or routes. A **legend** explains what the symbols mean. In this legend, different colors stand for different amounts of average yearly precipitation.

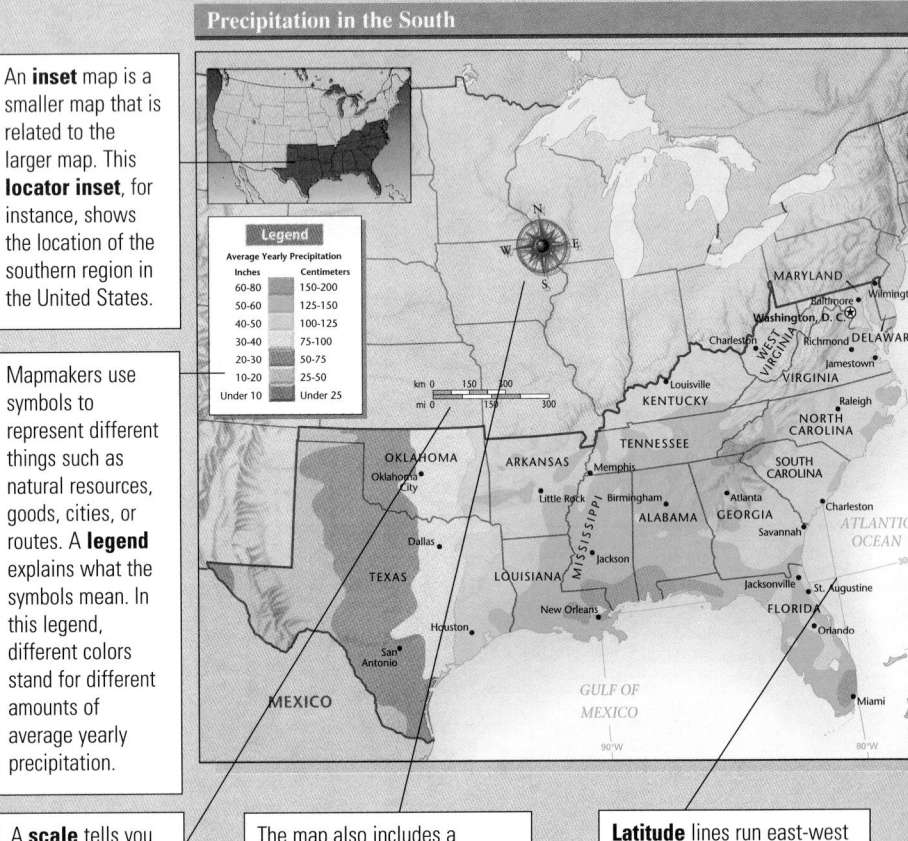

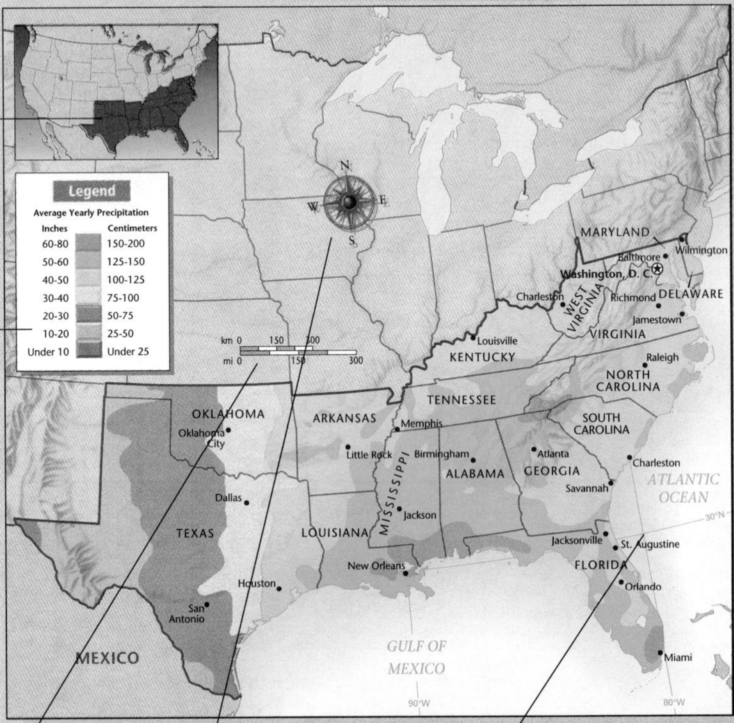

A **scale** tells you the ratio between distance on the map and the corresponding distance on the earth.

The map also includes a **compass rose** with the directions North (N), East (E), West (W), and South (S). Intermediate directions such as Northeast (NE) may also be displayed.

Latitude lines run east-west and are measured in degrees. **Longitude** lines run north-south. These imaginary latitude and longitude lines form a **grid** that helps us locate places on the map.

Objectives

1. Interpret basic map-reading features that are common to most maps. (Visual Learning 4/Map and Globe Skills 1–4)
2. Analyze specific information on a particular map. (Map and Globe Skills 1)

Making Maps

Introduce one of these activities into your classroom: If your state is not shown on the map on this page, have students make a map showing its precipitation; If your state is shown, then have students make maps of your state but omit one of the key elements of the map—either legend, inset, scale, compass rose, or grid. Direct them to exchange and then complete maps.

Access Strategy

Define the word *precipitation* as the amount of water that falls as rain, snow, or hail. You may want to have students draw their own legends for the map that incorporate symbols such as raindrops or snowflakes.

Jsing the Legend, Inset, and Grid

Have you ever heard of a disease called the plague, or the Black Death? the fourteenth century, the plague spread from Asia to Europe, and illions of people died. The map below traces the spread of the plague. ou can use the legend, inset, and grid to see the movement of the disease.

The Great Plague

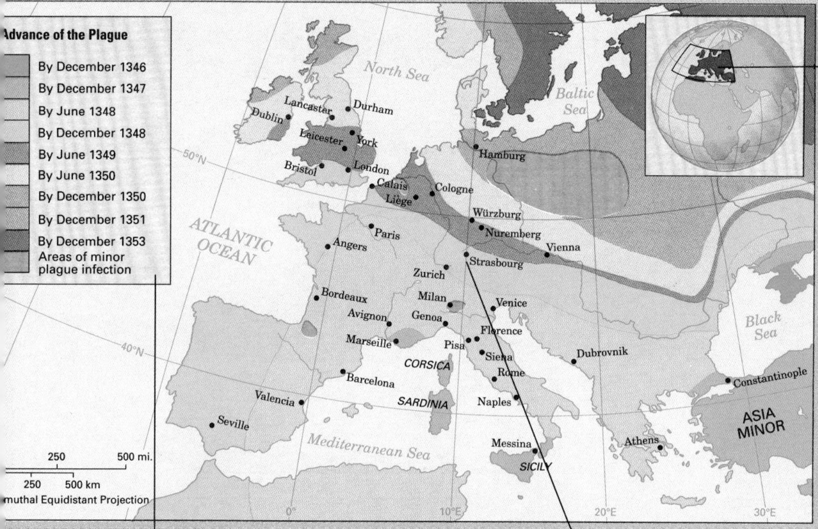

The inset locator map highlights the area of the earth that the larger map represents. As you can see, the map shows most of Europe and very little of Asia and Africa.

The legend uses color to show the spread of the disease. Each color stands or a different time period. By following he changes in color, you can easily see ow the plague spread.

The lines of latitude and longitude form a grid. Strasbourg, located at about 48°N, 10°E, was hit by the plague by December 1348. The plague arrived in Hamburg, located at 54°N, 10°E, by December 1350.

MAP SKILLS

REVIEW When did the plague arrive in London?

REVIEW Give the latitude and longitude of a city that was hit by the plague by December 1347.

3. THINK ABOUT IT Describe the spread of the plague in Great Britain and Ireland.
4. TRY IT Determine when the plague hit each city on the map. Then list the cities in order based on the time the plague arrived. In what direction did the plague travel?

CLASS ACTIVITY

Briefly explain to the class that more than 25 million people, about one-quarter of the population, died of the plague in Europe in the fourteenth century. The disease primarily affects rodents, but infected fleas can spread the plague to humans. It may have started in Africa or India. The disease was spread by traders to the Middle East and China. Mongol armies and traders carried it into Russia and then moved into Europe. The plague disappeared from Europe in the early eighteenth century, but there have been outbreaks since then in Turkey, the Middle East, Egypt, Greece, Russia, and China. Only Antarctica and Australia have not been infected. Today, improved sanitary conditions and antibiotics have dramatically cut the death rate of the disease.

Geography Theme: Movement

At the end of the nineteenth century, the plague traveled from the South China ports of Hong Kong and Canton to North and South America, and South Africa. Ask students how today's transportation and communication systems might affect the spread and control of disease.

Answers to Map Skills

1. by December 1348
2. Possible answers: 41°N, 29°E (Constantinople); 38°N, 15°E (Messina); 43°N, 5°E (Marseille)
3. It first hit southern Great Britain by December 1348. It spread from London to just below Lancaster in Great Britain and in southeastern Ireland by June 1349. Then it spread through half of Ireland and Great Britain by June 1350. By December 1350, the plague had spread throughout Great Britain and Ireland.
4. From earliest to latest: Constantinople, Messina, Marseille; Athens, Dubrovnik, Naples, Rome, Siena, Pisa, Florence, Venice, Genoa, Zurich, Avignon, Barcelona, Valencia, Bordeaux, Angers, Paris; Strasbourg, London, Bristol, Seville; Vienna, Nuremburg, Würzburg, Liege, Cologne, Calais, Leicester, York; Durham, Lancaster, Dublin; Hamburg. The plague traveled generally north, northeast.

Objectives

1. Understand and use legends, insets, and grids. (Visual Learning 4/Map and Globe Skills 1, 2)

2. Realize that a map can show movement. (Geography 4/Visual Learning 1/Map and Globe Skills 2/Critical Thinking 3)

CLASS ACTIVITY

Elicit from students different ways of describing the location of their community. If no one suggests it, give the latitude and longitude. Talk about the fact that although there may be other communities in the United States, or in the world, that possess the same name as yours, no other location has the same latitude and longitude. Provide globes, atlases, and world maps, and let students locate other communities that share the same latitude or longitude as yours. Discuss any characteristics that students think the communities might share such as climate, elevation, natural features, and so on.

GEOGRAPHY

Map and Globe Skills

Have students determine the easternmost, westernmost, northernmost, and southernmost points on the earth and give their latitudes and longitudes.

Understanding Latitude and Longitude

If someone asked you where Los Angeles is located, you'd probably say that it is in the state of California. You also could have answered, "thirty-four degrees north, one hundred eighteen degrees west." These numbers give Los Angeles's location by latitude and longitude. Use the grid of latitude and longitude lines to locate other places on the map below.

World: Latitude and Longitude

Latitude is measured in degrees. The **equator** is at 0°. Any location north of the equator is measured in degrees north, and any location south is measured in degrees south. At 34°N, Los Angeles is located north of the equator.

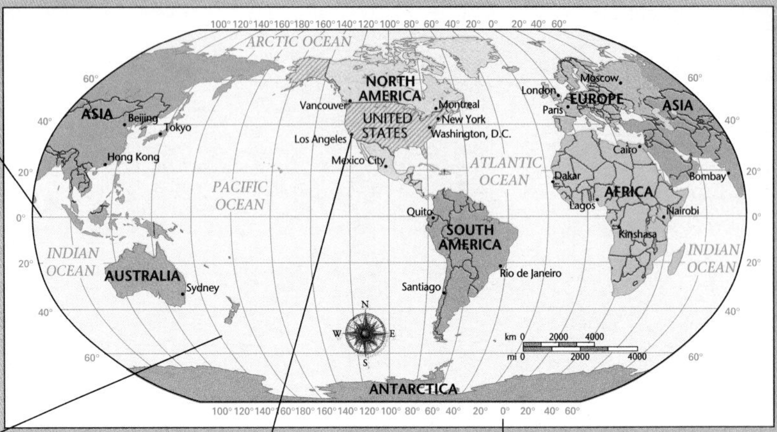

Because the earth is round, the lines of longitude curve as they approach either the North or the South Pole.

In giving the location of a place, the latitude always goes before the longitude. So we say Los Angeles is located at 34º N, 118º W.

Longitude is measured in degrees, too. The **prime meridian** is 0°. Locations are measured in degrees east or degrees west, depending upon their relationship to the prime meridian. For instance, Los Angeles is located 118 degrees west of the prime meridian.

MAP SKILLS

1. **REVIEW** What is the approximate latitude and longitude of Mexico City?
2. **REVIEW** Which city would you find at about 35°N, 139°E?
3. **THINK ABOUT IT** Which is farther east: Bombay, India or Nairobi, Kenya? How do yo know?
4. **TRY IT** At about what latitude and longitude i your community located?

Objective

Find the latitude and longitude of specific places. (Map and Globe Skills 2)

Answers to Map Skills

1. 19°N, 99°W
2. Tokyo, Japan
3. Bombay is farther east. It is located at a longitude that is farther east than the longitude of Nairobi.
4. Answers will vary.

Mathematics Connection

The length of each degree of latitude is about 69 miles. Use this measurement to find the distance between your community and at least four other communities in the world. Verify your results using a globe or a world map and its scale.

Making Hypotheses Using Maps

When you make a hypothesis, you're making an educated guess that can be tested. Usually, you make a hypothesis based on facts that you've read, or observed. Then you test your hypothesis to see if it is accurate.

This map shows the migration of African Americans from the South to the North between 1910 and 1920. At this time, so many African Americans moved north that the movement is known as the Great Migration. Why did so many African Americans move north? Follow the four steps below to make a hypothesis.

The Great Migration, 1910–1920

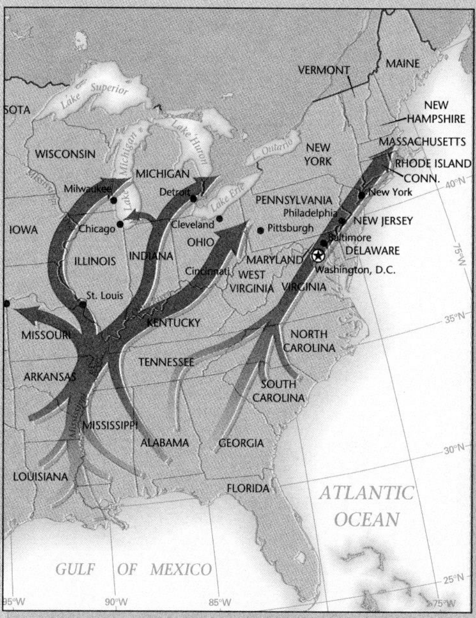

Step 1: Define the question. You know the map shows the movement of African Americans during the time period 1910–1920. You want to know why so many African Americans moved north.

Step 2: Gather evidence. You can see that African Americans moved from the rural South to large cities in the North. For instance, many African Americans moved from the coastal regions of the South, where few large cities are shown, to New York City. What other evidence can you see on the map?

Step 3: Make a hypothesis. Based on evidence from the map, you might conclude northern cities offered African Americans better jobs and living opportunities than the rural South.

Step 4: Test the hypothesis. Now you can do more research to back up your hypothesis. Look for facts in books, on the Internet, or in other sources. As you learn more, you may change your hypothesis.

MAP SKILLS

REVIEW Where did African Americans living in central Georgia tend to migrate?

REVIEW What southern states did African Americans who moved to Chicago come from?

3. **THINK ABOUT IT** What impact do you think segregation in the South had on the Great Migration?
4. **TRY IT** Research the Great Migration. Test the above hypothesis.

CLASS ACTIVITY

Make sure that students understand what a hypothesis is. If necessary, give several examples. Emphasize that a hypothesis is a well-reasoned guess that must be tested. Discuss the difference between an opinion and a hypothesis. Ask students to study the map and then choose one of the flow lines on which to concentrate. Have them describe in their own words the movement that that line shows.

Making Hypotheses Using Maps

Refer students to the map on page 194 of their textbooks. This map shows where free Blacks were living in the United States in 1810. Using that map in conjunction with the map on this page, what kind of hypothesis can they make about the Great Migration?

Answers to Map Skills

1. the Northeast
2. Possible answer: Louisiana, Arkansas, Mississippi, and Alabama
3. Possible answer: Segregation in the South may have made African Americans more likely to migrate to the North in hopes of finding better living and working conditions.
4. Students' research will prove that the search for better living and working conditions in northern cities was one reason for the Great Migration.

Language Connection

Ask students to imagine they are African Americans living in the North between 1910 and 1920. Have them write letters to a friend or relative convincing them to move North.

Objective

Make a hypothesis about migration based on a map. (Geography 4, 5/Visual Learning 1/Map and Globe Skills 3/Critical Thinking 3)

CLASS ACTIVITY

Discuss the differences between 2-dimensional and 3-dimensional shapes. Ask students to compare a 2-dimensional map to a 3-dimensional globe. What are the advantages and disadvantages of each?

GEOGRAPHY
Visual Learning

Direct students' attention to the grids on each projection. How would they describe the relationship of latitude to longitude in each projection? Encourage them to think in terms of right angles and straight, curved, parallel, and perpendicular lines.

Understanding Projections

Because globes are spheres, they accurately represent area, relative size and shape of physical features, the distance between points, and true compass directions. Maps, on the other hand, are accurate representations of the earth drawn on a flat piece of paper. But how can you accurately present the spherical earth on a flat surface? To deal with this problem, cartographers have come up with different kinds of projections. Four projections are displayed below.

Mercator Projection

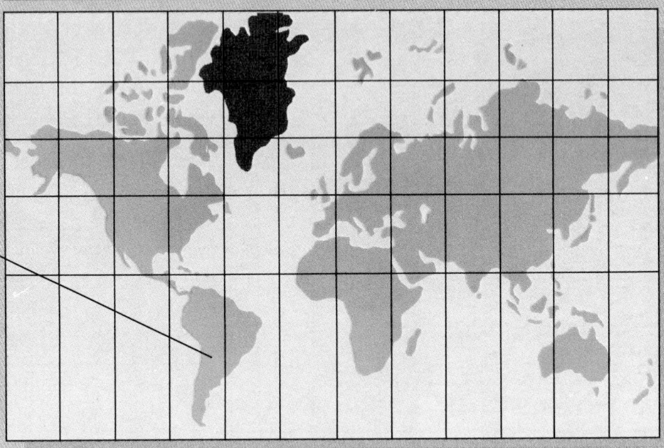

In 1569, the German cartographer Gerhardus Mercator first published this projection. A Mercator Projection maintains the shapes of the continents but distorts their sizes. The size distortion is particularly great near the poles. Find Greenland on a globe. Compare its size with South America. Which looks bigger? South America is more than eight times larger than Greenland.

Peters Projection

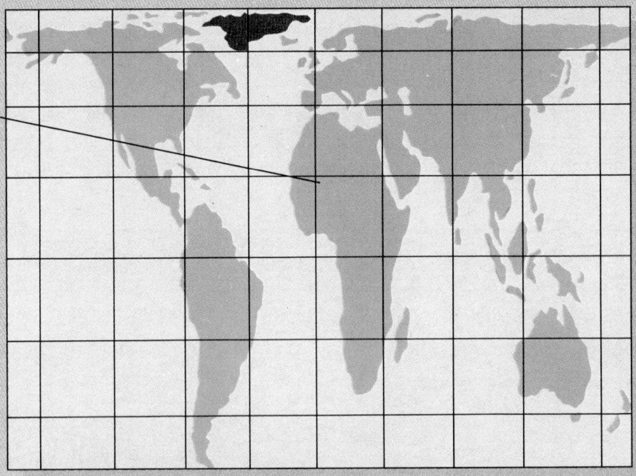

Arno Peters, a West German cartographer, created the Peters Projection in 1974. The sizes of the continents in relation to each other are accurate, but their shapes appear distorted. If you compare this projection to a globe, you'll see that Africa here is the correct size, but its shape is distorted.

Objectives

1. Understand how the shape of the Earth affects maps. (Critical Thinking 1/Visual Learning 1)

2. Compare map projections of the world. (Map and Globe Skills 1 and 5)

Critical Thinking

Pose the following question to students: *How and why does the location of Antarctica affect its appearance on the four different projections? Based upon each of the projections shown on these pages, what would you say about the size and shape of Antarctica?*

Goode Projection

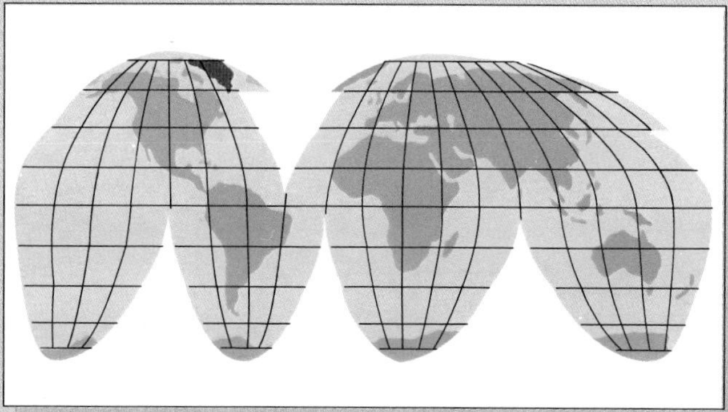

Paul Goode, a cartographer from the University of Chicago, combined elements from two other projections to create Goode's Interrupted Homolosine Projection in 1923. In order to show the continents accurately in both size and shape, Goode split the earth into sections. This projection, however, makes distances difficult to measure.

Robinson Projection

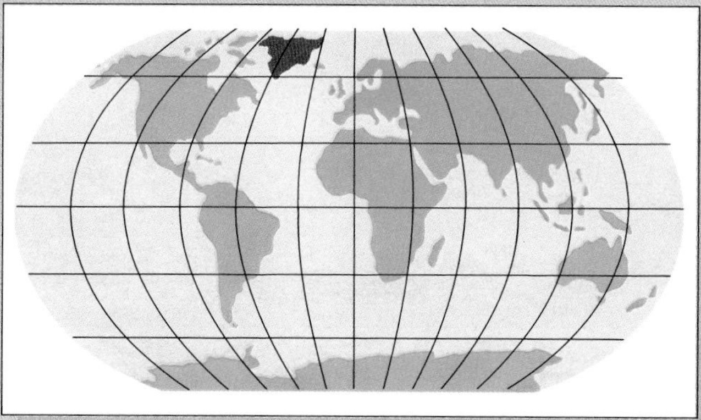

The Robinson Projection was designed by American cartographer Arthur Robinson in 1963. It portrays fairly accurately the sizes and shapes of the continents, and the distance between them. In this book, most of the world maps use the Robinson Projection as their base.

MAP SKILLS

1. **REVIEW** If you wanted to show continents' sizes and shapes most accurately, which projections would you use?
2. **REVIEW** Look at the map on page 19. What kind of projection was used?
3. **THINK ABOUT IT** Look at the different projections of maps in this book. Why do you think there are so many different kinds of projections?
4. **TRY IT** Use a sheet of tracing paper and a globe. Hold the paper up to the globe and try to trace two or three continents. What problems do you encounter?

CLASS ACTIVITY

Some sort of distortion always occurs in the transfer of a spherical surface to a flat surface. A mapmaker must decide which elements in a particular map must be the most accurate. Projections that distort shape and direction but convey the size correctly are called *equal-area,* or *equivalent, projections.* Projections that distort size but accurately present shape and direction are known as *conformal projections.* Still other projections aim for a balance among the elements.

Ask students to look through the textbook to find examples of other kinds of projections. They should select a country or continent on the map and compare its size and shape to the way in which it is presented on a globe. How does the projection distort the country or continent?

Background

Gerhardus Mercator was born in 1512 in what is now Belgium. After producing a series of maps, he was arrested for religious heresy in 1544 and held for seven months. To pursue his work in peace, Mercator moved to Germany where he created the Mercator projection in 1569. He also coined the word *atlas* to describe a collection of maps.

Answers to Map Skills

1. Goode Projection
2. Mercator Projection
3. Possible answer: Different projections focus on different things, such as size and shape or distance. Cartographers are still trying to perfect projections.
4. Possible answers are that the paper won't lie flat on the globe. Students may try to fold the paper to trace the continents, but they need to decide how to deal with the folds once they flatten the paper.

CLASS ACTIVITY

Bring in a variety of products such as canned goods and clothing. The labels should state where the products were made. Open a discussion of trade and how it can be represented as the flow of goods. Ask students to show on a map how one of the products would go from the place where it was produced to local stores and then into their homes. About how much distance would each product travel?

Looking Forward

The maps on pages 333 and 546 provide additional examples of maps using flow lines.

Interpreting Flow Lines

Suppose you lived in one of the British colonies in North America in the 1700s. If you wanted to sell your crop of wheat, tobacco, or rice, you would ship it to Great Britain or Ireland. Flow lines are arrows on maps that show where something came from and where it went. By varying the thickness of the lines, graduated flow lines show the quantity of what has moved.

Colonial Trade in the 1700s

Tobacco was the most popular crop shipped to Great Britain. The corresponding orange area in the British colonies shows where tobacco was grown.

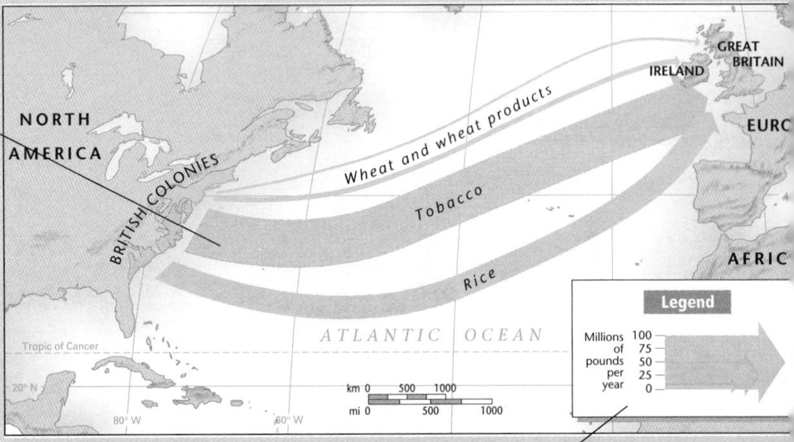

The green, purple, and orange lines are **graduated flow lines**. Their widths indicate the amount of goods traded to Great Britain and Ireland.

MAP SKILLS

1. **REVIEW** What was the total amount of wheat and wheat products, tobacco, and rice shipped by the colonies to Great Britain and Ireland in the 1700s?
2. **REVIEW** About how far did a shipment of rice travel from the colonies to Great Britain?
3. **THINK ABOUT IT** Which region of the British colonies was the most successful in trading its crops? Explain your answer.
4. **TRY IT** Use the legend to interpret each of the flow lines in your own words.

Objectives

1. Understand that a map can show the movement of people, goods, and ideas. (Map and Globe Skills 1 and 3)

2. Recognize the flow of trade between the American colonies and Great Britain and Ireland. (Visual Learning 4)

Answers to Map Skills

1. wheat and wheat products + tobacco + rice: 10 million + 5 million + 100 million + 50 million = 165 million pounds per year
2. about 4,600 miles
3. the upper South (the orange region); they used less land to produce more exports than the other two regions.
4. The New England colonies shipped about 5 million pounds of wheat and wheat products to Great Britain, and about 10 million pounds to Ireland. The Middle Colonies shipped about 100 million pounds of tobacco to Great Britain. The Southern Colonies shipped about 50 million pounds of rice to Great Britain.

Reading Different Kinds of Maps

By now, you should know that maps can do more than show the physical shape of the earth. On the following pages, you'll see how to use some different kinds of map, including maps of historical events, maps of wind and ocean currents, and even maps that show statistics.

A Time Zone Map

Suppose you have a friend who lives in Reykjavik, Iceland. You live in San Diego, California. If you called your friend at a reasonable time for you, say 8 P.M., your friend may not want to speak to you. After all, it's 2 A.M. in Reykjavik! The map below shows half of the world's 24 time zones.

Time Zones of the Western Hemisphere

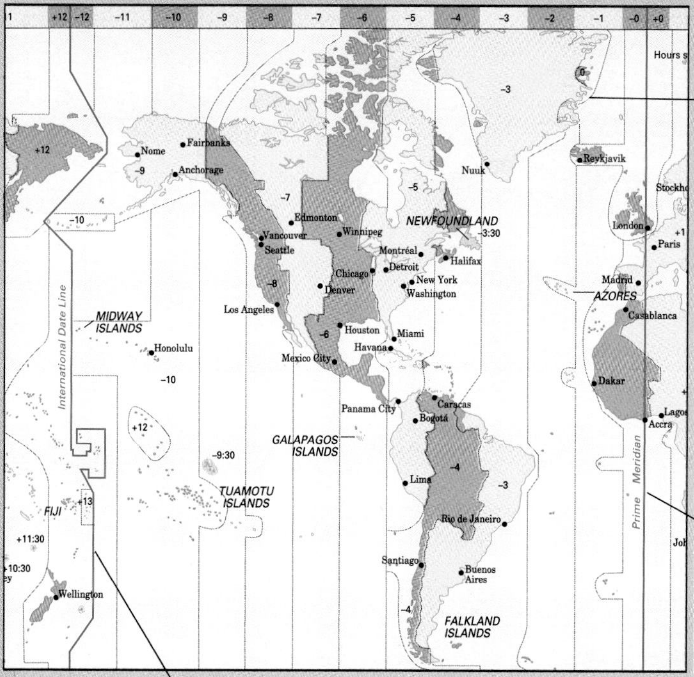

Because of political borders, the time zone lines aren't always straight. This curved line allows more of Greenland to be in the same time zone.

The time zone that includes the prime meridian is the starting point. It gets one hour earlier as you move west through each time zone. Chicago, Illinois is in the time zone that is six hours earlier than the prime meridian time zone.

When you cross the international date line, the date immediately becomes one day later or earlier. It is noon on Saturday in the time zone west of the date line at the same time that it is noon on Friday in the zone east of the line.

CLASS ACTIVITY

Take a moment to review the different kinds of maps students have learned about in the Handbook so far. Explain that in the coming pages students will find a time zone map, a historical map with a parallel timeline, a physical map of Africa with a vertical profile, a cartogram, and a wind and current map.

GEOGRAPHY

Map and Globe Skills

Put students in charge of Time Zone Managers, a company that makes calls for businesses. For instance, a business in New York wants to contact a business in Tokyo. Time Zone Managers decides when the best time to call Japan is and makes the call at the appropriate time. Have pairs work together. One partner will decide where to call, and the other partner will decide when to call.

Making a Map

Ask students to suppose that time zones followed lines of longitude and that political boundaries were never taken into account. How would they use longitude to divide the United States, including Alaska and Hawaii, into time zones? They should trace a map of the United States, outlining each state, and draw the longitude lines that will divide the time zones. What problems do they foresee with their systems of time zones?

Objectives

1. Identify time zones by reading a map. (Visual Learning 1/Map and Globe Skills 1)

2. Understand a time zone map. (Visual Learning 4/Map and Globe Skills 2)

CLASS ACTIVITY

Display a map of Central America. Ask the class to compare the place names on it to the map on this page. Remind students that maps can show present-day boundaries and empires from the past such as the Aztec Empire. Allow time for them to study the map. Then have students characterize the changes in the Aztec Empire in each 13-year period from 1427 to 1519 as shown by the legend.

Geography Themes: Relationships Within Places

People depend up their environment for survival. In many cases, they also must adapt to their environment—and sometimes, they change their environment. The island Tenochtitlan in the middle of Lake Texcoco was swamp. The Aztec learned to farm this land by using chinampas, or floating gardens. Discuss with students how they depend up, have adapted to, and changed their environment.

A Historical Map and Parallel Timeline

Although the Aztec Empire no longer exists, we know how its territory expanded and then disappeared. The map below shows how the Aztec Empire grew from 1427 to 1519. The timelines on the following page tell how events on two different continents changed the fate of the Aztecs.

Five different time periods are represented by different colors so you can see the expansion of the Aztec Empire. In the years from 1427 to 1440, the Aztecs settled around the swampy area of Lake Texcoco.

Expansion of the Aztec Empire

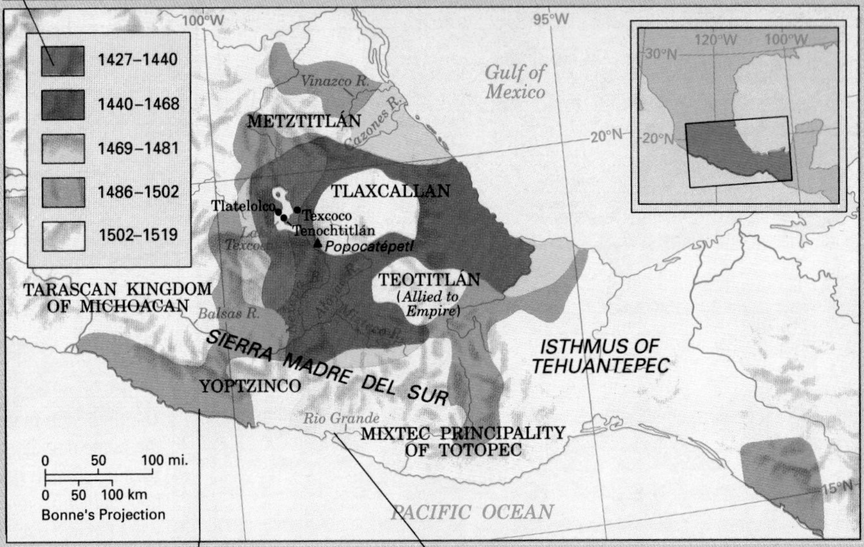

Between the years 1486 and 1502, the Aztec Empire acquired more distant territory. Led by the ruler Ahuitzotl *(ah WEE soh tl),* Aztec warriors conquered land throughout present-day Mexico and Central America.

By 1519, the Aztec Empire reached its greatest size, and had a population of about 25 million people. During which period shown on the map did the empire gain the most territory?

Objectives

1. Realize that maps can show historical events. (Geography 5/Visual Learning 1/Map and Globe Skills 1, 4)

2. Interpret historical maps. (Geography 5/Visual Learning 4/Map and Globe Skills 3)

Answers to Captions

Bottom right caption: The empire gained the most territory between 14986 and 1502.

Parallel timelines show events that happened at the same time in different cultures or places. The first timeline below shows some important events for the Aztec Empire. The second timeline shows some European actions and events, around the same time. Looking at both timelines can help you see how events on different continents were related.

It took a long time for the Aztecs to build their empire. About how many years after they first settled on Lake Texcoco did they form an alliance with two other tribes?

Ahuitzotl came to power in 1486. Compare the dates on the timeline to the dates on the map legend. How does that comparison help you to know that Ahuitzotl was a powerful leader?

Aztecs and Europeans

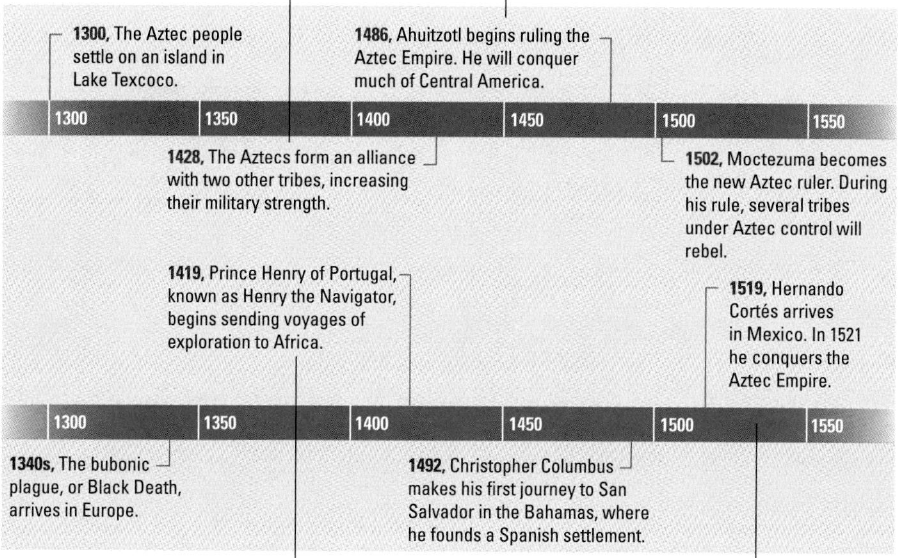

1300, The Aztec people settle on an island in Lake Texcoco.
1486, Ahuitzotl begins ruling the Aztec Empire. He will conquer much of Central America.
1300
1350
1400
1450
1500
1550
1428, The Aztecs form an alliance with two other tribes, increasing their military strength.
1502, Moctezuma becomes the new Aztec ruler. During his rule, several tribes under Aztec control will rebel.
1419, Prince Henry of Portugal, known as Henry the Navigator, begins sending voyages of exploration to Africa.
1519, Hernando Cortés arrives in Mexico. In 1521 he conquers the Aztec Empire.
1300
1350
1400
1450
1500
1550
1340s, The bubonic plague, or Black Death, arrives in Europe.
1492, Christopher Columbus makes his first journey to San Salvador in the Bahamas, where he founds a Spanish settlement.

Prince Henry's interest in exploring Africa increased Europeans' knowledge about sailing. This helped later voyages to the Americas. How long after Henry began sending ships to Africa did Columbus first travel to the Americas?

Look at both timelines. What was happening in the Aztec Empire when Cortés arrived there? How might the 1502 event on the top timeline have affected the 1519 event on the bottom timeline?

CLASS ACTIVITY

Lead students in a discussion of how events in other parts of the world affect this country. List a series of parallel events on the board. Remind students that different cultures have always had an impact on each other. Parallel timelines are one way to show that impact.

Looking Forward

For a more in-depth examination of parallel timelines, turn to Chapter 2, pages 60–61. This Skills lesson uses parallel timelines to look at pre-Revolutionary acts in the colonies and England that precipitated the war.

HISTORY

Visual Learning

For each hundred-year increment on the timelines, have students draw conclusions about the connection of the events to each other, and to the map on the previous page. Introduce some conclusions that are far-fetched. Can students explain why the conclusions may be false?

Answers to Captions

Top left caption: about 120 years later

Top right caption: The years of greatest growth for the empire coincide with Ahuitzotl's rule.

Bottom left caption: 73 years

Bottom right caption: At the time that Cortés arrived, several tribes under Aztec control were rebelling. That could have weakened Moctezuma's power and made it easier for Cortés to conquer the Aztecs.

Collaborative Learning

Challenge groups of students to add more levels to the parallel timelines by researching the same time periods in Asia and Africa.

CLASS ACTIVITY

Strengthen students' map-reading skills by calling on volunteers to give elevation readings of various locations. Identify locations in a variety of ways, such as by latitude and longitude, place name, and landforms. Students should then use the legend to determine the elevation of that location. Also ask comparative questions about locations.

GEOGRAPHY

Visual Learning

The range of elevations on the map go from a high above 6,560 feet to a low of below 18,000 feet. Challenge students to replace the numbers in the legend with descriptive words. For instance, they might describe below 18,000 feet as "the very bottom of the sea." Encourage them to be as creative as possible in their use of language.

GEOGRAPHY

Map and Globe Skills

Direct students to select another location for the profile line and then create a new vertical profile for Africa.

A Relief Map with a Vertical Profile

The map of Africa, shown below, is a relief map. It uses color to indica[te] the elevation, or height above sea level, of the landforms of the continent. The vertical profile is a diagram that presents a side view of a profile line drawn across the map. It shows how the elevation changes along that line.

Africa: Relief Map and Vertical Profile

Before making the profile, the cartographer had to decide where to place the profile line. In this case, the profile line is drawn at 3°S.

The ten colors in the legend show the different elevations across the continent. An elevation of 0 means the land is at sea level.

If you cut through Africa at 3°S, this is what the profile would look like. Notice how the scale from the elevation legend is reproduced in the profile. What would the profile look like if the profile line were drawn at 15°S?

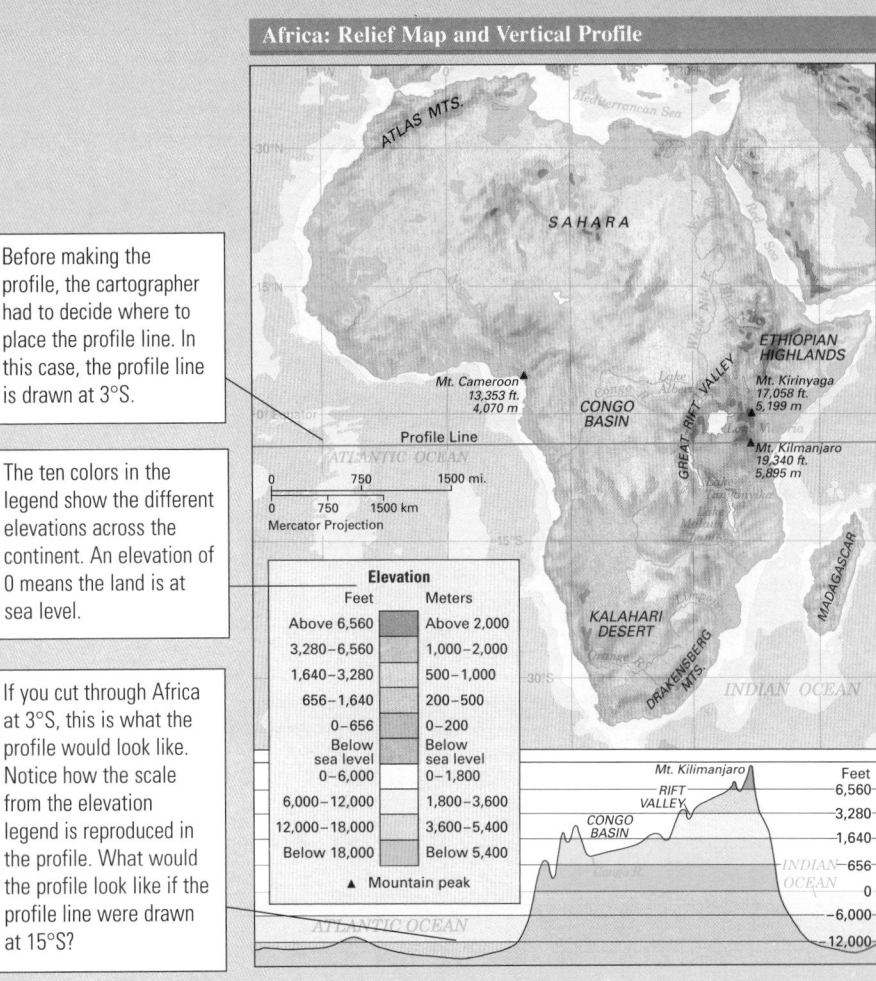

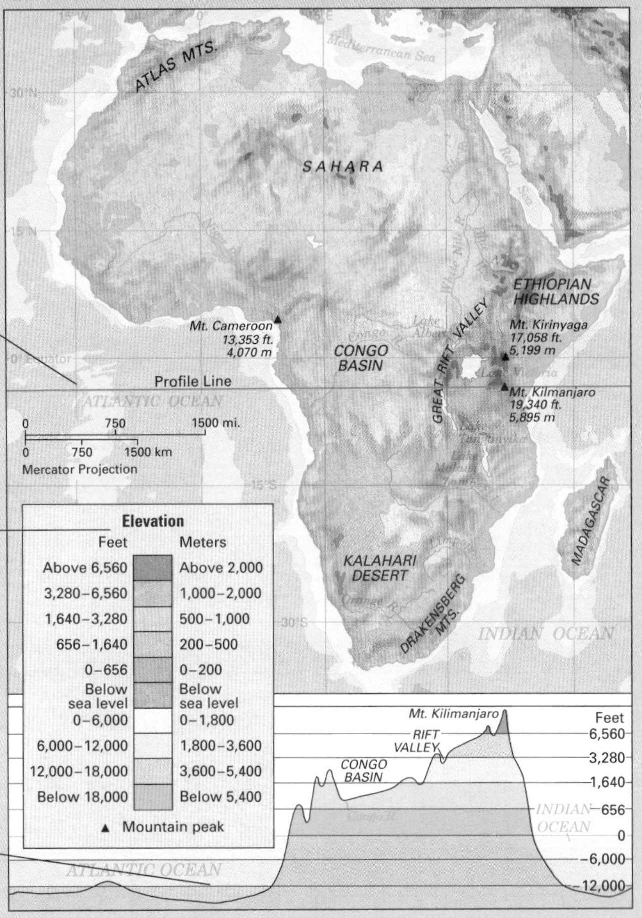

Objectives

1. Determine the elevation of a country. (Geography 1/Visual Learning 1, 4/Map and Globe Skills 1, 4)
2. Understand what a vertical profile is. (Map and Globe Skills 1, 4)

Answers to Captions

Bottom caption: Changing the profile line to 15°S would produce a flatter profile than the one shown here.

Mapping the Classroom

Divide the class into groups of three or four students and charge them with the task of creating a vertical profile of the classroom. Give each group a length of string to use as their profile line.

A Wind and Current Map

Hundreds of years ago, Arab trade ships had no motors, only sails, and the direction and speed of the wind and the ocean currents speeded or slowed travel. The Arabs planned their trips based on the motion of these currents. The map below, showing wind and ocean currents, would have greatly helped them. Today, maps like these are used by anyone traveling by boat.

Wind and Ocean Currents, January

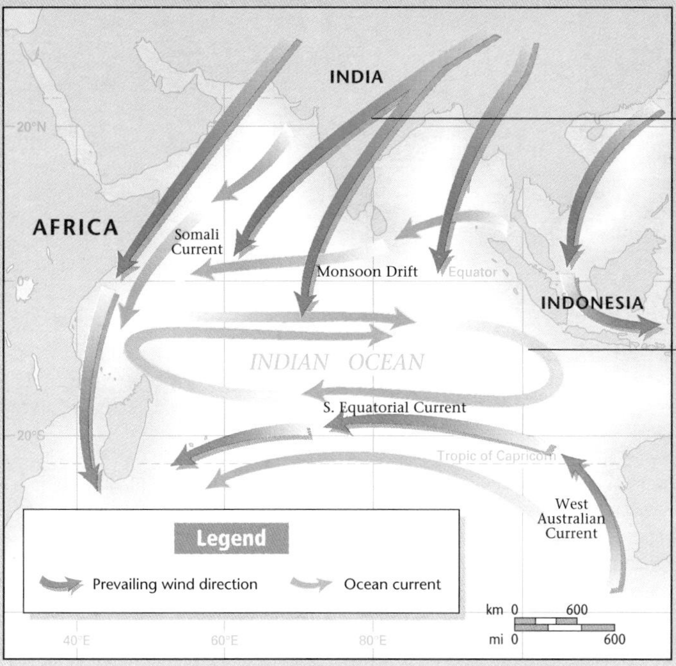

The red arrows represent prevailing winds, which means winds that blow mostly in a certain direction. In January, in what direction do the prevailing winds blow near India?

Ocean currents tend to move in the same direction as wind currents. In January, the currents around India flow away from land. In July, when the prevailing winds blow toward land, in what direction do you think the ocean currents flow?

Because the prevailing winds in Southwest Asia in the winter blow from the cool land to the warm ocean, the land gets little rain during that time. In the summer months, when the land warms up, the winds blow from the cooler ocean to the warmer lands. During the summer months, these winds bring heavy "monsoon" rains.

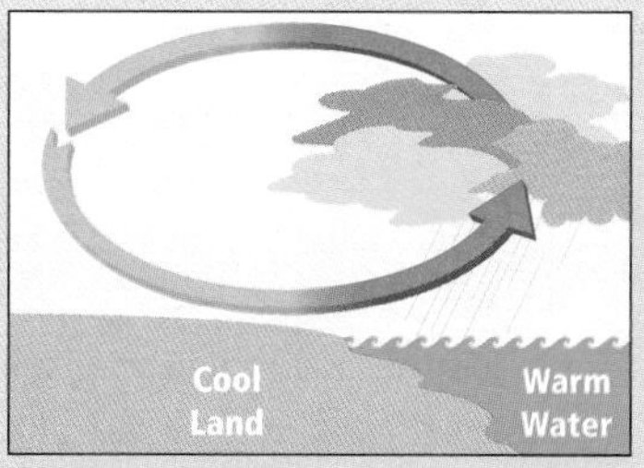

CLASS ACTIVITY

For a week, have your class record wind direction in your community. You may assign pairs of students different times of the day to go outside and record wind direction and/or you may ask them to gather the information from newspapers, radio, or television. What conclusions can they draw about wind direction from their data?

GEOGRAPHY

Map and Globe Skills

Suppose a trader wanted to travel from Africa to Australia in January. What would be the best ocean route to take? How would wind and ocean currents be both helpful and troublesome? Have students repeat the activity for travel between India and Africa.

Answers to Captions

Top caption: southwest, from the land to the ocean

Bottom caption: Ocean currents probably flow northeast, toward the land.

Mapping Winds

Give students the opportunity to create a "Winds from A to Z" atlas. List the following winds on the board: baguio (Philippines), chinook (Rocky Mountains), foehn (Alps), harmattan (Africa), pampero (Argentina), and zephyr (Mediterranean). Students should add to the list and create maps showing where and how these winds blow.

Objective

Form hypotheses from information on a special-purpose map. (Map and Globe Skills 1/ Critical Thinking 2)

CLASS ACTIVITY

Share the following world population figures with students: North America, more than 100 million people; Canada and Mexico, 20–100 million people; Australia, 10–20 million people; Ireland, less than 10 million people. Ask how they could present this statistical data. Students may suggest using a table or a bar graph. Then have them think about how to present the same data on a map. Students may suggest using different colors for different ranges of numbers. Tell them that a cartogram is a type of map that displays statistical data.

Looking Forward

A cartogram showing the gross national product of the countries of the world appears in the Atlas on page 708.

Geography Theme: Places

The cartogram clearly shows that some countries produce far more oil than other countries. Ask students to find out why some places are more oil-rich than others.

A Cartogram

When you first see a cartogram, you may think the mapmaker who created the map needs glasses! Cartograms are maps that show statistical data. As you can see from the cartogram below, the actual shape of a country or continent is usually distorted on these maps. The size of the place is related to the statistical information.

World: Petroleum Resources

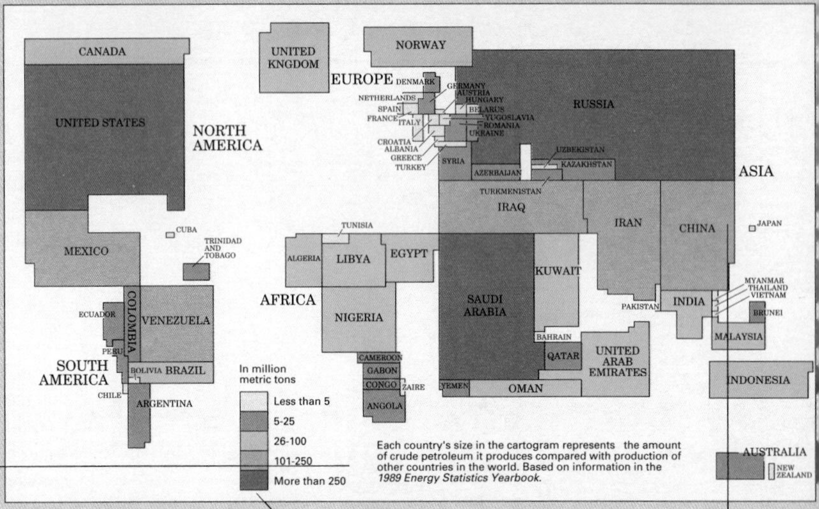

Cartograms don't contain scales of miles or kilometers. Instead, the scale tells what the size of each country represents. In this case, size reflects the amount of crude petroleum each country produces.

The legend gives specific information about how much petroleum each country produces. About how many million metric tons of petroleum does Nigeria produce?

Japan, the United Kingdom, and the United States are three major industrial nations. How do their petroleum resources compare? How might that difference affect the people of these three nations?

MAP SKILLS

1. **REVIEW** If it is 8:00 A.M. in Buenos Aires, Argentina, what time is it in Fairbanks, Alaska?
2. **REVIEW** If you wanted to sail along the northeast coast of Africa in January, in what direction would it be easiest to travel? Why?
3. **THINK ABOUT IT** Why might you want to have a vertical profile of a region?
4. **TRY IT** Look at the map on page 702. Compare the sizes of the United States, Canada, and Mexico to this cartogram. How does each country's actual size compare to its petroleum production?

Objective

Use a cartogram to show the world's production of oil. (Map and Globe Skills 1/ Visual Learning 1)

Answers to Captions and Map Skills

Far left caption: between 26 and 100 million metric tons

Far right caption: Possible answer: Of the three nations, the United States has the greatest oil production, then the United Kingdom, then Japan. This may mean that the people of the United States and the United Kingdom have to import less oil and could be less affected by international oil crises.

1. 2:00 A.M.
2. You should sail southwest. That is the direction of the prevailing winds, which would make sailing easier.
3. Possible answer: Vertical profiles give a better understanding of topography. You can see how the land rises and falls.
4. In comparison to its area, Canada produces very little petroleum. In comparison to their areas, the United States and Mexico produce a great amount of petroleum.

Jsing Geographic References

In which country is the Laurentian Shield located? Where in the world Tenochtitlán? How would you describe what a delta is? If you're stumped any of these questions, turn to the Time/Space Databank at the back of ur book on pages 694–713.

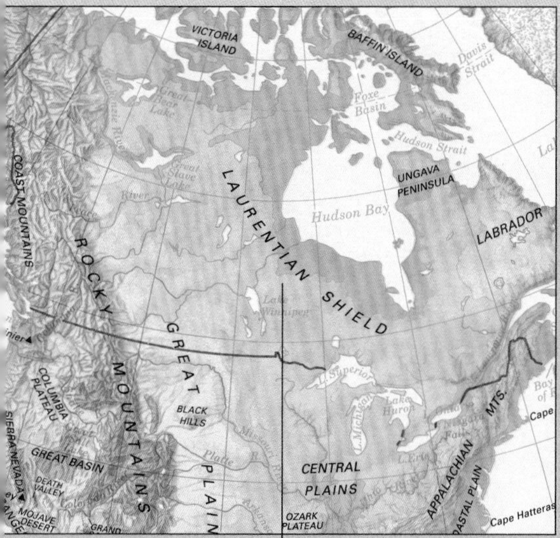

he Atlas, pages 694–708, contains maps of the world, North merica, and the United States. This map section shows anada and a portion of the northern United States. The aurentian Shield is located in Canada.

T

Tenochtitlán (Aztec name for Mexico City) 19°N 99°W

Trenton (capital of New Jersey) 40°N 74°W

The Gazetteer, pages 709–711, describes locations, their latitude and longitude, and gives page numbers where they can be found in this book. Tenochtitlán was the Aztec name for Mexico City. It was located at 19°N, 99°W.

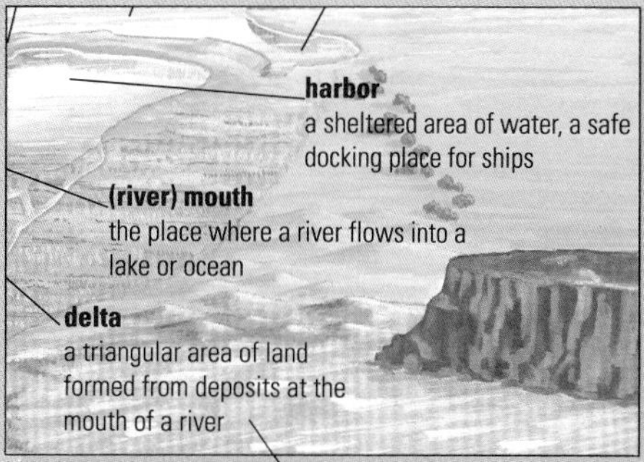

In the Glossary of Geographic Terms, pages 712–713, you'll find drawings and definitions of terms such as "delta." As you can see, a delta is an area of land deposited at the mouth of a river.

MAP SKILLS

REVIEW Where in the Time/Space Databank would you look to find the population density of the United States in 1790?

REVIEW Where are the Badlands located? How would you find that location in the Time/Space Databank?

3. **THINK ABOUT IT** What is the difference between a bay and a harbor? Where would you look to find the answer?
4. **TRY IT** You've been asked to add a map of your community to the Atlas. Draw and label the map. Then create a Gazetteer entry for it.

CLASS ACTIVITY

Divide the class into three teams. Have Team 1 find a map showing the world's climate, Team 2 find the latitude and longitude of Juneau, and Team 3 define the geographic term *steppe* using words and illustrations. Each team member should work independently. When teams have completed their tasks, talk about how each member found the information. Can students form a consensus about which reference material was most helpful?

GEOGRAPHY
Study Skills

Look through pp. 694–713 of the Time/Space Databank. Focus briefly on each of the three sections—the Atlas, the Glossary of Geographic Terms, and the Gazetteer. Encourage volunteers to suggest questions that could be answered by turning to these sections.

Answers to Map Skills

1. Look at the Atlas, page 704.
2. The Badlands are in South Dakota at 43°N, 102°W. You could find that information in the Gazetteer on page 709.
3. A bay is part of the ocean or a lake that extends into land. A harbor is a sheltered area of water; a safe docking place for ships. A bay can be a harbor. The answer is in the Glossary of Geographic Terms.
4. Check students' maps and Gazetteer entries.

Objectives

1. Use Atlas maps to find geography information (Map and Globe Skills 1)
2. Use the Gazetteer to identify places and to find them on maps using latitude and longitude coordinates. (Visual Learning 2)
3. Use the Glossary of Geographic Terms to find definitions and of geographic features. (Visual Learning 1)

Unit 1
A Land of Promise

America was different promises to different people. For Columbus, it was the hope of a faster trade route to Asia. For the Spanish explorers, it was an opportunity for fame and fortune. For the Pilgrims, it was a refuge from religious persecution. And for thousands of European settlers, it was a chance for political freedom and economic opportunity. Whatever the promise, the wilderness land that greeted these newcomers seemed as large and grand as their dreams.

1492

The Rocky Mountains in Colorado. Photograph by Grant Heilman.

UNIT OVERVIEW

After students have read the title of the unit and the narrative underneath it, ask them to imagine that they are explorers or settlers from a small, densely populated European town. How might they feel upon encountering this view of the American landscape? *(Excited; maybe frightened or overwhelmed)* In what ways are the Rocky Mountains representative of the New World? How does the photograph reflect the spirit of the unit title? *(The expansive mountain scene looks inviting; it looks as though it could fulfill people's hopes.)*

Looking Forward

Tell students that they will be reviewing their knowledge of the settlement of the New World and the beginnings of the United States in the next two chapters:

Chapter 1 *Reviewing Exploration and Settlement*
Chapter 2 *Reviewing the American Revolution*

GEOGRAPHY PROJECT

Land and History

Geography Skill **Reading a Regional U.S. Map**
Students use the skills of Acquiring and Analyzing geographic information.

Geography Themes Physical Systems/Environment and Society

Geography Standard 4, physical and human characteristics of places

Activity ***Create Region Reports***

Materials writing paper, construction paper, pencils, markers or crayons

Management Individual/Small Group

Select one of the four regions discussed in the text and write a short report about the physical geography and cultural characteristics before and after European settlement.

Have students:

- write reports and/or create a diorama showing one region's physical geography, the Native Americans living in the region before European settlement, European settlers in the region, or the effects of the American Revolution.
- include a map of the selected region at different time periods.

Understanding the Photograph

Using the physical map of the United States on pp. 700–701, have students locate the Rocky Mountains. Point out that the Rocky Mountains are the largest mountain system in North America. The mountains extend more than 3,000 miles through the United States and Canada. Several United States national parks are located throughout the mountain chain. Refer students to pp. 678–679 in the minipedia.

Understanding Chronology

Point out that Unit 1 covers a nearly 300-year span—from the discovery and exploration of the New World to the end of the American Revolution. What is the significance of the beginning date of the unit—the year 1492? *(It is the year that Christopher Columbus first arrived in the Americas.)*

For research support activities, see the *Research Handbook.*

For simulations correlated to this unit, see *Citizenship Simulations*, p. viii.

HOUGHTON MIFFLIN SOCIAL STUDIES

Bookshelf II

An Enemy Among Them

by Deborah DeFord and Harry S. Stout

In this historical fiction story, Margaret and her Patriot family become tied to Revolutionary War events through a Hessian soldier who fought on the side of Great Britain.

Motivate Read aloud pp. 54–60 (through second paragraph), the hospital scene, in which Margaret meets a wounded Hessian soldier who was brought to the same room as her wounded brother after the Battle of Trenton. Ask students why a soldier fighting for Great Britain would not be welcomed among Patriot communities. Have students predict some of the causes and events of the American Revolution that they will read about in this first unit.

To connect this book with the unit content, use the planning guide and student activity blackline masters beginning on p. iv of the *Bookshelf II Teacher's Resources.*

For additional books that are Easy, Average, and Challenging, see the Unit Bibliography on p. T43. See bibliography updates at www.eduplace.com/ss/hmss.

CHAPTER 1

Planning at a Glance

Reviewing Exploration and Settlement

	Objectives	Reading Support and Other Resources	Diverse Learning Strategies
Lesson 1 The American Land *pp. 4–13* 2–3 days	• Explain why geography is important in the study of history. • Describe the main geographic features of the eastern and southern United States, the central interior of the U.S., and the western U.S.	• **Workbook** or **Reading Support:** pp. 2–5 Review p. 1 Lesson Support/Transition p. 1 Multi-lang. Sum. pp. 1–2 • **Other Resources:** Posters 4, 6; Study Guide p. 1; Study Print 1	Map and Globe Skills **(Visual)** TE p. 7 Music Connection **(Auditory)** TE p. 8 Writing a Description **(Visual)** TE p. 11 Audiotapes of Multi-language Lesson Summaries **(Auditory)**
Making Decisions: Environment or Energy *pp. 14–15*		• **Other Resources:** Poster 8	Activities **(Auditory)** TE p. 14
Lesson 2 European Exploration and Settlement *pp. 16–23* 1–2 days **Literature** "Seven Devil's Mountain" *pp. 24–25*	• Identify the motives behind the European exploration of the Americas. • Explain the significance of European–especially Spanish–exploration of North America. • Summarize the major events in the early European settement of North America.	• **Workbook** or **Reading Support:** pp. 6–9 Review p. 2 Lesson Support/Transition p. 2 Multi-lang. Sum. pp. 3–4 • **Other Resources:** Geography Kit, Poster 2, Study Guide p. 2	Access Strat. **(Extra Support)** TE p. 17 Map and Globe Skills **(Kinesthetic)** TE p. 19 Art Connection **(Visual)** TE p. 21 Audiotapes of Multi-language Lesson Summaries **(Auditory)**
Lesson 3 European and Native Peoples *pp. 26–31* 1–2 days	• Describe how the native peoples of the Americas lived before the arrival of the Europeans. • Explain the impact of early contacts and relations between Europeans and American Indians.	• **Workbook** or **Reading Support:** pp. 10–13 Review p. 3 Lesson Support/Transition p. 3 Multi-lang. Sum. pp. 5–6 • **Other Resources:** Geography Kit, Study Guide p. 3	Access Strat. **(SDAIE)** TE p. 27 Health Connection **(GATE)** TE p. 29 Debate **(Auditory)** TE p. 30 Audiotapes of Multi-language Lesson Summaries **(Auditory)**
Skill: Using Specialized Resources *p. 32*	• Use historical atlases, chronologies, and statistical sources as reference resources.	• **Other Resources:** Study Guide p. 4	
Lesson 4 Life in the English Colonies *pp. 33–39* 2–3 days **Literature** "The Witch of Blackbird Pond" *pp. 40–43*	• Explain how the demand for labor in colonial America led to the growth of both indentured servitude and slavery. • Summarize the chief differences and similarities between the New England, Middle, and Southern colonies.	• **Workbook** or **Reading Support:** pp. 14–17 Review p. 4 Lesson Support/Transition p. 4 Multi-lang. Sum. pp. 7–8 • **Other Resources:** Geography Kit, Poster 1, Study Guide p. 5, Study Print 2	Access Act. **(SDAIE)** TE p. 34 Art Connection **(Visual)** TE p. 36 Homework Options **(GATE)** TE p. 39 Audiotapes of Multi-language Lesson Summaries **(Auditory)**
Chapter Review *pp. 44–45* 1 day		Chapter 1 Test pp. 1–4 *(See facsimiles on TE p. 749.)*	Assessment Multiple-Use Masters pp. 81–88

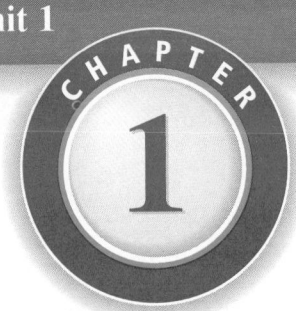

Reading Support Resources *for Every Lesson*

Reading and Review

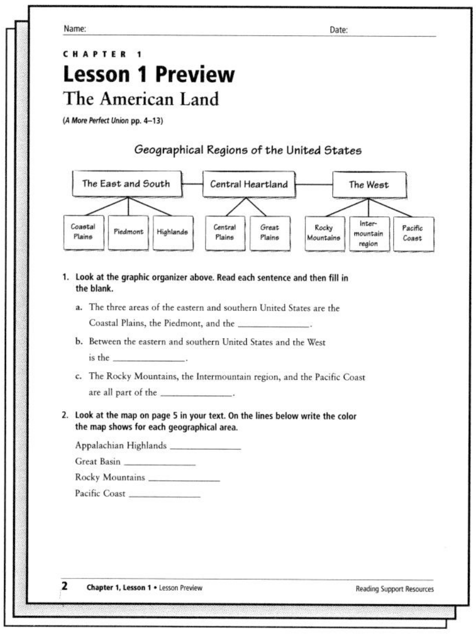
Name: Date:

CHAPTER 1

Lesson 1 Preview

The American Land

(A More Perfect Union pp. 4–13)

Geographical Regions of the United States

The East and South — Central Heartland — The West

Coastal Plains | Piedmont | Highlands | Central Plains | Great Plains | Rocky Mountains | Inter-mountain region | Pacific Coast

1. Look at the graphic organizer above. Read each sentence and then fill in the blank.
   a. The three areas of the eastern and southern United States are the Coastal Plains, the Piedmont, and the ______.
   b. Between the eastern and southern United States and the West is the ______.
   c. The Rocky Mountains, the Intermountain region, and the Pacific Coast are all part of the ______.
2. Look at the map on page 5 in your text. On the lines below write the color the map shows for each geographical area.
   Appalachian Highlands ______
   Great Basin ______
   Rocky Mountains ______
   Pacific Coast ______

2 Chapter 1, Lesson 1 • Lesson Preview — Reading Support Resources

- **Chapter Overview*** p. 1
- **Lesson Previews*** using graphic organizers from the Teacher's Edition pp. 2, 6, 10, 14
- **Reading Strategies*** pp. 3, 7, 11, 15
- **Lesson Summaries*** pp. 4–5, 8–9, 12–13, 16–17
- **Lesson Reviews** pp. 1, 2, 3, 4

* **Workbook** includes starred items.

Multi-language Summaries

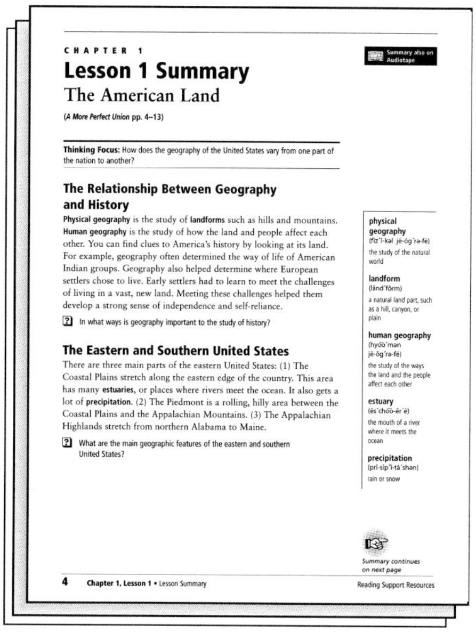
CHAPTER 1

Lesson 1 Summary

The American Land

(A More Perfect Union pp. 4–13)

Summary also on Audiotape

Thinking Focus: How does the geography of the United States vary from one part of the nation to another?

The Relationship Between Geography and History

Physical geography is the study of landforms such as hills and mountains. Human geography is the study of how the land and people affect each other. You can find clues to America's history by looking at its land. For example, geography often determined the way of life of American Indian groups. Geography also helped determine where European settlers chose to live. Early settlers had to learn to meet the challenges of living in a vast, new land. Meeting these challenges helped them develop a strong sense of independence and self-reliance.

In what ways is geography important to the study of history?

The Eastern and Southern United States

There are three main parts of the eastern United States: (1) The Coastal Plains stretch along the eastern edge of the country. This area has many estuaries, or places where rivers meet the ocean. It also gets a lot of precipitation. (2) The Piedmont is a rolling, hilly area between the Coastal Plains and the Appalachian Mountains. (3) The Appalachian Highlands stretch from northern Alabama to Maine.

What are the main geographic features of the eastern and southern United States?

physical geography — the study of the natural world

landform — a natural land part, such as a hill, canyon, or plain

human geography — the study of the ways the land and the people affect each other

estuary — the mouth of a river where it meets the ocean

precipitation — rain or snow

Summary continues on next page

4 Chapter 1, Lesson 1 • Lesson Summary — Reading Support Resources

Lesson Summaries in:

- English (See Reading and Review.)
- Spanish pp. 4–5, 8–9, 12–13, 16–17
- Chinese pp. 1–8
- Hmong pp. 1–8
- Khmer pp. 1–8
- Vietnamese pp. 1–8

Summaries available on audiotapes

Lesson Support / Transition

S D A I E

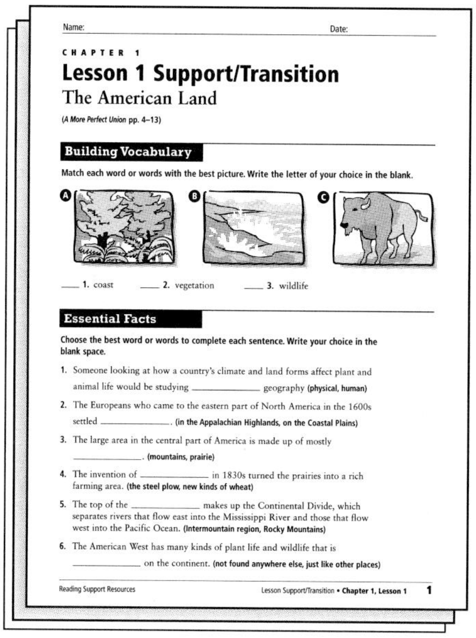
Name: Date:

CHAPTER 1

Lesson 1 Support/Transition

The American Land

(A More Perfect Union pp. 4–13)

Building Vocabulary

Match each word or words with the best picture. Write the letter of your choice in the blank.

A B C

___ 1. coast ___ 2. vegetation ___ 3. wildlife

Essential Facts

Choose the best word or words to complete each sentence. Write your choice in the blank space.

1. Someone looking at how a country's climate and land forms affect plant and animal life would be studying ______ geography (physical, human)
2. The Europeans who came to the eastern part of North America in the 1600s settled ______. (in the Appalachian Highlands, on the Coastal Plains)
3. The large area in the central part of America is made up of mostly ______. (mountains, prairie)
4. The invention of ______ in 1830s turned the prairies into a rich farming area. (the steel plow, new kinds of wheat)
5. The top of the ______ makes up the Continental Divide, which separates rivers that flow east into the Mississippi River and those that flow west into the Pacific Ocean. (Intermountain region, Rocky Mountains)
6. The American West has many kinds of plant life and wildlife that is ______ on the continent. (not found anywhere else, just like other places)

Reading Support Resources — Lesson Support/Transition • Chapter 1, Lesson 1 1

Activities for SDAIE
Specially **D**esigned **A**cademic **I**nstruction in **E**nglish

- **Lesson Support/Transition** pp. 1, 2, 3, 4

Technology Options

Internet Support

http://www.eduplace.com

Social Studies Center at Education Place

Internet support for Chapter 1:

- ***Lesson at a Glance***
- ***The Colonial Farm***

Videotape/Videodisc

We the People:
Supports and enhances major topics: **Themes: *America the Beautiful; Native Americans***

Software

Student Writing Center® (CD-ROM) (Macintosh® or Windows®)
An Odyssey of Discovery™: Continent Explorer II (CD-ROM)

School to Career

Millions have long viewed America as a land of opportunity Career possibilities are virtually limitless. Have small groups of students brainstorm different types of careers. Then, help students organize a classroom career fair, with each group creating a booth spotlighting a specific career.

Character Education

People came to America for a variety of reasons, but for most a great deal of hard work lay ahead. Ask the class for examples of individuals they know who have worked hard and whether such efforts have contributed to that person's success in life.

CHAPTER PREVIEW

After students have read the chapter title and the narrative under it, ask them to explain how the visuals on the page reflect the people who travelled to the New World. *(The map, ships, and the quadrant represent explorers and the photograph of Plimoth Plantation represents settlers.)*

Looking Forward

Tell students that as they read the lessons in this chapter—The American Land, European Exploration and Settlement, Europeans and Native Peoples, and Life in the English Colonies—they will learn how many different groups of people together created the new identity and culture of America.

Chapter 1
Reviewing Exploration and Settlement

European explorers set sail with dreams of glory and discovery in the late 1400s. What they hoped to find was a quicker trade route to Asia. Instead they found a land and a people whose existence had not been known to Europeans. By the 1600s, thousands of Europeans were taking the long ocean voyage to the Americas, drawn by the excitement of discovery and the promise of life in a New World.

1543-45 Battista Agnese's world map includes both the New World and the routes of Spanish explorers.

1450	1500	1550	1600

1492

BACKGROUND

The desire for new trade routes to Asia led Europeans to explore and settle in the New World. This brought them into contact—and sometimes conflict— with the native peoples of the Americas. Thirteen colonies eventually emerged along the Atlantic Coast, colonies with both regional differences and shared characteristics.

Pocahontas

Pocahontas, daughter of the chief of the Powhatan Confederacy of Indian tribes, was an ambassador between the Jamestown colonists and the Indians. Initial contact between the two groups was hostile. An advocate for the settlers, she intervened to save the life of Captain John Smith after he was captured by the Indians and sentenced to death. During the winter of 1607–1608, she supplied the starving colonists with food and provisions. Her marriage to John Rolfe in 1613 sealed an agreement between the Indians and colonists, giving military support to Powhatan in exchange for settlement privileges to the English.

The Lost Colony of Roanoke

The fate of the Roanoke colony has never been determined. Some people speculate that Indians killed the colonists; others think the Indians adopted them. Walter Raleigh made little effort to find them. His land grant was protected only as long as a colony existed; therefore, assuming that they were alive protected his interests.

The development of a new kind of ship, the Portuguese caravel pictured in the 16th century painting above, made the long voyages of the early explorers possible. These explorers used navigational instruments such as the quadrant, shown at left, to chart their courses.

The Pilgrims founded a small settlement in Massachusetts called Plymouth, shown above in a modern reconstruction.

1650	1700	1750	1800

1775

Understanding the Visuals

The sixteenth century painting shows a fleet of Portuguese caravels—vessels used in sixteenth century exploration—sailing up the Tagus River to Lisbon, a center of trade in the 1400s and 1500s.

Draw attention to the Agnese map. Point out that the route shown is Magellan's route around the world. Notice how the map fades near the unexplored areas at the top of North America. The figures blowing the wind represent different races of people.

In the photo of Plimoth Plantation, point out to students that the settlement was located on a hill, giving the settlers a clear view of the harbor. The settlement also included a fort and was surrounded by a barricade.

Understanding Chronology

Draw students' attention to the chapter timeline. Point out that this chapter covers nearly 300 years of history and is designed to review students' knowledge of the exploration and settlement of the New World.

The Salem Witch Trials

Changing social and economic conditions in colonial America were basic factors leading to the Salem witch trials in 1692. The rise of a merchant economy challenged the resources and social status of small-scale subsistence farmers. Factions developed as merchants became wealthier and more powerful.

The judicial system had been suspended in the three years before the Salem witch hysteria, leaving people with no place to air legal complaints. When a special court was created in 1692 to judge witchcraft cases, people used this avenue of redress to state their grievances. Religious changes also led to social divisions. Different religious groups began to appear on the scene challenging the orthodoxy of the Congregational Church. Among them were the Quakers and Baptists. Many of the people killed in the Salem witch trials had social connections or were relatives of members of such dissenting groups. (See also the Literature selection on pages 40–41, which is a fictional account of a witch hunt.)

INTRODUCE

Once students have read the Thinking Focus, ask them to describe the major geographical features of their community and state. Then have them name several places in the United States that have very different landscapes. How would they describe the landscape in these places?

Key Terms

Vocabulary strategies: T36–37

landform—a natural feature of the earth's surface, such as a mountain, hill, plateau, or plain

physical geography—the study of the natural world, including the earth's climate, landforms, water bodies, plants, animals, and resources

human geography—the study of how human beings and places interact with and influence one another

estuary—the mouth of a river whose current is met and partly submerged by the tide of the ocean

precipitation—moisture, condensed in the atmosphere, that falls to the earth in the form of rain or snow

prairie—an area of rolling grassland

plateau—an expanse of high, flat land

LESSON 1

The American Land

THINKING FOCUS

How does the geography of the United States vary from one part of the nation to another?

Key Terms

- landform
- physical geography
- human geography
- estuary
- precipitation
- prairie
- plateau

Even after hundreds of years of exploring, Americans continue to make many discoveries about the land they inhabit. In 1974, for example, a team of archaeologists working in southeastern Missouri unearthed the remains of a culture of people who lived along the Mississippi River centuries ago. The tools, weapons, and broken pottery they found shed new light on the lives of the mound builders of the Mississippi Valley.

Mound builders were not a single group of people. They were many groups of early North American Indians who built monuments out of earth. The mounds they constructed served as burial places and as platforms to hold either temples or the homes of their leaders. Most mound builders lived in the Great Lakes region or in the valleys of the Ohio and Mississippi rivers, where thousands of burial mounds still stand.

The culture of the Mississippian mound builders lasted from roughly 700 to 1600 A.D. In addition to raising livestock and growing crops, these Indians built some of the earliest cities in North America. Cahokia, which is located in present-day Illinois, was the largest of these cities with a population of nearly 40,000.

Like the Mexican Indians, the Mississippian mound builders built their flat-topped mounds in the center of their cities and used them for religious ceremonies. The largest of these temple mounds, Monk's Mound in Cahokia, has a larger base than the Great Pyramid of Egypt and stands 100 feet tall.

By the time the Spanish explorers arrived in the early 1500s, the civilization of the mound builders was already in serious decline. Diseases brought by the Spanish wiped out most of the remaining mound builders in the Mississippi Valley. Although the 1974 discovery in Missouri added another piece to the story of this fascinating people, much remains to be learned about the early inhabitants of the central river valley of North America.

The Relationship Between Geography and History

Like the history of the mound builders, the history of the United States is a story filled with discoveries: the discovery of the New World; the discovery of a previously unknown race of human beings; the discovery of the Pacific Ocean; the discovery of the St. Lawrence, Hudson, and Mississippi Rivers; the discovery of the Great Lakes and the Rocky Mountains; the discovery of corn, tomatoes, potatoes, and squash; the discovery of buffalo, mountain lions, and coyotes—the list could go on for pages. Unlike Europe, which contained no more wilderness, America was a land of mystery—the great unknown. The people who settled there became a nation of explorers, continually looking beyond the next river or hill for new adventures.

Objectives

1. Explain why geography is important in the study of history.
2. Describe the main geographic features of the eastern and southern United States.
3. Describe the main geographic features of the central interior of the United States.
4. Describe the main geographic features of the western United States.

Graphic Overview

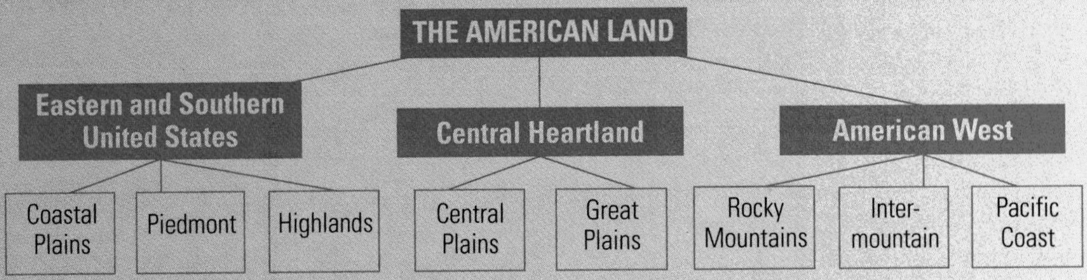

Geography: History's Stage

Any list of the most important discoveries in American history will share a central element: geography. Geography is the place where history happens. Just as the events of a play take place on a specially designed stage, the events of history occur in a specific geographic setting from which they cannot be separated.

Geography involves more than just the study of **landforms** such as mountains, plains, and valleys. In fact, geographers have divided their field into two main branches to take into account geography's varied concerns. **Physical geography** involves the study of the natural world, including the earth's climate, landforms, bodies of water, plants, animals, and resources. **Human geography**, on the other hand, explores how people and places influence one another. Someone interested in the human geography of a region, for instance, might look at the growth and movement of the population, the use of resources, land-use patterns, and the impact of such human-made objects as cities, reservoirs, dams, highways, mines, bridges, and canals.

Geography and American History

To understand American history, then, one must also have a solid grasp of the geography of North America. The briefest survey of U.S. history soon illustrates this point.

For example, geography was partly responsible for the variation in custom and lifestyle that distinguished American Indian societies from one another. Geography also influenced how North America was settled and the particular way in which the continent's population spread westward after 1492. In addition, geography played a role in determining why some towns grew and prospered while others failed.

Geography did more, however, than simply influence certain events and patterns of the nation's history. It also helped shape the character of the American people. Few Europeans knew what to expect when they came to America in the 1600s, and they were continually surprised by what

▲ *Mountain lions like the one pictured above were among the many new animals Europeans encountered in the New World.*

▼ *The map below indicates the most significant physical regions of the United States.*

Geographical Regions of the United States.

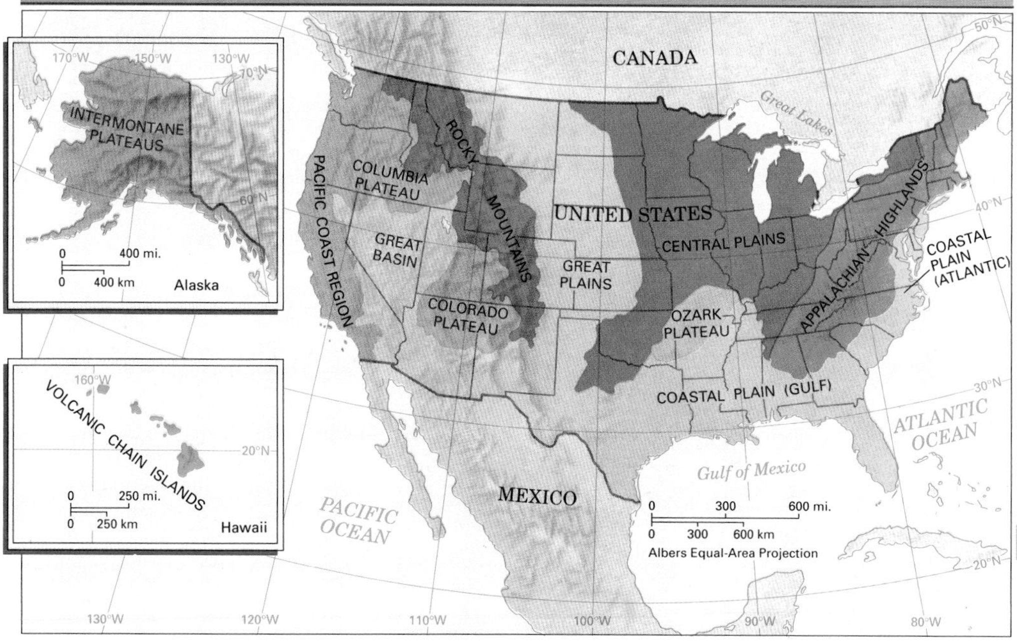

DEVELOP

Copy on the board the Graphic Overview from page 4 and suggest that students make an organization chart for each of the areas described in the lesson. The subheads could include: Landforms, Bodies of Water, Climate, Plants, Animals. Encourage students to fill in details for each region as they read the lesson.

GEOGRAPHY

Critical Thinking

The text on this page compares geography to the setting of a play—"Just as the events of a play take place on a specially designed stage, the events of history occur in a specific geographic setting from which they cannot be separated." Ask students to give examples to support this statement. *(Sample answer: Many towns grew up near good harbors.)*

Access Strategy

Help students become familiar with the concept of physical geography by asking the following questions. What is the climate like where you live? Does it change very much in different seasons? What landforms are around you? Are there hills and mountains, or is the land flat? Are there bodies of water, such as lakes, rivers, or streams? Do you live near a seacoast, or are you inland? What kinds of trees grow in your area? What kinds of animals live there? Have one student write the class's responses to these questions on the board.

Explain that in this lesson students will be reading about the landforms, bodies of water, and plants and animals that are evident throughout the country. They will also learn how geography has affected history.

Access Activity

Have students describe the landscapes shown on pages 6, 7, 9, 11, and 12. Then ask them to use the captions to find the location of each landscape. They can then locate each of these areas on the map on page 5.

CULTURE

Critical Thinking

Have students reread the MacLeish quotation on this page and explain the meaning of *forever* in this context. *(Unlimited possibilities, the unknown)* In what way does the quotation express the ideas of early settlers in the New World? *(The land offered unlimited possibilities.)* In what way was the belief in unlimited possibilities false? *(There was not an unlimited supply of land and natural resources; some possibilities could be realized only at the expense of the American Indians.)*

■ *Geography is important because it plays a role in the development of customs, lifestyles, and political events.*

■ *In what ways is geography important to the study of history?*

they found here. Despite its rich and varied resources, the land proved a constant challenge to these new settlers, demanding all their courage, ingenuity, hard work and perseverance. It is not really surprising, therefore, that while learning to live in this new landscape, these settlers developed a strong sense of self-reliance and independence.

Above all, the sheer size and diversity of the American land amazed most newcomers from Europe. And while the vastness of the land was in one sense yet another challenge, it also fired the imaginations of those who chose to settle in the New World. Just as there seemed no limit to the land, there seemed no limit to the freedom and discoveries it promised. Or, as Archibald MacLeish put it in his 1938 poem, "Land of the Free": "We looked west from a rise and we saw forever." ■

The Eastern and Southern United States

Three major physical regions dominate the eastern portion of the United States: the Atlantic and Gulf Coastal Plains, the Piedmont, and the Appalachian Highlands. Stretching from Maine to Texas, these regions include the original 13 colonies that eventually became the United States.

As you read further in this lesson, refer regularly to the physical map of the United States on pages 700–701 in the Atlas. Refer also to the climate and vegetation maps on page 706 and the precipitation and land use maps on page 707.

Early settlers from Europe made their homes along the Atlantic seaboard. Pictured below is the rocky coast of Maine.

Coastal Plains

From Maine southward, the Atlantic seaboard has a steadily widening coastal plain. Much of the immediate coast is low-lying and swampy, with many offshore islands. Further inland, the coastal plain is a bit higher and better drained.

The jagged shoreline of the east coast contains many natural harbors. In addition, a rise in sea level centuries ago formed numerous **estuaries**, or submerged river mouths, which also provide excellent shelter for ships. Two of the most important of these estuaries are the Chesapeake and Delaware bays.

The Europeans who settled the eastern seaboard in the early 1600s stayed close to the coast. Their chief reason for living by the ocean was to be near the harbors that brought people, supplies, and news from Europe. But the abundance of sea life in coastal waters also provided a steady supply of food for these settlers.

A low, flat continuation of the coastal plain begins in Florida and extends through the South, along the

Visual Learning

Have students look at the picture on this page and explain what it shows about the Maine coast. Then ask what information about the landscape cannot be learned from the picture. *(Seasonal changes, animals, human population)*

Geographic Context

As students read the lesson, they will become increasingly aware of the connection between geography and political and social developments.

The Pilgrims, for example, almost perished at Plymouth because of the rocky terrain and the harsh winter climate. Because of the rocky soil and abundant trees, these northern coast settlers eventually focused on fishing, lumbering, and shipbuilding rather than on farming. Later, the Northeast became the center of industry because of the accessibility of fast-moving streams and waterfalls needed to power factory machinery.

Europeans who settled in Virginia and areas farther south had a different experience. Malnutrition was a problem for Virginia colonists, who were not familiar with the crops and farming methods most suitable to the climate. Virginians became sick and died from diseases borne by insects from the swampy area around their settlement. Their

Gulf of Mexico, to Texas. This area was the site of many Spanish settlements in the 16th and 17th centuries. Although similar to the plain along the Atlantic seaboard, the Gulf Coastal Plain is lower and swampier and contains fewer excellent harbors.

The Piedmont

Inland from the coastal plain lies the "Upper Country," or Piedmont ("foot of the mountains"), as it was later named. This rolling, hilly area—running from New Jersey to Alabama—forms a transition between the plains to the east and the mountains to the west. The place where the harder rocks of the Piedmont meet the softer coastal plain was the former Atlantic shoreline, referred to as the "fall line." The streams flowing out of the hills onto the flat plain produce small waterfalls, which early settlers turned into a source of energy by building waterwheels.

The Appalachian Highlands

West of the Piedmont is the most prominent feature of the eastern section of the country. The Appalachian Highlands, as this region is called, extend from northern Alabama to Maine. At first these mountains were thought to be a barrier to communication and movement, but frontiersmen found "gaps," such as the Cumberland Gap in Kentucky, through which westward movement took place.

A northern section of the Appalachians covers much of New England, meeting the Atlantic Coast in Maine. Because the thin, stony soil was poor for farming, New England's economy depended more on trade and fishing than agriculture in colonial times.

Climate

The Europeans who settled the eastern section of North America encountered greater extremes of temperature than they were accustomed to in Europe. The summers were longer and much hotter, while the winters were colder and harsher.

The entire east coast was said to

▲ *The Appalachian Mountains made western expansion difficult for the English colonists.*

▼ *A low coastal plain and wet climate have created many swamps in the southeastern United States. Alligators like the one shown below populate many of these swamps.*

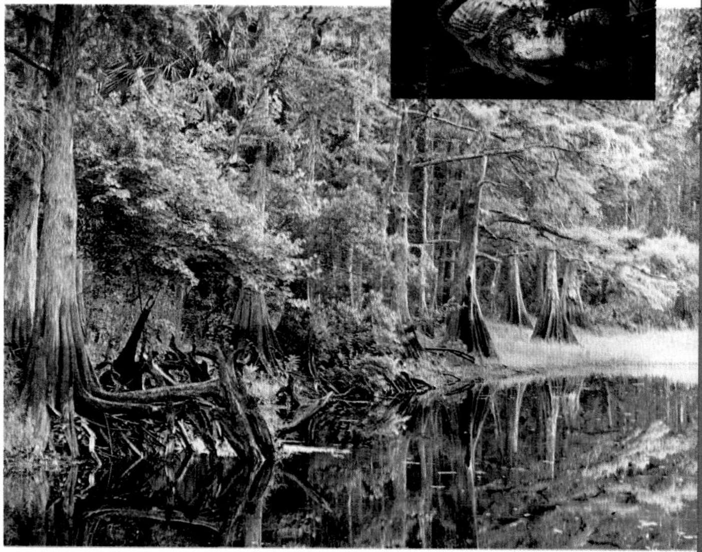

GEOGRAPHY

Critical Thinking

Early European settlers on the northeast coast of America had to learn many new skills to survive. Have students use the map on pages 700–701 and 706–707 in the Atlas to predict answers to the following questions: What kinds of shelter would the settlers need to build? How would they get food? Would they need to navigate rivers or climb mountains? *(Sample answers: Sturdy shelters; farming, fishing, and also hunting; they would need to ford rivers.)*

water supply—salty water from the river estuary—also caused many deaths, although most of the settlers were unaware of the connection.

Although the early Virginians could have started farming right away, serious planting did not take place until they discovered that a type of tobacco popular in Europe grew easily in the Virginia soil. Southern settlers soon became cash crop growers—not only of tobacco, but also of rice, cotton, and indigo. To make a profit, Southern farmers grew large amounts of these crops and therefore required a large labor force. For this reason, indentured servants, and eventually black slaves, were brought to the South. The existence of slavery in the South and the absence of it in the North resulted in part from differences in geography.

Map and Globe Skills

Ask students to find the area where they live on the physical map of the United States on pages 700–701 in the Atlas. What does the map tell them about the landforms in their state? Have them find additional information about their area by looking at the map on pages 706–707 in the Atlas.

GEOGRAPHY

Critical Thinking

In what ways did the geography of the eastern coast of the United States make farming easy? *(Plenty of land and water)* In what ways did it make farming difficult? *(Land had to be cleared; it was too cold for crops in winter in some areas.)*

■ *The main geographic features are the Coastal Plains, the hills inland from the Coastal Plains (the Piedmont), and the Appalachian Highlands.*

▲ *Black bears were a common sight in the forests of the eastern United States in the 1600s and 1700s.*

be "well watered," meaning that there was adequate and dependable rainfall. While western Europe received **precipitation**, or rainfall, in fairly even amounts throughout the year, the settlers found heavier precipitation in the warmer months, coinciding with the growing season.

The further south you go along the eastern seaboard of the United States, the warmer the climate becomes and the milder the winters. The Gulf Coast Plain has a humid subtropical climate. The weather there is hotter and rainier than that found along the Atlantic coast. These conditions provide a longer growing season for such crops as cotton.

Vegetation and Wildlife

Forests were the dominant vegetation in the eastern and southern United States in the early 1600s. Plentiful lumber made the log cabin the most practical form of housing for many settlers. Coniferous, or needleleaf, trees such as cedar, spruce, and pine mixed with deciduous, or leaf-shedding, hardwoods such as elm, oak, maple, ash, and hickory in the colder north. Broadleaf hardwoods were dominant in the middle section of the eastern seaboard and gradually gave way to pines and cypress along the sandy southern coasts. Thicker, tropical vegetation thrived in the swamps of the Gulf Coast.

The first settlers went to work clearing thousands of acres of land for their farms. Despite the massive amounts of land clearing that occurred in the 17th and 18th centuries, new forests now cover large portions of the eastern and southern United States that were once farmland.

In the same way that the rich sea life in the Atlantic attracted people to the coast, the abundant wildlife in the forests soon drew many settlers further inland. French and Dutch fur traders were the first to venture westward in search of beaver, mink, and otter. They soon discovered that the eastern forests of the New World were teeming with such wildlife as black bears, deer, moose, foxes, wildcats, and muskrats. ■

➤ *Deer provided the early settlers with an important source of food.*

■ *What are the main geographic features of the eastern and southern United States?*

The Central Heartland

In the 1700s, the first brave settlers pushed their way westward over the Appalachian Mountains into present-day Kentucky, Ohio, and Indiana. Eventually some of these settlers moved farther west to what is now Indiana and Illinois. What they found was the enormous plain that forms the central heartland of America. Most of this plain consisted of **prairie**, an expanse of flat or rolling grassland.

Writer Washington Irving captured the landscape of the prairie in his 1835 book *A Tour on the Prairies:*

> After a toilsome march of some distance through a country cut up by ravines and brooks, and entangled by thickets, we emerged upon a grand prairie. Here one of the characteristic scenes of the Far West broke upon us. An immense extent of grassy, undulating, or, as it is termed, rolling country, with here and there a clump of trees, dimly seen in the distance like a ship at sea; the landscape deriving sublimity (majesty) from its vastness and simplicity.

Critical Thinking

What physical conditions do you think were new for the British settlers on the Atlantic Coast of the United States. *(Sample answer: Climates more harsh, denser forests, more wild animals)* How do you think these conditions affected their lifestyle? *(Sample answer: They had to build sturdy houses and clear land in order to farm.)*

Music Connection

The geography of America has been celebrated in many musical works, one of the most popular being Woody Guthrie's folk national anthem, "This Land Is Your Land." Provide the lyrics and play a recording of the song in class, if possible. Encourage students to discuss the meaning of the lyrics. Ask them to think of other songs whose lyrics relate to the physical or human geography of the land. *("America the Beautiful," "Old Man River," "Home On The Range," "Old Cape Cod," "The Sidewalks of New York"; songs sung by pioneers, cowhands, and black slaves)*

You may also wish to point out that the landscape of North America has inspired orchestral music as well. If possible, play recordings of Sergei Grofé's *Grand Canyon Suite,* Antonín Dvořák's *Symphony No. 9* ("New World"), and *Appalachian Spring* by Aaron Copland.

The Central and Great Plains

From the Appalachians westward to the Rockies lies the region drained by the Mississippi River system. Geographers generally divide this great interior plain into two areas: the Central Plains in the east and the Great Plains in the west.

The early explorers of the Central Plains either came north from the mouth of the Mississippi River or south from the Great Lakes. What they discovered was a huge expanse of rolling grasslands that rose gradually toward the forested foothills of the Appalachian Mountains in the east.

The south-central portion of the Central Plains is interrupted by the Ozark Mountains, which cover a wide area of present-day Arkansas and Missouri. The northern reaches of this interior region are occupied by the Great Lakes, the enormous water system that allowed early explorers and traders to penetrate the interior.

Like the Central Plains, the Great Plains are an enormous expanse of grassland, though they are bleaker and emptier than the eastern prairies. From their starting point in the western sections of the Dakotas, Nebraska, and Kansas, the Great Plains rise gradually to meet the Rocky Mountains in the west. Stretching from North Dakota to Texas, the Great Plains are briefly interrupted in South Dakota by a series of steep hills and gullies known as the Badlands.

Climate

The climate of the central heartlands is a climate of extremes. In the summer, temperatures often top 100° F. In the winter, they may drop as low as -40° F. The distance of the plains from any oceans, which have a moderating influence on weather patterns, is largely responsible for these extreme temperatures.

The average annual rainfall in the Central Plains is moderate, though it is less plentiful than that found along the Atlantic seaboard. To the west of the Mississippi, however, the amount of rainfall diminishes steadily. Rainfall

Coyotes like the one shown below roamed the tall grasslands of the prairies long before the first Europeans arrived on the scene.

GEOGRAPHY

Critical Thinking

Refer students to the text on this page and to the maps on pages 700–701 and 706–707 of the Atlas. Have them imagine being newly arrived settlers in the Central Plains in the 1700s. Ask them to predict the problems they will have building shelters, finding food, and preparing the land for farming. *(Few trees for wood; different game animals; very tall grass—probably with very deep roots)*

Language Arts Connection

America's geography has also been celebrated in folktales. Ask students to recall the stories of Johnny Appleseed and Paul Bunyan and to point out how these tales relate to geography. Use a folklore anthology to help them remember the details.

Many popular works of American literature and poetry have also focused on people's interaction with or feelings about the land. Have groups of students look through an anthology of literature to find poems that express sentiments about the land. Each group can introduce one poem to the rest of the class. Suggestions include: Vachel Lindsay's "An Indian Summer Day in the Prairie," Langston Hughes's "The Negro Speaks of Rivers," Robert Frost's "Birches," and Edna St. Vincent Millay's "Exiled."

Visual Learning

Have students make a list of words describing the prairie in the picture on this page. *(Endless, empty, rolling)* Then have them explain how living on the prairie would be different from living in the Appalachian Mountains (as described on page 7).

GEOGRAPHY

Critical Thinking

Remind students that millions of bison lived on the Great Plains in the 1700s and 1800s. Based on what they know about the Great Plains, what inferences could they make about the dietary needs of bison and the conditions in which they can survive? *(Bison feed on grass and need wide open spaces for grazing.)*

■ *Geographic features of the central interior of the U.S. include prairies (Central Plains and Great Plains), Ozark Mountains, Great Lakes, and Badlands.*

The bison, or buffalo, has come to symbolize the romance and adventure of the frontier more than any other animal.

■ *What are the main geographic features of the central interior of the United States?*

in the Great Plains is so limited that parts of that region are semidesert.

Vegetation and Wildlife

The humid, wetter areas just west of the Appalachians supported forests of broadleaf hardwoods. The Great Lakes territory and the Ozark Highlands were also heavily forested. But starting in Indiana and Illinois, the forests gave way to grasslands.

The first pioneers who saw the prairies described them as a "sea of grass." This description particularly suited the prairies of the Central Plains, which received sufficient rainfall to support a lush cover of tall grass that was often higher than a horse's back. In addition, the streams and rivers of the eastern plains were lined in many places with trees.

To the west, the limited moisture of the Great Plains provided only enough moisture for shorter grasses, one to two feet high. But these "buffalo" grasses, as the early settlers called them, played a crucial role in the environment of the plains. By holding the soil in place, they kept the Great Plains from becoming a real desert.

Early visitors to the prairies did not realize the rich agricultural potential of these grasslands. In addition, the wooden plow of that time was not capable of cutting through the thick root system of the grasses. The invention of the steel plow in the 1830s enabled the pioneers of that era to subdue and farm the land of the Central Plains. Even the Great Plains, once called the "Great American Desert," became prime grazing land for cattle and a major producer of wheat in the late 1800s.

Before 1800, the American bison, or buffalo, roamed as far east as Ohio and Kentucky. As late as the 1870s, millions of buffalo still crowded the western plains, along with a number of other forms of wildlife unique to that region. The pronghorn (American antelope), prairie dog, ground squirrel, jack rabbit, coyote, mountain lion, and wolf were some of the wildlife encountered by pioneers on their western journeys. ■

The American West

The American West, or Far West as it is sometimes called, contains three major physical regions: the Rocky Mountains, the Intermountain region, and the Pacific Coast. It also contains some of the most dramatic and varied landscape in the United States.

The Rocky Mountains

Running more than 3,000 miles, north and south, through the United States and Canada, the Rocky Mountains cover parts of New Mexico, Colorado, Utah, Wyoming, Idaho, Montana, Washington, and Alaska. They were long seen as an immense barrier between the eastern two-thirds of the United States and the western coast. Tall and rugged, the Rockies contain 52 peaks that are higher than 14,000 feet. Crossing these mountains created many hardships for pioneers in the 1800s.

The crest of the Rockies forms an important dividing line on the North

Study Skills

Have each student choose a national park from the map on pages 678–679 in the Minipedia and then write to the National Park Service for more information: Department of the Interior, National Park Service, Rm. 1013, P.O. Box 37127, Washington, D.C., 20013–7127

Oral Report

Remind students that when settlers arrived in America, many people were already living across the land. Put students in groups to research how different groups of American Indians interacted with the land. Each group of students can research the lifestyle, customs, and beliefs of one group of American Indians by looking in encyclopedias and other reference books. They can then report their findings to the rest of the class. You could suggest the following American Indian groups: Wampanoag, Powhatan, Seminole, Pawnee, Hopi, Kennebec, Chinook, Pueblo, Sioux, and Cherokee.

American continent. Called the Continental Divide, this ridge separates rivers that flow east into the Mississippi and the Gulf of Mexico—the Missouri, the Arkansas, the Platte, the Rio Grande—from those that flow west into the Pacific Ocean—the Colorado and the Columbia.

The Intermountain Region

The Intermountain region, as the area between the Rockies and the Sierra Nevada is sometimes called, contains high plateaus and basins, deep canyons, and wide deserts. The largest and most important geographical areas in the Intermountain region are the Great Basin and the Colorado Plateau.

Although the term basin often applies to a low-relief, low-elevation landscape, such is not the case with the Great Basin, whose average elevation is 4,000–5,000 feet above sea level. Located as it is between the Rocky Mountains on the east and the even taller Sierra Nevada on the west, however, the Great Basin does have the appearance of an enormous bowl.

Because the region is an interior basin, rivers flowing into the Great Basin from the surrounding mountains have no outlet to the ocean. As a result, these streams either dry up, disappear underground, or flow into lakes that become salty. The most famous of these lakes is Great Salt Lake in Utah.

A **plateau** is an area of high, flat land. One of the largest plateaus in the United States is the Colorado Plateau, which includes much of Arizona, parts of Utah, and smaller areas of Colorado and New Mexico. Long the home of the Hopi, Navajo, and Zuni Indians, this region was later settled by the Spanish and Mexicans.

Rugged deserts and deep canyons make up most of the land in the Colorado Plateau. Among the most famous natural features of the region are the Grand Canyon of the Colorado River and the Painted Desert.

The Pacific Coast

Unlike the eastern seaboard, the Pacific Coast contains few natural harbors. But with its rugged coastline and nearby mountain ranges, it does possess some of the most dramatic scenery in North America.

Apart from a break at San Francisco Bay, the mountains of the Coastal Ranges run parallel to the coast from central California through Oregon to Washington state. Further inland are the much higher peaks of the Klamath Mountains and the Sierra Nevada in California, and the Cascades in California, Oregon, and Washington. The most important rivers in the region—the Columbia, the Sacramento, the San Joaquin, and

Across Time & Space

Today the states in the Great Plains produce more wheat than any other region in the world. In addition to being the "breadbasket" of the United States, this area provides wheat to many other nations as well.

The Rocky Mountains proved to be a serious obstacle for pioneers traveling west. The region is still rich in wildlife such as the elk pictured below.

GEOGRAPHY

Critical Thinking

Point out that both the Intermountain region in the West and the Piedmont region in the East are located between mountain ranges and coastal areas. Ask students to contrast these two areas. *(Piedmont—rolling hills, plains, waterfalls; Intermountain—high plateaus, basins, deep canyons, deserts)*

Writing a Description

Artists have portrayed the American landscape in many different ways. Have students choose a landscape painting or photograph by one of the following artists: William Sidney Mount, George C. Bingham, Thomas Cole, Frederick Church, Albert Bierstadt, Fitz Hugh Lane, Winslow Homer, Edward Hopper, Georgia O'Keeffe, Ansel Adams, or David Muench. They can use art history books, encyclopedias, and magazines to find paintings or photographs by these artists. Then have them write one or two paragraphs describing the picture they have chosen. Have them refer to the excerpt on page 8 for an example of a vivid description. Some students may be interested in drawing or painting a landscape based on one they have researched.

Critical Thinking

Point out that 200 years ago the Rocky Mountains were considered a barrier between the west coast and the rest of the United States. Ask students why these mountains are no longer considered to be a barrier. *(Roads, trains, and airplanes have made it easy to get over the mountains.)*

GEOGRAPHY

Visual Learning

Ask students to study the picture of the Pacific coast on this page and compare and contrast it to the Atlantic coast in the picture on page 6. *(Both coasts are rocky—jagged on the Atlantic coast and stepped on the Pacific coast; trees on both coasts)*

▲ *Although the Pacific Coast contains many dramatic cliffs and beautiful beaches, it has few natural harbors.*

the Colorado—are important sources of water and water power. The Grand Coulee Dam on the Columbia River and the Hoover Dam on the Colorado produce a large portion of the region's electrical power.

The other significant landform in the region is the great Central Valley of California. This valley runs more than half the length of the state. Many of California's early settlers chose the rich land of the Central Valley for their new home.

Climate

The highlands climate of the Rocky Mountains is characterized by cool, short summers and cold winters. Rainfall varies with elevation, with the higher elevations receiving heavy amounts of precipitation.

The chief climatic feature of the Intermountain region is the lack of rainfall. In fact, roughly half of the land in this area is actual desert, more suitable for mining than for agriculture. Temperature ranges from summer to winter are extreme throughout the region, particularly in the Great Basin.

▼ *Seals are among the most common form of marine life found in the waters off the California coast.*

Much of California has a Mediterranean climate, with mild, wet winters, and sunny, dry summers. Since it mirrored the weather patterns of Spain, this climate was especially attractive to Spanish settlers.

The Pacific Northwest, which includes northern California and the Oregon and Washington coasts, has what is known as a marine climate. Although this climate is cooler and wetter than that of central and southern California, it is also much milder than the climate of New England.

Vegetation and Wildlife

The lower slopes of the Rocky Mountains are covered with junipers, piñon pines, and aspen. At higher elevations, coniferous forests of fir, pine, and spruce flourish. Above a certain point called the "tree line," however, the climate is too harsh to support trees.

Because of the lack of rainfall there, the vegetation of the Great Basin is sparse. Plant life consists mainly of scrub, broken here and there by occasional patches of steppe grasses. Trees are rare and are confined to narrow strips along riverbanks.

In addition to scrub, sagebrush,

Study Skills

Have groups of students choose from the lesson an animal that lives in the West. Each group should research the animal's characteristics, habitat, and feeding patterns. Are there obvious reasons why the animal is most comfortable living in that particular environment? Have groups share their information.

Writing a Travelogue

Ask students to imagine taking a trip across America by small airplane—flying over several of the regions discussed in this lesson. Their assignment is to gather details about the physical geography of the land over which they pass. Where do they see mountains, lakes, rivers, plains, and plateaus? Have students plan their routes and gather the details. Students can then put this information into a travelogue describing the geographic details of the imaginary route that they took across the country. Ask volunteers to read their descriptive travelogues to the rest of the class. Some students may wish to substitute an annotated or illustrated map in place of a written travelogue.

and mesquite trees, the deserts of the Colorado Plateau support a variety of species of cactus. During dry periods, the vegetation of the desert is sparse. But after a rainfall, colorful flowers and lush vegetation may cover parts of the desert for a brief period.

The Pacific Coast supports a wide variety of plant life. In the southern sections of California, for example, tropical plants such as palm trees thrive. In the Central Valley, on the other hand, Mediterranean crops such as grapes and olives have replaced the earlier cover of short grasses. Scrub vegetation and coniferous forests of fir and redwoods cover the mountains of the Coastal Ranges, while coniferous forests of fir and pine are the rule in the higher Sierra Nevada and Cascades. The thick forests of the Pacific Northwest are a major source of timber for the United States.

The American West contains numerous forms of wildlife that are not found elsewhere on the continent. The Rocky Mountains, for example, serve as the home for grizzly bears, wild goats, and bighorn sheep. The deserts of the American Southwest contain such wildlife as roadrunners, peccaries (wild pigs), kangaroo rats, Gila monsters, and many other species of birds and lizards that are unique to the desert. Columbian black-tailed deer and Roosevelt elk are unique to the Pacific Coast. The rich marine life of the west coast includes salmon, abalones, otters, and sea lions.

In the mid-1800s, thousands of pioneers traveling west thought of the Pacific Coast as a kind of promised land. Two centuries earlier, many Europeans viewed the East Coast of North America in exactly the same way. In the late 1400s, however, most Europeans did not even dream, let alone know, of the existence of new continents to their west. For them, America was still a wilderness land waiting to be explored. ■

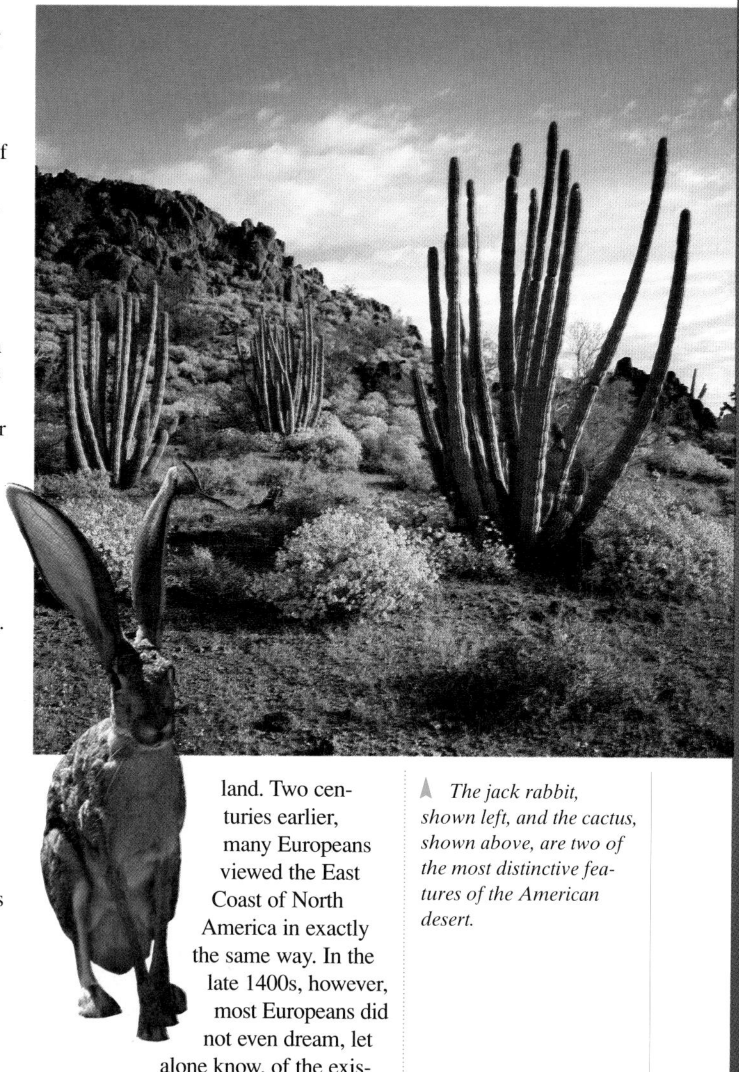

The jack rabbit, shown left, and the cactus, shown above, are two of the most distinctive features of the American desert.

■ *What are the main geographic features of the western United States?*

■ *The main geographic features of the western United States are the Rocky Mountains, the Intermountain region, and the Pacific Coast.*

REVIEW

1. **FOCUS** How does the geography of the United States vary from one part of the nation to another?
2. **GEOGRAPHY** In what kinds of events or objects would a human geographer be interested?
3. **GEOGRAPHY** How did geography influence the way the eastern section of the United States was settled?
4. **CRITICAL THINKING** Look at the population density map for 1990 on page 705 in the Atlas. How did geography contribute to the creation of both the most densely and least densely populated regions of the United States?
5. **WRITING ACTIVITY** Imagine you are a pioneer who has moved from New England to the Great Plains. Write a journal entry in which you compare your new life to your old and explain how it is influenced by geography.

CLOSE

Ask students to share the details that they collected for their organization charts. Have them combine their findings into one organization chart on the board. They can then use the chart to make sentences describing the different regions. To summarize the lesson, have students answer the Thinking Focus.

Answers to Review Questions

1. The geography of the United States varies from low-lying, swampy coastal plains to rolling hills and highlands, rolling grasslands, prairies, high mountains, deep canyons, plateaus, and coastal mountains.
2. Sample answer: A human geographer would be interested in how people use the land and how human settlement affects the land.
3. Good harbors and fishing encouraged people to stay along the coast.
4. Sample answer: Many people live near natural transportation routes (rivers), good harbors, and in comfortable climates. Fewer people live in areas that are isolated by natural barriers. Allow for personal opinion.
5. Encourage students to use details about the geography of the area.

Homework Options

Ask students to investigate a current situation in which geography is affecting the course of events. *(Desertification in Africa)*

Study Guide: page 1.

DECISION-MAKING PROCESS

1. Recognize the need for a decision.
2. Define the goals and values involved.
3. Acquire and evaluate necessary information.
4. Identify and analyze possible alternatives.
5. Choose the best alternative.

This Making Decisions lesson, Environment or Energy, will focus on steps 1 and 2 of the decision-making process.

CITIZENSHIP

Critical Thinking

Discuss the reasons why Congress would want to set aside certain lands, such as the ANWR, for the protection of wildlife. Ask students why they think protecting wildlife is a goal of the U.S. Government. *(To enjoy the beauty of wildlife, for scientific study, as a reminder of the natural state of land before settlement and development)*

MAKING DECISIONS

Environment or Energy

The facts point to the urgent need to open 1.5 million acres of the Coastal Plain of the Arctic National Wildlife Refuge [ANWR] to exploration. The facts also highlight the industry's ability to develop arctic oil in an environmentally sound manner.

Oil Company Publication, Winter 1989

If we're going to develop this [the ANWR coastal plain] we might as well go ahead and dam the Grand Canyon. You can make the same arguments for national energy needs. So why don't we? Because the nation has decided it's in its own best interest to preserve the Grand Canyon and find our energy elsewhere.

Tim Mahoney, "An Arctic Dilemma," *National Geographic*, December 1980

Background

Environmentalists say that exploration of the coastal plain could harm the habitats of wildlife such as the Dall sheep.

The wild and remote lands of northeast Alaska are home to a variety of wildlife—grizzly bears, wolverines, Dall sheep, foxes, moose, and North America's largest caribou herd. These lands are also the summer nesting places of snowy owls, peregrine falcons, golden eagles, and many other birds.

In 1960, to protect the wildlife in this unspoiled region, Congress set aside 8.9 million acres as the Arctic National Wildlife Range. Twenty years later, in 1980, Congress added 10 million acres to the protected area, and renamed it the Arctic National Wildlife Refuge (ANWR). Congress also said that 1.5 million acres of the refuge could be studied as a possible source of oil and gas. The area to be studied was the coastal plain—the flat, marshy land between the rugged mountains of the Brooks Range and the Arctic Ocean.

In early 1987, the U.S. Department of the Interior released the results of a six-year study of the ANWR coastal plain. Their report stated that the region might contain as much as 9.2 billion barrels of oil.

Objectives

1. Identify the issues involved in a conflict over land use in Alaska. (Critical Thinking 1)
2. Define the goals and values of both sides in an environment v. energy conflict. (Citizenship 5)

Activities

Divide the class into pairs. Ask one student of each pair to take a pro-environment view in a debate (assuming that any oil drilling on the coastal plain will disturb the wildlife). Ask the other student to take a pro-drilling view (assuming that drilling creates benefits for Alaskans as well as supplying energy for many people). Give the students time to research their positions.

Have students take on the different roles of concerned people, animals, and even inanimate objects and share with the rest of the class how the issues look from each perspective. (Sample roles: the head of an oil company, a grizzly bear, an average consumer, coastal marsh lands).

Conflict Over the Land

The report recommended beginning oil exploration as soon as possible, and touched off a heated debate between oil companies and environmentalists. Producers argue that the nation needs the energy and that the ANWR region is the most promising oil exploration site in the country. Developing the site, they say, would eliminate the need to purchase imported oil. It would also help the Alaskan economy by bringing in money and jobs. They cite polls showing that most Alaskans want to develop the state's mineral resources.

Environmentalists argue that oil drilling would be harmful to the environment, destroy wildlife habitats, and disturb the fragile balance of the Alaskan wilderness. The oil industry cannot be trusted to protect the environment, they say, pointing to the oil spills that happened around the world, despite the industry's assurances that such events will not happen.

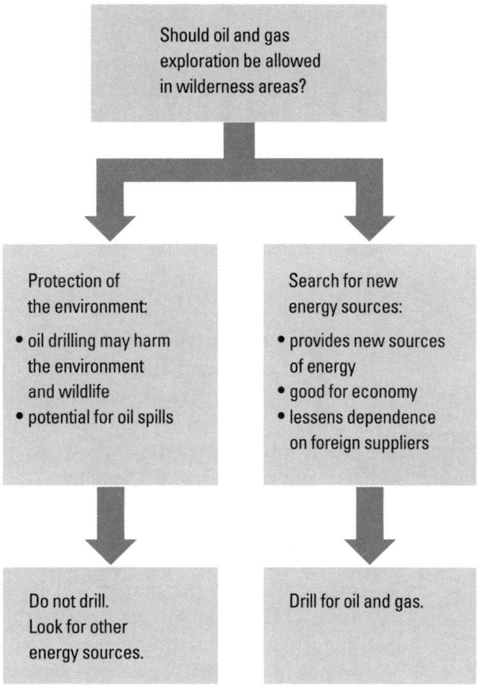

Should oil and gas exploration be allowed in wilderness areas?
Protection of the environment:
• oil drilling may harm the environment and wildlife
• potential for oil spills
Search for new energy sources:
• provides new sources of energy
• good for economy
• lessens dependence on foreign suppliers
Do not drill. Look for other energy sources.
Drill for oil and gas.

Decision Point

1. What are the benefits of drilling for oil on the coastal plain?
2. What are the benefits of leaving the coastal plain undisturbed?
3. If you were going to vote on whether drilling should be allowed on the coastal plain, what other information would you want?
4. What alternatives to drilling can you think of that would be good for the economy and less harmful to the environment? Discuss this question in small groups, then report to your class.

Oil producers believe that the ANWR region offers the most promising oil exploration site in the United States.

CITIZENSHIP
Visual Learning

Have students identify in the decision-making chart the main issue that involves a conflict, the goal of each of the two sides, and the values implied by those two goals.

ECONOMICS
Critical Thinking

Discuss the reasons why Congress would agree to study the wildlife refuge as a possible source of oil and gas. Why are these resources important economically? *(Large energy needs of an industrial society; oil and gas becoming increasingly scarce resources)*

Answers to Decision Point

1. The area might contain as much as 9.2 billion barrels of oil that we would not have to import.
2. The natural habitats and nesting areas of numerous species would remain protected.
3. Sample answers: Are there alternative sources of energy and how costly are these? How good have the oil producers been at avoiding environmental catastrophes? What evidence do environmentalists give to support the claim of possible harm to wildlife? What are the exact results of the polls of Alaskans?
4. Sample answers: Renewable energy sources such as solar and wind power should be researched, as well as decreases in the use of plastics that are manufactured from oil.

Collaborative Strategy

A recommended strategy for this lesson is pair-debate. For more details about collaborative learning strategies, see pages T34–35.

INTRODUCE

Point out the lesson title and explain that exploration in the New World went on for over a hundred years before Europeans began to settle there. Have one student read aloud the Thinking Focus. Then ask students to predict why people would leave their homes to explore new lands. Have them read to confirm or reject their predicitons.

Key Terms

Vocabulary strategies: T36–37
navigation—practice of plotting the course of a ship
conquistador—a Spanish word meaning "conqueror"
sect—a small religious group that has separated from a larger denomination

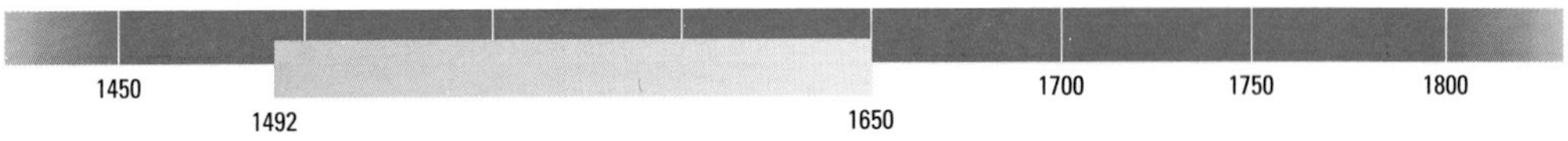

L E S S O N 2

European Exploration and Settlement

THINKING FOCUS

Why did Europeans leave their homes in the 1500s and 1600s to explore and settle new continents?

Key Terms

- navigation
- conquistador
- sect

Thunderclouds rise like mountains off to the east. The once calm ocean has suddenly grown restless, loudly thumping the ship's prow.

You're crossing the Atlantic Ocean in the mid-1500s. Nearby you can hear the crew member on watch calling out worried instructions to the man at the helm. Already the sky has turned black, and the seas begin to run high. Suddenly the storm erupts. You witness a wild fury you've never seen before in nature.

Indeed, dangerous storms were just one of the hardships facing the brave women and men who left Europe in search of new lives in a New World. They came in boats not much longer than your classroom. The ships had weak rigging and small hulls. To plot their course, sailors depended on simple navigational equipment such as the astrolabe, an instrument used to calculate the position of the sun and stars. Conditions on board these early ships were not pleasant. A Spanish priest named Father Thomas de la Torre, who made the long voyage to America in 1544, described his experience in this way:

We soon realized that the sea was not man's natural habitat. Everyone became so seasick that nothing in the world could induce us to move from where we lay. A more befouled hospital and one so filled with the moans of the sick can hardly be imagined. Some sufferers were cooked alive in the heat below decks. The sun roasted others, where they were trod upon and trampled, and where they were so filthy that words cannot describe the scene. . . .

Europeans Look to New Worlds

Despite the hardships of the two-month Atlantic crossing, Europeans made it their business to stretch the boundaries of their world. The hunger for new lands came in many forms and for many reasons.

First of all, a revival of classical art, literature, and learning known as the Renaissance *(REHN i sahns)*, was taking place in Europe in the 15th and 16th centuries. It sparked people's imaginations and made them more eager to explore the world around them. At roughly the same time there was a revolution in religion known as the Protestant Reformation. This movement challenged the Catholic religious authorities, who in turn persecuted the Protestants. The Protestants longed for a place where they could worship as they thought best.

Objectives

1. Identify the motives behind the European exploration of the Americas.
2. Describe the role Spain played in exploring the New World.
3. Explain the significance of the English, French, and Dutch exploration of North America.
4. Summarize the major events in the early European settlement of North America.

Graphic Overview

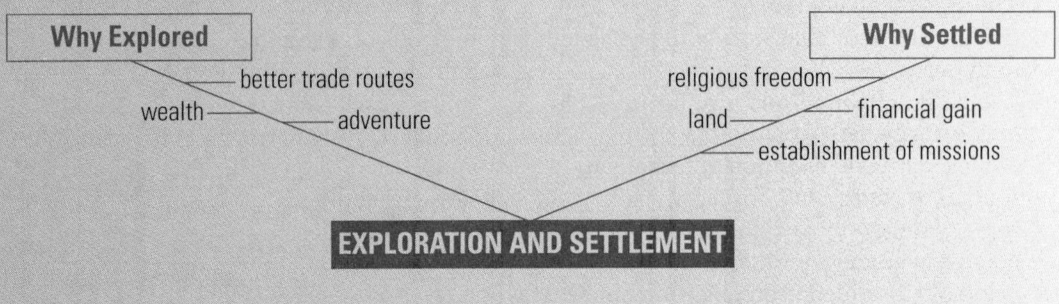

Several European nations also began to form strong, stable governments during this period. Spain, Portugal, France, England, and the Netherlands gradually resolved internal power struggles that had weakened and preoccupied them. They also gathered the wealth, ships, and armies needed to take ambitious leaps into new worlds.

These nations wanted to find quicker routes to Asia. Contact with Muslim traders brought wealth and improved technology and **navigation,** the charting of a course at sea. Through advances in measurement and mathematics, Muslims had improved map making. Their study of ancient cultures allowed them to pass along technologies, like the astrolabe, to the Europeans. Europeans also developed their own technologies, like the Portuguese *caravel*, shown below. This ship could sail with or against the wind. Instruments like the quadrant and the cross-staff helped sailors to navigate on long voyages. ■

◄ *The astrolabe, shown at left, was first invented by the ancient Greeks. Its rediscovery by Muslims led to increased sea travel, because it was used to determine the location of ships at sea.*

■ *What historical events and developments led Europeans to explore the world beyond their borders?*

Spain Leads the Way

Even more than the desire for exploration, the search for wealth turned Spain into the leading nation of what is now called the Age of Discovery. Spanish rulers and merchants desperately wanted to find a way around the land routes to Asia. They had become tired of paying the middlemen who were raking large profits from overland caravans to the Far East. They desired not only exotic goods such as gold, silk, and jewels, but also Asian spices to enhance their plain European diet.

Some people thought there might be a better and faster way to Asia. One of them was an Italian named Christopher Columbus.

Columbus Stumbles on a New World

Many educated people in the 1400s knew that the world was round. Christopher Columbus set out to prove this fact to those Europeans who still had doubts. First he tried to persuade the rulers of Portugal, France, and England to provide the men and ships needed to make a trip to Asia. When they turned him down, he moved to Spain, where he took his case to the Spanish court. Here, too, he almost gave up. But after six years of indecision, Queen Isabella agreed to arrange an expedition for the 41-year-old navigator.

Two of Columbus's ships—the Nina and the Pinta—were only 50 feet long. The flagship, the Santa Maria, was much larger but less maneuverable. In all, 90 men went on the voyage. Favorable winds carried them westward from the time they set sail on August 3, 1492.

After two months at sea, Columbus's men became restless. Because he feared mutiny, Columbus concealed from his men the distance they

DEVELOP

Copy on the board the heads of the Graphic Overview from page 16. Explain that Europeans explored and later settled the New World for a number of different reasons. Encourage students to make notes under each head as they read the lesson.

CULTURE

Critical Thinking

Ask students how improvements in technology (the development of the astrolabe and caravel, for example) affected exploration. *(Improved technology made exploration safer, more efficient, and faster.)*

■ *Exploration was spurred by the Renaissance, the Reformation, the development of strong nations, and new improvements in sea travel.*

Access Strategy

Have students find Spain, Portugal, France, England, and the Netherlands on a globe. Point out that in the 1400s and 1500s competition between these countries was strong, especially for trade routes to India and China. Explain that each of these countries had access to the Atlantic Ocean and wanted to use it as a trade route to India and China. Have students trace on the globe several possible routes from Spain to India and China (overland and by water). Then tell them that Vasco da Gama reached India by water, following the coast of Africa. Have students trace his route.

Access Activity

Ask students to describe the sculpture on page 18 and to then imagine how Europeans reacted to these treasures from the New World. *(Sample answer: They admired them and wanted more.)* How could Europeans acquire valuable items such as this from the New World? *(By trading or by plunder)*

HISTORY

Critical Thinking

Explain that many people, especially American Indians, see Columbus negatively because he enslaved Taino people and saw the Americas as a place to conquer for European profit. His journeys also began the period of exploration that ultimately destroyed the lives and cultures of thousands of Native Americans. Ask students to discuss the pros and cons of Columbus's journeys. *(Sample answer: Pros: His journeys gained territory and wealth for Spain. They led to the creation of the United States. Cons: They led to death, enslavement, and loss of land for many American Indians.)*

Sebastiano del Piombo painted this famous portrait of Christopher Columbus after the explorer's death.

had traveled. Finally, he agreed that if they did not reach Asia in three days, he would turn back.

On the third day, October 12, they sighted land. Columbus mistakenly believed that they had reached India, so he called the native people there Indians. In reality, they were Tainos and he had landed on an island in the Bahamas that he named San Salvador. When Columbus returned to Spain, he brought gold and several Tainos he had kidnapped as slaves. On his three later voyages, he brought more Spanish people to the Caribbean and more enslaved Indians to Spain, changing the lives of both groups forever.

Seekers of Gold and Glory

Columbus's discovery set off a wave of exploration. As the map on page 19 shows, other daring explorers soon followed in his wake, drawn by the promise of wealth and fame.

In 1499, an Italian merchant named Amerigo Vespucci *(vehs POOT chee)* made the first of two voyages to the New World. Vespucci soon realized that the land he had explored was not Asia but "a very great continent, until [now] unknown." A few years later a mapmaker named this new continent "America" in Vespucci's honor.

Vasco Núñez de Balboa, a Spanish explorer, confirmed Vespucci's conclusion in 1513. That year Balboa led a party across the Isthmus of Panama, the narrow strip of land connecting North and South America. After weeks of hacking through thick rain forest, Balboa emerged on a cliff and became the first European to look out upon the Pacific Ocean.

The discoveries explorers made were often accidental. Explorers were more interested in acquiring gold and power than in finding new lands. New World or old, they were set on plundering it. Armed with swords, firearms, and lances, these Spanish **conquistadors** *(kohn KEES tah dohrs)*, or conquerors, subdued whole civilizations of native peoples.

Conquistador Hernando Cortés presented this Aztec sculpture, a double-headed snake made of turquoise mosaic, to Emperor Charles V of Spain.

Critical Thinking

Each major country in Europe wanted to be the first to find a shorter route to Asia. Ask students to suggest reasons why this was so. *(Sample answer: The first country would have trading advantages.)* Why might it have been important to find a shorter trade route? *(Sample answer: To save time and money, for safety reasons)*

Political Context

Spain and Portugal were the first nations to begin exploration and expansion westward. Their geographic position on the Atlantic coast and their stable governments gave them an early advantage. The discoveries of navigators such as Columbus, who worked for Spain and Portugal, created a shift in power and influence away from the Italian city-states of Genoa and Venice.

England was a latecomer to westward expansion because of internal religious and political conflicts. England emerged as a strong nation in the mid-1500s largely because of Elizabeth I, who was willing to compete with Spain for world dominance. Under Queen Elizabeth, English explorers challenged Spanish explorers in the New World. In 1588, the English challenged—and defeated—the Spanish Armada, up to then the most powerful naval force in existence. As a whole, however, the English people looked to the New World less for strategic

The most famous of the Spanish conquistadors was Hernando Cortés (*kohr TESS*), who in 1519 marched into Mexico with 600 men, including several Africans. There he found a thriving civilization with huge pyramids in its elaborate capital city, Tenochtitlán (*tay noch tee TLAHN*). More than 150,000 people lived in the Aztec capital, which was larger than any Spanish city at that time. The Emperor Moctezuma ruled over these people. In a few short years, Cortés used his superior arms and the discontent of many of Moctezuma's subjects to destroy much of Tenochtitlán and topple the Aztec Empire.

Another Spanish conqueror, Francisco Pizarro, led 180 men southward into the heart of Peru in 1531. Pizarro soon captured the Incas' ruler, Atahualpa, and by 1535 had brought down the entire Incan empire.

A steady stream of explorers and warriors followed these early conquistadors. They were men bent on conquest and the discovery of gold. Focusing first on Central and South America, they eventually reached the southern regions of North America.

Two such Spanish explorers were Francisco Vásquez de Coronado and Hernando de Soto. On an expedition through the American Southwest in 1540–1542, a party of Coronado's men were the first Europeans to see the Grand Canyon. De Soto explored what is now the southern United States and was the first European to reach the Mississippi River.

Although their names and discoveries live on in romantic stories, most of the conquistadors acted ruthlessly in their search for riches and power. They treated the native inhabitants of America cruelly, enslaving them and often killing them. The conquistadors left a trail of slaughter as they searched for lost cities of gold. Nobody ever found a single city of gold, but the silver and gold the conquistadors did find—and the sugar they grew—made them and Spain fabulously wealthy. At the same time, they opened up a vast area for Spanish settlement. ■

■ *What was the chief motive of Spanish explorers in going to the New World?*

▼ *As the exploration map below illustrates, geography played a key role in determining the pattern of European exploration. Explorers from southern Europe tended to focus on Central and South America, while explorers from northern Europe tended to concentrate on North America.*

European Exploration of the New World, 1492–1610

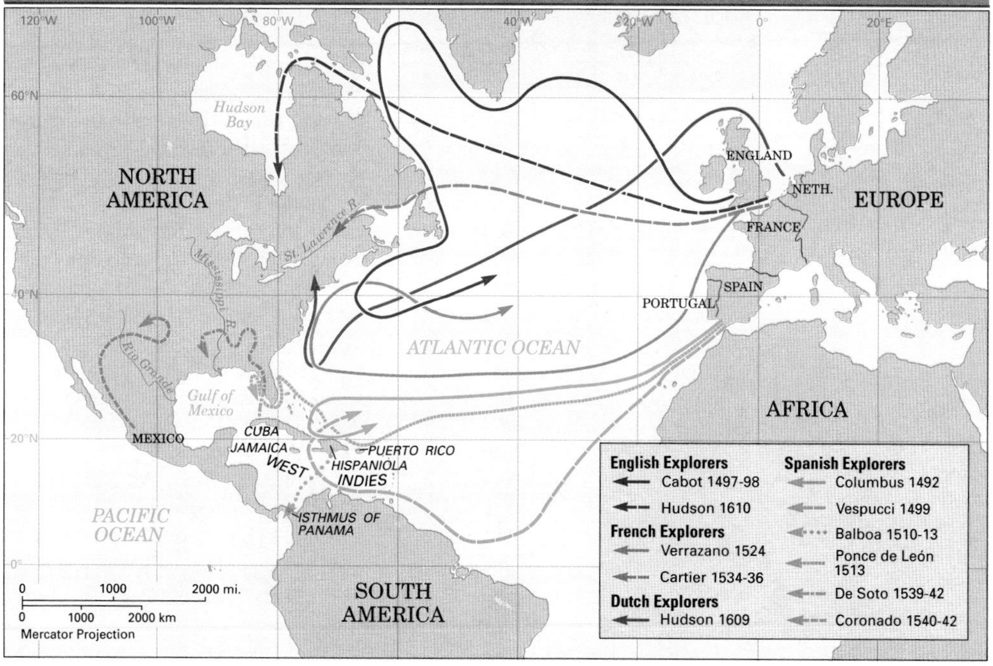

HISTORY

Critical Thinking

What factors gave Cortés and Pizarro a huge advantage over the Aztecs and Incas? *(The Aztecs and Incas had no weapons that were a match for Spanish cannons and pistols.)* How might the discontent of Moctezuma's subjects have helped Cortés to overthrow the Aztec Empire? *(Unhappy subjects would not fight as hard.)*

■ *Spaniards chiefly sought gold in the New World.*

GEOGRAPHY

Map and Globe Skills

Have students use the map on this page to compare the routes taken by an explorer from a northern country (England, France, Netherlands) and an explorer from a southern country (Spain, Portugal). What differences do you see in the routes? *(Northern countries explored New England and Canada; southern countries explored the West Indies, Mexico, and the Southwest.)*

military positions than for trade and for a place to settle.

By 1650, the Atlantic powers of western Europe—Spain, England, France, and the Netherlands—occupied parts of North America. Spanish military power was still sufficiently great to force that country's enemies to settle at a distance from the Caribbean—the center of Spain's colonial empire. Both Roanoke and Jamestown were located far enough north to be out of the range of Spanish forces in Florida but near enough to strike if opportunities arose.

Geography and resources also influenced settlement. The French—and later the English—were drawn to New England by the abundant fish and furs offered by local Indians. The Dutch, English, and French were also interested in locating and controlling the fabled Northwest Passage—a water route that would lead through North America to Asia. No such route existed, but the search led to exploration of the Hudson, St. Lawrence, and James rivers.

Map and Globe Skills

Have students use a ruler and the map scale on this page to find the number of kilometers represented by one inch. *(1 inch = 2000 km)* Ask students to determine how many miles one explorer traveled to get to the New World. Using a piece of string will make it easier to measure the routes. *(Sample answer: Cartier, roughly 5000 km.)*

HISTORY

Critical Thinking

European explorers "raced" to find a quick trade route to Asia. Although they never found it, other benefits came out of the race. What were these benefits? *(While looking for a trade route they explored much of North America. This exploration laid the basis for later settlement.)*

■ *In addition to trying to check Spain's growing power, they wanted to find the Northwest Passage.*

England, France, and the Netherlands Stake Claims

Spain had caught the rest of the world napping. Most of Europe was too entangled in its own internal problems to conquer new worlds. But Spain's growing power made the rest of Europe nervous—especially England, a Protestant nation and Catholic Spain's chief rival. Spain might soon take over most of the New World, leaving no room for other nations to stake a claim.

➤ *This engraving shows John Cabot somewhere off the coast of Canada during his 1497 voyage.*

The Search for the Northwest Passage

Like the Spanish, other Europeans wanted to find a quick trade route to Asia. They hoped to find a Northwest Passage, a northern waterway connecting the Atlantic Ocean and the Pacific Ocean. Even after they knew more about the New World, European explorers kept on searching for a northern shortcut to Asia. As late as 1847, the British explorer John Franklin and all his men died while trying to find their way through the Northwest Passage. But it was not until 1906 that the first successful trip through the frozen waters north of Canada occurred.

■ *Why did European nations other than Spain begin sending explorers to the New World?*

A Series of Discoveries

England's first exploration had limited results. John Cabot, an Italian working for the English king, sailed to Newfoundland and Nova Scotia in 1497. Cabot found waters teeming with fish, highly valuable in Europe. However, England was too preoccupied with internal affairs to take advantage of his discoveries.

Two explorers, Giovanni da Verrazano of Italy and Jacques Cartier *(kahr tee YAY)* of France, voyaged even farther than Cabot. In 1524, Verrazano explored the eastern coastline of North America from what is now North Carolina to Newfoundland. Eleven years later, in 1535, Cartier explored the Gulf of St. Lawrence. His discovery of the St. Lawrence River on a second voyage marked the beginning of France's dominance of the territory that later became Canada.

Henry Hudson, an Englishman, made several trips to the New World. On a 1609 voyage for the Dutch, Hudson found the river now named after him. His discovery planted the seeds of New Netherland, the powerful Dutch settlement in what is now New York. On later voyages for the English, Hudson discovered two more bodies of water that bear his name: Hudson's Strait and Hudson's Bay.

Hudson's desire to find a Northwest Passage led to his downfall. After a long, hard winter, during which Hudson's ship became trapped in the ice, his men mutinied. When they broke free from the ice in June 1611, the crew set Hudson, his son John, and seven other sailors adrift without food in a tiny boat. Hudson and his party were never seen again.

Explorers blaze paths. But if the lands are promising, settlers soon move in. This pattern of exploration and settlement is exactly what happened in North America. ■

Map and Globe Skills

Have students use the maps on pages 696–697 and 703 in the Atlas to find places on the coast of North America that might have seemed likely routes for a Northwest passage. Then have students explain why a sailing route around Canada was impractical in the 1500s. *(Weather and ice made it impossible for sailing vessels.)*

Language Arts Connection

Place names often reflect the early history of an area. Have students find the meaning of place names in and around their own community. They may find this information from a local historian, in the local history collection of the public library, or in foreign language dictionaries. Have students report their findings to the rest of the class. Students may wish to publish what they have learned in a dictionary or on a chart.

Science Connection

Have students find out about the navigation instruments used in the era of European exploration of the New World, such as the astrolabe (pictured on page 17), the quadrant, and the cross-staff. Have volunteers explain how these instruments worked.

Europeans Settle the New World

Many problems in Europe drove people to seek a new life across the ocean in the late 1500s and early 1600s. A new spurt in population growth crowded European cities. Religious intolerance led to the persecution of minority **sects,** small religious groups that had separated from larger denominations. In addition, changing economic conditions had left many people without jobs or land.

Thus, when news of a new continent with limitless opportunities spread throughout Europe, many people responded. Despite the dangers and uncertainties, Europeans began to leave their homelands—first in a trickle and then in a steady stream—to begin a challenging life in the New World. The map below shows where they settled.

Spanish Settlements

Spain was the first nation to settle the New World, and it had been the first to conquer parts of it. Following the conquistadors, Spanish missionaries brought their religious faith to the New World. These Catholic priests established missions in South America, Central America, and Mexico in the 1500s. During the next two centuries they expanded their activities into the American Southwest and West. The Spanish priests forced many American Indians into labor and

How Do We Know?

HISTORY *Explorers who crossed the Atlantic to the New World plotted their courses carefully on navigational charts. Captains and others on board also kept logs and diaries during these journeys. Piecing together information from this evidence, historians have painstakingly reconstructed the exact routes that early explorers took to the Americas.*

Settlements in the New World, 1650

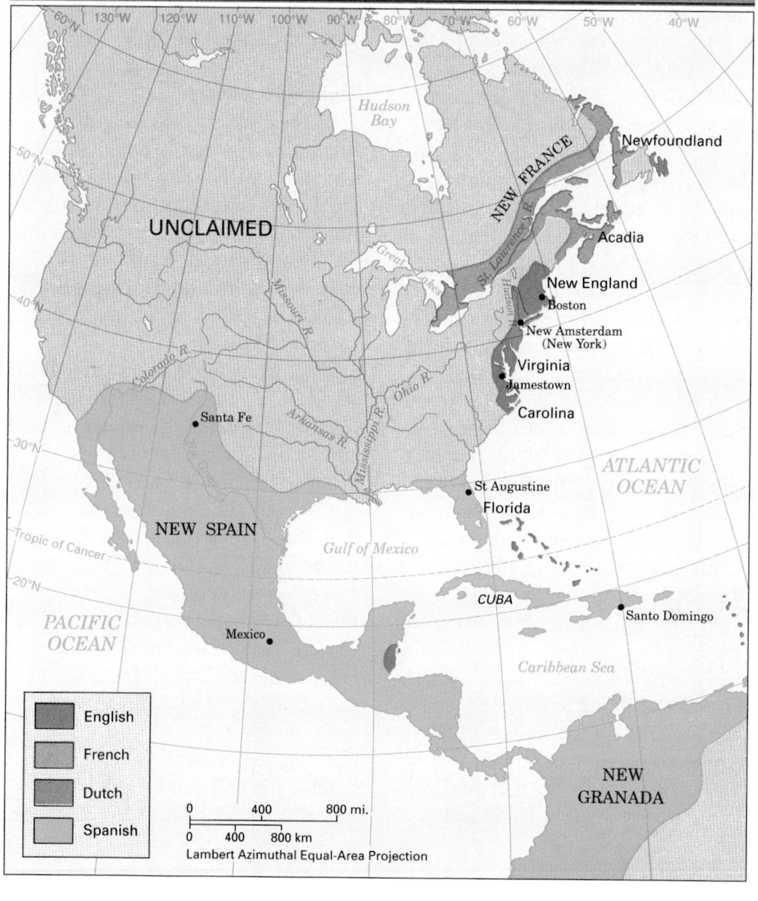

◄ *Compare the map at left with the European exploration map on page 19. Notice that European nations tended to settle those areas of the New World where they had originally sent explorers.*

HISTORY

Critical Thinking

Remind students that the Spanish conquistadors destroyed many American Indian settlements and much of their culture. Given the Spanish view of Indians as potential converts to Christianity, what possibility remained for Indians to preserve their own culture and religion? *(Sample answer: The Indians would have to break free from Spanish domination or else be forced to maintain their customs secretly.)*

Science Connection

The weapons used by the Spanish conquistadors gave them a tremendous advantage over the Aztec and Inca warriors. Have interested students find information on the Spanish cannons of the time. Tell students that pistols became practical as weapons of war around 1515 with the invention of the wheel lock. Ask a volunteer to find out what the wheel lock was, how it worked, and why it made the pistol a practical weapon.

Art Connection

Have students use library references—history books, encyclopedias, books on the history of fashion and jewelry—to find examples of the influence of South and Central American Indians on clothing and jewelry design. Students can demonstrate what they have learned by making captioned drawings or diagrams and displaying them in class.

Map and Globe Skills

Have students use the map on this page to compare the land areas controlled by each country. Which countries controlled the largest and smallest areas? *(Spain, the largest; the Netherlands, the smallest)*

GEOGRAPHY

Study Skills

Have students identify the colonies of the Spanish, French, Dutch, and English on the map on page 21. Students should make a chart identifying each colony, the date it was founded, who held it, and why it was settled. Have them use the modern United States political map in the Atlas on page 698–699 to add to their chart the name of the present state or country where each colony was located.

ECONOMICS

Critical Thinking

In the Dutch colony of New Netherlands, a person who brought 50 settlers to the colony received a large tract of land. What two classes of people were created as a result of this form of economic organization? *(Landowners and the people who worked the land for them)* What significance might this have had on the Dutch settlement? *(Sample answer: It might have caused a division into two social groups, one of which controlled the other.)*

Early Spanish and English settlements differed greatly in physical appearance. On these two pages are shown the English settlement at Jamestown (facing page) *and the Spanish mission at San Carlos de Rio Carmelo* (above).

taught them Christianity. The missions became the centers of the Spanish settlements.

The Spanish established armed presidios, or forts, wherever they needed to defend their claims to new lands. But the Spanish mission played a larger role in the history of Spanish settlement. The founder of many of these missions was Padre Junípero Serra, a Franciscan friar. Serra lived among the Indians in Baja California for twenty years. Then he journeyed into Alta (upper) California, establishing nine missions and teaching Christianity along the way.

Because of Serra's strong religious faith, he believed he was saving the souls of the California Indians by bringing them into the Catholic Church. In doing so, however, he and other missionaries forced these Indians to give up much of their own culture and way of life. Today, historians disagree about whether Serra had a positive or negative effect on California's history, but all agree that the missions were an important step in Spain's settlement of the American West.

French and Dutch Settlements

The first French settlers in North America hoped to make their fortunes. They sought the fish that swam in the waters of the Atlantic and the furs of animals that scurried through the inland forests. Like the Spanish, the French taught Christianity, but their settlements were trading posts and forts, not missions. These settlements sprang up along the St. Lawrence River. Later the French expanded into the Great Lakes region and the Mississippi River Valley.

Following Henry Hudson's 1609 voyage, the Dutch established a powerful colony in what is now New York State. Settling first on Manhattan Island in 1623, the Dutch established the city of New Amsterdam there. By offering large tracts of land to anyone who brought fifty or more settlers with them, the Dutch soon extended their colony up the Hudson River Valley to the present-day city of Albany. They called this colony New Netherland. The Dutch held New Netherland until the English fleet seized the colony in 1664.

English Settlements

Mystery surrounds an early attempt by England to establish a settlement in the New World. In 1584, Sir Walter Raleigh received permission from Queen Elizabeth to found a colony on Roanoke Island off the coast of North Carolina. Raleigh sent a group of settlers to colonize the island in 1587.

Unfortunately, Spain's attempt to invade England in 1588 prevented Raleigh from sending supplies to this new colony for nearly three years. When a ship finally reached Roanoke in 1590, the settlers were gone. The only clue to their disappearance was the word *CROATOAN* that had been carved on the door post of the ruined fort. Some people speculated that the settlers had fled to another island or had joined the Croatan Indians. But the fate of the "Lost Colony" was never discovered.

England's first permanent settlement in the new continent was small and nearly as ill-fated as the Roanoke

Visual Learning

Have students compare the Spanish and English settlements in the pictures on pages 22 and 23. *(Spanish—Organized around church, separated from surroundings; English—spread out, no dominant building)* How does the layout relate to the colony's purpose? *(Dominant church building relates to the Spanish goal of bringing Christianity to the New World.)*

Collaborative Learning

Divide the class into two groups to research either the Aztecs or the Incas. Several students in each group should work together to research and report on one of the following topics: social organization and government; achievements; and religion. Then have the students in each group work together to organize a presentation for the class.

Writing a Diary

Have students research the first years of the Jamestown settlement and write two diary entries from the point of view of a Jamestown settler. Encourage them to write about the problems in the settlement (malarial swamp and dense forest, mismanagement, stealing by the Indians, lack of food) and how they personally reacted to them. Interested students might want to read Scott O'Dell's *The Serpent Never Sleeps* (Boston: Houghton Mifflin Co., 1987).

Colony. The settlement of Jamestown survived, but at a great cost in human suffering.

On May 14, 1607, native inhabitants of what is now Virginia saw the first permanent European settlers heave their boats up onto the beaches of Jamestown Island. These colonists had come seeking economic gain. However, the settlement they founded, Jamestown, sat in marshy land that was not only poor farmland but was also a breeding ground for malaria-carrying mosquitoes.

As a result of malnutrition and disease, only 32 of the 105 original settlers at Jamestown survived the first seven months. To make matters worse, relations with surrounding American Indians quickly deteriorated, often as a result of harsh treatment by the new white settlers. Almost the entire colony perished in "the starving time" during the winter of 1609–1610.

During the next twenty years, the Jamestown settlers scratched out a living for themselves, endured hostile Indian attacks, and struggled with deadly diseases. By the 1630s, they had driven the Indians out of eastern Virginia and built a successful colony based on growing tobacco.

▲ *Founded in 1607, Jamestown (shown above) was the first successful English settlement in North America.*

Religious Influences

Like the towns that started as Spanish missions, several English settlements were founded for religious reasons. The Pilgrims who sailed on the *Mayflower* in 1620 left England because of religious persecution. They had opposed many practices of the Church of England, and needed a place to start their own church. They settled in Plymouth, Massachusetts, and faced conditions that were as harsh as those in Jamestown.

The Pilgrim settlement at Plymouth survived, but became part of the larger Puritan settlement to its north. The Puritans left England with roughly one thousand settlers in 1630, searching for a place to establish a strict religious community. They had been persecuted in England for their religious practices, and wanted to start a model community of people who shared the same beliefs. By 1642, about 12,000 of them had settled in the Massachusetts Bay Colony near today's city of Boston. They, too, faced death in their first winter, but their settlement soon took root, grew, and flourished. Like the other European colonies in the New World, it would continue to grow. ■

■ *What factors led English settlers to leave their home for the New World?*

REVIEW

1. **FOCUS** Why did Europeans leave their homes in the 1500s and 1600s to explore and settle new continents?
2. **CONNECT** How did the geography of the New World frustrate early European explorers in their attempts to find a new trade route to East Asia?
3. **GEOGRAPHY** If land routes to Asia had been shorter and safer, would the Age of Discovery have occurred sooner or later than it did?
4. **CRITICAL THINKING** Judging from their behavior, what can you infer about the way the Spanish conquistadors viewed the native inhabitants of the Americas?
5. **ACTIVITY** Imagine you are a European farm laborer in the mid-1600s. Years of bad crops have left you with no work. Make a list of the pros and cons of leaving your homeland.

BELIEF SYSTEMS

Critical Thinking

The Spanish and the English both had religious motives for settling in the New World. Have students compare and contrast those motives. *(Both believed strongly in their religion, and wanted to live according to their faith. The Spanish wanted to convert the Indians to Catholicism, Spain's established religion. The Pilgrims and Puritans faced persecution in England for opposing the Anglican Church of England and sought a place to practice their faith freely.)*

■ *Overpopulation, religious intolerance, and economic difficulties led Europeans to seek new opportunities in the New World.*

CLOSE

Copy on the board the heads of the Graphic Overview from page 16. Have students work together to complete the Overview using the notes that they took while reading the text. They can then use the information in this chart to answer the Thinking Focus and evaluate their predictions. As an extension activity, have students do the Writing a Diary activity on page 22.

Answers to Review Questions

1. The Renaissance, the Reformation, the development of strong nations, and new technology led to exploration. Overpopulation, religious intolerance, and economic difficulties in Europe led to settlement in the New World.
2. The New World blocked possible trade routes between Europe and Asia via the Atlantic Ocean.
3. The Age of Discovery would have been delayed because many explorers were motivated by the desire to find a shortcut to Asia.
4. Sample answer: The conquistadors seemed to view the native inhabitants as inferior people in need of their help. Allow for personal opinion.
5. After making individual lists, students may compare ideas.

Homework Options

Have students write a one-page essay about an area of the world—or universe—that they would like to explore. Why would they choose that area? What would they want to do there?

Study Guide: page 2.

INTRODUCE

Discuss with students what they learned about American Indians in Lesson 2. Ask them what kind of story this selection is. *(An American Indian creation story)* Point out that many cultures have myths and legends to explain the forces of nature. Explain that American Indians felt close to nature because everything they needed and used, from clothing to food, came directly from nature.

READ AND RESPOND

After students read the selection independently, have them share their responses to the legend. As students answer the purpose-setting question, make sure they give reasons for their answers.

As you read in Lesson 2, there were dozens of different American Indian cultures in North America at the time of European settlement. Each of these Indian cultures had its own myths and legends, one of which is reprinted here.

LITERATURE

The Seven Devils Mountains

An American Indian Creation Story

The Seven Devils Mountains are a series of high mountain peaks along the border between Oregon and Idaho. Caleb Whitman, a Nez Perce on the Umatilla Reservation, told the legend of these mountains to Ella E. Clark, the editor of a collection of Indian legends, in 1950. Creation stories are an important part of Indian oral tradition, and Coyote appears in the legends of many Indian peoples. Coyote is often a trickster who outwits other creatures to survive and creates parts of the natural world.

Long, long ago, when the world was very young, seven giant brothers lived in the Blue Mountains. These giant monsters were taller than the tallest pines and stronger than the strongest oaks.

The ancient people feared these brothers greatly because they ate children. Each year the brothers traveled eastward and devoured all the little ones they could find. Mothers fled with their children and hid them, but still many were seized by the giants. The headmen in the villages feared that the tribe would soon be wiped out. But no one was big enough and strong enough to fight with seven giants at a time.

At last the headmen of the tribe decided to ask Coyote to help them. "Coyote is our friend," they said. "He has defeated other monsters. He will free us from the seven giants."

So they sent a messenger to Coyote. "Yes, I will help you," he promised. "I will free you from the seven giants."

But Coyote really did not know what to do. He had fought with giants. He had fought with monsters of the lakes and the rivers. But he knew he could not defeat seven giants at one time. So he asked his good friend Fox for advice.

"We will first dig seven holes," said his good friend Fox. "We will dig them very deep, in a place the giants always pass over when they travel to the east. Then we will fill the holes with boiling liquid."

So Coyote called together all the animals with claws—the beavers, the whistling marmots, the cougars—the bears, and even the rats and mice and moles—to dig seven deep holes. Then Coyote filled each hole with a reddish-yellow liquid. His good friend Fox helped him keep the liquid boiling by dropping hot rocks into it.

Soon the time came for the giants' journey eastward. They marched along, all seven of them, their heads held high in the air. They were sure

Thematic Connections

Social Studies: American Indian legends

Houghton Mifflin Literary Readers: Oral Traditions

Background

In many American Indian legends, the coyote plays a central role. He was often seen as a mediator between humans and nature, as in this creation story. The coyote's habit of howling at the moon at night caused awe in both American Indians and cowboys of the West. American Indians often kept dogs, which are relatives of the coyote, as pets. Coyotes are sometimes called "wild dogs."

that no one dared to attack them. Coyote and Fox watched from behind some rocks and shrubs.

Down, down, down the seven giants went into the seven deep holes of boiling liquid. They struggled and struggled to get out, but the holes were very deep. They fumed and roared and splashed. As they struggled, they scattered the reddish liquid around them as far as a man can travel in a day.

Then Coyote came out from his hiding place. The seven giants stood still. They knew Coyote.

"You are being punished for your wickedness," Coyote said to the seven giants. "I will punish you even more by changing you into seven mountains. I will make you very high, so that everyone can see you. You will stand here forever, to remind people that punishment comes from wrongdoing.

"And I will make a deep gash in the earth here, so that no more of your family can get across to trouble my people."

Coyote caused the seven giants to grow taller, and then he changed them into seven mountain peaks. He struck the earth a hard blow and so opened up a deep canyon at the feet of the giant peaks.

Today the mountain peaks are called the Seven Devils. The deep gorge at their feet is known as Hell's Canyon of the Snake River. And the copper scattered by the splashings of the seven giants is still being mined.

Further Reading

Indian Legends of the Pacific Northwest. Ella E. Clark. The legend reprinted above as well as other Indian legends are contained in this book.

A Girl Who Married a Ghost and Other Tales of North American Indians. John Bierhorst.

Doctor Coyote: A Native American Aesop's Fables. John Bierhorst. These two books contain more American Indian legends.

What was the problem that the ancient people faced? *(Seven giant brothers ate their children.)*

What happened to the liquid scattered by the splashing of the giants? *(It became the copper that is still being mined today.)*

EXTEND

Have students find other examples of American Indian legends and myths in which Coyote plays a leading role. Discuss what kind of character he appears to be in most of these legends.

Further Reading

You may want to ask students to find books in the school or local library with more American Indian legends.

INTRODUCE

Have students read the lesson title and recall from Lesson 2 how the Spanish conquistadors treated the native peoples of the New World. *(Brutally; they enslaved or killed many.)* After students read the Thinking Focus, have them predict ways in which Indians and colonists helped each other and reasons why they were in conflict. Have them read the lesson to confirm or reject their predictions.

Key Terms

Vocabulary strategies: T36–37
nomad—one who moves from place to place rather than settling in one location
alliance—an organization or agreement to promote common interests among its members

1450 1492 1700 1750 1800

LESSON 3

Europeans and Native Peoples

THINKING FOCUS

What impact did European exploration and settlement have on the native inhabitants of the Americas?

Key Terms

- nomad
- alliance

You are standing in the empty expanses of the Great Plains on a hot summer afternoon in the late 1600s. The sun hangs low in the sky, and the heat rises in eerie waves off the land.

Suddenly a thundering noise arises in the west, and black specks appear along the horizon. A few minutes later a herd of buffalo sweeps past you, followed by several men riding on the backs of strange beasts. With their hair streaming behind them, these men look like gods who have captured the wind.

As you may have realized, the men described in the above passage were riding horses. But if you had been a Plains Indian in the 1600s, you might have been seeing a horse for the first time. Before the Spanish conquistador Hernando Cortés brought horses to the New World in 1519, Indians did not even know that these animals existed. Soon, however, horses changed the way Plains Indians had lived for centuries.

Before the arrival of the horse, Plains Indians lived in villages along the Missouri River and its tributaries. The men hunted on foot, and the women cultivated crops. Horses changed all that. They gave Plains Indians the ability to move around more easily and turned them into full-time buffalo hunters. Before long, these Indians adopted new methods of hunting and developed new rituals. Their entire way of life came to center around the great shaggy beasts that blanketed the plains. The meeting of two cultures had dramatically transformed the lives of a people.

The horse helped Plains Indians become efficient buffalo hunters.

Objectives

1. Describe how the native peoples of the Americas lived before the arrival of the Europeans.
2. Explain the impact of early contacts between Europeans and American Indians.
3. Trace the history of the relations between native peoples and European colonists.

Graphic Overview

Cause
European colonists settle America

→

New Crops
Horses
Diseases
Trade

→

Effects
- competition for land
- conflict
- alliances
- death from disease

The First Americans

The Plains Indians were only one of hundreds of Indian cultures that existed in the Americas before Europeans arrived. The Anasazi, who lived in what is now the southwestern United States, built multilevel cliff dwellings, irrigated their crops, and developed trading networks. They were only one of many North American tribal groups that were as different as any of the nations of Europe. In Mexico, Central America, and South America, too, the Mayas, the Incas, and the Aztecs developed sophisticated civilizations and elaborate cities.

◄ *English settler John White painted this watercolor of an Indian village in 1585.*

Different Ways of Life

Some Indians were **nomads,** moving through the countryside in search of water and wild food rather than establishing a home in one place. Many more settled down near lakes and streams, living off the fruits, berries, roots, and game they could gather and hunt near their camps.

However, most Indian groups became very successful farmers. Indians developed almost half the crops grown for food in the world today, including potatoes, corn, squash, pumpkins, and a variety of beans. Some Indian nations built irrigation systems to provide water for their crops, and many Indian societies cleared land for farming.

A Variety of Cultures

Whether they were farmers or hunters, the native inhabitants of the Americas did not see themselves as a single unified people. A Hopi was not a Blackfoot, who was not an Ojibwa, who was not a Shawnee. They spoke languages as foreign to each other as French is to Russian. They formed **alliances**—organizations to promote the common interests or defense of their members—fought wars, and recognized their cultural differences. Some of their alliances were highly complex. In the east, five tribes—the Mohawk, Seneca, Oneida, Onondaga, and Cayuga—joined together in the 1500s to form the Iroquois League, an alliance based on their common languages and interests.

More often, language differences and competition maintained sharp divisions between the peoples of the Americas. In time, European colonists would exploit these differences. ■

How Do We Know?

HISTORY *To find out how American Indians lived before Europeans arrived in the New World, archaeologists often turn to "middens," literally garbage dumps of ancient villages. Generally, these middens are buried beneath layers of soil and gravel. By excavating and examining middens, archaeologists learn a great deal about the customs and cultures of America's first inhabitants.*

■ *In what ways were Indian tribes similar to European nations?*

Early Contacts with American Indians

The first meetings between Indians and Europeans varied greatly from place to place. In some places Indians kept a cautious distance from the intruders. Elsewhere, they came forward eagerly to greet and trade with the strange new people who came on giant boats from across the ocean. Whenever they did make contact with Europeans, Indians got something they hadn't counted on: deadly diseases.

DEVELOP

Point out that this lesson has a cause-and-effect structure. As they read, students should look for key developments that occurred during early settlement and for the major effects of these developments on relationships between settlers and American Indians.

◄ *John White was a leader of the Roanoke Colony and grandfather of Virginia Dare, the first white child born in North America.*

CULTURE

Visual Learning

Ask students to analyze the painting of an Indian village on this page. What does it reveal about how people lived and worked? *(The people lived together. Large crop areas are close to the houses.)*

■ *The Indian tribes were not a single, unified people but many separate groups that formed alliances, fought wars, spoke different languages, and developed different cultures.*

Access Strategy

Ask students to imagine that a large group of aliens from another galaxy lands on Earth in a strange-looking spacecraft. The aliens are dressed in garments vastly different from our own, speak a language we do not understand, and move around in small airships. They are clearly perplexed about things they hear and see on Earth, such as our music, food, and technology. Have students suggest what might happen when the aliens first have contact with Earth people. What kinds of things might the two groups learn from one another? *(They could probably teach us about their galaxy; we could teach them how to survive on this planet.)* What kinds of problems might arise? *(How to communicate, how to balance what they want and what we want)*

Tell students that a similar situation occurred when Europeans first settled in the New World. To the native inhabitants, the Europeans seemed like aliens.

Access Activity

Have students look at the picture on page 26. Tell them there were once millions of buffalo in the United States. Ask students to describe what is happening in the picture. Why would the Indians have hunted buffalo? *(For food and hides)* Could the Indians have hunted as successfully without horses? *(No. They needed horses to move quickly over large distances.)*

HISTORY

Critical Thinking

How did the spread of smallpox work to the advantage of the European colonists? *(The colonists had fewer Indian competitors for land and less threat of Indian attacks.)* Even if all contact between Europeans and Indians had remained friendly, would Indian peoples and their cultures have survived with limited change? *(Probably not. Too many European settlers came bringing a strong impetus for change.)*

CULTURE

Critical Thinking

Point out that although United States citizens are generally referred to as "Americans," Canadians, Mexicans, or Venezuelans will remind United States citizens that they, too, are Americans. Imagine that you are from a Latin American country. How might you react to the term *American* being used only for United States citizens? *(Sample answer: You might feel resentful.)*

Destructive New Diseases

A great, invisible death walked among the Indians of the Americas after the Europeans came to stay. For many centuries, Europeans had been building up immunity to typhoid, diphtheria, smallpox, and other plagues. But Indians had lived untouched by these diseases, until the European settlers brought the germs to the New World. With no immunity against the silent killers, many Indians died of such mild diseases as influenza and the common cold.

By far, the deadliest of the diseases Europeans brought to the Americas was smallpox. Spanish conquistadors spread smallpox throughout Central and South America. The results were devastating. During the century after Columbus arrived in the New World, the Indian population of Central America and Mexico dropped from more than 25 million to just one million people. Although warfare and enslavement caused some of these deaths, many more were the result of disease.

Smallpox also nearly wiped out the Indians of North America. Everywhere it touched, the disease killed Indians by the thousands. It is said to have slain over half the Indian population of North America. When the time came to defend their lands against the spread of European invaders, many Indian societies found themselves so weakened in numbers by various plagues that they were unable even to defend themselves in war.

Religion and Trade

Europeans brought more than just diseases to the New World. They brought Christianity and European goods as well.

You have already read how the Spanish sent hundreds of missionaries to the Americas in the 1600s and

Understanding Eurocentrism and Racism

When Europeans first reached the Western Hemisphere, they called it the New World. It was new to them, but it wasn't new to the native peoples who had lived there for thousands of years. Europeans called them "Indians" because the first explorers had thought they had arrived in India.

Terms such as "New World" and "Indians" reflect a European point of view. The word Eurocentrism means seeing things in terms of European culture and civilization. People with Eurocentric views ignore the accomplishments of other cultures and peoples.

Racism

In addition to Eurocentric beliefs, many Europeans and Americans have also had racist beliefs. When Europeans began founding colonies, they divided up the people of the world based on skin color, with dark-skinned Africans seen as the opposite of light-skinned Europeans. They believed in the cultural superiority of whites, and used it to justify slavery based on race in the Americas. Slavery had existed for thousands of years throughout the world, but in the Americas, race became its determining factor.

Effects of These Attitudes

In the United States, Africans, Native Americans, Asians, and Latin Americans, as well as many European groups, have all faced different forms of discrimination because of their race, religion, or culture.

As you read more about American history, think about how the beliefs of Eurocentrism and racism have affected laws and government policies as well as individuals' actions. Then think about the world you live in now. Do you see examples of these attitudes today?

Map and Globe Skills

In small groups, have students use an encyclopedia and a world map to identify and locate the former colonies that belonged to Spain, Portugal, England, and France. Then have them list what resources the European countries gained from each colony. Finally, have them list when and how each colony gained its independence.

Religious Context

From its beginning, Christianity spread quickly due in part to the efforts of missionaries. Within 300 years of its foundation, Christianity was practiced throughout the Roman Empire and, by the Middle Ages, throughout Europe.

In the 1500s and 1600s, religion played an important role in the political policies and in the daily life of most European nations. Converting non-Christians soon became a goal for these nations. Early Spanish explorers, for example, spread "the word" as they searched for trade routes to Asia. The government sent friars on every expedition.

Foreign missions are still active in Africa, Asia, Central and South America, and the Pacific islands. Some American churches even send missionaries to Europe. Modern missionaries are less zealous than the Spanish missionaries were, exerting much effort in the fields of education and health.

1700s to bring the Roman Catholic faith to the New World. The Spanish saw the Indians as souls to be saved by Christianity, but also as potential slaves. The Spanish used both religion and force to control the Indians.

The French also sent missionaries to the New World, though they had less impact than the Spanish missions. The most famous of the French missionaries was a Jesuit named Jacques Marquette *(mahr KEHT)*, who explored much of the Missouri and Mississippi rivers in the early 1670s. Marquette won converts from Quebec to Arkansas.

Marquette traveled with a fur trader named Louis Joliet. In fact, wherever the French, Spanish, and English went in the New World, they brought trade with them. It wasn't long before tools such as fishhooks, kettles, knives, needles, and guns were introduced into the daily life of many Indian villages. In return, Europeans were transporting beaver and deer hides back across the ocean. They were also growing crops and eating foods they had never tasted in their homelands.

Where trade flourished, European settlers and Indians often got along quite well; they had a mutual interest in remaining friendly in these situations. But relations between settlers and Indians varied widely from region to region, and from time to time, from group to group. ■

■ *How did trade between whites and native peoples affect the daily lives of both Europeans and Indians?*

Relations with English Colonists

The Pilgrims struggled through the terrible winter of 1620–1621 at Plymouth, half of them dying in the process. They did not seek contact with Indians, whom they feared and mistrusted. When spring came, they had run out of food and were too weak to begin planting.

Just as the Pilgrims' situation was getting desperate, Samoset, a Pemaquid Indian, made his appearance. To the Pilgrims' astonishment, he spoke some English, which he said he had learned from English fishermen. He made his tribe's peaceful intentions known and introduced them to Squanto, an Indian who had been enslaved in Spain and had spent two years in England. Squanto showed the colonists where to fish and hunt and taught them to plant native crops such as corn, beans, and squash.

After the 1621 harvest, the Pilgrims wanted to give thanks to God, whom they felt had provided them with plentiful crops. Consequently, they invited their Indian neighbors to a common feast of "thanksgiving," as the colony's governor, William Bradford, proclaimed it. The peaceful relations between the Pilgrims and the Pemaquids lasted for years, and Americans have continued to celebrate Thanksgiving to this day.

Friendship and Cooperation

Peace wasn't always won that easily. Generally, disagreements about land were the cause of the tension between European settlers and native inhabitants. When the leaders of the Massachusetts Bay Colony wanted Indian land, for instance, they simply decided to take it.

Roger Williams, a fiery, religious man from Salem, accused the colonists of

The Pilgrims learned about new vegetables such as maize (corn) and squash. These foods helped the Pilgrims survive the cold New England winters.

CULTURE

Critical Thinking

What role did religion play in relations between Europeans and American Indians? *(Sample answer: Religion provided some ties between Europeans and Indians, though the Spanish could be said to have enslaved the Indians. Also, it was a one-way exchange because Europeans did not adopt Indian religions.)*

■ *American Indians gained iron tools that made some of their work easier; Europeans got furs they could sell as well as foods and information that helped them to survive.*

Health Connection

This lesson provides many opportunities for students to learn more about diseases and how they are transmitted. Have several students find out how smallpox came to be controlled, beginning with Lady Mary Wortley Montagu's contribution in 1718 and including Edward Jenner's discoveries. Have other students look in an encyclopedia or medical handbook to find out the diseases that people can be inoculated against today. Students could also research the history of the germ theory. When did people first understand how diseases were transmitted? Another group of students could research and write a report on how the body develops immunity to a disease.

Critical Thinking

Ask students how the corn, beans, and squash shown on this page symbolize the contribution of the Indians to the Plymouth colony. How did these "simple gifts" change the course of events at Plymouth? *(The colonists were ill-prepared for winter. The Indians helped them to survive by giving gifts of food and teaching them to hunt and fish.)*

BELIEF SYSTEMS

Critical Thinking

What did Penn's promise to the Indians reveal about the Quaker attitude toward American Indians? How was Roger Williams's attitude similar? *(Both felt that the Indian peoples had an equal right to their land and were equal to white people in the eyes of God. Both groups lived in peace with the Indians.)* Ask students why different groups of Europeans had different relations with the American Indian. *(Different religious beliefs and different attitudes towards other humans, individual differences, different goals)*

taking what the Indians had every right to keep. Because they didn't like his attitude toward the Indians and his belief in religious tolerance, the Puritans banished Williams from the colony. He went south with his followers to live in Rhode Island, where they lived peacefully with the Narragansett Indians.

Probably the greatest success story of European-Indian cooperation was the colony of William Penn and the Quakers. A Quaker leader, Penn recived a vast grant of land in what is now Pennsylvania from King Charles II in 1681. The Quakers, a sect much persecuted in England, respected Indians as fellow children of God. It was not surprising, therefore, that Penn set out to establish a colony in which Indians and colonists could live together in peace. Penn promised never to occupy any land without the agreement of the Indians. Remarkably, Quakers and Indians did live in peace for almost 70 years.

Competition for Land

In the early 1600s, Virginia settlers staked out huge tracts of land to build tobacco plantations, thereby creating tension with local Indians. When the colonists murdered a popular Indian religious leader, his people sought revenge. The Indians' surprise raid in 1622 killed one-third of Virginia's white settlers and devastated the colony's economy. The colonists responded by slaughtering the inhabitants of many Indian villages.

The fighting in Virginia was only one battle in a complicated pattern of wars that would engulf the English colonies. In 1637, for example, English settlers in New England, helped by their Narragansett allies, set fire to the main village of the Pequot on the Mystic River. This battle destroyed the Pequot tribe. The Pequot War had begun over a series of land disputes.

Several decades later, in 1675, the Narragansett found themselves in the

American painter William Hicks's "The Peaceable Kingdom" shows William Penn signing a peace treaty with Pennsylvania's Indians.

Critical Thinking

Explain that the Indians believed that land should be shared by all the people in a community. What was the European attitude toward land? *(Europeans believed that individuals could own land.)* Why might the Indians have been willing to give Europeans rights to some land? *(The Indians thought they would be sharing the land, not losing it.)*

Collaborative Learning

Many Indian groups formed alliances such as the Iroquois Confederacy in the East. Ask a group of students to use library resources to find examples of other Indian alliances at the time of early European settlement in the New World. Then have individual students find out which Indian nations belonged to each alliance, what brought each alliance together, when it was formed, and how long it lasted. Have them pool their findings on a chart.

Debate

Much of the friction between American Indians and Europeans was centered on land use. Questions of land use still cause friction between people. Divide the class into two groups to debate whether or not a piece of undeveloped land should be developed or purchased by your town and left as open land. The debate teams should consider how their use of the land would affect the natural environment and serve the needs of the surrounding community.

same position as the Pequot. To defend themselves against advancing English settlers, the Narragansett allied themselves with the Wampanoag in Metacom's War. This war is known as King Philip's War, since the Wampanoag leader, Metacom, was called King Philip by the English. The Indians destroyed 13 Puritan towns and killed thousands of settlers, but the Narragansett were nearly wiped out. When Metacom died in battle in 1676, his head was brought back to Plymouth and put on display for 25 years.

While Metacom's War was being fought in New England, friction between poor frontier farmers and rich coastal planters started a civil war in Virginia. Virginia's native inhabitants were the final losers of this war.

The small planters of Virginia's frontier desired the rich lands that belonged to the Susquehannock and other Indian nations. These settlers strongly opposed the colonial governor's policy of peaceful relations with Virginia's Indian tribes. In 1676, a group of these planters decided to take matters into their own hands. Led by a hot-tempered immigrant named Nathaniel Bacon, they began to attack any Indians they could find, friendly or hostile.

When the colonial governor spoke against these attacks, Bacon led his forces against Jamestown. After burning much of the capital to the ground, the rebels took control of Virginia's government. However, their victory was short-lived. Six months later, Bacon lay dead of fever, the colonial governor had returned to power, and 23 of Bacon's followers were hanging from the gallows.

Even though Bacon's Rebellion failed, the backcountry planters had made their point. In the years following the rebellion, the colonial government allowed the white settlers of the frontier to conduct a war of extermination against local Indians.

A Variety of Alliances

In many of the conflicts between European settlers and native inhabitants, the colonists turned Indian nations against each other. Often they tried to make alliances that led Indians to do much of the colonists' fighting for them. The clearest example of this strategy occurred during the 1715 Yamasee War. During this conflict, the English in the Carolinas persuaded the Cherokee to join them in fending off the Yamasee and their allied nations. Only two years earlier, these same Yamasee had helped the colonists wipe out the Tuscarora. By dividing their Indian enemies, white settlers often succeeded in conquering and eliminating their chief competitors for land.

By the late 1600s, a pattern had been established. Whether sold into slavery, killed or dispersed, the native inhabitants of the English colonies fell victim to the settlers' seemingly endless hunger for land. ■

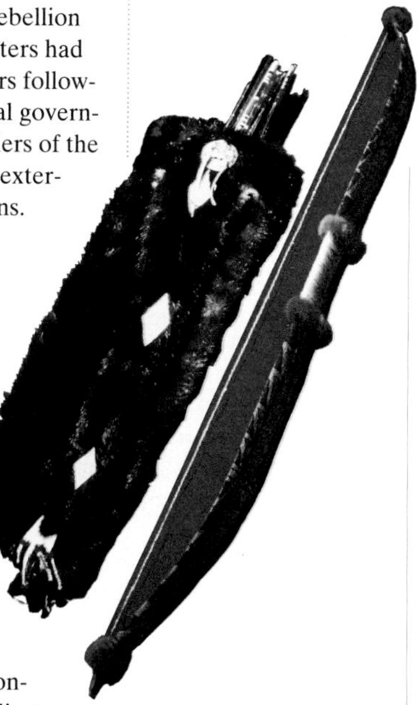

▲ *Using mostly primitive weapons American Indians lost most battles with colonists.*

■ *What caused most of the conflicts between European colonists and American Indians?*

REVIEW

1. **FOCUS** What impact did European exploration and settlement have on the native inhabitants of the Americas?
2. **CONNECT** European explorers and settlers did not hesitate to claim large expanses of land in the New World for themselves. How do you think this attitude affected relations with the Indians of these regions?
3. **CULTURE** What European objects soon became a part of the daily lives of many American Indian societies?
4. **CRITICAL THINKING** If the native peoples of the Americas had not been so susceptible to European diseases, how might the history of the colonial settlement of the New World have been different?
5. **WRITING ACTIVITY** Imagine that you are an American Indian watching the arrival of a European ship. Write a paragraph describing the ship and the landing of the settlers inside it. How do you feel about these people?

HISTORY

Critical Thinking

Ask students how Bacon's Rebellion, a conflict among settlers, affected the relations between settlers and Indians. *(The rebellion warned government officials not to interfere with settlers' violent treatment of the Indians.)*

■ *Most of their conflicts were over land.*

CLOSE

Have students use their notes on the key developments of the period of early settlement to make a cause-and-effect chart similar to the Graphic Overview on page 26. They can then use the chart to answer the Thinking Focus and to evaluate their predictions. As a reteaching activity, ask students how the colonists' reasons for settling affected their attitude toward the American Indians and their treatment of them.

Answers to Review Questions

1. In addition to bringing trade and Christianity to the native inhabitants, Europeans brought deadly diseases and wars over land.
2. It caused conflict with the native inhabitants of the land.
3. Kettles, knives, fishhooks, guns, needles were adopted from the Europeans.
4. Sample answer: If European diseases had not wiped out such a large percentage of the American Indian population, European colonists would not have been able to dominate the New World. Allow for personal opinion.
5. Encourage students to raise questions as they imagine this event. Allow for personal opinion.

Homework Options

Have students use library resources to find groups other than Puritans and Quakers who settled with Roger Williams in Rhode Island and William Penn in Pennsylvania.

Study Guide: page 3.

UNDERSTANDING REFERENCE MATERIALS

This skill lesson will give students the opportunity to go beyond the more familiar reference sources.

HISTORY

Study Skills

Students will benefit from a trip to the school library in conjunction with this lesson. Have the librarian show students where the reference materials mentioned on this page are kept. If reference materials are not available on open shelves, encourage students to ask the librarian for help.

After students have located the reference books mentioned, show how each book is organized. Extend the lesson by having students use these books to find the specific items listed in Try It and to locate the information that will help them develop the topics they chose for Apply It.

UNDERSTANDING REFERENCE MATERIALS

Using Specialized Resources

Here's Why

As you have read in this chapter, the history of the United States is still being written. Each time archaeologists find unfamiliar tools, weapons, or pieces of pottery, they uncover more information about the background of this country. In order to keep track of both historical information and new information, historians use a number of different reference sources.

As a student of American history, you too will need to use a number of different reference sources. The most familiar reference sources are dictionaries and encyclopedias. You may also use the card catalog to locate books on a specific topic. In addition, however, most libraries have special reference materials that contain a wealth of information about American history.

Suppose you want to research a particular topic, such as the origin and use of the hoe pictured on this page. Becoming familiar with these references can help you find answers quickly and also expand your ability to locate information and documents that you need.

Here's How

Spend some time in the reference section of your school or local library. Locate one or more of the following kinds of reference materials:

Historical Atlases: In a historical atlas, you can find maps that show information about people, events, and conditions at different points in history. Some atlases, such as the *National Geographic Historical Atlas of American History,* also contain timelines and informative articles.

Chronologies: If you need to verify a date or find out about the important events that happened in a particular year, you might use a chronology like the one in Richard Morris's *Encyclopedia of American History.* Morris's book contains a summary chronology of the major events of American history plus separate chronologies on such topics as territorial expansion, transportation, and communication. The final section of the book presents biographical information about 500 notable Americans.

Statistical Sources: Often you may want statistical information about the population or economic activities at specific times in our past. Each year since 1878 the United States Bureau of the Census has published a *Statistical Abstract of the United States.* This book provides data about more than 30 topics. Much of it is about the United States today, but the book also includes much statistical information from as far back as 1790, when the first census was conducted. Many almanacs also provide some limited data about United States history.

Try It

Below is a list of items to research. Identify which of the reference sources described above would be the best source for information about each of the following items:

1. the text of a speech by an Indian leader
2. a map of areas of European settlement in 1700
3. a list of the U. S. cities with the largest populations in 1800
4. a summary of the key events in Metacom's War
5. William Penn's date and place of birth
6. the text of the Articles of Confederation

Apply It

Consider what you have read about the geography of the United States and about the Indians and colonists in the 1600s and 1700s. Choose a topic that interests you for further research. Write a short paragraph that defines the topic and outlines what specialized history references you would use in your school or community library.

Objective

Use historical atlases, chronologies, and statistical sources as reference resources. (Study Skills 1)

Answers to Try It

1. Chronology
2. Historical atlas
3. Statistical sources
4. Chronology or historical atlas
5. Chronology
6. Chronology

Answers to Apply It

Encourage students to be as specific as possible in defining the topic. If they have visited the library, have them cite the specific titles of reference works they would use to research the topic further.

1450 1500 1550 1600 1650 1700 1775 1800

L E S S O N 4

Life in the English Colonies

The summer heat turned the forest into an open oven. Lifting an ax high across his shoulders, the farmer swung it into the trunk of the tree and then wrestled it out again. Lift, stroke, heave, pull—this backbreaking work went on hour after hour, until the farmer was aching and drenched with sweat.

The stumps of fallen trees lay on the ground until spring, when the felled wood was burned and the stumps set on fire. Settlers all over the English colonies used this process to clear away forests and prepare the land for farming.

Farther south, in the Chesapeake region, farmers used a system called girdling. First, they cut a deep notch all the way around the trunk of a tree and pulled away the bark around this notch. Because the tree could no longer grow leaves and block the sun, farmers could plant crops sooner. A year later, they would chop down the ghostly gray trees that stood dead in their fields.

Whatever method a farmer chose, clearing the land was a slow process. In a year, a man could clear only one or two acres. If he worked alone, he could spend a lifetime clearing enough ground to make a decent-sized farm.

Intermingled with the many other daily tasks of colonial farm life, the clearing of ground became a grueling chore, always waiting to be done. It could not be left undone, because in those days you "bought" your farmland from the wilderness—that is, you carved it out with your own bare hands.

THINKING FOCUS

What were some of the main characteristics of daily life in the English colonies in the early 1700s?

Key Terms

- indentured servant
- subsistence farmer

The painting at left shows settlers burning trees that they had "girdled" the previous year.

INTRODUCE

Point out the lesson title and ask students to recall from the previous lesson some of the problems of the early colonists. *(Lack of food, illness, weather)* After students read the Thinking Focus, point out that their answer to it depends in part on the regional, social, and economic position of each colony. Ask students to read the lesson to find out why there were similarities and differences between the colonies in the different regions.

Key Terms

Vocabulary strategies: T36–37

indentured servant—a person who agreed to work for a specified period of time in exchange for passage from Europe to the colonies

subsistence farmer—a person who grows just enough food for his or her family's needs

Graphic Overview

	New England	Middle	Southern
Heritage	English, Scots	most diverse	moderately diverse
Community	small towns	spread out	plantations, backcountry
Livelihood	subsistence farming, fishing	cash crops, manufacturing	large-scale farming
Labor	mostly self, a few slaves	self, indentured servants, slaves	self, indentured servants, slaves

Objectives

1. Explain how the demand for labor in colonial America led to the growth of both indentured servitude and slavery.
2. Summarize the chief differences between the New England, Middle, and Southern colonies.
3. Describe some of the features of colonial life shared by all the English colonies.

DEVELOP

Tell students that this lesson looks at daily life in the American colonies. Copy on the board the top and side heads of the Graphic Overview from page 33. Have students fill in the blanks in the chart as they read the lesson.

HISTORY

Critical Thinking

Why would anyone sign a contract of indenture? Have students suggest reasons why. *(Economic conditions in much of Europe were not good; many people wanted to leave but had little money. A contract of indenture may have been the only way they could afford passage to the colonies.)*

The Demand for Labor

Clearing the land, tilling, planting, and harvesting the crops all required weeks and months of labor. The labor-intensive plantations of the South had a special need for workers to keep them going. Plantation owners relied first on indentured servants and then on slaves to do much of this work.

Indentured Servants

Indentured servants were people who agreed to work for a specified period of time in exchange for payment of their passage from Europe to the English colonies and for food, clothing, and shelter. Their period of servitude could last anywhere from four to seven years. The contract indentured servants signed promised them tools, seed, and sometimes even land when the period of indenture was over.

In the 1600s, most indentured servants settled in the Southern colonies where their labor was most needed. For example, as many as 80 percent of the immigrants to Virginia and Maryland were indentured servants at this time. In fact, these workers accounted for more than one-third of the immigrants to the English colonies during that century.

Indentured servants could be bought and sold like property. Some planters even gambled them away in card games. Often, they were worked hard and fed poorly. Given these conditions, it is not surprising that many indentured servants died before they finished their servitude. Still, however bad their lot in life, it was generally much better than that of the African slave.

The Growth of Slavery

As late as 1671, white indentured servants outnumbered black slaves in Virginia by three to one. But three factors combined to convince planters to invest money in African slaves rather than in white indentured servants. First, England became increasingly involved in the slave trade during the late 1600s, making it easier for planters to acquire slaves. At the same time, the supply of white indentured servants began to decline sharply as economic conditions improved in England. Finally, wealthy planters feared that a growing population of bitter ex-servants would increase the likelihood of uprisings like Bacon's rebellion.

To meet the growing demand by Southern planters for slaves, England set up the Royal African Company in 1672. Colonial merchants, many from New England, also entered the business of transporting slaves to the colonies. These merchants traveled to the coast of West Africa to trade for slaves. Then began the terrible "middle passage"—the journey across the Atlantic. Packed into the holds of ships like cargo and chained together like criminals, slaves suffered through intense heat, painful illnesses, and rough seas. Not surprisingly, one out of every seven died on these grueling journeys of four to six weeks.

The Africans who did survive were quickly sold at slave auctions.

Slave traders used loading plans like the one shown below right to pack as many African slaves into the smallest space possible. The poster announces the auction of a new cargo of slaves.

Charlestown, July 24th, 1769.
TO BE SOLD,
On THURSDAY the third Day of AUGUST next,
A CARGO
OF
NINETY-FOUR
PRIME, HEALTHY
NEGROES,
CONSISTING OF
Thirty-nine MEN, Fifteen BOYS,
Twenty-four WOMEN, and
Sixteen GIRLS.
JUST ARRIVED,
In the Brigantine DEMBIA, Francis Bare, Maſter, from SIERRA-LEON, by
DAVID & JOHN DEAS.

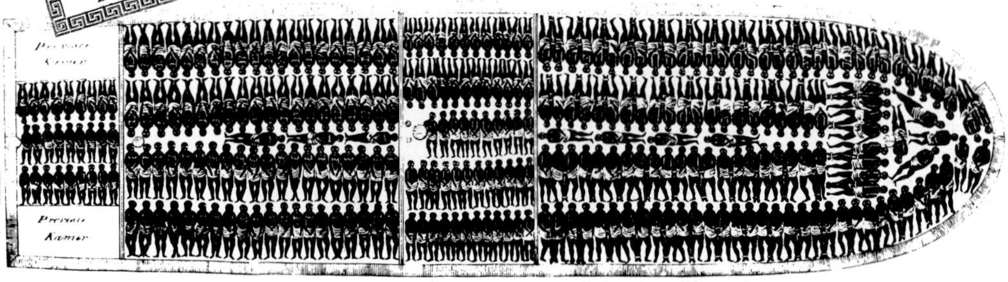

Access Activity

Have students examine the diagram of the slave ship on this page while you read the caption aloud. Tell students that in some cases, slaves were taken on deck to exercise but their chains were never removed. Ask students what were some of the dangers and problems of living in this manner for four weeks. *(Illness could spread easily; painfully uncomfortable)*

Access Strategy

Have students point to the Atlantic seaboard on a wall map, and ask them what they know about this area. How does the climate in New England differ from that of Virginia? *(Much colder, shorter growing season)* What do they know about the landforms in New England? *(Rocky coast, inland mountains, rocky soil)* You may want to refer them to the maps on pages 700–701 and 706–707 in the Atlas. Have students think about how the geography of New England influenced the way settlers got food, earned a living, and housed themselves. Have a volunteer write the students' answers on the boards. *(Sample answer: The geography made basic survival difficult; close communities resulted because people needed each other's help and protection.)*

> The sale began—young girls were there,
> Defenceless in their wretchedness,
> Whose stifled sobs of deep despair
> Revealed their anguish and distress.
> And mothers stood with streaming eyes,
> And saw their dearest children sold;
> Unheeded rose their bitter cries,
> While tyrants bartered them for gold.
>
> Frances Harper from *Slave Auction*

In her 1854 poem, "Slave Auction" (above), reformer and author Frances Harper captured the sense of grief that slaves experienced.

Torn from their homelands and loved ones, most slaves ended up on Southern plantations where their numbers increased rapidly in the late 1600s. Whereas fewer than 5,000 slaves lived in the English colonies in 1670, three decades later that number had jumped to 28,000. Still, the slave trade did not reach its peak until around 1730. By that time slave traders were bringing roughly 5,000 new slaves to the colonies each year. By 1775, roughly 500,000 slaves toiled in the colonies. ■

■ *What factors led to the rapid growth of slavery in the English colonies?*

Regional Differences

The Northern colonies had far fewer slaves than the Southern colonies. But this was just one of many differences in the way life was lived from colony to colony.

New England Colonies

Most New Englanders shared a common heritage. The great majority of the settlers there came from England or Scotland. As a result, the colonies of New England—New Hampshire, Massachusetts, Connecticut, and Rhode Island—all developed in similar ways.

Despite the region's poor, rocky soil, many New Englanders were farmers. Both to promote a sense of religious community and to protect themselves from Indians, New England farmers settled in small villages rather than scattered farms. While they went out to work in their fields during the day, their cattle grazed on the common, a shared area of land in the middle of the village. These hardy settlers were **subsistence farmers**, producing just enough food for their own needs. The Closer Look on pages 36–37 shows more about these farms.

◄ *Linton Park's painting, "The Scutching Bee," shows that scutching flax could be fun as well as work.*

■ *England's involvement in the slave trade made it easy for colonists to acquire slaves. As England's economy improved, fewer white people were willing to become indentured servants; slaves filled the need.*

CULTURE

Visual Learning

Point out that the text on page 36 describes scutching as the breaking of flax stalks into fibers. Have students look at the picture on this page to learn how this is done. *(The flax is beaten with clubs or mallets.)* What other things are people in the painting doing? Why do you think group work projects were important to the colonists? *(Group projects gave the colonists a chance to visit with and get help from neighbors.)*

Economic Context

Tobacco was the first major cash crop in the Southern colonies. But like rice, indigo, and cotton—crops later grown in the South on a large scale—tobacco demanded intensive labor. To meet this need for labor, southern planters acquired more slaves. Thus, slaves became valued property. A colony with many slaves had an advantage over one with only a few. The entire economy of the South depended on the slave trade.

Geographic Context

The slash-and-burn method used by many Indians and colonists to clear land entailed cutting down the trees and burning them. They used the ashes to fertilize the soil and then planted their crops among the remaining stumps. This method is still used in undeveloped areas of the world, but it is now a subject of political and environmental controversy.

Critical Thinking

Discuss with students the excerpt on this page from *Slave Auction* by Francis Harper. What did she mean by "defenceless in their wretchedness"? *(There was nothing they could do to change their situation.)* Why were the mothers' cries unheeded? *(The slave owners weren't interested in their sorrow.)*

Many of those who weren't farmers lived in one of the busy seaports that dotted New England's coast. Shipbuilding flourished in these seaports, as did the fishing and whaling industries. Soon, the cutting and shipping of timber became a major commercial activity as well.

As elsewhere in the colonies, life in New England was often difficult and primitive. Cutting and dragging wood, working the fields, tending the livestock, making and fixing clothes, mending the fences—all these tasks made life a constant round of toil for men, women, and children.

Even the popular forms of entertainment tended to involve work. Groups of farm women would often get together in a quilting bee where they made large quilted blankets. Or men, women, and children would gather for a scutching bee, in which the participants would break stalks of flax, a cotton-like plant, into fiber.

Music and dancing generally enlivened all these gatherings.

Middle Colonies

Life wasn't much easier in the Middle colonies—Pennsylvania, Delaware, New Jersey, and New York—with two important exceptions. The soil was richer, and much of the land had already been cleared by Indian farmers. As a result, the farmers in these colonies were able to grow small surpluses, or cash crops, which they could then sell to others. Travelers along the country roads of the Middle colonies could see farmers bringing corn, wheat, beef, and pork to trade in cities like New York and Philadelphia, the largest seaport in America at the time.

Unlike farmers in New England, farmers in the Middle colonies did not settle in small villages. Relations with the Indians in this part of the colonies were generally friendly, and good land

A CLOSER LOOK

The Colonial Farm

Imagine the Pennsylvania farmers' rough hands. Women's were blistered from churning butter. Men's stung with splinters from chopping wood. On colonial farms, men and women filled clearly defined roles.

Women used decorative butter molds to stamp butter with garden designs such as strawberries or wheat.

Women cooked meals in iron pots over coals and flames.

Women spun cotton and wool to make the family's clothes.

It took three to four hours to churn three pounds of butter.

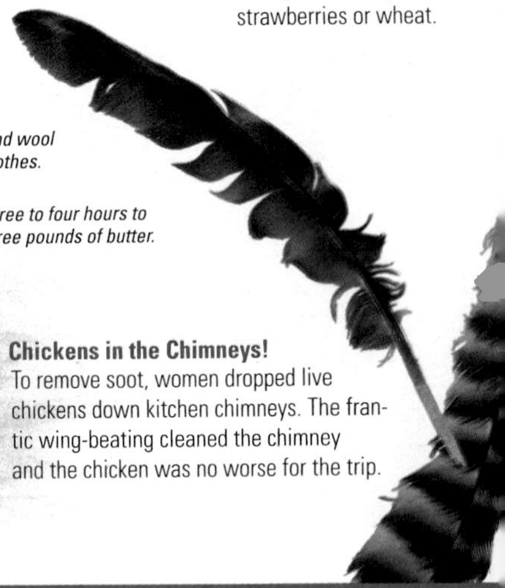

Chickens in the Chimneys!
To remove soot, women dropped live chickens down kitchen chimneys. The frantic wing-beating cleaned the chimney and the chicken was no worse for the trip.

36

Note: You may wish to use A Closer Look to review this lesson.

Critical Thinking

Refer students to A Closer Look and ask them to look for items that the farming family probably had to buy or have made by someone outside of the family. *(Butter mold, kettle)* What items did they probably make themselves? *(Clothes, yoke, plow, butter)*

More About the Role of Women
On an ordinary day, a farm woman might have to milk cows, spin thread, make soap, dip candles, fetch water, weed the garden, slaughter a hog, wash floors, smoke meat, milk cows again, weave cloth, mend socks, clean a big kettle, and sweep the kitchen.

Critical Thinking

Have students use the images and captions in A Closer Look to brainstorm a list of qualities for a successful colonial farmer. What kind of person would most likely succeed in these living conditions? *(Independent, resourceful, hardworking)*

Science Connection

Have students check an encyclopedia or almanac to find out what crops are grown in the New England, Middle Atlantic, and Southern states today. How do these crops correspond to the crops grown in the original thirteen colonies? Which crops from that time are no longer available?

Art Connection

The Pennsylvania Dutch, who settled much of southeastern Pennsylvania, have a heritage rich in the folk arts. Have students find examples of Pennsylvania Dutch designs in books on folk art. Some students may want to use some of these designs to decorate a book cover or wall hanging.

was more abundant. As a result, settlers built up large farms in the fertile, rolling countryside.

Farming wasn't the only way to make a living in the Middle colonies. The region also employed a large number of workers in a variety of manufacturing jobs involving the production of glass, textiles, and paper. In addition to working in shipyards and iron mines, thousands worked as craftsmen—shoemakers, tailors, blacksmiths, carpenters, watchmakers, printers, and many others.

Whereas most New Englanders came from England or Scotland, people from a variety of different nations settled in the Middle colonies. Immigrants from England, Ireland, Germany, Scotland, Sweden, and the Netherlands made the population of this region more diverse than anywhere else in the English colonies. Some of these immigrants chose to settle inland, on the eastern slopes of the Appalachian Mountains, an area that came to be known as the backcountry. Life in the backcountry was rough and dangerous, but the people who settled on the frontier enjoyed an unusual degree of independence.

Southern Colonies

The contrast between life along the coast and life in the backcountry was even sharper in the Southern colonies. In the tidewater region of the South—the rich coastal plains where ocean tides swept up the rivers—a system of large plantations grew up in the 1600s. In the forested backcountry, on the other hand, a society of small farmers emerged.

Settlers in Virginia began to grow tobacco in the early 1600s. Soon they discovered that they could increase profits by cultivating tobacco on a large scale. The great tobacco plantations that resulted became the hallmark not only of the Chesapeake

Across Time & Space

Today developers in Brazil use great earth-moving machines to gouge out huge bites from the nation's forests. In an effort to obtain rich farmlands, these developers displace native peoples, destroy habitats, and threaten the extinction of innumerable species.

From sunrise to sunset, men worked, butchering livestock, chopping wood, and tending fields. With a wooden plow, two horses, and a yoke such as this, one man could plant and harvest ten to twelve acres of wheat per year.

Wheat was stored and used as cash to buy tools and spices.

Threshing involved beating stems and husks to free the small pieces of grain.

Plows loosened the soil, making it easier for plants to grow.

ECONOMICS

Critical Thinking

How was life easier for Middle colony farmers than for New England farmers? *(In the Middle colonies, more and better land was available, and some of it had already been cleared by Indians. Because relations with the Indians were peaceful, farmers had more freedom in choosing where to farm.)*

More About the Plow Plowing was slow work because soil clung to the wooden plow; a man working with a wooden plow and two draft animals could turn over about an acre of soil a day. A ten-to-twelve-acre farm was about as much as one person could handle.

Writing a Diary

Have students imagine that they live on the farm pictured in A Closer Look. After studying the pictures and thinking about life on the farm, students can write several diary entries. Encourage them to include detailed information about the farm, their responsibilities on the farm, and the activities of family members. Put the students in groups and have them share their diary entries. Then have each group choose a diary entry to role play for the rest of the class.

Critical Thinking

Despite the fact that living and working conditions in New England were difficult, many people chose to live there. Have students consider why. *(It provided a religious community; it was even harder to move; it was familiar; they didn't know much about other areas.)*

GEOGRAPHY

Map and Globe Skills

Have students locate the port cities of Boston, Newport, New York, Philadelphia, and Charlestown on the map on this page as well as on the political map of the United States on pages 698–699 of the Atlas. Then have them identify the colonies in each of the three regions described in the text.

SOCIAL SYSTEMS

Critical Thinking

Why do you think backcountry farmers might have resented plantation owners? *(The farmers were poor and some had been badly exploited as indentured servants of the planters. They now resented the power of the planters in the state legislature.)* Why were some colonists in the South able to become plantation owners while others were not? *(They may have come to the colonies with more wealth or at least not as indentured servants. Some may have been better farmers and business people.)*

Although they shared certain characteristics, the English colonies were divided by distinct regional differences. The map at left shows the different regions of the colonies.

colonies of Virginia and Maryland, but of the Upper South colony of North Carolina as well.

A plantation system also developed in the Lower South colonies of South Carolina and Georgia. Here the chief crop was not tobacco but rice, which thrived in the swampy lowlands of the coast. In the 1740s, Eliza Lucas Pinckney, wife of a rich planter, successfully cultivated indigo, a plant from which blue dye is made. Indigo soon joined rice as a staple crop in the economy of the Lower South.

The typical Southern plantation was a more self-sufficient community than an ordinary farm. The planter and his family lived in a mansion known as the Great House. Other buildings on the plantation might include stables, a blacksmith's shop, a schoolhouse, a dairy, a bakehouse, a brickworks, and quarters for indentured servants or slaves.

Most planters managed the operation of the plantation themselves. Some hired overseers, or supervisors, to help them direct a work force of anywhere from 10 to 100 or more slaves. Women also played a major role in running the plantation. The planter's wife organized the household and supervised the house slaves and servants who worked there.

For the immigrants and former indentured servants who settled in the Southern backcountry, life was a continual struggle. Most backcountry people lived in log cabins or shacks and farmed at a subsistence level. Though some farmers earned a little money raising cattle and pigs, many more waged a constant fight against poverty. Schools, churches, and towns were few and far between.

Backcountry settlers did not hide their hostility toward the wealthy colonists who lived along the coasts.

The English Colonies, 1750

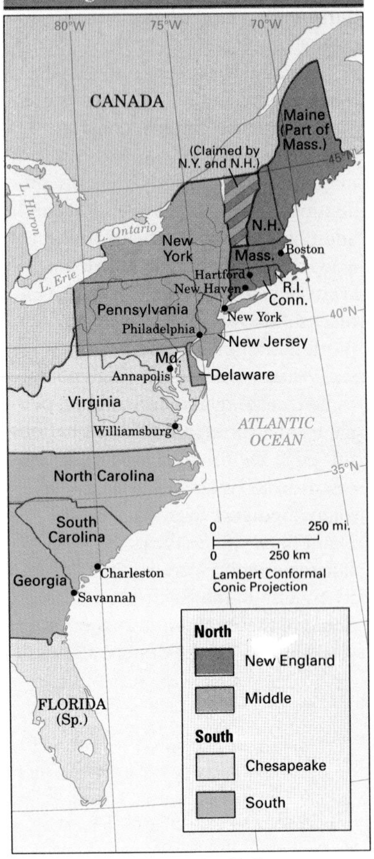

As this 1720 painting by Peter Cooper shows, Philadelphia was already a bustling port city by the early 1700s.

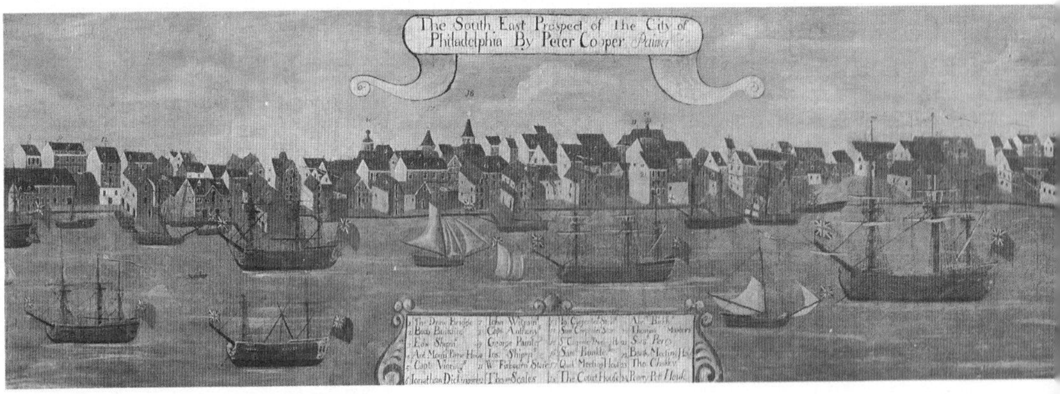

Social Participation

Many country taverns or inns in colonial times served as communication centers for the community. Have students describe such a gathering place near the school—a place where they go to hear "what's happening." Have them explain why such meeting places are important.

Writing a Report

Have students research and report on early newspapers in the colonies. Encourage them to use the card catalog to locate books on the history of newspapers. Public libraries may also have copies on microfilm of newspapers from the 1700s. Their report can describe how these newspapers were different from modern ones.

Reader's Theater

Have students work together to create a one-act play based on a chapter from Alex Haley's *Roots* (New York: Doubleday, 1976). Suggest that they use material from an early chapter that describes some aspect of Kunta Kinte's African heritage. Have other students recreate a scene from Paula Fox's *The Slave Dancer* (New York: Bradbury Press, 1973), the story of a 13-year-old girl who is kidnapped and taken aboard a slave boat to play music for the slaves.

These poor farmers felt they were not fairly represented in the colonial governments and resented the taxes these governments imposed on them. Sometimes their resentment boiled over into open revolt, as in the case of Bacon's rebellion.

Although the population of the Southern colonies was less varied than that of the Middle colonies, it was more diverse than that of New England. The most distinctive feature of the South's population was, of course, the large number of African slaves living there—roughly 35 percent of the region's total population in 1750. The other distinctive feature was the sharp split between the coast and the backcountry in terms of national origins. The large plantation owners tended to be English, while the small farmers of the frontier were mainly Germans and Scots-Irish, with a few English and French Protestants mixed in. ■

■ *What were the chief differences between life in the New England, Middle, and Southern colonies?*

Patterns of Colonial Life

Despite the distinct differences among the ways of life in the New England, Middle, and Southern colonies, these regions shared some important characteristics as well. Many of these shared characteristics involved transportation and communication.

The most common denominator of colonial life was travel. And travelers in the 1700s were often on their way to or from a port city. During the first half of the 18th century, many small trading villages blossomed into bustling port cities. The most important of these were Boston, Newport, New York, Philadelphia, and Charleston.

Port cities were centers of trade and consequently the lifeblood of the colonial economy. Out of them flowed the goods that the colonists exported to England and the Caribbean: tobacco, rice, indigo, fish, timber, and wheat, to name a few. Into the port cities came English goods that the colonists needed, including glass, paper, iron tools, cloth, and spices.

Port cities also became centers of transportation and communication. They were the hubs through which public coaches passed. They also published the most important colonial newspapers and were the places where news from the rest of the world arrived first. Farmers returning home from port cities would bring important information, which they would then pass on to their neighbors.

On a much smaller scale, the colonial tavern was the rural equivalent of the port city. Dotting lonely stretches of road, colonial taverns served as lodgings, restaurants, and gathering places. Travelers often had to put up with uncomfortable beds and simple meals in these taverns. Like port cities, however, these stopping-over places became centers of transportation and communication. They formed a complex network that bound the colonies closer together. ■

▲ *The signs hung outside colonial taverns were often distinctive and colorful, as the tavern sign above illustrates.*

■ *What features of daily life were common to all the English colonies?*

REVIEW

1. **FOCUS** What were some of the main characteristics of daily life in the English colonies in the early 1700s?
2. **CONNECT** Look at the exploration map on page 19. How did the routes English explorers took affect the way England settled the New World?
3. **ECONOMICS** Why did Southern planters prefer to use slaves rather than indentured servants as laborers?
4. **CRITICAL THINKING** Why do you think some people chose to live in the backcountry of the Southern colonies rather than on the coastal plains?
5. **WRITING ACTIVITY** Write an eyewitness account of conditions on a slave ship in the late 1600s.

■ *New England had a homogeneous population, subsistence farms, villages, and seaports; the Middle colonies had a diverse population, large farms, cash crops, manufacturing; the Southern colonies had a diverse population, plantations, slave labor, backcountry farms.*

GEOGRAPHY

Critical Thinking

Ask students what the port cities of Boston, New York, and Charleston had in common. *(They were centers of communication, travel, export, import)* Why were these port cities valuable? *(They gave the colonies access to England, continental Europe, and the Caribbean.)*

■ *Travel to and from port cities and reliance on taverns as centers of communication.*

CLOSE

Have small groups of students compare the information that they collected for the chart comparing colonial life in the three regions. When the students have agreed on the information in the chart, have them answer the Thinking Focus. As a reteaching activity, have students review the map on page 38.

Answers to Review Questions

1. Daily life in the early 1700s was filled with hard work, new challenges, and few forms of entertainment.
2. The English tended to settle in the areas visited by English explorers—that is, the northern parts of the country.
3. England's involvement in the slave trade made it easier to get slaves; the supply of indentured servants declined sharply; plantation owners feared uprisings of bitter ex-servants.
4. They could not compete with the wealthy planters; they were from different cultures and preferred to stay with their own people. Allow for personal opinion.
5. Students should use the details mentioned in the lesson in their answer.

Homework Options

Colonies in outer space may exist in the lifetime of these students. Have them write a one-page essay on why they would or would not want to be part of a space colonization program.

Study Guide: page 5.

INTRODUCE

Discuss what students learned about the Puritans in Lesson 2. Explain to them that in the 1630s, a group of Puritans established a colony in Connecticut. That colony is the subject of the historical work of fiction from which this excerpt is taken. You may wish to discuss the common superstitious belief of those times that men and women could be "witches."

READ AND RESPOND

After students read the selection independently, discuss why people are often suspicious of those who are different in some way from themselves. Point out that this fear of difference is one cause of prejudice. As students answer the purpose-setting question, make sure they give reasons for their answers.

In Lesson 2 you learned about the Puritan settlement of New England, and in Lesson 3 you read about the Puritans' treatment of Roger Williams. In this story you will read about life in a Puritan village.

LITERATURE

The Witch of Blackbird Pond

Elizabeth G. Speare

Having grown up in exotic Barbados, 16-year-old Kit Taylor comes to live with relatives in Puritan Wethersfield, in the colony of Connecticut, in the late 1600s. There, she has a difficult time fitting in. She befriends an elderly woman, Hannah, who lives near Blackbird Pond with her cat and memories of her husband, Thomas. When an epidemic kills many in Wethersfield, the townspeople think there is witchcraft at work. As you read this excerpt from Elizabeth G. Speare's book, ask yourself why Kit , a young girl, shows so much compassion for Hannah, when the "religious" people of Wethersfield do not.

From without the house there was an approaching sound of stamping feet and murmuring voices, gathering volume in the roadway outside. There was a crashing knock on the outer door. The three women's eyes met in consternation. Matthew Wood reached the door in one stride and flung it open.

"How dare you?" he demanded in low-voiced anger. "Know you not there is illness here?"

"Aye, we know right enough," a voice replied. "There's illness everywhere. We need your help to put a stop to it."

"What do you want?"

"We want you to come along with us. We're going for the witch."

"Get away from my house at once," ordered Matthew.

"You'll listen to us first," shouted another voice, "if you know what's good for your daughter."

"Keep your voices down, then, and be quick," warned Matthew. "I've no time to listen to foolishness."

"Is it foolishness that there's scarce a house in this town but has a sick child in it? You'd do well to heed what we say, Matthew Wood. John Wetherell's boy died today. That makes three dead, and it's the witch's doing!"

"Whose doing? What are you driving at, man?"

"The Quaker woman's. Down by Blackbird Pond. She's been a curse on this town for years with her witchcraft!"

The voices sounded hysterical. "We should have run her out long ago."

"Time and again she's been seen consorting with the devil down in that meadow!"

"Now she's put a curse on our children. God knows how many

Thematic Connections

Social Studies: The witchcraft hysteria

Houghton Mifflin Literary Readers: Challenging Dilemmas

Background

The first large-scale settlement in Connecticut began in 1636, when Puritan minister Thomas Hooker led a group overland from Massachusetts. Inspired by Hooker's ideas of self-government, these colonists wrote *The Fundamental Orders of Connecticut,* which served as the basis of government there for almost 200 years.

Charges of witchcraft were taken seriously in the 1600s. In the 1690s, the accusations of several teen-age girls prompted a wave of hysteria in the Massachusetts Colony. Fourteen women and six men were executed on suspicion of witchcraft before the Salem witch trials ended. Although Speare's story is entirely fictional, it demonstrates what could happen when a community turns against someone whose only real crime is being different.

more will be dead before morning!"

"This is nonsense,"scoffed Matthew Wood impatiently. "There's no old woman, and no witchcraft either could bring on a plague like this."

"What is it then?" shrilled a woman's voice.

Matthew passed a hand over his forehead. "The will of God—" he began helplessly.

"The curse of God, you mean!" another voice screamed. "His judgment on us for harboring an infidel and a Quaker."

"You'd better come with us, Matthew. Your own daughter's like to die. You can't deny it."

"I'll have naught to do with it," said Matthew firmly. "I'll hold with no witch hunt."

"You'd better hold with it!" the woman's voice shrilled suddenly. "You'd better look to the witch in your own household!"

"Ask that high and mighty niece of yours where she spends her time!" another woman shouted from the darkness. "Ask her what she knows about your Mercy's sickness!"

The weariness dropped suddenly from Matthew Wood. With his shoulders thrown back he seemed to tower in the doorway.

"Begone from my house!" he roared, his caution drowned in anger. "How dare you speak the name of a good, God-fearing girl? Any man who slanders one of my family has me to reckon with!"

There was a silence. "No harm meant," a man's voice said uneasily. "'Tis only woman's talk."

"If you won't come there's plenty more in the town who will," said another. "What are we wasting our time for?"

The voices receded down the pathway, rising again in the darkness beyond. Matthew bolted the door and dashed back to the dumbfounded women.

"Did they wake her?" he asked dully.

"No," sighed Rachel. "Even that could not disturb the poor child."

For a moment there was no sound but that torrid breathing. Kit had risen to her feet and stood clinging to the table's edge. Now the new fear that was stifling her broke from her lips in an anguished whisper.

"What will they do to her?"

Her aunt looked up in alarm. Matthew's black brows drew together darkly. "What concern is that of yours?"

"I know her!" she cried. "She's just a poor helpless old woman! Oh, please tell me! Will they harm her?"

"This is Connecticut," answered Matthew sternly. "They will abide by the law. They will bring her to trial, I suppose. If she can prove herself innocent she is safe enough."

"But what will they do with her now —tonight —before the trial?"

"How do I know? Leave off your questions, girl. Is there not trouble enough in our own house tonight?" He lowered himself into a chair and sunk his head in his hands.

"Go get some sleep, Kit," urged Rachel, dreading any more disturbance. "We may need you later on."

Kit stared from one to the other, half frantic with helplessness. They were not going to do anything. Unable to stop herself she burst into tears and ran from the room.

Why did the townspeople think a witch was at work? *(Many children fell sick, and three died.)*

In what way was the old woman who lived by Blackbird Pond different from other people in the community? *(She was a Quaker; they were Puritans.)*

Upstairs, in her own room, she stood leaning against the door, trying to collect her wits. She would have to get to Hannah. No matter what happened, she could not stay here and leave Hannah to face the mob alone. If she could get there in time to warn her—that was as far as she could see just now.

She snatched her cloak from the peg and, carrying her leather boots in her hand, crept down the stairs. She dared not try to unbolt the great front door but instead tiptoed cautiously through the cold company room into the back chamber and let herself out the shed door into the garden. She could hear shouts in the distance, and slipping hurriedly into her boots she fled along the roadway.

In Meeting House Square she leaned against a tree for an instant to get her bearing. The crowd was gathering, a good twenty men and boys and a few women, carrying flaring pine torches. In the hoarse shouting and the heedless screaming of the women there was a mounting violence, and a terror she had never known before closed over Kit's mind like a fog. For a moment her knees sagged and she caught at the tree for support. Then her mind cleared again, and skirting the square, darting from tree to tree like a savage, she made her way down Broad Street and out onto South Road.

She had never before seen the Meadows by moon light. They lay serene and still, wrapped in thin veils of drifting mist. She found the path easily, passed the dark clump of willows, and saw ahead the deep shining pool that was Blackbird Pond and a faint reddish glow that must be Hannah's window.

Hannah's door was not even bolted. Inside, by the still-flickering embers of the hearth, Hannah sat nodding in her chair, fast asleep. Kit touched the woman's shoulder gently.

"Hannah dear," she said, struggling to control her panting breath. "Wake up! 'Tis Kit. You've got to come with me, quickly."

"What is it?" Hannah jerked instantly awake. "Is it a flood?"

"Don't talk, Hannah. Just get into this cloak. Where are your shoes? Here, hold out your foot, quick! Now—"

There was not a moment to spare. As they stepped into the darkness the clamor of voices struck against them. The torches looked very near.

"Not that way! Down the path to the river!"

In the shelter of the dark bushes Hannah faltered, clutching at Kit's arms. She could not be budged. "Kit! Why are those people coming?"

"Hush! Hannah, dear, please—"

"I know that sound. I've heard it before. They're coming for the Quakers."

"No, Hannah, come—I—"

"Shame on thee, Kit. Thee knows a Quaker does not run away. Thomas will take care of us."

Desperately Kit shook the old woman's shoulders. "Oh, Hannah! What shall I do with you?" Of all times for Hannah to turn vague!

But Hannah's brief resolution suddenly gave way, and all at once she clung to Kit, sobbing like a child.

"Don't let them take me again," she pleaded. "Where is Thomas? I can't face it again without Thomas."

➤ What did Kit decide to do? *(Go to warn Hannah, the old woman)*

Why didn't Hannah want to run away? *(She said a Quaker does not run away.)*

Writing Activity

Tell students about Joseph McCarthy's activities in the early 1950s and the phenomenon known as McCarthyism. Then ask students to write an essay that compares McCarthyism to the witch hunts that occurred during Puritan times. Read aloud and discuss these essays with the class.

This time Kit succeeded in half dragging the sobbing woman through the underbrush. They made a terrible rustling and snapping of twigs as they went, but the noise behind them was still louder. The crowd had reached the cottage now. There was a crashing, as though the furniture were being hurled to splinters against the walls.

"She was here! The fire is still burning!"

"Look behind the woodpile. She can't have got far."

"There's the cat!" screeched a woman in terror. "Look out!"

There was a shot, then two more.

"It got away. Disappeared into thin air."

"There's no bullet could kill that cat."

"Here's the goats. Get rid of them too!"

"Hold on there! I'll take the goats. Witched or no, goats is worth twenty shillings apiece."

"Scotch the witch out!"

"Fire the house! Give us a light to search by!"

Desperately the two women pushed on, over a marshy bog that dragged at their feet, through a cornfield where the neglected shocks hid their scurrying figures, past a brambly tangle, to the shelter of the poplar trees and the broad moonlit stretch of the river. There they had to halt, crouching against a fallen log.

Behind them a flare of light, redder than the moonlight, lit up the meadows. There was a hissing and crackling.

"My house!" cried out Hannah, so heedlessly that Kit clapped a hand over her mouth. "Our own house that Thomas built!" With the tears running down her own cheeks, Kit flung both arms around the trembling woman, and together they huddled against the log and watched till the red glow lessened and died away.

For a long time the thrashing in the woods continued. Once voices came very close, and the search party went thwacking through the cornfield. Two men came out on the beach, not twenty feet from where they hid.

"Could she swim the river, think you?"

"Not likely. No use going on like this all night, Jem. I've had enough. There's another day coming." The men climbed back up the river bank.

When the voices died away it was very still. Serenity flowed back over the meadows. The veil of mist was again unbroken. After a long time, Kit dared to stretch her aching muscles. It was bitterly cold and damp here by the river's edge. She drew Hannah's slight figure closer against her, like a child's, and presently the woman's shuddering ceased, and Hannah drifted into the shallow napping of the very old.

Further Reading

The Seekers. Eilis Dillon. Based on firsthand accounts, this is the story of a young boy who sails to a Puritan colony in 1632 to follow his beloved to the New World.

Everyday Life in Colonial America. David Freemen Hawke. Diary accounts, curious facts, and illustrations give insight into the life of coionial Americans.

◄ Why didn't the townspeople kill Hannah's goats? *(They were worth money, so they stole them instead.)*

Was Uncle Matthew correct when he said the townspeople would abide by the law? *(No)*

EXTEND

Have students research and write a report on the Salem witch trials. Ask them to pay special attention to the causes of the witch hysteria.

Further Reading

You may want to ask students to go to the school or local library to find more books to read about the Salem witch trials.

Answers to Reviewing Key Terms

A. Sample answers:

1. The physical geography of a region shapes the human geography, or the way people relate to the land.
2. Some indentured servants eventually became subsistence farmers.
3. The low, flat prairie surrounded the high, level plane of the plateau.
4. In the navigation of the Atlantic seaboard, sailors often found estuaries to be safe harbors.
5. Nomadic tribes that traveled from place to place in search of food had little opportunity to form alliances with other tribes.

B. Answers:

1. False. Conquistadors explored Mexico, Central America, and South America.
2. False. Human geography involves how people and places influence one another.
3. True. The astrolabe, quadrant, and cross-staff improved navigation.
4. True. Landforms are natural features of the earth's surface.
5. False. New England states offer a range of geographic features, including mountains, flatlands, and a jagged coastline.
6. False. Indentured servants had their passage to America paid by someone else in exchange for an agreement to work for a specific period of time.

Answers to Exploring Concepts

A. Answers:

Jamestown founded—1607
Cabot sails to new World—1497
Mass. Colony founded—1630
Hudson River discovered—1609
Cartier discovers Gulf of St. Lawrence—1535
Columbus's first voyage—1492
Plymouth founded—1620
Verrazano to New World—1524
Balboa finds Pacific—1513
Roanoke colony begun—1587

B. Sample answers:

1. Students could include the difficulties associated with small boats, primitive navigational equipment, seasickness, filth, and too much heat below deck
2. Answers may include the influence of the Renaissance, the search for religious freedom, the search for short routes to Asia, and the search for wealth.
3. The geography includes prairies, hills, deserts, rocky coastlines, lakes and rivers, mountains, swamps, and forests.
4. Indians showed the Pilgrims where to fish and hunt and taught them to plant native crops such as corn, beans, and squash.
5. The Aztecs had established a thriving culture with more than 150,000 people living in an elaborate city with pyramids.
6. Slaves were packed tightly into the holds of ships, chained like criminals, and faced intense heat, illness, and rough seas.

Chapter Review

Reviewing Key Terms

alliance (p. 27)
conquistador (p. 18)
estuary (p. 6)
human geography (p. 5)
indentured servant (p. 34)
landform (p. 5)
navigation (p. 17)
nomad (p. 27)
physical geography (p. 5)
plateau (p. 11)
prairie (p. 8)
precipitation (p. 8)
sect (p. 21)
subsistence farmer (p. 35)

A. In each of the following pairs, the two terms are related in some way. Write a sentence for each pair that clearly explains the relationship between the two terms.

1. human geography, physical geography
2. indentured servant, subsistence farmer
3. prairie, plateau
4. navigation, estuary
5. nomad, alliance

B. Based on what you have read in the chapter, decide whether each of the following statements is accurate. Write an explanation of each decision.

1. Conquistadors settled the New England colonies.
2. Human geography involves the study of the natural world, such as climate and rainfall.
3. Because of improvements in navigation, sailors were able to make more accurate and longer voyages.
4. Mountains, plains, and valleys are examples of landforms.
5. Most of the New England states consist of prairies.
6. Indentured servants paid someone else's passage to the New World in exchange for labor.

Exploring Concepts

A. Copy the timeline below on a separate sheet of paper. Use the information below to complete your timeline. Insert the name of each event in the correct time position.

- Jamestown founded
- John Cabot sails to New World
- Massachusetts Bay Colony founded
- Henry Hudson discovers Hudson River
- Cartier discovers Gulf of St. Lawrence
- Columbus's first voyage for Spain
- Plymouth founded
- Verrazano sails to New World
- Balboa finds Pacific
- Roanoke colony begun

B. Support each of the following statements with facts and details from the chapter.

1. The crossing of the Atlantic was usually a voyage filled with hardship.
2. Explorers had many reasons for braving the unknown.
3. The continental United States has a dramatically varied geographic landscape.
4. The Pilgrims owed their survival to the help of Indians.
5. The civilization Cortés founded in Mexico was a flourishing one.
6. The "middle passage" was a voyage of endless misery.

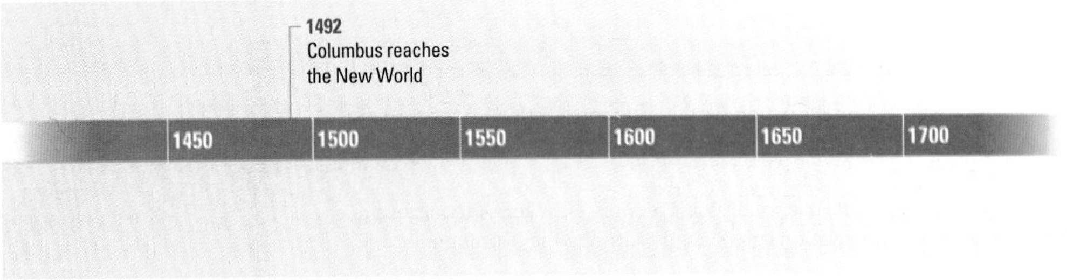

Reviewing Skills

1. What is the difference between a historical atlas and a world atlas?
2. The hoe pictured on page 32 was handmade by a colonial farmer or blacksmith. How might you find out (a) the date when factories began producing hoes and (b) the cost of handmade and factory-made hoes?
3. Which of the references listed on page 32 would help you to determine how the geography and climate of the area in which you live affected the way the area developed?
4. Suppose you wanted to find the state census for the year you were born, as well as a map that shows your state during that year. Which of the reference materials listed on page 32 could you use?

Using Critical Thinking

1. Are people in modern American society as ruled by geographic conditions as people in colonial society were? Keep in mind such considerations as modes of travel, how food is acquired, and types of houses built.
2. Do geography and climate affect the ways people in your town or city make their living? Explain your answer.
3. Which Europeans, in your opinion, treated the native inhabitants of America worse, the Spanish conquistadors or the English settlers? Why?
4. Did an indentured servant have basically the same status as a slave? Why or why not?
5. Even though the English colonies were all controlled by England, important differences soon arose among the colonies' various regions. Explain how the geography of each region—New England, the Middle Colonies, and the South—contributed to its distinctive qualities.

Europeans' treatment of Indians ranged from enslavement to acceptance of them as equals. What factors contributed to the Europeans' harsh treatment of the Indians? Why didn't more Europeans follow the example of William Penn and Roger Williams?

Preparing for Citizenship

1. **WRITING ACTIVITY** Many laws of colonial New England seem harsh to us today, but the leaders of communities believed that those laws were necessary to maintain order in an untamed land. Research and write a report on colonial laws and punishments.
2. **WRITING ACTIVITY** Imagine you have won a roundtrip one-day time-travel ticket to colonial New England. Keep a travel journal of what you eat, activities you engage in, clothes you wear, etc. Then write a short paper comparing your day in colonial New England with a typical day as a modern teenager.
3. **COLLECTING INFORMATION** Indians occupied most areas of North America at the time Europeans first came here. Traces of Indian life still survive in many communities. For example, New York City's major street, called Broadway, was originally an Indian path on Manhattan Island. Many place names also reflect the Indian heritage. Find out if any groups of Indians lived in your area. Report on their way of life and what happened to them. Include in your report any examples of the Indian heritage that still survive.
4. **ART ACTIVITY** Imagine you are an enterprising Englishman who wants to start your own colony in one of the three major areas of colonial America. Choose an area, and design an advertisement convincing people to leave their homes and settle in the New World.
5. **ART ACTIVITY** Conduct a class quilting bee. Make the quilt out of paper by having each student make a square of paper nine inches on each side. Decorate the square with a picture of one of the persons, events, or scenes from the chapter. When all are finished, paste them together in a large quilt for display.
6. **COLLABORATIVE LEARNING** As a class, make a list on the board of the landforms, climate, and major geographic features of the community in which you live. Then determine how people today control, change, utilize, or simply adapt to their geographic surroundings. Do we have greater control over geography than the colonists did?

Answers to Reviewing Skills

1. A historical atlas includes information about people, events, and conditions at different times in history; a world atlas focuses on geography and location.
2. a) Look in a chronology of agricultural development.
   b) Look in a statistical source on economic activities.
3. A historical atlas would be the most helpful because it can include topographical and climatic maps.
4. Students could use the *Statistical Abstract of the United States for the state census and a historical atlas for the map.*

Answers to Using Critical Thinking

1. Students might consider how often they think about the geography of their area in the course of one day.
2. Ask students to consider how many occupations today are dependent on weather conditions.
3. Students should support their answers with specific details.
4. Point out that indentured servants had the promise of freedom and that they made the voyage to America voluntarily.
5. Students should point out how the physical geography of each area determined how the colonists could make a living.
6. Point out that many Europeans were fleeing harsh treatment themselves.

Answers to Preparing for Citizenship

1. **WRITING ACTIVITY** Refer students to Understanding Reference Materials on page 32.
2. **WRITING ACTIVITY** Students should use details from the chapter in their comparison.
3. **COLLECTING INFORMATION** Students may want to contact the Bureau of Indian Affairs for information.
4. **ART ACTIVITY** Ask students to include information on the physical and human geography of the area they are advertising.
5. **ART ACTIVITY** This activity can also be used for a community history display.
6. **COLLABORATIVE LEARNING** Supporting material for this activity can be found in John McPhee's book *The Control of Nature* (New York: Farrar, Straus & Giroux, Inc., 1989) and in journals of the Audubon society.

CHAPTER 2

Planning at a Glance

Reviewing the American Revolution

	Objectives	Reading Support *and* Other Resources	Diverse Learning Strategies
Lesson 1 An Emerging American Identity *pp. 48–53* 1–2 days	• Explain how a large and increasingly varied population helped to produce a distinct American culture and identity. • Demonstrate how the colonists developed their own political institutions and gained experience in the exercise of power.	• **Workbook** or **Reading Support:** pp. 19–22 Review p. 5 Extra Support/Transition p. 5 Multi-lang. Sum. pp. 9–10 • **Other Resources:** Geography Kit, Poster I, Study Guide p. 6	Access Strat. **(SDAIE)** TE p. 49 Math Connection **(GATE)** TE p. 51 Collaborative Act. **(Visual)** TE p. 52 Audiotapes of Multi-langauge Lesson Summaries **(Auditory)**
Lesson 2 Growing Conflict with England *pp. 54–59* 2–3 days	• Summarize the background and outcome of the Seven Years' War. • Identify the reasons why tension developed and led to violent clashes between England and the American colonies after the Seven Years' War.	• **Workbook** or **Reading Support:** pp. 23–26 Review p. 6 Extra Support/Transition p. 6 Multi-lang. Sum. pp. 11–12 • **Other Resources:** Study Guide p. 7	Access Strat. **(SDAIE)** TE p. 55 Social Participation **(Auditory)** TE p. 56 Art Connection **(Visual)** TE p. 57 Audiotapes of Multi-langauge Lesson Summaries **(Auditory)**
Skill: Charting Pre-Revolutionary Events *pp. 60–61*	• Use parallel timelines to determine relationships between events in England and events in the colonies.	• **Other Resources:** Study Guide p. 8	Making a Timeline **(Visual)** TE p. 60
Lesson 3 Fighting the American Revolution *pp. 62–70* 2–3 days	• Trace the steps that led to the Declaration of Independence, including early military encounters. • Identify the main events of the Revolution in the North, the West, and the South. • Describe the provisions of the Treaty of Paris.	• **Workbook** or **Reading Support:** pp. 27–30 Review p. 7 Extra Support/Transition p. 7 Multi-lang. Sum. pp. 13–14 • **Other Resources:** Geography Kit, Study Guide p. 9	Music Connection **(Auditory)** TE p. 66 Map and Globe Skills **(Visual)** TE p. 67 Writing Historical Fiction **(GATE)** TE p. 69 Audiotapes of Multi-langauge Lesson Summaries **(Auditory)**
Lesson 4 Fighting the War at Home *pp. 71–75* 1–2 days	• Describe the impact of the American Revolution on the civilian population, including specific groups of people. • Explain why the new state governments worked well during the war but were not as effective in governing a new nation in peacetime.	• **Workbook** or **Reading Support:** pp. 31–34 Review p. 8 Extra Support/Transition p. 8 Multi-lang. Sum. pp. 15–16 • **Other Resources:** Study Guide p. 10	Access Strat. **(SDAIE)** TE p. 72 Map and Globe Skills **(Visual)** TE p. 74 Homework Options **(Auditory)** TE p. 75 Audiotapes of Multi-langauge Lesson Summaries **(Auditory)**
Chapter Review *pp. 76–77* 1 day		Chapter 2 Test pp. 5–8 *(See facsimiles on TE p. 750.)*	Assessment Multiple-Use Masters pp. 81–88

Reading Support Resources *for Every Lesson*

Reading and Review

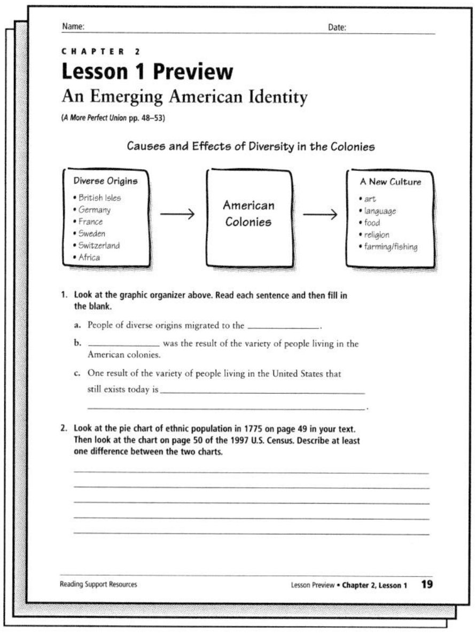
Name: Date:

CHAPTER 2

Lesson 1 Preview

An Emerging American Identity

(A More Perfect Union pp. 48–53)

Causes and Effects of Diversity in the Colonies

Diverse Origins: • British Isles • Germany • France • Sweden • Switzerland • Africa → American Colonies → A New Culture: • art • language • food • religion • farming/fishing

1. Look at the graphic organizer above. Read each sentence and then fill in the blank.
   a. People of diverse origins migrated to the ________.
   b. ________ was the result of the variety of people living in the American colonies.
   c. One result of the variety of people living in the United States that still exists today is ________
2. Look at the pie chart of ethnic population in 1775 on page 49 in your text. Then look at the chart on page 50 of the 1997 U.S. Census. Describe at least one difference between the two charts.

Reading Support Resources — Lesson Preview • Chapter 2, Lesson 1 — 19

- **Chapter Overview*** p. 18
- **Lesson Previews*** using graphic organizers from the Teacher's Edition pp. 19, 23, 27, 31
- **Reading Strategies*** pp. 20, 24, 28, 32
- **Lesson Summaries*** pp. 21–22, 25–26, 29–30, 33–34
- **Lesson Reviews** pp. 5, 6, 7, 8

* **Workbook** includes starred items.

Multi-language Summaries

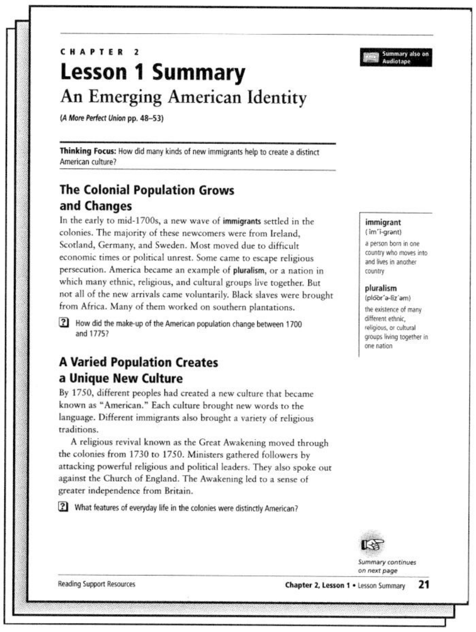
CHAPTER 2

Lesson 1 Summary

Summary also on Audiotape

An Emerging American Identity

(A More Perfect Union pp. 48–53)

Thinking Focus: How did many kinds of new immigrants help to create a distinct American culture?

The Colonial Population Grows and Changes

In the early to mid-1700s, a new wave of **immigrants** settled in the colonies. The majority of these newcomers were from Ireland, Scotland, Germany, and Sweden. Most moved due to difficult economic times or political unrest. Some came to escape religious persecution. America became an example of **pluralism**, or a nation in which many ethnic, religious, and cultural groups live together. But not all of the new arrivals came voluntarily. Black slaves were brought from Africa. Many of them worked on southern plantations.

How did the make-up of the American population change between 1700 and 1775?

immigrant (ĭm'ĭ-grənt) a person born in one country who moves into and lives in another country

pluralism (plŏor'ə-lĭz'əm) the existence of many different ethnic, religious, or cultural groups living together in one nation

A Varied Population Creates a Unique New Culture

By 1750, different peoples had created a new culture that became known as "American." Each culture brought new words to the language. Different immigrants also brought a variety of religious traditions.

A religious revival known as the Great Awakening moved through the colonies from 1730 to 1750. Ministers gathered followers by attacking powerful religious and political leaders. They also spoke out against the Church of England. The Awakening led to a sense of greater independence from Britain.

What features of everyday life in the colonies were distinctly American?

Summary continues on next page

Reading Support Resources — Chapter 2, Lesson 1 • Lesson Summary — 21

Lesson Summaries in:

- English (See Reading and Review.)
- Spanish pp. 21–22, 25–26, 29–30, 33–34
- Chinese pp. 9–16
- Hmong pp. 9–16
- Khmer pp. 9–16
- Vietnamese pp. 9–16

Summaries available on audiotapes

Lesson Support / Transition

S D A I E

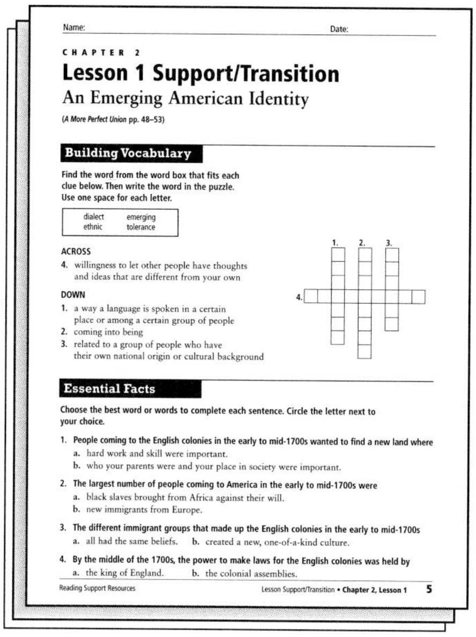
Name: Date:

CHAPTER 2

Lesson 1 Support/Transition

An Emerging American Identity

(A More Perfect Union pp. 48–53)

Building Vocabulary

Find the word from the word box that fits each clue below. Then write the word in the puzzle. Use one space for each letter.

dialect, emerging, ethnic, tolerance

ACROSS
4. willingness to let other people have thoughts and ideas that are different from your own

DOWN
1. a way a language is spoken in a certain place or among a certain group of people
2. coming into being
3. related to a group of people who have their own national origin or cultural background

Essential Facts

Choose the best word or words to complete each sentence. Circle the letter next to your choice.

1. People coming to the English colonies in the early to mid-1700s wanted to find a new land where
   a. hard work and skill were important.
   b. who your parents were and your place in society were important.
2. The largest number of people coming to America in the early to mid-1700s were
   a. black slaves brought from Africa against their will.
   b. new immigrants from Europe.
3. The different immigrant groups that made up the English colonies in the early to mid-1700s
   a. all had the same beliefs. b. created a new, one-of-a-kind culture.
4. By the middle of the 1700s, the power to make laws for the English colonies was held by
   a. the king of England. b. the colonial assemblies.

Reading Support Resources — Lesson Support/Transition • Chapter 2, Lesson 1 — 5

Activities for SDAIE
Specially **D**esigned **A**cademic **I**nstruction in **E**nglish

- **Lesson Support/Transition** pp. 5, 6, 7, 8

Technology Options

Internet Support

http://www.eduplace.com

Social Studies Center at Education Place

Internet support for Chapter 2:

- ***Lesson at a Glance***
- ***A Minuteman***

Software

Student Writing Center® (CD-ROM) (Macintosh® or Windows®)

School to Career

The American Revolution was fought by brave men and women on both sides of the conflict. Have students discuss the role and nature of the military in national life then and today. What sorts of careers are possible for persons joining each of the branches of the military today?

Character Education

Immigrants who came to America for political and religious freedom led lives of **courage** and **self-sacrifice.** Ask students to discuss what these terms mean to them and to find examples in the text. Then divide the class into small groups and have find an example from the current local, national, or international news in which an individual acts with courage or self-sacrifice.

CHAPTER
PREVIEW

After students have read the chapter title and the narrative under it, ask them to compare the Allan Ramsey portrait of King George III (1760) with Willard's painting *The Spirit of '76* and John Wesley Jarvis's portrait of Thomas Paine, 1806. *(The king is in regal attire and looks aloof; the patriots are dressed in rugged uniforms and convey a spirit of cooperation and determination. Paine looks more open and approachable than the King.)* How do these differences represent the differences between the colonies and England? *(Colonies wanted a more democratic government.)*

Looking Back

Ask students what they have learned about the first Europeans who settled in America. Have students suggest one word that best describes these early settlers. *(Independent)*

Looking Forward

Tell students that they will be studying the American Revolution in the following four lessons: An Emerging American Identity, Growing Conflict with England, Fighting the American Revolution, and Fighting the War at Home.

Chapter 2

Reviewing the American Revolution

By the mid-1770s, a distinct American identity had begun to emerge. Along with this new identity came a growing spirit of independence from George III and the English government. When England tried to assert its authority over the colonies, the colonists first resisted and then rebelled. Out of the revolution a new nation emerged.

George III reigned as King of England from 1760 to 1811. His unpopular political and economic policies eventually stirred the colonists to revolt against British rule.

Thomas Paine's popular and influential pamphlet, *Common Sense*, aroused the colonists in the winter and spring of 1776 and prepared the way for revolution.

1690 | 1710 | 1730

1700

BACKGROUND

During the 1700s the colonial population grew larger and more diverse, and a distinct American culture, outlook, and sense of independence developed. This spirit of independence led, in turn, to growing tension with Great Britain and eventually open rebellion.

Tribal Strategies in the Seven Years' War

During the Seven Years' War, both the British and the French tried to persuade the Iroquois Confederacy—the Mohawk, Oneida, Onondaga, Cayuga, Seneca, and Tuscarora tribes—to join their side by offering gifts or by showing their power. The gifts were important, and the British offered the most gifts. The Confederacy, however, had its own plan. The policy of the American Indians was to analyze the balance of military power as it shifted between the European nations and to give their support to the stronger nation. In the first three years of the war, the French were victorious, therefore winning also the American Indians' support. But after 1759, British victories persuaded the Iroquois to abandon the French. The Confederacy knew that an alliance with the winner would help them to get a treaty that honored their claims to land.

Deborah Sampson

Deborah Sampson disguised herself as a man to serve in the Continental Army. Sampson's unusual but dedicated service in the

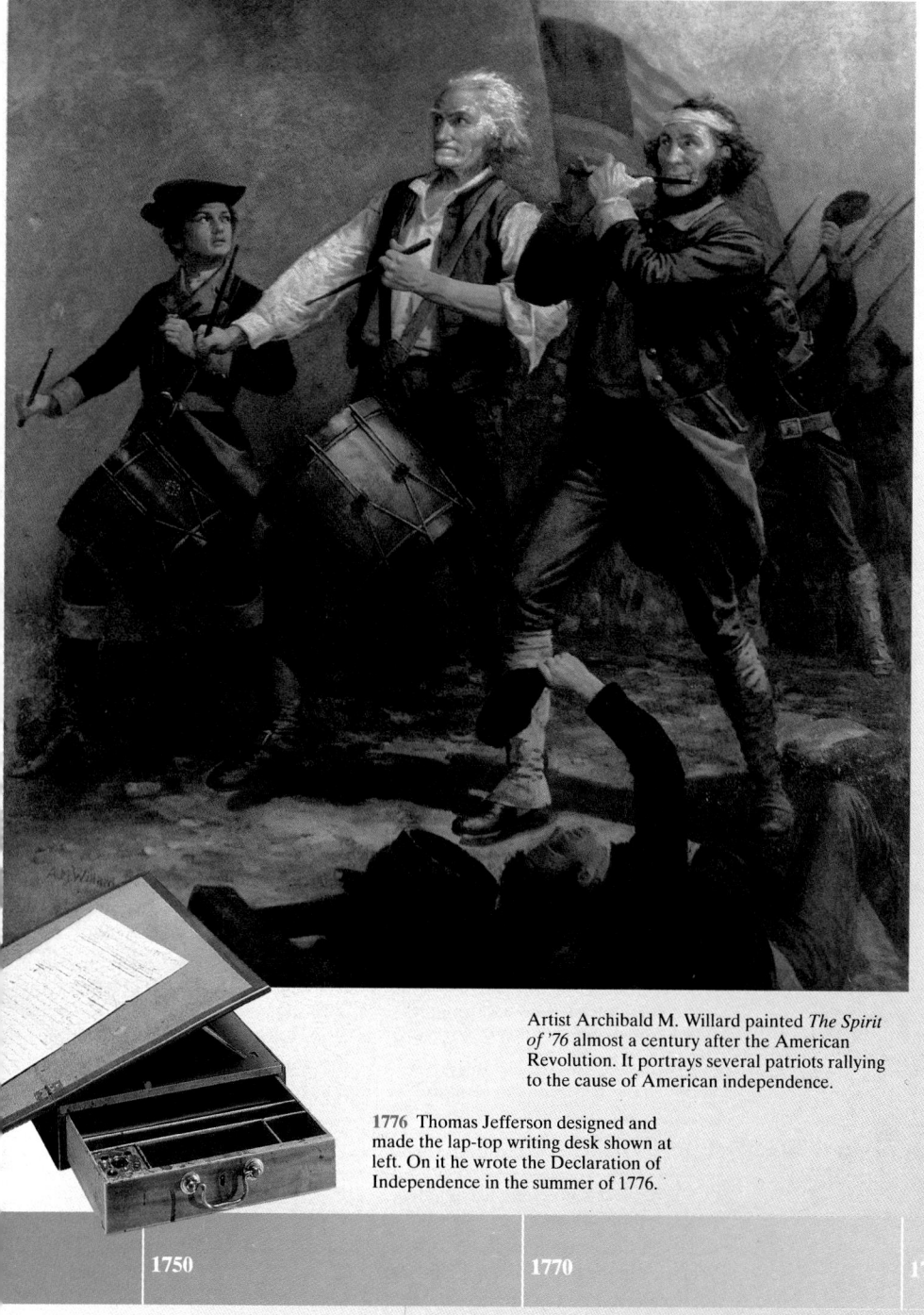

Artist Archibald M. Willard painted *The Spirit of '76* almost a century after the American Revolution. It portrays several patriots rallying to the cause of American independence.

1776 Thomas Jefferson designed and made the lap-top writing desk shown at left. On it he wrote the Declaration of Independence in the summer of 1776.

1750 | 1770 | 1790

1783

Understanding the Visuals

Refer students to the *Spirit of '76*. Does Willard capture a realistic or romantic image of the American revolution? *(Romantic, because the painting does not show the harsh realities of war, but instead celebrates American patriotism)*

Draw attention to the lap desk and point out that Thomas Jefferson, in addition to being an important statesman, was also an inventor. Among his useful devices were an odometer, a swivel chair, a dumbwaiter, and a compass connected to a weathervane, which told him inside his house, the direction of the wind outside.

Understanding Chronology

Use the timeline to review students' prior knowledge of the period. What was happening in the colonies in the early 1700s? *(Colonies were maturing, becoming "American.")* Mid-1700s? *(England begins to pass laws and demand taxes that anger colonists.)* Late 1700s? *(War breaks out between England and the colonies.)*

Fourth Massachusetts Regiment was officially recognized by the United States Government. In 1792 the government granted her, along with the men who fought with her, a small pension. Leaders like General John Paterson, her former commanding officer, and Paul Revere helped her gain this recognition and support.

In 1838, eleven years after her death, Congress passed an Act "for the relief of the heirs of Deborah Gannet" (Sampson's married name). The cost of medical care to treat injuries she received in the war had impoverished her family. To ease the family's hardship, the government awarded her three children $466.66, the equivalent of a full military pension.

INTRODUCE

Read the lesson title. Discuss with students the meaning of *identity* and what might make up a person's or a country's identity. *(Form of government, geography, social customs, ethnic makeup, and history)* Have students read the Thinking Focus and ask them to predict what kind of culture might emerge in a society made up of people from different nations. Have them read to confirm or reject their predictions.

Key Terms

Vocabulary strategies: T36–37

immigrant—a person born in one country who moves to and takes up residence in another country

pluralism—a condition of society in which numerous distinct ethnic, religious, or cultural groups coexist within one nation

salutary neglect—the hands-off policy with which England governed the American colonies for much of the late 1600s and early 1700s

veto—to forbid or prevent authoritatively a legislative bill from becoming law

1700 1775 1780 1790

LESSON 1

An Emerging American Identity

THINKING FOCUS

How did many kinds of new immigrants help to create a distinct American culture?

Key Terms

- immigrant
- pluralism
- salutary neglect
- veto

When a young Scottish doctor named Alexander Hamilton visited Philadelphia for the first time in 1744, he was surprised by what he found there, as his diary entry illustrates:

> *I dined at a tavern with a very mixed company of different nations and religions. There were Scots, English, Dutch, Germans, and Irish; there were Roman Catholics, Church men [Anglicans], Presbyterians, Quakers, Methodists, Seventh-Day men, Moravians, Anabaptists, and one Jew."*

At the time of Hamilton's visit, Philadelphia was already the largest city in the colonies, and it was growing and changing fast. The city's population doubled from 15,000 to 30,000 between 1740 and 1775. It attracted people from Ireland, the German states, and Scotland, as well as from other colonies.

Newcomers to Philadelphia found a booming, prosperous city. They marveled at its stone-paved streets, lit at night by whale oil lamps. The city's many rooming houses provided lodging for its fast-growing population. Wealthy merchants built great homes and decorated them with paintings, helping to make Philadelphia the cultural center of the colonies.

Dr. Hamilton was not the only European visitor to notice how many different kinds of people were living in Philadelphia in the mid-1700s. Through the city's streets, Quakers in their broad black hats walked side by side with Shawnee or Delaware Indians from the surrounding countryside. Free blacks traded with shopkeepers who spoke German and French. Boasting many of the features of a large European city, Philadelphia was also uniquely American in the variety of its inhabitants.

The Colonial Population Grows and Changes

What was happening in Philadelphia symbolized what was happening in all the English colonies of North America in the early to mid-1700s. An increasing number of **immigrants** arrived daily. They were people eager to find a home in a new land that valued hard work and ability more than high birth or position. Over time, the presence of a variety of new peoples worked to change the character of the colonial population.

A New Wave of Immigrants

The largest group of new immigrants came from Northern Ireland. These were Scottish farmers whose families had moved to Ireland a

Objectives

1. Describe how the colonial population grew and changed during the 1700s.
2. Explain how an increasingly varied population helped to produce a distinct American culture and identity.
3. Demonstrate how the colonists developed their own political institutions and gained experience in the exercise of power.

Graphic Overview

Diverse Origins
- British Isles
- Germany
- France
- Sweden
- Switzerland
- Africa

→ **American Colonies** →

Cultural Effects
- art
- language
- food
- religion
- farming/fishing

This engraving shows the downtown area of colonial Philadelphia. Philadelphia was one of the fastest growing cities in colonial times.

century earlier. As a result of drought and disputes with the English government in the early 1700s, many of these Scots-Irish chose to try their luck in America. A majority of them settled in Pennsylvania, but the hardiest pushed farther west into the frontier.

Some crossed the Appalachians into what is now West Virginia. Others moved south to North Carolina and South Carolina.

Crop failures and constant wars in Europe drove many Germans to America. Germans soon developed improved versions of the rifle and the iron stove. Their efficient methods of farming were copied by other colonists. Swedes also moved to the timber-covered new land. They introduced the log cabin to the North American wilderness.

America was always a safe place for those running from religious persecution as well. French Protestants, or Huguenots, settled in cities along the coast. Jews from Portuguese colonies set up synagogues in the major port cities. Catholics made homes in Maryland. Lutherans from Germany and Sweden, Calvinists from Switzerland, and Quakers from England also enriched the American mix. The word **pluralism** describes a nation in which many ethnic, religious, and cultural groups live together. As the chart below shows, American society became more pluralistic in the 1700s. See Understanding Pluralism on page 50.

A Growing Population of Slaves

The largest number of newcomers to America were black slaves brought from Africa against their will. As Southern plantations grew in size, the demand for slaves increased.

Ethnic Population, 1775

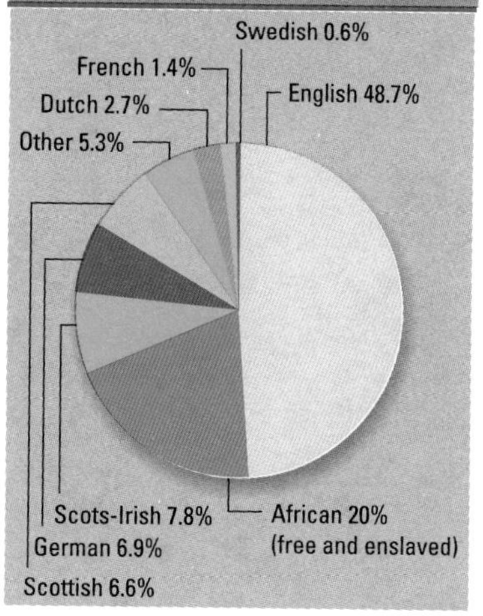

This chart shows the great diversity in the population of the colonies. Notice that by 1775 less than half of the colonists were of English background. Why do you think Native Americans are missing from this graph?

DEVELOP

Point out to students the cause-and-effect structure of the lesson. Explain that the culture in the American colonies was a direct product (effect) of the diversity of its settlers (cause). Tell students to list the effects of this diversity as they read the lesson.

HISTORY

Study Skills

Have students use the information in the lesson to make a chart showing both the forces that caused many people to migrate and settle in the colonies and the contributions these immigrants made to the emerging society. Remind students to draw on what they learned in Chapter 1 about the forces that caused the initial English migration.

Access Strategy

Ask students what family traditions they have, such as traditions for celebrating birthdays or for sharing household chores among family members. Do they participate in any religious or ethnic traditions? Were these learned from parents or relatives? Ask them about traditions practiced by their friends or neighbors. Have they adopted any aspects of those traditions as their own? Then ask students to decide which traditions have been passed to them vertically (down through the generations) or horizontally (from friend to friend and neighbor to neighbor). Tell students that in this lesson they will see that as the colonists adapted to their new lives, they borrowed a great deal from each other's cultures.

Access Activity

Direct students to the chart of ethnic diversity on this page. How did the German and Scottish populations compare? *(About the same size)* How much of the total population was made up of Africans, and how did this group compare with the English? *(20 per cent, about half as large as the English)*

HISTORY

Critical Thinking

Ask students why the pluralistic nature of the colonies might lead to weakened ties with the British government. *(Colonists from other countries might feel no loyalty to England.)* For what reasons did the British government allow so many different types of people to settle in the new colonies? *(Perhaps because many people were needed to populate the vast new land and because more people allowed the British to make more money from the colonies)*

Understanding Pluralism

Since colonial times, first-time visitors to America have marveled at the broad diversity of its people. For many years, America has prided itself on its ability to accept—and to borrow from—the lifestyles and values of many different nationalities. It has also recognized and respected the practice of many different languages and religions. This belief that many cultures can co-exist in one country is called pluralism. In fact, our national motto expresses this fundamental belief: *E pluribus unum*, Latin for "out of many, one."

Many nations in the world are not pluralistic. For example, Japan has a very homogeneous population. That is, most of the Japanese people share the same language, customs, and ancestry. The Japanese celebrate their likeness rather than their differences. For more than 1,200 years, the Japanese have discouraged immigration to their country. They believe that their sameness—their *nihonjinron* or "Japaneseness" binds them together and makes them strong.

Present Day Pluralism

Because of large-scale immigration, especially from Asia and Latin America, the United States has become more pluralistic than ever before. The fastest growing ethnic group in the United States is Hispanics. According to official census data, Hispanics made up 6.4 percent of the U.S. population in 1980, and grew to 10.9 percent of the population in 1997. At the same time, the percentage of whites in the population has decreased from 78.8 percent in 1980 to 72.7 percent in 1997.

American Life Enriched

What does pluralism mean to the United States as a democratic society? It means that citizens of all cultural groups have a voice in the decision-making process of government. It means that people must compromise, or settle their differences by yielding on certain points. In addition, our pluralistic society challenges Americans to exercise tolerance, or respect, for the opinions, customs, traditions, and lifestyles of others. Today, as in the past, the diversity of our people greatly enriches American life and strengthens the nation.

The 1997 U.S. Population

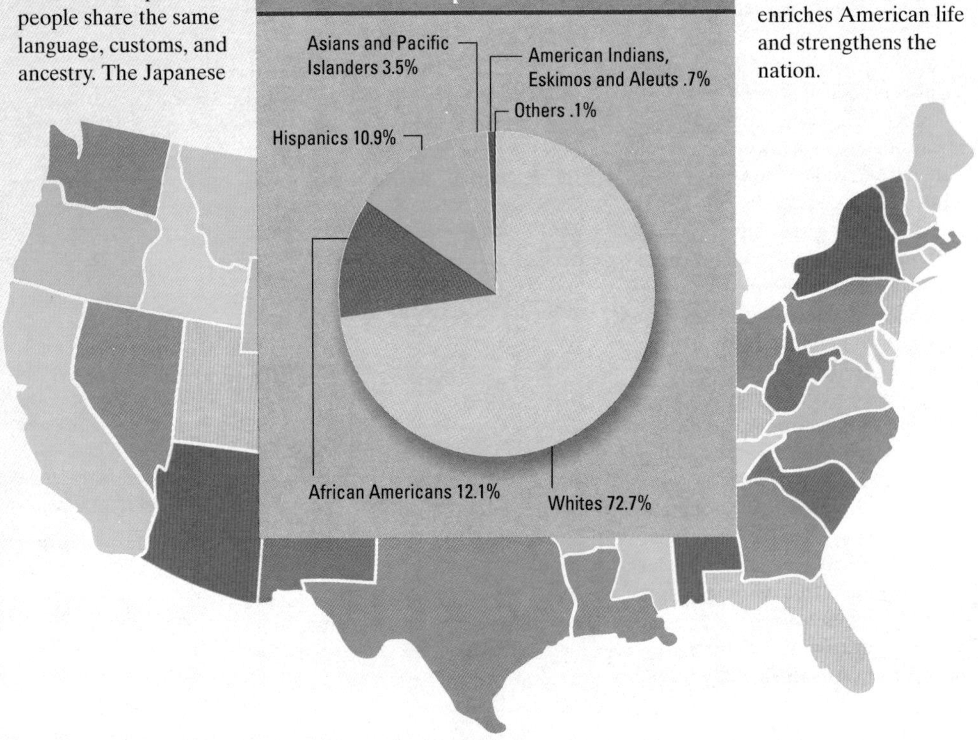

Social Participation

Encourage students to analyze the pluralistic nature of their class. Ask a volunteer to record on the board the ethnic heritage of class members.

Social Context

In the early 1700s, most Americans were farmers. Their idea of success was to live comfortably and securely on their own land and to provide everything for themselves. Because most colonists had escaped some form of hardship in Europe, they wanted to be as self-sufficient as possible.

Men and women brought separate skills to a household. Farms required the work of both husband and wife, as well as the children. There was very little hired labor available. Women provided for the family's food and clothing. They tended dairy animals, made cheese and butter, spun and wove wool and flax for cloth. Men did not help in these demanding jobs.

Men worked long hours clearing land for crops and pastures, as well as planting, harvesting, and storing crops. This work was done by hand, often without the use of horses or oxen.

Slave traders brought over 250,000 Africans to the colonies between 1700 and 1775. On the eve of the Revolution, one in five Americans was black.

A few African Americans won their freedom and became farmers, artisans, and shopkeepers. In most places, however, laws limited the rights of free blacks, denying them full equality with whites.

African Americans made many valuable contributions to American life. They showed planters how to grow rice, which became South Carolina's most important food crop and product. They also brought improved methods for herding cattle and introduced African-style boats, baskets, and fishing nets. Many Africans blended parts of Christian beliefs with traditional African religious beliefs. Black Christian churches would later become an important institution in the black community in the United States. ■

■ *How did the make-up of the American population change between 1700 and 1775?*

A Varied Population Creates a Unique New Culture

Different immigrant groups brought their own special cultural traditions to America. Living closely together, people from different lands began to form a very distinct new culture. Most colonists continued to think of themselves as residents of a particular colony. By 1750, however, the term *American* was widely used to describe both the colonists and their culture.

A New American Dialect

Although English remained the principal language of the colonies, an "American" English began to evolve. Colonists often used the American Indian names for towns, rivers, and mountains. They also borrowed Indian words such as *squash, chipmunk, raccoon, skunk,* and *woodchuck* for new plants and animals.

New words from many different cultures became part of Americans' everyday speech. From African languages came the words *banjo, yam,* and *okra*. From the German language came *sauerkraut* and *beer*. Dutch settlers added *cole slaw, cookies,* and *waffles,* together with the words *boss, Santa Claus,* and *Yankee* to the American vocabulary. The Scots contributed *brae* and *plaid.* On top of all this, Americans made new words by combining older ones in new ways, such as *bullfrog* and *snowshoe*. In 1756, Dr. Samuel Johnson, the English author and dictionary writer, called the colonists' speech an "American dialect." The New World had produced a new form of English.

Growing Religious Tolerance

The great variety of religious traditions carried on in the colonies led to a growing spirit of toleration in the 1700s. A Swedish traveler, Peter Kalm, was impressed by the religious freedom he found in America. Such freedom was not easy to find in Europe at that time. "There are many Jews settled in New York, who possess great privileges," he wrote. "They have great synagogues and houses . . . and are allowed to keep shops. . . . They enjoy all the privileges common to the other inhabitants."

Even so, Jews, Catholics, and atheists could not hold office or vote in most colonies. But, for the most part, religious persecution had almost disappeared by the mid-1700s.

The Great Awakening

Between 1730 and 1750, a religious revival known as the Great Awakening swept through the colonies. Ministers responded to a long decline in church membership with a

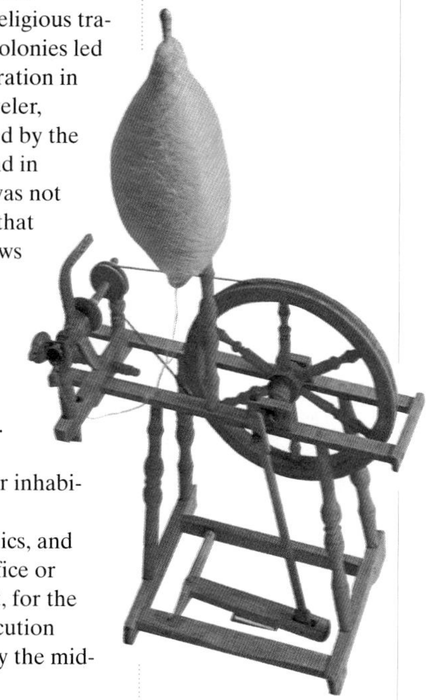

▲ *The colonies had little industry. New arrivals found they needed a spinning wheel like this one to make yarn and thread.*

■ *American society became pluralistic with the influx of immigrants from Europe and slaves from Africa.*

BELIEF SYSTEMS

Critical Thinking

After they read about the Great Awakening on pages 51–52, ask students how it may have affected people's social relationships. *(By emphasizing individuals' relationships with God, the Awakening gave many people a new sense of self-worth. Because some preachers stressed the equality of all people, and attacked the wealthy and powerful, the Awakening encouraged people to challenge authority, both in secular and religious arenas.)*

Language Arts Connection

European colonists borrowed from American Indians the names of four common small mammals: *chipmunk, raccoon, skunk,* and *woodchuck*. Have students check an encyclopedia or a reference book about mammals to find out why the colonists borrowed these names. *(Those animals are native only to this continent.)* Suggest that they look in an unabridged dictionary to find out which Indian languages the words came from.

Mathematics Connection

Have students research the current make-up of the American population by ethnic group. Population figures can be obtained from a census report. Have students refer to the pie chart on page 49 and compare the ethnic diversity percentages of 1775 with current figures. How has the ethnic make-up of the United States changed?

Critical Thinking

Why might Kalm have been so impressed by the religious freedom that he found in America? *(Other nations restricted the practice of religion.)* What conditions must he have seen in other places he visited or must he have been used to at home? *(Discrimination against people because of their religion)*

■ *Both language and religious tolerance were distinctly American. In addition, the role of lay people in the Great Awakening was uniquely American.*

CONSTITUTIONAL HERITAGE

Critical Thinking

Have students discuss how the colonial governments might have developed had the British not practiced the policy of salutary neglect. *(The colonies would probably have been tied culturally and economically to England. Colonial assemblies may have followed more closely the dictates of Parliament and the king.)*

This needlepoint showing a colonial wedding scene was made in the period of the Great Awakening.

■ *What features of everyday life in the colonies were distinctly American?*

new approach. They attempted to reach the hearts as well as the minds of their listeners.

In New England, Jonathan Edwards was the leading figure of the Awakening. He warned his congregation that sin placed their very souls in great danger: "O sinner! . . . You hang by a slender thread, with the flames of divine wrath flashing about it." His vivid description of the horrors of hell caused members of his congregation to rush to be "born again." They renewed their faith by declaring themselves newly converted.

George Whitefield *(WIT feeld)*, a British preacher, stormed through the colonies in 1739 and 1740. His outdoor sermons drew huge crowds. Whitefield was a powerful speaker, and spellbound audiences followed his exhortation to "fly to Christ."

During the Great Awakening, lay people, or non-clergy, played a greater role in religious matters. They rose in church to speak of their conversion. They even spread the Christian message as lay preachers. Some preachers stressed the equality of all people and attacked religious and political leaders who had great wealth and power.

The Great Awakening had a very strong effect on the colonies, influencing slaves as well as white colonists. By attacking the authority of the official church of England, it strengthened other religions. For the same reason, it wore down ties between church and state. The Awakening gave people a new sense of self-worth. They had been part of a powerful experience. They had challenged the authority of the established church beliefs. These experiences helped the colonists develop a greater sense of independence and helped to pave the way for the American Revolution. ■

Colonial Governments Seek Greater Independence

The 3,000-mile-wide Atlantic Ocean separated England from the colonies. It took five weeks or longer for a message to arrive from Great Britain. The gap in space and time allowed early American colonial governments to develop an important role.

In the first half of the 1700s, the British government was busy with European conflicts. It took little interest in its colonies. England seldom enforced the rules it set for its colonies, a policy known as **salutary neglect.** For example, in 1733, England set a tax on molasses that the colonies imported from outside the British Empire. The colonists bribed customs officials to ignore the tax. The English government did nothing.

A governor, a council, and an assembly shared political power in each colony. Usually the governor received his appointment from the king. In turn, the governor named a

Study Skills

How did the Great Awakening affect the connection between church and state in the colonies? Have students go to a library card catalog to answer this question. They should check the subject index in each source to find exact page references for the information.

Collaborative Learning

In the early 1700s, the population of the colonies grew dramatically and became more ethnically diverse. In some areas, however, ways of life and social customs were kept up without changes. Assign different colonies or regions to individual students. Have them research which ethnic groups settled in their particular area. (Pennsylvania, for instance, was formed by William Penn, who set up the colony as a haven for persecuted Quakers.) Then have students pool their knowledge to develop a map showing the ethnic make-up of the colonies. You may also wish to have them give brief oral reports on their findings.

◄ *This scene shows the Boston Common in Massachusetts in 1768. As conflict with England increased, the Common became a meeting place for revolutionaries like the Sons of Liberty.*

council of advisers. The colonists elected members to an assembly that represented them.

Not everybody could vote for the assembly. That right was limited to free white males over the age of 21. Voters also had to own land and, in some colonies, meet religious qualifications as well. These voting requirements were very much like England's. But because land ownership was more common in the colonies than in England, so was the right to vote. In New England, up to 75 percent of the white male population could vote. The percentage of eligible voters was generally smaller in the South.

Through the years, as the royal power grew weaker, the power of colonial assemblies increased. By the 1730s, they had won the right to approve plans for spending money. This right, "the power of the purse," was crucial. For example, if a colonial assembly did not vote funds for a road, the road would not be built. If a governor wanted to raise troops for the colony's defense, he had to ask the assembly to provide the money to make this possible.

In all colonies except Virginia, the assembly also controlled the salary of the governor. This power often made the governor less willing to oppose the assembly's demands.

The king had to approve any law passed by the assemblies. But a **veto**, or rejection of a bill from a colonial assembly, meant the assembly would often pass another bill that was similar to the one vetoed. Gradually it became clear that the assemblies held most of the power to make the colonies' laws. When England tried to reassert its authority in the 1760s, serious conflict resulted. ■

■ *How did the British policy of salutary neglect contribute to the development of colonial governments?*

■ *It contributed to the independence of colonial government, in which assemblies held most of the power.*

REVIEW

1. **FOCUS** How did many kinds of new immigrants help to create a distinct American culture?
2. **CONNECT** In what ways were the English colonies different in the 1750s from what they had been in the 1650s?
3. **POLITICAL SYSTEMS** What was the "power of the purse," and how did it affect colonial politics?
4. **CRITICAL THINKING** How do you think the colonial leaders of the Anglican Church felt about the Great Awakening? Why?
5. **ACTIVITY** Using the maps on pages 672 and 698–699, make a list of at least 10 place names that are of American Indian origin.

53

CLOSE

Tell students to evaluate the predictions they made in response to the Thinking Focus. Copy on the board the structure and main heads from the Graphic Overview on page 48. Have students work as a group to fill in the causes and effects using the lists they made while reading the lesson. As an extension exercise, assign the Mathematics Connection on page 51.

Answers to Review Questions

1. Varied immigrant groups living together mixed their unique cultural traditions, forming a distinct American culture.
2. They had a greater sense of independence from England.
3. Because the assemblies had to approve plans for spending money, governors had to be responsive to the demands of the assemblies.
4. Sample answer: They probably felt threatened by the break from the Anglican Church and the break from the authority of the clergy. Allow for personal opinion.
5. Encourage students to speculate. They can follow up with research.

Homework Options

Ask students to list five ways in which a diversity of cultures within the United States has affected their lives.

Study Guide: page 60.

INTRODUCE

Read the lesson title aloud. Ask students what problems existed between the colonies and England in 1754. What can they recall from Lesson 1 that might explain what the conflict will be about? *(A unique colonial culture was growing; colonial governments sought independence.)* Have students read the Thinking Focus. Ask them what some of the causes for resentment might be.

Key Terms

Vocabulary strategies: T36–37

writs of assistance—documents issued by the British government in the colonial period that allowed officials to conduct unrestricted searches

boycott—an organized refusal to buy or use a product to express protest or to force a government, company, or person to take some action

embargo—a ban on trade with another nation

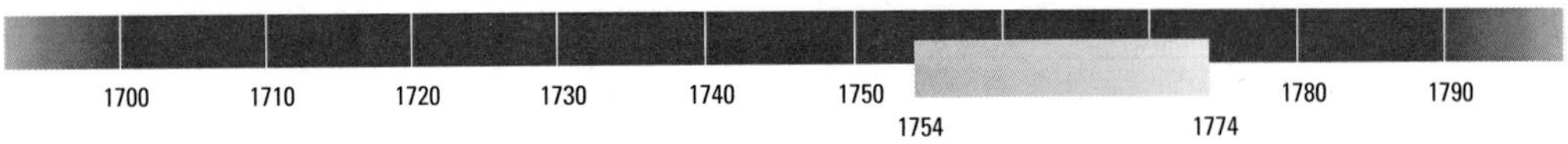

LESSON 2

Growing Conflict with England

THINKING FOCUS

What were the causes of the colonists' growing resentment of British rule?

Key Terms

- writs of assistance
- boycott
- embargo

As the sun rose over Boston on August 14, 1765, a scarecrow-like figure clad in rags dangled from a large oak tree. This hanging effigy, or dummy, represented Andrew Oliver, stamp distributor for Boston. Underneath was a warning: "He that takes this down is an enemy to his country." The display was a protest against the Stamp Act, due to be enforced in November, which required stamps on nearly all printed materials. The colonists were enraged that they should be taxed without their consent or, at the very least, without their representation.

Throughout the day, Bostonians gathered at the spot to view the protest. At one point the sheriff arrived with orders to remove the effigy. But when a threatening crowd surrounded him, he quickly retreated.

At the end of a tense afternoon, the leaders of the mob cut down the figure of Oliver and nailed it to a board. Four men carried it through the streets, heading for a new brick building on the docks of Boston's South End. Word on the street said that this would be Oliver's office for distributing the hated stamps. In less than an hour, the mob tore the building down.

Led by Ebenezer MacIntosh, a poor 28-year-old shoemaker, the crowd then marched to Oliver's home. Warned by the sheriff, Oliver and his family had just slipped out the back way when the protesters arrived. While one group cut off the head of the effigy, others destroyed Oliver's stable and coach. Breaking into the house, the mob smashed the windows and tore apart the furniture. They emptied the bottles from Oliver's large and elegant wine cellar and tore up his gardens. Oliver got the message and resigned as stamp distributor the next day.

Boston was not alone in its hatred of the Stamp Act. More protests followed in other colonial towns and cities. The colonists would stoutly resist the efforts of the British government to tax them. "No taxation without representation" became their rallying cry.

➤ *To show their disapproval of the 1765 Stamp Act, these citizens from Boston seized and burned stacks of the British government's official stamps.*

Objectives

1. Summarize the background and outcome of the Seven Years' War.
2. Identify the reasons why tension developed between England and the American colonies after the Seven Years' War.
3. Explain how tension led to violent clashes between colonists and the representatives of English authority.

Graphic Overview

Cause
British war debt

→

Stamp Act
Townshend Acts
Tea Act
Intolerable Acts

→

Effects
- boycotts
- Boston Tea Party
- First Continental Congress

Rivalry for North America Leads to Seven Years' War

To understand the reasons for the Stamp Act riots, you must first look at the Seven Years' War, also called the French and Indian War. This war was actually one in a series of wars fought between England and France beginning in the late 1600s. While competing for North American territory on the one hand, the two European nations were also battling for dominance of Europe.

Both England and France claimed territory along the Ohio River Valley. As English colonists from Virginia began to settle this area, they faced resistance from both the French and the Indians. In 1755, England sent soldiers under General Edward Braddock to the region, but the French and their Indian allies drove them back.

George Washington, a young Virginian, was part of Braddock's force. He noted that British soldiers in their bright red coats were easy targets for Indians who fired from hiding places in the forest. Washington was later able to put this knowledge to use during the American Revolution.

Braddock's defeat did not discourage the British. They sent the full might of their military force against the French empire in America. In 1759, three years after the war started, the British took the French outpost at Quebec, Canada. The following year, all of Canada was in British hands.

By the Treaty of Paris in 1763, England gained Canada and the French lands east of the Mississippi River, (as the map below shows). Because Spain had unwisely entered the war on France's side, it lost Florida to England. But Spain received French territory west of the Mississippi as compensation, or payment, for this loss. ■

■ *What did England gain as a result of the Seven Years' War?*

European Land Claims in North America, 1763

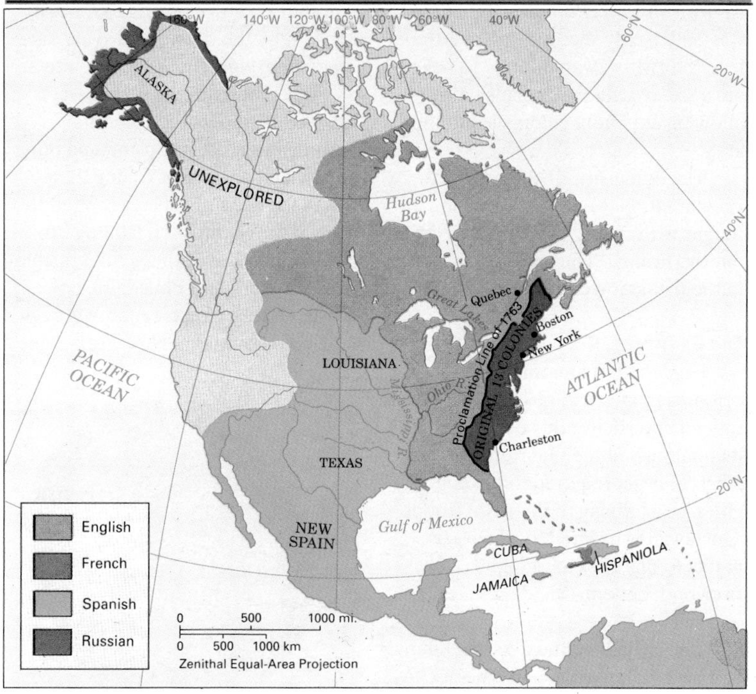

After defeating the French in the Seven Years' War, England controlled the entire eastern half of North America. Spain claimed much of what was left of the continent.

DEVELOP

Explain that this lesson, like Lesson 1, is structured by cause and effect. As students read, they should look for the effects of England's attempts to tax the colonies to pay off its war debt.

■ *England gained Canada, Florida, and the French lands east of the Mississippi River.*

HISTORY

Map and Globe Skills

Ask students to use the map on this page to locate the territory disputed in the Seven Years' War. *(Ohio River Valley, Quebec, Caribbean Islands)* Have them compare the area gained by England after the war with the total area of Europe. Refer students to the political map of the world on pages 694–695. *(Europe is only a little larger.)*

Access Strategy

Ask students to think about the free time they have during the school day, such as lunch or recess, when they can choose what to do with their time. Then have them imagine that the state government suddenly passed new laws requiring that they work during their lunch break, go to their lockers for only one minute before and after school, and attend school on Saturday. What if they also had to follow a strict dress and grooming code? How would they feel about these laws? Would they go along willingly or would they be resentful? Would they protest? How? Tell students they will learn in this lesson why some colonists felt that their lives were being controlled by England in a similar way.

Access Activity

Refer students to the picture on page 54 of colonists protesting the Stamp Act. What kinds of feelings do they see expressed in people's faces and body posture? If the picture showed representatives of the English government, how might this artist have depicted them? What kinds of actions or facial expressions might have been shown?

ECONOMICS

Critical Thinking

Have students analyze why colonists reacted so strongly to the Stamp Act. Why did the Stamp Act particularly affect lawyers, tavern owners, merchants, and printers? *(The Stamp Act put a tax on legal documents and printed matter.)*

British Policies Stir Colonial Protests

As a result of the war, England's North American territory was doubled, but the war also plunged England into a huge debt. The British government believed the colonies should help pay this debt, but first England had to assert its right to control the colonists' economic affairs.

The Proclamation of 1763

The colonists expected to benefit from England's control over the western frontier. Many colonial farmers wanted to move into the area. They received a rude shock when the king issued the Proclamation of 1763. This act closed the newly won territory west of the Appalachians to all colonists. You can find the Proclamation Line on the map on page 55.

Chief Pontiac of the Ottawas was indirectly responsible for the Proclamation. Seeing the new British rulers as a threat, he had organized many tribes in a widespread attack on British forts in 1762. Pontiac's Rebellion was only partly successful. Nevertheless, the British wanted time to negotiate a treaty with the Indians before allowing any more colonists into the area.

The colonists felt cheated by the Proclamation. Many of them had fought with the British troops to drive out the French. They wanted to share in the fruits of victory.

The Quartering Act

England left an army in the colonies to guard the frontier. In order to feed and shelter those troops, Parliament passed the Quartering Act in 1765. This act required that colonial cities give lodging to the royal troops. The law also ordered local governments to pay for such supplies as firewood, bedding, candles, vinegar, and salt.

The British military commander had his headquarters in New York. At first, the New York Assembly refused to vote any money for his troops, saying that the Quartering Act placed an unfair burden on the colony. But when Parliament threatened to take away the powers of the assembly, it finally gave up the money.

The Stamp Act

Parliament also passed the Stamp Act in 1765—the most hated of its attempts to raise money. The act required colonists to buy a revenue stamp each time they registered a legal document or bought newspapers, pamphlets, almanacs, liquor licenses, or playing cards. Two revenue stamps are shown here. Another is shown on page 57. Most hard hit by the tax were lawyers, tavern owners, merchants, and printers.

When news of the Stamp Act reached America, the colonists became enraged. In Boston and other colonial cities, groups calling themselves the Sons of Liberty formed to protest the Stamp Act. Rioting broke out in a number of these cities, including New York and Philadelphia.

In October, representatives from nine colonies met in New York at the

Social Participation

Divide the class into groups to role play a debate on whether the colonies should help pay England's debt after the Seven Years' War. Have one side represent the colonies who wanted no part of the debt. Have the other side represent England.

Political Context

The conflict between England and the American colonies began as England changed its mercantile colonial policy to an imperialist colonial policy. Under the mercantile policy, England acquired colonies whose exports would pay for the colonies' own development and defense. Under the imperialist policy, England used colonies as markets for manufactured goods and as sources of tax revenue. Before the Seven Years' War, English merchants were becoming rich from rice, tobacco, indigo, and lumber from the colonies. After 1763, England became imperialistic because English landowners, who paid most of the taxes, did not want to pay for the war expenses. In addition, England now had Canada to administer as well. Imperialists saw the American colonies as a source of money, but their efforts to tax the colonies were seen by many colonists as unreasonable.

This British political cartoon, which pictures a funeral procession for the recently repealed Stamp Act, pokes fun at Parliament and British Prime Minister George Grenville (fourth from left).

Stamp Act Congress. There they wrote a Declaration of Rights. This declaration expressed their opposition both to taxation without representation in Parliament and to trial without jury in the courts. They asked the king to repeal the Stamp Act. They claimed that only colonial assemblies could legally impose taxes on them, except taxes meant to regulate trade.

In the face of strong colonial opposition, the British government backed down. Before the petition even reached England, Parliament repealed the Stamp Act in March 1766. When the news reached the colonies, people paraded in the streets. ■

■ *How did the Seven Years' War change the relationship between England and the colonies?*

Tensions Reach the Breaking Point

Despite the failure of the Stamp Act, England kept trying to control and tax the colonies. In 1767, Parliament passed the Townshend Acts, which taxed paint, glass, lead, paper, and tea. To enforce the act, customs officials were granted **writs of assistance.** These documents, issued by a court, gave them the power to enter private homes and businesses at any time, with no reasonable suspicion, to look for smuggled goods.

In response, men and women in the colonies launched a **boycott**—that is, they refused to buy the newly taxed goods. Colonists made their own clothes, paper, and paint. Women organized the Daughters of Liberty and held public spinning bees to make American cloth. The boycott helped create a sense of unity.

The Boston Massacre

Anti-British feeling ran highest in the city of Boston where British troops had been stationed since 1768. Samuel Adams, a leader of the Sons of Liberty, whipped up crowds of protesters and wrote inflammatory newspaper articles.

■ *As England tried to force the colonies to help pay for the war debt, conflict arose.*

ECONOMICS

Critical Thinking

Tell students to list British goods that colonists boycotted. *(Paint, glass, lead, paper, and tea)* Why would such boycotts increase tension between England and the colonies? *(England denied revenue it felt entitled to; colonists encouraged to become less dependent on England)*

Language Arts Connection

The colonists burned British tax representatives in effigy, boycotted British goods, and later placed an embargo on British trade. Have students check the *Oxford English Dictionary* or any unabridged dictionary to find the word histories of *effigy, boycott,* and *embargo.* Were these words in use in the 1770s? How did they become part of the English language?

Art Connection

Political cartoons have long been a powerful way of expressing a point of view about an issue. Suggest that students pick an issue from the lesson—such as the Quartering Act or the Boston Massacre—and draw a political cartoon supporting either the British or the American side. Students might also look in an encyclopedia or a history book to find out when and where political cartooning began.

Visual Learning

Have students look at the cartoon on this page and analyze its elements. What is the cartoon's point of view? How does this cartoon make fun of the British government? *(It shows them as mourners.)* Why does the cartoonist use a funeral procession to illustrate the repeal of the Stamp Act? *(To show that the tax had been "killed")*

HISTORY

Visual Learning

Tell students to study the engraving of the Boston Massacre on this page and identify the elements mentioned in the caption. Ask them to compare the description of the massacre in the lesson with Revere's engraving. How are the two different? How might a British artist have shown the scene? *(The lesson says there was a scuffle and "someone" fired. The rioters are shown standing passively in the engraving, but the lesson points out that they were throwing things at the soldiers. A British artist might have shown the British defending themselves against the rioters.)*

▲ *Silversmith Paul Revere's famous engraving of Boston's "Bloody Massacre" circulated widely in the colonies and stirred up anger against the British. A propaganda piece, Revere's picture refers to the British-controlled Customs House as "Butcher's Hall" and shows the British captain giving the order to fire.*

Tensions came to a head on March 5, 1770. On that day a band of unemployed laborers attacked the guard of the Boston Customs House. When British soldiers came to his aid, the crowd pelted them with oyster shells and snowballs. In the scuffle that followed, someone started to shoot and five rioters were killed. The first to die was Crispus Attucks, of African and Indian parentage, who had gained his freedom by running away from his master years earlier.

Patriots branded the incident a "massacre" to gain sympathy for their cause. Adams's articles about the incident spread news of the Boston Massacre throughout the colonies.

The Boston Tea Party

As a result of the colonists' boycott, the British government repealed the Townshend taxes on all items except tea in 1770. The news calmed most colonists.

However, Samuel Adams formed a Committee of Correspondence in Boston in 1772 to keep American complaints against England in the public eye. Towns in other colonies followed his lead and exchanged written complaints about British actions.

In 1773, Parliament passed the Tea Act, which allowed the British East India Company to sell tea directly to the colonists. Previously the company sold tea to British wholesalers,

Critical Thinking

The Continental Congress called for more protests against the Intolerable Acts but, at the same time, sent a petition to the British Parliament. Ask students what this shows about the different points of view among the delegates. *(It shows that some still acknowledged England's authority, but others did not.)*

Writing an Editorial

After the Boston Tea Party, the British king said, "We must master them or totally leave them to themselves and treat them as aliens." Have students write a newspaper editorial responding to King George's statement, either agreeing or disagreeing with his position. Students may consult current newspaper editorials as models for style. Encourage students to use a typewriter or word processor to produce their editorials in columns.

Research

Tea seems an unusual cause for a political protest. Why did the tax on tea cause such a bitter reaction in America in 1773? How and where is tea grown? What is its history? What role did it have in the economy and the social life of England and the colonies? Assign some students to research these questions and report their findings to the class.

who in turn sold tea to the colonists. By selling more tea at lower prices, England expected to benefit more from its tax on imported tea.

Protest was immediate. In Charleston, colonists locked the tea in warehouses. In North Carolina, women burned their tea in public. In some colonies, Americans prevented tea ships from landing.

On December 16, 1773, a band of men disguised as Indians boarded three tea ships in Boston harbor. While a crowd looked on, the leaders of the "Boston Tea Party" threw hundreds of chests of tea overboard.

King George III was furious. He said of the colonists, "We must master them or totally leave them to themselves and treat them as aliens."

The Intolerable Acts

In 1774, Parliament passed a series of measures designed to punish the colonists. It closed the port of Boston until the city paid for the destroyed tea. It increased the powers of the governor to the point that he could even ban town meetings. At the same time, a new Quartering Act allowed British commanders to station troops in private homes. Finally, the Quebec Act put much of the Ohio River Valley into the province of Quebec, cutting off this land from New York, Pennsylvania, and Virginia.

Colonists called these measures the Intolerable Acts. The Committees of Correspondence urged the colonies to hold a meeting about the crisis. Within months, the colonies had agreed to meet.

The First Continental Congress

Delegates from all 13 colonies except Georgia met at Carpenter's Hall in Philadelphia from September 5 to October 26, 1774. Calling themselves the First Continental Congress, they agreed to support Massachusetts and passed a resolution that declared the Intolerable Acts null and void. They also called for further acts of protest. But to soothe those who wanted to settle the crisis peacefully, the delegates sent a petition of their grievances to the British government.

The Congress also set up the Continental Association to enforce an **embargo,** or ban on trade, against England. The Congress set the stage for future developments when it called on each colony to begin training soldiers for defense.

Before the delegates adjourned, they scheduled another Congress for May of the following year. By the time the Second Continental Congress met, fighting had already begun. ■

◄ This wooden chest, typical of the beautifully decorated tea chests of the period, was recovered from Boston harbor after the Boston Tea Party.

■ What actions taken by Parliament contributed to the growing tension between England and the colonies?

REVIEW

1. **FOCUS** What were the causes of the colonists' growing resentment of British rule?
2. **CONNECT** Did England continue its policy of salutary neglect after the Seven Years' War? Explain.
3. **ECONOMICS** In what sense were economic issues responsible for the outbreak of the American Revolution?
4. **CRITICAL THINKING** Why do you think it was so difficult for the British government to maintain tight control over the colonies?
5. **WRITING ACTIVITY** Imagine that you are a colonial printer. Write a letter to the King of England stating why you think the Stamp Act is unfair.

■ The Townshend Acts and the Intolerable Acts increased the tension between England and the colonies.

CLOSE

Copy on the board the Graphic Overview from page 54 to help students summarize the lesson and to outline the events leading to the Revolutionary War. Point out that each act passed by the British caused a reaction by the colonists.

As a reteaching activity, divide the class into two groups to debate "taxation without representation." Why did the English feel they had a right to tax the colonies, and why did the colonists think the English had no such right?

Answers to Review Questions

1. Their resentment grew with the Proclamation of 1763, the Quartering Act, the Stamp Act, the Townshend Acts, and the Intolerable Acts.
2. England abandoned its policy of salutary neglect when it tried to get funds to pay the debt from the war.
3. The growing tension between England and the colonies was due to taxation, import controls, and trade embargoes.
4. Sample answer: The geographic location of the colonies fostered their independence. Allow for personal opinion.
5. Students should include in their letters the reasons why printers were especially burdened by the Stamp Act.

Homework Options

Have students use library resources to research taxes in their state and special-use fees and licenses.

Study Guide: page 7.

UNDERSTANDING TIMELINES

This skill lesson will give students practice in interpreting the historical relationships displayed in timelines.

HISTORY

Visual Learning

Point out that students should be careful in drawing cause-and-effect relationships from a timeline alone. For example, can students conclude that the petition sent to King George III by colonial representatives after the Stamp Act Congress of October 1765 caused Parliament to repeal the Act in March 1766? Have students check the facts on page 57. *(Parliament repealed the Act before the petition reached England. It was not the petition but earlier protests of colonists, like the one shown in the picture, that moved Parliament.)*

UNDERSTANDING TIMELINES

Charting Pre-Revolutionary Events

Here's Why

Timelines allow you to see a sequence of events and then to understand how these events affect one another. In this chapter you have read about a number of events that took place in England and the colonies before the Revolutionary War. The distance between England and the colonies delayed communication by months. There was often a definite connection, however, between what happened in one place and what happened in the other.

Suppose you wanted to find out how various events related to the onset of the war. Two parallel timelines—one of events in England and the other of events in the colonies—would help you to see the order and frequency of events on both sides of the conflict. By comparing the two timelines, you could more clearly see the relationship of one event to another. You could also see the progression of related events within that time period.

Here's How

Look at the two timelines on page 61. They are marked off in decades from 1740 to 1776. The events on the top timeline occurred in England, while the events in the line below occurred in the colonies.

You can see that a number of events in England and the colonies were happening at the same time. Identify the relationship between those events. For example, in 1765, Parliament passed the Stamp Act. That same year the colonists staged protests and petitioned for repeal of the act (see A. B. Frost's picture at the left of colonists in New York burning seized stamped papers). When England passed the Stamp Act, the colonies were quick to respond. By the next year, the act was repealed. There was a direct relationship between the colonists' protests and the act's repeal.

Now look at the frequency of events. Notice that there are more events listed on the timeline after 1760 than before. That could mean that conflicts between England the colonies were increasing at that time. Remember, however, that the analysis that you can conduct by using a timeline is dependent on the information that it contains. You need to be sure that all the information on the timeline is accurate and that all the relevant events that occurred between the colonies and England appear on the timeline.

60

Objective

Use parallel timelines to determine relationships between events in England and events in the colonies. (Visual Learning 2)

Making a Timeline

Have students use the events described in Chapter 1 to make a timeline of the European exploration and settlement of America, including dates reflecting contact with American Indians and life in the English colonies. The timeline should begin with the year 1492 and end with the year 1740. Students should then make a parallel timeline of major events occurring in Europe. They should choose the countries that financed exploration or were the birthplace of some of the explorers—Spain, Portugal, France, Holland, Italy, and England. Students may use an encyclopedia for necessary research. What relationships can they see between their two timelines?

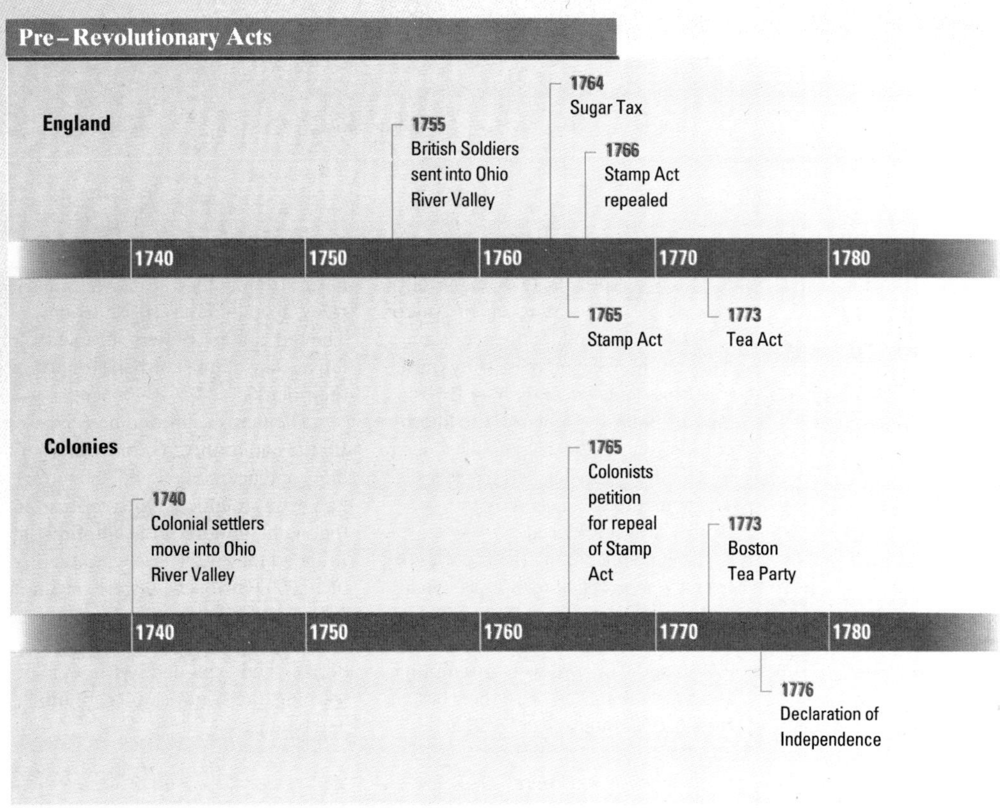

Try It

Copy the timelines above onto a piece of paper. Read the following list of events, and go back to the chapter to find the dates of each event. Decide on which timeline they belong and enter them on your copy.

- Proclamation of 1763
- Quartering Act
- Stamp Act Congress
- Townshend Acts
- Boston Massacre
- Committees of Correspondence
- First Continental Congress
- Green Mountain Boys take Ticonderoga

Can you see that adding events to the timeline changes the conclusions you are able to reach? This new timeline now includes your researched additions. Which events happened first? Which events appear to be reactions to other events? What relationships do you see between the events you entered on the England timeline and those you entered on the colonies timeline?

Apply It

Create a pair of parallel timelines for the past year. Mark each one off in one-month segments. On one timeline enter important national events such as presidential elections, Supreme Court decisions, or scientific discoveries.

On the other timeline enter important events in the life of your family over the same time period. Can you see a relationship between the national events and your personal life?

HISTORY

Visual Learning

Note the first event shown on each timeline. Discuss the relationship between colonial settlers moving into the Ohio Valley in 1740 and British soldiers being sent there in 1755. *(As more settlers moved there, they needed protection against the French.)* What major event resulted that could be shown on the timeline? *(Sample answers: Seven Years' War, Treaty of Paris)* Point out that the more information a timeline shows, the more useful it will be as a mirror of the time shown.

Answers to Try It

England timeline: 1763—Proclamation of 1763; 1765—Quartering Act; 1767—Townshend Acts

Colonies timeline: 1765—Stamp Act Congress; 1770—Boston Massacre; 1772—Committees of Correspondence; 1774—First Continental Congress; 1777—Green Mountain Boys take Ticonderoga

Students should recognize a connection between the Townshend Acts and the Boston Massacre.

Answers to Apply It

Check to see that students have created two timelines that are parallel in time, although they are not parallel in events. Few students will find a causal relationship between national events and their personal lives.

Study Skills

Divide the class into six groups. Assign each group to do further research on one of the decades on either timeline. One group, for example, may study England during the 1760s. Students should prepare a group report expanding on the events in England during that time period.

INTRODUCE

Have a student read the lesson title aloud. Ask students to define the word *revolution* (see Access Strategy, page 63). Considering the situation in the colonies at the end of Lesson 2, was a revolution necessary?

Ask students to read the Thinking Focus and predict what difficulties the colonies might face in a war against a powerful nation. Students should read to evaluate their predictions.

Key Terms

Vocabulary strategies: T36–37

militia—a group of armed citizens who are prepared for military service if called to defend their town, state, or country

minuteman—a member of the colonial Massachusetts militia ready to fight the British at a minute's notice

republic—a form of government in which the people exercise power through their chosen representatives

1700 1710 1720 1730 1740 1750 1760 1770 1775 1783 1790

LESSON 3

Fighting the American Revolution

THINKING FOCUS

How did the colonies manage to defeat the most powerful nation in the world?

Key Terms

- militia
- minuteman
- republic

On the afternoon of April 19, 1775, eight Patriots—supporters of American independence—lay dead on the village green at Lexington, Massachusetts, killed by British musket-balls. In Concord, the liberty pole—a symbol of the colonists' desire for freedom—lay hacked to pieces. The courthouse, burned by the British, still smoldered.

Meanwhile, along the bloody road from Concord back to Boston, curses and screams filled the air. The 700 British troops that had overrun Lexington and Concord were attempting an orderly march back to their base in Boston. But hundreds of enraged colonists, firing from houses and barns, from behind stone walls and trees, assaulted the British troops. The red-coated soldiers shrieked and fell as Patriot musket-balls found their marks.

The British suffered heavy losses. By the end of the day, 70 British soldiers had been killed and 200 more had been wounded. Outside Boston that night, hundreds of campfires surrounded the city. These were the fires of 16,000 Patriots who were beginning an armed vigil.

A spark had flown, and the powder keg had exploded. Without plan or warning, the American Revolution had begun.

In this color print of the Battle of Lexington, British soldiers and colonial minutemen engage in the first military encounter of what would be a seven-year war.

Objectives

1. Evaluate early military encounters of the Revolution.
2. Trace the steps that led to the Declaration of Independence.
3. Identify the main events of the Revolution in the North.
4. Summarize the course of the Revolution in the West and the South.
5. Describe the provisions of the Treaty of Paris.

Graphic Overview

Stage 1
- Lexington/Concord
- Fort Ticonderoga
- Breed's Hill

➤ **Stage 2**
- Long Island, N.Y.
- Trenton, N.J.

➤ **Stage 3**
- Saratoga
- Valley Forge

➤ **Stage 4**
Western Front

➤ **Stage 5**
- Southern Front
- Yorktown

Early Battles of the Revolution

The outbreak of armed conflict took many in the colonies by surprise. Less than a month before the fighting in Lexington and Concord, members of the Virginia Assembly had been shocked when they heard a proposal by Patrick Henry, politician and colonial leader, to prepare Virginia for war. Nevertheless, Henry's words proved to be prophetic:

> *Gentlemen may cry peace, peace—but there is no peace. The war is actually begun! The next gale that sweeps from the north will bring to our ears the clash of resounding arms! Our brethren are already in the field! Why stand we here idle? . . . I know not what course others may take; but as for me, give me liberty, or give me death!*

Lexington and Concord

In the fall of 1774, a group of middle-class Massachusetts colonists—including John Hancock and Paul Revere—met at Concord and decided to prepare for a possible war with Britain. They named Hancock, a wealthy merchant, to organize an armed force. His **militia,** or citizen army, called themselves **minutemen,** because they were ready to fight at a minute's notice. (See Moment in Time on page 64.)

The royal governor of Massachusetts, stationed at Boston, was General Thomas Gage. In April 1775, he sent 700 soldiers to Concord to arrest the Patriot leaders. Paul Revere learned of the plan. On the night of April 18, 1775, he prepared to warn the Patriots.

Boston was already an armed camp. Yet Revere slipped out of town and rode off on his horse down the road the British would travel. He shouted the alarm as he passed the houses of minutemen along the way.

A little before midnight, Revere reached Lexington, where Hancock was hiding. True to their name, 70 of Lexington's minutemen were waiting on the village green when the British marched in at dawn on April 19.

When the colonists refused to lay down their arms, the British soldiers rushed forward, firing several volleys. They killed eight minutemen and wounded ten others.

By noon, a larger force of minutemen had assembled at Concord. They blocked the North Bridge and this time fired from behind walls and trees. The "shot heard 'round the world" dealt the British their first casualties. Philosopher and poet Ralph Waldo Emerson later captured this moment in the following stanzas of his 1837 poem, "Concord Hymn":

> By the rude bridge that arched the flood,
> Their flag to April's breeze unfurled,
> Here once the embattled farmers stood
> And fired the shot heard 'round the world.
>
> Spirit that made those heroes dare
> To die, and leave their children free,
> Bid Time and Nature gently spare
> The shaft we raise to them and thee.

Ticonderoga

In the area that is now Vermont, Ethan Allen organized a group of tough frontiersmen called the Green Mountain Boys. In May 1775, they surprised the sleeping British troops at Fort Ticonderoga in New York. Allen captured the fort's 50 cannons. His Green Mountain Boys slowly dragged these cannon along backwoods trails to the Patriot forces in Boston, where Washington later used them to drive the British from the city.

This lantern, hung from the belfry of the Old North Church, sent Paul Revere on his midnight ride.

How Do We Know?

Some of Patrick Henry's speeches–including his most famous "Give Me Liberty or Give Me Death" address–were never formally written down. The speeches exist only as they were remembered by people who heard them. A reconstruction of Henry's 'Liberty or Death' speech appears on page 664.

DEVELOP

Tell students that the revolution began as a skirmish and grew to be a full-fledged war. Suggest that as they read, they not only keep track of the war by finding each battle location on the map on page 69, but also note the changes in the size of the armies and areas involved.

HISTORY

Critical Thinking

Have students analyze Patrick Henry's speech, excerpted on this page. Was he serious in saying "give me liberty or give me death?" Why did he put the choice in such extreme terms? *(Students should realize that Henry used powerful language because he also wanted to persuade his audience.)* Students can read the full text of his speech on pages 664–665.

Access Strategy

Ask students how the meanings of the words *revolution* and *rebellion* are both similar and different. A *rebellion* is any open defiance of authority with the intention of bringing about a change. A *revolution* usually describes a sudden social or political change, such as a political overthrow from within a nation. The difference is in the results. A revolution is usually an accomplished fact. A rebellion can have any outcome and often leads to reform rather than a new order. Ask students to speculate why the colonists' rebellion escalated to revolution, based on what they learned in Lesson 2. Tell students that they will read in this lesson about the American Revolution.

Access Activity

The British army was professional, disciplined, and very well supplied. They fought in rank and followed orders. The Patriots' army was largely an untrained army of citizens who signed on for short periods of duty. They knew little of military tactics and relied heavily on surprise. Have students name the advantages and disadvantages of each army.

Note: You may wish to use this Moment in Time to preview Lesson 3.

POLITICAL SYSTEMS

Visual Learning

Would the colonies have had militias had there been no conflict with England? *(Yes, since the first Pilgrim set foot on North America, colonists had taken defensive measures. Nearly every town had its own militia.)*

More About the Musket Until the 1800s, all guns were entirely handmade and unique. Gunsmiths made longer guns for taller people and shorter guns for shorter people. At the time of the Revolution, the rifle was coming into more common use. With its grooved barrel, a rifle could shoot farther and more accurately than any musket.

A MOMENT IN TIME

A Minuteman

11:12 A.M. April 19, 1775
Near the North Bridge
in Concord, Massachusetts

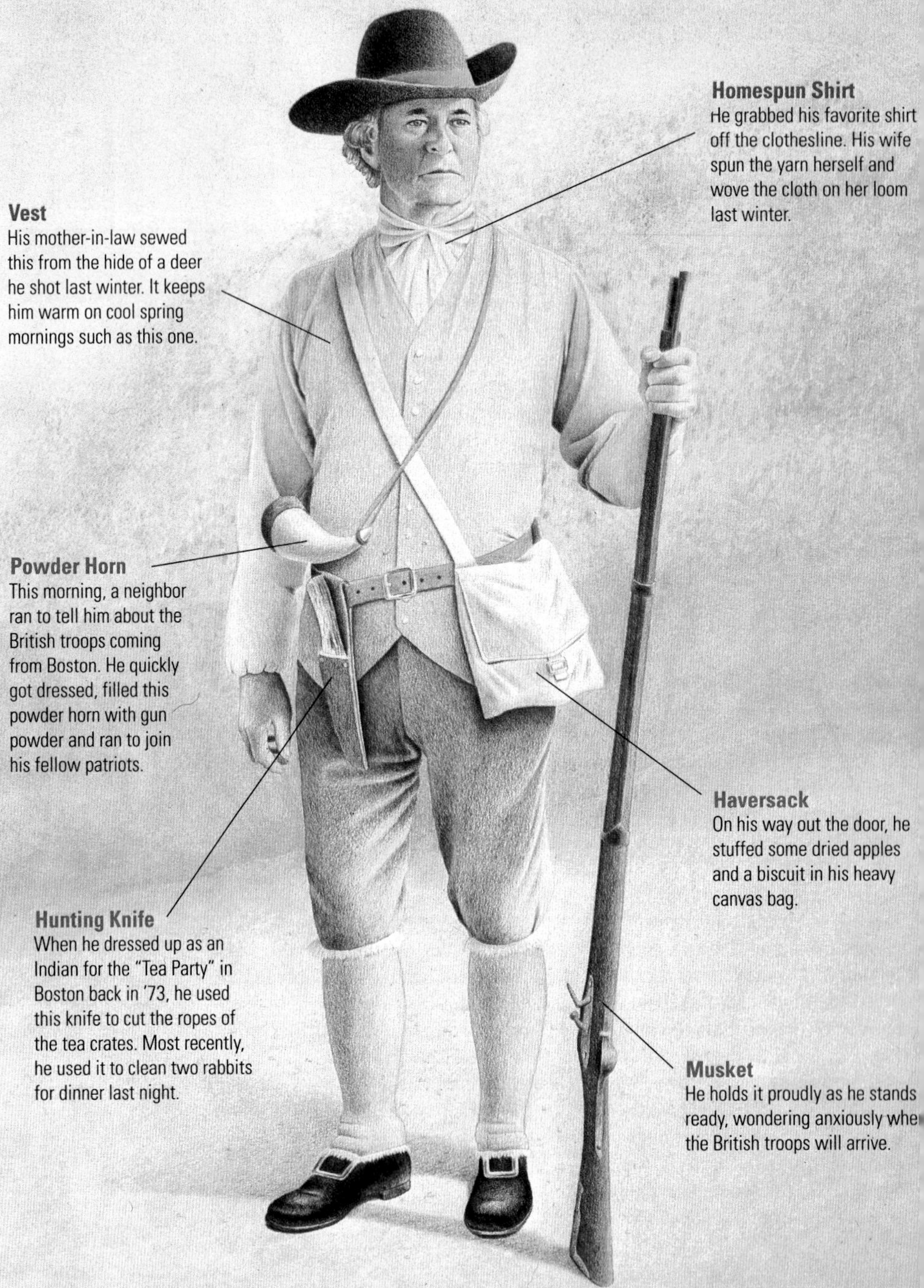

Homespun Shirt
He grabbed his favorite shirt off the clothesline. His wife spun the yarn herself and wove the cloth on her loom last winter.
Vest
His mother-in-law sewed this from the hide of a deer he shot last winter. It keeps him warm on cool spring mornings such as this one.
Powder Horn
This morning, a neighbor ran to tell him about the British troops coming from Boston. He quickly got dressed, filled this powder horn with gun powder and ran to join his fellow patriots.
Haversack
On his way out the door, he stuffed some dried apples and a biscuit in his heavy canvas bag.
Hunting Knife
When he dressed up as an Indian for the "Tea Party" in Boston back in '73, he used this knife to cut the ropes of the tea crates. Most recently, he used it to clean two rabbits for dinner last night.
Musket
He holds it proudly as he stands ready, wondering anxiously whe the British troops will arrive.

Study Skills

Have students use an encyclopedia or other library reference to organize information about Paul Revere into an outline with these main heads: I. Early Life; II. Contributions During the American Revolution; III. Livelihood. For each main head, students should find three subheads, each containing at least two details.

Historical Context

Trouble between the colonists and England began in Boston, largely because Boston was an economically troubled city. British troops, which were sent to Boston to calm unruly citizens fed the idea that the British were conspiring for more power in the colonies.

Colonists began stockpiling arms and ammunition but moved their base to Concord because the British army controlled Boston. The intent of the British troops in April 1775 was to seize those military supplies, a plan that failed because of the warnings of Paul Revere and others.

After the Battle of Lexington and Concord, British troops remained in Boston, looking for revenge. Loyalist support was slight, however, and General Howe moved the troops to New York where there was more support. New York was also more centrally located, and Howe felt he could control the colonies better from there. His aim was

"Don't fire until you see the whites of their eyes" was the order given by an American general at the Battle of Bunker Hill, pictured here.

The Battle of Bunker Hill

In order to defend Boston, General Thomas Gage decided to place troops on Bunker Hill. Once more the Americans learned of his plans. On the night of June 16, over a thousand Patriots moved to nearby Breed's Hill. Gage ordered his men to drive them off. "Don't fire until you see the whites of their eyes," ordered American General Israel Putnam, in an attempt to conserve ammunition. When the British troops were 100 feet away, the American guns roared, and the British front ranks fell. Yet the British surged forward, again and again, until the Patriots ran out of ammunition and retreated.

After the Battle of Bunker Hill, over 1,000 British soldiers lay dead or wounded, while the Americans lost only 397 men. Although the British technically won the battle because they forced the Patriots to retreat, the Americans had shown that the British faced a hard fight. ■

■ *Find evidence to support the following statement: The early battles showed that the Revolution was likely to be a long and difficult war.*

The Road to the Declaration of Independence

Despite the fighting, many colonists still wanted to avoid war. In July 1775, the Second Continental Congress sent the Olive Branch Petition to King George III. It blamed Parliament for the trouble and urged the king to intervene. Instead, he proclaimed that the colonies were in rebellion and gave orders "to bring the traitors to justice."

Common Sense Stirs Colonists

In January 1776, a pamphlet titled *Common Sense* appeared in the colonies. Its author, Thomas Paine, had moved to America from England only a year before. But the news of Lexington and Concord had inflamed him. Calling George III "the Royal Brute of Britain," Paine declared, "A government of our own is our natural right. . . ." He then urged the colonists to establish a **republic**, or system of representative government.

Common Sense sold half a million copies in six months. Arguments about the legality of Parliament's acts seemed pale and fussy in the face of Paine's outright demand for independence.

Across Time & Space

Since the early 1800s, Americans have celebrated Independence Day with fireworks, picnics, and parades. Amazingly, two heroes of the Revolution—Thomas Jefferson and John Adams—both died on July 4, 1826, the 50th anniversary of the signing of the Declaration of Independence.

■ *The early battles reflected the persistence of each side and resulted in casualties for both.*

BELIEF SYSTEMS

Critical Thinking

Have students analyze what Thomas Paine meant when he said, "A government of our own is our natural right . . . ." *(The colonists had no direct representation in Parliament, which held the power of taxation over them.)* Ask why Paine's *Common Sense* helped convince the Continental Congress to declare independence from England. *(It helped people see that negotiations with England were useless.)* Students can read a longer excerpt from *Common Sense* on pages 666–667.

to destroy, disperse, and demoralize the rebels. He caused many to flee, but George Washington, using untrained local militiamen and relying heavily on surprise attacks and on the locals' knowledge of the land, persevered with his small group of Patriots.

The British capture of the largest colonial city, Philadelphia, did not defeat the colonists, and a month later, the British war strategy was thrown into confusion when they were defeated at Saratoga. They pulled back to New York and Rhode Island to reevaluate their stand. Support was absolutely necessary, and at that time the South was the largest Loyalist stronghold left. The British army moved south, hoping to gain military control of one colony, then another, ultimately gaining control of the entire South. But it was a tactic that failed.

Critical Thinking

Encourage students to consider how the fact that the colonists were fighting on and for control of their own land might have affected the course of the war. Were the Americans at an advantage or a disadvantage? *(Advantages—knew the land, strong attachment to it motivated them; disadvantages—many people lost homes, property, and businesses.)*

■ *The king's rejection of the Olive Branch Petition and the publication of Paine's* Common Sense *swayed many to push for a declaration of independence.*

HISTORY

Visual Learning

After students study the timeline on this page and on page 67, have them compare the two battle pictures shown in the timeline. What similarities do they see in the two pictures? *(They both show American victories.)* What differences? *(At Saratoga the armies fought in the wilderness; at Yorktown the British had built up fortifications.)* What conclusion could be drawn about the development of the war? *(Sample answer: By the end of the war, the American army was large and disciplined enough to make a conventional attack on the British.)*

Writing the Declaration

In the late spring of 1776, public sentiment finally persuaded the Continental Congress to take the final step. The delegates named Thomas Jefferson to head a committee to write a declaration of independence. Jefferson, a brilliant young lawyer from Virginia, took pen in hand and wrote a first draft.

Jefferson's words stirred the colonists: "All men are created equal . . . with certain unalienable rights; that among these are life, liberty, and the pursuit of happiness."

On July 4, 1776, John Hancock, the president of the Congress, signed his name to the Declaration. Legend said he wrote it large enough for King George to read without his glasses. The delegates from the remaining colonies added their names. The English colonies had become the United States of America. (For the full text of the Declaration of Independence, see pages 656–659.) ■

■ *What events finally convinced many colonists that they should declare their independence from England?*

War in the North

If the Declaration were to become more than a piece of paper, an army had to defend its bold words. The year before, in 1775, Congress had asked George Washington to organize a Continental Army.

Washington's Early Campaign

When Washington led his small force toward Boston in March 1776, the British withdrew. But Washington knew that the British commander, General William Howe, eyed a bigger prize: New York City.

Howe's troops landed on Long Island in August 1776. By this time Washington had managed to assemble an army of roughly 20,000 men representing nearly every colony. When Washington tried to block Howe's forces, however, the experienced British troops routed the Americans. Only a desperate nighttime retreat saved the Continental Army.

▼ *Progress in the war was slow for both sides. The conflict dragged on for seven years.*

Major Battles of the Revolution

1775 | 1776 | 1777 | 1778

Lexington and Concord
April 19. Minutemen, warned by Paul Revere, open the war by confronting 700 British soldiers and forcing them to retreat to Boston.

Trenton
Dec. 26. Having crossed the icy Delaware river, George Washington and 2,400 men strike Hessian mercenaries and take 900 prisoners.

Bunker Hill
June 17. Colonial militia (see drum at left), dug in on the hill overlooking Boston harbor, are ousted by British soldiers. But in the process, the British suffer twice the losses of the colonists.

Ticonderoga
May 10. Surprise attack by Ethan Allen and his "Green Mountain Boys" on the British fort results in the capture of much-needed cannons. It also marks the first surrender by a British commander.

Saratoga
Oct. 17. British plans to isolate New England are thwarted when commander Burgoyne has to surrender to General Horatio Gates (below).

66

Music Connection

A fife and drum corps was a part of most militia organizations. Find recordings of fife and drum music to play for the class. Ask students to research in a library these two musical instruments. Have them also research the role a fife and drum corps played in colonial militias.

Language Arts Connection

Have students look back at the two stanzas from Ralph Waldo Emerson's "Concord Hymn" on page 63. Ask them to think about and discuss why Emerson called it "Concord Hymn." Who were the "embattled farmers" and what is the significance of the phrase "and fired the shot heard round the world"?

As winter came on, Howe rested his army in New Jersey. Washington struck back in a sneak attack. On Christmas night, 1776, he led his forces across the Delaware River to Trenton, New Jersey. Washington's men surprised and captured many Hessian mercenaries—German soldiers—hired to help the British. Ten days later, Washington captured Princeton, New Jersey. These victories raised the colonists' spirits.

Victory Brings French Support

In 1777, British General John Burgoyne worked out a plan to isolate New England by bringing his army south from Quebec to Albany, recapturing Fort Ticonderoga on the way. According to Burgoyne's ambitious plan, General Howe and his army would sail up the Hudson from New York City, thereby cutting off all land routes from New England to the other colonies.

A gambler, "Gentleman Johnny" Burgoyne had placed a bet of 50 pounds with a friend in London that he would return victorious from America by Christmas of 1777. After successfully retaking Fort Ticonderoga, however, Burgoyne experienced a summer of disastrous encounters in the wilderness of upper New York. But Howe had gone to Philadelphia. Burgoyne was left stranded.

At Saratoga, New York, American General Horatio Gates attacked Burgoyne's poorly positioned forces. Moving swiftly, Gates surrounded the British, cutting them off from supplies. On October 17, 1777, Burgoyne had to surrender his entire army of 6,000 men to General Gates.

At the time of the American victory at Saratoga, Benjamin Franklin was in Paris, trying to persuade the French government to help the colonies. The French wanted to see their British enemy defeated, but they also needed proof that the Americans could win the war. The news of Saratoga provided a convincing argument. Before long, French ships were carrying soldiers and supplies to the war-torn colonies.

Cowpens, S.C.
Jan 17. After the defeats of Savannah and Charleston, this battle is a crucial victory for the colonists under the brilliant Daniel Morgan, who receives the medal at left for his efforts.

1779 | **1780** | **1781** | **1782**

Charleston
May 12. The situation at first looks bleak for the colonists in the second, Southern phase of the war. The British, having conquered Savannah in December 1779, now capture Charleston and its entire garrison.

Yorktown
Oct. 19. The war comes to an end when General Cornwallis, entrenched on the peninsula of Yorktown, is surrounded by Washington's troops on land and French ships on sea. "My God! It is all over," is the British response to the news of his surrender.

HISTORY

Visual Learning

Tell students to study the timeline on page 66 and on this page as well as the map on page 69. Have them note the time intervals between the major battles. Why were battles so far apart in time? *(Each side had to move its armies on foot or by boat. The British kept changing their military goals from one section of the country to another.)* Students can also refer to the chronology and map of the Revolutionary War on pages 684–685 in the Minipedia.

Science Connection

The weapons used by the British and Patriot armies were different from those used today. Suggest that students find out what types of weapons and ammunition the armies used, how and where the guns were manufactured, how the guns were loaded, and how reliable they were. Students might also draw a diagram of a typical Patriot musket, labeling each part. Finally, some students may want to compare weapons of the 1700s to those used today.

Health Connection

General Washington complained often of the lack of discipline within his troops. The problem was not confined to the battlefield but existed in camps that were dirty and ill-kept. Partially as a result of these conditions, more soldiers died of diseases such as smallpox and bacterial infection than died in battle. Have students research in an encyclopedia or other library reference book the history of camp sanitation and battlefield medicine.

Map and Globe Skills

Students can compare the military locations on the map on page 69 with the map of National Parks on pages 678–679 in the Minipedia. Suggest that they list each battle area from the lesson map and note whether it is now a National Monument, Historic Site, Military Park, Historic Park, Memorial, or Battlefield.

■ *Benjamin Franklin's persuasion and the victory at Saratoga led the French to support the colonies in war.*

GEOGRAPHY

Critical Thinking

Ask students why the battles of the West and the South were so important to the outcome of the Revolution. *(Winning the western frontier was important because it shut off the Indians and gave farmers a transportation route to the sea. Beating the British in the South was important because Loyalist support centered there.)*

■ *Why did the French decide to enter the Revolution on the side of the colonists?*

Valley Forge—a Low Point

Despite the victory at Saratoga, the winter of 1777–1778 proved to be a difficult time for the Continental Army. That winter, while the British occupied Philadelphia, Washington's men set up camp and endured the bitter cold in Valley Forge, Pennsylvania. The Continental Congress had no money left to feed and clothe its army, and many soldiers did not even have shoes. According to General Washington, "you might have tracked the army . . . to Valley Forge by the blood of their feet" Over 2,500 men died of disease or starvation that winter. Sometimes the troops had only bread and water to eat. Some began to slip away, heading for families and farms they had neglected in what now seemed like a lost cause.

Washington told his men they had to stay together. Each day he rode around the camp, reminding them of the cause for which they were fighting. By the sheer force of his personality, he kept his ragtag army from falling apart. ■

War in the West and South

Across Time & Space

The Americans received another blow in the summer of 1780 when Benedict Arnold, one of the most talented generals in the Continental Army, switched sides and joined the British cause. Apparently Arnold felt that he had not received sufficient credit for his military successes. Today Americans use the name Benedict Arnold as a synonym for traitor.

Valley Forge marked a turning point in the war. After the spring of 1778, as the map on the opposite page shows, the major fighting in the Revolution turned to the West and South.

Clark Drives British from the West

On the Ohio frontier, Lieutenant Colonel George Rogers Clark raised the money to supply an American force in early 1778. His aim was to take the British wilderness outposts. Clark's frontier fighters knew the paths through the forests and mountains. They marched down the Ohio River Valley and appeared without warning to attack British camps. When Clark's men captured the British fort at Vincennes in February 1779, their victory virtually ended British control of the frontier.

▼ *This is a typical cannon of the Revolutionary period.*

British Successes in the South

Late in 1778, the British captured Savannah, Georgia. Then, on May 12, 1780, they won in their second try to take Charleston, South Carolina. England continued to build on these successes in the following months. General Gates, the hero of Saratoga, took command of the American army in the South. But in August 1780, British General Charles Cornwallis dealt him a disastrous defeat at Camden, South Carolina. Cornwallis then moved west, plundering the large plantations as he went.

His only opposition came from Francis Marion, known as the Swamp Fox. Marion led a band of Carolina men in hit-and-run attacks on the British. Marion and his men harassed Cornwallis by destroying supplies, then disappearing into secret lairs.

In December 1780, Washington named General Nathanael Greene to replace Gates as head of the army in the South. General Greene followed Washington's strategy: strike the British where they were weak and retreat where they were strong. Greene lured Cornwallis into battle at carefully chosen spots, handing heavy losses to the British.

Critical Thinking

During the winter at Valley Forge, Washington held his troops together by inspiring loyalty and respect in them. What things might Washington have said to his troops to encourage them to stay? Discuss charisma with the students—the quality of personality that draws the devotion of other people.

Writing an Essay

In drafting the Declaration of Independence, Thomas Jefferson said he did not "invent new ideas" but merely expressed "the American mind." Have students read the Declaration (starting on page 656) and write a two-page essay about what the phrase "unalienable rights" means to them and what it might have meant to the colonists.

Reader's Theater

Although it contains historical inaccuracies, Henry Wadsworth Longfellow's poem "Paul Revere's Ride" lives as the story of how the minutemen were warned of an impending British attack. Provide students with a copy of the poem; assign each stanza to a volunteer to prepare as a dramatic reading.

ajor Battles of the Revolutionary War

HISTORY

Map and Globe Skills

Using the map on this page, students should examine the three sections of the colonies—North—New England and New York; Middle—New Jersey, Pennsylvania, Delaware, Maryland; South—Virginia and southward. Which section was affected by actual fighting or troop occupation for the longest time? *(Middle)* How does this area compare in size with the other two? *(Smallest)* How far north did fighting occur? *(Quebec)* How far south? *(Savannah)* West? *(Vincennes)* Where did the fighting begin? *(Lexington)* End? *(Yorktown)*

Research

After the battle in Concord in April 1775, he courthouse was burning and the liberty ›ole lay hacked to pieces. Have a few stu-lents research and report orally what a liber-y pole was, how it was constructed, what it ›ymbolized, who erected it, and what purpose t served.

Writing Historical Fiction

Action surrounding the American Revolution has long been a source for historical fiction. Suggest students try to create their own historical fiction. Have them choose an incident from the lesson on which to base a first-person "I was there" account. They should research their subject in a library or encyclopedia to obtain more facts as well as another point of view.

Critical Thinking

Have students evaluate the effectiveness of Francis Marion's and General Greene's military tactics, described on page 68. How did the combined efforts of these men force the British army to move to Virginia? *(They dealt heavy losses to the British.)* Why did their strategy succeed? *(The British force was trained only for large, open offensives.)*

■ *Washington and his men blocked the town's entrance, and French ships prevented British rescue by sea; Cornwallis's troops would have starved if they had not surrendered.*

POLITICAL SYSTEMS

Critical Thinking

Tell students to analyze the role Spain played in the Treaty of Paris. How did Spain work against the interests of the United States? *(Spain had major holdings in America and was not eager for a strong United States.)*

■ *Because France wanted a treaty that would satisfy Spain, Americans met secretly with the British.*

CLOSE

Ask students to answer the Thinking Focus and to evaluate the predictions they made before reading the lesson. Copy on the board the Graphic Overview on page 62 and use it along with the maps on page 69 and 685 to review the progression of the war.

▲ *This painting shows General Washington receiving the surrender of the British at Yorktown.*

■ *What factors led to Cornwallis's surrender at Yorktown?*

Technically, Cornwallis won several victories over Greene's army, but he lost so many men that he eventually abandoned South Carolina. He then moved north to Virginia, where one final battle awaited him.

Victory at Yorktown

By 1781, French aid had strengthened the American cause. Washington's troops were now well fed and well armed. His close friend, the Marquis de Lafayette, a French nobleman inspired by the ideals of freedom, led a combined French-American army in Virginia. When Lafayette learned that Cornwallis's army was in Yorktown, he sent an urgent message to Washington. Yorktown was located on a peninsula. With enough men, the Americans could bottle up Cornwallis's forces and starve them out.

Washington led 7,000 soldiers south from his headquarters in New York. He marched them hard, knowing that this was a chance for a major victory. In September 1781, the trap snapped shut. Washington stood outside Yorktown with more than twice as many men as Cornwallis had.

British ships tried to rescue Cornwallis by sea, but French warships drove them off. Finally, on October 19, the British soldiers marched out of Yorktown and lay down their arms. ■

The Treaty of Paris

■ *Why did the delegates for the United States meet secretly with the British to negotiate the Treaty of Paris?*

Yorktown spelled the end of British control over the colonies. The defeat forced the British to ask for peace terms. In Paris, Benjamin Franklin and John Jay met with a British representative. They demanded independence and the withdrawal of all British troops. The Americans found that France wanted a treaty that would satisfy Spain, its ally. Spain did not want a strong United States to threaten its own American empire. Consequently, France tried to limit the territory that Britain would give up.

Meeting in secret, the Americans quickly hammered out an agreement with the British. It set the United States' western boundary at the Mississippi River. Franklin had hoped to get all of Canada as well, but he settled for the border that still exists between the two countries.

The Treaty of Paris, signed on September 3, 1783, officially ended the war. On December 4, the last British troops left their former colonies. The United States became the world's newest nation. ■

REVIEW

1. **FOCUS** How did the colonies manage to defeat the most powerful nation in the world?
2. **CONNECT** How did the emergence of an American "identity" in the mid-1700s contribute to the colonists' decision to make the break from England?
3. **CITIZENSHIP** Why is the Declaration of Independence considered such an important American document?
4. **CRITICAL THINKING** How might the course of the Revolutionary War have been different if France had not entered the war on the side of the colonists?
5. **ACTIVITY** Imagine you are a member of the Second Continental Congress. Then make a chart listing the pros and cons of declaring the colonies' independence from England.

Homework Options

Have students research the background and basic issues of a revolution or rebellion currently in the news.

Study Guide: page 9.

Answers to Review Questions

1. By staging battles in carefully chosen spots and using French support, the Americans defeated the British.
2. Prior to the 1650s, the colonies were composed mainly of people with a common heritage and were more dependent on England.
3. It expresses the essential political ideals on which the United States was founded.
4. Sample answer: Without French support, Americans might have been unable to win a war against the powerful British nation. Allow for personal opinion.
5. Students' charts should address the question of whether to sign the Declaration of Independence.

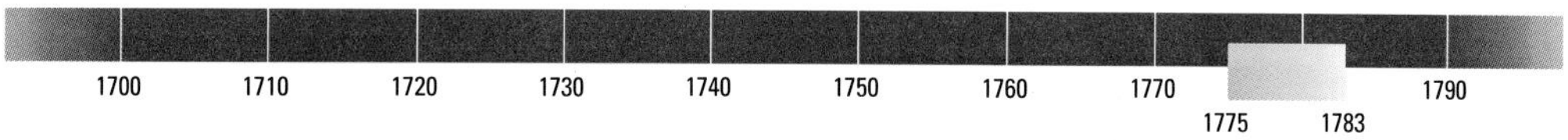

L E S S O N 4

Fighting the War at Home

Elizabeth Sandwith Drinker's 1777 diary account could have been written by thousands of women who survived the seven-year struggle for independence:

> *November 1: . . . The Hessians go on plundering at a great rate such things as wood, potatoes, turnips, etc. Provisions are scarce among us.*
>
> *November 5: A soldier came to demand blankets. . . . Notwithstanding my refusal, he went upstairs and took one, and with seeming good nature begged I would excuse his borrowing it, as it was by Gen. Howe's orders.*

As the Revolution wore on, the hardships of war intruded more and more deeply into domestic life:

> *I will tell you what I have done. . . . retrenched [cut back on] every superfluous [extra] expense in my table and family; tea I have not drunk since last Christmas, nor bought a new gown. . . . I have learned to knit and am now making stockings of American wool for my servants, and this way do I throw in the mite [do a small part] to the public good. I know this, that as free I can die but once, but [unfree] I shall not be worthy of life.*

So wrote a Philadelphia woman in a letter to a family member during the Revolution.

These women were not alone in their sacrifices. During the Revolution, daily life changed for nearly everyone. Women throughout the colonies shared the hardships of war. Women who stayed home plowed fields and harvested crops to keep farms going while their men went off to fight. They took over their husbands' businesses as shopkeepers and traders, becoming quite expert in traditionally masculine activities. After the war, many women were reluctant to give up their new roles.

When women took men's jobs, they found a new sense of self-reliance. Some learned to use guns to defend their homes. Many melted their pewter cups and plates to make bullets. Women sometimes took a direct role in the fighting to defend their homes. Nancy Morgan Hart lived in the back country of Georgia. She singlehandedly captured five British soldiers who had come to her home demanding a meal. She managed to grab one of their rifles, kill one soldier, and hold the others at bay while her daughter ran for help.

Mary Ludwig Hays, nicknamed Molly Pitcher, also became famous for her role as a fighter. When her husband fell at the Battle of Monmouth, she took his place and kept the Patriot cannon firing.

THINKING FOCUS

How did the American Revolution affect the people of the colonies?

Key Terms

- currency
- inflation
- cede

INTRODUCE

Point out the lesson title and then have students read the Thinking Focus. Ask students to recall the events of the previous lesson and help them to distinguish between "fighting battles" and "fighting the war at home."

Key Terms

Vocabulary strategies: T36–37

currency—coins and paper bills that serve as money

inflation—a rapid rise in prices over a given period of time

cede—to grant or surrender possession through a formal agreement

Graphic Overview

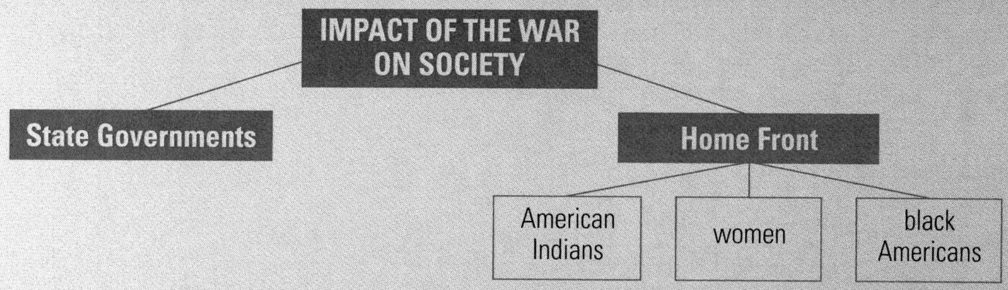

Objectives

1. Describe the impact of the American Revolution on the civilian population as a whole.
2. Compare the ways in which the war affected specific population groups.
3. Explain why the new state governments worked well during the war but were not as effective in governing a new nation in peacetime.

DEVELOP

Copy on the board the Graphic Overview from page 71. Encourage students to refer to it as they read and to add notes appropriate to each heading.

HISTORY

Critical Thinking

Tell students to evaluate the impact the war had on families and communities, including the conflicts between Patriots and Loyalists and the effects on business and property. *(Many colonists sided with the British, so communities that had worked together were split apart. Many people lost lives and property because of the battles, the taking of supplies by both armies, and the sudden drop in foreign trade.)*

Local Impact of the War

The revolution was a destructive civil war as well as a rebellion against England. States, counties, towns, and even families were torn apart as Americans chose sides. About 10 to 20 percent of the colonists remained loyal to Britain. They called themselves Loyalists, but the Patriots called them Tories.

Loyalists Versus Patriots

Patriots jeered their Loyalist neighbors in the street and sometimes vandalized and burned their houses. Those suspected of aiding the British were often tarred and feathered by angry Patriots.

Patriots also formed organizations called Committees of Safety, which took the law into their own hands to find and to harass Loyalists. They demanded oaths of allegiance to the Revolution and jailed those who refused to take them. In 1777, the Continental Congress ordered that all Loyalist land be seized. If a family was split between Loyalists and Patriots, the Patriot members often lost their land anyway.

Some Loyalists fled to areas under British occupation. Others went to Canada, the British West Indies, or England. About 80,000 Loyalists had left the colonies by the end of the war. Some later regretted leaving home. One loyalist, Hannah Winslow, sadly wrote in England: "Sincerely wish I had never left Boston, but it is now too late and my unhappy fate is fix't."

Physical Devastation

As the fighting spread, civilians experienced the horrors of war firsthand. The armies lived off the land, taking what they needed and showing little mercy to those who opposed them. British and American troops burned settlements and crops. They committed brutal acts against civilians, driving many settlers from their homes.

The more populated coastal areas suffered the most damage during the war. The British attacked the tidewater region of Virginia, destroying plantations and capturing slaves. Ships raided New England towns. What the British could not take, they torched.

Many civilians lost their homes and belongings during the Revolution. In the painting below, British troops plunder and burn a colonial farm.

Access Activity

Read aloud the diary entries in the lesson opener on page 71. Refer students to the picture on this page. What might the writer of the diary have said if it had been her farm that was destroyed? How might it have affected colonists' feelings toward the British?

Access Strategy

Encourage students to think about the members in their family, the daily family routine, the activities done with each member, and the household tasks each is responsible for. Then have them imagine that one member of the family who normally lives at home will be away for several months. How will the family routine be altered? What will happen to the shared activities? Who will do that person's household tasks? Explain to students that nearly every family in the colonies faced a similar situation. The war also had a dramatic effect on white, black, and American Indian population groups.

At some time during the war, British troops occupied all the major colonial cities—Boston, New York, Philadelphia, Charleston, and Savannah. When the British marched into New York in 1777, half of the city's population fled. The occupation troops plundered the city, taking the best housing and food for themselves. Poor citizens lived in makeshift huts made of sailcloth and timbers. A "canvas town" stretched along Broadway, New York's main street. When American troops entered New York at the end of the war, a soldier complained: "We took possession of a ruined city."

Economic Consequences

The loss of the major port cities dealt an economic blow to the Americans. These centers of shipping and trade had been the colonies' lifeline.

The colonies had enjoyed the benefits of being part of a great empire. Now they were cut off from their traditional trading partners. England and the West Indies would not buy New England fish, Pennsylvania grain, or Virginia tobacco. The British fleet no longer protected colonial trade. Instead it tried to sweep American merchant ships from the seas.

The American economy fell into chaos. The collapse of foreign trade wrecked once prosperous industries such as shipbuilding. It also affected farmers who produced goods for export. Many farms and shops were abandoned when people left to fight the war or to flee opposing armies.

During the Revolution the Continental Congress printed its own **currency**, or money, called a Continental dollar. As more money was printed, the value of the dollar decreased, causing rising prices, or **inflation**. Since the value of each dollar was less and the cost of goods higher, inflation caused more economic hardship.

In Massachusetts, the cost of a bushel of corn soared from less than a dollar to $80 in the first two years of the war. Angry women in Boston protested high prices by tossing a merchant into a cart and dragging him through the streets. Throughout the colonies, inflation made the wages of workers and soldiers virtually worthless. "Not worth a Continental" was a common complaint of the period. ■

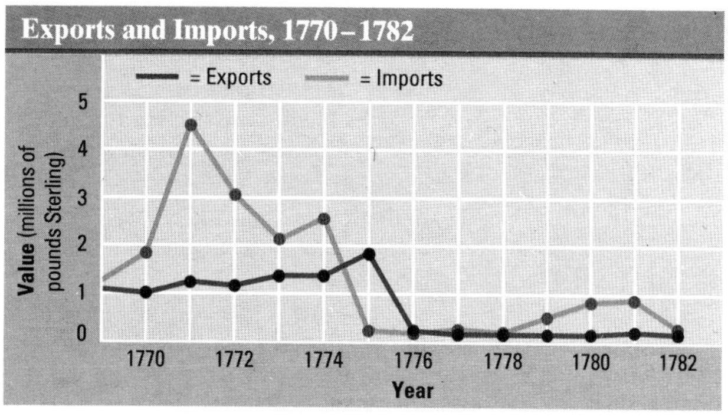

▲ *What does this graph show about the growth or decline in imports and exports during the war?*

▲ *Shown here is Continental currency with a face value of eight dollars. Wartime inflation, however, made this paper money almost worthless.*

■ *How did the war affect American agriculture, manufacturing, and trade?*

The War's Impact on Some Social Groups

Although few Americans completely escaped the impact of the Revolution, the war affected different groups in the population in different ways. For example, the war had a unique impact on black Americans, American Indians, and women.

Black Soldiers Aid the Fight

African Americans took part in most of the battles of the Revolution. Ten black Minutemen fought at Lexington and Concord. Salem Poor was commended for bravery at Bunker Hill, and Peter Salem received credit for killing the British commander in the battle. Despite this impressive record, the Continental Army barred blacks in November 1775.

The British attempted to win the support of blacks as soon as the war broke out. In 1775, the royal governor of Virginia, Lord Dunmore, promised freedom to all slaves who were "will-

ECONOMICS

Visual Learning

Tell students to study the graph on imports and exports on this page and to compare the levels of each before and during the war. *(Both imports and exports nearly came to a halt once the war started.)* How must this have affected the colonial economy? *(Most businesses must have been hurt badly, but the lack of imports may have forced the colonies to make more of their own goods.)*

◄ *Both imports and exports declined.*

■ *Agriculture, manufacturing, and trade suffered greatly during the war. Port cities and plantations were burned. People abandoned farms and ships. Trade connections were cut off.*

Economic Context

Money, in and of itself, has no actual value. Its value comes from what it represents. When there is too much money relative to the amount of available goods, inflation follows and prices rise. This often occurs during or after a war.

Several things cause inflation. The scarcity of goods—as with corn and other farm produce during the Revolution—is the primary source, but the scarcity of services is also a factor. Particularly after the kind of economic surge that often follows a war, businesses cannot produce as much as the public wants to buy.

During the revolutionary period, inflation and uncertainty about money ran high. Prices changed rapidly, from day to day, and it became difficult to determine what goods or services were actually worth. Business slowed down, which further reduced the amount of money in circulation. Serious financial losses followed.

Critical Thinking

Ask students to explain what the phrase "not worth a continental" means and how it came into use. *(Inflation made the paper money printed by the Continental Congress nearly worthless. When something was "not worth a continental," it had no value.)*

HISTORY

Critical Thinking

Ask students to explain how the war both helped and hindered the attempts of black Americans to win their freedom. *(Many black Americans were freed because of their service during the war, and their dedication increased antislavery support in the North. Americans' hard-won independence, however, did not generally apply to slaves.)*

The portrait (below) *of Mercy Otis Warren, author and Patriot, was painted by John Singleton Copley, the finest colonial portrait painter. Among the writings of Warren were two short plays in which the British and the Loyalists were the targets of her sharp wit.*

ing to bear arms." Many slaves rushed to enlist, wearing sashes bearing the motto "Liberty to Slaves."

Lord Dunmore's action forced the Continental Army to accept free blacks in January 1776. About 5,000 of them served during the war, and African Americans saw action in every major battle.

The valuable service of blacks in the military nourished antislavery sentiments in the North, but little was done to improve the condition of blacks. Thousands of slaves took advantage of the war to flee their masters or to gain freedom through military service.

Whether slave or free, however, few blacks benefited from the high ideals set forth in the Declaration of Independence.

American Indians Lose an Ally

For the native inhabitants of North America, the American Revolution was a disaster. Most sympathized with the British, who had brought them trade and gifts and kept American settlers out of their lands.

In the South in 1776, Cherokees raided the farms of settlers who had moved into their territory. Carolina and Virginia militia retaliated by destroying Cherokee towns.

The most powerful American Indian group, the Iroquois Confederacy, split apart at the start of the war. All but the Oneidas and Tuscaroras joined the British side. British and Iroquois forces pillaged towns in central New York and along the Pennsylvania border. In revenge, the Americans burned Iroquois villages and killed men, women, and children.

After the war, the British withdrew from land they had formerly held and abandoned their Indian allies in the process. Both the Iroquois and Cherokees were forced to **cede,** or give, much of their territory to the new government of the United States.

Women Join the Battle

As many as 20,000 women marched with the armies of both sides. They served as cooks, laundresses, nurses, guides, and porters. One observer of American troops noticed "great numbers of women, who seemed to be the beasts of burden, having a bushel basket on their back, by which they were bent double. The contents seemed to be pots and kettles, various sorts of furniture." Some women disguised themselves as men in order to join the army. Deborah Sampson took a man's name and enlisted in the Continental Army. She was wounded twice but escaped detection and received an honorable discharge.

Mercy Otis Warren, shown here, published political pamphlets on the issues of the day. A friend of many

Map and Globe Skills

Have students refer to Chapter 1 (page 27) to find out what groups made up the Iroquois Confederacy. Then have them turn to the map of Native American cultures in the Atlas on page 672 and locate the areas held by the Iroquois Confederacy and the Cherokee tribe.

Mathematics Connection

Between 1775 and 1777, a bushel of corn in Massachusetts increased in cost from less than a dollar to $80. Have students figure out this rate of inflation. *(About 8000 per cent over two years)* Have them compare that figure with the current rate of inflation to see what an economic burden the war was. (Check newspapers for current inflation rate.)

Writing an Essay

The colonies survived the war largely because they had a bond of shared experiences. Vermont, for example, had more in common with Georgia than with its Canadian neighbor, Quebec. Students may recall from earlier lessons experiences that bound the colonies together. Ask them to write a one-page essay describing the common experiences and analyzing what would have happened if the bond among the colonies had not been so strong.

leaders of the Revolution, including Thomas Jefferson and Sam Adams, she was a strong supporter of American independence. She also wrote the first complete history of the Revolution, published in 1805. ■

■ *What impact did the war have on the Iroquois Confederacy?*

■ *The alliance split, most siding with the British.*

Colonies Form New Governments

During the war, the former colonies formed new state governments, a process that often divided people with different views about government. The first duty of these governments was to help fight the war. Each state formed its own militia. The states also turned over some of their tax revenues to the war effort. Like the Continental Congress, the state governments issued paper currency.

The states gave more people the right to vote by reducing property requirements for voters. In a few states, almost every white male over the age of 21 could vote.

The state governments set up during the war faced a new problem once the war ended: how to govern effectively in peacetime. The economy had to be pulled back together, and important matters of law had to be decided.

The particular traditions of government in each colony ran deep. Most colonists identified themselves as Virginians, New Yorkers, and so forth, rather than as Americans. Accustomed to acting as independent units, state governments resisted the compromises necessary to establish an effective central government. For a while, it looked as if the 13 states might split into many tiny nations. Some time would be required before they put aside their differences and formed a true national government. ■

POLITICAL SYSTEMS

Critical Thinking

Ask students to compare the conditions and problems facing state governments during the war and after it. *(During the war each colony needed to raise and support a militia. After the war, states had to cooperate to form a national government and rebuild the economy.)*

■ *Why was it more difficult for the colonies to work together after the war than during the war?*

■ *During the war the colonies drew together in a common cause; after the war, states acted independently, intent on their own interests.*

Independence Hall, Philadelphia, was built in 1732 as Pennsylvania's colonial state house. It was here that the Declaration of Independence (1776), the Articles of Confederation (1781), and the United States Constitution (1787) were adopted.

REVIEW

1. **FOCUS** How did the American Revolution affect the people of the colonies?
2. **CONNECT** Which group do you think the Revolution hurt more: farmers in New England or farmers in the Middle Colonies? Explain.
3. **ECONOMICS** Discuss at least three ways in which the Revolution might have affected a wealthy merchant living in Philadelphia.
4. **CRITICAL THINKING** Do you think slaves would have been better off fighting for the British or the Americans during the American Revolution?
5. **ACTIVITY** Make a list of activities women engaged in during the American Revolution that were not part of their usual role in society. Share your list with the class.

CLOSE

Have students answer the Thinking Focus. Copy on the board the Graphic Overview from page 71. Summarize the lesson by having students fill in details from the notes they took as they read the lesson.

Answers to Review Questions

1. The war affected most of the population negatively. American Indians lost their land; a few male slaves gained freedom, but for most slaves, men and women, the war did not change their status. Women suffered hardships but also took on new roles as they filled in for men.
2. Sample answer: Because farmers in the Middle Colonies were more dependent on trading their produce, they were hurt more. Allow for personal opinion.
3. A Philadelphia merchant might have had fewer goods to trade, might have been cut off from trading partners, and might have suffered from inflation.
4. Sample answer: They were better off fighting for the Americans because the ideals of the Declaration of Independence would eventually apply to them. Allow for personal opinion.
5. Students should realize the differences in women's roles then and now.

Homework Options

Encourage students to talk with a relative or neighbor who experienced World War II or the oil crisis of the 1970s, and report to the class how that person coped with the shortages and rationing.

Study Guide: page 10.

Answers to Reviewing Key Terms

A. Sample answers:

1. The colonists boycotted England by not buying tea and by setting up an embargo to make trading with England illegal.
2. A minuteman was a soldier in the army of citizens called the militia.
3. Printing too much currency can cause inflation, as the value of each dollar declines.

B. Answers:

1. True. Immigrants came from many countries and practiced many different religions.
2. False. The British adopted a policy of salutary neglect, but they never asked people to salute statues.
3. True. The assemblies often passed new laws to get around the king's vetoes.
4. False. The writs of assistance allowed customs officials to enter homes to search for smuggled goods. The quartering act forced people to lodge British troops.
5. True. In a republic, people vote for the rulers of the country.
6. True. The colonists thought the taxes they had to pay England were unfair.

Answers to Exploring Concepts

A. Answers:

Great Awakening: broke down ties between church and state and made society more open to different religions

Seven Years' War: England gained Canada, land east of the Mississippi River and Florida

Passage of Stamp Act: made the colonists angry enough to riot and organize Stamp Act Congress

First Continental Congress: colonists organized to protest British policies

Battle of Lexington: first time colonists stood up to British forces

Battle of Concord: colonists fought back, letting the world know they were prepared to battle England

Battle of Saratoga: Victory convinced French that Americans could win war.

Battle of Yorktown: Washington won the war with the help of the French

B. Sample answers:

1. Immigrants came from Scotland, Ireland, the German States, Ireland, and France.
2. Indian, African, German, Dutch and Scottish words shaped the American "dialect."
3. The assemblies approved uses of money and controlled the governor's salary.
4. The colonists wanted to move to the new land right away, but England issued the Proclamation of 1763, banning the move.
5. British troops had been stationed in Boston for a long time, causing great tension between the Bostonians and the British soldiers.
6. Thomas Paine's *Common Sense* and the Declaration of Independence stirred the colonists to act.
7. Women tended farms and businesses, defended their homes, and sometimes fought in the war.
8. England and the West Indies ended trade with America. Many people could not make money.
9. Most American Indians backed the British who had kept colonists off their lands. Black soldiers fought for the colonists or for the British, hoping to gain freedom.

Chapter Review

Reviewing Key Terms

boycott (p. 57)
cede (p. 74)
currency (p. 73)
embargo (p. 59)
immigrant (p. 48)
inflation (p. 73)
militia (p. 63)
minuteman (p. 63)
pluralism (p. 49)
republic (p. 65)
salutary neglect (p. 52)
veto (p. 53)
writs of assistance (p. 57)

A. In each of the following pairs, the two terms are related in some way. Write a sentence for each pair that clearly explains the relationship between the terms.

1. boycott, embargo
2. militia, minuteman
3. currency, inflation

B. Based on your reading in the chapter, decide whether each of the following statements is accurate. Write an explanation for each decision.

1. People of many nations and religious groups contributed to the pluralism of the colonies.
2. The British followed a policy of salutary neglect by not requiring colonists to salute statues and paintings of the king.
3. Colonial assemblies often responded to a veto by passing a law similar to the one that had been rejected.
4. The writs of assistance required colonial officials to provide food and shelter to British troops.
5. In a republic, elected officials represent the people.
6. The American Revolution broke out because the colonists refused to pay taxes to England.

Exploring Concepts

A. On a separate sheet of paper, make a chart like the one shown below. Complete it by identifying the contributions each event made to society .

Event	Contribution
Great Awakening	
Seven Years' War	
Passage of Stamp Act	
First Continental Congress	
Battle of Lexington	
Battle of Concord	
Battle of Saratoga	
Battle of Yorktown	

B. Support each of the following statements with facts and details from the chapter.

1. In the 1700s, new immigrants came to the colonies from many places besides England.
2. The American "dialect" reflected the wide variety of peoples who lived in the colonies.
3. The colonial assemblies increased their power in a variety of ways in the 1700s.
4. Although England won the Seven Years' War, the effects of the war created conflict between England and the colonies.
5. Opposition to British policies was stronger in Boston, Massachusetts than anywhere else in the colonies.
6. The written word proved as powerful a tool for the cause of independence as the muskets of the minutemen.
7. Women made important contributions to the revolutionary cause.
8. The newly independent nation faced serious economic problems as a result of the war.
9. Blacks and Indians took part in the war on both sides.

Reviewing Skills

1. Look at the timeline on pages 46-47. Identify the time period it covers. What is the earliest date shown on the timeline? What is the latest date? Into what segments of time is it divided?
2. Identify two different kinds of information you can gather from timelines. Explain how timelines provide that information.
3. Create a timeline of current events in the past month. Ask a friend or classmate to create his or her own timeline of current events. What are the similarities and differences between your timelines? Why do you think such differences occur?
4. What specialized resource would you use if you wanted to find out how much of North America Spain laid claim to after the Seven Years' War?
5. Suppose you wanted to see how all the events that have occurred in your life this month compare to all the events in your life this year. What kind of a timeline would you use?

Using Critical Thinking

1. The Boston Tea Party was an act of civil disobedience—the refusal to obey civil laws considered unjust. In many other parts of the colonies, people deliberately broke what they considered to be unjust laws as a way of protesting British policies. Can you suggest any recent examples of civil disobedience used by protesters? Do you agree that people should not obey laws they believe are unjust? Explain your answer.
2. Many colonists felt that they could obtain their demands through peaceful means. What do you think would have had to happen to prevent war between England and the colonies? Would the colonists have ever been content to remain part of the British Empire? How would our nation be different today if the American Revolution had not occurred?
3. The only colonists who benefited from the American Revolution were wealthy white males. Do you agree or disagree with this statement? Explain your answer, using specific examples from the chapter.
4. It has often been said, "The pen is mightier than the sword." Think about the writings of Thomas Paine and Thomas Jefferson. What effect did their publications have on the growing split with England? With that in mind, explain the quote above.

Preparing for Citizenship

1. **WRITING ACTIVITY** Imagine you are a colonist in 1776 reading the Declaration of Independence for the first time. (Turn to page 656 and read the complete text of the Declaration.) Then write a letter to the editor detailing what you think of the Declaration. Be specific in explaining whether you think the idea of breaking ties with England will be good or bad for the colonies.
2. **COLLECTING INFORMATION** In the 1760s and 1770s, the colonists formed citizens' groups such as the Sons of Liberty and the Committees of Correspondence. The purpose of these groups was to keep a close watch on the actions of the British government and protest those actions when they hurt the colonists' interests. Go to the library and do some research on modern citizens groups, such as Common Cause. Compare and contrast the methods used by today's groups with those used by the Sons of Liberty and the Committees of Correspondence.
3. **COLLABORATIVE LEARNING** Select eight or ten important leaders in the Revolutionary days and prepare a "clues" program for the class. Divide the class into two teams. Give each team a list of five leaders, and have each team then develop a set of ten or more clues to the identity of each leader. A spokesperson from each team then gives one clue at a time to the other team. See how many clues it takes to identify each Revolutionary leader.
4. **COLLABORATIVE LEARNING** Prepare a class trial of George III based on the list of accusations in the Declaration of Independence. Choose a judge, a jury, a committee for the prosecution, and a committee for the defense. Research the background of each accusation and prepare your case carefully before staging the trial.

Answers to Reviewing Skills

1. The timeline shows what years are covered in the chapter: 1690 to 1790. It is divided into twenty-year segments.
2. A timeline shows when events happened and how events are related to each other. Timelines do this by arranging information visually.
3. Encourage students to discuss how a person's point of view influences the importance of events.
4. A historical atlas.
5. You would use a telescoping timeline, which shows a highly detailed, short period as part of a less detailed, longer period.

Answers to Using Critical Thinking

1. Students might discuss animal rights protestors releasing laboratory animals, Rosa Parks sitting in the front of the bus, or people who do not pay taxes for political reasons. Ask students to consider what, if any, issues would be important enough for them to commit civil disobedience. Why might it be dangerous to commit civil disobedience?
2. Students should consider the kinds of compromises England and colonists might have made. They may also want to look at Canada as a country that has remained a member of the British Commonwealth.
3. Encourage students to consider that there were positive and negative results of the war. On the one hand, after the war more white men could vote as property requirements were lowered. On the other hand, American Indians lost a lot of territory to the Americans when the British no longer protected them.
4. Students should discuss how Paine and Jefferson articulated the colonists' anger and desires. Such documents united the colonists against the British.

Answers to Preparing for Citizenship

1. **WRITING ACTIVITY** Encourage students to use quotations from the Declaration of Independence to illustrate the arguments in their letters. Students may want to read the letters aloud.
2. **COLLECTING INFORMATION** The Committees of Correspondence and the Sons of Liberty were illegal groups who sometimes used violent means of protest. Discuss whether or not those methods are used today. Discuss the difference between citizens' groups that promote revolution and groups that promote reform.
3. **COLLABORATIVE LEARNING** Keep track of the scores on the board. After the game, discuss current leaders and the clues that future generations may use to identify them.
4. **COLLABORATIVE LEARNING** Explain how a trial works. The prosecution will have an easier job, using the Declaration of Independence. Help the defense to imagine good reasons for George III's actions.

UNIT OVERVIEW

After students have read the unit title and the narrative underneath it, ask them to imagine what it was like for the colonies to be on their own as a new nation faced with the task of having to set up a government. What might it have been like to create a constitution—a set of governing principles and basic laws—for the new government? What were some of the choices that the new states had to make? *(Who would lead; who would choose the leaders)*

Looking Back

How might the principles for which the Revolution was fought influence the kind of government that the American people would set up? *(No monarch; emphasis on participation in government)*

Looking Forward

Tell students that they will be finding out how our form of government came into being in the next two chapters:

Chapter 3 *Toward the Constitution*

Chapter 4 *The Constitutional Convention*

Unit 2

The Constitution of the United States

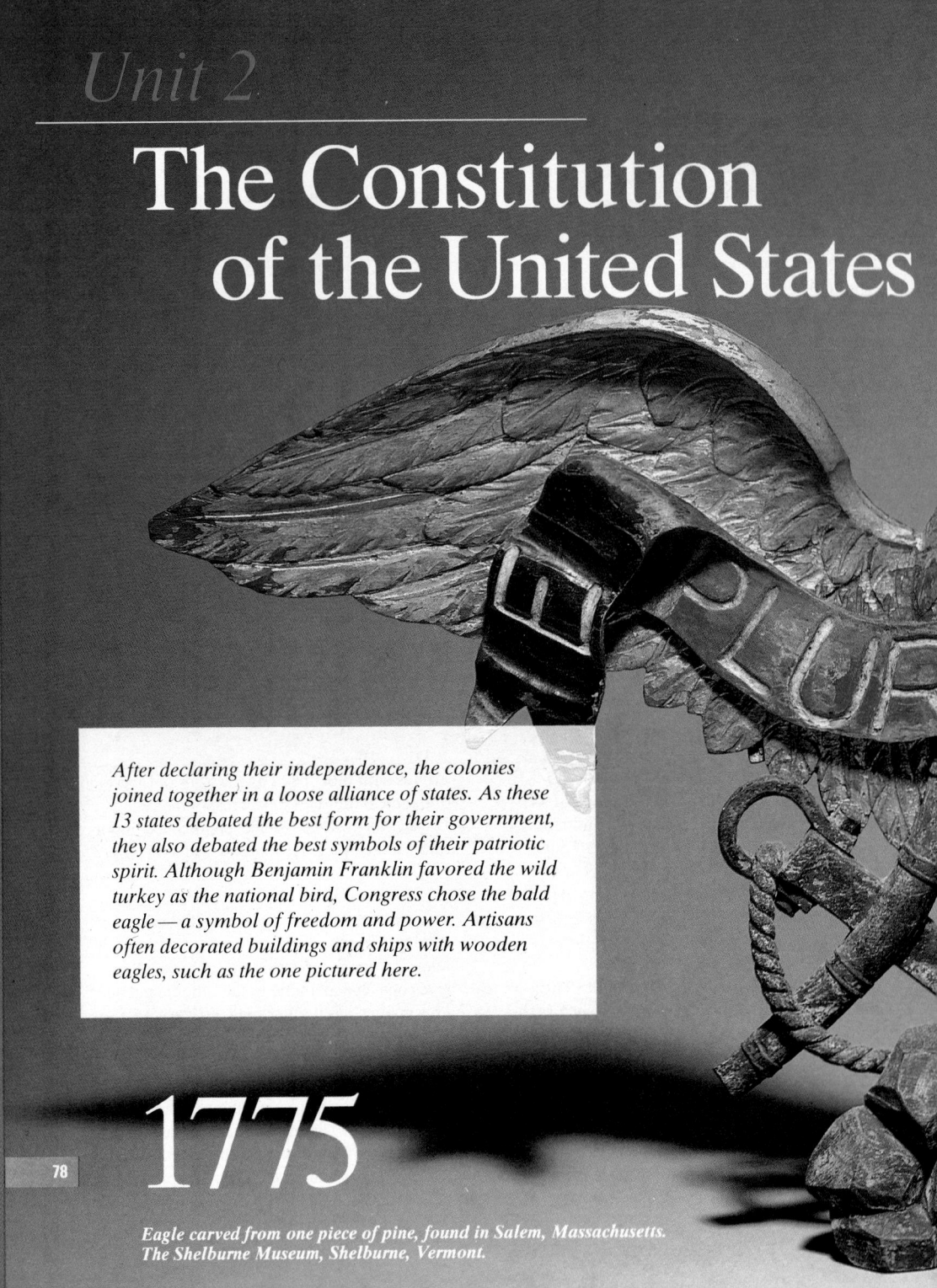

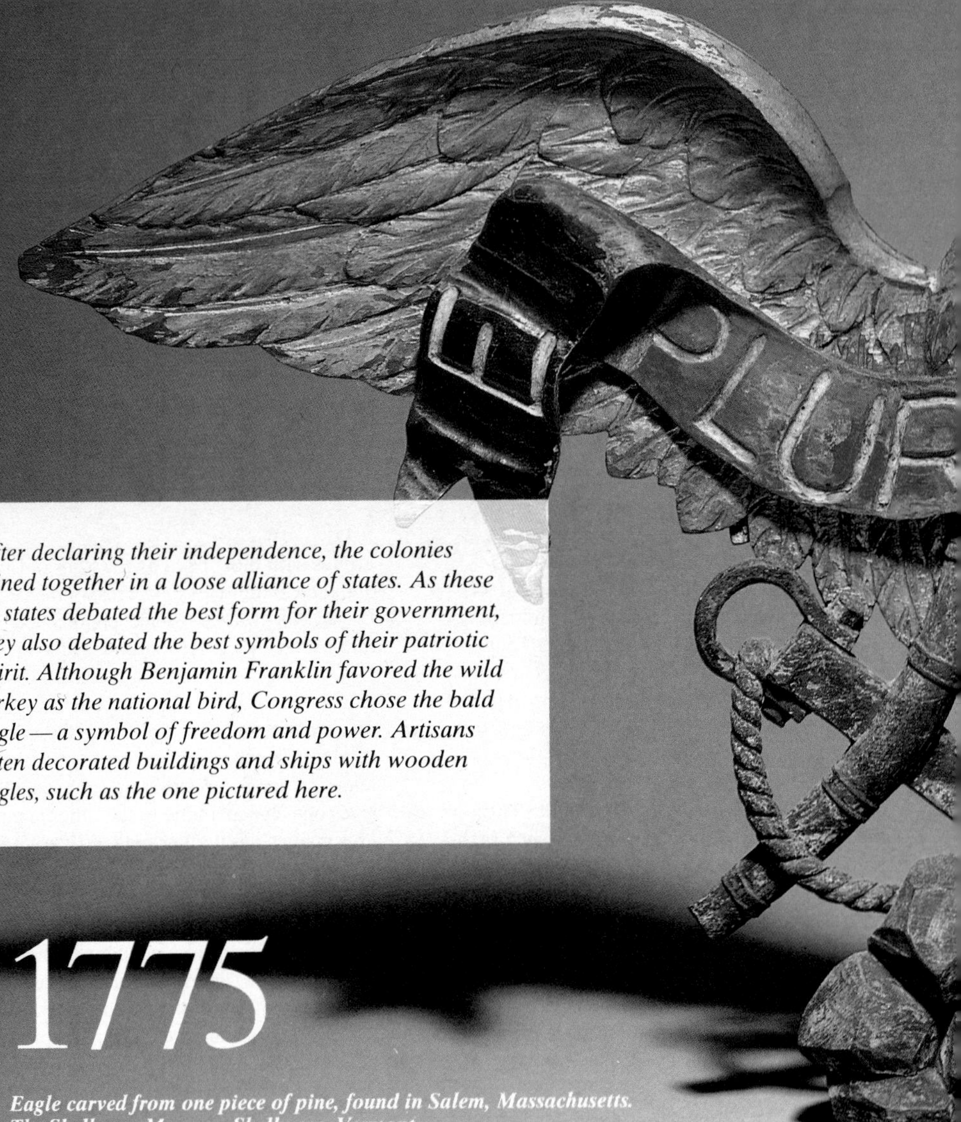

After declaring their independence, the colonies joined together in a loose alliance of states. As these 13 states debated the best form for their government, they also debated the best symbols of their patriotic spirit. Although Benjamin Franklin favored the wild turkey as the national bird, Congress chose the bald eagle — a symbol of freedom and power. Artisans often decorated buildings and ships with wooden eagles, such as the one pictured here.

1775

Eagle carved from one piece of pine, found in Salem, Massachusetts. The Shelburne Museum, Shelburne, Vermont.

GEOGRAPHY • PROJECT

Regional Representative

Geography Skill **Comparing Area on Maps**
Students use the skill of Asking and Answering geographic questions.

Geography Theme Regions

Geography Standard 13, conflict among people influences the control of earth's surfaces

Activity ***Create a Chart***

Materials construction paper, pencils and markers

Management Whole Class/Small Group

Imagine you are a 1787 representative from one of the thirteen original states, the American frontier, or the non-American West. List problems and solutions as they relate to the new U.S. Constitution.

Have students:

- list the problems and solutions on a chart and/or hold a panel discussion about the effect of the Constitution on problems/solutions in your region.
- add to the chart the ways in which the Constitution affected regional geography.

Understanding the Sculpture

The United States chose the eagle as its national bird in 1782. Eagles were then—and continue to be—popular adornments on many household objects, including brass door knockers and weather vanes. Eagles have also been sewn on emblems, woven into coverlets, and painted on chinaware.

Understanding Chronology

Point out that in 1775, a year before the Declaration of Independence was signed, Benjamin Franklin first proposed the idea of a union of the states. In 1791, the Bill of Rights, the finishing touch to the new Constitution, was ratified.

For research support activities, see the *Research Handbook.*

For simulations correlated to this unit, see *Citizenship Simulations*, p. viii.

HOUGHTON MIFFLIN SOCIAL STUDIES

Bookshelf II

A Young Patriot: The American Revolution as Experienced by One Boy

by Jim Murphy

This biography of Joseph Plumb Martin takes place during the time Joseph was an enlisted soldier in the Continental Army during the Revolutionary War.

Motivate Read pp. 49–56 about a young soldier's days at Valley Forge. Ask students why they think the Continental Army had untrained soldiers and so few supplies. Remind them that prior to the writing of the Constitution, there was a loose organization of thirteen colonies, each wanting to exert its own authority. Have students study the photo on this page and predict what they will study in this unit about the Constitution.

To connect this book with the unit content, use the planning guide and student activity blackline masters beginning on p. iv of the *Bookshelf II Teacher's Resources.*

For additional books that are Easy, Average, and Challenging, see the Unit Bibliography on p. T43. See bibliography updates at www.eduplace.com/ss/hmss.

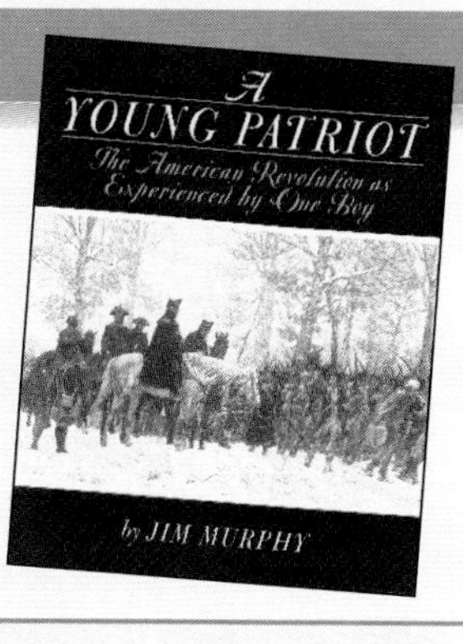

CHAPTER 3

Planning at a Glance

Toward the Constitution

	Objectives	Reading Support and Other Resources	Diverse Learning Strategies
Lesson 1 Roots of Government *pp. 82–87* 2–3 days	• Trace the history that favored establishing the United States as a republican government with a written constitution. • Explain why Americans first chose to establish a weak central government. • Describe the democratic features of the Pennsylvania and Massachusetts constitutions.	• **Workbook** or **Reading Support:** pp. 36–39 Review p. 9 Extra Support/Transition p. 9 Multi-lang. Sum. pp. 17–18 • **Other Resources:** Study Guide p. 11, Study Print 3	Access Strat. **(SDAIE)** TE p. 83 Music Connection **(Auditory)** TE p. 85 Mathematics Connection **(Visual)** TE p. 85 Audiotapes of Multi-language Lesson Summaries **(Auditory)**
Skill: Reading Abigail Adams's Letters *pp. 88–89*	• Use correspondence between Abigail and John Adams to evaluate primary source materials.	• **Other Resources:** Study Guide p. 12	Role Playing **(Auditory)** TE p. 88
Lesson 2 The Articles of Confederation *pp. 90–94* 1–2 days	• Explain how European acceptance of the Articles of Confederation helped Americans win the Revolutionary War. • Compare some aspects of the confederation government in 1783 with the federal government today. • Relate the government's inability to pay soldiers to currency problems.	• **Workbook** or **Reading Support:** pp. 40–43 Review p. 10 Extra Support/Transition p. 10 Multi-lang. Sum. pp. 19–20 • **Other Resources:** Geography Kit, Study Guide p. 13	Access Strat. **(Extra Support)** TE p. 91 Access Act. **(SDAIE)** TE p. 91 Visual Learning **(Visual)** TE p. 92 Audiotapes of Multi-language Lesson Summaries **(Auditory)**
Lesson 3 The Crisis of Confederation *pp. 95–99* 2–3 days	• Describe conflicts between the new national government and the 13 states. • Explain the significance of the Northwest Ordinance. • Analyze the factors leading up to the Annapolis Convention.	• **Workbook** or **Reading Support:** pp. 44–47 Review p. 11 Extra Support/Transition p. 11 Multi-lang. Sum. pp. 21–22 • **Other Resources:** Poster 10, Study Guide p. 14	Access Strat. **(Extra Support)** TE p. 96 Map and Globe Skills **(Visual)** TE p. 98 Writing a Letter **(GATE)** TE p. 98 Audiotapes of Multi-language Lesson Summaries **(Auditory)**
Exploring: Educating Americans *pp. 100–101*	• Use library resources to identify and describe some recent educational changes and issues. • Explain the need for educated citizens in a democratic society.		Activity **(Visual)** TE p. 100
Chapter Review *pp. 102–103* 1 day		Chapter 3 Test pp. 9–12 *(See facsimiles on TE p. 751.)*	Assessment Multiple-Use Masters pp. 81–88

Reading Support Resources *for Every Lesson*

Reading and Review

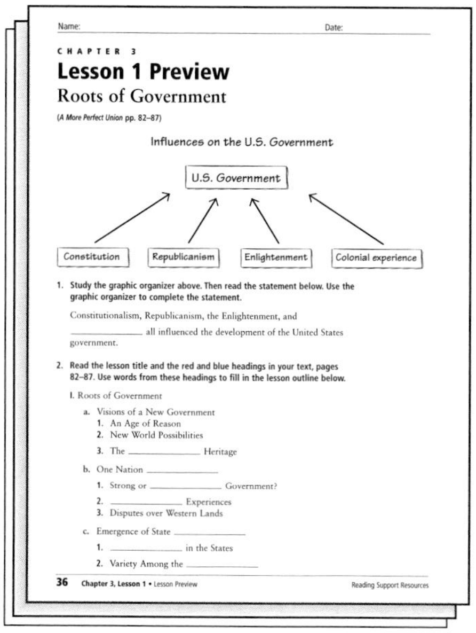

Name: Date:

CHAPTER 3

Lesson 1 Preview

Roots of Government

(*A More Perfect Union* pp. 82–87)

1. **Study the graphic organizer above. Then read the statement below. Use the graphic organizer to complete the statement.**

   Constitutionalism, Republicanism, the Enlightenment, and ______ all influenced the development of the United States government.

2. **Read the lesson title and the red and blue headings in your text, pages 82–87. Use words from these headings to fill in the lesson outline below.**

   I. Roots of Government
   - a. Visions of a New Government
     1. An Age of Reason
     2. New World Possibilities
     3. The ______ Heritage
   - b. One Nation ______
     1. Strong or ______ Government?
     2. ______ Experiences
     3. Disputes over Western Lands
   - c. Emergence of State ______
     1. ______ in the States
     2. Variety Among the ______

36 Chapter 3, Lesson 1 • Lesson Preview — Reading Support Resources

- **Chapter Overview*** p. 35
- **Lesson Previews*** using graphic organizers from the Teacher's Edition pp. 36, 40, 44
- **Reading Strategies*** pp. 37, 41, 45
- **Lesson Summaries*** pp. 38–39, 42–43, 46–47
- **Lesson Reviews** pp. 9, 10, 11

* **Workbook** includes starred items.

Multi-language Summaries

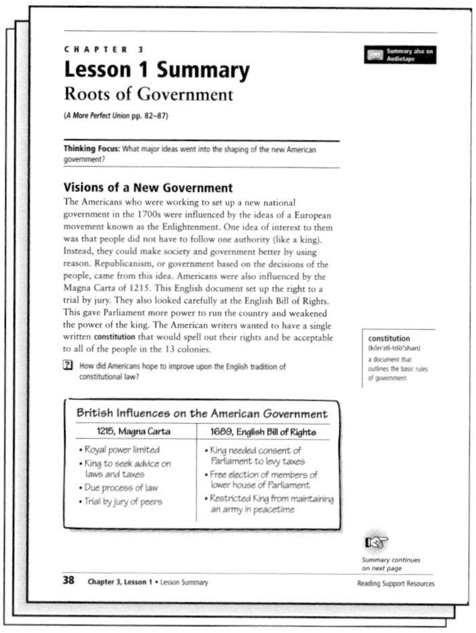

CHAPTER 3

Lesson 1 Summary

Roots of Government

(*A More Perfect Union* pp. 82–87)

Summary also on Audiotape

Thinking Focus: What major ideas went into the shaping of the new American government?

Visions of a New Government

The Americans who were working to set up a new national government in the 1700s were influenced by the ideas of a European movement known as the Enlightenment. One idea of interest to them was that people did not have to follow one authority (like a king). Instead, they could make society and government better by using reason. Republicanism, or government based on the decisions of the people, came from this idea. Americans were also influenced by the Magna Carta of 1215. This English document set up the right to a trial by jury. They also looked carefully at the English Bill of Rights. This gave Parliament more power to run the country and weakened the power of the king. The American writers wanted to have a single written **constitution** that would spell out their rights and be acceptable to all of the people in the 13 colonies.

constitution (kŏn′stĭ-tōō′shən) a document that outlines the basic rules of government

? How did Americans hope to improve upon the English tradition of constitutional law?

British Influences on the American Government

1215, Magna Carta	1689, English Bill of Rights
• Royal power limited • King to seek advice on laws and taxes • Due process of law • Trial by jury of peers	• King needed consent of Parliament to levy taxes • Free election of members of lower house of Parliament • Restricted King from maintaining an army in peacetime

Summary continues on next page

38 Chapter 3, Lesson 1 • Lesson Summary — Reading Support Resources

Lesson Summaries in:

- English (See Reading and Review.)
- Spanish pp. 38–39, 42–43, 46–47
- Chinese pp. 17–22
- Hmong pp. 17–22
- Khmer pp. 17–22
- Vietnamese pp. 17–22

Summaries available on audiotapes

Lesson Support / Transition

S D A I E

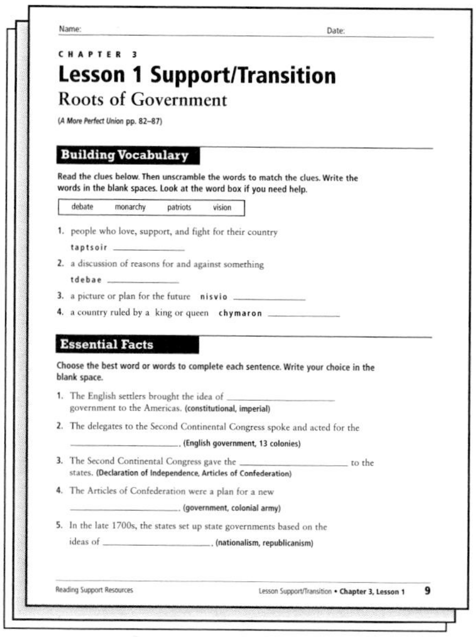

Name: Date:

CHAPTER 3

Lesson 1 Support/Transition

Roots of Government

(*A More Perfect Union* pp. 82–87)

Building Vocabulary

Read the clues below. Then unscramble the words to match the clues. Write the words in the blank spaces. Look at the word box if you need help.

debate monarchy patriots vision

1. people who love, support, and fight for their country **taptsoir** ______
2. a discussion of reasons for and against something **tdebae** ______
3. a picture or plan for the future **nisvio** ______
4. a country ruled by a king or queen **chymaron** ______

Essential Facts

Choose the best word or words to complete each sentence. Write your choice in the blank space.

1. The English settlers brought the idea of ______ government to the Americas. **(constitutional, imperial)**
2. The delegates to the Second Continental Congress spoke and acted for the ______. **(English government, 13 colonies)**
3. The Second Continental Congress gave the ______ to the states. **(Declaration of Independence, Articles of Confederation)**
4. The Articles of Confederation were a plan for a new ______. **(government, colonial army)**
5. In the late 1700s, the states set up state governments based on the ideas of ______. **(nationalism, republicanism)**

Reading Support Resources — Lesson Support/Transition • Chapter 3, Lesson 1 — 9

Activities for SDAIE
Specially **D**esigned **A**cademic **I**nstruction in **E**nglish

- **Lesson Support/Transition** pp. 9, 10, 11

Technology Options

Internet Support

http://www.eduplace.com

Social Studies Center at Education Place

Internet support for Chapter 3:

- ***Lesson at a Glance***
- ***A China-Bound Sailor***

Software

***Student Writing Center*®** (CD-ROM) (Macintosh® or Windows®)

School to Career

A national currency is a strong symbol of unity for a country. Have students research how money is coined or printed and create a flow chart showing the process and the jobs involved. What skills are needed at each step to carry out this process?

Character Education

Writing letters used to be the only way people living far from each other could communicate. Today, there are other ways, such as e-mailing and telephoning. No matter what the method, however, privacy is very important. Have students write a brief essay explaining why personal communication between individuals should be respected.

CHAPTER
PREVIEW

After students have read the chapter title and the narrative under it, explain that while we know the U.S. Government is based on the Constitution (thus the title of the chapter), the people at the time did not. In this chapter students will read about the first attempts to establish a central government.

Have students look at the Articles of Confederation document and read the caption. What does it mean to form a government? *(To establish rules that everyone must obey; to establish people's responsibilities and rights)* What makes a good government? *(People represented equally; no person given too much power)*

Looking Back

Have student recall that the last chapter focuses on war. This chapter, covering part of the same time period, focuses on setting up a government.

Looking Forward

Tell students that they will be learning about the United States's first attempts at forming a national government in the next three lessons: Roots of Government, The Articles of Confederation, and The Crisis of Confederation.

Chapter 3
Toward the Constitution

The former colonists were now on their own as a new nation. Cautiously, the thirteen states joined together under a weak government. Having just fought a war over individual freedoms, the states were reluctant to surrender hard-won rights to their own central government. Could the new nation succeed—separate as states, but together as a country?

1776 The people of Pennsylvania ratify their first state constitution at a convention held in the Pennsylvania State House in Philadelphia.

Robert Morris, a Pennsylvania merchant and banker (shown below, right), raised money to support the American Revolution. In 1782, he established the Bank of North America.

1775

1779

1775

BACKGROUND

Having declared independence, the colonies (now states) had to form a national government during military conflict. The Articles of Confederation were weak and imperfect, but they were important as a first constitution and led to the Constitution of 1787.

Virginia and Massachusetts Self-government

The Virginia House of Burgesses grew out of the Virginia Company, whose main interest was in the tobacco economy. By 1619, the company was bringing skilled craftsmen to Virginia and promising them both a share in self-government and the full rights of Englishmen, as the original 1606 charter from the King of England had provided.

Delegates from the various communities met as the House of Burgesses on July 30, 1619, in Jamestown, Virginia. This was the first meeting of an elected legislature in the colonial settlements in America.

The General Court of Massachusetts grew out of the Massachusetts Bay Company, whose members were a group of Puritan merchants who came from England in 1630. These stockholders wanted both economic growth and religious freedom. The company charter provided guidelines for stockholders of the Massachusetts Bay Company to adopt officers and rules for the corporation.

The General Court, which at first involved only the corporation, quickly changed to a political body that included all free male

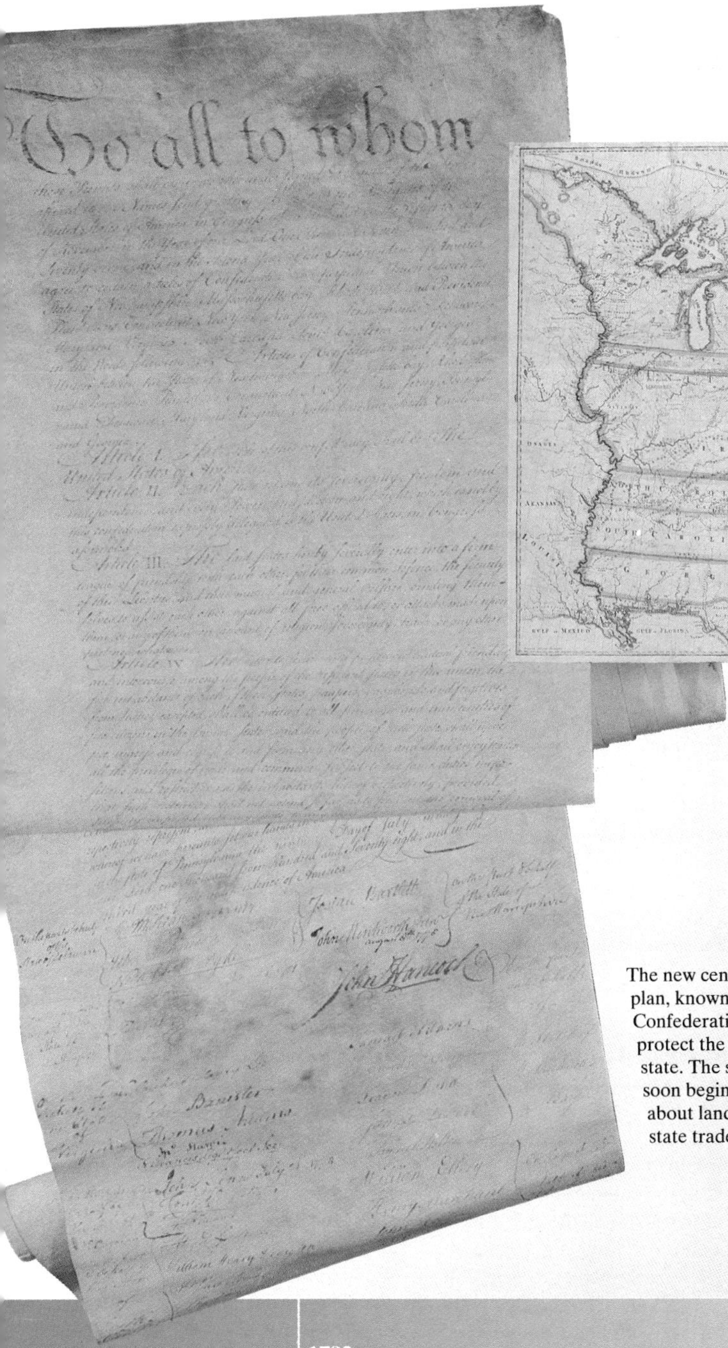

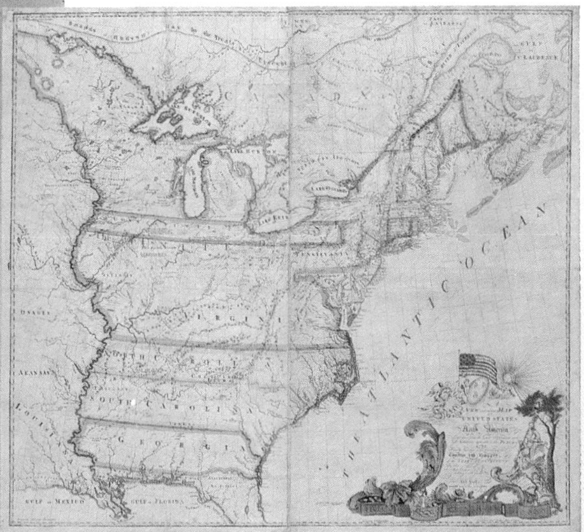

The first map of the new nation drawn by an American, Abel Buell, is based on the boundaries established by the Treaty of Paris in 1783.

The new central government plan, known as the Articles of Confederation, is designed to protect the power of each state. The states, however, soon begin to quarrel bitterly about land rights and interstate trade.

1783

1787

1787

Understanding the Visuals

Ask students to look carefully at the park depicted in this print. What do they see? *(People greeting each other; a group of American Indians walking together; children playing with a dog)* How is this park similar to and different from parks that they visit?

William Birch's print of Philadelphia shows what city life was like in America in the late 1700s. Explain to students that just as the government was being developed, so too were the nation's cities. Philadelphia was one of the most important cities.

Understanding Chronology

Ask students to recall when the first fighting of the revolution took place *(1775)*, and when the war ended *(1781)*. Point out that the Articles of Confederation, shown on this page and discussed in this chapter, were first approved by Congress during the war, in 1777, but didn't go into effect until 1781, about six months before the war ended.

property owners. By 1644, the General Court became a bicameral legislature, with a lower House of Deputies and an upper chamber that included the governor and his board.

Interstate Commerce

Many of the coastal merchants who traded with the British were influential in state government, intensifying the conflict of the states over the Articles of the Confederation. The merchants imported and sold to inland storekeepers items such as glass, iron, medicine, and gunpowder. These storekeepers traded the imported goods with farmers for bartered items such as grains, vegetables, and animals. The inland storekeepers were more willing than coastal merchants to barter with the farmers.

After the war, with many American goods banned from British markets but American markets open to British goods, American coastal merchants imported more from the British than they exported. The British suppliers demanded payment of this debt in coin. The coastal merchants required the same of the inland storekeepers, who then refused to barter with the farmers. With higher property taxes also having to be paid in coin, the farmers found themselves in a state of crisis at the end of a chain of debt.

INTRODUCE

Point out the lesson title and discuss with students the concept of roots. Have students read the Thinking Focus and name the ideas that Americans have valued up to this point. *(For example, fair representation and liberty)* Ask them to predict whether people with such ideas would be likely to form a government with a powerful or a weak central authority. Have them read the lesson to confirm or reject their predictions.

Key Terms

Vocabulary strategies: T36–37

constitution—a document that defines the main principles and framework of a government

federal—relating to a system of government that divides power between a central authority and a number of smaller states

confederation—a group of states joined loosely for a common purpose

executive—a person or group having administrative or managerial authority

legislature—an officially selected body responsible for making the laws for a political unit

1775 1781 1783 1785 1787 1789

L E S S O N 1

Roots of Government

THINKING FOCUS

What major ideas went into the shaping of the new American government?

Key Terms

- constitution
- federal
- confederation
- executive
- legislature

➤ *American painter John Trumbull probably copied a French engraving to produce this oil portrait of Benjamin Franklin.*

Benjamin Franklin wore a rustic fur hat when he arrived in Paris in 1776 as the representative of his new nation. The Parisians saw Franklin as a self-taught frontiersman, and he charmed them with his witty conversation. Considered something of a curiosity, he was followed by crowds throughout Paris. Poets wrote flattering rhymes in his honor. And French shopkeepers sold snuffboxes and other trinkets bearing his portrait.

To the French, Franklin stood for a new citizen of the world—the American. During his long life he worked as a printer, author, inventor, philosopher, scientist, and diplomat. More than anything else, Franklin was a patriot, one of the first to dream that the colonies could become one nation.

In July 1775—a full year before the signing of the Declaration of Independence—he presented to the Second Continental Congress a plan of government called "The Articles of Confederation and Perpetual Union." Most delegates to the Congress considered Franklin's proposal for a unifying central government too radical for the time. Many people still hoped that the colonies could settle their disputes with Britain and be left to rule themselves, individually.

Visions of a New Government

Franklin's ideas circulated throughout the colonies during the Revolutionary War as the colonists thought about creating a government. "We have it in our power to begin the world over again," Thomas Paine, the author of the pamphlet *Common Sense*, wrote enthusiastically.

An Age of Reason

Franklin and Paine, as well as Thomas Jefferson, were greatly influenced by the revolutionary ideas of the Enlightenment—the philosophical movement taking place in Europe at that time. Its most important idea was that people could approach religious, social, political, and economic issues through reason and science. This meant that people should not follow authority blindly. Instead, progress and a better life—for both individuals and society—were possible through putting thoughts into action. According to Enlightenment thinkers, the right of people to revolt against

Objectives

1. Trace the history that favored establishing the United States as a republican government with a written constitution.
2. Explain why Americans first chose to establish a weak central government.
3. Describe the democratic features of the Pennsylvania and Massachusetts constitutions.

Graphic Overview

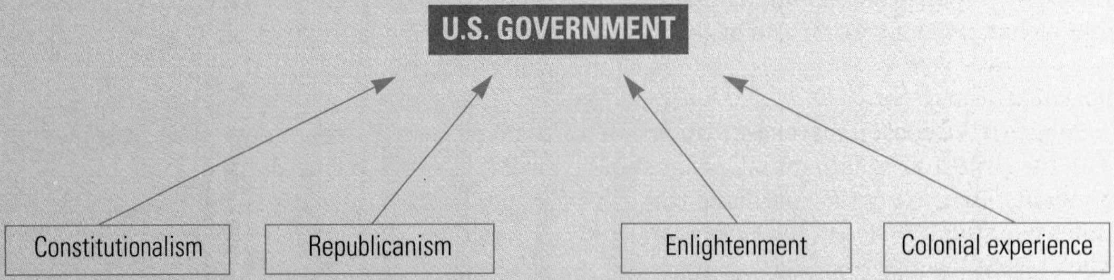

oppressive authority followed from the use of individual reasoning.

Enlightenment thinkers in the American colonies were excited. Here they were, the first people in history to have the chance to create an entirely new government based on Enlightenment principles. But what form should the new American government be given in order to serve the different needs and desires of people in 13 separate colonies?

New World Possibilities

Today it is difficult to appreciate just how rare republicanism, or government based on the consent of the people, was in the late 1700s. At that time, kings and emperors ruled most of the world. The only models for republics were a few small countries such as Switzerland, Holland, and the city-states of Italy.

A group of George Washington's officers wanted him to become King of America. Imagine what our nation would be like now if the patriots had chosen to have a monarch! At the creation of an entirely new government, almost anything was possible. The familiar shape of the United States map in the Atlas on page 702 might even have been different if Great Britain's colonies in Canada had accepted a U.S. invitation to agree "to this confederation, joining in the measures of the united states" to become additional states.

The English Heritage

Even though they rejected the idea of having a monarchy, Americans did look to England for ideas for their new political system. Their English tradition had given the colonists a respect for government based on legal documents. In addition, many English writers of the time lent their voices to Enlightenment ideas. Americans naturally tried to adapt English tradition to suit their new country.

England did not have a single written **constitution**, or document that defined its fundamental principles of government. But several historical documents contributed to English political structure. One such document was the Magna Carta of 1215. English nobles had won from King John the right to trial by people of a rank equal to their own. This early law formed the basis of what we know as trial by jury.

In 1689, the English Bill of Rights further limited the power of the monarchy and increased Parliament's say in ruling the country. Parliament gained the right to approve plans to spend money, and the king was forbidden to keep a standing, or permanent, army.

The English settlers had brought the idea of constitutional government to the New World. Before the *Mayflower* landed in 1620, 41 of the men on board had agreed to abide by cer-

▲ *This crown, used for British coronations to this day, has long been a symbol of the British monarchy.*

▼ *Although the United States left the door open for Canada to "be admitted into, and entitled to all the advantages of this union," the invitation was rejected. This map never became real.*

An Imaginary United States, 1777

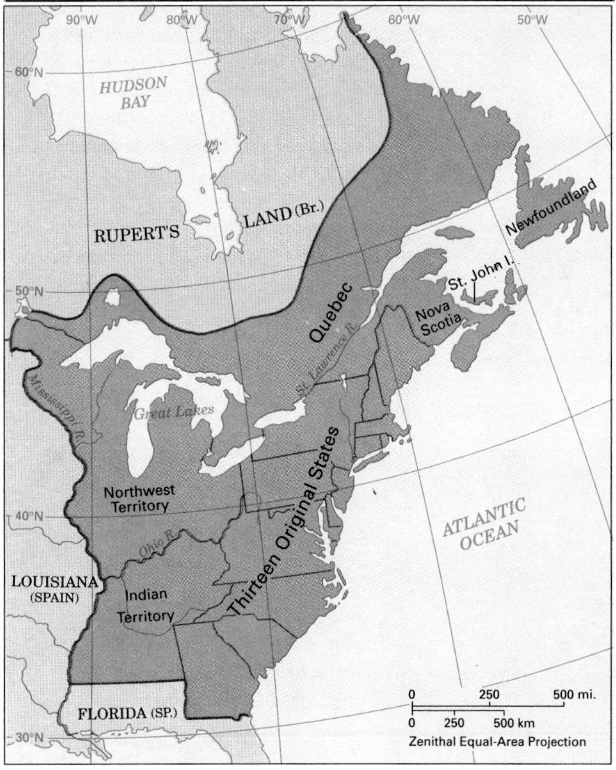

DEVELOP

Copy on the board the main head and structure of the Graphic Overview from page 82. Tell students to look for the four "roots" of American government as they read the lesson and to list details about each "root."

HISTORY

Critical Thinking

Why did Thomas Paine write "We have it in our power to begin the world over again" and what did he mean? *(Exciting opportunity to apply Enlightenment ideals to a new government)* For an excerpt from *Common Sense*, refer students to pages 666–667.

Access Strategy

Have students imagine that they are setting up a new club. You may wish to divide the class into small heterogeneous groups for this discussion. To help make their discussion concrete, ask them to agree on a purpose for their club. Discuss with them what type of structure their club will have. How will decisions be made? Who will be responsible for running meetings? How will they raise funds for club activities?

Tell students that the founders of the new nation had a similar decision to make—what kind of structure the new government should have. This lesson explains how the colonists' earlier experiences with government influenced them as they formed a new government after Independence.

Access Activity

What does the map on this page show about the uncertainty that existed when Americans began forming a government? *(Country's boundaries not yet set)* Point out the southern border of Quebec *(Ohio River)* and discuss the consequences of Canada's joining the Confederation. *(Canada's large territory would have given them a strong influence.)*

CONSTITUTIONAL HERITAGE

Visual Learning

Refer students to the timeline on this page. Ask students to identify the earliest written statement of people's rights in England. *(Magna Carta)* How many years are there between this document and the English Bill of Rights? *(474)*

■ *They wanted to have a single document that would spell out in writing their rights and the country's governing principles.*

POLITICAL SYSTEMS

Critical Thinking

Students may have heard of the Confederacy or the Confederate States in connection with the Civil War. Ask students to define the words *Confederacy (The 11 Southern states that fought to secede from the United States)* and *confederation (A group of states joined loosely for a common purpose).* Be sure that they can distinguish between the American government under the Articles of Confederation in the 1770s and 1780s and the Confederacy in the 1860s.

British Influences on the American Government

1215, Magna Carta
- Checked royal power.
- Required King to seek advice on laws and taxes.
- Granted due process of law.
- Provided for trial by jury of peers.

1620, Mayflower Compact
- Agreed to form a self-governing body.
- Promised to frame, constitute, and enact just and equal laws.
- Agreed to promote general order and the good of all.

1628, Petition of Rights
- Rejected idea of absolute monarchy by divine right.
- Established supremacy of law over personal wishes.
- Forbade King from housing soldiers in private homes, setting up martial law, and imprisoning citizens illegally.

1689, English Bill of Rights
- Required King to have consent of Parliament to levy taxes.
- Provided for free election of members of lower house of Parliament.
- Restricted King from maintaining an army in peacetime.

1200 | 1300 | 1400 | 1500 | 1600 | 1700 | 1800

▲ *Unlike the other constitutional documents, which restricted powers of the king, the Mayflower Compact was written for life in an unknown wilderness.*

tain rules for the general good of all. This Mayflower Compact was the most basic form of a constitution.

As Americans prepared to set up their own government in the late 1700s, they wanted a single document that would spell out their rights in clear terms. They hoped that by defining clearly their governing principles they could avoid the kinds of problems that had troubled the American colonies—such as the disputes they had had with the King and English Parliament. ■

■ *How did Americans hope to improve upon the English tradition of constitutional law?*

One Nation United

In 1775, the delegates to the Second Continental Congress still represented 13 separate colonies. When John Adams said "our country," he meant his own state of Massachusetts. But in declaring their own independence, the states took a risk as one nation together. The concept of "Union" began as a military necessity, the united effort needed to defeat Great Britain—the greatest military power of the time. Soon the shared experience of fighting the Revolution would more closely bind the colonists.

Strong or Weak Government?

In June 1776 — just a few weeks before the Declaration of Independence would be signed—the Second Continental Congress appointed a committee to write a blueprint for a new government. Thirteen members were chosen—one from each "state," as the former colonies now called themselves.

A month later the committee presented a draft calling for a **federal** government, to be given a strong central authority by the states. They used Franklin's old title: "Articles of Confederation and Perpetual Union." As members of Congress debated, disagreements surfaced. Delegates feared a tyrannical national government might be too much like a monarchy. They therefore proposed that the new government be a **confederation**—a loose alliance of states.

The delegates argued about how to structure a congress. If the new congress were to represent the people of the new nation, large states should have more representatives. But as Roger Sherman of Connecticut argued, "We are representatives of states, not individuals."

After over a year of debate during which war raged, the Second Continental Congress adopted a list of thirteen items in 1777. Article III

Critical Thinking

Ask students to read the excerpt on page 85 from the Articles of Confederation, focusing especially on the words *severally* and *league of friendship*. Do the states actually think of themselves as one nation? *(No)* What do they agree to do? *(To help protect each other.)*

Cultural Context

Enlightenment philosophers were inspired by the discoveries of scientists, such as the Italian astronomer Galileo Galilei (1564–1642) and the English mathematician and scientist Sir Isaac Newton (1642–1727). The discovery of scientific laws led to a main point of Enlightenment philosophy—the belief in an orderly world governed by the laws of nature. These laws could be discovered by the rational mind by applying the scientific method of first forming a hypothesis and then gathering evidence that supports or disproves it.

Enlightenment philosophers were committed to freedom of the mind to pursue the teachings of science and reason. They believed that passion (such as jealousy) leads to vice but that reason leads to virtue. They also believed that government should help people to be happy. Their hopeful goal was to create a society in which error and evil would disappear.

of the Articles of Confederation described the states' new relationship:

> *The said states hereby severally enter into a firm league of friendship with each other, for their common defence, the security of their Liberties, and their mutual and general welfare, binding themselves to assist each other, against all force offered to, or attacks made upon them, or any of them, on account of religion, sovereignty, trade, or any other pretence whatever.*

Each state would have equal power in the new congress. There was no national **executive**—that is, no one person in the government was given administrative authority. And there was no national court system.

Colonial Experiences

Based on their experience as colonial subjects of Great Britain, Americans were afraid of a centralized government. They were especially suspicious of any strong executive, such as the governor appointed by the king for each colony. Tensions often flared between these royal governors and many of the elected **legislatures** responsible for making some of the laws within the colonies. In New Jersey, for example, Governor William Franklin was imprisoned during the Revolutionary War because of his staunch Loyalist sympathies. Ironically, he was the son of patriot Benjamin Franklin.

In their first attempts at representative government, the colonists made sure that their local governments were strong. Throughout New England, local government took the form of town meetings—annual gatherings called to establish rules for each community. Although the New England colonies had elected legislatures, such as the Great and General Court of Massachusetts, the people felt that they had additional control over their daily lives through participation in their town meetings. These annual town meetings still go on today.

In Virginia, laws were passed by the elected members of the colony's legislature, which was called the House of Burgesses. But Virginia law was also made at the local level by justices of the peace who met in county courts.

Disputes over Western Lands

In November 1777, the Second Continental Congress presented the Articles of Confederation to the states. For the Articles to go into effect, all 13 states would have to approve them. But long-standing disputes over western lands delayed the Articles' passage.

The old colonial charters had granted states such as Massachusetts and the Carolinas all the land stretching westward from the Atlantic Ocean. Virginia's charter mentioned land to the northwest as well. New York's land claims stretched from the Great Lakes south to Georgia. Look at the map on page 86 to find land claimed by more than one state.

The states that lacked such western lands were not willing to let these

Across Time & Space

After the war, the American branch of the Church of England cut its ties to the British monarchy and became the Episcopal Church. In 1786, Thomas Jefferson urged Virginia to pass a law separating all churches from state control and the state legislature did. Today, separation of church and state is an established American principle.

Colonel Nathaniel Heard and his militia, under orders of the New Jersey state provincial congress, arrested royal governor William Franklin in June 1776.

HISTORY

Critical Thinking

In the colonies many conflicts had occurred between elected state legislatures and royal governors. What effect did this history of conflict have on the structure of the Confederation government? *(Led to their decision not to have a national executive)*

Mathematics Connection

Have students use the scale on the map on page 86 to estimate the area of the land belonging to the 13 states after western land claims were ceded to the United States *(1800 square miles)* and the area of the land that became territories after the cessions *(2700 square miles)*. What was the approximate ratio of the area of the states' own land to the area of the land in the territories? *(2:3)* What percentage of U.S. land lay in the territories? *(60 percent)*

Music Connection

An evening's entertainment in the 1770s for Benjamin Franklin, Thomas Jefferson, and other Americans in Paris might have included a performance of music. Have students look at the painting on page 91 and listen to chamber music by Handel, Haydn, Mozart, Gluck, and other composers of the period. Show them portraits of eighteenth century Europeans to help them visualize the scene. Art books and illustrated European history books are good sources for visuals.

Critical Thinking

Remind students that because of British neglect, Americans had developed strong local governments. Have students name preexisting government powers that remained unchanged after the Articles of Confederation went into effect. *(For example, town meetings' making rules for their communities, and elected legislatures' making laws for states.)*

Western Land Claims and Cessions

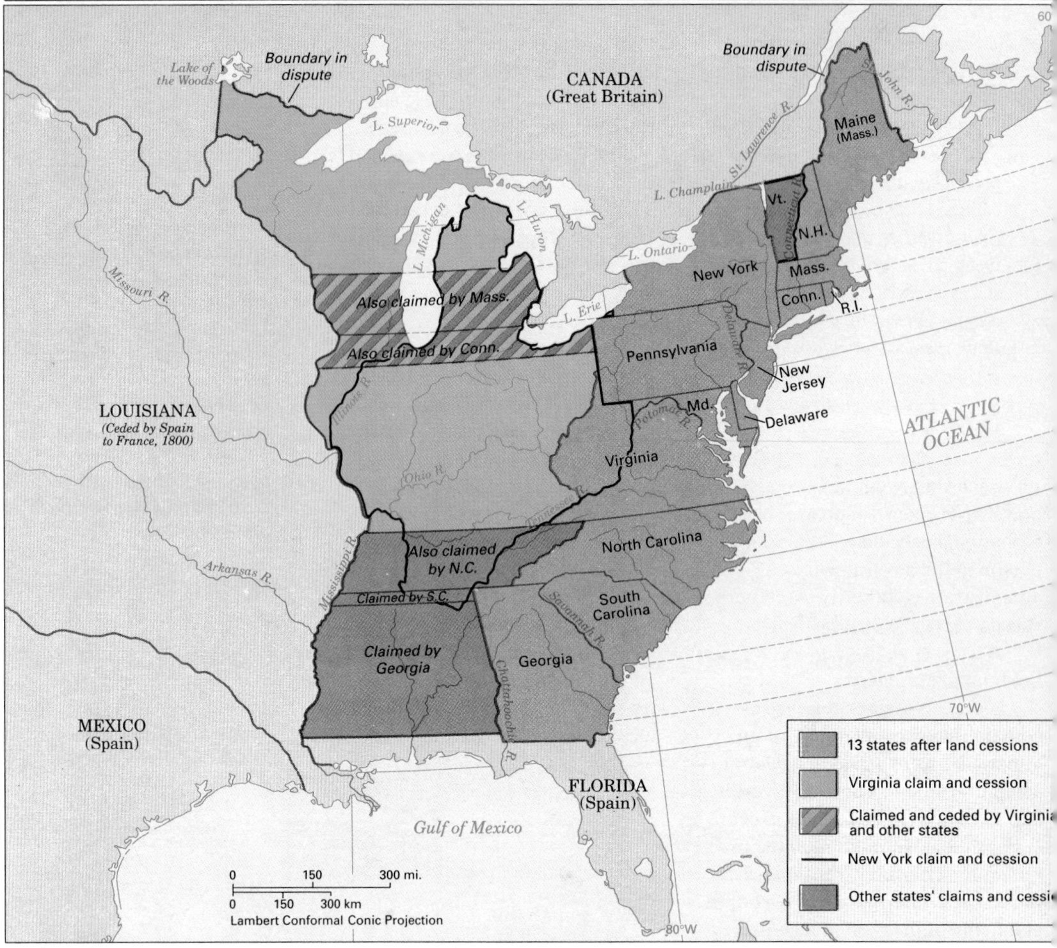

▲ *Seven states ceded land claims in the western territories. New York and New Hampshire also ceded claims to Vermont in 1791.*

claims stand. They argued that the western lands were "wrested from the common enemy by the blood and treasure of the thirteen states." Therefore, the states as one union should share the frontier territory.

Maryland refused to approve the Articles unless all western lands were ceded, or transferred, to the central government. In 1781, after New York and Virginia agreed to the cession of their lands, Maryland accepted the proposal for a new government. The Articles were finally approved. ■

■ *What issues contributed to the reluctance of Americans to establish a strong national government?*

Emergence of State Governments

After declaring independence from Great Britain, the states tried not only to establish an effective national government. Each had to set up its own new government also. This was indeed an exciting time—a chance to develop plans for the future. "We are," said Benjamin Franklin, "on the right road to improvement, for we are making experiments."

Republicanism in the States

Speaking to a state convention—made up of former members of the Virginia House of Burgesses—James Madison praised the emerging

■ *Because of their experience with Great Britain, they feared tyranny, believed in republicanism, and favored state over national government.*

POLITICAL SYSTEMS

Critical Thinking

Ask students why they do or do not share James Madison's faith in the republican principle that people will have the virtue and intelligence to select the best people to govern them. *(Some may believe more in people's common sense, others in their selfishness.)*

Map and Globe Skills

Have students refer to the map on this page. Which states had overlapping claims? *(Sample answer: Mass. and Conn. overlap with Va. and N.Y.)* Which states ceded land to the union? *(Mass., Conn., Ga., N.C., S.C., N.Y., N.H.)* Which state continued to hold western lands that eventually became a new state? *(Part of Va. became W. Va.)*

Collaborative Learning

Divide students into teams to debate the question whether a weak or strong central government would be the best choice for the new nation. Give the teams time in class to prepare their strategies, to plan who will present each argument, and to practice. Remind students to base their arguments only on information that was known in 1776. After the debate, have students discuss any insights that they gained.

republican governments. "I go on this great republican principle, that the people will have the virtue and intelligence to select men of virtue and wisdom."

All the new state governments had elected legislatures. Republicanism demanded that the representatives had to be close to the voters who elected them. In most states, representatives had to stand for election annually. They had to live in the community they represented and have a stake in it by owning property there.

The state legislatures were usually more powerful than the executives of the states, the governors. In more than half the states, the legislature chose the governor, making him accountable to the wishes of the representatives.

Variety Among the States

Although the early state constitutions shared features of republicanism, some were more creative than others. Only Connecticut and Rhode Island kept their original colonial charters, after omitting references to the King and Parliament.

In 1776, Pennsylvania's new constitution eliminated the state executive so that there would be no governor at all, and established a unicameral, or one-house, legislature. Supporters of this constitution saw no need for an upper house—like the House of Lords in the English Parliament—to represent the wealthier people of the community. Pennsylvania, along with North Carolina, dropped any requirement for owning property in order to vote—a radical concept for the time.

Conservative political leaders were appalled by these democratic innovations. They succeeded in 1790 in replacing the first Pennsylvania constitution with a more moderate one.

Massachusetts established a two-step procedure for democratically adopting a new government. In the first step, a special convention gathered to write a constitution. In the second step, all Massachusetts voters—not just members of the state legislature—decided whether to approve their new constitution. Massachusetts' constitution, approved in 1780, stated that all men were "born free and equal" and it was used in a 1783 court case to outlaw slavery in that state.

The creation of the early state constitutions was a critical step in the evolution of a successful national government. Through their state governments, Americans learned more about the workings of republicanism as well as about ways to improve their national government. ■

▲ After the British dissolved the House of Burgesses in 1774, many former members worked to create Virginia's constitution and became part of the new state government. The House of Burgesses is pictured above as it might have looked in the 1600s.

■ Predict which aspects of the early state constitutions would eventually be adopted for the national government.

CITIZENSHIP
Critical Thinking

Have students name the democratic features of Pennsylvania's 1776 constitution. *(No governor, no "upper house," no property requirements for voting)* What was unusually democratic about the Massachusetts constitution of 1780? *(It stated that all men were "born free and equal" and became the basis for ending slavery in that state.)*

■ *Sample predictions: Representatives had to live in the community they represented; no property requirement to vote; election of an executive by all the voters.*

CLOSE

After students answer the Thinking Focus, have them evaluate the predictions they made before reading the lesson. Copy on the board the main head and structure of the Graphic Overview from page 82. Have students fill in the four "roots" and name details about each based on the lists that they made while reading the lesson.

R E V I E W

1. **FOCUS** What major ideas went into the shaping of the new American government?
2. **CONNECT** Why were one-year terms for political offices thought to be a way to avoid a tyrannical government?
3. **POLITICAL SYSTEMS** How was Pennsylvania's constitution unusually democratic for the time?
4. **CRITICAL THINKING** Why would a politician like John Adams refer to his home state of Massachusetts as "his country"?
5. **WRITING ACTIVITY** Imagine that you represent Maryland in Congress in 1781. Prepare a brief speech arguing against approval of the Articles of Confederation while states still hold western land.

Toward the Constitution

Answers to Review Questions

1. The new American government was shaped by belief in republicanism, in the philosophies of the Enlightenment, in a written constitution, and in limited power for the central government.
2. One-year terms would make the representatives accountable to the people.
3. Pennsylvania's constitution eliminated the state executive, established a unicameral legislature, and made it unnecessary to own land in order to vote.
4. Sample answer: He identified more with his particular state than with the states as a group. Allow for personal opinion.
5. Students should argue for sharing the western territories as one union. They should remember that Maryland lacked western lands of its own.

Homework Options

Have students list ways in which their daily lives are affected by local, state, and national government. *(Paying a sales tax, going to public school)*

Study Guide: page 11.

UNDERSTANDING PRIMARY SOURCES

This skill lesson will give students techniques for using primary sources, such as the letters of historical figures.

SOCIAL SYSTEMS

Study Skills

After students read Abigail Adams's letter, ask them what they can infer about the relationship between husbands and wives in the colonies. Have them cite evidence from the letter to support their answers. *(Sample answer: Husbands probably had a great deal of power over their wives, since Abigail asks her husband to make laws that would "be more generous and favorable" to women than those of his ancestors. Even though some men voluntarily gave up "the harsh title of master," others were "vicious" husbands who treated their wives "with cruelty and indignity.")*

UNDERSTANDING PRIMARY SOURCES

Reading Abigail Adams's Letters

Here's Why

Primary sources are the raw materials of history. Any document of daily life—a news article, a personal letter, even a laundry list—provides information about how people lived. Knowing how to use such primary sources is one way to get a view of individual people and events of the past.

In this chapter you read about the roots of our nation and how men like Benjamin Franklin, James Madison, and John Adams shaped our government. Primary sources are extremely useful because they give us a record of events by people who were there, and in their own words.

Suppose you wanted to get a closer perspective on the personal lives of the people affected by events in this chapter. Reading letters written by John Adams and by his wife Abigail Adams would provide that information.

Here's How

In order to use a particular item for historical information, you need to evaluate it as a primary source. On this page is a letter that Abigail Adams sent her husband in 1776. (Above the letter is what is traditionally thought to be a portrait of Abigail Adams). Ask the following questions to determine the accuracy and usefulness of this document.

1. **Who was the writer?** Abigail Adams educated herself by reading literature and history. She was a woman who took an

Abigail to John
March 31, 1776

I long to hear that you have declared an independency—and, by the way, in the new code of laws, which I suppose it will be necessary for you to make, I desire you would remember the ladies, and be more generous and favorable to them than [were] your ancestors. Do not put such unlimited power into the hands of the husbands. Remember all men would be tyrants if they could. If particular care and attention is not paid to the ladies, we are determined to [instigate] a rebellion, and will not hold ourselves bound by any laws in which we have no voice or representation. That your sex are naturally tyrannical is a truth so thoroughly established as to admit of no dispute. But such of you as wish to be happy willingly give up the harsh title of master for the more tender and endearing one of friend. Why, then, not put it out of the power of the vicious and the lawless to use us with cruelty and indignity. . . ? Men of sense in all ages abhor those customs which treat us only as the vassals of your sex. Regard us then as beings, placed by providence under your protection, and in imitation of the Supreme Being make us of that power only for our happiness.

Objective

Use correspondence between Abigail and John Adams to evaluate primary source material. (Study Skills 2)

Role Playing

After students have read the letters, assign pairs of students (one boy, one girl) to continue the discussion orally. The girl in each pair should respond as Abigail might have responded to John's letter. The boy should then continue with John's possible reply.

Research

The Adams family was quite a lively one. Encourage students to find out more about them and to make a short report to the class. *John Adams and the American Revolution*, by Catherine Drinker Bowen (Boston: Little Brown, 1949), is a classic work which students will find very readable.

active interest in her husband's work. Since women of that time did not vote or work outside the home and usually did not attend political meetings, this letter does not present the ideas and feelings of the average woman of that time.

John to Abigail
April 14, 1776

As to your extraordinary code of laws, I cannot but laugh. We have been told that our struggle has loosened the bands of government everywhere. . . .
Depend upon it, we know better than to repeal our masculine systems. Although they are in full force, you know they are little more than theory. We dare not exert our power in its full latitude. We are obliged to go fair and softly, and in practice, you know, we are the subjects. We have only the name of masters, and rather than give up this, which would completely subject us to the despotism of the petticoat, I hope General Washington, and all our brave heroes would fight. . . .

2. **When was the letter written?**
Notice that Adams wrote her letter in the same year that the Declaration of Independence was signed. It gives the reader a unique look at the issues that were being discussed. As a primary source, the letter provides more detailed information about the decisions involved in producing the Declaration than a document written many months or years later.

3. **Why was it written?**
The letter reveals that Abigail Adams hoped to convince her husband that he should create a certain kind of policy. She wanted him to grant rights to women, to "remember the ladies," and to treat women as friends rather than as possessions.

4. **What difficulties does this source present?**
Some sources present difficulties because they are incomplete or because they require special knowledge in order to be understood. In Adam's letter, the language may prove difficult. Look up the words *instigate*, *tyrannical*, and *vassals* in the dictionary. When you examine primary sources, you need to determine if the vocabulary or spelling were common for that time period. In this case, the vocabulary that Adams uses is an indication of how well-educated she was.

Try It

Now read the letter that John Adams sent to Abigail on April 14, 1776. Following the steps outlined above, answer the following questions. What is his first response? What does he think about his wife's concern for women's rights? Do you think that he shares her opinions? What does he mean when he says "We have only the name of masters . . .?" Compare John Adams's letter with Abigail Adams's. What do you think about the roles of men and women during that time?

Apply It

Ask your parents, grandparents, or other older relatives for a letter they have saved. Read through it several times. Look for information in the letter that helps you to learn about the writer and about the person being addressed, as well as about any event to which the letter refers.

SOCIAL SYSTEMS

Study Skills

From these letters, what can the students infer about the relationship between John and Abigail Adams? *(Sample answers: They were comfortable expressing their feelings to each other and probably regarded each other with fondness and respect. There is humor in both letters, despite the more serious tone of Abigail's.)*

HISTORY

Critical Thinking

Point out that people do not write personal letters as frequently today as they did in the 1700s. What are the reasons for this change? *(New technologies, such as the telephone, make it easier to communicate in different ways. People have more recreational distractions, such as television and movies.)* What kinds of primary sources, other than letters, would help people of the future to know about the students and their families? *(Photographs, home movies and videotapes, audio tapes, computer records)*

Answers to Try It

Students should consider what they know about John Adams and what he was doing in April 1776 (delegate to the Second Continental Congress). John's first response is to laugh. He does not share his wife's concerns for women's rights. When he says, "We have only the name of masters," he means that men are actually the subjects of their wives. Students' evaluations of the roles of men and women will depend on whether they identify with John or with Abigail.

Answers to Apply It

Encourage students to find dates, references to events, and other information that will help them place the letter writer in a certain time frame. Ask them to look for references that indicate the difference between past and present, particularly in the social system. These references may include technology, transportation, and the roles of men and women in the family and at work.

Visual Learning

Paintings can also be primary sources, if they were done by a painter who had seen the subject. What can students infer about Abigail Adams from her portrait? *(She was a serious, determined person, careful about her dress and grooming, but not vain about her appearance or her position.)*

INTRODUCE

Have students read the lesson title and discuss its meaning. Point out that the word *articles* in this context refers to items in a written contract. The Articles of Confederation is a list of the conditions agreed to by the members of the confederation.

Tell students to read the Thinking Focus and recall what they learned about the division of power between the states and the national government in Lesson 1. Ask students to read the lesson to find out the problems caused by the weakness of the central government.

Key Terms

Vocabulary strategies: T36–37

sovereignty—the supreme power or authority that an independent country or state has within its borders

term of office—a limited period of time during which an elected official serves the public

1775 1777 1785 1787 1789

LESSON 2

The Articles of Confederation

THINKING FOCUS

How did the Articles of Confederation divide power between the new national government and the state governments?

Key Terms

- sovereignty
- term of office

Imagine that you are a merchant in the new nation. One morning in 1785 as the tide goes out, your two-masted schooner slips away from a busy Philadelphia dock. It is bound for Charleston, South Carolina.

Your ship hugs the coastline during the trip south. With some of the profit from selling a cargo of wheat flour from Pennsylvania mills, you plan to buy indigo—a plant that produces a beautiful deep blue dye.

After a week, the ship finally docks in Charleston. Unlike Europe, where travel is restricted, the new nation allows you to enter another state freely without a passport.

Despite any differences between you and the people in Charleston, you will be doing business together as citizens of the same nation. The Articles of Confederation promise the "free inhabitants of each of these states . . . all privileges and immunities of free citizens in the several states."

You are anticipating difficulties, however. You can now trade freely with merchants from different states, without excessive import taxes and regulations. But you still face the problem of doing business with different money issued by each state. You worry that the money you will receive will not be equal to the value of your cargo, and you will not be able to spend it when you return home to Philadelphia. Often money issued by the states is worth only a fraction of its face value. You believe that the need for uniform currency—worth the same amount wherever it is spent—points to the need for a strong central government to issue that currency and to vouch for its value.

➤ *The docks and shipyards of the Philadelphia waterfront spread out along the banks of the Delaware River.*

Objectives

1. Explain how European acceptance of the Articles of Confederation helped Americans win the Revolutionary War.
2. Compare some aspects of the confederation government in 1783 with the federal government today.
3. Relate the government's inability to pay soldiers to currency problems.

Graphic Overview

	Central Government	State Government
Diplomacy	control foreign affairs	enforce treaties
Finance and Commerce	set value of coins, weights, and measures	tax citizens, imports, and exports
Military	appoint army officers	
Law	negotiate between states	direct court system

Confederation Works for Wartime

Even before all the states accepted the Articles, Congress had used them as a working plan of government. Americans desperately needed a system by which to raise and pay an army to fight Great Britain.

No member of Congress played a more important role in funding the Revolutionary army than the prominent Philadelphia merchant Robert Morris. As superintendent of finance, he borrowed money and bought supplies to keep Washington's troops on the battlefield. Morris was dedicated to strengthening the Confederation, at the same time making a profit for himself and his friends.

Congress also sent diplomats to Europe to gain support for the Confederation's military efforts against Great Britain. After the colonists' victory at Saratoga in 1777, American diplomats showed off a French translation of the Articles to demonstrate that the United States had a serious new government worthy of aid. Benjamin Franklin, John Adams, Thomas Jefferson, and John Jay impressed Europeans with their arguments. They gained diplomatic and financial support from France, Holland, Russia, and Spain.

After the war ended in 1781, the Confederation government sent three seasoned diplomats—Franklin, Adams, and Jay—to Paris to negotiate a peace treaty. They won not only Great Britain's recognition of American independence but also all British territory south of the Great Lakes and east of the Mississippi River, the Northwest Territory, and the old Southwest Territory. The victory at the peace table in 1783 was as stunning as the battle at Yorktown. ■

This painting shows Franklin in the French royal court at Versailles surrounded by a crowd of admirers.

■ *How did the Articles help win support from Europeans for the American cause?*

The Articles Define Government

At first, most Americans found it difficult to think of their new confederation as a true union. The Articles were an attempt to create a national government that would unite 13 very diverse colonies. Although the new government was weak, Thomas Jefferson regarded it as a model—the best government "existing or that ever did exist."

Congressional Powers

The Articles did give the Congress a few of the powers typical of an independent, sovereign nation. For example, Congress alone had the **sovereignty**—the supreme authority and power—to conduct foreign affairs, send ambassadors, and negotiate treaties. The individual states had given up such powers when they signed the Articles. Congress controlled the national army and appointed its officers. It held the sole right to coin money, to establish weights and measures, and to operate a national postal system. The chart on the following page shows how the postal system worked.

The national government con-

DEVELOP

Have students write on a sheet of paper "Powers of Confederation Government" and "Powers of State Governments." Ask them to list the powers of each as they read.

The woman in the painting is placing on Franklin's head a laurel wreath, a symbol of honor and glory.

HISTORY

Critical Thinking

Ask students to explain why gaining European support was so important to the United States. *(England was powerful, the United States lacked financial resources.)* Ask them to speculate whether Americans could have won the war on their own.

■ *The Articles showed that the states had a central government with the authority to raise an army and to make treaties.*

Access Strategy

Ask students to imagine that a field trip for tomorrow has just been announced. Because there is no time to raise money before the trip, the class agrees to borrow the money and raise the funds to repay the debt as soon as possible. How will the class treasurer make sure that everyone helps raise funds? What can be done if some students refuse to help or others do less than their share? Have one student write on the board the class responses to these questions.

Repaying the war debt created a similar problem for the Confederation government after the Revolutionary War. Tell students that this lesson will explain how the government dealt with the problem.

Access Activity

Ask student to name situations that have mandatory attendance requirements. *(Students attending school, adults showing up at work)* What would happen if attendance were voluntary? *(Some people would only attend when they felt like it.)* What would happen if paying taxes became voluntary in this country? *(The government would not have enough money.)*

POLITICAL SYSTEMS

Visual Learning

Using the diagram on this page, have students describe differences between the mail system of the 1780s and the mail system of today. *(Used to be slower and more expensive; recipient paid postage)* How would the lives of people in the 1700s have been different if a speedier means of communication had existed? *(People would have been more informed about events in distant areas.)*

■ *It lacked the power to enforce its decisions.*

Delivery! The Journey of a Letter in 1790

Write
Sender writes in cramped script with a quill pen on single sheet because of paper shortage. No envelopes. The letter is folded, addressed and sealed with wax.

Post
Sender goes into town to hand letter to appointed post master, usually an innkeeper or merchant.

Deliver
Post rider travels between towns on the post road, often through wilderness. Road-side mile markers are used for setting postage.

Receive
Recipient claims letter from closest post-master, paying the postage at the rate of 6 cents per single sheet per 25 miles.

Parts of the postal system shown in the diagram were inherited from the British colonial system. This milestone was located along the old post road between New York and Boston.

■ *What was the national government's most serious weakness under the Articles of Confederation?*

sisted only of Congress and the agencies created by it. Congress established four important departments: foreign affairs, war, finance, and the post office. These were forerunners of executive agencies that exist in the federal government today.

Limited Sovereignty

The Articles deliberately kept the central government weak so that the freedom of each state was not threatened. There was no executive branch to enforce the will of Congress. The "president" was merely a member of Congress appointed to preside over each congressional session. The lack of a national court meant that disputes between states had to be settled either through negotiation in interstate commissions or in state courts. Because each state court tended to favor its own state, this policy did not work well.

All important decisions in Congress required the approval of at least nine states. Even so, resolutions of Congress were merely recommendations to the states, unless the resolution dealt with matters over which Congress had total control. For example, although Congress could make treaties, it could not enforce them. When New York took away lands owned by British Loyalists—a violation of the 1783 treaty—Congress could do nothing.

In addition, members of Congress were elected for only a year-long **term of office** and could not serve more than three of these limited periods within six years. Thus, by the time a delegate had acquired enough experience to be effective in Congress, he was forced to leave Congress for at least three years. ■

Morris Funds the National Treasury

Robert Morris had to deal with the government's biggest problem: Congress lacked the power under the Articles to tax its citizens directly. Congress assigned to each state a share of the funds needed by the national government. The share was based on the value of that state's land. Congress could only hope that the state governments would be cooperative and collect money for them. The national government was often fortunate to receive even one-fourth of the funds requested from the states.

Critical Thinking

Ask students to compare the role of the president of the Congress under the Articles of Confederation with the role of the President of the United States today. *(Formerly only "presided" over Congress; not an "executive")*

Economic Context

The following facts help to explain the new nation's severe money problems. Congress requested $10 million from the states for 1782 and 1783 but received less than 15 percent of this amount. By 1784, the nation's war debt was $35 million and growing. Congress could not raise enough money even to pay the interest on the debt.

The nation's debt led to a scarcity of hard currency—silver and gold—especially among the poor. Because many merchants refused to accept paper money, farmers were unable to pay their debts or to buy seeds and tools.

Furthermore, during the war Congress had said that when peace came, every army officer would receive half pay for life and every enlisted soldier would be given a bonus based on length of service. Because there was no money, Congress could only give papers promising later payment. Poor veterans, desperate for cash, sold them to speculators for a fraction of their face value.

Understanding Government Revenues

Robert Morris, the first Superintendent of Finance of the new Confederation, was the first to juggle one of the most challenging checkbooks around—that of the United States government. Morris had a hard time gathering enough funds to pay the bills, and things haven't changed since then. Today, the President, his financial advisers, and the Congress spend much time and energy trying to finance the needs of the American society. The money needed and spent by the government is called revenues.

Incoming Revenues

The term income refers to money collected, whether it be the income of an individual worker or of a huge government. The national and state governments receive their income from various sources. For example, some state government funds come from fees charged for the use of parks, for driver's licenses, or for permission to operate a business. The national, or federal, government can sell or lease some of the millions of acres of land it owns.

By far, the largest source of government income is taxes. Taxes take many forms. For example, many state and local governments collect sales tax, a percentage of each purchase made by citizens added on to the price of goods. Property owners pay taxes on their homes, cars, and land. In 1913, the Sixteenth Amendment to the Constitution allowed the federal government to make citizens pay a tax on a portion of their incomes. Today, this income tax is the chief source of income for the federal government.

Federal Government Funding, 1997

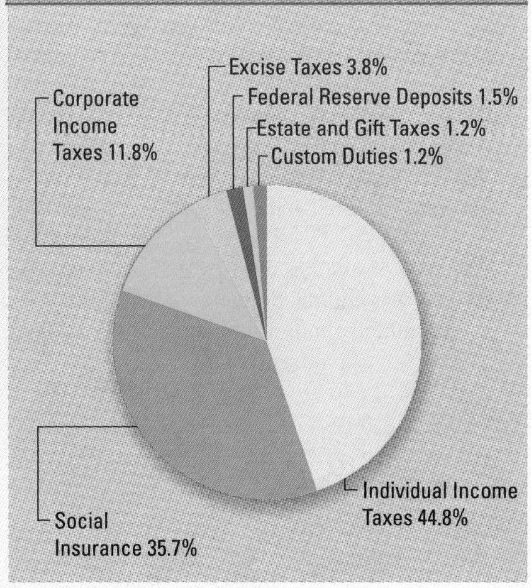

Outgoing Revenues

From this variety of sources, the federal government collects many billions of dollars each year. In fact, by the late 1980s, the national budget exceeded $1 trillion per year. Deciding how to spend all this money is one of the principal jobs of the Congress. Each year, Congress and the President must decide the relative importance, for example, of military spending, stopping the drug problem, or cleaning up the environment. These decisions affect all of our lives.

The Problem of Debt

Since the 1950s, Congress has been spending more money than it takes in. The government makes up the difference by borrowing money. By 1995, the national debt had ballooned to about $5 trillion. That translates to about $19,000 for every man, woman, and child in the country.

In one sense, government funding has improved since Morris's time. Today, taxes provide a huge and dependable source of income for our nation's government. On the other hand, we have overspent our budgets for many years. As a result, about $233 billion, or about 15 percent of the federal government's income, goes simply to pay the interest on our debt. The growth of this debt has created a financial situation that Robert Morris could never have imagined.

ECONOMICS

Critical Thinking

Government funding remains as much an issue today as it was during the early years of the nation. What problem with funding does the government face today? *(For many years, we have spent more than we have taken in, so we have a huge national debt.)* If students were to try to resolve some of the national debt problems, what questions might they ask as they first approach the task? *(How much money do we have to spend? How much do government services cost? Where does the money come from? Is there any way we could save money? Is there any way we could raise more money?)*

Science Connection

"Not worth a continental" is a phrase that came into use because of the devaluing of paper currency issued by the Continental Congress. Many people regarded paper money as worthless. They wanted coins—especially gold and silver. Have students research the properties of these two metals to find out what makes them so valuable. What other metals are used for coins? How are coins minted?

Research

Although Congress had sovereignty in foreign affairs, the weakness of the government under the Articles of Confederation allowed pirates to flourish. The Barbary Coast pirates reached the height of their power during the 1600s, but they were still active into the 1800s. Have students research the history of these pirates. What were their ships like? What countries did they come from, and why did some sultans encourage piracy? Students can report orally to the class.

Study Skills

Have students read the pie chart on this page. On a separate sheet of paper, students should list the sources of federal government funding in decreasing order. In small groups, students can use government publications to research one source of funding.

ECONOMICS

Critical Thinking

Call a bank or check the newspaper to find out the current rate of exchange of U.S. dollars to German marks and Japanese yen. Present this information to the class. How would a change in the rate of exchange affect travel to each country? Trade with each? *(It would affect how much a dollar can buy.)*

■ *People would have to change money whenever they crossed state borders. States would have to agree on rates of exchange.*

CLOSE

Tell students to answer the Thinking Focus. Copy on the board the structure of the Graphic Overview on page 90. Have students complete the chart by using the lists that they made as they read. As a reteaching of the lesson, have students name the problems of the Confederation and the reasons for these problems.

Morris worked heroically to keep the government financially solvent, sometimes purchasing army supplies with his personal funds. Still, the national treasury was often bare. In a letter sent to Morris in 1783, General Washington wrote:

> *I have often reflected, with much Solicitude, upon the disagreeableness of your Situation and the Negligence of the several States, in not enabling you to do that Justice to the public Creditors, which their Demands require. I wish the Step you have taken, may sound the Alarm to their inmost Souls, and rouse them to a just Sense of their own Interest, honor and Credit.*

Matters worsened as the Revolutionary War was ending. Soldiers grumbled about not being paid, and many feared that they would never receive their promised wages.

In March 1783, a group of soldiers and officers in Newburgh, New York, plotted to overthrow the government. General Washington had to use his prestige to stop this revolt. As he put on his spectacles before speaking to the men at Newburgh, he said: "Gentlemen, I have grown gray in your service, and now I am going blind." He silenced the protesters, at least temporarily. Even so, other soldiers marched on Philadelphia three months later to demand payment for their services, forcing the government to flee to Princeton, New Jersey.

During this time, Congress had been printing money to pay for military supplies and salaries without having the gold to back up the paper. Many people would not accept the national government's paper currency —basically worthless—as payment for debts. So the states issued their own paper currency, backed only by "full faith and credit"—that is, people's confidence that the state could pay its debts. People who traveled from state to state had to carry or obtain different kinds of paper money. Naturally, this hampered trade between the states.

Many states wanted to create a strong currency, but the lack of gold and silver in circulation made this task difficult. The states set limits on the amount of currency that they put into circulation. They also raised taxes to pay their debts promptly. These measures made borrowing expensive and led to a crisis in western Massachusetts. Indeed, the problems of banking and currency would not be resolved for another 100 years. ■

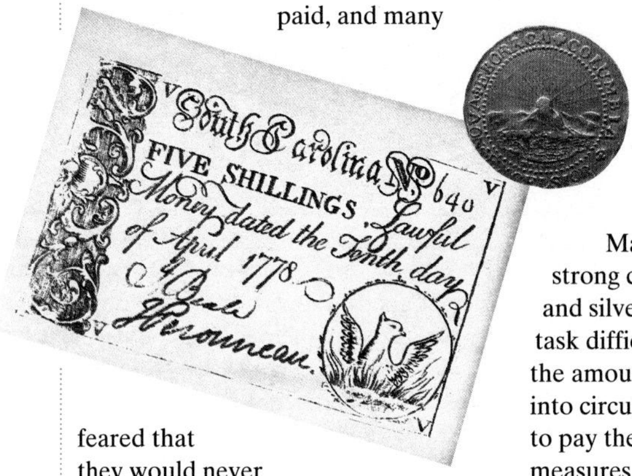

➤ *This gold coin, minted by New York in 1787, was called a doubloon. The face value of this paper money, printed by South Carolina in 1778, was five shillings. The names doubloon and shilling came from European money of the time.*

■ *If the states still issued their own money today, how would trade and travel within the country be different?*

REVIEW

1. **FOCUS** How did the Articles of Confederation divide power between the new national government and the state governments?
2. **CONNECT** Relate Washington's point of view in his letter to Morris to Washington's problems with feeding and clothing his army during the Revolutionary War.
3. **POLITICAL SYSTEMS** What are some aspects of the early government that have been carried over into the twentieth century?
4. **CRITICAL THINKING** What are some advantages and disadvantages of a weak central government?
5. **WRITING ACTIVITY** Imagine that you are Robert Morris trying to persuade the states to pay their shares into the treasury. Write a convincing letter to them.

Homework Options

Ask students to look at an encyclopedia to find out about the history of the postal system. Have them write a brief report on their findings.

Study Guide: page 13.

Answers to Review Questions

1. Congress had the power to conduct foreign affairs, raise an army, coin money, establish weights and measures, and run the postal system. The states controlled commerce, the courts, taxation, and law enforcement.
2. Because of his own experience with a starving, freezing army, Washington could sympathize with Morris.
3. We still have a national postal system and government departments for defense, finance, and foreign affairs.
4. Sample answer: A weak central government cannot interfere with states' rights, nor can it enforce its laws or unify the states. Allow for personal opinion.
5. Students should base their letters on the lesson.

1775 1777 1779 1781 1782 1787 1789

LESSON 3

The Crisis of Confederation

Five hundred angry farmers, armed with pitchforks and wooden boards, stood with their leader Daniel Shays, near Springfield, in western Massachusetts. They were attempting to intimidate the state's supreme court, which was hearing cases against farmers who could not pay their private debts and state property taxes.

It was September 1786, and the end of the war had not brought prosperity. The states were taxing the farmers heavily—in the gold and silver no one had—to pay off war debts. Turning to wealthy merchants, the farmers had borrowed the money they needed to pay their taxes. Then, unable to pay these private debts, many farmers faced having their farms auctioned off. Their many petitions for relief to the merchant-dominated state legislature in Boston had gone unanswered.

Daniel Shays had fought at Bunker Hill and Saratoga. In 1780, he had returned home to wait for payment for his military service. No payment came, and his debts piled up. He feared "the spectre of debtor's jail always . . . close by." Most of the men with him at Springfield were also angry veterans and, like him, were in debt.

The Massachusetts governor ordered the protesters to disband. When they refused, he called out a special militia financed by the state's rich merchants. Four months later, in January 1787, Shays again led his band, now over two thousand strong, to the federal arsenal in Springfield. Its defenders opened fire, killing four of the rebels, and Shays's force fled.

The governor's militia chased down the rebels—taking away for a period of three years their right to vote, hold elective office, and serve as jurors. By March 1787, six months after the rebellion began, it was over.

Shock waves from Shays's Rebellion spread beyond Massachusetts. Wealthy creditors around the nation wanted protection against future armed rebellion. Under the Articles of Confederation, the national government could not supply it.

THINKING FOCUS

Why did the Articles of Confederation fail?

Key Terms

- commerce
- territory

This engraving shows a group of angry farmers seizing a Massachusetts court house during Shays's Rebellion.

INTRODUCE

Point out the title and discuss the concept of crisis. Students should understand that a crisis in political affairs is an unstable condition. During a crisis, change often occurs.

Have students read the Thinking Focus and predict the reasons for the failure of the Articles of Confederation. Have them read to confirm or reject their predictions.

Key Terms

Vocabulary strategies: T36–37

commerce—the buying and selling of goods on a large scale

territory—an area belonging to the United States but not included within any existing state

Graphic Overview

Causes
- no power to tax
- no power to regulate commerce

→

Worthless Money

No Import Taxes

→

Effects
- can't pay soldiers
- farmers' rebellion
- little income
- states compete
- U.S. can't retaliate against Britain

Objectives

1. Describe conflicts between the new national government and the 13 states.
2. Explain the significance of the Northwest Ordinance.
3. Analyze the factors leading up to the Annapolis Convention.

DEVELOP

As students read, have them list the achievements of the Confederation government and the reasons it ultimately failed.

HISTORY

Critical Thinking

Why did the Barbary Coast pirates cause more problems for American ships after the Revolution than before? *(No longer British protection)*

■ *They feared that the national government would make trade policies that would hurt their own particular states.*

How Do We Know?

ECONOMICS *Today, many objects from the China trade are preserved in museums such as the Peabody Museum in Salem, Massachusetts. Visitors to the museum can see the work of skilled Chinese artisans who crafted porcelain bowls and plates, jade and ivory carvings, and beautifully painted fans.*

A Critical Period in Finance and Trade

Without a strong national government, each state went its own way under the Articles of Confederation. For example, trade among the states would have benefited if everyone had agreed to accept the uniform paper money of the national government. Instead, the states' paper money, each with a different rate of exchange, caused confusion and arguments. Often, currency issued by a state bank was nearly worthless and merchants would not accept it as payment for goods. Sometimes they would allow only $0.25 for a note with a face value of $1.00.

Congress Lacks Power

The states would not allow Congress to regulate **commerce**—the buying and selling of goods among states and with foreign nations. In the area of commerce, the states retained complete sovereignty. When Great Britain closed its West Indian colonies to American trade, Congress had no power to retaliate by banning British ships from American ports.

Nor could Congress collect import taxes on foreign goods. The states had kept this right for themselves. "Easy states" took trade from the others by offering lower import tax rates to importers.

Furthermore, the states resisted any plans for national taxation. Without the power to tax, the national government could not raise enough money to function effectively.

The weakness of the government under the Articles of Confederation also showed in foreign affairs. The Barbary Coast pirates had, since the 1500s, freely accepted payments in exchange for letting any merchant ships pass through the Mediterranean Sea. The pirates operated out of the region of North Africa that includes present-day Libya and Tunisia. They captured many American ships and sold their sailors into slavery. The U.S. Government was too poor to buy back its citizens' freedom and too weak to prevent such hostile acts.

International Trade Grows

Still, the new United States was able to develop trade with France, the Netherlands, and Morocco. American ships also began to travel to the markets of the Dutch and French West Indies.

A year after the Treaty of Paris ended the Revolutionary War, the ship *Empress of China* sailed from Philadelphia to Canton, China, with a cargo of cotton and fur. Its voyage opened what became known as the China trade. The China trade would become increasingly important to the United States in the 1800s. ■

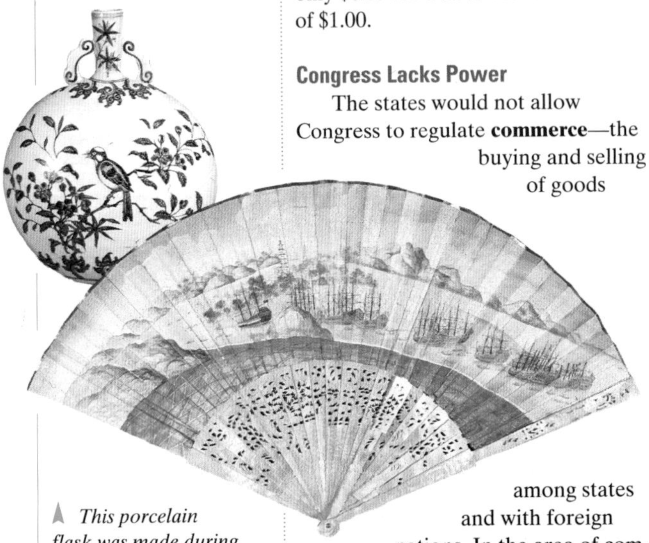

▲ *This porcelain flask was made during the Ming Dynasty, 1300s–1600s. The Chinese fan carries the only image known to exist of the* Empress of China*–the ship on the far left.*

■ *Why did the states refuse to allow the national government to regulate commerce between states and foreign countries?*

Success in Land Policy

In the midst of financial chaos, the Confederation government achieved its greatest success. After two years of debate, Congress agreed on how to develop the Northwest Territory.

In 1785 Congress issued a land ordinance, a legal order subdividing the western **territories**—possessions of the United States that were not states—into pieces called townships.

Access Activity

Read aloud the lesson opener on page 95 and discuss it with students. Were Shays and his followers justified in rebelling? Should they have been punished? Why or why not? *(Answers should weigh the farmers' rights against the government's authority.)*

Access Strategy

Ask students to raise their hands if they think there should be no school on Saturday. *(Presumably all hands go up.)* Inform students that they are unanimous, explaining that a decision is not unanimous unless every participant agrees to it. Move on to questions that will not receive a unanimous response. (Should there be school only two months per year?) Why is it difficult to achieve unanimous decisions? *(People have different needs, goals, and beliefs.)*

Explain that changing the Articles of Confederation required a unanimous vote of the states. Discuss why this might cause difficulties in solving the government's problems. *(States have different needs, goals, priorities, and beliefs.)*

A Moment in Time

A China-bound Sailor

10:16 A.M., August 18, 1789
Whampoa Beach, 4 miles from Canton, China

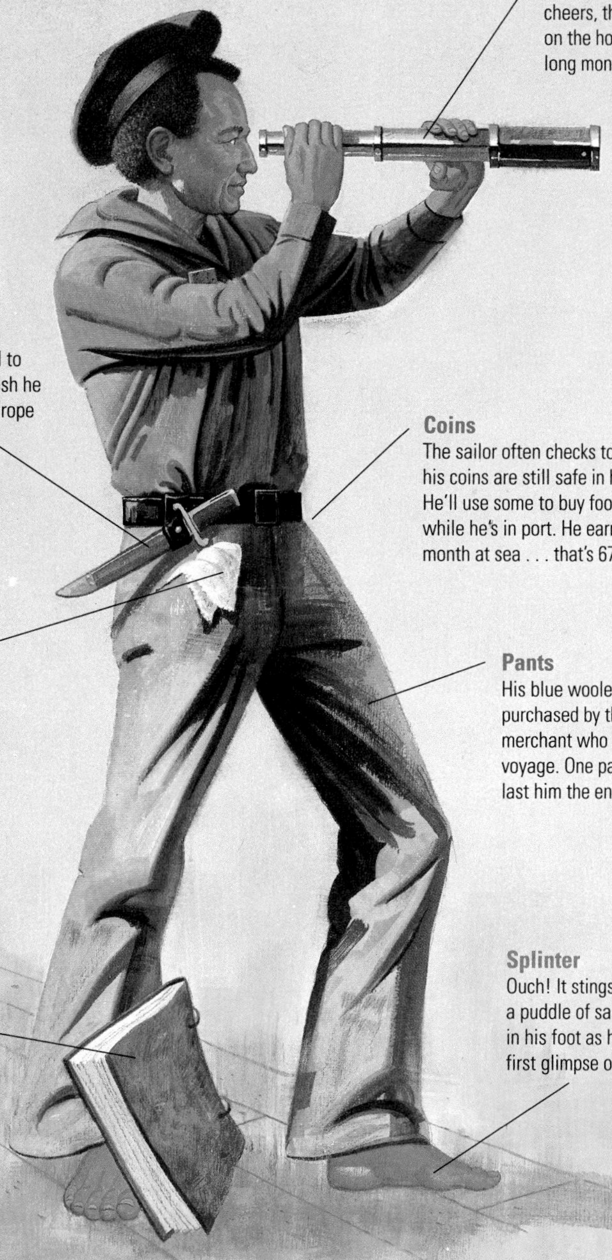

Spyglass
Land ho! He grabs the spyglass and runs to the side of the ship. The crew cheers, thrilled to see land on the horizon after eight long months at sea.

Knife
He uses this utensil to eat with, to clean fish he catches, and to cut rope for his hammock.

Coins
The sailor often checks to make sure his coins are still safe in his pocket. He'll use some to buy food and drink while he's in port. He earns $20 a month at sea . . . that's 67 cents a day.

Handkerchief
His girlfriend embroidered this linen handkerchief. With the money he makes from this voyage, they'll marry.

Pants
His blue woolen uniform was purchased by the New York merchant who financed this voyage. One pair of pants must last him the entire 14-month trip.

Splinter
Ouch! It stings as he stands in a puddle of salty water. It stuck in his foot as he ran to catch his first glimpse of China.

Sketchbook
With simple charcoal, he has drawn portraits of other crew members. After they reach Whompoa Beach, he'll draw temples, dragons, and chopsticks.

Note: Refer your students to this Moment in Time after they have read on page 96 about the beginning of the China Trade.

CULTURE

Visual Learning

Encourage students to imagine the reaction of American sailors upon their first exposure to Chinese civilization. *(Amazed by clothing, art, and food that were foreign to American experience; eager to tell families back home)*

More About the Sailor There were many black sailors on American ships from the late 1700s through the early 1800s. As many as one fourth of the seamen who served during the Revolutionary War were black.

Political Context

News of Shays's Rebellion spread shock waves throughout the new nation. To many, it seemed that "rule by the mob" was just around the corner. George Washington expressed such fears. "We are fast verging on anarchy and confusion," he wrote. "There are combustibles in every state which a spark might set fire to."

Most of the Founding Fathers shared Washington's concerns, but not Thomas Jefferson. From France, he wrote to his friends that he hoped "the spirit of resistance to government" would always be kept alive. "A little rebellion now and then is a good thing, and as necessary in the political world as storms in the physical. It prevents the degeneracy of government, and nourishes a general attention to the public affairs."

Visual Learning

Call students' attention to the caption in A Moment in Time on coins. Who will grow rich from the lucrative China Trade? *(Not the sailors; possibly the merchants who financed the voyage)*

GEOGRAPHY

Map and Globe Skills

Have students compare the map on this page with the political map of the United States on page 698 of the Atlas . What are some of the differences? *(For example, the Great Lakes were distorted in size and shape in the old map.)*

■ *Congress set up a system for accepting new territories as states.*

This 1785 map shows the territories affected by the land ordinances. In the words in the upper right corner, the mapmaker apologizes for the quality of his work.

To encourage education, some land in each of the townships was set aside for schools. The western territories shown on the map are the same lands earlier claimed by some of the states. These also included the lands ceded by Britain in the Treaty of Paris.

The Northwest Ordinance

Two years later, in 1787, Congress passed the Northwest Ordinance, thereby creating the three-step process by which territories could become new states. In the first step, Congress appointed a governor, secretary, and three judges for a territory.

After 5,000 free male inhabitants moved into the territory, the second step went into effect. The people elected a legislature and nonvoting delegates to Congress. When a territory had a population of 60,000 free male inhabitants, step three was to apply to become a state. The Northwest Territory could eventually be divided into no more than five and no fewer than three states. The Northwest Territory included the present states of Ohio, Michigan, Indiana, Illinois, Wisconsin, and part of Minnesota.

Any new states would be on an equal footing with the original states. In addition, Congress promised to protect rights and liberties in the new states and territories. Therefore, people who moved west were guaranteed freedom of religion, the first time that the national government stood for what later became a basic American right.

The Northwest Ordinance was a very enlightened piece of legislation. By defining in writing a policy to accept new territories as states equal to the others, Congress avoided the problem of governing colonies. It also avoided conflicts between the East and the West.

Promises Made

In the Northwest Ordinance, the United States promised that "utmost good faith shall always be observed toward the Indians; their land and property shall never be taken from them without their consent." With these words, the U.S. Government guaranteed sovereignty rights to the American Indians and respect for their territory. This promise would be broken in less than 10 years.

The ordinance also stated, "There shall be neither slavery nor involuntary servitude in the . . . territory." This had little effect on the slaves in the Northwest, but it encouraged antislavery feelings among most of the settlers. The states north of the Ohio River and east of the Mississippi River would later oppose extension of slavery into newer territories. ■

■ *Why was the Northwest Ordinance the crowning achievement of the Confederation?*

Visual Learning

Have students study the Great Seal of the United States, pictured on page 99. What is the eagle holding? *(13 arrows and an olive branch with 13 leaves)* Point out that the olive branch is a traditional symbol of peace. Which way is the eagle facing? *(Toward the olive branch)* What is the symbolism of this image? *(The desire for peace but the ability to wage war)*

Language Arts Connection

The term *E pluribus unum* is Latin for "one out of many." Have students find this phrase on the gold doubloon pictured on page 94 and on the coins and bills that we use today. In the Middle Ages, Latin had been the language of scholars; in the 1770s, well-educated people used Latin for mottoes. Encourage students to find the meanings of other Latin mottoes and phrases, such as *ex libris* (from the library of) and *caveat emptor* (let the buyer beware).

Writing a Letter

Ask students to imagine being an American in 1787—a member of a state legislature, a merchant, a farmer, or a war widow. They have just heard about Shays's Rebellion. Ask them to write a letter about the rebellion from the point of view of the person they have chosen to imagine. Have students read their letters aloud to the class.

Government at a Standstill

While Congress was passing the Northwest Ordinance, Americans were also attempting to strengthen the government under the Articles. Even former supporters of the Articles now admitted that the government was too weak. The states regularly ignored resolutions of the Congress. George Washington remarked that the Confederation was "little more than the shadow without the substance."

Tax Plans Blocked

In 1783, Congress proposed a national tax based on state populations—an act for which it had no specific authority under the Articles. In addition, in 1784 Congress asked for two revisions to the Articles that would give the national government some control over commerce. In 1786, New York rejected the national tax plan. The commercial revisions did not come close to being approved.

All states had to agree unanimously on any revision of the original Articles. A single state could block change, making it difficult to come to agreement on any issue.

Reforms Attempted

James Madison, a delegate to Congress from Virginia, worked to reform the Articles. However, he could serve as a delegate for only three years. Returning to Virginia, he was elected to the state assembly in 1785. At his urging, Virginia organized a national convention on the problems of interstate commerce.

The commission chose Annapolis, Maryland, as the site. Yet when the Annapolis Convention opened in September 1786, only five states sent delegates. The few delegates who attended felt unable to proceed.

Alarmed by crises such as Shays's Rebellion, Madison and the other Virginia delegates tried again. They enlisted the support of Alexander Hamilton, a politically minded New York lawyer and an important wartime aide to General Washington, to call another convention the following spring. The experience of ineffective government under the Articles of Confederation made it clear to more Americans that they needed a stronger national authority. Congress, therefore, authorized a convention to meet in Philadelphia in May 1787, to consider all the defects of the Articles of Confederation.

Despite the problems of this first American attempt at a national government, the Articles did serve as the first constitution of the new nation. The Articles' greatest legacies were the victory in the Revolutionary War and the peace with Great Britain and especially Benjamin Franklin's concept of "perpetual union." In adopting this phrase, Congress fostered the idea that they had produced an unbreakable union out of many states —*E pluribus unum.* ■

▲ *On June 20, 1782, Congress adopted the seal still used today. On the scroll in the eagle's beak is written* E pluribus unum—*also the motto on the gold coin minted by the state of New York (page 94).*

■ *Find evidence to support this statement: the Confederation was an inefficient and largely ineffective government.*

REVIEW

1. **FOCUS** Why did the Articles of Confederation fail?
2. **CONNECT** According to Benjamin Franklin, Americans were "on the right road to improvement, for we are making experiments." Why was government under the Articles a useful experiment in the long run?
3. **HISTORY** Explain how the three-step process of statehood in the Northwest Ordinance was far-sighted.
4. **CRITICAL THINKING** Why was it so difficult for Congress to move forward with its proposals for the government under the Confederation?
5. **WRITING ACTIVITY** Imagine you are a farmer in western Massachusetts in 1786 who has decided to participate in Shays's Rebellion. Write a petition to the governor that you want to pass around to your friends to sign.

CONSTITUTIONAL HERITAGE

Critical Thinking

In his Fourth of July oration of 1787, Dr. Benjamin Rush said, "The American War is over; but this is far from being the case with the American Revolution. On the contrary, nothing but the first act of the great drama is closed." Ask students to predict changes that they think will be made when the states meet in Philadelphia in 1787.

■ *Congress had difficulty in raising needed funds, in changing the Articles, and in getting states to accept its resolutions.*

CLOSE

Have students answer the Thinking Focus and evaluate the predictions they made before reading the lesson. Copy on the board the Graphic Overview from page 95 to help students review the lesson. Ask students to name the major accomplishments of the United States under the Articles of Confederation. *(Victory in war, peace treaty with Britain, passage of Northwest Ordinance, the concept of perpetual union)*

Answers to Review Questions

1. The central government was not given enough power to function effectively.
2. As the first constitution of the new nation, the Articles led to our Constitution.
3. By creating an orderly system for territories to become states, Congress avoided the problems inherent in governing colonies and conflicts between western settlers and eastern government.
4. Sample answer: Congress received little cooperation from the states, who wanted to protect their own interests. Allow for personal opinion.
5. Students should present effective arguments for participating in the rebellion.

Homework Options

Students can research safety in international travel today (for example, terrorist attacks) in newspapers and magazines.

Study Guide: page 14.

DISCOVERY PROCESS

Students will use the following steps in the discovery process to complete the activity.

Get Ready Have a notebook to organize information about an educational innovation today.

Find Out Discuss with parents or other adults how schools today are different from schools a generation ago.

Move Ahead Choose one educational change or reform, and research it in the library, using newspapers, magazines, or journals. Share what you've learned with the class.

Explore Some More Attend a local school board meeting to learn more about educational issues in your community.

Materials needed: books, newspapers, journals, schedule of local school board meetings

HISTORY
Critical Thinking

After the revolution, leaders began to see formal education as important for more people than just the upper classes. Why did leaders think that more Americans should be well educated? *(Sample answers: Citizens would be choosing leaders and needed to be informed. Educated people would help the United States to compete, economically, with other countries.)*

100

EXPLORING
Educating Americans

The leaders of the new nation knew that their republic couldn't survive without educated citizens. That's why the early years of the United States were a period of growth and change for American education. How has education changed in recent years to reflect today's society?

Get Ready

In the colonial period, many religious leaders started schools so people could learn to read the Bible and understand the word of God. Most colonists believed that only upper class children needed an academic education, but that everyone needed moral and practical education. To get that practical education, some boys became apprentices, and worked for an adult to learn a skill, like farming or printing, until they were old enough to make a living on their own.

In the years after the Revolution, people found another reason to sup-

➤ *A primer is another word for a textbook. This primer was published in the 1780s to help Mohawk children learn to read and write both English and their own language.*

(A)
P R I M E R,
FOR THE USE OF THE
MOHAWK CHILDREN,

To acquire the SPELLING and READING of their own, as well as to get acquainted with the ENGLISH, Tongue; which for that Purpose is put on the opposite Page.

WAERIGHWAGHSAWE
IKSAONGOENWA

Tsiwaondad-derighhonny Kaghyadoghsera; Nayon-deweyestaghk ayeweanaghnódon ayeghyádow Ka-niyenkehàga Kaweanondaghkouh; Dyorheaf-hàga oni tsinihadiweanotea.

(OO)
O

LONDON,
PRINTED BY C.BUCKTON, GREAT PULTNEY-STREET.
1786.

100

Chapter 3

Objectives

1. Use library resources to identify recent educational changes and issues. (Study Skills 1)
2. Explain the need for educated citizens in a democratic society. (Citizenship 2)

Activity

Have students discuss the names of different schools in their community. If schools are named after people, have them research those people. Then discuss the values that are reflected by the name of each school. Do they honor local or national leaders? Are they named for some geographic element of their community? Finally, ask students to think of a new name for their school, and explain why they chose it.

Have students work in small groups. Ask each group to decide what will be most important for them to know when they are adults. Then have each group create a high school curriculum to meet those needs. Their curriculum should be a list and short description of courses for grades 9–12. Groups should then compare curricula, and discuss how and why they differ from the real high school curriculum in their community.

port education. They believed that if the United States was going to be a democracy, its citizens needed to be well educated. Because citizens had a role in choosing their leaders, they needed to understand the political issues of the day.

People believed that educated minds were necessary both for scientific advances and for the democracy to grow. As a result, many schools, colleges, and state universities were founded. A few of the colleges that opened at this time were the University of North Carolina, Georgetown University, and Williams College. Schools also began to teach "practical" subjects, like modern languages, algebra, and the sciences. Some people recommended dropping traditional courses, like Latin and Greek.

The number of public schools that were supported by taxes or state subsidies increased at this time. Churches and charitable associations also ran schools for children whose parents could not pay for their education. John Adams reflected a growing sentiment when he said he wanted education for "every class and rank of people, down to the lowest and poorest."

New schools for young women also opened as Americans began to believe the country needed educated women to raise good citizens. Women's colleges did not yet exist, but a number of academies for girls opened. Schools for black students, often run by black churches, also increased at this time. As Northern states began doing away with slavery, schools for free blacks opened in those states.

Find Out

Many of these new schools and ideas about education were a reaction to changes in the society and government. Do you know of any new ideas or policies for education that reflect changes that have occurred in our society? (The use of computers is one example.)

One important innovation in education today is technology. This class, for example, is part of a teleconference, in which they can see and talk with someone many miles away.

One way to start your research is to talk to your parents or other adults about what their schools were like, and to find out how what you study or do in school is different from what they did. You might also discuss how other educational issues in the news reflect today's society and politics.

Move Ahead

You'll need to go to the library to find information, probably in articles from newspapers or magazines, about an educational issue you're interested in. Your librarian or teacher can give you the names of publications focusing on teaching and education. Once you've found more information, share what you've learned with your class and see if anyone else has information on your topic.

Explore Some More

To learn about even more educational issues, plan a group or class trip to a school board meeting in your community. By going to a meeting of your own school board, you can learn of proposed changes in education that might affect you. You will probably even have a chance to tell the board your opinions.

CITIZENSHIP

Critical Thinking

Ask students to think about how education in the United States has changed in the past 200 years. *(Sample answer: Free public education is available to all students, schools provide programs to meet the needs of diverse learners)* Then ask how the changes in education have reflected changes in American society. *(All adult citizens, not just white men, participate in government. As a nation, we value the contributions of all groups of people, schools try to provide everyone with the tools they need to succeed.)*

Collaborative Strategy

A recommended strategy for this lesson is heterogeneous grouping. For more details about collaborative strategies, see pages T34–35.

Answers to Reviewing Key Terms

A. Sample answers:

1. Some colonists wanted a federal government with strong central authority while others wanted a confederation, a more informal group of states.
2. Colonists who wanted a confederation were afraid to give sovereignty, or absolute power, to the national government.
3. Today our executive, the President, has a four-year term of office that can be repeated once.

B. Answers:

1. False. The idea of limited sovereignty appealed to people who wanted to have a say in their own government.
2. True.
3. False. The Congress made the laws.
4. True.
5. False. The Northwest Ordinance provided clear steps for becoming a state.

Answers to Exploring Concepts

A. Answers:

Strengths: 2-No authoritarian monarch like George III; 3-Postal service was more dependable; 4-Strong defense of country; 5-Citizens voted for their rulers; 9-Avoided conflicts between East and West.

Weaknesses: 1-No way to settle disputes between states; 6-Delegates had to leave just as they gained experience; 7-Government did not have enough money; 8-Congress could not respond to problems with foreign countries; 10-One state could block changes.

Chapter Review

Reviewing Key Terms

commerce (p. 96)
confederation (p. 84)
constitution (p. 83)
executive (p. 85)
federal (p. 84)
legislature (p. 85)
sovereignty (p. 91)
term of office (p. 92)
territory (p. 96)

A. In each of the following pairs, the two terms are related in some way. Write a sentence for each pair that clearly explains the relationship between the two terms.

1. federal, confederation
2. confederation, sovereignty
3. executive, term of office

B. Based on what you have read in the chapter, decide whether each of the following statements is true or false. If it is false, change the sentence to a true statement.

1. The idea of sovereignty appealed to people who wanted to have a say in their own government.
2. A constitution could provide for either a weak or a strong central government.
3. Under the Articles of Confederation, the executive branch made the laws for the government.
4. Every member of the legislative branch was allowed to serve for a certain term.
5. The people in the western territory had no way of developing state governments.

Exploring Concepts

A. On a separate sheet of paper make a table like the one below. Decide whether each of the phrases listed at right belongs in either the "strengths" or "weaknesses" column. Place the number of the phrase in the proper column. Then next to the number , write a short explanation of your choice. For example, Number 1, "no national court," has been placed in the "weaknesses" box because without a national court there was no way for the government to settle disputes between states.

Articles of Confederation

Strengths	Weaknesses
	1. No way to settle disputes between states.

1. no national court
2. no executive branch
3. Congress operates national postal service
4. Congress controls national army
5. republican form of government
6. member of Congress limited to three-year term
7. Congress unable to tax citizens directly
8. Congress unable to regulate commerce
9. Congress decides use of western territories
10. changes in the Articles required unanimous state agreement

B. Support each of the following statements with facts and details from the chapter. Then use your responses to write a statement about the beliefs and values people at that time had about government.

1. In creating a written plan of government, Americans found different models in their English and colonial heritages.
2. When the Articles of Confederation were written, Americans had several reasons for wanting a weak central government.
3. The new state governments provided additional models of republicanism.
4. Congress successfully used its few powers in several ways.

B. Sample answers:

1. Americans borrowed from England's Magna Carta and Bill of Rights, and from the Mayflower Compact.
2. Americans feared a tyrannical government with strong executives like King George III or the governors of the colonies. They wanted their local and state governments to make most of the decisions.
3. Many states required legislators to live and own property in the community they represented. Legislators were usually elected annually. In about half of the states the legislature chose the governor.
4. Congress sent diplomats to Paris to negotiate a successful peace treaty with England, developed trade with other countries, and passed the Northwest Ordinance to develop the new territories.

Written statement: Students should review their answers to the four questions above and then write a clear statement about the views of government at that time.

Reviewing Skills

> *I cannot say that I think you very generous to the ladies. For, whilst you are proclaiming peace and good will to men, emancipating all nations, you insist upon retaining an absolute power over wives. But you must remember that arbitrary power is like most other things which are very hard—very liable to be broken; and, notwithstanding all your wise laws and maxims, we have it in our power not only to free ourselves but to subdue our masters, and without violence throw both your natural and legal authority at our feet.*
>
> Abigail to John, May 7, 1776

1. What type of primary source material is shown above? Why are such documents important to historians?
2. Read the letter shown above from Abigail Adams to her husband John dated May 7, 1776. Look up any unfamiliar words such as *emancipating, arbitrary* and *liable*. As a primary source, what does this letter tell you about the relationship between John Adams and his wife?
3. In Abigail Adams's letter to her husband John dated March 31, 1776 (page 88), she asks him to "Regard us then as beings, placed by providence under your protection, and in imitation of the Supreme Being make use of that power only for our happiness." As a primary source, what does this letter tell you about how Abigail Adams felt about the roles of women at that time?
4. Create a timeline for the events in this chapter. Then identify any relationships you see among the events shown on your timeline.
5. Suppose you wanted to find out what daily life was like for a British soldier living in the colonies. What kind of source would you look for in your library?

Using Critical Thinking

1. Some people have suggested that the terms of today's Representative and Senators should be limited, as were those of the members of Congress under the Articles of Confederation. What would be the advantages and disadvantages of setting a limit on the number of terms someone could serve in Congress?
2. What important powers does the national government have today under the Constitution that it did not have under the Articles of Confederation?
3. Under the Articles of Confederation, states had to agree unanimously on any revision of the original Articles. Do you think this was fair? Why or why not? What are advantages and disadvantages of unanimous rule?
4. The United States has had two major political parties since the early 1800s. What are the advantages and disadvantages of a two-party system of government?

Preparing for Citizenship

1. **WRITING ACTIVITY** Robert Morris, once one of the richest men in the colonies, died penniless and forgotten. Find out more about his life and the contributions he made to the nation in its earliest years. Write a report on your findings.
2. **ART ACTIVITY** The United States flag has gone through a number of changes throughout its history. On June 14, 1777, the Second Continental Congress passed a flag resolution. It said that the flag of the United States would have 13 alternating red and white stripes and 13 white stars on a field of blue, but it did not say exactly how the stars should be arranged. Design your own flag for the United States, based on the information given in the flag resolution.
3. **COLLABORATIVE LEARNING** In small groups, make a list of expenses for which the government attempted to collect taxes during the time period covered in this chapter. Then research the range of programs and other efforts for which present-day federal taxes are paid.
4. **COLLABORATIVE LEARNING** Stage a class debate over the Articles of Confederation. One team will support the Articles, and the other will argue that they need to be changed. Follow Robert's Rules of Order in managing the debate.

Answers to Reviewing Skills

1. It is a personal letter; historians read letters to see how a particular person thought and felt about events.
2. Her tone suggests that she felt comfortable enough to criticize him and felt confident that he would listen.
3. She thought that woman's relationship to man was somewhat like the relationship of humans to God. She wanted men to take care of women but not to misuse the power they had.
4. Students should include these events: The Articles of Confederation and Perpetual Union presented to the Second Continental Congress (1775); Articles of Confederation adopted by the Second Continental Congress (1777); Revolutionary War ends and Articles of Confederation approved (1781); peace treaty signed (1783); Shays's Rebellion (1786–1787); Northwest Ordinance and Constitutional Convention (1787).
5. Students may suggest a diary, a book of letters, or a book of artifacts and drawings from that period.

Answers to Using Critical Thinking

1. Suggest that students do research to find the longest terms ever held by representatives and senators. Students may also want to look at the events that led to limiting the number of presidential terms.
2. Students should read the Constitution, beginning on page 636, and compare it with the Articles of Confederation.
3. Ask students to describe experiences in which they have had to make decisions in a group.
4. Point out that in a class discussion there are often more than two points of view on a subject. Ask students to research third political parties and find out what kinds of successes and failures they have had.

Answers to Preparing for Citizenship

1. **WRITING ACTIVITY** Encourage students to look for primary sources and to use quotations in their reports. Refer students to "Understanding Government Revenues" on page 93.
2. **ART ACTIVITY** Compare student designs with the flags shown on page 127. Are there common patterns that students have used?
3. **COLLABORATIVE LEARNING** Encourage students to find newspaper articles on the federal budget and to discuss how federal money should be used.
4. **COLLABORATIVE LEARNING** Prepare a handout explaining Robert's Rules of Order. Suggest that students review their responses to the chart in Exploring Concepts.

CHAPTER 4

Planning at a Glance

The Constitutional Convention

	Objectives	Reading Support *and* Other Resources	Diverse Learning Strategies
Lesson 1 The Constitutional Convention *pp. 108–113* 2–3 days **Literature** **"Autobiography of Ben Franklin" and "Poor Richard's Almanac"** *pp. 114–117*	• Explain how the Constitution was the result of compromises. • Describe the debates between small and large states regarding representation. • Summarize the disagreements between Northern and Southern states at the Convention. • Evaluate the personal role of major delegates in the Convention's outcome.	• **Workbook** or **Reading Support:** pp. 49–52 Review p. 12 Extra Support/Transition p. 12 Multi-lang. Sum. pp. 23–24 • **Other Resources:** Geography Kit, Poster 1, Study Guide p. 15	Access Strat. **(SDAIE)** TE p. 107 Map and Globe Skills **(Visual)** TE p. 112 Collaborative Act. **(Visual)** TE p. 112 Audiotapes of Multi-language Lesson Summaries **(Auditory)**
Lesson 2 The Ratification Debate *pp. 118–122* 1–2 days	• State the basic arguments of the Federalists and the Antifederalists for and against ratification. • Describe the political process that led to the states' ratification of the Constitution. • Explain why many people thought the Constitution was incomplete.	• **Workbook** or **Reading Support:** pp. 53–56 Review p. 13 Extra Support/Transition p. 13 Multi-lang. Sum. pp. 25–26 • **Other Resources:** Study Guide p. 16	Access Strat. **(Extra Support)** TE p. 119 Visual Learning **(Visual)** TE pp. 121, 122 Audiotapes of Multi-language Lesson Summaries **(Auditory)**
Skill: **Reaching a Compromise** *p. 123*	• Use group plans for a surprise party to practice compromise.	• **Other Resources:** Study Guide p. 17	
Lesson 3 The Bill of Rights *pp. 124–127* 1–2 days	• Identify the Bill of Rights and its relevance to everyday life. • Explain why a bill of rights was left out of the Constitution and why many people thought it was necessary. • Describe the process by which the Bill of Rights was added to the Constitution.	• **Workbook** or **Reading Support:** pp. 57–60 Review p. 14 Extra Support/Transition p. 14 Multi-lang. Sum. pp. 27–28 • **Other Resources:** Study Guide p. 18	Access Strat. **(Extra Support)** TE p. 125 Access Act. **(SDAIE)** TE p. 125 Collaborative Act. **(Multi-Age)** TE p. 126 Audiotapes of Multi-language Lesson Summaries **(Auditory)**
Chapter Review *pp. 128–129* 1 day		Chapter 4 Test pp. 13–16 *(See facsimiles on TE p. 752.)*	Assessment Multiple-Use Masters pp. 81–88

Reading Support Resources *for Every Lesson*

Reading and Review

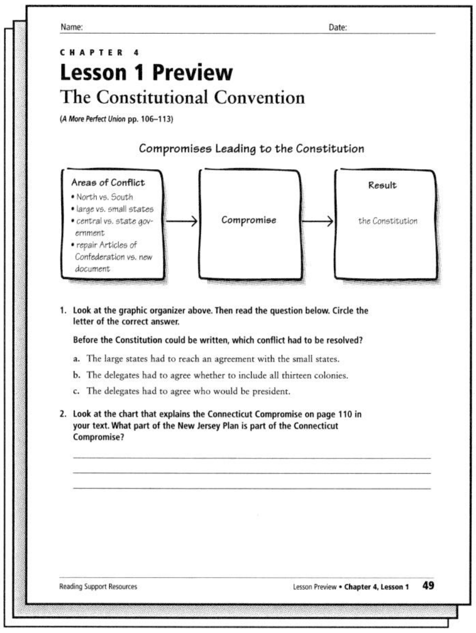
Name: Date:

CHAPTER 4

Lesson 1 Preview

The Constitutional Convention

(A More Perfect Union pp. 106–113)

Compromises Leading to the Constitution

1. Look at the graphic organizer above. Then read the question below. Circle the letter of the correct answer.
Before the Constitution could be written, which conflict had to be resolved?
a. The large states had to reach an agreement with the small states.
b. The delegates had to agree whether to include all thirteen colonies.
c. The delegates had to agree who would be president.

2. Look at the chart that explains the Connecticut Compromise on page 110 in your text. What part of the New Jersey Plan is part of the Connecticut Compromise?

Reading Support Resources — Lesson Preview • Chapter 4, Lesson 1 — 49

- **Chapter Overview*** p. 48
- **Lesson Previews*** using graphic organizers from the Teacher's Edition pp. 49, 53, 57
- **Reading Strategies*** pp. 50, 54, 58
- **Lesson Summaries*** pp. 51–52, 55–56, 59–60
- **Lesson Reviews** pp. 12, 13, 14

* **Workbook** includes starred items.

Multi-language Summaries

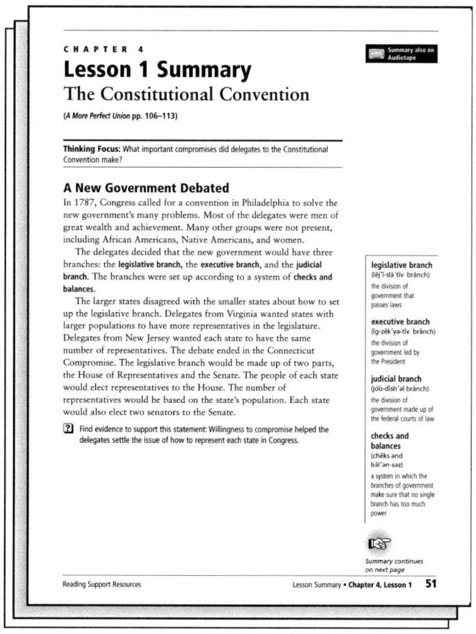
CHAPTER 4

Lesson 1 Summary

The Constitutional Convention

(A More Perfect Union pp. 106–113)

Summary also on Audiotape

Thinking Focus: What important compromises did delegates to the Constitutional Convention make?

A New Government Debated

In 1787, Congress called for a convention in Philadelphia to solve the new government's many problems. Most of the delegates were men of great wealth and achievement. Many other groups were not present, including African Americans, Native Americans, and women.

The delegates decided that the new government would have three branches: the **legislative branch**, the **executive branch**, and the **judicial branch**. The branches were set up according to a system of **checks and balances**.

The larger states disagreed with the smaller states about how to set up the legislative branch. Delegates from Virginia wanted states with larger populations to have more representatives in the legislature. Delegates from New Jersey wanted each state to have the same number of representatives. The debate ended in the Connecticut Compromise. The legislative branch would be made up of two parts, the House of Representatives and the Senate. The people of each state would elect representatives to the House. The number of representatives would be based on the state's population. Each state would also elect two senators to the Senate.

Find evidence to support this statement: Willingness to compromise helped the delegates settle the issue of how to represent each state in Congress.

legislative branch the division of government that passes laws

executive branch the division of government led by the President

judicial branch the division of government made up of the federal courts of law

checks and balances a system in which the branches of government make sure that no single branch has too much power

Summary continues on next page

Reading Support Resources — Lesson Summary • Chapter 4, Lesson 1 — 51

Lesson Summaries in:

- English (See Reading and Review.)
- Spanish pp. 51–52, 55–56, 59–60
- Chinese pp. 23–28
- Hmong pp. 23–28
- Khmer pp. 23–28
- Vietnamese pp. 23–28

Summaries available on audiotapes

Lesson Support / Transition

S D A I E

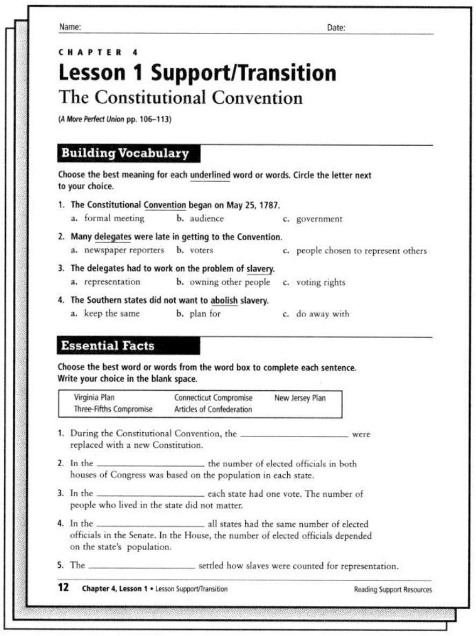
Name: Date:

CHAPTER 4

Lesson 1 Support/Transition

The Constitutional Convention

(A More Perfect Union pp. 106–113)

Building Vocabulary

Choose the best meaning for each underlined word or words. Circle the letter next to your choice.

1. The Constitutional Convention began on May 25, 1787.
a. formal meeting b. audience c. government
2. Many delegates were late in getting to the Convention.
a. newspaper reporters b. voters c. people chosen to represent others
3. The delegates had to work on the problem of slavery.
a. representation b. owning other people c. voting rights
4. The Southern states did not want to abolish slavery.
a. keep the same b. plan for c. do away with

Essential Facts

Choose the best word or words from the word box to complete each sentence. Write your choice in the blank space.

Virginia Plan — Connecticut Compromise — New Jersey Plan — Three-Fifths Compromise — Articles of Confederation

1. During the Constitutional Convention, the ______ were replaced with a new Constitution.
2. In the ______ the number of elected officials in both houses of Congress was based on the population in each state.
3. In the ______ each state had one vote. The number of people who lived in the state did not matter.
4. In the ______ all states had the same number of elected officials in the Senate. In the House, the number of elected officials depended on the state's population.
5. The ______ settled how slaves were counted for representation.

12 Chapter 4, Lesson 1 • Lesson Support/Transition — Reading Support Resources

Activities for SDAIE
Specially **D**esigned **A**cademic **I**nstruction in **E**nglish

- **Lesson Support/Transition** pp. 12, 13, 14

Technology Options

Internet Support

http://www.eduplace.com

Social Studies Center at Education Place

Internet support for Chapter 4:

- ***Lesson at a Glance***
- ***The Federalist Papers***

Software

Student Writing Center® (CD-ROM) (Macintosh® or Windows®)

School to Career

The Constitution may never have been ratified if its supporters hadn't waged a war in the press. The media has always played an important role in this country. Have students select a form of media (radio, television, print, Internet) and research the jobs involved in taking a story from idea through completion.

Character Education

Service Learning: Divide the class into small groups, and ask each to select a community service project in which they would like the class to take part. Then, have each group present their idea so the class can select one. Afterward, have students discuss what compromises they had to make within their groups and as a class in order to choose a project.

CHAPTER PREVIEW

Have students read the chapter title and the narrative under it. Point out the uncertainty of the time. Although we know that a new government would be adopted, the men at the Convention did not.

Refer students to the map of Philadelphia on this page and the painting of the Convention next to it. Just as the map was a plan for the city, the Constitutional Convention established a plan for a new government.

Looking Back

Why was the national government under the Articles of Confederation weak? What problems resulted from the weakness of the Congress? *(States wanted to keep own sovereignty; Congress could not tax, regulate commerce, or make changes)*

Looking Forward

Tell students that they will be learning about the conflict over creating a strengthened national government in the next three lessons: The Constitutional Convention, The Ratification Debate, and The Bill of Rights.

Chapter 4
The Constitutional Convention

The plan was to meet in Philadelphia in 1787 to patch up an ailing government. But when the 55 delegates met, the arguments began. Tempers flared and bargains were made. The result? The new Constitution. The signing of the Constitution was only the beginning of even more debate.

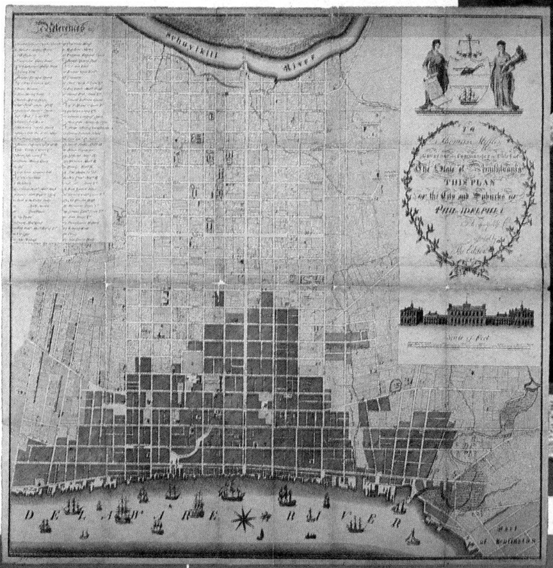

1787 The Constitutional Convention begins at the Pennsylvania State House, now Independence Hall. On the 1794 map at right, the State House is the red building on the gray block above the last E in Delaware.

1787 | 1788 | 1789

1787

BACKGROUND

When the Articles of Confederation proved to be inadequate, representatives from the states made a new plan that gave more power to the national government. State ratification debates on the new Constitution revealed the need to include a bill of rights to guarantee citizens' basic liberties.

National and Federal

The words *national* and *federal* had different connotations in 1787 than they do today. *Federal* was used to refer to sovereign states joined together for mutual benefit, with local and state levels holding most of the power. *National*, which described the British system of central control, was associated with tyranny. People feared that a strong national government would be no better than British rule.

The Parliament in Great Britain had sovereign authority. It could create, fund, and dissolve local governments. The delegates wanted a different system, in which states give the national government its power.

Distrust of Democracy

It may surprise students to learn that some of the nation's founders feared democracy. Believing that the common people could not make good decisions, some delegates argued that the President and senators should not be elected directly by the people. For example, Roger Sherman of Connecticut stated that the people "should have as little to do as may be about the government. They want [lack]

With the inkstand shown here, which had also been used for the signing of the Declaration of Independence, 39 delegates signed their names to the Constitution. The flag above commemorates the adoption of the Constitution by the new nation.

1790	1791	1792

1792

Understanding the Visuals

The historic, elaborate silver inkstand tells us that the signers of the Constitution realized that this was an important event. The banner was carried by the New York Society of Pewterers in a New York City parade in 1788 to celebrate the ratification of the Constitution. The picture in the center is a detail from the "Signing of the Constitution" (page 108), painted by Louis S. Glanzman in 1987.

Understanding Chronology

Draw students' attention to the chapter timeline. The Articles of Confederation were actually in effect until 1789, when the Constitution had been ratified by enough states to be valid. Point out that the Congress established by the Articles was meeting in New York while the Constitutional Convention met in Philadelphia. The Northwest Ordinance was enacted in July 1787. Discuss reasons for devoting an entire chapter to such a short period of time. *(Turning point in history, a new government formed)*

information and are constantly liable to be misled."

In contrast to this negative attitude about the common people, delegates such as James Wilson thought a strong government must "flow immediately from the legitimate source of all authority—the people." Sherman and like-minded delegates influenced the Constitution in two ways: senators would be elected by state legislators, and the president would be elected by the Electoral College, made up of elected representatives from the states. Senators are now elected by popular vote, but the president is still, at least nominally, chosen by electors.

Regional Economics

Votes on whether to allow slavery often split on the basis of which states were dependent on slave labor and which were not. The following percentages of slaves out of the total state populations shows how dependent some states were on slavery:

New Hampshire—0.55
Massachusetts—1.44
Connecticut—2.33
Pennsylvania—2.37
Rhode Island—6.40
New York—7.64
New Jersey—7.70
Delaware—21.64
North Carolina—26.80
Maryland—34.74
Georgia—35.93
Virginia—40.92
South Carolina—43.72

INTRODUCE

Point out the lesson title and tell students that in 1787 the convention was called the Federal Convention, not the Constitutional Convention. Ask them to guess why. *(The delegates intended to repair the Articles of Confederation; they did not plan to write a new Constitution.)*

Have students read the Thinking Focus and define the word *compromise. (Settling differences by each side giving something up)* Ask students to recall Chapter 3 and predict what compromises might be necessary. Have students read to confirm or reject their predictions.

Key Terms

Vocabulary strategies: T36–37

checks and balances—a system in which branches of government balance each other in order to guard against abuses

legislative branch—Congress, the division of government that passes laws

executive branch—the division of government that is led by the President

judicial branch—the division of government made up of the federal courts of law

bill of rights—a list of the basic liberties of citizens

1787 May — 1788 September — 1789 — 1790 — 1791 — 1792

LESSON 1

The Constitutional Convention

THINKING FOCUS

What important compromises did delegates to the Constitutional Convention make?

Key Terms

- checks and balances
- legislative branch
- executive branch
- judicial branch
- bill of rights

James Madison of Virginia was always early. A short man with a serious expression, he was the first delegate to ride into Philadelphia in May 1787. Deeply concerned about the politics of the new nation, Madison had been reading and reflecting on the subject of constitutional government day and night. He entered the city well prepared for the work ahead.

Madison worried that a national crisis was at hand. In its call for a federal convention, Congress had specified that this convention should have the "sole and express purpose of revising the Articles of Confederation." But Madison thought that simple changes could not solve the many problems of the ineffective Confederation government. He was planning to propose a totally new government at the convention—and he was worried that the other delegates would consider his plan to be radical, that is, too extreme for the time.

Madison planned his strategy carefully. To prepare for the convention, he asked his friend Thomas Jefferson to send him books about earlier confederations and other forms of government. Jefferson, who was serving as ambassador to France, responded by sending Madison more than 100 volumes by French and English philosophers. These books covered a wide range of political theory and the history of governments.

Involved in politics since the 1770s, James Madison helped draft a new Virginia constitution and the Virginia Declaration of Rights.

In the days before the convention began, Madison continued to work on his plans for the new government. But he worried about his chances for success. Could 13 states really come to agreement despite all their differences—different concepts of government, different natural resources, different cultural backgrounds, even different money?

Madison expected most of the delegates to be loyal to their own regions. He anticipated that many would be firmly committed to preserving the independence their states had enjoyed under the Articles of Confederation. But where were the other delegates? What if nobody showed up?

Objectives

1. Explain how the Constitution was the result of compromises.
2. Describe the debates between small and large states regarding representation.
3. Summarize the disagreements between Northern and Southern states at the Convention.
4. Evaluate the personal role of major delegates in the Convention's outcome.

Graphic Overview

Areas of Conflict
- North v. South
- large v. small states
- central v. state government
- repair articles v. new document

→ **Compromise** →

Result
the Constitution

A New Government Debated

On May 13, the day before the federal convention was scheduled to begin, George Washington arrived in Philadelphia. Bells rang and cannons boomed to welcome him. The city's troops escorted him to the home of 81-year-old Benjamin Franklin, who was the "elder statesman" of the nation. General Washington, at the age of 55, was the most highly respected American of his time. His participation in the convention lent a special dignity to the proceedings.

The Delegates

The other delegates, too, were men of great achievement and wealth. Many had fought in the Revolution, and some had signed the Declaration of Independence. The group included Alexander Hamilton, an intelligent young lawyer from New York, Gouverneur Morris, the Pennsylvania delegate who spoke more times than anyone else at the convention, and Roger Sherman, a former farmer and shoemaker who was called "honest as an angel."

Some key people were missing. Thomas Jefferson and John Adams were absent because they were serving as ambassadors overseas. Patrick Henry was chosen as a delegate, but refused to attend because he opposed strengthening the national government and limiting states' powers. Also missing were any of the nation's nearly two million women, 700,000 African Americans, or tens of thousands of Native Americans. The absence of these groups allowed the white male delegates to remain silent about important issues of the day.

Slowly Delegates Gather

Most of the 55 delegates chosen to attend the convention were not there on May 14, its scheduled beginning date. Some delegates had to travel hundreds of miles to Philadelphia, and weeks of rain and mud had delayed many of them. The convention could not begin until at least seven of the thirteen states were represented. So all that the early arrivals could do was wait and wonder what would happen.

Finally, on May 25, delegates from seven states had arrived, and the convention began. The delegates unanimously elected George Washington as president of the convention. They also established rules for their debates, including a rule of strict secrecy. No one was to make the proceedings public until a final agreement had been reached.

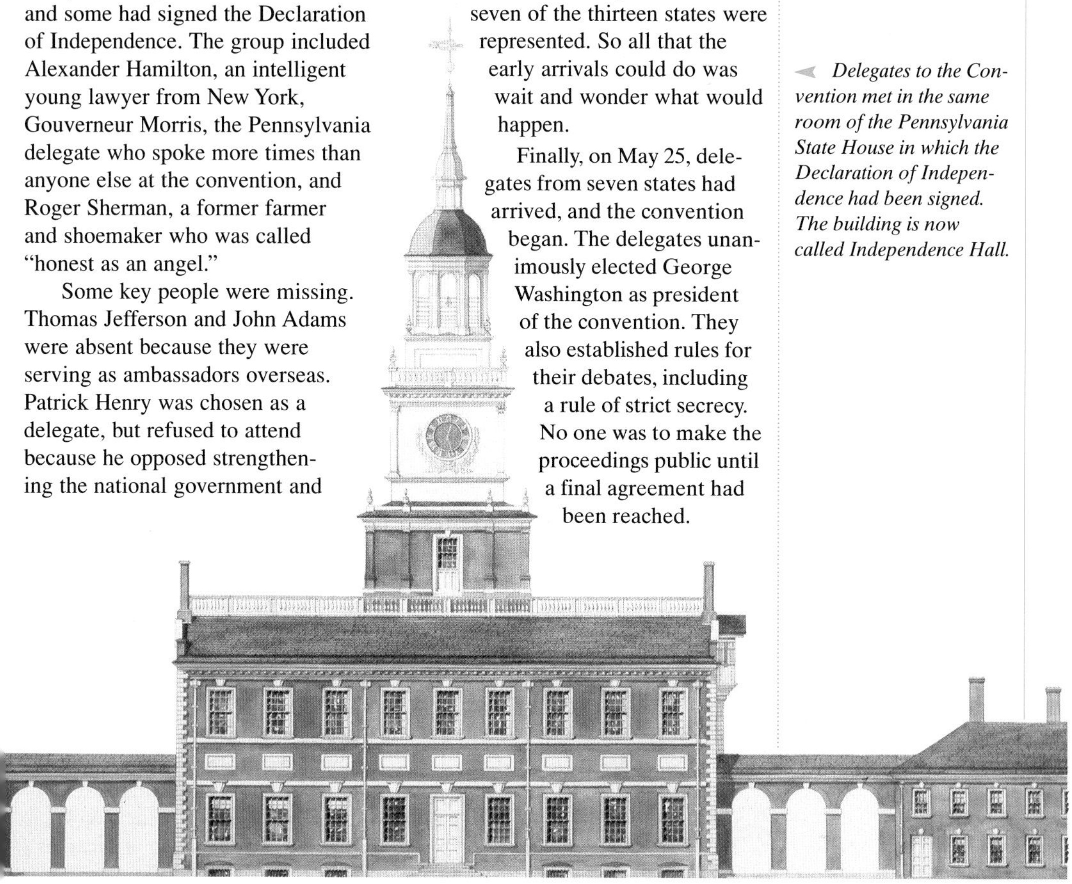

Delegates to the Convention met in the same room of the Pennsylvania State House in which the Declaration of Independence had been signed. The building is now called Independence Hall.

DEVELOP

Before students read the lesson, have them scan the heads and visuals for the word *compromise* and also for words associated with arriving at a compromise, such as *debate, react,* and *counterproposals.* Have students read to find out how several differences at the convention were resolved by compromise.

HISTORY

Critical Thinking

Ask students to identify the groups who were not represented at the Convention. *(women, African Americans, American Indians)* What issues might these people have brought up if they had been there? *(Sample answers: slavery, voting and other rights for women, settler violation of land treaties with American Indians)* As students continue reading this lesson, ask them to see which of these issues actually were discussed at the Convention. *(only slavery)*

Access Strategy

Have students imagine that their class has no central authority. Each student can make individual decisions on class attendance, homework, and grading. Point out that although students may initially enjoy this freedom, they will soon see that little is accomplished in class because they do not agree with each other's decisions.

Ask students how they will decide how the class should be run. Should each student have an equal vote? What will they do if the vote is divided? On what are they willing to compromise for the good of the class as a whole? Have one student write class responses to these questions on the board.

Tell students that in this lesson they will read about how representatives of the states in 1787 made decisions on the rules that states would have as a group and the kind of central government they would need.

Access Activity

Ask students to explain why Convention delegates might have chosen to keep proceedings secret. *(The pressures of public opinion might have limited delegates' freedom to change their minds or make compromises.)* Ask them for examples of times when they have felt the need for secrecy. *(Planning a surprise birthday party, keeping a friend's confidence)*

CONSTITUTIONAL HERITAGE

Critical Thinking

Ask students to name at least two major differences between the Articles of Confederation and the Virginia Plan. Students may refer to Chapter 3. *(The Virginia Plan gave greater authority to the federal government and proposed three branches of government rather than just a Congress.)*

➤ *He was the most respected and trusted man in the country. His presence gave the proceedings dignity.*

▲ *Even though Washington presided over the Convention, he was silent in debates. Why was his presence so important?*

The Virginia Plan

On the third day of the convention, Edmund Randolph took the floor to present 15 resolves, or formal proposals, drafted by the Virginia delegation. Why Randolph, when many of the ideas were actually those of Madison? The handsome, six-foot Randolph, governor of Virginia and the head of his delegation, made a more imposing figure than the shy, slight Madison.

"An individual independence of the States is utterly irreconcilable," Randolph announced. "Let national Government be armed with positive and complete authority."

➤ *Edmund Randolph's family had been prominent in Virginia ever since his ancestors arrived from England in 1673.*

As Randolph read his speech, the words *complete authority* sent shock waves through the hall. Although most of the delegates agreed that the nation needed a stronger central government, most were not ready to give up the sovereignty, or independence, of the states.

The Virginia Plan, as it came to be known, proposed a supreme national government. The basis of this entirely new government would be three branches with a system of built-in **checks and balances**. Each branch of government would balance the power of the others in order to check, or protect, against any abuses of power. Although stunned by the far-reaching changes proposed, the delegates had been frustrated with the weaknesses of the Articles of Confederation. Most delegates agreed that the new plan had merit.

Reactions and Counterproposals

Charles Pinckney, a wealthy planter from South Carolina, started the debate by challenging the Virginia Plan. Did Randolph, asked Pinckney, mean to abolish state governments altogether? Many delegates were concerned that a strong central government would overpower the individual states. But they voted for a national government, despite their concerns.

Visual Learning

Refer students to the painting on this page of the Convention, commissioned by the Daughters of the American Revolution for the 1987 bicentennial of the Convention. Do the people in the painting look natural or posed? Why might the artist have chosen to make the proceedings look dignified? *(To celebrate an important moment in history)*

Social Context

At the time of the Convention, Philadelphia, with a population of about 40,000, was the largest city in the United States. Congress had met there earlier. Philadelphia was a good location for such meetings because it was roughly at the geographic center of the thirteen states. It was also a city of commerce, shipping, science, politics, and art.

Philadelphia's most prominent citizen was Benjamin Franklin, who had returned to the United States in 1785 after living many years in Paris, France. Franklin was president of the Pennsylvania Assembly, a position equivalent to governor of the state. At the age of 81, he was the oldest member of the Constitutional Convention.

Franklin was ill at the time of the Convention, and he found traveling by coach agonizing. Instead, he came to the State House each day in a sedan chair carried by four prisoners from the local jail. Although he was too weak to speak before the Convention, he was able

Understanding Origins of the Constitution

As they considered creating a new form of government, the writers of the Constitution had many models. The one closest to home was the Iroquois League, a union of five nations that had formed an alliance in the 1500s. Each nation had its own leaders, but it also sent representatives to a Council to deal with issues common to all the tribes. Along with this local model, the delegates were familiar with some of the European theories of confederated government of the time.

British and European Origins

All of the delegates to the Constitutional Convention were once British citizens. The 35 lawyers and 8 judges among them were all steeped in the tradition of British law. Thus, it would not be surprising to find similarities between British and European traditions and the new U.S. Constitution.

To answer the question of who the most influential writers were among the colonists, a recent study looked at more than 15,000 political writings published in America between 1760 and 1805. A tally was made of the authors who were referred to or cited most often. Topping the list, cited three or four times more often than any other, was the French philosopher Baron de Montesquieu. The English philosophers David Hume and John Locke were the next two runners up.

The Enlightenment

All three writers were a part of the Enlightenment, an intellectual movement that began in Europe in the eighteenth century. The Enlightenment is also sometimes called the Age of Reason. A central idea in this movement was the optimistic notion that humankind, by exercising its ability to use reason, could solve the problems of society.

The Enlightenment thinkers also gave a great deal of power to the individual. They believed that people should participate directly in their government. People had natural rights, they said, that belonged to them as a condition of being human, as part of the natural order of things. Locke identified these rights as life itself, liberty, and property. Note how closely this follows the wording of the Declaration of Independence:

"That all men . . . are endowed by their Creator with certain unalienable Rights, that among these are Life, Liberty and the pursuit of Happiness."

Locke, in his book *Two Theories of Government* (1690), wrote that government was a contract between the people and their ruler. If the ruler did not honor the contract and live up to its provisions, then the people had the right to replace him with another ruler.

At the time Locke wrote his book, England was working out an agreement known as the Bill of Rights of 1689. It guaranteed the right of the nobles and the gentry—the upper middle class—against the crown. Although some similarities can be seen between the English Bill of Rights and the U.S. Bill of Rights a century later, there are also some strong differences. The U.S. document goes much further in guaranteeing the rights of the individual, not just of a single class of people.

Checks and Balances

A point that Montesquieu was fond of making was that "power should be a check to power." Therefore he was interested in looking for ways of maintaining checks and balances between powers. This also concerned the authors of the U.S. Constitution.

Montesquieu identified three centers of power: the legislative, the executive, and the executive in regard to civil law (what is called in this country the judiciary). The Constitution, in its first three Articles, lays out the power of the legislative, the executive, and the judicial. The Constitution also establishes a system of checks and balances, so that each of the branches of government has some control over the others.

Here are some examples of how this works: Congress, the legislative branch, has the power to make the laws, but the President has the power to veto them—a check by the executive on the legislative. Congress, however, can override the veto—a check by the legislative on the executive. The Supreme Court can declare laws or executive actions unconstitutional—a check by the judicial on the legislative and the executive. The President appoints the Supreme Court justices and the Senate confirms the appointments—a check by the execu-tive and the legislative on the judicial.

CONSTITUTIONAL HERITAGE

Critical Thinking

Have students analyze Locke's idea of government as a contract. What is a contract? *(An agreement between people)* Because a government was a contract between people and their ruler, Locke wrote, the ruler could be replaced if the people were unhappy with his rule. Why didn't this idea of a contract apply to European monarchies? *(Monarchs could not be replaced.)* In what ways was the Constitution a contract among citizens? *(The people agreed among themselves to a form of government. No ruler was involved.)*

to contribute his wisdom through a fellow delegate who read his words.

The delegates generally met from 10 A.M to about 3 P.M. The street in front of the State House was paved with cobblestones. Carriages going by made such a clatter that members of the convention persuaded the people of Philadelphia to cover the cobblestones with gravel so that passing carriages would make less noise.

Since most delegates had come from out of town, they needed to pay for lodgings. Many chose to stay at the Indian Queen Tavern near the State House, where they often held private meetings to plan their strategies for the debates. As weeks stretched into months, they tried to keep alive businesses and farms back home. Some had their families join them in Philadelphia. Most communicated with their families by mail. Some left Philadelphia for various periods of time to attend to personal matters.

Social Participation

Ask students to draw up a contract between themselves and another individual. For example, students could agree to clean a neighbor's home once a week for a month in exchange for money or some other service. Contracts should be evaluated and signed by the other party. Have students share their contracts with the class.

CONSTITUTIONAL HERITAGE

Visual Learning

The diagram on this page shows how the Virginia and New Jersey plans were combined to form the Connecticut Compromise. Have students use the diagram to determine what the large states won and what the small states won in the compromise. *(Large states—representation in the House according to population; small states—equal representation in the Senate)*

■ *The Connecticut Compromise provided a system in which both large and small states could feel that they were represented fairly.*

➤ *The Connecticut Compromise was so important to the writing of the Constitution that it often has been called the Great Compromise.*

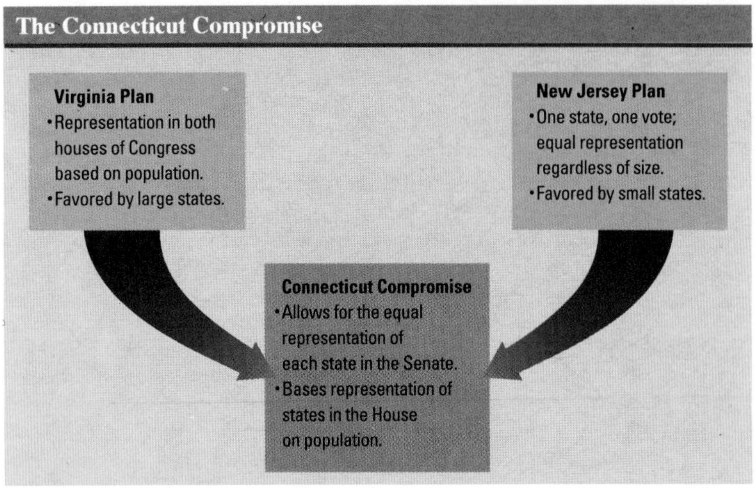

The Connecticut Compromise
Virginia Plan
•Representation in both houses of Congress based on population.
•Favored by large states.
New Jersey Plan
•One state, one vote; equal representation regardless of size.
•Favored by small states.
Connecticut Compromise
•Allows for the equal representation of each state in the Senate.
•Bases representation of states in the House on population.

The new government would consist of a **legislative branch** (the Congress), an **executive branch** headed by the President, and a **judicial branch** (a national system of courts of law). Clearly the convention was no longer repairing the old Articles of Confederation. Instead the delegates were replacing the Articles with a constitution, a document defining a new government.

The delegates agreed quickly to a bicameral, or two-house, legislature. The Virginia Plan had proposed a lower house, the House of Representatives, to be elected by the people of each state. In turn, this lower house would select an upper, more selective house, the Senate. But a major disagreement arose between the states with large populations and the states with small populations. It concerned the election of representatives. Then the real struggle began.

Madison believed that representation in both houses should be proportional to population rather than equal for each state. This meant that a large state would have more representatives than a small state. James Wilson of Pennsylvania agreed. "We must bury all local interests and distinctions," he argued. The delegates from smaller states objected. They feared that they would lose their ability to prevent Congress from making any decisions the small states opposed.

William Paterson of New Jersey warned that his state would never give up its political independence. He then countered the Virginia Plan by proposing the New Jersey, or small-state, Plan. This plan was similar to the old Articles of Confederation in that each state—large or small—would get one vote in Congress. After three days of sharp debate, the delegates defeated the New Jersey Plan.

The Great Compromise

Spring gave way to summer, and the delegates still had many decisions to make. After the New Jersey defeat, the Connecticut delegation proposed a compromise. The people of each state would directly elect representatives to one house of Congress, the House of Representatives. The number of representatives for each state would be based on population. For the other house of Congress, each state legislature would choose two senators. After many days of impassioned debate, the delegates accepted the Connecticut Compromise. With this compromise all states were represented equally in the Senate, but representation in the House varied with each state's population. ■

■ *Find evidence to support this statement: Willingness to compromise helped the delegates settle the issue of how to represent each state in Congress.*

Social Participation

Ask students to explain how compromise is used to resolve conflicts in daily life. For example, how is it used in making decisions at club meetings or in resolving disagreements among friends or neighbors? Have them name examples of compromise from their own lives.

Mathematics Connection

Point out to students that the ratio between a state's size and its population reflects how densely populated the state is. The map on page 112 gives the relative sizes of states and indicates which had populations over or under 250,000. Have students use the map to estimate which states were the most densely populated in 1787 and which were least densely populated. *(Maryland was densely populated; Georgia and South Carolina, sparsely populated.)*

Language Arts Connection

After students have read the account of Franklin's "rising sun" story on page 113 from James Madison's *Records of the Federal Convention of 1787,* discuss the symbolism with them. What did the image of the rising sun stand for? What would a setting sun have meant? *(Rising sun—hope and a new beginning for the confederation; setting sun—the opposite)*

The Slavery Issue

As the debate in the Pennsylvania State House heated up, so did the summer weather. The windows were sealed tight to protect the secrecy of the convention and to keep out flies, so the air in the meeting room became incredibly warm.

Debate soon turned to the issue of exactly how many representatives each state could send to the House of Representatives. As delegates argued their points of view, Madison observed that the states were "divided into different interests not by their difference of size . . . but principally from their having or not having slaves." How would populations be counted, especially in states with large numbers of slaves?

So far, the word *slavery* had been avoided at the convention. The delegates knew that a confrontation over this issue might ruin any chance they had of reaching a consensus. But it was impossible to avoid the issue of slavery entirely.

How to Count Slaves

Delegates from New England proposed that representation be based on the number of free inhabitants only. Delegates from the South wanted to increase their representation by counting everyone, including slaves.

The debate on this issue was lengthy. It touched on many concerns, including how to count a state's population for the purpose of setting that state's share of national taxes. During these debates, the Southern states defended their right to keep slaves.

The Three-Fifths Compromise

Eventually the delegates compromised. Representation would be in proportion to the whole number of white and other free citizens and three-fifths of all other persons. The

Taverns, such as the one shown in this John Lewis Krimmel oil painting of a Philadelphia inn, were often a gathering place for political discussion.

ECONOMICS

Critical Thinking

Why did Southern delegates want to defend the institution of slavery at all costs? *(Southern economy was dependent on plantations; slaves made up a large percentage of plantation workers.)*

Art Connection

Ask students to write reports on famous painters of the 1770s and 1780s, such as Americans John Singleton Copley, Benjamin West, and Charles Wilson Peale (who painted the portrait of Madison on the first page of this lesson); English Sir Joshua Reynolds, George Romney, Thomas Gainsborough, and J.M.W. Turner; and French Jacques-Louis David.

Other students may report on American architecture of the period. The major eighteenth-century architectural style in the English colonies before the Revolutionary War is called Georgian. Examples of this style include Independence Hall in Philadelphia and the buildings in colonial Williamsburg, Virginia. This style was followed by the Federal style, a more ornamental style used mainly for residential architecture (1780–1820). An example of this style is the State House in Boston, Massachusetts.

Critical Thinking

Many delegates opposed to slavery agreed to compromises on slavery issues in order to keep the states united as one nation. Ask students if they think the delegates should have taken a stronger stand against slavery. What might have been the result at the Constitutional Convention if they had? *(Sample answer: States may have formed two nations rather than one.)*

■ *The Northern states wanted the Southern states to agree to the Constitution.*

■ *Why did the Northern states agree to postpone a vote on the slave trade, despite their antislavery feelings?*

"other persons" were, of course, slaves. For purposes of representation, all population counts included women.

The delegates reached two other compromises concerning slavery. Southerners insisted on treating slaves as property. They bought them to expand the labor force on their plantations. Delegates finally agreed to stop Congress from voting to end the slave trade until after 1808. This Slave Trade Clause was included in the text of the Constitution. The Fugitive Slave Clause, which allowed for the arrest of runaway slaves in any state, was also included. ■

The Constitution Is Signed

Throughout the four long months of debate, delegates came and went. Rhode Island had refused to send any delegates at all. At one point, two of the New York delegates walked out because they disagreed with the direction of the Convention. The third, Alexander Hamilton—one of the original organizers of the federal convention—left also but later returned. As the map below shows, other delegates had various reasons for being absent.

Finally, on September 17, 1787, a completed document was ready for signing. Of the 55 delegates who had attended at one time or another, 42 were present for the signing. Benjamin Franklin set the tone for the day: "I confess that there are several parts of

As shown in the map, the "large states" referred to in the text are the most populous states but not necessarily the states with greatest land area.

GEOGRAPHY

Map Skills

Using the map of the states in 1787 on this page together with the political map of the United States today found in the Atlas as on pages 698–699, have students name which of the original thirteen states were larger in land area than they are today. *(Massachusetts, Virginia)*

The Constitutional Convention: Delegates From Each State

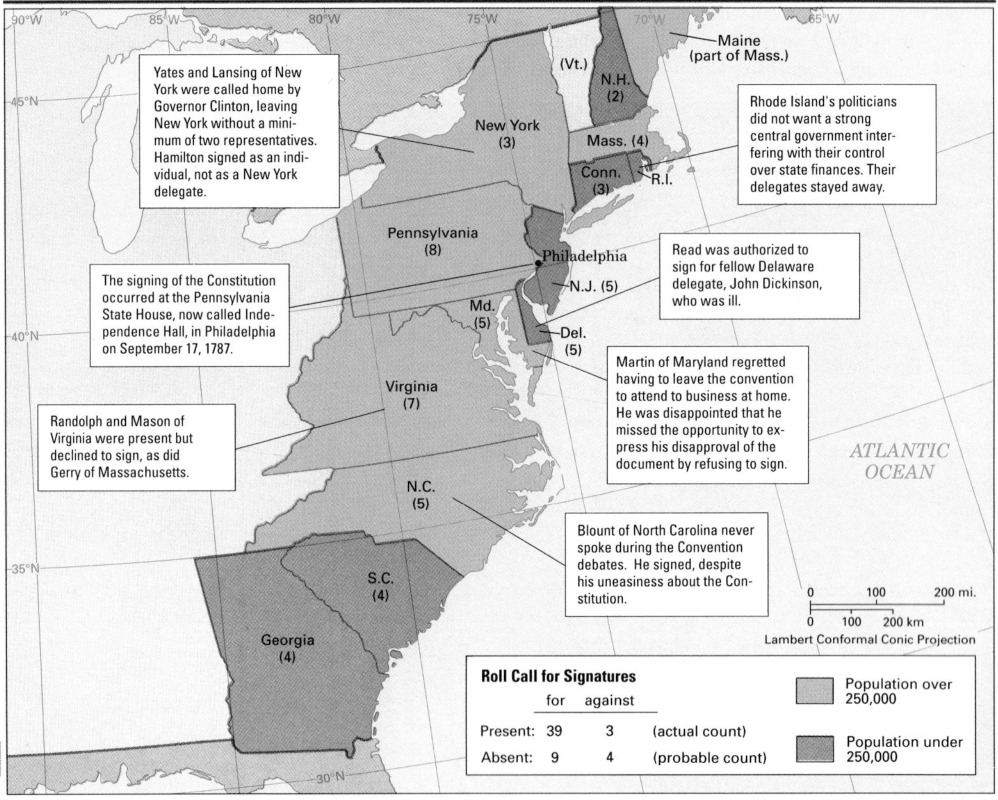

90°W
85°W
80°W
75°W
70°W
65°W
45°N
40°N
35°N
30°N
Maine (part of Mass.)
(Vt.)
N.H. (2)
New York (3)
Mass. (4)
Conn. (3)
R.I.
Pennsylvania (8)
Philadelphia
N.J. (5)
Md. (5)
Del. (5)
Virginia (7)
N.C. (5)
S.C. (4)
Georgia (4)
ATLANTIC OCEAN
Yates and Lansing of New York were called home by Governor Clinton, leaving New York without a minimum of two representatives. Hamilton signed as an individual, not as a New York delegate.
Rhode Island's politicians did not want a strong central government interfering with their control over state finances. Their delegates stayed away.
Read was authorized to sign for fellow Delaware delegate, John Dickinson, who was ill.
The signing of the Constitution occurred at the Pennsylvania State House, now called Independence Hall, in Philadelphia on September 17, 1787.
Martin of Maryland regretted having to leave the convention to attend to business at home. He was disappointed that he missed the opportunity to express his disapproval of the document by refusing to sign.
Randolph and Mason of Virginia were present but declined to sign, as did Gerry of Massachusetts.
Blount of North Carolina never spoke during the Convention debates. He signed, despite his uneasiness about the Constitution.
0 100 200 mi.
0 100 200 km
Lambert Conformal Conic Projection
Roll Call for Signatures
for against
Present: 39 3 (actual count)
Absent: 9 4 (probable count)
Population over 250,000
Population under 250,000

Map and Globe Skills

Point out that the figures on the map indicate the number of delegates sent by each state. Which states sent the most delegates? *(Pennsylvania with 8, followed by Virginia with 7)* Call students' attention to the use of color: green for states with large populations, orange for smaller states, and beige for areas not yet part of the Union (such as Vermont).

Collaborative Learning

Have students work in pairs to create diagrams that compare the different structures of government under the Articles of Confederation and under the Constitution. Each student should first work individually to diagram both structures. Next, students should discuss, compare, and adjust their drawings, finally combining their diagrams to illustrate the comparison.

Debate

Divide students into debate teams to argue questions that are of current interest to them, such as proposed changes in the school cafeteria or budget cuts in certain school programs. Give the teams time to do research as a homework assignment and to formulate strong arguments during class. After the debate, encourage students to think of ways that the two sides of the issue might be resolved by compromise.

this constitution which I do not at present approve. . . ." But he went on to explain why he would sign it anyway, and he finished by offering a motion that the Constitution be accepted by unanimous consent of "the States."

> *Whilst the last members were signing it, Doctr. Franklin looking towards the President's chair, at the back of which a rising sun happened to be painted, observed to a few members near him, that painters had found it difficult to distinguish in their art a rising from a setting sun. I have, said he, often and often in the course of the session . . . looked at that [sun] behind the President without being able to tell whether it was rising or setting: But now at length I have the happiness to know that it is a rising and not a setting sun.*
>
> James Madison, in *The Records of the Federal Convention of 1787*

Only three of the members present that day refused to sign. Edmund Randolph, who had proposed the Virginia Plan, wanted to remain uncommitted until his state had a chance to debate the Constitution. George Mason, a fellow Virginian, particularly objected to the absence of a **bill of rights**, a summary of the basic rights and liberties of the people. Elbridge Gerry of Massachusetts also refused to sign the Constitution without a bill of rights. He feared that the debate in

the states would result in civil war and said he "could not . . . pledge himself to abide by it at all events."

That night, according to Washington's diary, the delegates dined together at the City Tavern and then parted on friendly terms. After months of secret meetings, they felt relieved that a new constitution existed. But they also felt rather uneasy. The Congress—still operating under the Articles of Confederation—would now have to send the Constitution to the states. At least nine of the thirteen states would have to approve it.

In the minds of the delegates the question remained: what if no one agreed with what the delegates had worked out? There was still a chance that all those hot days and long hours of debate would add up to nothing. ■

In objecting to the Constitution, George Mason said, "We are not indeed constituting a British Government, but a more dangerous monarchy, an elective one."

How Do We Know?

HISTORY *We learned about the secret discussions at the Convention from the notes kept by a few delegates. Each night, after the long, tiring meetings, James Madison carefully wrote out in longhand his notes of what took place that day. Madison's journal was made public after his death in 1836.*

■ *Why didn't the signing of a document on September 17 finish the business of creating the Constitution?*

REVIEW

1. **FOCUS** What important compromises did the delegates to the Constitutional Convention make?
2. **CONNECT** Considering the many problems with the Articles of Confederation, why were some delegates upset by the prospect of a supreme national government?
3. **SOCIAL SYSTEMS** How did the 13 states' differences on the issue of slavery contribute to the outcome of the Constitutional Convention?
4. **CRITICAL THINKING** Why did the disagreement among delegates over the election of representatives result in the Connecticut Compromise? Can you think of a different solution to the problem of representation?
5. **ACTIVITY** Assume the role of a delegate to the Convention of 1787 from a small state in the North or a large state in the South. Prepare a two-minute speech in which you report to your state legislature on the outcome of the Convention. Use an outline to organize your speech.

■ *It had to be ratified by at least nine states.*

CLOSE

Have students answer the Thinking Focus and evaluate the predictions they made before reading the lesson. Copy on the board the Graphic Overview from page 106 to review the differences that led to compromise. As a reteaching activity, ask students to use information from the lesson to explain the role of each of these men at the Constitutional Convention: James Madison, George Washington, Edmund Randolph, William Paterson, Benjamin Franklin, James Wilson, Charles Pinckney, George Mason, Elbridge Gerry, Luther Martin, Alexander Hamilton.

Answers to Review Questions

1. They agreed to the Great Compromise, to the three-fifths compromise, and to delaying the vote on slavery.
2. Although delegates knew a stronger government was needed, they feared the possibility of tyranny and did not want to give up independence.
3. Differences on the issue of slavery led to the three-fifths compromise, which determined representation in Congress.
4. One house was to be based on population and the other would have equal representation, making both the small states and the large states happy. Student solutions should reflect their understanding of the debates and the idea of compromise.
5. Student speeches should reflect the point of view of the states they represent on the issues of slavery and how states should be represented in Congress.

Homework Options

Have students look at the annotated Constitution starting on page 636 and find the specific articles and clauses that contain the Connecticut Compromise and the three-fifths Compromise.

Study Guide: page 15.

INTRODUCE

Students will recall from Lesson 1 that by the time of the Constitutional Convention in 1787, Benjamin Franklin was one of the most famous and respected men in America. This excerpt from his *Autobiography* makes clear that he started life with few advantages. Point out that Joseph Priestly, the recipient of Franklin's letter entitled "Moral Algebra," was the famous British scientist who discovered oxygen. Explain that the maxims, or wise sayings, Franklin wrote for *Poor Richard's Almanac* were quoted throughout the colonies.

READ AND RESPOND

The first two selections lend themselves well to the study of primary sources. Students can read these selections independently. Ask volunteers to read the maxims aloud. Discuss the meaning of each one. Ask students how they would follow Franklin's advice. As students answer the purpose-setting question, make sure they give reasons for their answers.

In Chapter 3, Lesson 1, you read about Benjamin Franklin's contributions and his ideas about the form that a new government could take in America. In this selection you will meet the young Ben Franklin.

LITERATURE

First Day in Philadelphia

Benjamin Franklin

Benjamin Franklin (1706-1790) was an inventor, scientist, and statesman as well as a diplomat, editor, and publisher. Franklin was also a dedicated author whose writings about his thoughts, ideas, and accomplishments are both educational and entertaining. Below is a selection from his Autobiography. *It captures the thoughts of the young Ben Franklin as he arrives, alone, in Philadelphia for the first time. The second selection, a letter to Joseph Priestley written in 1772, is Franklin's practical reply to a request for his advice on decision-making. While reading these selections, think about what sort of person might have written these words.*

I have been the more particular in this description of my journey, and shall be so of my first entry into that city, that you may in your mind compare such unlikely beginnings with the figure I have since made there. I was in my working dress, my best clothes being to come round by sea. I was dirty from my journey; my pockets were stuff'd out with shirts and stockings, and I knew no soul nor where to look for lodging. I was fatigued with travelling, rowing, and want of rest, I was very hungry; and my whole stock of cash consisted of a Dutch dollar, and about a shilling in copper. The latter I gave the people of the boat for my passage, who at first refus'd it, on account of my rowing; but I insisted on their taking it. A man being sometimes more generous when he has but a little money than when he has plenty, perhaps thro' fear of being thought to have but little.

Then I walked up the street, gazing about till near the market-house I met a boy with bread. I had made many a meal on bread, and, inquiring where he got it, I went immediately to the baker's he directed me to, in Second-street, and ask'd for bisket, intending such as we had in Boston; but they, it seems, were not made in Philadelphia. Then I asked for a three-penny loaf, and was told they had none such. So not considering or knowing the difference of money, and the greater cheapness nor the names of his bread, I bad him give me three-penny worth of any sort. He gave me, accordingly, three great puffy rolls. I was surpriz'd at the quantity, but took it, and, having no room in my pockets, walk'd off with a roll under each arm, and eating the other. Thus I went up Market-street as far as Fourth-street, passing by the door of Mr. Read, my future wife's father; when she, standing at the door, saw me, and thought I made, as I certainly did, a most awkward, ridiculous appearance. Then I turned and went down Chestnut-street and part of Walnut-street, eating my roll all the way, and, coming round, found myself again at Market-street wharf, near the boat I came in, to which I went for a draught of the

bad asked

draught drink

114

Thematic Connections

Social Studies: Life of Benjamin Franklin

Houghton Mifflin Literary Readers: Seeking Identity

Background

At the age of 12, Benjamin Franklin began working as an apprentice in his brother's printing shop. When he moved to Philadelphia in 1723, he soon found another job as a printer, and by the time he was 26 he owned his own newspaper. He also began to publish the yearly *Poor Richard's Almanac*, which became a best-seller.

Franklin was Philadelphia's leading citizen. He founded the first circulating library in the colonies, the school that later became the University of Pennsylvania, a hospital, and a fire company. His endless curiosity led him to conduct many experiments, including the famous (and dangerous) one of flying a kite in a thunderstorm to show that lightning and electricity were the same.

river water; and, being filled with one of my rolls, gave the other two to a woman and her child that came down the river in the boat with us, and were waiting to go farther.

Thus refreshed, I walked again up the street, which by this time had many clean-dressed people in it, who were all walking the same way. I joined them and thereby was led into the great meeting-house of the Quakers near the market. I sat down among them, and, after looking round awhile and hearing nothing said, being very drowsy thro' labor and want of rest the preceding night, I fell fast asleep, and continued so till the meeting broke up, when one was kind enough to rouse me. This was, therefore, the first house I was in or slept in, in Philadelphia.

Why did Franklin insist (in the first selection) that the people on the boat take his payment? *(He was afraid of being thought too poor to pay.)*

Moral Algebra

Dear Sir:

In the affair of so much importance to you, wherein you ask my advice, I cannot, for want of sufficient premises, advise you *what* to determine; but, if you please, I will tell you *how*. When these difficult cases occur, they are difficult, chiefly because, while we have them under consideration, all the reasons *pro* and *con* are not present to the mind at the same time; but sometimes one set present themselves, and at other times another, the first being out of sight. Hence the various purposes or inclinations that alternately prevail, and the uncertainty that perplexes us.

premises details

alternately prevail take turns in being uppermost in one's mind

To get over this, my way is to divide half a sheet of paper by a line into two columns; writing over the one *pro*, and over the other *con*; then during three or four days' consideration, I put down under the different heads short hints of the different motives that at different times occur to me, *for* or *against* the measure. When I have thus got them all together in one view, I endeavor to estimate their respective weights; and, where I find two (one on each side) that seem equal, I strike them both out. If I find a reason *pro* equal to some two reasons *con*, I strike out the three. If I judge some two reasons *con*, equal to some three reasons *pro*, I strike out the five; and thus proceeding I find at length where the balance lies; and if, after a day or two of further consideration, nothing new that is of importance occurs on either side, I come to a determination accordingly. And though the weight of reasons cannot be taken with the precision of algebraic quantities, yet, when each is thus considered separately and comparatively, and the whole lies before me, I think I can judge better, and am less likely to make a rash step; and in fact I have found great advantage from this kind of equation, in what may be called *moral* or *prudential algebra*.

endeavor try

Wishing sincerely that you may determine for the best, I am ever, my dear friend, yours most affectionately,

—B. Franklin

Why is the letter entitled "Moral Algebra"? *(Franklin's method of making a decision —a moral judgment—was the same as setting up a mathematical equation.)*

Maxims

This selection is from Poor Richard's Almanac, *a book written and published by Benjamin Franklin. An almanac provides practical advice, poems, jokes, and weather predictions. The practical advice is expressed in short sayings called maxims. The maxims selected here reflect Benjamin Franklin's ideas on thrift, hard work, and simplicity.*

Keep conscience clear,
Then never fear.

Half the truth is often a great lie.

Blessed is he that expects nothing, for he shall never be disappointed.

Eat to live, and not live to eat.

There are three things extremely hard: steel, a diamond, and to know one's self.

To lengthen thy life, lessen thy meals.

He that lieth down with dogs shall rise up with fleas.

He that falls in love with himself will have no rivals.

A flatterer never seems absurd;
The flattered always takes his word.

The rotten apple spoils his companion.

Tart words make no friends: a spoonful of honey will catch more flies than a gallon of vinegar.

If you'd lose a troublesome visitor, lend him money.

He's a fool that makes his doctor his heir.

Three may keep a secret, if two of them are dead.

➤What is Franklin's attitude toward eating? *(He thinks that one should eat in moderation.)*

What is Franklin's advice for those who criticize others? *(If they wish to make friends, they should use kind rather than harsh words.)*

Writing Activity

Students should choose one of Franklin's maxims that most interests them. Then ask students to write a brief story, real or imaginary, that illustrates the wisdom of this maxim. Read and discuss these stories with the class.

All would live long, but none would be old.

❦

Dost thou love life? Then do not squander time;
for that's the stuff life is made of.

❦

Doing an injury puts you below your enemy;
Revenging one makes you but even with him;
Forgiving it sets you above him.

❦

If your head is wax, don't walk in the sun.

❦

Learn of the skilful: He that teaches himself
hath a fool for his master.

❦

For want of a nail the shoe is lost; for want of a shoe the horse is lost;
for want of a horse the rider is lost.

❦

Man's tongue is soft, and bone doth lack;
Yet a stroke therewith may break a man's back.

❦

Lost time is never found again.

❦

Time is an herb that cures all diseases.

❦

Better slip with foot than tongue.

Further Reading

The Autobiography and Other Writings. Benjamin Franklin. Edited and with an introduction by Peter Shaw. The three excerpts given here appear in this book along with many other of Franklin's writings.

The Many Worlds of Ben Franklin. Frank R. Donovan.

Benjamin Franklin. Robin McKowan. These two books contain biographical information about the life of this great man.

What does Franklin think about making good use of time? *(He thinks that time is the one thing we should never waste.)*

What kind of person was Benjamin Franklin? *(Sample answer: A very practical person, who believed in hard work and thinking carefully before making a decision.)*

EXTEND

Ask students to write at least five maxims of their own. They should think about their own rules for life and express them in a simple or humorous way. Collect the maxims and make a classroom *Poor Richard's Almanac.*

Further Reading.

You may want to ask students to go to the school or local library to find more books to read about Benjamin Franklin.

INTRODUCE

Read aloud the lesson title and ask students what the main topics of debate might be. Have students read the Thinking Focus and discuss why the Constitution signed in Philadelphia was not yet "official." Ask students to read to find out who opposed the Constitution and what their arguments were.

Key Terms

Vocabulary strategies: T36–37
Federalist—one who supported ratifying the Constitution
Antifederalist—one who opposed ratifying the Constitution
ratify—to approve formally

1787 | September | August | 1789 | 1790 | 1791 | 1792

LESSON 2

The Ratification Debate

THINKING FOCUS

How did the ratification of the Constitution depend on the debates in each of the states?

Key Terms

- Federalist
- Antifederalist
- ratify

This proposal of altering our federal government is of a most alarming nature. You ought to be extremely cautious, watchful, jealous of your liberty, for instead of securing your rights, you may lose them forever. If a wrong step be now made, the republic may be lost forever.

The great orator Patrick Henry was speaking at Virginia's state convention. It was a sweltering June day in Richmond. Nine months had gone by since the delegates in Philadelphia had signed the Constitution, but Patrick Henry was still dead-set against its approval. In a thundering voice, he warned a roomful of his fellow Virginians about the dangers the Constitution presented.

Referring to the delegates at the Philadelphia Convention, he asked: "Who authorized them to speak the language of 'We, the People' instead of 'We, the States'? States are the characteristics and the soul of a confederation."

Henry feared that the national government could overpower the ability of the states to protect their own citizens. He asked his fellow Virginians to consider the rights they valued, such as trial by jury. "Will the abandonment of your most sacred rights tend to the security of your liberty?"

Speaking directly to the state convention's chairman, Henry compared the Constitution to the human face:

This Constitution is said to have beautiful features, but when I come to examine these features, sir, they appear to me horridly frightful. Among other deformities, it has an awful squinting; it squints [is inclined to a bias] towards monarchy.

In the noted 1763 lawsuit called the "Parson's cause," shown here in this painting, Patrick Henry first won fame as a brilliant speaker.

Objectives

1. State the basic arguments of the Federalists and the Antifederalists for and against ratification.
2. Describe the political process that led to the states' ratification of the Constitution.
3. Explain why many people thought the Constitution was incomplete.

Graphic Overview

	Federalists	Antifederalists
Power balance	wanted strong central government	wanted state sovereignty
Finances	wanted to pay foreign debts	feared taxes
General Concerns	feared factions	feared tyranny

The Debate Goes Public

Similar objections were raised in all the state conventions. After four months of secret deliberations, the Constitution had become the subject of widespread public debate.

When the Philadelphia Convention had submitted the Constitution to the Congress still meeting in New York City under the old Articles of Confederation, the document was accompanied by a letter signed by George Washington. He firmly supported the Constitution, writing:

> *It is obviously impracticable, in the federal government of these states, to secure all rights of independent sovereignty to each, and yet provide for the interest and safety of all: Individuals entering into society must give up a share of liberty to preserve the rest.*

After Congress agreed to turn the Constitution over to the states for ratification, newspapers throughout the country printed its full text. (You can read the Constitution starting on page 636.) Though Washington's stamp of approval carried great weight, opponents of a constitution rallied to defeat it at the state conventions.

Antifederalist Fears

The word *federal* refers to a union of states under a government with central authority. People who supported the Constitution were called **Federalists**. People who opposed the Constitution were called **Antifederalists**. Although their specific concerns varied, most Antifederalists looked to the historical legacy of the English Bill of Rights, designed to protect the basic liberties of the king's subjects. Why, asked the Antifederalists, had the framers of the Constitution failed to include an American bill of rights to protect individual citizens?

The Antifederalists also questioned the legality of the Constitution. What right had the Convention to go so far beyond its original purpose, which was simply to revise the Articles of Confederation?

Among the first Antifederalists to explain his position publicly was Elbridge Gerry. "Conceiving as I did that the liberties of America were not secured by the system," he wrote the Massachusetts legislature in October 1787, "it was my duty to oppose it."

Some of the most powerful leaders within the states—including George Clinton, governor of New York—had long opposed the idea of a strong central government. These men did not want the national government to have more power than the states.

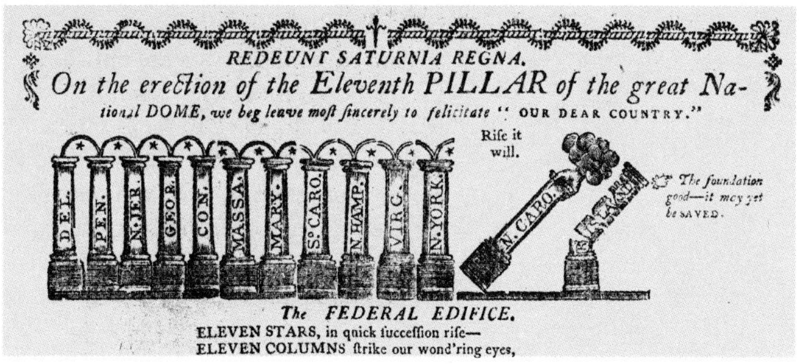

In building the federal government, each state had to formally approve the new Constitution. This 1788 cartoon shows 11 columns—states—supporting approval. Two columns remained unsteady.

They had begun to publish the reasons for their opposition in newspapers and pamphlets as soon as the Constitution was in print.

Antifederalist writers aroused people's fears that a strong central government could not be trusted. Among the threats to personal freedom, argued the Antifederalists, were taxes, government regulations, and a standing army. A strong central government could take away the liberties they had fought so hard to achieve in the war against Great Britain.

Some Antifederalists believed that the Constitution established a government in which a small, select group would protect its own interests

DEVELOP

Draw on the board the structure and main heads of the Graphic Overview on page 118. Ask students to copy it in their notes and, as they read, to list under the appropriate head the desires and fears that caused Federalists and Antifederalists to support or oppose the Constitution.

NATIONAL IDENTITY

Social Participation

Ask students to discuss how they would react if one of their classmates stated that the United States Constitution were out-of-date and ought to be changed. Is the freedom to express such an opinion important in a democracy?

Access Strategy

To help students analyze why people vote as they do, tell them the results of a recent local, state, or national election (for example, a referendum or initiative petition that was passed or defeated). Ask them why some people vote for candidates and ballot questions that promise change. Why do other people vote for candidates and ballot questions that will not "rock the boat"?

Tell students that in this lesson they will learn that the issues that made people vote for and against the Constitution are not very different from the reasons why people vote for and against new laws today. Politicians then and now had to figure out ways to "sell" their views to the public.

Access Activity

Read aloud the excerpts of Patrick Henry's speech on page 118. Have students paraphrase his speech. *(We could lose liberties. The power of states is important. We risk a return to monarchy.)* Ask students how they would persuade people to see the Constitution's "beautiful features." *(Point out that unity provides benefits for the states.)*

CONSTITUTIONAL HERITAGE

Critical Thinking

Have students explain the main arguments of the Antifederalists against the Constitution. *(The Constitution did not guarantee states' rights nor did it protect individual liberties; the Convention went too far by writing the Constitution.)*

■ *They ridiculed the Antifederalists by portraying their fears as irrational.*

Across Time & Space

At the time The Federalist *papers first appeared, they were similar to Letters to the Editor in today's newspapers. Letters to the Editor provide an opportunity for private citizens to express their views to a large audience.*

■ *Explain how the Federalists used ridicule to respond to the arguments of the Antifederalists.*

more than those of the common people. In their deepest fears, the Antifederalists worried that an elected government could turn out to be even worse than a monarchy. Publishing their "Reasons for Dissent" in the *Pennsylvania Packet and Daily Advertiser,* some delegates to the Pennsylvania convention claimed:

> *The power of direct taxation will apply to every individual.... However oppressive, the people will have but this alternative, except to pay the tax, or let their property be taken, for all resistance will be in vain. The standing army and select militia would enforce the collection.*

Selling the Constitution

The Federalists, on the other hand, did not share this sense of mistrust. They believed that a strong, central government was the only hope for the new nation. They soon realized that they would have to wage a war in the press to answer the charges made by the Antifederalists. To win support for the ratification of the Constitution, the Federalists resorted to newspaper articles and pamphlets. The page on the right shows how political arguments were debated in print.

Alexander Hamilton enlisted the aid of John Jay, another Federalist from New York, and James Madison. Together they wrote a series of letters, starting in October 1787, that were printed in a New York newspaper under the name *Publius.* Political writers often used classical pen names, and Hamilton chose *Publius,* the hero who established a stable republican government in Rome.

The letters from *Publius* were later collected and republished in book form under the title *The Federalist.* In Number 29 of *The Federalist,* Alexander Hamilton ridiculed the Antifederalists' fears:

> *There is something so far-fetched and so extravagant in the idea of danger to liberty from the militia that one is at a loss whether to treat it with gravity or with raillery [humor].... Where in the name of common sense are our fears to end if we may not trust our sons, our brothers, our neighbors, our fellow-citizens?*

The Federalist essays were an eloquent defense of the newly created Constitution, but they were only one of many political strategies used to win votes for the ratification of the document. The decisive battles were fought state by state in the ratifying conventions. ■

Ratification—Just Barely

The Federalists acted quickly to bring the Constitution to a vote in states in which they had a clear majority. The first states to debate the Constitution were Delaware and Pennsylvania. Delaware was the first state to **ratify**, or formally approve, with a unanimous vote on December 7, 1787. Pennsylvania followed with its approval in less than a week.

Those who opposed the Constitution were angry. They believed that the first state conventions had been called too hastily. Antifederalists tried to delay the process.

The next three state conventions —in New Jersey, Georgia, and Connecticut—ratified the Constitution with little opposition. Massachusetts proved to be the first serious problem. Antifederalists probably had a majority in the state, but they lacked leadership. Massachusetts, after debating from early January to early February 1788, became the sixth state to ratify the Constitution by a vote of 187-168.

Social Participation

Using the excerpt from "Reasons for Dissent" on this page and the accompanying text, have students analyze the Antifederalists' fears. *(Liberties not protected, oppressive taxes)* Then ask students why politicians often emphasize issues that arouse people's fears. *(People will vote to avoid something they fear.)*

Political Context

The way Federalists in Pennsylvania called for a state ratifying convention upset the Antifederalists in other states. It contributed to their decision to delay state ratifying conventions whenever possible. When the text of the Constitution became public, feelings for and against it ran very high in Pennsylvania. Enthusiastic Federalists in the Pennsylvania Assembly, the state's unicameral legislature, were quick to propose a state convention for ratification of the Constitution. Assemblymen with Antifederalist views did not want to rush into it. They stayed away from the State House on the day the vote was scheduled so that the required number of representatives would not be present. The next day a sergeant-at-arms, aided by a mob, forcibly carried two of the absent assemblymen to the State House and held them in their seats. By this violent method, the question of calling a convention to ratify the Constitution was voted on and approved 45 to 2.

A Closer Look

The Federalist Papers

Federalists versus Antifederalists. Alexander Hamilton wondered how to win people over to his Federalist thinking. How about a newspaper devoted to the cause? If the essays were persuasive enough, the new nation might choose to establish a strong central government.

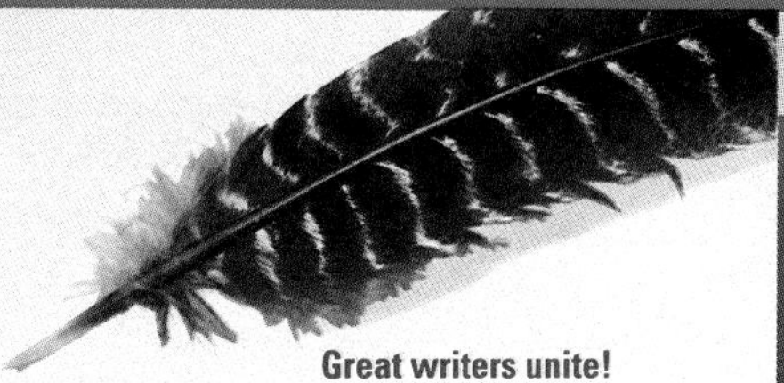

Great writers unite! For eight months, anonymous essays by some of America's greatest political thinkers—Alexander Hamilton, James Madison, and John Jay—sparked the attention of readers. Together, these essays explained why their authors thought the Constitution should be ratified.

The Federalist was printed on a press such as this. The printer set individual letters of type into a form by hand. Then the type was inked, and a piece of paper was placed on it. The printer pushed down on a lever so that a wooden block pressed the type to the paper.

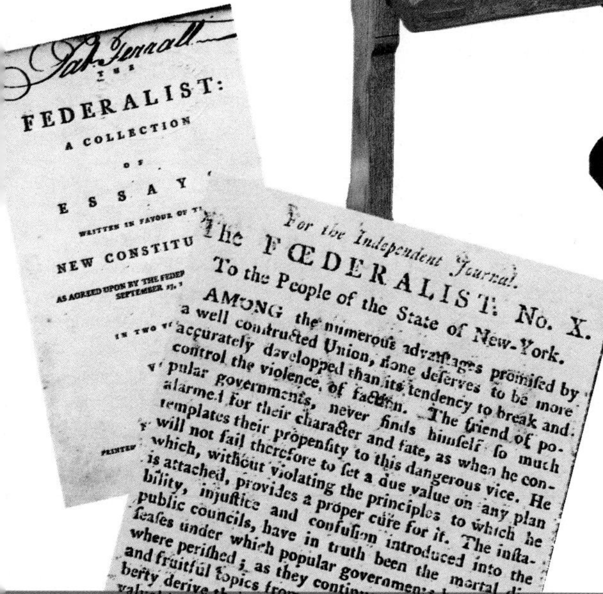

THE FEDERALIST: A COLLECTION OF ESSAYS, WRITTEN IN FAVOUR OF THE NEW CONSTITUTION

For the Independent Journal.

The FŒDERALIST. No. X.

To the People of the State of New-York.

AMONG the numerous advantages promised by a well constructed Union, none deserves to be more accurately developed than its tendency to break and control the violence of faction. The friend of popular governments, never finds himself so much alarmed for their character and fate, as when he contemplates their propensity to this dangerous vice. He will not fail therefore to set a due value on any plan which, without violating the principles to which he is attached, provides a proper cure for it. The instability, injustice and confusion introduced into the public councils, have in truth been the mortal diseases under which popular governments have every where perished; as they continue ...

Only 300 copies were printed because printers knew that people would post them on public buildings and read them aloud at public meetings. Soon after the newspapers were published, *The Federalist* was published as a book. Today, the essays are still studied around the world.

HISTORY

Visual Learning

Have students refer to the pictures of the Federalist Papers on this page and read the accompanying caption. Why is it significant that such essays were posted and often read aloud in public places? *(Might cause people to discuss the issues together; might reach people who could not read)*

More About the Printing Press
Each sheet of the newspaper had to be "pulled" twice. In order to "pull" each sheet, a printer had to use his weight and his strength in order to put an adequate amount of pressure on the lever.

Speaking and Listening

Have students read aloud parts of the annotated text of the Constitution, starting on page 636, and discuss the meaning of each section. Begin by having one student read aloud the Preamble. Others may read aloud the parts about the powers of Congress and the states *(Article 1, Sections 6, 8, 9)*, the President *(Article 2, Sections 2, 3)*, or the Supreme Court *(Article 3, Section 1)*.

Language Arts Connection

Discuss propaganda techniques with your students, particularly the use of *loaded words*—words that have strongly positive or negative associations. Have students look for the loaded words in the Federalist and Antifederalist arguments presented in this lesson. *(Positive words:* liberty, sacred rights, brothers, neighbors; *negative words:* monarchy, taxation, standing army*)*

Visual Learning

Have students examine the pictures of the quill pen and the Federalist Papers, as well as the captions on this page. Why might people in 1787 be more excited about the publication of a new newspaper than people would be today? *(They had less access to news—no television, no radio, fewer newspapers.)*

POLITICAL SYSTEMS

Visual Learning

Ask students to look at the "Road to Ratification" timeline on this page. How long did it take for all 13 states to ratify the Constitution? *(From September 1787 to May 1790)* Which states decided to ratify in the months immediately after the February 1788 proposal of the Bill of Rights? *(Mass., Md., S.C., N.H., Va., N.Y.)*

■ *Both used debate as well as newspapers and pamphlets. Antifederalists tried to delay the conventions. Federalists pushed for quick votes.*

CLOSE

Have students answer the Thinking Focus. Draw the structure of the Graphic Overview from page 118 on the board. Have students complete it, based on the lists they made while reading the lesson.

The Road to Ratification: 1787–1790

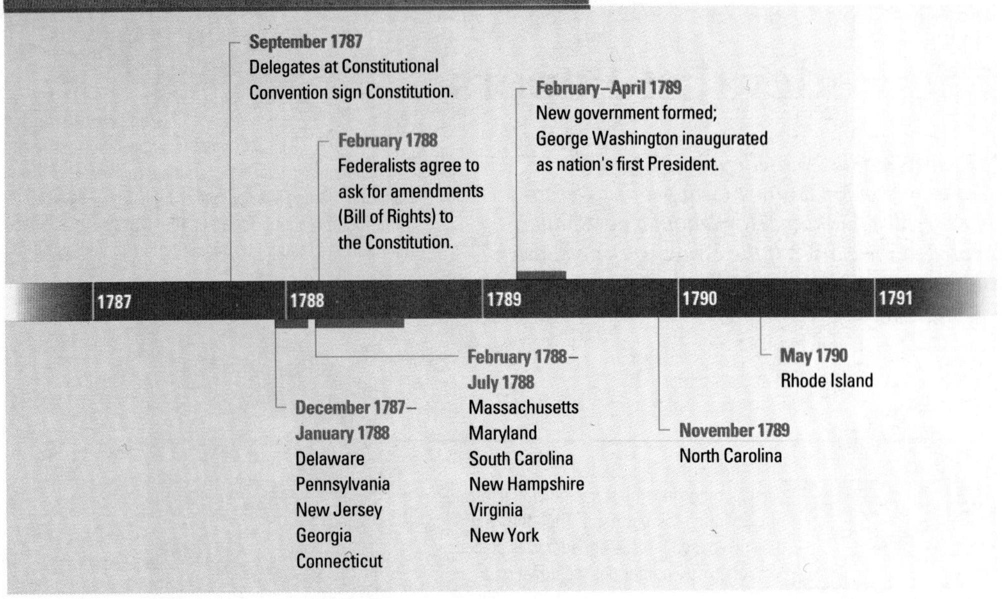
September 1787
Delegates at Constitutional Convention sign Constitution.
February 1788
Federalists agree to ask for amendments (Bill of Rights) to the Constitution.
February–April 1789
New government formed; George Washington inaugurated as nation's first President.
1787
1788
1789
1790
1791
December 1787–January 1788
Delaware
Pennsylvania
New Jersey
Georgia
Connecticut
February 1788–July 1788
Massachusetts
Maryland
South Carolina
New Hampshire
Virginia
New York
November 1789
North Carolina
May 1790
Rhode Island

North Carolina and Rhode Island finally ratified the Constitution after George Washington was sworn into office in April 1789 as the first President.

After overcoming strong opposition, New Hampshire — on June 21, 1788 — became the ninth and decisive state to ratify the Constitution.

Meanwhile, a grand debate was taking place in Richmond, Virginia, between James Madison, often called the Father of the Constitution, and Patrick Henry, its most articulate opponent. The vote for ratification was close: 89-79.

If the Antifederalists had moved more quickly in Virginia and New York, where they had strong leaders and much support, the Constitution might never have been ratified. In fact, the Antifederalists' decision to delay worked against them. Another factor was that less than 10 percent of the newspapers supported them.

The Federalists had needed the approval of only nine states—not all thirteen. The fact that ratification did not require a unanimous vote, which had been a problem with the Articles of Confederation, kept the Constitution alive.

Even though the Antifederalists were defeated, they had won some support for the idea that the Constitution was not complete without a bill of rights. Still to be added to the Constitution was an official promise that the national government would not infringe on dearly valued liberties. Whether the Antifederalists would get such an addition to the Constitution was still uncertain. ■

■ *What were the strategies of the Federalists and the Antifederalists for winning votes in the states?*

REVIEW

1. **FOCUS** How did the ratification of the Constitution depend on the debates in each of the states?
2. **CONNECT** How did Patrick Henry and other Antifederalists appeal to Americans' long-standing fear of the British monarchy?
3. **POLITICAL SYSTEMS** Examine the Federalist and Antifederalist positions. Which position gave greater value to the sovereignty of the nation and which gave greater value to the independence of the states?
4. **CRITICAL THINKING** Explain how printing political arguments in the newspapers of 1787–1788 was essential to carrying out the ratification debates.
5. **CRITICAL THINKING** Why do you think the Constitution was, in the end, ratified?
6. **ACTIVITY** Take a Federalist or an Antifederalist position, and draw and caption your own cartoon to illustrate your viewpoint. What sort of publication do you think would print your cartoon?

Homework Options

Ask students to find examples of persuasive writing in newspapers. Have them describe the techniques—such as humor or loaded words—that the writers use to make their points.

Study Guide: page 16.

Answers to Review Questions

1. Whether each state convention ratified the Constitution depended on the outcome of debates between Federalists and Antifederalists
2. They suggested that an elected government could be as tyrannical as a monarchy.
3. Federalists considered national sovereignty most important; Antifederalists valued the independence of states above all else.
4. Both sides used the press to explain their views to the public.
5. Sample answer: The Federalists were able to move quickly to get ratification. They did not give the Antifederalists a chance to organize against ratification. Allow for personal opinion.
6. Students' cartoons should have an obvious point of view.

UNDERSTANDING GROUP ACTIVITIES

Reaching a Compromise

Here's Why

A compromise is a settlement of differences by agreement. Sometimes a number of people have to work together on a project, but each of them has different ideas about how to do the work. In order to finish the project, the group has to reach an agreement on how to do the work. The agreement they reach is called a compromise.

For example, although the delegates to the Constitutional Convention of 1787 wanted to do the best they could for America's 13 states, each had a very different idea of what should be done. The delegates had to reach a compromise in order to do the work of the convention. Families, businesses, and friends all use the process of compromise.

Suppose your class decided to have a surprise party for your teacher, but everyone had different ideas about how to do it. You would need to find a way for everyone to agree on the plans for the party.

Here's How

Each person in a group has to be willing to give up something in order for a group to reach an agreement. Therefore one of the most important parts of the compromise process is your individual decision on what you will go along with and what you won't.

Asking yourself questions is often a good way to decide where you stand on an issue. If you need to work with a group to plan a party for your teacher, you might want to ask yourself these questions:

1. **What part of this project is most important to me?**
   You may decide that the decorations are the most important part of the project for you.

2. **How many other people think that part of the project is important?**
   If many people want to do the decorating, it may be difficult for everyone to agree on who should be responsible for it.

3. **Why is that part important to me?**
   You need to evaluate how important decorating is for you, in order to see if it is something you can give up. Perhaps the decorations are the most important part for you because you enjoy drawing and making them. Or perhaps it is the only part of the project you feel you can do well.

4. **What is best for the group?**
   At this point, you need to look at the whole project. If you love decorating, but the party will not happen unless there are more people making food than decorating, you need to decide if it would be better for you to give up doing the decorating in order to get the job done. On the other hand, if you feel decorating is the only thing you could do well for the group, you may want to stick to your original goal of doing the decorating.

Try It

Whenever students work together in groups in the classroom, they have to agree on who will do what. Assume that your class has to produce a play. Use the questions to decide which part of the production you would choose to work on and how you would work with the group to reach an agreement.

Apply It

Choose an issue important to your class, such as the choice of school lunch menus. Make your individual decision, then divide into groups and go through the process of compromise. Write a short paragraph outlining what your original decision was, what the group decision was, and how the compromise was reached.

UNDERSTANDING GROUP ACTIVITIES

This skill lesson will give students an opportunity to develop the skill of compromise through several class projects.

CITIZENSHIP

Social Participation

After they analyze the four questions suggested in Here's How, ask students which of the four they think is most important. *(Sample answer: Questions 1 and 3 relate to the individual's preferences, while 2 relates to the preferences of others. Question 4 is probably most important.)* Why? *(Because it leads to a solution that will unite the group in support of the proposed project)* Encourage students to consider why the ability to compromise is important in everyday life. *(Sample answer: Our society often uses groups to achieve goals. Group activity works best when group members realize that they cannot get their own way all of the time.)*

Answers to Try It

Students should be able to provide an answer to each of the four questions. You may suggest possible roles they would each like to play, such as acting, writing, directing, lighting, scenery preparation, or publicity.

Answers to Apply It

To encourage lively group discussion, have each student write down his or her favorite lunch choices before beginning to work with their group on a compromise menu. Have the groups refer to the four questions in Here's How to guide their discussions. Students should apply the four questions in their descriptions of how their group operates.

Objective

Use group plans for a surprise party to practice compromise. (Social Participation 2)

INTRODUCE

Point out the lesson title and ask students why the Constitution seemed incomplete to the Antifederalists without a bill of rights. Have them read the Thinking Focus and predict what kinds of rights will be protected in the Bill of Rights. Have them read the lesson to confirm or reject their predictions.

Key Terms

Vocabulary strategies: T36–37

free press—the right to publish anything, including criticism of the government in power

amendment—an addition or change to the Constitution, made into law through the process of ratification

➤The word *gerrymandering*—reshaping voting districts to favor the party in power—was coined in 1812. It was based on the name of Elbridge Gerry, then governor of Massachusetts, and the salamander-shape of one particular voting district.

1787 September — 1792 December

LESSON 3

The Bill of Rights

THINKING FOCUS

How does the Bill of Rights balance governmental powers with the rights of individuals?

Key Terms

- free press
- amendment

▲ *Antifederalist Elbridge Gerry warned citizens that a bill of rights was necessary to protect individual liberties.*

Helping to fuel the strong feelings for the bill of rights in the 1780s were Americans' memories of New Yorker John Peter Zenger's fight for freedom of the press fifty years earlier. Every Monday in 1733, Zenger's *New York Weekly Journal* would appear with stinging articles criticizing the British colonial government: Governor William Cosby is a tyrant! An enemy of justice!

Government officials were outraged. Roughly one year after the newspaper was first published, British officials jailed Zenger for his criticism of the colonial government in New York. Although Zenger wrote few of the articles himself, he was held solely responsible since he was the newspaper's publisher. Zenger was kept in jail for more than 11 months since he could not afford to pay the bail. Still the newspaper appeared every Monday. With whispered instructions she received through a hole in the prison door, Zenger's wife, Anna, continued to publish the newspaper so hated by the British.

Finally, the case was brought to trial. The financial backers of Zenger's newspaper hired Andrew Hamilton of Philadelphia to represent Zenger. Hamilton was considered one of the most brilliant lawyers in the colonies. Hamilton argued that Zenger had only published the truth, and that he should not be punished for publishing the truth. The jury agreed and they found Zenger not guilty. After his release, Zenger printed a complete account of his trial and the British authorities didn't stop him. This was considered the first major victory for a **free press** that is, news media such as newspapers and magazines that are unrestricted by the government.

Americans did not forget the case. Nor did they forget other memories of British rule. The British army had forced the owners of private homes to house soldiers. Colonial customs officials had invaded homes to search for and seize smuggled goods. With a bill of rights, the new Constitution would guarantee that such governmental practices would be only memories of the past.

Why Massachusetts Resisted

"There is no declaration of rights." This was how George Mason had objected to the Constitution in 1787. And these words became the rallying cry of the Antifederalists back in the states. The debates at the Massachusetts state ratifying convention would prove to be the turning point for the adoption of the bill of rights.

"Beware! beware!—you are forging chains for yourselves and your children—your liberties are at stake," exclaimed Elbridge Gerry in November 1787, after he had returned to Massachusetts. The lack of a bill of rights was the most serious obstacle to winning the support of old patriots such as Samuel Adams and John

Objectives

1. Identify the Bill of Rights and its relevance to everyday life.
2. Explain why a bill of rights was left out of the Constitution and why many people thought it was necessary.
3 Describe the process by which the Bill of Rights was added to the Constitution.

Graphic Overview

Problem potential abuse of power by central government → **Solution** add Bill of Rights to Constitution → **Result** protection of rights of individuals and states

Hancock. Adams planned to oppose the Constitution at the Massachusetts state convention, because he was determined "to protect and cover the rights of Mankind" against the threat of a strong central government.

Wanted: Guaranteed Rights

After the Philadelphia Convention, most of the men who had written the Constitution could not understand why a bill of rights was a serious issue for many states. They believed that the Constitution, as it was, could stand on its own. On the last day of the Convention, George Mason proposed that a bill of rights be added to the Constitution. Elbridge Gerry agreed with him but other delegates had argued that the states' own declarations of rights would be sufficient to protect individual liberties. They had voted against the motion to add a bill of rights at the Convention.

A Winning Strategy

Although many Federalists continued to consider a bill of rights unnecessary, some were willing to compromise on this issue in order to establish a new government. The Federalists had already used compromise as a unifying force in Philadelphia. Because they feared defeat in the Massachusetts ratifying convention, Federalist leaders decided to gain support by drafting a list of **amendments,** additions meant to improve the Constitution. They persuaded John Hancock, the most popular man in Massachusetts, to present these amendments to the state convention. The proposed amendments made the Constitution acceptable to many who had formerly opposed ratification.

The winning strategy of the Massachusetts Federalists turned the tide of ratification. As other states debated the Constitution, they too insisted on amendments that would guarantee a person's rights. ■

▲ *The British army occupied Boston in 1768 to enforce the writs of assistance, which gave officials blanket authority to carry out searches at any time and any place.*

■ *What made some Federalists change their minds about including a bill of rights in the Constitution?*

Balancing the Constitution

The framers of the Constitution had worked hard to create a system that balanced the powers of the three branches of government—legislative, executive, and judicial. The amendments proposed by the state ratifying conventions were aimed at another kind of balance: balancing the rights of the states and of individual citizens against the powers of the central government.

James Madison was one of the Federalists who had expressed concerns about the protection of basic rights, through his part in writing *The Federalist*. During the debates in

DEVELOP

Suggest that students make a list of the rights that are protected in the Bill of Rights as they read this lesson.

HISTORY

Critical Thinking

Ask students how British rule in America led to the demand for a bill of rights as part of the Constitution. *(Colonists were aware of what could happen when their rights were not protected, as in the Zenger trial.)*

■ *They realized that a bill of rights would make the Constitution acceptable to more states.*

Access Strategy

Have students recall their role playing in the Access Strategy in Lesson 1. Remind them that almost any organization—families, schools, organized sports, town governments—has rules. In order for groups to be fair to all members, everyone—including people with less power—must have rights that are protected.

Encourage students to name some of the rules and rights they have as students. Have them discuss how they would feel if they lost some of their rights. For example, how would they respond if they were told they could no longer talk, even quietly, with any of their friends in the hallways or cafeteria? You may wish to divide the class into heterogeneous groups for this discussion.

Tell students that many people in the United States in 1787 were worried that the government might take away many of their rights. This lesson will explain what the people did to protect their rights.

Access Activity

Use the illustration on this page to begin a discussion of ways in which governments sometimes take away people's rights. What might the colonists and British soldiers be saying to each other? *(Colonists protesting that their rights are being violated, soldiers asserting their authority)*

CONSTITUTIONAL HERITAGE

Critical Thinking

Ask students to review the procedure for amending the Constitution. *(An amendment can be proposed by either two-thirds of both houses of Congress or the legislatures of two-thirds of the states; it must be ratified by three-fourths of the states.)* Have them discuss why including a method for amending the Constitution was and continues to be an important strength of the original document. *(Writers of the Constitution were not perfect; they could not predict changes necessary in the future.)*

Virginia, Madison promised to work for a bill of rights once the Constitution was ratified. After he was elected in 1789 to the first Congress, he pressed for passage of a series of amendments to the new Constitution.

Rights for the People

The amendments drafted at the state conventions listed the rights of individual citizens and the rights of the states. These were rights the national government could not take away. Many advocates of a bill of rights also wanted the Constitution to state clearly that any rights not given to the national government by the states be reserved to the states or to the people.

The first Congress under the Constitution met in New York in March 1789. Most men elected to Congress had been delegates to the Convention of 1787 or to the state ratifying conventions. Madison and other members of the first Congress combined the many proposed amendments into a list of twelve. Some amendments included more than one right. For example, the First Amendment was written to protect freedom of speech, press, assembly, and petition. Congress voted in favor of the twelve amendments in September 1789 and sent them to the states for ratification.

Ratification of Ten Amendments

Although the men who framed the original Constitution had not included a bill of rights at first, they did have the foresight to include ways to amend the Constitution. Americans are able to change the Constitution or add to it. An amendment may be proposed by two-thirds of both houses of

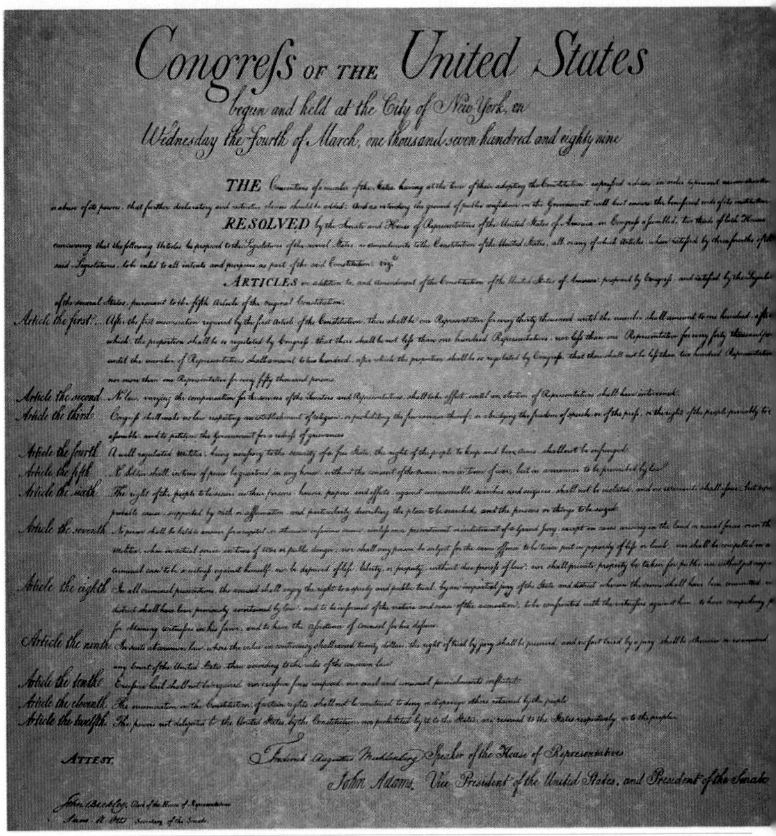
Congress of the United States
begun and held at the City of New-York, on
Wednesday the fourth of March, one thousand seven hundred and eighty nine

THE ...
RESOLVED ...
ARTICLES ...

Article the first ...
Article the second ...
Article the third ...
Article the fourth ...
Article the fifth ...
Article the sixth ...
Article the seventh ...
Article the eighth ...
Article the ninth ...
Article the tenth ...
Article the eleventh ...
Article the twelfth ...

ATTEST,
Speaker of the House of Representatives
John Adams, Vice President of the United States, and President of the Senate

➤ *Of the twelve amendments proposed for a bill of rights, two were not ratified. One limited the size of the House of Representatives; the other forbade members of the House and Senate to raise their own salaries.*

Visual Learning

Have students look at the copy of the Bill of Rights on this page. Ask them to point out evidence that our use of the English language has changed in two hundred years. *(An s in the middle of a word looks like an f. Many nouns that would not be capitalized now were capitalized then.)*

Historical Context

Originally the Bill of Rights applied only to the federal government. It did not require the state governments to respect an individual's basic rights. The Fourteenth Amendment, added in 1868, limits the states' power. It forbids any state to deny any person "life, liberty, or property without due process of law" or to "deny any person . . . equal protection of its laws."

Collaborative Learning

Tell students to recall their discussion in the Access Strategy. Have them work in groups of four or five students to draft a "bill of rights" for the students in their school. Within each group, students should make suggestions, discuss, and agree upon a list of rights. Then, a representative from each group should share the group's bill of rights with the class.

Congress, or the legislatures of two-thirds of the states can propose a constitutional convention. If three-fourths of the states ratify a proposed amendment, it then becomes part of the Constitution.

Thomas Jefferson observed this amendment process from France. He commented proudly that "the example of changing a constitution by assembling the wise men of the state instead of assembling armies" would be worth "much to the world."

The system worked remarkably well. By December 15, 1791, the states had ratified ten out of the twelve proposed amendments to the Constitution, and the United States had its Bill of Rights. Look at page 647 of this book and find where the Bill of Rights now appears in the Constitution along with more recent amendments.

The Framework Completed

The Bill of Rights balances the Constitution by giving people legal protection against abuses of power. The First Amendment, for example, prohibits the government from attempting to control what people think, say, or write. It grants people the right to worship according to their own beliefs, without interference from the government. The Fourth Amendment protects people from unreasonable searches and seizures of their private property. The Sixth Amendment guarantees the right to a speedy and fair trial by jury. The Eighth Amendment prohibits cruel and unusual punishment. When these or any other declared rights are violated, individuals may appeal to the courts.

The first ten amendments brought the nation together under one federal government by removing most of the Antifederalists' fears. Now that the Constitution included the Bill of Rights, many Antifederalists became active in the new government. Edmund Randolph was named the first attorney general by Washington. George Clinton became Vice President under Jefferson and again under Madison. And James Monroe, an Antifederalist from Virginia, eventually became the fifth President of the United States.

The government created by the Constitutional Convention of 1787 has worked for more than 200 years because its wise authors made it both strong and flexible. With the addition of the Bill of Rights, the Constitution has also protected the basic freedoms and rights that Americans cherish.

The framers could not have foreseen all the conflicts, problems, and needs of a growing nation. The Constitution was indeed sketchy. But with its amendment procedure, it has provided a means to accommodate changes. As the U.S. Supreme Court's Chief Justice John Marshall once stated, the Constitution was "intended to endure for ages to come, and, consequently to be adapted to the various *crises* of human affairs. ■

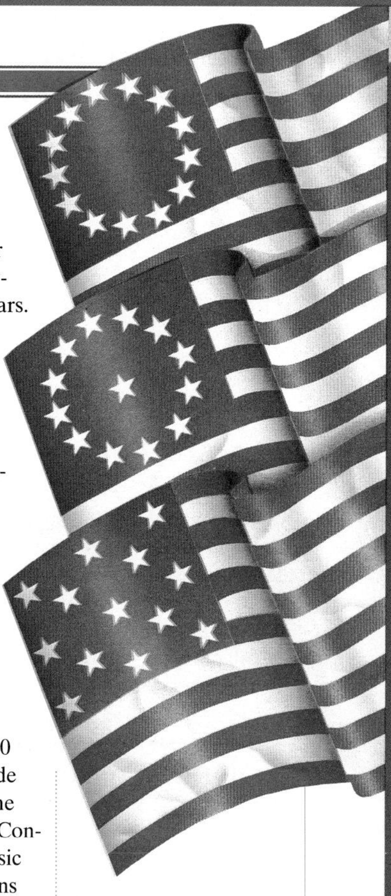

The states still had to work out many details. There was not yet an official arrangement of the stars in the U.S. flag.

■ *How did the amendment process provide the flexibility to make the Constitution strong?*

R E V I E W

1. **FOCUS** How does the Bill of Rights balance governmental powers with the rights of individuals?
2. **CONNECT** Why did Federalists first oppose the addition of a bill of rights? Why did most Antifederalists believe such a bill was absolutely necesssary?
3. **HISTORY** Explain why the strategy of the Federalists to compromise in Massachusetts also helped the Antifederalists in the other states.
4. **CONSTITUTIONAL HERITAGE** Describe the process by which the Bill of Rights was added to the Constitution.
5. **CRITICAL THINKING** In 1791, the Bill of Rights was ratified. Since then 16 amendments have been ratified. Why do you think Americans have continued to revise the Constitution?
6. **ACTIVITY** Prepare and deliver a one-minute presentation on the basic rights guaranteed by the Bill of Rights.

CONSTITUTIONAL HERITAGE

Social Participation

Ask students how our country might be different if we lacked the protections of the Bill of Rights. Which amendment in the Bill of Rights do they value the most? Why? *(Students should consult the Bill of Rights in the annotated Constitution that begins on page 636.)*

■ *It provided a peaceful and orderly process for settling conflicts about the Constitution.*

C L O S E

Have students answer the Thinking Focus. Copy on the board the Graphic Overview from page 124. Ask students to evaluate their predictions and compare the lists they made while reading the lesson with the Bill of Rights, found in the annotated Constitution beginning on page 636. As an extension activity, have them read the amendments aloud and discuss the meaning of each one.

Answers to Review Questions

1. It guarantees that the federal government cannot abuse the rights of individuals.
2. Federalists thought individual rights were already protected by the states' declaration of rights, but Antifederalists believed that a strong federal government could take away these rights.
3. Federalists and Antifederalists in other states began to compromise on the issue of a bill of rights.
4. Congress proposed twelve amendments. Ten were ratified by three-fourths of the states.
5. Sample answer: Americans have adapted the Constitution to the changing times, in some cases giving civil rights to those people denied them in the original document. Allow for personal opinion.
6. Students' presentations should explain the rights clearly and concisely.

Homework Option

Have students bring to class newspaper or magazine articles or letters to the editor that refer to proposed amendments to the Constitution.

Study Guide: page 18.

Answers to Reviewing Key Terms

A. Sample answers:

1. The Federalists supported a strong central government while the Anti-Federalists wanted states to have more power.
2. The first ten amendments to the Constitution are called the Bill of Rights.
3. Americans are guaranteed a free press in the First Amendment of the Bill of Rights.

B. Answers:

1. True. Each branch—legislative, judicial and executive—had certain powers to check the other two and prevent abuses.
2. False. The executive branch is headed by the President.
3. True. Congress, which makes laws, is the legislative branch.
4. False. The framers of the Constitution provided rules for passing amendments in order to change the Constitution.

Answers to Exploring Concepts

A. Answers:

Power of state government: strong / weaker than national government but with specific powers

Power of central government: weak, mostly advisory / strong

Importance of Bill of Rights: very important to protect rights / not very important because state laws would protect rights

Legality of the Constitution: illegal because the framers made bigger changes than they were supposed to / legal and necessary to make a strong nation

Chapter Review

Reviewing Key Terms

amendment (p. 125)
Antifederalist (p. 119)
bill of rights (p. 113)
checks and balances (p. 108)
executive branch (p. 110)
Federalist (p. 119)
free press (p. 124)
judicial branch (p. 110)
legislative branch (p. 110)
ratify (p. 120)

A. In each of the following pairs, the two terms are related in some way. Write a sentence for each pair that clearly explains the relationship between the two terms.

1. Antifederalist, Federalist
2. bill of rights, amendment
3. free press, bill of rights

B. Based on what you have read in the chapter, decide whether each of the following statements is accurate. Write an explanation for each decision.

1. The Constitution created a system of checks and balances to keep any one branch of government from becoming more powerful than the other two.
2. The judicial branch of the government is headed by the President.
3. The legislative branch of the government is made up of the Congress.
4. The framers of the Constitution provided for the passage of amendments to make sure that its provisions would never change.

Exploring Concepts

A. On a separate sheet of paper make a table like the one shown below. Then complete the table by briefly describing the Antifederalist position and the Federalist position on each of the issues listed on the left.

Issues	Anti-Federalist Position	Federalist Position
The power of state government		
The power of central government		
Importance of Bill of Rights		
Legality of the Constitution		

B. Decide whether each of the following statements is true or false. If it is false, correct the statement and provide facts from the chapter to support your correction.

1. A series of compromises helped the delegates to the Constitutional Convention agree on a final document.
2. Even though most of the delegates signed the Constitution, they were not sure it would be adopted.
3. Many people thought the Constitution was incomplete.
4. There were many reasons why people feared a strong central government.
5. The Federalists' actions won several quick victories in favor of the Constitution.
6. The Antifederalists' decision to delay votes worked for them.
7. The Antifederalists did not want the Constitution to have a bill of rights.
8. In order to gain ratification, the Federalists agreed they would soon add a bill of rights.
9. The decision to include a procedure for amending the Constitution was a mistake.
10. The delegates to the Constitutional Convention reached an easy compromise.

B. Answers:

1. True.
2. True.
3. True.
4. True.
5. True.
6. False. Although the Anti-Federalists tried to delay the process, the Federalists quickly got the Constitution ratified in several states, which helped them gain support in other states.
7. False. The main objection the Anti-Federalists had to the Constitution was that it lacked a bill of rights.
8. True.
9. False. The framers of the Constitution had no way of knowing what the future held; therefore, providing a means for change was a good thing.
10. False. The delegates debated for a long time before they made the compromises that led to the Constitution.

Reviewing Skills

1. Identify three situations in which you would want to use the process of compromise.
2. Using the process of reaching a compromise that you learned on page 123, write a short paragraph describing how you would decide whether you would have wanted to support the Federalist position on the Constitution or the Antifederalist position.
3. What compromise did the delegates to the Constitutional Convention of 1787 reach?
4. If you were looking for detailed information on the Constitutional Convention what kind of primary sources could you use?
5. Suppose you and your family are planning a vacation. You want to go someplace where you can go swimming, another person wants to go skiing, and another wants to go horseback riding. How would you reach a compromise?

Using Critical Thinking

1. If you had lived during the development of the Constitution, would you have been a Federalist or an Antifederalist? Explain your answer.
2. Why do you think the framers of the Constitution included a provision that ensured that there would be a free press?
3. Federalist Alexander Hamilton wrote that those who fought the Revolution "sought to obtain liberty for no particular state, but for the whole Union. . . connected under one controlling and supreme head." Do you agree with his position in this statement? Explain your answer.
4. Antifederalists in Pennsylvania wrote that "the powers vested in Congress by this Constitution must necessarily annihilate [wipe out] and absorb the legislative, executive, and judicial powers of the several states." Did this prediction come true? Explain your answer.
5. Read the Bill of Rights which begins on page 647 in the back of this book. Which of the rights or freedoms in the Bill of Rights is the most important to you? Why?
6. Thomas Jefferson, writing from France, said that "the example of changing a constitution by assembling the wise men of the state instead of assembling armies" was "worth much to the world." Find out what was happening in France at the time of the Constitutional Convention. With that information in mind, explain Jefferson's statement.

Preparing for Citizenship

1. **WRITING ACTIVITY** The Bill of Rights still causes controversy today. Choose one of the rights listed in the first ten amendments to the Constitution. Find some recent newspaper stories or magazine articles that describe disputes over its meaning. Write a summary of the arguments, giving both sides of the issue, and stating your position on the issue.
2. **COLLECTING INFORMATION** The Constitution originally allowed the state legislatures to choose the Senators for their state. Read the amendments to the Constitution, beginning on page 647 at the back of this book, and find which amendment changed the election process for the Senate. Write a paragraph explaining how the Senators are elected today and stating why you think the amendment was changed.
3. **ART ACTIVITY** Throughout history documents have been important graphic symbols as well as legal papers. Find a copy of the original Constitution. Create a contemporary design for the document. You may use advanced artistic techniques, such as computer graphics, if you would like.
4. **ART ACTIVITY** Make a chart showing the members of the national government who represent you. Include the President and Vice President as well as the senators and representatives from your district. If possible, include a picture of each one and a short biography.
5. **COLLABORATIVE LEARNING** Create a constitution for your class. Assuming that the teacher is the executive, create a system of checks and balances to ensure that necessary class work is done. Class duties such as cleaning the room, decorating the bulletin boards, and monitoring assignments should be taken into account. Make provisions for a free press, for individual rights, and for resolving disputes that may arise among classmates.

Answers to Reviewing Skills

1. Ask students to remember situations in which a decision had to be made. Did the participants compromise? Or did one person or a few people make the decision?
2. Refer students to the chart they made in Exploring Concepts.
3. The Three-fifths Compromise or the Connecticut Compromise.
4. Students may suggest diaries, notes, newspaper accounts, and letters.
5. Encourage students to consider all the parts of the vacation that might be important to discuss.

Answers to Using Critical Thinking

1. Ask students to consider how occupation and home state might have affected their opinion of the Constitution.
2. Encourage students to research Supreme Court decisions on the freedom of the press and to learn about the development of this freedom in the years since it became part of the Constitution.
3. Students who agree should point out that the colonists fought as one country, intending to create one nation. Students who disagree may point out that many patriots, such as Sam Adams, wanted the states to keep their own power and identities.
4. Students should recognize that each state still has its own legislature, governor, and court; therefore, the prediction did not come true.
5. Encourage students to consider examples from their own lives, such as freedom of expression in wearing clothes and freedom of choice in reading books and listening to music.
6. Students should look up the French Revolution and the Reign of Terror.

Answers to Preparing for Citizenship

1. **WRITING ACTIVITY** Students may be interested in recent decisions on student rights, such as the right of schools to censor student newspapers and to search lockers.
2. **COLLECTING INFORMATION** Students should consider the advantages of allowing the people to elect Senators directly.
3. **ART ACTIVITY** Refer students to the proposed Bill of Rights shown on page 126. Suggest that they compare the appearance of the printing with examples of modern design, such as newsletters and brochures.
4. **ART ACTIVITY** Refer students to congressional directories in the local library. Also encourage students to contact their representatives for brochures with photos and information.
5. **COLLABORATIVE LEARNING** Once the constitution is agreed upon, students can divide up the tasks of writing and editing, designing and producing the final draft (by hand or on a typewriter or computer). Each student can sign it and then copies can be made for each student.

UNIT
OVERVIEW

Draw students' attention to the unit title and the narrative underneath it. Ask students to name what they think are distinctly "American" characteristics. Point out that decisions made by people in the early days of the nation have helped to establish many of the ideas we consider American today.

Have students examine the painting. Ask them to explain how it might relate to the unit title and the narrative. *(The July 4th celebration helps to establish a national identity.)*

Looking Back

Remind students that they have just learned about the creation of the Constitution and what its authors intended to decide—or not decide—before the nation tried to apply the Constitution to day-to-day governing.

Looking Forward

Tell students that they will be studying the unfolding of the American drama in the next three chapters:

Chapter 5 *The Creation of a Party System*
Chapter 6 *The Maturing Republic*
Chapter 7 *People of the New Nation*

Unit 3 Establishing the New Nation

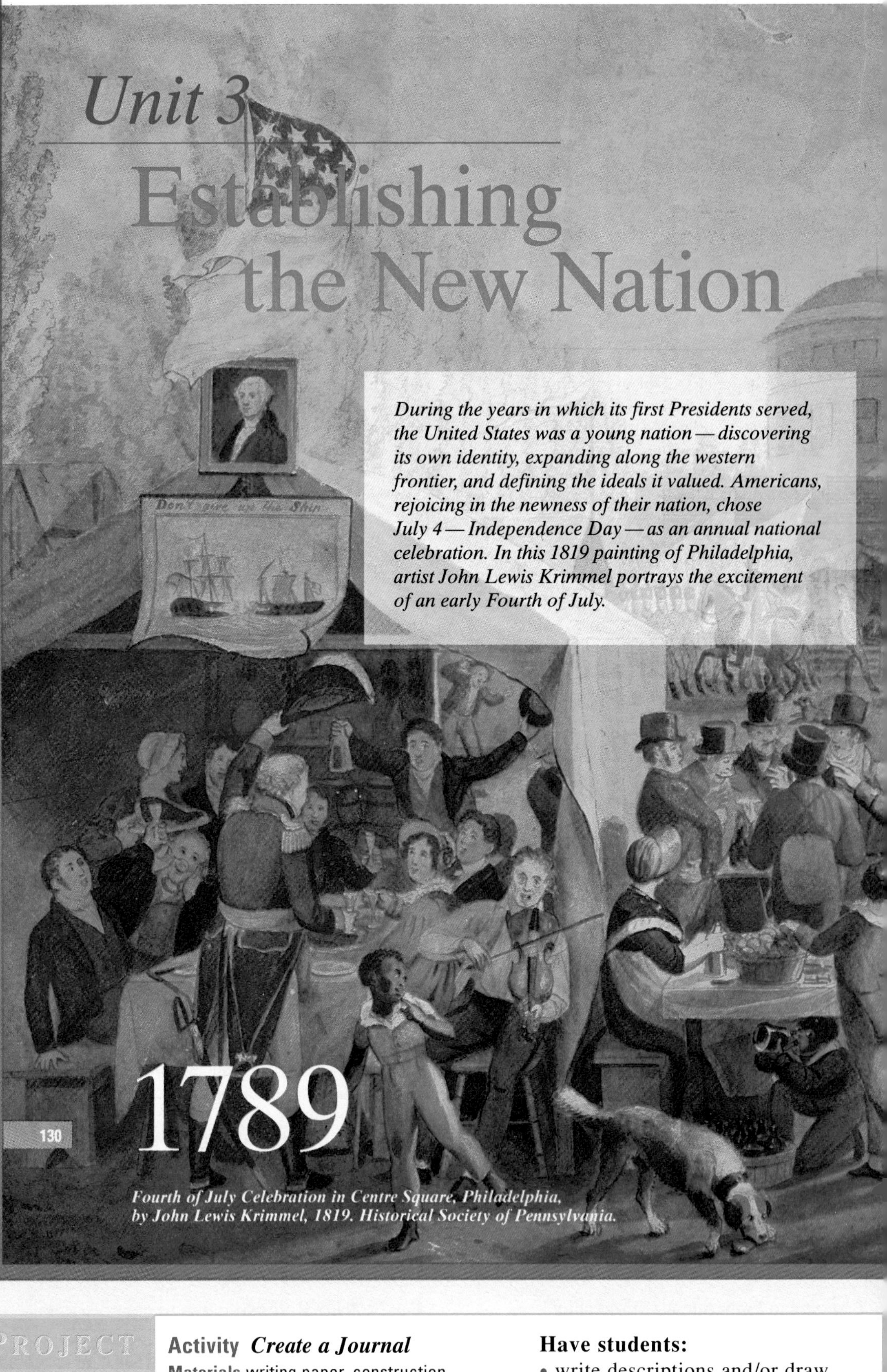

During the years in which its first Presidents served, the United States was a young nation—discovering its own identity, expanding along the western frontier, and defining the ideals it valued. Americans, rejoicing in the newness of their nation, chose July 4—Independence Day—as an annual national celebration. In this 1819 painting of Philadelphia, artist John Lewis Krimmel portrays the excitement of an early Fourth of July.

1789

Fourth of July Celebration in Centre Square, Philadelphia, by John Lewis Krimmel, 1819. Historical Society of Pennsylvania.

GEOGRAPHY PROJECT

Traveler in America

Geography Skill **Compare Routes on a Map**
Students use the skills of Acquiring, Organizing, and Analyzing geographic information.

Geography Theme Movement

Geography Standards 4, 12 physical and human characteristics of places; humans modify environments

Activity ***Create a Journal***

Materials writing paper, construction paper, pencils and markers

Management Individual

Look through the unit maps and select four places that a traveler might have visited in crossing the new nation between the years 1789–1860. Record in a journal what a visitor might have seen in these places.

Have students:

- write descriptions and/or draw illustrations of the places they want to visit.
- include a map in the journal, showing the route traveled.
- include illustrations or captions to accompany the text or pictures.
- comment on both the physical and human geography of the places.

Understanding the Painting

John Lewis Krimmel (1789–1821) was a German immigrant who settled in Philadelphia. He is known for his vivid sketches and paintings of ordinary people in familiar settings. Ask students to point out the details in the painting that set the mood for a national celebration. *(People eating, drinking; patriotic symbols such as the flags and the portrait of George Washington; military parade)*

Understanding Chronology

Explain that Unit 3 begins with events that immediately followed the ratification of the Constitution in 1789 and continues into the years just before the Civil War, which began in 1861.

For research support activities, see the *Research Handbook.*

For simulations correlated to this unit, see *Citizenship Simulations*, p. viii.

HOUGHTON MIFFLIN SOCIAL STUDIES

Bookshelf II

On the Long Trail Home

by Elisabeth J. Stewart

A Cherokee sister and brother escape from soldiers guarding their people as they walk along the Trail of Tears. They face many dangers as they make their way back to their village.

Motivate Read the opening pp. 1–9 of the book telling about a Cherokee girl and her family who endure the harsh treatment of soldiers guarding them as they rest during their long forced march from their homelands. Ask students how they think the Cherokee and the soldiers feel about this long march. Have students look at this page and predict what other events they will read about in this unit.

To connect this book with the unit content, use the planning guide and student activity blackline masters beginning on p. iv of the *Bookshelf II Teacher's Resources.*

For additional books that are Easy, Average, and Challenging, see the Unit Bibliography on p. T43. See bibliography updates at www.eduplace.com/ss/hmss.

CHAPTER 5

Planning at a Glance

The Creation of a Party System

	Objectives	Reading Support and Other Resources	Diverse Learning Strategies
Lesson 1 Internal Conflict *pp. 134–139* 2–3 days **Literature** **"Rip Van Winkle"** *pp. 140–145*	• Illustrate the differences between Federalist and Republican ideals. • Explain why there was disagreement over Hamilton's financial programs. • Summarize the events that led the Federalist-controlled Congress to pass the Alien and Sedition acts.	• **Workbook** or **Reading Support:** pp. 62–65 Review p. 15 Extra Support/Transition p. 15 Multi-lang. Sum. pp. 29–30 • **Other Resources:** Poster 1, Study Guide p. 19	Access Act. **(SDAIE)** TE p. 135 Writing a Letter **(GATE)** TE p. 137 Interviewing **(Auditory)** TE p. 138 Homework Options **(Visual)** TE p. 139 Audiotapes of Multi-language Lesson Summaries **(Auditory)**
Lesson 2 Jefferson and the Republicans *pp. 146–151* 2–3 days	• Analyze Jefferson's strategy in absorbing the Federalists into his Republican administration. • Explain how the Louisiana Purchase contributed to American independence. • Summarize the main idea behind the *Marbury v. Madison* decision.	• **Workbook** or **Reading Support:** pp. 66–69 Review p. 16 Extra Support/Transition p. 16 Multi-lang. Sum. pp. 31–32 • **Other Resources:** Geography Kit, Poster 3, Study Guide p. 20	Visual Learning **(Visual)** TE pp. 147, 148 Science Connection **(GATE)** TE p. 149 Making a Speech **(Auditory)** TE p. 150 Map and Globe Skills **(Visual)** TE p. 150 Audiotapes of Multi-language Lesson Summaries **(Auditory)**
Skill: **Researching Aaron Burr** *p. 152*	• Use the title page from the book on Aaron Burr to create bibliography cards.	• **Other Resources:** Study Guide p. 21	
Lesson 3 The United States and The World *pp. 153–159* 2–3 days	• Trace the beginnings of international disturbances that led to the War of 1812. • Explain why the Federalist party collapsed as a national political force. • Describe how the United States, strengthened and unified by the War of 1812, asserted its independence from Europe.	• **Workbook** or **Reading Support:** pp. 70–73 Review p. 17 Extra Support/Transition p. 17 Multi-lang. Sum. pp. 33–34 • **Other Resources:** Geography Kit, Study Guide p. 22	Access Act. **(SDAIE)** TE p. 154 Access Strat. **(Extra Support)** TE p. 154 Music Connection **(Auditory)** TE p. 156 Writing a News Account **(GATE)** TE p. 158 Audiotapes of Multi-language Lesson Summaries **(Auditory)**
Chapter Review *pp. 160–161* 1 day		Chapter 5 Test pp. 17–20 *(See facsimiles on TE p. 753.)*	Assessment Multiple-Use Masters pp. 81–88

Reading Support Resources *for Every Lesson*

Reading and Review

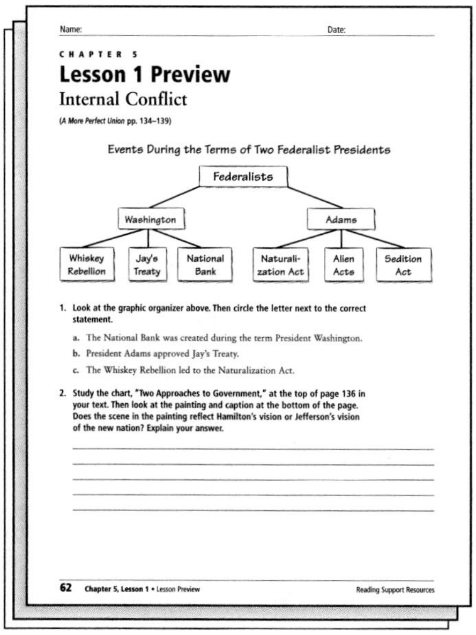
Name: Date:

CHAPTER 5
Lesson 1 Preview
Internal Conflict
(*A More Perfect Union* pp. 134–139)

Events During the Terms of Two Federalist Presidents

Federalists
Washington
Adams
Whiskey Rebellion
Jay's Treaty
National Bank
Naturalization Act
Alien Acts
Sedition Act

1. Look at the graphic organizer above. Then circle the letter next to the correct statement.
a. The National Bank was created during the term President Washington.
b. President Adams approved Jay's Treaty.
c. The Whiskey Rebellion led to the Naturalization Act.

2. Study the chart, "Two Approaches to Government," at the top of page 136 in your text. Then look at the painting and caption at the bottom of the page. Does the scene in the painting reflect Hamilton's vision or Jefferson's vision of the new nation? Explain your answer.

62 Chapter 5, Lesson 1 • Lesson Preview — Reading Support Resources

- **Chapter Overview*** p. 61
- **Lesson Previews*** using graphic organizers from the Teacher's Edition pp. 62, 66, 70
- **Reading Strategies*** pp. 63, 67, 71
- **Lesson Summaries*** pp. 64–65, 68–69, 72–73
- **Lesson Reviews** pp. 15, 16, 17

* **Workbook** includes starred items.

Multi-language Summaries

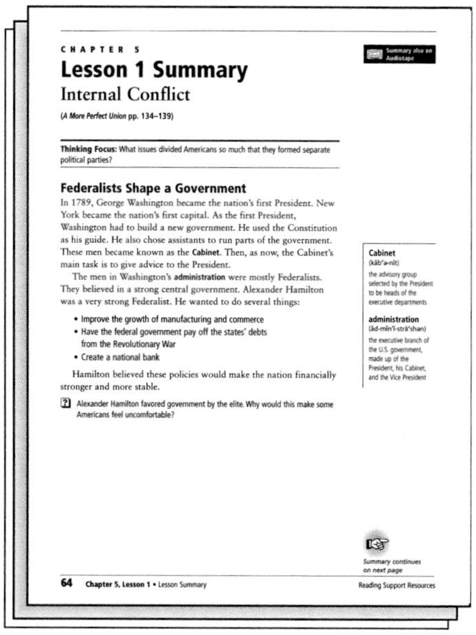
CHAPTER 5
Lesson 1 Summary
Internal Conflict
(*A More Perfect Union* pp. 134–139)

Summary also on Audiotape

Thinking Focus: What issues divided Americans so much that they formed separate political parties?

Federalists Shape a Government

In 1789, George Washington became the nation's first President. New York became the nation's first capital. As the first President, Washington had to build a new government. He used the Constitution as his guide. He also chose assistants to run parts of the government. These men became known as the **Cabinet**. Then, as now, the Cabinet's main task is to give advice to the President.

The men in Washington's **administration** were mostly Federalists. They believed in a strong central government. Alexander Hamilton was a very strong Federalist. He wanted to do several things:

- Improve the growth of manufacturing and commerce
- Have the federal government pay off the states' debts from the Revolutionary War
- Create a national bank

Hamilton believed these policies would make the nation financially stronger and more stable.

Alexander Hamilton favored government by the elite. Why would this make some Americans feel uncomfortable?

Cabinet (kăb'ə-nĭt) the advisory group selected by the President to be heads of the executive departments

administration (ăd-mĭn'ĭ-strā'shən) the executive branch of the U.S. government, made up of the President, his Cabinet, and the Vice President

Summary continues on next page

64 Chapter 5, Lesson 1 • Lesson Summary — Reading Support Resources

Lesson Summaries in:

- English (See Reading and Review.)
- Spanish pp. 64–65, 68–69, 72–73
- Chinese pp. 29–34
- Hmong pp. 29–34
- Khmer pp. 29–34
- Vietnamese pp. 29–34

Summaries available on audiotapes

Lesson Support / Transition

S D A I E

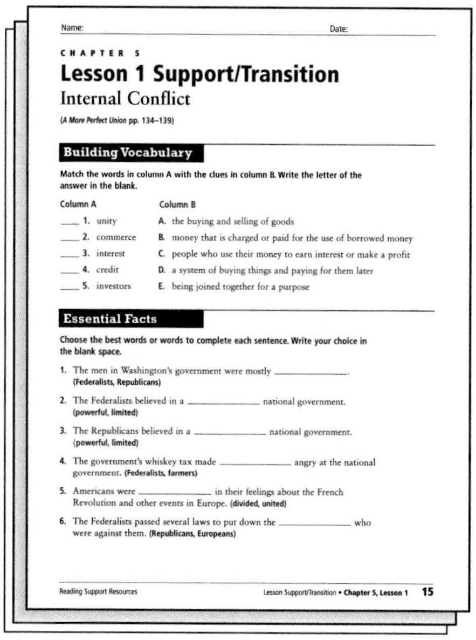
Name: Date:

CHAPTER 5
Lesson 1 Support/Transition
Internal Conflict
(*A More Perfect Union* pp. 134–139)

Building Vocabulary

Match the words in column A with the clues in column B. Write the letter of the answer in the blank.

Column A
___ 1. unity
___ 2. commerce
___ 3. interest
___ 4. credit
___ 5. investors

Column B
A. the buying and selling of goods
B. money that is charged or paid for the use of borrowed money
C. people who use their money to earn interest or make a profit
D. a system of buying things and paying for them later
E. being joined together for a purpose

Essential Facts

Choose the best words or words to complete each sentence. Write your choice in the blank space.

1. The men in Washington's government were mostly ________. (Federalists, Republicans)
2. The Federalists believed in a ________ national government. (powerful, limited)
3. The Republicans believed in a ________ national government. (powerful, limited)
4. The government's whiskey tax made ________ angry at the national government. (Federalists, farmers)
5. Americans were ________ in their feelings about the French Revolution and other events in Europe. (divided, united)
6. The Federalists passed several laws to put down the ________ who were against them. (Republicans, Europeans)

Reading Support Resources — Lesson Support/Transition • Chapter 5, Lesson 1 15

Activities for SDAIE
Specially **D**esigned **A**cademic **I**nstruction in **E**nglish

- **Lesson Support/Transition** pp. 15, 16, 17

Technology Options

Internet Support

http://www.eduplace.com

Social Studies Center at Education Place

Internet support for Chapter 5:

- ***Lesson at a Glance***
- ***The Battle of New Orleans***

Software

Student Writing Center® (CD-ROM) (Macintosh® or Windows®)

School to Career

Even with the use of airplanes today, ships are still an important mode of transporting products, just as they were in the early years of the United States. Have students create a chart showing how they believe jobs on cargo ships have changed or stayed the same from long ago to today.

Character Education

The Founding Fathers of our country may have had different ideas about how the nation should be governed and how it should develop, but ultimately, they all wanted to see the United States succeed. How does the class define "patriotism"? How do people show their patriotism today?

CHAPTER

PREVIEW

After they have read the chapter title and the narrative under it, ask students to name the major political parties today. Direct students' attention to the portraits of Thomas Jefferson and Alexander Hamilton, leaders of opposing political parties. Who are considered the leaders of today's political parties?

Looking Back

Remind students that the delegates to the Constitutional Convention disagreed over many issues. What were some of the issues over which they debated? *(States' rights, the power of the central government, slavery)*

Looking Forward

Explain that in the following three lessons the new country tests its new powers: Internal Conflict, Jefferson and the Republicans, and The United States and the World.

Chapter 5

The Creation of a Party System

The people had launched a new government under the Constitution. The early Presidents worked to establish the nation at home and abroad. Many issues needed to be solved. What goals were best for the country? What role should the government play? Not all people agreed on one plan, and political parties began to form.

Thomas Jefferson (right) led the opposition to the policies of Alexander Hamilton, (left). Two separate political parties formed as a result of their differences.

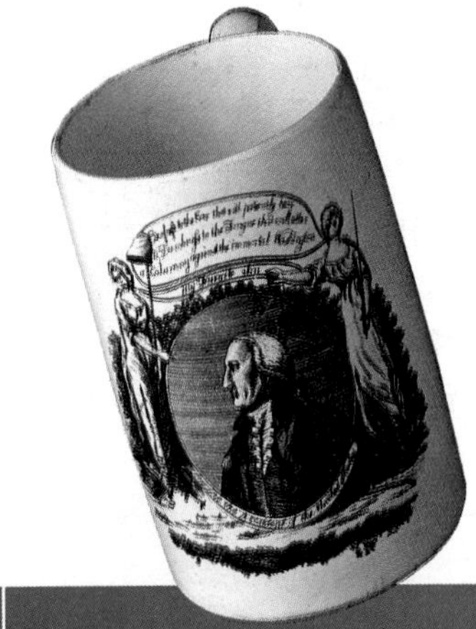

1789 President Washington, shown on the button above, laid the foundation for a powerful central government. This mug commemorated Washington's first presidential inauguration.

1780 | 1790 | 1800

Presidents

1789-1797 Washington

1797-1801 Adams

1801-1809 Jefferson

1789

BACKGROUND

In the 35 years following ratification of the Constitution, political parties threatened to split the nation, the American territory expanded to the Pacific Ocean, and European affairs pulled the nation into war. By meeting these challenges in domestic and foreign affairs, the country proved itself to be a strong, independent nation.

Foreign Affairs Under President Adams

President John Adams considered his work with France to be among his best achievements, despite criticism from both Federalists and Republicans. Although Federalists favored war with France, Adams tried to make a peaceful settlement. When this effort failed, Adams began raising money for war and authorized American ships to seize French vessels. This action angered Republicans, who didn't want to fight a country that had been the ally of the United States in the American Revolution. Eventually Adams negotiated a peace settlement with Napoleon Bonaparte, the new ruler of France. Years later Adams wrote, "I desire no other inscription over my gravestone than: 'Here lies John Adams, who took upon himself the responsibility of the peace with France in the year 1800.' "

John Marshall Strengthens the Supreme Court

When John Marshall was appointed chief justice of the Supreme Court in 1800, the Court was the weakest, least respected branch of government. A series of rulings,

The map on this handkerchief shows Pierre L'Enfant's plan for the city of Washington. At this time, though, the site is still mostly swamps and trees.

1810 | 1820 | 1830

1809-1817
Madison

1817-1825
Monroe

1823

Understanding the Visuals

On the mug commemorating Washington's inauguration appear the words, "Long live the President of the United States." The mug's message seems to reflect the cry often heard in Europe: "Long live the King!"

The souvenir map of the city of Washington by Andrew Ellicott shows broad, tree-lined boulevards and grand open spaces, much like those seen in many European cities of the time.

The portrait of Alexander Hamilton was painted by John Trumbull in 1775. The one of Thomas Jefferson was done in 1805 by Rembrandt Peale.

Understanding Chronology

Refer students to the chapter timeline. The chapter begins in 1789, the year that George Washington was inaugurated. Point out that two of the original thirteen states, North Carolina and Rhode Island, ratified the Constitution after Washington was elected the nation's first President.

beginning with *Marbury* v. *Madison*, considerably strengthened the court during Marshall's thirty-five year tenure. *McCulloch* v. *Maryland* (1819) gave the federal government powers—with regard to establishing a national bank—beyond those specifically stated in the Constitution. *Dartmouth College* v. *Woodward* (1819) denied states the right to interfere with private charters. *Cohens* v. *Virginia* (1821) allowed individuals convicted by states to appeal to federal courts, and *Gibbons* v. *Ogden* (1824) placed interstate commerce under federal jurisdiction.

John Quincy Adams and the Monroe Doctrine

John Quincy Adams played a valuable role in negotiating the treaty that ended the War of 1812 and in developing the Monroe doctrine. Adams was able to respond with personal knowledge of the Russian government and culture when Russia claimed the Alaskan-Canadian coastline in 1821. He had lived there first as a fourteen-year-old secretary to the foreign minister and later as foreign minister himself. His statement on Russia's claims to land expresses the philosophy that would become the Monroe Doctrine: "(W)e should contest the right of Russia to any territorial establishment on this continent, and . . . we should assume distinctly the principle that the American continents are no longer subjects for any new European colonial establishments."

INTRODUCE

Have students recall examples of people or groups that were in conflict in the period before the Constitution was ratified. *(Colonists* v. *British; states* v. *Congress; the North* v. *the South)* Have a student read the Thinking Focus aloud. What controversial issues might divide Americans after the first President takes office? *(Role of people in government, role of individual states in government)*

Key Terms

Vocabulary strategies: T36–37

Cabinet—the advisory group selected by the President, made up of the heads of the executive departments

administration—the executive branch of the U.S. government, consisting of the President, his Cabinet, and the Vice President

agrarian—having to do with land, its ownership, and its cultivation

alien—an unnaturalized foreign resident of a country

sedition—rebellion against the authority of the government

L E S S O N 1

Internal Conflict

THINKING FOCUS

What issues divided Americans so much that they formed separate political parties?

Key Terms

- Cabinet
- administration
- agrarian
- alien
- sedition

George Washington felt a mixture of dread and nervous anticipation as he left Mount Vernon for New York City on April 16, 1789. In New York, the first U. S. capital under the Constitution, he was to be inaugurated President of the United States. Great crowds along the way cheered the first President-elect. Unanimously elected on February 4, 1789, Washington had accepted the office only reluctantly. He doubted his ability as a political leader, but he felt he had a duty to serve the new nation.

On April 30, Washington, standing on the balcony of Federal Hall, took the oath of office and gave his inaugural address. He shared his feelings about taking on "the weighty and untried cares" before him. "The magnitude and difficulty of the trust to which the voice of my country called me," the President confessed, were overwhelming.

Washington's uneasiness was clear to everyone who heard him speak that day. Washington trembled as he spoke and at times seemed barely able to make out the speech he had in front of him. One senator remarked, "This great man was agitated and embarrassed more than ever he was by the leveled cannon or pcinted musket."

Federalists Shape a Government

Imagine the burden on the first President. He had to work out the many details of the government's operation. He had to solve problems that had not been anticipated by the framers of the Constitution. An entire country depended on him to make the new system work.

The Constitution gave Washington a strong foundation for a new government. He wanted unity and stability for the United States, and the Constitution was his only guide. But what direction should the nation take? And how should it proceed?

Quest for Political Unity

As provided by law, Washington appointed assistants to head the departments of government: a secretary of state, a secretary of the treasury, a secretary of war, and a postmaster general. Together, these assistants who advise the President came to be known as the **Cabinet**. Since Washington's time, the President together with the Cabinet and the Vice President have been called the **administration.**

The men in the Washington administration were mostly Federalists. They believed in a powerful central government run by the elite, that is, men of wealth, education, and special talent. In their opinion, only such men were able to promote the public good and to make the wisest policies in government.

The Founding Fathers neither expected nor welcomed political parties. They believed that parties represented selfish interests that worked against the public good. "A division of

Objectives

1. Illustrate the differences between Federalist and Republican ideals.
2. Explain why there was disagreement over Hamilton's financial programs.
3. Summarize the events that led the Federalist-controlled Congress to pass the Alien and Sedition Acts.

Graphic Overview

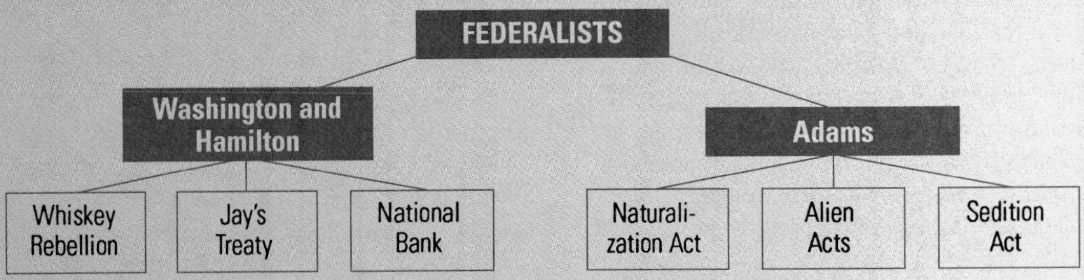

the republic into two great parties," Vice President John Adams said, "is to be dreaded as the greatest political evil under our Constitution." But parties proved unavoidable. Soon it became clear that Alexander Hamilton was leading a party of Federalists.

▲ *The National Bank is shown at its location on Third Street in New York City.*

Hamilton's Proposals

George Washington had named Hamilton as secretary of the treasury. Hamilton's extraordinary intelligence and ambition helped him become the most powerful figure in Washington's Cabinet. An unshakable Federalist, he favored a powerful national government. As secretary of the treasury he wanted to strengthen and stabilize the nation's economy by encouraging the growth of manufacturing and commerce as well as farming.

In his Report on Public Credit of 1790, Hamilton recommended that the national government pay off the debt left over from the Revolutionary War, including the debts of the states. Much of the debt took the form of government bonds, or notes, which had been given to soldiers as pay or bought by patriotic citizens. Hamilton proposed that anyone holding a government bond be paid in full, plus interest. Most of the original owners, however, had sold their bonds for hard money at far less than their face value. In addition, the real value of the debt had decreased. Nonetheless, Hamilton argued that the program would establish the nation's credit and would give investors a good feeling about the new government.

Hamilton also called for the creation of a national bank. The bank would keep deposits of money for the government, regulate the state banks, and print bank notes that could be turned in for gold or silver. He believed that such a bank would strengthen the ties between rich Americans and the federal government. In other words, a national bank would lead to a more stable financial base for the country. ■

■ *Hamilton favored government by the elite. Why would this make some Americans feel uncomfortable?*

Some Oppose Federalist Centralization

James Madison, who was known as the architect of the Constitution, now served as a congressman from Virginia. He questioned the fairness of Hamilton's credit proposals. He thought the national bank was not legal.

The credit program seemed to favor Northerners over Southerners, speculators over original bond holders, and the federal government over individual states. Merchants and investors from the North had bought up most of the nation's bonds, often at low cost from the first holder. These Northerners would profit tremendously from the plan. Hamilton had also called for a federal tax on imported goods to pay off both federal and state debts. Madison felt that this tax was unfair to the Southern states, which generally had smaller debts than the Northern states. And nowhere, he claimed, did the Constitution give the federal government the power to create banks.

DEVELOP

Point out that this lesson highlights several issues that created conflict. Have students preview the heads for words associated with conflict. *(Oppose, tension)* As they read, students should list the issues that divided Americans and the position that each political party supported.

HISTORY

Critical Thinking

Remind students that George Washington fought in the Revolution and presided over the Constitutional Convention in Philadelphia. Ask students to describe what some of his feelings and hopes for the new government and nation might be. What problems might he face?

■ *Some might feel that wealthy, educated leaders would not fairly represent the interests of the common people.*

Access Strategy

Begin by having students suggest ways that people can buy things without using cash. *(Bank loan, credit card, check)* Next have students explain why a person or group might need to borrow money from a bank. *(To buy something, to pay a bill, because they ran out of money)* Ask why banks are willing to make loans. *(Banks earn interest.)*

Explain that a bond is a kind of loan. In the American Revolution, the government had sold bonds to raise money for the war. It also had paid soldiers in bonds. Be sure that students understand who had borrowed money to pay for the Revolution and from whom. *(The government borrowed initially from soldiers, merchants, and farmers, but then Northern speculators bought up many bonds, often for pennies on the dollar.)* Tell students that they will learn in this lesson how the new U.S. Government dealt with paying back these loans.

Access Activity

Have students name reasons why a government might need to borrow money. *(To pay employees; to pay for buildings, printing, supplies; to provide national defense)* Then have them list ways the government could earn money to pay back the loans. *(Mostly through different kinds of taxes)*

POLITICAL SYSTEMS

Critical Thinking

Have students refer to the excerpt of Jefferson's letter to John Jay on this page. Tell them to put the quote into their own words. Why did Jefferson see the "Cultivators of the Earth" as important citizens? Ask them to consider what current issues Jefferson might support. *(Sample answers: Loans for farmers, federal funds for agricultural schools, land preservation programs)*

Two Approaches to Government

Federalists
(Hamilton)

- Favored strong, centralized government
- Advocated regulation of foreign and interstate trade
- Created national bank
- Promoted industry and manufacturing

Republicans
(Jefferson)

- Favored limited federal government
- Supported states' rights
- Encouraged western expansion
- Emphasized agricultural society

The Federalists and the Republicans held different views on most subjects.

The painting below, made in 1822, idealizes the agrarian republic so dear to Jefferson.

Jefferson's Vision

People who hated the favors that Hamilton's programs gave to Northern businessmen looked to Thomas Jefferson as their leader. As Washington's secretary of state, Jefferson believed in limited government and wished for a nation of landholding farmers. His ideal of a peaceful **agrarian,** or farm-based, nation seemed a sharp contrast to Hamilton's ideal of a complex, industrialized nation. In a letter to John Jay in 1785 Jefferson expressed his confidence in the common people:

> *Cultivators of the earth are the most valuable citizens. They are the most vigorous, the most independent, the most virtuous, and they are tied to their country and wedded to its liberty and interests by the most lasting bonds.*

Jefferson had greater faith in the people's ability to govern than Hamilton had. "The whole mass of the people," he believed, "are the only sure reliance for the preservation of our liberty."

The Rise of Republicanism

As tension mounted over Hamilton's financial program in 1790, Madison and Jefferson tried to discredit Hamilton. They even charged Hamilton with planning to replace republicanism with monarchy. To show their loyalty, Jefferson, Madison, and their followers began calling themselves Republicans. Meanwhile, Hamilton and his Federalist friends, claiming to be the correct followers of the Constitution, also started to form a party.

By 1791, Congress had approved Hamilton's credit program, and the Bank of the United States—the national bank suggested by him—had

Visual Learning

Have students look at the painting on page 137 of George Washington leading the army against the Whiskey Rebellion. Ask them to make a list of words or phrases that describe Washington and the army in this picture. *(Powerful, organized)* How might an artist who favored farmers have painted the event? *(Might have shown farmers greatly outnumbered)*

Political Context

The founders of the country were familiar with political parties. The Whig and Tory parties had opposed each other for many years in England. The Tories favored the continued reign of the Stuart monarchs, while the Whigs opposed the increasing power of royalty. As the American Revolution began, the Tories were just coming into power. They were firmly in power from 1783 to 1794 and were united with landowning Whigs against popular reforms until 1830.

Historical Context

"Wheeling and dealing" played a role in choosing the location of the nation's capital city. Hamilton, as Secretary of the Treasury, needed enough members of Congress to vote to assume the states' existing debts. To get these votes, Hamilton made a deal with Jefferson and Madison. If they would get some Southern congressmen to change their votes in favor of Hamilton's plan, the capital would stay in Philadelphia for ten years and then be moved near the Potomac.

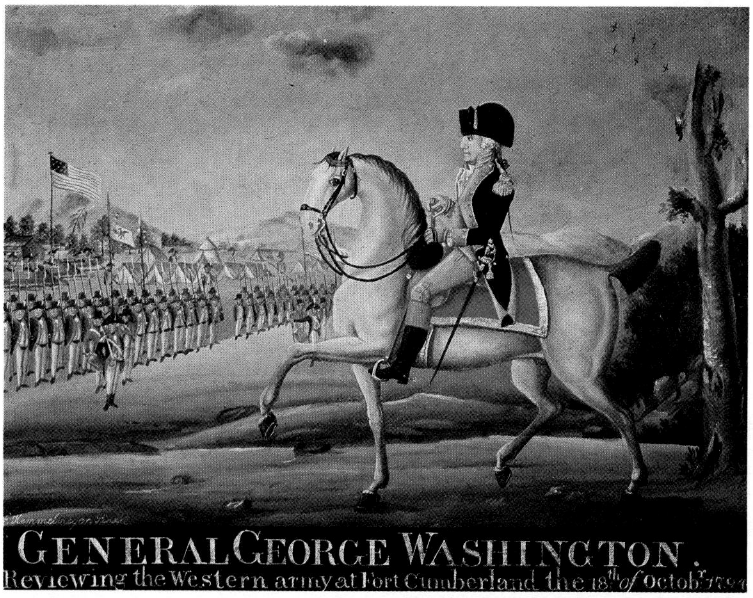

GENERAL GEORGE WASHINGTON.
Reviewing the Western army at Fort Cumberland the 18th of October

◄ *The President also acts as Commander-in-Chief of the armed forces. President Washington actually led the army on the field against the Whiskey Rebellion.*

been established. Nevertheless, President Washington feared that the growing opposition to these changes threatened the strength of the government. He tried to promote unity by seeking a second term of office, and in 1792 he was re-elected without opposition. John Adams also won re-election as Vice President.

Despite Washington's leadership, a full-scale revolt was beginning. To get money to pay off the war debt, Hamilton had convinced Congress in 1791 to pass a 25 percent tax on whiskey. Many farmers made their grain into whiskey because it was easier to bring to market. Also, whiskey took the place of money in some places. Farmers felt they were being unfairly singled out to pay for Hamilton's programs. In protest, the angry farmers of western Pennsylvania tarred and feathered tax collectors, destroyed the whiskey stills of those who paid the tax, and stopped court proceedings. Frightened by the violence of the farmers, one chief collector of the whiskey tax quit his job.

President Washington was angry and shocked at the farmers' defiance of the federal government. In 1794, he led nearly 13,000 militia to Pennsylvania to make them obey. But the farmers were not an organized force. Washington found no army to fight against. Only a few rioters were arrested, and these were pardoned. The government's show of arms against the people helped to make the Republicans more popular. Understanding Concepts on page 138 explores the importance of leadership. ■

How Do We Know

HISTORY *Though they did not dislike each other personally, Jefferson and Hamilton were each convinced that the other's ideas were the source of all political evil. Their letters to each other and to friends about each other still exist—providing historians with plenty of evidence of their strong disagreements.*

■ *The policies Hamilton proposed were designed to create national unity. But instead they divided people. Why?*

Events in Europe Cause Tension at Home

The political events in Europe during this time served to divide the nation even more. Officially, the United States held a neutral position in all European wars. That is, it did not take sides. But in truth, Americans usually had strong feelings about European matters.

When the French Revolution began in 1789, almost all Americans rejoiced. The ideals of the American Revolution, it seemed, had spread to

ECONOMICS

Critical Thinking

Ask students what seem to be the advantages of taxing whiskey. *(Easy to administer and collect; whiskey considered more of a luxury than a necessity)* Why did the tax on whiskey backfire? *(It singled out one class of people, the farmers, to carry the burden for all.)*

■ *Hamilton's proposals seemed to favor Northerners over Southerners, speculators over the original bond holders, and the federal government over the states and individuals.*

Art Connection

Have students refer to the painting of the idealized agrarian republic on page 136. Bring in art history books showing landscape paintings of agricultural areas. (Ask the school art teacher for suggestions of paintings.) Have pairs of students choose a painting to study. Each pair should decide if the painting is communicating a pro-agrarian or an anti-agrarian view. Ask students to give specific examples to support their decision.

Writing a Letter

Tell students to imagine that a friend has been sent to jail under the Alien and Sedition acts for printing a criticism of the government. Have each student write a letter defending free speech to the editor of a newspaper. Students should support their arguments with details from the lesson. Have volunteers read their letters aloud to the class.

Critical Thinking

Have students recall why some Americans were for the French Revolution. *(Fighting for a noble cause)* Why were some against it? *(Too much killing)* Have students suggest other reasons why Americans might be for or against revolution in another country. *(It might open trade; it might bring in a government hostile to us.)*

France, where peasants lacked adequate land and the middle class lacked adequate political power. Dissatisfaction with the monarchy was growing. However, American feelings changed when the French beheaded King Louis XVI in 1793 and declared war on Great Britain. Federalists were horrified by the bloodiness of the revolution and sided with Great Britain. Republicans, however, refused to abandon the cause of liberty and remained sympathetic to France.

The French Revolution was not the only international event to concern the United States during this time. Americans were angry about Great Britain's harassment of American ships during its war with France. British occupation of American northwestern forts after the Revolutionary War also added to the tension. In 1794, Washington sent Chief Justice John Jay to London to negotiate a settlement of the nations' differences and thus to prevent war.

UNDERSTANDING LEADERSHIP

The early days of the new nation saw the rise of many political leaders: Washington, Hamilton, Jefferson, Franklin. What qualities did they possess that allowed them to become effective leaders? In other words, what is meant by leadership? To define the word very simply, leadership is both the position (or role) of a leader and the ability to lead.

Leadership exists at many levels: in schools; in your community, state, and nation; and in other nations. In addition, leadership is found in all kinds of groups and organizations.

Leadership Qualities

What qualities do people look for in a good leader? Some qualities of effective leaders are listed below. Think about these qualities. Are there any qualities you might add?

- knowledge of the responsibilities of his or her role
- ability to set goals, communicate a vision, and use effective plans to carry out goals and visions
- receptiveness to the ideas, viewpoints, and visions of others
- ability to organize and communicate ideas
- self-confidence and decisiveness
- willingness to let other people assume responsibility
- ability to weigh decisions carefully
- ability to get along well with people
- fairness and honesty

Washington's Leadership

George Washington stands out as an example of an effective leader. He served in many important leadership roles in the new nation, including Commander of the Continental Army, president of the Constitutional Convention, and first President of the United States. Through his responsible leadership in all three roles, Washington inspired people and won their respect and confidence.

Leadership Today

When you think of modern leaders, what names come to mind? Some popular responses are Martin Luther King, Jr., John F. Kennedy, Mohandas Gandhi, Cesar Chavez, Ronald Reagan, and Mikhail Gorbachev. In the past only men held positions of political leadership. But in this century, many women have held important positions of world leadership. The most outstanding examples include Margaret Thatcher of Great Britain, Golda Meir of Israel, and Indira Gandhi of India.

Any leader is a representative of the large group that he or she leads. For that reason, people in the United States from the days of George Washington to today try to choose leaders carefully. Our leaders are people who not only "get the job done" but also represent beliefs in the present and hopes for the future.

POLITICAL SYSTEMS

Critical Thinking

The new nation relied heavily on its leaders. What responsibilities of today's leaders are similar to those of the nation's first leaders? *(Ensuring military defense, providing and funding government services, handling foreign relations)* What responsibilities are different? *(First leaders had to set up many of the government structures; today's leaders deal with more complicated international issues and represent more people.)*

Social Participation

Divide students into groups of three or four. Have each group list what it considers to be the ten major challenges facing United States leaders today. One representative from each group should write the group's list on the board. Then the class should analyze together which issues seem to be the most important.

Research

For most of its history, the United States has had a two-party political system. In some countries, such as Italy or Israel, many political parties compete for control of the government. Have the students research and write a two-page report on how a country with a multi-party system governs itself. Some students could research and report on a country with a one-party system, such as Mexico. Alternatively, have students present their findings in a chart.

Interviewing

Have students interview leaders of local political party units and report on what they learn. To prepare for the interviews, the class should generate a list of questions that will get the leaders to talk about the differences among parties, for example: Are you in favor of raising taxes? Why?

The British agreed to take their troops out of the forts by 1796, but they refused to accept the U.S. demand for freedom of the seas. When the treaty's terms became known, protest swept the country and added to the growing power of the Republicans.

Vice President John Adams, a Federalist, narrowly won the presidential election of 1796, the first to have rival candidates for the presidency. As soon as Adams was inaugurated, he faced a problem with France. Angry because the United States had signed a treaty with Great Britain, the French took American ships and refused to talk with American officials. In 1798 Adams responded by ordering American ships to seize French vessels, thus starting an undeclared war at sea. Republicans protested and called for peace.

This cartoon illustrates a famous brawl that took place in Congress in 1798. Federalist Roger Griswold is at the right; Republican Matthew Lyon is in the center.

Suppression by Federalists

The battle for control of the nation went on. The Federalist-controlled Congress passed several laws meant to put down the Republican opposition. Immigrants, especially French ones, were suspected of being Republicans. The Naturalization Act lengthened the time required for foreigners—mostly common people supporting the Republicans—to gain citizenship. Naturalization, or the granting of full citizenship to foreigners, now took fourteen years instead of five. The Alien Acts authorized the President to imprison or expel any **aliens,** or foreigners, he considered dangerous.

The Sedition Act repressed **sedition**—rebellion against the government—by restricting freedom of speech and of the press. Anyone who wrote, printed, or said anything false or critical about the government of the United States could be fined or put in jail. Under this law Federalists imprisoned the editors of the five largest pro-Republican newspapers.

Republicans tried to block the Alien and Sedition Acts. The Virginia and Kentucky governments passed resolutions stating that the acts went against the Bill of Rights. Since the Constitution "resulted from the compact to which the states are parties," they argued, "the states have the right and . . . duty" to stop the federal government from using powers not allowed by the Constitution. Both states declared the Alien and Sedition Acts "altogether void and of no effect" and urged other states to join them in protest. The resolutions received no positive replies, but they served to rally Republicans everywhere in the country. ■

■ *What motivated the Federalist Congress to pass the Alien and Sedition Acts—and why did they cause problems?*

REVIEW

1. **FOCUS** What issues divided Americans so much that they formed separate political parties?
2. **CONNECT** How were the Virginia and Kentucky Resolutions related to the positions taken by the Antifederalists ten years earlier?
3. **GEOGRAPHY** Why were Hamilton's programs not well received in the South?
4. **CRITICAL THINKING** In what ways might Jefferson's agrarian ideal have been short-sighted?
5. **WRITING ACTIVITY** Imagine you are a western Pennsylvania farmer and write an account of your experiences in the Whiskey Rebellion.

POLITICAL SYSTEMS

Critical Thinking

Encourage students to express their views on the Alien and Sedition Acts. Were these acts justified in light of the events leading up to them? Under what conditions today, if any, would such acts be justifiable? *(Encourage students to give reasons for their answers.)*

■ *The Federalist Congress used these acts to limit Republican opposition, but both acts were seen as violating the Bill of Rights.*

CLOSE

To answer the Thinking Focus, have students compare the lists that they made of divisive issues and the positions of political parties. Then students may contribute to one master list. As a reteaching activity, read aloud one position at a time from the table on page 136 and call on students to identify the position as part of the Federalist or the Republican approach.

Answers to Review Questions

1. Americans were divided over who should run the government—the elite or the common people. They also disagreed on whether the national government or the states and the people should hold the most power.
2. Like the Antifederalists' earlier positions, these resolutions defended states' rights against abuses by the federal government.
3. Northern merchants and investors benefited by buying bonds at a low cost from Southern holders.
4. Sample answer: This ideal did not consider what would happen when the population increased or when industry began to grow. Allow for personal opinion.
5. Encourage students to reflect the emotions of the farmers regarding the rebellion and their feeling of being singled out to provide revenue for the whole country.

Homework Options

Have students create parallel timelines showing domestic and foreign developments from 1789–1799. A good source is *The Timetables of History* by Bernard Grun (New York: Simon and Schuster, 1982).

Study Guide: page 19.

INTRODUCE

Explain that in the earlier part of this short story, Rip Van Winkle had gone hunting in the Catskill Mountains. He met a strange group of men, who cast a spell on him. He fell asleep before the American Revolution and woke up twenty years later during an election campaign. Discuss what students learned about the development of the party system in Lesson 1.

READ AND RESPOND

Before they read the story independently, ask students to think about the changes they think Rip Van Winkle will find. As students answer the purpose-setting question, make sure they give reasons for their answers.

During the first decades of the new republic, politics, economics, and social life all changed dramatically. The story of Rip Van Winkle cautions us not to fall out of touch with the changing world around us.

LITERATURE

Rip Van Winkle

Washington Irving

Washington Irving (1783-1859) was born in New York City and lived in this country until he was 32. He went to Europe in 1815 and stayed there for 15 years. During this time he traveled to many countries, collecting fairy tales from each one he visited. The story of Rip Van Winkle is loosely based on the German folktale "Peter Klaus." Irving set his story of Rip Van Winkle in the Revolutionary War period. He added descriptions of local customs and settings to create a uniquely American story of colonial life in the Catskill Mountains of New York. This tale of a ne'er-do-well who sleeps for 20 years helped the short story become established as a popular literary form. As you read this short story, ask yourself why fairy tales continue to be a part of our literary tradition.

As he approached the village he met a number of people, but none whom he knew, which somewhat surprised him, for he had thought himself acquainted with every one in the country round. Their dress, too, was of a different fashion from that to which he was accustomed. They all stared at him with equal marks of surprise, and whenever they cast their eyes upon him, invariably stroked their chins. The constant recurrence of this gesture induced Rip, involuntarily, to do the same, when, to his astonishment, he found his beard had grown a foot long!

He had now entered the skirts of the village. A troop of strange children ran at his heels, hooting after him, and pointing at his gray beard. The dogs, too, not one of which he recognized for an old acquaintance, barked at him as he passed. The very village was altered; it was larger and more populous. There were rows of houses which he had never seen before, and those which had been his familiar haunts had disappeared. Strange names were over the doors—strange faces at the windows—every thing was strange. His mind now misgave him; he began to doubt whether both he and the world around him were not bewitched. Surely this was his native village, which he had left but the day before. There stood the Kaatskill mountains—there ran the silver Hudson at a distance—there was every hill and dale precisely as it had always been—Rip was sorely perplexed—"That flagon last night," thought he, "has addled my poor head sadly!"

flagon jug

It was with some difficulty that he found the way to his own house, which he approached with silent awe, expecting every moment to hear the shrill voice of Dame Van Winkle. He found the house gone to decay—the roof fallen in, the windows shattered, and the doors off the

Thematic Connections

Social Studies: The new nation

Houghton Mifflin Literary Readers: Mysterious Happenings

Background

Born the son of a New York merchant, Washington Irving was named after the nation's first President. When his family's business failed, Irving turned to writing full time. His first work was a satirical portrayal of the Dutch era of New York history. His collection of stories *The Sketch Book*, which includes "Rip Van Winkle," was widely praised in Europe as the first evidence of real American literature.

In 1826, Irving accepted the offer of a post in the U.S. embassy in Spain. While he was there, he turned out histories of Columbus and his voyages, along with collections of Spanish tales. Returning to the United States after 17 years abroad, Irving traveled to the frontier and continued to write books based on his travels and experiences. He capped his career with a series of biographies, including a five-volume set of books about George Washington.

hinges. A half-starved dog that looked like Wolf was skulking about it. Rip called him by name, but the cur snarled, showed his teeth, and passed on. This was an unkind cut indeed—"My very dog," sighed poor Rip, "has forgotten me!"

He entered the house, which, to tell the truth, Dame Van Winkle had always kept in neat order. It was empty, forlorn, and apparently abandoned. This desolateness overcame all his connubial fears—he called loudly for his wife and children—the lonely chambers rang for a moment with his voice, and then all again was silence.

He now hurried forth, and hastened to his old resort, the village inn—but it too was gone. A large rickety wooden building stood in its place, with great gaping windows, some of them broken and mended with old hats and petticoats, and over the door was painted, "the Union Hotel, by Jonathan Doolittle." Instead of the great tree that used to shelter the quiet little Dutch inn of yore, there now was reared a tall naked pole, with something on the top that looked like a red night-cap, and from it was fluttering a flag, on which was a singular assemblage of stars and stripes—all this was strange and incomprehensible. He recognized on the sign, however, the ruby face of King George, under which he had smoked so many a peaceful pipe; but even this was singularly metamorphosed. The red coat was changed for one of blue and buff, a sword was held in the hand instead of a sceptre, the head was decorated with a cocked hat, and underneath was painted in large characters, GENERAL WASHINGTON.

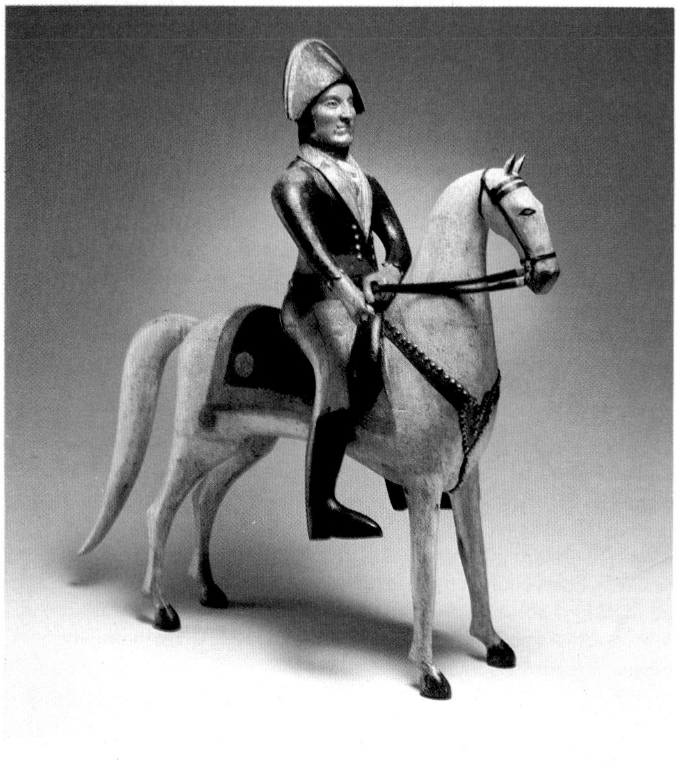

connubial marital

yore time past
The "liberty cap," symbol of the French Revolution, was often displayed during the revolutionary period.
assemblage arrangement
buff pale yellow
sceptre a staff symbolizing a king's authority

◄ What were the first two signs that indicated Rip had been gone for a very long time? *(The people in the village did not recognize him; their clothing styles were quite different from what he was used to.)*

What did Rip find when he returned to his house? *(The house was in decay and seemed to be abandoned. His dog did not remember him.)*

disputatious inclined to dispute
phlegm lack of energy

There was, as usual, a crowd of folk about the door, but none that Rip recollected. The very character of the people seemed changed. There was a busy, bustling, disputatious tone about it, instead of the accustomed phlegm and drowsy tranquillity. He looked in vain for the sage Nicholas Vedder, with his broad face, double chin and fair long pipe, uttering clouds of tobacco-smoke instead of idle speeches; or Van Bummel, the schoolmaster, doling forth the contents of an ancient newspaper. In place of these, a lean, bilious looking fellow, with his pockets full of handbills, was haranguing vehemently about rights of citizens—elections—members of congress—liberty—Bunker's Hill—heroes of seventy-six—and other words, which were a perfect Babylonish jargon to the bewildered Van Winkle.

The appearance of Rip, with his long grizzled beard, his rusty fowling-piece, his uncouth dress, and an army of women and children at his heels, soon attracted the attention of the tavern politicians. They crowded round him, eyeing him from head to foot with great curiosity. The orator bustled up to him, and, drawing him partly aside, inquired "on which side he voted?" Rip stared in vacant stupidity. Another short but busy little fellow pulled him by the arm, and, rising on tiptoe, inquired in his ear, "Whether he was Federal or Democrat?" Rip was equally at a loss to comprehend the question; when a knowing, self-important old gentleman, in a sharp cocked hat, made his way through the crowd, putting them to the right and left with his elbows as he passed, and planting himself before Van Winkle, with one arm akimbo, the other resting on his cane, his keen eyes and sharp hat penetrating, as it were, into his very soul, demanded in an austere tone, "what brought him to the election with a gun on his shoulder, and a mob at his heels, and whether he meant to breed a riot in the village?"—"Alas! gentlemen," cried Rip, somewhat dismayed, "I am a poor quiet man, a native of the place, and a loyal subject of the king, God bless him!"

akimbo hand on hip and elbow bowed outward

Here a general shout burst from the by-standers—"A tory! a tory! a spy! a refugee! hustle him! away with him!" It was with great difficulty that the self-important man in the cocked hat restored order; and, having assumed a tenfold austerity of brow, demanded again of the unknown culprit, what he came there for, and whom he was seeking? The poor man humbly assured him that he meant no harm, but merely came there in search of some of his neighbors, who used to keep about the tavern.

austerity severity

➤ What is the first question Rip was asked? *(For which political party did he vote in the election?)*

What did Rip say that angered the crowd? *(He said he was a loyal subject of the king.)*

"Well—who are they?—name them."

Rip bethought himself a moment, and inquired, "Where's Nicholas Vedder?"

There was a silence for a little while, when an old man replied, in a thin piping voice, "Nicholas Vedder! why, he is dead and gone these eighteen years! There was a wooden tombstone in the churchyard that used to tell all about him, but that's rotten and gone too."

"Where's Brom Dutcher?"

"Oh, he went off to the army in the beginning of the war; some say he was killed at the storming of Stony Point—others say he was drowned in a squall at the foot of Antony's Nose. I don't know—he never came back again."

"Where's Van Bummel, the schoolmaster?"

142

Bulletin Board

Have students find out what major events, inventions, social changes, and fashion changes have occurred in the last 20 years. Ask them to find pictures of the familiar things we have today that would be new to a person who had slept for the past 20 years. Display the pictures on the class bulletin board.

"He went off to the wars too, was a great militia general, and is now in congress."

Rip's heart died away at hearing of these sad changes in his home and friends, and finding himself thus alone in the world. Every answer puzzled him too, by treating of such enormous lapses of time, and of matters which he could not understand: war—congress—Stony Point;—he had no courage to ask after any more friends, but cried out in despair, "Does nobody here know Rip Van Winkle?"

"Oh, Rip Van Winkle!" exclaimed two or three, "Oh, to be sure! that's Rip Van Winkle yonder, leaning against the tree."

Rip looked, and beheld a precise counterpart of himself, as he went up the mountain: apparently as lazy, and certainly as ragged. The poor fellow was now completely confounded. He doubted his own identity, and whether he was himself or another man. In the midst of his bewilderment, the man in the cocked hat demanded who he was, and what was his name?

"God knows," exclaimed he at his wit's end; "I'm not myself—I'm somebody else—that's me yonder—no—that's somebody else got into my shoes—I was myself last night, but I fell asleep on the mountain, and they've changed my gun, and every thing's changed, and I'm changed, and I can't tell what's my name, or who I am!"

The by-standers began now to look at each other, nod, wink significantly, and tap their fingers against their foreheads. There was a whisper, also, about securing the gun, and keeping the old fellow from doing mischief, at the very suggestion of which the self-important man in the cocked hat retired with some precipitation. At this critical moment a fresh comely woman passed through the throng to get a peep at the gray-bearded man. She had a chubby child in her arms, which, frightened at his looks, began to cry. "Hush, Rip," cried she, "hush, you little

What did Rip learn about his former friends? *(One was dead, one went to war and did not return, and the third became a general and was elected to Congress.)*

fool; the old man won't hurt you." The name of the child, the air of the mother, the tone of her voice, all awakened a train of recollections in his mind. "What is your name, my good woman?" asked he.

"Judith Gardenier."

"And your father's name?"

"Ah, poor man, Rip Van Winkle was his name, but it's twenty years since he went away from home with his gun, and never has been heard of since—his dog came home without him; but whether he shot himself, or was carried away by the Indians, nobody can tell. I was then but a little girl."

Rip had but one question more to ask; but he put it with a faltering voice:

"Where's your mother?"

"Oh, she too had died but a short time since; she broke a blood-vessel in a fit of passion at a New-England peddler."

There was a drop of comfort, at least, in this intelligence. The honest man could contain himself no longer. He caught his daughter and her child in his arms. "I am your father!" cried he—"Young Rip Van Winkle once—old Rip Van Winkle now!—Does nobody know poor Rip Van Winkle?"

All stood amazed, until an old woman, tottering out from among the crowd, put her hand to her brow, and peering under it in his face for a moment, exclaimed, "Sure enough! it is Rip Van Winkle—it is himself! Welcome home again, old neighbor—Why, where have you been these twenty long years?"

Rip's story was soon told, for the whole twenty years had been to him but as one night. The neighbors stared when they heard it; some were seen to wink at each other, and put their tongues in their cheeks: and the self-important man in the cocked hat, who, when the alarm was over, had returned to the field, screwed down the corners of his mouth, and shook his head—upon which there was a general shaking of the head throughout the assemblage.

It was determined, however, to take the opinion of old Peter Vanderdonk, who was seen slowly advancing up the road. He was a descendant of the historian of that name, who wrote one of the earliest accounts of the province. Peter was the most ancient inhabitant of the village, and well versed in all the wonderful events and traditions of the neighborhood. He recollected Rip at once, and corroborated his story in the most satisfactory manner. He assured the company that it was a fact, handed down from his ancestor the historian, that the Kaatskill mountains had always been haunted by strange beings. That it was affirmed that the great Hendrick Hudson, the first discoverer of the river and country, kept a kind of vigil there every twenty years, with his crew of the Halfmoon; being permitted in this way to revisit the scenes of his enterprise, and keep a guardian eye upon the river, and the great city called by his name. That his father had once seen them in their old Dutch dresses playing at nine-pins in a hollow of the mountain; and that he himself had heard, one summer afternoon, the sound of their balls, like distant peals of thunder.

To make a long story short, the company broke up, and returned to

➤ How do we know that the neighbors did not believe Rip's story? *(They winked, put their tongues in their cheeks, and shook their heads.)*

Why did the villagers finally believe Rip? *(The oldest person in the village confirmed Rip's story.)*

Language Arts

Washington Irving uses the name *Kaatskill* for the mountain range that we know today as *Catskill.* Explain that *Kaatskill* was the spelling used by Dutch settlers. The Dutch word *kaat* means "cat" and *kill* means "stream." Have students research names of natural features, streets, or neighborhoods in and around their communities to find out what languages they came from and what they originally meant.

the more important concerns of the election. Rip's daughter took him home to live with her; she had a snug, well-furnished house, and a stout cheery farmer for a husband, whom Rip recollected for one of the urchins that used to climb upon his back. As to Rip's son and heir, who was the ditto of himself, seen leaning against the tree, he was employed to work on the farm; but evinced an hereditary disposition to attend to any thing else but his business.

ditto exact copy
evinced demonstrated clearly

Rip now resumed his old walks and habits; he soon found many of his former cronies, though all rather the worse for the wear and tear of time; and preferred making friends among the rising generation, with whom he soon grew into great favor.

Having nothing to do at home, and being arrived at that happy age when a man can be idle with impunity, he took his place once more on the bench at the inn door, and was reverenced as one of the patriarchs of the village, and a chronicle of the old times "before the war." It was some time before he could get into the regular track of gossip, or could be made to comprehend the strange events that had taken place during his torpor. How that there had been a revolutionary war—that the country had thrown off the yoke of old England—and that, instead of being a subject of His Majesty George the Third, he was now a free citizen of the United States.

impunity exemption from punishment

Further Reading

The Legend of Sleepy Hollow. Washington Irving. A short story about a poor schoolmaster, Ichabod Crane, and his encounter with a headless horseman.

Knickerbocker's History of New York (A History of New York from the Beginning of the World to the End of the Dutch Dynasty). Washington Irving. A satirical account of New York state during the eighteenth and early nineteenth centuries, written under the pen name Diedrich Knickerbocker.

Whom did Rip prefer as new friends? *(The rising generation of young people)*

How did Rip come to see himself? *(As a free citizen of the United States)*

EXTEND

Have the class suggest what changes they would expect to find if they fell asleep for 20 years. After making a list of their ideas, interested students could create a short play in which a modern Rip Van Winkle returns to their community 20 years in the future.

Further Reading

You may want to ask students to go to the school or local library to find more books to read by Washington Irving.

INTRODUCE

Have students read the Thinking Focus. Remind them that Jefferson's Republican Party differs from today's Republican Party, established in 1857. Have students recall from Lesson 1 the Federalist policies that Republicans opposed. *(Strong central government, Alien and Sedition Acts, national bank)* Ask what they think Jefferson will do with these Federalist policies when he is President. Have the students read to discover the problems that Jefferson faced and how he solved them.

Key Terms

Vocabulary strategies: T36–37

electoral vote—the vote cast by the persons chosen by each state to elect the President

judicial review—the power of a court, especially the Supreme Court, to decide on the constitutionality of a law or an executive act

constitutional—in agreement with the principles established by the Constitution

1780 | 1790 | 1796 | 1803 | 1810 | 1820 | 1830

L E S S O N 2

Jefferson and the Republicans

THINKING FOCUS

How did the transfer of power to the Republicans in 1800 make a difference for the nation?

Key Terms

- electoral vote
- judicial review
- constitutional

President John Adams: "a fool, a gross hypocrite, and an unprincipled oppressor." His opponent, Thomas Jefferson: "an uncivilized atheist, anti-American, a tool for the godless French." The presidential election of 1800 was dirty business, with ugly insults coming from both sides. Newspapers of the time followed strict party lines. They printed nasty statements meant to entertain as well as persuade—like political bumper stickers and TV ads today.

Federalists urged their followers to join together and save their government "from the fangs of those who are tearing it to pieces." Republicans came back with the warning, "Now is the time when the heads of federal robbers shall be hunted from their den, when public indignation shall overtake them. . . ."

➤ *This political cartoon from the election of 1800 shows Jefferson throwing the Constitution into the flames of "Gallic Despotism" (France). The eagle symbolizes the Federalists, who save the Constitution.*

The worst attack came from a Federalist newspaper in Baltimore. Trying to dash Republican hopes, it printed a false rumor that Jefferson had died.

Jefferson Takes the Reins

The Republicans had begun soon after the election in 1796 to build a national party organization. They started state and local political groups everywhere in the nation. Federalists also tried to develop and coordinate local party organizations. But conflicts inside their party limited the Federalists' success. Alexander Hamilton disliked and disagreed with President Adams. As leader of the Federalist party, Hamilton tried to persuade the Federalists to elect Charles C. Pinckney President. Adams would then become Vice President. But Hamilton's plan failed.

Close Presidential Race

Presidents are not elected directly by the people. Instead, **electoral votes**, cast by specially chosen people in each state, determine who gets elected. The people chosen to cast electoral votes are called electors. Each state has the

Objectives

1. Analyze Jefferson's strategy in absorbing the Federalists into his Republican administration.
2. Explain how the Louisiana Purchase contributed to American independence.
3. Summarize the main idea behind the *Marbury* v. *Madison* decision.

Graphic Overview

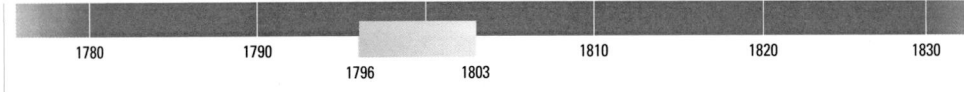

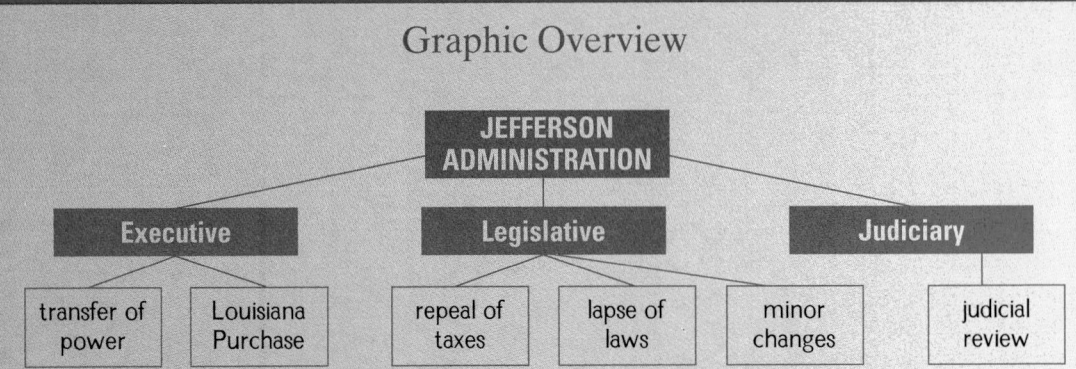

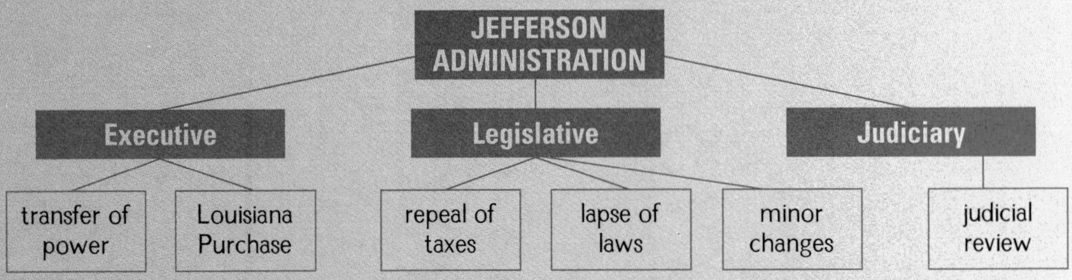

same number of electors as it has representatives in Congress.

In the election of 1800, Jefferson and another Republican, Aaron Burr of New York, won the majority of electoral votes. They each had 73 votes, compared with 65 for John Adams and 64 for Charles C. Pinckney. In these early presidential elections, the person with the most votes became President and the first runner-up was made Vice President. The election showed that the people were tired of Federalist rule. The majority of ballots had been cast for the Republicans. But which Republican—Jefferson or Burr—would lead the country?

Because of the tie, the decision went to the House of Representatives. There the Federalists tried to give the presidency to Burr. Thirty-five times the representatives voted, and thirty-five times the ballots remained tied. Some feared that the government would dissolve. Delaware Federalist James Bayard finally broke the tie, and Jefferson became President.

Peaceful Transfer of Power

"I have this morning witnessed one of the most interesting scenes a free people can ever witness," Margaret B. Smith wrote to her sister-in-law after observing the inauguration ceremony of Thomas Jefferson. "The changes of administration, which in every government and in every age have most generally been epochs of confusion, villainy, and bloodshed, in this our happy country take place without any species of distraction or disorder."

Jefferson viewed his election as the "Revolution of 1800." But unlike the French Revolution, and contrary to the fears publicized by the Federalists only a short time before, it was not followed by a period of violence and political chaos. Indeed, the fact that Jefferson's inauguration was an occasion when control of the government was transferred peacefully from one political party to another may have been the most revolutionary thing about it.

On March 4, 1801, Jefferson became the first President to be inaugurated in Washington, D.C., the nation's new capital. At that time, Washington consisted of unfinished government buildings, boarding houses, muddy roads, and large tracts of wilderness. The building we know as the White House was called the President's House and was not white at all. The capitol building was less than

◄ *Through an oversight, the voting laws of New Jersey allowed women to vote until 1808. Republican wives and daughters helped Jefferson win New Jersey in 1800.*

Across Time & Space

Throughout history other countries and places have experienced dramatic political changes without violence. On July 1, 1997, jurisdiction over Hong Kong changed. Hong Kong had been a dependent territory of Great Britain since the 1800s. In 1898, Great Britain leased most of the territory from China for 99 years, and ruled it until 1997, when Hong Kong was returned to China.

DEVELOP

Have students divide a sheet of paper into two columns and label one *Problems* and the other one *Solutions*. Encourage students to make a list as they read of each problem Jefferson faced when he took office and each solution tried during his presidency.

SOCIAL SYSTEMS

Visual Learning

Ask the students to describe what the people in the picture are doing. *(Gathering at a voting place)* What clue in the picture tells roughly what time period it is? *(It must be after the Revolutionary War because the sign says state, not colony, of New Jersey.)* What appears unusual in the picture? *(Women are voting.)* Have students consider how an Adams Federalist might react to the picture. *(Perhaps would be opposed to women voting)*

Access Strategy

Tell students to list some of the things that usually happen when a new President takes office in this country. Have a volunteer list the class responses on the board. *(A party, a parade, an inauguration speech, people appointed to some jobs)* Have students describe what they may have seen or heard on TV news about the ways power sometimes changes hands in other countries (for example, through a violent coup d'etat). Have a student read aloud Across Time and Space on page 147. Explain that internal unrest and violence have marred domestic transitions of power at various points in the history of England, Spain, Italy, Mexico, Argentina, China, India, and Korea. Tell students that in this lesson they will be learning about a transfer of power in 1800 that was "revolutionary" because it was peaceful.

Access Activity

Ask students what Jefferson meant when he said in his inaugural address: "Let us . . . unite with one heart and one mind. . . . Every difference of opinion is not a difference of principle. . . . We are all republicans—we are all federalists. . . ." *(Sample answer: The political parties should work together to advance the goals of the country.)*

■ *As in a revolution, the control of government was passed from one party to another. Unlike most revolutions, it was done peacefully (revolutionary in itself).*

POLITICAL SYSTEMS

Critical Thinking

Have students discuss why a new President might keep some of the policies of the opposing political party. *(To maintain harmony, to gain support for other policies)* Why did Jefferson keep some of the Federalist policies? *(To bring the Federalists into the Republican Party)* Why did Jefferson want to absorb the Federalists? *(Disliked political parties, wanted unity, aware that Federalists feared chaos)*

➤ *This watercolor from 1800 shows that by then only the north wing of the Capitol had been finished. Note the unpaved road beside the building.*

■ *Why did Jefferson think of his election as the Revolution of 1800?*

half-finished. Only the chamber for the House of Representatives was ready to be used. One British diplomat thought the primitive new capital was "scarce any better than a mere swamp." ■

The Republicans Make Some Changes

In his first inaugural address, Jefferson tried to play down his differences with the Federalists. "Every difference of opinion is not a difference of principle," he said. "We are all republicans, we are all federalists." Now that the election had been decided, all must "unite in common efforts for the common good."

▲ *This flag celebrates the victory of Thomas Jefferson in the election of 1800.*

Jefferson's goal was not to coexist peacefully with the Federalists, but to draw them into the Republican Party. Sharing the Federalists' dislike for parties, Jefferson hoped that all parties would sooner or later disappear. "Nothing shall be spared on my part to obliterate the traces of party and consolidate the nation," Jefferson wrote shortly after he was inaugurated.

The heart of Jefferson's strategy was not in what he did, but in what he did not do. Even though he disliked the Hamiltonian national bank, for example, he did not do away with it. Hamilton's system for paying off the debt remained in place, and the national bank went on operating until its charter ran out in 1811. Jefferson's moderation convinced many Federalists that the Republicans were not a danger to the nation.

Yet Jefferson, with the help of his Congress, reshaped the government to fit Republican goals. Most notably he appointed Republican judges. When the Alien and Sedition acts ran out in 1801, Congress refused to renew them. A new liberal naturalization law was adopted. Jefferson pardoned prisoners and gave back fines to those who had already been convicted under the Sedition Act. He also persuaded Congress to shorten the residency requirement for naturalization of citizens to its old level of five years. Once again, Jefferson hoped, the nation could serve as a new home for "oppressed humanity."

The new President trimmed a

Visual Learning

Have students bring in pictures from news magazines or newspapers that show the U.S. Capitol and other Washington buildings. Students can compare these to the picture on this page. Have them list several ways in which the Capitol and the surrounding area differs today from the way it was in 1800. *(No dome, rough roads, more countrylike)*

Historical Context

At the time of the Louisiana Purchase, Napoleon Bonaparte had conquered most of western Europe and was just two years away from being proclaimed emperor. Jefferson was not eager to have so powerful a neighbor on his western doorstep. When the sale took place, Napoleon was desperate for money. He was about to go to war with England, and his first attempts to establish himself in the New World had ended in disaster.

Political Context

Because the election of 1800 had resulted in a deadlock in the House of Representatives, Congress passed the Twelfth Amendment in 1804. This amendment changed the electoral process by making electors vote separately for President and Vice President. The candidate with the majority in each category would be the winner. If no candidate received a majority, the presidency would be decided in the House and the vice presidency in the Senate.

great deal from the budget, particularly military costs. He also did away with all taxes on U.S.-made goods, including the tax on whiskey.

Jefferson set a tone of simplicity in the new Republican government and got rid of most of the stiff, formal ceremony that had characterized Federalist administrations. He liked to shake hands rather than bow, for example, and he rode around Washington on horseback instead of by carriage. He also paid no attention to the rules of protocol that gave a rank of dignity to every senator, representative, and diplomat. "When brought together in society, all are perfectly equal," Jefferson insisted. ■

■ *How did Jefferson earn the cooperation of the Federalists?*

■ *Jefferson kept important Federalist programs even though he disagreed with them.*

The Nation Matures Under Jefferson

After cutting out Federalist excesses, Jeffersonian Republicans began to put in place a policy that worked toward their goal of a strong agrarian republic. The greatest accomplishment of the Jefferson administration was a major land purchase that helped make the new nation more independent. Other actions, especially an important Supreme Court case, tested and made clear procedures set up by the Constitution.

The Louisiana Purchase

Republicans believed the strength of a nation depended on liberty and on land ownership for all. Jefferson wanted to stop the concentration of wealth and power linked with manufacturing and big cities. He believed the answer lay in gaining new lands for farming.

When Jefferson learned that Spain had given Louisiana to France by a secret treaty in 1800, he was greatly upset. The presence in Louisiana of a powerful foreign country like France threatened future expansion by the United States. American trade on the Mississippi River could be endangered if the French owned New Orleans, the city at the river's mouth. Jefferson had always looked upon France as the nation's "natural friend." But even he

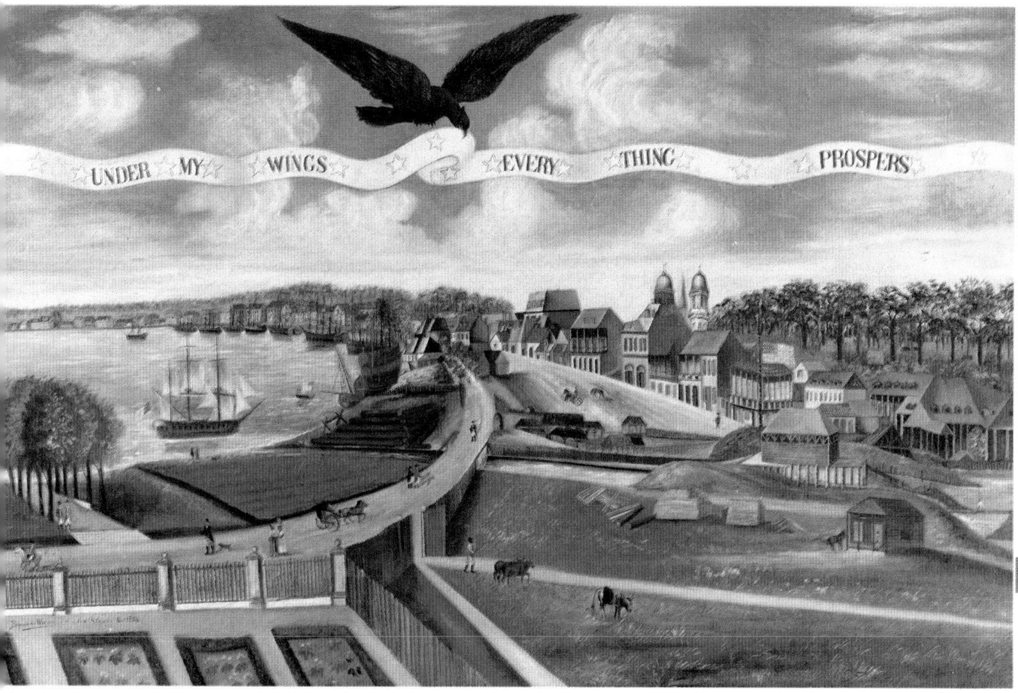
UNDER MY WINGS EVERY THING PROSPERS

This 1803 painting of New Orleans celebrates the Louisiana Purchase. The eagle symbolizes the United States. Note the American flags on the ships and buildings. New Orleans gave the United States control of the Mississippi River, the most important transportation route for Western farmers.

GEOGRAPHY

Visual Learning

Have students compare the picture on this page of New Orleans with the picture in A Closer Look at the Battle of New Orleans on page 157. *(Sample answers: Mississippi River and flat landscapes are featured in both pictures, which commemorate key events in the city's history.)*

Mathematics Connection

The Louisiana Purchase doubled the territory of the United States, adding 827,192 square miles of area. Have students calculate how many acres this represents, using 640 acres = 1 square mile. *(529,402,880)* At the price of $15 million, how much did the United States pay per acre? *(Less than 3 cents)* Have students find out the current cost per acre of undeveloped land and calculate what the Louisiana Purchase would cost today.

Science Connection

Tell students that Jefferson once said, "Science is my passion, politics my duty." His scientific curiosity led to many inventions. Have students research and report on one or more of Jefferson's inventions, such as the revolving chair, a pedometer for measuring the distance one has walked, a walking stick that unfolded to become a chair, and even a plow, which won a gold medal at a French exhibition.

Study Skills

Have students consult an encyclopedia or biographical dictionary to discover more about Thomas Jefferson. They might look specifically for information about his views on government, his retirement to Monticello, or his work habits and personality. Have the class make a profile of Jefferson by combining their findings in a list of facts on the board.

considered an alliance with Britain to remove the French from Louisiana. As he told Robert Livingston, the American minister to France, "there is on the globe one single spot the possessor of which is our natural and habitual enemy. . . . The day that France takes possession of New Orleans, . . . we must marry ourselves to the British fleet and nation."

Jefferson tried to solve the problem through peaceful means. He had Livingston offer to buy New Orleans from France. Jefferson sent James Monroe to Paris in 1803 to help Livingston. To the surprise of the Americans, the French minister offered to sell the whole Louisiana Territory. It just happened that the French Emperor Napoleon needed money to fight Great Britain. Livingston and Monroe both jumped at the chance. For $15 million, the United States bought all of the Louisiana Territory. The

The Mississippi River provided transportation for the large and fertile interior of North America. This map shows the importance of the river to trappers and farmers.

Mississippi River Valley, 1803

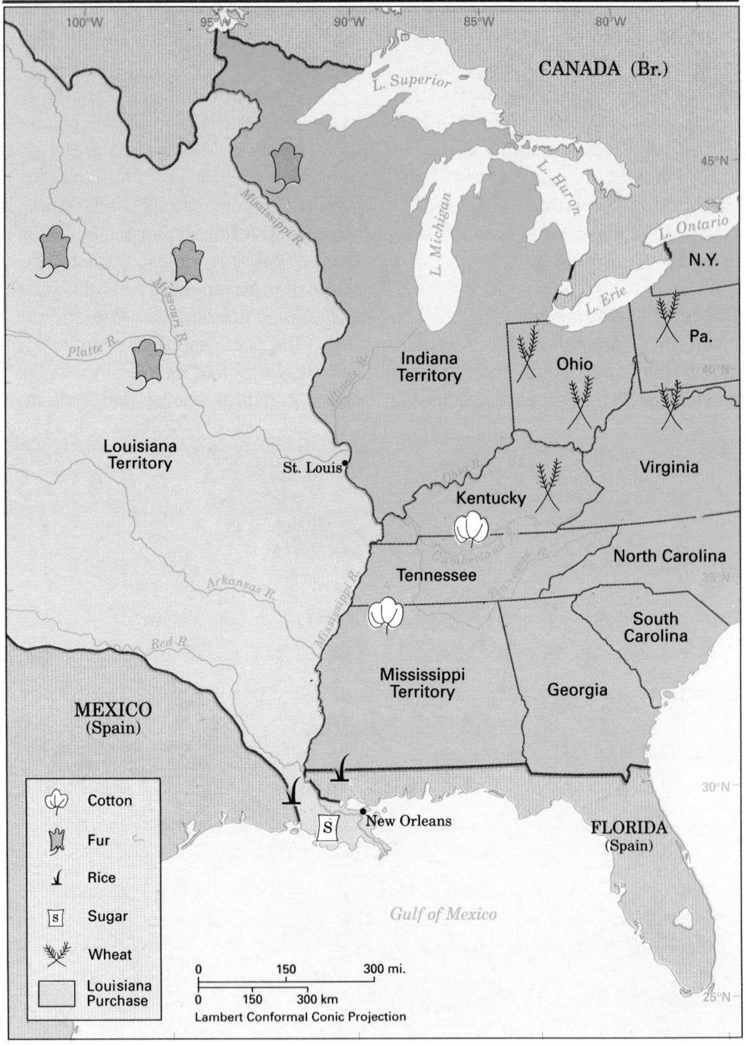

ECONOMICS

Map and Globe Skills

Tell students to use the map on this page to find two natural or man-made features that the Louisiana Territory added to the country. *(For example, the Mississippi River, the port of New Orleans)* Have students explain some of the economic benefits of the Louisiana Purchase by identifying the location of each kind of symbol representing goods transported along the Mississippi to New Orleans. *(Sample answers: wheat along the Ohio River, cotton in Mississippi Territory)*

Map and Globe Skills

Waterways such as the Mississippi River were vital to the growth of the United States. Have students draw a map or fill in an outline map showing other principal rivers and canals in the continental United States. Students may refer to the physical map of the United States in the Atlas on pages 700–701.

Making a Speech

Divide the class into two groups. Have one side prepare two-minute speeches in favor of Jefferson's moderation after his inauguration. Have the other side prepare two-minute speeches in favor of a more drastic overturning of Federalist policies. Then have the sides alternately present their speeches.

Writing a Report

Have each student research an example of the Supreme Court's use of judicial review, such as *McCulloch* v. *Maryland* (1819), *Dartmouth College* v. *Woodward* (1819), *Cohens* v. *Virginia* (1821), or *Gibbons* v. *Ogden* (1824). Ask students to write a one-page report describing the main points of the issue involved and the ruling of the court.

purchase secured American control of the Mississippi River and provided transportation routes for the crops of western farmers. As you can see on the map on page 150, the purchase doubled the nation's land area and allowed Jefferson's vision of an agrarian republic to live on.

Strong Supreme Court

Also during Jefferson's administration, the Supreme Court decision in the case *Marbury* v. (versus) *Madison* made clear the part of the Constitution that defines the Court's powers. As a result, the Supreme Court became an equal branch of government, in fact as well as in theory.

Shortly before leaving office in 1800, President Adams had appointed a large number of Federalist judges, including John Marshall as chief justice of the Supreme Court and William Marbury justice of the peace in the District of Columbia. However, Marbury's commission, the paper entitling him to his job, had not been given to him before Jefferson became President. Jefferson wanted to appoint a Republican and thus asked his secretary of state, James Madison, to hold on to the paper. Marbury filed a suit against Madison. He wanted the court to order Madison to deliver the commission. A law passed by Congress had given the federal courts the power to order such an action by the executive branch.

Chief Justice Marshall dismissed the suit. He observed that Marbury had a right to his commission and that Jefferson and Madison had no right to keep it. More importantly, however, Marshall stated that the Supreme Court did not have the power to order the President to turn over the commission. Marshall ruled that the law giving the Supreme Court power to make such an order went against the Constitution and was therefore invalid.

By denying Marbury's request, Marshall handed Jefferson a victory. At the same time, he defined the process of **judicial review** as the Supreme Court's key function in the system of checks and balances. Through judicial review, the Court decides whether laws are **constitutional**—that is, in agreement with the principles and powers established by the Constitution. With Republicans controlling the other branches of government beginning in 1800, the heavily Federalist Supreme Court asserted its power as an independent and equal part of the government. ■

Judicial Review Process

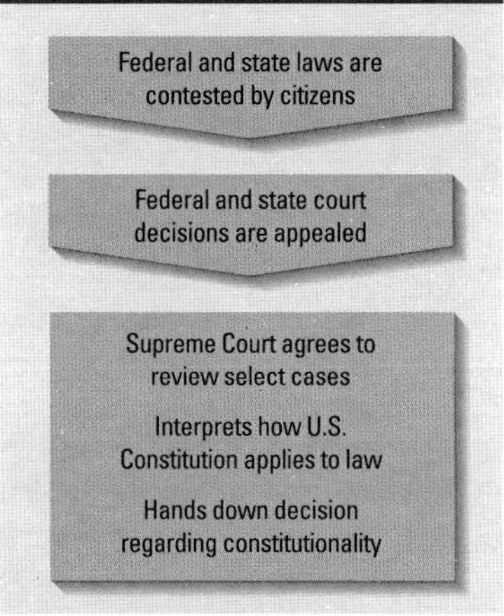

Federal and state laws are contested by citizens
Federal and state court decisions are appealed
Supreme Court agrees to review select cases
Interprets how U.S. Constitution applies to law
Hands down decision regarding constitutionality

◄ This chart shows how questions of constitutionality are resolved. Note that the Supreme Court only reviews laws that have been contested in lower courts.

■ *Why did Americans consider control of the Mississippi River so important?*

REVIEW

1. **FOCUS** How did the transfer of power to the Republicans in 1800 make a difference for the nation?
2. **CONNECT** Were Jefferson's actions as President consistent with the views he expressed while the Federalists were in power? Explain your answer.
3. **HISTORY** Explain how the Republican vice presidential candidate Aaron Burr was almost elected President.
4. **CRITICAL THINKING** What was the most important result of the *Marbury* v. *Madison* case?
5. **WRITING ACTIVITY** Write a news story for a television broadcast about the purchase of the Louisiana territory. Include in your story imaginary interviews with citizens of both the United States and France who give their opinions about the purchase and sale.

POLITICAL SYSTEMS

Critical Thinking

Pose the following question to the class: If Marshall agreed that Marbury was entitled to his commission, why didn't the Court insist that Madison give it to Marbury? *(The Court found that the law giving the Court the power to order a President to perform his duty was unconstitutional.)*

■ *Control of the Mississippi River was important because it was a major route for goods traveling from north to south and west to east.*

CLOSE

Have students answer the Thinking Focus. Then have them combine the lists they made while reading the lesson into a master list on the board. As a reteaching activity, copy on the board the three heads of the Graphic Overview on page 146. Allow students to add examples of actions taken by each branch of government.

Answers to Review Questions

1. Under Jefferson the Republicans kept some of the Federalist policies, got rid of the most extreme Federalist policies, and set up a program for a strong agrarian republic.
2. President Jefferson continued to work for his ideal of an agrarian nation free of political parties. He kept some Federalist programs to try to bring the Federalist party into the Republican party.
3. Because both Jefferson and Burr received 73 electoral votes, the decision went to the House of Representatives. The House voted 35 times before breaking the tie.
4. Sample answer: It established the power of the Supreme Court to decide whether laws are constitutional. Allow for personal opinion.
5. Students should write their news stories in a journalistic style. Encourage students to consider the price, the value, and popular feelings about the French.

Homework Options

Encourage students to read more about the Louisiana Purchase and list the states or parts of states that were formed from the Louisiana Territory.

Study Guide: page 20.

UNDERSTANDING BIBLIOGRAPHY CARDS

This skill lesson will get students started on a research report by giving them practice with bibliography cards and note cards.

HISTORY

Study Skills

Show the students a sample bibliography from a book in the library. Point out that each entry lists the name of the author or editor first. Entries are arranged in alphabetical order by the last name of the author or editor. Remind students that when they assemble their index cards for a final bibilography, they should order them alphabetically by the author's or editor's last name.

Researching Aaron Burr

Here's Why

Doing research is like being a private investigator. You have to follow clues. An article you read in a magazine may mention a book with more information on the subject. That book may refer to a news article. One step leads to another until you have found enough information on the topic to write a report.

Sometimes you can use short cuts. Researchers create bibliographies, or lists of books and articles they used in their research. You can use these bibliographies to do your own research. In turn, you should create a bibliography of your research for other investigators to use.

Suppose you were writing a report on Aaron Burr (pictured above), Thomas Jefferson's vice president, who was tried for treason. You would need to create bibliography cards to keep track of your sources.

Here's How

1. Begin by using the library to locate information on Aaron Burr. Then use an index card to record the following bibliographic information on each card:
   - the title of the book or article
   - the author(s) or editor(s)
   - the publisher
   - the city of publication
   - the date of publication

   The publisher and publication dates are important, because they tell the reader exactly which edition of a book you used and how old the information is.
2. Now use index cards to take notes. At the top of each card, record the title of the book, magazine, or reference article from which you are taking information, along with the number of the page with which you are working.
3. Use as many cards as necessary. Just remember to write the title of your source and its page number at the top.

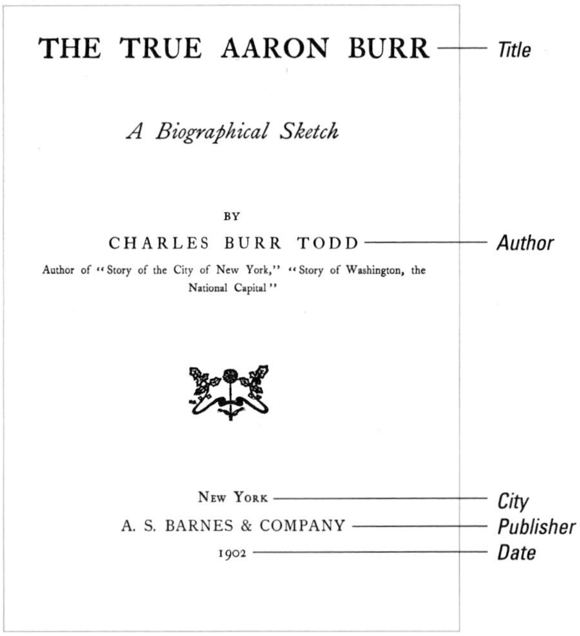
THE TRUE AARON BURR
Title
A Biographical Sketch
BY
CHARLES BURR TODD
Author
Author of "Story of the City of New York," "Story of Washington, the National Capital"
NEW YORK
City
A. S. BARNES & COMPANY
Publisher
1902
Date

Try It

Look at the title page at left. Use it to create a bibliography card and a note card.

Apply It

Choose a contemporary political figure of interest to you. Follow the steps above to locate sources, create bibliography cards, and take notes.

Objective

Use the title page from the book on Aaron Burr to create bibliography cards. (Study Skills 2)

Answers to Try It

Bibliography card: *The True Aaron Burr,* Charles Burr Todd, A.S. Barnes & Company, New York, 1902.

Note card: *The True Aaron Burr*, p. 00. Notes with relevant information.

Answers to Apply It

Make sure that each student creates several bibliography cards and uses at least one note card for each bibliography card. Check to see that they have used the note cards to write down a specific item of information from the source.

1780 1790 1800 1803 1823 1830

L E S S O N 3

The United States and the World

Smoke and flames engulfed the city of Washington, D.C., on the evening of August 24, 1814. British soldiers had stormed into the city, driving the small American army into the Virginia woods. In what became an unforgettable insult to the young nation, the troops set fire to all but one of the government buildings in the capital. The President's House and the Capitol survived but were scarred by smoke and flames.

When the attack began, First Lady Dolley Madison quickly gathered some of the treasures from the President's House and fled to Virginia. Among the things she saved were some important Cabinet papers, the most famous portrait of George Washington, and the presidential silver service. President Madison also fled, finding shelter in houses and inns.

Americans were devastated by the loss of their capital. One woman declared, "Already in one night have hundreds of our citizens been reduced from affluence to poverty, for it is not to be expected Washington will ever again be the seat of Government." What had happened between the end of Jefferson's presidency and the beginning of Madison's to cause this humiliating attack by the British?

THINKING FOCUS

How well did the United States handle international conflicts?

Key Terms

- neutrality
- impressment

The portrait above is of First Lady Dolley Madison.

This English engraving shows the burning city of Washington, D.C., in 1814.

INTRODUCE

Remind students that when Jefferson became President, the United States was officially a neutral country. Have students read the lesson title and recall some instances when the United States was pulled into world events. *(The French Revolution, the undeclared war with France in 1798)* Ask students to read the Thinking Focus and predict different ways the United States might act in international conflicts. Have them read to confirm or reject their predictions.

Key Terms

Vocabulary strategies: T36–37

neutrality—the state of being a nonparticipant in a war or other conflict

impressment—the forcing of someone into naval service

Graphic Overview

	Jefferson	Madison	Monroe
Event	Embargo Act Non-Intercourse Act	War of 1812	Adams–Onís Treaty Monroe Doctrine
Evaluation	ineffective against France and Britain	increased nationalistic pride	gained new territory, earned respect

Objectives

1. Trace the beginnings of international disturbances that led to the War of 1812.
2. Explain why the Federalist party collapsed as a national political force.
3. Describe how the United States, strengthened and unified by the War of 1812, asserted its independence from Europe.

DEVELOP

Explain that this lesson will show how the foreign policy of the United States slowly changed. Have the students preview the headings in this lesson to look for any evidence of a trend. As they read the lesson, students can list the ways in which the United States responded to each major international event.

HISTORY

Critical Thinking

Have students analyze why it is difficult for a nation to maintain a state of neutrality. *(Loyalty to allies, interruption of trade)* Which U.S. Presidents before Jefferson struggled to maintain neutrality? *(Washington, Adams)*

Jefferson's Foreign Policy Is Challenged

As President of a neutral nation during a period of European wars in the early 1800s, Jefferson had struggled to defend American freedom of the seas. He knew that overseas markets for agricultural exports were crucial; the prosperity of American farmers depended upon them. At the same time, manufactured goods from Europe were also important. The United States was then mostly a farming nation, unable to supply its own manufactured goods.

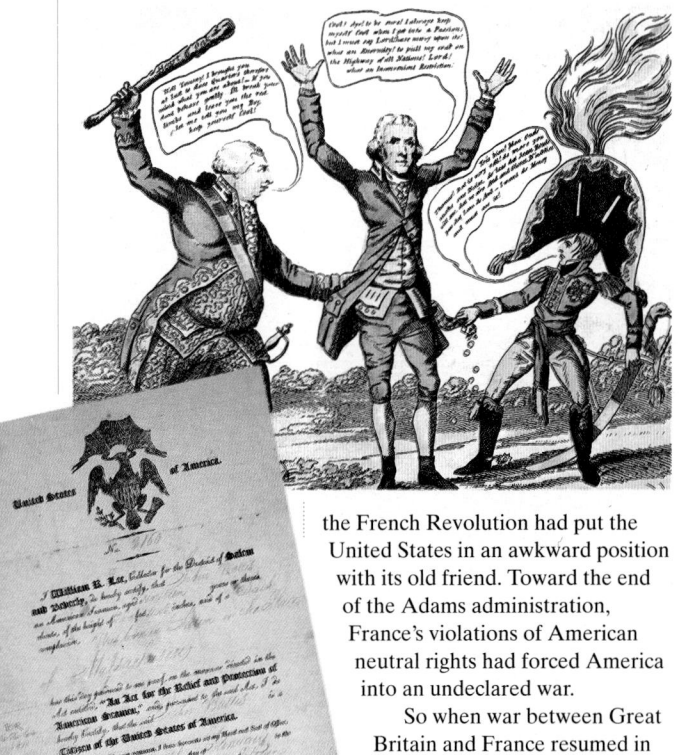

Caught in the Middle Again

America's struggle to maintain **neutrality,** the state of being a nonparticipant in war, was not a new issue. During Washington's presidency, the French Revolution had put the United States in an awkward position with its old friend. Toward the end of the Adams administration, France's violations of American neutral rights had forced America into an undeclared war.

So when war between Great Britain and France resumed in 1803, American neutrality faced familiar challenges. Thanks to its powerful navy, Great Britain ruled the seas. French armies quickly took control of the European continent. As a new country with little diplomatic or military power, the United States gained little respect from either side.

To keep its enemies from receiving goods by ship, Great Britain began a blockade of the European coast. In a blockade, hostile ships keep all other ships, usually neutrals, from going into or out of enemy ports. Sometimes only ships carrying war supplies are kept out. Ships caught in the British blockade were often taken for use by the British Navy. The French responded by blockading the British Isles. The French also seized neutral ships. Further restrictions from both Great Britain and France made it impossible for American ships to trade safely with either side. If American ships obeyed the wishes of one nation, they were subject to seizure by the other. By 1812, Great Britain had taken nearly 1,000 American ships; France had taken about 500.

The crisis was made worse by the policy of British **impressment.** This was the taking from American ships of sailors who might have been British deserters. The sailors were made to serve in the Royal Navy, which needed men to fight France. Although American sailors started to carry certificates of American citizenship with them, they were not safe from British impressment. As long as America was too weak to stop the British, the sailors would never be safe.

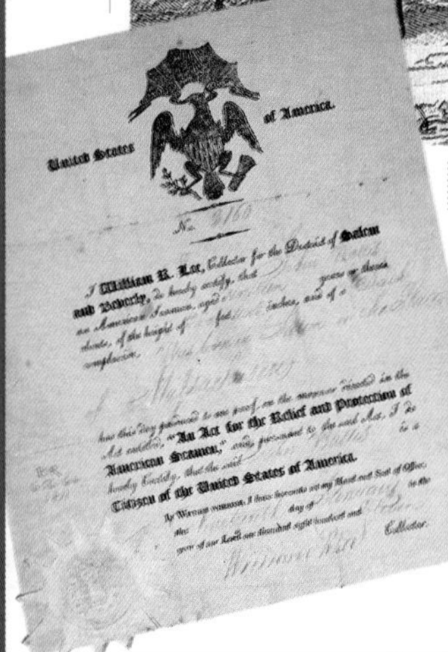

In this political cartoon, President Jefferson is robbed by King George of Great Britain and Emperor Napoleon of France (top). *Certificates of citizenship like this one were issued to American sailors while Great Britain was at war with France* (bottom).

The Failure of Diplomacy

Jefferson answered British and French aggression by cutting off American trade. In 1807 he had Congress pass the Embargo Act, which prohibited American ships from sailing to any foreign ports. This kept Great Britain and France from getting

Access Activity

Direct students to the political cartoon on this page and ask them to explain what King George and Napoleon are doing *(Picking Jefferson's pockets)* and how Jefferson is reacting *(Doing nothing)*. Ask students to suggest a word describing each character. *(Jefferson—passive; King George—rough; Napoleon—eager)*

Access Strategy

Ask students if they have ever been caught in the middle of an argument between two friends. Was it possible to remain neutral? Have three students role play the following situation: two students accuse each other of losing something. Finally, they each ask a third student to join their respective sides. Have the rest of the class suggest different ways the third student could respond. *(Join one side, walk away, give an opinion, pretend not to notice)*

To help students understand the events leading up to the War of 1812, emphasize that Great Britain and France were the countries originally at war. The United States was merely caught in the middle when its ships were captured by both sides. Tell students that they learn in this lesson how being "caught in the middle" affected U.S. foreign policy.

American goods even by buying them through neutral countries. But the law left American ships by the hundreds rotting at their wharves and sent the economy into a bad slump. Bitter opposition arose among farmers and merchants. As a result, Congress repealed the Embargo Act in 1809 and replaced it with the Non-Intercourse Act, which opened trade with all nations except France and Great Britain.

Both the Embargo Act and the Non-Intercourse Act failed as foreign policy measures. The government was not able to enforce the acts. Also, the European nations were able to get their supplies from other countries. ■

■ *Why was the war between Great Britain and France so harmful to the United States?*

■ *The war stopped trade between the United States and its overseas markets. This hurt the economy of the United States.*

Madison Pressured into War

In the election of 1808, James Madison won the presidency with no trouble. As President, he faced many of the same foreign policy dilemmas that had troubled Jefferson. Great Britain, the worst violator of neutral rights, went on to become the chief enemy of the United States during Madison's administration.

Madison also had troubles along the frontiers of the Northwest Territory. Shawnee chief Tecumseh had united many Indian tribes to resist white settlers who violated treaty boundaries. The growing militancy of the Indians alarmed the governor of the Indiana Territory, William Henry Harrison. At the Battle of Tippecanoe in 1811, Harrison destroyed the Indians' stronghold. The Indians fought back with devastating attacks all across the northwestern frontier.

Although the hostility of the Indians was largely due to their real anger about the whites' invasion of Indian lands, the attacks increased anti-British feelings. "I can have no doubt of the influence of British agents in keeping up Indian hostility," a Kentucky congressman said.

The trouble at sea and the perceived British influence on Indians led to an increase in war fever, particularly in the West and the South. A new group of Republican congressmen called War Hawks criticized Madison's ineffective diplomacy and called for stronger measures against the British. In June 1812, Madison tired of "the injuries and indignities which have been heaped upon our country." He then asked Congress for the nation's first declaration of war. Had news traveled faster, he might not have.

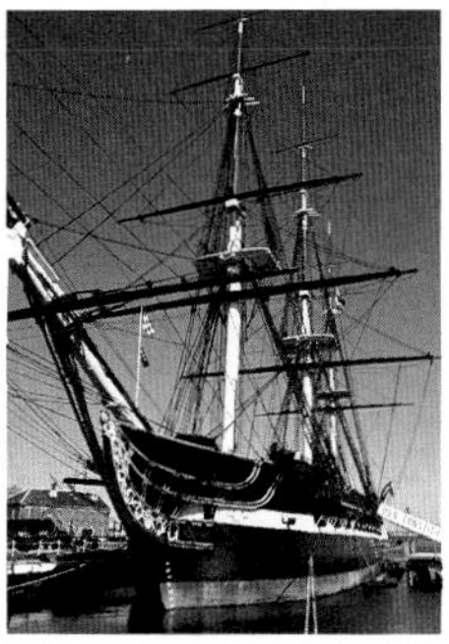

◄ *The U.S.S.* Constitution, *or "Old Ironsides," as it became known, is shown engaging the British frigate* Guerrière. *The* Guerrière *surrendered in half an hour. Today the* Constitution *is based at the Charlestown Naval Yard in Boston, Massachusetts. It has been restored and is now available for visits by the public. It sails on Independence Day.*

HISTORY

Critical Thinking

Have students work together to list the events that pressured Madison into asking Congress to declare war in 1812. *(British violations of neutral rights, influence of the British on the Indians)* Ask students what argument, if any, might have convinced Madison not to declare war in 1812. *(That the British are going to stop impressment, that Americans are not prepared for war)*

155

Cultural Context

Francis Scott Key was neither a poet nor a musician, but a lawyer. He was part of a group sent to the commander of the British naval fleet to negotiate the release of a friend, Dr. Beanes. The British commander, Admiral Cockburn, agreed to release Beanes. Key returned to his own ship in time to see the Admiral start bombarding Fort McHenry.

Key watched the British bombardment, which lasted 25 hours. As dawn came, Key wrote the first stanza of a poem on the back of an envelope. Later in his hotel room, he added three more stanzas. He gave the poem—"The Defense of Fort McHenry"—to his brother-in-law, J.H. Nicholson. Nicholson suggested a well-known British tune, "Anacreon in Heaven," as a setting for the poem. Together, the poem and tune have become "The Star-Spangled Banner."

Visual Learning

Refer students to the painting and the photo on this page of the *U.S.S. Constitution.* Why did the painter choose to show the ship in action? *(Probably to glorify the U.S. Navy)* Why does the U.S. Navy maintain the ship in Boston? *(Pride in national heritage)*

GEOGRAPHY

Map and Globe Skills

On the U.S. political map on pages 698–699 in the Atlas, have students point out the locations of the battles of the War of 1812. They should include the naval battle on Lake Erie, routes of the three-pronged British attack, the Battle of Tippecanoe, the sacking of Washington, D.C., the siege of Fort McHenry, and the Battle of New Orleans.

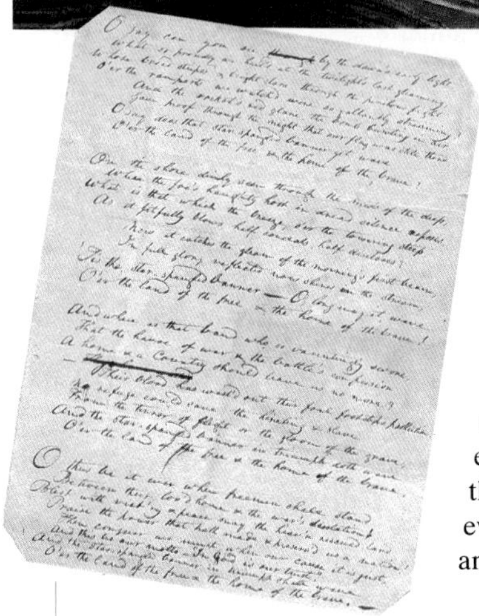

Fort McHenry survived after suffering 400 direct hits during the bombardment of September 13–14, 1814. This painting shows the British launching huge 190-pound bombs at the fort (top). *Francis Scott Key's original manuscript of "The Star Spangled Banner"* (bottom).

Unknown to Madison, the British had already officially ended their policy of impressment.

Americans Face the British

Americans were hopelessly unprepared for the War of 1812, but they still felt very sure of victory. To acquire new territory and to eliminate British support for the Indians, some Americans even wanted to conquer and annex Canada.

The first year of the war was a gloomy one for the United States. But in 1813, Captain Oliver Hazard Perry defeated the British on Lake Erie. "We have met the enemy and they are ours," he reported. By securing control of Lake Erie, Perry enabled an American general to capture part of Canada temporarily from the British. However, other invasions of Canada were failures.

After defeating French Emperor Napoleon in 1814, Great Britain strengthened its North American military force and planned a three-pronged invasion of the United States. In the north, British troops came from Canada by way of Lake Champlain. On the Atlantic coast they came through the Chesapeake Bay into Washington and Baltimore, and in the south they attacked from the Gulf of Mexico into New Orleans.

During the British attack on Fort McHenry outside Baltimore, Francis Scott Key spent the night watching "bombs bursting in air," afraid for the lives of his fellow Americans. At dawn, the sight that "our flag was still there" inspired Key to write the verses to "The Star Spangled Banner." Popular for many years, the song became the national anthem in 1931.

O say, can you see, by the
dawn's early light,
What so proudly we hail'd at the
twilight's last gleaming?
Whose broad stripes and bright
stars, thro' the perilous fight,
O'er the ramparts we watch'd,
were so gallantly streaming.

And the rockets' red glare, the
bombs bursting in air,
Gave proof thro' the night, that
our flag was still there . . .

Finally, in January 1815, a scrappy army of American militiamen, including many free blacks, surprised the British in New Orleans. It would be the last battle of the war. Led by General Andrew Jackson, the Americans boldly fought off the British troops. For more details about the Battle of New Orleans, see A Closer Look.

New Englanders Resist

The decision to declare war had divided the nation. Even though the War of 1812 was fought to defend the rights of Americans on the seas, support for the war came from the agrarian states of the Mid-Atlantic, South, and West. New England, led by its merchants, was against the war. Mostly Federalists, New Englanders felt betrayed by the Republicans in power. The war had put an end to the illegal trade New Englanders had been carrying on.

Social Participation

Tell students to name occasions when they have heard "The Star-Spangled Banner." *(Opening of baseball games, when an American citizen gets a gold medal at the Olympics)* Why do countries have national songs? *(To bring people together, to create national pride)*

Music Connection

Point out that many Americans don't know "The Star-Spangled Banner" very well and almost no one knows all four verses. Play a recording of the anthem and provide students with a copy of the words, which can be found in most almanacs.

Some people claim that "The Star-Spangled Banner" is difficult to sing well and is too militaristic. Have students decide which of the following patriotic songs, if any, might be suitable for a national anthem: "God Bless America," "America the Beautiful," "Columbia, the Gem of the Ocean," and "My Country 'Tis of Thee." Provide copies of the words and play recordings for the students.

A CLOSER LOOK

The Battle of New Orleans

When rumors of a British attack reached General Jackson in Mobile, he led his soldiers through the swamps to defend New Orleans. The British invaded, amid cattails and hanging moss, to fight for access to the Mississippi River. Ironically, the battle should never have happened: it actually took place after the Treaty of Ghent was signed.

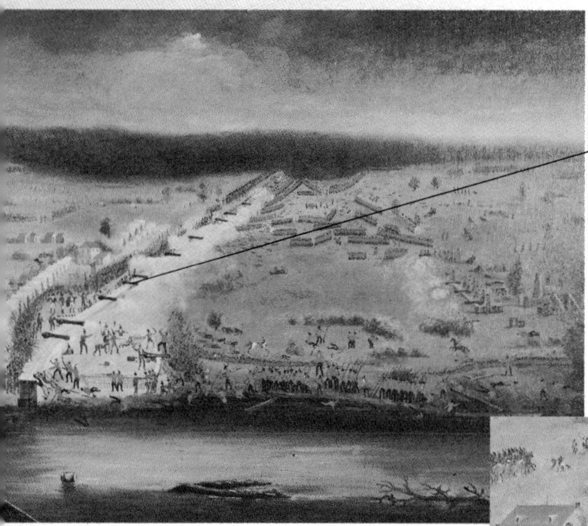

American troops cut down bayou trees to block access to the city. They stacked them and added cotton bales for extra height. As this painting shows, most of the combat was hand-to-hand, but both sides used cannons to rip through enemy walls.

"Old Hickory" triumphs! Under the command of rough and determined Andrew Jackson, the Americans killed more than 2,600 British soldiers while losing only 21 men of their own.

Bales go up in thick black smoke. Americans discovered just how flammable cotton could be in this, the last battle of the War of 1812. Bales sizzled and hissed in the muddy water, sending thick smoke into the air. After this battle, soldiers always covered cotton bales with mud to prevent them from going up in flames.

Note: Point out the strategic importance of New Orleans. Not only did it provide access to the Mississippi, but it also could be used as a bartering chip in peace negotiations. The city's warehouses held commodities, worth over four million pounds sterling, that could not be shipped because of the British blockade.

HISTORY

Visual Learning

In what way might the environment of the battle have worked to the American soldiers' advantage? *(Could hide behind the cattails and hanging moss in the swamp in order to surprise the British)* What nontraditional strategies had Americans used in the Revolutionary War? *(Hid behind trees and rocks rather than advancing in line as the British did)*

157

Health Connection

Impressment, hard work and the likelihood of battle made the sailor's job a dangerous one. Added to this were health problems caused by the sailors' poor diet. Have students find out about one common health problem among sailors—scurvy. Suggest that students research both its cause and cure. Based on this information, they can suggest a healthier diet for sailors who are on board a ship without refrigeration.

Science Connection

In the 25-hour bombardment of Ft. McHenry, the British used more than 1,500 shells, some weighing up to 220 pounds. Have students use an encyclopedia to find out more about typical artillery of the day: what types of guns and explosives were used, how far a ship-mounted cannon could fire, and what the dangers were.

Visual Learning

Have students examine the pictures of the battle and the captions on this page. How did American soldiers use cotton bales? *(To build walls for protection)* What would have caused the bales to go up in flames? *(Fire from cannon shot)*

HISTORY

Critical Thinking

Have students explain why the Federalists held the Hartford Convention in 1814. *(To air their grievances about the War of 1812)* Also have them review what was proposed. *(Limiting the power of the South, withdrawing from the Union)* What other ways could the Federalists have reacted with a less damaging effect? *(Sample answer: By restricting debates to within Congress)*

■ *The War of 1812 united Americans against a common enemy. Americans saw that the nation could defend and protect itself.*

HISTORY

Critical Thinking

Ask students to identify means of trans-Atlantic communication in the 1800s *(Letters by sailing ship)* and today *(Satellites and trans-Atlantic cable)*. How might events of the War of 1812 have differed with faster communications? *(Battle of New Orleans might not have happened; Hartford Convention might not have taken place.)*

In December 1814, while the last battles were being fought, New England delegates were holding a convention in Hartford, Connecticut, to discuss "public grievances and concerns" over Republican conduct of the war. A few extremists recommended withdrawing from the Union and forging a separate peace with Great Britain. Most, however, called for amendments to the Constitution designed to limit the power of the South, the West, and the Republican Party.

The Hartford Convention backfired fatally on the Federalists. In those days news could take weeks to reach the United States from Europe. The nation learned all at once of Andrew Jackson's incredible victory at New Orleans and of the signing of a peace treaty in Ghent, Belgium. The Federalists looked disloyal and foolish when the good news arrived. Soon afterwards, Federalism collapsed as a national political force.

War Ends, Problems Remain

The Treaty of Ghent had been signed on Christmas Eve, 1814—before the Battle of New Orleans. The treaty formally ended the war between Great Britain and the United States. But it included no statement about impressment and neutral rights. The treaty simply restored British-American relations and boundaries to what they had been before the war.

Although American military goals had not been met, nationalist goals had. In this way, the war was a success. An outpouring of national pride went on for 10 years after the war. Many people thought of the War of 1812 as a second war of independence. ■

■ *How did the War of 1812 help to bring Americans together?*

American Influence Expands

In the presidential election of 1816, Madison's secretary of state, James Monroe, easily defeated his Federalist opponent, Rufus King. When Monroe became President, the nation was at peace, feeling stronger, and ready to assert itself at home and abroad. Unlike earlier Presidents, Monroe made his greatest achievements in foreign affairs.

➤ *This engraving shows James Monroe, a President noted for foreign policy achievements.*

A Continental Nation

The negotiations with Spain after the War of 1812 dealt with both Florida and the western boundary of the Louisiana Territory. Monroe sent Secretary of State John Quincy Adams to bargain with the Spanish leader Luis de Onis. At the meeting, Spain agreed to the sale of the territory for $5 million. On February 22, 1819, Spain ceded Florida to the United States. In the boundary agreement, Spain gave up its claim to the Oregon country but held on to the lands of the Southwest. This area included what is now California, Texas, Arizona, and New Mexico. The resulting Transcontinental Treaty—also known as the Adams-Onis Treaty—transferred Florida to the United States and extended American territorial claims to the Pacific Ocean. In 1819, the United States became recognized as a continental nation.

Critical Thinking

Point out that Jackson's victory in the Battle of New Orleans was an occasion for great national pride. Have students list some positive and negative consequences of this growing national pride. *(Positive—greater loyalty to government, willingness to serve the common good; Negative—dislike of outsiders, willingness to make war)*

Writing a News Account

After students have read A Closer Look on page 157, have them research the Battle of New Orleans and write a newspaper account of the battle. Students should study a daily newspaper or weekly news magazine to help them choose a writing style. Encourage them to use a typewriter or word processor to produce their articles in columns.

Writing a Letter

Tell students to write letters to a family member or government official from the point of view of one person in the following list:

- a sailor who has just been kidnapped by the British Navy
- a settler at the western frontier
- a citizen of Washington, D.C., during the British attack
- a British soldier at the Battle of New Orleans

The Monroe Doctrine

Just two years later, Mexico's colonial revolution shifted control of the southwestern territory from Spain to Mexico. Indeed, successful independence movements in Colombia, Mexico, Chile, Argentina, and Peru caused the Spanish empire to fall apart very rapidly during the early 1800s. Sympathizing with the newly independent republics, Monroe in 1822 suggested that the United States officially recognize them as nations. Congress quickly agreed.

The possibility that France or its friends would help Spain once again get control of these Latin American nations worried Monroe and Secretary of State Adams. The British foreign secretary suggested a joint Anglo-American policy to address the question. But Adams did not like the idea and called for independent action. The time for the United States to play the junior partner to Great Britain was over.

Monroe made Adams's ideas the official policy of the United States in a speech he delivered to the Congress of the United States on December 2, 1823. The Monroe Doctrine, as it came to be called, laid down two American foreign policy ideals: noncolonization and nonintervention. "The American continents," Monroe said, are closed to "future colonization by any European powers." Monroe further warned Europe against trying to oppress, or control the destiny of, the newly independent Latin American nations. In return, the United States promised "not to interfere in the internal concerns" of the European powers.

The Monroe Doctrine stated in clear terms the longstanding belief that the New World was separate from the Old World. It also stated that American ideals and interests in the Western Hemisphere were more important than European interests. Such a statement of diplomatic nationalism by the United States would have been impossible during Jefferson's administration of 1800 or even during the War of 1812. The nation had finally won the respect of Europe. ■

The Americas Emerge from European Ownership, 1823

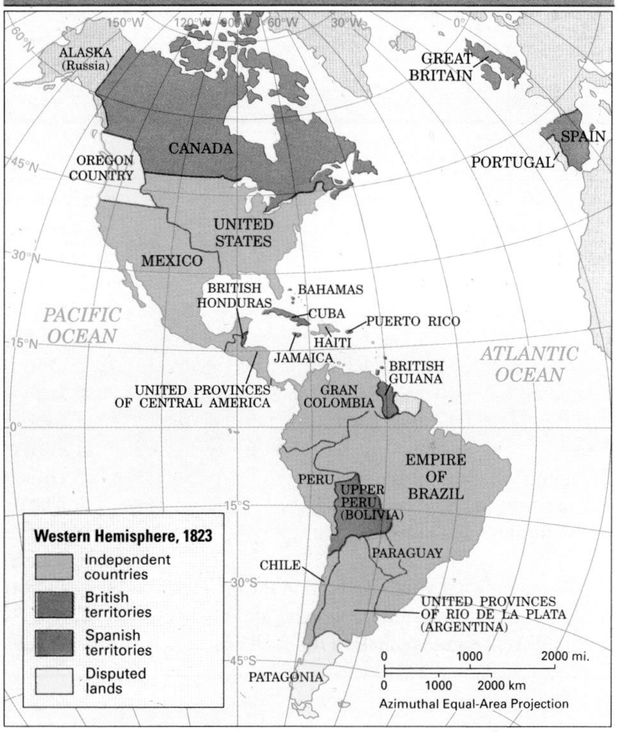

▲ *By 1823 much of the New World was free from European control.*

■ *Why was John Quincy Adams determined not to form a joint foreign policy with Great Britain?*

REVIEW

1. **FOCUS** How well did the United States handle international conflicts?
2. **CONNECT** Why do you think many Americans considered the War of 1812 a second War of Independence?
3. **ECONOMICS** Explain the role of commerce in the origin of the War of 1812.
4. **GEOGRAPHY** Why did the British choose New Orleans as one of the targets in their three-pronged invasion?
5. **CRITICAL THINKING** Why was Monroe's foreign policy more successful than that of earlier Presidents?
6. **ACTIVITY** Draw a political cartoon that illustrates one of the policies established by the Monroe Doctrine.

GEOGRAPHY
Map and Globe Skills

Have students study the map on this page and compare it with the world political map on pages 694–695 in the Atlas. Have them state the modern names of the countries protected by the Monroe Doctrine. *(Sample answer: Gran Colombia is now Colombia, Venezuela, and Ecuador.)*

■ *He did not want the United States to be tied forever to Britain. The new nation had to act independently.*

CLOSE

Copy the structure and main heads of the Graphic Overview on page 153 on the board. Have students complete the chart by referring to the lists they made while reading the lesson. Small groups of students can work together to evaluate the effects of each of these responses, evaluate the predictions they made before reading the lesson, and then answer the Thinking Focus.

Answers to Review Questions

1. The United States became better able to handle international conflicts, starting with the threatened state of neutrality, the War of 1812, and then the successful Monroe Doctrine.
2. Once again Americans were able to defend their rights against the British.
3. American ships had to be able to cross the Atlantic freely to reach overseas markets and bring back needed manufactured goods.
4. It was possible to get to the interior of the United States via the Mississippi River from this Southern city.
5. Sample answer: By this time the nation was more respected by Europe. Allow for personal opinion.
6. Students may include captions with their cartoons.

Homework Options

Ask students to write a new verse for the national anthem or to write an entirely new poem that could serve as lyrics for a national anthem.

Study Guide: page 22.

Answers to Reviewing Key Terms

A. Sample answers:
1. The President and the Cabinet make up the administration of the national government.
2. The government tried to keep out foreigners and to stop rebellion against the government with the Alien and Sedition Acts.
3. The Supreme Court uses judicial review to decide if laws are constitutional.

B. Answers:
1. False. An agrarian society is made up mostly of farms.
2. False. *Sedition* means rebellion against the government.
3. True. Jefferson did not support one foreign nation over another during his term in office.
4. True. The Supreme Court's job is to make sure laws follow the terms of the Constitution.
5. False. Electoral votes are cast by specially chosen people.
6. False. The American army did not use impressment.
7. False. The Cabinet is made up of assistants who are chosen by the President to help make decisions.
8. False. The Supreme Court reviews laws when they are made or challenged in the courts.

Chapter Review

Reviewing Key Terms

administration (p. 134)
agrarian (p. 136)
alien (p. 139)
Cabinet (p. 134)
constitutional (p. 151)
electoral vote (p. 146)
impressment (p. 154)
judicial review (p. 151)
neutrality (p. 154)
sedition (p. 139)

A. In each of the following pairs, the two terms are related in some way. Write a sentence for each pair that clearly explains the relationship between the terms.
1. administration, Cabinet
2. sedition, alien
3. judicial review, constitutional

B. Based on what you have read in the chapter, decide whether each of the following statements is accurate. Write an explanation for each decision.
1. Jefferson wanted the United States to be an agrarian society in which most people worked and lived in cities.
2. Those who plan sedition are usually loyal to their government.
3. The United States maintained its neutrality during Jefferson's administration.
4. If a law is constitutional, you can find support for it in the language of the Constitution.
5. As a citizen of the United States, you are entitled to an electoral vote.
6. The army built up its forces by using impressment.
7. The Cabinet is where the President stores important foreign documents.
8. The Supreme Court conducts a judicial review of all laws every four years.

Exploring Concepts

A. On a separate sheet of paper, copy the timeline below. Complete your timeline by placing each of the following events in the correct time position.

- End of the Whiskey Rebellion
- Outbreak of the French Revolution
- Alien and Sedition Acts passed
- Louisiana Purchase
- Embargo Act
- Madison asks for declaration of war
- Battle of New Orleans
- Treaty of Ghent
- Adams-Onis Treaty
- Monroe Doctrine

B. Support each of the following statements with facts and details from the chapter.
1. Two different political parties grew up during Washington's administration.
2. In his administration Jefferson combined the programs of both the Federalists and Republicans.
3. Government policies between 1789 and 1814 caused differences of opinion between sections of the United States.
4. Support for the Alien and Sedition Acts dwindled as the Federalists lost power.
5. The causes of the War of 1812 developed during the Washington and Jefferson administrations.

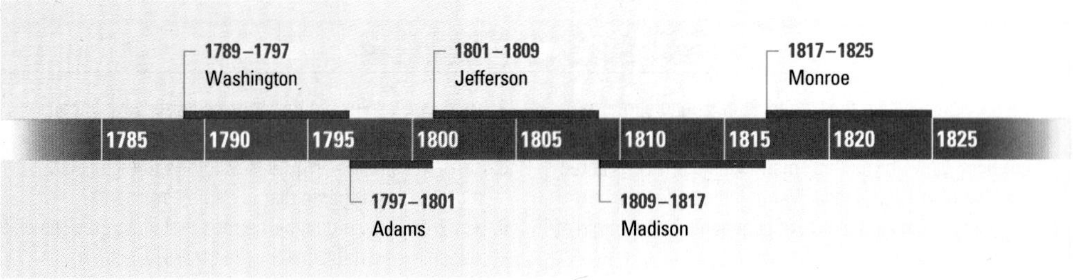

Answers to Exploring Concepts

A. Answers:
1. Whiskey Rebellion: 1794
2. French Revolution: 1789
3. Alien and Sedition Acts: 1798
4. Louisiana Purchase: 1803
5. Embargo Act: 1807
6. Madison asks for war: 1812
7. Battle of New Orleans: 1815
8. Treaty of Ghent: 1814
9. Adams-Onís Treaty: 1819
10. Monroe Doctrine: 1823

B. Sample answers:
1. The Federalist and Republican parties developed during Washington's administration.
2. Jefferson shared the Federalists' preference for one efficient political group. He did not abolish the Federalist financial system or the system for funding the debt, but he did appoint Republican judges and strived for a strong, agrarian republic.
3. Hamilton's credit and taxation programs seemed to favor Northerners, so Southerners opposed the programs. Farmers in western Pennsylvania rebelled against the whiskey tax.
4. Jefferson allowed the laws to lapse and pardoned those who had been convicted under the Sedition Act.
5. During Washington's administration, Americans were angry about Britain's occupation of American forts. During Jefferson's term, British ships kidnapped British subjects from American ships.

Reviewing Skills

1. Look at the bibliography card at right. Identify each item and state where you would find it.
2. Create a bibliography card for this textbook.
3. Read the following passage taken from page 7 of the book *The True Aaron Burr* (shown on page 152). Look up any unfamiliar words and create a note card based on this passage:

   "It was here [New York City], while the army lay in New York, that Burr and Hamilton first met, and here began that unfriendliness which culminated twenty-eight years later in the action on the fatal shelf at Weehawken."

Wagons to the West Jesse Wells Houghton Mifflin Company Boston 1982

4. Suppose you wanted to find out more information about the feud between Burr and Hamilton. Identify different ways you could do research on the feud.

Using Critical Thinking

1. In his inaugural address, Thomas Jefferson said, "Having banished from our land that religious intolerance under which mankind so long bled and suffered, we have yet gained little if we countenance [allow] a political intolerance as . . . capable of as bitter and bloody persecutions." What was the political situation Jefferson sought to correct? Are conflicts between political parties today as bitter as those Jefferson warned against? Give examples to support your answer.
2. Senator Samuel White of Delaware called the Louisiana Purchase "the greatest curse that could . . . befall us." White felt that Louisiana would draw settlers, draining the United States of its population. He feared that these settlers, separated by thousands of miles from Washington, D.C., would lose their loyalty to the United States. He preferred that France or Spain keep Louisiana, on condition that no United States citizens be allowed to settle there. What would the United States be like today if White's proposal had been adopted? Why didn't White's prediction come true?
3. Think about the expansion of the United States and the beliefs of certain political parties. Can you see any relationship between the concerns about the development of political parties and the policies the new government pursued?

Preparing for Citizenship

1. **WRITING ACTIVITY** Martha Washington, Abigail Adams, and Dolley Madison were wives of the presidents during the period covered in this chapter. Each became famous in her own right. Research and write a short biographical report on Martha Washington, Abigail Adams, or Dolley Madison. Explain how your subject contributed to the nation during those early years. Include quotations from the writings of the first lady to illustrate what she thought about the events of the time in which she lived.
2. **ART ACTIVITY** Draw a map that shows the territory controlled by the United States in 1824. Use colors to shade in the areas of the Louisiana Purchase and of the territory gained by the Adams-Onis Treaty. Use the map to predict any possible problems expansion could create for the United States.
3. **ART ACTIVITY** Make a chart that lists each presidential election from 1788 to 1820. Show who was elected President and Vice President in each election. Write a brief description of the major events of each president's administration.
4. **COLLABORATIVE LEARNING** As a class, write a skit about one or more of the events of the War of 1812. For example, you may choose the events leading to President Madison's decision to declare war, the burning of Washington, D.C., the bombardment of Fort McHenry, or the Battle of New Orleans. Then present the skit for another class or for a parents' evening.

Answers to Reviewing Skills

1. Title, author, publisher, city, and date of publication. All items would be found on the copyright page, and at least the title and author would be found on the title page.
2. Students should consult the title and copyright pages of the textbook.
3. To help students with the form of a notecard, refer students to Understanding Bibliography Cards on page 152.
4. Students may suggest looking up books, using bibliographies, or finding primary sources in letters and diaries.

Answers to Using Critical Thinking

1. Jefferson worried about the conflict between Federalists and Republicans that led to measures such as the Alien and Sedition Acts.
2. More than half the land area of today's country would be another nation if White had had his way. His prediction did not come true because the U.S. population grew, and the settlers in the Louisiana territory eventually formed their own states.
3. Jefferson clearly pursued his party's goals of limited government in an agrarian society by cutting the military budget, abolishing taxes on U.S. goods, and buying Louisiana. Because he also was afraid of the divisiveness of two parties, he allowed certain Federalist policies to continue.

Answers to Preparing for Citizenship

1. **WRITING ACTIVITY** Many biographies on these three women are available. Late in her life, Dolley Madison was photographed. Students may be interested in the strength of character that is depicted in her portrait.
2. **ART ACTIVITY** Students should consider issues of slavery, transportation, and the use of Indian lands.
3. **ART ACTIVITY** Direct students to a current almanac. The major events of these administrations are included in the chapter.
4. **COLLABORATIVE LEARNING** Encourage students to do further research on one of the events of the war. Divide roles among students—editing the play, making scenery, or creating light and sound effects.

CHAPTER 6

Planning at a Glance

The Maturing Republic

	Objectives	Reading Support *and* Other Resources	Diverse Learning Strategies
Lesson 1 Republicanism and Culture *pp. 164–169* 2–3 days	• Identify the republican ideals of early American society. • Describe how the ideals of the self-made man and market-oriented individualism developed as the nation expanded westward. • Compare the Second Great Awakening with the growing political awareness as responses to changing American values.	• **Workbook** or **Reading Support:** pp. 75–78 Review p. 18 Extra Support/Transition p. 18 Multi-lang. Sum. pp. 35–36 • **Other Resources:** Geography Kit; Posters 1, 3; Study Guide p. 23	Access Strat. **(Extra Support)** TE p. 165 Access Act. **(SDAIE)** TE p. 165 Role Playing **(Auditory)** TE p. 168 Audiotapes of Multi-language Lesson Summaries **(Auditory)**
Exploring: The Role of the First Lady *pp. 170–171*	• Identify different ways in which women have filled the role of First Lady. • Use library resources to research the role of the First Lady.		Activities **(Auditory)** TE p. 170
Lesson 2 The First Western President *pp. 172–178* 1–2 days	• Explain how 1800s politics reflected popular notions of individualism and expansion. • Describe how Jackson used his power as President to make widespread changes. • Summarize the opposing points of view in the issue of protective tariffs: strong federal union vs. state's rights.	• **Workbook** or **Reading Support:** pp. 79–82 Review p. 19 Extra Support/Transition p. 19 Multi-lang. Sum. pp. 37–38 • **Other Resources:** Geography Kit, Study Guide p. 24	Access Act. **(SDAIE)** TE p. 173 Study Skills **(Visual)** TE pp. 174, 176 Music Connection **(Auditory)** TE p. 177 Writing a Political Jingle **(GATE)** TE p. 177 Audiotapes of Multi-language Lesson Summaries **(Auditory)**
Lesson 3 How Others Saw Us *pp. 179–183* 2–3 days	• Summarize how four European visitors described the American citizens they observed. • Distinguish between the negative and positive aspects of American democracy observed by the Europeans. • Evaluate the contrasting views of Crèvecoeur, Trollope, Martineau, and Tocqueville for fairness.	• **Workbook** or **Reading Support:** pp. 83–86 Review p. 20 Extra Support/Transition p. 20 Multi-lang. Sum. pp. 39–40 • **Other Resources:** Study Guide p. 25	Access Act. **(SDAIE)** TE p. 180 Visual Learning **(Visual)** TE p. 181 Drawing **(Kinesthetic)** TE p. 182 Audiotapes of Multi-language Lesson Summaries **(Auditory)**
Skill: Understanding Political Cartoons *pp. 184–185*	• Use political cartoons to analyze the Jackson-Clay controversy.	• **Other Resources:** Study Guide p. 26	Bulletin Board **(Visual)** TE p. 184 Visual Learning **(Visual)** TE p. 185
Chapter Review *pp. 186–187* 1 day		Chapter 6 Test pp. 21–24 *(See facsimiles on TE p. 754.)*	Assessment Multiple-Use Masters pp. 81–88

Reading Support Resources *for Every Lesson*

Reading and Review

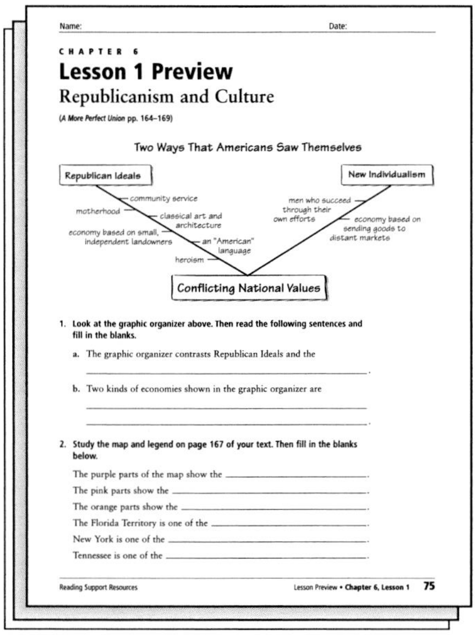
Name: Date:

CHAPTER 6

Lesson 1 Preview

Republicanism and Culture

(*A More Perfect Union* pp. 164–169)

Two Ways That Americans Saw Themselves

1. Look at the graphic organizer above. Then read the following sentences and fill in the blanks.

a. The graphic organizer contrasts Republican Ideals and the ______.

b. Two kinds of economies shown in the graphic organizer are ______ ______.

2. Study the map and legend on page 167 of your text. Then fill in the blanks below.

The purple parts of the map show the ______.
The pink parts show the ______.
The orange parts show the ______.
The Florida Territory is one of the ______.
New York is one of the ______.
Tennessee is one of the ______.

Reading Support Resources — Lesson Preview • **Chapter 6, Lesson 1** 75

- **Chapter Overview*** p. 74
- **Lesson Previews*** using graphic organizers from the Teacher's Edition pp. 75, 79, 83
- **Reading Strategies*** pp. 76, 80, 84
- **Lesson Summaries*** pp. 77–78, 81–82, 85–86
- **Lesson Reviews** pp. 18, 19, 20

* **Workbook** includes starred items.

Multi-language Summaries

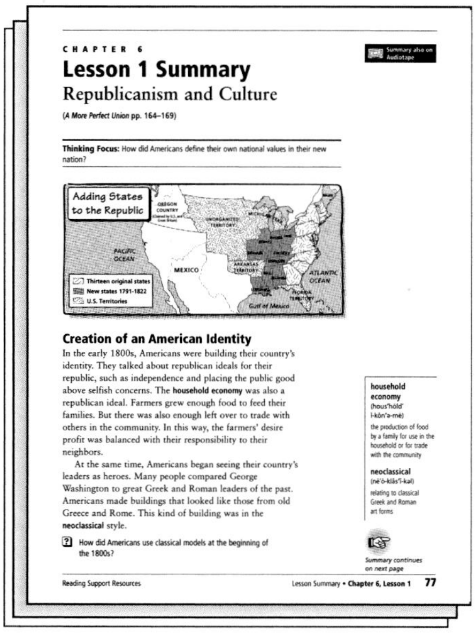
CHAPTER 6

Lesson 1 Summary

Republicanism and Culture

(*A More Perfect Union* pp. 164–169)

Summary also on Audiotape

Thinking Focus: How did Americans define their own national values in their new nation?

Creation of an American Identity

In the early 1800s, Americans were building their country's identity. They talked about republican ideals for their republic, such as independence and placing the public good above selfish concerns. The **household economy** was also a republican ideal. Farmers grew enough food to feed their families. But there was also enough left over to trade with others in the community. In this way, the farmers' desire profit was balanced with their responsibility to their neighbors.

At the same time, Americans began seeing their country's leaders as heroes. Many people compared George Washington to great Greek and Roman leaders of the past. Americans made buildings that looked like those from old Greece and Rome. This kind of building was in the **neoclassical** style.

? How did Americans use classical models at the beginning of the 1800s?

household economy (hous'hōld' ĭ-kŏn'ə-mē) the production of food by a family for use in the household or for trade with the community

neoclassical (nē'ō-klăs'ĭ-kəl) relating to classical Greek and Roman art forms

Summary continues on next page

Reading Support Resources — Lesson Summary • **Chapter 6, Lesson 1** 77

Lesson Summaries in:

- English (See Reading and Review.)
- Spanish pp. 77–78, 81–82, 85–86
- Chinese pp. 35–40
- Hmong pp. 35–40
- Khmer pp. 35–40
- Vietnamese pp. 35–40

Summaries available on audiotapes

Lesson Support / Transition

S D A I E

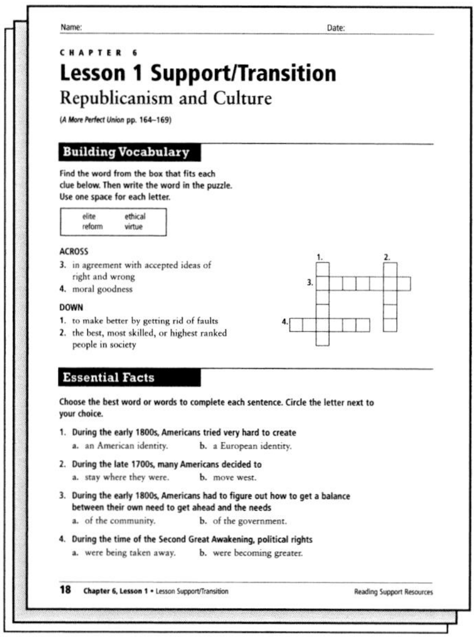
Name: Date:

CHAPTER 6

Lesson 1 Support/Transition

Republicanism and Culture

(*A More Perfect Union* pp. 164–169)

Building Vocabulary

Find the word from the box that fits each clue below. Then write the word in the puzzle. Use one space for each letter.

elite, ethical, reform, virtue

ACROSS
3. in agreement with accepted ideas of right and wrong
4. moral goodness

DOWN
1. to make better by getting rid of faults
2. the best, most skilled, or highest ranked people in society

Essential Facts

Choose the best word or words to complete each sentence. Circle the letter next to your choice.

1. During the early 1800s, Americans tried very hard to create
   a. an American identity. b. a European identity.
2. During the late 1700s, many Americans decided to
   a. stay where they were. b. move west.
3. During the early 1800s, Americans had to figure out how to get a balance between their own need to get ahead and the needs
   a. of the community. b. of the government.
4. During the time of the Second Great Awakening, political rights
   a. were being taken away. b. were becoming greater.

18 **Chapter 6, Lesson 1** • Lesson Support/Transition — Reading Support Resources

Activities for SDAIE
Specially **D**esigned **A**cademic **I**nstruction in **E**nglish

- **Lesson Support/Transition** pp. 18, 19, 20

Technology Options

Internet Support

http://www.eduplace.com

Social Studies Center at Education Place

Internet support for Chapter 6:

- ***Lesson at a Glance***
- ***Cities—Old and New***

Software

Student Writing Center® (CD-ROM) (Macintosh® or Windows®)

School to Career

Not long ago, factory-made goods were unheard of. People made their own goods or traded for something they needed. Ask students to think of types of products that are still made on a small scale, perhaps by hand. How are these businesses different from large-scale, mass-market industries?

Character Education

During the Second Great Awakening, individuals were encouraged to volunteer their time and resources to the cause. Volunteerism is still important today. Have students select a non-profit organization and report on the role volunteers play in it. They may even wish to become involved with the organization they choose to research.

CHAPTER
PREVIEW

Have students read the chapter title and the narrative under it. What does the word *mature* mean? *(To develop fully; to become older and wiser)* Discuss the decisions that maturing people make about themselves.

Compare and contrast the University of Virginia photograph and the folk art on this page. How does the art reflect the choices that faced the nation? *(The University of Virginia building looks very formal and serious; the folk art seems more relaxed and fun. The nation had to establish its national image: formal or free-spirited?)*

Looking Back

In Chapter 5 students learned how the United States established itself abroad through the War of 1812 and the Monroe Doctrine. This chapter focuses on how Americans established themselves at home.

Looking Forward

Tell students that they will learn about the United States' national identity in the next three lessons: Republicanism and Culture, The First Western President, and How Others Saw Us.

Chapter 6
The Maturing Republic

"Who is this new person, the American?" foreigners asked. The young nation asked itself this same question. Who are we? What are our ideals? Everyone had a different opinion. Classical ideas from ancient civilizations competed with the rugged individualism of the frontier. Which cultural traditions would people keep? Which traditions would they throw aside in favor of new American values?

Creating schools was important to the Americans. Thomas Jefferson's architectural design for the University of Virginia reflected his love of classical ideas and values.

1775 — 1800

Presidents
1789-1797 Washington
1797-1801 J. Adams
1801-1809 Jefferson
180[illegible] Ma[illegible]

1782

BACKGROUND

A national culture that valued the welfare of the community and the agricultural way of life developed after the Revolutionary War. As the new nation expanded, this culture changed to one that stressed individualism and a market economy. Expanding suffrage led to Jacksonian democracy.

From Household to Market Economy

Nearly 90 percent of Americans were involved in agriculture at the beginning of the 1800s. Farmers raised food for their families and traded the surplus for the few items that they could not produce, such as tea, sugar, and glass. Many farmers supplemented their income by producing goods such as shoes and clothing or operating sawmills and forges. Self-reliance was seen as a virtue; as one European traveler notes: "The great effort was for every farmer to produce anything he required within his own family; and he was esteemed the best farmer, to use a phrase of the day, 'who did everything within himself.'"

This household economy changed as transportation by roads and canals made it easier to trade beyond local communities. Merchants opened factories, which would eventually replace artisans. Francis Cabot Lowell established the first American textile factory that converted raw cotton into cloth in 1813. The new market economy would change the United States from an agrarian to an industrial nation.

American women gathered at quilting bees. Quilts like these embodied the patriotic spirit in a traditional craft.

New forms of music helped to define the American identity. This banjo, a uniquely American instrument that had its roots in Africa, was among the possessions of President Andrew Jackson's family.

1825

1817-1825 Monroe

1825-1829 J. Q. Adams

1829-1837 Jackson

1837-1841 Van Buren

1840

Understanding the Visuals

Draw students' attention to *The Quilting Party* by an unknown American artist. The original piece is oil and pencil on paper adhered to plywood.

Quilting bees such as the one depicted here were much more than a women's sewing get-togther. What else is happening here? *(Young people are meeting; a grandfather is playing with a baby; men are drinking in a corner.)* At quilting bees, gossip, music, dancing and other diversions all speeded the sewing chore and made for an enjoyable event. The result of their labors is a beautiful quilt such as the colorful cotton appliquéd one shown here.

Understanding Chronology

Have students look at the chapter timeline. Remind them that many of the cultural developments discussed in this chapter happened at the same time as many of the political events discussed in Chapter 5.

John C. Calhoun

John C. Calhoun began his political career in the South Carolina legislature in 1808. Just three years later, he was elected to the House of Representatives, where he served for six years. He distinguished himself there as a leader of the group of men known as War Hawks—supporters of the War of 1812.

In the controversial election of 1824, Calhoun ran as vice presidential candidate for both Jackson and Adams. He won by a landslide. Jackson supported him again as Vice President in the election of 1828, but soon after the election they began to disagree. Calhoun's loyalty to South Carolina and the South conflicted with Jackson's nationalism. By 1831, Jackson took opportunities to appoint Cabinet members who disagreed with Calhoun.

Calhoun's position on states' rights made it impossible for him to continue as Vice President. His resignation ensured that he would never become President, a fact that he bitterly resented. Calhoun went on to serve South Carolina in the Senate, and in 1844 he was appointed secretary of state under President John Tyler. In his later years he advocated slavery in the South and worked for the annexation of Texas.

INTRODUCE

Discuss with students the words in the lesson title. Ask them to recall from Chapter 3 the meaning of *republicanism*. Ask students what they think of when they hear the word *culture. (Some may associate it only with plays, classical music, the ballet.)* Help them to see that culture reflects the values and ideals shared by a population or community. Then have a student read aloud the Thinking Focus. Ask students to look in the lesson to see how American national values were reflected in their culture.

Key Terms

Vocabulary strategies: T36–37

household economy—production of food and other necessary items by a family for use within the household or for exchange within the immediate community

neoclassical—pertaining to the revival of classical art forms

market economy—production of food and other goods and services for cash sale, often in distant markets

suffrage—the right or privilege of voting

1770 1780 1790 1839

LESSON 1

Republicanism and Culture

THINKING FOCUS

How did Americans define their own national values in their new nation?

Key Terms

- household economy
- neoclassical
- market economy
- suffrage

"I am attached to America by berth, education, and habit. . . . I uze words that are most comon and generally understood. . . . I rite from feeling, from obzervation, from experience." So wrote Noah Webster in 1800. This man, who compiled a spelling book and wrote the first American dictionary (shown at right), would certainly have trouble passing a spelling test today. But in 1800, spelling was a matter of individual preference.

Webster, like other Americans in the early republic, wanted to create a truly American version of the English language. He redefined words such as *congress* and *court*—words that had meant something different back in England. Before he started to experiment with his spellings, he wrote, "As an independent nation, our honor requires us to have a system of our own, in language as well as government." Webster wanted to break cultural ties with England. He also saw that a standardized language—in spelling and pronunciation—would help to unify the new nation.

Many of Webster's spelling changes are still in use today. He worked to simplify language so that words were spelled phonetically—that is, the way they are pronounced. For example, he changed the British *centre* to *center, colour* to *color,* and *shoppe* to *shop*. He was less successful with other changes; Americans would not accept *meen* for *mean* or *frend* for *friend*.

Creation of an American Identity

During the early 1800s, Americans deliberately went about establishing a national identity—through art and education as well as through Webster's American language. They talked about ideals for their republic, such as virtue and placing the public good above selfish interests. Americans valued the ideal of independence, the right to make their own decisions. But even after the Revolutionary War, they also accepted men from an elite social group as their political leaders. These leaders were nearly always the wealthiest and best educated members of society. Common people were not likely to run for office.

The household economy was yet another republican ideal. In the **household economy**, small, independent owners of land grew food for their own families and for exchange with others within their community. These farmers usually knew most of

Objectives

1. Identify the republican ideals of early American society.
2. Describe how the ideals of the self-made man and market-oriented individualism developed as the nation expanded westward.
3. Compare the Second Great Awakening with the growing political awareness as responses to changing American values.

Graphic Overview

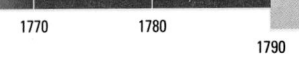

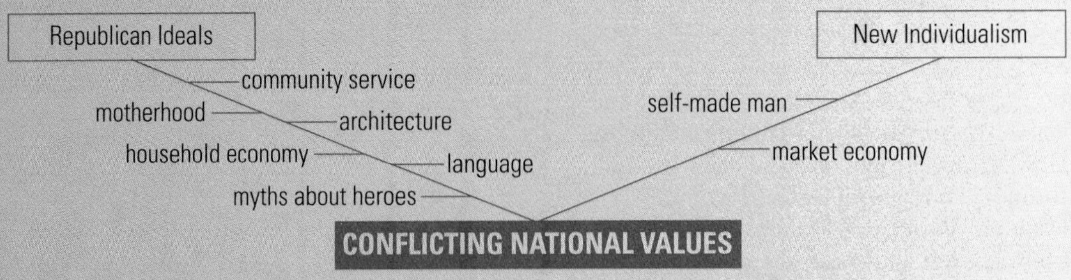

the people with whom they did business. Thus their desire for profit was balanced by a strong sense of responsibility to their neighbors and to their community's needs.

Washington: A Classical Hero

In establishing their own identity and values, well-educated Americans looked to classical models—those of the ancient republics of Greece and Rome. Writers at the time often compared their heroes to classical figures. George Washington was compared to Cincinnatus, the Roman general who returned to his farm after defending his country. Many statues of Washington were made that showed him in a Roman toga, wearing the classical hero's laurel-leaf crown.

In 1800, Mason Weems, a clergyman often referred to as "Parson" Weems, wrote a best-selling biography of Washington. Weems portrayed Washington as the perfect republican citizen. He made up many tall tales for his book, including the story of Washington and the cherry tree. In another tale, which used Washington's real experiences in the Seven Years' War to create a larger-than-life hero, Weems wrote:

> A famous Indian warrior . . . was often heard to swear, that "Washington was not born to be killed by a bullet! For," continued he, "I had seventeen fair fires at him with my rifle, and after all could not bring him to the ground!" And indeed whoever considers that a good rifle, levelled by a proper marksman, hardly ever misses its aim, will readily conclude . . . that there was some invisible hand, which turned aside his bullets.

The real George Washington was, of course, not invulnerable to bullets. He also never said, "I can't tell a lie." But Weems made Washington seem an example of heroic virtue. Adults of the time used such moral tales to teach their children republican ideals.

Washington was held up as a nearly godlike hero. In this work, the artist shows Washington entering heaven after his death.

Republican Architecture

To help express the ideals of their new nation, some Americans adopted classical art and architecture. By adapting elements of the style of ancient Greece and Rome, they tried to forge a link with the ideals of those great republics. Thomas Jefferson was very impressed by the classical style buildings he had seen in Europe. In fact, Jefferson patterned his designs for the University of Virginia and his own home, Monticello, after classical buildings. Throughout the nation, people built town halls and state

DEVELOP

Copy on the board the skeletal structure and main headings of the Graphic Overview from page 164. Have students copy it in their notes and fill in the examples of American values as they read the lesson.

CULTURE

Visual Learning

Refer students to the painting on this page. What symbols in the painting make George Washington seem godlike? *(Angels, heavenly lights)* Point out that this type of imagery was common to the period.

Access Strategy

Ask students if they have ever wanted to be more independent from their parents. What kinds of freedoms have they gained as they have grown older? In what ways do they express their differences from their parents? Lead students to understand that the desire for independence and self-expression is a natural part of growing up, but that it also often often leads to conflict.

Tell students that in this lesson they will read about ways in which the young nation tried to express its differences from its "parent," England. They will also learn about some of the conflicts that developed within the young nation.

Access Activity

To help students grasp the conflict between community and individuality, ask them to bring to class magazine advertisements that appeal to people's personal interests or their need for community. *(Cosmetics, cars, public service, environmental protection)* Discuss with students how advertising can both reflect and affect people's values.

➤ *Emma Hart Willard established the Troy Female Seminary in Troy, New York, in 1821. The school was renamed the Emma Willard School in 1895 and continues to educate young women to this day.*

■ *Jefferson and other Americans used classical models when they designed new buildings; writers compared popular figures to classical figures.*

ECONOMICS

Critical Thinking

Help students distinguish between household and market economy. *(Defined on pages 164 and 166)* What caused the shift to a market economy? *(Better transportation networks increased mobility)* Why would a market economy lead to individualism? *(Less direct connection to customers, success measured in personal wealth rather than in community standing)*

▲ *Emma Hart Willard promoted better education for young women.*

■ *How did Americans use classical models at the beginning of the 1800s?*

capitols in what was called the **neoclassical,** or new classical, style. Majestic columns and bold , simple forms replaced the swirls and curves so popular in Europe in the earlier period of Rococo art. Read Understanding Concepts on page 168 for more about this art style.

Republican Motherhood

What role did women play in the new republic? The Constitution did not allow women to vote or to hold office. Instead, they were encouraged to be virtuous citizens within their own homes. The role of women in the new republic took shape through the ideal of "republican motherhood." Every patriotic woman's aim was to instill in her family the values that would make the republic strong.

"Who knows how great and good a race of men may yet arise from the forming hand of mothers . . .?" So wrote Emma Hart Willard in 1819. She was arguing the case for better women's education—education that would help young women become republican mothers. In the new nation, women were respected for the moral instruction they provided to guide their children into ethical public service. Although some women began to form associations to reform society, republican motherhood also served to limit their opportunities in the world outside the home. ■

The New Individualism

During this period of a strengthening American identity, many people of the new republic began to move farther westward. Pioneers settled Kentucky and Tennessee in the 1790s. At the same time people started exploring the lands of the Old Northwest—the area that would become the states of Ohio, Indiana, Illinois, Michigan, and Wisconsin. Southern settlers moved into the Old Southwest—the area that would soon become the states of Alabama, Mississippi, and Louisiana.

Better transportation networks led to expanding American mobility and helped the nation grow. State governments had built some of the first roads, and under President Jefferson, the U.S. government began to build the National Road. It started in Cumberland, Maryland, and in 1818 reached Wheeling—now in West Virginia—on the Ohio River. An expanding canal system linked lakes and rivers. The newly invented steamboats moved along these waterways, making shipping quicker and cheaper than with hand-powered boats.

These changes brought about a great increase in trade and aided the growth of a **market economy**. That is, people began to send their goods to distant markets to be sold for cash.

Critical Thinking

Have students analyze the quote by Emma Willard on this page. In what way was the role of women meaningful in the furthering of republican ideals? *(Influenced children in the home)* What could women accomplish with more education? *(Could teach their children better)*

Religious Context

In the early 1800s, many Americans were Protestant. The two major denominations were Anglicans and Puritans (or Congregationalists). Other denominations included Presbyterians, Quakers, Moravians, Baptists, Dunkers, Lutherans, and Mennonites. The First Great Awakening caused the Baptists and Presbyterians to gain many members; it also decreased the tension of religious pluralism. George Whitefield pointed out the validity of all denominations: "Father Abraham, whom have you in heaven? Any Episcopalians? And the answer came back, No! Any Presbyterians? No! Any Independents or Methodists? No, no, no! Whom have you there? And the final answer came down from heaven, We don't know the names here. All who are here are Christians." The Second Great Awakening affected most denominations, the Methodists and the Baptists in particular. Black churches also gained many new members.

Adding States to the Republic

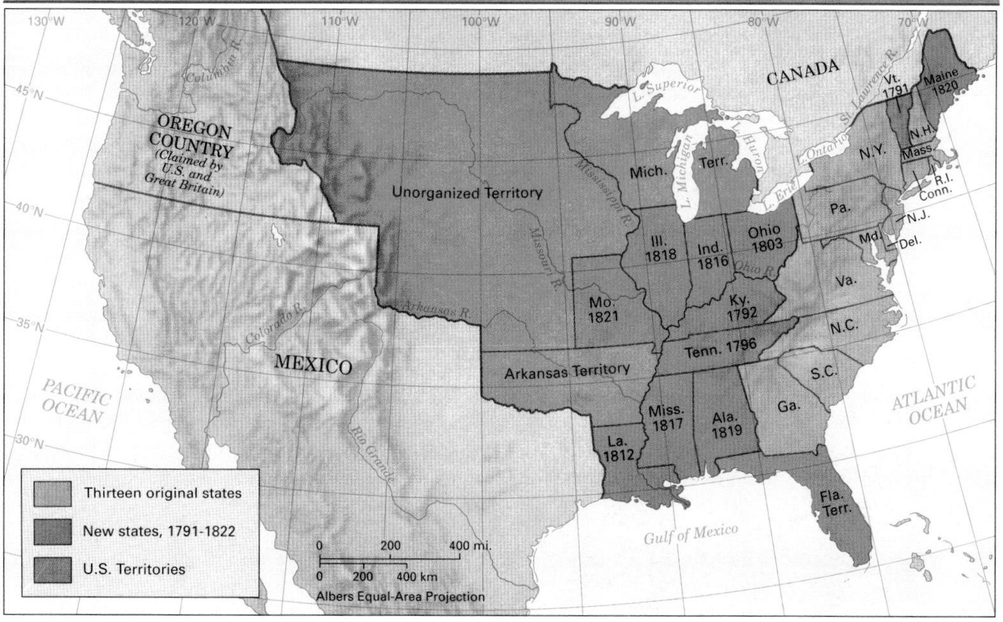

▲ *How many states did the United States add to the original 13 during 1791-1821?*

The market economy was quickly replacing the household economy. People's social ties to their own community grew weaker, since buyers and sellers often no longer exchanged their goods face to face. As a result, individual material success was fast becoming more important than a person's responsibility to the community. ■

■ *Summarize the economic changes that led to the weakening of people's ties to their communities.*

Values in Conflict

One ideal that grew out of the new emphasis on individual success was the "self-made man." This was the man who succeeded through his own efforts. Self-help books, with titles such as *A Good Foundation for Riches and Honor*, became popular across the United States. Both religion and politics were beginning to reflect the conflict between the wish for personal gain and the need to sacrifice for the good of the community.

The Second Great Awakening

This clash of values was at the heart of a religious revival now known as the Second Great Awakening, which followed the Great Awakening by about 70 years. Church membership had gone down during the Revolutionary War. Now clergymen wanted to bring people back into a more active religious life. At huge outdoor revival meetings, preachers excited the crowds by calling on them to renew their dedication to Christianity. This plea appealed to people's growing self-awareness.

The first Great Awakening in the 1700s had added members to several religious denominations, such as Baptists and Presbyterians. During the Second Great Awakening, all denominations, especially Methodists and Baptists, attracted new members. Black churches also increased membership. Denominations such as Methodists, which had grown in white communities since the 1760s, gained members in black communities during this period.

The revival movement found its greatest success in western New York. This area was called the "burnt-over

◄ *Ten states, including Vermont, joined the Union between 1791 and 1821.*

■ *Improvement in transportation and the growth of a market economy served to weaken community ties.*

BELIEF SYSTEMS

Critical Thinking

Ask students to respond to Finney's definition of sin as selfishness and his advice to be "useful in the highest degree possible" found on page 168. Do his ideas reflect the republican ideal or the individualism of the "self-made man"? *(The republican ideal)*

Historical Context

Cincinnatus was an important hero to the new republic because he stood for the citizen-soldier who fought when there was need and then returned to civilian life. The Society of the Cincinnati was founded by former Revolutionary War officers in May 1783. Its emblem showed three Roman senators presenting Cincinnatus with a sword, signifying that military power was under the control of the state. Its motto was *Omnia relinquit servare,* or "He left all to serve the republic."

Language Arts Connection

Have students look up the words *court* and *congress* in an unabridged dictionary, such as the Oxford English Dictionary. Ask them to figure out how each word may have been used in England in the 1700s and how they were redefined by Noah Webster in 1806 in his Compendious Dictionary of the English Language.

Map Skills

Have students fill in an outline map of the United States with the names of the states not shown on the map on this page and the dates of their entry into the Union. Have students use the the U.S. political map in the Atlas on pages 698–699 for the names of these states and an almanac for their dates of entry into the Union.

district" because revivalism spread through it like a fire. The most popular and inspiring of the preachers was Charles Grandison Finney. Throughout the North, thousands gathered to hear him preach "perfectionism." Finney defined sin simply as selfishness. He stressed the emotional nature of religion and told his converts to try to be "useful in the highest degree possible."

The Second Great Awakening also inspired church members to become missionaries. "Penny" societies, whose members gave a penny a week, sought to Christianize the poor and the uneducated. Such groups sent missionaries to western cities, to communities of American Indians, and even to Hawaii and China.

In addition, the revival movement gave young women—and many teenage girls—the chance to take a more active role in society. Some women formed female associations to carry the religious message. The wives of the well-to-do also formed groups to raise money for the revival ministries.

Expansion of Political Rights

The Second Great Awakening affected American society in many ways, such as the growth of voluntary and reform groups. And as Protestants renewed their faith through this

Understanding Neoclassicism

By 1750, Europeans had grown weary of the very ornate style of art known as rococo that had been popular for 50 years. They began examining ancient Roman and Greek sources for their art. Soon a new art movement, called neoclassicism, emerged and swept through Europe. Later it would reach the United States and greatly influence the architecture of many of the nation's public and private buildings. The movement was popular in America from about 1750 to 1830.

The neoclassical style was restrained and dignified, with simple, well-proportioned form and symmetrical parts. Color was either absent or in very light hues. Greek columns—the Doric, Ionic, and Corinthian—were common. Some buildings had a rectangular ground plan; others had a central plan with a dome. The style was popular in the design of large structures, especially public buildings, like capitals and courthouses.

Origins

Neoclassicism was a "new classical" form of art in that it tried to imitate characteristics of classical Greek and Roman art and architecture. Interest in neoclassicism was sparked by archaeological excavations that began in 1738 at Herculaneum and in 1763 at Pompeii. People in these Roman towns were buried alive by the eruption of a volcano, Mount Vesuvius. The excavations revealed well-preserved towns and provided an opportunity to view many aspects of life in ancient Rome.

Examples

Thomas Jefferson designed several outstanding examples of neoclassical architecture. They include the Virginia State Capitol in Richmond, the University of Virginia at Charlottesville, and Jefferson's own home, Monticello, in central Virginia (shown below). Two architects, Charles Bulfinch and Benjamin Latrobe, transformed parts of the Capitol in Washington, D.C. to the new style. Neoclassicism is also seen in the Missouri State Capitol and in President James Polk's mansion in Tennessee.

CULTURE

Critical Thinking

As you have read, neoclassical architecture was used to foster the idea that the new American nation was a continuation of ancient Greek ideals. What sorts of ideas might modern skyscrapers or office buildings represent? *(The power of technology in our lives, the drive to conquer nature, the importance of the companies in the buildings, the smallness of the individual)*

Critical Thinking

How does Monticello reflect the origins of Americans' republican ideals? *(Its classical architecture reflects the way in which Americans saw their origins coming from classical Greece and Rome.)*

Role Playing

Divide the class into pairs to role play the following situation. A merchant in another town tries to convince a farmer to trade with him rather than with local buyers. The merchant is self-reliant, motivated by the profit he sees in a large market; the farmer values his community and feels a responsibility to help out his neighbors. Students should base their arguments on information presented in the lesson.

Writing a Tall Tale

Have students read the Weems anecdote about Washington and the seventeen bullets on page 165. Ask students to think of other people who have been made larger than life through stories. *(Daniel Boone, Davy Crockett, Johnny Appleseed, Betsy Ross)* Have students write a tall tale about a modern political leader, sports great, or rock star.

This painting shows an audience listening to a preacher on a temporary platform at an 1839 religious camp meeting.

movement, Jews and Catholics in the United States gained and held onto new political rights.

Beginning with Virginia, state after state struck down the old practice of supporting churches with tax money. Laws that discriminated against people because of their religion were changed. States that had kept Jews and Catholics from holding public office stopped the practice. A 1790 letter from George Washington (See column 2) to a Jewish congregation in Newport, Rhode Island, reflected the growth of tolerance in the United States.

All over the nation, barriers to **suffrage**, or the right to vote, were removed, at least for white males. For example, some states no longer required voters to own land. The new self-made men began to seek political power. Many were elected to national and local offices.

> The Government of the United States, which gives to bigotry no factions [support], to persecution no assistance, requires only that they who live under its protection should demean themselves [act] as good citizens in giving it on all occasions their effectual support.

Those who clung to the old republican values looked down on these independent men, calling them "coonskin Congressmen" because of their frontier caps made of raccoon skins. But the new breed of politician paid attention to public opinion. The growing number of voters rewarded those who shared their views. ■

Across Time & Space

In 1920, an amendment to the Constitution prohibited the states from denying suffrage to women. Many Northern states had given free blacks the right to vote after the Revolutionary War but took away the right by the mid-1800s. Although a constitutional amendment in 1870 granted all African Americans the right to vote, many were prevented from exercising that right until the mid-1960s.

■ *What national values did the preachers of the Second Great Awakening draw on to revive their ministries?*

REVIEW

1. **FOCUS** How did Americans define their own national values in their new nation?
2. **CONNECT** How well did the change from a household economy to a market economy match Jefferson's vision of an agrarian republic?
3. **BELIEF SYSTEMS** Explain what characteristics the Second Great Awakening and the growth of people's politics have in common.
4. **CRITICAL THINKING** Why was it so important that the United States establish it own identity?
5. **ACTIVITY** Look around your community for examples of neoclassical architecture. You might also do some research on the buildings in your state capital. Compare your list of buildings with those of your classmates.

POLITICAL SYSTEMS

Critical Thinking

In what way did political rights expand? *(Laws that discriminated against people because of their religion were changed. Jews and Catholics could now hold public office. In some states voters no longer had to own land.)* Who did not benefit from this expanded suffrage? *(Women, black Americans, American Indians)*

■ *They encouraged making personal sacrifices for the benefit of others.*

CLOSE

After reading this lesson, have students answer the Thinking Focus. Draw on the board the skeletal structure of the Graphic Overview on page 164 and have them complete it, using the graphic organizers that they made as they read the lesson. As a reteaching of the lesson, have students do the role playing described on page 168.

Answers to Review Questions

1. Americans established a national identity through art, education, and language. They looked to classical models to express their republican ideals such as independence and public service.
2. The change to a market economy was a departure from Jefferson's vision of a peaceful agrarian republic, in which landowning farmers would feel ties to the country.
3. They both appealed to people's growing self-awareness and encouraged active participation.
4. Sample answer: To become completely independent of Great Britain, the United States had to develop its own national character. Allow for personal opinion.
5. Encourage students to look at libraries and government buildings for samples of neoclassical architecture. Their observations should include color, shape, and the relative dimensions of the buildings.

Homework Options

Have students research the role of religious revivals from 1850 to the present. *(For example, the Chautauqua Movement or evangelical preachers such as Dwight L. Moody)*

Study Guide: page 23.

DISCOVERY PROCESS

Students will use the following steps in the discovery process to complete the activity:
Get Ready Have a notebook to organize information about a First Lady.
Find Out Choose a First Lady and look in an encyclopedia for information about her. Try to find things that she wrote.
Move Ahead Report what you found out about your First Lady to the rest of the class.
Explore Some More Use the daily newspaper to find out about the current First Lady.

Materials needed: encyclopedia, biographical dictionary, biographies, historical magazines, newspapers, addresses of presidential museums

CITIZENSHIP

Critical Thinking

Ask students to imagine that they are the wife or husband of the President. What sorts of projects would they plan to take on? Would a man fill the role of supporting the President differently from a woman? If so, how? Could the spouse of a president have a separate full-time, paid career? *(Encourage discussion of the question.)*

EXPLORING

The Role of the First Lady

They are not elected. They have no official job description. Still, these women, the wives of the Presidents, have filled one of the most demanding positions in the United States. By searching in the spotlight and in the shadows, you can find how each defined her role to fit her unique personality.

Martha Washington served as this nation's first First Lady.

Dolley Madison was famous for being a very outgoing and fashionable Washington hostess.

Get Ready

You will be researching the lives of some fascinating American women. To learn about more than just their public lives, however, you will need to look behind the headlines, beyond the publicity photographs, and into primary sources — letters, personal memoirs, and biographies. Keep a notebook handy to organize your information.

Find Out

Your school library or local public library will be the place to begin your research. Choose one First Lady and concentrate on her. Look in a good encyclopedia and read what it has to say about her. If there is a list of additional resources, make a note of them for future use. Did your First Lady ever write anything about herself? Look up those materials, if any are available to you. Check the biography shelves to see if someone else wrote about her life.

Move Ahead

Several of you can report on your First Ladies and then compare them. Did they seem to enjoy their role? Were they shy? Did their husbands consult with them? What were their interests?

Explore Some More

You can use the daily newspaper as a way to keep track of the current First Lady. Write down any direct quotes. What does she seem to be most interested in? Compare her to the First Lady you researched. Are there ways they are similar? How are they different?

Some First Ladies

The first First Lady, Martha Washington, did not have even the example of previous First Ladies to guide her, but

Objectives

1. Identify different ways in which women have filled the role of First Lady. (History 1)
2. Use library resources to research the role of the First Lady. (Study Skills 1)

Activities

Divide students into small groups. Have each group use the resources mentioned above to research a different First Lady and the times in which she lived. Have students imagine a conversation between the First Lady and the President about an issue that she felt was important. Each group will then write a script of that conversation. The groups will then have the opportunity to read the scripts to the rest of the class.

Some First Ladies, like Nancy Reagan and Eleanor Roosevelt, have written extensively about themselves and the things that concerned them. Have students read the personal correspondence, an autobiography, or book by a First Lady and discuss what sort of person her own writings reflect. Have students compare the First Lady's own perceptions about a subject to those found in history books, magazines, or newspaper articles.

she was still an effective partner to the first President. Throughout the Revolutionary War and the first presidency, she used her considerable charm, wit, intellect, and social skills to smooth over political differences between her husband and other early leaders. Although she defined the role of First Lady and carried it out enthusiastically, she treasured her privacy. On leaving office after President Washington's second term she wrote, "The General and I felt like children just released from school. . . ."

For marrying a non-Quaker, Dolley Madison was expelled from the Society of Friends (Quakers) and she made up for the long years of modest living by becoming the most fashionable and elegant hostess in Washington, establishing a tradition that continues today. She occasionally filled in as official hostess for the widowed Thomas Jefferson as well.

Perhaps the most remarkable of all the First Ladies, Eleanor Roosevelt devoted herself to a wide variety of social causes on behalf of minorities and the poor, becoming a public leader in her own right. During her husband's presidency, she became so active in the country's affairs that one political opponent complained that the people were getting two Presidents instead of one. Following her husband's death in office, the new President (Truman) appointed Mrs. Roosevelt U.S. delegate to the United Nations, where she chaired the Commission on Human Rights, and was called by some, "First Lady of the World."

After Ellen Wilson died in 1914, President Woodrow Wilson met and married Edith Bolling Galt. When he became too ill to perform the duties of the presidency, she and a presidential aide took over many of them, without constitutional authority. The episode was called by her critics, "Mrs. Wilson's First Regency" and she herself was referred to as "acting First Man."

Barbara Bush, an active woman whose many interests include literacy, cancer research, and education, is an example of a contemporary First Lady. Her personal interest in literacy led her to write a book to help promote her efforts. The 1953 death of her four-year-old daughter from cancer led to her involvement in medical activities. Known for her warm, easy-going manner and clever sense of humor, Barbara Bush has faced the challenge of her role as our nation's First Lady with an energy and grace all her own.

▲ *Edith Wilson angered people when she took over presidential duties while her husband was ill.*

◄ *Public service has characterized the careers of Eleanor Roosevelt (above) and Barbara Bush.*

CULTURE

Critical Thinking

How has the role of the First Lady changed since the advent of television? *(The First Lady has become much more of a public figure.)* What images are First Ladies now called upon to project? *(A strong family leader, a spokesperson for various groups such as women and minorities, an advocate of health and education of children and the elderly)*

Collaborative Strategy

A recommended strategy for this lesson is the jigsaw approach. For more details about collaborative learning strategies, see pages T34–35.

INTRODUCE

Discuss what the word *western* means in the context of the title. *(Not the stereotypical "Wild West," but merely west of the original colonies)* Have students read the Thinking Focus. Ask them to recall what they learned about Andrew Jackson in Lesson 3 of Chapter 5. *(He was a war hero.)* Tell students to read this lesson to find out more about this fascinating president.

Key Terms

Vocabulary strategies: T36–37

tariff—a duty imposed by a government on imported or exported goods

popular vote—the total number of votes by the people within each state

caucus—a closed meeting of political leaders to select candidates for office

spoils system—the rewarding of the supporters of a winning candidate with appointment to public office after the election

states' rights—a political position favoring limitation of federal power and autonomy of states, according to strict interpretation of the Constitution

nullify—to refuse to recognize or enforce a law (a federal law within a state)

LESSON 2

The First Western President

THINKING FOCUS

How did Andrew Jackson's presidency reflect the politics of his time?

Key Terms

- tariff
- popular vote
- caucus
- spoils system
- states' rights
- nullify

Throngs of well-wishers lined the streets of Washington, D.C., on Inauguration Day March 4, 1829—many of them dressed in rough, frontier clothing. With his white mane of hair blowing in the wind, the tall, lean Andrew Jackson—61 years old—took the oath of office as President. After reading his inaugural address, Jackson bowed to the roaring crowd and rode to the White House for a public reception.

Hordes of people swarmed into the White House. Ice cream, cake, and lemonade awaited the guests. In the scramble to get to the food, the crowd overturned tables, broke china, and stained satin-covered furniture with their muddy boots. Jackson had to escape the crush of people through a back door. Fistfights broke out and noses were bloodied. The White House was cleared only after servants placed tubs of punch on the lawn, and some of the men jumped out of windows to get at it.

Washington had never seen anything like this party. "It was a proud day for the people," reported a Kentucky newspaper. "General Jackson is their own President." Many others, however, were horrified. For Supreme Court Justice Joseph Story, "the reign of King Mob seemed triumphant."

➤ *In another mob gathering at the White House in 1837, visitors carved up the 1600-pound cheese sent to Andrew Jackson by some admirers. None of the cheese was left for the President.*

Objectives

1. Explain how 1800s politics reflected popular notions of individualism and expansion.
2. Describe how Jackson used his power as President to make widespread changes.
3. Summarize the opposing points of view in the issue of protective tariffs: strong federal union *v.* states' rights.

Graphic Overview

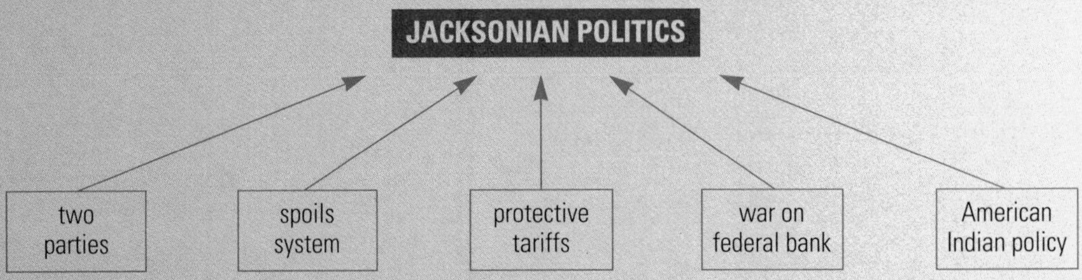

The Rise of Jacksonian Politics

Andrew Jackson's election in 1828—after his second presidential campaign—was the triumph of the self-made man. Born into a poor family in South Carolina, Jackson became wealthy through a successful law practice and the shrewd buying and selling of land. He had fought in the Revolutionary War at the age of 13, and he would always carry the scars from a British sword. Active in Tennessee politics, Jackson served briefly as its first congressman when Tennessee became a state in 1796. He won national fame in 1815 as a heroic

general at the Battle of New Orleans. Because of his toughness, his admiring soldiers called him "Old Hickory."

At the Hermitage, his luxurious mansion outside Nashville, Tennessee, Jackson kept many slaves. Yet he became the symbol of the common man in national politics. As a war hero and a Westerner from the land west of the original colonies, Jackson represented the new American ideal.

The 1824 Election

Jackson had first run unsuccessfully for the presidency in 1824. The presidential campaign that year was a free-for-all that attracted several other ambitious men: Secretary of State John Quincy Adams of Massachusetts, Speaker of the House Henry Clay of Kentucky, and Secretary of the Treasury William Crawford of Georgia. When the votes of the presidential

electors were counted, Jackson had more electoral votes than anyone else. But he did not have a majority. Again, as in the election of 1800, the House of Representatives would have to decide the election.

Through the influence of Henry Clay, the House elected Adams. When Adams then picked Clay to be his secretary of state, the Jackson supporters cried, "Corrupt bargain!" The Tennessee state legislature quickly made Jackson a candidate for the next election.

In the meantime, Adams was the President for the next four years. Adams stood for the old republican values. As John Adams's son he represented the ruling elite, the wealthy, and the well educated at a time when political values were changing. He was known as a harsh, stubborn person. As President, Adams wanted a high tax on imported goods, called a **tariff,** to raise money for important improvements such as roads and canals. He wanted to establish a national university.

◄ *After the election of 1824 Andrew Jackson* (portrait on left) *considered John Quincy Adams* (portrait on right) *to be his personal enemy as well as his political rival.*

DEVELOP

Point out to students that this lesson describes different aspects of one important period of history. As students read the lesson, have them list the main features of Jackson's presidency.

POLITICAL SYSTEMS

Critical Thinking

How did the 1824 election necessarily set the stage for Jackson's 1828 landslide victory? *(The 1824 "theft" of the presidency inspired Jackson's supporters to campaign in 1828.)* How did the popular ideas of individualism and expansion help Jackson in 1828? *(Jackson—a Westerner, a war hero, a self-made man—represented these ideas.)*

Access Strategy

Review Lesson 1 briefly with students. What barriers to suffrage were lifted? *(Voters no longer had to own land.)* Ask students which candidate the new voters in the early 1800s would most likely choose—an aristocratic, college-educated man who behaved formally or someone who became wealthy through hard work and who acted like a frontiersman. *(The self-made man)* How would the candidates campaign to appeal to the new voters? *(With loud and rowdy rallies)*

Explain that in this lesson students will read about the presidential elections of two very different men. They will learn how Jackson represented the ideals of the time.

Access Activity

Read aloud the lesson opener on page 172. Have students look at the picture and caption also on that page and name the ways in which this scene reflected the popularity of Jackson. *(Huge crowd, frontier clothing, "enthusiasm" at the reception)* Why did some people, like Joseph Story, disapprove? *(People seen as out of control)*

He also wanted the government to give money for scientific studies. Despite these new ideas, Adams was not a strong leader because he received no popular support from the people.

The 1828 Campaign

In 1828, Adams faced Jackson again. Jackson's followers staged barbecues, picnics, and torchlight parades to bring new voters to the polls. Campaign songs put down Adams and praised "our Jackson." Sung to the tune of "Auld Lang Syne," the "Jackson Toast" began:

> Though Adams now misrules the land,
> And strives t'oppress the free,
> He soon must yield his high command
> Unto "Old Hickory."
>
> *Chorus:*
> Then toast our Jackson, good and great,
> The man whom we admire,
> He soon will mount the chair of state,
> Which patriots desire.
>
> And though Corruption's baleful voice
> Did formerly prevail—
> Once more he'll be the people's choice,
> Though demagogues assail.
>
> Now Johnny Q. and Henry Clay,
> With all the people's foes,
> Are giving as they pass away,
> Their last convulsive throes.

Still angry about the 1824 "theft" of the presidency, Jackson supporters attacked Adams's reputation. Pro-Adams newspapers countered with false stories about Jackson's wife Rachel and about his mother. Adams supporters also handed out the so-called Coffin Handbill, which pictured the coffins of six men allegedly murdered by Jackson.

As a candidate, Jackson took stands favoring the common people over the rich and powerful. He did not like large banks and large factories. He believed such businesses would strengthen the national government and take power from the people. Settlers out west liked Jackson for his support of westward expansion. He swept to victory with 56 percent of the **popular vote**—the total number of votes by the people in all the states. He also won a large majority of the electoral votes.

Adams found it hard to accept his defeat. "It seemed," he said, "as if I was deserted by all Mankind."

The Second American Party System

Two new parties arose out of the bitter campaign of 1828. The Republican Party of Jefferson and Madison split. Jackson's followers became known as Democratic-Republicans, or Democrats. Those who opposed him formed the National-Republican Party, later called the Whig Party. The Whigs included business leaders

➤ Note in the first bar of the graph that the Republican Party had not yet split into two parties in 1824. Notice the increase in the number of people who voted in the 1828 national election.

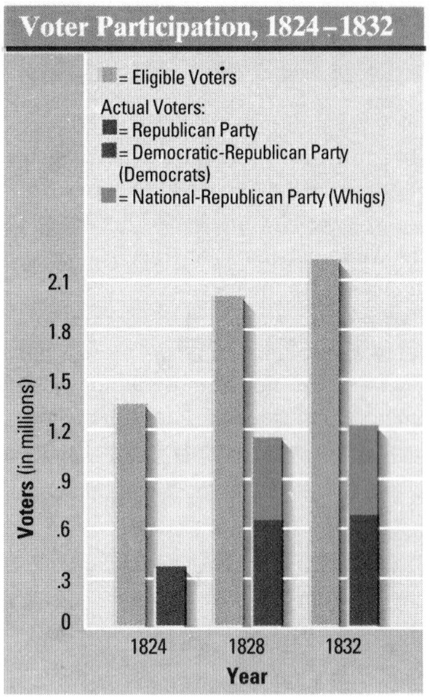

HISTORY

Visual Learning

Have students look at the bar graph and read the caption on this page. Does the increase in the number of eligible voters from 1824 to 1828 account entirely for the increase in the number of people who actually voted in the national election? *(No, a higher percentage of eligible voters actually voted.)*

Study Skills

Have students use an almanac to compile the results of a recent election and to construct a bar graph of some aspects of it: voter turnout; percentage of voter participation; popular versus electoral vote; a comparison of the votes in your state with nationwide votes on key issues or for national candidates.

Geographic Context

During the first 50 years of its independence, the United States had grown to be three times its original size and had more than doubled the original number of states. The thirteen colonies had been inhabited since the mid-1600s, but the land to the west of the Appalachians was unknown to most people.

Settlers of the western lands faced many of the same hardships and dangers as the colonists of the 1600s—for example, an uncertain food supply; scattered, isolated farms and towns; the threat of Indian attack; and poor communication with the rest of the country.

Jackson's Landslide Victory, 1828

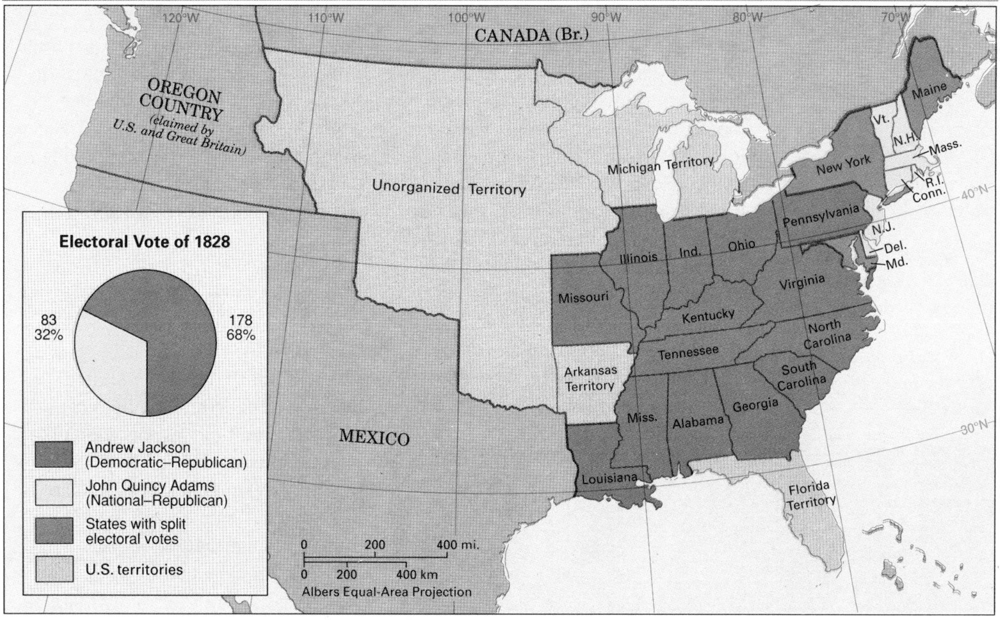

from the North as well as the South, and many Protestant religious reformers. Among the Whig leaders were Henry Clay and Massachusetts senator Daniel Webster. After losing his reelection campaign for the presidency, John Quincy Adams—himself a Whig—won election to the House of Representatives and served there for 17 years. Adams was the only President to have served as an elected official after his presidential term.

Political procedures in national elections became more democratic in Jackson's time. The public was no longer willing to leave the nomination in the hands of the **caucus.** This group of Congressional leaders had met in secret to pick the presidential candidates. By the 1832 election, both parties would hold national nominating conventions that ensured greater participation, at least by the delegates from state party committees. ■

▲ *From what regions of the United States did Andrew Jackson draw his support in the election of 1828?*

■ *Find evidence to support this statement: The American people were ready for Jacksonian politics.*

A Strong Presidency

After his overwhelming victory in 1828, Jackson entered office determined to take charge of the national government. He believed he had the people's support to put in place all of his own programs.

Political Supporters Rewarded

"To the victors belong the spoils" claimed a friend of Jackson after the election. The **spoils system** gave public jobs to the members of the party in power. The name that Jackson gave to his replacement of government officials was "rotation in office." He defended it, claiming that it simply allowed more people to serve their country. Government jobs were "so plain and simple," said Jackson. "No one man has any more . . . right to official station than another."

Jackson rewarded some of his friends with Cabinet posts. But the President's Tennessee "buddies" were his most important advisers. These men, who met informally with Jackson in the White House, were known as "the kitchen cabinet."

GEOGRAPHY

Map and Globe Skills

Point out that although the popular vote was in favor of Jackson by a margin of only 56 percent to 44 percent, the electoral vote was in favor of Jackson by a margin of 68 percent to 32 percent. Ask students to find which states on the map split their electoral vote. *(Maine, New York, Maryland)*

◄ *The Western and Southern states—the agrarian regions.*

■ *People showed their dissatisfaction with Adams and their overwhelming support of Jackson in the 1828 campaign, election, and inauguration.*

Social Context

Jackson had a strong temper. He challenged many opponents to duels, sometimes simply because a friend was making fun of him. Many of his duels were fought over his wife, Rachel. When she married Jackson, her divorce from her first husband was not final, though she thought it was. News of the scandal spread quickly. As soon as the divorce was final, Jackson married Rachel a second time. To protect both his wife's honor and his political future, Jackson fought dozens of duels. He was injured seriously twice; in 1806 he killed a man. Attacks on Rachel's reputation increased in the 1828 campaign. The prospect of going to Washington as First Lady brought her to the edge of a nervous breakdown. She died at 61 of a heart attack before Jackson took office; he blamed his political opponents for her death.

Social Participation

Have students discuss how they think people today would react to an election in which the House of Representatives picked a candidate who did not get the most electoral votes, as they did in 1824. Would people have demonstrations of protest? Point out that such an occurrence would be legal under the Constitution.

POLITICAL SYSTEMS

Critical Thinking

Have the students list on the board some of the noteworthy features of Jackson's terms in office and the positive and negative consequences of each. *(Opposition to the federal bank: eliminated abuse by large central bank but almost ruined economy; westward expansion: opened the West to exploration but did so at expense of Indians; spoils system: rewarded faithful supporters but created disorganization in government)*

CONSTITUTIONAL HERITAGE

Critical Thinking

Point out that in the *Worcester v. Georgia* case, the Supreme Court ruled that a state law can't violate a federal treaty. How did that decision reflect one of the principles of the U.S. Constitution? *(In the question of federal versus state powers, the federal government is supreme.)* When Jackson decided to ignore the Supreme Court decision, what constitutional principle was he violating? *(The idea that each branch is able to "check" the power of the other branches.)* Have students discuss the significance of Jackson's actions.

Jackson, famed as an Indian fighter, is shown in this print accepting the surrender of a Creek chief, Red Eagle, in 1814 after the Battle of Horseshoe Bend.

Jackson's Indian Policy

President Jackson had strong feelings about Indian policy. To make room for white settlers, he wanted to force American Indians who remained in the area east of the Mississippi River to move farther west. Jackson had built his reputation on his successful battles against the Muscogee (Creek) and the Seminole. He and his selfish supporters turned a deaf ear to all arguments about Indian rights.

Under U.S. treaties, the Cherokee in western Georgia—like other Indian peoples—were treated as an independent nation. A 1791 treaty with the United States had guaranteed the Cherokee their lands in Georgia. When Georgians tried to take over Cherokee land, the Cherokee brought several unsuccessful legal actions against the state of Georgia to the Supreme Court. In the 1832 *Worcester* v. *Georgia* case, Chief Justice John Marshall ruled that state laws that violated federal treaties with Indians were invalid.

Jackson, however, encouraged Georgia to ignore the Court's ruling. "John Marshall has made his decision; now let him enforce it," he said. Only a few years later, the U.S. government brutally forced the Cherokee and other Indians east of the Mississippi from their lands. By ignoring the Supreme Court's ruling, Jackson violated the federal government's system of checks and balances. As a result, the Indians' rights to their homelands were ignored and they faced terrible suffering, which you will read more about in Chapter 7.

War on the Federal Bank

As the common people's champion against the rich, Jackson went to war with the Bank of the United States. The federal bank held deposits of government money, on which it paid no interest. It used the money to pay the government's bills. It also printed paper money and loaned money to other banks.

Jackson called the federal bank the "moneyed monster," and claimed it treated common people unfairly. Nicholas Biddle, the wealthy head of the bank, had long been Jackson's enemy.

In 1832 Henry Clay was planning a presidential race. He had Nicholas Biddle ask Congress to renew the federal bank's charter early. Clay expected Jackson to veto, or reject the charter renewal. Hoping such a show of Jackson's power would result in a good campaign issue, Clay felt he would then win the votes of the

BORN TO COMMAND.
OF VETO MEMORY.
HAD I BEEN CONSULTED.
KING ANDREW THE FIRST.

This political cartoon shows Jackson in an emperor's robe, complete with crown and scepter. The Constitution lies shredded at his feet.

Study Skills

Have students organize the information in the text about the war on the federal bank in an outline or a flow chart. Remind them to include information on the people involved, the dates, the actions taken, and the consequences of the actions.

Music Connection

This lesson contains a political song on page 174 based on "Auld Lang Syne." Have students research political songs used in this century. (For example, "Happy Days are Here Again," used by the Democrats since 1932.) Have students give oral reports and play recordings of the songs.

Health Connection

Jackson carried scars from his participation in the Revolutionary War. He also harbored two bullets from various duels and brawls he engaged in. One of the bullets was successfully removed, but the other was too close to his heart. Have students research and write a report on American medical practices in Jackson's time. Possible topics include available medicines, surgical techniques, and the year that anesthetics, antiseptics, and disinfectants were first used.

In this 1832 cartoon Jackson strikes at the many-headed monster of the Bank of the United States with his veto rod. The face with top hat is bank president Nicholas Biddle, and the monster's other heads represent bank branch directors. Jackson is being helped by Vice President Martin Van Buren (in the middle), *while fictional backwoodsman Major Jack* Downing (on the right), *sneaks up on Biddle.*

federal bank supporters. Jackson did veto the rechartering, but as a campaign issue, the veto worked to Jackson's advantage. He won the election in 1832 by an even larger margin than in 1828.

Thinking the people were supporting his policies, Jackson began to deposit government money in state banks run by his friends. Congress let the federal bank's charter run out in 1836. Clearly, Jackson had won his battle—but with disastrous results for the economy. No longer held in check by the federal bank, the state banks began to give out too many loans, printing a flood of almost worthless paper money. Eventually the economy crashed in what was called the Panic of 1837. It was up to Jackson's successor, Martin Van Buren, to deal with the financial crisis. ■

■ *What specific attitudes serve to identify Jackson as a Western President?*

The Federal Union Put to the Test

At the same time that he was waging war against Biddle and the Bank of the United States, Andrew Jackson also found himself engaged in a struggle with some of his own old supporters. At a Democratic Party dinner in 1830, President Jackson lifted his glass to offer a toast: "Our Union—it must be preserved." All eyes turned to Vice President John Calhoun of South Carolina. "The Union—next to our liberty, the most dear! May we always remember that it can only be preserved by distributing equally the benefits and burdens of the Union," answered Calhoun. This exchange made public their intense disagreement over how much power the federal government should hold over the states.

The Tariff of Abominations

In 1828, during the Adams administration, Congress had passed the highest tariff bill ever. The purpose of taxing imports so highly was to protect American industries from foreign competition.

ECONOMICS

Visual Learning

Guide the students through an analysis of the federal bank cartoon on this page, asking them to point to each element of the cartoon described in the caption. Why would the cartoonist show the federal bank as a monster? *(Federal bank seen as hateful, destructive)*

■ *Jackson's support of western expansion for white settlers and of the removal of the Indians identify him as a Western President.*

Music Connection

Have students perform the political song on page 174. Encourage any students who have musical ability to accompany the song on instruments or to find the sheet music for "Auld Lang Syne" and sing the harmony parts.

Writing a Political Jingle

Have students write a poem or political jingle in support of or in opposition to a real or imaginary candidate. Point out that successful political jingles are catchy and usually have a simple rhyme scheme. Remind students that such a poem need not be particularly fair or kind to a candidate's opponents. Some students may set their poems or jingles to a contemporary tune.

Critical Thinking

Point out that tariffs are used today to protect U.S. industries from foreign competition. Have students name imported goods they or their family use. *(Electronic equipment, cars, clothing)* What would higher tariffs mean to them as consumers? *(Paying higher prices for imported goods)* To domestic industries? *(Imported goods less competitive)*

POLITICAL SYSTEMS

Critical Thinking

Ask students why the tariff issue became a states' rights issue. *(South Carolina acted against the tariff by nullifying it.)* Why do we hear very little about states' rights today? *(People less fearful of powerful central government today)*

■ *Southern states nullified the tariff laws, claiming that they had the right to refuse to enforce federal laws. Jackson supported the rights of the federal government over the rights of the states.*

CLOSE

Have students answer the Thinking Focus. What did Jackson do that favored western expansion? *(Allowed the Cherokee to be removed; encouraged system of pet banks that loaned money freely)* Draw on the board the skeletal structure of the Graphic Overview on page 172 and have students use their lists to complete it together. You may use the Critical Thinking activity on page 176 as a reteaching exercise.

➤ *One commentator described John Calhoun as "the cast iron man who looks as if he had never been born, and never could be extinguished."*

Across Time & Space

Protecting American manufacturing from foreign competition—especially that of Japanese industry—is an important economic issue today. Since the 1970s Congress has debated various measures, such as setting protective tariffs, limiting the number of Japanese cars sold in the United States, and guaranteeing that Japanese markets are open to American products.

■ *How did the nullification crisis test the doctrine of states' rights?*

Factory owners and workers in the North liked the bill because it protected their growing textile and clothing industries. Jackson himself supported it. But the South had few industries and imported manufactured goods. Southerners resented the high prices caused by what they called the "Tariff of Abominations."

As spokesman for the Southern point of view, Calhoun wrote a document called the *South Carolina Exposition* in 1828. In it he claimed that the final source of government power came from the states. This was the first time that anyone had clearly spelled out the doctrine of **states' rights**. From this doctrine came another idea that the states could **nullify,** or refuse to enforce, laws of Congress within their state boundaries.

In January 1830, the Senate debated the issue of states' rights. Robert Y. Haynes from South Carolina defended the idea of nullification. Daniel Webster, the most gifted speaker in the Senate, replied in defense of the federal government in a speech that lasted four hours. He ended with the ringing words, "Liberty and Union, now and for ever, one and inseparable."

Jackson had supported the principle of states' rights with respect to his Indian policy. But on the nullification problem, he chose instead to support the rights of the federal government over the rights of the states.

Defense of the Union

In 1832, Congress lowered tariff rates slightly. South Carolinians were not satisfied, however, and Calhoun resigned the vice presidency to lead the anti-tariff fight. South Carolina called a state convention that ruled for nullification of the tariffs of 1828 and 1832 and prevented the collection of tariffs in the state.

Jackson was outraged. In private, he threatened to hang Calhoun. Publicly, he said that nullification was treason. "The laws of the United States must be executed," Jackson said, and he strengthened the federal forts in South Carolina.

In 1833, under Henry Clay's leadership, Congress worked out a compromise that substantially reduced tariffs over a 10-year period. At the same time, Congress passed the Force Bill, which allowed the President to use the army and navy to enforce the laws. The South Carolina convention repealed its nullification ordinance. But to have the last word, the convention also nullified the Force Bill. The nullification crisis had passed. Jackson had temporarily silenced the Southerners and held the Union intact. ■

REVIEW

1. **FOCUS** How did Andrew Jackson's presidency reflect the politics of his time?
2. **CONNECT** Compare the presidential campaign of 1828 with the election of 1800.
3. **ECONOMICS** Explain how the federal bank's role in the economy became a political issue.
4. **CRITICAL THINKING** How did Jackson's position in the Georgia-Cherokee conflict exemplify his Indian policy?
5. **ACTIVITY** Make a chart to illustrate the argument over states' rights. List in two separate columns the positions of South Carolina and the federal government.

Homework Options

Students can investigate and report on the importance of banks in people's everyday lives—for example, making loans for business growth and buying houses and managing retirement accounts.

Study Guide: page 24.

Answers to Review Questions

1. Jackson's presidency reflected faith in a self-made, self-reliant frontiersman; he was a friend of the common person.
2. Both elections, which included personal attacks against both candidates, highlighted the division of the country into two political parties.
3. Jackson supported state banks because he saw the federal bank as an enemy of the common people in its loan policy and its control of the availability of paper money.
4. Sample answer: Supporting white settlers over American Indians, Jackson encouraged Georgia to ignore the Court's ruling which protected the Cherokee. Allow for personal opinion.
5. The South Carolina position should argue that the states are the ultimate source of power. The federal union position should claim supremacy of federal government in issues of commerce and trade.

1770 1782 1840

LESSON 3

How Others Saw Us

How dare she slander and belittle us Americans!" This is probably how you would have reacted in 1832 if you had seen the new book everyone in the United States was reading. Copies of *Domestic Manners of the Americans* had just arrived in the United States from its London publisher.

The book's author, an Englishwoman named Frances Trollope (*TRAHL uhp*) did not mince words. Of Americans in general, she wrote, "I do not like them. I do not like their principles, I do not like their manners, I do not like their opinions." Who did this Mrs. Trollope think she was anyway?

Trollope had come to the United States in 1827. She opened a store in the bustling frontier town of Cincinnati, hoping that Americans would buy fine clothing from London and Paris. After her shop failed, she returned to England to write books.

Almost all Americans, Trollope declared, showed a "total and universal want of manners, both in males and females." She complained about their bad posture and poor manners:

> The loathsome spitting... the frightful manner of feeding with their knives, till the whole blade seemed to enter into the mouth; and the still more frightful manner of cleaning the teeth afterwards with a pocket knife...

As for American women, she wrote, they "powder themselves immoderately, face, neck, and arms, with pulverized starch; the effect is disagreeable by day-light and not very favorable at any time."

Trollope had been used to the social life of Europe, where age-old traditions and formalities dictated what people could say and how they could act. Trollope had found little to admire about the United States, and most Americans were outraged by the criticisms in her book. They fought back with nasty cartoons and stinging **satires**—witty literary pieces that put down "Dame Trollope" by showing her as old, ugly, and crazy.

THINKING FOCUS

What can we learn about our history from Europeans who visited the young United States?

Key Terms

- satire
- social class

◄ *This illustration in Trollope's book was drawn by Auguste de Hervieu (air VYUH). Here he pictures an American woman who, according to Trollope, wears too much make-up.*

INTRODUCE

Read the lesson title and point out that many accounts of history are given by "outsiders." Have a student read aloud the Thinking Focus. Ask students to predict, using lessons 1 and 2 as a basis, what a European "outsider" might observe about the United States. Have students read to confirm or reject their predictions.

Key Terms

Vocabulary strategies: T36–37

satire—a literary work in which human faults are ridiculed through irony or wit

social class—a level of society characterized by certain cultural and economic traits

Graphic Overview

	Behavior	Social Equality	Beliefs
Trollope	rude manners		
Crèvecoeur	lawless frontier	lack of social classes	respect for laws
Martineau	too talkative	hypocrisy of slavery	worship of opinion
Tocqueville	feverish activity	social mobility	reign of the people

Objectives

1. Summarize how four European visitors described the American citizens they observed.
2. Distinguish between the negative and positive aspects of American democracy observed by the Europeans.
3. Evaluate the contrasting views of Crèvecoeur, Trollope, Martineau, and Tocqueville for fairness.

DEVELOP

Copy on the board the skeletal structure and heads of the Graphic Overview on page 179. Have students copy it in their notes and, as they read, list the Europeans' observations about Americans.

CULTURE

Critical Thinking

Both Trollope and Crèvecoeur had lived and worked in the United States. Ask students to name the different experiences that may have biased their observations. *(Trollope had tried to bring European culture to a rough frontier town; Crèvecoeur had married an American but left during the Revolutionary War.)*

■ *The new American was a law-abiding member of a nearly classless society, but on the frontier he could be selfish and lawless.*

The American Defined

Trollope was only one of many curious foreigners who sailed across the ocean to see the new country. A Frenchman named Michel-Guillaume Jean de Crèvecoeur (*krehv KUR*) had arrived in 1759. (His pen name was J. Hector St. John.) After many travels, Crèvecoeur married an American and settled on a farm in New York. But his support for Great Britain caused him to leave this country during the Revolutionary War. He did not return until 1783, when France appointed him consul in Boston.

Meanwhile, Crèvecoeur had published *Letters from an American Farmer* in London in 1782. He wrote the book as a series of letters from "James," a fictional Pennsylvania farmer, to a fictional English friend. Crèvecoeur's work was popular in Europe because it tried to answer the question that puzzled Europeans of that time: "What, then, is the American—this new man?"

Crèvecoeur found much to admire in American society. Unlike Europe, the United States was not composed "of great lords who possess everything and of a herd of people who have nothing." In Europe, **social class,** the grouping of people according to their status in society, was much more rigidly defined. People were either born into the upper class or the lower class, and they usually remained at that level of society all their lives. Crèvecoeur believed that what united Americans was a respect for laws, because American laws applied equally to rich and to poor.

Crèvecoeur's "James" also saw disturbing situations in the new nation. He described the horrors of slavery and found the frontier a lawless place, where isolation dissolved the bonds of community. He warned against the trend toward selfishness.

To Crèvecoeur, the greatness of the new country was that "individuals of all nations are melted into a new race of men." What emerged was the American—"a new man, who acts upon new principles; he must therefore entertain new ideas and form new opinions." ■

How Do We Know?

HISTORY *While photography was not invented until 1839, artists like Hervieu and Beaumont did provide a visual record of what life was like in the early republic.*

■ *Summarize Crèvecoeur's definition of the new American.*

➤ *The landscape of the United States was mostly rural at the time Crèvecoeur lived here, as shown in this painting of Poestenkill, New York.*

Access Activity

Tell students to observe people—other than school friends or family members—for a few days. Ask them to write statements that summarize what they observe. *(For example, people are often in a hurry.)* Have students share their observations about people's habits, manners, and attitudes. Then discuss with them what biases may have colored their perceptions.

Access Strategy

Tell students the fable of the four blind men and the elephant. One felt the tail and thought elephants were like rope. One felt the leg and said that elephants were like trees. One felt the side and claimed that elephants were like walls. And one felt the trunk and said that elephants were a kind of snake.

Discuss with students how any observer of a situation or event would have a kind of "blindness" or "bias," along with a tendency to overgeneralize. Explain to your students that they will see examples of bias as they read in the lesson about how foreign observers viewed Americans.

Criticism of America

Harriet Martineau (*MAHR tuh noh*), yet another foreign observer, brought a different point of view. Martineau was already a well-known English author when she arrived in New York in 1834. Two years before, Americans had been stung by Trollope's book. This time they wanted to make a good impression. The U.S. newspapers warned their readers not to chew tobacco or praise themselves while Martineau was present.

But the Englishwoman assured her hosts that she had come to "rough it." Since she was almost deaf, Martineau had to ask people to shout into her ear horn. She dealt with Americans cordially, even though she thought that many of them talked too much and were hungry for flattery.

Americans, Martineau observed, were very aware of the opinions of others."Worship of opinion" was the religion of the United States. Though Americans respected individualism, they were really conformists.

It was the practice of slavery that struck Martineau more than anything else. She wrote forcibly about what she saw as a hypocritical, or insincere, attitude toward slaves in the South: "A common question put to me by amiable ladies was, 'Do not you find the slaves generally very happy?' " To this, the outraged Englishwoman would answer, "Would you be happy with their means?"

▲ *Shown above is a drawing of a slave auction. Many auctions were actually much more cruel, with slaves bound hand and foot.*

Martineau wrote, "Much that is dreadful ensues from the negro being subjected to toil and lash." She questioned the foundations of American society in her book *Society in America*:

> *This discrepancy between principles and practice needs no more words. But the institution of slavery exists; and what we have to see is what the morals are of the society which is subject to it. What social virtues are possible in a society of which injustice is the primary characteristic? in a society which is divided into two classes, the servile [slavish] and the imperious [domineering]?*

■ *In what ways was Martineau critical of American society?*

Tocqueville's America

In 1831, the Frenchman Alexis de Tocqueville (*TOHK vihl*) and his friend Gustave de Beaumont (*BOH mahn*) traveled throughout the United States to report on American prisons. Later, with that business done and out of the way, Tocqueville wrote a book about life in the new republic, *Democracy in America: 1835-39*. A historian and lawyer from an aristocratic French family, Tocqueville brought a fresh point of view and proved to be a sharp observer of the American scene. His outsider's view told Americans much about their own national identity. Look at the following Closer Look for more on the European viewpoint on American architecture, work habits, and social values.

■ *She criticized Americans for being talkative. She pointed out that although they respected individualism, they were really conformists. Most of all, she condemned their acceptance of slavery.*

CULTURE

Critical Thinking

Which of the four observers were, in general, favorably impressed with Americans? *(Crèvecoeur, Tocqueville)* Which observers were generally negative in their impressions? *(Trollope, Martineau)*

Historical Context

What were the Europeans to think of the United States? Their own countries had existed for centuries; their strong cultural traditions gave them expectations about what proper behavior was.

The United States, on the other hand, had declared its own independence, won a war of revolution, and, after the War of 1812, established itself as a world power in about 36 years. The United States seemed to be in the process of inventing its own culture.

The "self-made man" must have seemed both exciting and strange to Europeans. Some observers were appalled, but Tocqueville was impressed. He praised Americans' "enlightened regard for themselves" and asserted that "self-interest rightly understood produces no great acts of self-sacrifice, but it suggests daily small acts of self-denial." He points out that "it is the interest of every man to be virtuous."

Visual Learning

Review the illustrations in this chapter: Washington ascending to heaven; Monticello; a revival meeting; Jackson's cheese; Jackson in various political cartoons; American manners; the Hudson Valley; a slave auction; camping in the woods. Ask students to summarize their understanding of the American character, based just on these illustrations.

Note: You may wish to refer students to A Closer Look before they read this lesson.

CULTURE

Visual Learning

Compare the established Old World splendor of Venice with the new, unfinished nature of Cincinnati. How do you think the building of new American cities reflected republican values? *(Scaled-down, simpler)*

A CLOSER LOOK

Cities—Old and New

In 1859, Charles Dickens published a novel called A Tale of Two Cities. *It portrayed London and Paris, two of Europe's grandest cities. Yet another kind of city was growing up across the sea in America, one with a unique look, character, and charm.*

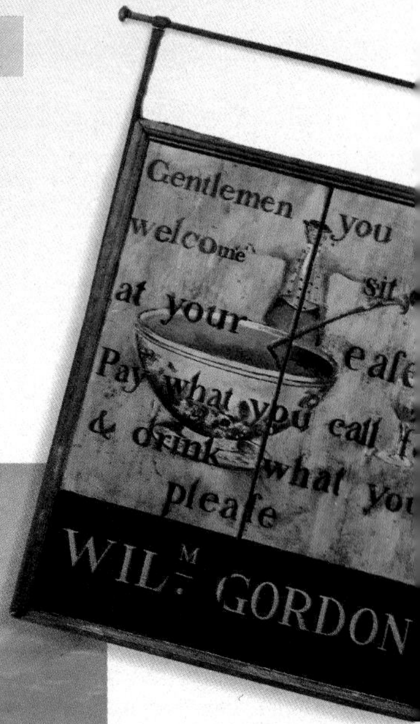

Hang Out Your Shingle! To newcomers from Europe, the United States held out the promise of prosperity. Anyone could "hang out a shingle," that is, start a new business, just like this innkeeper.

Wide open spaces were a feature of many cities on this side of the Atlantic. This painting of Cincinnati shows simple, colonial architecture and low, square buildings. Streets were dirt or cobblestone; sidewalks were made of wooden planks. Practical Americans were busy building a country for themselves. They had no use for the architecture of kings.

Palaces, cathedrals, and towers graced the streets and squares of European cities. Tall columns, sculpted gardens and stately villas were a familiar sight. They were designed to impress passers-by with the majesty of kings and noblemen, the power of the church, or the sheer wealth of a city such as Venice.

Visual Learning

Refer students to the captions on this page. Starting out anew in America meant for many "hanging out a shingle" of their own and leaving behind certain European customs and traditions. How did that affect the way people earned a living? *(Americans were not limited to traditional class-centered occupations.)*

Drawing

Have students work individually or together to draw a composite man and woman of the early 1800s. Students may use images throughout this chapter as a basis for their drawings as well as illustrations from library books about this period.

Reader's Theater

Ask students to give dramatic readings of some excerpts from the works of the European observers, such as Tocqueville's "Author's Introduction" to *Democracy in America* or portions of Trollope's *Domestic Manners of the Americas*. Students may string together several excerpts, using different voices to show comparisons and contrasts among the observers.

Though Tocqueville did write about the horrors of slavery, he was also impressed by the lack of class distinctions he saw in rural white society. "Among the novel objects that attracted my attention," he wrote, "nothing struck me more forcibly than the general equality of condition among the people." This equality, he continued, "gives birth to new sentiments, founds novel customs, and modifies whatever it does not produce."

It was this new American society, in which all social classes "melted into a middle class," that caused Tocqueville to remark, "We are in a different world here." It was a world of constant change. The poor today could be rich tomorrow. And new ways and "feverish activity" prevailed.

As an example, Tocqueville wrote about this conversation :

> *I accost an American sailor and inquire why the ships of his country are built so as to last for only a short time; he answers without hesitation that the art of navigation is every day making such rapid progress that the finest vessel would become almost useless if it lasted beyond a few years.*

Tocqueville saw the quest for perfection, whether in a better ship or in a better system of government, as a typically American trait.

Another result of the democratic climate in the United States, according to Tocqueville, was a new attitude toward women. American women received greater respect and esteem than women in Europe, though Tocqueville admitted that social inferiority of women did still continue in America. He wrote, "Although the women of the United States are confined within the narrow circle of domestic life, . . . I have nowhere seen women occupying a loftier position."

Like Martineau, Tocqueville found that public opinion ruled American thought, determining what the general will was at the moment. In Tocqueville's words, "the people reign in the American political world as the Deity does in the Universe."

That the people reigned, as Tocqueville put it, was reflected in everyday values as well as in the growing influence of Jacksonian politics. The United States, a self-made nation defined by its commitment to democracy, was finally coming of age.

Tocqueville and the other foreign visitors helped Americans to see themselves. Their outsiders' observations still provide historians with insights into American character. ■

Tocqueville's traveling companion Gustave de Beaumont kept a sketchbook of their 1831 trip. In this drawing he sketched their American Indian guide in the forests of Saginaw, now Michigan.

■ *List four features that Tocqueville chose to describe as characteristic of American democracy.*

REVIEW

1. **FOCUS** What can we learn about our history from Europeans who visited the young United States?
2. **CONNECT** According to European observers, how well did Americans in the early 1800s live up to the special ideals which they set for themselves? Explain your answer.
3. **SOCIAL SYSTEMS** What biases did the foreign travelers show in comparing American society to European?
4. **CRITICAL THINKING** How do modern-day Americans exhibit what Tocqueville saw as a "quest for perfection"?
5. **WRITING ACTIVITY** Assume the role of a foreigner in the United States today. Write a description of the society.

HISTORY

Study Skills

Ask students to write a paraphrase of the excerpt from Martineau on page 181. *(Slavery provides evidence of Americans' lack of morals.)* Have them paraphrase the main idea in the excerpt from Tocqueville on this page. *(Americans are constantly improving their technology.)*

■ *Tocqueville describes the lack of class distinctions, the quest for perfection, the respect for women, and the importance of public opinion in American politics.*

CLOSE

After students have read the lesson, have them answer the Thinking Focus and evaluate their predictions. Copy on the board the structure and heads of the Graphic Overview on page 179. Then have them complete it by using the chart they made while reading the lesson. As an extension of the lesson, discuss how Americans' sense of themselves might have been different from the Europeans' observations. Might some Americans have agreed with the criticisms of these Europeans?

Answers to Review Questions

1. Europeans saw the United States as a study in contrasts: the relatively classless society that allowed slavery; the people who believed in individualism yet conformed to public opinion.
2. The condoning of slavery and obsession with public opinion seem at odds with their republican ideals of equality and individualism.
3. They judged American customs by European standards.
4. Sample answer: Because of scientific and technological advances, products are constantly improved and replaced. Allow for personal opinion.
5. Encourage students to reflect the point of view of the country that they represent. Emphasize the importance of supporting their opinions with details.

Homework Options

Ask students to write a paragraph telling why they would or would not have wanted to live in the United States during the early 1800s.

Study Guide: page 25.

UNDERSTANDING POLITICAL CARTOONS

This skill lesson will teach students how to analyze political cartoons.

HISTORY

Visual Learning

The artist who drew the cartoon on this page seems to be pro-Clay and anti-Jackson. Discuss how a pro-Jackson cartoonist would portray the same situation that is described in the text. *(Sample answer: A pro-Jackson cartoonist would show Clay as a cruel person trying to thwart the power of a noble, honest president.)* Should we take cartoons as accurate representations of a situation? *(Not always. They are most useful in showing how some people regarded a situation.)*

UNDERSTANDING POLITICAL CARTOONS

Analyzing Jackson-Clay Cartoons

Here's Why

Reading political cartoons is an amusing way to uncover the politics that accompanied a particular event. Historical accounts of people and events relate when and where a particular situation occurred and usually also present why it occurred. What is often missing in such accounts is the general flavor of the times—the way the people and the press viewed the personalities of their day. Editorial drawings, or political cartoons, can provide that information while also giving a more detailed picture of what actually happened.

Cartoonists use dramatic symbols and characters and often exaggerate the images to make strong statements about events. As you have learned in this chapter, Andrew Jackson was a colorful and controversial president. His striking looks, strong personality, and decisive opinions on the issues of the day made him an easy target for the editorial cartoonists of his time.

PLAIN SEWING DONE HERE
SYMPTOMS OF A LOCKED JAW
"CLAY
"Might stop a hole, to keep the wind away"

Suppose you wanted to find out how events during Jackson's presidency were viewed by the people and the press. One good way to begin would be to examine how he was portrayed in the editorial cartoons of that era.

Here's How

You can use the following three steps to understand a political cartoon:

1. Identify the action in the cartoon.
2. Identify the symbols and possible exaggeration in the cartoon.
3. Interpret the cartoonist's purpose.

Look at the cartoon on this page, which was first published in 1834. The action here is Senator Henry Clay sewing President Jackson's mouth shut. Jackson was a very outspoken person who often did what he wanted without consulting Congress. The cartoonist was exaggerating how difficult it would be to change Jackson's behavior. You would have to wrestle him into a chair and sew his mouth shut.

Objective

Use political cartoons to analyze the Jackson-Clay controversy. (Visual Learning 3)

Bulletin Board

Ask students to make a bulletin board collection of current political cartoons. You may wish to group the cartoons according to the current issue they describe. Encourage students to find as many cartoons as possible to represent different points of view. News magazines sometimes print cartoons from a variety of newspapers to show the pros and cons of an issue.

Race over Uncle Sam's Course.
4th March 1833

By showing Clay as the one doing the sewing, the cartoonist was making a statement about who wanted to silence Jackson. In March 1834 the Senate voted to censure, or officially express disapproval of, President Jackson for taking government money out of the bank without congressional approval. Clay was the person who pushed the Senate to censure Jackson. Censuring a person is one way of reducing that person's power.

In this cartoon Jackson's mouth is a symbol of his power. Clay's use of a needle and thread to sew the mouth shut is a symbol of Clay's use of the Senate vote against Jackson to shut off his power. The cartoonist is saying that Clay was trying to stop Jackson from taking action without consulting Congress.

Notice the quotation from Shakespeare's play *Hamlet*: "Might stop a hole, to keep the wind away." Wind can be very damaging if allowed to blow. Sewing up holes in clothing or stopping up holes in walls is one way of preventing the damage that wind can do. The quotation indicates that the cartoonist thinks Clay's action was good. Clay's attempt to "stop up the hole" (Jackson's power) kept Jackson's "wind" (or damaging actions) away.

Try It

Look at the political cartoon above. It shows Clay and Jackson racing toward the White House. Jackson's horse is shown running into a rock called the Bank U S. while Clay's horse pulls ahead. In the cartoon, Nicholas Biddle, head of the federal bank, is a monkey riding on the back of Jackson's horse, and Jackson is swinging a club labeled "veto."

Now go back to page 176, read "The War on the National Bank," and answer the following questions. Why did the cartoonist label the rock "Bank U S."? Why is Biddle portrayed as a monkey on Jackson's back? What was the cartoonist saying about the election of 1832? Was he right?

Apply It

Newspapers and magazines today are filled with editorial cartoons about colorful figures. Find a cartoon of a current event or national leader. Write a short paragraph identifying the use of symbols and exaggeration and explaining the cartoonist's purpose.

HISTORY

Visual Learning

Have students study the cartoon on page 177. Point out that it portrays a different view of Jackson's struggle with the Bank of the United States. Contrast it with the cartoons on page 184 and this page. How does the cartoon on page 177 depict Jackson? *(Favorably, as a noble figure fighting a monster)* Does the cartoonist think Jackson's opposition to the bank would help or hurt his campaign for president? *(Help)*

Answers to Try It

The rock is labeled "Bank U. S." because it stands for the Bank of the United States, which Clay thought would be a stumbling block to Jackson's re-election. Biddle, the head of the bank, was an opponent of Jackson and sought to defeat him. The cartoonist was predicting that Jackson's veto of the bank's re-charter would defeat him; the cartoonist, however, was wrong.

Answers to Apply It

Make sure that students use the three-step process in analyzing the cartoons which they select. They should identify the action, the symbols, the possible exaggeration, and the cartoonist's purpose and meaning.

Visual Learning

Divide students into four groups. Each group should choose a current issue and create a cartoon showing their view of it. Display their cartoons on the bulletin board. Have the class analyze the cartoons using the three steps in Here's How.

Answers to Reviewing Key Terms

A. Sample answers:
1. Because he admired Greek and Roman architecture, Jefferson built his house in a similar, neoclassical style.
2. Women and blacks have become part of the political process by gaining suffrage.
3. Calhoun wanted the states to be able to nullify federal laws and follow their own rules.
4. Americans who did not like Trollope used satire to make fun of her.
5. Adams wanted a tariff imposed on imported goods to pay for roads and canals.
6. Congressional leaders used to form a caucus to choose the nominees for President.

B. Answers:
1. False. Because women did not have suffrage, they could not vote in the early years of the nation.
2. True.
3. False. In the caucus system, only a few Congressional leaders could decide on the nomination of a presidential candidate.
4. True.
5. True.
6. True.

Answers to Exploring Concepts

A. Sample answers:
Students may include: virtue / promotion of the public good over selfish interests / independence / elite rulers / household economy / morals and ethics.

Chapter Review

Reviewing Key Terms

caucus (p. 175)
household economy (p. 164)
market economy (p. 166)
neoclassical (p. 166)
nullify (p. 178)
popular vote (p. 174)
satire (p. 179)
social class (p. 180)
spoils system (p. 175)
states' rights (p. 178)
suffrage (p. 169)
tariff (p. 173)

A. Use a dictionary to look up the meaning and derivation of each of the following key terms. Then write a complete sentence for each term, using the term correctly.
1. neoclassical
2. suffrage
3. nullify
4. satire
5. tarjff
6. caucus

B. Based on what you have read in the chapter, decide whether each of the following statements is true or false. If a statement is false, rewrite it to make it true.
1. Because women had suffrage, they could not vote in the early years of the nation.
2. The tariff placed on imported goods made them more expensive for American shoppers.
3. In the caucus system, all voters could decide on the nomination of a presidential candidate.
4. The spoils system let a winning candidate reward his supporters.
5. Americans enjoyed reading satire about Mrs. Trollope and felt that it defended their government.
6. Tocqueville felt that because most Americans belonged to the middle class, there were no social class differences in the United States.

Exploring Concepts

A. On a separate sheet of paper, copy the cluster diagram shown below and fill in the empty circles with additional Republican Ideas and Values. Two circles have been already been filled in. You may add as many circles as you would like to your copy of the diagram.

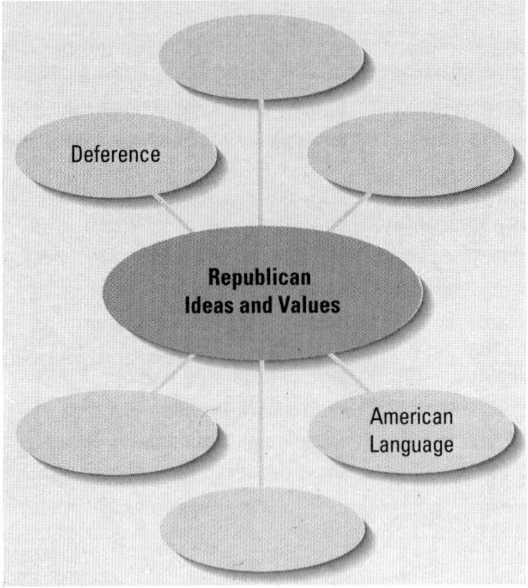

B. Support each of the following statements with facts and details from the chapter. Then write a short paragraph outlining connections among the categories of information presented in the statements below. For example, what did the new spirit of individualism, the Great Awakening, and the election of Andrew Jackson all have in common? How were they different?
1. The new spirit of individualism created values that conflicted with republican ideas.
2. Better means of transportation produced an increase in trade.
3. The Great Awakening increased people's participation in religion.
4. The election of Andrew Jackson as president stood for the triumph of the common man over the elite.
5. As president, Jackson used his power to make sweeping changes.

B. Sample answers:
1. As people began sending their goods to faraway markets, they became more interested in their personal successes than in the good of the community.
2. Roads, canals, and steamboats made it easier to travel, and therefore easier to sell goods far away from where they were made.
3. Church membership increased greatly with the revival movement and the development of independent black churches.
4. Andrew Jackson had risen from poverty to the presidency. He worked against large banks and businesses.
5. Jackson destroyed the federal bank and opened western lands to settlers by illegally forcing American Indians westward.

Paragraph: Students should explore the common spirit of self-help and individualism involved in participating in mass religious revivals, settling new lands, and seeking political power. Jackson believed that he should have the power to do as he wished, even to the extent of breaking laws. He was popular because people identified with his spirit of individualism.

Reviewing Skills

1. Look at the cartoon on page 185. Why is the hat labeled "New Orleans"? Why is the box behind Clay labeled "American System"?
2. Look at the cartoon on page 176. It shows Andrew Jackson dressed as a king. Identify the symbols in the cartoon. What is the action in the cartoon? Define the major points in the cartoon and write a short paragraph explaining how the cartoon relates to an issue in Jackson's presidency.
3. Find a cartoon of a current event or a national personality in a newspaper or magazine. Mount the cartoon on a sheet of paper, and write your interpretation of the cartoon next to it, pointing out the symbols and action.
4. Thomas Nast was a famous political cartoonist. Use your library to find information on Nast. Take notes on the information you find, and create a bibliography card.
5. Suppose you wanted to look at political cartoons from other countries. In what kinds of publications would you look?

Using Critical Thinking

1. "Andrew Jackson was the first president who really represented the common man." Do you agree or disagree with this statement? Does Jackson's background and personality indicate that the spirit of American politics was changing in the 1820s? If so, how?
2. Andrew Jackson felt that the House should have elected him president in 1824, because he had received more electoral votes than any of his opponents. Do you agree? State your reasons. How do you think people would react today if the House of Representatives decided an election in favor of a candidate who did not receive the most electoral votes?
3. Frances Trollope wrote that in the United States, "Any man's son may become the equal of any other man's son." What did she mean by this statement? Based on her observation, how do you think the society of her country differed from that of the United States? Explain your answer.

Preparing for Citizenship

1. **WRITING ACTIVITY** Many people consider George Washington to be the first American hero. Identify someone you consider to be a modern American hero. What characteristics or deeds make a person a hero? Is your hero similar in any way to George Washington? Write a short essay defining *hero*, and explaining the similarities and differences between your choice of a modern hero and George Washington.
2. **WRITING ACTIVITY** The idea of the "self-made man" that became popular in the United States during the early 1800s, is still alive today. Identify current men or women who have achieved individual success in their lives. Choose one who interests you, and look up recent newspaper and magazine articles about the person. Write a short report defining the person's success and identifying how that success was "self-made."
3. **ART ACTIVITY** Cut out magazine images of events and people that you believe are examples of basic American values. Then create a collage or poster that illustrates how those values have or have not changed since the early 1800s.
4. **COLLABORATIVE LEARNING** Divide into groups and choose a school or community law you would like to see changed. Determine what the consequences would be if you "nullified," or refused to obey, that law. Then decide what steps would need to be taken in order to change that law. Compare group decisions.
5. **COLLABORATIVE LEARNING** Divide into four groups representing the car manufacturing and trade situation in the United States: Group 1 will be government representatives, Group 2 will be a consumer interest group, Group 3 will be foreign car dealers, and Group 4 will be American car manufacturers. Each group should come up with a list of arguments to support or oppose a proposed tariff on foreign cars. When the groups have finished, one representative from each group should state the group's position. Then the representatives should work together to reach a compromise.

Answers to Reviewing Skills

1. "New Orleans" refers to the Battle of New Orleans. Clay is seen as a defender of the American system.
2. Jackson wears the robe and crown of a king, which symbolizes the all-powerful monarch. He is standing on the Constitution as if it is unimportant and he will do whatever he chooses, legal or not. In his left hand is a slip of paper which says "veto," to symbolize his veto of the federal bank charter and his overriding of the laws of Congress. He is using the eagle, symbol of America, to prop up his table, suggesting that America is serving him instead of his serving America.
3. This can be used as a bulletin board activity.
4. Refer students to Understanding Bibliography Cards on page 152.
5. Direct students to the library for books on political cartoons.

Answers to Using Critical Thinking

1. Discuss what it means to represent the common man. Does it refer to the President's background or policies, or both?
2. Discuss the way this controversy relates to controversies over the difference between the popular and electoral vote.
3. Discuss the class system in England, and ask students to consider if society in the United States today is classless.

Answers to Preparing for Citizenship

1. **WRITING ACTIVITY** Encourage students to consider people from sports, science, politics, the arts, or their local communities.
2. **WRITING ACTIVITY** Ask students to give their definitions of personal success and to relate their own goals in life to those of the successful person on whom they report.
3. **ART ACTIVITY** Suggest students draw a cluster diagram of modern American values and compare it with the diagram in Exploring Concepts.
4. **COLLABORATIVE LEARNING** Discuss the different ways in which laws can be changed.
5. **COLLABORATIVE LEARNING** Designate a secretary to write down the list and a speaker to explain it. Decide whether the representatives will have the authority to compromise on their own or if they will need to get the approval of their groups before agreeing to anything.

Chapter 7 Planning at a Glance

People of the New Nation

	Objectives	Reading Support and Other Resources	Diverse Learning Strategies
Lesson 1 Life Changes Along the Atlantic Seaboard *pp. 190–195* 2–3 days	• Describe changes in the American economy, including the increasing profitibility of family farms and the importance of port cities. • Analyze the effect of economic and social changes on free blacks.	• **Workbook** or **Reading Support:** pp. 88–91 Review p. 21 Extra Support/Transition p. 21 Multi-lang. Sum. pp. 41–42 • **Other Resources:** Posters 1, 3; Study Guide p. 27; Study Print 4	Access Strat. **(Extra Support)** TE p. 191 Access Act. **(SDAIE)** TE p. 191 Visual Learning **(Visual)** TE p. 191 Math Connection **(Visual)** TE p. 193 Audiotapes of Multi-language Lesson Summaries **(Auditory)**
Lesson 2 The Trans-Appalachian Frontier *pp. 196–200* 1–2 days	• Describe the trans-Appalachian frontier, the routes by which pioneers traveled there, and their reasons for migrating. • Trace the developments of townships, institutions, and services during the settlement of the frontier.	• **Workbook** or **Reading Support:** pp. 92–95 Review p. 22 Extra Support/Transition p. 22 Multi-lang. Sum. pp. 43–44 • **Other Resources:** Geography Kit, Study Guide p. 28	Access Act. **(SDAIE)** TE p. 197 Map and Globe Skills **(Visual)** TE pp. 198, 199 Making a Grid System **(Kinesthetic)** TE p. 199 Audiotapes of Multi-language Lesson Summaries **(Auditory)**
Lesson 3 The Changing World of American Indians *pp. 201–207* 2–3 days	• Describe the westward migration of whites into Indian territories. • Evaluate various Indian response to the white invasion: armed resistance, revitalization, and cultural accommodation. • Trace Cherokee experiences before and after their forced removal.	• **Workbook** or **Reading Support:** pp. 96–99 Review p. 23 Extra Support/Transition p. 23 Multi-lang. Sum. pp. 45–46 • **Other Resources:** Geography Kit, Study Guide p. 29	Access Act. **(SDAIE)** TE p. 202 Study Skills **(GATE)** TE p. 205 Drawing **(Visual)** TE p. 206 Audiotapes of Multi-language Lesson Summaries **(Auditory)**
Skill: Designing a City Map *pp. 208–209*	• Use scale and distance, symbols, and oral directions to design a map.	• **Other Resources:** Geography Kit, Study Guide p. 30	Map and Globe Skills **(Visual)** TE p. 209
Lesson 4 The Next Wave of Immigrants *pp. 210–215* 1–2 days	• Compare and contrast German and Irish immigrants' reasons for immigrating, as well as their experiences in the U.S. during their integration into the U.S. economy. • Define *nativism,* describe its sources in the 1850s, and explain its impact.	• **Workbook** or **Reading Support:** pp. 100–103 Review p. 24 Extra Support/Transition p. 24 Multi-lang. Sum. pp. 47–48 • **Other Resources:** Poster 5, Study Guide p. 31	Access Act. **(SDAIE)** TE p. 211 Music Connection **(Auditory)** TE p. 213 Role Playing **(Auditory)** TE p. 214 Audiotapes of Multi-language Lesson Summaries **(Auditory)**
Chapter Review *pp. 216–217* 1 day		Chapter 7 Test pp. 25–28 *(See facsimiles on TE p. 755.)*	Assessment Multiple-Use Masters pp. 81–88

Reading Support Resources *for Every Lesson*

Reading and Review

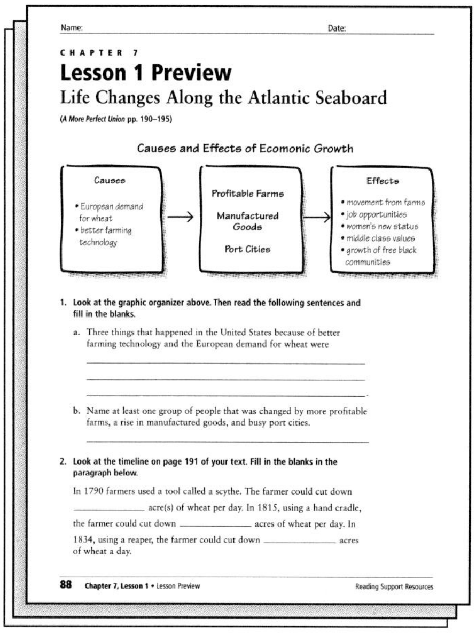
Name: Date:

CHAPTER 7

Lesson 1 Preview

Life Changes Along the Atlantic Seaboard

(*A More Perfect Union* pp. 190–195)

Causes and Effects of Ecomonic Growth

Causes: • European demand for wheat • better farming technology → Profitable Farms; Manufactured Goods; Port Cities → Effects: • movement from farms • job opportunities • women's new status • middle class values • growth of free black communities

1. Look at the graphic organizer above. Then read the following sentences and fill in the blanks.

a. Three things that happened in the United States because of better farming technology and the European demand for wheat were ______ ______ ______.

b. Name at least one group of people that was changed by more profitable farms, a rise in manufactured goods, and busy port cities. ______

2. Look at the timeline on page 191 of your text. Fill in the blanks in the paragraph below.

In 1790 farmers used a tool called a scythe. The farmer could cut down ______ acre(s) of wheat per day. In 1815, using a hand cradle, the farmer could cut down ______ acres of wheat per day. In 1834, using a reaper, the farmer could cut down ______ acres of wheat a day.

88 Chapter 7, Lesson 1 • Lesson Preview — Reading Support Resources

- **Chapter Overview*** p. 87
- **Lesson Previews*** using graphic organizers from the Teacher's Edition pp. 88, 92, 96, 100
- **Reading Strategies*** pp. 89, 93, 97, 101
- **Lesson Summaries*** pp. 90–91, 94–95, 98–99, 102–103
- **Lesson Reviews** pp. 21, 22, 23, 24

* **Workbook** includes starred items.

Multi-language Summaries

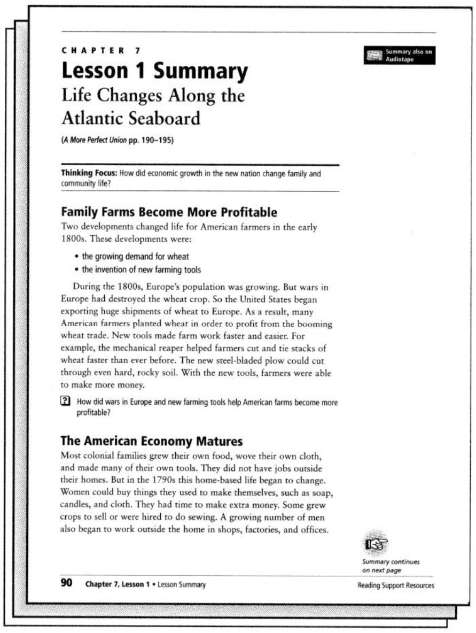
CHAPTER 7

Summary also on Audiotape

Lesson 1 Summary

Life Changes Along the Atlantic Seaboard

(*A More Perfect Union* pp. 190–195)

Thinking Focus: How did economic growth in the new nation change family and community life?

Family Farms Become More Profitable

Two developments changed life for American farmers in the early 1800s. These developments were:

- the growing demand for wheat
- the invention of new farming tools

During the 1800s, Europe's population was growing. But wars in Europe had destroyed the wheat crop. So the United States began exporting huge shipments of wheat to Europe. As a result, many American farmers planted wheat in order to profit from the booming wheat trade. New tools made farm work faster and easier. For example, the mechanical reaper helped farmers cut and tie stacks of wheat faster than ever before. The new steel-bladed plow could cut through even hard, rocky soil. With the new tools, farmers were able to make more money.

? How did wars in Europe and new farming tools help American farms become more profitable?

The American Economy Matures

Most colonial families grew their own food, wove their own cloth, and made many of their own tools. They did not have jobs outside their homes. But in the 1790s this home-based life began to change. Women could buy things they used to make themselves, such as soap, candles, and cloth. They had time to make extra money. Some grew crops to sell or were hired to do sewing. A growing number of men also began to work outside the home in shops, factories, and offices.

Summary continues on next page

90 Chapter 7, Lesson 1 • Lesson Summary — Reading Support Resources

Lesson Summaries in:

- English (See Reading and Review.)
- Spanish pp. 90–91, 94–95, 98–99, 102–103
- Chinese pp. 41–48
- Hmong pp. 41–48
- Khmer pp. 41–48
- Vietnamese pp. 41–48

Summaries available on audiotapes

Lesson Support / Transition

S D A I E

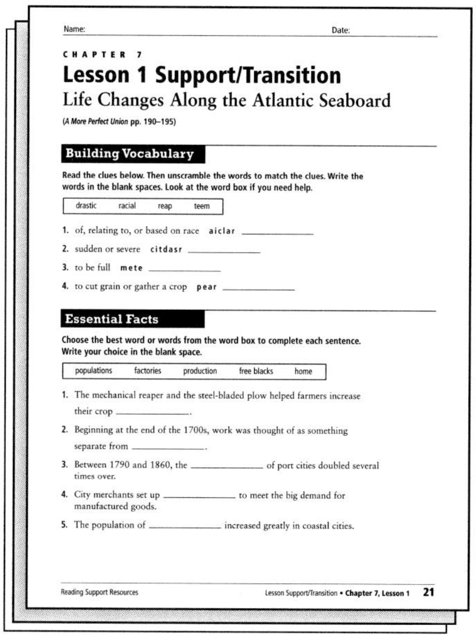
Name: Date:

CHAPTER 7

Lesson 1 Support/Transition

Life Changes Along the Atlantic Seaboard

(*A More Perfect Union* pp. 190–195)

Building Vocabulary

Read the clues below. Then unscramble the words to match the clues. Write the words in the blank spaces. Look at the word box if you need help.

drastic racial reap teem

1. of, relating to, or based on race **aiclar** ______
2. sudden or severe **citdasr** ______
3. to be full **mete** ______
4. to cut grain or gather a crop **pear** ______

Essential Facts

Choose the best word or words from the word box to complete each sentence. Write your choice in the blank space.

populations factories production free blacks home

1. The mechanical reaper and the steel-bladed plow helped farmers increase their crop ______.
2. Beginning at the end of the 1700s, work was thought of as something separate from ______.
3. Between 1790 and 1860, the ______ of port cities doubled several times over.
4. City merchants set up ______ to meet the big demand for manufactured goods.
5. The population of ______ increased greatly in coastal cities.

Reading Support Resources — Lesson Support/Transition • Chapter 7, Lesson 1 21

Activities for SDAIE

Specially **D**esigned **A**cademic **I**nstruction in **E**nglish

- **Lesson Support/Transition** pp. 21, 22, 23, 24

Technology Options

Internet Support

http://www.eduplace.com

Social Studies Center at Education Place

Internet support for Chapter 7:

- ***Lesson at a Glance***
- ***A Cherokee Mother and Son***

Videotape/Videodisc

We the People:

Supports and enhances major topics: **Theme:** ***The Immigrants***

Software

***Student Writing Center*®** (CD-ROM) (Macintosh® or Windows®)

School to Career

Surveyors help establish borders and determine boundaries. If possible, arrange for a surveyor to visit the class to demonstrate surveying techniques and perhaps give students a hands-on opportunity to survey an area.

Character Education

People often fear what they don't understand about a culture other than their own. Have each student write an editorial piece that could be run in a local newspaper dealing with his or her views on how intolerance, misjudgment, and distrust of others affects a community. What suggestions do they have to change this?

CHAPTER
PREVIEW

After students have read the chapter title and the narrative underneath it, emphasize that the study of history involves the study of ordinary people as well as political events. Direct students' attention to the painting *Landscape with Stagecoach* and the Absalom Jones portrait. In this chapter students will learn about the importance of ordinary people in the development of the frontier and the already established cities.

Looking Back

Remind students that the United States had doubled the original number of states in its first fifty years and that much of the country was frontier waiting to be settled. Ask students to predict how the American government will handle the inevitable conflicts with American Indians. *(War, treaties, reservations)*

Looking Forward

Have students read the titles of the lessons and explain what they might mean: Life Changes Along the Atlantic Seaboard, The Trans-Appalachian Frontier, The Changing World of American Indians, and The Next Wave of Immigrants.

Chapter 7
People of the New Nation

The political and economic freedom won in the Revolution released a torrent of creative energy in the new nation. The spirit of independence was reflected in rapid territorial expansion, population growth, and technological advances. Although people who had come from many nations enjoyed the benefit of this growth, the American Indians found that the growth was often at their expense.

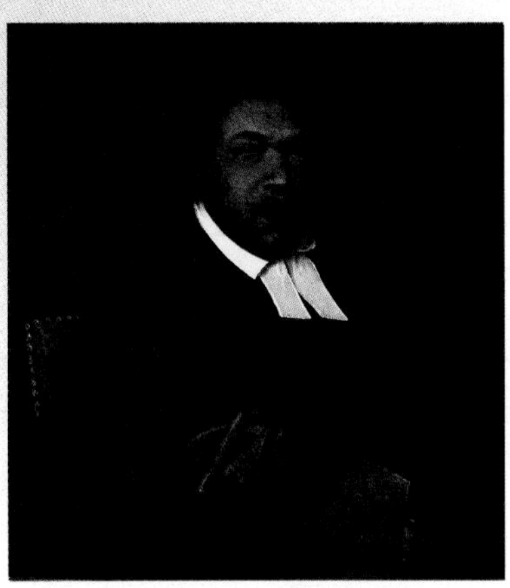

Led by such men as former slave Absalom Jones (here in a painting by Raphael Peale), communities of free blacks formed in cities throughout the United States.

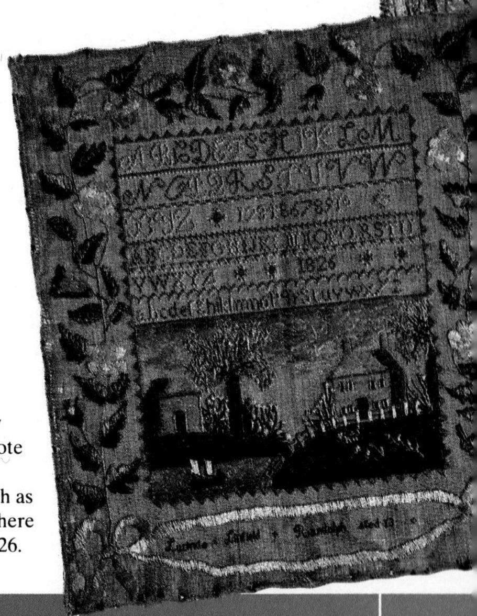

Increased prosperity freed women to devote themselves to more refined activities such as embroidery. Shown here is a sampler from 1826.

1790	1800	1810	1820

Presidents

- 1789-1797 Washington
- 1797-1801 J. Adams
- 1801-1809 Jefferson
- 1809-1817 Madison
- 1817-1825 Monroe

1790

BACKGROUND

The United States changed rapidly after the Revolutionary War. Contributing to economic and social changes were the migration of white and black Americans to the trans-Appalachian frontier, the removal of American Indians from areas east of the Mississippi River, and the immigration of millions of Germans and Irish.

Paternal Authority

Until the end of the 1700s, traditions of inheritance reinforced paternal authority in the family. The father's decision of how to distribute the family's property among his children had an important impact on their futures. Children had to remain obedient to their father's will because they were dependent on him for support and assistance in getting a start in life. He could exercise great control over his children's choice of career, marriage, and place of residence.

The Ohio River

Due to its navigability, the Ohio River served as a great national highway between the East and the West in the United States without the expense of cutting a canal. The increase in grain production in the Old Northwest and the introduction of steamboat travel for river transport after 1811 helped the Northwest Territory to grow into the important economic role of America's granary or "bread basket" in the early 1800s.

Cincinnati, the "Queen City of the West," was the major trading center on the Ohio

1856 From the Atlantic to the Great Plains, the country was dotted with towns and farms and crisscrossed by roads, canals, and railroads. Painter Henry Boese depicted this "Landscape with Stagecoach" in 1856.

1830 1840 1850 1860

825-1829 . Q. Adams
1829-1837 Jackson
1837-1841 Van Buren
1841 W. Harrison
1841-1845 Tyler
1845-1849 Polk
1849-1850 Taylor
1850-1853 Fillmore
1853-1857 Pierce
1857-1861 Buchanan

1860

Understanding the Visuals

The portrait of Absalom Jones was done in 1810 by Raphael Peale, a well-known Philadelphia artist. The portrait was commissioned, possibly by Jones's Philadelphia church, St. Thomas African Episcopal Church.

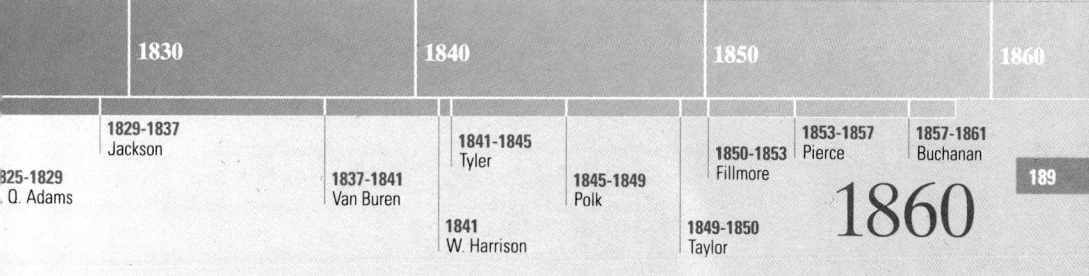

Understanding Chronology

Direct students to the chapter timeline. Remind them that, as they read this chapter, they should make a mental note of the U.S. Presidents listed on the timeline. In this way, they can relate presidential terms to changes in society.

River. In 1819, the agricultural items grown in the fertile Miami Valley outside the city accounted for 90 percent of the trade moving out of the city's ports.

Indian Removal

Not only the Cherokee, but also the Creek, Choctaw, and Chickasaw were forced to relocate from their Southern homelands to Indian Territory west of the Mississippi. Although these Indian peoples tried to negotiate their right to stay, the Seminole of Florida decided to fight for their land. The eight year long Seminole War cost the U. S. Government $20 million and 1,500 lives.

The war lingered on because of the Seminole's strategic advantage in knowing the Florida swamps. By the 1840s, though, the Seminole recognized that they were a tiny group against a large nation with great resources. When the Seminole surrendered, they were arrested and later removed.

INTRODUCE

Ask students what the Atlantic seaboard is. Have a volunteer point it out on a map. Have students read the Thinking Focus and recall, from previous chapters, different areas in which the new nation began to change. *(In government, in national identity, in adding of new territory)* Tell students that they will be reading about changes in the lives of various groups of people.

Key Terms

Vocabulary strategies: T36–37

middle class—members of society who have a better than average education and income and who share common values, especially regarding education

working class—members of society who are employed for hourly wages, usually in manual labor

LESSON 1

Life Changes Along the Atlantic Seaboard

THINKING FOCUS

How did economic growth in the new nation change family and community life?

Key Terms

- middle class
- working class

In the late 1700s, a 77-year-old farmer in Andover, Massachusetts, sat with quill in hand, putting the finishing touches on his will. This farmer was John Abbot. For three generations, members of his family had divided the Abbot farmland among their sons.

"And here let it be further Observed that it is upon mature Deliberation and for Sundry good & weighty Reasons that I have [Bequeathed] & Willed to my Said Eldest Son as above Expressed," wrote John Abbot. By this will, Abbot transferred all of his land together with any buildings to his oldest son, John, Jr.

With the words "mature Deliberation" and "good & weighty Reasons," the elder Abbot apologized for not dividing the family homestead among all his sons. It had long been a tradition to give each son a sizeable portion of land. But John Abbot knew that if he divided his farm among all four of his boys, each portion would be too small to support a family. Therefore his second son, Barachias, had already received some cash and training as a shoemaker. Abiel, the third son, had been given an education at Harvard College. And Joseph, the youngest, was given some livestock and a few farm tools. He had already been given money for farmland in New Hampshire.

As the population of New England grew, many farmers found themselves in John Abbot's position.

Family Farms Become More Profitable

The Abbot family's experience was shared by many farm families in the northeastern United States. Well into the 1800s, farmers worked their land by hand, with the help of a few family members. But life was also changing for other American farmers. Two developments would drastically alter their way of life: the growing worldwide demand for wheat and the invention of new farming tools.

The Wheat Boom

Population growth and wars throughout Europe had a direct effect on the American farm economy. Before the 1740s, European countries had been able to feed themselves. But the Napoleonic wars destroyed most of Europe's wheat crop. European demand for wheat increased greatly. As a result, wheat prices in the United States skyrocketed. Now huge quantities of grain and other farm produce were exported to Europe.

Farmers in the North and South planted as much wheat as they could. All wanted to make money on the booming wheat trade. Thousands of Americans sank their fortunes and

Objectives

1. Identify the factors that helped American family farms become more profitable.
2. Relate changing patterns of everyday life to changes in the American economy.
3. List the contributions of port cities to the changing economy.
4. Analyze the effect of economic and social changes on free blacks.

Graphic Overview

Causes
- European demand for wheat
- better farming technology

→

Profitable Farms
Manufactured Goods
Port Cities

→

Effects
- movement from farms
- job opportunities
- women's status
- middle class values
- growth of free black communities

Advances in Wheat Production

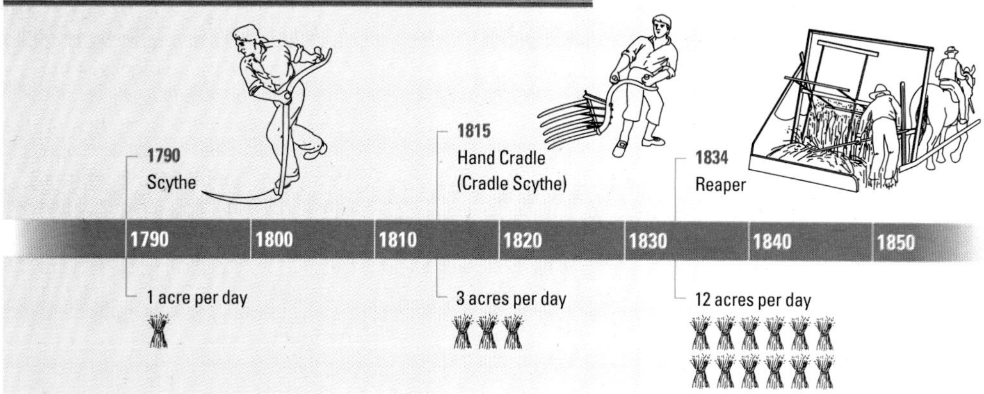

▲ *This graph compares how many acres of wheat one man could harvest in one day using a sickle, a scythe with a cradle, and a McCormick reaper.*

their plows into the fertile land of western New York, Pennsylvania, Virginia, and the territories of Tennessee and Kentucky. The grain trade, long the cornerstone of the nation's market economy, quickly made farmland of the old frontier.

Improved Farming Methods

Long after the turn of the 19th century, American farmers used the same simple tools and methods used by European farmers for hundreds of years. Typically, farmers had harvested their grain with the old-fashioned scythe, a single-edged blade on the end of a long, curved wooden handle.

In the 1830s, however, the way farmers worked the land changed very quickly. A new age began as machines entered the everyday world of nearly all Americans. With Cyrus McCormick's revolutionary mechanical reaper, developed in 1831, farmers cut and tied wheat twelve times faster than they had with some traditional tools. The tough steel-bladed plow, like the one shown below, was developed by John Deere in 1837. The plow sliced through even hard, rocky soil and turned it over into neat furrows.

With these machines American farms became more efficient and more profitable. It was now possible to plant many more acres of grain than before. With the cash from selling surplus wheat, farmers could afford to buy more ready-made products. Farm families were eager to buy items such as soap, shoes, pottery, and clothing. The merchants and craftspeople who made and sold these goods prospered as well. ■

■ *How did wars in Europe and new farming tools help American farms become more profitable?*

▲ *One of the first steel-bladed plows, made by John Deere himself in 1838.*

The American Economy Matures

Since colonial times, American farmers had been mostly self-sufficient. Most families grew their own food, wove their own cloth, and even made many of their own household tools. Boots, wooden plows, carved wooden utensils, and straw brooms were all homemade.

For these early American families, "work" was any farm or household task that had to be done. Very few people had jobs in the sense we now understand. And although men and women might have had different chores, their work was considered equally important.

DEVELOP

Remind students that most changes have causes. Point out that this lesson has a cause-and-effect structure. Tell them to list the causes, the key developments, and the effects of economic growth as they read this lesson.

ECONOMICS

Visual Learning

Have students study the graph on this page. How much more wheat could a farmer harvest with a hand cradle than with a scythe? *(Three times as much)* With a reaper? *(Four times as much as with a hand cradle, 12 times as much as with a scythe)*

■ *The wars in Europe caused an increase in the demand for wheat. The efficient new tools, the mechanical reaper and the plow, helped farmers increase their production.*

Access Strategy

To help students understand the changes that took place in the late 1700s and early 1800s, have them recall what they read about the household economy in Chapter 6. Ask students to imagine being farmers in 1800—having to produce almost all the necessities of daily life. What would they have to do to produce food? *(Grow crops, raise animals)* To make clothing? *(Shear, clean, card, spin, weave, cut, and sew wool)* To build shelter? *(Cut down trees or gather stones to put up homes, board by board or stone by stone with their own hands)*

Then have students recall what they read about the shift to a market economy in Chapter 6. How would their lives change if they could produce enough food to sell the surplus for cash? *(Could buy rather than produce some necessities; would have more leisure time)* Tell students that in this lesson they will learn about some of the ways in which people's lives changed with the new economy.

Access Activity

Ask students to name necessities that their families produce at home. *(Students might mention raising vegetables in home gardens, sewing clothes, and making furniture.)* What necessities do they buy? *(Most of their food items, clothing, and shelter)* Point out the extent to which families today are part of the market economy.

CULTURE

Visual Learning

Ask students how the etching on this page portrays the role of women in the 1800s. *(Woman shown raising and educating children, taking care of the home)* Ask students what kind of picture they might use to portray one of women's roles before the rise of a middle class. *(Woman dipping candles)*

■ *Because they could buy manufactured goods, farm women did "outwork" and sold dairy products and vegetables to townsfolk. The home became a "haven" ruled by women.*

Home and Workplace Divide

This home-based life began changing during the 1790s. Manufactured goods such as soap, candles, linen, and boots became cheaper and more readily available. As a result, American women spent fewer hours making these household goods. Farm women were then able to produce surplus dairy products and homegrown vegetables for sale to townspeople.

▲ *Etchings like this emphasized the importance of the woman's role as homemaker.*

Many women took on "outwork" in their homes. They stitched and sewed raw materials provided by storekeepers. Women in one New Hampshire town made hats from imported palm leaves provided by a local merchant. Outwork paid little, but it enabled families to save some money. Often the savings bought farmland for the children.

Better transportation, increased manufacturing, and labor-saving inventions changed the work of men as well. A growing number of men, like John Abbot's younger sons, found work outside the home—in shops, factories, and offices. Manufacturers, especially of shoes and textiles, began to organize work into hourly units. Gradually men's work came to be viewed as something separate from the home. More and more work took place in well-defined blocks of time away from the family.

The home, in contrast, became idealized as a sheltered, harmonious place away from the harsh working world. It was to be a haven shaped by women, just as public life would be ruled by men.

Women Acquire New Status

The rise in manufacturing helped create a growing **middle class**—a group of people of better-than-average education and income. This class held certain values in common. Chief among these middle-class values was education. For young women in financially stable families in the early 1800s, childrearing was now thought of as an educational mission.

Publishers offered hundreds of "how-to" books and articles for housewives. They covered topics such as cooking, family health, and infant care. Catharine Beecher's *A Treatise on Domestic Economy*, published in 1841, dealt with the noble task of children's education.

Surely it is a ...mistaken idea, that the duties which tax a woman's mind are petty, trivial, or unworthy of the highest grade of intellect and moral worth. Instead of allowing this feeling, every woman should imbibe, from early youth, the impression that she is training for the discharge of the most important, the most difficult, and the most sacred and interesting duties....

Literature such as Beecher's book was very popular at the time. It helped shape the ideals of generations of middle-class American women. These publications were also popular with women who were members of the **working class**—those who labored in mills and workshops for hourly wages. ■

■ *How were women and the American home affected by economic changes?*

Critical Thinking

Have students read the excerpt from Catharine Beecher's book on this page. What attitude was Beecher opposed to? *(The attitude that women's tasks are not important and did not require intelligence)* How did she want women's intellects to be used? *(To educate their children)*

Social Context

The economic changes in the 1800s had a major effect on women. As farm families began to buy household items formerly made at home, there were fewer farm chores to do. Many Northern young women went to work in the mills and married men from town rather than from their own villages. A large number of women moved to the western frontier to farm.

As the differences between male and female roles increased, a "Cult of Domesticity" arose among the middle class. Women were expected to keep a peaceful home and to be "republican mothers," educating their children with the knowledge and morals necessary to maintain a free republic (Chapter 6). Many middle-class women extended the realm of "true womanhood" into the public realm by joining, and frequently leading, the many reform movements of 1820–1860 (Chapter 9).

ECONOMICS
Critical Thinking

Ask students to explain how the opening of the frontier and the changes in the farm economy and in manufacturing led to the growth of port cities such as Boston and Charleston. *(Demand for crafted goods increased, ports needed to export an increased amount of goods, factories provided job opportunities)*

■ *Unable to keep up with the increasing demand for crafted goods, many master craftsmen were replaced by factories, which used less-skilled workers and a production line to produce goods cheaply.*

Port Cities Provide Economic Opportunity

Just as life was changing for young women, young men were gaining opportunities. Younger sons of farming families often left home to pioneer new land farther west. Others of these young men were drawn to busy seaports like Baltimore, Philadelphia, and New York. In the years between 1790 and 1860, Boston, Charleston, and other port cities grew dramatically. Their populations doubled several times over.

In New England, a rise in textile manufacturing fueled the rapid growth of the port of Boston. Boston's harbor could hold up to 500 ships at a time, and its 80 wharves teemed with dockworkers, sailors, and peddlers. In addition to textiles, Boston ships carried grain, lumber, horses, onions, butter, cheese, and beeswax to European ports. This thriving city opened the first free public schools in the United States.

In the South, Charleston became an important center for trade and business. Lively banter in French and Spanish could be heard near the docks. In the markets the smells of Brazilian coffee, New England dried fish, and Cuban tobacco mingled.

During this period a change occurred in the way goods were produced in the port cities. Traditionally, goods were made by master craftsmen with years of experience. As they worked, they trained others in their craft. But this system broke down. The opening of the Old Northwest and of the southwest frontier, plus the inflow of immigrants, created a huge demand for crafted goods. When the craftsmen were not able to keep up, city merchants set up factories of their own. They hired less-skilled workers and used a crude production line to make the goods. Though not as good as products made by master craftsmen, they were cheaper.

By the 1840s, few craftsmen could compete with the factories. Factory workers earned more than some trainees. But few would ever become their own master. ■

■ *How were master craftsmen affected by the booming economy in the port cities?*

Some African Americans Experience Changes

The coastal cities were the scene of important changes for many African Americans. Free blacks, African Americans who were no longer enslaved or had never been slaves, were drawn to Philadelphia, New York, and Baltimore. The population of free blacks increased greatly, though not as greatly as the slave population. Of the 1,800,000 African Americans in 1820, free blacks numbered 233,000, or 13 percent. In 1860, 488,000 out of 4,400,000 African Americans, or 11 percent, were free.

No Rights for Slaves

Most African Americans living in the first half of the 1800s were slaves, however. Legally, they were property, with no more legal rights than a horse or cow. A child's status—slave or free—was inherited from the mother. Unless a slaveholder chose to free his or her slave, a slave's status would not

◄ *African Americans in Philadelphia formed a large and thriving community. Dating from 1800, this painting shows a black street vendor selling oysters.*

Mathematics Connection

Have students translate the information in the graph on page 191 into a table with numbers. Challenge students to find other economic or historical data in tabular form in an almanac or encyclopedia and translate them into a graph. Depending on the data they find, they may want to use bar graphs, circle graphs, or line graphs.

Science Connection

In addition to the McCormick reaper and the Deere steel plow, many other items were invented between 1790 and 1860. Have students research and write a report on one or more of the other inventions of the period. Possibilities include carbon paper, rubber bands, shorthand writing, friction matches, paved roads, and bicycles.

Critical Thinking

After students have read pages 193–194, have them name the legal rights that slaves lacked. *(Could not marry, relocate, testify in court)* Ask students to evaluate the fairness of holding slaves responsible for their crimes yet not giving them any legal rights.

GEOGRAPHY

Map and Globe Skills

Ask students to compare the map on this page with the maps on page 213. *(Greatest population of free blacks and German and Irish immigrants coincide geographically.)* Ask students to predict what problems might arise in the future between free blacks and immigrant populations. *(Competition for jobs, housing)*

BELIEF SYSTEMS

Critical Thinking

After students have read about Richard Allen and the growth of black churches on page 195, ask what reasons African Americans might have had for founding their own churches. *(Sample answers: African Americans wanted to worship in ways that combined African modes of expression with American Christian traditions; they were not treated as equals in white churches; black churches were a source of support for the free black community.)*

change. Slaves could be bought or sold as their slaveholder wished.

Slaves could not legally marry. Nor could they testify in court—not even at an owner's request or in an owner's defense. Even though a slave had no legal rights, in most states a slave was held responsible for any crimes he or she might commit.

Slow Steps Toward Freedom

Slavery was far less profitable in the North than in the South because the northern climate did not permit year-round labor on farms. In addition, many reformers who wanted to do away with slavery lived in northern cities.

Slavery was abolished by the state constitution in Vermont in 1777, by a judicial decision in Massachusetts in 1783, and by laws in Pennsylvania in 1780 and in Rhode Island in 1784. Politicians in other northern states tried to make up a legal system for freeing slaves. Such laws were hard to pass. Slaveholders fought hard to protect the rights they believed they had as "property owners."

Often, free black men worked on the docks or as seamen on merchant and naval ships. In fact, in the mid-1820s officials in South Carolina were afraid of the influence that free blacks from the crews of northern ships might have on plantation slaves. These fearful South Carolinians ordered that all black sailors be kept in prison while their ships were in port.

In Pennsylvania, politicians argued for two years before passing a law in 1780 to free slaves gradually. New York and New Jersey would later pass laws that were very much like the Pennsylvania law.

Such laws, however, meant little to existing slaves. Pennsylvania's law, for example, stated that slaves born before March 1, 1780, would remain slaves for life. Those born after that date were required to work as slaves until the age of 28. Slaveholders maintained that 28 years of service would pay them for the money they had spent to raise the slave. Once they received their freedom papers, free blacks worked hard to earn enough money to buy the freedom of their families and loved ones still in slavery.

African Americans Form Communities

Despite these problems, communities of African Americans continued to grow in American cities. Black families organized groups for protection and support, founding societies—such as the Boston African Society and the Free African Society in Philadelphia—to help with medical and funeral costs.

Free blacks started their own fraternal organizations, like the Black Freemasons. These groups did charitable work and the members took part in social activities. Blacks created their own schools. Until then, the Quaker religious groups had run the only schools that were open to black students.

Most free blacks lived in the upper South and the Middle Atlantic states. But as this map shows, by 1810 free blacks lived in every state and territory of the nation.

Where Free Blacks Were Living, 1810

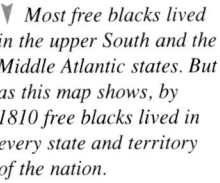

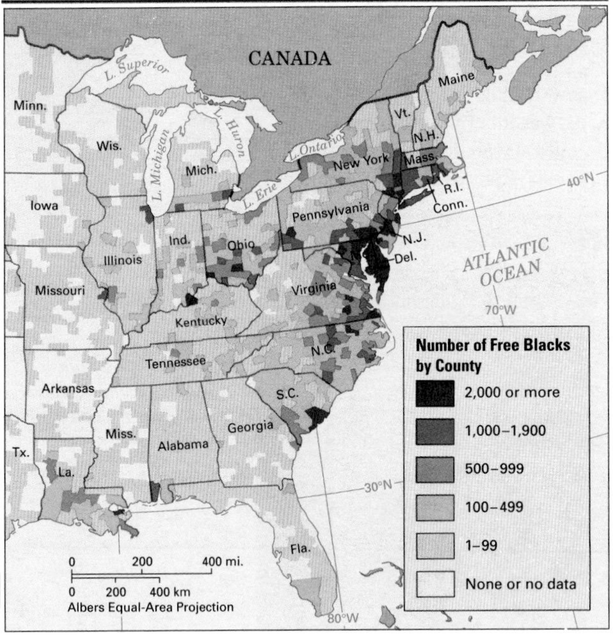

Critical Thinking

Have students compare the problems of free blacks to those of slaves. *(Slaves had no legal rights; free black Americans were restricted in job opportunities, education, housing, and politics.)* What changes would be necessary to improve the situation of free blacks? *(Creating civil rights laws, eliminating racial prejudice)*

Research

Catharine Beecher, quoted in this lesson and mentioned again in Lesson 2 as a champion of education for women, was one of thirteen children of Lyman Beecher. One contemporary said of Lyman Beecher that he was "the father of more brains than any other man in America." Have students research and write a report on Catharine Beecher or one of her siblings: Harriet Beecher Stowe, a noted suffragist and author of *Uncle Tom's Cabin* (Chapter 11); Henry Ward Beecher, a Congregational minister who became one of the most influential Protestant preachers of his time; Edward Beecher, a minister and college president; Charles Beecher, the superintendent of public instruction in Florida; or Isabella Beecher, a women's rights crusader.

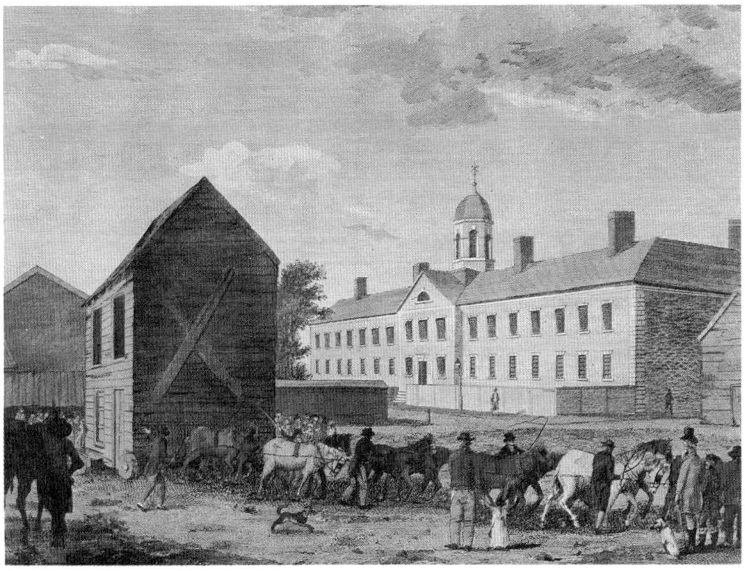

This blacksmith's shop is shown being moved to a new location, where it will function as Richard Allen's church. Allen is shown above.

Schools for free blacks educated both children and adults who wanted to learn to read.

Free blacks also started their own churches. Richard Allen and Absalom Jones were former slaves who became leaders of Philadelphia's free black community. They wanted African churches to be able to support themselves. They did not want to be dependent on the well-meaning charity of their white friends. In time, African churches, such as the African Methodist Episcopal Church founded in 1816 by Allen, became a powerful voice for African American rights and freedom.

The dreams of many of the nation's free blacks were crushed by restricted opportunities for jobs and education. Their social mobility and participation in politics were limited by many hostile white people. As the two groups competed for jobs and housing, many free blacks met violence at the hands of poor white job seekers. During the 1820s and 1830s, for example, race riots broke out against free blacks in New York, Philadelphia, and other cities.

Not surprisingly, many free blacks headed west. Yet, even on the frontier, they met with hostility from white settlers. In Cincinnati, Ohio, racial tension almost led to the total expulsion of many of the city's free blacks in 1829. Nevertheless, westbound African Americans continued to seek the same opportunities enjoyed by white pioneers. ■

■ *Describe the process, as in the 1780 Pennsylvania law, by which slaves in some Northern states were freed.*

REVIEW

1. **FOCUS** How did economic growth in the new nation change family and community life?
2. **CONNECT** Explain why a "republican mother" of the early 1800s would have been a member of the middle class.
3. **CONNECT** How do you think the Embargo Act of 1807 affected the price of American wheat?
4. **CULTURE** Name several of the social and economic problems faced by free blacks before the Civil War.
5. **CRITICAL THINKING** Why did women become more widely seen as "homemakers" in the years between 1790 and 1840? Give evidence to support your answer.
6. **WRITING ACTIVITY** Imagine that you are a great-grandchild of John Abbot's. Make a family tree giving dates and places of birth for all of your relatives. Create any characters and details that you may need for a realistic family tree.

CULTURE

Study Skills

Using information on pages 193–195, students can make a list of the changes in the lives of free blacks in the early 1800s. *(Their numbers increased; free black communities founded cultural institutions; limited opportunities sent many free blacks west.)*

■ *Slaves born after March 1, 1780, were freed after they worked 28 years to pay their owners for raising them.*

CLOSE

Have students answer the Thinking Focus. Copy the structure of the Graphic Overview from page 190 on the board and have students complete it, using the lists of causes, key developments, and effects that they made while they read the lesson. Add to the chart on the board items from page 190 as necessary.

Answers to Review Questions

1. Economic growth led to greater profit on family farms, the division of home and workplace, changes in women's roles, and development of free black communities.
2. Since they were supposed to devote most of their time to raising their children, the ideal "republican mothers" usually had above average income and education.
3. By cutting off European markets, Jefferson's Embargo Act would have caused a drastic drop in farm prices.
4. Free blacks experienced limited opportunities for employment, education, social mobility, and political involvement.
5. Sample answer: The role was encouraged by books and by the fact that men worked outside of the home, leaving women in charge of domestic matters. Allow for personal opinion.
6. Students' work should reflect changing employment and the movement of people away from farms.

Homework Options

Ask students to write an essay comparing the role of the housewives, as described by Catharine Beecher, with the role of women today. How do today's ideals regarding women differ from those of the 1800s?

Study Guide: page 27.

INTRODUCE

Have students read the lesson title and point out that *trans* means "across." Ask a volunteer to identify the Appalachian Mountains, the Mississippi River, and the states in between them on a classroom map or on the United States political map on pages 698–699 in the Atlas. Also have students refer to the historical map on page 98, which shows the territory under the Northwest Ordinance of 1787. Ask them to read the Thinking Focus, and tell them to note the sequence of events as they read the lesson.

Key Terms

Vocabulary strategies: T36–37

migrate—to move from one region to settle in another

institution—established organization dedicated to providing important social functions

1790 — 1860

LESSON 2

The Trans-Appalachian Frontier

THINKING FOCUS

What was the sequence of events leading to established, settled communities in the trans-Appalachian frontier?

Key Terms

- migrate
- institution

Buchanan's Station was one of several small settlements on Tennessee's remote Cumberland frontier in 1792. Eight pioneer families, some with slaves, clustered within the high timber walls of its stockade—afraid of yet another Indian attack. They would go out to feed the horses, milk the cows, or work the fields, but always within running distance of the stockade's gates.

Sometime after midnight on September 30, an Indian war party attacked. Within seconds, all 17 men in the settlement were firing from scattered positions along the wooden walls. Through the dust and smoke they could see a ring of hundreds of Chickamauga and Creek warriors. From as little as 10 feet away, Indian bullets and arrows poured into the stockade.

The pioneers fired back, no one even pausing to clean a gun barrel between shots. The yells of Indians and the roar of rifles filled the air. The women huddled in the small log houses, their children under the beds. All except for Sally Ridley Buchanan, wife of the settlement's leader. Nine months pregnant, she raced bravely through the moonlight from defender to defender, passing out bullets and spreading good cheer. All night long she repeated her rounds.

Suddenly, an explosion rocked the air. A spark from a misloaded weapon set off the powder and ammunition stored in a blockhouse, sending flames and bullets down on the startled Indian warriors. The blockhouse explosion took the fight out of the attackers, and they finally retreated shortly after dawn. The siege at Buchanan's Station was over.

➤ *Settling the trans-Appalachian frontier caused conflicts between settlers and American Indians. This engraving shows an attack on a Cumberland Valley settlement.*

Objectives

1. Analyze the reasons why many Americans migrated westward.
2. Describe the trans-Appalachian frontier and the routes by which pioneers traveled there.
3. Trace the development of townships, institutions, and services during the settlement of the frontier.

Graphic Overview

travel to frontier ➤ establish boundaries ➤ start farms and businesses ➤ build institutions ➤ cultivate farms and develop cities

People Move Westward for New Opportunities

Several events occurred before 1790 that led up to the incident you just read about. White families had begun settling parts of what is now Tennessee in the late 1760s. As in most places in the Americas, they began moving onto the land without making any treaties or agreements with the Indians who lived and hunted there. Although the settlers did lease land from the Cherokee in 1772, Indians and settlers kept trying to drive each other out of the area. In 1782, white settlers destroyed several Chickamauga towns.

Most Americans moving to the trans-Appalachian frontier—the region between the Appalachian Mountains and the Mississippi River—were not interested in the history of conflicts with the Indians. Most of them believed they could settle wherever they wanted to, and relished tales of heroes like Sally Ridley Buchanan and better-known frontiersmen like Davy Crockett. In real life, a hunter, soldier, scout, and Tennessee congressman, Crockett himself wrote some of the stories on which his reputation was based. He jokingly claimed to be "half horse, half alligator."

Frontier scout Daniel Boone was another living legend. Boone led the first groups of pioneers across the Appalachian Mountains through the Cumberland Gap and into Kentucky. Boone was famous for his knowledge of the American Indians. He had been captured by the Shawnee and had lived for a time as an adopted son of their chief, Blackfish.

Author James Fenimore Cooper modeled Natty Bumppo, the hero of his hugely popular series of novels, *The Leatherstocking Tales*, on Daniel Boone. Also known by the names "Deerslayer," "Hawkeye," and "Pathfinder," Natty dressed like his Indian friends. He wore "a hunting-shirt of forest-green, fringed with faded yellow" and a "summer cap of skins." His moccasins were decorated in the "fashion of the natives," and he wore "a pair of buckskin leggings that laced at the sides."

Readers everywhere admired Cooper's hero. In fact, Natty Bumppo helped inspire thousands to join what Cooper called "that band of pioneers . . . opening the way for the march of the nation across the continent."

Along the Frontier

This westward march rapidly changed the frontier of the United States into settled land. As a result, the nation's population center, that point at which equal numbers of people could be found to the north, south, east, and west, shifted westward. In 1790, the population center of the United States was in Baltimore, Maryland, just 50 miles from the Atlantic Ocean.

Over the next 25 years, two million pioneers moved into two main areas of the trans-Appalachian frontier: the Old Northwest and the southern frontier. By 1820, newly formed states included Ohio, Indiana, and Illinois in the Old Northwest and Alabama, Mississippi, and Louisiana on the southern frontier. By 1860, the country's population center had shifted all the way to Chillicothe, Ohio, 500 miles from the Atlantic.

Why did so many people **migrate**—that is, move great distances—within the United States to take on the uncertain life of the frontier? Most pioneers sought land and better economic opportunity. For

James Fenimore Cooper's exciting tales encouraged many Americans to try life on the frontier.

This powder horn, used to store gun powder, belonged to Daniel Boone, the legendary hunter.

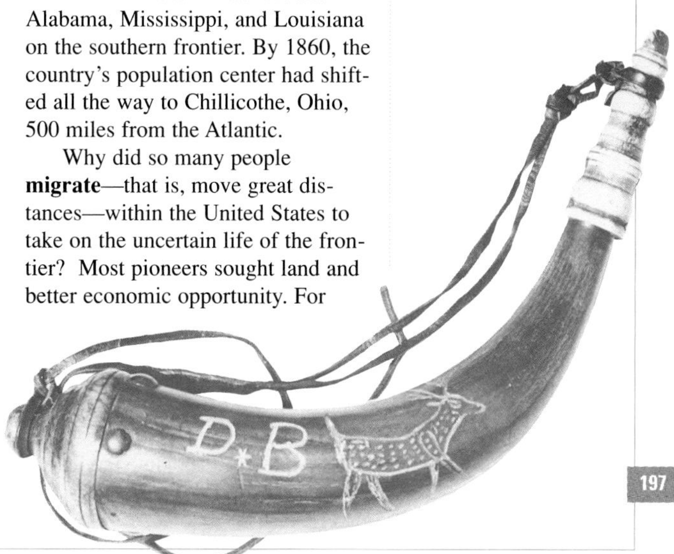

DEVELOP

Suggest that students structure their reading by looking for answers to the following six questions: Who are the principal actors? What did they do? Where? When? Why? How?

GEOGRAPHY

Critical Thinking

Have students find support in the lesson for the following statement: Geography is more than the study of maps; it also includes the movements of people between regions and the ways people interact with their environment. *(The lesson deals with people migrating, creating boundaries, building roads, and setting up social institutions.)*

Access Strategy

To help students identify with the trans-Appalachian pioneers, have them imagine that they are going to create a brand new community. Ask them to name basic institutions and services that they would need to build this community. *(Students may mention schools, libraries, churches, government, communications, roads, waste and sewage removal.)* Ask them to prioritize the items on their list. Which institutions or services would they need first? Which ones could wait awhile? Have a volunteer write their responses on the board. Tell students that they will read in this lesson about settlers who had to make similar decisions.

Access Activity

Read aloud the story of Buchanan's Station in the lesson opener on page 196. Ask students why people would leave their homes to go to a wild and often dangerous frontier. *(To escape religious or social persecution, for financial gain, for adventure)* Why do people migrate today? *(Similar reasons)*

GEOGRAPHY

Map and Globe Skills

Have students look at the map on this page. Ask them which road reached the farthest west and what states or territories it crossed. *(The National Road crossed Maryland, Virginia, Ohio, Indiana, and Illinois.)* Ask students to identify the physical barriers that influenced the routes. *(The Appalachian Mountains; no river valleys to cross from east to west)* Have them compare the map on this page with the United States political map on pages 698–699 in the Atlas to find one state in the region that did not exist at the time the National Road was built. *(West Virginia)*

The First Roads West, 1755-1838

The first federally funded road was the stone-paved National Road, begun in 1811. Paid for in irregular installments by Congress, it began in Cumberland, Maryland and eventually ended, in 1830, in Vandalia, Illinois (then the state capital).

example, New Englanders, like the sons of John Abbot in Lesson 1, left small farms that could not be further divided among family members. And Southern planters migrated west to grow cotton in the rich lower Mississippi River Valley.

Many pioneers such as Colonel Ridley, father of the heroine of the siege at Buchanan's Station, were veterans of the Revolutionary War. Soldiers had often been rewarded with land in Tennessee and Kentucky instead of being paid in cash for their military service.

The pioneers also included many African Americans. Southern planters took tens of thousands of slaves across the Appalachians to hack cotton plantations out of the wilderness. But hundreds of free blacks also migrated, especially into the Old Northwest and beyond the Mississippi into the Far West. There, they farmed or took jobs as cowhands and miners.

Roads to the West

For all Americans, westward overland travel was slow and difficult. At first, pioneers followed narrow pathways across the Appalachian Mountains. Even after roads were built, a full day's journey through dust or mud would cover fewer than 25 miles—as long as there were no rivers to cross. The first east-west roads are shown on the map above.

Many of the early roads were toll roads, built by private investors. Travelers had to stop at toll gates spaced every 6 to 10 miles to pay up to 25 cents per wagon. The first toll road, the Lancaster Turnpike, opened in 1794, between Philadelphia and Lancaster, Pennsylvania. The Lancaster Turnpike was surfaced with stone and gravel. It was the best road of its day. Many "roads," however, were only narrow dirt passages, with tree stumps cut off at 16 inches—just low enough for wagon axles to clear.

Map and Globe Skills

Students can locate on a modern road map of the United States the highways that follow the same routes as the first westward roads, canals, and riverways shown on the map on this page. *(National Road—U.S. Route 70; Lancaster Turnpike—U.S. Route 76)* Why are these roads still important today? *(Used for transporting goods, for traveling by car)*

Historical Context

Share with students a description of a typical one-room schoolhouse, such as this one, from Clifton Johnson's *Old Time Schools and Schoolbooks*: "The structure was generally roughly clapboarded, and it might possibly receive a coat of red or yellow paint, but more likely paint was lacking outside and in. The schoolroom was lathed and plastered, and was lighted by five or six small windows of twelve panes each. The glass in the windows was often broken, and during school hours, in cool weather, the place of the missing panes was apt to be supplied with hats. . . . at [the] end of the room was the master's desk or table—usually a table in the early days; but later a desk specially contrived by the carpenter, on a slight platform, was customary. Besides serving the ordinary purposes of a desk, it was a repository for confiscated tops, balls, penknives, marbles . . . and was frequently a perfect curiosity shop."

Transportation routes were not limited to roads. Canals and rivers carried both settlers and cargo to the West. At first flatboats, which had to have oarsmen, crossed the Mississippi and Ohio rivers. After 1810, the flatboats were being replaced by the first crude steamboats. ■

■ *List four reasons for the migration of Americans into the trans-Appalachian frontier.*

Pioneers Settle the West

The frontier did not remain untamed for long. New settlers set about clearing the land, planting crops, and putting up houses and barns. In their new environment, settlers often had to find different ways to solve old problems.

Mapping and Planning Towns

Since the 1600s, Americans had been using an old surveying method called "metes and bounds." This meant that surveyors described the boundaries of a piece of land in terms of natural landmarks. These were often trees, rivers, and other pieces of property. For example, surveyors in 1784 used a huge black oak and 26 other large trees to define William Few's 887 acres in Georgia. Such boundaries were often unclear. Misunderstandings sometimes led to lawsuits that cost far more than the land itself was worth.

To do away with this confusion in the Northwest Territory, Thomas Jefferson suggested a new system for describing boundaries. Put into use by the Land Ordinance of 1785, this system set boundaries according to the lines of longitude and latitude. These measurements were internationally recognized, but they ignored natural boundaries such as rivers, lakes, and mountains.

Land of the Northwest Territory was divided first into townships, areas that were six miles on each side. Townships were divided into thirty-six square "sections" of 640 acres. Each section was further divided into 320-acre "halves," 160-acre "quarters," and even 40-acre "quarter quarters."

This system gave the Old Northwest square fields and arrow-straight city streets. As seen from above today, this regularity contrasts with the odd lots created by the old "metes and bounds" system.

The township system allowed pioneers to buy government land with clearly defined boundaries. Abraham Lincoln's father, for example, had lost his Kentucky farm in a lawsuit over boundaries. In 1816, the Lincoln family could settle in Indiana with clear borders for their land.

Building Schools and Churches

Establishing boundaries was just the beginning of settling the West. Newly arrived families found no public **institutions**—schools, churches, and governing bodies—waiting for them. The settlers had to build their own social organizations.

One of the first businesses in a new township was often a mill where corn and wheat could be ground into flour. Blacksmiths, wheelwrights, and

How Do We Know?

GEOGRAPHY *Town, county, and state governments have preserved millions of documents that help us understand how earlier Americans divided up the frontier. These documents, which include old maps, surveyors' records, and deeds showing property transfer, are kept in archives.*

▼ *This map shows the survey of lands near Dayton, Ohio, under the Land Ordinance of 1785.*

■ *New England farms had become too small to be further divided among family members, cotton growers needed more land, Revolutionary War soldiers had been paid in land, and free blacks wanted greater opportunity.*

GEOGRAPHY

Visual Learning

Have students examine the historical map on this page. Remind them of the Land Ordinances of 1785, which they read about in Chapter 3, and point out that this map was drawn at that time. Ask what disadvantages the grid system would have had when mapping the land shown in the historical map. *(A boundary might be in the middle of a lake or gully.)*

Mathematics Connection

Help students understand the size of a township in the Northwest Territory. Ask them to calculate the number of acres in a township, given that the number of acres in a square mile is 640. *(If a township is 6 miles on a side, it is 36 square miles in area. Thus, 640 x 36 = 23,040 acres.)* Point out that it is possible to park about 100 cars in an acre of land, leaving aisles for them to get in and out of the area. Ask them how many townships their city or town occupies.

Making a Grid System

Using graph paper, students can devise a grid system for mapping the classroom. They should make measurements using tape measures or by pacing off the distances. The classroom represents a township, which they divide into 36 square "sections." They can also divide each section into "quarters." They should indicate on the graph paper the measurements, in feet and inches, for the side of both a square section and a quarter section.

Map and Globe Skills

Examine with students a map of their local area. Were any of the boundaries based on the grid system set? You might also supply U.S. Geodetic Survey maps so that students can assess how well the political boundaries correspond to natural ones.

SOCIAL SYSTEMS

Critical Thinking

Ask students to recall from Chapter 1 the hardships faced by the first settlers in New England and Jamestown. Have them compare the experiences of the Pilgrims and the first Virginians with those of the trans-Appalachian pioneers. *(Similar process of establishing a society, complete with cultural institutions and commercial services)*

■ *The township system allowed pioneers to buy government land with clearly defined boundaries.*

CLOSE

To help students review the lesson, have them answer the six questions posed in Develop. Who? *(Eastern pioneers, slaves, free black Americans)* What? *(Migration to the frontier)* Where? *(The Old Northwest, the Southern frontier)* Why? *(Better opportunities, farms too small to support families)* How? *(Over newly built roads to places that had been surveyed and planned)* Have students answer the Thinking Focus. To review the sequence of events, copy on the board the Graphic Overview from page 196.

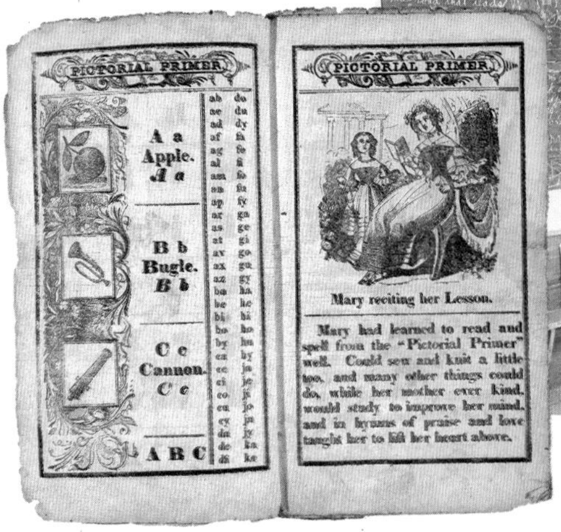

According to the Northwest Ordinance of 1787, a parcel of land in every township area was set aside for schools. This 1820 schoolhouse is actually a display from the Smithsonian Institute in Washington, D.C. Students used readers like this American Pictorial Primer in their daily studies.

■ *How did the township system benefit the pioneers who moved west?*

doctors soon followed, providing important services. Such service businesses were a very important and necessary part of maintaining a community. They answered the many needs of settlers who worked the land.

The Northwest Ordinance of 1787 had set aside pieces of land in the new townships for public education. As soon as schools could be built, frontier children received a basic education in the 3 R's—"reading, 'riting, and 'rithmetic." Few teachers were available in the West, however. Well-known lecturer and writer Catharine Beecher dedicated herself to the goal of sending New England teachers westward. She also devoted her efforts to organizing "female colleges" in Wisconsin and nearby states, to train the teachers needed by the new communities.

Churches grew slowly during the early years of the trans-Appalachian frontier. "Circuit riders"—preachers riding from place to place on horseback—began to appear in small towns. Pioneers also went to "camp meetings," which became important religious and social events. Later, when the population could support a priest or a minister on a more regular basis, these loose congregations became organized churches.

By the 1840s, pioneers had turned the farmlands and forests of the Cherokee, Creek, Pawnee, and Kickapoo into heavily cultivated farms and growing cities. The valleys of the Cumberland, Ohio, and Mississippi rivers now had the same institutions and services that the settlers had known in the East. But there were still opportunities for more settlers, soon to include the next wave of immigrants from Europe. ■

REVIEW

1. **FOCUS** What was the sequence of events leading to established, settled communities in the trans-Appalachian frontier?
2. **CONNECT** Relate the economic and social changes on the family farm of the early 1800s to the migration of Americans to the frontier.
3. **GEOGRAPHY** Explain how township lines affected the landscape of the Old Northwest, especially in terms of natural boundaries such as forests, mountains, and rivers.
4. **CRITICAL THINKING** Predict how later generations of settlers to the Old Northwest will benefit from the established township system.
5. **WRITING ACTIVITY** Write a news story for radio or TV broadcast about the completion of the Lancaster Turnpike.

Homework Options

Have students find the population center of the United States for various dates by looking in the current *Statistical Abstract of the United States* in the library.

Study Guide: page 28.

Answers to Review Questions

1. The settlers migrated, established boundaries, cleared land, planted crops, built houses and barns, set up mills and other business services, and established churches and schools.
2. As the population in New England grew and the demand for wheat increased, many farmers moved west in order to have sufficient land and to produce surplus crops to sell.
3. Based on the lines of longitude and latitude rather than on natural boundaries, the township system divided the Old Northwest into square fields and straight city streets.
4. Sample answer: Later generations will experience fewer disputes over boundaries. Allow for personal opinion.
5. Encourage students to play up the sense of progress and the potential for economic development and migration.

1790 1839 1850 1860

L E S S O N 3

The Changing World of American Indians

*T*he only way to check and stop this evil is for all the red men to unite in claiming a common and equal right in the land . . . for it never was divided, but belongs to all, for the use of each.... No part has a right to sell, even to each other, much less to strangers.

So spoke Shawnee chief Tecumseh (*ti KUM se*) as he condemned and canceled the sale of Indian land to the U.S. government in 1809. Tecumseh had enlisted southern and northern warriors along the Mississippi Valley for a major united effort to recover lands lost to the white people. He was determined to hold the Ohio River as the boundary dividing the United States and Indian country.

As governor of the Indiana Territory, William Henry Harrison was also determined to defend white pioneers who invaded and settled in Indian territories. In 1810, Harrison met the Shawnee leader face to face at Vincennes, Indiana. As their talks began, Harrison's interpreter told Tecumseh, "Your father requests you to take a chair." Angrily Tecumseh replied, "My father! The sun is my father, and the earth is my mother…" Tecumseh spoke forcefully to Harrison of the position of the Indians.

He argued that the U.S. government had no real right to lands ceded, or transferred, to whites without the consent of all American Indians. Tecumseh shouted, "Sell a country! Why not sell the air, the clouds, and the great sea?"

*T*he Great Spirit gave this great island to his red children. He placed the whites on the other side of the big water. They were not contented with their own, but came to take ours from us. They have driven us from the sea to the lakes—we can go no farther."

THINKING FOCUS

What were the different responses of the various American Indian peoples when their ancestral lands were threatened?

Key Terms

- revitalization
- cultural accommodation

◄ *Tecumseh is shown here saving American prisoners during the War of 1812.*

INTRODUCE

Have a student read aloud the title and the Thinking Focus. Point out that *world* in the title refers not only to the trans-Appalachian region, but also to the way of life of the American Indians. Remind students that the American Indian peoples were made up of many different nations. Have students predict what the U.S. Government will do to acquire the Indians' land and read to confirm or reject their predictions.

Key Terms

Vocabulary strategies: T36–37

revitalization—the effort to bring new life and strength to a people or culture

cultural accommodation—the reconciliation or compromise of opposing cultures

Graphic Overview

RESPONSES TO WHITE SETTLERS

- **Resistance**
  - Little Turtle
  - Tecumseh
- **Revitalization**
  - The Prophet
- **Cultural Accommodation**
  - John and Lewis Ross
  - Sequoya

Objectives

1. Show how the westward migration of whites into Indian territories involved both military conflict and treaty negotiation.
2. Evaluate various Indian responses to the white invasion: armed resistance, revitalization, and cultural accommodation.
3. Trace Cherokee experiences before and after their forced removal.

DEVELOP

Tell students that this lesson, like Lesson 2, is about migration, but it is a different kind of migration—the forced relocation of Indians. Have students preview the maps on pages 203 and 207 to see the extent of the relocation. Tell students to read the lesson to find out the different ways in which the Indians responded when their lands were being threatened.

HISTORY

Critical Thinking

Have students contrast how Little Turtle's confederacy might have viewed the Treaty of Greenville with how General Wayne probably viewed it. *(Little Turtle's confederacy—as a document that legalized their lands being stolen from them; General Wayne—as a fair negotiation after victory in battle)*

Indian Territories Invaded by the Push Westward

Ever since the first Europeans arrived, whites had gotten land by defeating American Indians. By the 1780s, few of the Indian tribes that had once flourished along the Atlantic seaboard survived. Entire tribal groups had been killed off by war, starvation, and disease.

Farther inland, however, Indian tribes still occupied much of the land. Many wanted to make sure that they would not share the fate of the coastal Indian peoples. The Shawnee, Delaware, Miami, and Potawatomi *(POT a WOT a mee)* of the Old Northwest, for example, formed a confederacy at the time of the Revolutionary War.

Led by Miami chief Little Turtle, the warriors of this powerful alliance raided white settlements on Indian lands. In the late 1780s and early 1790s, they were able to halt white advances. The Indians defeated the territorial militias that marched into their lands.

Then in 1793, President Washington sent federal troops commanded by the Revolutionary War hero General Anthony Wayne. In 1794, at the Battle of Fallen Timbers in what is now northern Ohio, General Wayne defeated Little Turtle's allied warriors. The next year, members of the confederacy were forced to sign the Treaty of Greenville. As a result, the Indians ceded to the United States the southeastern quarter of the Northwest Territory—about half the present state of Ohio.

Hunger for Land

In the Treaty of Greenville, the United States broke a promise it had made to the Indian peoples only eight years before. The Northwest Ordinance of 1787 had promised security for the Indians in their ancestral lands. But the policy of the U.S. government from the 1790s onward was to recognize the Indian tribes as independent nations. Each "nation" was seen as the sole "owner" of distinct territories. The Indians did not see themselves this way. But this policy enabled the government to obtain land by negotiating treaties with each separate Indian "nation."

And so began a series of treaties whereby the Indian tribes "freely consented" to cede their lands, sometimes receiving only pennies an acre for it. By making treaties, the U.S. government made it seem as though the Indians were voluntarily moving off the land. In fact, many treaties were obtained through the use of fraud and violence. Many treaties were signed by individuals who did not speak for all of the Indians or who had no authority to sign over the land. The U.S. government used any means to force Indian

The land Tecumseh defended was long ago divided up among individuals. Now only a little land of the Old Northwest, like this state park, is "for the use of all."

Access Activity

Ask students to imagine that a group of people is forcing their family to leave the land that they have lived on for generations and to move across the country. How would they first react? *(Probably try to negotiate)* What would they do if their efforts failed? *(Fight back, give in)*

Access Strategy

Read aloud the lesson opener on page 201. Ask students what Tecumseh meant when he shouted, "Sell a country! Why not sell the air, the clouds, and the great sea?" *(The American Indians did not live in nature; they were part of nature. Tecumseh might as easily have said, "Why not sell our hands, our hearts?")*

Then discuss the concept of private ownership. May owners of land do absolutely anything with it? If students answer *yes*, ask if owners may pollute land. If they answer *no*, ask them to name what limitations would be appropriate. Tell students that they will read in this lesson about the conflicting ideas that the American Indians and white settlers had concerning land ownership.

Relocation of Several American Indian Tribes, 1800-1840

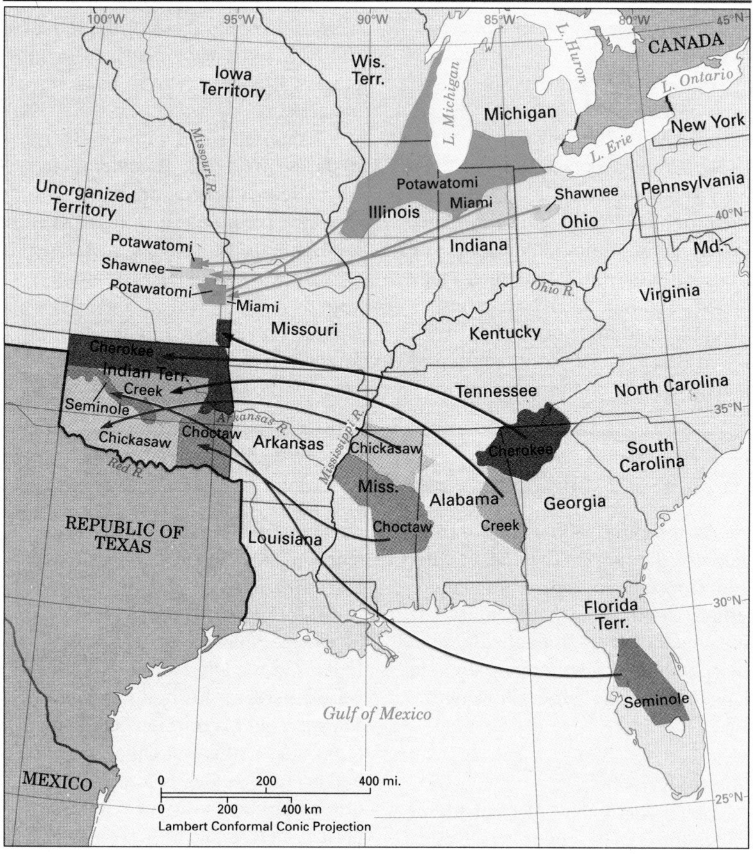

These lines show the relocation of selected Indian tribes to the new Indian Territory. Few Indians could pursue their traditional ways of living in the Indian Territory.

tribes off desirable frontier land onto more distant, less desirable land. "Indian Territory," as it is shown on the map, got smaller and smaller.

After the Treaty of Fort Wayne was signed in 1809, all of the Northwest Territory was legally open to white settlement. Tens of thousands of settlers were now entering yet another environment where Indians had lived for centuries. The ways of the Indians had been closely connected to the plants, the animals, the rivers, and the soil of a particular area. When white settlers cut down many square miles of forest to clear new farmland, they destroyed a way of life. They drove off the game—bear, deer, and buffalo—that had been a major food source for the Indian. Settlement of Indian lands also broke up networks of intertribal trade. But the pioneers did not particularly care what happened to the former inhabitants of the land.

Indian Resistance

Realizing that only drastic measures could save them, many Indian leaders saw the War of 1812 as an opportunity to strike out against the settlers. Along the southern frontier, more than 2,000 militant Creeks, called "Red Sticks," rose up as a unified force of warriors. But in 1814, after months of bloody fighting, General Andrew Jackson finally defeated the Red Sticks in Tennessee. The treaty that ended the conflict brought

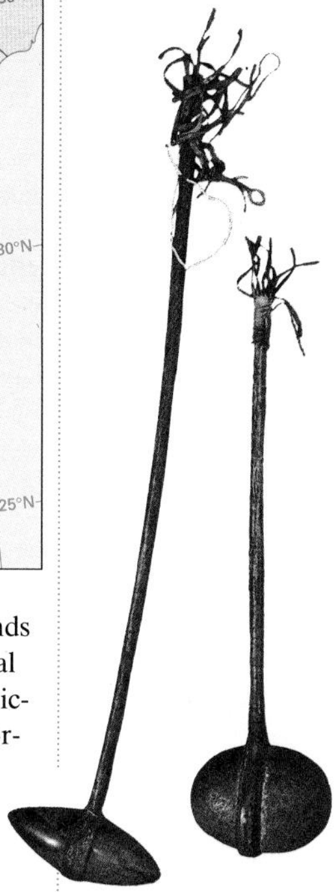

These war clubs were used by Tecumseh's warriors in defending their lands.

GEOGRAPHY

Map and Globe Skills

Have students compare the Indians' homeland with the land to which they were relocated by looking at the map on this page and the climate, vegetation, and precipitation maps on pages 706–707 in the Atlas. What was the difference in vegetation? *(From the forest to grasslands)* In precipitation? *(To a drier region)* To what difference in climate would the Seminole have to adjust? *(Cold winter)* How would such a move change the lifestyle of the Indian peoples? *(Change ways of getting food, clothing, and shelter; alter generations of customs)*

HISTORY

Critical Thinking

What techniques did the U.S. government use to take over the Indians' land? *(Manipulated Indian leaders, forced them to sign treaties, used military power)* Ask students to predict how Indians will respond in the second half of the 1800s as the white settlers push even farther west. *(Fight back, surrender)*

Social Context

Tecumseh's motivation as a warrior probably stemmed from his boyhood, when he saw his father killed by white frontiersmen. He had at one time, however, close ties with a white pioneer family, the Galloways. He even wanted to marry Rebecca Galloway, who taught him how to read and speak English. Her father gave his permission on condition that Tecumseh adopt the ways of the white man. Tecumseh deliberated, finally deciding that he could not give up his culture.

Historical Context

Governor Harrison, trying to weaken the influence of Tecumseh's brother Tenskwatawa, wrote to some Indians that Tenskwatawa was no prophet unless he could make the sun stand still. Learning that a solar eclipse was due, Tenskwatawa gathered a crowd to watch as he made the sun go away and then come back. News of this "miracle" reached many groups of Indians, who pledged their loyalty to Tecumseh and his brother.

Map and Globe Skills

Have students examine the map on this page and the one of American Indian cultures in the Minipedia on page 672 to find the historical locations of the American Indian peoples mentioned in the lesson. *(Southeast—Cherokee, Creek; Northeast—Shawnee, Delaware, Miami, Potawatomi)* To where were they forced to move? *(Plains)*

■ *Many treaties were gained through fraud and violence. Often the signers were not authorized representatives of the Indian peoples.*

CULTURE

Critical Thinking

Have students explain how the personal experiences of the Prophet might have caused him to lead the revitalization movement. *(His alcoholism and recovery from it may have helped him see that white culture could harm his people. Either his own personal spiritual experiences or the settlers' religious revivals of the time may have led him to see that his people needed to be more spiritual and return to their own traditions.)*

■ *Find evidence to support this statement: The U. S. government did not deal fairly when signing land cession treaties with American Indians.*

two-thirds of the Creek lands into the United States. The remaining Creeks withdrew to southern and western Alabama.

In the Old Northwest, the alliance led by Shawnee chief Tecumseh and his brother Tenskwatawa *(ten skwa TA wa),* known as "the Prophet," also tried to push back white settlement. Tecumseh believed that if different Indian nations united, they could stop white settlers from taking their lands. In 1811, William Henry Harrison fought a large force of the Prophet's warriors at Prophetstown, a group of Indian villages on the Tippecanoe *(tip ee ka NOO)* River, while Tecumseh was away. White losses were higher than those of the Indians. But Harrison's army managed to burn most of Prophetstown, so he claimed a victory.

Tecumseh sided with the British in the War of 1812. Together their forces scored several dramatic victories. But Tecumseh died in 1813, at the Battle of the Thames *(temz)* in Ontario, Canada. This loss, along with the 1832 defeat of Black Hawk and the Fox and Sauk Indians in Wisconsin ended most Indian resistance in the Old Northwest. ■

Various Indian Responses

By the early 1800s, more was at stake for the Indians than land ownership. Constant pressure from white settlers and the U.S. government threatened their traditional culture and their livelihood. The Indians stood in danger of losing their entire way of life.

This drawing of the Prophet shows him in the traditional dress of the Shawnee warrior. The Prophet shunned white culture.

Cultural Revival

In his youth, the Prophet had fallen "victim," as he saw it, to the evils of white culture. He had become an alcoholic and had abandoned his people's customs. As a result of wars and invasions from whites, many Indians had given up their traditions. But the Prophet, possibly influenced by religious revivals that occurred among white settlers, recovered from alcoholism and changed his ways.

The Prophet began a new religious movement, and told his followers to give up alcohol and other behaviors. At first these behaviors included some white and some traditional Indian activities. Over time, however, the Prophet began focusing on the importance of traditional Indian ways. He preached that Indians could regain their power if they rejected all white cultural habits and white trading goods. This effort to renew a people's culture is called **revitalization.**

The Prophet converted many Shawnee, Potawatomi, and other Indians of the Old Northwest, who were bitter over losing their land. They trusted his religious movement to provide a solution. Other warriors, however, looked to Tecumseh, who offered political unity as a way to protect their homelands. Tecumseh's political movement dissolved after his death in battle in 1813. Escaping the same battle, the Prophet fled to Canada, where his influence diminished over time.

Cultural Compromises

Other Indians believed that violent opposition to whites was no solution. The Cherokee, for example, recognized that the white presence in America was permanent. The Cherokee favored **cultural accommodation**, or peaceful compromises, with white society. They tried to combine the best features of both European and Cherokee culture.

Cultural accommodation brought about a remarkable period in Cherokee history. During the early 1800s,

Social Participation

Have students evaluate both revitalization and cultural accommodation. Is it more effective to strengthen one's traditional culture or to make compromises and blend cultures? *(Make it clear that there is no "right" answer.)*

Language Arts Connection

Sequoya is the only person in history to invent and perfect an entire alphabet. Divide students into groups to try to invent their own alphabets. Point out that Sequoya took twelve years to create his alphabet, and caution that theirs need not be so complete.

Each group should first discuss its goals. Should the letters be very distinct from one another or should they show some kind of relationship? (For example, should all vowels have a line through them?) Will the alphabet merely replace the letters of the Roman alphabet we use, or should it represent the sounds of English more directly? (For example, should a single letter represent the sound *sh*?)

Have each group present its alphabet to the class. Encourage groups to include a brief sample of text written in their alphabets on the overhead projector or on the board. After the presentations, discuss the similarities and differences of their alphabets.

many Cherokee gave up hunting to become farmers. Some even became rich plantation owners with dozens of black slaves. Other Cherokee turned to commerce—managing stores, mills, and other businesses.

At this time, boarding schools run by Christian missionaries taught Cherokee children everything from geography to arithmetic. But the Cherokee educational system took even greater steps forward because of the achievements of Sequoya *(si KWOI a),* a Cherokee silversmith.

Sequoya saw the advantages whites enjoyed because of their ability to read and write. He set out to make an alphabet for writing the Cherokee language. After years of work, he made an alphabet of 85 symbols that stood for the different syllables of the Cherokee language.

Sequoya's system was easy to learn. In fact, most Cherokee were able to read and write effectively in about a week. The Cherokee also adopted English as a second language. By the 1820s, they had established written laws and a democratic constitution. They founded their own newspaper, the *Cherokee Phoenix,* which printed every article in Cherokee and English, side by side.

Cherokee leadership was very strong at this time. The tribal and central councils were run by strong leaders like John and Lewis Ross, who helped govern the Cherokee people for almost forty years. ■

Sequoya is shown here with his alphabet. Note that his clothes are like those of the white settlers of the time.

■ *Compare and contrast the attitudes of The Prophet and Sequoya toward American society.*

Defeat of the Cherokee

The Cherokee hoped their policy of accommodation would allow them to live peacefully with the whites but this did not happen. They also tried to use their status as an independent nation to improve their situation. Their white neighbors tried equally hard to prevent them.

Legal Battle over Removal

White settlers on the southern frontier hungered for Cherokee lands. As cotton production increased the value of southern land, whites fought even harder for Indian removal.

Arguments went on for years, as did lawsuits. In time, some groups of Cherokee were pressured to give up their land and to move west. Others, under the leadership of John Ross, would not leave. They took their case all the way to the Supreme Court. Finally, in the 1832 case of *Worcester v. Georgia,* the Cherokee seemed to win. Chief Justice John Marshall recognized the right of the Cherokee people to their own nation and laws.

The victory, however, was hollow. Georgia, with the support of President Andrew Jackson, ignored Marshall and the Court. Other states joined Georgia in calling for the final removal of the remaining Cherokee from the southern frontier.

HISTORY

Critical Thinking

Ask students why they think the Cherokee decided to try cultural accommodation. *(Saw that military resistance didn't work; thought they would benefit from it, particularly from reading and writing)*

■ *The Prophet wanted to preserve American Indian culture through revitalization; Sequoya favored cultural accommodation, seeing some advantages in white culture for his people.*

Science Connection

American Indians lived in close communion with the land, depending on it for food, clothing, and shelter. This lifestyle is now so rare in America that such "survival skills" are taught in Scouting, in outdoors manuals and in special "adventure" schools.

Have students research some Scouting or other survival manuals and write a few paragraphs on how someone might survive in the outdoors. Then discuss with the class how the survival techniques they learned about could become a way of life. What kinds of knowledge would be necessary to go beyond mere survival to building a thriving culture? *(How to plan ahead to deal with natural disaster, how to build social structures)* How would the knowledge be passed on through the generations? *(By adults' educating children)*

Study Skills

Have students consider where they can find information on American Indian peoples. *(Libraries, natural history museums, historical societies, tribal authorities)* Have them research and write a report on one of the Indian nations mentioned in this lesson, including its prominent leaders, location, and culture.

Note: You may want to use A Moment in Time at the end of the lesson.

CULTURE

Visual Learning

Refer students to the picture and the captions on this page. Ask them to explain some of the difficulties, both emotional and physical, that the Indians had to deal with on the Trail of Tears. *(Cold, lack of proper clothing, increasing distance from home)* Explain that the Indians could take only a few things with them. Have them look to find the types of things that this Cherokee woman chose to take. Which items have practical value? Which have sentimental value?

A MOMENT IN TIME

A Cherokee Mother and Son

1:37 P.M. December 15, 1838
Along the Trail of Tears, on a frozen dirt path outside Greenville, Missouri

Leg Rattles
At the Green Corn Dance, she created loud rhythms by dancing while wearing these. She carries them in an oak basket to remind her of happier times.
Blowgun
This morning, the boy shot a pheasant with this simple gun. Georgia wild turkey is his favorite target.
Basket
An expert basket-maker, the boy's mother has taught many young girls to weave. In this basket, he now carries a few tools and dried fruit.
Hymnal
Methodist missionaries gave her this book of hymns. It is printed in Cherokee, so she can use it to teach her son to read after they reach Oklahoma.
Copper Pan
She had many fine pieces of copper cookware at home, but she can only carry one as she walks.
Red Clay
By carrying a handful of clay from Georgia and mixing it with the soil of his new home, the boy will keep part of his past alive.

Study Skills

Have students recall from Chapter 6 President Jackson's attitude and actions toward Indians. *(Reputation as an Indian fighter, favored westward expansion for white settlers at Indians' expense, ignored Supreme Court's ruling that Cherokee had a right to their land)* Help students see that these actions made the removal of the Indians inevitable.

Writing an Editorial

Students can write an editorial about the forced relocation of the Cherokee to Oklahoma for an American newspaper in 1839. Students should decide whether they approve or disapprove of President Van Buren's action before they start writing. Encourage students to use a typewriter or word processor to produce their editorials in columns. Have students with opposing points of view read aloud their editorials.

Drawing

Encourage students to draw pictures of and write captions for the Cherokee removal based on their reading of the lesson. Students should choose events leading to and taking place during the Trail of Tears. This activity can be incorporated into the timeline in the Review activity, which chronicles the events leading to the Trail of Tears.

Cherokee Trail of Tears, 1838–1840

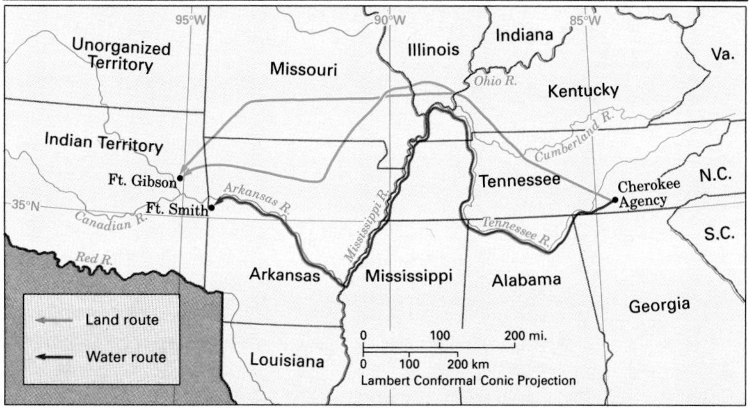

A rich civilization all but died on the 600-mile Trail of Tears. Most Cherokee were moved over land. Others went by flatboat along rivers.

A minority party of Cherokee, led by Major Ridge and his son John, gave in to white harassment. They finally signed a treaty giving up all rights to their land in 1835.

The Trail of Tears

Many Cherokee continued to resist removal even after this treaty was signed. President Martin Van Buren finally gave the order in 1838 to round up the Cherokee, at the point of a gun or a bayonet if need be. "The Cherokees are nearly all prisoners," one Baptist minister reported. "They have been dragged from their houses and encamped at the forts and military posts."

The U.S. Army moved over 15,000 Cherokee west during the winter of 1838–1839. More than 4,000 people died on what came to be known as the "Trail of Tears." The lands of what had been the remarkable Cherokee nation became the property of whites. Only a few scattered groups of Indian peoples, including the Seminoles of Florida, remained. Despite orders to treat the Cherokee humanely, they went without adequate clothing, shelter, or food. An Army private recalled the trail:

> The trail of the exiles was a trail of death. They had to sleep in the wagons and on the ground without fire. I have known as many as 22 of them to die in one night of pneumonia due to ill treatment, cold, and exposure.

The fate of the Cherokee suggested that there was little hope for the survival of Indian culture. No matter how they chose to approach the whites—with revitalization, resistance, or accommodation—Indians would eventually be overwhelmed by the white settlers flooding the West. ■

Across Time & Space

The United States has broken hundreds of treaties with American Indians. In 1946, the government set up the Indian Claims Commission. It heard and decided over 500 Indian claims against the United States for fraud and unfair treatment. Since 1978, the United States Claims Court has handled these claims. American Indians continue to fight for their legal rights.

■ *How was the Cherokee civilization finally destroyed?*

REVIEW

1. **FOCUS** What were the different responses of the various American Indian peoples when their ancestral lands were threatened?
2. **CONNECT** How did the U.S. policy toward American Indians from the 1790s onward differ from the policy of the British colonial governments? How were the Indians affected by this difference?
3. **CULTURE** What did the Cherokee lose or leave behind in western Georgia at the time of their removal?
4. **CRITICAL THINKING** Do you think that the possibility ever existed for the settlers and the American Indians to coexist peacefully? Explain your answer.
5. **ACTIVITY** Make a time line, beginning in 1827, that charts the events leading to the Trail of Tears.

HISTORY

Map and Globe Skills

Students can trace the Trail of Tears on the map on this page and calculate how many miles the Cherokee were moved. *(Approximately 600 miles)* Using 10 to 20 miles a day as an average rate of travel, how long did the journey take? *(About 30 to 60 days)*

■ *Cherokee civilization was destroyed by forced relocation, disruption of its culture, and the elimination of a large percent of the population.*

CLOSE

Have students answer the Thinking Focus and evaluate their predictions. Copy on the board the Graphic Overview on page 201. Ask students to explain why each response to the white invasion was insufficient. *(Revitalization—failed when Tecumseh was killed and the Prophet was forced to flee to Canada; cultural accommodation—backfired when it was too successful; armed resistance—could not overcome U.S. forces)*

Answers to Review Questions

1. Responses included war, revitalization, and cultural accommodation.
2. The British worked with the Indians, making them their allies. Because the Americans simply wanted to remove the Indians, they used any means to do so. Consequently, many Indians died and their culture was destroyed.
3. The Cherokee lost land and property, farm animals, burial places of their ancestors, and a large part of their cultural identity.
4. Sample answer: Because the cultural values of the settlers and the Indians were very much at odds, it would have been difficult for them to coexist peacefully. Allow for personal opinion.
5. Timeline should include entries for 1827, 1832, 1835, 1838, and 1839.

Homework Options

Ask students to research "Mad Anthony" Wayne and write a paragraph about him.

Study Guide: page 29.

UNDERSTANDING MAPMAKING

This skill lesson will give students an opportunity to practice basic mapmaking skills.

GEOGRAPHY

Map and Globe Skills

Show the students how to determine the scale in designing a map. Draw a 12-inch square on the board. Suggest that you will use it to make a map of an area 12 miles by 12 miles. What would the scale of the map be? *(One inch = one mile)* How long would one-half mile be on the map? *(One-half inch)* Vary the exercise by using the same square to represent other areas, such as six miles by six miles.

UNDERSTANDING MAPMAKING

Designing a City Map

Here's Why

You have already seen how maps play an important role in relating the history of an area to the actual land. In this chapter you have read that the Land Ordinance of 1785 changed the way cities were planned and mapped in the Old Northwest.

Knowing how to draw your own map can be useful for many purposes. You can present information about an area you know, show the distances between places, provide directions for someone else, illustrate a certain point in a report, or enhance the understanding of a project.

Suppose you wanted to draw a map of a city, like the port city shown on the facing page. First you would need to know what makes a successful map.

Here's How

You need to consider several steps in order to make an effective map.

1. **Scale**—In designing a map, scale is one of the most important things you need to consider. You must first decide the exact area you wish to show on the map, what size the map should be, and what information you need to include. The answers to these questions will help you determine the scale of the map. The smaller the area shown, the larger the scale.
2. **Orientation**—You need to place a compass on the map. The person reading the map may not know any of the places on the map. A compass will help the reader understand the direction of the map. In the map on the next page, you will notice that a compass has been included in the lower right-hand corner, so that you can see which direction is north.
3. **Labels**—You need to label the places, streets, land masses, waterways, countries, and cities, so that the person reading the map understands what is being shown. For example, notice in the port city map that the streets running northwest to southeast are numbered and that the streets running perpendicular to them are named.
4. **Symbols**—It is important to choose symbols that are easily understood. You can choose symbols that are direct representations like the lighthouse in the port city map. You can also choose ones that are more symbolic like the dollar sign representing the bank.

   Many symbols can change from one map to another. For example, a black dot may indicate a city on one map and an oil refinery on another. Therefore it is also important to draw a legend that includes all the symbols used on the map. On the port city map you will see that both highways and railroads are lines. It is necessary, then, to look at the colors on the legend to determine which is being shown.
5. **Distance**—It is important to be able to understand the distances between places on a map. So that these distances can be measured on your map, you need to include a scale. When you look at the port city map, you will see that the scale has been included in the lower right-hand corner. It shows that one-half mile in the city is represented by one inch on a ruler. Using a ruler, you will see that the distance between the center of the market and the city hall is two inches, or one mile.

Finally, it is important to be accurate when you use all of the above criteria to make your map. If you choose an appropriate scale for the area shown, orient your reader with a compass, give labels that are correct and easy to read, place your symbols accurately, and draw a correct scale for measuring distance, you will create a successful map.

Try It

Trace the map on the next page on another piece of paper. First choose names for the town and the bodies of water, and label them where they will be easy to read. Using the symbols

Objective

Use scale and distance symbols to design a map. (Map and Globe Skills 4)

Bulletin Board

If possible, find and display on the bulletin board an actual map of your city or town. Compare its scale and symbols with those on page 209. Encourage students to take turns describing a place they have been and using the map to demonstrate the route they took to get there.

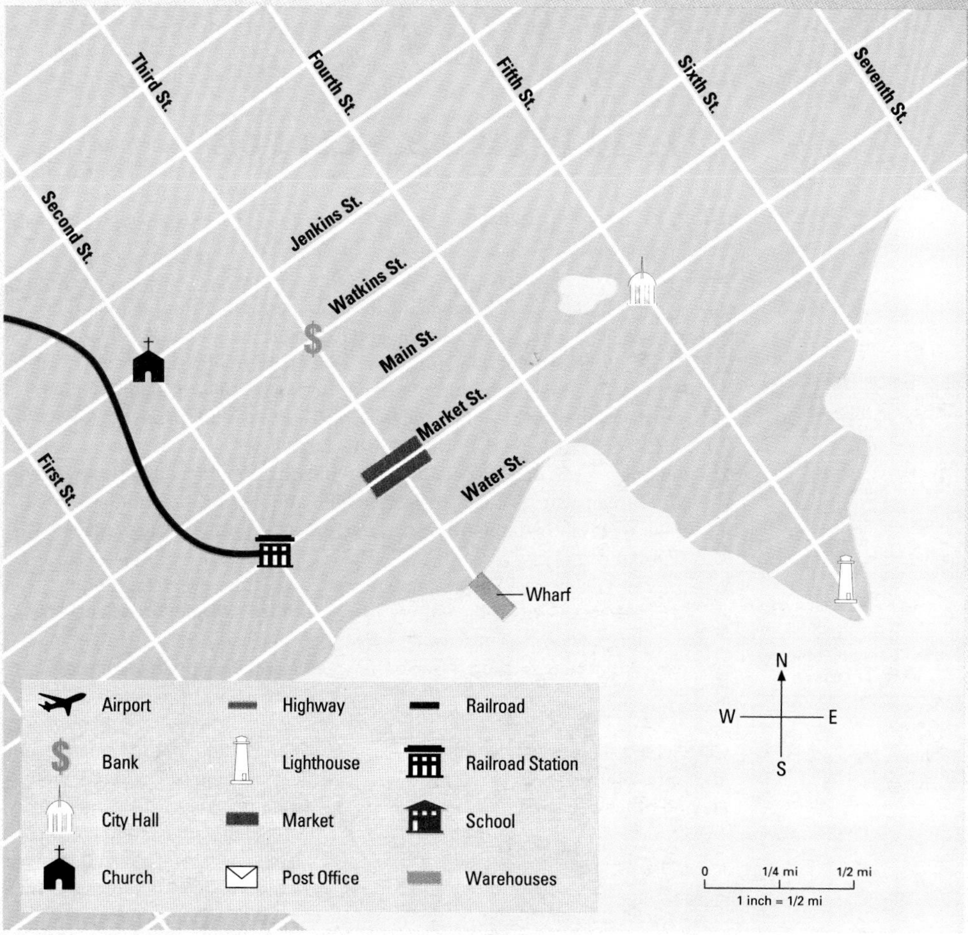

provided, add a school on Jenkins Street three-quarters of a mile from the church. Include an industrial section with warehouses, and have it take up most of the city block three-quarters to one mile northwest of the lighthouse between Fourth and Fifth Streets. Add an airport on Main Street two miles east of the intersection of Main and Third Street, and include a major highway that intersects with the airport. Choose a partner to work with, and decide what other places of interest should be included on the map. Have your partner give you directions about where these new places are, and add those places on the map. Remember to design appropriate symbols and to include them in your legend.

Apply It

Suppose you want to give directions to your house to a friend who has never been to your town. Make a map of your neighborhood using the steps outlined on the previous page. Exchange your map with a friend or classmate, and have them take a trip to your house by following your map to see if you have created a successful map.

GEOGRAPHY

Map and Globe Skills

To assist students in making maps of their town, help them determine direction. From which direction does the sun rise? *(East)* In which direction does it set? *(West)* After this basic orientation, students should be able to draw a compass rose on their maps.

Answers to Try It

Make sure that students place the additional symbols in the proper places on the map. Discuss the new symbols and the places that the pairs of students have added to their maps.

Answers to Apply It

Students can check their work by having a classmate analyze it. If students find that their map is not detailed enough for a friend to use it accurately, they should analyze why and make suitable additions to the map. Make sure that each map contains a compass rose, labels, symbols, and a distance scale.

Map and Globe Skills

Divide the class into groups of five. Have each group make a map that shows the school and also the home of each group member. Each member should then mark the route he or she uses to go to school and add symbols to show some of the places along the route. Groups should compare their maps to identify similarities and differences.

INTRODUCE

Have students read the lesson title and Thinking Focus to determine where the next wave of immigrants was to come from. *(Germany and Ireland)* Remind students that from 1620 to 1820 the majority of immigrants had been British.

Review the key terms *immigrant* (Chapter 2) and *migrate* (Lesson 2 of this chapter). Help students distinguish between *immigrant* and *emigrate*. (An immigrant is a person who comes into a place; a person emigrates when leaving a place) Ask students to read to find out why these people emigrated.

Key Terms

Vocabulary strategies: T36–37

emigrate—to leave one country forever to settle in another

famine—a drastic and wide-reaching shortage of food

nativism—a policy favoring the interests of native-born inhabitants over those of immigrants

1790 1800 1810 1820 1860

LESSON 4

The Next Wave of Immigrants

THINKING FOCUS

What experiences characterized German and Irish immigration to the United States in the 1840s and 1850s?

Key Terms

- emigrate
- famine
- nativism

On the 17th of September, 1852, my young wife and I entered the harbor of New York. . . . Having determined to make the United States my permanent home, I was resolved to look at everything from the brightest side, and not to permit myself to be discouraged by any disappointment. . . I remember well our first walk to see the town: —the very bustle on the principal streets; the men, old and young, mostly looking serious and preoccupied, and moving on with energetic rapidity; the women also appearing sober-minded and busy, although many of them were clothed in loud colors, red, green, yellow, or blue of a very pronounced glare.

We observed huge banners stretched across the street, upon which were inscribed the names of . . . candidates for the presidency and the vice-presidency—names which at that time had, to me, no meaning, except that they indicated the existence of competing political parties.

Carl Schurz, *The Reminiscences of Carl Schurz*

Carl Schurz fled his native Germany after a revolution there failed in 1849. He and other educated Germans had fought for a more democratic government. Defeated, many sailed for America.

Schurz adjusted quickly to American society, farming in Wisconsin and learning English by reading the newspapers. By 1858, Schurz had left farming to practice law. His legal knowledge impressed many of the more established Wisconsin politicians in the Republican Party. In 1861, Schurz was appointed ambassador to Spain by President Lincoln. Later he served as a senator from Missouri and as secretary of the interior in the administration of President Rutherford B. Hayes.

Carl Schurz and his wife, Margaretha Meyer Schurz, in 1852. Margaretha established the first kindergarten in the United States.

Objectives

1. Name the reasons for German and Irish immigration in the 1840s and 1850s.
2. Compare and contrast the experiences of German and Irish immigrants during their integration into the U.S. economy.
3. Define nativism, describe its sources in the 1850s, and explain its impact on Irish immigrants.

Graphic Overview

	Germans	Irish
Immigrants	artisans, middle class	tenant farmers, unskilled workers
Motivation	wanted political, economic freedom	fled poverty
U.S. Settlement	East and Midwest	Eastern cities
Life in U.S.	some economic success	remained poor, faced nativism

A New Generation of Europeans Arrives

During the 1820s, some 500,000 people arrived in the United States from Germany, Ireland, and other countries. But that number grew quickly. In the 1850s, 2.7 million people would **emigrate** from European countries. They left their homelands forever, to live in the United States. Like Schurz, many Germans who arrived after 1849 were running from the political turmoil of a failed revolution. But for the Irish, it was **famine,** a devastating food shortage, that drove them from their homeland.

While the situations in Germany and Ireland served to push people out of Europe, many also came because of what the United States had to offer. In America, as in few other places, people participated in their own government. There was plenty of land here and it was relatively easy to get. The discovery of gold in California in 1849 drew those who looked for riches. The rise of manufacturing promised the immigrants—the new arrivals—jobs and hope for a better life.

Germans Seek Democracy

By the mid-1800s, German intellectuals had lost patience with slow political reform in their country. Several years of bad crops and rising unemployment also caused great dissatisfaction. The intellectuals wanted a more democratic government, with representation for all Germans. But in 1849 their attempt to write a new constitution was put down. Government officials had rebels imprisoned, and soon afterward the "Parliament of Professors"—educated reformers—broke up. Intellectuals were not the only ones left discouraged. German tradespeople were not doing well because of competition from Great Britain's growing factory system.

The United States, especially the farmlands of the Midwest and the Great Plains, offered these immigrants political freedom and the chance for economic independence. Selling their belongings and withdrawing their savings, they set sail for the United States.

▲ *This print, titled* Helpless Mouths, *shows the conditions that caused many Irish people to come to America.*

Irish Flee Potato Famine

Economic conditions in Ireland had been getting worse for generations. It was not unusual for a person to live on a diet of half a dozen potatoes and a cup of milk each day. Sadly, this situation grew even more desperate. A destructive blight, or plant disease, struck the Irish potato fields in the 1840s and 1850s. The blight wiped out nearly the whole potato crop. In 1847, the Irish government sent agents into the countryside. One of them reported, "All I met told me they were going to give up the land, for they had neither food nor strength to till it."

With the mainstay of the Irish diet destroyed, hundreds of people died each month

▼ *The potato blight struck first at the plant below ground. The blight caused a major food shortage in Ireland in 1847.*

DEVELOP

Copy on the board the structure and main headings of the Graphic Overview from page 210 and have students copy it in their notes. As they read the lesson, students should list the differences in the experiences of German and Irish immigrants.

HISTORY

Critical Thinking

How did the motivations of the Germans and Irish differ? *(Germans—wanted political freedom and economic independence; Irish—flight from famine)* How were their motivations similar? *(Hoped for a better life in America)*

Access Strategy

Have students recall earlier examples in this book of people who left a homeland to travel, at considerable danger and expense, to an unknown land. *(The Pilgrims, the trans-Appalachian pioneers)* Ask students why people might want to come to America. *(To find religious or political freedom, to gain a better financial situation, to have a new beginning)* Explain that some of these motivations apply to the German and Irish immigrants they will read about in this lesson.

Access Activity

Ask students to imagine that they are emigrating from their homeland. How would they feel? *(Excited, scared, sad)* Have them name their hopes for life in the new land. *(New friends, good school)* What might their parents hope for? *(Good jobs, nice home)*

HISTORY

Visual Learning

Students can compare Liam O'Flaherty's description on this page with the print titled "Helpless Mouths" on page 211. Which elements in the picture match O'Flaherty's description? *(Extreme poverty—close quarters, dirt floor, no door, smoky fire)* Ask students to imagine all the items in O'Flaherty's description placed within the space in the print, which appears to be about eight by ten feet. What does the print reveal about why so many Irish emigrated? *(Terrible living conditions)*

■ *Economic hardships, political turmoil, and famine drove many people out of Europe.*

from starvation and disease. Families barely survived in houses like the one Liam O'Flaherty described in his novel *Famine:*

> The living-room was in a very sordid state, which was only natural on account of all those children romping about in a chamber that was only ten feet by eight, with a great deal of that space occupied by the furniture, cooking utensils, and farming tools. There was even some oat straw and a little heap of potatoes, all that was left of the year's crop.

Millions left Ireland, going anywhere that offered a chance for a better life. Over 1.5 million came to the United States.

Most Irish immigrants were poor tenant farmers and unskilled laborers. Since they had no land of their own to sell, most were not able to pay for their passage. But money came from relief organizations, relatives, and even local Irish governments. Some officials encouraged the poor to emigrate. This took some of the strain off public welfare budgets.

■ *What kind of hardships drove people from Europe to the United States?*

Immigrants Suffer En Route

No matter where they came from, most immigrants had a horrifying experience during their passage to the New World. A more prosperous passenger observed that the Irish people aboard his westbound ship were "full of wretchedness. Need and oppression stared within their eyes; upon their backs hung ragged misery. The world was not their friend."

They sailed in vessels known to people of the time as "plague ships" and "floating coffins." The trip could last three or four months. Hundreds of people crowded between the decks, and diseases spread rapidly. As of 1845, 20 percent of all those immigrating to America died during the voyage. One ship lost over 500 of the 1,100 German immigrants on board. ■

Immigrants Establish Themselves in the New Country

What awaited these immigrants when they finally stepped ashore? Their experiences would depend entirely on their individual situations.

Many Germans had worked in the old country as artisans or skilled laborers. They came to the United States with some savings and a valuable skill. In Germany, one's status was measured by the size of one's land holdings. Thus, many newly arrived Germans were eager to earn money quickly in order to buy land on the American frontier. Communities of

➤ *German immigrants tended to form close communities in their new home. In this 1856 drawing, German newcomers enjoy a Christmas gathering in an elegant New York building known as the Winter Garden.*

Map and Globe Skills

Have students use the world map in the Atlas on pages 694–695 to determine the distance from Ireland and Germany to the United States. *(4,000-5,000 miles)* Because many immigrants spent as much as three months on board ship, have students divide the distance by 90 to determine approximately how far ships traveled each day. *(44–55 miles a day)*

Historical Context

Although in 1997 the population of Ireland was less than four million, in 1840 it was 16 million, making it the most densely populated country in Europe. Some Irish emigrated for religious reasons. The Catholic majority in Ireland had been severely repressed since the late 1600s, when a Protestant was restored to the English throne. Catholics could neither vote nor hold office. Protestant landlords charged such high rents for farmland that making a living was very difficult.

Many Irish emigrated for financial reasons. The potato blight hit people who were already weakened from decades of extreme poverty. Thousands of Irish died from starvation, and over a million died from fevers that they had no strength to resist.

Between 1820 and 1850, over 42 percent of all immigrants to the United States were Irish. Today more than 30 million Americans trace their roots to Ireland.

Where German Immigrants Settled, 1860

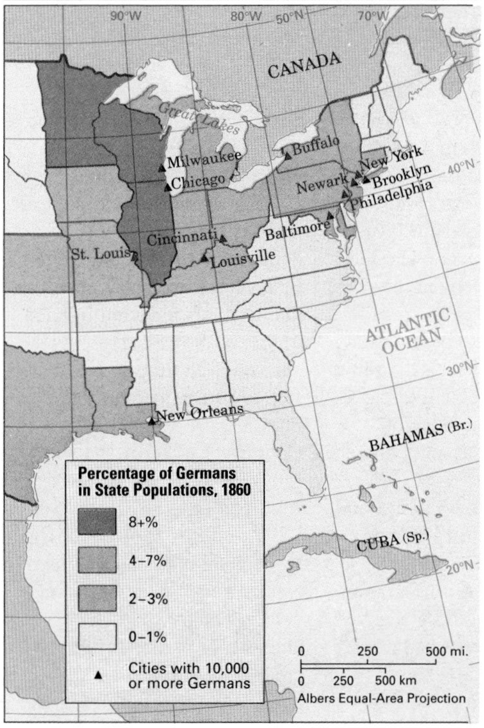

Where Irish Immigrants Settled, 1860

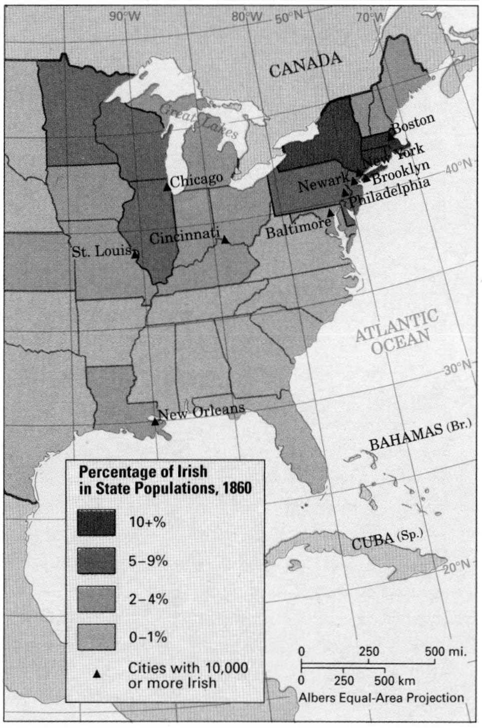

German immigrants tended to settle where good farm land was available. Generally, they stayed together as families. Irish immigrants tended to cluster in cities.

German immigrants grew in the seaport cities of the Northeast and in the midwestern cities of Cincinnati, St. Louis, Milwaukee, and Chicago.

Some immigrants already had cash from sales of their farms in Germany. They settled in the fertile countryside of Illinois, Michigan, Wisconsin, and the Great Plains.

For the most part, German immigrants were able to achieve a secure livelihood for themselves and their children. Though they sometimes met resentment from native-born Americans, they had little trouble with their neighbors.

The Irish, however, often had a far different experience. Penniless and unskilled, most Irish immigrants could not afford the cost of moving to the frontier of the United States. Compare the distribution of Irish and German immigrants in the two maps above.

The Irish immigrants often had to take whatever jobs they could find. Men collected rubbish, dug ditches and cellars, and labored in the building of canals and railroads. Women worked as cooks, laundresses, and servants. The housing they could afford was usually crowded and unhealthy. With hard work, Irish immigrants eventually gained some stability. ■

■ *Why did most Germans find it easier to establish themselves in America than did most Irish?*

New Americans Perceived as a Threat

The new immigrants had arrived with high hopes. Many native-born Americans accepted the immigrants and helped them adjust to American society. But a backlash of fear and resentment also developed.

The same Americans who found the Irish useful as cheap labor feared that the immigrants would take away their own jobs. Others worried that voting immigrants might become a powerful and dangerous political force.

GEOGRAPHY

Map and Globe Skills

Have students use the two maps on this page to identify the greatest concentrations of Germans and Irish in the United States. Which cities had both high German and high Irish populations? *(St. Louis, Chicago, Cincinnati, Newark, New York, Brooklyn, Philadelphia, Baltimore)* In which region did German immigrants form a significant percentage of the total population? *(In the Midwest)* Irish? *(In the East)* How could the two maps be combined into one? *(By using color coding)*

■ *Many German immigrants had skills and money; most Irish were unskilled and poor.*

Health Connection

Although the potato-and-milk diet of many Irish in the 1800s was inadequate, it was not as nutritionally deficient as one might think. Have students look in an encyclopedia to compare the nutritional composition of potatoes and milk with that of an adequate diet. Also, have students find out the caloric needs of the average person. *(1,800 to 4,000 a day)* Why did many Irish starve and succumb to disease? *(Dependence on a single crop; inadequate intake of calories)*

Music Connection

Immigrants brought their backgrounds and culture to this country. One part of that culture was the music. Have students find examples of Irish jigs and reels and German waltzes of the middle to late 1800s and play recordings of the music in class.

Critical Thinking

Ask students to recall why the trans-Appalachian pioneers migrated. *(Inadequate supply of land in the East)* Why did many German immigrants settle on the frontier? *(Same reason—to have enough land to farm)*

CULTURE

Critical Thinking

The movement of people has been a major theme of this chapter. Heighten students' empathy for migrating people by asking them to recall any experiences that they have had moving to a new place: a new country, state, city, even a neighborhood or school. Ask students how they first felt when they were in the new place. What experiences do they recall most vividly? What experiences helped them to become accustomed to the new place?

Understanding Immigration

In 1800, the population of Ohio was 45,365 people; in 1810, it was 230,760. The population of the state had grown to more than five times its size in only 10 years. The reasons for the state's enormous growth in such a short time are many, and included emigration from both the east coast and from other countries.

Terms for the movement of people can be confusing. The general term *migration* refers to any permanent movement of people from one country or region to settle in another. *Emigration* is the act of moving away from one's country or region to another (*e* means "out"). *Immigration* means entering or settling in a new country other than one's own (*im* means "in"). Thus newcomers to this country are always both emigrants (for example, from Ireland) and immigrants (into the United States).

Of course, everyone in the United States is a descendant of someone who once immigrated here. Only American Indians, Inuits, and Hawaiians are considered natives of this country.

Reasons for Immigration

Scholars who study migration movements worldwide speak of the "push-pull factors." What they mean is that sometimes the "push factor," such as the failure of the Irish potato crop in 1847, is a major cause of emigration. At other times, the "pull factor," such as the lure of gold in California in 1849, is the main reason for immigration. More frequently, the reasons are multiple, and are a combination of push and pull.

When reviewing the history of immigration to the United States, the push-pull factor is a useful tool of analysis. For example, the Quakers who left England and Europe in the 1660s were fleeing from religious and political persecution in their homelands. At the same time, they were pulled to the New World by the hope of achieving religious and political freedom here.

To economic, religious, and political reasons for immigration must be added a fourth factor—the forced immigration up until 1808 of Africans as slaves. The Africans had no choice in selecting whether to stay or to immigrate, so the push-pull factor did not work for them.

Immigration Today

The same push-pull factors can be applied to many foreigners who seek refuge in the United States today. The Jews and Pentecostal Christians who have left the Soviet Union for the United States exemplify the push-pull of religious persecution and opportunity. The displaced peoples of Southeast Asia and of Central America come because of political persecution at home and hope for political freedom here.

After one year's residence, refugees may change their status to that of permanent residents, which is a necessary first step toward naturalization, or becoming a citizen. In 1988, 110,721 refugees adjusted their status to permanent residents. This unusually high number was a result of changes in the immigration law that took effect during this period.

The economic and political reasons for entering a rich democracy such as the United States have been so compelling that millions have immigrated to this country illegally. As a correction to this, and as a first step toward remedying its immigration programs, Congress passed in 1986 an Immigration Reform and Control Act.

The IRCA allowed for legal registration of aliens who had resided here continuously since before January 1, 1982. This amnesty, or pardon for illegal entrance, combined with the annual acceptance of refugees, raised the number of immigrants during the 1980s to a new high.

Destinations of Immigrants

The largest number of immigrants today come to join family members who already live in the United States. This tradition has existed in America since its earliest days of settlement.

Most immigrants, in the past as well as today, headed for the large urban centers. In the cities, immigrants can attach themselves to communities of people who share the same ethnic background. Still later, they will change from immigrants to ethnic Americans. They will assume new identities by retaining some aspects of their ancestral heritage even as they adopt new practices and ways of thinking.

Critical Thinking

Discuss nativism (defined on page 215) with students. What are some of the effects of prejudice? *(Exclusion of population groups from voting; restricted economic opportunities when jobs are given only to native-born people; riots and violence)*

Role Playing

Divide the class into pairs to role play a conversation between an Irish immigrant and a native-born American employer. Students should discuss jobs, housing, and culture, using information from the lesson as a basis. After a few minutes, have partners change roles and continue their discussion.

Writing an Editorial

Have students write a newspaper editorial summarizing the history of the Know-Nothings and criticizing the party for being opposed to democratic principles. Students may support their arguments by citing statements from the Constitution guaranteeing equality. (An annotated version of the Constitution begins on page 636.)

Anti-Catholic Feelings

America was at that time a nation of Protestants. The Irish, who were Catholics, were widely feared and hated because of their strong ties to the Pope. Protestants feared that the Pope would gain political power in America through his Irish Catholic supporters. These feelings led to signs reading "No Irish Need Apply." Even worse, in some cities mobs attacked Catholic churches and schools.

This rise of strong feelings against immigrants formed part of a social movement called **nativism**. In this movement, established, native-born Americans glorified their own culture and condemned immigrant cultures. A number of societies whose aim was to control the new immigrants began to form. In the Northeast, the Native American Association was founded in 1837. It grew into the Native American Party, which gathered political support in the West and South by 1845.

Several of these societies united to form the Supreme Order of the Star Spangled Banner in 1850 and the American Party in 1854. Even though members of these groups met openly, all the proceedings were conducted under strict rules of secrecy. These societies had a number of undemocratic goals. They wanted to ban Catholics and aliens from elected office, to cut down on immigration, and to establish requirements that would limit immigrants' voting rights. Clearly, some Americans felt very threatened by the arrival of new people from foreign lands.

The Know-Nothings

Members of the American Party were called "Know-Nothings" because they answered "I don't know" when asked about their policies. The Know-Nothings influenced elections for several years. At one point, they even managed to control the Massachusetts government. But they remained weak in the West and never became a truly national political force.

By the late 1850s, the influence of the Know-Nothings was no longer very strong. The party's public image, it seemed, was hurt by its intense secrecy and hatred.The conflicts between native-born Americans and immigrants, between the East and the frontier, and between Indians and whites were being overshadowed by the great division between the Northern and Southern regions. ■

▲ *The Irish gradually overcame the troubles they found in America. This picture shows a lively St. Patrick's Day parade in New York City, a tradition that continues today.*

■ *Why did some Americans feel economically and politically threatened by the large immigrant population?*

R E V I E W

1. **FOCUS** What experiences characterized German and Irish immigration to the United States in the 1840s and 1850s?
2. **CONNECT** How was the social and economic position of Irish immigrants similar to that of free blacks?
3. **CRITICAL THINKING** Why might a German craftsman have been better off settling on the frontier than in Boston, New York, or Charleston?
4. **CULTURE** What advantages might immigrants gain by forming communities of their own? What might be the disadvantages?
5. **ACTIVITY** Prepare an oral report on an immigrant who has made important contributions to American society. Explain when and why the person came to the United States. Describe his or her achievements. Why was it possible for this person to succeed in the United States?

SOCIAL SYSTEMS

Critical Thinking

Ask students in what ways the feelings of the Know-Nothings were typical of supporters of nativism. *(Anti-Catholic, anti-immigrant)* Were the Know-Nothings truly "native" Americans? *(No; their ancestors were earlier immigrants.)*

■ *Immigrants caused more competition for jobs. They also had the potential for a strong voice in politics.*

C L O S E

Have students answer the Thinking Focus. Copy on the board the Graphic Overview on page 210 and have students compare it to the lists that they made while reading the lesson. As a review of the lesson, have students do the role play described on page 214 .

Answers to Review Questions

1. Middle-class Germans arrived with some money, settled in the Midwest, and generally found success. Poor Irish immigrants usually remained poor, settled in the East, and experienced discrimination.
2. Both Irish and free black Americans faced discrimination and economic restrictions.
3. Sample answer: The frontier offered many job opportunities and less competition than could be found in the East. Allow for personal opinion.
4. By forming their own communities, immigrants could pool their resources and find mutual support, but they might still face discrimination.
5. After students have given their reports, discuss with them the similarities and differences in the various immigrants' experiences.

Homework Options

Students can research the immigration of the Italians or Japanese to the United States, including why they emigrated, when they first arrived, and what their early experiences were.

Study Guide: page 31.

Answers to Reviewing Key Terms

A. Sample answers:

1. Catharine Beecher helped establish institutions and wrote "how-to" books that were popular with the middle and the working classes.
2. People who migrated moved from one area to another; those who emigrated left one country and moved to another.
3. Some Indian leaders favored the revitilization of their culture to resist the white settlers, but others wanted to keep peace through cultural accomodation.
4. Many Irish emigrated from Ireland to escape the famine.

B. Answers:

1. False. Some settlers floated down the Mississippi in crude steamboats.
2. True. Settlers started schools, churches and governments.
3. False. Working-class people worked in mills, factories, and workshops for hourly wages.
4. True. When crops fail, there can be severe food shortages.
5. False. People who believed in nativism condemned the most recent immigrants.

Answers to Exploring Concepts

A. Answers:

Young Eastern farmers: moved to the West / to farm their own land; to Atlantic seaports / to seek new business and trade

Free blacks: moved to coastal cities / to find jobs; to the West / to find land and escape discrimination

Creek Indians: moved to southern and western Alabama / driven off land in Tennessee

Cherokee Indians: moved to the West / driven off land in Georgia

German immigrants: moved to seaport cities in the Northeast and to farmlands of the Midwest and Great Plains / for greater opportunities

Irish immigrants: moved to the large Atlantic coastal cities / to escape famine in Ireland

B. Sample answers:

1. Both increased world demand for wheat, causing prices to rise and American trade to grow.
2. The McCormick reaper and the steel-blade plow helped American farmers to become more efficient and allowed them to increase trade.
3. Farm women spent less time making household goods. Some women worked in factories; others went West to teach.
4. They organized groups, like the Boston African Society and Free African Society.
5. Novels glorified life on the frontier, and better roads and other forms of transportation made migration easier.
6. The Indians lost land in the treaties of Greenville and Fort Wayne, and the treaty that ended the Red Stick uprising.
7. Indians were defeated in battle, their treaties were not respected, and the U. S. government allowed settlers to take their land.
8. Many German immigrants were educated and had marketable skills and some savings, so they were able to get good jobs. Because many Irish were poor and unskilled, they took menial jobs.
9. Many roads were dusty and muddy, some were narrow passages filled with tree stumps, and the best were only surfaced with stone and gravel.

Chapter Review

Reviewing Key Terms

cultural accommodation (p. 204)
emigrate (p. 211)
famine (p. 211)
institutions (p. 199)
middle class (p. 192)
migrate p. 197)
nativism (p. 215)
revitalization (p. 204)
working class (p. 192)

A. In each of the following pairs, the two terms are related in some way. Write a sentence for each pair that clearly explains the relationship between the two terms.

1. institutions, working class
2. migrate, emigrate
3. revitalization, cultural accommodation
4. famine, emigrate

B. Based on your reading of the chapter, decide which of the following statements are accurate. Write an explanation of each decision.

1. Some settlers floated down the Mississippi in large institutions.
2. On the frontier, the settlers had to establish their own public institutions.
3. People of the working class were those in between the Republican and Democratic parties.
4. When crops fail because of bad weather, a famine sometimes results.
5. People who believed in nativism supported the rights of American Indians.

Exploring Concepts

A. On a separate sheet of paper, make a chart like the one shown below. Then complete the chart by listing examples from the chapter that show where members of each group moved during the early 1800s and why they moved.

Group	Moved to	Reason
Young Eastern farmers		
Free blacks		
Creek Indians		
Cherokee Indians		
German immigrants		
Irish immigrants		

B. Support each of the following statements with facts and details from the chapter.

1. Population growth and wars in Europe had many effects on the United States economy.
2. New inventions contributed to changes in the United States' economy during the 1800s.
3. Women's roles at home and in society underwent great changes during the 1800s.
4. Free blacks who moved to the cities started to develop their own institutions.
5. Many factors attracted great numbers of settlers to the land across the Appalachians.
6. The United States government followed a policy of forcing Indians off their lands to make room for settlers.
7. No matter what policy the Indians followed, they were treated unfairly by the United States.
8. Immigrants' experiences in the United States were shaped by their cultural traditions and education level.
9. Westward overland travel was very difficult for the pioneers because roads were not well-constructed.

Reviewing Skills

1. Name five important elements in mapmaking.
2. Look at a map of your state in an atlas. Identify the symbols that are used in the map, such as the symbols for railroads, rivers, and cities.
3. Select a map from this book and study it carefully. Then choose a partner and give that person directions that would enable him or her to draw the map that you have studied
4. What kind of primary sources did the early cartographers use to design maps of the far west?
5. Today pictures can be taken of the earth from satellites. How is that information helpful in designing maps?

Using Critical Thinking

1. Throughout American history, people have always migrated to other areas where opportunities were greater. What effect did the migrations you read about in this chapter have on the nation? What areas of the country have people migrated to, and away from, in recent years? Are their reasons for migrating today similar to those in the past? Explain.
2. It is quite possible that within your lifetime certain areas of the United States could become as densely populated as Europe is now. What areas of the country attract the most immigrants today? Why? Do you think our government's policy toward immigrants will change? If so, explain what kinds of changes might take place and why.the government might enact them.
3. The United States' treatment of the Indians is one of the most shameful episodes in American history. What differences between the white and Indian ways of life caused conflict? Why was the United States government unsympathetic to the Indians? Do you think that if the Indians had been able to keep the lands on which they lived, they would have become part of American society as the immigrants did? Explain your answer.

Preparing for Citizenship

1. **WRITING ACTIVITY** Immigrants still come to the United States from all over the world. With a partner, gather information about current immigration from one country of your own choosing. Find out why the people are leaving their home country, why they chose the U.S. as their new home, what region of the U.S. they are settling in and why, and what kinds of jobs they are doing. Write a short report on your findings.
2. **COLLECTING INFORMATION** Interview three adults about your local community's policies toward immigrants. In your interview, ask your subjects to tell you what the policies are, as well as their own opinion of how those policies are working. Compare their responses with those of Americans of the 1850s. Do you see any similarities or differences? What are they?
3. **ART ACTIVITY** Make a copy of the family tree below. Enter the names and places of birth for your parents and grandparents. You may add onto the tree to go back further in your family history if you would like. Share your family tree with your classmates.

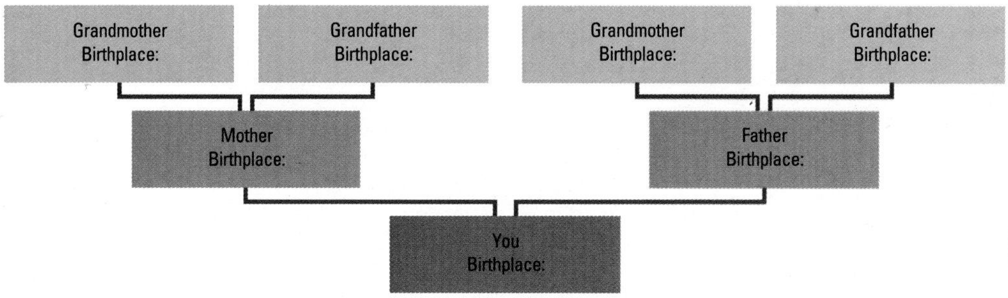

Answers to Reviewing Skills

1. Scale, orientation, labels, symbols, and distance
2. Students can also use this map to identify how the other elements are used.
3. Direct students to trace basic maps and then give directions for a particular route.
4. Refer students to Understanding Primary Sources on pages 88–89.
5. Encourage students to discuss how advances in technology can provide more detailed and accurate information.

Answers to Using Critical Thinking

1. Migrations caused Eastern seaboard cities to grow and created new settlements in the trans-Appalachian West. Students should consider how urban, suburban, and rural migration patterns have affected today's economy and politics.
2. Encourage students to compare the prejudice and hardships that German and Irish immigrants faced with how well immigrant groups are accepted today. Point out how difficult it is at first for new students in the classroom.
3. Discuss the fact that Indians did not believe that individuals could "own" land and that the government created opportunities for settlers to "earn" land.

Answers to Preparing for Citizenship

1. **WRITING ACTIVITY** Be sure students cover the political and religious beliefs as well as the economic factors for immigration.
2. **COLLECTING INFORMATION** Refer students to page 577 for interviewing skills. Students can also broaden the topic by comparing the local policies and attitudes to those on the national level.
3. **ART ACTIVITY** Be sensitive to the special concerns of adopted children and children from split homes. Students can add on other family members in addition to or in place of those on the tree. As an alternative activity, students can prepare a family tree for a friend's family or for a neighbor.

UNIT
OVERVIEW

Draw students' attention to the unit title and the narrative underneath it. Ask students if they can identify any specific regions in the United States. Encourage them to think of how these regions differ, naming factors that have contributed to the development of each region's unique identity.

Looking Back

Ask students to recall from Chapter 5 the Lousiana Purchase, which paved the way for the development of the West. Have them discuss the differences between the Northern and Southern colonies that they learned about in Chapter 1.

Looking Forward

Tell students that they will be reading about the development of America's regions in the following chapters:
Chapter 8 *The West*
Chapter 9 *The North*
Chapter 10 *The South*

Unit 4

The Development of America's Regions

The first half of the 1800s was a time of rapid expansion for the United States. The nation moved westward and acquired vast new territories. The economy grew as the nation became more industrialized. Rapid development of new roads, canals, and railroads produced a complex transportation network. As America grew, the nation's major regions developed as well. By 1860, the American West, North, and South each had its own special identity.

1790

Antique weathervanes from the 1800s.
The Shelburne Museum, Shelburne, Vermont.

GEOGRAPHY PROJECT

Comparing Maps

Geography Skill **Comparing Regions**
Students use the skill of Analyzing geographic information.

Geography Theme Place

Geography Standards 2, 6 Mental maps help people to organize information about places; experience influences people's perceptions

Activity ***Create a Brochure***

Materials construction paper, markers, crayons

Management Individual/Small Group

Select one place from each of the three regions covered in the unit: The West, The North, and The South. Then make a brochure for each place, describing its geographic characteristics and what life was like there between 1790–1860.

Have students:

- write clear, descriptive text for a brochure and/or postcards for the places selected in each region.
- make a regional map that includes the place selected in each region.
- include illustrations of what life was like in each place.
- share the brochures and/or the postcards with classmates.

Understanding the Weather Vanes

Ask students if they know the purpose that weather vanes serve. *(They point in the direction from which the wind comes.)* Point out that weather vanes are one of the oldest known weather instruments and are often ornamentally designed.

Understanding Chronology

Explain that Unit 4 covers the same time period as Unit 3 but focuses on the development of specific regions in the United States.

For research support activities, see the *Research Handbook.*

For simulations correlated to this unit, see *Citizenship Simulations*, p. iv.

HOUGHTON MIFFLIN SOCIAL STUDIES

Bookshelf II

The Underground Railroad

by Raymond Bial

Photographs and compelling text tell of the places and the heroic actions of those who traveled the Underground Railroad.

Motivate Read aloud the Foreword on pp. 3 –4 describing the impact felt by the author in telling the stories of enslaved people who traveled the Underground Railroad and those who risked arrest for harboring runaways. Ask students what caused enslaved people to risk their lives. Have students look at the chapter opener images on pp. 220–221, 251–252, and 282–283 to preview the content of Unit 4.

To connect this book with the unit content, use the planning guide and student activity blackline masters beginning on p. iv of the *Bookshelf II Teacher's Resources.*

For additional books that are Easy, Average, and Challenging, see the Unit Bibliography on page T43. See bibliography updates at www.eduplace.com/ss/hmss.

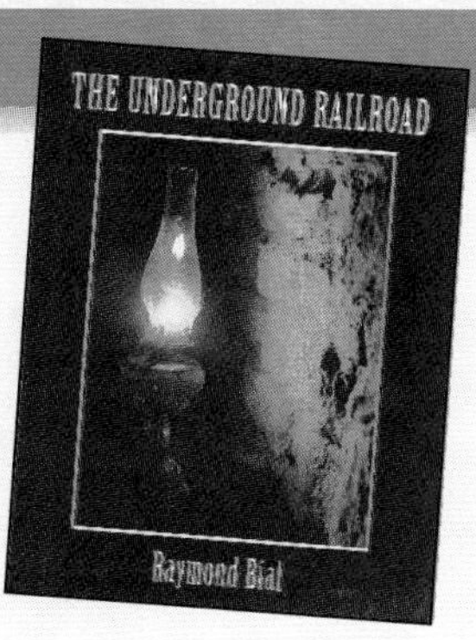

CHAPTER 8

Planning at a Glance

The West

	Objectives	Reading Support *and* Other Resources	Diverse Learning Strategies
Lesson 1 Exploring Beyond the Mississippi *pp. 222–227* 2–3 days	• Explain the importance of the exploration of the Louisiana Territory. • Evaluate how well the Lewis and Clark expedition achieved its goals. • Describe the role that the mountain men played in exploring the West.	• **Workbook** or **Reading Support:** pp. 105–108 Review p. 25 Extra Support/Transition p. 25 Multi-lang. Sum. pp. 49–50 • **Other Resources:** Geography Kit, Poster 3, Study Guide p. 32	Access Act. **(SDAIE)** TE p. 223 Interviewing **(Auditory)** TE p. 226 Making a Map **(Kinesthetic)** TE p. 226 Audiotapes of Multi-language Lesson Summaries **(Auditory)**
Skill: Outlining Lewis and Clark's Expedition *pp. 228–229*	• Use information about Lewis and Clark to develop a chronological outline.	• **Other Resources:** Study Guide p. 33	
Lesson 2 Achieving Manifest Destiny *pp. 230–235* 1–2 days	• Explain how war with Mexico helped the United States achieve its Manifest Destiny. • Explain how changes in relations between U.S. settlers in Texas and the Mexican government led to Texas' independence.	• **Workbook** or **Reading Support:** pp. 109–112 Review p. 26 Extra Support/Transition p. 26 Multi-lang. Sum. pp. 51–52 • **Other Resources:** Geography Kit, Study Guide p. 34	Access Strat. **(Extra Support)** TE p. 231 Language Arts Connection **(Visual)** TE p. 233 Writing a Narrative **(GATE)** TE p. 233 Audiotapes of Multi-language Lesson Summaries **(Auditory)**
Lesson 3 Settling the West *pp. 236–240* 1–2 days	• Describe life on the California missions and ranchos before and after the missions were secularized. • Compare the religious motives of the Mormons with those of the Oregon missionaries. • Explain how Oregon became part of the United States.	• **Workbook** or **Reading Support:** pp. 113–116 Review p. 27 Extra Support/Transition p. 27 Multi-lang. Sum. pp. 53–54 • **Other Resources:** Study Guide p. 35	Access Act. **(SDAIE)** TE p. 237 Map and Globe Skills **(Visual)** TE p. 239 Homework Options **(GATE)** TE p. 240 Audiotapes of Multi-language Lesson Summaries **(Auditory)**
Lesson 4 Surviving on the Frontier *pp. 241–247* 2–3 days **Literature** "The Oregon Trail" *pp. 248–249*	• Identify the impact of the California gold discovery on Californios, Indians, and pioneers. • Explain why mining towns appeared and disappeared. • Examine primary sources to infer the kind of life pioneers led.	• **Workbook** or **Reading Support:** pp. 117–120 Review p. 28 Extra Support/Transition p. 28 Multi-lang. Sum. pp. 55–56 • **Other Resources:** Poster 5; Study Guide p. 36; Study Prints 5, 6	Access Act. **(SDAIE)** TE p. 242 Art Connection **(Visual)** TE p. 244 Reader's Theatre **(Auditory)** TE p. 246 Audiotapes of Multi-language Lesson Summaries **(Auditory)**
Chapter Review *pp. 250–251* 1 day		Chapter 8 Test pp. 29–32 *(See facsimiles on TE p. 756.)*	Assessment Multiple-Use Masters pp. 81–88

Reading Support Resources *for Every Lesson*

Reading and Review

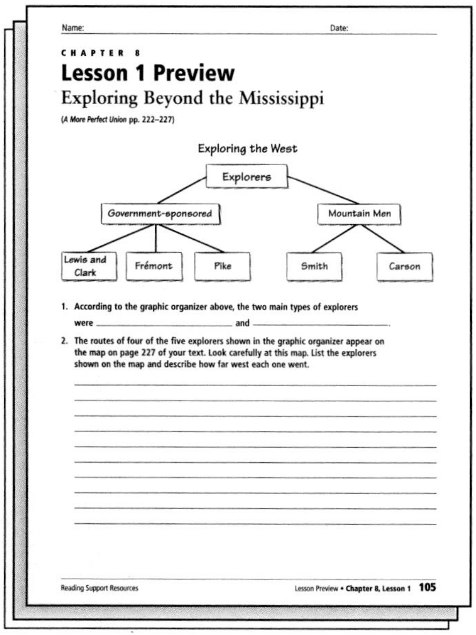
Name: Date:

CHAPTER 8

Lesson 1 Preview

Exploring Beyond the Mississippi

(*A More Perfect Union* pp. 222–227)

Exploring the West

Explorers — Government-sponsored: Lewis and Clark, Frémont, Pike; Mountain Men: Smith, Carson

1. According to the graphic organizer above, the two main types of explorers were ________ and ________.
2. The routes of four of the five explorers shown in the graphic organizer appear on the map on page 227 of your text. Look carefully at this map. List the explorers shown on the map and describe how far west each one went.

Reading Support Resources — Lesson Preview • Chapter 8, Lesson 1 — 105

- **Chapter Overview*** p. 104
- **Lesson Previews*** using graphic organizers from the Teacher's Edition pp. 105, 109, 113, 117
- **Reading Strategies*** pp. 106, 110, 114, 118
- **Lesson Summaries*** pp. 107–108, 111–112, 115–116, 119–120
- **Lesson Reviews** pp. 25, 26, 27, 28

* **Workbook** includes starred items.

Multi-language Summaries

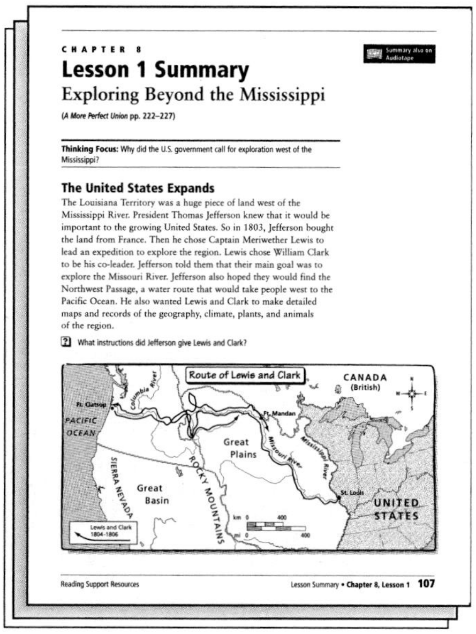
CHAPTER 8

Lesson 1 Summary

Summary also on Audiotape

Exploring Beyond the Mississippi

(*A More Perfect Union* pp. 222–227)

Thinking Focus: Why did the U.S. government call for exploration west of the Mississippi?

The United States Expands

The Louisiana Territory was a huge piece of land west of the Mississippi River. President Thomas Jefferson knew that it would be important to the growing United States. So in 1803, Jefferson bought the land from France. Then he chose Captain Meriwether Lewis to lead an expedition to explore the region. Lewis chose William Clark to be his co-leader. Jefferson told them that their main goal was to explore the Missouri River. Jefferson also hoped they would find the Northwest Passage, a water route that would take people west to the Pacific Ocean. He also wanted Lewis and Clark to make detailed maps and records of the geography, climate, plants, and animals of the region.

? What instructions did Jefferson give Lewis and Clark?

Reading Support Resources — Lesson Summary • Chapter 8, Lesson 1 — 107

Lesson Summaries in:

- English (See Reading and Review.)
- Spanish pp. 107–108, 111–112, 115–116, 119–120
- Chinese pp. 49–56
- Hmong pp. 49–56
- Khmer pp. 49–56
- Vietnamese pp. 49–56

Summaries available on audiotapes

Lesson Support / Transition

S D A I E

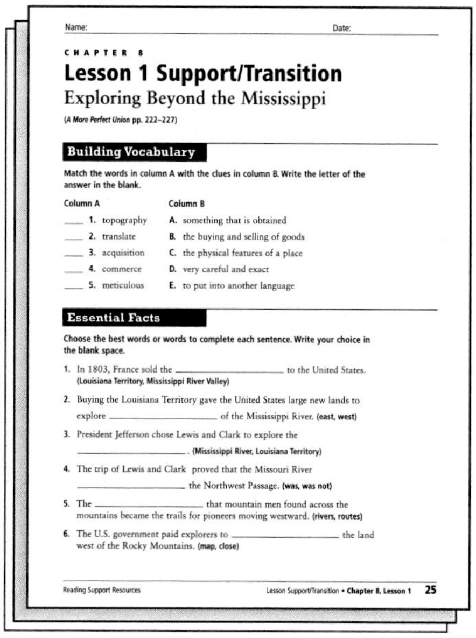
Name: Date:

CHAPTER 8

Lesson 1 Support/Transition

Exploring Beyond the Mississippi

(*A More Perfect Union* pp. 222–227)

Building Vocabulary

Match the words in column A with the clues in column B. Write the letter of the answer in the blank.

Column A	Column B
___ 1. topography	A. something that is obtained
___ 2. translate	B. the buying and selling of goods
___ 3. acquisition	C. the physical features of a place
___ 4. commerce	D. very careful and exact
___ 5. meticulous	E. to put into another language

Essential Facts

Choose the best words or words to complete each sentence. Write your choice in the blank space.

1. In 1803, France sold the ________ to the United States. (Louisiana Territory, Mississippi River Valley)
2. Buying the Louisiana Territory gave the United States large new lands to explore ________ of the Mississippi River. (east, west)
3. President Jefferson chose Lewis and Clark to explore the ________. (Mississippi River, Louisiana Territory)
4. The trip of Lewis and Clark proved that the Missouri River ________ the Northwest Passage. (was, was not)
5. The ________ that mountain men found across the mountains became the trails for pioneers moving westward. (rivers, routes)
6. The U.S. government paid explorers to ________ the land west of the Rocky Mountains. (map, close)

Reading Support Resources — Lesson Support/Transition • Chapter 8, Lesson 1 — 25

Activities for SDAIE
Specially **D**esigned **A**cademic **I**nstruction in **E**nglish

- **Lesson Support/Transition** pp. 25, 26, 27, 28

Technology Options

Internet Support

http://www.eduplace.com

Social Studies Center at Education Place

Internet support for Chapter 8:

- ***Lesson at a Glance***
- ***The Battle of the Alamo***

Videotape/Videodisc

We the People:
Supports and enhances major topics: **Theme: *Moving West***
Channel R.E.A.D.® Blue Jeans

Software

***Student Writing Center*®** (CD-ROM) (Macintosh® or Windows®)
***Oregon Trail II*®** (CD-ROM)

School to Career

Mining technology has advanced a great deal since the gold rush of 1848, but the search for most minerals still takes individuals deep beneath the earth's surface. Ask students to select a mineral that is mined and create a flow chart showing the process and listing the skills of the miners at each step.

Character Education

Travellers on the journey west to the frontier had to have courage, stamina, and determination. Accounts of these treks can be found in archives, libraries, and museums. Help students use these resources to write their own play or movie about the journey's adventures. Have them highlight the characteristics of the pioneers that made their journeys possible.

CHAPTER
PREVIEW

Direct students to read the chapter title and the narrative under it. Point out that at this time "the West" referred to almost anywhere west of the 13 colonies. Refer students to the Lewis and Clark compass and to the Frémont map on this page, emphasizing the vastness and mystery of the new frontier.

Looking Back

Have students recall from Chapter 5 why Jefferson thought the Louisiana Purchase was important. *(Assured access to Mississippi River, provided new land for farming)*

Looking Forward

Tell students that they will learn how the United States expanded westward in the following four lessons: Exploring Beyond the Mississippi, Achieving Manifest Destiny, Settling the West, and Surviving on the Frontier.

Chapter 8

The West

By 1850, the nation had pushed its boundaries to the shores of the Pacific Ocean. Explorers, eager to learn about the new land, crisscrossed unknown mountains and deserts. In their footsteps went daring men and women who built communities out of the wilderness.

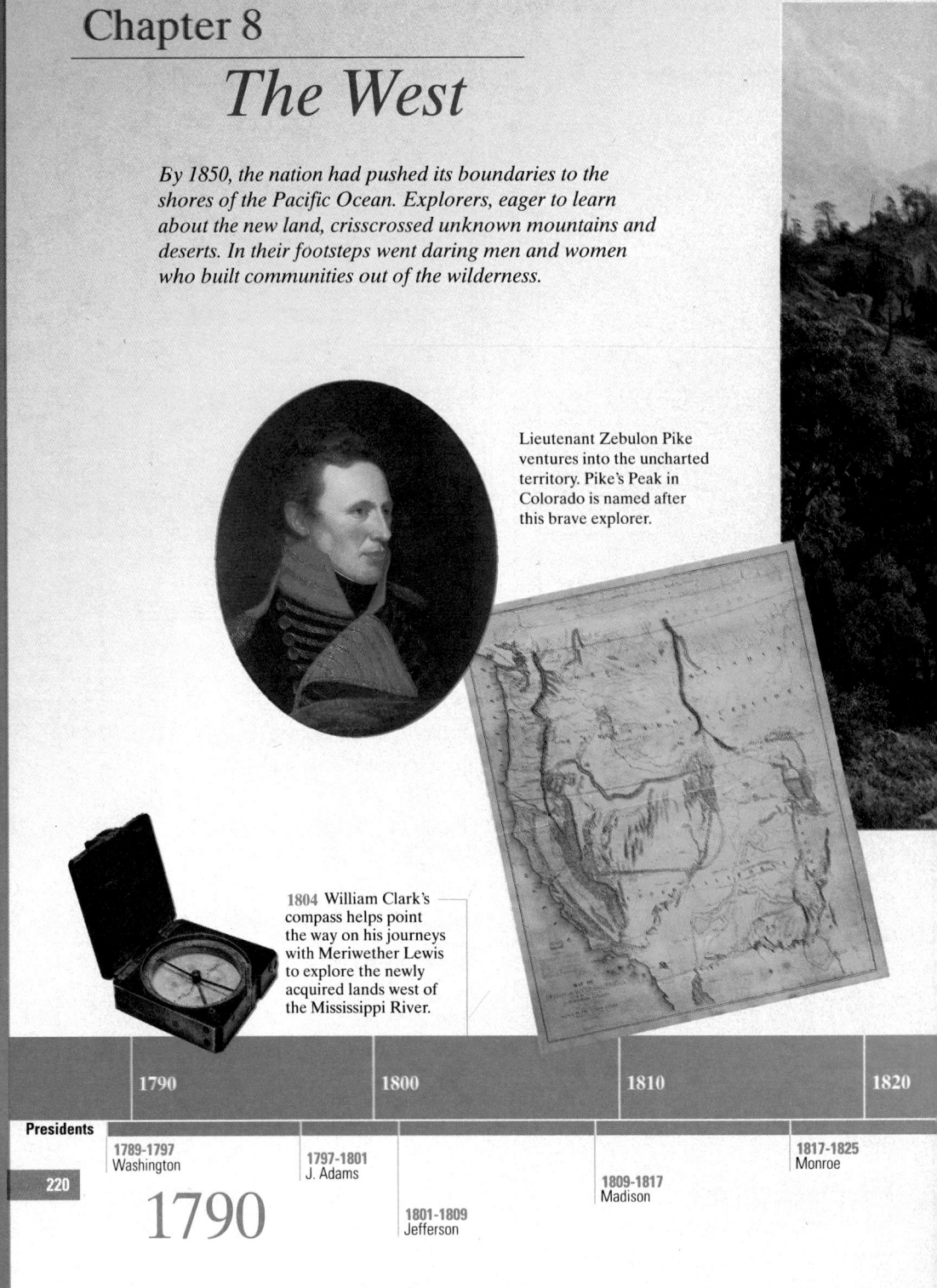

Lieutenant Zebulon Pike ventures into the uncharted territory. Pike's Peak in Colorado is named after this brave explorer.

1804 William Clark's compass helps point the way on his journeys with Meriwether Lewis to explore the newly acquired lands west of the Mississippi River.

1790 | 1800 | 1810 | 1820

Presidents

1789-1797 Washington

1797-1801 J. Adams

1801-1809 Jefferson

1809-1817 Madison

1817-1825 Monroe

1790

BACKGROUND

Through purchase and war, the United States acquired land west of the Mississippi River between 1800 and 1850. The mineral and agricultural resources of this territory encouraged thousands of Americans to move west. In the process, they developed a regional outlook that made the West distinct from other parts of the country.

The Mexican Border

The Treaty of Guadalupe Hidalgo ended the War between Mexico and the United States and set the Rio Grande as the border between the two countries. This border actually divided the city of El Paso del Norte into two sections. The northern section, which was part of the United States, became known as El Paso. Ciudad Juarez, the section south of the river, remained in Mexico.

In 1864, the Rio Grande overflowed and cut a new channel. Through this act of nature, over 600 acres of Ciudad Juarez became part of El Paso. When Mexico asked for the return of the property, the United States insisted that the river was still the boundary between the two countries. Mexico continued to protest what it thought was an unfair loss of property, but it was not until 1911 that the United States agreed to international arbitration. A Canadian tribunal returned two-thirds of the land to Mexico, but the United States ignored the decision.

People in El Paso forgot about the issue, but the Mexican government did not. In 1962, the American position changed. Eager

The majesty of the western landscape dominated the people who challenged it. This painting by Albert Bierstadt shows the vastness of the Sierra Nevada mountain range in California.

1848 Explorer John Charles Frémont's expeditions supplied information and valuable maps. This map shows Oregon and northern California.

1830 | 1840 | 1850

829 ams

1829-1837 Jackson

1837-1841 Van Buren

1841-1845 Tyler

1841 W. Harrison

1845-1849 Polk

1849-1850 Taylor

1850-1853 Fillmore

1853-1857 Pierce

1857-1861 Buchanan

1860

Understanding the Visuals

The portrait of Zebulon Pike is from the Independence National Historical Park collection. It is said that the explorer neither climbed nor named the mountain Pike's Peak.

The Bierstadt piece is a detail taken from his work *The Rocky Mountains, Lander's Peak,* 1863. Bierstadt is considered one of the finest American Romantic landscape artists. His combination of nature and theatrical effect helped make him one of the wealthiest painters of his day.

Understanding Chronology

Notice that the chapter timeline is the same as the Chapter 7 timeline. In this chapter, students will be studying a particular region, but they should keep in mind what was happening nationally during this period.

for Latin American support during the Cuban conflict, President Kennedy agreed to make a settlement with Mexico. Mexico regained 437 acres of land, and concrete was poured into the river channel to keep the border from ever moving again. Mexico's regained territory, known as El Chamizal (the thicket), is now a city park.

Early Settlement of California

Russian and British interest along the Pacific Coast alarmed Spain during the 1760s. In 1769, Spain sent sea and land expeditions to colonize California and to set up a presidio at the port of Monterey. Don Gaspar de Portolá, governor of Baja, California, led the land expedition. Father Junípero Serra, head of the Franciscan missions, was given the job of converting the Indian peoples.

Two land parties and two vessels met in San Diego in July 1769. Serra stayed in San Diego, where he set up the first of 21 Franciscan missions in California. Portolá headed north to Monterey with a small party of soldiers and Indians. They reached Monterey in August but failed to recognize the bay and continued north. A few months later, Portolá led a new expedition, and this time he was successful in identifying the bay. A sea expedition with Serra aboard reached Monterey a week later. The two parties established a mission and built a fort there. To colonize the territory between San Diego and Monterey, Serra founded seven more missions before his death in 1784.

INTRODUCE

Ask students to read the lesson title and define *exploring.* How is exploring different from traveling or visiting? Have students suggest places for modern-day explorations.

Have students read the Thinking Focus and give reasons why a nation would want to explore new territory. *(To learn about its size, boundaries, resources, natural features, and inhabitants)* Then have the students begin reading the lesson to find the reasons why Americans explored beyond the Mississippi.

Key Terms

Vocabulary strategies: T36–37

mountain man—a fur trapper of the West during the early 1800s

rendezvous—*(RAHN deh voo)* French word meaning "meeting place"; refers to a place where mountain men sold furs to traders

continental divide—line that divides the rivers that flow west from those that flow east

Manifest Destiny—the 19th century belief that the United States had a right and duty to expand throughout North America to spread white American culture

1790
1845
1850
1860

LESSON 1

Exploring Beyond the Mississippi

THINKING FOCUS

Why did the U.S. government call for exploration west of the Mississippi?

Key Terms

- mountain man
- rendezvous
- continental divide
- Manifest Destiny

➤ *Many statues exist of Sacajawea* (right), *who carried her baby son Jean Baptiste all the way to the Pacific and back on the Lewis and Clark expedition. She lived only a few years after the expedition ended. Jean Baptiste became a fur trapper and gold miner.*

Warily the explorers entered the Indian village at the foot of the Rockies. On every side women and children stared at the strangers in disbelief. Men muttered and reached for their knives. Never before had they seen such people. Dressed in deerskin like the village braves, the men had skins so light they must have "come from the clouds." The air vibrated with tension.

Then a small Indian woman appeared. On her back she carried a baby. A sigh of relief swept through the village. The woman's presence signaled that the strangers were not hostile. No enemy war party ever traveled with women and children.

The explorers were Lewis and Clark. The Indian woman was Sacajawea *(sak uh juh WE uh)*. Then probably 16 years old, she was part of the Corps of Discovery that made its way west to the Pacific Ocean between 1804 and 1805. On the way, Sacajawea was reunited with her own people, the Shoshone, from whom she had been captured during a raid. She played an important role as an interpreter. Without her, the historic expedition of discovery might have failed.

The United States Expands

Sacajawea's Shoshone were among the many American Indian tribes that lived west of the Mississippi. As the map shows, part of this western land was known as the Louisiana Territory. President Jefferson was convinced this area was vital to the nation. He predicted that one day it would yield much of the nation's farm produce and "contain more than half of our whole population."

Jefferson believed that the independent farmer was the backbone of the United States. Since farmers needed land and the population was doubling every 25 years, territorial growth seemed a natural goal for the nation. In fact, the U.S. frontier had been moving westward ever since colonial times. Some foresaw the day when the republic would stretch from the Atlantic Ocean to the Pacific.

Objectives

1. Locate the Louisiana Purchase.
2. Explain why exploration of the Louisiana Territory was important to the United States.
3. Evaluate how well the Lewis and Clark expedition achieved its goals.
4. Describe the role that the mountain men played in exploring the West.

Graphic Overview

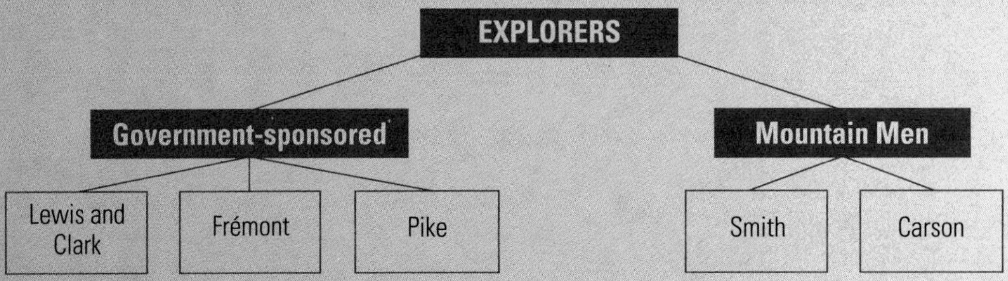
EXPLORERS
Government-sponsored
Mountain Men
Lewis and Clark
Frémont
Pike
Smith
Carson

Expanding United States, 1810

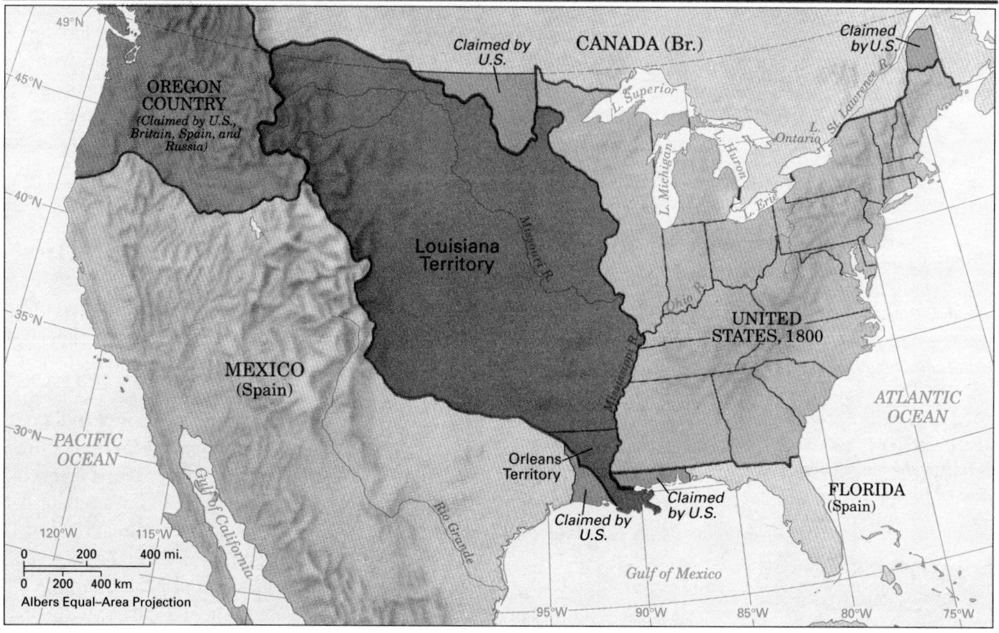

The western frontier in 1800 was east of the Mississippi River, although these lands were quickly settled in the next few years. By 1850 the United States had acquired enormous territory west of this river.

Preparing for Exploration

In 1803, Napoleon, France's powerful emperor, sold the Louisiana Territory to the United States for $15 million (Chapter 5). This acquisition protected the Western farmers who shipped their products down the Mississippi River to the port of New Orleans. It made sure that the port would remain open for commerce. The purchase also removed the threat of a powerful nation—France—that might stand in the way of U.S. expansion. Although the lands west of the Louisiana Territory were claimed by Spain, that country was weak and posed little threat to the United States. Finally, the purchase of the Louisiana Territory gave the United States vast new lands to explore.

Jefferson promptly called for an expedition to explore the new lands. He chose as its leader his private secretary and friend, Captain Meriwether Lewis, then on leave from his military duties. The 29-year-old Lewis was well educated, resourceful, and skilled at living in the wilderness, but he was subject to swift changes of mood. In contrast, William Clark, the co-leader that Lewis chose, was even-tempered. He was the youngest brother of George Rogers Clark, who had helped the United States acquire the territory known as the Old Northwest.

Jefferson gave Lewis detailed instructions about the goals of the expedition. Its main object was to explore the Missouri River and the smaller rivers that flowed into it. Jefferson hoped that one of these rivers reached the Pacific Ocean. He was looking for "the most direct & practicable water communication across this continent, for the purposes of commerce." The all-water route he sought was the fabled Northwest Passage that explorers had been seeking since the discovery of America.

Jefferson also instructed Lewis and Clark to make accurate maps and

▲ *Compare this map with the modern political map of the United States in the Atlas, pages 698–699. In 1810, what foreign nations held or claimed territory in what is now the United States?*

DEVELOP

Explain that this lesson is about some of the people who explored the land beyond the Mississippi. Ask students to read the lesson headings to preview these explorers and their explorations. Explain that some of the explorers were sponsored by the government while others were independent explorers. As they read, students should write down examples of these two types of explorers.

◄ *Spain, Britain, Russia*

GEOGRAPHY

Map and Globe Skills

Have students locate the Mississippi and Missouri rivers on the map on this page. Then have them use the physical map of the United States today on pages 700–701 in the Atlas to find other important natural features that were part of this area.

Access Strategy

Have students work in small groups to list supplies and materials that they would need for a two-year exploration of a huge and mostly wild territory in the early 1800s. Encourage them to consider the following when they make their list: they will travel by foot and small boat in an area with no roads and few paths; they will have to cross mountains, wide plains, and deep rivers; the climate will vary from the heat of summer to wintry blizzards; they may be able to hunt for food. Remind them that they will need clothing and shelter, some means of transporting the gear, food to supplement what they hunt, and equipment for cooking.

Assign one student in each group to write down the group's ideas. Then have the groups compare lists. Tell students that they will learn about important exploration expeditions the 1800s.

Access Activity

Ask students to look at the picture on page 225 of Lewis and Clark, York, and Sacajawea while you read the caption aloud. Have them identify the people in the picture. Then ask them to imagine what each person might be saying or thinking about the expedition. *(Sample answer: Sacajawea—"I'm getting closer to home.")*

GEOGRAPHY

Critical Thinking

One result of the Louisiana Purchase was that it doubled the size of the country with land that was basically unknown. Ask students to list the advantages and disadvantages of a large increase in the size of a country. *(Advantages—more land for agricultural development, new natural resources; disadvantages—confrontation with the inhabitants, cost of maintaining the land)*

■ *Jefferson instructed them to find the Northwest Passage and to make accurate maps and detailed notes on the region's geography, climate, plants, and animals.*

■ *What instructions did Jefferson give Lewis and Clark?*

detailed observations about the region's geography, climate, plants, and animals. They were also to record every detail that could be learned about the native peoples. By having the explorers treat the Indians with respect, Jefferson hoped to make ties that could be used to promote trade. ■

Lewis and Clark Explore the West

On May 14, 1804, the expedition of 44 men pushed their boats into the Missouri River where it met the Mississippi in St. Louis. They were setting off for the unknown. Lewis, who had studied botany, anatomy, medicine, and zoology to prepare for the journey, took charge of scientific discoveries. Clark acted as mapmaker, navigator, and journalist. Although an erratic speller, Clark kept meticulous records, as Jefferson had instructed.

Across the Plains

As the explorers pushed their boats into the waters of the Missouri, they had little idea of what lay ahead. How far south did the Rocky Mountains extend? Did the Pacific coast lie just a hundred miles west of the Missouri's source, as rumor said it did?

The explorers used the river to cross the nearly treeless Great Plains, which seemed to stretch endlessly before them. The men had few complaints, observed Clark, except "the Ticks & Musquiters are very troublesome." To drive away the pests, the explorers rubbed their bodies with cooking grease.

When the explorers met Indians, they presented items from their store of gifts—calico shirts, razors, colored glass beads, American flags, small hand mirrors, and medals. Jefferson had ordered that the medals be given to chiefs as a sign of peace, and the chiefs valued them highly.

Toward the end of October, the expedition reached the walled villages of the Mandan tribe in what is now North Dakota. Planning to stay the winter, they built a log structure and named it Fort Mandan. In preparation for the next spring, they hired the fur trader Toussaint Charbonneau *(too SAN shar bon NOH)* to be their interpreter. Charbonneau agreed to take along his Shoshone wife, Sacajawea, who had been sold to Charbonneau as a slave. In addition to helping her husband translate various Indian languages, she cooked meals for the expedition and found wild plants for them to eat and use for medicine.

Over the Mountains and Back

In April 1805, as the ice was breaking up on the rivers, the expedition left Fort Mandan. They crossed the plains that sloped gently upward to the barrier of the Rocky Mountains. The Rockies' jagged peaks glittered with ice and snow. They were an awesome sight to people familiar with the green, rounded peaks of eastern mountains.

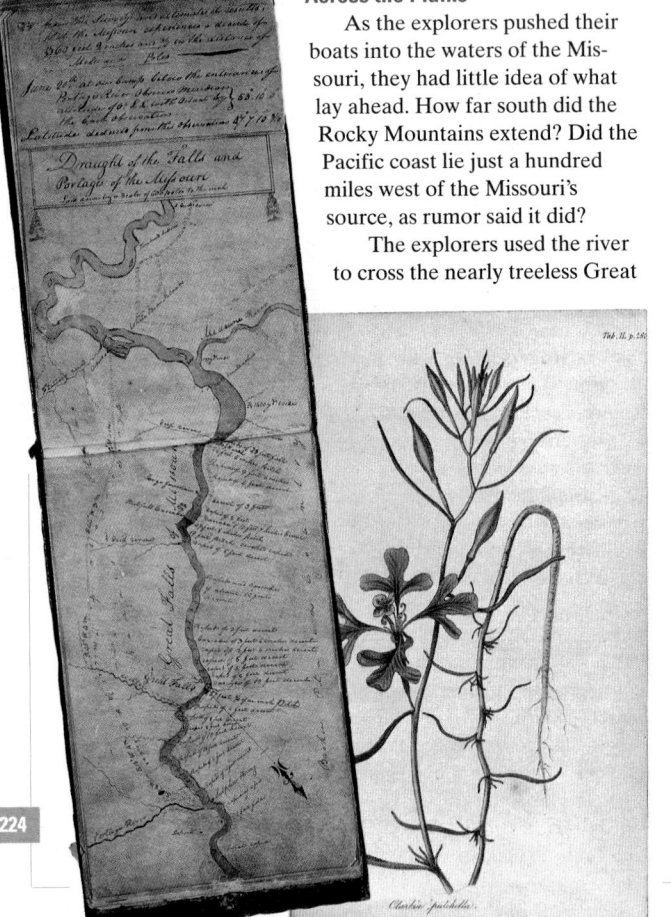

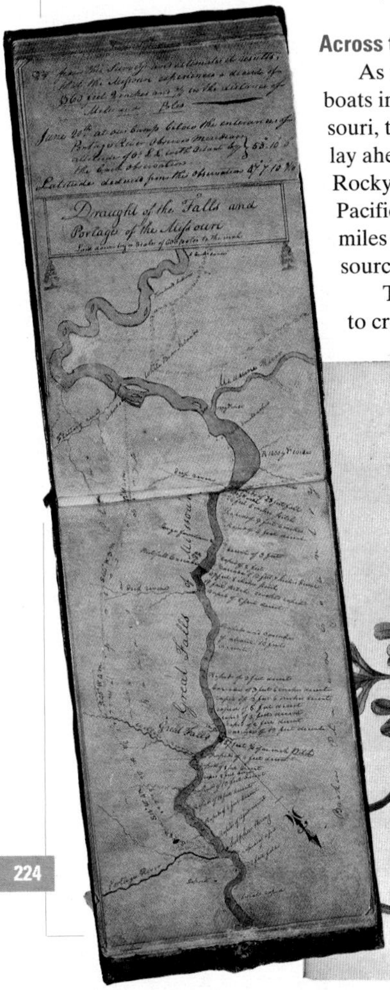

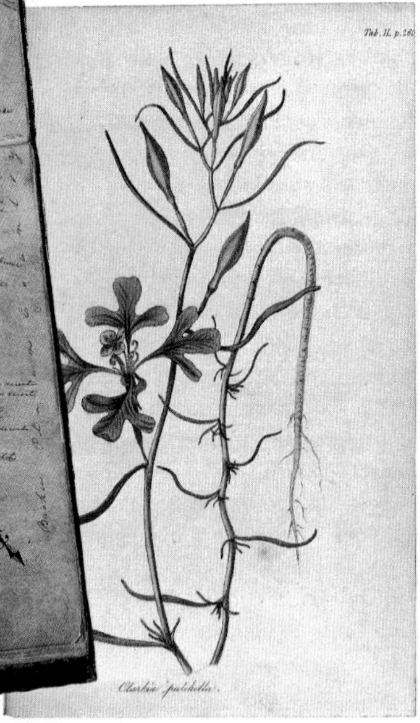

Clark's map of the great falls of the Missouri shows where the boats were carried around rapids and waterfalls. The evening primrose (clarkia palchella), *drawn from a specimen Lewis collected, is one of the new genera named for the explorers.*

Map and Globe Skills

Ask students to look at Clark's map on this page. What kinds of information did he include? *(Arrow to indicate north; location of falls and portages)* Why? *(Wanted to show future travellers how to navigate the river)* Have students work in teams to map a portion of the school grounds, including a scale and a north arrow on their maps.

Historical Context

Lewis and Clark's Corps of Discovery included 29 U.S. Army soldiers under the command of Captain Lewis. In addition, French trappers, who knew the area well, worked as boatmen and scouts for the expedition. Clark also brought his slave, York.

Although there was only one death on the expedition (probably caused by a ruptured appendix), many people became ill. Lewis ministered to them from a medicine chest containing dozens of drugs. His favorite was a cure-all called Rush's Thunderbolts. Sacajawea was of help, too, administering medicinal plants.

After the expedition, Clark took on the responsibility of educating Sacajawea's son, Jean Baptiste. After spending six years in Europe, the boy returned to America where he worked as a trapper, as a soldier in the Mexican war, and as a miner in the gold fields of California.

◄ *Olaf Seltze painted Lewis and Clark, Clark's servant York, and Sacajawea at Black Eagle Falls in Montana. The Friendship medals* (below) *were given to American Indian chiefs.*

When the expedition reached the great falls of the Missouri, the water was often rough. The boats had to be unloaded and carried around the roughest stretches. The men were in and out of the water all day. Sharp rocks on the shore cut their feet. Round pebbles in the stream threw them off balance and into the water.

A memorable meeting with the Shoshone made up for these trials. Mounted on fine horses, the warriors dashed up to the explorers at a gallop. The overjoyed Shoshone were now led by Sacajawea's brother. They hugged the members of the expedition, delighted to see Sacajawea again.

Using horses provided by the Shoshone, the explorers struggled over the mountains. They left the weary horses with some of the Nez Perce *(nez purs)*, who promised to keep them over the winter. After the explorers slowly descended the western slopes of the Rockies, they made new boats and followed the watershed of the Columbia River to the Pacific Ocean. They spent the winter of 1805–1806 near the shore at Fort Clatsop, which they had built.

The expedition had counted on four deer or one buffalo a day for food. In the early spring, however, game was scarce. At times the explorers were reduced to eating squirrels or crows. On the return journey, the group split up to make sure they had not missed an important waterway. Otherwise, the return trip was mostly a repeat of the outward journey. The weary explorers finally reached St. Louis on September 23, 1806. As they fired their guns in salute, cheering crowds rushed to the river bank. Months earlier, they had given the explorers up for lost.

Achievements of the Expedition

The Lewis and Clark expedition was one of the most successful journeys of exploration in U.S. history. Although it did not find the Northwest Passage, the expedition added enormously to knowledge of the Western lands. Lewis and Clark were the first to map the watershed of the Columbia River, thereby strengthening American claims to the Oregon country. Clark's descriptions of abundant game spurred American fur trappers to move west. Perhaps the most lasting achievement of the expedition was the great interest in the West that it aroused in a people who already had a tradition of westward expansion. Clark's map, which was the first to show the Northwest accurately, became invaluable to later explorers. ■

How Do We Know?

HISTORY *Archaeological findings indicate how greatly the peace medals were valued. Archaeologists have found the Jefferson medals included in chiefs' burials along with other objects important to those Indians.*

■ What were the achievements of the Lewis and Clark expedition?

225

GEOGRAPHY

Critical Thinking

Ask students how careful drawings and maps helped Lewis and Clark achieve their goals. *(Careful records helped them report scientific and geographical findings accurately; later explorers could follow Clark's map.)*

■ *They proved that the Missouri River was not the Northwest Passage; they established ties with American Indians; they provided the first accurate maps and descriptions of the land; and they aroused great interest in westward expansion.*

Science Connection

Have students suggest reasons why careful record keeping is important when exploring new land. Then ask students to gather and record data about an area near their home in a manner similar to Clark's. Have them first brainstorm categories about which they can make observations. *(Animal and vegetable life; geological features; people and their customs)* Have students prepare a one-page report of their observations.

Language Arts Connection

The names of many places in the United States derive from American Indian words. Have the students research and write a paragraph on the origin of one of the following names: *Missouri, Mississippi, Dakota, Nebraska.* Possible sources include unabridged dictionaries, encyclopedia articles, or etymological dictionaries.

Study Skills

Have students use library resources to locate primary and secondary sources of information on the Lewis and Clark expedition. These might include Clark's *History of the Expedition Under the Command of Captains Lewis and Clark*, published in 1814, and Bernard DeVoto's *Journals of Lewis and Clark* (Boston: Houghton Mifflin, 1953).

HISTORY

Critical Thinking

Ask students to explain why the mountain men were important to the exploration and settlement of the West. *(They knew the geography of the land and the routes through it; this information was used by government-sponsored explorers and later by the pioneers.)*

Mountain Men Blaze Trails

Lewis and Clark were soon followed by other explorers. Many of them were solitary trappers drawn to the wilderness of the Rockies by the chance to trap fur-bearing animals.

World of the Mountain Men

Each **mountain man**—as the fur trapper was called—was molded by hardship and constant danger. Like many Indians, he was a skilled tracker and pathfinder.

Like the American Indians, mountain men wore clothing of deerskin and elkskin and carried small items in pouches decorated with beadwork.

The mountain man spent much of the year alone or with a few companions, trapping animals such as mink, otter, and especially beaver, whose fur brought high prices in the East. Each spring he packed up his furs and headed for the **rendezvous** *(RAHN day voo,* a French word meaning "meeting place"*)*. Held each summer, the rendezvous took place at a location that was convenient for both fur trappers and traders. Instead of buying furs from the Indians, the traders hired a group of trappers and outfitted them.

As many as a hundred trappers and up to 5,000 Indians gathered at the rendezvous. For two or three weeks they swapped tall tales, caught up on the latest news, and enjoyed the rare chance to be sociable before returning to the wilderness trails.

Pathfinders of the West

Mountain men were colorful characters. Tall, gaunt Jedediah Smith carried a rifle in one hand and his Bible in the other. His face was deeply scarred because of his encounter with a grizzly bear that had tried to bite off his head. In 1824, he went through South Pass in what is now Wyoming and crossed the **continental divide**, the line that divides the rivers that flow west from those that flow east. Two years later Smith found the trail across the Great Basin to California. He also explored what are now the states of Oregon and Washington (see map, page 227).

Mountain men were keen observers, walking encyclopedias of the rivers, mountain passes, and Indian trails. The routes they found across the mountains and deserts in time became the overland trails for pioneers moving westward. Few mountain men, however, wrote down descriptions of the trails they knew. That task was done by U.S. government expeditions, which often used the mountain men as guides.

Government Expeditions

One of the first government explorers was General Zebulon Pike. In 1805–1806 Pike explored the upper Mississippi and the next year the land from central Colorado south. He also climbed halfway up Pikes Peak in Colorado, which is named in his honor.

John C. Frémont, a member of the U.S. Army topographical corps, led several government expeditions in the 1840s. Well-educated in mathematics and science, he was also married to Jessie Benton, the daughter of an important U.S. senator. In 1842, Frémont hired trapper Kit Carson, who spoke French, Spanish, and several Indian languages, to help on these journeys. Over the next few years, Frémont's group explored almost all of the West. His carefully prepared descriptions and maps gave concrete information to people who traveled west. His wife, Jessie, helped him turn his reports into dramatic accounts.

Despite his contributions to

Across Time & Space

Some of the land once explored by the mountain men remains in a wild state today. For example, the Jedediah Smith Wilderness covers over 116,500 acres in the Targhee National Forest in western Wyoming and eastern Idaho.

Critical Thinking

Have students name reasons why explorers and mountain men endured the danger and loneliness of the wilderness. *(Duty as soldiers on a mission; desire to become rich through trading and fur trapping; thirst for adventure; desire to get away from society)* Ask if any of these motives would be true of modern explorers, such as those in Antarctica or in space.

Interviewing

Have groups of students make a list of four questions Jefferson might have asked Lewis and Clark when they returned from the expedition. (Sample question: Did you find the Northwest Passage?) Have each group choose two students to role play Lewis and Clark. Have a representative from each group role play President Jefferson interviewing the pair. The activity can be extended by substituting Charbonneau or Sacajawea for Lewis and Clark.

Making a Map

Have students make a three-dimensional map showing the routes of exploration in this lesson, along with physical features the explorers had to negotiate. Students may refer to the maps in this lesson as well as the physical map of the United States in the Atlas on pages 700–701. They may use any suitable material, such as salt-and-flour dough or pâpier-maché.

Routes of Western Explorers, 1804–1845

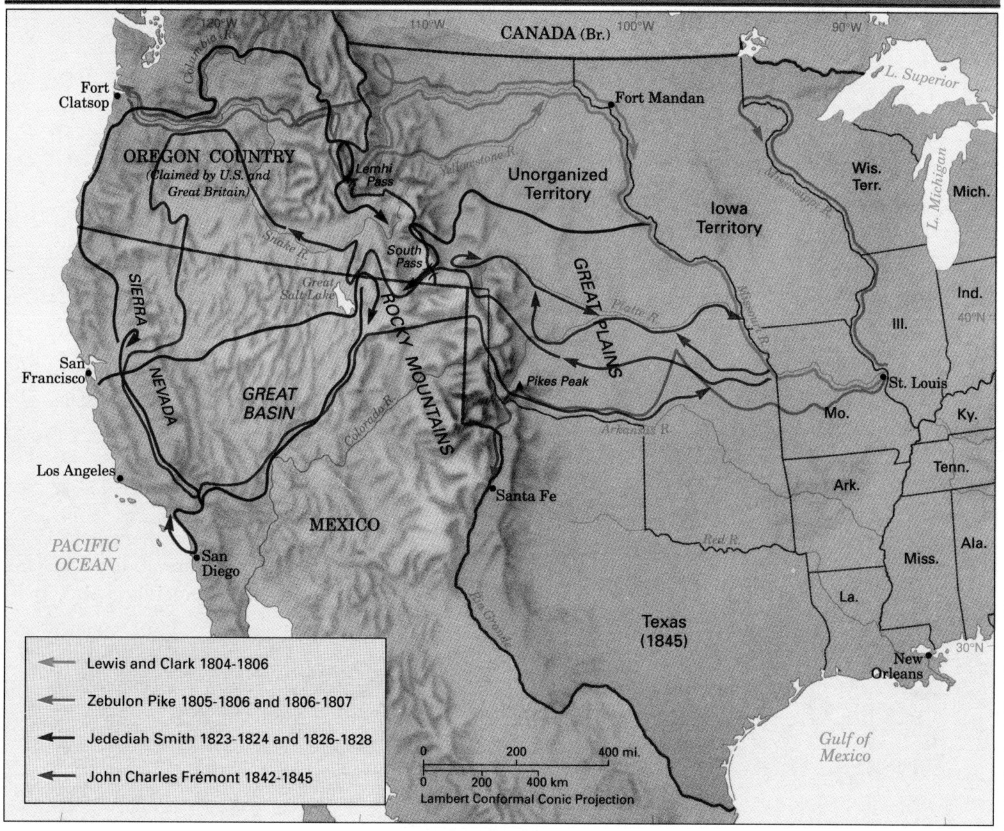

western exploration, however, Frémont had a brutal side. In 1846, he led an attack on a group of peaceful Maidu Indians, including women and children. He wanted to show them how powerful the whites were and to prevent any future aggression from the Indians.

Unfortunately, incidents like this one became more common as people explored more of the West. Over time, people came to believe that the United States had a duty to expand from the Atlantic to the Pacific. In 1845 this idea became known as **Manifest Destiny**. The Louisiana Purchase had been one step toward this goal. Between 1820 and 1850 the United States took other steps to achieve this objective. ■

The map shows some of the trails explorers found or made across the Rockies to the Pacific coast.

■ *How did the activities of the mountain men encourage U.S. expansion?*

REVIEW

1. **FOCUS** Why did the U.S. government call for exploration west of the Mississippi?
2. **CONNECT** How did Jefferson's policy toward the Indians contrast with the way Jackson had dealt with the Cherokee and other tribes in the Southeast?
3. **GEOGRAPHY** Use the physical map of North America in the Atlas to help you describe the many geographical obstacles that the Lewis and Clark expedition faced.
4. **ECONOMICS** Why was the fur trade important?
5. **CRITICAL THINKING** The reports of Lewis and Clark aroused interest in the West among people in the East. How do you think this interest might have affected the American Indians in the West?
6. **ACTIVITY** Prepare an oral report of the meeting between the Lewis and Clark expedition and the Shoshone. Include imaginary interviews with Sacajawea, various Shoshone, and expedition members.

GEOGRAPHY

Map and Globe Skills

Have students use the map legend on this page to identify the routes of Lewis and Clark, Pike, Smith, and Frémont. As an extension activity, also have students look at a map of a western state such as Wyoming and make a list of places named in honor of mountain men and other explorers.

■ *Their routes across mountains and deserts later provided trails for pioneers; they worked as guides for U.S. Government expeditions, and they provided valuable information for people traveling west.*

CLOSE

Have students summarize what they have learned by answering the Thinking Focus. Copy the structure and main heads of the Graphic Overview from page 222 on the board. Have students refer to the notes they made while reading the lesson to complete the chart. As a reteaching activity, have students point out the extent of the Louisiana Territory and the explorers' routes on a wall map of the United States.

Answers to Review Questions

1. The government wanted accurate information about the landforms, resources, and peoples of the area. Americans hoped to find the fabled Northwest Passage, to locate potential farmland, and to establish ties with American Indians.
2. Jefferson encouraged Lewis and Clark to treat Indians with respect, even giving them gifts, in order to foster ties that would promote future trade. Jackson had alienated the Cherokee and other tribes by pushing them farther west.
3. Obstacles included rivers with rapids and the Rocky Mountains
4. It was a profitable business because furs were highly valued in the East.
5. Sample answer: People were encouraged to move west. This westward movement of people might challenge Indian ownership of land. Allow for personal opinion.
6. Encourage students to use details and quotations to enliven their accounts.

Homework Options

Have the students explore a part of their own neighborhood and write a descriptive "Explorer's Journal." They may want to use the maps they developed in the Science Connection on page 225.

Study Guide: page 32.

UNDERSTANDING INFORMATION ORGANIZATION

This skill lesson will show students how to organize information in an outline.

Study Skills

When students write outlines, they often have trouble determining what information should be used for subtopics and what information should be used as supporting details. Review the outline shown on this page. Ask students why the four supporting details listed under subtopic I.C. were not considered subtopics. *(They are logically part of Jefferson's planning for the expedition. They are details that tell what those plans were.)*

Chronological Outlining

Here's Why

As a student, you are exposed to a great deal of information, both specific and general. You need to organize this information so that you can understand how the many facts relate to one another. Organizing information into an outline is one good way to do that. It is often helpful to list items chronologically, in the order in which they occurred.

In this chapter you have learned how Lewis and Clark were sent to explore the Louisiana Purchase territory and to take detailed notes on what they found there. (You can see pictures of their journey on page 229.)

Suppose you wanted to prepare a report based on their findings. You would need to organize information about where and when they traveled, and all the descriptions of what they found. One way that you could do that would be to prepare a chronological outline.

Here's How

Look at the outline below. It is based on the expeditions of Lewis and Clark. Notice how the outline is organized:

1. All major topics are marked with Roman numerals (I, II).
2. All subtopics are marked with capital letters (A, B, C, D).
3. All supporting details and information are marked with numerals (1, 2, 3, 4).

Lewis and Clark Expedition

Major Topics

I. Background
 A. Louisiana Purchase territory acquired - 1803
 B. Jefferson needs more information on territory
 C. Jefferson sends expedition to explore new land
 1. Names Meriwether Lewis as leader
 2. Lewis makes William Clark his lieutenant
 3. Budgets $2,500 for expedition
 4. 40 men leave on expedition

II. The Expedition

Subtopics

 A. Starts out from the Missouri River - Spring 1804
 B. Crosses the Great Plains
 C. Spends winter 1804 - 1805 at Fort Mandan
 D. Reaches Columbia River - November 1805
 E. Reaches Pacific Ocean - December 3, 1805
 F. Builds Fort Clatsop, spends winter 1805 - 1806 there
 G. Returns to St. Louis - September 1806

Supporting Details

 1. People surprised explorers survived
 2. Expedition traveled 8,000 miles in 28 months
 3. One of the most successful explorations ever

III. Results of the Lewis and Clark Expedition

228

Objective

Use information about Lewis and Clark to develop a chronological outline. (Study Skills 2)

Writing a Report

Have students use the outline on the page above to write a short report on the Lewis and Clark expedition. They may use additional information from the chapter or outside sources, but they should use the outline as the basis for the organization of their report.

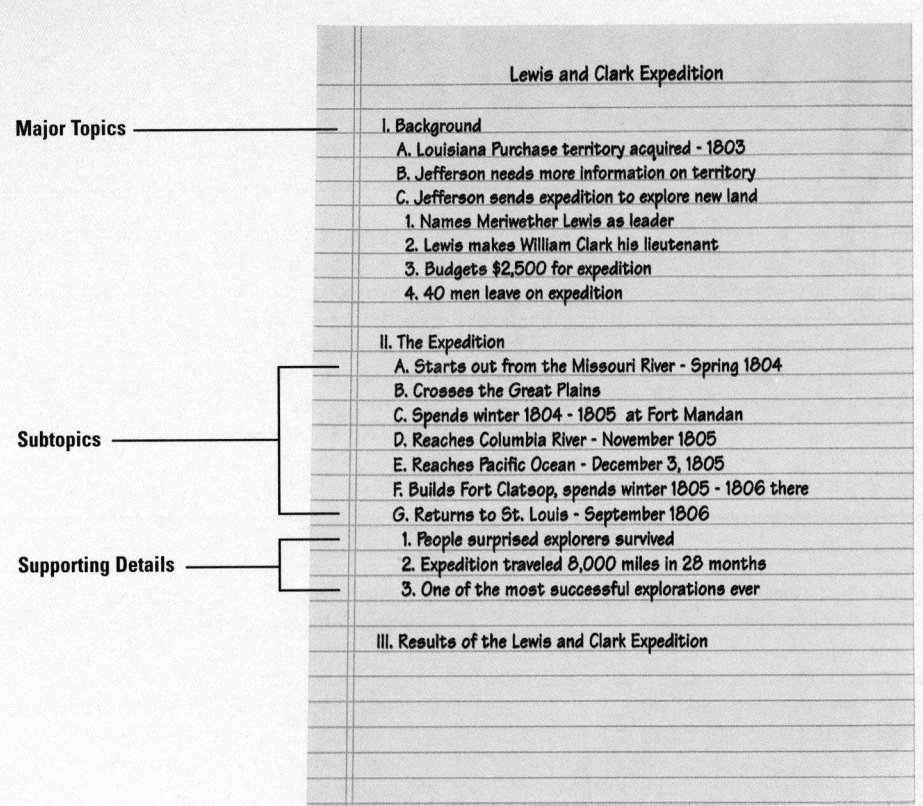

The outline is organized chronologically. First comes the background to the expedition, then the facts about the expedition itself, and then the results of the expedition. Within each of these major topics, subtopics are arranged. Supporting details are all arranged under their subtopics. When you are done arranging your information, this outline gives you all the facts that you need to write or present a report on this subject.

Try It

Look at the third major topic on the outline on page 228: "III. Results of the Lewis and Clark Expedition." Decide whether each fact in the following list is a subtopic or a detail. Label each subtopic with an "s" and each detail with a "d." Put all the facts in correct order. Then copy the outline from page 228 on a separate sheet of paper, and enter the facts in the proper place in the outline.

- The expedition confirmed the United States' claim to the Oregon region.
- William Clark carved the United States' claim to the Oregon region on the yellow pine tree.
- The expedition brought back the first maps to document the new land.
- Lewis's and Clark's maps showed that the Missouri River did not reach the Pacific Ocean.
- The Oregon region was first claimed by a Boston fur trapper, Robert Gray, who discovered the mouth of the Columbia River.
- The expedition brought back valuable information about the tribes of Indians living in the area.
- One map showed the watershed of the Columbia River.

Apply It

Research the life of a modern-day explorer or researcher such as Thor Heyerdahl, Jacques Cousteau, Sir Edmund Hillary, Jane Goodall, or another person who interests you. Organize the information that you find chronologically into an outline that includes at least three major topics.

HISTORY

Study Skills

Why does the Lewis and Clark expedition lend itself to a chronological outline? *(It had a clear period of preparation, clearly defined events, and the effects were apparent after the trip.)* Point out that not all subjects are best outlined or need to be outlined chronologically. How else could one organize the Exploration of the West? *(Sample answer: According to region)* Tell students that they should consider the topic and their purpose before deciding how to outline.

Answers to Try It

In order, the facts should be labeled s, d, s, d, d, s, d.

A. Confirmed U.S. claim to Oregon
   1. First claimed by Robt. Gray
   2. Clark carved claim on tree
B. First maps of the new land
   1. Extent of Missouri River
   2. Watershed of Columbia River
C. Brought information about Indians

Answers to Apply It

Make sure that the students' outlines have at least three major topics, make proper use of subtopics and supporting details, and are organized chronologically.

Study Skills

Divide the class into groups of three. Assign each group a subject from the chapter, such as "Settlement of Texas" or "History of the Mormons." One member of each group writes down three major topics. A second member then adds subtopics under each major topic. The third member provides suitable details. Check work for chronological order.

INTRODUCE

Ask students what they remember from Lesson 1 about the term *Manifest Destiny*. Have a volunteer read aloud the excerpt on this page from Davezac's speech and explain how it illustrates the meaning of Manifest Destiny. Who is "the young American buffalo"? *(The American settler or pioneer)*

After students read the Thinking Focus, have them look at the map on page 223 and identify the country that had claimed Texas. *(Spain)* Remind students that in the early 1800s, Mexico was called New Spain. Have students read to discover how the United States got involved in Texas.

Key Terms

Vocabulary strategies: T36–37

expansionist—one who calls for increasing a nation's territory

buffer zone—territory separating two opposing powers and lessening danger of conflict between them

annex—to increase the area of a country by incorporating other territory into it

1790 1800 1810 1821 1848 1860

L E S S O N 2

Achieving Manifest Destiny

THINKING FOCUS

How did Texas become the center of a conflict that gave the United States vast new lands?

Key Terms

- expansionist
- buffer zone
- annex

In a stirring speech in 1846, Democratic politician Major Auguste Davezac stated as follows his belief that the United States should expand:

> *Land enough—land enough! Make way, I say, for the young American buffalo—he has not yet got land enough; he wants more land as his cool shelter in summer—He wants more land for his beautiful pasture grounds. I tell you, we will give him Oregon for his summer shade, and the region of Texas as his winter pasture. [Applause] Like all of his race, he wants salt too. Well, he shall have the use of two oceans, the mighty Pacific and the turbulent Atlantic shall be his. He shall not stop his career until he slakes his thirst in the frozen ocean.*

Expansion was part of the concept of Manifest Destiny. Its roots went back to colonial days. In the mid-1600s, Governor John Winthrop of Massachusetts established the idea that if people did not improve land—that is, farm, mine, or change it in some way—they lost all right to it.

This idea grew into the view that the United States had the right to settle all of the continent of North America. **Expansionists**—those who wanted to increase U.S. territory—did not explain how the United States received the right to take over the entire North American continent.

Some people said Americans had the duty to extend white American culture—especially the ideals of democratic government, Christianity, and economic growth—to all who lacked them. From this idea it was but a short step to the claim that white American culture was superior to all others.

In 1845, editor John L. O'Sullivan came up with the name "Manifest Destiny" for the complex of expansionist ideas. Manifest Destiny was a thread that wove through the political fabric of the nation in the 1800s. Nowhere did it become more evident than in United States relations with Spain and later with Mexico.

Development of Texas

Spain claimed vast North American lands, among them what are now Texas, New Mexico, Arizona, and California. In a hundred years of colonization, however, few people had settled north of Mexico. Only 3,500 non-Indian people were scattered across the Southwest by 1820. In California and Texas, many were rancheros—cattle ranchers who grazed their herds on the unfenced range. In New Mexico, many colonists herded sheep.

Objectives

1. Explain how war with Mexico helped the United States achieve its Manifest Destiny.
2. Identify the reasons why the Mexican government allowed U.S. settlers in Texas.
3. Explain why relations between settlers in Texas and the Mexican government worsened.
4. Describe how Texas gained independence.

Graphic Overview

- land grant from Mexico to Moses Austin
- settlers brought by son Stephen

➤

- growth of Texas colony
- refusal of new settlers to uphold Austin's agreement

➤

- beginning of rebellion
- battle of the Alamo
- Lone Star Republic

➤

Texas admitted to Union

➤

- war with Mexico
- Mexican lands gained by United States

DEVELOP

Have students preview the heads to look for clues about the sequence of events in the development of Texas. As they read, students should list in order the events that took place in Texas.

HISTORY
Critical Thinking

Ask students to explain why Mexico allowed Americans to settle in its territory. *(To create a buffer zone settled by immigrants loyal to Mexico, to help develop its resources)* Why did the American settlers have few problems with the Mexican government? *(The settlers agreed to be loyal to Spain and to convert to Catholicism.)*

U.S. Settlers Welcomed

After the United States bought Louisiana, Americans had quickly settled the frontier along the Mississippi River. This rapid expansion caused Spain to fear for its northern lands. They had too few people and were too far away from Mexico City to be protected from adventurous settlers from the United States. For example, San Antonio de Bexar *(beh HAR)*, the center of government in Texas, had only 800 inhabitants in 1820.

Spain therefore agreed to a proposal made by a Missourian named Moses Austin. Austin wanted to settle a limited number of U.S. citizens in Texas. In exchange for low-priced land, he agreed that the U.S. settlers would be loyal to Spain and accept the Catholic religion. Spain felt that loyal colonists would help block U.S. expansion. It looked on the Texas colony as a **buffer zone**, a territory separating two opposing powers.

Moses Austin died before he could set up the colony, but his son Stephen took over the task. "I determined to fulfill rigidly all the duties of a Mexican citizen," he said, and remained faithful to his vow. The 300 settlers he brought from the United States in 1822 also lived up to the terms of the agreement.

Mexico gained its independence from Spain in 1821. It took Austin months to persuade the new government to maintain the grant in Texas.

Texas Towns: A Varied Heritage

San Antonio

- Founded as a Spanish mission and fort
- Named for Saint Anthony
- Planned around squares (plazas)
- Adobe buildings

Austin

- Founded as capital of Republic of Texas
- Named for Stephen F. Austin
- Planned along a grid of main streets and cross streets
- Log or wood frame buildings

Compare the two towns. Note what they tell about the mixture of cultures in Texas.

Growing Tensions

In the next few years Austin's colony in Texas prospered. As more and more U.S. settlers moved into Texas, however, relations with the Mexican government became strained. The settlements grew much more rapidly than the Mexican government had expected. By 1830, 15,000 white settlers and over 1,000 black slaves lived in Texas, outnumbering the Mexican settlers by about four to one. The explosive growth of people from the United States alarmed Mexico. Instead of serving as a buffer zone, Texas itself had become the threat.

In addition, many of the newer settlers refused to honor the original agreement. Protestants were annoyed by the religious requirement. The inefficiencies of the Mexican government, torn by quarrels between political parties, exasperated them. Many refused to obey Mexican laws. For example, Mexico tried to restrict U.S. settlement by abolishing slavery in Texas (and all of Mexico) in 1829. The settlers freed their slaves, then forced them to sign agreements that made them slaves in all but name. Austin's one-man rule also angered settlers accustomed to the democratic practices of the United States.

Control of Texas passed out of Austin's hands and into those of the newcomers, some of whom began to demand independence. To strengthen its control, the Mexican government sent troops to occupy Texas. It also forbade further immigration from the United States, but was unable to stop the flood of settlers. ■

■ *How did the white settlers' disregard for Mexican law and religion contribute to tension in Texas?*

■ *The settlers challenged Mexican authority by breaking their agreement to accept Catholicism. They defied Mexican laws by keeping slaves and by refusing to obey Mexico's immigration restrictions.*

Access Strategy

Ask the students to give examples of things that can be expanded. *(Balloons, rubber bands, houses, gardens)* Explain that an expansionist is a person who wants to increase U. S. territory. What famous expansionist can they think of from an earlier lesson? *(Jefferson)* Ask them what a store owner can do if he needs more space in his building. *(Move or enlarge the building)* Draw a square on the board to represent a store. Have one student add an attached building and label it *annex.* Ask what they think a country does when it annexes land. *(It adds land to the country.)* Tell students that they will read in this lesson how the United States expanded its territory by annexing Texas.

Access Activity

Have students give reasons why a country might want to expand. *(To respond to attack by another country, to add land and other natural resources, to protect economic interests, to promote nationalistic pride)* Then have them list some of the problems a country might have when trying to expand. *(Problems with neighboring countries, dealing with unknown land)*

POLITICAL SYSTEMS

Critical Thinking

Have students recall some of the problems that the United States faced in its first few years of independence. *(Security from foreign invasion, payment of war debts, establishment of relations with other countries)* Then ask them to list problems that the Lone Star Republic might have faced in its early years. *(Lack of security and money)*

Texas Gains Independence

On October 2, 1835, a group of volunteers refused an order to surrender a cannon to Mexican troops. Their refusal became the first step in a rebellion against Mexico. At first, the Texans acted as loyal Mexican citizens. They opposed not Mexico but its leader, General Antonio López de Santa Anna, who was doing away with the reforms of Mexico's constitution.

Battle of the Alamo

Early in December 1835, a group of 300 Texas volunteers drove 1,100 Mexican troops out of San Antonio. Santa Anna, vowing to crush the rebels, assembled an army. Few Texans took the threat seriously.

Some 180 rebels commanded by 26-year-old William Barret Travis occupied the Alamo, an old Spanish mission in San Antonio. On February 24, 1836, Santa Anna's army of more than a thousand men laid siege to the Alamo. As more troops joined the Mexicans, Travis realized the danger of his position:

▲ *Susanna Dickinson was one of the few survivors of the Battle of the Alamo. After the battle, Santa Anna sent the 18-year-old widow to Sam Houston to tell him that further revolt would be crushed like that at the Alamo.*

> *I am besieged by a thousand or more of the Mexicans under Santa Anna.* . . . I shall never surrender or retreat. . . . *I am determined to sustain myself as long as possible and die like a soldier who never forgets what is due to his own honor & that of his country—*
> *VICTORY OR DEATH.*

A Closer Look on the next page deals with the battle. The rebels held out until March 6. When the Mexicans finally broke into the Alamo, Santa Anna ordered the Texans killed.

Independence Proclaimed

While the Alamo was under siege, a group of delegates met to write a constitution for Texas. Deciding that Texas could no longer accept rule by Mexico, they proclaimed their independence and drew up a constitution based upon the U.S. document.

The new republic was in a desperate position. Santa Anna was determined to end opposition to his rule. After the victory at the Alamo, he succeeded in defeating the Texans at Goliad. Once again, he ordered all prisoners killed. Sam Houston, commander of the disorganized Texan army, led his grumbling troops on a steady retreat (they wanted to stop and fight). At San Jacinto on April 21, 1836, Houston decided the Texans were ready to attack. They caught Santa Anna by surprise and defeated the Mexican soldiers in minutes. The Texans then took a bloody revenge for the men killed at the Alamo and Goliad.

Lone Star Republic

The next day Santa Anna was captured and forced to recognize the independence of Texas. The Mexican government, however, stated that the treaty was worthless because it had been obtained by threat. Texas, the Mexicans insisted, was still part of Mexico.

At the same time the United States refused to **annex** Texas, that is, add it to the Union. Texas was a slave state; if it joined the Union, representatives argued, it would upset the balance between the 13 slave states and the 13 free states.

For almost 10 years Texas was an independent republic. The United States hesitated to annex it. The Mexicans, troubled by unrest at home, were powerless to bring it back under their control. Texans called their country the Lone Star Republic, symbolized by a single star on its flag. An uneasy peace prevailed. Bands of Comanche sometimes raided isolated settlements, and clashes with Mexico continued.

Critical Thinking

Ask students why some Texas settlers might have disagreed with Austin's promises to Mexico. *(Many favored slavery; Protestants didn't want to convert.)* Have students compare Austin's colonists to the American colonists just before the Revolutionary War. *(Both groups resented authoritarian rule, but Austin's colonists had actually experienced democracy.)*

Political Context

Mexico had a long tradition of absolute rule by the Roman Catholic Church and by the Spanish monarchy. When Mexico imported settlers from the United States, the U.S. tradition of democratic rule and self-determination also arrived in Texas. The clash between these two traditions was in part responsible for the war with Mexico. This war, however, was driven more by the concept of Manifest Destiny than by democratic principles.

Historical Context

Santa Anna brought 4,000 soldiers to the siege, according to some sources. Some of his recruits were teenagers from a nearby military academy. By the end of the siege, he had lost over 1,500 of his men—some of whom were shot by their fellow soldiers in the confusion and smoke.

A CLOSER LOOK

The Battle of the Alamo

When the Mexicans approached, the story goes, Colonel Travis drew a line in the dirt at the Alamo. He challenged his Texas volunteers, "I want everyone who's willing to die with me to come across this line. Who will be first?"

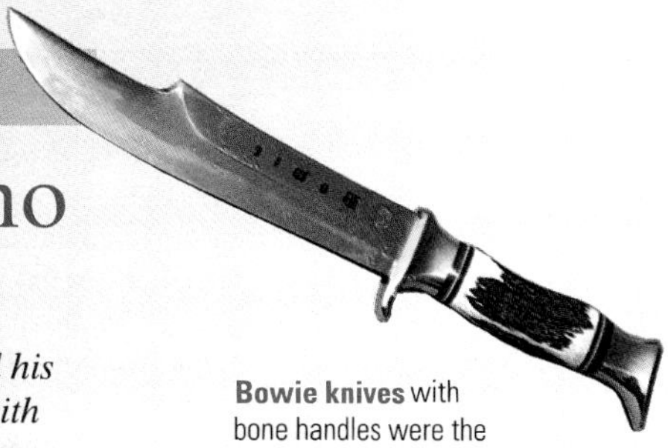

Bowie knives with bone handles were the weapons of the Texas volunteers. Popularized by adventurer Jim Bowie, they were no match for Mexican bayonets.

Sharpshooting and rugged, this percussion rifle was probably swung like a baseball bat during the hand-to-hand combat inside the fort.

After losing his life at the Alamo, Davy Crockett became a folk hero. Susanna Dickerson was one of only a few survivors of the battle. Afterward, she spread the news of the Alamo across the land.

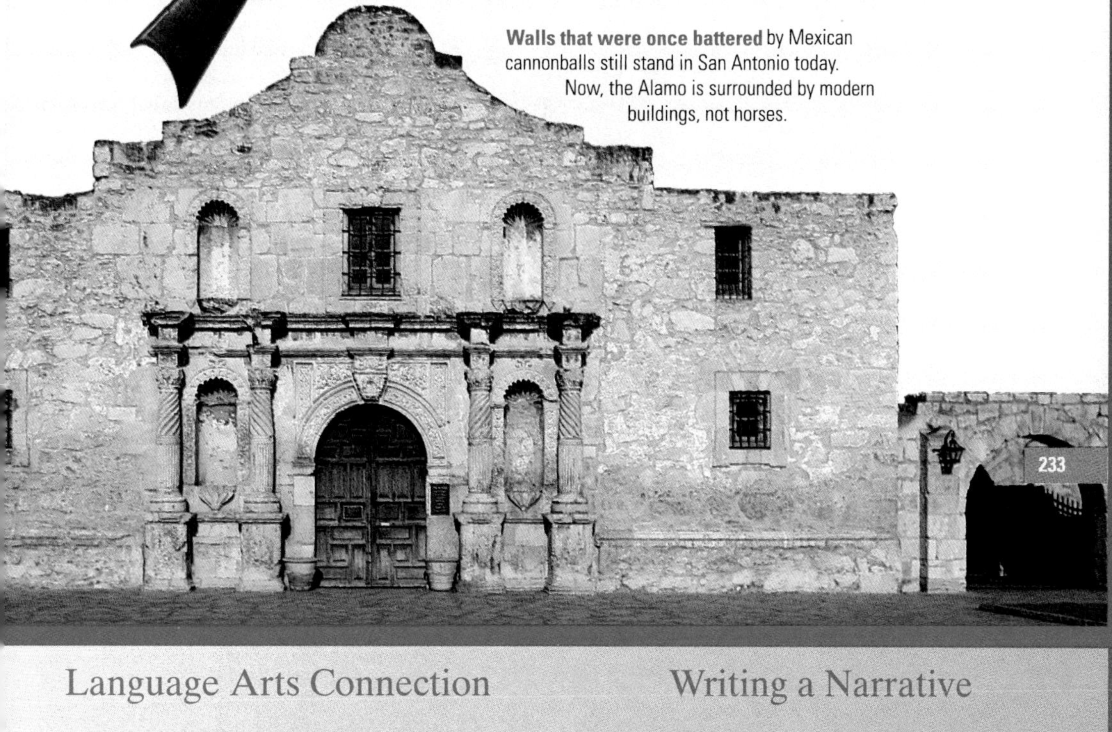

Walls that were once battered by Mexican cannonballs still stand in San Antonio today. Now, the Alamo is surrounded by modern buildings, not horses.

233

HISTORY

Visual Learning

Refer students to the pictures on this page of the battle and the Crockett almanac. Have them also read the captions. Ask them to analyze how accurate Susanna Dickinson's version of the massacre was likely to be. *(Probably accurate because she was an eyewitness; somewhat altered by her perspective, which probably favored the Texans)*

More About the Alamo The name *Alamo* comes from the cottonwood trees—*los alamos*—that lined the water ditches around the fort.

Language Arts Connection

Explain that some Spanish words used to describe land are also used in English. Divide students into groups of four or five and have each group look up one of the following geological words: *mesa, sierra, canyon,* and *arroyo.* Have them draw or find a picture illustrating the word and then share their findings with the rest of the class.

Writing a Narrative

Have students do research in the library to find out more about the battle at the Alamo. Then have them write an account of the siege, the massacre, and its aftermath. Students may write the account from the Mexican point of view or from the point of view of the U.S. government. Alternatively, they may draw illustrations for key events and write a caption for each.

Study Skills

Antonio Lopez de Santa Anna was a colorful figure in Mexican history. He was even brought to Washington by Texas president, Sam Houston, to plead the case for annexation. Have students find more information about Santa Anna in an encyclopedia or biographical dictionary and write one or two paragraphs about him.

■ *Settlers proclaimed independence from Mexico in 1835, Sam Houston defeated Santa Anna in 1836, and the United States refused to annex Texas.*

➤ *Through Corpus Christi, Matamoros, and Veracruz*

HISTORY

Critical Thinking

Have students identify some of the potential consequences of Mexico's refusal to recognize the Lone Star Republic. How, for instance, might Mexico view the United States's annexation of Texas? *(Annexation would be an act of war against Mexico. Mexico might see the settlers as disloyal rebels or illegal immigrants.)*

■ *What events made Texas the Lone Star Republic?*

Sam Houston, elected as first president, worked tirelessly to get rid of the huge debt. He encouraged people from the United States and Europe to move to Texas by offering them free land. The number of immigrants grew from 35,000 settlers in 1836 to about 147,000 people 10 years later. Most settled on the fertile land along the rivers and produced large cotton crops. Others raised cattle for their hides and meat. As settlements grew, the demand to be annexed to the United States continued. ■

War with Mexico

U.S. presidential candidate James K. Polk made the annexation of Texas a major issue in the election of 1844. Annexing Texas, he argued, would help the United States achieve its Manifest Destiny. Just before Polk took office in 1845, Congress voted Texas into the Union.

Mexico Defeated

Polk also had his eye on the rest of the Mexican lands reaching from Texas to the Pacific Ocean. The United States, he argued, had yet to reach its territorial limits. To achieve this goal, Polk made several attempts to buy the territory from Mexico. When diplomacy failed, he provoked a war by sending troops to the area of the Rio Grande. Texas claimed that river was its southern boundary. Mexico insisted that the boundary was the Nueces (*noo AY sis*) River, 150 miles farther north. In Mexican eyes, the United States had committed a hostile act. It had annexed Mexican land (Texas) and had moved troops there.

When Mexican and U.S. troops clashed, Polk used the incident as an excuse. He proclaimed that Mexicans had "shed American blood on American soil." Expansionists applauded his claim, and the U.S. Congress declared war on Mexico on May 13, 1846. Some representatives, however, protested. Abraham Lincoln, a congressman from Illinois, asked Polk to show exactly where on American soil the incident had occurred.

Although the Mexican soldiers fought bravely, the war went badly for Mexico. The U.S. forces were better organized and equipped. The Mexicans were weakened by civil war.

Santa Fe, the capital of New Mexico, was quickly occupied by U.S. troops. In California, just before the war broke out, a group of U.S. settlers in Sonoma had seized Mexican General Mariano Vallejo (*vah YEH hoh*). Raising a homemade flag showing a bear and a single star, they proclaimed California to be the Bear Flag Republic. When the U.S. navy occupied California ports in July 1846, the Bear Flaggers joined its forces. Some Californios and New Mexicans later rebelled, but their uprisings were quickly halted.

▼ *The Mexican forces, led by Santa Anna, faced U.S. troops commanded by experienced generals —Zachary Taylor, called "Old Rough and Ready," and Winfield Scott, "Old Fuss and Feathers." Find the invasion routes these generals took into Mexico.*

Mexican War, 1846-1848

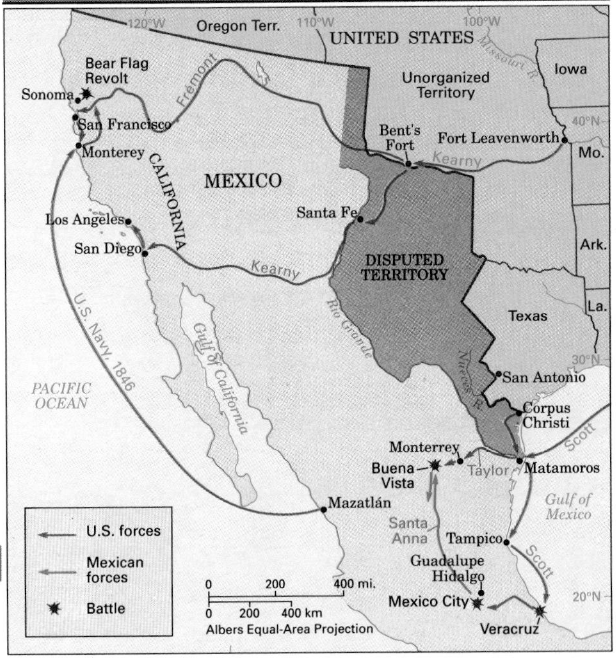

234

Critical Thinking

Point out that Polk was not expected to win the presidency in 1844. In his campaign, Polk made the annexation of Texas a major issue. Why was it to Polk's advantage to do this? *(Many Americans believed in Manifest Destiny and wanted a President who also supported expansionism.)*

Making a Map

Students can show the addition of land to the United States on a series of transparent overlays. Have students draw and label a base map of the original thirteen states. Using suitable transparent material, students may draw an overlay for each of the major additions of land: states added before the Louisiana Purchase, the Louisiana Purchase, the Spanish cession of 1819, the Transcontinental (Adams–Onís) Treaty, and the Mexican War.

Research

Have students research James Bowie, one of the heroes of the Battle of the Alamo. Ask them to find out where he was born, what country he was a citizen of, and why some people consider him a hero. Have students write a two-page profile of Bowie's life.

Expanding United States, 1853

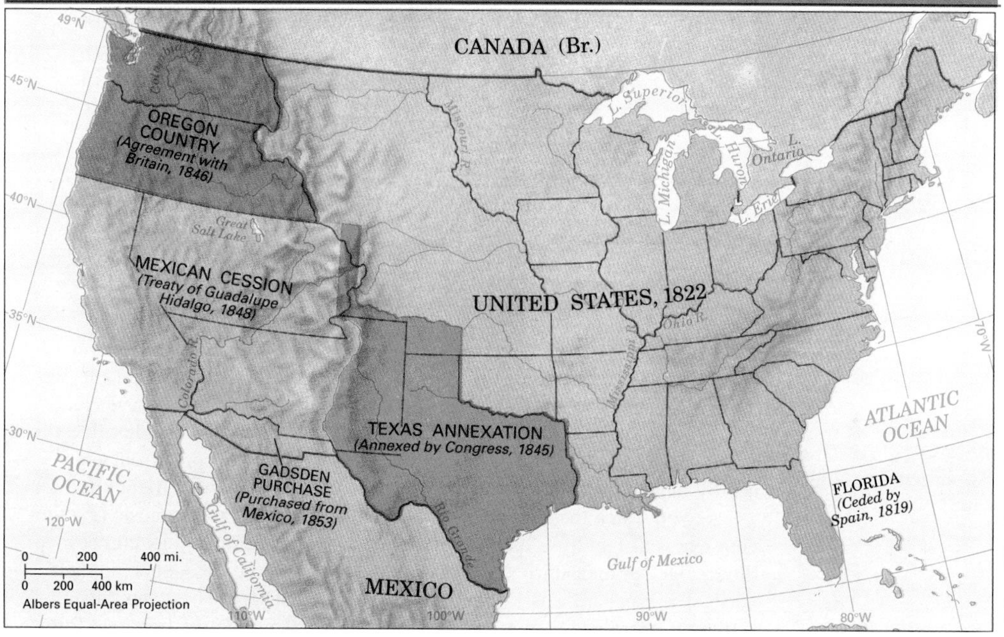

Manifest Destiny Achieved

U.S. troops also invaded Mexico south of the Rio Grande and won several victories (see map, page 234). After two years of war, the Mexican government conceded defeat.

In February 1848, Mexico and the United States signed the Treaty of Guadalupe Hidalgo. Under the terms of the treaty, the United States would pay Mexico $15 million and would assume up to $3.25 million in Mexican debts to American citizens. In return, Mexico would cede to the United States most of the land north of the Rio Grande. The Senate approved the treaty in March 1848. The United States had achieved its long-sought Manifest Destiny and now stretched "from sea to shining sea."

Although the nation had doubled in size, it had also acquired some new problems. The war caused hard feelings between Mexico and the United States. Mexico was humiliated by its defeat; U.S. expansionists were elated at their nation's victory. Some U.S. citizens, convinced that their civilization was superior, tended to look on Mexico as a backward nation, an attitude that has lasted into modern times. The land gained from Mexico included thousands of Mexicans who became U.S. citizens. As white settlers moved west, the treaty protecting Mexican Americans was often not enforced. ■

Included in the Mexican Cession were present-day Utah, California, Nevada, parts of Colorado and Wyoming, and most of New Mexico and Arizona. In 1853, Santa Anna sold the rest of New Mexico and Arizona to the United States.

■ *How did the United States achieve Manifest Destiny through war with Mexico?*

REVIEW

1. **FOCUS** How did Texas become the center of a conflict that gave the United States vast new lands?
2. **CONNECT** How did the concept of Manifest Destiny relate to Jefferson's territorial goals?
3. **CULTURE** List the factors that caused conflict between the U.S. settlers in Texas and the Mexican government.
4. **GEOGRAPHY** Compare the modern U.S. political map in the Atlas (pages 698–699) with the map above showing territory lost by Mexico. What present-day U.S. states were once part of Mexico?
5. **CRITICAL THINKING** What bias might result from the belief in Manifest Destiny?
6. **ACTIVITY** With a classmate, debate the desirability of Manifest Destiny. Be sure both sides of the argument are presented. Use relevant material from the lesson to support the presentation.

HISTORY
Map and Globe Skills

Using the map on this page, students may compare the areas of land added to the United States. Ask students which acquisitions allowed the United States to reach its Manifest Destiny of spreading from sea to sea. *(Oregon Country, 1846; Mexican Cession, 1848)*

■ *The land that Mexico ceded to the United States after the war gave the United States access to the Pacific Ocean. The nation now stretched "from sea to shining sea."*

CLOSE

Ask students to use the lists they made while reading the lesson to answer the Thinking Focus. Then copy on the board the Graphic Overview from page 230. As a reteaching activity, have students identify the people who played an important role in this part of Texas history. *(Moses Austin, Stephen Austin, Antonio de Santa Anna, Sam Houston, William Travis, and James Polk)*

Answers to Review Questions

1. Initially Texas was a buffer zone between the United States and Spain. Later, settlers arrived unwilling to uphold Austin's agreement with Spain. Texans rebelled against the rule of Santa Anna and proclaimed independence; U.S. provocation along the disputed border led to war with Mexico.
2. It supported Jefferson's ideals by saying that it was the duty and right of the country to expand its territory.
3. Many U.S. settlers remained Protestant, refused to free their slaves, and ignored Mexican restrictions on immigration.
4. California, Utah, Nevada, and parts of New Mexico, Arizona, Colorado, Wyoming, and Texas were originally part of Mexico.
5. Sample answer: It might contribute to the bias of white, American superiority. Allow for personal opinion.
6. Tell students to use modern examples and examples from the lesson as support.

Homework Options

Have students imagine that they live in 1836. Have them write a letter to a young soldier waiting out the siege from inside the Alamo or to a soldier in Santa Anna's army. Encourage them to give comfort and advice or to ask questions.

Study Guide: page 34.

INTRODUCE

Direct students' attention to the title of the lesson and then pose this question: Why would anyone other than an adventurer or explorer want to settle in an area with unfamiliar conditions and dangers? *(Promise of riches, land, employment)* Have one student read the Thinking Focus aloud. Have students read the lesson to learn some of the reasons why people settled in the West.

Key Term

Vocabulary strategies: T36–37

secularize—to convert from religious use or ownership to civil use or ownership

1790 1800 1810 1820 1830 1833 1848 1850 1860

LESSON 3

Settling the West

THINKING FOCUS

Why did U.S. citizens begin to settle in the lands west of the Mississippi River?

Key Terms

- secularize

Picture yourself a Yankee trader in the company of Walter Colton, a judge in Monterey, California. He has asked you to join him at a party on a nearby rancho or ranch.

As you watch the guests arrive, your eye is caught by a young couple riding together on a spirited chestnut horse. The ranchero's dark sombrero is tilted forward and tightly strapped under his chin. His dark blue suit shines with silver buttons, and his handsewn boots bear jingling spurs. The boots were probably part of the cargo a Yankee ship carried from New England. The leather for the boots may have originally come from hides of the ranchero's own cattle.

Sitting sideways in front of the ranchero is his wife, a wreath of tiny flowers in her dark braids, her dark eyes sparkling with excitement. Her rustling dress may also have come from New England, and her fine silk shawl may have come from China.

The couple greet friends and join others dancing to the music of a violin and guitar. In a quiet corner older women sit and gossip behind their fans. Rancheros boast about their horses. Children run back and forth, playing games and snatching tidbits from the table laden with food.

Although imaginary, the account above describes what a visitor to a rancho might have seen. The music, the food, the dress of the people, and the soft-spoken Spanish all indicate how California differed from New England in the 1830s.

On the veranda of a California rancho a couple dances a fandango to the music of a guitar.

Objectives

1. Describe life on the California missions and ranchos.
2. Explain how secularizing missions changed life in California.
3. Compare the religious motives of the Mormons with those of the Oregon missionaries.
4. Identify early U.S. contacts with California.
5. Explain how Oregon became part of the United States.

Graphic Overview

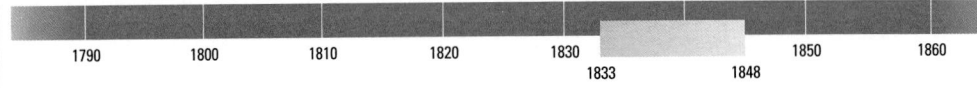

Spaniards Settle in California

The difference between California and New England lies in their colonial backgrounds. California was settled by people from Catholic Spain, whereas New England's early settlers were Protestant English.

Mission California

The colony in California was set up in 1769. When officials in New Spain (now Mexico) set up outposts in places such as California and Texas, they sent soldiers to build forts, priests to establish churches, and settlers to grow food for the soldiers. Walled presidios, or forts, had quarters for troops, a jail, and storage rooms.

Food for the presidios was supposed to be grown by the settlers. Since few people in New Spain wanted to migrate to California, the government gave them land as an encouragement. Some settlers became rancheros; others were townspeople who ran small businesses or served as government officials.

The missions were much more successful than the towns. Each mission included a church, workshops and storerooms, rooms for the priests, and houses for the Indians who lived there. By 1823, 21 missions, each a day's walk from the next, stretched 600 miles along the coast from San Diego in the south to Sonoma, north of San Francisco. These missions were home to several thousand Indians. Some Indians labored in the fields of wheat, the fruit orchards, and the vineyards. Others tended the herds of sheep and cattle or worked in the kitchens and workrooms, grinding meal into flour, tanning hides, making tiles and adobe bricks for building, and weaving blankets and clothing. Indian artists created religious carvings and paintings for the mission church.

Most Indians found it hard to adjust to mission life. They were used to living in small bands and moving from place to place to gather food. The Indians resented the hard work they were forced to do at the mission, and many of them ran away. Moreover, diseases brought by the Spaniards often proved fatal to the Indians. By 1833, the Indian population of California was three-fourths of what it had been in 1769 when the first mission was established.

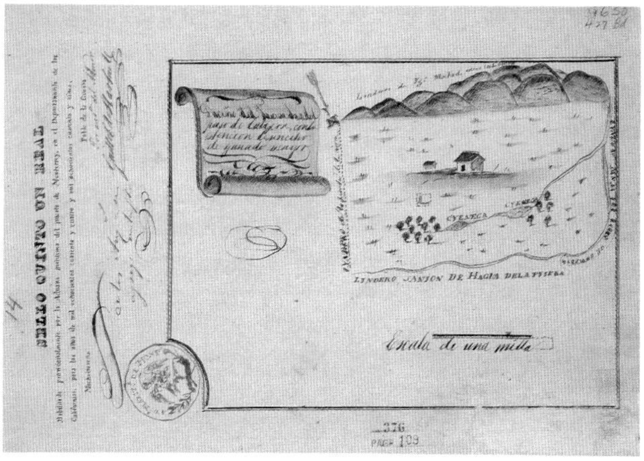

This plan of Rancho del Ciénaga (Marsh Ranch) was used to register the land claimed by the ranchero.

California Ranchos

When Mexico gained its independence from Spain, it took over California. In 1833, Mexico's government began to **secularize** the missions; that is, it took the mission lands away from the Catholic Church. By lessening the priests' power, the Mexicans hoped to weaken loyalty to Spain.

The lands were originally intended for the Indians, but most of them went to rancheros. Most Indians were unfamiliar with the idea of private property, and the few who got any land were then cheated out of it by settlers. To gain the land—and the hundreds of thousands of cattle already on it—a ranchero made a diseño (*dih SEH nyoh*), a drawing that identified the rancho. Each land grant was enormous, measured in square miles rather than in acres.

Although the ranchos were like

DEVELOP

Point out to students that they will have many opportunities to compare and contrast things in this lesson, such as mission life versus rancho life. Copy on the board the Graphic Overview from page 236 and ask students to look for each group mentioned as they read the lesson.

GEOGRAPHY
Visual Learning

Instruct students to examine the plan pictured on this page and identify the features that a ranchero could use to define the rancho's boundaries. *(Mountains, canyons, trees)*

Access Strategy

Have students imagine that they own a successful rancho in California in the year 1845. Ask them to brainstorm to create a list of the jobs or tasks necessary to run the rancho. Have a volunteer list class responses on the board. What sort of household jobs are there? How is clothing provided? Where does the food come from? Who takes care of the stock? What about building and repairs? How are things kept clean? Point out that most of the household work was done by American Indians, who were supervised by the ranchero's wife. Ask students what they think life would have been like for the Indians on the rancho and for the wife of the ranchero. Then explain that raising stock on unfenced land and selling it for hides involved little intensive work, except at round-up time. How might this affect the lifestyle of a ranchero? Tell students that in this lesson they will learn more about rancho life in California.

Access Activity

Have students look at the picture on page 236 and describe the setting and what the people are doing. Read the lesson opener aloud while students look at the picture. Tell them to listen for words that describe the objects in the picture. Ask the students to explain why they would or would not like to live on this rancho.

CULTURE

Critical Thinking

Ask students whether they would prefer to be a worker in a mission or on a rancho. Have them give specific reasons to support their answer. *(Sample answer: On a rancho because a vaquero's work sounds fun and exciting)*

■ *The rancheros became the important figures, like the mission priests before them.*

small kingdoms, the main house was usually a simple building of adobe (bricks of sun-dried clay) with dirt floors. On the wealthier ranchos, skilled horsemen called vaqueros (*vah KAIR ohs*) did most of the work for the rancheros. In springtime, the vaqueros rounded up and branded the newly born calves. In the fall, they rounded up full-grown cattle to slaughter for their hides and meat.

Yankee traders sailed their ships into the ports at San Diego, Monterey, and San Francisco. There they bought the cured hides and shipped them to New England shoe factories. In addition to hides, the ships took on tallow, a cattle by-product used in making soap and candles.

■ *How did taking the missions away from the church change life in California?*

The hide trade was profitable but irregular. In the winter of 1835–1836, Richard Henry Dana, the writer—in an account of his voyage from Boston around Cape Horn to California—reported that the port of San Francisco was nearly deserted. ■

All around was the stillness of nature. . . . To the westward of the landing-place, were dreary sandhills, with little grass to be seen, and few trees, and beyond them higher hills, steep and barren, their sides gullied [worn away] by the rains. Some five or six miles beyond the landing-place, to the right, was a ruinous presidio, and some three or four miles to the left was the Mission of Dolores, as ruinous as the presidio, almost deserted.

U.S. Citizens Go West

Although California and the east coast of the United States were linked by trade, California was a Mexican possession. Most westward-moving people from the United States headed for Oregon.

Californios traded tanned hides of the type shown below. At right is a carpetbag, the "suitcase" used by many pioneers.

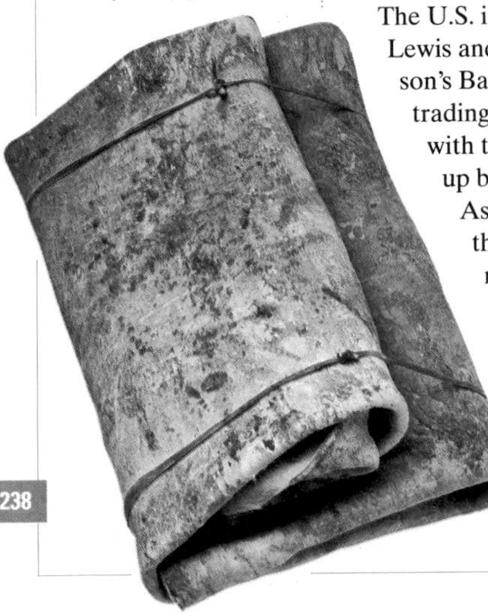

Overland to Oregon

The United States and Britain both claimed the Oregon country. The U.S. interest went back to the Lewis and Clark expedition. Hudson's Bay, a powerful British fur-trading company, competed with the fur-trading post set up by American John Jacob Astor. When Britain and the United States could not agree on the boundary between Oregon and Canada, they decided to let people from both countries settle in Oregon.

In 1835, the American Board for Foreign Missions strengthened the American claim by sending missionaries to the Northwest. Marcus and Narcissa Whitman and Henry and Eliza Spalding set up churches, schools, and mills, showed people of the Cayuse and Nez Perce tribes how to irrigate land, and taught them Christian ideas.

The descriptions by explorers, missionaries, and settlers helped to attract other U.S. citizens. By 1845, over 5,000 Americans had settled in Oregon. At his inauguration as President in 1845, Polk proclaimed that the United States had a "clear and unquestionable" title to Oregon. The following year Great Britain and the United States agreed to set the Oregon boundary at Latitude 49°N. Some expansionists had demanded a boundary at Latitude 54°40'N, but Polk did not feel the added territory was worth

Critical Thinking

Have students read aloud the excerpt from Richard Dana on this page. Have them refer to Chapter 7 and suggest how Dana might have described the port of Boston that he left in 1835. *(Very busy, lots of people, noisy)* Why were the two cities so different? *(San Francisco's presidio and mission were nearly deserted; the hide trade was irregular.)*

Political Context

Many immigrants to the original colonies had come because they disagreed with the official religion of their native countries. To avoid this problem in the United States, the framers of the Constitution had written the First Amendment, which separated church and state. The Mormons, however, disagreed with the separation of church and state. One of the principal reasons that they went west was to get outside of the United States so that they could make their own laws.

Cultural Context

The long and arduous journey west by wagon caused, in many cases, a change in traditional sex roles. Men traveling without families did their own washing and cooking. When necessary, women drove the wagons, served as lookouts, scouted for campgrounds, and shot game for food. One consequence of the blurring of traditional roles was that women demanded, and often got, a role in the management and decision making of the traveling company.

▲ *Some Mormon families included several wives, a practice that stopped in 1890. Note the spinning wheel and butter churn. What do these tools tell you about the pioneers' way of life?*

a dispute with Britain.

By 1847, the increasing number of white settlers was beginning to alarm the Cayuse and Nez Perce. When some settlers arrived with measles, the disease proved fatal to large numbers of the Cayuse because they had no immunity to it. Convinced the missionaries had poisoned their children, the Cayuse killed 14 white people, including the Whitmans. To protect other settlers, Congress made Oregon a territory in 1848.

The Mormon Promised Land

The Whitmans and Spaldings went west for religious reasons—to establish Protestant missions and to convert the Indians to Christianity. A group known as the Mormons also went west for religious reasons.

The Mormons were founded by a young New Englander named Joseph Smith. From the age of 15 on, Smith experienced religious visions. He believed he was chosen to head a new and purified Christian church. In 1830, he formally founded the Church of Jesus Christ of Latter-day Saints at Fayette, New York. Smith and his followers later moved west.

Smith's followers, known as Mormons, often met with hostility. People of other faiths objected to some practices such as the Mormons having several wives. Nevertheless, the Mormons built thriving communities in Ohio, Missouri, and Illinois. In Nauvoo, Illinois, Smith served as both mayor and religious leader. The Mormon community grew to 20,000, making Nauvoo the largest city in the state.

In 1844, however, some Mormons accused Smith of treason. This disagreement encouraged some anti-Mormons to attack the settlement at Nauvoo. An angry mob burst into the jail where Smith was held and murdered him and his brother Hyrum.

The horrified Mormons, led by Brigham Young, fled west, looking for a place to live that was outside the United States. The desert west of the Rockies, known as the Great Basin, seemed ideal.

Lured by the opportunity to worship freely, thousands of Mormons trekked west to the Great Basin and

HISTORY

Critical Thinking

Ask students why the United States made Oregon a territory in 1848. *(To provide U.S. protection to settlers)* Why else might Congress have wanted to make Oregon a territory? *(To keep the British out, to add valuable farmland and wildlife to the country)*

◄ *Pioneers had to make everything they needed for themselves.*

BELIEF SYSTEMS

Critical Thinking

Remind students of the Second Great Awakening discussed in Chapter 6. Why did Protestant missionaries and Mormons move westward? *(Both groups went for religious reasons: the Mormons wanted to get outside of U.S. law; many Protestants wanted to set up missions and make converts.)*

Research

Have students consider what else they could learn about Brigham Young, the Whitmans, or John Sutter. Have the class brainstorm a list of questions to research about each person. (Sample: Where did Brigham Young grow up?) Divide the class into three groups, each group researching a different person. The group can divide the questions among its members or research the answers as a group. Have a spokesperson from each group report their findings.

Map and Globe Skills

Have students study the physical and climatological maps of the United States in the Atlas on pages 700–701 and 706. Ask them to predict where the major routes westward would be. Point out that most of the overland trails followed river beds, which provided water and were flat. Refer students to the map on page 244 for an example of one route westward.

BELIEF SYSTEMS

Critical Thinking

Ask students why groups of people such as the Mormons might be persecuted for their beliefs. *(Sample answer: intolerance; threat to own beliefs; fear of unknown; conviction that own way is the only right way)*

➤ *The salt pyramid still exists today as a distinctive landmark.*

■ *After Lewis and Clark's expedition sparked U.S. interest in Oregon, other explorers, fur-traders, missionaries, and settlers went to Oregon.*

CLOSE

Encourage students to summarize what they have learned by answering the Thinking Focus. Copy the Graphic Overview from page 236 on the board again and, as a reteaching activity, have students add the reasons why each group of people settled in the West.

▲ *Like Great Salt Lake, Pyramid Lake in Nevada has no outlet. Compare the modern photograph (top) with the sketch made by Charles Preuss, Frémont's mapmaker, in 1844.*

■ *Briefly describe how U.S. settlements developed in Oregon.*

established a Mormon state named Deseret in 1849. By the next year the settlement at Great Salt Lake had over 11,000 inhabitants, most of them farmers. Their hard labor and discipline, combined with Young's irrigation scheme, made the desert blossom.

Other people admired the Mormons for their hard work and farming skills. But they were disturbed that Mormon religious leaders also headed the government. In the United States, in contrast, the Constitution called for separation of church and state. For more than 40 years the close relationship of Mormon religion and politics caused opposition to admitting the Mormon state to the Union. Utah did not become a state until 1896.

Early U.S. Settlers in California

U.S. citizens began settling in Mexico's colony of California in the 1820s. Occasionally sailors left ship to try ranching or storekeeping or to work as tinsmiths, carpenters, or lumberjacks. Some U.S. trappers drifted into the colony and settled down.

Among the early non-Mexican settlers was Swiss immigrant John Augustus Sutter, who arrived by way of Hawaii. Sutter convinced the Mexican government that he would build a fort to protect the colony. His settlement on the American River became a goal for people traveling to California. Soon it would play a major role in California's history. ■

REVIEW

1. **FOCUS** Why did U.S. citizens begin to settle in the lands west of the Mississippi River?
2. **CONNECT** How did the Mexican War influence Polk's position on Oregon?
3. **ECONOMICS** How did Yankee traders and California rancheros supply one another's needs?
4. **CULTURE** In what way were the motives of the Oregon missionaries and the Mormons similar? different?
5. **CRITICAL THINKING** Apply the concept of Manifest Destiny to California. How might U.S. expansion affect the rancheros?
6. **ACTIVITY** Imagine you are in charge of a group of people about to settle in Oregon. Plan a colony and decide what the settlers will need. Think of problems they may face and their economic and cultural needs. Write your plan in the form of an outline.

Homework Options

Have students write three diary entries about settling the West, from the point of view of either a missionary, a trapper, a Mormon settler, or an American Indian.

Study Guide: page 35.

Answers to Review Questions

1. Settlers were attracted to the West by descriptions of the land, trade opportunities, and the possibilities of religious freedom and mission work.
2. Because of the Mexican War, Polk compromised on the Oregon boundary to avoid a dispute with Britain.
3. Rancheros supplied traders with hides and tallow; traders supplied finished goods, such as shoes, boots, candles, soap, and clothing.
4. Oregon missionaries and Mormons both wanted to express their religion freely; the Oregon missionaries went to convert Indians to Christianity while Mormons wanted freedom from persecution.
5. Sample answer: Rancheros might lose their way of life and their land if U.S. settlers dominated California as they did Texas. Allow for personal opinion.
6. Have students base their outlines on resources mentioned in the lesson.

L E S S O N 4

Surviving on the Frontier

On January 24, 1848, James Marshall was working with a group of Maidu Indians at Sutter's sawmill on the American River in California. He described the day this way. "My eye was caught by something shiny in the bottom of the ditch. I reached my hand down and picked it up; it made my heart thump, for I was certain it was gold. . . . "

Although historians disagree whether it was Marshall or the Indians who found the gold, news of the discovery spread quickly.

According to one legend, storekeeper Sam Brannan went to San Francisco on May 12. Grasping a bottle of gold dust, he shouted words that electrified his listeners: "Gold! Gold! Gold from the American River!"

Fired by gold fever, thousands rushed to the gold fields. "The whole country," reported the *Californian* newspaper, "resounds to the sordid cry of gold, gold, GOLD! while the field is left half planted, the house half built and everything neglected but the manufacture of shovels and pickaxes."

THINKING FOCUS

What impact did the discovery of gold have on the West?

Key Terms

- ghost town
- regionalism

The Gold Fields

Forty-niners, as they were called, came to California from all over the world. Whites, free blacks, slaves, and Indians came from across the United States. Others came from Mexico, South America, and as far as China and Europe.

The Journey

Americans and Mexicans could travel to California by horseback or wagon, but those who came greater distances, from places like China or Chile, had to travel by boat. In spite of its high cost, boat travel was very unpleasant. People were jammed together for weeks of seasickness, bad food, and possibly dangerous storms.

Forty-niners traveling from the eastern United States had more options. Some sailed 13,000 miles around the tip of South America, while others went only as far south as Panama, crossed its jungles, and caught a ship headed north in the

Like these Chinese miners, people came from all over the world to seek their fortunes in California's gold fields.

INTRODUCE

Have students recall from previous lessons some of the problems of living on the frontier. After reading the Thinking Focus, students may predict some of the problems caused by the discovery of gold in the West. Have them read to confirm or reject their predictions.

Key Terms

Vocabulary strategies: T36–37

ghost town—a town that has been totally abandoned

regionalism—a sense of belonging to a distinct region

Graphic Overview

Cause
gold discovered in 1848

→ **Increased U.S. Settlement in the West** →

Effects
- loss of land grants
- displacement of rancheros
- reduced status of Californios

Objectives

1. Identify the impact of the gold discovery in California.
2. Explain why mining towns appeared and disappeared.
3. Describe the hardships that pioneers faced.
4. Examine primary sources to infer how pioneers lived.
5. Identify the impact of the gold rush on the Californios and California Indians.

DEVELOP

Have students preview the heads and scan the pictures in the lesson to find examples of how people traveled to the West. *(On foot, by boat)* Explain that the discovery of gold caused many things to happen in the West. As they read, have the students list the effects of the discovery of gold. Point out that some groups benefited more from the gold rush than others.

GEOGRAPHY

Critical Thinking

Ask students what they think would happen to the region they live in if gold were discovered in their home town. How would a discovery of gold today be different from the discovery of gold in California in the 1840s? *(Sample answer: Communications today would get the news to people quickly; people could travel to the area quickly and easily.)*

Prospectors shoveled water and gravel into a wood and iron rocker or cradle (below)*, then rocked it back and forth so that the heavier gold settled on the bottom. The rocker evolved into the Long Tom* (right)*, which made working a claim easier.*

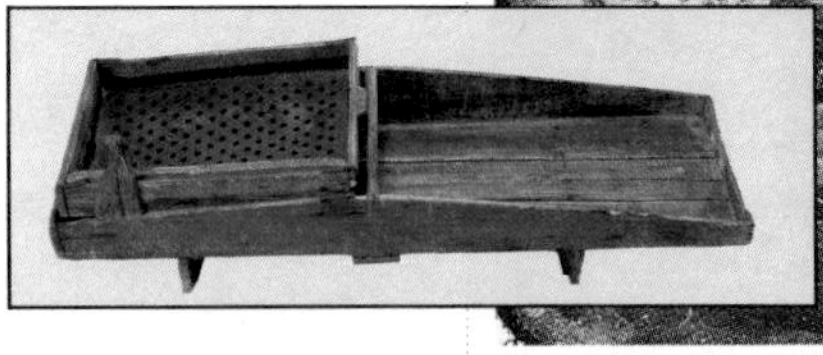

Across Time & Space

The California gold rush came back to life in 1987 when a group of divers found the wreck of the S.S. Central America, *a paddlewheel steamer that sank off the coast of Charleston, South Carolina, in 1857. Inside the wreck was California gold on its way from San Francisco to banks in New York. The value of the gold then was $1.2 million. Today it is worth about $450 million.*

Pacific. Most Americans traveled over land, which was the cheapest route. That journey was dangerous too, since travelers faced deserts, mountains, bad weather, and even diseases.

Indians from across the United States, as well as Mexicans and Indians from California, also took part in the gold rush. A small number of Indians benefited from mining on their own, but many California Indians were kidnapped and forced to work as slaves for miners. A number of Indians were killed by miners who were never punished for their crimes. As a result, the Indian population of California dropped from about 100,000 in 1849 to 35,000 in 1860.

Tales of Riches

For a few miners, arriving in California really did mean getting rich. One angry miner kicked a rock in disgust and found a gold nugget underneath it. Another prospector—one who seeks valuable natural deposits such as gold—claimed to have found gold under his doorstep. Not to be outdone was the miner who shot a bear and found gold where the animal fell onto a rocky ledge. As strange as it sounds, some of these stories were true!

Mining Camps

The mining camps were usually makeshift towns full of single men. Life was disorderly and rough, and brawls could break out at any time. Terrible living conditions at the gold fields, combined with a failure to strike it rich, made miners short-tempered.

Some of the worst violence was directed at Chinese and other foreign miners. Many white miners resented the Chinese immigrants who were willing to work hard, even in abandoned claims, in order to succeed. The Foreign Miners Tax, passed in 1852, made all foreign miners pay a tax of three dollars.

Another aspect of the camps was the outrageous prices charged for most goods. The cost of a shovel went from $1 to $50 in a month. A $2 cradle—the device used to separate gold from sand and pebbles—cost $100 at the mines.

In mining areas, towns seemed to appear almost overnight. In November 1848, there was not a house in

Access Activity

Have students look through the visuals in the lesson to find examples of the difficulties of life on the frontier. *(Outdoor cooking, poor roads)* Then direct their attention to the picture on page 243. What kind of difficulties might these people encounter traveling West on foot? *(Rivers, mountains, wild animals)*

Access Strategy

Bring catalogues of camping equipment to class and have the students familiarize themselves with some of the equipment used to camp in the outdoors today. Then have the students examine the pictures in this lesson and list some of the similarities and differences in the camping equipment used then and today. Encourage students who have gone camping to share their experiences. What modern equipment would have made the pioneers' trip easier or safer? *(Today's nylon and aluminum equipment is lighter.)* How was the clothing similar or different? *(Long dresses* v. *blue jeans)* Was their clothing, particularly that of the women, appropriate for the long westward journey? Tell students that they will read in the lesson about some of the hardships the pioneers experienced.

Sacramento. In 1849, it became a supply center for the gold fields. Its population soared to 12,000 people.

Mining towns might die out overnight. When miners heard of a rich strike somewhere else, they grabbed their belongings and left. Within weeks, their town might become a **ghost town**, a deserted place. Silence replaced the bustle. ■

■ *Why did few mining towns become permanent settlements?*

Hardships of the Overland Trail

In 1849, 30,000 people traveled the Overland Trail. The next year the number rose to 55,000. Numbers decreased after that year but by 1860, 145,000 more people had moved to the West.

These men, women, and children all shared the hardships of life on the trail. Their journey began with the emotional strain of parting with familiar places and loved ones. One pioneer woman mourned, "I am leaving my home, my early friends and associates, never to see them again."

Looking like ships against the rolling plains, the canvas-covered wagons were known as prairie schooners. Each was about ten feet long, and they followed one another in trains that could stretch for two to five miles.

An experienced scout guided the wagon train. Usually everyone rode horseback or walked beside the team of oxen pulling the wagon. Since each wagon might weight a ton or more when loaded, it needed three or four pair of oxen to pull it. Wagons contained tools, clothing, a few family treasures, and food for the journey.

A guidebook suggested pioneers carry 200 pounds of flour, 150 pounds of bacon, 10 pounds each of coffee and salt, and 20 pounds of sugar. To these staples the pioneers added dried fruit and beans. Slung beneath the wagon were spare wagon tongues, axles, spokes, and wheels for making the repairs that were often necessary.

Demanding Daily Chores

Travel by wagon train was physically taxing. The Overland Trail from Independence, Missouri, to Sutter's Fort in California was 2,000 miles long. Since wagons traveled only about two miles an hour, the trip took several months to complete. The map on the next page shows one man's journey across the United States.

During the trip, people had little privacy and no sanitary facilities. The journey was especially hard for the women because they were expected to cook, wash and mend clothes and the wagon canvas, take care of the children, and doctor the family. Women and children also spent part of the day walking in the choking dust behind the wagons, picking up dried buffalo droppings, called buffalo chips, to use in place of wood for fuel.

For a pregnant woman, it was even harder. One woman said, "It all seems like a jumble of jolting wagon, crying baby, dust, sagebrush, and the never ceasing pain."

▲ *C. C. A. Christensen painted this group of pioneers crossing the plains on foot and hauling their possessions in handcarts. Many Mormons used this method of traveling west.*

ECONOMICS

Critical Thinking

Have students name some of the jobs that were created when a mining town was built. Who was needed to keep the town operating? *(Storekeepers, cooks, suppliers)* Then ask them to identify the people who would be affected when a mine was tapped or proved empty. Why would the town become a ghost town? *(The town was dependent on the miners; without them, everyone had to leave.)*

■ *Miners left the towns as soon as the ore ran out or when they heard of a strike elsewhere.*

Historical Context

Edward Hargraves started a gold rush in Australia in 1851. He had just returned from the California rush when he discovered gold in Summerhill Creek. In 1896, George Carmack and two relatives discovered gold in the Klondike region of northwestern Canada just across the border from Alaska. By 1897, the Klondike and Alaska gold rush was on. Before it ended, over 100,000 prospectors went there; of those who survived, only about four percent struck gold.

Cultural Context

Among the immigrants to California were the Chinese, the largest group of Asians to arrive. Between 1850 and 1880, more than 100,000 Chinese people settled there. About a third stayed and worked in San Francisco or Sacramento. Others took over abandoned claims. The Chinese came up with many efficient methods of extracting gold, including special dams to reveal the river beds and a foot-operated pump for pumping water out of holes.

Social Participation

Encourage students to think about why they would or would not want to be pioneers and to list positive and negative aspects of pioneering. *(Negative—hardships of the trail, uprooting from home, many unknowns, and the near-impossibility of going back; positive—opportunity to get land, chance to see new things)*

GEOGRAPHY

Map and Globe Skills

Have the students study the map and read through the diary entries on this page. Have pairs of students expand on one caption on the map. Based on the location and time of year, students may add information about the climate and terrain at the various points on the map depicting Geiger's trip westward. Encourage them to use the physical and climatological maps of the United States on pages 700–701 and 706 of the Atlas.

➤ *Almost seven months*

In 1853, Charlotte Stearns Pengra recorded some routine evening chores she did:

> *I hung out what things were wet in the wagon, made griddle cakes, stewed berries, and made tea for supper. After that was over made two loaves of bread, stewed a pan of apples, prepared potatoes and meat for breakfast, and mended a pair of pants for Wm. pretty tired.*

She neglected to add that she unpacked the wagon when they halted and repacked it when they went on. Men's chores included repairing harnesses and wagons, caring for their animals, planning routes with the wagon train captain, hunting game, and standing guard at night.

Hazards of the Journey

Some of the pioneers, both men and women, were unable to bear the hardships of the trail and turned back. Others became sick and died from diseases such as cholera, smallpox, and dysentery that were brought on by poor diets.

At all times the pioneers were at the mercy of the weather. They lost time waiting to ford flooded streams or stopping to find cattle that had stampeded during a storm. As they crossed Oregon in 1847, Elizabeth Smith Geer wrote the following:

> *It rains and snows. We start this morning around the falls with our wagons. . . . I carry my babe and lead, or rather carry another through snow, mud and water, almost to my knees.*

Since heavy wagon loads could not be carried across the mountains, items such as furniture often had to be discarded. Some people died of dehydration on the deserts. Others found out too late that the water hole they had drunk from was poisonous. While Indians often intrigued travelers, they rarely posed a threat until later years on the Overland Trail.

On February 8, 1849, V. E. Geiger left Staunton, Virginia, and headed for California. How long did his journey take?

A Journey on the Overland Trail

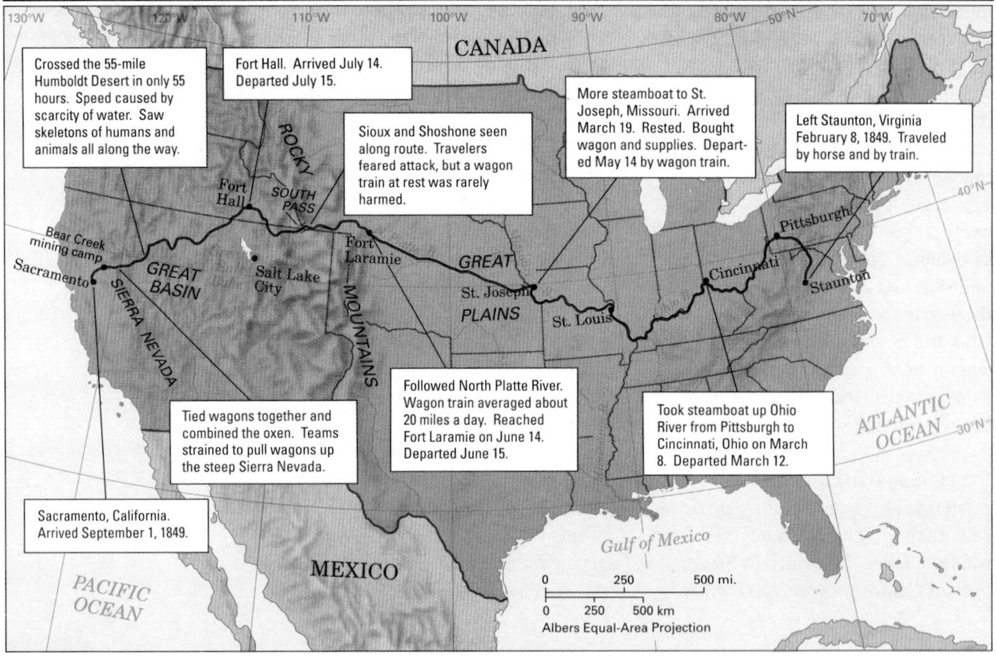

130°W
120°W
110°W
100°W
90°W
80°W
70°W
50°N
40°N
30°N
CANADA
Crossed the 55-mile Humboldt Desert in only 55 hours. Speed caused by scarcity of water. Saw skeletons of humans and animals all along the way.
Fort Hall. Arrived July 14. Departed July 15.
Sioux and Shoshone seen along route. Travelers feared attack, but a wagon train at rest was rarely harmed.
More steamboat to St. Joseph, Missouri. Arrived March 19. Rested. Bought wagon and supplies. Departed May 14 by wagon train.
Left Staunton, Virginia February 8, 1849. Traveled by horse and by train.
ROCKY
Fort Hall
SOUTH PASS
Bear Creek mining camp
Sacramento
GREAT BASIN
Salt Lake City
Fort Laramie
GREAT
St. Joseph
PLAINS
St. Louis
Cincinnati
Pittsburgh
Staunton
SIERRA NEVADA
MOUNTAINS
Followed North Platte River. Wagon train averaged about 20 miles a day. Reached Fort Laramie on June 14. Departed June 15.
Took steamboat up Ohio River from Pittsburgh to Cincinnati, Ohio on March 8. Departed March 12.
Tied wagons together and combined the oxen. Teams strained to pull wagons up the steep Sierra Nevada.
ATLANTIC OCEAN
Sacramento, California. Arrived September 1, 1849.
Gulf of Mexico
MEXICO
PACIFIC OCEAN
0 250 500 mi.
0 250 500 km
Albers Equal-Area Projection

Map and Globe Skills

Using the map on this page and the physical map of the United States on pages 700–701 in the Atlas, each student can write a diary entry describing the geography of a place on the Overland Trail not in Geiger's diary. Have students read their entries aloud while other students guess the general location.

Art Connection

Have students use an encyclopedia and other reference books to find more information about covered wagons. Then have them explore different techniques for conveying this information through drawings. Bring in books with examples of cross-sectional and detail drawings, such as David Macaulay's *Mill* (see page 219, Social Studies Bookshelf), to give students an idea of the different possibilities. Divide the students into small groups and have each group make several drawings of a covered wagon. Encourage them to make cross-sectional drawings at different cuts through the wagon. If students have been able to find out the materials with which the various parts of the wagon were made, ask them to indicate this information in their drawings.

"The Prairie Schooner Family" shows pioneers enjoying an evening meal on the Overland Trail. What made the preparation of meals difficult?

Meal preparation could not start until the wagons stopped in the evening. Fuel or game might not be available.

The settlers learned quickly that their trips must be well planned. Lack of food or equipment could be fatal.

Life on the Frontier

The hardships did not end when the pioneers reached their goal. It was difficult to part with the friends they had made while crossing the country. The pioneers missed those they had left behind. Because of the length of the trip, most pioneers reached Oregon or California in the fall. Despite their exhaustion, they had to build a shelter and start clearing fields.

Even for those who were experienced farmers, the new climate and growing conditions caused problems. The workday was a long one that ran from dawn to after dusk. Children matured quickly; they were expected to feed livestock, work in the fields, and care for younger sisters and brothers. A pioneer woman might stay up all night mending, making candles, preserving food, or caring for a sick family member. Men worked in their fields, helped others with farm chores, and took part in building the community school or church. ■

■ *What problems of weather and geography did the pioneers face?*

■ *Pioneers faced heat, dust, rain, mud, snow, ice, cold, steep mountains, and dry deserts.*

Impact of the Westward Movement

The hardships shared by people on the frontier gave them a sense of **regionalism**, of belonging to a distinct area. Gradually settlements grew into communities and then into towns with doctors, storekeepers, lawyers, sheriffs, and deputies. Towns that had existed before settlers from the United States arrived were often transformed.

In 1859, Richard Henry Dana returned to the port of San Francisco. Compare the following description of the port with his earlier account on page 238.

> We bore round the point towards the old anchoring-ground of the hide ships, and there, covering the sand-hills and the valleys, stretching from the water's edge to the base of the great hills, and from the old presidio to the mission, flickering all over with the lamps of its streets and houses, lay a city of one hundred thousand inhabitants. Clocks tolled the hour of midnight, . . . but the city was alive from the salute of our guns.
>
> Richard Henry Dana, Twenty Years After, 1859

HISTORY

Critical Thinking

Have students name geographical and psychological hardships of life on the frontier. *(New climate, isolation, farm work for children)* Which of these hardships would apply to modern pioneers?

HISTORY

Study Skills

Point out that excerpts from diaries and other books convey points of view. Ask students what they know about Pengra, Geer, and Dana. What is each writer's attitude about the West? *(Sample answer: Charlotte Stearns Pengra is traveling with someone named William (Wm.). They have a wagon and food, but she is tired from all her work.)*

Oral Report

Have students research and report on the role of women as pioneers, both on the trail westward and after they arrived. Encourage them to look for women who owned ranches. Two excellent sources are *Westering Women and the Frontier Experience 1800–1925*, by Sandra L. Myres (Albuquerque: University of New Mexico Press, 1982) and *Women's Diaries of the Westward Journey* by Lillian Schlissel (New York: Schocken Books, 1982).

Map and Globe Skills

Have students use a map scale to measure the distance by land or by sea from their home town, or from a major city in the East or Midwest, to San Francisco or to Portland, Oregon. They can consult either a large wall map or the modern United States map on pages 702–703 in the Atlas.

CULTURE

Critical Thinking

Have students analyze why improved transportation and mass communication might lessen regional distinctions. *(Sample answers: People would travel and relocate more frequently, causing cultures to mix. Through the radio and television, people of different regions hear information given in the same dialect, causing accents to weaken.)*

Understanding Regionalism

The common experiences of the people who settled the West suggest they might have formed a region that is somehow distinct from other regions in the country. What exactly is a region? How are its borders determined? Do the same regions that were forming in 1850 still exist today?

Defining a Region

A country as immense as the United States can be divided up in many ways, on the basis of geography, economics, or culture. A region is an area that shares some set of defined characteristics. Geographical division, for example, groups together states with similar physical features such as mountains or plains. A geographical division may also emphasize transportation routes, such as river systems. Economic division stresses local agriculture, such as the citrus belt; or manufacturing; or markets—who trades with whom.

In addition to these indicators, regions may also be defined by the people who live in an area. This can be termed *cultural regionalism*. People might live in similar areas and use the land differently. For example, the Great Plains stretches from the Dakotas into Texas. The people who live in the north tend to be descendants of New Englanders and of Scandinavians, interested in cooperative ventures. The people who live in the south are apt to be small-scale, independent farmers who probably migrated there from the South.

Culture, as you know, includes all learned behavior—all the kinds of knowledge and skills that are passed on from one generation to another. In looking at cultural variations across the country, you would want to consider a group's religion, politics, housing styles, and special ways of speaking. You might also look at a group's preferences in music, literature, food, and social behavior.

Cultural Variations

Let's look at some examples of regional cultural variations. Some of the most interesting are differences in dialects—how people speak. Many people who live in New England, New York City, the South, and Texas use the same words but pronounce them in different ways. Do you pronounce the letter "a" in "pass" like the "a" in "pat" or like the broad "a" in "father"? Do you sound the "r" in "car" or "hard" or do you let it drop ("cah" or "hahd")? If you do, there is a good chance that you live in New England or that you moved from there recently.

Differences in dialects can also be traced through the choice of words. In the North people carry water in a "pail"; in the Midwest and in the South water is carried in a "bucket." Researchers can draw a line on a map of the United States dividing those who say "barn lot" and those who call it a "barnyard."

Spread of Cultures

The spread of cultures across the United States parallels the migration of people in the late 1700s from the first coastal settlements inwards. The independent farmers of the Southern colonies were in the forefront of the migrants who entered Kentucky and Tennessee. The settlers on the Kentucky frontier, still restless, were among the first to travel along the Oregon Trail.

California in some ways is the most Americanized of all the states because its population is so diverse. Spaniards and Mexicans were of course the first to arrive. The explosive growth following the discovery of gold brought in settlers from every part of the country. Added to this were immigrants from both east and west—Irish and Chinese. Though in the East, immigrants typically headed for the big cities, in California many immigrants settled in the countryside to farm.

The Future of Regionalism

Some observers have predicted that regionalism is becoming less of a force in this country because of the achievements in transportation and in mass communication. They say that the distinctions between North, South, West, and East, are becoming blurred.

Others disagree. They point to the increased interest in folk cultures and in ethnic origins. Backing up this point of view are polls that suggest regional differences are even stronger among the population under 40 years of age than among the older population. Pride in regional variations, according to this point of view, will lead naturally to renewed pride in the country as a whole.

246

Critical Thinking

Have students identify the name and boundaries of the region in which they live. Have them list regional qualities that they share—food, manners of speech (such as local idioms or accent), and customs. If the class has any newcomers to your region, have them comment on the things that are new to them.

Reader's Theater

Divide the class into small groups and ask each group of students to choose a diary entry or series of entries from the sources on pioneer women mentioned in the Oral Report activity on page 245 or from other sources. Have each group prepare a short dramatic presentation based on the diary entry or entries. Students can use the voice of the person who wrote the diary or the voices of her family.

Impact on Inhabitants

Westward movement had a major impact on the Indians and Mexican citizens of the West. The Treaty of Guadalupe Hidalgo guaranteed the rights of Mexican citizens living on the lands ceded to the United States in 1848. Many Mexicans decided to stay and automatically became U.S. citizens. When thousands of forty-niners arrived, however, the Californios, as the Mexican inhabitants were called, had difficulty keeping their land.

Some prospectors simply moved in and took possession. Under U.S. law, landholders had to provide positive proof that the land belonged to them. The boundaries of the land grants, however, were often vague and ownership was not clear. Rancheros who fought white settlers' claims in court usually lost their land. Within a few years most of the great California ranchos were gone. In the following decades, landholders and villagers in New Mexico also lost their land grants. Many were reduced to working as hired hands on the lands they once owned.

The Indian peoples of the West grew increasingly alarmed as the waves of pioneers flooded through their hunting lands. They attacked some wagon trains and an occasional settlement. However, because the pioneers did not stop in the Great Plains, no major confrontation occurred between the Plains Indians and white people. That clash would come later.

▲ *William Henry Jackson, a photographer with U.S. surveyors, also made some watercolor sketches. In this scene he shows a family just getting settled on the frontier.*

Impact on Pioneers

Those who journeyed west found that the mountains were higher than those elsewhere in the nation, the plains more vast, the rivers more turbulent. In overcoming these obstacles, the pioneers learned to be tough, resourceful, and frugal. The experience of the trail was a forge on which they hammered out their character.

The common hardships the pioneers had shared in the journey westward and in settling the frontier gave them a sense of community. They learned to cooperate in building homes, schools, and churches. At the same time, Westerners were self-reliant individualists used to solving their own problems and supplying their own needs. People in other parts of the United States also developed a sense of belonging to a particular region. ■

■ *How did the westward movement affect those who already lived there?*

R E V I E W

1. **FOCUS** What impact did the discovery of gold have on the West?
2. **CONNECT** Compare and contrast the reasons why people moved west after 1848 with the reasons why the Whitmans and the Mormons had earlier moved to Oregon and Utah.
3. **SOCIAL** Describe the hardships people faced on the Overland Trail. How did life on the frontier differ from those hardships? How was it similar?
4. **CRITICAL THINKING** Review the concept of Manifest Destiny. What elements of Manifest Destiny can be seen in the way the Californios were treated after 1848?
5. **WRITING ACTIVITY** Imagine that the year is 1848 and that you are at Sutter's sawmill on the American River in California when gold is discovered. Interview the people who are there. How do they react at first? What do they do when they learn that gold has been found?

POLITICAL SYSTEMS

Critical Thinking

Have students describe how the Californios probably felt about the arrival of U.S. settlers. *(They probably felt angry about losing their land and their status.)*

■ *Californios lost their ranchos and also became U.S. citizens.*

C L O S E

To help students summarize the lesson, you may wish to copy on the board the Graphic Overview from page 241. Have students use the lists they made while reading the lesson to add to it. Then ask them to answer the Thinking Focus and evaluate the predictions they made before reading the lesson.

Answers to Review Questions

1. The promise of gold lured many people to move to the West, causing an increase in population and conflict between U.S. settlers and the Indians and Californios.
2. The Oregon missionaries and Mormons moved west for religious reasons; the people who moved west after 1848 did so mainly for economic reasons.
3. Differences include the companionship of the trail versus the loneliness of the farms. Similarities include continuous hard work, disease, and difficult weather conditions.
4. Sample answer: Settlers from the eastern United States took the Californios' land; they believed they had the right to North America and to any "unimproved" land. Allow for personal opinion.
5. Encourage students to use descriptive details based on information from this lesson.

Homework Options

Have students write an essay comparing the immigrants to the West in the mid-1800s with the immigrants to New England and Virginia in the 1600s.

Study Guide: page 36.

INTRODUCE

Discuss what students learned about the Treaty of Guadalupe Hidalgo and the treatment of Californios in Lessons 2 and 4. Explain to them that this petition was written nine years after California became a state, by a group of Californios who had lost much of their land to newly arrived settlers. They were petitioning the U.S. House of Representatives to uphold the terms of the Treaty of Guadalupe Hidalgo and to protect their property.

READ AND RESPOND

Before reading this text, students may want to read an excerpt from the Treaty of Guadalupe Hidalgo on page 662.

Because the formal language of the petition may be difficult for some students, you may want to have them read a paragraph at a time, and then discuss the paragraphs in small groups to be sure they understand the meaning.

In Lesson 4, you learned that Californios lost much of their land after California became a state. This petition was one reaction to that loss.

LITERATURE

Petition of the California Landowners

In the years following California statehood, the Californios (Mexican citizens living in California) lost much of their land to the U.S. citizens who moved to the new state. The petition below describes the promises that Americans made when California joined the United States. It then tells how the real conditions that Californios faced differed from those promises. As you read the petition, ask yourself what you might have done if you had been in the Californios' place.

To the Honorable Senate and House of Representatives of the United States of America

We, the undersigned, residents of the state of California, and some of us citizens of the United States, previously citizens of the Republic of Mexico, respectfully say:

That during the war between the United States and Mexico the officers of the United States, as commandants of the land and sea forces, on several occasions offered and promised in the most solemn manner to the inhabitants of California, protection and security of their persons and their property and the annexation of the said state of California to the American Union, impressing upon them the great advantages to be derived from their being citizens of the United Sates, as was promised them.

That, in consequence of such promises and representations, very few of the inhabitants of California opposed the invasion; some of them welcomed the invaders with open arms; a great number of them acclaimed the new order with joy, giving a warm reception to their guests, for those inhabitants had maintained very feeble relations with the government of Mexico and had looked with envy upon the development, greatness, prosperity, and glory of the great northern republic, to which they were bound for reasons of commercial and personal interests, and also because its principles of freedom had won their friendliness.

When peace was established between the two nations by the Treaty of Guadalupe Hidalgo, they joined in the general rejoicing with their new American fellow countrymen, even though some—a very few indeed—decided to remain in California as Mexican citizens, in conformity with the literal interpretation of that solemn instrument; they immediately assumed the position of American citizens that was offered them, and since then have conducted themselves with zeal and faithfulness and with no less loyalty than those whose great fortune it was to be born under the flag of the North American republic—believing, thus, that all their rights were insured in the treaty, which declares that *their property shall be inviolably protected and insured*; seeing the realization of the promises made to them by United

impressing upon describing in detail

in consequence of because of

feeble weak

in conformity with following

inviolably securely

Background

Part of the problem faced by California landowners occurred because Mexico and the United States had different concepts of land ownership. Many Californios had received grants of former mission lands by drawing up diseños, maps of their ranchos. The California government (when it was part of Mexico) had signed deeds granting these land to Californios, but the legality of claims was based on tradition or land occupation, not the written documents.

The California state government passed the Land Act of 1851, which created a commission to verify all Californio land claims. Californio landowners had to appear in American courts to prove their claims. Many landowners did not have the paperwork they needed, and lost all or part of their land. Even when they had solid legal claims, the legal fees were so high that they sometimes had to sell or mortgage parts of their land to pay them.

States officials; trusting and hoping to participate in the prosperity and happiness of the great nation of which they now had come to be an integral part, and in which, if it was true that they now found the value of their possessions increased, that was also to be considered compensation for their sufferings and privations. . . .

integral necessary

compensation payment

Scattered as the population was over a large territory, they could hardly hope that the titles under which their ancestors held and preserved their lands, in many cases for over half a century, would be able to withstand a scrupulously critical examination before a court. . . .

scrupulously very exact

The undersigned, ignorant, then, of the forms and proceedings of an American court of justice, were obliged to engage the services of American lawyers to present their claims, paying them enormous fees. Not having other means with which to meet those expenses but their lands, they were compelled to give up part of their property, in many cases as much as a fourth of it, and in other cases even more.

The discovery of gold attracted an immense number of immigrants to this country, and, when they perceived that the titles of the old inhabitants were considered doubtful and their validity questionable, they spread themselves over the land as though it were public property, taking possession of the improvements made by the inhabitants, many times seizing even their houses (where they had lived for many years with their families), taking and killing the cattle and destroying their crops; so that those who before had owned great numbers of cattle that could have been counted by the thousands, now found themselves without any, and the men who were the owners of many leagues of land now were deprived of the peaceful possession of even one vara. . . .

league a unit of measure, about three miles

vara a Spanish unit of measure; about 40 inches

Some, who at one time had been the richest landholders, today find themselves without a foot of ground, living as objects of charity—and even in sight of the many leagues of land which, with many a thousand head of cattle, they once had called their own; and those of us who, by means of strict economy and immense sacrifices, have been able to preserve a small portion of our property, have heard to our great dismay that new legal projects are being planned to keep us still longer in suspense, consuming, to the last iota, the property left us by our ancestors. . . .

iota very small amount

The manifest injustice of such an act must be clearly apparent to those honorable bodies when they consider that the native Californians were an agricultural people and that they have wished to continue so; but they have encountered the obstacle of the enterprising genius of the Americans, who have assumed possession of their lands, taken their cattle, and destroyed their woods, while the Californians have been thrown among those who were strangers to their language, customs, laws, and habits. . . .

manifest obvious

San Francisco, February 21, 1859

Further Reading

Walking Up a Rainbow. Theodore Taylor. In 1852, a courageous Iowa orphan embarks on a westward journey full of hardship, adventure, intrigue, and danger.

◄ What did the Mexican citizens of California expect would happen when California became a part of the United States? *(They thought they would get to keep their land.)* Why did they expect that? *(Because of U.S. government promises and the language of the Treaty of Guadalupe Hidalgo)*

◄ What happened to the Californios' land holdings after the discovery of gold? *(New settlers coming to California took possession of the Californios' property, and sometimes even their homes. American courts usually favored the American settlers, so Californios lost much of their land.)*

EXTEND

Have students use library or Internet resources to find out more about a specific Californio family or individual and what happened to them during the 1840s and 1850s. Ask students to give oral reports to the class about the family or person they researched.

Further Reading

You may want to ask students to find more books about the settlement of the West and its effects on the people who were already there—both Californios and American Indians.

Chapter Review

Reviewing Key Terms

annex (p. 232)
buffer zone (p. 231)
continental divide (p. 226)
expansionist (p. 230)
ghost town (p. 243)
Manifest Destiny (p. 227)
mountain man (p. 226)
regionalism (p. 245)
rendezvous (p. 226)
secularize (p. 237)

A. Define each of the following terms in your own words. Then use the term in a sentence that clearly shows the meaning of the term.

1. continental divide
2. Manifest Destiny
3. annex
4. expansionist
5. secularize
6. mountain man

B. Based on what you have read in the chapter, decide whether each of the following statements is true or false. If it is false, rewrite the sentence so that it is true.

1. A mountain man would spend much of the year in the wilderness and become a skilled tracker and pathfinder.
2. No settlers were allowed to go to Texas, which was a buffer zone between Mexico and the United States.
3. The Mexican government began to secularize the missions by putting them under the control of priests.
4. A ghost town only came alive at night, when the miners returned from the gold fields.

Exploring Concepts

A. On a separate sheet of paper, make a chart like the one shown below. Fill in the chart with information from the chapter. In the first column of your chart, list the areas explored or settled, along with dates of exploration or settlement. Then complete the chart by listing in the second column the reasons for the exploration or settlement. Write a short paragraph outlining the explorations and settlements that developed the West.

B. On your paper, answer each of the following questions in complete sentences.

1. What were the major effects of the Lewis and Clark expedition?
2. How did the work of the mountain men help later settlers?
3. How did Mexico's agreement to give free land to U.S. settlers in Texas backfire?
4. How did Texans turn the defeats at the Alamo and Goliad into victories?

Explorer/Settler	Dates and Territories Expanded/Settled	Reasons for Exploration/Settlement
Meriwether Lewis and William Clark		
Jedediah Smith		
Brigham Young		
Zebulon Pike		
Stephen Austin		
John C. Frémont		

Answers to Reviewing Key Terms

A. Sample answers:

1. The continental divide marks the point where rivers on one side flow west and those on the other flow east.
2. The idea of Manifest Destiny helped form the U. S. expansionist policies in the 1800s.
3. Many Texans wanted the U. S. Government to annex their republic so they could be part of the United States.
4. Expansionists wanted to extend U. S. territory from the Atlantic to the Pacific.
5. When Mexico secularized the missions in California, it took power away from the priests.
6. Mountain men often served as guides for government-sponsored explorers.

B. Answers:

1. True.
2. False. At first settlers were welcomed as long as they honored Mexican laws. Later Mexico unsuccessfully tried to stop immigration.
3. False. Secularization takes power away from the priests.
4. False. Ghost towns were abandoned towns.

Answers to Exploring Concepts

A. Answers:

Lewis and Clark: 1804–1806 / the Missouri River and its tributaries, the upper Great Plains and Rocky Mountains, Oregon country along the Columbia River to the Pacific / to find the Northwest passage

Smith: 1823–1824, 1826–1828 / the Great Plains, the Rocky Mountains, across the Great Basin to California, Oregon, and Washington / to find hunting grounds

Young: 1844–1849 / Utah and the Great Basin / religious freedom

Pike: 1805–1807 / the upper Mississippi River, the central Great Plains, and lands south of central Colorado / government-sponsored exploration

Austin: 1822 / the Texas territory / to set up a colony

Frémont: 1842–1845 / most of the West / scientific exploration

The paragraph should mention the idea of Manifest Destiny, the gathering of information about the land and inhabitants, the new economic opportunities (trapping, trade, gold), and the search for religious freedom.

B. Sample answers:

1. Their valuable information about the land, people, and animals and their accurate maps of the Northwest helped the country expand.
2. Mountain men carved out routes across the West and guided U. S. Government expeditions.
3. Many settlers refused to convert to Catholicism or to obey Mexican laws. They rebelled against Mexico and won independence.
4. They rallied their forces by reminding them that these defeats at the hands of Santa Anna's army were brutal and that the men who fought bravely to the very end were heroes.

Reviewing Skills

1. Outlines use roman numerals, capital letters, and numbers to note the difference between topics and details. Identify which parts of an outline use roman numerals, which use capital letters, and which use numbers.
2. Copy the outline on page 228. Decide whether the facts below are subtopics (S) or details (D), and put them in the correct order under the heading "III. Results of the Lewis and Clark Expedition."
   - New species were recorded, such as buffalo and Pacific salmon.
   - The expedition's samples of plants, animals, and rocks showed that the Louisiana Purchase territory was rich in natural resources.
   - The expedition catalogued in detail thousands of different plants and animals.
3. Zebulon Pike was exploring the upper Mississippi River at about the same time as the Lewis and Clark expedition. Use the information below to complete this outline:

   I. Zebulon Pike's Explorations
      A. Rocky Mountain Region
         1. Pike's Peak named after him.

   - Pike gives the government information about the number and kinds of troops Spain has in the New Mexico area.
   - New Mexico and Northern Mexico Region
   - Pike describes the wide sandy deserts of the Southwest.
4. Use the outline on page 228 to create a timeline of the Lewis and Clark expedition. Conduct your own research on the expedition, and add any information you find to your timeline.

Using Critical Thinking

1. In President Polk's inaugural address, he said, "None can fail to see the danger to our safety and future peace if Texas remains an independent state or becomes an ally . . . of some foreign nation." What do you think was the danger that Polk feared? Does that fear affect the United States' relationships with nearby countries today? Give examples to support your answer.
2. The Texans' defeat at the Alamo became one of our country's proudest stories. Why do you think a defeat became such a precious memory? Why are Texans and all Americans proud of it?
3. One historian has written of the Mexican War, "The vanquished Mexicans have never forgotten, or will they soon forget, that the northern 'gringos' tore away half of their country." Do you think the war was justified? What other means might have been used to settle the dispute?

Preparing for Citizenship

1. **WRITING ACTIVITY** Tales of the mountain men and their exploits became part of American folklore. Read through current newspapers and magazines, and identify people you think may become a part of our folklore. Write a short paper explaining what these people have done and how you think they will be seen by future generations.
2. **WRITING ACTIVITY** Many of the pioneers who made the journey across the plains kept diaries or wrote letters home. In the library, find some of these firsthand accounts. Write your favorite quotations in a notebook, and share them with the class.
3. **ART ACTIVITY** Draw a map of North America that shows how the idea of Manifest Destiny changed the boundaries in the Western United States during the 1800s.
4. **COLLABORATIVE LEARNING** The West was the frontier for Americans in the 1800s. The frontier for Americans today is outer space. Divide into groups and imagine that you are preparing to homestead on a new planet. What will you bring with you? What hardships might you face? Are your concerns different from or similar to those of the nineteenth-century pioneers? Compare your decisions with those of the other groups in your class.

Answers to Reviewing Skills

1. Roman numerals mark major topics, capital letters mark subtopics, and numbers mark supporting details.
2. A. The expedition catalogued in detail . . .
   1. New species were . . .
   2. The expedition's samples of plants . . .
3. B. New Mexico and Northern Mexico Region
   1. Pike describes the wide sandy deserts of the . . .
   2. Pike gives the government information . . .
4. Refer students to Understanding Timelines on pages 60–61.

Answers to Using Critical Thinking

1. Polk feared that other nations might use Texas as a base to attack the United States. Students should consider how such fears still influence our relationships with Cuba, Panama, and other countries in the Caribbean and in Central America.
2. The defeat was used as a slogan to inspire Texans to win their independence. Students may cite Travis's letter as evidence of the bravery of those who fought and died at the Alamo.
3. Point out that the dispute might have been settled through diplomacy. Ask students to consider the influences of individual leaders.

Answers to Preparing for Citizenship

1. **WRITING ACTIVITY** Discuss what makes a person or a story a part of a culture's folklore.
2. **WRITING ACTIVITY** Refer students to the many personal accounts of pioneers. Narcissa Whitman kept a journal that gives a lively picture of the journey and of her life in Oregon.
3. **ART ACTIVITY** This activity could be used as a class bulletin board activity.
4. **COLLABORATIVE LEARNING** The groups should discuss how early settlers reached decisions about their journeys and compare the hardships they might face today with those Americans in the 1800s faced.

Chapter 9 Planning at a Glance

The North

	Objectives	Reading Support *and* Other Resources	Diverse Learning Strategies
Lesson 1 The Industrial Revolution *pp. 254–260* 1–2 days	• Describe the advances in industrial production and in transportation systems. • Explain the relationship between industrialization and transportation. • Contrast the work of skilled craftspeople with the work of industrial workers.	• **Workbook** or **Reading Support:** pp. 122–125 Review p. 29 Extra Support/Transition p. 29 Multi-lang. Sum. pp. 57–58 • **Other Resources:** Posters 1, 3; Study Guide p. 37; Study Print 7	Access Strat. **(SDAIE)** TE p. 255 Study Skills **(Visual)** TE p. 256 Making Diagrams **(Visual)** TE p. 258 Social Participation **(Auditory)** TE p. 259 Audiotapes of Multi-language Lesson Summaries **(Auditory)**
Lesson 2 The Urban North *pp. 261–266* 1–2 days	• Describe the tremendous population growth in cities during the Industrial Revolution. • Link the growth in city population to the need for new kinds of housing and municipal services. • Compare and contrast the lives of the wealthy, the middle class, and the working poor in the cities.	• **Workbook** or **Reading Support:** pp. 126–129 Review p. 30 Extra Support/Transition p. 30 Multi-lang. Sum. pp. 59–60 • **Other Resources:** Geography Kit, Poster 5, Study Guide p. 38	Access Strat. **(Extra Support)** TE p. 262 Study Skills **(Visual)** TE p. 263 Map and Globe Skills **(Visual)** TE p. 264 Writing a Letter to the Editor **(GATE)** TE p. 264 Audiotapes of Multi-language Lesson Summaries **(Auditory)**
Lesson 3 Seeking a Better Way *pp. 267–273* 3–4 days **Literature** "Susan's Trial" *pp. 276–277*	• Identify the social problems that inspired social reform movements. • Explain the key role played by women in the temperance and other popular social reform movements. • Describe the beliefs and lifestyles of utopian communities.	• **Workbook** or **Reading Support:** pp. 130–133 Review p. 31 Extra Support/Transition p. 31 Multi-lang. Sum. pp. 61–62 • **Other Resources:** Study Guide p. 39	Access Strat. **(Extra Support)** TE p. 268 Research **(GATE)** TE p. 269 Collaborative Act. **(Multi-Age)** TE p. 271 Audiotapes of Multi-language Lesson Summaries **(Auditory)**
Skill: Using Computerized Resources *pp. 274–275*	• Use directions about computerized reference systems to locate library materials.	• **Other Resources:** Study Guide p. 40	Science Connection **(Auditory)** TE p. 274
Exploring: Sports in the United States *pp. 278–279*	• Trace the development and cultural importance of a sport. • Locate, select, and collect information about a sport by using appropriate reference materials.		
Chapter Review *pp. 280–281* 1 day		Chapter 9 Test pp. 33–36 *(See facsimiles on TE p. 757.)*	Assessment Multiple-Use Masters pp. 81–88

Reading Support Resources *for Every Lesson*

Reading and Review

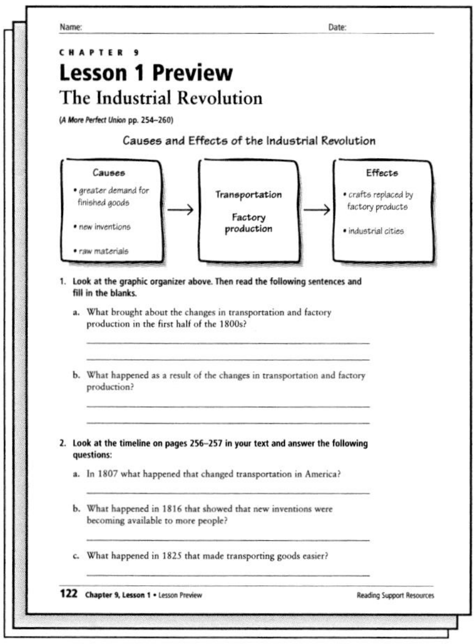
Name: Date:

CHAPTER 9

Lesson 1 Preview

The Industrial Revolution

(*A More Perfect Union* pp. 254–260)

Causes and Effects of the Industrial Revolution

Causes: • greater demand for finished goods • new inventions • raw materials → Transportation / Factory production → Effects: • crafts replaced by factory products • industrial cities

1. Look at the graphic organizer above. Then read the following sentences and fill in the blanks.
   a. What brought about the changes in transportation and factory production in the first half of the 1800s?
   b. What happened as a result of the changes in transportation and factory production?
2. Look at the timeline on pages 256–257 in your text and answer the following questions:
   a. In 1807 what happened that changed transportation in America?
   b. What happened in 1816 that showed that new inventions were becoming available to more people?
   c. What happened in 1825 that made transporting goods easier?

122 Chapter 9, Lesson 1 • Lesson Preview — Reading Support Resources

- **Chapter Overview*** p. 121
- **Lesson Previews*** using graphic organizers from the Teacher's Edition pp. 122, 126, 130
- **Reading Strategies*** pp. 123, 127, 131
- **Lesson Summaries*** pp. 124–125, 128–129, 132–133
- **Lesson Reviews** pp. 29, 30, 31

* **Workbook** includes starred items.

Multi-language Summaries

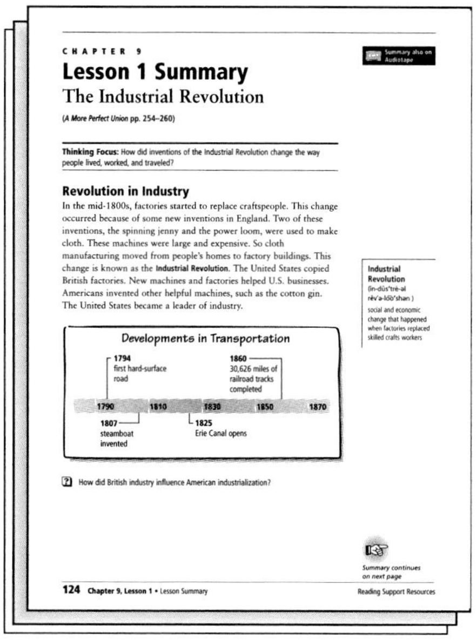
CHAPTER 9

Lesson 1 Summary

The Industrial Revolution

(*A More Perfect Union* pp. 254–260)

Summary also on Audiotape

Thinking Focus: How did inventions of the Industrial Revolution change the way people lived, worked, and traveled?

Revolution in Industry

In the mid-1800s, factories started to replace craftspeople. This change occurred because of some new inventions in England. Two of these inventions, the spinning jenny and the power loom, were used to make cloth. These machines were large and expensive. So cloth manufacturing moved from people's homes to factory buildings. This change is known as the **Industrial Revolution**. The United States copied British factories. New machines and factories helped U.S. businesses. Americans invented other helpful machines, such as the cotton gin. The United States became a leader of industry.

Industrial Revolution (in-dŭs'trē-əl rĕv'ə-lōō'shən) social and economic change that happened when factories replaced skilled crafts workers

Developments in Transportation: 1794 first hard-surface road; 1807 steamboat invented; 1825 Erie Canal opens; 1860 30,626 miles of railroad tracks completed (1790, 1810, 1830, 1850, 1870)

How did British industry influence American industrialization?

Summary continues on next page

124 Chapter 9, Lesson 1 • Lesson Summary — Reading Support Resources

Lesson Summaries in:

- English (See Reading and Review.)
- Spanish pp. 124–125, 128–129, 132–133
- Chinese pp. 57–62
- Hmong pp. 57–62
- Khmer pp. 57–62
- Vietnamese pp. 57–62

Summaries available on audiotapes

Lesson Support / Transition

S D A I E

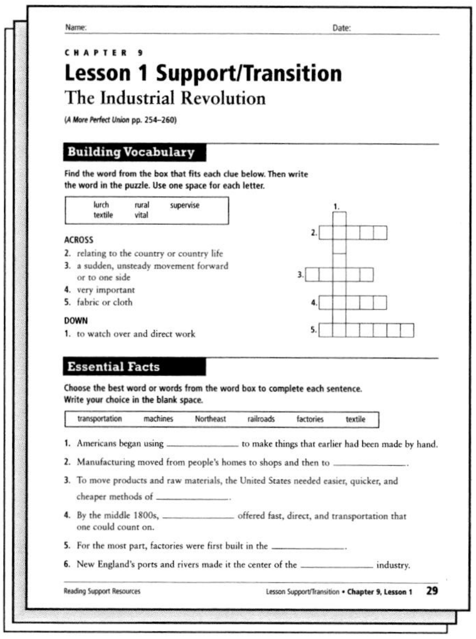
Name: Date:

CHAPTER 9

Lesson 1 Support/Transition

The Industrial Revolution

(*A More Perfect Union* pp. 254–260)

Building Vocabulary

Find the word from the box that fits each clue below. Then write the word in the puzzle. Use one space for each letter.

lurch rural supervise textile vital

ACROSS
2. relating to the country or country life
3. a sudden, unsteady movement forward or to one side
4. very important
5. fabric or cloth

DOWN
1. to watch over and direct work

Essential Facts

Choose the best word or words from the word box to complete each sentence. Write your choice in the blank space.

transportation machines Northeast railroads factories textile

1. Americans began using ______ to make things that earlier had been made by hand.
2. Manufacturing moved from people's homes to shops and then to ______.
3. To move products and raw materials, the United States needed easier, quicker, and cheaper methods of ______.
4. By the middle 1800s, ______ offered fast, direct, and transportation that one could count on.
5. For the most part, factories were first built in the ______.
6. New England's ports and rivers made it the center of the ______ industry.

Reading Support Resources — Lesson Support/Transition • Chapter 9, Lesson 1 29

Activities for SDAIE
Specially **D**esigned **A**cademic **I**nstruction in **E**nglish

- **Lesson Support/Transition** pp. 29, 30, 31

Technology Options

Internet Support

http://www.eduplace.com

Social Studies Center at Education Place

Internet support for Chapter 9:

- ***Lesson at a Glance***
- ***A Telegraph Operator***

Videotape/Videodisc

We the People:
Supports and enhances major topics: **Themes: *The Rise of the City; Transportation***

Software

Student Writing Center® (CD-ROM) (Macintosh® or Windows®)

School to Career

A public education was not always guaranteed to everyone in the United States. Only after determined individuals such as Emma Willard organized and protested, did cities and states begin to change. Open a discussion on careers in education by telling the class what brought you into the field.

Character Education

Ask students to list individuals whom they feel exercise social responsibility and improve the conditions of people who often can't help themselves. What contributions have they made to society? Create a certificate of appreciation to present to those individuals.

CHAPTER PREVIEW

Have students read the chapter title and the narrative underneath it. Using the U.S. political map in the Atlas on pages 698–699, locate the region designated the North in this chapter: the Northeast and the states bordering the Great Lakes. Compare the images of the North with those of the West from Chapter 8. How do the regions differ? *(The North is more developed and more densely populated; it has public services such as the fire department.)*

Looking Back

Remind students that in Chapter 7 they learned about changes in family farms in the Northeast and the rise of port cities along the Atlantic seaboard.

Looking Forward

Tell students that they will be building their knowledge of the North in the following lessons: The Industrial Revolution, The Urban North, and Seeking a Better Way.

Chapter 9
The North

One man built an entire mill from memory. Another man turned a "folly" into the first successful steam-powered boat. Women filled the factories and mills. The North was alive with invention and progress. Cities thrived and everywhere the character of Northern life was changing.

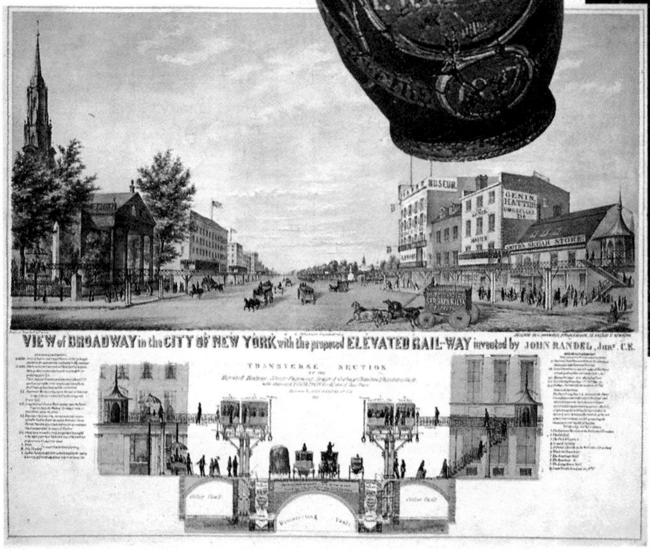

Cities grow quickly as canals, railroads, and telegraphs connect the nation. New York City even has elevated trains for mass transportation.

1790 | 1800 | 1810 | 1820

Presidents

1789-1797 Washington

1797-1801 J. Adams

1801-1809 Jefferson

1809-1817 Madison

1817-1825 Monroe

1790

252

BACKGROUND

After 1800, early industrialization brought about many changes in the lives of Americans living in the North. Factory workers replaced craftspeople, transportation became increasingly easy and less expensive, and large numbers of people began to live and work in the city. This, in turn, resulted in the need for reform movements.

The Steam Engine

Factories needed huge amounts of power to keep machinery running. Manufacturers located factories on rivers to take advantage of rushing water, but water was simply too unreliable. Floods produced too much power and droughts halted work completely. The steam engine provided an efficient, reliable source of power that could run machinery inexpensively on any site where fuel to generate steam was available.

Before the steamboat, travellers and shippers had to choose between barges, pulled by people and animals, and river sloops, which depended on wind. Neither worked well upstream. Steam engines gave boats the power to move quickly and easily up and down waterways. In addition, trees along the river provided a ready supply of fuel for steam engines.

The first modern-day steam engine, which pumped water out of mines, was patented by Thomas Savery in England in 1698. In 1712, Thomas Newcomen developed another steam engine pump. Both of these engines were quite inefficient because they used huge

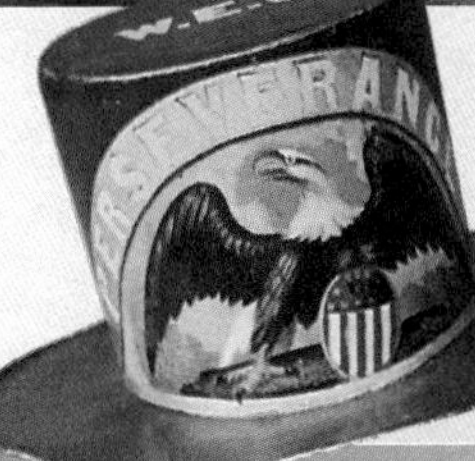

1827 Growing cities demand fire and police services. At right is a decorated hat worn by a firefighter in a parade. An equally ornate fire bucket from 1827 is shown at the top, left.

1860 Artist Henry Mosler depicts the bustling Canal Market in Cincinnati.

1830 | 1840 | 1850 | 1860

1829 Adams · 1829-1837 Jackson · 1837-1841 Van Buren · 1841 W. Harrison · 1841-1845 Tyler · 1845-1849 Polk · 1849-1850 Taylor · 1850-1853 Fillmore · 1853-1857 Pierce · 1857-1861 Buchanan

1860

Understanding the Visuals

Name the types of people represented in the painting of the Canal Street Market by J. Mosler, 1860. *(Young and old, black and white)* How does this market differ from supermarkets today?

Point out the elevated railway plan. Why might a plan for an elevated railway have been proposed? *(To ease traffic problems)* Explain that this plan was originally rejected because people feared that the railway would "destroy" the appearance of Broadway. New York City did finally build an elevated railway (not on Broadway) in 1870.

Understanding Chronology

Point out that the time period covered in this chapter is the same time period covered in Chapter 7. Ask students to recall some of the major events in Chapter 7. *(Family farms breaking up; American Indian relocation; settlement of trans-Appalachian frontier; immigration from Germany and Ireland)*

amounts of steam and, therefore, large amounts of fuel to heat the water. James Watt of Scotland, who is usually credited with inventing the steam engine, simply developed a more efficient engine that could have more applications. Improvements in manufacturing methods made much of his work possible. For example, a precise boring machine developed in 1775 enabled him to drill perfectly round holes to prevent steam from leaking.

One of the first uses of the steam engine in the United States was not in manufacturing or transportation, but in supplying a major city, Philadelphia, with its first adequate water supply for drinking, fighting fires, and cleaning streets (1801).

The Seneca Falls Convention

Elizabeth Cady Stanton met with Lucretia Mott and some other friends in July 1848 and challenged them "to do and dare anything." The next day an advertisement in a local newspaper announced a convention on women's rights to be held in Seneca Falls, New York, later in the week. Many reformers and factory workers attended. The convention's Declaration of Sentiments and Resolutions, an effective parody of the Declaration of Independence, proclaimed that "the history of mankind is a history of repeated injuries and usurpations on the part of man toward woman, having in direct object the establishment of tyranny over her." The convention formally launched the women's rights movement and spurred conventions in other states.

INTRODUCE

Have students read the Thinking Focus. Ask them to tell their associations with the word *revolution. (Students may mention the American and French revolutions.)* Help them define *revolution. (A sudden change in a situation)* Ask students to describe what an industrial revolution might be and what effects it might have. Tell students to read the lesson to confirm or reject their descriptions.

Key Terms

Vocabulary strategies: T36–37
Industrial Revolution—the social and economic changes that occurred when manufacturing shifted from people's homes and shops to factories
raw materials—unprocessed natural products used in manufacturing

1790 — 1860

L E S S O N 1

The Industrial Revolution

THINKING FOCUS

How did the inventions of the Industrial Revolution change the way people lived, worked, and traveled?

Key Terms

- Industrial Revolution
- raw materials

Randolph, Massachusetts, 1830. Gideon Howard awakes each morning to his new life as an independent craftsman. In earlier days, he was a farmer who made shoes in his spare time for extra money. Now Howard makes his living as a cordwainer, or shoemaker.

Because more people want to buy shoes, Howard needs help to make enough pairs. He does some of the skilled work himself and supervises the other workers. One cuts the leather for the uppers (the top of the shoe); another stretches the leather over a wooden mold shaped like a foot. A stitcher attaches the upper to the sole, and another worker tacks on the heels. The completed shoes are then taken to a store to be sold.

Individual shoemakers like Howard did a good business until the mid-1800s. Then the demand for shoes rose so rapidly they could not make shoes fast enough. Individual craftspeople lost business, and production moved from small shops to factories that used stitching machines and other new inventions. In the factories, each worker tended a machine that might do several tasks once done by skilled craftspeople working by hand. These advances made it possible to produce more shoes in a shorter time.

Howard's story illustrates how factories largely replaced craftspeople in the 1800s. A new industrial economy was emerging in America. Its growth was especially strong in the North.

Among a shoemaker's tools were knives for cutting leather, foot-shaped wooden casts for shaping leather, and hammers for tacking on the heels of shoes.

Objectives

1. Describe the advances in industrial production and transportation systems.
2. Explain the relationship between industrialization and transportation.
3. Contrast the work of skilled craftspeople with the work of industrial workers.

Graphic Overview

Causes
- greater demand for finished goods
- new inventions
- raw materials

→ **Transportation** / **Factory Production** →

Effects
- crafts replaced by factory products
- industrial cities

Revolution in Industry

The shift to factories in the United States grew out of a process that began in the British textile industry. In the late 1700s, British inventors developed machines to do tasks that had been done by hand. The spinning jenny, run by water power, replaced the spinning wheel, and the power loom replaced the hand loom. Because these machines were too expensive for most individuals, manufacturing moved from people's homes and shops to factories. This change in producing goods was so far-reaching and had such widespread effects that it is known as the **Industrial Revolution**. It changed not only the way goods were produced, but also how people lived and worked.

Americans copied, then modified, British industrial methods. To limit competition, however, British factory owners refused to allow any machinery or plans of machines to leave England. An ambitious British textile worker named Samuel Slater outwitted them by memorizing the plans. In 1790, Slater built a spinning mill in Pawtucket, Rhode Island, using machines based on these plans. It began a revolution in U.S. industry.

The use of the newest machinery and the newest techniques helped American industry succeed. One new method was the use of standard parts. Eli Whitney, a Connecticut inventor, developed tools and machinery to make parts that were exactly alike. For example, the bolt for one of Whitney's rifles would fit any of his rifles. Having interchangeable parts speeded up production and reduced costs.

Also important in America's success was its store of natural resources. Wood from its forests, coal and iron ore from its mines, and abundant water power were all vital in early industry.

Last, but certainly not least, were the American people. Skilled and resourceful, they provided the labor, the business leadership, and the inventiveness that made the United States an industrial leader. ■

■ *How did British industry influence American industrialization?*

◄ *As the Industrial Revolution swept the North, mills such as this one in Massachusetts were established. Americans began to make goods for themselves.*

DEVELOP

Point out that this lesson shows the causes for the shift from people working in homes to people working in factories as well as how that shift affected people's lives. Tell students to list the causes and effects of the shift from homes to factories as they read the lesson.

ECONOMICS

Critical Thinking

In addition to having British inventions to expand on, what other factors contributed to the success of the American Industrial Revolution? *(Interchangeable parts, abundant natural resources, skilled people)*

■ *Americans copied and modified British machines, which performed tasks previously done by hand.*

Access Strategy

Ask students if they are wearing or if they own any handmade clothes. Ask if they or if any people in their family do crafts, such as needlework or furniture making. Who produces most of their clothes and household products? *(Factories)* Why do some people prefer handmade over factory-made items? *(Handmade items are often of better quality.)* Why are handmade items generally more expensive? *(Take longer to produce)* Could today's consumer-demands be met by handmade goods alone? *(No)*

Have students imagine being workers who make clothing. Ask whether they would rather work in a factory or in a small shop. Why? Which would they enjoy more? In which would they be likely to make more money? Tell students that they will read in the lesson about the shift from handmade products to factory-made products.

Access Activity

Have students compare the picture of the shoemaker's shop on page 254 to the pictures of factories on this page and on page 259. What can they infer about differences between working in a shop and in a factory? *(Shop—small space, one or two people, use of hand tools; factory—large space, many people, use of machines)*

Building a Transportation Network

The enormous size of the young nation meant that transportation was difficult and expensive. The United States needed easier, quicker, and cheaper methods of transportation.

A System of Roads

In 1794, the Lancaster Turnpike, linking Philadelphia and Lancaster, Pennsylvania, became the first hard-surfaced road in the United States. In the following years, more than 10,000 miles of roads were built to link the major commercial centers of the North. Many roads were built by private companies which charged a toll, or fee, for their use. Although tolls were used for upkeep, the roads were rough. Travelers jounced and bumped over the uneven surfaces. They welcomed the development of canals.

A Canal Network

In 1825, the state of New York completed the Erie Canal, a 363-mile waterway joining Buffalo on Lake Erie with Troy and Albany on the Hudson River. The new waterway linked the Atlantic Coast to all of the Great Lakes for the first time. Ships sailed from New York City up the Hudson River to Albany; then their cargo and passengers shifted to canal boats. The canal helped New York become the nation's most important city.

The Erie Canal made travel into the heart of the country easier and less expensive. Goods that cost $100 a ton by road cost only $10 a ton by canal—and the trip was only a third as long. Western **raw materials**—products in their natural state, such as iron ore or cotton—were shipped by canal to the East. Manufactured goods were shipped to the western frontier.

The enormous success of the Erie Canal encouraged an era of canal building. By 1840, over 3,000 miles of canals had been built. Yet, within a few years, canal building virtually ended. Canals could not compete with less costly kinds of transportation.

New inventions and advances in technology helped fuel the growth of U.S. industry.

The First Industrial Revolution, 1790–1860

1790, U.S. Patent Office opens, issuing the first patent to Samuel Hopkins for a new kind of fertilizer ingredient.

1794, Eli Whitney's patent for the cotton gin is granted. Whitney's idea is stolen and copied by others despite his patent.

1816, Although Philadelphia tested street lights earlier, Baltimore becomes the first city to light its streets with gas lamps.

1790 | 1800 | 1810 | 1820

1807, Robert Fulton's steamboat *Clermont* makes its maiden voyage on the Hudson River, traveling from New York City to Albany.

1825, Water keg from which Gov. Clinton of New York poured water from Lake Erie into the Atlantic Ocean November 25, 1825, symbolizing the completion of the Erie Canal.

ECONOMICS

Visual Learning

Have students examine the timeline on this page and page 257. Ask them to list each new invention and technological advance in the timeline. *(Fertilizer ingredient, cotton gin, steamboat, gas street lamp, Erie Canal, Colt revolver, postage stamp, telegraph, bloomers)* Which one do they think will have the most dramatic consequences? *(Sample answer: Telegraph—will fill need for speedier communication, which will affect business, travel, and personal lives)*

Study Skills

On the bulletin board, reproduce on a long strip of paper the timeline on this page, leaving room for additions. Ask students to look in the lesson and in encyclopedias for other inventions and events from the period of the Industrial Revolution. Have students make drawings and captions for these inventions and events and add them to the timeline.

Social Context

Despite the good intentions of some factory builders to create ideal communities of "mill girls," entire families worked in many factories. Child labor became common, with children as young as six working under dangerous conditions for pennies a day. Some factory owners established stores where workers could buy necessities on credit. It often took the family's weekly paycheck to pay off the store debt, leading to an endless cycle that kept workers tied to the mill.

Economic Context

Although Jefferson's agrarian ideal (Chapter 5) was successful on the western frontier, it lowered food prices in the East, driving farmers into the cities to look for work. Factories were oversupplied with cheap labor, which led to the exploitation of workers. In more recent times, the techniques of mass production have come to agriculture, precipitating a decline in smaller farms that has approached crisis proportions, especially in the Midwest.

Speedy Clipper Ships

When trade with England was cut off during the War of 1812, New England merchants developed a highly profitable trade with Asia. Lean, fast clipper ships with sails billowing in the wind, sped southeast from Salem and Boston and plunged through the raging waters of Cape Horn at the tip of South America. On the northwest coast of North America they traded blankets and trinkets for furs brought by Indian peoples. The furs were exchanged in China for silk, tea, and fine porcelain. On the return journey, the American ships took on California hides for New England shoemakers (see Chapter 8).

Both the dumpy canal barges and the sleek clippers were important to trade. Yet neither could compete with new vehicles powered by steam—the steamboat and the railroad.

Travel by Steamboat

Credit for making the steamboat a success goes to inventor Robert Fulton. He launched the *Clermont*, the first commercially successful steamboat, on the Hudson River in 1807. Soon steamboats were puffing along U.S. rivers and lakes. They dominated transportation on American waterways from 1815 to 1860. Eventually, however, their use declined. They were replaced by the steam railroad, which did not depend on the fixed routes of natural waterways.

▲ *Horses and mules walked along the towpath beside a canal, towing boats and barges. This painting shows the Erie Canal at Pittsford, New York.*

1847, The first official U.S. gummed postage stamps are issued. Senders began to pay the costs of sending letters.

1853, The Crystal Palace Exhibition is held in New York to display and demonstrate new American inventions and industrial advances.

1830 | 1840 | 1850 | 1860

1833, Samuel Colt invents and patents this six-shooter revolver, the first gun that could be used effectively by a person on hourseback.

1844, The first telegraph message is sent from the U.S. Supreme Court in Washington, D.C. to Baltimore, Md. by Samuel Morse, inventor of the telegraph. A printing telegraph invented by David Hughes is shown here.

1851, Amelia Jenks Bloomer, editor of the women's rights magazine, *Lily,* gains attention by wearing trousers, later known as *bloomers.*

HISTORY

Critical Thinking

Have students recall Tocqueville's description of Americans' "quest for perfection" and his conversation with a sailor about building ships (page 183). In what way do the advances in transportation reflect Tocqueville's observations? *(Canals were replaced by clipper ships and steamboats, which, in turn, were replaced by railroads.)* Ask students why new methods of transportation actually replaced old methods rather than merely adding another way to travel. *(New methods usually quicker, easier, cheaper)*

257

Art Connection

With the Industrial Revolution, America saw the beginning of a golden age of invention. Ask students to think about something practical or fanciful that they would like to invent. Have them research the kinds of drawings made by inventors for patent applications. Ask each student to draw an invention and to write a description of how it would work and how it would change people's lives.

Health Connection

The Industrial Revolution marked the beginning of problems in industrial safety and health. Have students research some of the physical and chemical occupational hazards of the early years of industrialization—for example, brown lung disease (caused by inhaling textile dust) or mercury poisoning (caused by making felt). Have them also investigate occupational hazards of today, such as silicosis (caused by inhaling harmful fumes while making computer chips).

Critical Thinking

Tell students to explain how this lesson describes the changes they learned about in Lesson 1 of Chapter 7. *(Change from a home-based working life to working outside the home, new roles for women, the shift to living in cities)*

GEOGRAPHY

Map and Globe Skills

Ask students to compare the map on this page with the political map of the United States on pages 698–699 in the Atlas. What major cities were connected by the system of canals and railroads in 1836? *(Sample answers: Cleveland, Columbus, Pittsburgh, New York, Boston, Providence, Cincinnati)*

■ *Transportation changes include hard-surfaced roads, canal networks, clipper ships, steamboats, and railroads.*

Northern Railroad and Canal Network, 1850

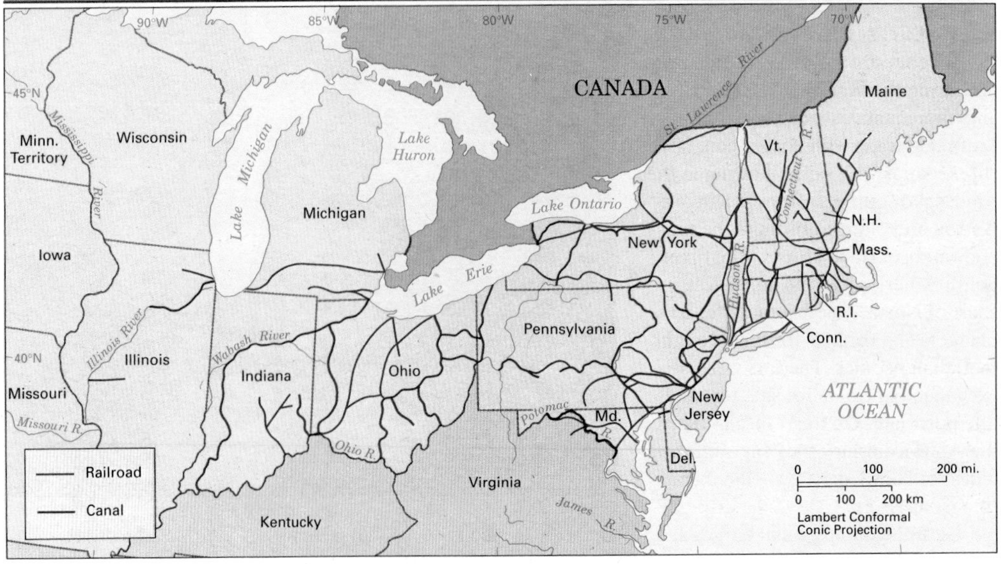

In 1790, an order sent from Boston to Philadelphia took two weeks to arrive. By 1836, because of expanded railroad services, a similar order took only 36 hours.

Railroads Revolutionize Travel

Railroads developed first in Britain but grew most dramatically in the United States. Between 1828 and 1840, American workers laid about 3,300 miles of track. By 1860, trains clattered over an incredible 30,626 miles of track.

Train travel was speedy but uncomfortable. Cinders from the wood-burning engine blew into people's eyes, and black soot covered their clothing. The train lurched and jolted over uneven tracks. Yet, because railroads could be built almost anywhere, growing numbers of people used them.

Railroads offered fast, direct, and dependable service. The newly invented telegraph, developed in 1837 by Samuel F. B. Morse, helped control train traffic.

Railroads also provided job opportunities. Unskilled workers, many of them immigrants, laid the tracks and maintained the rail lines. Factory workers manufactured the locomotives and rails needed.

Steamboats and railroads used a new kind of power—steam. By the mid-1800s, steam power was transforming industry as well as transportation in the United States. ■

■ *What changes occurred in transportation in the 1800s?*

Across Time & Space

Workers in the 1800s felt machines threatened their jobs. In the 1950s factories began to use electronic robots for boring or dangerous jobs. Some people fear that such machines will put them out of work; others say they create new jobs.

Production Revolutionized

For the most part, industrialization took place in the Northeast. The region had abundant water that could be used for power. The poor, stony soil of its hilly farms discouraged some farmers and sent them to the cities looking for work. Also New England already had a thriving trade by sea.

The New England textile mills were long brick buildings, three or four stories high, built beside a river that supplied power for the machines. Inside the factories, workers cared for machines that clattered and hummed as they spun thread and wove fabric.

In 1814, a Boston merchant named Francis Cabot Lowell founded a textile mill at Waltham, Massachusetts. In this mill, Lowell combined all the steps of textile production—from spinning the raw cotton into thread to weaving

Map and Globe Skills

Have students locate on a current national highway map the major routes of commerce. *(Interstate highways)* By comparing the map on this page to the highway map, students can determine which of the waterways and railroad lines of the 1830s are part of modern transportation today. *(Sample answers: The Hudson and the Mississippi rivers)*

Role Playing

Divide students into groups of five or six to role play a meeting between "mill girls" and the owner of a textile factory. Suggest that they discuss wages and working conditions in order to agree on a contract that satisfies both the workers and the owner. You may want to remind students that each factory owner had a virtually unlimited supply of labor. One person in each group should write down their group's contract provisions and read it aloud to the class.

Making Diagrams

Have students research the workings of the steam engine and make a series of diagrams that show how the steam is generated, is fed into the cylinder, moves the piston, and escapes through the exhaust. Good resources for the research are encyclopedias and David Macaulay's *Mill* (see the Social Studies Bookshelf, page 219) and *The Way Things Work* (Boston: Houghton Mifflin Co., 1988).

the finished cloth—under one roof for the first time.

Lowell had hoped to build an entire community around his mill, but died before he could complete his plan. After his death, a city based on his ideas was built by the falls on the broad Merrimack River. Named Lowell in his honor, by 1855 it had some 52 mills that employed more than 13,000 people. These mills produced over one million yards of cotton cloth each week. In a year that was "nearly enough to belt the globe twice over." Lowell and the other Merrimack River towns—nearby Lawrence and Merrimack, New Hampshire—were the center of the textile industry in New England.

Women Enter the Factories

During the early 1800s, most farm women remained at home, rearing the children and performing household tasks. This pattern began to change in about 1820. New England farmers found it difficult to compete with Western farmers who could grow grain and other crops more cheaply. Many farmers' sons left New England and headed for the more fertile farms in the West. Farm daughters tried to help their families by going to work in the textile factories.

Most American factory owners welcomed these young women. They were used to hard work on the farms, and the factory owners hoped they would prove to be a dependable, obedient work force.

To avoid the poverty and crime found in British factory towns, the owners paid wages in cash, set up company-run boarding houses, and provided social and cultural opportunities. Although the boarding houses had strict rules, they gave the young women a place to live where someone looked after their well-being.

Water power was used to operate mills. Flowing water turned a large, outdoor wheel. Gears then turned pulleys and belts that moved the factory's machines.

Lowell "Mill Girls"

Factory work tended to be repetitious and dull. Lucy Larcoom, who worked in the Lowell mills at a machine called a dressing frame, told how the machines sometimes seemed to overwhelm the workers.

> *It had to be watched in a dozen directions every minute . . . it was always getting itself and me into trouble. I felt as if the half-live creature . . . was aware of my incapacity to manage it.*

The women in the Lowell mills worked an average of 12 hours a day, six days a week. Men held all the

ECONOMICS

Visual Learning

Have students point to the parts of a factory shown in the picture and described in the caption on this page. *(Large outdoor wheel, gears, belts, pulleys, machinery)*

HISTORY

Critical Thinking

Ask a student to read aloud Lucy Larcom's description on this page of working with a dressing frame. Why was this particular machine difficult to monitor? *(Moved quickly in many directions)* How does her description reflect a rather personal battle with this machine? *(She calls it "the half-live creature," and says it seemed to realize she could not handle it.)*

Writing a Letter

Tell students to imagine that they are "mill girls" working and living at a textile mill in New England. Have them write a letter home, telling about the work itself, their fellow workers, their boss, their social lives, and their hopes for the future. Students may base their letters on information in the lesson as well as on other sources in the library, such as Bernice Selden's *The Mill Girls* (New York: Atheneum, 1983).

Research

Have students research and write a two- to three-page report on the steel or the textile industry today. They can concentrate on the mill process itself, or they can describe the route from raw materials to finished goods. Students can also report on the decline of these industries or the effect that foreign competition has had on the United States's finished steel and cloth markets.

Social Participation

After students have read the lesson, divide them into teams of four or five to debate one of the following questions: Did factory owners owe anything besides wages to the workers? Were they justified in paying women so much less than men?

CULTURE

Visual Learning

Ask students to relate the picture on this page to the quotation of Lucy Larcom on page 259. In what ways is her description reflected in the picture? *(Woman monitoring a machine)* How could the machine harm the operator? *(Hand or hair could get caught in moving parts.)*

■ *New England had a strong sea trade and a good water supply for power. Its poor soil drove many farmers to the city to look for work.*

CLOSE

Have students answer the Thinking Focus and evaluate how they described an industrial revolution and its effects before they had read the lesson. Copy on the board the structure of the Graphic Overview from page 254 and have students complete it by using the lists that they made while reading the lesson.

Lowell "mill girls" faced long work days for little pay.

How Do We Know?

HISTORY *We have learned a great deal about 19th century Lowell, Massachusetts through the work of archaeologists. They have uncovered foundations of factories and housing for workers. From bottles and jars they learn about the food and medicine people used. Coins and pieces of crockery provide dates.*

■ *What made New England the center of the textile industry?*

supervisory positions and received higher pay. In 1836, men's daily wages ranged between 85 cents and $2, while women earned from 40 cents to 80 cents. A worker could be fined or denied work for being late, working too slowly, or challenging a supervisor's authority. To increase production, some mills had each worker take care of more machines or speeded up the rate at which machines worked. Workers had little choice but to work faster if they wanted to keep their jobs.

Despite these disadvantages, the New England "mill girls" saw factory work as a chance to learn about a world that was different from their familiar rural surroundings. Most enjoyed meeting other young people, going to theaters and museums, and shopping in a variety of stores. They found the bustling throngs of the city an exciting change from the isolation of farm life.

Most "mill girls" looked on factory work as temporary. Most young women intended to work in the mills only until they married. When they felt conditions were too difficult, they left. In the mid-1800s, many farm women grew dissatisfied. Their place was taken by immigrant workers, most of them from Ireland.

Industry Inland

Not all the industrial cities were near the coast. When steam began to be used in factories as well as in transportation, industry could be set up closer to raw materials or markets. Pittsburgh, Pennsylvania, for example, was an inland city that grew up near supplies of coal and iron ore and cheap water transportation.

The Pittsburgh factories concentrated on metal working. The first factories made nails. Added to these were a steam engine factory and a mill using iron ore. At first, slabs of iron were rolled flat by hammers driven by country streams. In 1819, the Union Rolling Mill introduced a process that allowed the iron to be rolled in the factory. By making iron production more efficient, Pittsburgh became America's "Iron City."

The wave of industrial development sent ripples through every level of society in the United States. Centuries' old traditions were transformed as Americans faced new challenges of adjusting to city life. The country and the world would never again be the same. ■

REVIEW

1. **FOCUS** How did the inventions of the Industrial Revolution change the way people lived, worked, and traveled?
2. **CONNECT** How was settlement of the West spurred by the expansion of the railroad and canal networks?
3. **GEOGRAPHY** What factors determined where factories were built during the early 1800s?
4. **CRITICAL THINKING** What do you think are the advantages and disadvantages of products assembled by hand? Of manufactured goods?
5. **CRITICAL THINKING** "Mill girls" were subject to highly supervised, highly regulated work and social lives. Do you think this was an effective way to ensure productivity? Give reasons for your opinion.
6. **ACTIVITY** Ask your parents or other adults to tell you about their memories of a roadway being built. Ask them to explain how the road's construction affected the area in which it was built.

Homework Options

Have the students research and write a paragraph on the transition of one product, such as candles or furniture, from a craft workshop to factory production in the early 1800s.

Study Guide: page 37.

Answers to Review Questions

1. Because of the inventions, people began to live in cities, work in factories, and travel quickly and inexpensively.
2. The quicker, cheaper transportation stimulated commerce, which then increased settlement of the West.
3. Factories were built near power sources, raw materials, and transportation.
4. Sample answer: Handmade products are often expressions of the creator's individuality, but they take a relatively long time to make. Allow for personal opinion.
5. Sample answers: Yes, this method prevented them from wasting time. No, the girls would eventually quit because they would dislike having so little control over their own lives. Allow for personal opinion.
6. Encourage students to ask about the effects on personal lives as well as the effects on the business community.

LESSON 2

The Urban North

> *I think our governments will remain virtuous for many centuries as long as they are chiefly agricultural; and this will be as long as there shall be vacant lands in any part of America. When they get piled upon one another in large cities, as in Europe, they will become corrupt as in Europe.*
>
> Thomas Jefferson to James Madison, 1787

Thomas Jefferson believed that cities were a threat to American values. In Jefferson's mind, America was meant to be a land of sturdy, independent farmers (see Chapter 8). The land would be free of the factories, industrial cities, and crowds of people found in Europe.

By 1816, growing cities and spreading industrialism pointed to sweeping change in the nation's political, social, and economic life. Jefferson declared, "we must now place the manufacturer by the side of the agriculturalist." He had come to recognize that the United States was becoming an industrial nation.

Many Americans welcomed the shift toward an urban society. In 1833, Amasa Walker, a follower of Andrew Jackson, remarked that a time would come when cities would become "great fountains of healthful moral influence, sending forth streams that shall fertilize and bless the land."

THINKING FOCUS

How did the growth of cities affect American society?

Key Term

- municipal

Urban Growth

During the 1700s, American business had been based on trade with other countries. The major colonial cities in the North were located on the Atlantic Coast and their economy depended on shipping.

In the 1800s, advances in technology and transportation shifted the economic emphasis from trade to industry. This shift changed the way Americans lived and worked.

City Populations Grow

U.S. cities grew very quickly during the 1840s, their population expanded due to immigrants and people moving from the farms. In 1820, only 12 cities in the United States had populations of more than 10,000 people. By 1860, the United States had 101 cities of more than 10,000 people each. Eight of them were home to more than 100,000 people; one—New York City—had already topped one million inhabitants.

As the urban populations grew, city governments faced a number of problems. Housing the increase in people and protecting them were obviously important issues. The expanding cities also needed their own transportation systems.

Providing Housing

An important innovation in urban construction was the "balloon frame" house, introduced in the 1830s. Wood was sawed into thin pieces that were

INTRODUCE

Begin by having students read the lesson title and the Thinking Focus. Help students contrast *rural* (of the country) and *urban* (of the city). Tell students to name problems that some city dwellers face today. *(For example, poverty, crime, drugs, pollution)* Point out that these problems are not unique to cities but that city life does tend to heighten these problems. Ask students if they think similar problems existed a hundred years ago. Tell them to read the lesson to find out about the problems of growing cities in the 1800s.

Key Term

Vocabulary strategies: T36–37

municipal—of an urban political unit

Graphic Overview

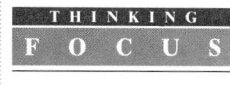

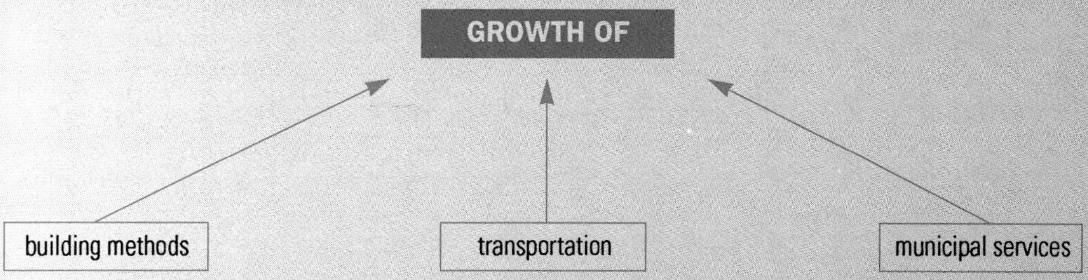

Objectives

1. Describe the tremendous population growth in cities during the Industrial Revolution.
2. Link the growth in city population to the need for new kinds of housing and municipal services.
3. Compare and contrast the lives of the wealthy, the middle class, and the working poor in the cities.

DEVELOP

Have students scan the heads in the lesson to preview some of the changes that have taken place in cities and in the lives of city residents. Encourage students to take notes as they read the lesson, using the lesson heads as main points in an outline.

HISTORY

Critical Thinking

Ask students to describe just how rapidly cities grew from 1820 to 1860. *(In 1820 there were only 12 cities with populations over 10,000; by 1860 there were 20 such cities.)* Why did this increase in population lead to the construction of "balloon frame" houses? *(Increasing numbers of people needed housing in the city. The balloon frame could be built quickly and inexpensively.)*

➤ *Cities include New York, Philadelphia, and St. Louis.*

nailed together to make a relatively light, inexpensive frame. Traditional structures used heavy jointed timbers in their frames and needed skilled carpenters to build them.

The balloon frame did not require special skills. It allowed people to build whole neighborhoods quickly and economically. This technique was especially useful farther west, where the cities had plenty of space to spread outward.

In the older areas of the Northeast, cities grew upward instead of outward. The wooden frames that were most commonly used could not support the weight of buildings that were over a few stories high.

To solve this problem, some architects combined cast-iron columns with stone buildings. James Bogardus pioneered this method in 1848 when he built a five-story factory in New York. Later, he used iron to make entire frames for buildings. Iron, however, was heavy, and it limited the height of buildings. Taller buildings were not possible until new technology came along in the late 1800s.

➤ *On this map the circles represent population, not the areas of the city. What cities had grown to over 300,000 people by 1860?*

Northern Population Increase 1800-1860

Access Activity

Have students use the two maps on this page to explain changes that took place between 1800 and 1856. *(Some cities didn't grow enough to be included in the 1856 map; more cities existed by 1856; some cities grew considerably; more state names on map)*

Access Strategy

Tell students to imagine what would happen if the enrollment in their school suddenly doubled. What problems would the school immediately face? *(Not enough teachers, classrooms, desks, sports equipment, lockers)* What problems would a city face if thousands of people looking for housing and jobs began to pour into it? *(Problems with housing, sanitation, safety, unemployment, increased crime)* Point out that both schools and cities would need some time to be able to figure out how to deal with such increases in population. Tell them that in this lesson they will find out how cities in the 1800s handled major population growth.

This 1803 painting, A Large View of Baltimore, *shows one of the rapidly growing American cities.*

Moving City People Around

In most cities before 1840, people could easily walk from one place to another. As these cities grew, the distances between different parts increased, and cities began to develop public transportation systems. Within the cities, horse-drawn vehicles called horsecars came into use in about 1850. Horsecars traveled on specific routes around the city, taking people from their homes to the places where they worked and shopped. By 1866, New York City had 16 horsecars with 800 cars and 8,000 horses to pull them. They carried about 35 million passengers a year.

As cities grew more crowded, however, the horsecars became less practical. Author Mark Twain commented that the cars were "getting left behind by fast walkers." He added that the cars were so crowded that "you will have to hang on by your eyelashes and your toenails."

Transportation was one **municipal**, or city-run, service. As city populations grew, the need increased for municipal services.

Protecting People

One problem facing the growing cities was a rising rate of crime. The part-time law officers were little more than watchmen who made scheduled rounds of the city. They were not organized or trained to enforce law and order. To protect law-abiding citizens, full-time municipal police forces were needed. In 1845, New York City set up the first modern police force. Philadelphia and Boston soon followed New York's example.

City dwellers also needed protection from fire. The large number of wooden frame buildings and the use of candles, fireplaces, and wood-burning stoves caused frequent fires. In the crowded cities these fires spread quickly and killed many people. At first, crews of volunteer firemen rushed through the streets pulling hose wagons and hand pumps. As cities grew, these volunteers were replaced by full-time professional firemen. About the same time, steam-powered pumps came into use. When the fire alarm sounded, horses dashed through the streets pulling steam pumps.

Another important concern in the cities were health problems. Most cities had no sanitation systems, and streets were clogged with garbage. Polluted water caused epidemics of deadly diseases. After a cholera epidemic in 1866, New York City set up the Metropolitan Board of Health. To make the city a more healthful place to

GEOGRAPHY

Visual Learning

Have students read the captions and study the 1803 painting of Baltimore on this page. How does the skyline of this growing city differ from a typical city skyline today? *(No skyscrapers or air traffic in 1803)*

POLITICAL SYSTEMS

Study Skills

Tell students to use the information in the lesson on this page and page 264 to make a chart of both the services provided by cities and the urban problems they were established to combat. *(Police—crime; fire departments—fire, often caused by candles and fireplaces; sanitation systems—disease, caused by polluted water, garbage, lack of ventilation)*

Economic Context

Many people who came to cities to escape rural poverty found urban poverty. They hoped to find jobs with good wages that would provide their families with adequate food and housing. Large numbers of immigrants and free blacks came to cities with similar hopes. Because such large numbers of people flooded into cities, business owners could be selective, hiring people who would accept the lowest possible wages. As a result, many working class people earned less than they needed to live on. Immigrants and black Americans often could not find work at any price because of discrimination against them.

Critical Thinking

Ask students to compare the urban transportation of the mid-1800s to today's. *(1800s—horse-drawn vehicles; today—subways, cars)* Ask them to name transportation problems similar to both time periods. *(Congestion, noise, pollution)* Have them suggest solutions to today's transportation problems. *(Ban cars in busy areas; improve public transportation)*

■ *Cities needed housing, transportation, police forces, fire departments, and sanitation systems.*

■ *What types of services did the growing cities need?*

live, it limited the number of people living in a room, banned throwing garbage in the streets, and required better ventilation of rooms and better connections between buildings and the city's sewer system. ■

People in the Cities

Most Americans considered the growth of cities a sign of success. Urban growth was so rapid, however, that it created numerous problems for people, especially the poor.

Social Classes

Within the cities lived wealthy factory owners and bankers, middle-class shopkeepers, and poor workers. The middle class included mill supervisors, shopkeepers, craftspeople, ministers, and school teachers. (The telegraph operator in A Moment in Time on page 265 was a member of the middle class.) Educated free blacks, usually ministers or teachers, made up a small proportion of the middle class.

The working poor included people who had moved from rural areas to the cities, immigrants, and unskilled free blacks. In the 1840s, over four million immigrants entered the United States; most of them settled in cities as unskilled laborers. Eventually some of the immigrants, through hard work and education, moved up into the middle class.

In many typical mill cities, the workers lived in crowded apartments or company-owned housing a short walk from the factories where they worked. They depended on the factory whistle to tell them the time of day. The middle class were scattered throughout the city. Many used the horsecars to travel about. On the outskirts of the city, or on hills overlooking the mills, stood the mansions of the wealthy. Private horse-drawn carriages took them around the city.

Changing Social Relationships

Although the same social classes had existed before, industrialism changed the relationships between them. The gap between the classes grew steadily wider. Factory owners, bankers, and railroad owners grew wealthier as their businesses prospered. People in the middle class also benefited.

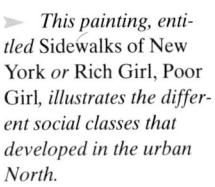

This painting, entitled Sidewalks of New York *or* Rich Girl, Poor Girl, *illustrates the different social classes that developed in the urban North.*

SOCIAL SYSTEMS

Critical Thinking

Ask students to contrast the observations about the United States made by the Europeans (Chapter 6) to the changes in the social classes described in this lesson. *(Crèvecoeur and Tocqueville were impressed by the lack of social distinctions, but the gaps between classes were widening in cities.)*

Map and Globe Skills

In this lesson, the two maps on page 262 are used to show population growth. Have students examine the maps in Chapter 7 (pages 194 and 213) and Chapter 19 (page 572) and the population map of the United States on pages 704–705 in the Atlas. What can be learned from such maps about populations? *(Population size, growth, location)*

Health Connection

In addition to cholera, which is mentioned in the lesson, typhoid and dysentery were other diseases common in cities in the 1800s. Ask students to find out what these three diseases are, how they are transmitted, and how they can be prevented. Suggest that they discover what role, if any, malnutrition plays in promoting these diseases. Students may also compare treatment of diseases in the 1800s with treatments today.

Writing a Letter to the Editor

Have students write a letter about the conditions of poverty in the city to the editor of a newspaper of the 1800s. They should choose details from the lesson to support their own or one of the following points of view—the urban poor deserve what they get; the urban poor are victims of an unjust system; or poverty is beyond anyone's control.

A MOMENT IN TIME

A Telegraph Operator

10:34 A.M., August 29, 1852
Office of the Pittsburgh, Cincinnati, and Louisville Telegraph Company in Pittsburgh, Pennsylvania

Starched Collar
This stiff collar irritates his neck. Six months ago he was on his family's farm in Marietta, Ohio. Now he's a telegraph operator in Pittsburgh. No more comfortable homespun shirts.

Message
"Largest gold shipment received in New York from San Francisco, worth over $2 million dollars." Someone run this message to the newspaper editor—now!

Telegraph
Dot, Dash, Dot . . . The telegraph taps out dots and dashes, each code signaling a different letter. It records the message on a strip of paper. His job is to transcribe the code into English.

Handkerchief
The summer air in the office is musty and hot. He reaches for this when the smells of oil lamps and ink make him sneeze.

Lunch Pail
With any luck, the boarding house matron packed him a big lunch. He came in at 6:00 this morning, and with all the excitement, he may be here until 9:00 tonight.

Note: You may wish to use A Moment in Time to help students better understand how middle class people lived.

HISTORY

Visual Learning

What skills would the telegraph operator need to do his job well? *(Be able to read and write, be able to interpret Morse code, work quickly)* What might make his job interesting? *(He'd be the first person in the area to receive important news.)*

More About the Message The message, tapped out at 40 words per minute, is 15 words long and costs 90 cents. A message boy will deliver the piece of paper to the newspaper editor for 3 cents.

Research

Have students find out more about balloon-frame houses and the tools needed to build them. Suggest that they contrast these houses and tools with wood-frame houses and power tools of today. Some students may also want to research how the houses were finished once they were framed (lathing, plaster, flooring, wall coverings).

Critical Thinking

Ask why the telegraph operator in A Moment in Time on this page was considered middle class rather than working class. *(The people of the middle class had specific skills.)*

CITIZENSHIP

Critical Thinking

Help students analyze Dix's motivation for promoting reform. Why were the mentally ill in prisons? *(There were not a sufficient number of mental hospitals. Perhaps people did not know what else to do with the mentally ill.)* How successful were her reforming efforts? *(She increased the number of state mental hospitals by over nine times.)*

■ *It increased the gap between the social classes.*

CLOSE

Have students answer the Thinking Focus. Copy on the board the Graphic Overview from page 261. Ask students to use the outlines that they made while reading the lesson to add examples to each head in the Graphic Overview.

The poor, however, faced a new situation. Before industrialization, they had worked on farms or in shops for their board and room. They usually lived where they worked or nearby. If poor workers became ill or could not work, their employer often helped them out.

With the coming of industrialization, workers received wages that had to be spent for rent, food, clothing, medicine, and other expenses. They lost their income if they lost their jobs. They had no unemployment benefits or health insurance to protect them. They might receive aid from private charities, such as church groups, but there were no government programs of aid. Unemployment was a real threat. Urban workers had little choice but to work 10 to 12 hours a day, plus six hours on Saturdays, for very little pay.

➤ *Social reformer Dorothea Dix worked throughout her lifetime to improve life for people who were mentally ill.*

■ *How did industrialization change the relationship between social classes?*

Beginnings of Reform

The problems that faced people in the industrializing cities led to several reform movements. At first, these were carried out by individuals or private groups. One individual who worked for reform was Dorothea Dix, a Massachusetts school teacher. When she visited a women's prison in 1841, she found several mentally ill women among the inmates. To help these unfortunate women became Dix's lifelong cause.

For the next 40 years she urged states to build more hospitals for the mentally ill. She was so persuasive that the number of state mental hospitals increased from 13 in 1843 to 123 in 1880.

Dorothea Dix had concentrated on a single area that needed reform. Other reformers became involved in wider social issues. ■

REVIEW

1. **FOCUS** How did the growth of cities affect American society?
2. **CONNECT** How did developments in transportation contribute to the rapid industrialization of the North?
3. **ECONOMICS** How did the move from an economy based on commerce and trade to one based on manufacturing affect the way Americans lived and worked?
4. **CRITICAL THINKING** Why are municipal services performed by city governments rather than private organizations?
5. **CRITICAL THINKING** How did the experience of the working poor in cities differ from that of the wealthy and middle classes?
6. **WRITING ACTIVITY** Imagine you are a factory worker who has moved from a rural area to find a job in the city. Write two or three short diary entries that describe your first impressions of city life.

Homework Options

Have students research and write a one-page report on the lifestyle of factory owners in the 1800s.

Study Guide: page 38.

Answers to Review Questions

1. It created the need for housing, transportation, and municipal services. It also widened the gaps among three distinct social classes.
2. Industries were able to grow because raw materials could be shipped quickly and inexpensively.
3. This change led many Americans to live and work in cities.
4. Sample answer: Municipal services require more funds than most private organizations could supply. Allow for personal opinion.
5. Sample answer: In contrast to many people in the wealthy and middle classes who benefitted from city life, many of the poor suffered various hardships—poor housing, lack of medical attention, and difficult working conditions. Allow for personal opinion.
6. Encourage students to use emotional and concrete details in their descriptions.

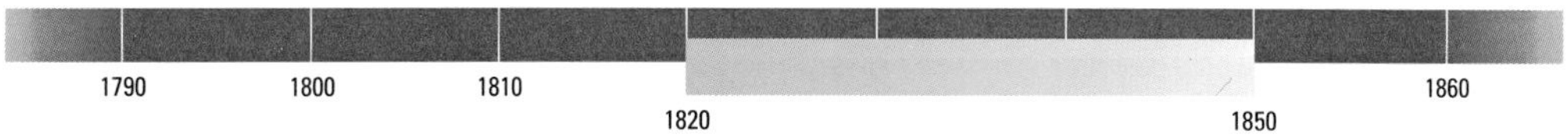

L E S S O N 3

Seeking a Better Way

"We hold these truths to be self-evident: that all men and women are created equal..."

Declaration of Sentiments,
Women's Rights Convention,
Seneca Falls, New York, 1848

These words sound familiar, but they are not the ones Thomas Jefferson wrote for the Declaration of Independence. Jefferson had mentioned only men when he wrote of equality. By the mid-1800s, some women were beginning to challenge this limitation of rights.

In 1848, no woman had the right to vote, and most women were denied property rights. If a woman was divorced, her husband had the unchallenged right to take the children.

In July 1848, more than 300 women met at the Wesleyan Methodist Church in Seneca Falls, New York. Their aim was to discuss "the social, civil, and religious condition and rights of women."

Among the organizers of the convention were Lucretia Mott and Elizabeth Cady Stanton. Both were active in the fight to end slavery. Their articles against slavery were welcomed by men who worked to end slavery. Yet, because they were women, they had not been allowed to make public speeches at the world antislavery convention in 1840. Angered by this rejection, Mott and Stanton decided to work to improve the status of women.

Some men supported the movement for women's rights. Most men, however, agreed with a male editor who called the Seneca Falls meeting "the most shocking and unnatural incident ever recorded in the history of womanity."

Despite this opposition, the movement for women's rights continued. In 1841, Elizabeth Cady Stanton met Susan B. Anthony, who was active in the antislavery movement. (To read more about Susan B. Anthony, see page 276.) The women became close friends and worked together for women's rights. This movement was just one of the social reforms that developed in the 1800s.

THINKING FOCUS

What types of social reform movements developed in the 1800s?

Key Terms

- temperance
- utopia

◄ *Elizabeth Cady Stanton, a homemaker in upstate New York, organized the women's rights meeting in Seneca Falls. Many people still consider Seneca Falls as the birthplace of the women's rights movement in the United States.*

INTRODUCE

After students have read the lesson title and Thinking Focus, ask them to recall the problems of urban life introduced in Lesson 2. *(Lack of adequate housing, transportation, and sanitation; crime; fire; poverty)* Also ask them to name an example of a reformer in Lesson 2. *(Dorothea Dix)* Suggest that students read the lesson to find out what sorts of reform movements were established to solve the problems of urban life.

Key Terms

Vocabulary strategies: T36–37

temperance—giving up the drinking of all alcoholic beverages

utopia—a community established to create social and political reform

Graphic Overview

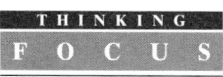

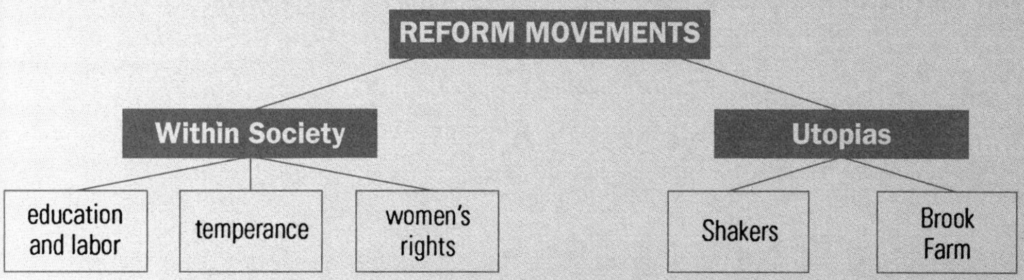

Objectives

1. Identify the social problems that inspired social reform movements.
2. Explain the key role played by women in the temperance and other popular social reform movements.
3. Describe the beliefs and lifestyles of utopian communities.

DEVELOP

Point out that people in the 1800s tried to change society in two main ways—by creating reform movements within society and by establishing new communities (called *utopias)* apart from society. Many people turned to religion as a source of comfort and support during this time. Copy on the board the structure and main heads of the Graphic Overview from page 267. Suggest that students list both the reform movements within society and those formed outside of society as they read the lesson.

SOCIAL SYSTEMS

Visual Learning

Have students answer the following questions about the temperance poster on this page. In what order are we to read the corner pictures? *(Clockwise from lower left)* Besides temperance, what virtues are represented? *(Faith, hope, and charity)* What do the women on the right and left represent? *(Temperance and truth)* Help students define *inebriate. (A drunk person)* What does the "Inebriate Express" represent? *(Rapid route to ruin through alcohol)*

Reform Takes Many Shapes

▲ *Social reformer Susan B. Anthony was active in the antislavery, temperance, and women's rights movements. Anthony pledged her life insurance money to the University of Rochester in Rochester, New York, so that women could attend the school.*

Americans both welcomed and feared the rapid changes society was undergoing during the 1800s. Industrialization and the growth of cities offered new opportunities, but many people wondered about the cost of progress. Problems such as alcoholism, illiteracy, and poor working conditions cried out for action.

Reform movements that tried to solve these problems were largely an outgrowth of the Second Great Awakening (see Chapter 6). Through that movement, people renewed their religious faith and came to believe that they could change the world. The educator Horace Mann expressed this desire to improve society, saying: "Be ashamed to die until you have won some victory for humanity."

The Temperance Movement

Reformers had the most success in their attempts to decrease alcoholism. Although alcohol abuse had existed throughout American history, the problem became more severe with industrialization. Many workers felt resentment because their lives seemed to be regulated by machines. Instead of feeling proud of the products they made, many workers grew bored from doing the same, repetitive task. They feared unemployment, illness, and old age. In despair, many workers sought to escape their misery with alcohol.

Alcoholism led to physical abuse and broke up many families. Recognizing this destructiveness of alcoholism, reformers called for **temperance**—giving up all drinking of alcoholic beverages. By 1833, there were 5,000 local temperance societies with a combined membership of over one million people. Members signed a pledge promising they would never drink alcoholic beverages.

In line with the ideals of the Second Great Awakening, temperance leaders looked on alcoholism as a moral problem rather that a social problem or an illness. To them, alcoholics were sinners who spent the Sabbath in drinking rather than in worship. Through the efforts of these temperance societies, alcoholism declined sharply in the 1840s.

Women played a major role in the temperance movement. First, they were expected by tradition to set a

➤ *Through drawings and posters that illustrated the results of alcoholism, temperance societies persuaded many to sign the pledge.*

Access Activity

Divide students into groups of four or five to brainstorm ideas for improving the difficult conditions in the work and home lives of the working poor of the mid 1800s. Have one student in each group write down the ideas. Then combine the groups so that they can share their ideas.

Access Strategy

To help students understand the value in people working together to bring about change, ask them to imagine the following modern situation: The manager of a fast-food restaurant is mistreating the part-time help. She cuts pay for minor tardiness, publicly humiliates workers whom she does not like, gives her "favorite" workers all the best hours, and fires people who complain about how they are treated. How could one person change this unfair situation? *(Organize a group of workers to talk to the manager's boss, seek help from a labor relations office, or get in touch with a union of restaurant workers)* Ask students to name examples of people working together to bring about change. *(Neighborhood crime-watch programs, MADD, Greenpeace)* How do people go about promoting change? *(Public demonstrations, petitions, letter-writing campaigns)* Tell students they will find out in this lesson how people in the 1800s tried to change society.

Many women used the education they gained to become teachers themselves.

moral example for other family members. Second, women had firsthand experience of excessive drinking. Many had suffered physical and mental abuse at the hands of drunken fathers or husbands. Third, women wanted to stop men from spending on alcohol the money that their families needed.

Education for Women

In addition to urging temperance, many women sought expanded educational opportunities for themselves. In the process, they helped bring about public education for all.

One of the early reformers was Emma Willard, who believed women should be allowed to study mathematics, science, and philosophy—subjects traditionally restricted to male students. Willard founded the Troy Female Seminary in Troy, New York, in 1821. Other pioneers in this area included Sarah Josepha Hale, one of the first female magazine editors in the United States, and Mary Lyon, who founded Mount Holyoke Female Seminary (later Mount Holyoke College) in 1837.

Through the efforts of people such as these, women became better educated and more aware of the world outside their homes. Many, however, continued to believe that a woman's place was in the home. Jobs such as teaching were seen as temporary positions that a woman would leave when she married.

Establishing Public Education

Before the 1820s, few children had the opportunity to go to school. From an early age they worked at trades or on the farm. The few public schools that did exist were understaffed; teachers were poorly paid and received little training. Students of all ages and abilities were crowded into one room. Schools had little money for textbooks or other supplies.

In 1837, lawyer Horace Mann became head of the newly formed Massachusetts State Board of Education. For the next 11 years, Mann worked with other reformers to establish a public educational system. Mann believed education was essential to democracy: "If we do not prepare children to become good citizens, if we do not develop their capacities, . . . then our republic must go down to destruction." His argument reinforced the idea that American constitutional democracy required citizens who were well informed.

Public education, Mann believed, would give children values—thrift, a sense of order, discipline, respect for authority—that would be useful in

CITIZENSHIP

Critical Thinking

Refer students to the quote by Horace Mann on this page. Why did he believe education was important for the future of the United States? *(Children must be prepared to become informed citizens.)* Ask students to explain why they agree or disagree with Mann. *(Students should consider the idea that citizens in a democracy need to be informed because they have a voice in the government.)* Have students name other benefits of education. *(Preparation for a good job, financial security, social skills)*

Research

Have students research and write a two- to three-page report on the role of one of the following women in the movement for women's rights: Emma Willard, Elizabeth Cady Stanton, Lucretia Mott, Mary Lyon, Susan B. Anthony, Sarah Josepha Hale. Alternatively, have students trace the women's movement from its roots in the 1800s to the present. What has the movement accomplished in the past? What is it working on now?

Critical Thinking

How is the role of women in reform similar to the role of the "republican mother" described in Chapters 6 and 7? *(In both, women maintain peace in the home and promote education.)* How is it different? *(Changed to more involvement outside the home and education for women)*

Understanding Cultural Institutions

The booming cities of the late nineteenth century had their share of problems: crime, fires, garbage, disease. But cities also had their share of pleasures. City-dwellers were less isolated than people living in the country. City people were able to get together to share ideas, entertainment, and common creative interests. Because the large populations were necessary to support libraries, theaters, museums, and art galleries, these cultural institutions first developed as part of the trend toward urbanization.

Reading Societies and Lyceums

The earliest cultural institutions weren't museums or concerts; they were discussion groups that met to exchange ideas and encourage learning. Benjamin Franklin started such a group, called the Junto, in the 1720s. Writer and critic Margaret Fuller also organized a group called "Conversations" in Boston from 1839 through 1844.

Discussions that featured a key speaker, often a famous figure, were known as lyceums. Begun in 1836 by Josiah Holbrook, lyceums offered the public the chance to hear lectures and debates. Later, the American Lyceum paid fees to lecturers who traveled around the entire country. Well-known speakers included Henry David Thoreau, Nathaniel Hawthorne, and Susan B. Anthony. Instead of gathering around the TV or going out to see a movie, as people do today, city-dwellers of the 1800s often spent a social evening at a public lecture.

Libraries

Some of these discussion groups and lyceums were known as "reading societies" because their members loaned each other books from their private collections. In this way, the meeting rooms became the earliest versions of public libraries. In 1731, for example, Benjamin Franklin started the Library Company of Philadelphia, a subscription library in which members' dues purchased books that members shared.

Other libraries began near colleges. For example, in 1638, John Harvard willed about 400 volumes to a newly formed school in Massachusetts, and the Harvard College Library was born. Today, this oldest U.S. library boasts over 11 million volumes.

The nation's commitment to free public education led naturally to its commitment to free public libraries. The first tax-supported public library opened in Peterborough, New Hampshire in 1833. In 1881, Andrew Carnegie, a leader in the steel industry, used part of his vast fortune to build more than 1,700 public libraries throughout the United States.

After the formation of the American Library Association in 1876, the institutions multiplied. Today, Americans have the opportunity to borrow books from over 6,000 public libraries across the country.

During the urbanization of the Industrial Revolution, people worked hard to improve the quality of their lives. This improvement included efforts to extend education beyond the confines of the schoolroom, into meeting places and libraries. In a sense, libraries were a small piece of the longed-for ideal city that actually became reality for cities and towns all across the nation.

CULTURE

Critical Thinking

The early discussion groups that were organized by people such as Benjamin Franklin helped give people in the United States a feeling of common identity and participation. Today, commercial television is the single most pervasive cultural influence in America. Can television today serve a function similar to the discussion groups of the 1700s? Why or why not? *(Encourage students to give specific reasons for their answers.)*

Critical Thinking

What does the last sentence on this page mean by "a longed for ideal of the city"? *(Libraries gave people the opportunity to improve the quality of their lives.)*

Health Connection

Intemperance, later called alcoholism, was probably the first drug-related public health problem in the United States. Since then other drugs—marijuana, heroin, cocaine, "crack"—have also been viewed as harmful to society. Have students research and write a two-page report on one of the illegal drugs commonly used today and the problems it causes. Alternatively have them research and report on one of the three legal, widely used addictives—alcohol, tobacco, and caffeine.

Mathematics Connection

Many people worked long hours in the 1800s. "Mill girls" worked a twelve-hour day, six days a week (72 hours per week). In this lesson, the Philadelphia trade societies demanded a ten-hour work day (60 hours a week, including Saturday). How many hours are there in the eight-hour, five-day work-week common today? *(40)* Assuming a fifty-week year, how many hours per year are represented by those weekly rates? *(3,600; 3,000; and 2,000 respectively)*

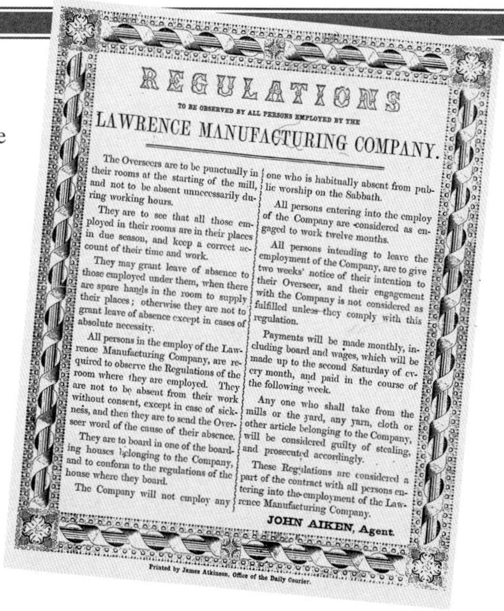

REGULATIONS

TO BE OBSERVED BY ALL PERSONS EMPLOYED BY THE

LAWRENCE MANUFACTURING COMPANY.

The Overseers are to be punctually in their rooms at the starting of the mill, and not to be absent unnecessarily during working hours.

They are to see that all those employed in their rooms are in their places in due season, and keep a correct account of their time and work.

They may grant leave of absence to those employed under them, when there are spare hands in the room to supply their places; otherwise they are not to grant leave of absence except in cases of absolute necessity.

All persons in the employ of the Lawrence Manufacturing Company, are required to observe the Regulations of the room where they are employed. They are not to be absent from their work without consent, except in case of sickness, and then they are to send the Overseer word of the cause of their absence.

They are to board in one of the boarding houses belonging to the Company, and to conform to the regulations of the house where they board.

The Company will not employ any one who is habitually absent from public worship on the Sabbath.

All persons entering into the employ of the Company are considered as engaged to work twelve months.

All persons intending to leave the employment of the Company, are to give two weeks' notice of their intention to their Overseer, and their engagement with the Company is not considered as fulfilled unless they comply with this regulation.

Payments will be made monthly, including board and wages, which will be made up to the second Saturday of every month, and paid in the course of the following week.

Any one who shall take from the mills or the yard, any yarn, cloth or other article belonging to the Company, will be considered guilty of stealing, and prosecuted accordingly.

These Regulations are considered a part of the contract with all persons entering into the employment of the Lawrence Manufacturing Company.

JOHN AIKEN, Agent.

Printed by James Atkinson, Office of the Daily Courier.

▲ *This list shows the strict regulations mill owners set for their workers.*

industrialized society.

Massachusetts set aside tax money for public education and made it compulsory for children to attend elementary school. To meet the need for better trained teachers, Mann established the first of the normal schools (now called teacher's colleges). Other states followed his example, and public education became widely available.

Men Protest Working Conditions

The roots of labor reform came during the early 1800s as skilled craftsmen such as carpenters, shoemakers, and printers formed "trade societies." They called for higher wages, shorter hours, and better working conditions.

In 1835, the Philadelphia trade societies called a citywide strike —that is, they stopped work until their demands were met. Their slogan, "6 to 6," called for a workday running from 6 A.M. to 6 P.M., with an hour for breakfast and an hour for lunch.

Woman Workers Organize

The trade unions did not include women, since most labor organizers felt women did only unskilled work. Women therefore formed unions of their own. New York seamstresses established a union in 1825. In the 1830s, a Philadelphia organization represented women working in a variety of occupations.

Like men, women workers also used strikes to make their demands clear. In 1828, when textile mill owners in Dover, New Hampshire, issued rules that women workers found unacceptable, the women went on strike. The huge textile factories in Lowell, Massachusetts, stood idle when women went on strike in 1834 to protest a wage cut of 25 percent. Another strike occurred in 1836 when Lowell boarding houses raised the rent they charged. Workers gained little through these early strikes. The mill owners could easily replace the strikers with newly arrived immigrants who would work for lower wages. For most workers, conditions improved little until the late 1800s.

In 1844, five mill workers set up the Lowell Female Reform Association, an influential labor group. In one year, about 500 women joined. The association led the way in the fight to win a 10-hour workday. Their agitation led to the first government investigation of working conditions. ■

■ *What part did women play in the reform movements of the 19th century?*

Utopian Societies

Most of the reform movements were practical attempts to improve life by eliminating such problems as poverty, illiteracy, and alcoholism. Other reform groups felt that a new society was needed. These groups tried to set up communities known as **utopias** *(yoo TOW pee uhz)*. The name came from Thomas More's book *Utopia*, published in 1516, which describes a perfect place where all people are equal, prosperous, educat-

ECONOMICS

Visual Learning

Have students compare the Lawrence regulations on this page with any requirements they may have to follow in school or at home (for example, being punctual, or receiving consent for a planned absence). Which of the Lawrence regulations would not be required in most jobs today? *(Living in a boardinghouse, attending church, making a twelve-month commitment)*

■ *Women were involved in the temperance movement as well as reforms in education, labor, slavery, and women's rights.*

Collaborative Learning

Divide students into groups of three or four to design a utopian school. Students should first discuss the goals of the new school. What rules would they establish in order to create a harmonious community? How would they design the school building, school government, the selection of classes? Each group should establish a specific plan, dividing up the following roles: researcher, diagram drawer, group coordinator, and class presenter.

Critical Thinking

Help students analyze the importance of technological inventions (such as the steam engine) and of social services (such as education and public health).Which do they think has helped humankind more? Do technological inventions and social services ever work together? *(Yes, for example, creating inexpensive, quality housing could be used to help the homeless.)*

CULTURE

Critical Thinking

Help students analyze why people established utopias. Why did some people decide to establish separate communities rather than working to reform the existing society? *(Sample answers: Saw the problems of society as being too complex to change; recognized that their goals were completely different from a large percentage of the population)* Ask students if they would be content to live in a group that was as isolated from society as most utopias in the 1800s were. Why or why not?

ed, and wise. Since utopia comes from Greek words meaning "no where," it clearly describes a place that does not exist. Nevertheless, many people in the 19th century believed perfection could be attained.

Utopian societies usually held ideas that differed greatly from those of the rest of the population. For example, many utopians were disturbed by the widening gap between rich and poor. Most utopians believed that people should set aside their private interests and work for the good of the community as a whole. They would thus share in both the work and the income of the community.

The Shakers

The Shakers, founded by Ann Lee in England, were the most famous of the religious utopian communities. Shaker ideals included purity, love, peace, and justice. In 1774, Ann Lee, known as Mother Ann, led eight followers to America. After the Shakers settled in upstate New York, they made many converts.

The largest Shaker community was founded in 1787 in New Lebanon, New York. The Shakers believed that all people were equal and should share in the benefits and responsibilities of life. Among the Shakers, property was owned by the community as a whole, not by the individual. Also, Shakers did not believe in marriage or bearing children. They therefore had to rely on converts to increase their numbers. By 1850, the number of Shakers had grown to about 6,000 people. Within a few years, however, the appeal of the Shakers diminished, and the number of their colonies declined. Today, only a handful of Shakers remain in New Hampshire and Maine.

Brook Farm

Some utopias were an attempt to create communities where people combined physical labor with intellectual curiosity. These communities were supposed to be "pure" compared to the cities. Though the structures and rules of groups varied, most consisted of members from several families living together and sharing the work.

The most famous of these utopian experiments was Brook Farm, established in 1841 in West Roxbury, Massachusetts. Brook Farm was planned as a community of thoughtful people who would lead harmonious lives by avoiding competition and greed.

Shaker religious communities, established during the early 1800s, were examples of utopian societies. This print shows the performance of a "wheel dance."

Critical Thinking

Point out to students that most of the utopian movements of the 1800s failed. Have students discuss why this might have happened. *(Sample answers: Set goals too high; assumed that people were much more alike than they are; lacked a sense of business; did not acknowledge people's selfish interests)*

Historical Context

In 1758, when Ann Lee was in her twenties, she helped form a society that came to be known as "Shakers" because of its style of worship, which included singing, shouting, dancing, and shaking. The Shakers prophesied that Christ would soon return, but they had no other specific beliefs at that time. Ann's relatives pressured her into marrying Abraham Standerin, one of her father's employees, in 1762. When all four of the children produced in the marriage died, she became convinced that marriage was an evil. Interestingly, her husband was one of the eight followers whom she led from England to the United States to spread her beliefs. Shortly after their arrival, however, Abraham deserted Ann and the Shakers. In New England the Shakers attracted many followers. In addition to advocating strict religious practices, Ann Lee promoted democracy and equal roles and rights for women in the group.

◄ *Artist Olof Krans presents a peaceful view of Bishop Hill, a utopian community in Illinois (1864). Such communities encouraged individual responsibility and cooperation among residents.*

Individuals became members of Brook Farm by buying shares of stock. Each member had one vote. Community members worked the same number of hours for the same wages and paid the same room and board. Brook Farm was noted for its fine school, which stressed personal responsibility and encouraged students to have questioning minds.

The most famous shareholder, author Nathaniel Hawthorne, served for a time as the colony's director of agriculture. Hawthorne's fictional account, *The Blithedale Romance*, describes the goal of the colonists as the desire to breathe "air that had not been spoken into words of falsehood, formality and error, like all the air of the dusky city!"

Like other utopian communities, Brook Farm failed, closing in 1847. Utopians claimed the failure was financial, but Hawthorne pointed out that life in a utopian community had as many problems as life in a city. By the mid-1800s, the North was characterized by industrial cities joined to one another by an efficient transportation network. The outlooks and reform movements that colored the region were responses to rapid industrialization and the problems it created. These problems were quite different from those faced by the agricultural South. ■

■ *What were the goals of utopian societies?*

REVIEW

1. **FOCUS** What types of social reform movements developed in the 1800s?
2. **CONNECT** How did the rapid growth of cities and industries spark the move for social reform in the United States?
3. **CITIZENSHIP** How did utopians attempt to create a new social order?
4. **HISTORY** Why did so many women become involved in the temperance movement?
5. **CRITICAL THINKING** Why do you think social reformers considered public education to be so important?
6. **ACTIVITY** Imagine you are seeking to create a modern-day utopia. Prepare and deliver a short speech about how your community would be organized. Mention the ideals that would govern it and how it would provide food, jobs, and shelter for its members.

GEOGRAPHY

Visual Learning

Refer students to the painting of Bishop Hill on this page. Why might utopians choose such a place to establish a community? *(Because it is away from the masses of people, industrialism, and problems of cities, it might be easier to start a new way of doing things.)* Why would it be difficult to establish a utopia in an urban setting? *(Hard to be "separate" in a crowded city)*

■ *Utopian societies tried to establish perfect communities in which all people were considered equal and worked together for the good of the community as a whole.*

CLOSE

Copy on the board the structure and main heads of the Graphic Overview from page 267. Have students complete it together, using the lists they made while reading the lesson. Have them answer the Thinking Focus. As an extension activity, have students discuss whether people could solve today's social problems by reform or if they should consider creating new utopias.

Answers to Review Questions

1. Reform movements included education, labor, women's rights, and temperance. Reform also occurred in utopian societies.
2. The rapid growth of cities led to many problems, including the lack of adequate housing, sanitation, education as well as poor working conditions.
3. Utopians tried to create an ideal society by escaping from city life.
4. Women were expected to set a moral example; they were often abused by alcoholic fathers or husbands; and they knew that their family could not spare the money men were spending on drink.
5. Sample answer: Through education, people could gain better jobs and living conditions. Allow for personal opinion.
6. Encourage students to consider what changes would help community members live in harmony.

Homework Options

Ask students to investigate the history of a local or state law regarding children, such as labor or school attendance laws.

Study Guide: page 39.

UNDERSTANDING REFERENCE MATERIALS

This skill lesson will introduce students to computerized reference systems and their use.

HISTORY

Study Skills

After students have read the lesson, ask the following: Why is entering the key word the first step in the process? *(The computer must know what you're looking for.)* Why must you spell the key word correctly? *(The computer will look for exactly what you type.)* Why must you press Enter after making each choice? *(It tells the computer to carry out your instructions.)* Why would you choose Search Titles or Search Topic Index? *(You only want items about Mary Lyon.)*

UNDERSTANDING REFERENCE MATERIALS

Using Computerized Sources

Here's Why

In order to make use of all possible resources when doing research, you need to understand and use computerized reference information. We are living in an age of "information explosion." Books, magazines, newspapers, radio, and television produce more and more information every day. In order to keep track of all that information, many libraries now use computerized systems to add to, or even to take the place of, the card catalog system.

Suppose you want to write a research paper on Mary Lyon, one of the educational leaders you have read about in this chapter. You could use a computer data bank to locate your reference material quickly and efficiently.

Here's How

A number of computerized reference systems are available today. Although they may vary in detail, most of them use menus and screens to organize the location and presentation of information. The following example uses features that are common to these systems. It does not show the detailed operations of an actual system, but instead serves as a guide for using these systems.

To begin your search on a computer data bank, you need to understand that the computer "interacts" with you. That is, information appears on the screen, you select what you want to know, and the computer screen changes as you make those selections.

When you begin the search, the computer screen will show a main "menu," or list of items for you to select. Look at the sample "Main Menu" shown on this page. This menu presents you with five choices.

Your first choice should be number 1 because you want to give the computer your topic first. When you type the number 1, the screen titled "Enter Key Words" will appear.

Now type the first word or phrase of your topic on the first line. Type "Mary Lyon" and then press Enter. Remember that the computer will match exactly what you type. If you misspell your key word, the computer will not be able to find exactly what you are looking for.

When you finish with this screen, press the escape key, and the computer will return to the "Main Menu" again. Now choose number 2, "Set Search

MAIN MENU

Functions:

1. Enter Keyword(s)
2. Set Search Options
3. Search
4. Print
5. Exit

Type the number of the function.

ENTER KEYWORDS

Keyword(s): ______________

Type one word or phrase on each line.
Press the <Esc> key to return to MAIN MENU.

274

Objective

Use directions for computerized reference systems to locate library materials. (Study Skills 1)

Science Connection

Emphasize that the computer is a tool which everyone should know how to use. Have the students think of jobs in which computers are useful. If the school has a computer, ask the person who operates it to demonstrate the use of menus for the class. As an alternative, students who have a computer at home can explain how they use it. Parents who use a computer in their work may be willing to explain how it helps them.

Have each student interview a person who uses computers on his or her job. Prepare by having the class brainstorm a list of possible questions to ask the person. These may include the specific job the person does, how the computer helps them, and how they learned to use the computer.

Option." The next screen that appears will give you a choice of three different ways to search for information—by title, by topic, or by text. That is, you can look for items that have your key word in the title, for items about your key word, or for items in which your key word appears in the text.

At this point, you may choose number 1 to look for items that have "Mary Lyon" in the title, number 2 to look for items that are about Mary Lyon, or number 3 to choose items that have the name Mary Lyon anywhere in their text. In this case, you would choose either number 1 or 2, since you want items that are specifically about Mary Lyon, not articles that may refer to her. Type the number 1, and press Escape to return to the "Main Menu" again.

This time you will want to choose number 3 to perform the search. The computer will search through its data to locate articles that match your key words and search options. If you typed number 1 in the "Set Search Option" menu, the next screen that appears will provide you with a list of sources in the library whose titles contain the key words "Mary Lyon."

Your search is complete: you now know that the library has a book about Mary Lyon. At this point you can return to the main menu. You can type number 4 to print a copy of the information for your own reference, or you can type number 5 to exit from the system.

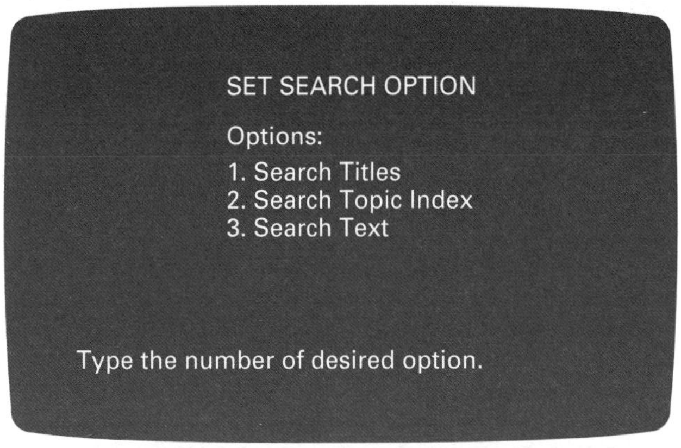

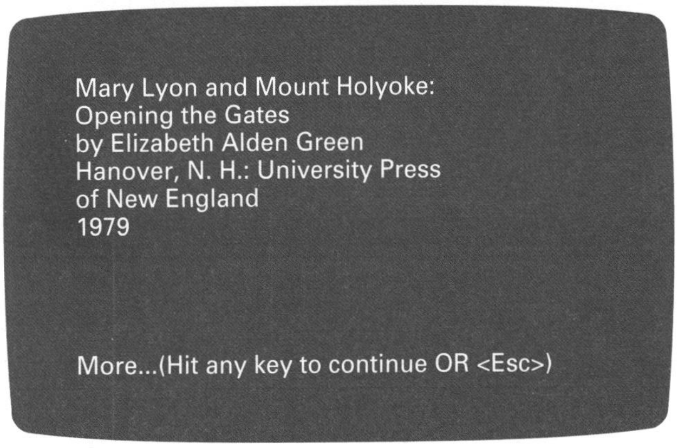

Mary Lyon and Mount Holyoke:
Opening the Gates
by Elizabeth Alden Green
Hanover, N. H.: University Press
of New England
1979
More...(Hit any key to continue OR <Esc>)

Try It

Suppose you wanted to research the Seneca Falls conference. Write down three words you could use to look for entries about your topic in a data bank. Then use a computer reference system in a library near you to do the research. Locate at least two entries on your topic using the computer.

Apply It

Think of a topic that you would like to learn about. Write down three ways you could look for information on this topic in a computerized reference system. Then use that system to locate one article on this topic.

HISTORY

Study Skills

Point out that the computer might search for the key word *Mary Lyon* without finding it. It will report that there are no titles or specific items about her in the library. What should the students do then? *(Students should use option 2 or option 3 to make their search.)*

Answers to Try It

Students should readily supply *Seneca Falls Conference* as one key word. Other key words may include *women's rights, woman suffrage, suffrage movement, Elizabeth Cady Stanton, Lucretia Mott*. You may direct students to large public libraries and libraries in local colleges and universities to find a computer reference system.

Answers to Apply It

Point out to students that the information they need may be stored in the computer's memory under several different key words. Thus, it is best to prepare a list of possible key words before beginning research on a computerized reference system. If the most obvious key word does not give them a list of titles, they can try the others.

Study Skills

Suggest that students look for five sources of information about a topic by using the card catalog. Ask students to keep track of the time it took them. Then have them look for five sources of information by using the computer. How much time were they able to save? Were there other benefits to using the computer?

INTRODUCE

Discuss what students learned about Susan B. Anthony in Lesson 3. Point out that although she was active in many reform movements, Susan B. Anthony is most closely associated with the woman suffrage movement. This excerpt from a historical novel describes her trial for breaking the law by voting in the 1872 presidential election.

READ AND RESPOND

After students read the selection independently, discuss it as a class. Point out that Susan B. Anthony argued that because she could not vote, she did not have to obey the law. As students answer the purpose-setting question, make sure they give reasons for their answers.

In Lesson 3, you read about Susan B. Anthony's involvement in various reform movements of the 1800s. Here is a story about her fight for women's suffrage.

LITERATURE

Susan's Trial

William Jay Jacobs

William Jay Jacobs' book Mother, Aunt Susan, and Me *tells the story of Elizabeth Cady Stanton (1815-1902) and Susan B. Anthony (1820-1906), and their organization of the women's suffrage movement. This move led to the introduction of the Nineteenth Amendment, which gave women the right to vote. As part of the struggle for this right, Anthony broke the law by voting in the 1872 presidential election and was subsequently arrested. This excerpt from* Mother, Aunt Susan, and Me *tells the story of Susan's trial. As you read, ask yourself, "Why would Susan B. Anthony be willing to break the law?"*

Justice Ward Hunt presided as trial judge. Henry B. Selden served as Susan B. Anthony's chief attorney. Mr. Selden said that when Susan voted she thought she had a right to vote. So what she did could not be considered a crime. She was putting her idea to a test. Susan B. Anthony was no criminal. Moreover, women legally did have the right to vote, he said, according to the Constitution.

Mr. Selden's speech was clear, logical, and to the point. For more than three hours he spoke eloquently.

But Judge Hunt hardly listened at all. Instead, he read a statement that he had prepared before coming into court–before he had heard the argument for the defense.

Then he ordered the all-male jury to find Susan B. Anthony guilty as charged.

Mr. Selden jumped to his feet. "I object! I object!" he shouted. "No judge has a right in a criminal case to tell a jury what to decide. I demand that the members of the jury be allowed to vote."

But Judge Hunt dismissed the jury without letting one of its members speak.

The next day Susan's lawyers asked for a new trial. Judge Hunt turned down the request. He then ordered Susan to stand for sentencing. "Has the prisoner anything to say why sentence shall not be pronounced?" asked Judge Hunt.

Susan, dressed in black except for a trimming of white lace at her neckline, paused for an instant. Then she spoke firmly and forcefully.

"Yes, Your Honor, I have many things to say: for in your ordered verdict of guilty you have trampled under foot every vital principle of our government. My natural rights, my civil rights, my political rights, my judicial rights are all alike ignored."

Judge Hunt, impatient, interrupted. Pointing at the accused, he declared, "The Court cannot allow the prisoner to go on."

Thematic Connections

Social Studies: Woman suffrage

Houghton Mifflin Literary Readers: Responding to Challenge

Background

Susan B. Anthony (1820–1906) was raised by Quaker parents. She learned of the 1848 Seneca Falls convention from her mother and sister, who had attended. She attended her first women's rights convention in Syracuse, New York, in 1852. Although she worked tirelessly for the feminist cause, Anthony feared speaking in public. She confided in her journal, "It is a terrible martyrdom for me to speak."

In 1872, Susan B. Anthony led more than a dozen women in Rochester, New York, to the polling place, where they cast their ballots. They were immediately charged with voting illegally. Anthony's defense was that the Fourteenth Amendment defined "citizens" as all persons born or naturalized in the United States.

But Susan would not stop. Since the day of her arrest she had been given no chance to defend herself. Judge Hunt had not even allowed her to be a witness for herself at the trial.

"The prisoner must sit down–the Court cannot allow it," bellowed Judge Hunt.

Susan continued: "Had Your Honor submitted my case to the jury, as was clearly your duty, even then I should have had just cause of protest, for not one of those men was my peer; but native or foreign born, white or black, rich or poor, educated or ignorant, sober or drunk, each and every man of them was my political superior. . . . Under such circumstances a commoner in England, tried before a jury of lords, would have far less cause to complain than have I, a woman, tried before a jury of men."

"The Court must insist," Judge Hunt interrupted again. "The prisoner has been tried according to the established forms of the law."

"Yes, Your Honor," answered Susan, "but by forms of law all made by men, interpreted by men, in favor of men, and against women."

"The Court orders the prisoner to sit down. It will not allow another word!" shouted Judge Hunt, banging his gavel for order.

Susan had a final word. She had expected, she said, a fair trial and justice. "But failing to get this justice . . . I ask not leniency at your hands but rather the full rigor of the law."

"The Court must insist . . ."started Judge Hunt. At that point Susan sat down.

"The prisoner will stand up," directed the judge.

Again she rose.

"The sentence of the Court is that you pay a fine of one hundred dollars and the costs of prosecution."

"May it please Your Honor," began Susan. "I will never pay a dollar of your unjust penalty. All I possess is a debt of ten thousand dollars incurred by publishing my paper–*The Revolution*–the sole object of which was to educate all women to do precisely as I have done, rebel against your man-made, unjust, unconstitutional forms of law, which tax, fine, imprison, and hang women, while denying them the right of representation in the government."

Susan, remaining calm, but with her voice rising in defiance, then concluded: "I will work on with might and main to pay every dollar of that honest debt, but not a penny shall go to this unjust claim. And I shall earnestly and persistently continue to urge all women to the practical recognition of the old Revolutionary maxim, 'Resistance to tyranny is obedience to God.'"

For a moment the courtroom was hushed in silence. Later we heard that even some members of the jury said they had felt like applauding, perhaps even cheering out loud.

Further Reading

The Story of the 19th Amendment. Conrad Stein. This book presents an overview of the women's suffrage movement with attention to the work of Elizabeth Stanton, Lucretia Mott, and Susan B. Anthony.

How do you know that Judge Hunt had made up his mind before he heard Mr. Selden's argument? *(He read a statement that he had prepared before coming to court.)*

What did Susan say about the established forms of law? *(They were "made by men, interpreted by men, in favor of men, and against women.")*

EXTEND

Reading aloud the dialogue between the judge and Susan can be very effective. Assign a pair of students the roles, having them start to read aloud from the point at which the judge asks, "Has the prisoner anything to say . . .?"

Further Reading

You may want to ask students to go to the school or local library to find more books about Susan B. Anthony or the woman suffrage movement.

DISCOVERY PROCESS

Students will use the following steps in the discovery process to complete the activity:
Get Ready Think of a sport that you would like to research, as well as questions you would like to ask.
Find Out Go to the library. Read articles about the history of the sport.
Move Ahead Organize your notes into categories.
Explore Some More Read about current changes being made in your sport.

Materials needed: Notebook, pen or pencil

CULTURE

Critical Thinking

Today's baseball teams grew out of local amateur teams. Have students imagine that they are fans of a local team in the 1860s. How would their relationship to their 1860s team differ from their relationship to a baseball team today? *(Fans might have known some of the players personally. Today local teams are made up of well-paid professionals.)*

EXPLORING

Sports in the United States

Did Abner Doubleday invent baseball? Or did baseball in fact develop from a game played by Egyptians in time of the Pharaohs? If you could ride a time machine back to the early days of your favorite game, you would probably find some surprises.

Get Ready

Take a trip to your local library and explore the history of a sport that interests you. Some sports you might consider exploring, besides football and baseball, include archery, billiards, auto racing, gymnastics, roller skating, basketball, or the sport originally played by the Indians, lacrosse.

Before you begin your research, decide which sport you will investigate and think of interesting questions to ask. You might seek answers to such questions as: Where did this sport come from? Who invented it? Who played it in the past? How has the game changed? You might also consider how this sport reflects certain American values. Then collect the tools you will need: a notebook and a pen or pencil.

Find Out

Stories about any sport are easy to come by, but remember—not all the stories you might read about or hear are true. For example, according to one popular story, a man named Abner Doubleday invented baseball in Cooperstown, New York. Supposedly, he did this one day in 1839. Historical records, however, show that baseball developed out of a British game called rounders, which was played at least as far back as the 1500s. Rounders, in turn, developed from other, older games. Some sources suggest that baseball may in fact have come from a game played by Egyptians in the time of the Pharaohs!

Lacrosse, a ball game played all across the United States and Canada, was invented centuries ago by the Huron Indians, who called it *bagataway.* The game was called *jeu de la crosse (zhe deh lah KRAWS)*, French for "game of the hooked stick" by a French Jesuit priest who saw the game played in 1636. In both

Objectives

1. Trace the development and cultural importance of a sport. (History 2)
2. Locate, select, and collect information about a sport by using appropriate reference materials. (Study Skills 2)

Activities

Spectator sports became an increasingly popular form of group entertainment around the turn of the century. Professional baseball had already been organized by this time. Basketball was introduced in 1891, and boxing was becoming more respectable as a spectator sport. Have students research and write reports on how and why spectator sports, or a particular spectator sport, developed, focusing on the period 1870–1920.

Many sports are played around the world that, although occasionally played here, are not popular in the United States. Have students do research and write papers on sports such as curling, boccie, and sumo wrestling. How do these sports reflect the people who play them and the societies in which they occur?

bagataway and lacrosse, two teams try to hurl a ball into each others' goals, using nets attached to sticks. Huron versions of the game sometimes involved hundreds of players and lasted for days. Modern lacrosse is played by two teams of 10 players each and lasts for one hour.

In 1891, James Naismith, a physical education teacher at the School for Christian Workers (now called Springfield College) in Massachusetts needed an indoor game for his students to play in times of bad weather. He hung some peach baskets on a gym rail and had his students compete to toss soccer balls into them. Naismith had just invented basketball. He would hardly recognize the fast-paced acrobatic game as it is played in the United States today, not just by professional, college, and high school teams, but by amateurs on playgrounds across the nation.

Separating fact from folklore takes research that is based on reliable sources. Begin by reading articles about your sport in some good encyclopedias. If the articles end with lists of recommended books on the subject, write down the titles and check for them in the card catalog. Also look for other books in the card catalog under under the category "sport" and under the name of the particular sport you are investigating. As you read, remember to jot down all interesting facts.

Move Ahead

Organize your notes in categories such as Original Game Form, Changes in Game Form, and Famous Players. If any other students have researched the same sport as you, compare your findings with theirs. Then work together to produce an oral report about your sport, complete with diagrams, pictures, and other interesting visuals.

Explore Some More

History doesn't just happen in the past. Changes like those of the past are happening right now. If you pay attention to sports news, you might see that the sport you have researched is changing today. (You might also want to consider how news coverage has influenced your sport.)

Take notes on changes you might see on television, hear on radio, or read about in newspapers or magazines that relate to the sport you are researching. If you play the sport yourself, notice what bothers you and your friends about the way it is set up. Your complaints may be the first signs of changes to come.

As you collect this information, compare the way the sport has evolved to the way it is changing now. Then shine your light into the future: write a description of the game as you predict it will be played 100 years from now.

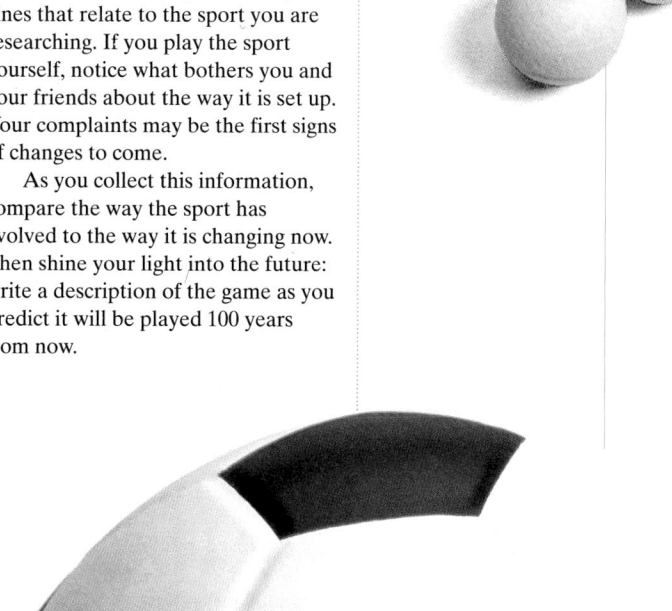

SOCIAL SYSTEMS

Critical Thinking

The role of sports in our society is undergoing a great deal of scrutiny. Problems include scandals over funding for athletes in some collegiate programs, the use of anabolic steroids and other drugs, bad sportsmanship, violence, and racism. What values or breakdown of values do these problems reflect? *(Some problems may be due to the drive to win at any cost. Allow for personal opinion.)*

Collaborative Strategy

A recommended strategy for this lesson is the jigsaw approach. For more details about collaborative learning strategies, see pages T34–35.

Chapter Review

Reviewing Key Terms

Industrial Revolution (p. 255)
municipal (p. 263)
raw materials (p. 256)
temperance (p. 268)
utopia (p. 271)

A. The sentences below have been started for you. Complete each sentence so that the meaning of the key term is clear.

1. The Industrial Revolution . . .
2. The temperance movement . . .
3. The idea of a utopia today . . .
4. Raw materials from the West . . .
5. A municipal . . .

B. Based on what you have read in the chapter, decide whether each of the following statements is accurate. Write an explanation of each decision.

1. Supporters of the temperance movement wanted to encourage the use of alcoholic beverages.
2. Some nineteenth-century reformers tried to create a utopia by starting new communities in which all people were considered equal.
3. The increase in city populations decreased the need for municipal services.
4. Factory workers often took home the raw materials left at the end of a day of work in the textile mills.
5. The Industrial Revolution that swept through the North in the early 1800s was the result of an earlier revolution in Britain.

Exploring Concepts

A. Copy the following paragraph onto a separate sheet of paper. Fill in the blank spaces with information from the chapter.

In order to avoid competition with the United States, British factory owners refused to allow _______ to leave England. However, _______ managed to build a spinning mill in Pawtucket, Rhode Island, that marked the start of a new Industrial Revolution. New machinery and _______ contributed to the success of America's industries. Transportation was another key to the Industrial Revolution. Clipper ships, steamboats, a system of _______ and networks of _______ and _______ helped move goods more easily. In addition, the nation's natural resources, like _______ power, helped revolutionize production.

B. On a separate sheet of paper, answer the following questions in complete sentences.

1. How did the role of women change with the rise of industry in the Northeast?
2. What municipal services did cities need to provide for their growing populations?
3. What were some of the changes made in public education after the 1820s, and what were the reasons for the changes?

C. Support each of the following statements with facts and details from the chapter.

1. When the Industrial Revolution occurred in the United States, Americans adapted and improved British industrial methods.
2. The Industrial Revolution led to improvements in transportation in the United States.
3. The Lowell mill owners took several steps to avoid the poverty and moral decay that had occurred in British industrial towns.
4. Industries no longer needed to be located near the nation's coasts.
5. New methods of construction helped cities to grow.
6. There was a wide gap between the lifestyles of the rich and poor in American cities.
7. The condition of the urban poor gave rise to many reform movements.
8. People who sought to create utopian societies had two different motives.
9. Women played a major role in many of the reform movements.

Answers to Reviewing Key Terms

A. Sample answers:

1. The Industrial Revolution changed the manufacturing process as more goods were produced in factories.
2. The temperance movement urged people to give up alcohol.
3. A utopia today would be a world of peace, justice, and equality.
4. Raw materials from the West, like iron ore and cotton, were sent to the East to be manufactured into products.
5. A municipal service is a service run by the city, such as garbage collection.

B. Answers:

1. False. Supporters of the temperance movement encouraged people to stop drinking.
2. True. A utopia is an ideal place.
3. False. More people in a city create a need for more municipal services.
4. False. Closely supervised workers were not allowed to take anything from the factory (see list of regulations on page 271).
5. True. The British invented the first industrial machines.

Answers to Exploring Concepts

A. Answers:

Machinery or plans; Samuel Slater; natural resources; roads; canals; railroads; water

B. Sample answers:

1. Instead of taking care of children and doing farm work, young women moved to cities to work in factories.
2. Cities needed to provide police officers, fire fighters, and public health services.
3. Reformers helped to start more schools. As women became politically active, they also opened colleges for women.

C. Sample answers:

1. Americans made the first interchangeable parts.
2. Factories needed cheap, efficient means of transportation to bring them raw materials and to take goods to markets. Roads, canals, steamboats and the steam railway made trade easier.
3. Owners paid workers cash wages and housed them in company-run boarding houses with strict rules, prepared meals, and cultural events.
4. With the development of steam power, factories could be built near the source of raw materials or the markets where products were sold.
5. It was cheaper and faster to build houses using the balloon frame. Cast-iron columns and metal frames were used for taller buildings.
6. Rich people lived in mansions and used horse-drawn carriages. The poor lived in crowded apartments and worked long hours in harsh environments.
7. Dorothea Dix helped found state mental hospitals. Other social reformers worked on the problems of crime, poverty, disease, workplace conditions, poor education, and alcohol abuse.
8. Some, like the Shakers, followed their religious beliefs. Others, like the founders of Brook Farm, wanted to create an ideal agricultural society in which everyone contributed to the community.
9. Women were involved in the movements for temperance, abolition, educational reform, and women's rights.

Reviewing Skills

1. Explain why libraries are increasing their use of computer data banks.
2. When conducting a search by computer, why is it important to define and enter your key words very carefully?
3. Look at the sample computer screen at right. What information should you type onto the computer screen after you have pressed key number 1?
4. After you have entered the exact title of a book that you need for your research, which key should you select to begin your search?
5. Look at the timeline on page 256. When was the first patent issued? When was gaslight first used to light city streets?
6. Suppose you were using a computerized reference system. Although you searched for your key words under titles, topics, and text, no references were located. What information would you need to continue your search?

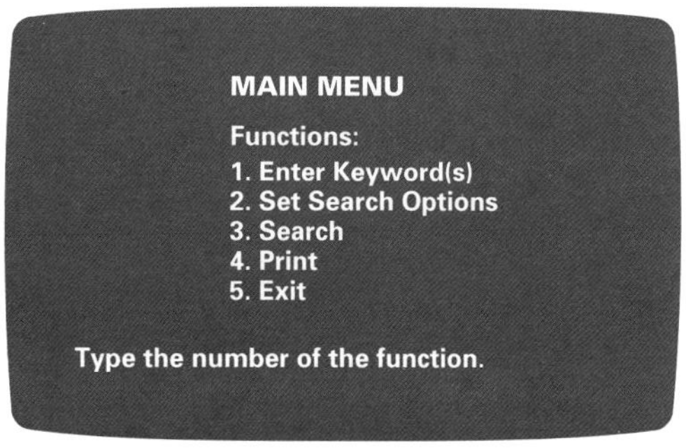

Using Critical Thinking

1. Private charitable groups took on the burden of caring for the needs of the poor during the early 1800s. Since the 1930s, the federal government has played a major part in helping the poor, but recently some politicians have said that private groups should do the job. Who do you think is better suited for this work—government agencies or private groups? Explain your answer.
2. Fanny Wright claimed that the wide gap between rich and poor contradicted the idea that all men are created equal. "The man possessed of a dollar feels himself to be, not merely 100 cents richer but also 100 cents better than the man who is penniless," she wrote. Do you agree with her? Explain your answer.
3. Many people recognized the need for universal education of both men and women. One teacher wrote, "Give the people knowledge . . . and you give them power. Education must ever be the grand safeguard of our liberties." Do you agree? Would our system of government be weakened if many people remained poorly educated? How?

Preparing for Citizenship

1. **WRITING ACTIVITY** Some Americans still live in communities that resemble utopias, in which people share tasks, grow their own food, and reject machinery. Research such groups as the Amish or Mennonites, and write a report on their beliefs and way of life.
2. **COLLECTING INFORMATION** Find out if there are any religious or charitable groups in your community that have programs to help those in need. Interview a person connected with the group to find out what they do. Are there any activities that the class can help with? Report on your findings.
3. **COLLECTING INFORMATION** Ask older people such as your parents or grandparents to describe the changes that have occurred in their community since they were children. What new buildings, roads, factories, shopping centers, or other changes have been made? Do they feel these changes have improved or harmed the community? Why? Compare your findings with those of other students.
4. **COLLABORATIVE LEARNING** Take a class trip through your community by walking or using public transportation. Look at different neighborhoods and parts of the community. Take notes on how your community is laid out in terms of housing, industry, parks, and municipal facilities. When you return, discuss what changes, if any, you would make to improve municipal services.

Answers to Reviewing Skills

1. There is so much information available today that libraries need a system that takes up little space and that can quickly search for information.
2. The computer searches the entries in its files for exactly what you type.
3. Students should enter the keyword or words.
4. Student should enter the number *3*.
5. The first patent was issued in 1790. Gaslights first lit city streets in 1816.
6. Students should first check their spelling of keywords and then look for other keywords or titles for their topic.

Answers to Using Critical Thinking

1. The advantage of government operation is that it receives funding from taxes and centralizes organization, possibly making it more efficient. It has the disadvantage of allowing legislators to decide which charities are most important. Private agencies may be less encumbered by bureaucracy and have more independence, but they spend a considerable amount of time fund-raising.
2. Explain that, like Lucretia Mott and Elizabeth Cady Stanton, Fanny Wright worked to abolish slavery. Students may want to discuss whether this gap between rich and poor still exists today. Would Fanny Wright say the same thing about modern society?
3. Discuss the relationship between knowledge and power. Students may want to list the kinds of activities that make people more powerful and that require education or knowledge, such as the ability to vote for presidential candidates. If possible, give students statistics on literacy rates in other countries.

Answers to Preparing for Citizenship

1. **WRITING ACTIVITY** Encourage students to use computer data banks available to them.
2. **COLLECTING INFORMATION** Students may want to share their findings on different groups and choose a project to work on, such as saving newspapers and cans for recycling, organizing a fundraising drive, or doing errands for people who need help.
3. **COLLECTING INFORMATION** Students can draw maps that show the way their area has changed. They may be able to find books with pictures of old streets and buildings.
4. **COLLABORATIVE LEARNING** Point out that new developments often spark controversy among businesses, neighbors and environmental activists. Ask students to consider long-term effects of changes. If students have worked on Collecting Information number 3, refer to the long-term consequences they have seen in some changes. Students may want to research a current controversy in their area and debate the proposed changes.

Chapter 10 Planning at a Glance

The South

	Objectives	Reading Support and Other Resources	Diverse Learning Strategies
Lesson 1 The Cotton Kingdom *pp. 284–289* 1–2 days	• Explain how the cotton gin revolutionized cotton production in the South. • Describe the slaves' work on the plantation. • Compare the economies of the antebellum South and the North during that period. • Identify three arguments used in support of slavery.	• **Workbook** or **Reading Support:** pp. 135–138 Review p. 32 Extra Support/Transition p. 32 Multi-lang. Sum. pp. 63–64 • **Other Resources:** Geography Kit; Posters 3, 5; Study Guide p. 41	Science Connection **(GATE)** TE p. 287 Drawing **(Kinesthetic)** TE p. 288 Map and Globe Skills **(Visual)** TE p. 288 Collaborative Act. **(Visual)** TE p. 288 Audiotapes of Multi-language Lesson Summaries **(Auditory)**
Lesson 2 Life on the Plantation *pp. 290–295* 1–2 days **Literature** **"Slave Life"** *pp. 296–297*	• Identify the responsibilities of both the planter and the plantation mistress. • Describe how slaves were treated on Southern plantations. • Identify at least three ways in which slaves maintained their identity and their African heritage. • Identify the means that slaves used to resist slavery.	• **Workbook** or **Reading Support:** pp. 139–142 Review p. 33 Extra Support/Transition p. 33 Multi-lang. Sum. pp. 65–66 • **Other Resources:** Geography Kit, Study Guide p. 42	Access Strat. **(Extra Support)** TE p. 291 Visual Learning **(Visual)** TE pp. 291, 292 Map and Globe Skills **(Visual)** TE p. 294 Research **(GATE)** TE p. 294 Audiotapes of Multi-language Lesson Summaries **(Auditory)**
Lesson 3 The Other Souths *pp. 298–305* 2–3 days	• Identify and describe the groups of Southerners who did not live on plantations. • Describe the diverse society that developed in Southern cities. • Compare education in the south with education in the North. • Discuss the status of free blacks in Southern society.	• **Workbook** or **Reading Support:** pp. 143–146 Review p. 34 Extra Support/Transition p. 34 Multi-lang. Sum. pp. 67–68 • **Other Resources:** Study Guide p. 43	Access Act. **(SDAIE)** TE p. 299 Art Connection **(Visual)** TE p. 302 Making a Model **(Kinesthetic)** TE p. 304 Audiotapes of Multi-language Lesson Summaries **(Auditory)**
Skill: Comparing Appropriate Graphs *pp. 306–307*	• Use information about line, bar, and circle graphs to choose appropriate graphs.	• **Other Resources:** Study Guide p. 44	Visual Learning **(Visual)** TE p. 307
Chapter Review *pp. 308–309* 1 day		Chapter 10 Test pp. 37–40 *(See facsimiles on TE p. 758.)*	Assessment Multiple-Use Masters pp. 81–88

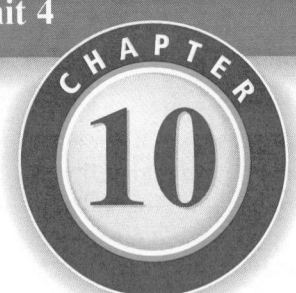

Reading Support Resources *for Every Lesson*

Reading and Review

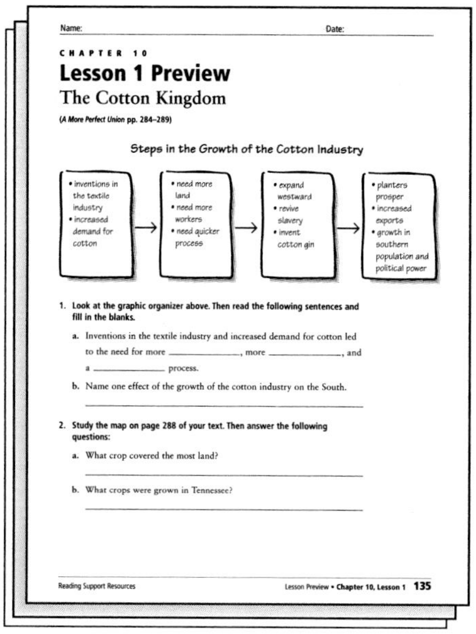
Name: Date:

CHAPTER 10

Lesson 1 Preview

The Cotton Kingdom

(*A More Perfect Union* pp. 284–289)

Steps in the Growth of the Cotton Industry

1. Look at the graphic organizer above. Then read the following sentences and fill in the blanks.

a. Inventions in the textile industry and increased demand for cotton led to the need for more ______, more ______, and a ______ process.

b. Name one effect of the growth of the cotton industry on the South.

______

2. Study the map on page 288 of your text. Then answer the following questions:

a. What crop covered the most land?

______

b. What crops were grown in Tennessee?

______

Reading Support Resources   Lesson Preview • **Chapter 10, Lesson 1** **135**

- **Chapter Overview*** p. 134
- **Lesson Previews*** using graphic organizers from the Teacher's Edition pp. 135, 139, 143
- **Reading Strategies*** pp. 136, 140, 144
- **Lesson Summaries*** pp. 137–138, 141–142, 145–146
- **Lesson Reviews** pp. 32, 33, 34

* **Workbook** includes starred items.

Multi-language Summaries

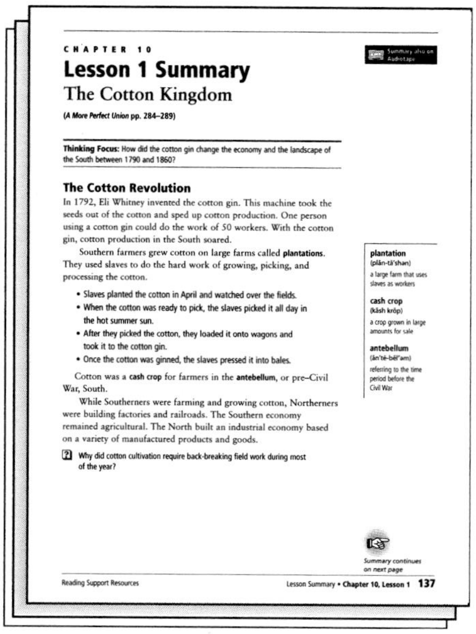
CHAPTER 10

Summary also on Audiotape

Lesson 1 Summary

The Cotton Kingdom

(*A More Perfect Union* pp. 284–289)

Thinking Focus: How did the cotton gin change the economy and the landscape of the South between 1790 and 1860?

The Cotton Revolution

In 1792, Eli Whitney invented the cotton gin. This machine took the seeds out of the cotton and sped up cotton production. One person using a cotton gin could do the work of 50 workers. With the cotton gin, cotton production in the South soared.

Southern farmers grew cotton on large farms called **plantations**. They used slaves to do the hard work of growing, picking, and processing the cotton.

- Slaves planted the cotton in April and watched over the fields.
- When the cotton was ready to pick, the slaves picked it all day in the hot summer sun.
- After they picked the cotton, they loaded it onto wagons and took it to the cotton gin.
- Once the cotton was ginned, the slaves pressed it into bales.

Cotton was a **cash crop** for farmers in the **antebellum**, or pre–Civil War, South.

While Southerners were farming and growing cotton, Northerners were building factories and railroads. The Southern economy remained agricultural. The North built an industrial economy based on a variety of manufactured products and goods.

? Why did cotton cultivation require back-breaking field work during most of the year?

plantation (plăn-tā'shən) a large farm that uses slaves as workers

cash crop (kăsh krŏp) a crop grown in large amounts for sale

antebellum (ăn'tē-bĕl'əm) referring to the time period before the Civil War

Summary continues on next page

Reading Support Resources   Lesson Summary • **Chapter 10, Lesson 1** **137**

Lesson Summaries in:

- English (See Reading and Review.)
- Spanish pp. 137–138, 141–142, 145–146
- Chinese pp. 63–68
- Hmong pp. 63–68
- Khmer pp. 63–68
- Vietnamese pp. 63–68

Summaries available on audiotapes

Lesson Support / Transition

S D A I E

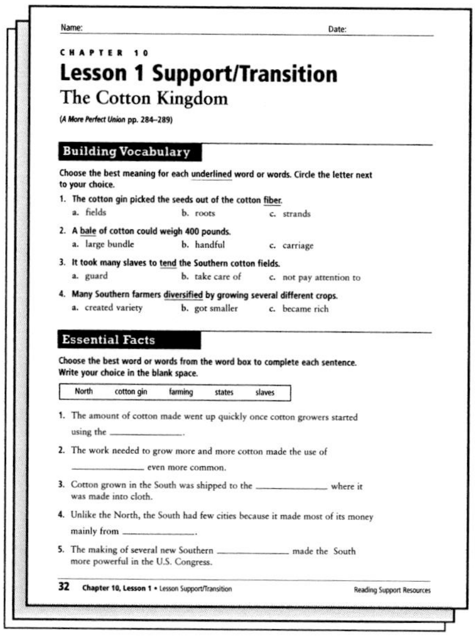
Name: Date:

CHAPTER 10

Lesson 1 Support/Transition

The Cotton Kingdom

(*A More Perfect Union* pp. 284–289)

Building Vocabulary

Choose the best meaning for each underlined word or words. Circle the letter next to your choice.

1. The cotton gin picked the seeds out of the cotton fiber.
a. fields b. roots c. strands

2. A bale of cotton could weigh 400 pounds.
a. large bundle b. handful c. carriage

3. It took many slaves to tend the Southern cotton fields.
a. guard b. take care of c. not pay attention to

4. Many Southern farmers diversified by growing several different crops.
a. created variety b. got smaller c. became rich

Essential Facts

Choose the best word or words from the word box to complete each sentence. Write your choice in the blank space.

North	cotton gin	farming	states	slaves

1. The amount of cotton made went up quickly once cotton growers started using the ______.
2. The work needed to grow more and more cotton made the use of ______ even more common.
3. Cotton grown in the South was shipped to the ______ where it was made into cloth.
4. Unlike the North, the South had few cities because it made most of its money mainly from ______.
5. The making of several new Southern ______ made the South more powerful in the U.S. Congress.

32 **Chapter 10, Lesson 1** • Lesson Support/Transition   Reading Support Resources

Activities for SDAIE

Specially **D**esigned **A**cademic **I**nstruction in **E**nglish

- **Lesson Support/Transition** pp. 32, 33, 34

Technology Options

Internet Support

http://www.eduplace.com

Social Studies Center at Education Place

Internet support for Chapter 10:

- ***Lesson at a Glance***
- ***Appalachian Crafts***

Software

Student Writing Center® (CD-ROM) (Macintosh® or Windows®)

School to Career

Throughout history, music has often been an important form of political, social, and economic statement for people for which no other form of expression is available. Ask students to select a musician who they feel makes a statement with his or her music. How did this musician achieve success?

Character Education

Enslaved Africans were deprived of basic human rights. Ask students to review the Bill of Rights and the Declaration of Independence. Have them take note of the rights guaranteed to the people of the United States in these documents. As a class, have students define what they feel to be basic human rights. Why are these important?

CHAPTER PREVIEW

Have students read the chapter title and the narrative under it. Ask them to use a wall map to locate the Southern region. Ask students to describe the South before the Civil War. Which image on these pages do they most readily identify with the South: the commercial port, the plantation, or the rustic cabin? Point out that impressions are a mixture of fact and opinion. As students read the chapter, have them think about the wrong impressions that they may have had about the South.

Looking Back

Review the concept of regionalism from Chapter 8. Tell students that Southerners at this time had a strong sense of regional identity, partly due to the institution of slavery.

Looking Forward

Tell students that they will learn more about the South in the era before the Civil War in the following lessons: The Cotton Kingdom, Life on the Plantation, and The Other Souths.

Chapter 10
The South

The South's rural landscape was filled with wide fields, elegant mansions, and small mountain farms. Down slow, winding rivers, boats carried cotton to ports on the coast. In the South, cotton was King. Grown by slave labor, cotton brought a thriving economy and a desire for more land.

The large, elegant home of a Southern landowner graces the rural landscape.

	1790	1800	1810	1820

Presidents

- 1789-1797 Washington
- 1797-1801 J. Adams
- 1801-1809 Jefferson
- 1809-1817 Madison
- 1817-1825 Monroe

1790

BACKGROUND

Emerging in the South in the 1800s was a regional culture distinct from the industrial culture of the North. A plantation system dependent on black slaves dominated this new culture. Although most white Southerners did not own slaves, they tended to support slavery and the social system that accompanied it.

The Development of Chattel Slavery

The South was not the first area to have slaves. From ancient times through the Crusades and later wars, captives were often enslaved rather than put to death. Some European countries in the 1600s enslaved debtors and vagabonds as well.

Economic conditions led other Europeans to become indentured servants in exchange for passage to the American colonies in the early 1600s (Chapter 1). Black servants, from as early as 1619, worked side by side in the fields with white servants. Both were freed following a specified term of service.

As the size of the black labor force increased, Southern colonies began to write slave codes that made legal distinctions between black and white servants. By 1700, black servitude was redefined as chattel slavery, a form of property to be bought and sold. Black slaves and their descendants, the laws insisted, would serve for life. This type of bondage was unknown under English law. Its development in America fueled racial prejudice and hostility.

Mountain people cleared the land, built log cabins, and protected their fields with split-rail fences. The soft, sweet music of the Appalachian dulcimer accompanied the folk music of the mountain people.

1840 The port of New Orleans bustles with trade to far off places.

1830 | 1840 | 1850 | 1860

1829 Adams

1829-1837 Jackson

1837-1841 Van Buren

1841 W. Harrison

1841-1845 Tyler

1845-1849 Polk

1849-1850 Taylor

1850-1853 Fillmore

1853-1857 Pierce

1857-1861 Buchanan

1860

Understanding the Visuals

Point out that the engraving on the right was done in 1841 by the artist W.J. Bennett. Tell the students that Bennett emphasized one important aspect of New Orleans in each part of the engraving: foreground, middle ground, and background. Have students look for the aspects of the city that he highlighted. *(The cosmopolitan population, shipping, the city's large buildings)* Have students look for evidence of the importance of cotton in the South in this engraving and in the painting on the left by an unidentified artist.

Understanding Chronology

Have students look at the chapter timeline. Recap with them the events that were happening in the West and the North during the time period of this chapter: exploration, pioneer settlement, and the Industrial Revolution.

283

Religion in the South

Many white people in the antebellum South used religion as a form of social control, believing that Christian lessons of humility and obedience would lead slaves to be submissive. Yet because black and white church services were segregated, especially during the 1800s, the slaves' religion became the center of their resistance. The services increased their psychological and cultural independence, provided a basis for self-respect, and generated faith in eventual deliverance.

INTRODUCE

Have students read the title and Thinking Focus. Refer them to the picture of a cotton boll on this page and ask them to imagine how difficult it would be to separate by hand the seeds that are buried within the boll. Tell students to read the lesson to learn about the dependence of the South on cotton and of the planters on slaves.

Key Terms

Vocabulary strategies: T36–37

plantation—a large farm on which crops are grown by slaves

antebellum—referring to the time period before the Civil War

cash crop—a crop grown in large quantities for sale

1790 1860

LESSON 1

The Cotton Kingdom

THINKING FOCUS

How did the cotton gin change the economy and the landscape of the South between 1790 and 1860?

Key Terms

- plantation
- antebellum
- cash crop

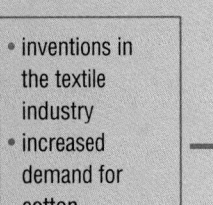

In 1792, wealthy Southerners gathered at Mulberry Grove, Georgia, the home of Catharine Littlefield Greene, widow of the Revolutionary War hero General Nathanael Greene. Imagine the scene: candles glowed in tall silver holders, a floral centerpiece lightly perfumed the air.

The dinner guests talked with animation of hunting, fine horses, and cotton, always cotton. Eli Whitney, a young tutor from the North, listened closely to their talk. The men's eyes sparkled when they described how machinery was changing the textile industry in New England and Britain. Since the mills needed more and more cotton, it looked like good times for the South.

Cotton grows in a pod or boll that pops open when it is ripe. Southern planters grew two kinds of cotton. Sea-island cotton was easy to clean but grew well only along the coast. Upland cotton had a wider growing range but was difficult to clean.

One of the cotton growers brought the conversation back to reality. It was all very well to talk about possible profits, he said. But how were they to meet the demand for cotton? Their slaves could barely clean enough cotton by hand to meet the present needs of industry.

The growers did have machines to clean cotton. However, these machines did not work well with upland cotton, which was the kind most of them grew. The seeds stuck to the fiber so that slaves had to finish the cleaning by hand.

Whitney, who loved to tinker with machines, was intrigued. He wrote his father:

> *I heard much said of the extreme difficulty of ginning Cotton, that is, separating it from its seeds. There were a number of very respectable gentlemen at Mrs. Greene's who all agreed that if a machine could be invented which could clean the cotton with expedition, it would be a great thing both to the Country and to the inventor. I involuntarily happened to be thinking on the Subject, and struck out a plan of a Machine in my mind. . . . In about ten days I made a little model. . . which required the labor of one man to turn it. . . . One man and a horse will do more than fifty men with the old machines.*

Whitney's cotton gin (gin is a shortened form of engine) was just what the Southern cotton growers needed. It rapidly cleaned the seeds from the short, sticky fibers of upland cotton, the variety that grew all over the South. The process was simple: a roller carried raw cotton along wooden slats. Sharp metal teeth thrust through the slats and quickly pulled the fibers from the seeds.

In 1794 Whitney obtained a patent—a license granting sole rights to make, use, or sell an invention—for his cotton gin. He himself earned little from his invention. The machine was so simple that manufacturers copied it without permission or paying a fee.

Objectives

1. Explain how the cotton gin revolutionized cotton production in the South.
2. Describe the slaves' work on the plantation.
3. Compare the economies of the antebellum South and the North during that period.
4. Identify arguments in support of and against slavery.

Graphic Overview

• inventions in the textile industry • increased demand for cotton →	• need more land • need more workers • need quicker process →	• expand westward • revive slavery • invent cotton gin →	• planters prosper • increased exports • growth in Southern population and political power

The Cotton Revolution

The cotton gin caused great changes in the Southern economy. Once cotton growers began using Whitney's invention, production soared. In the years after 1812, raw cotton accounted for one-third of all exports from the United States. By 1830, cotton had increased to half of all U.S. exports.

Because cotton was so valuable, planters (farmers who owned 20 slaves or more) put all their efforts into growing it. They cleared large areas in the western part of the South. Known as the "New South," this area included Arkansas, Louisiana, Mississippi, Alabama, western Georgia, and northern Florida (see map, page 288).

The long, hot summers and the rich soil of the river valleys in the "New South" created ideal conditions for growing cotton. **Plantations**—large farms on which crops were grown by slaves—produced ever larger amounts of cotton. This revived slavery, which had declined after the tobacco market shrank in the late 1700s.

▲ *After working from sunrise to sunset, these field slaves had to line up and carry the day's cotton to be weighed.*

Toiling in the Fields

Cotton needed a great deal of labor during the year. The backbreaking work was done by slaves—men, women, and children—who worked from dawn to dark under a broiling sun. They planted the fields in April and tended them constantly.

In his book *Twelve Years as a Slave* (1853) Solomon Northup, a free black man who had been kidnapped and sold into slavery, described labor in the cotton fields:

> During all [the] hoeings the overseer or driver follows the slaves on horseback with a whip. . . . The fastest hoer takes the lead row. He is usually about a rod in advance of his companions. If one of them passes him, he [the fastest hoer] is whipped. If one falls behind or is a moment idle, he is whipped. In fact, the lash is flying from morning until night. . . .
>
> When a new hand, one unaccustomed to [picking cotton], is sent for the first time into the field, he is whipped up smartly, and made for that day to pick as fast as he can possibly. At night [what he has picked] is weighed, so that his capability in cotton picking is known. He must bring in the same weight each night following. . . . The hands are required to be in the cotton field as soon as it is light in the morning, and, with the exception of 10 or 15 minutes, which is given them at noon to swallow their allowance of cold bacon, they are not permitted to be a moment idle until it is too dark to see.
>
> Solomon Northup, *Twelve Years As a Slave*

DEVELOP

Point out that this lesson is about a series of events caused by inventions in the textile industry and an increased demand for cotton. As students read, they may make notes on the effects of these two causes.

BELIEF SYSTEMS

Critical Thinking

Have a student read aloud the excerpt on this page from Solomon Northup's book. What conclusions might be drawn from the excerpt about how slaves were viewed and treated? *(Slaves were viewed and treated like livestock.)*

Access Strategy

Ask students to recall what they learned about the South in Chapter 1. *(Plantation system, backcountry farmers, indentured servants, slaves, variety in immigrant population)* Also have them recall what they read in Chapter 9 about the Industrial Revolution in the North. *(Inventions, mass production, factories, mills)* Have one student write class responses on the board. Introduce the term *cash crop*, a crop whose only value to the grower is the money it brings upon being sold. Tell students that new inventions in the Northern textile mills caused an increased demand for cotton, the main cash crop in the South. In this lesson they will learn how the increased demand for cotton affected the South.

Access Activity

Help students see how a region's main way of making a living might affect its culture. How might the rural, agricultural nature of the South affect its culture? *(The South is family-oriented; values practical skills more than book-learning; and pays attention to seasons and nature.)*

ECONOMICS

Visual Learning

Have students look at the picture on this page. What ages do the slaves seem to be? *(Young children to adults)* Why were slave children used as laborers? *(Because the supply of slaves was inadequate, even children were used.)* What do the ax and rake in the picture suggest about slaves' work? *(They worked in gardens, cleaned yards, and cut wood, in addition to working in fields.)*

William Henry Brown combined cutouts and watercolors to create this scene of slaves hauling cotton to the gin.

Other Plantation Chores

After the field work ended for the day, each slave still had tasks to do. "One feeds the mules," Northup wrote, "another the swine—another cuts the wood." Even then, the day was not over for the slaves. Evening was the only time they could return to their cabins, care for their families, and prepare the food they would need in the fields the next day.

Most slaveowners tried to get as much labor from their slaves as possible. The whip became the symbol of the slave regime, and few slaves escaped cruel punishments. Some masters used rewards like additional food to spur their slaves to further work. Slaves became more valuable because Great Britain banned the Atlantic slave trade, Congress ended the American slave trade in 1808, and six new slave states were created.

After picking the cotton, slaves loaded it onto wagons to haul the crop to a nearby gin. The ginned cotton was pressed into bales—400-pound bundles covered with coarse cloth and held together with rope. Each of the cotton gins at a ginning mill processed three or four bales a day.

The bundles were then shipped to Northern or European factories where the cotton was made into cloth. In 1814, Southern planters shipped 150,000 bales of cotton. In 1825, they shipped 600,000 bales.

Rural South, Industrial North

The plantation South differed greatly from the industrial North. In the 1700s, both the North and the South depended mainly on farming. The North began to develop industries in the early 1800s. In the **antebellum** period—the time before the Civil War—the South remained agricultural. Eighty percent of the labor force worked in farming. Planters dominated the Southern economy. In the North, on the other hand, the farm population dropped from 70 to 40 percent of the total labor force.

As their industries grew, Northerners built a canal and railroad system to carry raw materials and manufactured goods to the growing cities. Northerners also harnessed the rivers to get power for industry. In the South, planters were content to send their crops to market on the slow-flowing rivers and the waterways along the coast. Few were interested in developing factories or using water for power.

Because farming remained the chief economy, few cities developed in the South. The cities that did grow had very little industry. Small, scattered towns served as centers of marketing or transportation, mainly in the fall and winter when crops were being shipped. Southern industries tended to be small—cabinet making or iron-working or cotton ginning—and

Critical Thinking

Ask students what similarities they see between plantation owners and factory owners (Chapter 9). *(Both oversee large groups of workers and receive a large percentage of the financial benefit of their operations.)*

Economic Context

The cotton revolution had a major effect on Southern economy. The improvements in spinning and weaving machinery in New England and Britain caused a demand for cotton. Southern planters invested heavily in land and slaves, which led to sharp price increases. Between 1850 and 1860, the price of both slaves and agricultural lands rose 70 percent. Even if the South had wanted to increase manufacturing industries, the money was not available. Annual per capita investment in manufacturing was under 40 cents.

From 1850 to 1860, the average wealth of white slaveholders rose from $9,000 to $25,000; even nonslaveholders saw their income more than double, from $750 to $1,700.

Economic gain was not increasing evenly, however. The number of slaveholding households dropped between 1830 and 1860. Wealth was becoming concentrated in the hands of a few. (See the Economic Context on page 292 of Lesson 2.)

devoted to local needs. Southern towns were rarely manufacturing centers. The difference between South and North could be seen in the way people talked of the place where they lived. While Northerners spoke of living in or near a town, Southerners talked of their county.

Some Southern leaders worried that their economy was not varied enough. They thought that Southern income depended too heavily on cotton. Although other crops—tobacco, rice, sugar cane, corn, and other grains—were grown, cotton brought in the most money.

Other Southern leaders noted that the South depended on the North not only for manufactured goods, but also for much of its transportation. The South had few ocean-going ships. Its produce was shipped to New England and Europe in Northern vessels. Joseph W. Lesesne, an Alabama plantation owner, complained in 1847, "Our whole commerce except a small fraction is in the hands of Northern men. . . . financially we are more enslaved than our negroes."

Impact of the Cotton Economy

Between 1830 and 1860, new machinery in the textile industry made it possible to produce cloth more quickly. This advance increased the demand for raw cotton. As a result, the South's economy relied on cotton production and the need for slave labor to grow it.

Cotton was a **cash crop**—one grown mainly to sell for money. An economy based on a single cash crop can yield a high income. However, if the crop fails or market prices for it drop, there is nothing to fall back on.

For greater security, many farmers diversify. They grow several money-making crops. If something goes wrong with one crop, the others will still bring in income.

Growing a variety of crops is especially important in cotton-growing areas, because cotton wears out the

Across Time & Space

The cotton jeans and shirts people wear today come from one of the earliest crops people grew. One strain of cotton was developed in Pakistan in Asia about 5,000 years ago. The ancient Greeks called it the wool of lambs that grows on trees. Originally cotton was so rare in Europe that only the very rich could afford it.

▼ *Compare the factories and transportation in Springfield, Massachusetts, with those in New Orleans, Louisiana.*

Comparing the North and the South, around 1850

The North
- Transportation by railroads and canals
- Industrial economy, factories using water power
- Variety of manufactured products, textiles, and steel goods
- Voluntary labor force, many immigrants, low wages
- Few large cities and many mill towns

The South
- Transportation by steamboats on natural inland rivers
- Agricultural economy, centered on plantations
- Major crop concentration on cotton
- Slave labor force
- Few cities; river towns busy during harvest for shipping

ECONOMICS

Critical Thinking

Ask students to name the major differences between Northern (Chapter 9) and Southern economies. *(North—industrial, factories in cities, railroads; South—agricultural, plantations, steamboats)*

◄ *In Springfield, railroads were used and money was invested in factory buildings; in New Orleans, steamboats were used and wealth was found in bales and sacks of agricultural products.*

Science Connection

Have students research and write a two- to three-page report on cotton. They may write about cotton in the antebellum South, modern cotton-growing, or both. Reports may include varieties of cotton, germination time for the seed, natural pests of cotton, yield per acre, water and sun requirements, and kinds of fertilizer used. Alternatively, students may present their findings in a chart.

Research

Students can research and report on the technological advances in spinning and weaving that made the cotton revolution possible. They should trace the process from the baled, ginned cotton to fine finished goods from England. How was the cotton spun? What kind of loom did the weaving? How did English cotton fabrics differ from New England cotton fabrics? How was the cotton dyed?

Critical Thinking

Why might you choose to grow a single cash crop? *(Chance for high profit)* Why might you choose to diversify? *(Chance for reasonable profit from several crops)* What similar choices exist in modern stock market investment? *(Decision to invest money in one stock or several)*

Cash-Crop Economy of the South

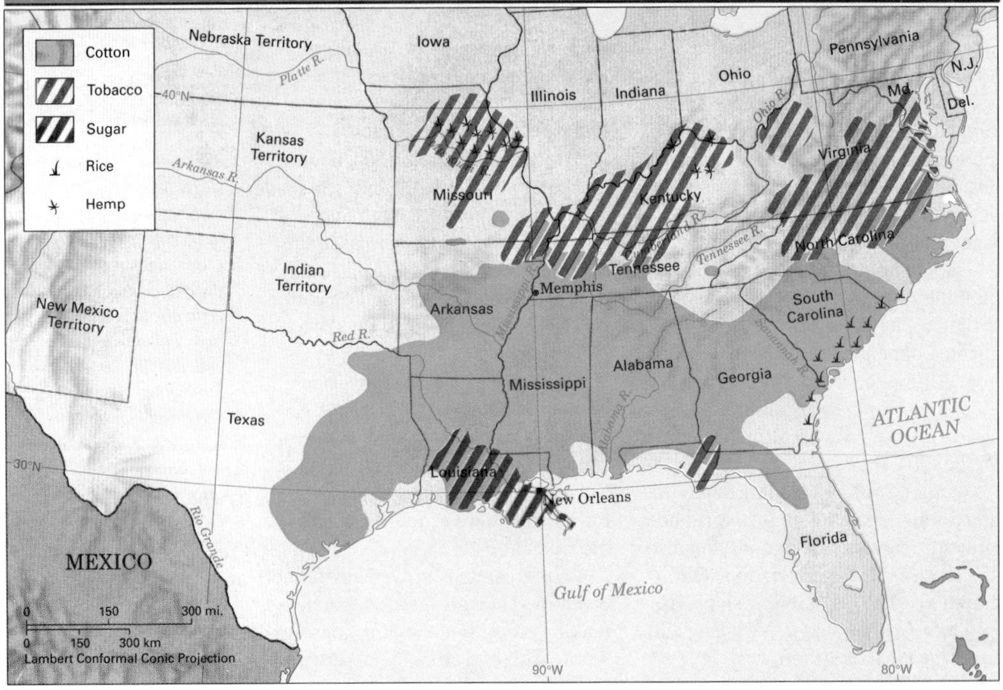

▲ *What cash crops were grown in the antebellum South? Coastal areas in the South are humid. What does that tell you about the rice and sugar cane grown there?*

➤ *Cotton, tobacco, sugar, rice, and hemp. Humidity is required to grow rice and sugar cane.*

soil rapidly. The land becomes useless unless it rests for a year between crops. Or soil can be improved by adding fertilizer or by alternating cotton with other crops. Before the 1830s, when planters began to use more fertilizer, they would abandon worn out fields and move to new land farther west.

Political Impact of Cotton

As planters in the "New South" turned more and more land to growing cotton, the economy could support more people. In 1790, the South had roughly one million white people, 657,000 black slaves, and 32,000 free black people. By 1860, some eight million white people, almost four million black slaves, and 262,000 free black people lived in the South. (Compare the Atlas maps on page 704 showing U.S. population density in 1790 and 1870.)

The rise in population brought statehood to the Southern territories. New states joined the Union in quick succession: Louisiana in 1812, Mississippi in 1817, Alabama in 1819, Arkansas in 1836, and Florida and Texas in 1845. The admission of these states greatly increased the power of the South in the United States Congress. ■

■ *Why did cotton cultivation require back-breaking field work during most of the year?*

■ *It required planting in April, constant tending throughout the growing season, and then picking and ginning.*

Proslavery Movement

Even white Southerners who did not own slaves took a proslavery stand during the antebellum years. Since most white Southerners benefited either directly or indirectly from the economy based on King Cotton, they supported slavery. Economic security was one powerful reason for the proslavery position in the South.

Some white Southerners also supported slavery out of fear. They believed that if slaves were freed and given legal rights, they would take control and white people would lose their property and even be in physical danger.

Map and Globe Skills

Ask students to compare the crop map on this page with the physical map of the United States in the Atlas on pages 700–701. Which states have portions of highland area? *(Tennessee, Kentucky, West Virginia)* Which cash crops were grown more in these areas than lowland areas? *(Tobacco, hemp)*

Drawing

Students can research the cotton gin and other antebellum cotton-farming implements to produce a drawing, painting, or collage. Some students may want to do a detailed drawing of the cotton gin, showing how it works. Display the artwork on a bulletin board with appropriate captions.

Collaborative Learning

Have groups of four or five students draw an economic map showing the route of cotton from field to finished product. Each student in a group should draw one step in the process—ginning, baling, spinning, weaving, and sewing. The group should then combine the drawings in a map that includes shipment to a Boston textile mill, to a New York factory for sewing into garments, and to England as exported products.

Arguments Defending Slavery

Many people defended slavery by arguing that the Bible recognized slavery, and that slavery had existed worldwide for thousands of years. They noted that by introducing Christianity to their slaves, planters had saved their souls.

Defenders of slavery also claimed that Northern industrial workers were not much better off than slaves. They were poorly paid, worked long hours, and lived in poverty. While Northern industrial workers often went hungry and cold, slaves got some food, a little clothing, and basic shelter from their white owners.

▲ *Slaves outside their homes on a South Carolina plantation share some time together. Those supporting slavery used pictures such as this as evidence of a master's concern for the slaves' well-being.*

Proslavery Refuted

A growing number of antislavery activists challenged these arguments. Quakers were one of many groups that opposed the biblical argument for slavery, saying that all people were equal before God, so it was sinful for one person to own another.

Activists also used political arguments against slavery, citing the Declaration of Independence, and pointing out that the United States could not be a democratic society as long as slavery existed. People argued that while some Northern working conditions needed to improve, they did not compare with being denied one's freedom for life.

Impact of Antislavery Movement

All Southerners did not support slavery, and all Northerners did not oppose it. Sarah and Angela Grimke, for example, were sisters who grew up on a South Carolina plantation and became active in the antislavery movement. Overall, however, the movement was strongest in the North, where many opponents of slavery helped Southern slaves to escape.

Resentful of this Northern interference, Southerners defended slavery more firmly. Extreme supporters of slavery wanted to go back to importing slaves from Africa. The goal of most white Southerners, however, was to maintain the white-dominated slave system as it existed. ■

■ *List two arguments people gave opposing slavery.*

REVIEW

1. **FOCUS** How did the cotton gin change the economy and the landscape of the South between 1790 and 1860?
2. **GEOGRAPHY** What made the "New South" suitable for growing cotton?
3. **CONNECT** What did Southern slaves harvest before 1790? What did they harvest after that date?
4. **ECONOMICS** Use the map on page 288 to make a chart listing each Southern state and its major cash crop(s).
5. **CRITICAL THINKING** If Whitney had not invented a practical cotton gin, what might have happened to slavery in the South? Explain your answer.
6. **WRITING ACTIVITY** Write a news story about the invention of the cotton gin. Include imaginary interviews with Eli Whitney and a plantation owner in your story.

BELIEF SYSTEMS

Critical Thinking

Why did proslavery advocates claim that Northern laborers were equally "enslaved" to factory owners who paid below-poverty wages? *(Both were unable to rise above their current position.)* Ask students to name differences between Northern laborers and slaves. *(Northern laborers had at least in theory, the option of walking away from a job or boss.)*

■ *They argued that the Bible recognizes the existence of slavery and that by introducing Christianity to slaves, planters had saved their souls; and that slaves were better off than Northern industrial workers.*

CLOSE

Have students answer the Thinking Focus and complete a flow chart, using the notes that they made while reading the lesson. Or, copy on the board the structure of the Graphic Overview on page 284. Ask students how dependent the South was on cotton and the planters on slaves. *(The economy of the South was highly dependent on cotton; slaves were an essential part of the work force.)*

Answers to Review Questions

1. The cotton gin increased production, increasing the need for labor. It expanded trade with the North and foreign countries. The landscape was characterized by plantations and steamboats on rivers.
2. The long, hot summers and the rich soil of the river valleys provided ideal growing conditions for cotton.
3. Prior to 1790, slaves harvested tobacco, indigo, and rice; after 1790, the main crop was cotton.
4. Louisiana: sugar, cotton; Arkansas, Mississippi, Alabama: cotton; Georgia, South Carolina: cotton, rice; North Carolina: tobacco, cotton, rice; Virginia, Maryland: tobacco; Kentucky, Missouri: tobacco, hemp.
5. Sample answer: Because the need for slavery had been declining, slavery might have ended. Allow for personal opinion.
6. Students should use a journalistic style, answering the questions: who? what? where? when? why? how?

Homework Options

Ask students to make a survey to find out what percentage of their clothing is made of cotton or contains cotton.

Study Guide: page 41.

INTRODUCE

Have the students read the Thinking Focus. Ask them to estimate how large the average plantation was and what percentage of white Southerners owned slaves. Also ask them to explain how they think slaves were treated. Tell students to read the lesson to confirm or disprove their ideas.

Key Term

Vocabulary strategies: T36–37

cultural heritage—a people's traditions of language, art, customs, and beliefs

1790 1860

LESSON 2

Life on the Plantation

THINKING FOCUS

Describe the responsibilities of the plantation owner, his wife, and the slaves they controlled.

Key Term

- cultural heritage

On the highest ground stood a large and handsome mansion. . . . the whole plantation, including the swamp land around it, and owned with it, covered several square miles. It was four miles from the settlement to the nearest neighbor's house. There were between thirteen and fourteen hundred acres under cultivation with cotton, corn, and other hoed crops, and two hundred hogs running at large in the swamp. . . . There were 135 slaves, big and little, of which 67 went to the field regularly. . . . We found in the field thirty ploughs [plows], moving together, turning the earth from the cotton plants, and from 30 to 40 hoers, the latter mainly women.

Frederick Law Olmsted published this account of a plantation after a Southern trip he made in 1856. Olmsted was a Northern journalist and travel writer who later became famous as the designer of Central Park in New York City.

A large plantation was not just cotton fields and a stately mansion at the end of a tree-lined road. It included many other buildings: the smokehouse where meat was preserved, the henhouse where poultry was raised, the barn where dairy cows and work animals were kept, and various buildings for storing tools, grain, and other goods. Stables sheltered purebred horses. In workshops, slaves made barrels and horseshoes, furniture, and cloth for use on the plantation.

Some plantations included a private chapel and a school for the planter's children. The kitchen was separate from the planter's home—known as the Big House—so that kitchen fires would not burn down the mansion. The Big House often had formal gardens. Vegetables and herbs were grown in other gardens for use in cooking and for herbal remedies.

Slave cabins were always separate from the Big House. A number of plantations included slave infirmaries, or hospitals, and a nursery where slave infants were cared for.

The Slave South

Olmsted's description of grand plantations with over 100 slaves continues to dominate most people's picture of the antebellum South. However, this portrait was the exception rather than the rule. Of the 50,000 plantations in the South in 1860, only 2,300 were owned by planters who held more than 100 slaves.

Most Southern farmers owned small farms and did not hold slaves. Nevertheless, these farmers tended to support slavery. They also acted as if they felt superior to all black people. Their support allowed the owners of large plantations to run the government and dominate the economy of the South.

Objectives

1. Identify the responsibilities of both the planter and the plantation mistress.
2. Describe how slaves were treated on Southern plantations.
3. Identify at least three ways in which slaves maintained their identity and their African heritage.
4. Identify the means that slaves used to resist slavery.

Graphic Overview

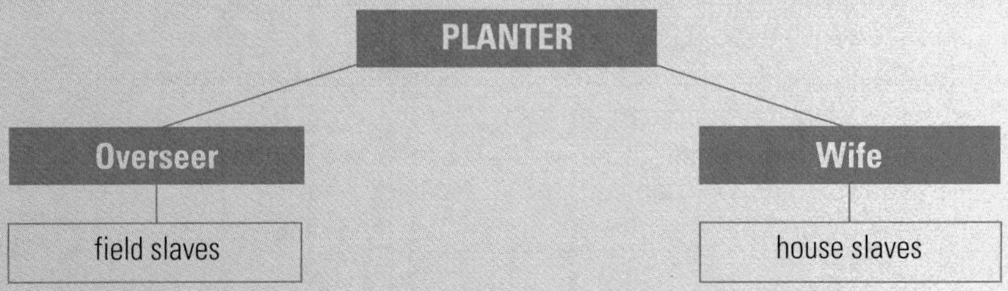

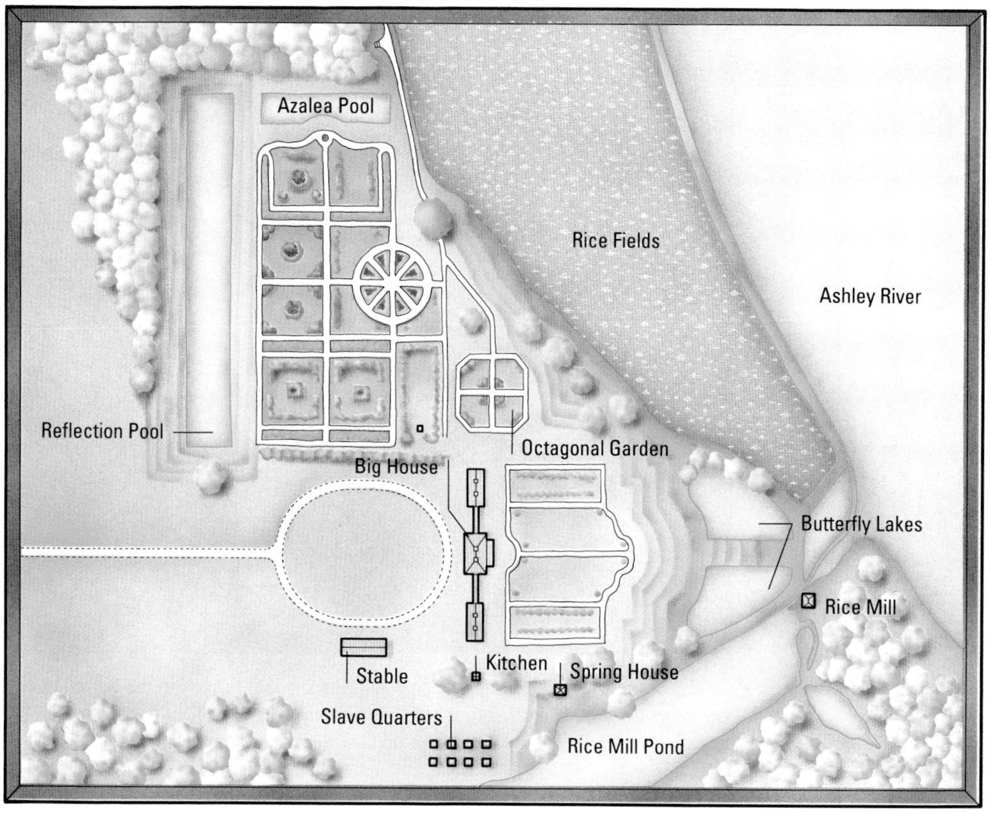

Master of the Land

A plantation was a self-contained world in which everyone—the planter, his wife and family, perhaps hired white workers, and slaves—played carefully assigned roles.

The plantation master had final authority over his land, his slaves, and his family. When problems arose among his slaves, the master acted as judge and jury. If a slave wanted to marry, the master had to grant permission. Planters had almost total power over their slaves. The way they treated slaves, however, was tempered by the realization that slaves were valuable possessions. Planters frequently overworked slaves and often treated them brutally—whipping them for failing to do their work, branding them, or otherwise disfiguring them. Planters often punished particularly difficult slaves by selling them away from their families.

Planters also took the law into their own hands in arguments with other white gentlemen. They lived by a "code of honor," settling disputes by "pistols at ten paces," in duels that were often deadly.

Some masters believed they had a duty to teach their slaves about Christianity. A planter might take his slaves to Sunday services with him, but they were seated in their own section in the back of the church or in a separate balcony. Other masters hired preachers to hold services on the plantation or took it upon themselves to read the Bible to their slaves.

Plantations had a strict ranking system. Although the planter ruled the entire estate, he might hire a white overseer to supervise work in the

This diagram is based on Middleton Plantation in South Carolina. What buildings can you identify? Why were gardens important?

DEVELOP

Have students skim the headings of the lesson. Ask them to explain how the lesson seems to be structured. *(Sections on the various people on a plantation)* Tell them that as they read the lesson they should list the responsibilities of the planter, the plantation mistress, the overseers, and the slaves on a plantation.

Buildings include a stable, a kitchen, a rice mill, the Big House, and the slave quarters. Gardens provided food in the self-sufficient community of the plantation.

ECONOMIC

Visual Learning

Ask the students to study the diagram of the plantation. How much space is devoted to the Big House and gardens? *(A large percentage)* To the slave quarters? *(A small amount)* Who maintained and cared for the grounds and buildings? *(The slaves)* What conclusion can be drawn about how much they benefited from their work? *(Very little benefit relative to the amount of work that they did)*

Access Strategy

Ask students to respond to the following questions. How would you feel if your life were completely controlled by someone else? How would you respond if someone forced you to do hard physical labor all day, threatening to beat or whip you if you slowed down? Would you cooperate or rebel? If you chose to rebel, would you do it openly or resist passively? Individually or with others in the same situation?

Then ask students how they would feel if the situation were reversed. How would you treat slaves who pretended to be sick or worked slowly? What would you do to get sufficient work from your slaves? Tell students that they will read in this lesson about the relationship between masters and their slaves.

Access Activity

Point out that slaves were either born to parents of slaves or they were purchased and brought to a plantation to live and work. Either way, slaves were regarded as personal property and generally treated harshly. Why do you suppose some slaves were able to survive whereas others were not?

SOCIAL SYSTEMS

Critical Thinking

Help students analyze the hierarchy of authority on a plantation. Over whom does the planter have authority? *(Over everyone)* The plantation mistress? *(Over everyone but her husband)* White overseers and black drivers? *(Over field hands)* Slaves? *(Over no one, under the authority of all)*

This photograph shows a group of plantation mistresses with some of their slaves.

fields. Some planters used trusted slaves as drivers, supervisors who made sure that the field hands kept up a fast pace.

The plantation mistress—usually the planter's wife—was second only to her husband in authority. However, she was expected to obey him without question.

Life in the Big House

The Big House was a visible symbol of a planter's wealth. It was usually a large two- or three-storied mansion. A wide entrance hall led into the dining room, parlor, library, and sitting room. Fine furniture, paintings, tapestries, and other fine objects, often imported from Europe, decorated the large, high-ceilinged rooms.

A wide staircase led to the second floor where there were several large bedrooms for family members and guests. In many homes the beds had headboards that were removed during hot weather. Because windows had no screens, mosquito netting was hung over beds to protect sleepers from the insects that thrived in the humid climate. Nurseries for the planter's children were on upper floors and could be reached by servants' stairs at the back of the house.

Women's Responsibilities

Running the Big House was the responsibility of the plantation mistress. She was responsible for all food preparation, including curing meats, churning butter, and baking. She was also supposed to see that the slaves had food, clothing, shelter, and medical attention, and possibly offer them advice or provide religious instruction. In addition, the mistress was usually left in charge of the entire plantation when the master was absent.

Many women took on the responsibilities of a plantation mistress at a young age. Daughters of planters usually married by age 22, and brides of 14 or 15 were not uncommon. Most women had little training for their new duties, and often learned their tasks from slaves on the plantation.

The obligations of plantation mis-

How Do We Know?

HISTORY *Letter writing was very important in the 19th century. Many plantation mistresses wrote daily or weekly letters to friends and family. Historians have found much detailed information about plantation society in such letters.*

Visual Learning

Have students study the photograph on this page. Why were black slave women included in the picture? *(Perhaps to show the status of the white women)* What is significant about their position in the photograph? *(In the rear of the group, reflecting their relative status)*

Economic Context

The majority of slaves—about 67 percent —planted and harvested cotton. Large cotton plantations ranged from North Carolina to Texas, including Alabama, Mississippi, Arkansas, and Louisiana. Employing about 15 percent of the slaves, tobacco plantations became established in eastern Maryland, Virginia, North Carolina, Kentucky, Tennessee, and Missouri.

Rice plantations were relatively large but few in number. They were situated along coastal North Carolina, South Carolina, Georgia, and along the banks of the Mississippi in the southern Louisiana delta. They used only about five percent of the slaves. The main investment for sugar cane, grown only in Louisiana, was in machinery; only six percent of the slaves were used in growing sugar cane. Hemp, a rope-making product, used only three percent of the slaves and was grown in Kentucky and northwest Missouri.

tresses were very different from those of enslaved women. Whether slave women worked in the Big House or the field, they also had to care for their own families. Mothers often brought their babies with them to the fields until the children could be left alone or with another adult. The only time that enslaved women could give to their families was at night and on Sundays. Even then, tasks like tending a garden and handling cabin chores usually filled the day. Enslaved women had little time for rest or for themselves. ■

■ *What were some of the skills a woman needed to learn when she became mistress of the plantation?*

■ *She had to oversee operations in the Big House and supervise slaves of the house. These white women were raised from birth to be masters of slaves.*

The Slave Community

Although slaves were a constant presence in the white household, they did not look on the master's house as their home. Rather, they found comfort and identity within their own slave community.

Slave Life

Myths about plantation life promote the idea that house slaves, slaves who did household chores such as cooking and caring for the planter's children, were too proud to do field work. In reality, most slaves were sent to the fields at harvest time. Only those who were too old or too young escaped working from sunup to sundown. Even the male slaves who were chosen to be drivers worked hard.

House slaves and drivers were set apart from the rest of the slave community. They had better food and clothing than field hands, but the costs were great. For example, a slave mother working in the Big House might be separated from her own child and have to sleep outside the door of her mistress's room. A driver might be forced to whip a member of his own family or a close friend.

When slaves were originally captured in Africa, they were separated from their families before being sold in America. To survive such inhumane treatment they often replaced their lost African families by "adopting" kin from among slaves with whom they were shipped to America. The Africans who suffered the journey to America together formed a new family.

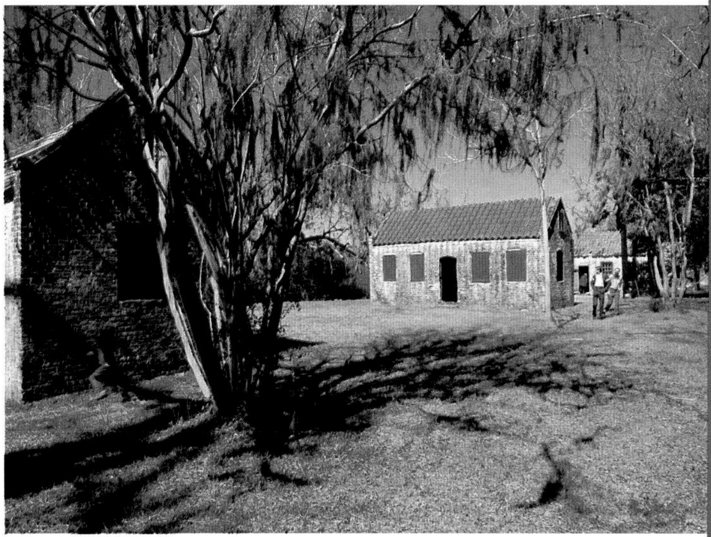

▲ *Slave cabins were a stark contrast to the elegant Big House. These cabins are on Boone Plantation in South Carolina. They are reported to be the only remaining row of slave cabins in the United States. Today they are visited by tourists.*

Slave Culture

Slaves strengthened their sense of identity by carefully preserving the African cultural heritage. A people's **cultural heritage** includes customs, language, art, and beliefs. For example, since slaves could not legally marry, they often performed a ceremony adapted from an African custom. By "jumping the broom," a couple was united in the eyes of the slave community. Such customs gave slaves support and helped them to resist their oppression.

Many slaves had two names: the English names that their masters assigned them at birth or when they were purchased, and African names used only among fellow slaves.

During the revival movements of the "Great Awakening" in the 1740s

SOCIAL SYSTEMS

Critical Thinking

Have students review the text and pictures in this lesson and in Lesson 1. What are the differences between the lives of the slaves and the lives of a planter and his family? *(Slaves—work hard, live in horrific quarters; planter and his family—supervise, live in relative luxury)*

Religious Context

Religious faith played an important role in the slave community and included various African religions combined with some of the elements of Christianity. The Christmas holidays, for example, were considered important by both masters and slaves. Christmas was one of the few times when slaves had the day off, visited relatives, and were not required to work. Slaves would tell different stories about Africa and often sing songs from Africa.

Health Connection

Since ancient times, herbal and other folk remedies have sometimes been quite effective. Have students research the use of herbal remedies today and in the past. Alternatively, have them research some modern medicines that are derived from herbal remedies. (For example, aspirin from willow bark, digitalis from foxglove)

Critical Thinking

Help students understand the importance of preserving one's cultural heritage. Ask students to name traditions that reflect their cultural heritage. *(Sample answer: Fourth of July celebrations)* If they were forced to move to a foreign country, how would they preserve their heritage? *(Continue some of their traditions)*

CULTURE

Critical Thinking

Encourage students to identify their own ethnic backgrounds and any food, music, and family customs that are traditional for that culture. How might their cultural heritage be important in their lives? *(Perhaps it provides a framework for their identity.)*

■ *Cultural activities included "jumping the broom," work songs and spirituals, and religious ceremonies based on African ritual.*

➤ *This quilt, one of two surviving coverlets made by former slave Harriet Powers, uses a West African technique known as appliqué—cutting out pieces of one material and sewing them to another.*

Across Time & Space

By the 1800s, African Americans had created a new sound in music. Based on the folk music of Southern slaves, it was transformed into a new style that came to be known as jazz. It remains America's greatest contribution to the world of music.

■ *Give three examples of cultural activities, separate from the white culture, in which plantation slaves participated.*

and the "Second Great Awakening" in the early 1820s, slaves were converted to Christianity by the thousands. Their church services combined African ritual with forms of American Protestantism. For example, the use of the ring shout echoed African ceremonies. Joyfully singing hymns, clapping, and stamping, worshippers circled in a shuffling dance, swaying to the rhythm of the music.

African cures for the sick sometimes proved more effective than white practices. For example, some white doctors used treatments that could be dangerous. Sometimes they drew blood from a patient, making the sick person weaker.

Slaves, on the other hand, tended to rely on natural cures and herbal medicines. For aches and pains they might use asper-root. It had an effect similar to that of today's aspirin.

Slaves also preserved African musical traditions. They created banjos and drums similar to African instruments by using hollowed gourds and stretched animal skins.

Slave work songs and spirituals combined African rhythms and musical tones with American hymns. From them grew new musical forms, such as spirituals, blues, and the forerunners of ragtime, Dixieland, and jazz.

Folktales, like music, provided relief. For example, the folktale character "Brer Rabbit" used his wits to outsmart his enemy. A symbol of the slaves' own condition, the rabbit stood for the dream of triumphing over slavery. You can read part of an account of one former slave's life on page 296. ■

Resistance to Slavery

Slaves found many ways to resist white control. Most forms of resistance were nonviolent.

Nonviolent Resistance

Slaves used songs not only to express their longings to be free, but also as a means of resisting slavery. For example, slaves might spread the news of a secret meeting by singing the refrain of the spiritual "Steal Away to Jesus":

"Steal away, steal away,
Steal away to Jesus.
Steal away, steal away home."

Made-up verses then indicated the place for a secret night meeting. White

Map and Globe Skills

Have students identify West and West Central Africa on the world political map on pages 694–695 in the Atlas. Point out that this part of Africa was the departure point for most slaves. Have students give the modern names of the countries where one could trace the roots of the black slaves in the United States. *(Guinea, Senegal, Nigeria, Cameroon)*

Research

Students can research one or more of the ways black slaves maintained their culture through music or storytelling. Ask students to find similarities to West African music or folktales. Students may also investigate modern examples of African elements in African American music, dress, art, religion, or folktales.

Writing a Letter to the Editor

Suggest that students write two letters to the editor of a Southern newspaper in the antebellum period. The first letter should make a case for continuing slavery, despite the fear of slave rebellions. The second letter should answer the first one, giving some of the reasons for the uprisings and questioning the fairness of slavery.

people who overheard the song were unaware of its special meaning.

Individual slaves resisted the planter's authority in various ways. Some pretended to be sick; some purposely broke tools; others worked as slowly as possible. Some slaves ran away often, even though they knew they would probably be caught and punished. By running away they were temporarily depriving the planter of their labor. Other slaves ran away to be with family members who did not live on their plantation.

Punishment for disobedience was harsh. Almost all runaways were whipped, some were branded, and some were actually maimed by having a leg tendon cut so that they could not run away again. For arson—the act of deliberately setting a fire—a slave might be hanged.

Such brutal punishments were not restricted to the South or to slaves. Captains of Northern ships often treated sailors with similar brutality. But nowhere outside the South was a labor force so cruelly exploited throughout their entire lives.

Slave Rebellions

Knowledge of plants might tempt a house slave to poison the master's food. This form of rebellion caused widespread fear among white Southerners. The most feared form of resistance, however, was organized, violent rebellion by a number of slaves.

Three major slave rebellions shook the South during the antebellum era, although only one of the three was an actual uprising. In 1800, white people in Richmond, Virginia, discovered a plot for a slave rebellion. Gabriel, an enslaved preacher and blacksmith, was plotting a general slave uprising. Betrayed by another slave, Gabriel and 35 others were hanged.

In 1822, Denmark Vesey, a free black carpenter in Charleston, South Carolina, planned to lead a rebellion on July 14, the anniversary of the French Revolution. He too was betrayed by a slave and was executed along with 35 other black men. Thirty-seven more were deported from the city.

The most terrifying rebellion of the era was Nat Turner's revolt in 1831. A slave preacher, Turner led 70 black men in an uprising in Southampton, Virginia. Before the three-day revolt was put down, 57 white people had been killed. White Southerners were in a panic. It was several weeks before Turner was caught, tried, and executed.

Most slaves did not revolt, and planters claimed they ruled their slaves generously. Although slaveholders were a minority in the South, they convinced millions of white Southerners to support slavery. ■

▲ *The shackles indicate the harsh treatment slaves often received. What does the poster suggest about the value of slaves?*

■ *Describe nonviolent methods that slaves used to resist the master's authority.*

REVIEW

1. **FOCUS** Describe the responsibilities of the plantation owner, his wife, and the slaves they controlled.
2. **ECONOMICS** Explain why the plantation could be called a "self-contained world." How was this different from the way people in the North lived and worked?
3. **CULTURE** Identify the African traditions that slaves preserved. Explain how those traditions helped slaves maintain a sense of identity.
4. **CONNECT** Compare the labor system in the Northern factories in Chapter 9 with the Southern plantation system.
5. **CRITICAL THINKING** Why do you think planters dominated Southern life?
6. **WRITING ACTIVITY** Write two short accounts of an event occurring on a plantation. One account should reflect the point of view of someone living in the Big House; the other should be from a slave's viewpoint.

HISTORY

Critical Thinking

Ask students to identify the effects of slave resistance on slaves. *(Often resulted in punishment; perhaps provided hope)* On their masters? *(Produced fear; decreased their profits)* What was the common purpose of nonviolent resistance and open rebellion? *(To fight back against slavery)* Which was more effective? *(Neither was very successful)*

◄ *It suggests that slaves were considered valuable possessions.*

■ *Slaves resisted by faking illness, working slowly, breaking tools, and running away.*

CLOSE

Have students evaluate the ideas that they had about plantation life before they read the lesson. Copy on the board the Graphic Overview from page 290 and have students answer the Thinking Focus by naming details about each person's role on a large plantation, using the lists that they made while reading the lesson.

Answers to Review Questions

1. The owner had authority over his family, the slaves, and the land. His wife supervised all the operations of the Big House, cared for her family, and tended to the physical and spiritual well-being of slaves. Most slaves worked in the fields and did jobs such as carpentry and gardening; some also did household chores.
2. The plantation included most of the institutions of a community. Some Northerners lived and worked in factories in the city. Others worked and lived on rural farms.
3. Slaves called each other by African names and used African customs in weddings, church services, and music to help preserve their African identity.
4. Like plantation slaves, Northern factory workers had harsh working conditions, but, unlike slaves, they were free to leave.
5. Sample answer: They held the financial and political power.
6. Encourage students to make clear the differences in perspective.

Homework Options

Students can research the slave rebellion of 1791 in Saint Domingue, Haiti.

Study Guide: p. 42.

INTRODUCE

Drawing on what students learned about plantation life in Lesson 2, discuss what it was like to be a slave. Point out to students that Frederick Douglass wrote his 1845 autobiography, from which this excerpt is taken, just seven years after he escaped from slavery at the age of 21. Douglass's autobiography is the most famous work in a genre, known as the slave narrative, which was popular in the mid-1800s.

READ AND RESPOND

Ask students to imagine, as they read the selection independently, how it would feel to be in Frederick Douglass's place. If you have LEP students, you might wish to read aloud the vocabulary words and their meanings noted in the margin. As students answer the purpose-setting question, make sure they give reasons for their answers.

LITERATURE

Slave Life

Frederick Douglass

In Lesson 2 you read about daily life on a Southern plantation. This selection is a firsthand account of slave life.

Frederick Douglass (1817?-1895) was a leading crusader for the rights of black Americans in the 1800s. An escaped slave, he knew the horrors of slavery and recorded his impressions in an autobiography, Narrative of the Life of Frederick Douglass. *His lifework included founding a newspaper, lecturing against slavery and inequality, and assisting with the Underground Railroad. As you read the selection, think about why the narrator feels both delight and sadness at seeing sailing ships.*

point of endurance: breaking point

fodder food for livestock

cunning skill at tricks

I lived with Mr. Covey one year. During the first six months, of that year, scarce a week passed without his whipping me. I was seldom free from a sore back. My awkwardness was almost always his excuse for whipping me. We were worked fully up to the point of endurance. Long before day we were up, our horses fed, and by the first approach of day we were off to the field with our hoes and ploughing teams. Mr. Covey gave us enough to eat, but scarce time to eat it. We were often less than five minutes taking our meals. We were often in the field from the first approach of day till its last lingering ray had left us; and at saving-fodder time, midnight often caught us in the field binding blades.

Covey would be out with us. The way he used to stand it, was this. He would spend the most of his afternoons in bed. He would then come out fresh in the evening, ready to urge us on with his words, example, and frequently with the whip. Mr. Covey was one of the few slaveholders who could and did work with his hands. He was a hard-working man. He knew by himself just what a man or a boy could do. There was no deceiving him. His work went on in his absence almost as well as in his presence; and he had the faculty of making us feel that he was ever present with us. This he did by surprising us. He seldom approached the spot where we were at work openly, if he could do it secretly. He always aimed at taking us by surprise. Such was his cunning, that we used to call him, among ourselves, "the snake." When we were at work in the cornfield, he would sometimes crawl on his hands and knees to avoid detection, and all at once he would rise nearly in our midst, and scream out, "Ha, ha! Come, come! Dash on, dash on!" This being his mode of attack, it was never safe to stop a single minute. . . .

If at any one time of my life more than another, I was made to drink the bitterest dregs of slavery, that time was during the first six months of my stay with Mr. Covey. We were worked in all weathers. It was never too hot or too cold; it could never rain, blow, hail, or snow, too hard for us to work in the field. Work, work, work, was scarcely more the order

Thematic Connections

Social Studies: Slave life

Houghton Mifflin Literary Readers: Finding Ways to Cope

Background

Frederick Douglass actually took a risk by writing this autobiography, for he named the slave owner from whom he escaped. Fearing that his former master would try to recapture him, Douglass left the country for two years and lectured in England. While there, he earned enough money to purchase his freedom and returned to the United States.

Because Douglass's newspaper and speeches showed such highly developed intellect, people claimed he had never been a slave at all. One reason Douglass wrote his autobiography was to disprove these claims. In fact, he had been taught the alphabet by a kindly mistress, and he had learned to read and write on his own.

of the day than of the night. The longest days were too short for him, and the shortest nights too long for him. I was somewhat unmanageable when I first went there, but a few months of this discipline tamed me. Mr. Covey succeeded in breaking me. I was broken in body, soul, and spirit. My natural elasticity was crushed, my intellect languished, the disposition to read departed, the cheerful spark that lingered about my eye died; the dark night of slavery closed in upon me; and behold a man transformed into a brute!

languish to go unused

Sunday was my only leisure time. I spent this in a sort of beast-like stupor, between sleep and wake, under some large tree. At times I would rise up, a flash of energetic freedom would dart through my soul, accompanied with a faint beam of hope, that flickered for a moment, and then vanished. I sank down again, mourning over my wretched condition. I was sometimes prompted to take my life, and that of Covey, but was prevented by a combination of hope and fear. My sufferings on this plantation seem now like a dream rather than a stern reality.

Our house stood within a few rods of the Chesapeake Bay, whose broad bosom was ever white with sails from every quarter of the habitable globe. Those beautiful vessels, robed in purest white, so delightful to the eye of freedom, were to me so many shrouded ghosts, to terrify and torment me with thoughts of my wretched condition. I have often, in the deep stillness of a summer's Sabbath, stood all alone upon the lofty banks of that noble bay, and traced, with saddened heart and tearful eye, the countless number of sails moving off to the mighty ocean. The sight of these always affected me powerfully. My thoughts would compel utterance; and there, with no audience but the Almighty, I would pour out my soul's complaint, in my rude way, with an apostrophe to the moving multitude of ships:—

shrouded covered

utterance speech

"You are loosed from your moorings, and are free; I am fast in my chains, and am a slave! You move merrily before the gentle gale, and I sadly before the bloody whip! You are freedom's swift-winged angels, that fly round the world; I am confined in bands of iron! O that I were free! . . ."

Further Reading

Narrative of the Life of Frederick Douglass. Frederick Douglass. In this famous autobiography, Douglass gives a vivid account of his life as a slave, his escape to freedom, and his work as an abolitionist.

Frederick Douglass and the Fight for Freedom. Shalman Russell. The story of Frederick Douglass comes to life in this thoughtful biography.

◄ Why was Mr. Covey able to work late with the slaves? *(He spent most of his afternoons in bed.)*

What effect did working for Mr. Covey have on Frederick Douglass? *(It broke his body, soul, and spirit.)*

EXTEND

Have students research slave narratives in the library. Then ask them to imagine that they had been slave and write their own story, describing some aspect of what it was like to be a slave.

Further Reading

You may want to ask students to go to the school or local library to find more books to read about Frederick Douglass or the daily life of slaves.

INTRODUCE

After students read the lesson title and the Thinking Focus, remind them that a fairly small number of white Southerners owned large plantations. Have students read the lesson to find out who the other Southerners were.

Key Terms

Vocabulary strategies: T36–37

yeoman farmer—owner of a small farm

artisan—worker trained in a skilled trade such as cabinet making or printing

➤ *Women did not have an active role in politics at that time.*

1790 1860

LESSON 3

The Other Souths

THINKING FOCUS

What groups made up the majority of Southerners who lived outside the plantation system?

Key Terms

- yeoman farmer
- artisan

Imagine the excitement as the people living in a small county in Georgia gathered at the town square on a Saturday morning in 1835. A robust man with a red face, white hair, and a booming voice stood on a tree stump and called out "Welcome! Welcome! Help yourself to our fresh-pressed cider, roast pig, and all the fixin's. We're gonna have a great time today! It will give you a taste of the great future for you all once I'm elected!"

The speaker, owner of the largest plantation in the county, looked out over the faces gathering around the stump he stood on, and smiled. Most of the people in his county had small farms. They lived far from one another in the scrubby pine woods. For them, a trip to the county seat (the town where government offices were located) was a major event. A full day of free food and entertainment would probably persuade most of the farmers to vote for this candidate.

The barbecue continued throughout the day with games, dances, and the constant hum of people gossiping with neighbors they hadn't seen for weeks. By nightfall, the plantation owner had shaken hands with each person in the crowd, kissed every baby in sight, and made sure that even those who couldn't read or write would be able to mark the ballot with an X beside his name.

Although this account is imaginary, it describes a common event in the South. Since most farm families had no slaves for large projects, they would get together at day-long parties to build barns or husk corn. Politicians in rural areas depended on such gatherings to gain political support. In this way, white Southerners mixed pleasure with politics or with cooperative labor.

➤ *George Caleb Bingham did a series of paintings about Southern political life. Why did he omit women?*

Objectives

1. Identify and describe the groups of Southerners who did not live on plantations.
2. Describe the diverse society that developed in Southern cities.
3. Compare education in the South with education in the North.
4. Discuss the status of free blacks in Southern society.

Graphic Overview

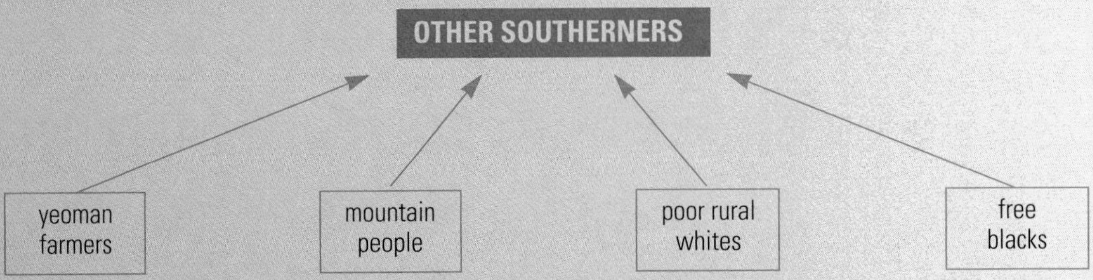

The Neglected Majority

The majority of white Southerners did not own slaves. They included **yeoman farmers**—owners of small farms—and mountain settlers. The mountain people lived by hunting, fishing, and gathering wild vegetables as well as by maintaining small farms. In addition, there were some very poor rural white people who owned no land and earned their living in whatever way they could.

Yeoman Farmers

Yeoman farmers usually grew an acre or so of cotton or another cash crop. They also grew crops and raised livestock for their own needs. The farmer and the farmer's family performed the work, perhaps with the help of a few hired white laborers. During the planting and harvesting seasons they might borrow several slaves. And, as noted, neighboring farm families shared work on large projects such as building a house.

Many yeoman farmers, although illiterate, had a strong oral tradition of songs and folk stories. The church played an important part in their social life, and many could quote long passages from the Bible.

Although they were not slaveholders and did not directly benefit from the slave economy, yeoman farmers generally supported the proslavery position of the ruling minority of planters.

Appalachian Culture

The people of the Appalachians—from the Smoky Mountains of Virginia to the Cumberland region of Tennessee—had much in common. Unlike yeoman farmers who might grow a small cash crop, these families often were completely cut off from the market economy. Most were hunters who managed to grow enough food for their family, but not enough for trade. Although mountain families lived isolated lives, they enjoyed a rich culture.

A Closer Look shows some of the objects the mountain people used. Music was important in their lives. Many of the earliest settlers came to the United States from England, Wales, and the Scottish Highlands, where ancient ballads and dances were handed down from one generation to the next. Mountain musicians played the dulcimer (a stringed instrument), the fiddle, the bagpipe, and a small instrument known as the "mouth harp."

People in the mountains enjoyed opportunities to get together. Church meetings, harvest suppers, and Fourth of July celebrations provided a chance to display folk dances. Monthly county court sessions also served as a social event. Women met there to exchange recipes while men talked politics.

The mists formed by a humid atmosphere gave the Great Smoky Mountains (above) *their name. Mountain people built their sturdy cabins with long sloping roofs that provide protection from the damp climate.*

DEVELOP

Tell students to preview the pictures in the lesson, including A Closer Look, without reading any text or headings. What conclusions can they draw about the South just from this brief glance? *(Students should notice the diversityof its people.)* As students read, have them list characteristics of each of the main groups of Southerners who lived outside of the plantation system.

GEOGRAPHY

Visual Learning

Refer students to the picture of the Appalachians on this page and the diagram of a large plantation on page 291. Ask students to explain why it would be difficult to create a plantation in the Appalachians. *(Isolation, land difficult to till)* Share with students the information from the Geographic Context on page 301.

Access Strategy

To help students understand the diversity of the people of the antebellum South, have them analyze the people of their own community. Divide the students into small, heterogeneous groups. Are there common features that people in their community share? *(Such as a recognizable accent)* What differences exist among the people? *(Different jobs, incomes, living accommodations, ethnic backgrounds, ages)* Why is it misleading to generalize about a community or region? *(Diversity)* Tell students that in this lesson they will learn about the diversity of people in the antebellum South.

Access Activity

Have students locate the Appalachians, including the Great Smoky Mountains, on the physical map of the United States on pages 700–701 in the Atlas. Also have them use the political map of the United States on pages 698–699 to find the main cities of the South today. *(Savannah, Richmond, Charleston, New Orleans, Atlanta)*

CULTURE

Critical Thinking

Refer students to the pictures and captions in A Closer Look. Explain that the people of the Appalachians found creative ways to use many of the things in their natural environment. Ask students to look for examples of this. *(Carved wood for walking sticks, roots and bark for dyes, vines for baskets, wood for instruments)*

More About the Quilts Before the 1850s, quilts were made with homemade material, either wool scraps or homespun linsey-woolsey (flax and wool woven together) left over after clothing had been made. After the 1850s, peddlers began to reach these communities on a regular basis, selling factory-made cloth, including calico and unbleached muslin.

A CLOSER LOOK

Appalachian Crafts

Travel into the Appalachians—over hills and streams to cabins nestled in forests and grassy knolls. One observer commented, "Everywhere you go, it's climb, scramble, clamber down, and climb again." Here, people use what nature gives them to craft charming and practical items.

"Dipper gourds" are perfect for scooping water out of a stream, and "bottle gourds" are handy for storing seeds. Nimble fingers turn corn husks into useful articles: hats, shopping bags, doormats, or pretty painted dolls.

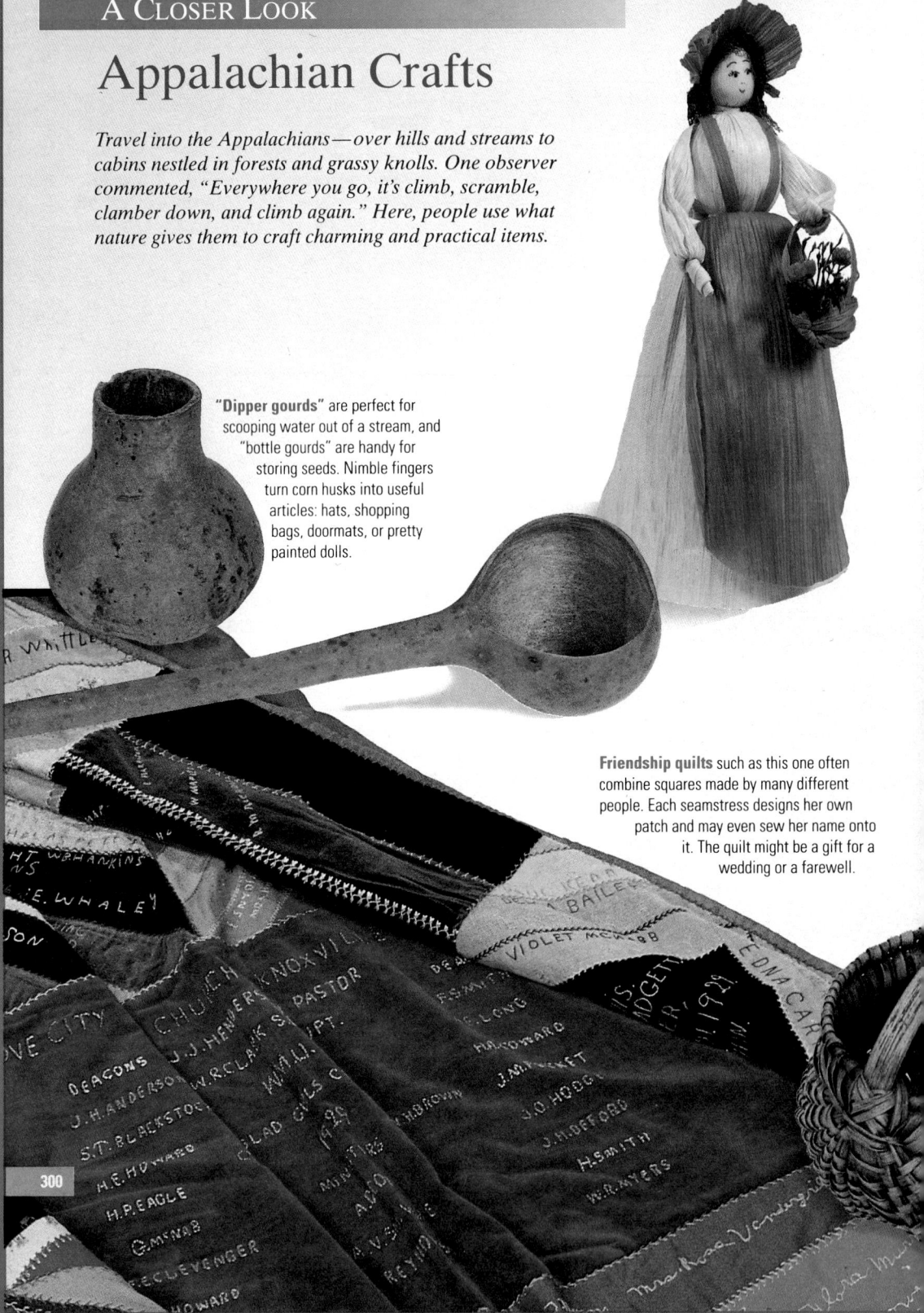

Friendship quilts such as this one often combine squares made by many different people. Each seamstress designs her own patch and may even sew her name onto it. The quilt might be a gift for a wedding or a farewell.

300

Social Participation

Ask students to recall the lesson opener. What kinds of projects did yeoman farmers do cooperatively? *(Built barns and houses, husked corn)* Why? *(By dividing a task among a group of people, the project could be done quickly.)* How can social studies projects be done cooperatively? *(Divide tasks—research, find resources, make a model)*

Cultural Context

The musical heritage of Appalachia can be traced back to England and Scotland. Musicologists have discovered identical or nearly identical ballads on both sides of the Atlantic. Chief among the collectors were Cecil Sharp, John Jacob Niles, Alan Lomax, and Jean Ritchie. Ritchie, from eastern Kentucky, told of a family song with the words *Killy Kranky* that they thought was nonsense. Then one day she got lost in Scotland and chanced upon the town of Killy Kranky.

Religious Context

New Orleans, once a French city, maintains a tradition that dates back to its European origins. The Mardi Gras celebration, on the Tuesday before Ash Wednesday, includes colorful parades in bright costumes, music, merriment, and food. The words *Mardi Gras* mean "fat Tuesday," signifying a last party before Lent, the forty days of fasting and penitence leading up to Easter. Mardi Gras is the last day of Carnival. *Carnival* literally means "good-bye to meat."

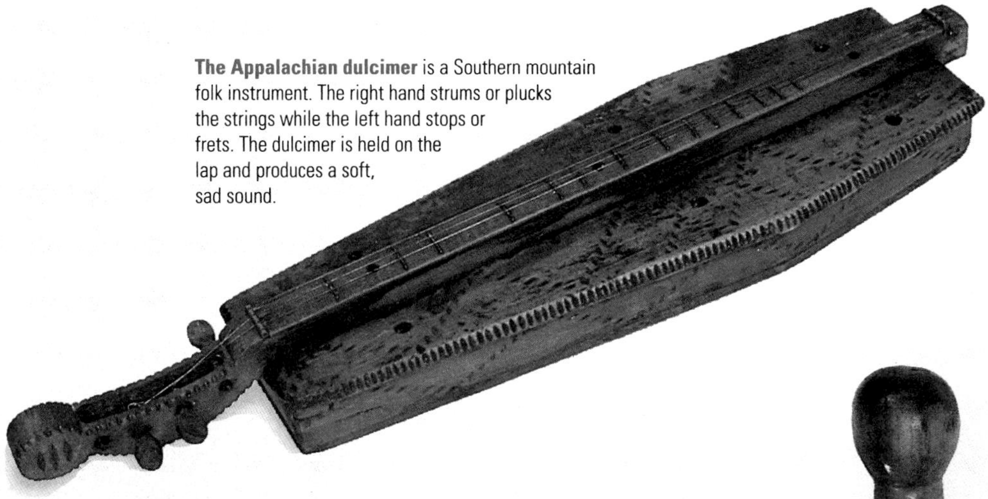

The Appalachian dulcimer is a Southern mountain folk instrument. The right hand strums or plucks the strings while the left hand stops or frets. The dulcimer is held on the lap and produces a soft, sad sound.

Snakes slither through folktales and folk art. A whittler had a good time carving this one on a walking stick.

Cornhusks, willow wands, cattail leaves, and honeysuckle vines all make fine baskets. These baskets are woven from oak splints shaved off an oak log with an axe. Basket dyes are made from roots and barks, such as walnut, willow, and sassafras.

CULTURE

Critical Thinking

After looking at the examples of Appalachian crafts in A Closer Look, students can infer how the people of the Appalachians might have handled other aspects of their work. *(They probably took advantage of what was around them, found creative ways to do things, paid attention to detail, and added ornament to work tools.)*

More About Baskets To prepare the honeysuckle vines for weaving, the runners were gathered when the sap was down, wound into balls, and then boiled for four hours. After peeling off the bark and soaking the vines in cold water overnight, they would then be hung to dry in the sun. Once the vines were dry, the weaving could begin.

Geographic Context

The Appalachian foothills ensure the isolation of small farms and towns even today. Fast-running streams pouring off the mountainsides cut deep valleys or "hollers," making road building, or even horseback travel, difficult. This isolation limits Appalachian farmers' contact with each other and with the outside world.

Critical Thinking

Point out that the ways of many Appalachian peoples have changed very little in 200 years. The musical instruments, dances, and even speech patterns and vocabulary still survive. Why would these aspects of the culture survive in such an area? *(Limited contacts with outside world caused community to turn inward.)*

■ *Plantations were part of the market economy. In contrast, yeoman farmers grew just a small cash crop, and mountain settlers hunted and grew food only for their own families.*

SOCIAL SYSTEMS

Critical Thinking

Have students compare the diversity of Southern cities with Northern cities (Chapter 9). *(Both had a variety of immigrant populations, job opportunities, and social activities.)*

■ *How did the lives of yeoman farmers and mountain settlers differ from life on the plantations?*

At county fairs people exhibited their best quilts, vegetables, and livestock, and sold stock at fairs and "mule days." Horse races gave the mountain people another chance for social contact, as well as an opportunity to show off the thoroughbred horses for which the South was famous. ■

The Urban South

The South was overwhelmingly rural. Social life in the rural South usually took place on the great plantations. Small Southern towns were active during the fall harvest and shipping season, but offered no year-round amusements such as theaters, lecture halls, or even inns for temporary hospitality. Only the larger cities could be called true metropolitan cultural centers.

Southern towns grew slowly, although there were some exceptions: Louisville, Kentucky, and New Orleans, Louisiana, almost doubled in size in the 10 years preceding the Civil War. The population of Mobile, Alabama, grew by 155 percent.

Urban Centers

Cities such as Savannah in Georgia, Richmond in Virginia, Charleston in South Carolina, and New Orleans had as varied a lifestyle as any Northern city. Planters and their wives often spent part of the year in cities. White **artisans**—workers trained in skilled trades such as printing and cabinet making—lived in the cities. So did most former slaves, who had either been granted their freedom or had bought it.

Many Southern cities had a diverse society. St. Augustine, Florida, had Spanish roots; Jamestown, Virginia, had been settled by the English. New Orleans, which had been settled by the French, gained Spanish colonists during the years it was ruled by Spain. The influence of these origins persisted and blended with the cultures of such later arrivals as white and black Southerners and German and Irish immigrants. Farmers from the Ohio River Valley and the South shipped their produce down the Mississippi through the busy port at its mouth. By 1860 New Orleans was the largest city in the South, and the fifth largest in the United States.

➤ *Eastman Johnson called this painting "Old Kentucky Home." The actual scene was the backyard of his father's home in Washington, D.C.*

Visual Learning

Refer students to the painting on this page and ask them what in the painting indicates that the scene is in an urban setting. *(Black and white Southerners living side by side)*

Music Connection

Have students bring to class recordings of Appalachian ballads or perform the ballads themselves. Some students may bring in English, Welsh, and Scottish tunes for comparison. (See the Cultural Context on page 300.)

Art Connection

The folk art of the rural South consisted of practical things such as wooden buckets, oxen yokes, and quilts, as well as wooden toys for the children. Have students find pictures of these objects (in addition to the ones in A Closer Look) or the objects themselves, if possible, and combine them to make a bulletin board display or an exhibit on a table.

Southern Education

Cities such as New Orleans had fine colleges, and wealthy white people in the South were generally well-educated. They were tutored at home or were sent to private boarding schools or military academies. In 1850, the Southern states led the nation in number of private schools. The first state universities in the United States were the University of North Carolina, founded in 1795, and the University of Georgia, opened in 1808. Many Southern colleges were large by comparison with Northern schools. In 1856, for example, the University of Virginia had 568 students to the 361 at Harvard in Massachusetts.

Public education in the South, however, lagged behind the North, and many Southerners could not read and write. Many rural schools were open only those few months a year when children could be released from farm work. Southern farmers, like farmers in the North, did not feel formal education was a necessity for farm work.

Education for Black People

In a democracy, educated citizens are a necessity for the government to work. Education is also necessary for individuals to grow and prosper in their lives. The fact that slaves were forbidden to read or write shows that slaveholders understood that education gives people power. They feared education would unite slaves and teach them dangerous ideas about freedom. In fact, two of the three major slave revolts were launched in cities, where more black men and women were literate.

Some slaves did learn to read and write. Among them was Frederick Douglass, who was enslaved at birth on a Maryland plantation. Douglass taught himself to write by copying letters marked on timber in the shipyard where he worked. Eventually, he became one of the greatest leaders in the struggle for black freedom. In his autobiography, he explains how he cleverly expanded his knowledge. ■

◄ *Frederick Douglass escaped slavery in Maryland by running away to Massachusetts.*

When I met any boy who I knew could write, I would tell him I could write as well as he. The next word would be, "I don't believe you. Let me see you try it." I would then make the letters which I had been so fortunate as to learn and ask him to beat that. In this way I got a good many lessons in writing, which it is quite possible I should never have gotten in any other way.

During this time, my copy-book was the board fence, brick wall, and pavement; my pen and ink was a lump of chalk. . . . By this time my little master Thomas had gone to school and learned how to write and had written over a number of copy-books. . . . When left [to take care of the house], I used to spend the time in writing in the places left in Master Thomas' copy-book, copying what he had written.

Narrative of the Life of Frederick Douglass, 1845

■ *What made most Southern cities different from cities in the North during the antebellum period?*

303

SOCIAL SYSTEMS

Critical Thinking

Have students compare the education system in the North with education in the antebellum South. *(Public education encouraged and highly valued in the North; little or no public education in the self-contained plantation and rural South, but private schools for wealthy white Southerners)*

■ *Because the South was so rural, its cities were smaller and active only during the fall harvest and the shipping season.*

ECONOMICS

Critical Thinking

Ask students why white Southerners favored laws restricting free blacks as well as opposing their being freed at all. *(White Southerners worried that free blacks would become educated and have a powerful influence on slaves. Frederick Douglass, for example, taught himself to read and write and eventually became one of the greatest leaders for black freedom.)*

Free Blacks

Thousands of free blacks—slaves who had been granted or had bought their freedom—lived in the cities below the Mason-Dixon line—the line that divided the North from the South. Some free black Southerners purchased land and a small number owned slaves.

Job Opportunities

Many free blacks used the skills they had learned as slaves to earn a living as blacksmiths, carpenters, masons, barbers, and tailors. In 1860, for example, free black men made up 40 percent of the tailors and 25 percent of the carpenters in Charleston, South Carolina.

The majority of free blacks in Southern towns and cities were women. By 1850, some cities had as many as 140 free black women for every 100 free black men. These women usually faced harsher lives than free black men because they lacked skills that paid well. Some

UNDERSTANDING SOCIAL CLASSES

Southern society in the 1860s was not just one society but was made up of several social classes that had a clear order of rank. A social class is a group of people that share similar economic and cultural characteristics.

Southern Class Structure

Not everyone in white Southern society owned slaves, but because ownership of slaves indicated wealth, most everyone wanted to. A social hierarchy means that one social class is ranked above another. At the top of the white Southern hierarchy were the small number—about 2,300—who owned 100 or more slaves. Below them were the slightly larger group who owned 10 to 50 slaves. An even larger group—about 270,000 families—owned fewer than 10 slaves.

Three-quarters of Southern families, the yeoman farmers, did not own slaves. Yet they supported the right to own slaves, and might have bought slaves if they could have afforded to. Slave ownership was not economically profitable for poor landowners.

At the bottom of this white social hierarchy were the very poor who owned no land at all. In a way, they felt better about their own position, because as long as slavery existed, there was someone else who was worse off than they were. On the other hand, the existence of slavery allowed white plantation holders to accumulate large holdings of land, and made it harder for the landless to own property.

Other Class Hierarchies

The social ranking of white Southern society was not as rigid as the hierarchy of feudal society. Moving into a new rank was easier in principle in the South than it had been in feudal times.

Yet there were important differences between Southern society and feudal society. Although medieval serfs, or peasants, could not leave the land, they could not be sold. Their families could not be split up among masters, as happened with slave families.

African Americans

Free blacks and black slaves lived outside the white class structure, even though Southern society could not have existed without them. A part of the American social philosophy, then—as now—was that everyone had the same opportunity for social and economic advancement. In theory, landless whites could buy land, whites who didn't own slaves could one day buy them, and white farmers could become plantation owners. The only people who could not move to another group were blacks. With very few exceptions, blacks, free or enslaved, could not break out of the system that depended on their labor.

SOCIAL SYSTEMS

Critical Thinking

Highlight the importance of social class in the antebellum South. Where might the differences in Southern social class have been more apparent: on the plantation or in the Southern urban areas? Have students explain their answers. *(Social class would probably be more apparent on the plantation because of the obvious difference between master and slave; urban areas have a greater mixture of people from different social classes and professions.)*

Critical Thinking

Have students discuss why some white Southerners preferred to keep slaves from gaining literacy. *(Some white Southerners worried that learning to read and write could help slaves become independent thinkers and thus become more powerful as a group.)*

Making a Model

Appalachian parents were talented in making toys for their children, often using bits of wood or other materials that they had at hand. Have the students research these folk toys and perhaps try to make some of their own. Instruction for 100 toys and games can be found in the sixth volume of the *Foxfire* series (Garden City, N.Y.: Anchor Press/Doubleday, 1980).

Writing a Letter

Have students imagine that they are a free black person who has just learned to write after moving to one of the major Southern cities. Have them write a letter to their former church minister, describing life as a free person and contrasting it with life on the plantation. Students should use details in this chapter to give an accurate account of city and plantation life.

worked as laundresses and nurses, and a large number ran small boarding houses. Many free black women worked as domestic servants.

Restrictions on Free Blacks

Despite their status, free blacks were subject to harsh laws. They were not allowed to vote. Their wages were unequal to those of whites and many jobs were closed to them. State and local laws restricted their travel, and allowed white authorities to search their houses without legal permits.

When Virginia prisons became too crowded in 1822, the state decided not to imprison free blacks accused of crimes. Instead, officials whipped them or sold them into slavery as punishment for serious crimes.

Although masters often granted freedom to a faithful servant, white Southerners continued to be fearful and suspicious of the influence of free blacks on slaves. This attitude made it dangerous for free blacks to socialize with slaves.

In the early 1800s many whites supported the idea of shipping free blacks to Africa. Colonization societies were formed to accomplish this goal. But most free blacks, whether they were first-, second- or third-generation Americans, had no desire to "return" to Africa. By the late antebellum period, it was clear that the colonization plan did not work. By the 1850s, the great demand for slaves and the white fear of free blacks caused many planters to resist granting freedom to their slaves.

Resistance to Freeing Slaves

Slavery created ties that bound together the many Souths. The system of servitude provided the foundation for plantation life, fueled the cotton revolution that enriched New England mill owners, and helped to keep the Southern economy rural. White Southerners also tended to support slavery out of fear. The slave rebellions of the early 1800s created alarm at the possibility that freed slaves might gain power and destroy the Southern plantation system, as slaves had done in the country of Haiti.

As the South's dependence on slavery increased between 1790 and 1860, the gulf between the Southern cotton economy and the industrial economy of the North widened. The opposing goals and needs of the North and the South would create a deeper conflict—a conflict that would eventually lead to war. ■

■ *In what ways were free blacks' rights limited?*

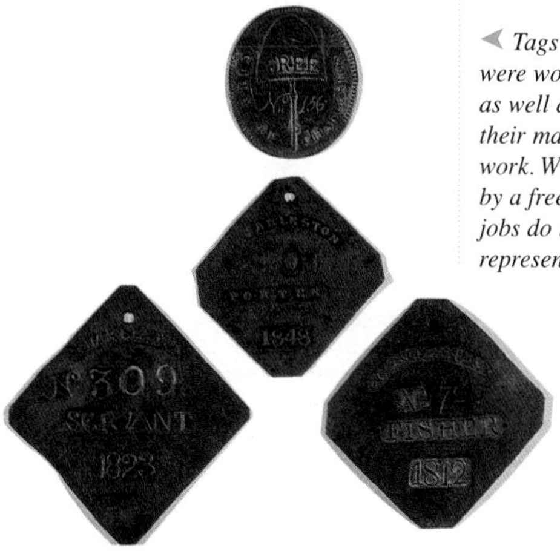

Tags such as these were worn by free blacks as well as by slaves whom their masters hired out for work. Which tag was worn by a free black? What jobs do the other tags represent?

REVIEW

1. **FOCUS** What groups made up the majority of Southerners who lived outside the plantation system?
2. **CONNECT** How did the lives of Southern free blacks differ from those of slaves? In what ways were their lives similar?
3. **GEOGRAPHY** How did the mountain people's crafts reflect the natural surroundings?
4. **CRITICAL THINKING** Why do you think schooling did not seem as important to yeoman farmers in the rural South as it did to the working classes of the urban North?
5. **ACTIVITY** Draw a picture of an Appalachian event such as a harvest supper, a Fourth of July celebration, or a county fair. Be sure to include distinctly Appalachian objects and activities.

Porter, fisher, servant.

SOCIAL SYSTEMS

Critical Thinking

Ask students to compare the rights and restrictions for free black persons with those for slaves. *(Comparison could include freedom to move about, source of food and shelter, payment for work.)*

■ *Free blacks were not allowed to vote, read and write, live in certain areas, attend schools, have certain jobs, or travel without restrictions; they could be whipped or sold into slavery.*

CLOSE

Have students answer the Thinking Focus. Copy on the board the Graphic Overview from page 298 and have students add characteristics describing each group, using the lists that they made while reading the lesson.

Answers to Review Questions

1. The majority of Southerners who lived outside the plantation system were yeomen farmers, mountain settlers, poor rural whites who owned no land, and free blacks.
2. Both slaves and free blacks experienced discrimination by whites, but some free blacks could own land and work for themselves.
3. The mountain people got inspiration for designs from nature and used natural materials available locally.
4. Sample answer: Southern yeoman farmers needed their children to work in the fields and did not think formal education was important for farming. Northern urban workers valued education as a means to rise in the industrial world. Allow for personal opinion.
5. Remind students to consult the lesson opener as well as A Closer Look for details.

Homework Options

Ask students to find a Southern folktale and share it with the class.

Study Guide: page 43.

UNDERSTANDING GRAPHS

This skill lesson will show students which kinds of graphs are appropriate for displaying different information.

HISTORY

Visual Learning

Ask students to add up the percentages shown for each slice of the circle graph. Point out that every circle graph represents all, or 100 percent, of something. What fact about Southern slave ownership is immediately obvious from a glance at the graph? *(A large majority of Southerners owned no slaves.)*

HISTORY

Visual Learning

To reinforce the idea that different kinds of graphs are useful for showing different information, ask students to think about how the information on the bar graph in their book would appear on a circle graph. How many circle graphs would be needed to show the same information? *(Three; one for each of the years shown on the bar graph)*

UNDERSTANDING GRAPHS

Choosing Appropriate Graphs

Here's Why

Graphs are an excellent way to present numerical information so that it is easier to understand. It is much easier to "see" what was happening over a certain time period by looking at graphs rather than at lists of numbers.

For example, in this chapter you have read about the dramatic increase in cotton production after the invention of the cotton gin. Suppose you wanted to show this information with a graph. In order to determine which kind of graph—line, bar, or circle graph—would be most appropriate, you first need to understand what each of these graphs does.

Here's How

Look at each of the graphs on this page and on the next. Bar graphs, like the one below, show information in columns and are best for presenting numbers and comparing quantities. Circle graphs, like the one on the right, indicate percentages and are useful for showing the relationship between parts and the whole. You also can use two or more circle graphs to compare different subjects, such as products or groups of people, or to show the difference in percentages over a period of time. The graphs on page 307 are line graphs, which are best for presenting statistics over a period of time. By reading the plotted points on a line graph, you can follow the curve to determine a trend in the information being given.

In order to choose which of these graphs is most appropriate for your purposes, you can follow the steps outlined below:

1. Ask yourself, "What is the main point I wish to communicate?"
2. Decide whether this point involves comparing the quantities of similar things (bar graph), showing percentages or the relationship of parts to a whole (circle graph), or showing a change or trend over time (line graph).
3. Choose the type of graph that can most effectively convey your information based on your answer in step two.

Look at the bar graph, which shows the growth of the nation's urban and rural populations in the North and South. This graph is effective in showing the overall growth in population from 1820 to 1860, but if you just wanted to show this change, you could use a line

Southern Slave Ownership, 1860

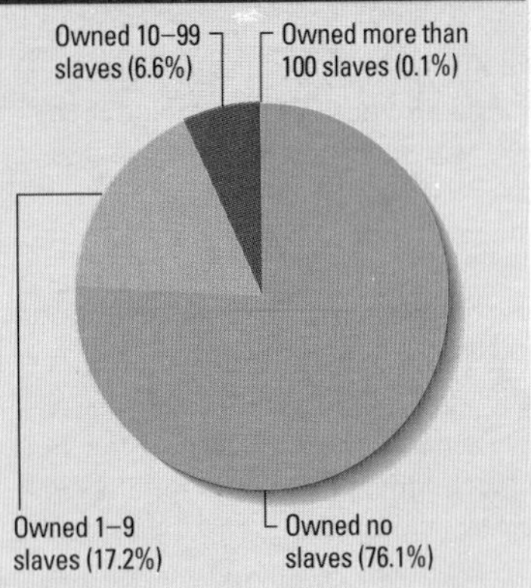

Northern and Southern Populations, 1820–1860

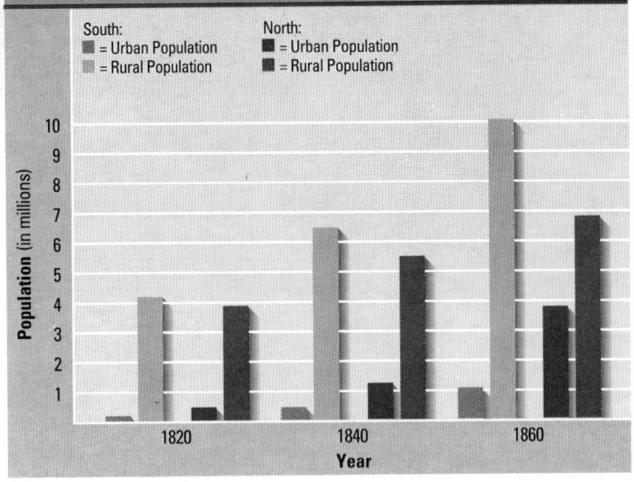

Objective

Use information about line, bar, and circle graphs to choose appropriate graphs. (Visual Learning 2)

Science Connection

Tell students to find other examples of these three types of graphs in their science textbooks. Discuss what information each graph shows and why the authors of the textbook chose that particular type of graph.

Bulletin Board

Have students use the newspaper to record the high temperatures in your area each day for a week. Prepare a line graph for the bulletin board to show the information. Fill in one segment of the line each day.

Note: You may wish to have graph paper available for your students to use.

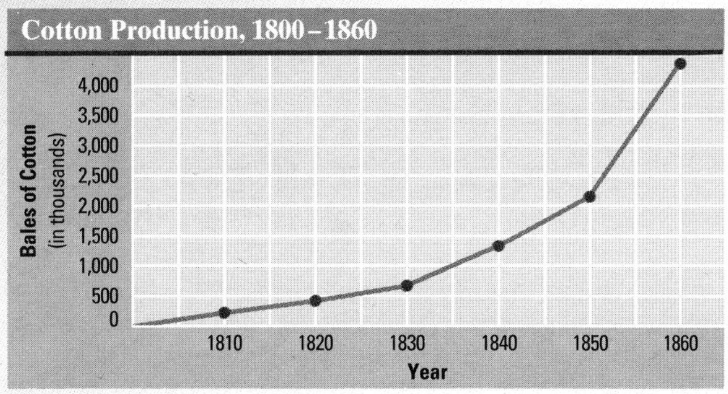

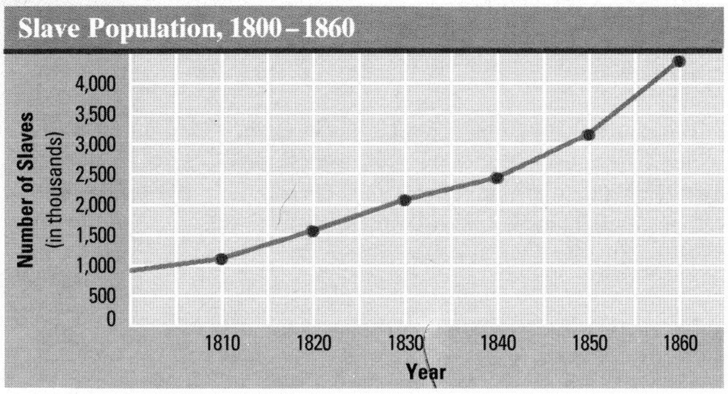

graph. By using different colored columns for urban and rural populations, this graph emphasizes the actual population numbers and more specifically outlines the differences in the population growth between the North and the South. You can see that in 1820 each region had similar populations in rural areas and in urban areas. However by 1860, the urban population in the North was triple that of the South, and the South had ten times the amount of people living on farms as they did in the cities.

Look at the circle graph on page 306 showing what percentage of Southern white people owned slaves. Although it seems that many people before the Civil War owned slaves, you've read that few planters owned more than 100 slaves. A circle graph is effective here since it gives you a dramatic picture of what those numbers mean and shows that three-quarters of the Southern white population owned no slaves at all.

Next look at the line graphs, which show cotton production and slave population from 1800 to 1860. Here the emphasis is in showing not just the numbers or quantities for these subjects, but also the trends over a period time that these figures represent. By comparing two graphs of the same kind, you can see whether these two sets of statistics follow the same trend.

The cotton production graph shows growth, or an upward trend, since production increased from over 73,000 bales in 1800 to almost four million in 1860. You will notice an upward trend in the slave population graph as well, since the number of slaves rose significantly from 1800 to 1860. By comparing these two line graphs, you can see whether there was a relationship between cotton production and slavery.

Try It

Now go back to Lesson 1 of this chapter, and find the statistics about how many white people, slaves, and free blacks lived in the South in 1790 and in 1860. Following the process outlined on page 306, decide which type of graph—line, bar, or circle—is most appropriate to show this information, and then create that graph.

Apply It

You may look forward to the weekend all week long, but then once the weekend arrives, the hours just fly by. Suppose you wanted an accurate account of how you spend that free time. Write down how many hours of your weekend days you spend on different activities like sleeping, eating, studying, watching television, playing sports, or visiting with friends. Then choose two different graphs to present this information, and create those graphs, noting the difference in how this information is presented in each graph.

HISTORY

Visual Learning

Point out that the information on the bar graph on page 306 could also be shown on a line graph. How many lines would be needed? *(Four)* Let volunteers make the line graph on the board. Discuss why the bar graph is easier to read. *(Sample answer: The number of lines makes the line graph confusing. On the bar graph, it is easier to see at a glance that in the South, the difference between rural and urban populations was much greater than in the North.)*

Answers to Try It

Two circle graphs would be needed to show the information. If the information were put on a line graph, there would be three lines, and only two points of reference. Thus, the most useful graph would be a bar graph. It would show three bars for each of the two years—one for white people, one for slaves, and one for free blacks.

Answers to Apply It

After students have prepared their graphs, display and discuss them. Ask which graphs show the information most effectively. Students should see that a circle graph will be the most concise form for showing the information. However, if there are many different categories, a bar graph might be best.

Visual Learning

Divide the class into four groups. Assign each group to find out information about the class. The information could be about such things as students' height, favorite subjects, birth months, the year in which they first attended your school. Then have students prepare graphs that show this information.

Answers to Reviewing Key Terms

A. Sample answers:

1. Yeoman farmers worked small farms in the rural South, while artisans were skilled tradesmen in the city.
2. Cash crops, such as cotton, were grown on huge farms called plantations.
3. The cultural heritage of slaves during the antebellum period included customs from Africa.

B. Answers:

1. False. Antebellum refers to the South before the Civil War.
2. False. A yeoman farmer lived on a small farm.
3. True. Cultural heritage includes people's language, art, beliefs, and customs.
4. False. A yeoman farmer did not own slaves.
5. False. An artisan is a worker who knows a skilled trade.
6. True. Free blacks worked as blacksmiths, carpenters, masons, barbers, and tailors.
7. False. In a cash crop economy, farmers grow large quantities of one crop to sell to many different markets.
8. True. Plantations included farm buildings and the owner's large home.

Answers to Exploring Concepts

A. Sample answers:

cotton gin / slaves / yeoman farmers / government / plantation / resisted / punished / ran away / rebellion / free / slaves

Chapter Review

Reviewing Key Terms

antebellum (p. 286) cultural heritage (p. 293)
artisan (p. 302) plantation (p. 285)
cash crop (p. 287) yeoman farmer (p. 299)

A. In each of the following pairs, the two terms are related in some way. Write a sentence for each pair that clearly explains the meaning of the two terms.

1. artisan, yeoman farmer
2. cash crop, plantation
3. cultural heritage, antebellum

B. Based on what you have read in the chapter, decide whether each of the following sentences is accurate. Write an explanation of each decision.

1. The antebellum South grew quite rapidly in the years after the Civil War.
2. A yeoman farmer usually lived on a large plantation and spent all his time running it.
3. The cultural heritage of the South can be determined by studying the language, art, and beliefs of the people who lived there.
4. A yeoman farmer usually owned many slaves.
5. An artisan was an unskilled worker who traveled from place to place.
6. Some free blacks worked as artisans in the North and South before the Civil War.
7. In a cash crop economy, most farmers grow food for their own use and for sale to their neighbors.
8. Southern plantations were working farms with large, elegant homes for the white owners.

Exploring Concepts

A. Copy the following paragraph onto a separate sheet of paper. Fill in the blank spaces with information from the chapter.

With the invention of the ________ , cotton became the single most important crop of the South. Because growing cotton required many workers, the Southern economy became more dependent on ________. Though most Southern whites were ________ with few or no slaves, large planters controlled the ________ and economy of the South. The master of a ________ had final authority over his land, his slaves, and his family. The life of a slave was one of constant work, but slaves ________ their masters in various ways. Even though slaves were brutally ________ , some worked as slowly as possible or ________ from the plantation. Slaves were not allowed to learn to read or write, for their masters thought that would encourage ________ . Laws even restricted the activities of ________ blacks, because whites feared their influence on ________ .

B. Support each of the following statements with facts and details from the chapter.

1. Whitney's cotton gin revolutionized the economy of the antebellum South.
2. The South's economy depended on the North.
3. The South became important in the United States Congress because the expansion of cotton growing territories increased the number of Southern representatives in Congress.
4. Southerners used both economic and religious arguments to defend slavery.
5. Everyone on a plantation played a specific role in this self-contained world.
6. Slaves had many ways of preserving their sense of identity and culture.
7. The majority of Southern whites were not owners of large plantations, but made up a diverse mix of people.
8. Most free blacks in the South were deprived of their full rights as citizens.

B. Sample answers:

1. Cotton imports increased, which revived slavery.
2. Goods were manufactured and transported by the Northern industries. Southern cotton was marketed to Northern mills.
3. The increased population created new states, which raised the number of Southern representatives to Congress.
4. Southerners said the Bible recognized the rights of masters to own slaves and that Northern workers were treated no better than slaves.
5. Students should identify any of the following: master, mistress, overseer, drivers, slaves.
6. Slaves kept their medical practices and musical traditions. They used African names among themselves and created their own church services.
7. White Southerners included yeoman farmers, white mountain settlers, poor rural whites, white professionals, and artisans.
8. Laws kept free blacks from voting and traveling freely. Their homes could be searched at any time, and they were often kept from socializing with slaves.

Reviewing Skills

1. The table at right gives U.S. population figures for 1800-1860. Decide which kind of graph—circle, line, or bar—would be the most appropriate way to present this information. Then draw the graph of your choice.
2. If you wanted to show the percentage of tailors who were free blacks in Charleston, South Carolina in 1860, what kind of graph would you choose?
3. Look at the quilt on page 294. What kind of a primary source is it? Make a list of all the information you can gather from that source.
4. In what kind of publications would you find graphs that present statistics on currency rates, population trends, and budget figures?

Northern and Southern Populations, 1800–1860

	1800	1820	1840	1860
North	2,636,000	4,360,000	6,761,000	10,594,000
South	2,622,000	4,419,000	6,951,000	11,133,000

Using Critical Thinking

1. In 1835, the governor of South Carolina said of the slaves, "There is not upon the face of the earth any class of people, high or low, so perfectly free from care and anxiety. . . . Our slaves are cheerful, contented, and happy, [unlike] the general condition of the human race." Put yourself in the place of a slave. How would you respond to this statement? Do people today still claim that the disadvantaged are content with their lives? Explain your answer?
2. An ex-slave recalled the religious teaching of his master, "Be nice to massa and missus; don't be mean; be obedient, and work hard. That was all the Sunday school lesson they taught us." Why do you think slaveowners sought to use religion as justification for slavery? How did the slaves respond?
3. Alexis de Tocqueville claimed that whites in the slave states were not as industrious as those in free states. In his opinion, slavery had a bad effect on the slaveholders, making them lazy and interested only in pleasure. Using examples from the chapter, explain why you agree or disagree with Tocqueville's statement.
4. Abraham Lincoln suggested that if "A" could enslave "B," then it stood to reason that "B" could enslave "A." If color were the reason for slavery, he went on, then "you are to be slave to the first man you meet with a fairer skin than your own." How would Southerners answer this argument? What was their main justification for slavery? Are there any places in the world where this argument is still used?

Preparing for Citizenship

1. **WRITING ACTIVITY** Many ex-slaves wrote about their experiences. Find some accounts of slavery in your library. Write a report describing the life of a slave.
2. **ART ACTIVITY** Look at the site plan for the plantation shown on page 291. Design your own plan, taking into account all that you have learned about the working and living conditions on large Southern plantations. If you choose, you may design a modern plantation, adding any modern conveniences that you think would have replaced slavery had the plantation culture survived.
3. **ART ACTIVITY** Both the white Appalachian mountain families of the South and the slaves created music that is part of American culture today. Find some recordings of mountain music or black spirituals and play them for the class. Discuss how they reflect the culture of the people who created them. Which kinds do you enjoy most? Why? Make up your own dances to perform with the music.
4. **COLLABORATIVE LEARNING** Create a short skit of a day in the life of a large plantation. Use details described in the chapter to role-play the people who lived there. Each student should have a chance to be a master, a mistress, an overseer, and a slave. Does your attitude toward the project change as your role changes?

Answers to Reviewing Skills

1. Although students may draw a line graph, a bar graph that shows quantities of similar things, would be more appropriate.
2. Students should choose a circle graph.
3. The quilt is an artifact. Students can gather information about the daily life of the person who made it.
4. Direct students to government publications, as well as to news magazines and newspapers.

Answers to Using Critical Thinking

1. Answers will vary. Ask students to find examples of the governor's comments in the chapter. Discuss contemporary views of welfare recipients and the homeless.
2. Students should recall that the chapter refers to slavery proponents who cited the Bible as justification (see page 289).
3. Answers will vary. Students may agree that slavery allows white people to let others do the work.
4. Southerners thought that black people were less intelligent than white people.

Answers to Preparing for Citizenship

1. **WRITING ACTIVITY** Julius Lester's book, *To Be a Slave,* is one of many collections of slave narratives that students may look for.
2. **ART ACTIVITY** Students can make blueprint plans, or cardboard constructions. An alternative activity would be to make the plan a class project.
3. **ART ACTIVITY** Direct students to libraries for musical collections. Ask students to research simple musical instruments such as the mouth harp.
4. **COLLABORATIVE LEARNING** Point out that all the work performed by the slaves benefited the planter and his family in some way. Ask students to discuss their feelings about the roles they played.

UNIT
OVERVIEW

Draw students' attention to the unit title and the narrative underneath it. Ask them to imagine how a civil war would affect a country's loyalties, economics, and family relationships.

Ask students what *reconstruct* means. *(To build again)* Discuss the meaning of *Reconstruction* in the context of the Civil War. *(The reorganization and reestablishment of the seceded states in the Union)*

Looking Back

Ask students to recap briefly what they learned about the North and the South in the last unit. How might the different ways of life and economies of each region affect the outcome of the Civil War? *(The Union's decisive advantage in population, railroad mileage, and industrial goods gave it a superior position.)*

Looking Forward

Tell students they will learn in the following chapters about the conflicts between North and South, how war erupted when they couldn't agree, and Reconstruction:

Chapter 11 *Causes of the Civil War*
Chapter 12 *A Nation Divided*
Chapter 13 *Reconstruction*

Unit 5

The Nation Divides and Reunites

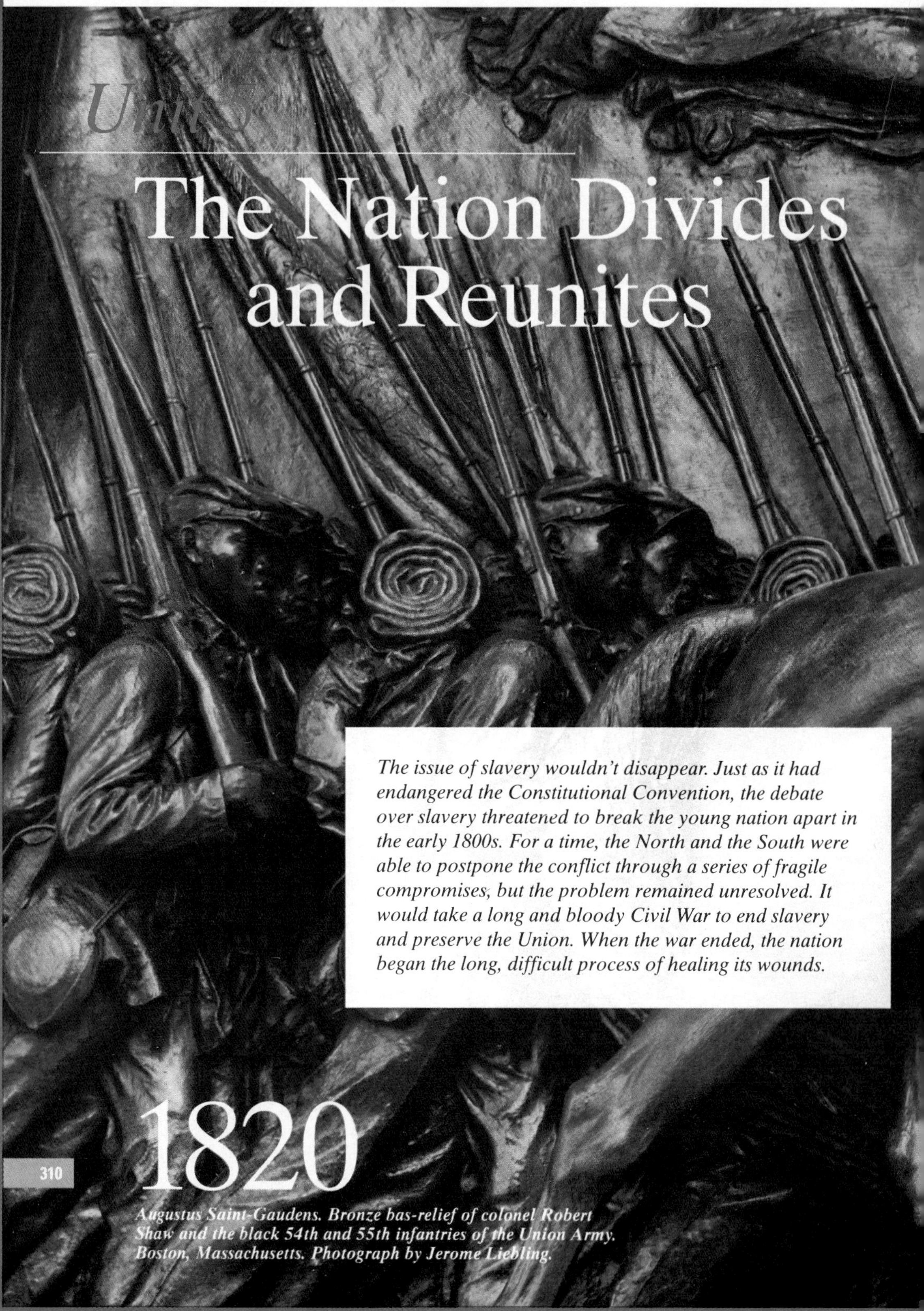

The issue of slavery wouldn't disappear. Just as it had endangered the Constitutional Convention, the debate over slavery threatened to break the young nation apart in the early 1800s. For a time, the North and the South were able to postpone the conflict through a series of fragile compromises, but the problem remained unresolved. It would take a long and bloody Civil War to end slavery and preserve the Union. When the war ended, the nation began the long, difficult process of healing its wounds.

1820

Augustus Saint-Gaudens. Bronze bas-relief of colonel Robert Shaw and the black 54th and 55th infantries of the Union Army. Boston, Massachusetts. Photograph by Jerome Liebling.

GEOGRAPHY PROJECT

Mapping the Civil War

Geography Skill **Making Maps**
Students use the skills of Asking, Organizing, and Answering geographic questions.

Geography Themes Location, Human/Environment Interaction

Geography Standard 1, maps help people report geographic information

Activity ***Create an Annotated Map***

Materials construction paper, pencils, pens, markers

Management Individual/Small Group

Select a combination of three places such as battle sites, cities, rivers or mountains that played a role in the events of the Civil War. Create an annotated map that includes these important places.

Have students:

- draw an annotated map of Civil War locations and/or draw an illustrated map of Civil War locations.
- write clear, concise annotations to explain the importance of each Civil War site or geographic location.
- include a legend and compass rose on the map.

Understanding the Monument

Tell students that allowing black men into the Union army was a controversial issue in the early years of the war. The men shown in this memorial were the first regiment of free black volunteers to face combat and were led by Colonel Shaw. Their story is told in the 1990 film *Glory*.

The artist, Augustus Saint Gaudens, one of the finest American sculptors of the late 19th century, worked 13 years on the memorial. He originally wanted to depict just Shaw, but Shaw's family insisted that the black troops be honored also.

Understanding Chronology

Point out that Unit 5 covers 60 years of ill will between the North and the South. The problems leading up to the Civil War were deeply rooted in the nation's history; hence the beginning date for this unit of 1820. The war itself lasted from 1861 to 1865. The last federal troops left the South in 1877, the end of Reconstruction.

For research support activities, see the *Research Handbook*.

For simulations correlated to this unit, see *Citizenship Simulations*, p. viii.

HOUGHTON MIFFLIN SOCIAL STUDIES

Bookshelf II

The Gettysburg Address

by Abraham Lincoln

This illustrated text of the Gettysburg Address gives a vivid picture of Civil War people and events inspired by the memorable words of Lincoln's speech.

Motivate Show students the pictures in the book prior to reading it aloud. Let students study the images. Ask them to explain the major ideas that the pictures convey about the Civil War and the people who lived at that time. Then have students look at the photograph on this page and write questions they have about the Civil War. Have them look for the answers as they read this unit.

To connect this book with the unit content, use the planning guide and student activity blackline masters beginning on p. iv of the *Bookshelf II Teacher's Resources*.

For additional books that are Easy, Average, and Challenging, see the Unit Bibliography on p. T43. See bibliography updates at www.eduplace.com/ss/hmss.

CHAPTER 11

Planning at a Glance

The Causes of the Civil War

	Objectives	Reading Support and Other Resources	Diverse Learning Strategies
Lesson 1 The Sectional Conflict *pp. 314–319* 1–2 days	• Explain how the lands gained in the Mexican War caused conflict between the North and the South. • Assess why the Missouri Compromise and the Compromise of 1850 failed to resolve the debate over slavery.	• **Workbook** or **Reading Support:** pp. 148–151 Review p. 35 Extra Support/Transition p. 35 Multi-lang. Sum. pp. 69–70 • **Other Resources:** Poster 3, Study Guide p. 45, Study Print 8	Access Act. **(SDAIE)** TE p. 315 Language Arts Connection **(Visual)** TE p. 317 Social Participation **(Auditory)** TE p. 317 Audiotapes of Multi-language Lesson Summaries **(Auditory)**
Lesson 2 The Antislavery Movement *pp. 320–324* 1–2 days	• Explain the role of slaves, blacks, and women in the antislavery movement. • Identify the diverse motives and beliefs held by abolitionists. • Evaluate the impact of Harriet Beecher Stowe's *Uncle Tom's Cabin.*	• **Workbook** or **Reading Support:** pp. 152–155 Review p. 36 Extra Support/Transition p. 36 Multi-lang. Sum. pp. 71–72 • **Other Resources:** Geography Kit, Poster 5, Study Guide p. 46	Access Act. **(SDAIE)** TE p. 321 Music Connection **(Auditory)** TE p. 323 Writing a Persuasive Article **(GATE)** TE p. 323 Audiotapes of Multi-language Lesson Summaries **(Auditory)**
Lesson 3 The Road to Bleeding Kansas *pp. 325–329* 1–2 days	• Explain why violence broke out in the Kansas territories. • State the political positions of the Republican, Democratic, and Know-Nothing parties. • Define popular sovereignty, and explain why the South supported it.	• **Workbook** or **Reading Support:** pp. 156–159 Review p. 37 Extra Support/Transition p. 37 Multi-lang. Sum. pp. 73–74 • **Other Resources:** Geography Kit, Study Guide p. 47	Access Strat. **(SDAIE)** TE p. 326 Map and Globe Skills **(Visual)** TE p. 327 Science Connection **(GATE)** TE p. 328 Collaborative Act. **(Auditory)** TE p. 328 Audiotapes of Multi-language Lesson Summaries **(Auditory)**
Lesson 4 The House Divided *pp. 330–335* 2–3 days	• Review the impact of the Dred Scott case. • Explain the provisions of the Lecompton Constitution and why it was illegal. • Describe the Underground Railroad. • Assess the Southern reaction to Lincoln's election.	• **Workbook** or **Reading Support:** pp. 160–163 Review p. 38 Extra Support/Transition p. 38 Multi-lang. Sum. pp. 75–76 • **Other Resources:** Geography Kit, Study Guide p. 48	Reader's Theatre **(Auditory)** TE p. 333 Map and Globe Skills **(Visual)** TE p. 333 Making a Poster **(Visual)** TE p. 334 Audiotapes of Multi-language Lesson Summaries **(Auditory)**
Skill: Analyzing Viewpoints on Slavery *pp. 336–337*	• Use antebellum primary sources to determine point of view.	• **Other Resources:** Study Guide p. 49	
Chapter Review *pp. 338–339* 1 day		Chapter 11 Test pp. 41–44 *(See facsimiles on TE p. 759.)*	Assessment Multiple-Use Masters pp. 81–88

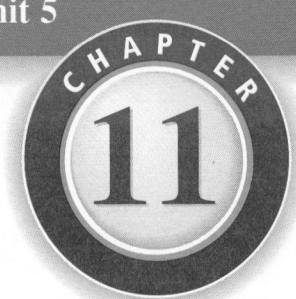

Reading Support Resources *for Every Lesson*

Reading and Review

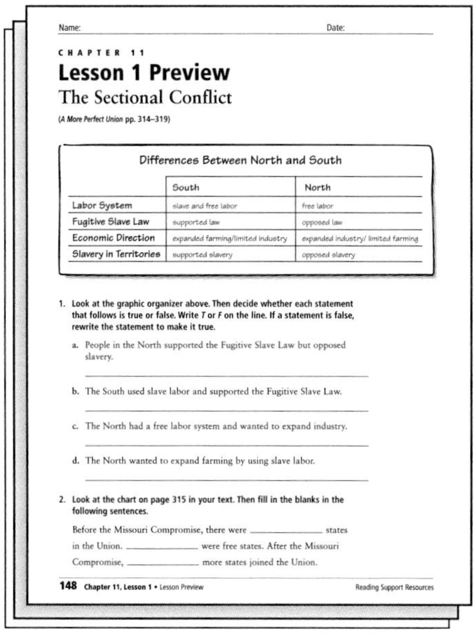

Name: Date:

CHAPTER 11

Lesson 1 Preview

The Sectional Conflict

(*A More Perfect Union* pp. 314–319)

Differences Between North and South

	South	North
Labor System	slave and free labor	free labor
Fugitive Slave Law	supported law	opposed law
Economic Direction	expanded farming/limited industry	expanded industry/ limited farming
Slavery in Territories	supported slavery	opposed slavery

1. **Look at the graphic organizer above. Then decide whether each statement that follows is true or false. Write *T* or *F* on the line. If a statement is false, rewrite the statement to make it true.**
   a. People in the North supported the Fugitive Slave Law but opposed slavery. ______
   b. The South used slave labor and supported the Fugitive Slave Law. ______
   c. The North had a free labor system and wanted to expand industry. ______
   d. The North wanted to expand farming by using slave labor. ______
2. **Look at the chart on page 315 in your text. Then fill in the blanks in the following sentences.**
   Before the Missouri Compromise, there were ______ states in the Union. ______ were free states. After the Missouri Compromise, ______ more states joined the Union.

148 **Chapter 11, Lesson 1** • Lesson Preview Reading Support Resources

- **Chapter Overview*** p. 147
- **Lesson Previews*** using graphic organizers from the Teacher's Edition pp. 148, 152, 156, 160
- **Reading Strategies*** pp. 149, 153, 157, 161
- **Lesson Summaries*** pp. 150–151, 154–155, 158–159, 162–163
- **Lesson Reviews** pp. 35, 36, 37, 38

* **Workbook** includes starred items.

Multi-language Summaries

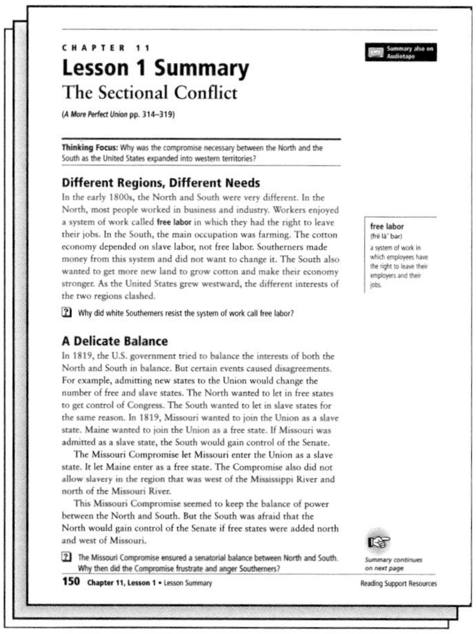

CHAPTER 11

Lesson 1 Summary

The Sectional Conflict

(*A More Perfect Union* pp. 314–319)

Summary also on Audiotape

Thinking Focus: Why was the compromise necessary between the North and the South as the United States expanded into western territories?

Different Regions, Different Needs

In the early 1800s, the North and South were very different. In the North, most people worked in business and industry. Workers enjoyed a system of work called **free labor** in which they had the right to leave their jobs. In the South, the main occupation was farming. The cotton economy depended on slave labor, not free labor. Southerners made money from this system and did not want to change it. The South also wanted to get more new land to grow cotton and make their economy stronger. As the United States grew westward, the different interests of the two regions clashed.

free labor (frē lā' bər) a system of work in which employees have the right to leave their employers and their jobs.

? Why did white Southerners resist the system of work call free labor?

A Delicate Balance

In 1819, the U.S. government tried to balance the interests of both the North and South in balance. But certain events caused disagreements. For example, admitting new states to the Union would change the number of free and slave states. The North wanted to let in free states to get control of Congress. The South wanted to let in slave states for the same reason. In 1819, Missouri wanted to join the Union as a slave state. Maine wanted to join the Union as a free state. If Missouri was admitted as a slave state, the South would gain control of the Senate.

The Missouri Compromise let Missouri enter the Union as a slave state. It let Maine enter as a free state. The Compromise also did not allow slavery in the region that was west of the Mississippi River and north of the Missouri River.

This Missouri Compromise seemed to keep the balance of power between the North and South. But the South was afraid that the North would gain control of the Senate if free states were added north and west of Missouri.

? The Missouri Compromise ensured a senatorial balance between North and South. Why then did the Compromise frustrate and anger Southerners?

Summary continues on next page

150 **Chapter 11, Lesson 1** • Lesson Summary Reading Support Resources

Lesson Summaries in:

- English (See Reading and Review.)
- Spanish pp. 150–151, 154–155, 158–159, 162–163
- Chinese pp. 69–76
- Hmong pp. 69–76
- Khmer pp. 69–76
- Vietnamese pp. 69–76

Summaries available on audiotapes

Lesson Support / Transition

S D A I E

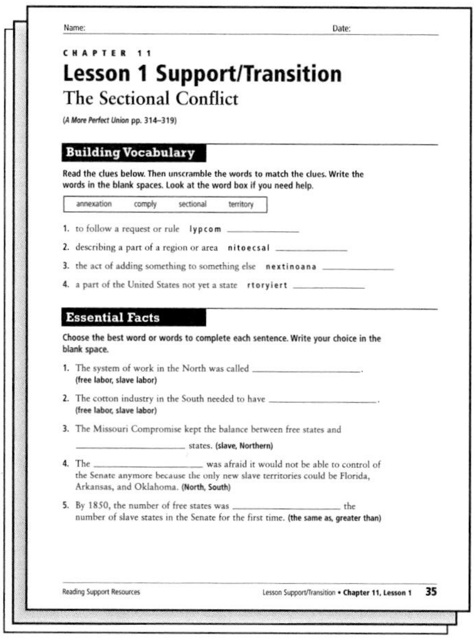

Name: Date:

CHAPTER 11

Lesson 1 Support/Transition

The Sectional Conflict

(*A More Perfect Union* pp. 314–319)

Building Vocabulary

Read the clues below. Then unscramble the words to match the clues. Write the words in the blank spaces. Look at the word box if you need help.

annexation comply sectional territory

1. to follow a request or rule **lypcom** ______
2. describing a part of a region or area **nitoecsal** ______
3. the act of adding something to something else **nextinoana** ______
4. a part of the United States not yet a state **rtoryiert** ______

Essential Facts

Choose the best word or words to complete each sentence. Write your choice in the blank space.

1. The system of work in the North was called ______. **(free labor, slave labor)**
2. The cotton industry in the South needed to have ______. **(free labor, slave labor)**
3. The Missouri Compromise kept the balance between free states and ______ states. **(slave, Northern)**
4. The ______ was afraid it would not be able to control of the Senate anymore because the only new slave territories could be Florida, Arkansas, and Oklahoma. **(North, South)**
5. By 1850, the number of free states was ______ the number of slave states in the Senate for the first time. **(the same as, greater than)**

Reading Support Resources Lesson Support/Transition • **Chapter 11, Lesson 1** **35**

Activities for SDAIE

Specially **D**esigned **A**cademic **I**nstruction in **E**nglish

- **Lesson Support/Transition** pp. 35, 36, 37, 38

Technology Options

Internet Support

http://www.eduplace.com

Social Studies Center at Education Place

Internet support for Chapter 11:

- ***Lesson at a Glance***
- ***A Quaker Abolitionist***

Videotape/Videodisc

We the People:

Supports and enhances major topics: **Theme: *The Civil War***

Software

Student Writing Center® (CD-ROM) (Macintosh® or Windows®)

School to Career

Politicians in the pre-Civil War United States had the difficult task of trying to reconcile the needs of the North and South. These politicians had a variety of backgrounds and occupations. Have students research current state or federal leaders to find out what types of careers they held before they entered office.

Character Education

Abolitionists fought to end slavery through political means, private actions, and public outcries. Eventually, their persistence and determination began to make a difference. Divide students into small groups. Have each group select an abolitionist to research. Then have the groups create a presentation to share with the class.

CHAPTER PREVIEW

Have students read the chapter title and the narrative underneath it. What mood is reflected on these pages? *(Tension, conflict)* Point out that the debate over slavery dominated the national scene since the beginning of the 1800s.

Draw attention to the Garrison banner. Help students define *equivocate. (To avoid committing oneself to what one says)* What does Garrison mean when he says he will not equivocate? *(He will not back down.)*

Looking Back

Review with students the long-standing differences between the North and the South: the compromises on slavery in the Constitution (Chapter 4), the nullification crisis led by Calhoun (Chapter 6), and the disagreements about the Mexican War (Chapter 8).

Looking Forward

Tell students they will read about the increasing conflict between the North and the South in the next four lessons: The Sectional Conflict, The Antislavery Movement, The Road to Bleeding Kansas, and The House Divided.

Chapter 11

Causes of the Civil War

Slave or free? For decades, politicians from the North and the South tried to resolve the slavery issue through compromise. Now, new lands gained through purchase and battle brought the question into even sharper focus: Slave or free? The compromises failed. The antislavery movement gained momentum. And tensions grew.

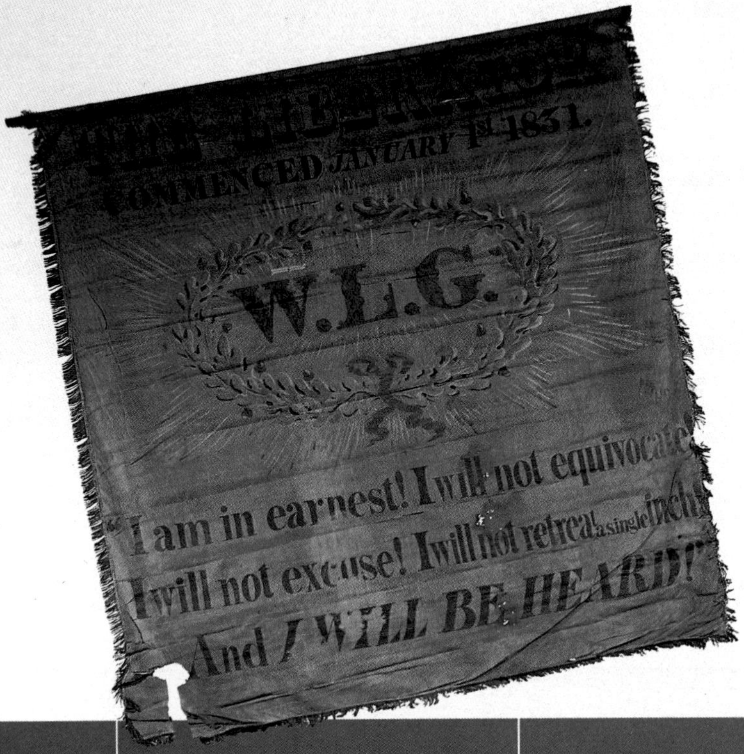

1831 Antislavery activists demand an immediate and no-compromise end to slavery. This banner shows the devotion of William Lloyd Garrison—publisher of the antislavery newspaper, *The Liberator*—to the cause.

Harriet Tubman, at the far left of the photograph opposite, helped hundreds of slaves escape to freedom through the Underground Railroad.

1815 | 1825 | 1835

Presidents

1817-1825 Monroe

1825-1829 J. Q. Adams

1829-1837 Jackson

1837-18 Van Bure

1820

BACKGROUND

Tensions over political power and the issue of slavery caused the North and South to look westward for new territories in which to gain strongholds. Irreconcilable differences between the North and the South led to political and physical clashes and eventually to the Civil War.

The Lincoln-Douglas Debates

In his campaign for re-election in 1858, Senator Stephen A. Douglas agreed to a series of seven debates with the Republican contender Abraham Lincoln. Thousands of farmers, clerks, lawyers, and others came to listen. Covered heavily by the press, the debates were followed by a large national readership as well.

Appealing to the listeners' racial prejudices, Douglas tried to portray his opponent as a dangerous radical and an advocate of racial equality. Lincoln responded that he believed black people were "entitled to all the natural rights enumerated in the Declaration of Independence, the right to life, liberty, and the pursuit of happiness." He protested, however, "against that counterfeit logic which presumes that because I do not want a Negro woman for a slave, I do necessarily want her for a wife."

In one debate, Douglas defended his position on popular sovereignty by saying that the states had the right to decide for themselves whether to allow slavery. Lincoln challenged him saying, "This government was

1858 Democrat Stephen A. Douglas and Republican Abraham Lincoln run for the Senate. Slavery in the new territories is a main issue. Douglas favors letting the people decide; Lincoln wants to end slavery in the territories. Douglas wins, but the issue remains.

1845 1855 1865

1841-1845 Tyler

1845-1849 Polk

1850-1853 Fillmore

1857-1861 Buchanan

Harrison

1849-1850 Taylor

1853-1857 Pierce

1861

Understanding the Visuals

Point out that Harriet Tubman is pictured here with a former slave family whom she helped escape to freedom.

The portraits of Douglas and Lincoln are mounted on pins that men and women would wear on their lapels. It is interesting that women could wear them, given that they couldn't vote.

Understanding Chronology

Draw student attention to the timeline. Emphasize that the bitter debate and disagreements between the North and the South brewed for nearly 50 years before the Civil War broke out.

nstituted to secure the blessings of freeom." And he went on to say, "Slavery is an nqualified evil to the Negro, to the white nan, to the soil, and to the State."

olitical Parties

During the 1850s, America's two-party ystem disintegrated rapidly. Controversy ver territorial issues caused the Whig Party o disappear; the Democrats acquired domiance in the South but suffered disastrous osses in the North.

The Democratic Party's opposition to the Wilmot Proviso in 1847 caused many Northerners to leave the party and organize the Free Soil Party. While Free Soilers believed that slavery should be kept out of the territories, they did not call for abolition of slavery or equal rights for black Americans.

When division over the Kansas-Nebraska Act killed the Whig Party in 1854, Northern Whigs joined Free Soilers to form the Republican Party. Moving beyond the single-issue appeal of the Free-Soil Party, the Republicans gained additional supporters by advocating a homestead act, a high protective tariff, and a liberal immigration policy. By 1856, the Republican Party had become the dominant alternative to the Democratic Party. It was not, however, a national organization; it appealed to Northerners only.

INTRODUCE

Have students recall from previous lessons the differences between the North and the South. *(Industrial* v. *agricultural, non-slave-based economy* v. *slave-based)*

Ask students to read the Thinking Focus and have them suggest reasons why compromise might be necessary. *(To prevent a war, to give something to both sides, to save lives)* Have students read to find out why compromise was necessary between the North and the South.

Key Term

Vocabulary strategies: T36–37

free labor—a system of work in which employees have the right to leave their employers and their jobs for better opportunities

■ *White Southerners resisted free labor because their cotton economy was dependent on slave labor.*

1820 1850 1860 1870

LESSON 1

The Sectional Conflict

THINKING FOCUS

Why was compromise necessary between the North and the South as the United States expanded into western territories?

Key Term

- free labor

> *We have the wolf by the ears, and we can neither hold him, nor safely let him go. Justice is in one scale and self-preservation in the other.*
>
> Thomas Jefferson

The fearsome "wolf" to which Thomas Jefferson referred in 1820 was slavery in the United States. Politicians had tried to maintain a balance between slaveholding and nonslaveholding states. Expansion into the West, however, deepened disagreement between North and South. When the territory of Missouri applied for admission to the Union in 1819, it was assumed that this slaveholding territory would become a slave state. Instead, a full-scale congressional debate began in which slavery became a question of sectional, or regional, power.

The retired Jefferson, who had owned slaves all his life, saw both the good sense and the danger in ending slavery. "The Missouri debate, like a firebell in the night, awakened and filled me with terror," he wrote to a Massachusetts congressman who had requested the elder statesman's advice. The same man who penned the Declaration of Independence 44 years earlier, declaring "all men are created equal," could offer no solutions to the slavery issue. Politicians were faced with the great challenge of compromise in handling this growing national problem.

Different Regions, Different Needs

The North and the South of the early 1800s differed greatly in their economies and ways of life. Busy commercial regions filled with cities and factories characterized the North. Immigrants joined the Northern workforce, settling in cities and farmlands. Northern workers received pay for their labor, as well as the chance to improve their lives. They had the right to leave their employers and jobs for better opportunities.This system of work was called **free labor**.

In the South, the thriving cotton economy depended on slave labor. Owners of large and small plantations saw little reason to change a system that brought great profit. Talk among Northerners of new farming methods, growing cities, and improved manufacturing must have sounded foolish to white Southerners. The South wanted new land for cotton—not a plan for remodeling its economy based on Northern ideas about industry.

Most white Southerners, even those who owned few slaves or none, believed in the economic need for slavery. And as the United States expanded into the territories it gained from the Louisiana Purchase, it was clear that the different interests of the two regions would cause serious conflict. How would Northerners and Southerners ever agree on such an important issue? ■

■ *Why did white Southerners resist the system of work called free labor?*

Objectives

1. Assess why the Missouri Compromise failed to resolve the debate over slavery.
2. Explain how the lands gained in the Mexican War caused conflict between the North and the South.
3. Describe what the Wilmot Proviso was supposed to achieve.
4. Explain the significance of the Compromise of 1850.

Graphic Overview

	South	North
Labor System	slave and free labor	free labor
Fugitive Slave Law	supported law	opposed law
Economic Direction	expanded farming/ limited industry	expanded industry/ limited farming
Slavery in Territories	supported slavery	opposed salvery

A Delicate Balance

When Missouri sought admission to the Union in 1819, it proposed a state constitution that would protect slavery. At the time, there were exactly as many slave states as free states in the Union. The House of Representatives was dominated by the North, and Southerners stood to gain control of the Senate if Missouri was admitted as a slave state. Most important, however, was the issue of extending slavery to the West.

Before the Missouri debate began, Congress used the Northwest Ordinance, legislation adopted in 1787 under the old Articles of Confederation, to prohibit slavery north and west of the Ohio River.

Now the political balance was in danger of being upset. Although the balance had been upset before, it had been easy to decide whether states east of the Mississippi should be slave or free. Mason and Dixon's line and the Ohio River had formed a natural and easily defined boundary between the two sections. But a line had not been drawn west of the Mississippi River. To complicate matters further, parts of the Missouri Territory lay to the north of the Ohio River, while other parts lay to the south.

Forging a Compromise

The debate in Congress grew heated. Some lawmakers wanted to forbid slavery in the new state. Others believed the Congress should not have authority over such matters. As the debate continued, Maine (then a northern portion of Massachusetts) applied for statehood.

In 1820, the Missouri Compromise was worked out and gained congressional approval, in part because of statesman Henry Clay's support. Missouri was to be admitted as a slave state. Maine would enter the Union as a free state. The balance had been preserved. The Compromise also prohibited slavery in other American territories west of the Mississippi River and north of Missouri's southern boundary.

While Northerners and Southerners had each gained from the Compromise, people from both regions remained concerned. Southerners grew more distrustful of Northerners and feared further legislation against slavery. An angry editorial in the *Richmond Enquirer* remarked about the Compromise, "We scarcely ever recollect to ever have tasted a bitterer cup. . . . What is a territorial restriction today becomes a state restriction tomorrow."

Thomas Jefferson, reflecting on the need to draw boundaries,

▲ *Statesman Henry Clay lent his support to the Missouri Compromise.*

▼ *The balance of slave and free states was threatened in 1819 when the Missouri Territory sought admission to the Union.*

Missouri Compromise

■ = Original Thirteen States
■ = States entering the Union, 1791–1819
■ = States entering after the Missouri Compromise

Slave States		Free States	
Missouri	(1821)	Maine	(1820)
Alabama	(1819)	Illinois	(1818)
Mississippi	(1817)	Indiana	(1816)
Louisiana	(1812)	Ohio	(1803)
Tennessee	(1796)	Vermont	(1791)
Kentucky	(1792)	Pennsylvania	
Georgia		New Jersey	
South Carolina		New York	
North Carolina		Connecticut	
Virginia		Rhode Island	
Maryland		Massachusetts	
Delaware		New Hampshire	

DEVELOP

Explain that the Civil War became unavoidable when the North and South were unable to resolve the basic issues that divided them. Copy on the board the structure of the Graphic Overview from page 314 with only the heads *North* and *South* written in. As they read the lesson, students can look for examples of the issues dividing the North and the South and add this information to the chart.

POLITICAL SYSTEMS

Visual Learning

Refer students to the chart on this page. Ask them how the 24 states were divided after the Missouri Compromise. *(Into 12 slave states and 12 free states)* Of the original 13 states, how many were slave and how many free? *(6 slave, 7 free)*

Access Strategy

To build on students' prior understanding of compromise, have them recall from Chapter 4 examples of compromise between Northern and Southern states. What compromises did the framers of the Constitution make? (*Three-fifths Compromise, Fugitive Slave Clause, clause postponing vote on abolishing slave trade until 1808*) Students should understand that a compromise can only succeed if both parties can accept the loss of some of their goals. Review with students Understanding Group Activities: Reaching a Compromise (page 123). Tell them they will read in this lesson about the need for the North and the South to compromise.

Access Activity

Ask students to think of an argument that they had recently. Did people stay calm or did they get excited? Did they really listen to each other? Remind students that in the years before the Civil War, the North and the South found it increasingly difficult to discuss solutions to their problems.

GEOGRAPHY

Map and Globe Skills

Refer students to the map on this page. Ask them to find the categories in the map legend and then to name the states in each category.

HISTORY

Critical Thinking

Do you think Northerners or Southerners had more to lose by the annexation of Texas? *(Sample answer: Northerners had more to lose because it would add another slave state, thus disrupting the balance between the North and the South.)* Why did Congress agree to annex Texas? *(The country would gain land.)*

■ *Because of its larger population, the North already controlled the House of Representatives. Because the North could expand into the area north and west of Missouri, it would in time also control the Senate.*

Missouri Compromise, 1820

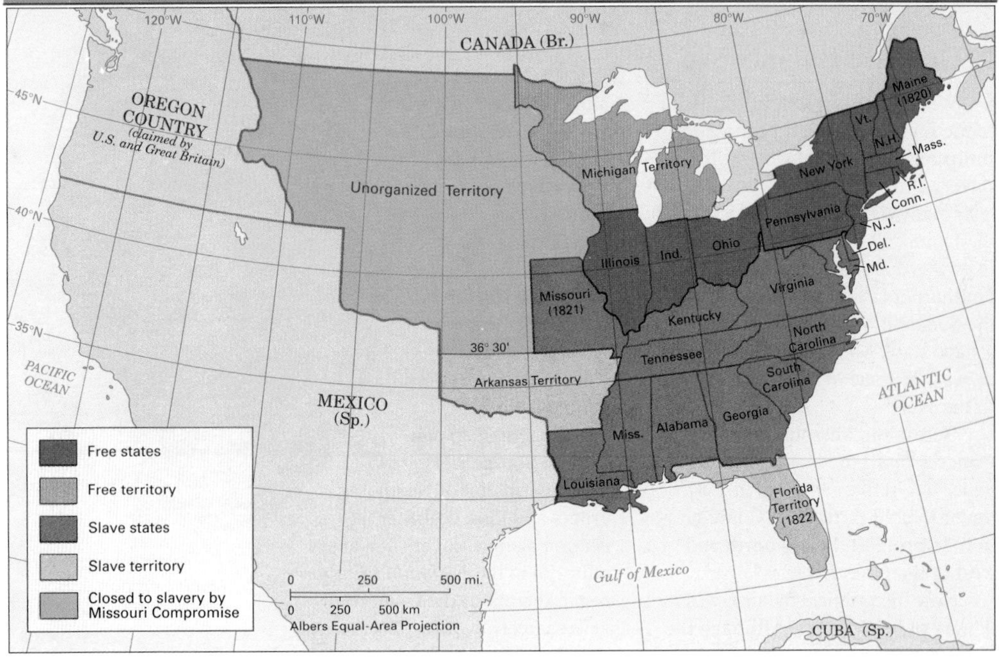

The United States acquired new territories with the Louisiana Purchase. White Southerners wished to extend slavery to the western territories, but Northerners opposed the idea. The Missouri Compromise was an attempt to strike a balance.

■ *The Missouri Compromise ensured a senatorial balance between North and South. Why then did the Compromise frustrate and anger Southerners?*

observed, "A geographical line, coinciding with a marked principle, moral and political, once conceived and held up to the angry passions of men, will never be obliterated; and every new irritation will mark it deeper and deeper." Jefferson's remark predicted the bitter struggle that was yet to come.

South Relies on Senatorial Power

From 1820 to 1850 the South fought to maintain equality with the North in the Senate, and the two sections kept a delicate balance in that lawmaking body. As the South sought to bring new slave states into the Union, this balance in the Senate provided the basis of the South's political power.

The North, because of its larger population, controlled the House of Representatives. It seemed only a matter of time before the North would control the nation's entire political process, including the Senate. This appeared especially true since the North could expand into the area north and west of Missouri—the area that would eventually become Minnesota, Iowa, the Dakotas, Montana, Idaho, Kansas, Nebraska, and Wyoming. The South, it seemed, could expand only into Florida, Arkansas, and Oklahoma.

South Eyes Texas for Slavery

In the early 1800s, Texas was a part of Mexico, although many American settlers lived there. These settlers considered themselves Americans, not Mexicans, and declared their independence in 1836.

As you learned in Chapter 8, Texans then set up their expansive Southern region as a slaveholding republic and sought to join the Union. But the United States, realizing the threat of war with Mexico, refused to annex, or take over, Texas. To do so would mean stirring resentment in Mexico and creating a new slave state, a step the North was eager to avoid. Mexico still did not accept the independence of Texas. In 1845, however, Congress bowed to Southern pressure and passed a bill allowing annexation. ■

Map and Globe Skills

Have students compare the map on this page with the modern political map of the United States found on pages 698–699 in the Atlas. What states were carved out of land that belonged to Mexico? *(California, Arizona, New Mexico, Utah, Nevada, and parts of Colorado)* What states were carved out of the Oregon Country? *(Oregon, Washington, Idaho)*

Historical Context

In much the same way that the Spanish Civil War in 1936 was a training ground for the military tactics of World War II, the war with Mexico in 1846–1848 was a training ground for the Civil War. Many important leaders of the Civil War fought side-by-side, including the future Union commander, Ulysses S. Grant, and six future Union generals. Also serving in Mexico were the future Confederate commander, General Robert E. Lee; five future Confederate generals; and the future president of the Confederacy, Jefferson Davis.

Some Civil War historians argue that the casualties in the Civil War were so high because frontal attacks worked against Mexico and were therefore tried in the Civil War. The strategy failed, however, and produced many casualties. Also, many Northerners thought they would win easily over the South because the U.S. victory over Mexico had been quick and relatively bloodless.

Understanding Sectionalism

By the mid-1800s, the United States had grown through the addition of the Louisiana Purchase, Florida, Texas, the Oregon Territory, and the territory ceded by Mexico. With an area of 2,992,620 square miles, the United States was enormous compared to such nations as Great Britain, France, and Spain.

How could such a huge nation be ruled by one government? How could people living thousands of miles away from each other agree on political and social issues? The truth is that they often didn't. Citizens in various parts of the country developed their own interests, economies, and causes. The result was sectionalism, the devotion to the political and economic interest of a region or section of the country. Unlike regionalism, which divides the country culturally, sectionalism divides it politically and economically—often with serious consequences.

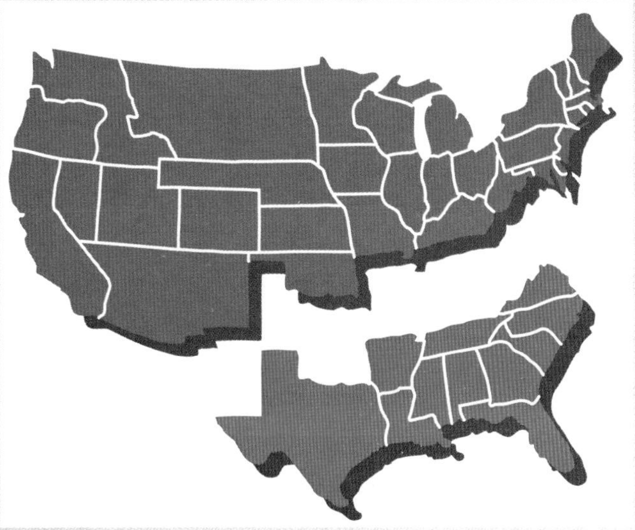

Early Sectionalism

Although sectionalism rose to a peak during the years before the Civil War, it was apparent even to the writers of the Constitution. There was strong sectional debate during the Constitutional Convention. The debate involved several issues, including ending the slave trade, passing export taxes, and giving Congress the power to allow only American ships to carry goods to and from America's ports.

Delegates from the Southern states objected to all of these measures. The region depended on slaves, the delegates argued. The South also wanted no taxes or shipping laws to interfere with their profitable exports. Delegates from the Northern states favored these measures, and the seeds of sectionalism were sown.

At the Constitutional Convention, delegates worked out a compromise. The slave trade would remain, they decided, but after 20 years it would again be put to a vote. Congress was given the power to tax imports, but export taxes were forbidden. Throughout American history, compromises such as this often solve sectional differences in constructive ways.

Sectionalism Continues

By the 1850s, sectionalism manifested itself almost entirely in the issues of slavery and states' rights. The North and the South were bitter enemies, rather than two parts of one whole. During these bitter years, citizens' loyalties to their section seemed more fierce than their loyalties to their nation.

America's regions have continued to clash politically and economically. In the late 1800s, the farmers in the West and the South joined together to form the Populist party. The Populists aimed to compete against what they saw as overwhelming northeastern and industrial political groups.

Even today, this sectionalism can be seen in the halls of Congress. Representatives of largely agricultural areas of the South and the West compete against the more industrial areas of the country for federal money. Despite their disagreements, however, there is little doubt that today's conflicts will never be as bitter or the result as serious as a Civil War that cost the nation hundreds of thousands of lives.

HISTORY

Critical Thinking

Sectionalism is unlikely to cause another serious division in the nation. There are, however social and political conflicts causing division in our society today. Ask students to make a list of divisive forces in the country that should concern national leaders. *(Racism, homelessness, the disappearance of the family farm)*

Language Arts Connection

Have students study the handbill on page 319. How did the writer get the reader's attention? *(Chose shocking words, used varied type sizes and styles)* Point out that the basic message is in the large, bold type. Then have students design their own handbills notifying people of a local problem or issue. Display them on a bulletin board.

Art Connection

Have students look at the portrait of Henry Clay on page 315. What can they tell about Clay's personality from the photograph? *(Looks friendly)* Next have students look back at the painting of Calhoun on page 118. What can they tell about Calhoun from this painting? *(Seems fiery)* Have students search through history books for portraits of other American leaders of the mid-1800s. Assign them to write a one-paragraph description of one portrait.

Social Participation

Divide students into small groups. Have them imagine that they are a special committee whose job is to settle the conflict between the North and the South. Have each group write and present a proposal that will prevent the Civil War.

HISTORY

Critical Thinking

The Wilmot Proviso failed because it was not acceptable to Southerners. What compromise might Southerners have agreed to? *(Sample answer: Land in new territories could be divided evenly between slave and nonslave states.)*

HISTORY

Map and Globe Skills

Have students compare the map on this page with the map on page 316. What trends do they see? *(The pieces of land are getting broken into smaller pieces; five more territories have become states.)*

Sectionalism Deepens

In March 1845, Mexico, angered by the plan to annex Texas, broke diplomatic relations with the United States. By May 1846, Mexico and the United States were engaged in battle. President James Polk believed wholeheartedly that American settlers should expand westward. Some people suspected that his desire to gain new territory made him exaggerate reports of border conflicts and push for war with Mexico.

The Mexican-American War lasted until 1848, ending in an American victory. During these two years, the United States acquired vast territories. The new U.S. lands included areas that today make up California, Arizona, New Mexico, Utah, Nevada, and parts of Colorado.

Americans held strong views on the Mexican-American War. Support split along party lines and geographic lines. Democrats generally supported the war as a necessary step in the nation's westward expansion, but Northern Democrats were in a difficult position. They believed, with the rest of their party, in a policy of territorial expansion. But support of the war might appear to be support of slavery. Whigs tended to oppose becoming involved in a battle with Mexico.

North Backs the Wilmot Proviso

Congressman David Wilmot, a Pennsylvania Democrat and previous Polk supporter, had an answer to the dilemma of Northern Democrats. In 1846, he introduced the Wilmot Proviso, an amendment to a bill to finance the war. The amendment prohibited slavery in any territories won from Mexico. It allowed Northern Democrats to support the war without appearing to be proslavery. The amendment easily passed in the

The United States gained new lands from the Mexican-American War. These new territories sparked more disagreement over westward expansion and slavery.

Compromise of 1850

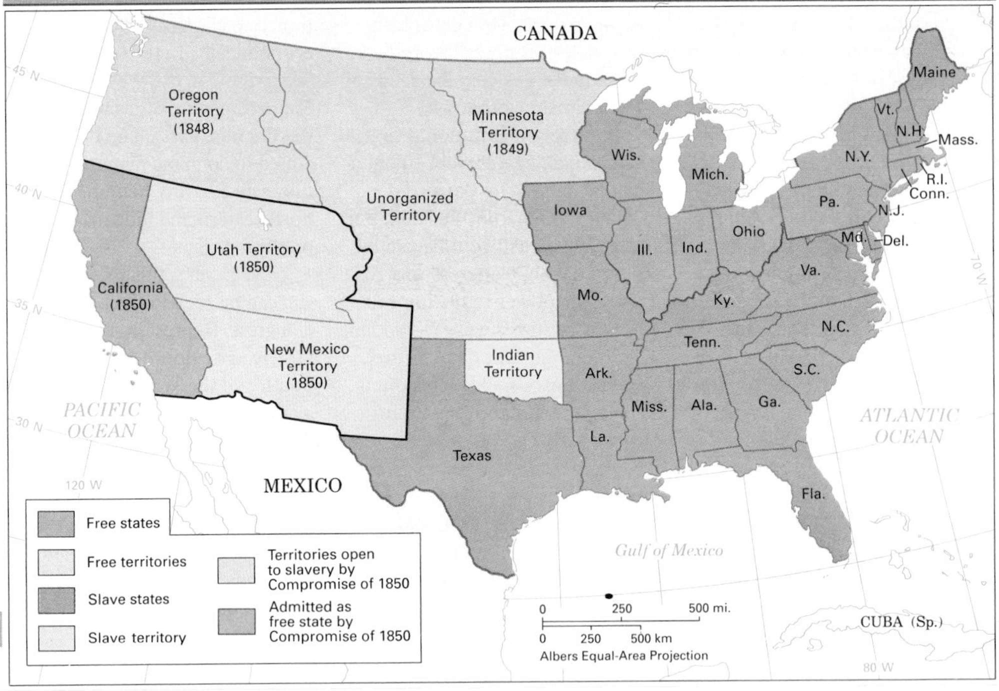

Critical Thinking

Ask students to recall what they learned in Chapter 8 about American settlers in Texas. Point out that although Texas belonged to Mexico, the settlers declared themselves independent. Were the Texans justified in declaring their independence? Why or why not? *(Students should give reasons for their answers.)*

Research

Henry Clay (1777–1852), a leading American statesman for almost 40 years, tried to hold the Union together by forging compromises between the North and the South. Because of his work in producing the Missouri Compromise and the Compromise of 1850, he was known as the "Great Compromiser." Have students refer to Chapter 6 and other sources and write a two-page research report on why Clay was known by this title.

Collaborative Learning

Have students identify the areas of conflict between North and South at the end of this lesson (page 319). Divide the class into pairs, and have the students in each pair take opposing sides in debating the Fugitive Slave Law. Ask each pair of students to suggest a compromise that would make the Fugitive Slave Law more acceptable to both the North and the South. Then have each pair report back to the class to compare the compromise ideas.

House, thanks to the support of Northern Whigs and Democrats. But it failed in the Senate. This voting pattern was repeated in 1847. The South had won a legislative victory. But the voting—along rigid geographical lines—told another story, that of a nation where the hope of peace seemed lost.

Compromise of 1850 Reopens Wounds

Should the lands won from Mexico be open to slavery? By 1850, this question paralyzed national politics. Southerners said yes; they wanted more land for cotton cultivation. Northerners said no; their free labor system could not compete with slave labor in the territories. They insisted that if slavery took root in the territories, Northerners would be unable to settle there.

Meanwhile, another controversy developed. In the 1842 Prigg Decision, the Supreme court relieved Northern law officials of the responsibility of catching runaway slaves. Southerners were furious. As many as 1,000 slaves escaped each year. Slaveholders wanted a stronger federal law to regain their "property." Congress addressed these issues in a series of bills supported by Daniel Webster, Henry Clay, and Stephen A. Douglas. The Compromise of 1850 handed the South a new, harsher Fugitive Slave Law and created two slave territories: Utah and New Mexico.

The Compromise of 1850 offered the admission of California as a free state. It also ended the public sale of slaves in Washington, D. C. Now, for the first time since the Missouri Compromise, the free states outnumbered the slave states in the Senate.

The harsher Fugitive Slave Law created great hostility in the North and even led to violent riots. Northerners refused to help slaveholders capture runaway slaves. The North's failure to comply with the law only made the South more intent on defending its way of life. ■

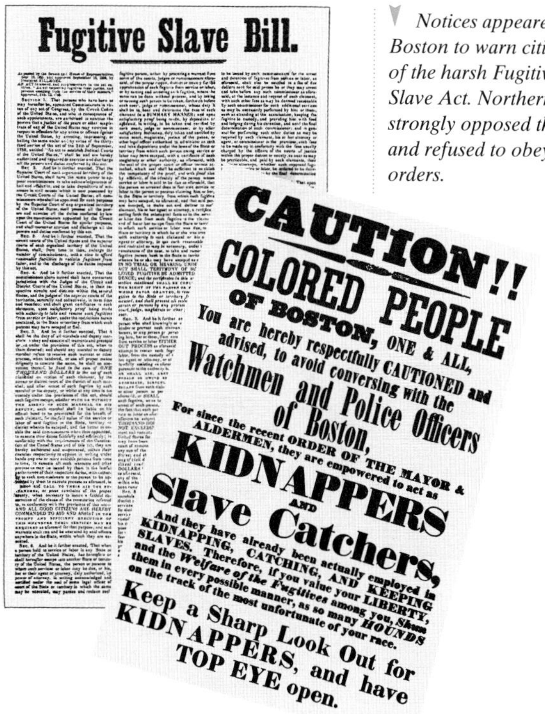

Fugitive Slave Bill.
CAUTION!!
COLORED PEOPLE
OF BOSTON, ONE & ALL,
You are hereby respectfully CAUTIONED and advised, to avoid conversing with the
Watchmen and Police Officers of Boston,
For since the recent ORDER OF THE MAYOR & ALDERMEN, they are empowered to act as
KIDNAPPERS
AND
Slave Catchers,
And they have already been actually employed in KIDNAPPING, CATCHING, AND KEEPING SLAVES. Therefore, if you value your LIBERTY, and the Welfare of the Fugitives among you, Shun them in every possible manner, as so many HOUNDS on the track of the most unfortunate of your race.
Keep a Sharp Look Out for KIDNAPPERS, and have TOP EYE open.

Notices appeared in Boston to warn citizens of the harsh Fugitive Slave Act. Northerners strongly opposed the law and refused to obey its orders.

■ *The Compromise of 1850 gave the South a tougher fugitive slave law and two new territories. The North gained a free state. Why did both sides feel the Compromise was unacceptable?*

REVIEW

1. **FOCUS** Why was compromise necessary between the North and the South as the United States expanded into western territories?
2. **CONNECT** Why did the North develop into an industrial economy while the South remained an agricultural economy?
3. **GEOGRAPHY** What effect did the Mexican-American War have on the acquisition of new land?
4. **CRITICAL THINKING** Why did the Missouri Compromise of 1820 fail to resolve the slavery debate?
5. **CRITICAL THINKING** What was the aim of the Wilmot Proviso?
6. **WRITING ACTIVITY** Write a "Letter to the Editor" from a Northerner, and another from a Southerner, stating your views on the Compromise of 1850. Do you approve or disapprove?

HISTORY

Critical Thinking

Ask students what provisions in the Compromise of 1850 favored the North. *(Admission of California as a free state gave the North a majority in the Senate.)* The South? *(Utah and New Mexico became slave territories, and the Fugitive Slave Law was made harsher.)*

■ *The South was unhappy that the free states outnumbered the slave states; the North found the harsher Fugitive Slave Law unacceptable and refused to comply with it.*

CLOSE

Copy on the board the structure of the Graphic Overview from page 314 and have students use their notes to add information to the chart. To summarize the lesson, have students answer the Thinking Focus. As an extension activity, you may wish to have students do the Research activity on page 318.

Answers to Review Questions

1. Compromise was necessary to preserve the balance between North and South, which differed so greatly in their economies and their ways of life.
2. Free labor helped the growth of factories in the North, while slave labor made agriculture profitable in the South.
3. It led to the acquisition of much land, including what is now California, Arizona, New Mexico, Utah, Nevada, and parts of Colorado.
4. Sample answer: The 1820 Missouri Compromise provided only a temporary solution. Allow for personal opinion.
5. Sample answer: The aim of the Wilmot Proviso was to allow Northern Democrats to support the Mexican-American War without appearing to be proslavery. Allow for personal opinion.
6. Students should clearly reflect the differences in perspective in their letters.

Homework Options

Have students select an issue being debated in their town or before the Supreme Court and list the arguments on each side. What would they decide? Why?

Study Guide: page 45.

CHAPTER
INTRODUCE

Have students recall what they learned in previous lessons about the antislavery movement. *(Nonviolent resistance of slaves, slave revolts, Frederick Douglass, Nat Turner)*

After one student reads the Thinking Focus aloud, explain that the goal of the abolitionist movement was to end slavery. Ask students to predict some of the things that abolitionists would do to end slavery. Have students read to confirm or reject their predictions.

Key Term

Vocabulary strategies: T36–T37

abolitionism—the advocacy of the end of slavery in the United States

LESSON 2

The Antislavery Movement

THINKING FOCUS

How did the abolitionist movement contribute to the ongoing conflict between the North and the South?

Key Term

- abolitionism

Sojourner Truth, a famous activist in the antislavery movement, helped hundreds of slaves to escape.

Outrageous! Dangerous! High treason! These were the typical reactions of Southern whites who read a pamphlet that mysteriously appeared in Southern cities. "How would they like for us to hold them in cruel slavery, and murder them as they do to us?" the publication demanded.

People all over the South were shocked when, in 1830, they were faced with such questions in a pamphlet titled *Appeal to the Colored Citizens of the World.* David Walker, a free black man who worked as a tailor in Boston, published the piece in 1829. It was not long afterward that the state of Georgia offered a $1,000 reward for Walker's arrest. Georgia enacted laws that made it a crime to hand out such incendiary, or inflammatory, publications. Teaching blacks to read or write became a crime in Georgia. Walker continued his mission, but died mysteriously in 1830, the possible victim of murder.

Born a free man in the slave state of North Carolina, Walker had witnessed blacks being bought and sold as human property. He considered the supporters of slavery "avaricious [greedy] and unmerciful wretches."

Many of Walker's customers were sailors, and he would slip copies of his *Appeal* inside their duffel bags. Then his pamphlets would be carried to Southern port cities, where they would be passed along. In this way, Walker's bold call to insurrection, or open revolt, spread to slaves and slaveholders alike. Walker's message was the topic of many religious sermons in the South. The antislavery movement had found an urgent and compelling voice in David Walker. But his *Appeal* was just one of the many ways that abolitionists, those opposed to slavery, presented their views. Soon, men and women across the nation would be working for the antislavery movement.

Antislavery Movement Speaks with Many Voices

Many slaves sought their freedom at every opportunity. They tried risky escapes, they disobeyed their day-to-day orders, and they occasionally rose up violently against the slaveholders. Nat Turner's violent revolt of 1831 in Virginia, together with scores of smaller uprisings, made slaveowners fear their own slaves. Southerners' distrust of the North also grew because they believed that antislavery agitation in the North encouraged slave rebellions.

Northern free blacks launched a crusade to liberate their "brothers" and "sisters" from slavery. One of the most famous activists was Sojourner Truth, who discarded her slave name of Isabella Baumfree. Expressing her belief that people best show love for God by love and concern for others,

Objectives

1. Explain the role of slaves and free black people in the antislavery movement.
2. Identify the diverse motives and beliefs held by abolitionists.
3. Describe the role of women in the abolitionist movement.
4. Evaluate the impact of Harriet Beecher Stowe's *Uncle Tom's Cabin* on the nation.

Graphic Overview

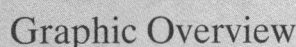

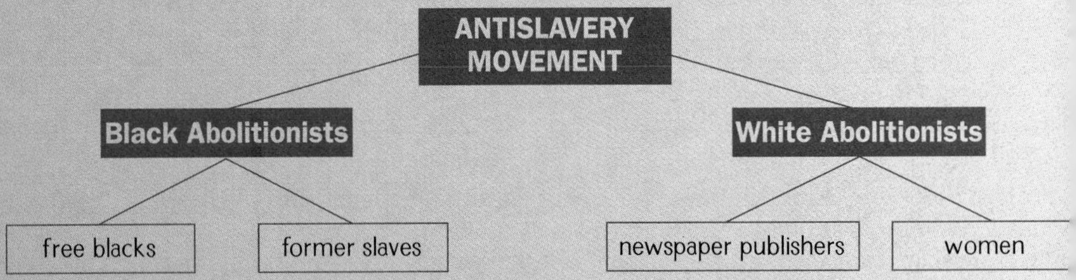

she helped hundreds of slaves escape and spread her word throughout the North. She even visited President Abraham Lincoln at the White House to deliver her message personally.

Antislavery Roots

Before the 1830s, the white antislavery movement was disorganized and ineffective. One group, the American Colonization Society, proposed to send free blacks and emancipated slaves to settle in the African land of Liberia. The first settlement of American blacks took place there in 1822. This group posed no threat to slaveholders who were happy to get rid of free blacks and troublesome slaves. Other groups believed that slavery should be ended gradually.

Then, on New Year's Day of 1831, a new and fiery brand of antislavery was born. On that day Boston publisher William Lloyd Garrison began a newspaper called the *Liberator.* The *Liberator* supported **abolitionism**, a movement that demanded an immediate and no-compromise end to slavery.

In 1834, Garrison helped found the American Antislavery Society. This new group worked to spread the abolition movement across the nation through the mails, lectures, and petitions to Congress.

Louder Voices

Among the many voices speaking against slavery during the 1800s was that of Frederick Douglass. A former slave from Maryland, Douglass became a leading spokesman for black freedom. He was a gifted writer and speaker who devoted his life to ending slavery and fighting for black rights.

Born Frederick Augustus Washington Bailey, he fled his Baltimore, Maryland, master as a young man in 1838. He settled in New Bedford, Massachusetts, and changed his name to avoid being captured. Douglass found work in a shipyard, but other men refused to work with him because he was black. He found other jobs collecting trash and digging cellars.

At a meeting of the Massachusetts Antislavery Society in 1841, Douglass described what freedom meant to him. His speech impressed the audience and he was hired by the society to lecture about his experiences as a slave. In addition to lecturing, Douglass actively protested the racial segregation that was common in public places, even churches. He was once dragged from a railroad car reserved for white people.

In 1845, Douglass published the first of two autobiographies, or life accounts, *Narrative of the Life of Frederick Douglass.* You have already read two stories from this book in Chapter 10. Fearing that his identity as a runaway slave would be revealed, Douglass went to England for two years. While there, he continued to speak against slavery. When he returned to America in 1847, he founded an antislavery newspaper, the *North Star,* in Rochester, New York. ■

THE LIBERATOR.
OUR COUNTRY IS THE WORLD—OUR COUNTRYMEN ARE ALL MANKIND.
VOL. VII.
BOSTON, MASSACHUSETTS.]
[SATURDAY, JANU
SLAVERY.
THE LIBERATOR
IS PUBLISHED WEEKLY
EDITOR.

Across Time & Space

Freedom's Journal began a long tradition of black newspapers in the United States. Today there are a number of black papers across the nation, including the Daily Challenge (Brooklyn, New York), the Chicago Daily Defender, and the Atlanta Daily World. The Challenge reaches more than 70,000 readers, while about 39,000 read the Defender and the World.

■ *What techniques did abolitionists Sojourner Truth, William Lloyd Garrison, and Frederick Douglass use to gain support for the antislavery movement?*

◄ *William Lloyd Garrison published a newspaper, the Liberator, to support the abolitionist movement.*

DEVELOP

Have students preview the lesson headings to look for clues about the individuals and groups who worked to abolish slavery. As they read the lesson, have them write down the names of the key people in abolitionism.

■ *They used mailings, lectures, and petitions to Congress.*

BELIEF SYSTEMS

Critical Thinking

Point out that many black and white Northerners worked in the antislavery movement, even though their lives were not directly affected by slavery. Have students suggest reasons why people from the North became involved in this issue. *(Sample answers: Desire for equal rights for everyone, sense of brotherhood, religious reasons)*

Access Strategy

To help students understand why people worked so hard to abolish slavery, give them an example of someone today who is working to change a political or social situation. (For example, Candy Lightner and MADD) Have them suggest reasons why some people are willing to become actively involved in working for change. *(Feel an obligation, religious reasons, or the belief that they can make a difference)*

Encourage students to talk about people whom they know or have heard about who have worked to achieve a specific goal of social or political change, either by themselves or through an organization. Why is this person working on behalf of his or her particular cause? What is the person working to achieve? Tell students they will read in this lesson about people who worked to end slavery in the 1800s.

Access Activity

Ask students to choose as a group a school problem that interests them. Have them decide on a solution to the problem and then brainstorm a list of ways to get support, such as making posters, passing out fliers, or organizing meetings. Tell them to keep these tactics in mind as they read the lesson.

SOCIAL SYSTEMS

Critical Thinking

Refer students to page 267 to find examples of the inequalities experienced by women such as Lucretia Mott and Elizabeth Cady Stanton. Why do you think so many women were abolitionists? *(Sample answer: Women were concerned with equality and human rights for everyone.)*

POLITICAL SYSTEMS

Critical Thinking

Have students list some of the things women did in the abolitionist movement. *(Organized gatherings, circulated petitions, recruited members, hid runaway slaves)* Then ask them to analyze the importance of each of these in a political movement.

Women Play a Crucial Role

From the beginning of the abolition movement, women joined in large numbers. At first, they had to work in separate women's organizations. Many people believed that it was improper for women and men to work together. Some of the women's duties included organizing social gatherings to recruit new members and to circulate petitions. Some women even hid runaway slaves in their homes.

Early in the abolition movement, women saw their work as a religious crusade against the "sinful" and "un-Christian" slaveholders. Over time, however, many began to think of abolitionism as a broader movement toward equal rights—not only for blacks but for women as well.

The Grimké sisters, Angelina and Sarah, were two Southerners who went against all notions of "proper behavior" for women. They dared to lecture against slavery, not just to other women, but to audiences of both men and women—a practice unheard of in those days. "My idea," wrote Angelina, "is that whatever is morally right for a man to do is morally right for a woman to do."

Lucretia Mott and Elizabeth Cady Stanton traveled overseas in 1840 to attend the World Antislavery Convention in London. As women, they were required to sit apart from the men at meetings. And in all the Convention's plans, they noticed that women were forced into secondary roles.

One of the most forceful voices among white women fighting slavery belonged to novelist Harriet Beecher Stowe.

Uncle Tom's Cabin Stirs the Nation

Imagine a Northern family in the 1850s, gathered around the fireplace, listening to a tale of incredible cruelty and unhappiness. They are reading a novel about the horrors of slavery. The main character, Tom, a slave, has just been sold. The novel that stirred the country was *Uncle Tom's Cabin,* written by Harriet Beecher Stowe and published in 1852. Stowe hated slavery and was especially appalled by the harsh new Fugitive Slave Act of 1850, which called on Northerners to help catch runaway slaves. Even worse, the

Lucretia Mott, seated second from the right (front row), is shown here with other members of the Pennsylvania Antislavery Society.

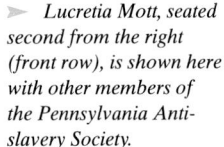

322

Critical Thinking

Thomas Jefferson, who owned slaves, wrote "All men are created equal." Have students offer explanations for this apparent contradiction.

Historical Context

At the age of 46, Isabella Baumbee changed her name to Sojourner Truth and started traveling around the country giving speeches and raising money for the abolitionist cause. She shared the speaking platform with Frederick Douglass and other leaders of the movement and stayed at the home of Harriet Beecher Stowe.

Later, Sojourner Truth began to speak out on the issue of equal rights for women. In her 1851 "Ain't I a Woman" speech, she responded to a man's statement that a woman needed to be helped by saying, "Nobody ever helps me into carriages, or over mud-puddles, or gives me any best place! And ain't I a woman? Look at me! Look at my arm! I have ploughed and planted, and gathered into barns, and no man could head me! And ain't I a woman? I could work as much and eat as much as a man—when I could get it—and bear the lash as well! And ain't I a woman?"

A Moment in Time

A Quaker Abolitionist

5:47 P.M., October 29, 1839
On a path in the woods in Union, Ohio

Bonnet
It would be improper for her to leave home with her head uncovered. Hats are signs of modesty for Quaker women.
Woolen Shawl
As she walks to a meeting of the Union Female Antislavery Society, the shawl shields her from the wind. Like other Quaker women, she dresses plainly and practically.
Antislavery Petition
At tonight's meeting, her petition signed by 18 of her neighbors will be mailed with other petitions to President Van Buren.
Coins
Saved from her teaching pay, 17 cents is tucked in her dress pocket. Tonight, she'll give the coins to the Antislavery pamphlet fund. The money will help mail pamphlets to U.S. Senators.
Bread
This morning, she picked herbs from her garden to bake into the loaf. Tomorrow, it will be sold with many others at the Society Fair.
Newspaper
This copy of *The Liberator*, published in Boston by William Lloyd Garrison, contains antislavery articles she will share at the meeting.
Muddy Shoes
She just finished feeding vegetable scraps to the pigs. Mud from the pen sticks to her shoes. No matter—there are plenty of puddles between home and the meeting house.

BELIEF SYSTEMS

Visual Learning

Explain that people often used the words *practical, plain,* and *modest* to describe Quakers. Ask students how the picture on this page reflects these words. *(Sample answer: She's nearly completely covered; her clothes are simple.)*

More About the Shawl Many non-Quakers of this period wore embroidered shawls, colored skirts, and fancy hats—attire shunned by Quaker women.

Music Connection

Ask students if they are familiar with spirituals—songs originally written and sung by black slaves—that have become part of our musical heritage. Remind them that many spirituals are songs of freedom. Bring in tapes or records of freedom songs such as "Go Down, Moses" and "Follow the Drinking Gourd," and play them for the class. Ask students to pay close attention to the lyrics. Also have them note how the tone and cadence of the music reflect the lyrics.

Writing a Persuasive Article

Assign the students to write a one-page persuasive article for David Walker's pamphlet described on page 320. Remind students that persuasive articles can sometimes be very emotional. Encourage them to use both logic and emotion in their persuasive article.

Critical Thinking

Explain that Quakers have been pioneers in areas such as equal rights, nonviolence, and peace education. Ask students to name political issues that religious groups are fighting for today. Have them brainstorm a list of the pros and cons of religious groups' advocating political change.

CULTURE

Critical Thinking

Read aloud the excerpt from *Uncle Tom's Cabin* on this page. Ask students to describe the kind of person Tom is. *(Submissive to his master, well-liked and respected by other slaves, religious)* Is he a sympathetic or unsympathetic character? *(Sympathetic)* Then have students consider how Harriet Beecher Stowe would have portrayed an unsympathetic character. *(Sample answer: Cruel, unpopular)*

■ *They first saw it as a religious crusade but later saw it as a broader movement toward equal rights for women as well as for black Americans.*

CLOSE

Copy on the board the Graphic Overview from page 320. Ask students to add the names of the key people and organizations involved with the abolitionist movement. Then have students answer the Thinking Focus and evaluate the predictions they made before reading the lesson.

Harriet Beecher Stowe hoped her novel, Uncle Tom's Cabin, *would help bring about a peaceful end to slavery. Published in 1852, the book was very popular.*

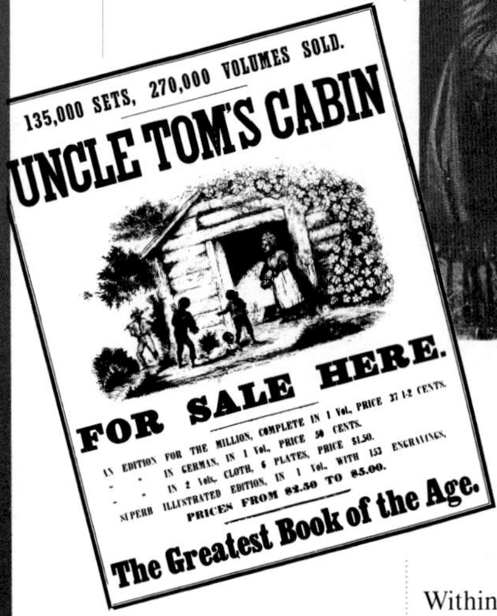
135,000 SETS, 270,000 VOLUMES SOLD.
UNCLE TOM'S CABIN
FOR SALE HERE.
The Greatest Book of the Age.

act did not allow accused runaways to defend themselves in court.

Stowe decided to "write something that would make this whole nation feel what an accursed thing slavery is." Within days after the book came out, 10,000 people had bought copies. Within a year, readers had bought 300,000 copies of *Uncle Tom's Cabin*. A dramatic play inspired by the book was performed in New York, London, and Paris. Audiences were moved to tears. Popular skits loosely based on the book were widely performed in towns throughout the North. Everywhere the book went, *Uncle Tom's Cabin* carried its powerful message of the evils of slavery.

Through this work of fiction, millions learned of the nightmare that individual slaves lived. People who had paid little attention to Garrison's political pleas read each word of Stowe's more emotional appeal. Many Americans became convinced that slavery was a great national sin.

Stowe had hoped that her book would bring a peaceful end to slavery, but instead, it just seemed to bring the nation closer to war. Northerners hated the South more than ever, and Southerners considered the book an elaborate lie, an unforgivable insult to their way of life. ■

Tom rose up meekly, to follow his new master, and raised up his heavy box on his shoulder. His wife took the baby in her arms to go with him to the wagon, and the children, still crying, trailed on behind.

Mrs. Shelby, walking up to the trader, detained him for a few moments, talking with him in an earnest manner; and while she was thus talking, the whole family party proceeded to a wagon, that stood ready harnessed at the door. A crowd of all the old and young hands on the place stood gathered around it, to bid farewell to their old associates. Tom had been looked up to, both as a head servant and a Christian teacher, by all the place, and there was much honest sympathy and grief about him, particularly among the women.

Harriet Beecher Stowe, *Uncle Tom's Cabin*

■ *Why did women join the abolitionist movement? How did their reasons change in time?*

REVIEW

1. **FOCUS** How did the abolitionist movement contribute to the ongoing conflict between the North and the South?
2. **CONNECT** What social, political, and economic forces led the nation to question slavery?
3. **CITIZENSHIP** Name some of the methods people used in their fight against slavery.
4. **HISTORY** Why did slave rebellions make Southerners distrust Northerners?
5. **CRITICAL THINKING** Why do you think Harriet Beecher Stowe's novel was so effective in demonstrating to the American public the evils of slavery?
6. **WRITING ACTIVITY** Write a news story that describes a white Southerner's reactions to finding a copy of David Walker's Appeal. Write it as a Southern reporter might view the experience.

Homework Options

Ask students to research and write a two-page report on someone who is fighting for equal rights today.

Study Guide: page 46.

Answers to Review Questions

1. Because they demanded an immediate end to slavery and refused to compromise, the abolitionists intensified the conflict between the North and the South.
2. The abolitionists, the failure of compromises to settle issues between the North and the South, and the cruelty of slave labor led the nation to question slavery.
3. Methods included writing pamphlets and books, giving lectures, and helping slaves to escape.
4. Many Southerners blamed Northerners for assisting in slave rebellions.
5. Sample answer: Her novel helped people see and feel the horror of slavery. Allow for personal opinion.
6. Students should reflect a proslavery bias in their news stories.

1820 1830 1840 1860 1870

LESSON 3

The Road to Bleeding Kansas

Crack! Crack! Congressman Brooks's wooden cane landed its solid blows across the back of Senator Sumner's head. Crack! Crack! Again and again, Brooks brandished his cane against his victim. Onlookers felt helpless because a friend of Brooks held them off with a pistol. Crack! Crack! The cane broke, yet Brooks kept swinging.

Sumner sat trapped behind his desk, which stood bolted to the floor. He couldn't move to defend himself. Finally, Sumner ripped his desk out of its very bolts and arose. He stumbled groggily and collapsed as the enraged Brooks kept swinging the broken walking stick. A few men at last rushed in to stop the savage beating. Why would a congressman attack a United States senator?

It was May 1856. Two days earlier Senator Charles Sumner of Massachusetts, one of the most outspoken enemies of slavery, had given a seething antislavery speech. Proslavery Congressman Preston Brooks of South Carolina became angered because the speech targeted Brooks's uncle, Senator Andrew Butler. Both the issue of slavery and Brooks's family honor were at stake. Brooks had at last found a chance to vent his rage at Senator Sumner.

Brooks's shocking attack symbolized the nation's growing split over slavery. No longer, it seemed, could lawmakers negotiate or compromise on this explosive issue. No longer could the nation hope for a peaceful solution to the conflict over slavery.

The Kansas-Nebraska Act Paves the Way

The strain between North and South that exploded in the Senate also continued to affect the race to settle new territories. By the late 1840s, a westward migration had pushed past the Mississippi River and the lands bordering it. The rich, fertile lands of Kansas and Nebraska drew thousands of farmers onto the prairies. Many other settlers flocked to California for gold. Politicians saw that the growing nation needed to be linked by a transcontinental railroad that would stretch from Chicago to California.

Lawmakers knew that a bill was needed to set up a territorial government for Kansas. And in order to build the railroad, land had to be set aside for the railroad companies.

Yet the issue of slavery blocked these promising plans. Kansas and Nebraska were both closed to slavery under the Missouri Compromise of 1820. Southerners would not go along with the railroad unless they saw hope for slavery in these territories. They felt they had to overturn the Missouri Compromise.

THINKING FOCUS

In what ways did the slavery issue continue to affect the American political process?

Key Terms

- popular sovereignty
- guerrilla

How Do We Know?

HISTORY *Newspapers from the past give historians and students alike a valuable, first-hand view of history. Most large libraries have extensive microfilm files of newspapers. How can we find out, for example, about the South's view of the attack on Senator Sumner? In a Southern proslavery newspaper, the beating was called "an elegant and effectual [effective] caning."*

INTRODUCE

Ask students to recall from Lesson 1 what the Missouri Compromise established for the lands west of the Mississippi River. *(It prohibited slavery there.)* Have them read the lesson title and the Thinking Focus. Ask students to read the lesson to find out why Kansas might be at the center of a political conflict.

Key Terms

Vocabulary strategies: T36–37

popular sovereignty—self-government of a state by its own elected officials

guerrilla—describing irregular warfare by independent forces

325

Graphic Overview

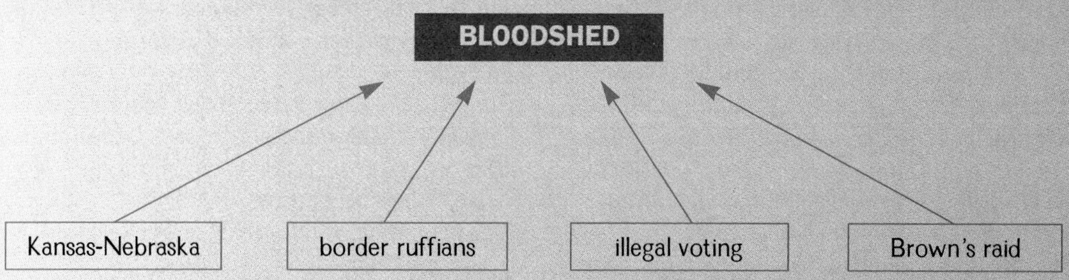

Objectives

1. Explain why violence broke out in the Kansas territories.
2. State the political positions of the Republican, Democratic, and Know-Nothing parties.
3. Define popular sovereignty, and explain why the South supported it.
4. Assess the impact of Buchanan's victory on slavery-related dissension.

DEVELOP

Tell students that they are going to read about some events leading to bloodshed in Kansas. Ask them to preview the lesson heads to find clues to these events. Copy on the board the Graphic Overview from page 325, leaving out the contributing causes in the four lower boxes. As they read the lesson, students can note the important events leading to the outbreak of violence in Kansas.

HISTORY

Visual Learning

Refer students to the chart on this page. Ask them on which political issues the parties agreed and on which they disagreed. *(Sample answer: Republican and Know-Nothing parties were against slavery.)*

The Republican party was established in 1854 as the result of an "anti-Nebraska" meeting, and attracted members from many different groups.

A Northerner, Democratic Senator Stephen A. Douglas of Illinois, started the new debate rolling. Douglas introduced the Nebraska Bill in 1854 to organize a territorial government, which could then open the way to lay down railroad tracks. Southern senators, however, balked at any bill that would allow the ban on slavery in the territories to continue.

Douglas reworked his bill. His new proposal divided the area into two territories: that of Kansas and that of Nebraska. It was implied, but not stated, that Kansas would become a slave state, and Nebraska would be free of slavery. Douglas also proposed an idea called **popular sovereignty**, or the right of the voters in each territory to decide whether to become a free or slave state. The new bill rendered the Missouri Compromise meaningless.

Congress passed the Kansas-Nebraska Act in 1854. Antislavery people, Democrats and Whigs included, held rallies, demonstrations, and meetings throughout the North to condemn the Kansas-Nebraska Act. These gatherings helped to form a new political party. (The chart below will help your understanding of the many political parties and their beliefs during this time period.)

Political Parties

Party	Platform
Democratic Formed in 1830	• Members mainly Southerners • Proslavery • Favored Western expansion, popular sovereignty, and states' rights
Whig Popular during 1840s–1850s	• Members mainly Easterners • Opposed Mexican War • Most opposed slavery in Western territories • Many joined Republican Party
American (Know-Nothing) Popular during 1850s	• Members promoted interests of native-born Americans • Anti-immigration • Opposed slavery • Ceased after 1856 election; many joined Republican Party
Republican Formed in 1854	• Members mainly Northerners • Antislavery • Favored Western expansion, strong federal government • Attracted Whigs and Know-Nothings

Republicans Oppose Slavery

In February 1854, even before the Kansas-Nebraska Act passed, an "anti-Nebraska" meeting assembled in Ripon, Wisconsin. The participants called it a "Republican" meeting. The name was then kept when a new political party grew out of this meeting and was joined by many similar groups emerging throughout the North.

Antislavery people of all sorts joined the Republican Party. People who had supported the antislavery Free Soil Party in 1848 joined, as did many members of the Whig Party. Some Democrats embraced Republicanism, splitting from the proslavery forces in their own party.

As members of the Whigs and Democrats shifted to the Republican Party, another party—the Know-Nothings—grew in power for a short time. The Know-Nothing Party was dedicated to stopping immigration into the United States. Most Know-Nothing party members eventually joined the Republican party.

With the rise of the Republican Party, the nation's widening split became official. Their slogan—"Free Soil, Free Labor, Free Speech, Free Men" clearly identified Republicans as the antislavery party.

Self-Government for States?

Democrats needed an issue to strengthen their identity, an issue that would win the vote of the South. Yet they could not appear to be proslavery for fear of losing Northern votes.

The Democrats rallied behind

Access Activity

Have students imagine that a person with a gun is standing outside a voting booth telling them how to vote. How would they act in this situation? *(Refuse to vote, change their vote, ignore the person)* Ask how they would feel voting against the person's orders. *(Probably afraid)* Explain that they will read about a similar situation in the lesson.

Access Strategy

Ask students to imagine that their town is having an election for a new mayor. Two people are running: Ms. Green and Mr. Orange. On the day of the election, hundreds of Mr. Orange's friends from other towns arrive carrying weapons and making threats. Ask students how this might affect the election. *(It could frighten Ms. Green's supporters.)*

Your town decides that the election results are invalid. Mr. Orange, however, insists that he is now mayor. What could the people of your town do? *(Ask for a new election)* What kind of compromise might be possible? *(The candidates might agree that the winner would guarantee the loser a place in the government.)* Tell students that they will be reading about a similar situation that occurred in Kansas when proslavery outsiders tried to elect illegally a proslavery legislature.

Free and Slave States and Territories, 1854

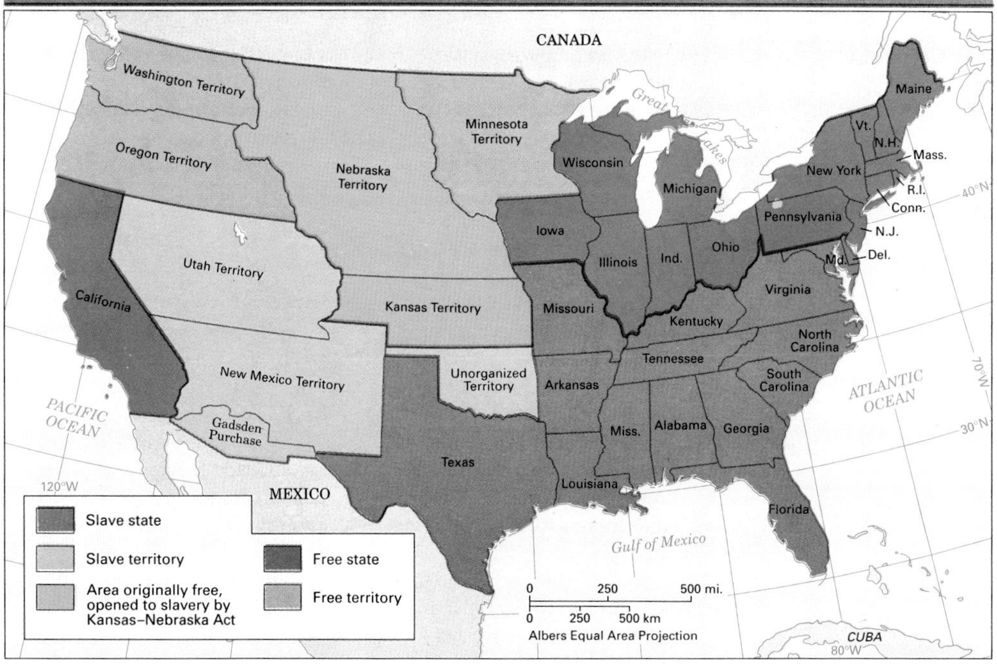

The slavery issue caused many problems in settling new western territories. The Kansas-Nebraska Act of 1854 overturned the Missouri Compromise.

popular sovereignty, which allowed the settlers of any new territory to decide for themselves, through the vote, whether or not slavery would exist in that territory.

With this issue, the Democrats hoped to appeal to the age-old American ideal of self-government. Popular sovereignty truly seemed like an idea that all Americans could understand and support.

Split Over Popular Sovereignty

Southerners doubted that anyone would oppose the right of Western settlers to have a voice in their own government. Yet they also knew the concrete rewards of this "patriotic" idea. Popular sovereignty gave Southerners the opportunity to extend slavery westward. This was still an important concern for white Southerners who wanted more land for cotton.

Many Northerners scoffed at popular sovereignty. They would never agree to slavery in the territories, even if Western settlers had voted for it. Northerners believed that slave territories would turn away free laborers who were looking for new opportunities. Popular sovereignty, they feared, would close off new territories to settlers who did not have slaves. Settlement of the western territories was important to the Northern free labor economy as well. With such different economic concerns, and ways of life that seemed worlds apart, how could the North and the South avoid an all-out conflict? ■

■ *The Kansas-Nebraska Act implied that Congress could no longer decide whether or not a state or territory would allow slavery. How did this Act conflict with the earlier Missouri Compromise?*

Kansas Bleeds Under Western Expansion

The battle over slavery extended to the sprawling wheat fields and cattle country of Kansas. This time, however, the opposing forces used guns, swords, and cannons. Antislavery fighters carried rifles known as "Beecher's Bibles," named for Henry Ward Beecher (Harriet Beecher Stowe's brother). Beecher was a leading antislavery minister who helped to raise money to send guns to the antislavery settlers in Kansas.

HISTORY

Critical Thinking

Ask students to define *popular sovereignty*. (See definitions of key terms, page 325.) How did this concept relate to John Calhoun's doctrine of states' rights explained in Chapter 6? *(The two concepts were in agreement on states' rights. Calhoun claimed that the states had the ultimate power and could nullify the laws of Congress within their state boundaries.)*

■ *It overturned the Missouri Compromise, which prohibited slavery in the new territories.*

Political Context

Even Northerners who didn't support Senator Sumner were angry at Brooks for his beating of Sumner. The South, one Northern newspaper declared, "cannot tolerate free speech anywhere, and would stifle it in Washington with the bludgeon and the bowie-knife, as they are now trying to stifle it in Kansas by massacre, rapine, and murder." "Has it come to this," asked poet and editor William Cullen Bryant, "that we must speak with bated breath in the presence of our Southern masters? Are we to be chastised as they chastised their slaves? Are we, too, slaves, slaves for life, a target for their brutal blows, when we do not comport ourselves to please them?"

The South, however, revered Brooks. *The Richmond Enquirer* declared "the act good in conception, better in execution, and best of all in consequence . . . [the abolitionists] must be lashed into submission."

Map and Globe Skills

Have students compare the map on this page with the map on page 318. Have them use the maps to identify the changes that took place in the West between 1850 and 1854. *(Sample answer: Utah Territory became a slave territory.)*

CITIZENSHIP

Social Participation

Point out that when the people of Kansas were faced with an illegally elected government, they formed a second government that represented the majority of people in Kansas. Have students suggest possible motivations of the people. *(Belief in freedom and in the United States Constitution; desire for self-determination as a state; refusal to be intimidated by force)*

John Brown took matters into his own hands when he led a violent four-month fight in Kansas against pro-slavery forces.

The battle erupted over settlement of the vast new territory. Each side wanted to populate Kansas. Yet few slaveowners actually moved to Kansas. They preferred raising cotton in the warmer South or Southwest. Northerners flocked to the area to start small farms on the territory's rich soil. By 1855, the majority of settlers in Kansas were from the North. Popular sovereignty, it seemed, would surely make Kansas a free state. But Southerners had a plan.

During the first territorial election in 1854, Kansans were to elect nonvoting delegates to Congress. Before the elections, 1,700 proslavery men stormed into Kansas from neighboring Missouri.

These "border ruffians" came to cast illegal votes and frighten the antislavery voters. The next year 5,000 border ruffians voted for the territorial legislature. Their votes elected a proslavery government.

The election was illegal, yet proslavery forces took over the territory and wrote slavery into the constitution. Antislavery forces felt cheated. They banded together and formed their own government, representing the majority of Kansas. The territory now had two opposing governments. Kansas had become a powder keg, ready to explode.

Kansans Shed Blood

The antislavery forces, based in the city of Lawrence, armed themselves against the border ruffians. At first small skirmishes broke out, but both sides avoided a major battle. Then in May 1856, seven hundred proslavery men from Missouri and Kansas attacked Lawrence. These raiders burned the hotel, destroyed two newspaper offices, and looted the stores.

Abolitionist John Brown and his sons immediately staged a raid on proslavery settlers along the Pottawatomie River. Brown's men killed five settlers, splitting their heads open with swords.

Brown's raid launched four months of **guerrilla**, or independent, war in Kansas. As the violence dragged on, "Bleeding Kansas"

This photograph shows "free-staters" in Kansas preparing for battle.

Visual Learning

Have students look at the picture of "free-staters" on this page. Then ask them to scan the text on this page to find out whom these people are preparing to fight. *(Proslavery people)*

Science Connection

Few Southerners settled in Kansas because the conditions there were not favorable for growing cotton. Have students research in the encyclopedia to find information on the soil and climate conditions in Kansas and in a cotton-growing state such as Mississippi or Georgia. Have them compare this information to understand why Kansas became a wheat-growing rather than a cotton-growing state.

Collaborative Learning

Have pairs of students debate the issue of states' rights from the point of view of Americans of the 1850s. Have one student take the point of view that states should have the right to decide whether to become slave or free; have the other student argue that the federal government should make the decision. Encourage students to use states' rights ideas introduced by John Calhoun (Chapter 6) for the pro-popular sovereignty side. Have students switch sides and debate again.

became a slogan for antislavery forces around the nation.

Finally, federal troops were sent to end the fighting in Kansas. In just a few months, two hundred people had died fighting over slavery. And while "Bleeding Kansas" was no longer bleeding, the issue of slavery in the territories, the future of Kansas and the future of the nation were far from certain.

Violence Erupts in Congress

Perhaps some Americans could shrug off the violence in Kansas because it took place so far from their own homes. Perhaps they felt that such rugged frontier areas always attracted desperadoes, gunfighters, and other violent sorts. But they couldn't ignore the shocking attack that took place on the floor of the United States Senate. It took Senator Sumner three years to recover from the beating. Meanwhile, the statesman of Massachusetts left his Senate seat empty, a symbol of the aggressive and dangerous nature of "slave power."

The guerrilla warfare in Kansas and the violence in the Senate showed that Americans were clearly unable to resolve the debate over slavery. Northerners and Southerners alike held out little hope for a peaceful solution. Nevertheless, the political debate continued as the 1856 presidential election drew near. ■

■ More than two hundred fighters died during the skirmishes in "Bleeding Kansas." Why was this territory fought over so violently?

Buchanan Gains a Narrow Victory

The presidential election of 1856 became a three-way race over the issue of slavery in the territories. Republicans nominated John C. Frémont, a famous western explorer. Democrats named James Buchanan as their candidate. The Know-Nothing Party nominated former President Millard Fillmore.

The Republicans, a party of the North, stood firmly against slavery in the territories. The Democrats hoped to win Northern and Southern votes by standing for the "patriotic" popular sovereignty.

The Democrats won the election, but the Republicans made a very strong showing. Democrat Buchanan won only 45 percent of the popular vote, and the Republicans finished far ahead of the third-place Know-Nothing candidate.

The South appeared to have won this election—the nation had supported popular sovereignty. Yet the vote did little to heal the nation's wounds. Antislavery forces, inspired by the strong Republican showing, were ready to fight even harder. ■

◄ Democrat James Buchanan won the 1856 presidential election.

■ The Republicans lost the presidential election of 1856. Yet in many ways the campaign was a success for them. How can a losing election campaign still benefit a candidate or party?

R E V I E W

1. **FOCUS** In what ways did the slavery issue continue to affect the American political process?
2. **CONNECT** Make a list of all the factors that led to the overturn of the Missouri Compromise. What was the reason it was overturned?
3. **CITIZENSHIP** Give a description of someone who might have joined the Republican Party. What were some of the ideas the party supported?
4. **BELIEF SYSTEMS** How were "Bleeding Kansas" and the violence that erupted in Congress linked?
5. **CRITICAL THINKING** Why do you think that the presidential election of 1856 was not a simple two-way race between a proslavery and an antislavery candidate?
6. **WRITING ACTIVITY** Imagine you are a white Southern Democrat in the 1850s. Write a speech defending the idea of popular sovereignty.

■ Both slavery and antislavery forces wanted to claim this territory.

POLITICAL SYSTEMS

Critical Thinking

Point out that Buchanan won the election with 45 percent of the national vote, yet the South was unhappy with the election results. Why? *(The antislavery Republicans made a surprisingly strong showing.)*

■ Losing by a small margin can inspire people to fight harder in the future.

C L O S E

Have students use their notes on the events in this lesson that contributed to bloodshed in Kansas to make a chart similar to the Graphic Overview on page 325. Have students answer the Thinking Focus.

Answers to Review Questions

1. The slavery issue led to the argument over popular sovereignty, to border raids, to the rise of the Republican Party, and to the close 1856 presidential race.
2. Sample answer: Northerners desired a railway line through the area. It was overturned because neither the North nor the South could accept it.
3. The person might have supported the Free Soil Party in 1848 or been a former member of the Whig or Democratic party. The Republicans were the antislavery party; their slogan was "Free Soil, Free Labor, Free Speech."
4. Both were violent, and both resulted from the clash between proslavery and antislavery forces.
5. Sample answer: Slavery was not the only issue of the day. Allow for personal opinion.
6. Encourage several students to give their speeches to the class.

Homework Options

Ask students to look through newspapers to find an account of someone being verbally attacked for views that he or she holds.

Study Guide: page 52.

INTRODUCE

Begin by asking students to suggest what the lesson title means. *(The country divided over the issue of slavery)* Ask them to recall from previous lessons some of the events that revealed the intense conflict between North and South. *(Fighting in Kansas, antislavery movement, Brown's raid)* Then have them read the Thinking Focus, and suggest that they read the lesson to find out about other events that might reveal that this conflict would never be resolved peacefully.

Key Term

Vocabulary strategies: T36–37
Underground Railroad—a network of people who helped escaped slaves to travel north

1820 1830 1840 1850 1861 1870

LESSON 4

The House Divided

THINKING FOCUS

What events during the 1850s revealed that the conflict between the North and the South would never be resolved peacefully?

Key Term

- Underground Railroad

From the jail emerged a man of distinguished features. With head held high, the prisoner walked unhesitantly on a cool Virginia morning in 1859 to the field where he was to be hanged.

"This is a beautiful country," he declared. "I have never had the pleasure of seeing it before." A few minutes later, he was dead.

To antislavery supporters, John Brown's massacre of five slaveholders in Kansas in 1856 and his bold defense of the antislavery town of Osawatomie had been heroic acts.

John Brown had angrily witnessed victory after victory for the proslavery forces—in the courts, in Congress, and in the territories. He decided to fight back with a vengeance. In October 1859, with 21 of his followers, Brown raided a federal arsenal at Harpers Ferry with plans to seize guns stored there and to pass out guns and ammunition to slaves in the area. The success of his rebellion depended almost entirely on the help of slaves.

At first Brown and his men were able to hold the arsenal. They even held off the local militia throughout the next day and night. Yet no local slaves came to Brown's aid. Few had even heard of his revolt. U.S. marines soon stormed the arsenal. After losing many men, including two of his sons, Brown surrendered. Brown was tried and convicted for insurrection, treason, and murder. The sentence called for his speedy death. He was hanged on December 2, 1859. His death touched off a wave of sympathy and admiration in the North.

Now the hangman and soldiers guarding him looked on at the man who was soon to become legend. The words he had written in a note to his jailer would prove all too true: "The crimes of this guilty land will never be purged away, but with blood."

This oil painting by Thomas Hovenden is entitled The Last Moments of John Brown. *Brown's death inspired strong antislavery feelings in the North.*

Objectives

1. Review the conclusions of the Dred Scott case, its impact on slaves, and reactions to it.
2. Explain the provisions of the Lecompton Constitution and why it was illegal.
3. Describe the methods of the Underground Railroad.
4. Assess the reaction of the South to Lincoln's election.

Graphic Overview

Causes
- Harpers Ferry
- Dred Scott decision
- Lecompton Constitution
- Underground Railroad

→ **Election of 1860** →

Effects
- secession by Southern states
- rebel fire on Fort Sumter

Slavery Battled on All Fronts

John Brown's bloody raid at Harpers Ferry angered many people. But events during the late 1850s convinced passionate abolitionists that they had to take matters into their own hands.

The Supreme Court decision against Dred Scott strengthened the harsh Fugitive Slave Law.

The Dred Scott Case

Two days after President Buchanan's inauguration in 1857, the Supreme Court released its decision in an important case known as *Dred Scott* v. *Sandford.* Dred Scott had been the slave of John Emerson, an army doctor from Missouri. During his military career, Emerson had taken Scott with him as a personal servant. On one assignment, Emerson lived at Fort Snelling in the present-day state of Minnesota. At that time, Fort Snelling was in a part of the territories declared free by the Missouri Compromise. After more than a year, the two men returned to Missouri.

When Emerson died in 1846, Scott was determined to gain his freedom. Some white friends helped Scott find a lawyer, and the slave sued for his freedom in the courts. He argued that he had become free the moment his master brought him into the territory designated nonslavery by the Missouri Compromise.

A Missouri court agreed with Scott's argument and declared him free. The Missouri Supreme Court, however, reversed the decision. Dred Scott then took his case to the United States Supreme Court.

The Supreme Court Decision

In 1857, the Supreme Court voted 7 to 2 that Scott must remain a slave. Writing the Supreme Court's opinion on the Dred Scott case, Chief Justice Roger B. Taney reached two important conclusions. Blacks, he insisted, had no right to sue in the federal courts because they could never be considered citizens of the United States. Even when the Constitution was written, Taney argued, blacks could not vote and had no rights. Taney was mistaken. Free blacks could in fact vote in 8 of the 13 states.

Taney and the Court also asserted that the Missouri Compromise was unconstitutional because it denied white Southerners the right to take their human property with them into the territories. In addition, Taney stated, Congress had no power to pass such a law for the territories. The Dred Scott case seemed to open all federal territories to slavery.

Republicans, now the majority party in the North, shook their heads in disbelief and anger. They considered Taney's opinion unjust and unsound. The one-sided, proslavery decision shattered their confidence in the Supreme Court.

Southerners and many Northern Democrats, however, applauded Taney's decision. They hoped it would finally end the great controversy over slavery in the territories. But the decision only added more fuel to the burning issue of slavery.

DEVELOP

Tell students that this lesson is about the increasing conflict between the North and the South that finally resulted in the Civil War. Have them preview the lesson heads to find examples of this conflict. As they read the lesson, students can make a list of examples of conflict between the North and the South.

CONSTITUTIONAL HERITAGE

Critical Thinking

Ask students how the Supreme Court ruling in the Dred Scott case was consistent with Justice John Marshall's concept of judicial review that they studied in Chapter 5. *(According to judicial review, the Supreme Court decides whether laws are constitutional; in the Dred Scott case, the Court said that it was unconstitutional for Congress to make laws for the territories.)*

Access Strategy

Have students recall some of the examples of compromise from Lesson 1. *(Missouri Compromise, Wilmot Proviso, Compromise of 1850)* Then ask students if they know of a current international, national, or local issue in which compromise seems impossible. *(Examples might include the Middle East or abortion.)* If both sides are unwilling to compromise, what might happen? *(Sample answer: continuing conflict resulting in demonstrations, petitions, possible violence, work stoppages, war)* Tell students that they will learn in this lesson how compromise over the slavery issue completely broke down between the North and the South, resulting finally in war.

Access Activity

Read the lesson opener on page 330 aloud and have students look at the painting of John Brown on that page. Have students suggest reasons why Brown became a legend. *(Sample answer: Northerners thought his acts were heroic.)*

HISTORY

Critical Thinking

Have students explain why the Lecompton Constitution was illegal. *(It was written by an illegally elected legislature.)* Why was this constitution passed easily? *(Many antislavery settlers refused to vote on the issue, allowing the proslavery advocates, who voted, to pass it.)* Is abstaining from voting ever an effective strategy? Why or why not?

■ *The antislavery movement was already so strong that it refused to acknowledge the rulings, declaring them unjust.*

■ *Alleged fugitives were often seized secretly, were not allowed to testify, and usually had no lawyer. Often the word of the slaveholder alone settled the case.*

Kansans Create a Constitution

The debate over slavery still raged in Kansas, where fraudulent elections had been held and where an illegal proslavery legislature reigned. In 1857, this legislature called for a constitutional convention to make Kansas a slave state. The convention, meeting at the town of Lecompton, wrote a proslavery constitution.

Antislavery Kansas settlers refused to participate in the vote for the new constitution, but their action backfired. With only proslavery people voting, the constitution passed easily.

President Buchanan didn't want to anger Southern Democrats. He accepted this fraudulent "Lecompton Constitution," and the Senate, with its large Democratic majority, passed a Kansas statehood bill. The House, however, defeated it. The issue of slavery in Kansas remained unsettled. ■

■ *Why didn't Chief Justice Taney's rulings dissolve the antislavery movement?*

Antislavery Movement Forges Ahead

Despite setbacks in the courts, antislavery forces continued their work. Neither the harsh Fugitive Slave Act of 1850 nor the Dred Scott Decision could stop the movement.

Proslavery resistance was powerful. In 1854, the federal government spent almost $100,000 to return just one fugitive slave, Anthony Burns, from Boston. Burns's master later sold the slave for $905. Such was the determination of the proslavery forces.

Northerners argued that the whole Fugitive Slave Act was unfair. Marshals often seized accused slaves secretly and hurried them off to a commissioner before anyone knew what had happened. The accused person usually had no lawyer. Just the word of the slaveholder was often enough to settle the case. The alleged fugitive slave could not testify at all. Antislavery forces stood up to resist such unfair laws.

Picture this scene. Onto the streets of Christiana, Pennsylvania, in 1851, walk a group of black men, escaped slaves. They are cautious and are armed with pistols and rifles. Their former owner is now close on the trail of the runaways. The fugitives, finally in Pennsylvania, feel that their former master has surely given them up for lost.

But he hasn't. Suddenly, in Christiana, he and his men appear. In a flash, guns blaze. The slaves are determined to die before they will return. When the smoke clears, the slaveholder himself lies dead. His former slaves head for Canada and freedom.

In a number of Northern cities there were similar shootouts and crowd actions to prevent the return of fugitive slaves. Often the mobs included whites and blacks side by side. These actions made Southerners distrust the North more than ever. ■

■ *Why did Northerners think the Fugitive Slave Act was unfair?*

▼ *Southern states held 70 percent of the nation's total slave population in 1860.*

Slave Population, 1860

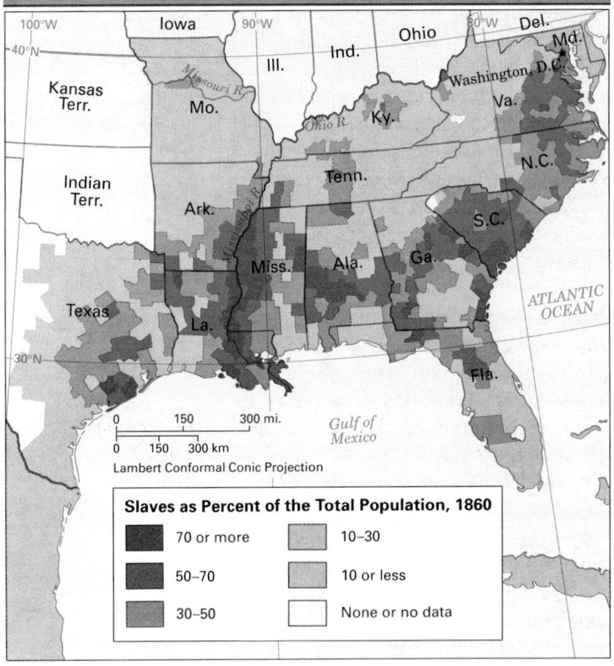

Map and Globe Skills

Have students compare the map on this page to the economic map on page 288. In what areas of the South were slaves the largest part of the population? *(Through the cotton belt, along the Mississippi River, in some cities)*

Political Context

Although the North was considered free soil, black Americans still did not have full equality in most Northern states. In the state of Illinois, for example, black Northerners paid taxes but could not vote, hold political office, serve on juries, or testify in court. Some who couldn't find jobs sold themselves as "indentures" for a period of twenty years. However, black Americans did have the right to vote in six New England states and, under some circumstances, in New York and Michigan. They could also own property, pursue professions, and educate their children.

Slave Routes to Freedom, 1860

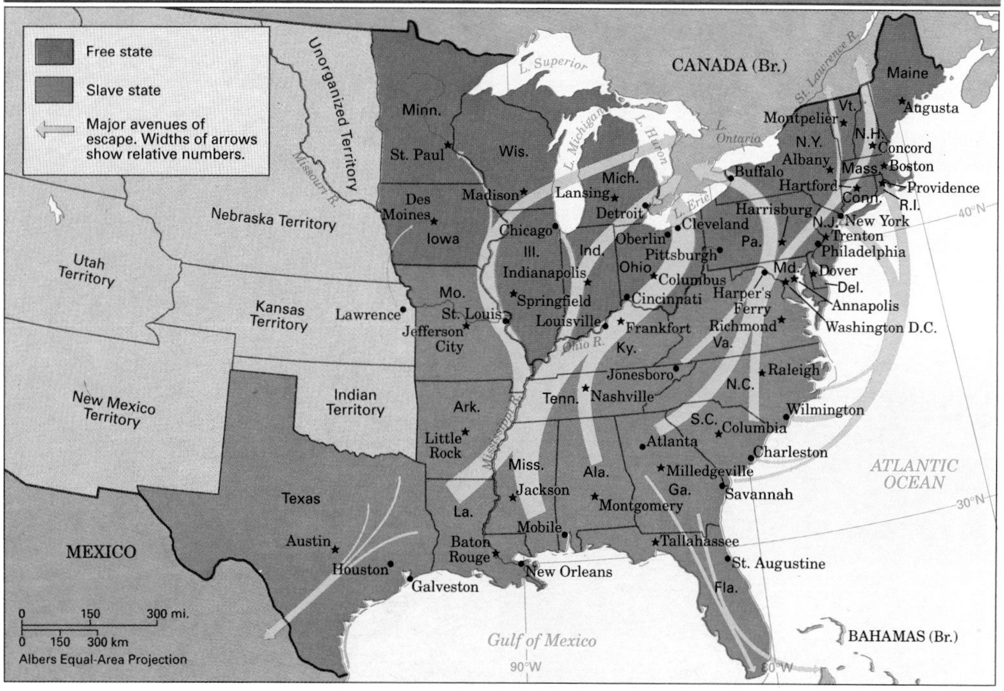

The Underground Railroad relied on thousands of "conductors" operating secretly throughout the North and the South.

Slaves Ride the Underground Railroad

Antislavery forces did more than protect and rescue runaway slaves. In fact, they helped many slaves escape. A secret network known as the **Underground Railroad** guided some 100,000 fugitive slaves to freedom between 1780 and 1865.

What was the Underground Railroad? It was not a railroad, and it did not move underground. The Underground Railroad was a complex system of about 3,000 people—both blacks and whites—who helped transport escaped slaves. Under the cover of night, "conductors" led runaways to freedom, providing food and safe hiding places. They risked great danger in aiding slaves.

The means of transportation in the Underground Railroad varied. Slaves traveled on foot, in covered wagons, in boxes shipped by rail or in small boats gliding silently through the water by night. At the stations, slaves hid in attics, barns, cellars, and even secret rooms. Finally, at the end of the perilous journey, the runaway slave would settle in one of the 14 free states or in Canada.

Probably the most famous Underground Railroad "conductor" was a heroic black woman named Harriet Tubman, who had herself escaped from slavery. Harriet Tubman guided more than 300 slaves to freedom.

Harriet Tubman was known to blacks as "Moses." Like that Old-Testament leader, she brought her people out of slavery.

■ *How did some abolitionists break the law to help the slaves?*

HISTORY

Critical Thinking

What problems and difficulties do you think people would have in running a system like the Underground Railroad? *(Sample answer: Organizational problems, secrecy)* How might conditions in the 1800s have made it more difficult or easier to run the Underground Railroad? *(Sample answer: Poor communications might have made it more difficult to coordinate the effort.)*

Language Arts Connection

Tell students that Stephen Vincent Benét wrote a poem called "John Brown's Body" about the famous abolitionist. Ask them to read the poem and then write an additional verse that tells how John Brown's life and heroic death are still meaningful in today's world.

Reader's Theater

Have students research, write, and produce a brief dramatization about the Underground Railroad. One good source is Ann Petry's *Harriet Tubman: Conductor on the Underground Railroad* (New York: Pocket Books, 1971). Students can dramatize selected chapters from the book.

Map and Globe Skills

Refer students to the map on this page and ask them to use the arrows to determine which escape route was used the most. The least? *(The route used most often went north along the Mississippi and Ohio rivers to Lake Erie and Canada. A few slaves also escaped through Texas to Mexico and through Florida to the Caribbean.)*

■ *Some abolitionists broke the law by helping slaves to escape.*

POLITICAL SYSTEMS

Critical Thinking

How did the public debates help Lincoln to get nominated as the Republican presidential candidate? (*They got him public attention; he was able to impress people with his speaking ability.*) What are some of the advantages and disadvantages of public debates? *(Sample answer: They bring attention to important issues, but too much attention can be given to the way a person speaks rather than what he or she says.)*

The woman shown below is Lear Green. She escaped slavery by shipping herself to Philadelphia in a sailor's chest. Many other slaves faced the danger of being caught while trying to escape.

■ *How did some abolitionists break the law to help the slaves?*

The raids, the rescues, and the Underground Railroad all convinced the South even more that the North was their enemy. But the raids and the Underground Railroad were not enough to topple slavery. The abolitionist movement alone did not have that much power.

Instead, antislavery forces needed a powerful spokesperson to state their case in the political arena. During the late 1850s just such a leader emerged. He was a country lawyer with just one term in Congress to his credit. His name was Abraham Lincoln. ■

Lincoln Inspires the Republicans

What should have been a routine election took a surprising turn. It was 1858, time for Illinois voters to reelect Democrat Stephen A. Douglas to the U.S. Senate. (Actually, the voters selected a state legislature, which then selected the senator.) Douglas's Republican opponent, Abraham Lincoln, had little political experience compared with Douglas.

Lincoln had an exciting idea. He would challenge the senator to a series of debates. Crowds who came to hear Douglas would also see and hear the less well known Lincoln.

Lincoln's focus in the debates was on slavery in the territories. Douglas, he insisted, did not care if slavery was voted "up" or "down" in the territories. Lincoln, however, voiced strong opposition to the spread of slavery. Throughout Illinois in the summer and fall of 1858, crowds were fascinated by the spirited exchanges between the two chief candidates. Lincoln's speaking abilities particularly impressed the audience.

Lincoln lost the election of 1858. But the Republicans now had a forceful leader who had shown up well against the likely Democratic presidential candidate of 1860.

When the 1860 presidential campaign got under way, the Republicans did indeed nominate Lincoln as their candidate. The Democrats broke into

Visual Learning

Refer students to the pictures on this page and ask them to describe two ways that people tried to escape slavery. *(In a crate, by boat)* Have students speculate on how the woman in the larger picture was caught and what might happen to her next. *(Someone spotted her and told the slaveowner. She might be whipped and sent back to her owner.)*

Writing a News Broadcast

Have students imagine that they are radio reporters who were given advance notice of John Brown's raid on Harpers Ferry. Tell them to research and write an account as if they were eyewitnesses. Have volunteers read their broadcasts aloud to the class.

Making a Poster

Have students write and design a poster for Abraham Lincoln's campaign for the Senate. Encourage them to consider the issues that he raised in his campaign and then brainstorm different ways in which the poster could appeal to the voters. *(Make an emotional appeal, make negative statements about his opponent, give facts)*

South Carolina rebels fired on Fort Sumter near Charleston, South Carolina on April 12, 1861. This action triggered the secession of four states and the start of the Civil War.

two groups. Northern Democrats nominated Stephen A. Douglas. Southern Democrats chose their own candidate, John C. Breckenridge. A third party, the Constitutional Union Party, nominated John Bell.

Lincoln won the four-way race, sweeping the Northern states. Although he won only 39 percent of the popular vote, he gained more than enough electoral votes. Antislavery forces had elected a President, and white Southerners were horrified.

The South Chooses Secession

White Southerners did not want to be part of a nation that could elect Lincoln as its President. They called the new President a "black radical Republican" and a "friend of John Brown." Even before Lincoln took office, South Carolina, Mississippi, Florida, Alabama, Georgia, Louisiana, and Texas had decided to **secede**, or leave the Union. These states even proposed starting their own government, the Confederate government.

War seemed unavoidable. Then, on April 12, 1861, Southern rebel forces fired on a federal outpost, Fort Sumter, in the harbor of Charleston, South Carolina. Immediately, the Southern states of Virginia, Arkansas, Tennessee, and North Carolina seceded and joined the Confederates. The tragic "firebell in the night" imagined by Jefferson had finally rung. The Missouri Compromise had failed. Proslavery and antislavery civilians clashed in the streets and took up arms. Thousands of Northerners and Southerners alike were to die for their beliefs. The Civil War had begun. The states were at war with each other. ■

■ *Abraham Lincoln lost the senatorial race of 1858 in Illinois but won the presidential election in 1860. Who elected him president?*

REVIEW

1. **FOCUS** What events during the 1850s revealed that the conflict between the North and the South would never be resolved peacefully?
2. **CONNECT** How did the political system fail to resolve the slavery issue?
3. **GEOGRAPHY** Look at the map on page 333 of this lesson. List two routes the Underground Railroad used in bringing runaway slaves to freedom.
4. **BELIEF SYSTEMS** What conclusions were a result of the Dred Scott case? How did Northerners react?
5. **CRITICAL THINKING** What event marked the beginning of the Civil War? Why were Southern states so determined to secede?
6. **WRITING ACTIVITY** Imagine you are a Northerner who refuses to obey the Fugitive Slave Act of 1850. Write a diary entry that plans the route of escape you would take from your home if a runaway slave were to approach you for help.

POLITICAL CONTEXT

Critical Thinking

What did the South fear would happen when Lincoln was elected? *(That the North would pass antislavery measures)* As President, what could Lincoln have actually done to pass antislavery measures? *(Sample answer: He might have rallied Northerners to work for change; he could have asked Congress to make new laws.)*

■ *Lincoln was elected by Northern antislavery forces.*

CLOSE

Have students answer the Thinking Focus. Copy on the board the Graphic Overview from page 330 or review with students the lists that they made while reading the lesson.

Answers to Review Questions

1. Events included the Harpers Ferry raid, the Dred Scott decision, the Lecompton Constitution, the Fugitive Slave Law riots, and the election of Lincoln.
2. It failed to come up with a compromise acceptable to both the North and the South.
3. One route followed the Mississippi and Ohio rivers; one moved through the mid-Atlantic states to New England.
4. The Supreme Court ruled that black Americans were not citizens and declared the Missouri Compromise unconstitutional. Many Northerners were shocked by the court's decision.
5. Sample answer: The firing on Fort Sumter marked the beginning of the Civil War. Southern states did not want to be part of a nation with antislavery Lincoln as president. Allow for personal opinion.
6. Remind students to refer to the map on page 333 as they write their entries.

Homework Options

Have students research and write a two-page report on John Brown, Dred Scott, Justice Roger B. Taney, or Harriet Tubman.

Study Guide: page 48.

UNDERSTANDING POINT OF VIEW

This skill lesson will use nineteenth-century writings on slavery to show students how to analyze points of view.

HISTORY

Critical Thinking

Could some facts presented in each selection be "true" even though the authors advocate opposing ideas? *(Yes)* Would an abolitionist ever have made the point that slaves led pleasant lives? Why or why not? *(Sample answer: Probably not, because that would imply that there might be something positive about slavery)* If the statements given in the second quote were sometimes true, what does the quote imply about its author's point of view? *(Sample answer: The author believed that slavery was a good institution.)* How did the authors come to such opposite conclusions? *(Sample answer: They selected facts that supported their own points of view.)*

UNDERSTANDING POINT OF VIEW

Analyzing Viewpoints on Slavery

Here's Why

Learning how to recognize the point of view that shapes a piece of writing helps us to know what influenced the writer to present information in a certain way. That knowledge can then help us to determine the extent to which the piece is based on the writer's emotional response to the subject.

Objective information is based on facts—statements that record an event without inserting personal opinion. Points of view, on the other hand, are subjective. That means that they involve the writer's opinions, attitudes, beliefs, or feelings. Historians are careful to analyze point of view when studying documents from the past. It is important for you, as a student, to recognize bias (personal preference) when you read any historical document.

In this chapter you learned that differences over slavery were so severe that they led to war between the North and South. You read that abolitionists demanded an immediate end to slavery, and that most white Southerners believed slavery to be a good and economically necessary way of life. First-person accounts and artifacts from that time period allow you to expand the knowledge you gained from the chapter. The actual written words of those who supported and those who opposed slavery offer an opportunity to learn how real people felt about the issue.

Suppose you are researching two very different documents that relate to slavery. Identifying and understanding the point of view of each document will help you to decide how the writers reached their conclusions.

Here's How

Read the following passages, and follow the steps to identify and analyze point of view. Be sure to look up any unfamiliar words.

1. **What is the subject?**
   The subject of both passages is slavery.

2. **Who is the writer?**
   The writer of the first passage is Lucretia Mott, a spokesperson for the abolitionist movement. The second passage is taken from an artifact. The author of the second passage is unknown; it appears on the

We have watched the accounts that had been furnished—some in the daily papers and some in letters and communications directly to us, and in personal visits of the cruelty that has been practiced in the South; and those accounts have come to us with the express desire that we should keep on and not resign the organization. They have told that the time has not come, while the slave in so many instances is only nominally and legally free, while in fact the almost unlimited power of his oppressor continues; and that in many parts of our Southland large numbers of families of slaves are still actually held in bondage, and their labor extorted from them by the lash, as formerly; that while, so far as the law is concerned, they may no longer be publicly bought and sold, yet they have been actually sold and transferred from place to place. All these facts show the necessity of our cause, and the continued existence of the Anti-Slavery Society, notwithstanding the legal abolition of the accursed system. All this has kept us on the watch, and has kept our interest alive in the great cause.

Lucretia Mott

Objective

Use antebellum primary sources to determine point of view. (Critical Thinking 1)

Writing a Paragraph

Illustrate the concept of bias in a written selection by asking students to write paragraphs of their own. They should present their point of view on any current issue of interest. Let volunteers read their paragraphs and ask the other students to listen carefully for evidence of bias in the form of unstated assumptions. When the author of the paragraph reads something that shows an unstated assumption, the listeners should raise their hands.

This picture represents the Negro Quarters of a plantation, as taken in 1860. It is a true picture of life on a well organized Plantation in South Carolina. Old and young are assembled after the heads of the families have finished their tasks, to partake of their meals, prepared by those selected for that purpose by their owner, in consequence of their inability to do field work. The task of the industrious and provident slave was often finished by mid-day. After which they were permitted to work for themselves in a garden patch attached to their quarters. Many frequently made considerable sums of money in this way, which the more provident appropriated to the purchase of useful atricles, whilst others squandered theirs on things of no value, either for comfort or luxury.

Anonymous

back of the photograph shown on page 289.

3. **Who is the audience? That is, for whom is the piece written?**
Lucretia Mott was writing for fellow abolitionists. The passage is part of a speech she gave in September 1858 in Yardleyville, Pennsylvania.
The second passage describes a photograph of comfortable slaves on a plantation. It appears to have been written for proslavery white people.

4. **What is the purpose?**
Lucretia Mott's speech was written to convince people to join the fight against slavery. The other passage was written to convince people that slaves had a good life.

5. **What is the writer's attitude, or tone? Is it angry, sympathetic, humorous, or serious?**
Lucretia Mott's speech is urgent. She does not feel that there is any room for more than one opinion on slavery, but declares it is a "sin." She speaks of the "necessity of our cause."
The other writer takes a tone of authority, presenting all of the information in the description as fact. For instance, the phrase, "many frequently made considerable sums of money" is not backed by any examples, but the tone makes it sound like a well-researched fact. This piece also has a critical tone. When the writer says that "others squandered theirs on things of no value, either for comfort or luxury," a criticism of slaves is implied.

Try It

Now read the passage below. It is Abraham Lincoln's response to the demands of the abolitionists.

Use the five questions listed above to analyze the point of view in Lincoln's reply. Compare and contrast his point of view with that of the other two writers. What differences or similarities do you find?

My [foremost] object in this struggle is to save the Union. . . . if I could save the Union without freeing any slave, I would do it; if I could save it by freeing all the slaves, I would do it; and if I could save it by freeing some and leaving others alone, I would also do that.

Abraham Lincoln

Apply It

Locate a first-person account of a contemporary event or issue, such as a political rally, a debate, or a proposed law. Follow the steps outlined above to identify the writer's point of view. Analyze the information, and write a short paragraph outlining the writer's point of view.

HISTORY

Critical Thinking

Why is it important to recognize and analyze viewpoints in historical accounts? *(Sample answer: It can help the reader determine an author's reliability.)* Does Lucretia Mott's membership in an antislavery group necessarily make her statements unreliable? *(Sample answers: No, she may have come to her position by carefully weighing the evidence of slavery. Yes, her advocacy locks her into her point of view.)*

Answers to Try It

1. How to save the union 2. Lincoln 3. Citizens of the United States, in particular abolitionists 4. To persuade people that saving the Union is more important than the issue of slavery 5. Matter-of-fact, very plain-spoken tone

Differences: Lincoln does not appear as emotional as the other writers; he does not seek to persuade as much as to declare his purpose. Similarity: All three display certainty about the correctness of their positions.

Answers to Apply It

Suggest that students choose a source likely to provide a viewpoint, such as a newspaper opinion column or a magazine article. Make sure that students apply the five-step process to determine the author's point of view.

Social Participation

Divide the students into groups of five, and let each group choose a current topic of interest. Have each student tell one thing he or she knows about the topic. The others should then judge whether the statement shows what the speaker's viewpoint is.

Answers to Reviewing Key Terms

A. Sample answers:

1. Northern workers were paid for their work under the free labor system.
2. William Lloyd Garrison and Lucretia Mott were people who actively supported abolitionism.
3. Allowing voters in new territories to decide whether their state should become a free or slave state was the concept behind popular sovereignty.
4. John Brown's raid in Kansas was an example of guerrilla war.
5. Harriet Tubman worked on the Underground Railroad to lead slaves to freedom.

B. Answers:

1. False. Blacks hoped abolitionism would help them gain their freedom.
2. True. Northern workers could look for better employment opportunities when they wanted.
3. False. Popular sovereignty allowed each territory to decide the issue of slavery.
4. False. The Underground Railroad was a secret network that helped guide slaves to freedom in the North.
5. True. Douglass spent his life speaking and writing against slavery.

Answers to Exploring Concepts

A. Answers:

Missouri Compromise—1820
Texas becomes a state—1845
Uncle Tom's Cabin—1852
Kansas-Nebraska Act—1854
Raid on Lawrence, Kansas—1856
Dred Scott decision—1857
John Brown's raid—1859
Lincoln elected—1860

Chapter Review

Reviewing Key Terms

abolitionism (p. 321)
free labor (p. 314)
guerrilla (p. 328)
popular sovereignty (p. 326)
Underground Railroad (p. 333)

A. The sentences below have been started for you. Use the key terms above to complete each sentence correctly.

1. Northern workers were paid . . .
2. William Lloyd Garrison and Lucretia Mott were people who . . .
3. Allowing voters in new territories . . .
4. John Brown's raid in Kansas . . .
5. Harriet Tubman worked . . .

B. Based on what you have read in the chapter, decide whether each of the following statements is accurate. Write an explanation of each decision.

1. Blacks feared that abolitionism would deny them their right to freedom.
2. The free labor economy in the North allowed workers to change jobs whenever they wanted.
3. Those who favored popular sovereignty felt that Congress should decide the issue of slavery for the nation.
4. The Underground Railroad was the first intercontinental railroad.
5. Frederick Douglass spoke out against slavery and was a strong proponent of abolitionism.

Exploring Concepts

A. On a separate sheet of paper, copy the timeline below. Use the events listed below to complete your timeline. Insert each event in the correct time position, and give the date it occurred (two of the events have been entered on the timeline as examples.)

- *Uncle Tom's Cabin* published
- Missouri Compromise
- Raid on Lawrence, Kansas
- Attack on Fort Sumter
- Texas becomes a state
- Kansas-Nebraska Act
- Dred Scott decision
- John Brown's raid on Harpers Ferry
- Lincoln elected president
- Fugitive Slave Act

B. Support each of the following statements with facts and details from the chapter.

1. In the early 1800s, the North and South differed greatly in their economies and their ways of life.
2. The Missouri Compromise settled one dispute, but contained a provision that began another battle.
3. The issue of the Mexican War divided the North and South.
4. The Compromise of 1850 further added to the divisions within the nation.
5. During the 1830s, several events frightened Southerners who supported slavery.
6. Women played a crucial role in the antislavery movement.
7. The Supreme Court's decision in the Dred Scott case was a great victory for slavery.

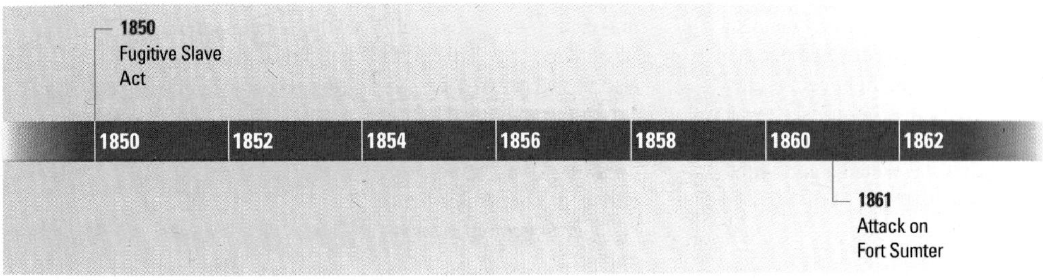

B. Sample answers:

1. The North had factories and growing industrial cities where immigrants worked as free labor. In the South the economy depended on slave labor and plantations.
2. The compromise kept the balance of free states to slave states, but it prohibited slavery west of the Mississippi and north of Missouri's southern border.
3. The North opposed adding new slave territory. Southerners saw the war as a chance to gain new territory.
4. Although the compromise offered the admission of California as a free state, it also included a Fugitive Slave Act and created two new slave territories.
5. David Walker's pamphlet urged slaves to revolt; Nat Turner led a slave rebellion; and William Lloyd Garrison began his abolitionist newspaper and founded the American Antislavery Society.
6. Women organized gatherings to recruit new abolitionist members, and some hid runaway slaves in their homes.
7. The decision prevented blacks from suing for their freedom in federal courts; it declared the Missouri Compromise unconstitutional; and it said that Congress had no power to pass an antislavery law for the territories.

Reviewing Skills

In the South, where slavery still exists, the Negroes are less carefully kept apart; they sometimes share the labors and the recreations of the whites; the whites consent to intermix with them to a certain extent, and although legislation treats them more harshly, the habits of the people are more tolerant and compassionate. In the South the master is not afraid to raise his slave to his own standing, because he knows that he can in a moment reduce him to the dust at pleasure. In the North the white no longer distinctly perceives the barrier that separates him from the degraded race, and he shuns the Negro with the more pertinacity [stubbornness] since he fears lest they should some day be confounded [mixed] together.

Alexis de Tocqueville, *Democracy in America*

1. Read the above passage from *Democracy in America* by Alexis de Tocqueville. Tocqueville was a French politician who was sent by his government in 1831 to study the prison system in the United States. He became so fascinated with the social structure of the United States that he wrote two volumes about it.
2. Look up any unfamiliar terms that you find in the passage. In your own words, explain what Tocqueville is saying in the passage.
3. What difference does Tocqueville point out between the way Northerners and Southerners treat black people?
4. Study the table on page 315 that shows Slave States and Free States after the Missouri Compromise. Use the information provided in that table to create two pie charts. One chart should show the percentages of free and slave states after the Missouri Compromise. The other should show the percentages of original states, states that entered the union between 1791 and 1819, and states that entered after the Missouri Compromise.

Using Critical Thinking

1. At the time of the Missouri Compromise, former President John Quincy Adams said that it would have been wiser to hold a new constitutional convention to outlaw slavery. He said, "This would have produced a new Union of 13 or 14 states, unpolluted with slavery." The slave states would have formed a separate government. How would Adams's plan have changed the history of the United States? What would the United States be like today?
2. William Lloyd Garrison said that even the states that had outlawed slavery were "involved in the guilt of slavery" because they allowed it to exist in the slave states. Do you agree or disagree? Explain your reasons.
3. People who disobeyed the Fugitive Slave Act by helping runaway slaves were breaking the law. They argued that the law was so unjust that they did not have to obey it. Do you think they were right or wrong? Explain your response.

Preparing for Citizenship

1. **WRITING ACTIVITY** William Lloyd Garrison's newspaper, *The Liberator*, was published in order to support abolitionism. Identify a current newspaper or magazine that is pubished in order to support a cause. Read the publication and choose an article on a subject that interests you. Write a letter to the editor in response to the article.
2. **WRITING ACTIVITY** Our system of law is based on precedent. That is, lawyers look at previous court decisions and use them to support their cases. Groups such as the abolitionists have tried to set a precedent by winning a court case, such as the Dred Scott case, in order to change the laws. Interest groups today still support individual legal cases in order to promote their point of view. Identify a current lawsuit in which an individual or group of individuals is trying to make a change through the courts. Write a brief outline of their cause and the case they are taking to court.
3. **COLLABORATIVE LEARNING** Stage a class debate on one of the issues in the Lincoln-Douglas debates, role-playing the two candidates. Then take a class vote to decide which side "won" the debate.

Answers to Reviewing Skills

1. Suggest that students look up more information on Alexis de Tocqueville.
2. Refer students to Understanding Point of View on pages 336–337.
3. Tocqueville notes that although Northerners more actively advocated abolitionism, they treated black people poorly on an everyday basis out of fear. On the other hand, because Southerners knew they had legal power over slaves, they could afford at times to be more compassionate.
4. The first circle graph should show a 50-50 split. The second graph can be divided into 24 sections with the breakdown being 13 original states, nine added between 1791 and 1819, and two after the Missouri Compromise.

Answers to Using Critical Thinking

1. Students should note that the Civil War might not have occurred. On the other hand, the two separate nations might have fought over territory. Today's United States would not be as large, or probably as strong, as it is.
2. Students could agree because the Congressional representatives of the free states voted to allow slavery in some of the territories. However, they were powerless to outlaw slavery in every state without causing war. This question could open up discussion of states' rights versus federal rights.
3. Encourage students to consider modern examples of civil disobedience. Allow for personal opinion.

Answers to Preparing for Citizenship

1. **WRITING ACTIVITY** Ask students to look at newsletters and magazines by consumer groups.
2. **WRITING ACTIVITY** Students may consider environmental or civil rights cases.
3. **COLLABORATIVE LEARNING** Point out that although these were complicated issues, they created strong emotional responses on both sides.

CHAPTER 12

Planning at a Glance

A Nation Divided

	Objectives	Reading Support and Other Resources	Diverse Learning Strategies
Lesson 1 North Versus South *pp. 342–346* 1–2 days	• State the differences between the North and the South that led to civil war. • Explain the concept of secession. • Assess the military strengths and weaknesses of the Union and the Confederacy.	• **Workbook** or **Reading Support:** pp. 165–168 Review p. 39 Extra Support/Transition p. 39 Multi-lang. Sum. pp. 77–78 • **Other Resources:** Geography Kit, Poster 5, Study Guide 50	Access Act. **(SDAIE)** TE p. 343 Social Participation **(Auditory)** TE p. 344 Visual Learning **(Visual)** TE p. 346 Audiotapes of Multi-language Lesson Summaries **(Auditory)**
Lesson 2 The Nation at War *pp. 347–354* 2–3 days	• Compare the Union and Confederate commanders-in-chief. • Explain why the war lasted four years. • Explain the impact of the Emancipation Proclamation. • Evaluate the effects of the battles of Vicksburg and Gettysburg.	• **Workbook** or **Reading Support:** pp. 169–172 Review p. 40 Extra Support/Transition p. 40 Multi-lang. Sum. pp. 79–80 • **Other Resources:** Geography Kit, Study Guide p. 51, Study Print 13	Access Act. **(SDAIE)** TE p. 348 Visual Learning **(Visual)** TE p. 349–350 Homework Options **(GATE)** TE p. 354 Audiotapes of Multi-language Lesson Summaries **(Auditory)**
Lesson 3 War on the Homefront *pp. 355–359* 2–3 days	• Identify the difficulties in maintaining social, economic, and political order during the war. • Name the roles taken by young men in the Civil War. • Show how the war created new roles for women.	• **Workbook** or **Reading Support:** pp. 173–176 Review p. 41 Extra Support/Transition p. 41 Multi-lang. Sum. pp. 81–82 • **Other Resources:** Study Guide p. 52	Access Strat. **(Extra Support)** TE p. 356 Visual Learning **(Visual)** TE p. 358 Health Connection **(Auditory)** TE p. 358 Audiotapes of Multi-language Lesson Summaries **(Auditory)**
Making Decisions: The Shakers and Civil Obedience *pp. 360–361*	• Identify the alternatives in the issues facing Lincoln and the Shakers in a debate on pacifism.	• **Other Resources:** Poster 8	Activities **(Auditory)** TE p. 360
Lesson 4 The Long March to Surrender *pp. 362–367* 2–3 days **Literature** "The Slopes of War" *pp. 370–371*	• Summarize the toll of the Civil War. • Evaluate how new weaponry and the lack of medical advantages contributed to the high death tolls. • Describe the concluding battles and the "total war" that finally forced the South's surrender.	• **Workbook** or **Reading Support:** pp. 177–180 Review p. 42 Extra Support/Transition p. 42 Multi-lang. Sum. pp. 83–84 • **Other Resources:** Study Guide p. 53	Access Act. **(Extra Support)** TE p. 363 Math Connection **(Visual)** TE p. 365 Writing a News Account **(GATE)** TE p. 366 Audiotapes of Multi-language Lesson Summaries **(Auditory)**
Skill: Reporting on the Battle of Antietam *pp. 368–369*	• Use reference materials, notecards, and outlines to create a written report.	• **Other Resources:** Study Guide p. 54	
Chapter Review *pp. 372–373* 1 day		Chapter 12 Test pp. 45-48 *(See facsimiles on TE p. 760.)*	Assessment Multiple-Use Masters pp. 81–88

Reading Support Resources *for Every Lesson*

Reading and Review

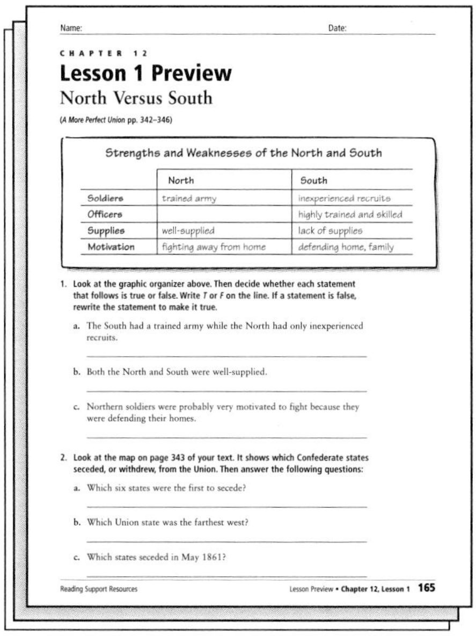
Name: Date:

CHAPTER 12
Lesson 1 Preview
North Versus South
(*A More Perfect Union* pp. 342–346)

Strengths and Weaknesses of the North and South

	North	South
Soldiers	trained army	inexperienced recruits
Officers		highly trained and skilled
Supplies	well-supplied	lack of supplies
Motivation	fighting away from home	defending home, family

1. Look at the graphic organizer above. Then decide whether each statement that follows is true or false. Write *T* or *F* on the line. If a statement is false, rewrite the statement to make it true.
   a. The South had a trained army while the North had only inexperienced recruits.
   b. Both the North and South were well-supplied.
   c. Northern soldiers were probably very motivated to fight because they were defending their homes.
2. Look at the map on page 343 of your text. It shows which Confederate states seceded, or withdrew, from the Union. Then answer the following questions:
   a. Which six states were the first to secede?
   b. Which Union state was the farthest west?
   c. Which states seceded in May 1861?

Reading Support Resources — Lesson Preview • Chapter 12, Lesson 1 165

- **Chapter Overview*** p. 164
- **Lesson Previews*** using graphic organizers from the Teacher's Edition pp. 165, 169, 173, 177
- **Reading Strategies*** pp. 166, 170, 174, 178
- **Lesson Summaries*** pp. 167–168, 171–172, 175–176, 179–180
- **Lesson Reviews** pp. 39, 40, 41, 42

* **Workbook** includes starred items.

Multi-language Summaries

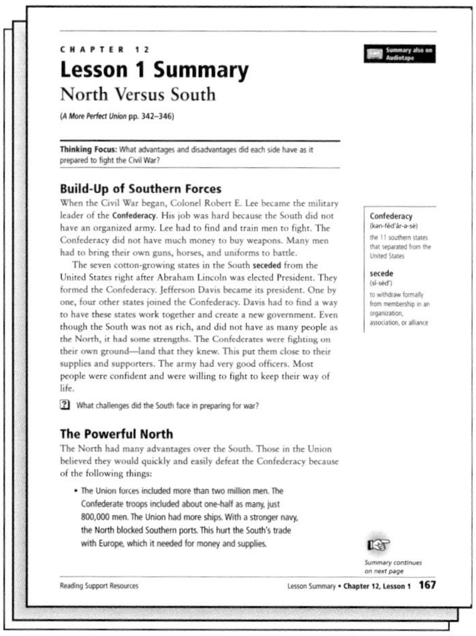
CHAPTER 12
Lesson 1 Summary
North Versus South
(*A More Perfect Union* pp. 342–346)

Summary also on Audiotape

Thinking Focus: What advantages and disadvantages did each side have as it prepared to fight the Civil War?

Build-Up of Southern Forces
When the Civil War began, Colonel Robert E. Lee became the military leader of the **Confederacy**. His job was hard because the South did not have an organized army. Lee had to find and train men to fight. The Confederacy did not have much money to buy weapons. Many men had to bring their own guns, horses, and uniforms to battle.
The seven cotton-growing states in the South **seceded** from the United States right after Abraham Lincoln was elected President. They formed the Confederacy. Jefferson Davis became its president. One by one, four other states joined the Confederacy. Davis had to find a way to have these states work together and create a new government. Even though the South was not as rich, and did not have as many people as the North, it had some strengths. The Confederates were fighting on their own ground—land that they knew. This put them close to their supplies and supporters. The army had very good officers. Most people were confident and were willing to fight to keep their way of life.

What challenges did the South face in preparing for war?

Confederacy (kan-fĕd'ăr-a-sē) the 11 southern states that separated from the United States
secede (sĭ-sēd') to withdraw formally from membership in an organization, association, or alliance

The Powerful North
The North had many advantages over the South. Those in the Union believed they would quickly and easily defeat the Confederacy because of the following things:
- The Union forces included more than two million men. The Confederate troops included about one-half as many, just 800,000 men. The Union had more ships. With a stronger navy, the North blocked Southern ports. This hurt the South's trade with Europe, which it needed for money and supplies.

Summary continues on next page

Reading Support Resources — Lesson Summary • Chapter 12, Lesson 1 167

Lesson Summaries in:

- English (See Reading and Review.)
- Spanish pp. 167–168, 171–172, 175–176, 179–180
- Chinese pp. 77–84
- Hmong pp. 77–84
- Khmer pp. 77–84
- Vietnamese pp. 77–84

Summaries available on audiotapes

Lesson Support / Transition

S D A I E

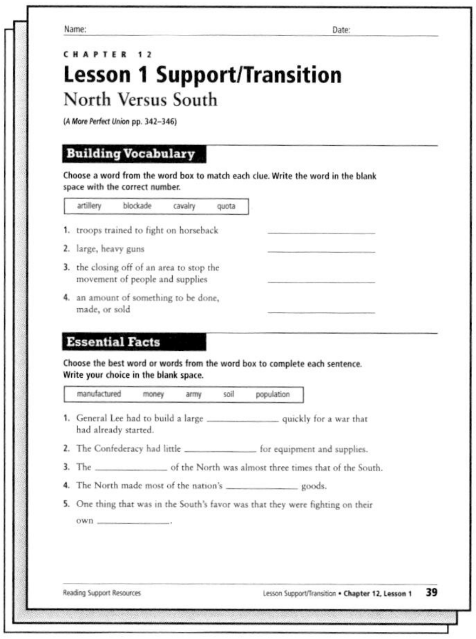
Name: Date:

CHAPTER 12
Lesson 1 Support/Transition
North Versus South
(*A More Perfect Union* pp. 342–346)

Building Vocabulary
Choose a word from the word box to match each clue. Write the word in the blank space with the correct number.

artillery blockade cavalry quota

1. troops trained to fight on horseback
2. large, heavy guns
3. the closing off of an area to stop the movement of people and supplies
4. an amount of something to be done, made, or sold

Essential Facts
Choose the best word or words from the word box to complete each sentence. Write your choice in the blank space.

manufactured money army soil population

1. General Lee had to build a large ________ quickly for a war that had already started.
2. The Confederacy had little ________ for equipment and supplies.
3. The ________ of the North was almost three times that of the South.
4. The North made most of the nation's ________ goods.
5. One thing that was in the South's favor was that they were fighting on their own ________.

Reading Support Resources — Lesson Support/Transition • Chapter 12, Lesson 1 39

Activities for SDAIE
Specially **D**esigned **A**cademic **I**nstruction in **E**nglish

- **Lesson Support/Transition** pp. 39, 40, 41, 42

Technology Options

Internet Support

http://www.eduplace.com

Social Studies Center at Education Place

Internet support for Chapter 12:

- ***Lesson at a Glance***
- ***Civil War Technology***

Videotape/Videodisc

We the People:

Supports and enhances major topics: **Theme:** ***The Civil War***

Software

Student Writing Center® (CD-ROM) (Macintosh® or Windows®)

School to Career

Today, technology and research help medical professionals save thousands of patients every year. Ask a physician or nurse from a local clinic or hospital to come speak to the class. Have students prepare questions about the knowledge and skills needed by today's medical personnel.

Character Education

Despite the grief and hardship of war, the examples of great humanity and generosity during war are many. Divide students into small groups, and ask them to find a current example of an individual or organization involved in humanitarian efforts in a part of the world divided by conflict.

CHAPTER
PREVIEW

Have the students read the chapter title and the narrative below it. Refer them to the photos of the Union and Confederate soldiers. Who else appears in the photos besides the soldiers? (*Members of their families*) Emphasize the terrible political and personal toll this war took on the nation.

Looking Back

Have students recall the causes of the Civil War, such as differences of beliefs on slavery, the election of Lincoln, and the decision of 11 Southern states to secede.

Looking Forward

Tell students they will be reading about the Civil War in the following lessons: North versus South, A Nation at War, War on the Home Front, and The Long March to Surrender.

Chapter 12
A Nation Divided

Lincoln became President. The Southern states left the Union. Soon a bloody conflict ripped the nation apart. Both sides were confident of a quick victory. But just as the slavery issue offered no easy answers, this war yielded no easy victories. The war dragged on for four years, leaving hundreds of thousands dead and a way of life destroyed.

Before the war, either a Northern or a Southern soldier could have worn this U.S. Army hat. Once the war began, only Northerners would wear it.

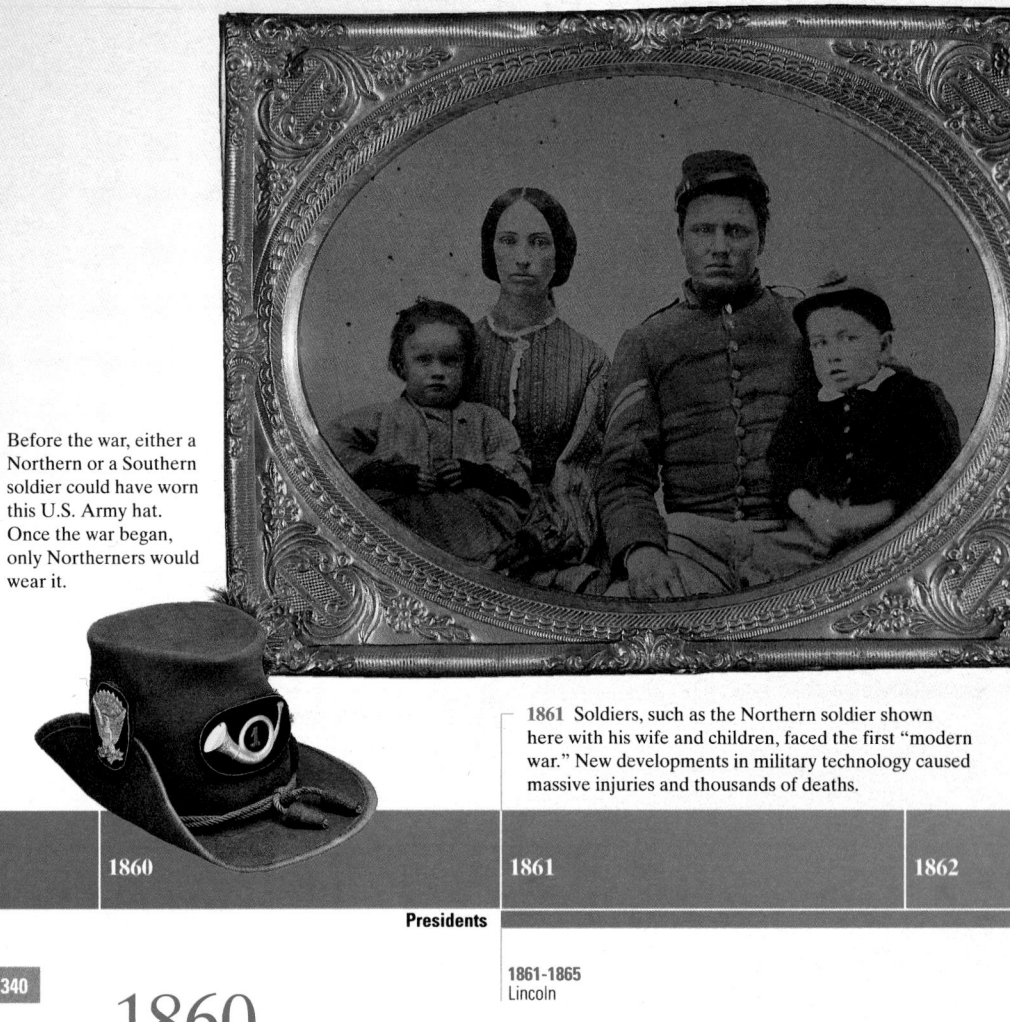

1861 Soldiers, such as the Northern soldier shown here with his wife and children, faced the first "modern war." New developments in military technology caused massive injuries and thousands of deaths.

1860	1861	1862
Presidents	1861-1865 Lincoln	

1860

BACKGROUND

When the Civil War began, both sides were confident of a quick, easy victory. The First Battle of Bull Run made it clear that despite distinct Northern advantages, the war would be a long, grueling series of battles. By the time the war ended, much of the South was destroyed and both sides suffered huge death tolls.

The Confederate Constitution

The Confederate states created a constitution based on the United States Constitution, except that it emphasized states' rights and popular sovereignty. The preamble of the Confederate constitution stated that this document was established by "each State acting in its sovereign and independent character."

The leaders of the seceding states had seen the United States Constitution as a compact, or agreement, that authorized the federal government to act as the states' agent. They believed that since a state had delegated this authority by the ratifying act of a convention, it could also withdraw from the compact and reassert its full sovereignty through another convention. The Confederate states did just that in 1861 by seceding and then preserving the idea of state sovereignty in their own constitution.

Black Americans in the Union Army

After the Emancipation Proclamation, both Northern and Southern blacks were recruited to serve in the Union army. By the end of the war, 180,000 black soldiers and

Confederate soldiers, though fewer in number than Union soldiers, proved to be powerful opponents in a war that would pit brother against brother.

This drum belonged to a young New York state volunteer. Many of the nation's youth joined the war effort.

1863 | 1864 | 1865

1865

Understanding the Visuals

The soldiers pictured in these photos are unidentified. Point out that photography in the United States was developed during the Civil War. In this chapter, and in the chapters following, illustrations will be primarily photographs.

Draw attention to the child's drum. Point out that many young boys participated in the Civil War as drummer boys. Their music inspired the men on the field and provided entertainment at the camp. Sometimes Confederate and Union musicians engaged in musical duels during the battles.

Understanding Chronology

Point out that the last five chapters have covered the same basic time period, 1790–1860. The Civil War, 1861–1865, is considered a major turning point in American history.

sailors had enlisted—ten percent of the Union forces. Black soldiers faced discrimination in pay, in work assignments and combat duty, and in denial of officer commissions. In addition, they were segregated in "colored" regiments led by white directors.

After black soldiers protested pay inequities and appealed to be involved directly in the fighting, eighteen months later Congress passed laws in June 1864 making black soldiers' pay equal to white soldiers' and requiring that the heavy labor of building fortifications be shared equally among black and white soldiers.

Despite many requests, eligible blacks were regularly denied officer commissions during the war. Excluding chaplains, not more than 100 black soldiers were made officers. Army regiments would remain segregated until World War II.

INTRODUCE

Point out the lesson title and have students recall the ways in which the North and the South differed in economy and lifestyle. *(North—industrial, urban; South—agricultural, rural)* Have students recall the meaning of *confederation* (Chapter 3). Help them distinguish the term *confederation* (used for the pre-Constitution government) from the terms *Confederacy* and *Confederates* (used for the Civil War period).

Have students read the Thinking Focus and predict how prepared each side might be for the war. Have them read the lesson to confirm or reject their predictions.

Key Terms

Vocabulary strategies: T36–37

Confederacy—the 11 Southern states that separated from the United States

secede—to withdraw formally from membership in an organization, association, or alliance

1860 1865

LESSON 1

North Versus South

THINKING FOCUS

What advantages and disadvantages did each side have as it prepared to fight the Civil War?

Key Terms

- Confederacy
- secede

The battle cry echoed across the many fields and cities of the North and South: "The Confederates have taken Fort Sumter!" On April 12, 1861, the day of the attack, Col. Robert E. Lee faced a painful choice. Earlier, he had called slavery "a moral and political evil in any society." Lee had to decide whether to defend states' rights and slavery by defending his homeland, the South.

President Lincoln had hoped to use Lee's military skills, and with good reason. Lee had 30 years of experience in the United States Army. He had heroically defended his country in the Mexican-American War, and his friendship with fellow officers went back to his college years at the military academy at West Point, New York. For generations his family had been deeply patriotic.

Yet Lee's Southern loyalties also ran deep. Both his family and his wife's family had lived and prospered in Virginia since the 1600s. From 1791 to 1794, Lee's father governed the state. The thought of a divided nation pained him.

➤ *In the painting* (above right) *General Robert E. Lee is sitting astride his horse, Traveller. Lee considered "duty" the most important word in the English language.*

Which had the greater claim on his loyalty: state or nation? Lee found it difficult to decide the matter. Then on April 19, 1861, he learned that Virginia was planning to leave the Union. That evening, in a letter to his son, he resolved: "I shall return to my native state and share the miseries of my people." Lee took command of the military and naval forces of Virginia. He was to prove an able and much respected military leader.

Build-Up of Southern Forces

Lee faced the difficult task of building a large army from scratch for a war that had already started. Enlisting enough men was the easiest part, because war fever ran high. Lee soon filled his quota of 51,000. Many of the best officers from the United States Army—some of whom had fought in the Mexican-American war—joined the forces of the **Confederacy,** those Southern states that separated from the United States.

Thousands of Confederate recruits lacked experience, however, and had to be trained rapidly. Gathering supplies posed an even greater

Objectives

1. State the differences that led the North and the South to engage in a civil war.
2. Explain and clarify the concept of secession.
3. Assess the strengths and weaknesses of the Union and the Confederacy in waging war.

Graphic Overview

	North	South
Soldiers	trained army	inexperienced recruits
Officers		highly trained and skilled
Supplies	well-supplied	lack of supplies
Motivation	fighting away from home	defending home, family

challenge. Heavy artillery was scarce, and the Confederacy had little money to provide equipment and uniforms. Volunteers furnished their own clothes and brought along their own hunting guns. Most of the cavalry even supplied their own horses. Amazingly, Lee's army was functioning within a month.

The Southern Viewpoint

In the three months that followed the election of President Lincoln in 1860, the seven cotton-growing states of the Deep South decided to **secede,** or withdraw formally, from the Union. These states were South Carolina, Mississippi, Florida, Alabama, Georgia, Louisiana, and Texas.

Jefferson Davis, the President of the new Southern Confederacy, had to establish not only an army but also a government. The fact that Southern states seceded one at a time over a six-month period did not make these tasks easy. The Confederacy had to pull these states together to form a solid government.

The states of Virginia, Arkansas, and North Carolina remained in the Union until after the Confederates captured Fort Sumter in Charleston, South Carolina, on April 14, 1861. Tennessee did not join the Confederacy until June 1861. Many from Tennessee and from the western part of Virginia were pro-Union (they supported the government), and thousands of people from these states fought for the Union.

The states of Maryland, Delaware, Kentucky, and Missouri never seceded, although great numbers of their citizens fought for the South. Family loyalties in the slave states that did not secede were often divided.

Eleven Southern states decided to form their own government and call themselves the Confederate States of America.

Secession of Confederate States, 1861

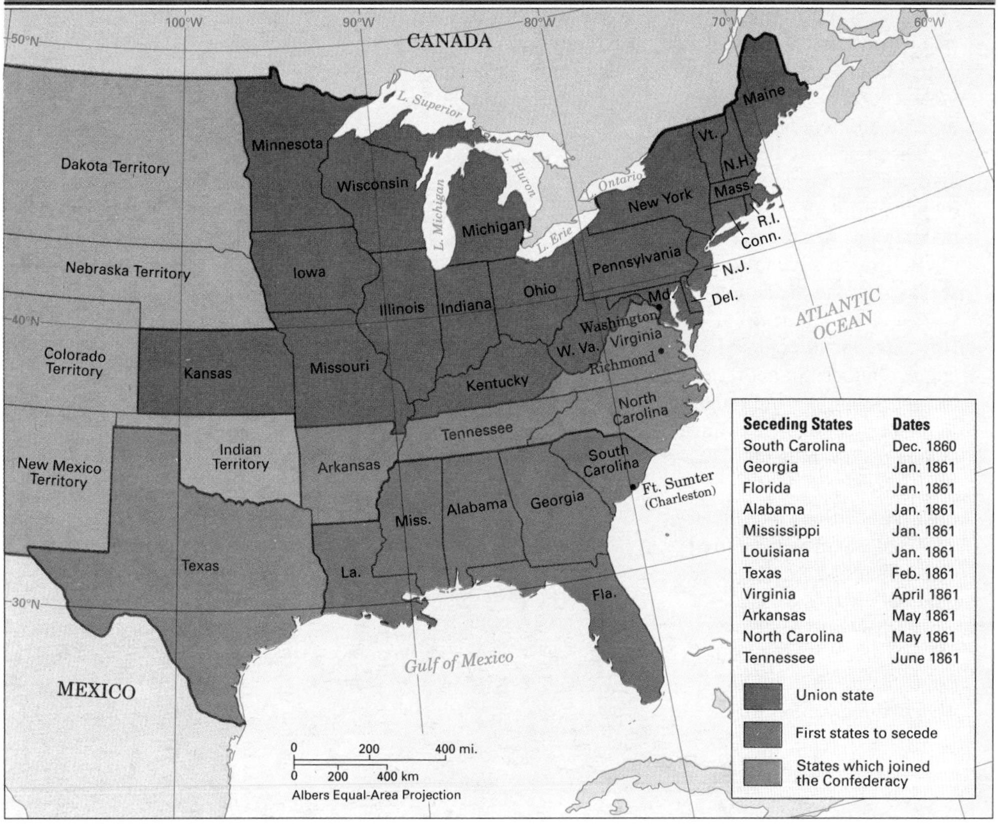

DEVELOP

Point out to students that this lesson portrays the advantages of both the North and the South at the outset of the Civil War. Copy on the board the structure and top and side headings of the Graphic Overview from page 342. Have students copy the chart in their notes and complete it as they read the lesson.

HISTORY

Critical Thinking

What are the implications of secession for the 11 Southern states and their citizens? *(States—form a new country and get ready for war; citizens—cut business and social relations with the North and sometimes within their own families)*

Access Strategy

To build background for the lesson, have students imagine that their state has just declared itself to be a new country, separate from the United States. Would they support their state's decision? Would they move to another state to be part of the United States? What would they gain by staying? *(Remain with family and friends, stay in the same school, live in the same community)* What would they lose by their state's secession? *(Benefits from being part of the United States's economy, strength in military defense)* If the secession led to a war, how would they feel if they had to face some of their friends in battle? Tell students they will read in this lesson about how Southerners faced similar issues as they prepared for the Civil War.

Access Activity

Have students look at the map on this page to find the geographical location of the states that joined the Confederacy after January 1861. *(On the fringes of the South)* How might this location have affected the timing of their secession? *(Probably delayed by more disagreement because of their close geographical ties with the North)*

POLITICAL SYSTEMS

Critical Thinking

The way we label events reflects how we view them. For example, the Civil War might be labelled "the War Between the States" or "the War of Rebellion." A person one side refers to as a "terrorist" may be called a "freedom fighter" by the other side. What are the effects of putting labels on events? *(Sample answer: Labels can keep us from understanding or appreciating the other side's point of view.)*

UNDERSTANDING CIVIL WAR

Alexander Stephens, the Vice President of the Confederacy, called the conflict the "War Between the States." This name emphasized the Southern view that the war was based on states' rights. In U.S. government records, the conflict was called the "War of Rebellion," reflecting the Northern view that the Confederates had no right to secede and were therefore rebels. However, most Americans know the war best as the Civil War.

America has suffered only one civil war, but the term applies to many conflicts in history. The term civil war refers to any war between two organized groups within the same nation seeking power. In this way, a civil war clearly differs from wars that involve violent conflict between two or more different nations.

Distinguishing between a civil war and a revolution is a bit more difficult. In general, a revolution is a particular kind of civil war in which one side seeks to change the nation's system of government. However, not all civil wars are revolutions. Sometimes the opposing sides are fighting for power within the existing system of government.

Civil Wars Throughout History

Civil wars have occurred throughout history whenever a group of citizens organizes a rebellion against the government in power. In China, for example, regional military leaders often battled for the right to establish a new dynasty. In the 1600s, a civil war took place in England. In that war, the common people fought the ruling class of the English court. Eventually, the king was executed and the power shifted to the common people for a brief period.

In the twentieth century, the Spanish Civil War foreshadowed World War II. From 1936 to 1939, Republicans staged a military revolt against the Nationalist government. As sometimes happens in civil war, each side received support from outside their nation. Volunteers from the Soviet Union, Europe, and the United States supported the Republicans, while the Nationalists were aided by Nazi Germany and Italy. Eventually, the Nationalists drove the Republicans from Spain.

Internal Conflicts Today

Fighting within a country still occurs today, but it is not always called a civil war. Many of today's internal conflicts occur among several different groups.

In the former nation of Yugoslavia, several republics, (which are like states) declared their independence in the last decade. These republics are made up of different ethnic groups. In some republics, there has been terrible fighting between the new governments and the ethnic groups that want to stay tied to what's left of Yugoslavia.

Internal conflict has also occurred in Somalia, in Africa, where a group of rebels overthrew the government in 1991. Then several different rebel groups began fighting among themselves for power, which led to food shortages throughout the country.

Sadness of Civil War

All wars are terrible and destructive. However, civil wars are perhaps the saddest of human conflicts because they pit brother against brother. They determine the future of countries and usually bring about dramatic change, no matter who wins or loses. Their resolutions are often unclear and may leave a heritage of hatred. Today, more than 130 years after the U.S. Civil War, the bitterness left by the war has not yet totally disappeared.

344

Social Participation

The Civil War often divided families. Have students write a script and role play a scene in which family members take opposite sides on the issues of slavery, secession, or war.

Historical Context

Although slavery was the primary moral issue separating the North and the South, its existence was not what first caused hundreds of thousands of young men to sign up to fight in the early days of the war. Most white Northerners did not agree with abolitionism and viewed the war as a struggle to preserve the Union. In fact, many Northern Republicans supported a proposed amendment prohibiting the U.S. Government from abolishing slavery in any state that wanted it.

Similarly, most white Southerners, including non-slaveholders, saw the newly formed Confederate States of America as the means of keeping rights they were entitled to under the Constitution, rights they believed were threatened by Republicans who were in control of the national government. Indeed, as J.B.D. DeBow, editor of the prestigious *DeBow's Review* explained, "We are upholding the true doctrines of the Constitution. We are conservative."

The family of President Lincoln's wife, Mary Todd Lincoln, had brothers, sisters, and other relatives who were loyal to the South. In fact, President Lincoln himself was forced to make an official denial that any member of his family was loyal to the South.

The North was a mighty opponent. It had the advantages of a much larger population and greater economic strength. Even so, at the start of the war, Southerners were self-confident. They compared themselves to the small number of colonists in the Revolutionary War who had defeated the vast powers of Great Britain.

Southerners, in fact, did have advantages. First, they were fighting on their own ground. This meant they were familiar with the land and accustomed to the climate. They were also nearer to their sources of supply and could count on local inhabitants for help. And they had a very important reason to fight. They were defending their families, their homes, and their way of life.

White Southerners believed in being prepared to defend themselves. Military schools across the South supported this tradition by training men to be skilled and daring soldiers.

▲ *President Davis and his generals are, from left: P. G. T. Beauregard, Thomas "Stonewall" Jackson, Jefferson Davis, Jeb Stuart, and Joe Johnston. Downhill, to the right of the figures, an encampment is pictured.*

Officers and Gentlemen

The Confederacy had reason to pride itself on its officers. After the war, both Northerners and Southerners could agree that Confederate Generals Robert E. Lee and Thomas "Stonewall" Jackson were among the greatest strategists of all time.

A close-knit corps of officers who had been trained at West Point as well as at military schools in the South provided valuable support. In addition, soldiers shared a friendship and deep pride that helped them to fight, and often to win, against overwhelming odds. ■

■ *What challenges did the South face in preparing for war?*

The Powerful North

Because of the Union's superior size and economic strength, both Northern leaders and the populace were convinced that they could defeat the Confederacy within a few months. They believed that democracy, both at home and abroad, would be threatened unless America was reunified. The North, in fact, appeared to have many real advantages over their opponents.

Strength in Numbers

The population of the 22 Union states was almost three times that of the 11 states of the Confederacy. Furthermore, one-third of the South's population were slaves, who were not allowed to serve in battle. Over the course of the war, these figures translated to some 2 million men who fought for the Union, compared with 800,000 for the Confederacy.

Although the Union army and navy were poorly prepared for war, they were strong compared with the armed troops of the Confederate forces, which at first had no navy. The North also had a larger fleet of ships and more shipyards. A strong Union navy enabled the North to block Southern ports, preventing Confeder-

POLITICAL SYSTEMS

Critical Thinking

Have students name the similarities in the political positions of Lincoln and Lee as they entered the conflict between the North and the South. *(Both opposed slavery, both patriotic)* Differences? *(Lincoln—supported a strong Union; Lee—decided to support his native state)*

■ *Challenges included building an army for a war that had already started, training inexperienced recruits, and gathering supplies despite a shortage of money.*

Language Arts Connection

Explain that the concept of being "an officer and a gentleman" (see the heading on this page) was especially embedded in Southern culture. Today the concept is still part of the training philosophy for all U.S. military officers. Have students write a one-page essay defining this phrase and evaluating the idea that a military officer has an obligation to kill his enemy and at the same time to behave like a gentleman. Is "fair play" possible or even desirable when an officer's life is on the line?

Making a Speech

Have students imagine they are recruiters, convincing young men in the border state of Missouri to join the army. Divide the class into two groups, one recruiting for the Union and the other for the Confederacy. Have the groups make their speeches to each other. Both groups should address the issue of states' rights.

Visual Learning

Point out that the picture on this page is a painting, not a photograph. It is unlikely that the five men actually posed for the painting, so why might the artist have chosen to portray them all in the same picture? *(To portray their unity)* Why did he portray them on horseback? *(Perhaps to show them as men of action)*

HISTORY

Visual Learning

Ask students to use the information in the pie charts on this page to evaluate the advantages of the Union and the Confederacy in war. *(The Union had more miles of railroad track, more manufacturing plants, a larger population, more money, and more firearms manufactured.)*

■ *A strong navy could control river traffic, blocking the delivery of vital supplies to the South.*

CLOSE

Copy on the board the structure and top and side headings of the Graphic Overview from page 342. Encourage students to complete it by referring to the charts they made while reading the lesson. Then have students use the Graphic Overview on the board to answer the Thinking Focus and to evaluate the predictions they made before reading the lesson.

Union and Confederate Resources, 1860

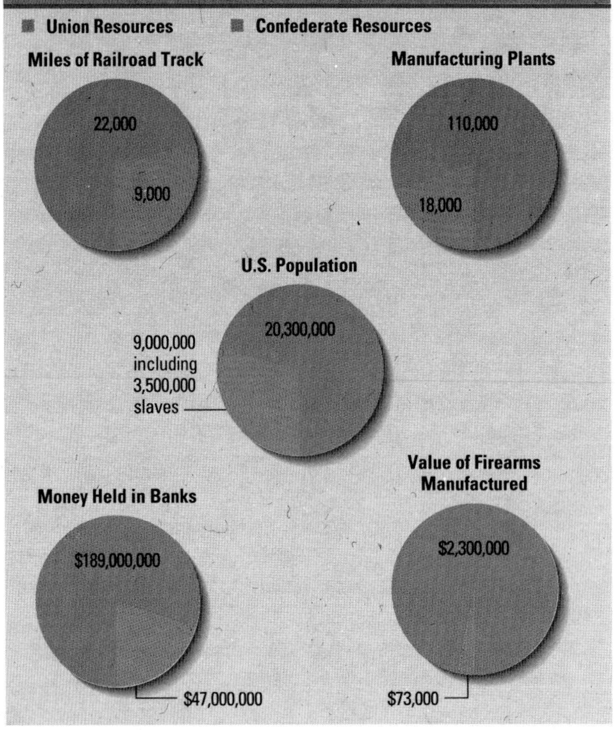

Although the North had more supplies and resources than the South, both sides felt confident about winning the war.

■ *Why was a strong navy so important to the North's military success?*

ate ships from moving goods and trading with Europe.

Upper Hand in Industry

In the 1860s, the North produced most of the nation's manufactured goods, while the South remained mainly agricultural. The South's economy had always depended on the sale of farm products to Europe and the North in exchange for manufactured goods. These markets were cut off as a result of the war, causing the South severe shortages of all kinds.

Control of all rail and water traffic was vital to both sides to move supplies and troops. When the war began, the North had 70 percent of all the railroads. The North's naval strength also enabled it to take charge of much of the Southern river traffic.

The Financial Edge

Prior to the war, the South had also depended on the North's experience in handling money and business matters. During the war, both North and South issued their own paper money to pay expenses. But many people felt that these paper bills were less valuable than silver and gold. The paper dollar in the North was worth only about 50 cents. Toward the end of the war, the Southern dollar had a value of three cents. By the spring of 1864, prices in the South were 46 times higher than pre-war levels. For instance, it took five Confederate dollars to buy a cup of coffee. Many Southerners found it hard to feed their families.

At the beginning of the war, the Confederates hoped for support from Great Britain because it needed Southern cotton for its textile mills. Britain, however, was not prepared to become involved in the war. This denied the Confederacy the help of Britain's powerful navy to break the crippling Northern blockade.

In 1861, a quick and easy victory seemed possible to Northerners. Their optimism proved totally false. Four years of destruction were to pass before the North forced the South to surrender. ■

REVIEW

1. **FOCUS** What advantages and disadvantages did each side have as it prepared to fight the Civil War?
2. **CONNECT** How did the North and South's inability to compromise on slavery lead to the Civil War?
3. **CITIZENSHIP** Why was Robert E. Lee so torn about which side to defend in the war?
4. **CRITICAL THINKING** Secession divided America into two separate governments. Why do you think President Lincoln feared foreign reaction to secession?
5. **ACTIVITY** Create a drawing or political cartoon showing the firing at Fort Sumter as though you witnessed the event. In a caption, describe how this attack brings the nation to war, and summarize the positions of both the North and the South.

Homework Options

Ask students to write a one-page paper on the psychological factors that helped the South.

Study Guide: page 50.

Answers to Review Questions

1. Southern advantages included fighting on their own territory and having a strong reason to fight—to defend their families, homes, and way of life. Northern advantages included a larger population, greater economic strength, and a better-prepared army and navy.
2. Because all attempts at compromise failed, many people saw war as the only way to resolve the conflict.
3. Lee had defended the Union in the war with Mexico and was friendly with many Union officers, but his family had deep loyalties to the South. Although he was opposed to slavery, he also believed in states' rights.
4. Sample answer: He was probably afraid that foreign countries would see democracy in the United States as a failure. Allow for personal opinion.
5. Students should try to portray a clear point of view.

1860 | 1861 | 1863 | 1864 | 1865

L E S S O N 2

The Nation at War

Sunday, July 21, 1861, was a steamy midsummer day in Washington, D.C., but the nation's capital was festive. For more than a week, thousands of Union and Confederate troops had gathered in northern Virginia. Now the greatest battle yet to take place on American soil was about to begin. Politicians, along with hundreds of other Washingtonians, expected that Union troops would crush the rebel forces. They loaded their horse-drawn buggies and headed for the battle site, ready for a picnic and an exciting and brief battle.

The Confederate troops, headed by General P. G. T. Beauregard, awaited the Yankees near Manassas Junction on the river of Bull Run. Both the Confederate and Union troops had employed almost 30,000 troops on the field. Few of these men had battle experience.

The soldiers on both sides had been up since before dawn. By noon, when the main battle began, they were hungry, thirsty, and tired. As the black smoke from cannons thickened and round after round of bullets battered the soldiers, neither side was at an advantage. Confederate troops held their ground, however, and General Thomas J. Jackson earned his nickname, "Stonewall," because his men held the line "like a stone wall."

By 4:30 that afternoon, the inexperienced Union troops retreated, shocked by the fighting ability of their opponent. Union soldiers struggled back toward Washington. Even sightseers ran for their lives. Several, including a congressman, were captured by the Confederates.

However, the Confederates were too exhausted and disorganized to chase the enemy to Washington and capture the Union capital. Some 600 men on each side died or were mortally wounded. Clearly, this war was going to be more of a struggle than either side had anticipated.

THINKING FOCUS

How did ideas about the nature of war change from the First Battle of Bull Run in 1861 to the Battle of Gettysburg of 1863?

Key Terms

- moderate
- emancipation

At the First Battle of Bull Run, soldiers from both sides discovered the grim reality of combat.

INTRODUCE

Have students read the Thinking Focus. Ask them to recall how both sides viewed their chances in the war. *(Both were optimistic about winning.)* Tell students to read the lesson to find out how the views of both the Northerners and the Southerners would change in the next two years.

Key Terms

Vocabulary strategies: T36–37
moderate—an individual opposed to extreme views or measures in politics or religion
emancipation—a condition of being freed from oppression, bondage, or restraint

Graphic Overview

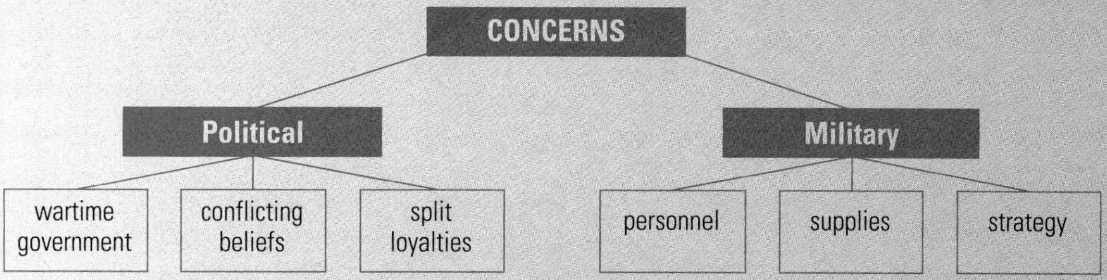

Objectives

1. Compare the two commanders-in-chief—their backgrounds and their challenges.
2. Explain why a war that was supposed to be short-lived lasted four years.
3. Explain the impact of the Emancipation Proclamation.
4. Evaluate the effects of the battles of Vicksburg and Gettysburg on the course of the war.

DEVELOP

Explain that this lesson portrays the course of the Civil War, including the concerns of the Union and Confederate leaders. Copy on the board the structure and main heads of the Graphic Overview on page 347. Have students copy these in their notes and add the concerns as they read.

▲ *In 1861, Presidents Abraham Lincoln* (top) *and Jefferson Davis were challenged to provide strong leadership for their governments.*

▼ *This photograph shows the living quarters of General McClellan at his military camp at Yorktown, Virginia.*

Two Commanders-in-Chief Take Stock

In 1861, as the war began, the leadership of both governments was disorganized, just as their armies were. Confederate President Jefferson Davis faced the enormous challenge of having to quickly build a new Confederate government. President Lincoln had the difficult task of uniting a number of groups within the Union government.

The two Presidents came from very different backgrounds. Lincoln came from a poor frontier family. Davis grew up on his father's large Mississippi cotton plantation and became a successful planter himself. Lincoln was largely self-educated and began his career as a country lawyer. Davis graduated from West Point and had a distinguished military career. However, while their backgrounds and points of view were totally opposed, they shared a position as **moderates,** people who disapproved of extreme political views within their own political parties.

Davis's Challenge

Davis was elected President of the Confederacy as a compromise candidate. As a moderate, he had always supported the idea of states' rights. Now he also had to form a strong, united government if the Confederacy was going to survive the war. This meant gathering troops, forming battle plans, and raising taxes to run the war. Opponents of Davis said that he was limiting states' rights rather than saving and strengthening the ideas for which the South was fighting.

Davis's cold manner caused resentment in his Confederate Congress and led many people to resign. His strongest critics accused Davis of taking part in military business without really knowing much about the battlefield.

Lincoln's Task

Lincoln also had troubles in running the war, especially in the early years. Both political and military problems demanded the Union President's attentions.

Following the First Battle of Bull Run, Lincoln replaced General Irwin McDowell, whom Lincoln believed was too cautious, with General George B. McClellan, who had cleared western Virginia of Confederate troops. The following year, howev-

Access Activity

Point out to students that brothers, fathers, and sons fought on opposite sides during the Civil War. Ask students to imagine facing a family member in battle. To whom would they be loyal? Their family? Their government? How would they feel betraying either?

Access Strategy

Ask students to think of examples of an individual, team, or group that engaged in a struggle or contest and succeeded despite certain disadvantages. *(For example, someone in a wheelchair who completed a marathon, or a sports team that beat the current champion)* Why do some people make a great effort to win against all odds? *(To achieve an important goal; to prove to themselves or others that they can do it)* Is the "will to win" always enough? *(No, disadvantages often lead to losing.)* Tell students that in this lesson they will read about how the Confederacy, despite a tremendous will to win, faltered when it faced the Union forces.

er, Lincoln removed General McClellan for his lack of forcefulness. Although an excellent organizer, McClellan, who was known as the "Little Napoleon" of the Civil War, was often slow—too slow at times—in making decisions.

Not until early 1864, when Lincoln put Ulysses S. Grant in charge of all Union forces, did the President feel he had found a bold and competent military leader. Grant's fighting ability pushed him to the rank of lieutenant general—a rank which, in the past, was held only by President George Washington. His bold and daring leadership also earned him the name "Unconditional Surrender" Grant.

Political problems also troubled the Union President. Early in his administration, Lincoln said that the war was a fight to save the nation rather than to end slavery. This idea angered the abolitionists, people working to end slavery in the United States.

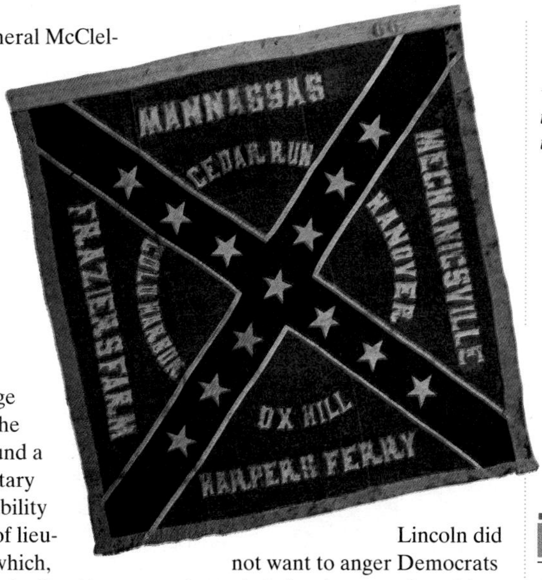

◄ *The Confederate troops carried flags like this one into battle.*

Lincoln did not want to anger Democrats and people in border states by taking a total stand against slavery. At the same time, Lincoln supported Congress in freeing the District of Columbia slaves, which angered proslavery groups. With great caution, and after weighing proslavery and abolitionist arguments, Lincoln gained antislavery support by saying slavery was morally wrong. He made this bold move at a time when most of the nation still did not want to free the slaves. ■

Across Time & Space

What issues should be regulated, or controlled by the federal government? Today, issues such as gun control and the death penalty are covered by state-based legislation.

■ *What were the similarities and differences between President Lincoln and President Davis?*

HISTORY

Critical Thinking

Remind students that Lincoln and Davis held moderate beliefs. What problems did both men face in making their views prevail during a time of crisis? *(Both the North and the South were polarized; extreme views were popular.)*

■ *Lincoln was from a poor frontier family, was self-educated, and had been a country lawyer. In contrast, Davis was from a successful plantation family, had graduated from West Point, and had a distinguished military career. Both men were moderates.*

Historical Context

The Quartermaster Bureau of the Union Army supplied its soldiers with almost everything they needed except weapons and food. It supplied uniforms, shoes, knapsacks, canteens, mess gear, blankets, tents, barracks, horses, mules, horseshoes, and portable blacksmith shops. Since most of the war was fought in the South, the Northern army had to maintain long supply lines of wagon trains, railroads, and port facilities. A campaigning army of 100,000 men needed 2,500 supply wagons and at least 34,000 animals. It needed some 600 tons of supplies every day. Union Quartermaster General Montgomery Meigs substituted portable tents known as "dog tents" (now called pup tents) for the heavy tents that had been used in the past. His bureau also furnished clothing manufacturers with standard measurements for uniforms, introducing the concept of size, which was applied to men's clothing after the war.

Visual Learning

Have students study the photographs on the bottom of page 348 and this page. Why might the photographer have chosen to place this series of photographs side by side? *(Perhaps to create a single picture that portrays the vastness of military forces, to make the viewer feel overwhelmed)*

HISTORY

Visual Learning

Have students use the map on this page to trace the direction of the battle lines in the North and in the South: In which direction is the battle line moving on the east coast? *(north)* Which side is advancing? *(the Confederacy)* In which direction is the battle line moving in the west? *(south)* Which side is advancing? *(the Union)*

Major Battles of the Civil War

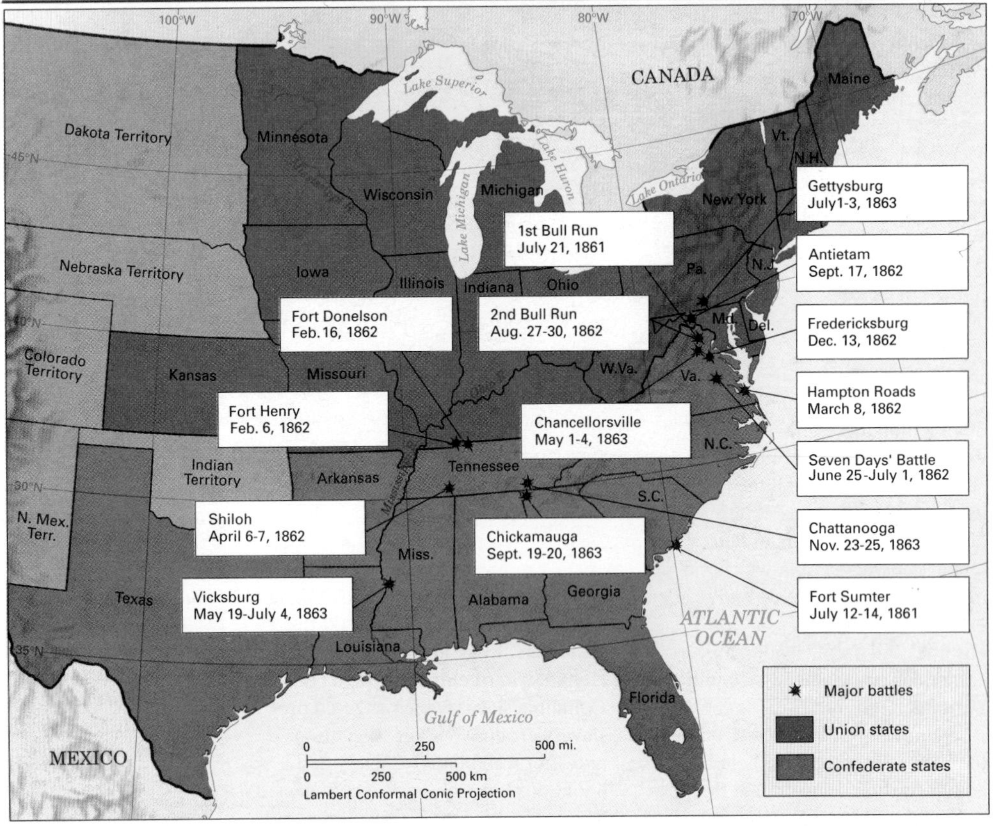

Major Battles of the Civil War

Battle	Significance	Battle	Significance
Fort Sumter July 12–14, 1861	Opening shots fired. Civil War declared.	**Second Bull Run** August 27–30, 1862	Grant's army forced to retreat to Washington.
First Bull Run July 21, 1861	First Civil War battle; Confederates prove their strength.	**Antietam** September 17, 1862	Bloodiest one-day battle of the Civil War: combined casualties of 23,000.
Fort Henry February 6, 1862	Grant's new ironclad gunboats batter and flood the fort.	**Fredericksburg** December 13, 1862	Confederate gunfire forces Union troops to retreat from attempts to cross river.
Fort Donelson February 16, 1862	Union victory. Grant demands "immediate and unconditional surrender."	**Chancellorsville** May 1–4, 1863	"Stonewall" Jackson wages successful offensive, but later dies from wounds.
Hampton Roads March 8, 1862	First major U.S. naval encounter: the North's *Monitor* fought the South's *Merrimac*.	**Vicksburg** May 19–July 4, 1863	Union victory. Opens Mississippi R. supply route to Union.
		Gettysburg July 1–3, 1863	Union victory. "Pickett's Charge" exposes Confederate troops to heavy fire.
Battle of Shiloh April 6–7, 1862	Union victory. Heavy combined casualties; 23,000 soldiers killed.	**Chickamauga** September 19–20, 1863	Confederate victory. Union army retreats to Chattanooga.
Seven Days' Battle June 25–July 1, 1862	Confederates launch seven-day offensive; suffer heavy casualties, but save Richmond.	**Chattanooga** November 23–25, 1863	Union reinforcements arrive by railroad and are victorious.

Map and Globe Skills

Refer students to the map on this page. Which Southern states suffered the most battles? *(Virginia, Tennessee)* Which had no major battles within its borders? *(Florida, Alabama, Louisiana, North Carolina, and Arkansas)*

Historical Context

Clara Barton, who later founded the American Red Cross, served as a volunteer nurse during the Civil War (Lesson 4). After a bloody battle she wrote, "The men were brot down from the field and laid on the ground beside the train and so back up the hill 'till they covered acres . . . . By midnight there must have been three thousand helpless men lying in the [beds of] hay . . . . All night we made compresses and slings—and bound up and wet wounds, when we could get water, fed what we could, travelled miles in that dark over these poor helpless wretches, in terror lest some one's candle fall into the hay and consume them all."

War Rages On

By the fall of 1862, the war had been raging for over a year, with no end in sight. On September 17, 1862, at Antietam Creek in Maryland, one of the bloodiest battles of the war took place. In a single day of fighting, the combined death counts of Confederate and Union men numbered over 20,000. This number exceeds the deaths from the War of 1812, the Mexican War, and the Spanish-American War combined.

Although Lincoln claimed Antietam as a victory for the North, in truth, neither side was victorious. The day after the slaughter, the Union forces under McClellan did not attack, and the Confederate troops, hungry and tired, retreated to Virginia.

Both sides suffered much loss of life, property, and of family unity. For example, Franklin Buchanan, commander of the Confederate ship *Merrimac*, sank the Union ship *Congress* on March 8, 1862. Later he learned that his brother, McKean, had drowned on the *Congress*. Mary Vaughan, a Missouri woman, became a prisoner of the Union government, who accused her of being a Confederate sympathizer. Speaking in her own defense, she said: "Except for my own sons and son-in-law, whom I willingly fed, I never willingly furnished the rebels anything. . . . I have tried hard to act as a loyal woman."

All People Fight

No group of Americans was able to escape the war. Thousands of American Indians fought, for both the North and the South. General Ely Samuel Parker, also known as Hasanoanda, was a Seneca chief who served as General Grant's military secretary. In the West, many Cherokee fought for the Confederacy. General Stand Watie, a Cherokee chief, did not lay down his arms until a month after the Confederates surrendered.

Mexican Americans also fought in the war. Santos Benavides, a member of the 33rd Texas Cavalry, recruited Mexican Americans to fight for the South, and protected the important cotton trade with Mexico. He was promoted to colonel, the highest rank of any Mexican American in the war. ■

▲ *General Ely Samuel Parker, a Seneca, was an aide to General Grant. At Appomattox, Grant was too nervous to write clearly, so Parker wrote the final copy of the surrender agreement.*

■ *Evaluate how the battle at Antietam helped to convince citizens that the nature of the Civil War would be neither glorious nor short-lived.*

◄ *Santos Benavides (shown on the right) was a member of the 33rd Texas Cavalry who recruited Mexican Americans to fight for the South.*

More on the American Indian Involvement During the Civil War

Before the Civil War, the Indian tribes of Oklahoma developed their own governments and achieved a high level of economic prosperity. When the Civil War began, some tribes fought for the North, but more sided with the South. A number of tribal members owned slaves and sided with the Confederacy. Other tribes, such as the Muscogee Creek, Seminole, and Cherokee, although politically divided, made treaties with the South and fought on the side of the South. After the war, Indian nations were forced to cede western portions of their territory, abolish slavery, and grant railroad rights of way.

■ *The large death count, over 20,000, showed that neither side would find an easy victory.*

Reader's Theater

Ask students to create a reader's theater using excerpts of N.A. Perez's historical novel *The Slopes of War* (see the Social Studies Bookshelf, page 311). Students should string together selections that represent the perspectives of Union soldier Buck Summerhill, his sister in Gettysburg, and their Southern cousin, Curtis Walker.

Critical Thinking

Have a student read aloud the quotation of Mary Vaughan on this page. Does she seem to be honest? Did the Union government rightfully imprison her? To whom has she tried to be "a loyal woman"? *(The Union government)* In what way are her loyalties divided? *(Between the Union government and her Confederate sons and son-in-law)*

POLITICAL CONTEXT

Critical Thinking

Ask students which slaves were affected by the Emancipation Proclamation. *(Slaves in the Confederacy, not those in the Union or in Union-controlled areas in the Confederacy)* What impact did it have on Southern economy? *(Slaves left plantations, depriving planters of a labor force.)*

■ *It strengthened the North by supplying Union forces with a new source of troops.*

The President Proclaims an End to Slavery

Following the bloodshed at Antietam, Lincoln needed to broaden the reasons for remaining at war. He was still very serious about saving the Union, but now he took a firm stand on slavery as well. Linking the Union with the abolition of slavery in the South would strengthen his support in the North by pointing out the need to protect the country and to make it a country where freedom held great value. On September 22, 1862, he issued his first **Emancipation** (the act of freeing) Proclamation.

➤ *A young black man is shown as a slave* (left) *and in his Union uniform* (right) *after the Emancipation Proclamation.*

The Emancipation Proclamation would free "all slaves in areas still in rebellion." It was a statement of intent instead of a law, and slaveholders refused to accept it. But the Proclamation caused many people to realize that, along with moral reasons, other good reasons existed for freeing the four million slaves in the Confederacy. Emancipation would take away the South's major source of labor and give Union forces a new source of troops.

The proclamation did not affect slaveholders in the Union nor in parts of the Confederacy in Union hands. However, it would become effective in the regions that remained rebellious on January 1, 1863. When the Confederacy failed to agree, Lincoln signed a second Proclamation on New Year's Day. Many blacks took advantage of the proclamation and other Union antislavery policies to go to Union lines and freedom.

Blacks Can Enlist

The proclamation allowed former slaves to join the armed troops and opened the way for Northern free blacks to join the army. The army was already unofficially using both Northern blacks and escaped slaves to do low-paying jobs, and sometimes to fight. Large numbers of free blacks signed up, both because they wanted to support their country and because they needed work. At first they were paid less than white soldiers, but after they protested this discrimination, the pay was made equal.

During the war, 186,000 blacks served in the Union army and 29,000 in the Union navy. Sixteen blacks earned the Congressional Medal of Honor, the nation's highest military award. Overall, black military service created great pride among black citizens. Many Northern whites felt a debt of thanks to blacks as well. ■

■ *With the enactment of the Emancipation Proclamation, blacks could enlist in the military. How did this new policy influence the North's military strength?*

Critical Thinking

The Emancipation Proclamation is often seen as Lincoln's moral command to free slaves. Have students explain why the Emancipation was as much a political action as a moral one. Why did Lincoln free only the slaves in the seceded states and not those in Union hands? *(Could then justify the action as a way to weaken the South)*

Oral Report

Proportionately, the Civil War took the highest death toll of any American war—one of every 50 Americans died. Today almost every town in what was then the North and the South has a monument to its Civil War dead. If your community has such a memorial, ask students to visit it and give an oral report to the class on its location, design, and commemorative plaque. Alternatively, ask students to research and present an oral report on the current status of different Civil War battlefields, such as Gettysburg or Antietam. Have they been made into parks? Tourist attractions? What artifacts survive?

The Hinge of Fate

In the summer of 1863, the South began to back off before the powerful and persistent Union troops. Until then, the Confederacy had held its own despite limited resources. In 1861 and 1862, the two sides had each won and lost major battles, and, in many instances, there was no clear winner.

Basic military plans used by the South and the North differed widely. The South's plan called for its troops to protect its home soil and fight until the North gave up the idea of winning and accepted secession.

Union plans focused on blocking all major waterways used by the South and capturing Richmond, Virginia, the Confederate capital. In April 1862, Grant's Union troops began a bold campaign at Shiloh, Tennessee, in which the South lost its last chance for an important victory in the West. In July, Lee held back Union troops attempting to capture Richmond. In September, Lee's march into Maryland was stopped at Antietam.

Then in December 1862, the Confederates won a victory against General Joseph Hooker and his men at Fredericksburg, Virginia, and again in May 1863 at Chancellorsville, Virginia. At the battle of Chancellorsville General Thomas "Stonewall" Jackson was accidentally shot and killed by one of his own men.

Meanwhile, in April 1862 on the western front, Union Admiral David Farragut captured New Orleans and continued up the Mississippi River, taking Baton Rouge, Louisiana, and Natchez, Mississippi. He was not, however, able to take Vicksburg, Mississippi. In June, the navy succeeded in capturing Memphis, Tennessee. Only Vicksburg prevented the Union from controlling the entire river.

The Battle of Vicksburg

Union attempts to overtake Vicksburg by land at the end of 1862 also failed. Situated on high bluffs above the river, the city was seemingly impossible to capture. In the spring of 1863, Union General Grant surrounded the city by land, while his navy attacked it from the river.

Beginning May 22, Grant bombarded Vicksburg day and night for six weeks. The townspeople lived in quickly dug caves and many had to eat rats to survive. Vicksburg surrendered

▲ *This doll was used to smuggle medicine across state borders.*

▼ *The seventeen battle-scarred acres that became Cemetery Hill today have a peaceful air, as in this contemporary photograph.*

HISTORY

Critical Thinking

Have students explain why, against all expectations, the war dragged on for so long. *(Although the South had fewer soldiers and economic resources, it had talented commanders and a will to win because its soldiers were defending their homes.)*

HISTORY

Critical Thinking

Have students recall the 1815 Battle of New Orleans, between American and British forces (Chapter 5). Ask students to compare previous British strategy with the Union assault on the Mississippi River during the Civil War. *(British wanted access to the Mississippi River; the Union saw the importance of controlling the river.)*

Research

Students can research and write a one-page report on the *Merrimac*, the ironclad Confederate ship used to attack a Northern blockade of wooden ships. Some students may wish to focus on the technology of the time that made possible the production of an ironclad ship.

Writing a Diary Entry

Ask students to write diary entries by people on opposing sides at the Battle of Vicksburg. One entry will be from the perspective of a soldier in a Union artillery unit outside the city. The other entry will be from the viewpoint of a woman in Vicksburg who is experiencing terror and hunger during the bombardment. Have students read their entries aloud to the class.

Map and Globe Skills

Refer students to the map on page 350 and the political map of the United States in the Atlas on pages 698–699 to trace the path of the Mississippi River. How did the surrender of Vicksburg affect the course of the war? *(The Union could then control the entire river and block Southern trade and supplies.)*

HISTORY

Critical Thinking

Evaluate what might have happened had the Union lost the battles of Vicksburg and Gettysburg. *(The Union would have been unable to blockade trade along the Mississippi River if Vicksburg had not surrendered. Confederate forces could have advanced into the North if they had won the battle of Gettysburg.)*

■ *These two battles determined the Union's ultimate victory.*

CLOSE

After they read the lesson, students should answer the Thinking Focus. Copy on the board the structure and main heads of the Graphic Overview from page 347. Have students complete it together, using the notes they made while reading the lesson. As a reteaching activity, trace the ups and downs of the war by referring to the charts on page 350 in the lesson and page 671 in the Minipedia.

➤ *A Confederate sharpshooter is killed while defending his post.*

on July 4, 1863. This major victory for the Union enabled Union troops to blockade crucial Southern trade along the Mississippi River.

The Battle of Gettysburg

On the same day that the Union won a victory at Vicksburg in the west, it won another great battle in the east. In July 1863, General Lee invaded the North for the second time, crossing the Potomac River and ranging into Pennsylvania. On July 1, his army met the Union army under General George Meade at the town of Gettysburg. Lee succeeded in driving Meade back from the town. Unfortunately for Lee, Union forces took up a strong position along a high ridge of land. For three days, Lee's men, time after time, charged up from the valley toward the Union lines above them, and were forced back. At the end of the third day, 23,000 Union men lay dead or wounded. The Confederates suffered 25,000 casualties.

On July 4 in a rainstorm, Lee's men faced the fire of Union forces and the shattered Confederate army stumbled back across the Potomac.

The number of dead resulting from the bloody Gettysburg battle reached 7,000 more than had died in the Revolutionary War and the War of 1812 combined. The Union was slowly headed for victory. (For a view of the battle of Gettysburg, read the literature selection on page 370.) ■

■ *Why were the battles at Vicksburg and Gettysburg referred to as "the Hinge of Fate"?*

REVIEW

1. **FOCUS** How did ideas about the nature of the war change from the First Battle of Bull Run in 1861 to the Battle at Gettysburg in 1863?
2. **CONNECT** Why did Southerners see their role in the Civil War as similar to that of the colonists in the Revolutionary War?
3. **CIVIC VALUES, RIGHTS, AND RESPONSIBILITIES** What difficulties did Presidents Lincoln and Davis face as leaders during the Civil War?
4. **CRITICAL THINKING** What might have been President Lincoln's reason(s) for allowing Union slaveholders to keep their slaves under the terms of the Emancipation Proclamation?
5. **WRITING ACTIVITY** Imagine two people in the same family who support opposite sides in the Civil War. Write a letter from the point of view of each person, in which that person explains his/her opinions and feelings about the war to the other.

Homework Options

Have students select one military or political action taken by Lincoln or Davis with which they disagree. Ask them to write a one-page essay explaining what they would have done and why.

Study Guide: page 51.

Answers to Review Questions

1. Originally believing the war would be a short, glorious battle, people began to see that it was to be a long, demanding series of battles in which both sides would lose many lives.
2. Southerners, like the colonists, were a relatively small group attempting to defeat a stronger power.
3. Davis's challenges included organizing a strong, united government while still preserving states' rights. Lincoln's difficulties included finding a good general and getting support from both abolitionist and pro-slavery groups.
4. Sample answer: He probably did not want to lose the support of Union slaveholders. Allow for personal opinion.
5. The second letter should respond to specific points in the first letter.

LESSON 3

War on the Homefront

Following the Battle of Gettysburg, a group of Pennsylvanians made a cemetery out of part of the battleground to honor both Union and Confederate soldiers who died there. On November 19, 1863, a ceremony was held to dedicate the cemetery. Edward Everett, a prominent scholar and politician, made a two-hour speech.

Then President Lincoln rose and gave the Gettysburg Address. He spoke for just two minutes, but that speech, printed below, is still thought to be one of the greatest speeches in American history.

In defending the Civil War, President Lincoln urged Americans to "make common cause to save the good old ship of the Union."

THINKING FOCUS

What major changes took place in American society as a result of the Civil War?

Key Terms

- civil rights
- draft

Fourscore and seven years ago our fathers brought forth upon this continent a new nation, conceived in liberty, and dedicated to the proposition that all men are created equal.

Now we are engaged in a great civil war, testing whether that nation, or any nation so conceived and so dedicated, can long endure. We are met on a great battlefield of that war. We have come to dedicate a portion of that field as a final resting place for those who here gave their lives that that nation might live. It is altogether fitting and proper that we should do this.

But in a larger sense we cannot dedicate, we cannot consecrate, we cannot hallow this ground. The brave men, living and dead, who struggled here, have consecrated it, far above our poor power to add or detract. The world will little note, nor long remember what we say here; but it can never forget what they did here. It is for us, the living, rather to be dedicated here to the unfinished work which they who fought here have thus far so nobly advanced. It is rather for us to be here dedicated to the great task remaining before us, that from these honored dead we take increased devotion to that cause for which they gave the last full measure of devotion; that we here highly resolve that these dead shall not have died in vain; that this nation, under God, shall have a new birth of freedom, and the government of the people, by the people, and for the people shall not perish from the earth.

–The Gettysburg Address, delivered by Abraham Lincoln, November 19, 1863

INTRODUCE

Students should read the lesson title and Thinking Focus. Basing their predictions on what they read in Lessons 1 and 2, have students name the ways the Civil War might change daily life in American society. Tell them to read the lesson to confirm or reject their predictions.

Key Terms

Vocabulary strategies: T36–37

civil rights—rights belonging to a person because of his or her status as a citizen or as a member of society

draft—a call to military service

Graphic Overview

Cause	→		→	Effects
lengthy war		**New Taxes** **Civil Rights Restricted** **Food Shortages** **Draft**		• riots • guerilla bands • desertion by soldiers

Objectives

1. Identify the difficulties of the nation in maintaining social, economic, and political order during the Civil War.
2. Name the roles taken by young men in the Civil War.
3. Show how the war created new social and economic roles for women.

DEVELOP

Point out to students that this lesson portrays how the war affected American society. Tell them to list, as they read the lesson, the key developments and effects of the lengthy war on daily life.

POLITICAL SYSTEMS

Critical Thinking

Ask students to explain why it is more difficult to maintain law and order in times of upheaval (during natural catastrophes, such as hurricanes or earthquakes, or during a war) than in times of peace. *(Lack of food, housing, and jobs causes people to act in desperation. When their civil rights are restricted, people resist.)*

Crisis of Wartime Leadership

Lincoln's stirring speech at Gettysburg called for "a new birth of freedom." That was easier said than done. True, some slaves had been freed, but their freedom was still very limited because of racial prejudice. In addition, the **civil rights** of Union citizens had been greatly restricted by Lincoln and Congress in their push to win the war. Civil rights are the rights and freedoms (including freedom of speech, of the press, and of religion) of people as citizens. Freedom of the people of the Confederacy had also been limited by the need to keep economic and social order in a time of war.

These bills are an example of the variety of privately-issued paper money in use in the early war years. In 1863, the National Bank Act made Confederate money worthless.

War Taxes Create Dissent

Federal spending rose to new heights during the war. The government imposed heavy taxes, which Union citizens deeply disliked. People paid these taxes every time they bought, sold, or distributed goods. In addition, Congress started an income tax to help raise money. It was small compared to today's taxes: 3 percent on income over $800. But this figure rose to 10 percent on incomes over $10,000 by the end of the war.

Confederate citizens paid even heavier taxes. In addition to creating income and sales taxes, the government took a percentage of all food crops. When these supplies rotted in warehouses because of the lack of transportation, hungry citizens and angry farmers became upset.

Civil Liberties Threatened

In wartime, governments often restrict civil rights. They did so during the Civil War. In April 1861, Lincoln first suspended the writ of habeas corpus—a law that protected people from being arrested and held without a trial—in certain parts of the Union. By September 1862, the suspension applied to the whole nation. Lincoln said that the Constitution gave him the power to take any steps he needed for the nation during wartime. Under Lincoln's order, the Union military could arrest "all Rebels and Insurgents, their aiders and abettors within the United States." They could also arrest "all persons discouraging volunteer enlistments, resisting the militia **draft** [a call to military service], or guilty of any disloyal practice." This especially affected newspapers and politicians who disliked the draft and Southern sympathizers in the border states.

In 1863, soldiers arrested Clement L. Vallandigham, a popular congressman from Ohio, for his antigovernment positions as leader of the Peace Democrats. (Opponents, who did not trust the Peace Democrats, called them "Copperheads" after the poisonous snake.) However, government law was not always enforced. Vallandigham's supporters raised an outcry over his arrest, and he was merely released to the Confederacy.

Southerners Accused as Spies

Thousands of civilian men and women in the South faced arrest for suspected spying or for aiding the enemy. Once arrested, they could be sent to jail, without ever being officially charged. Feeding or caring for guerrillas—bands of civilians who fought against the Union—carried the risk of being arrested as a spy.

Guerrilla bands controlled whole areas in the South and sometimes destroyed enemy communications and supply lines. For the most part, however, they were considered outlaws. They often attacked citizens who were not directly involved in the war. Deserters often joined these bands.

Access Activity

Read aloud the Gettysburg Address on page 355. Have students name the phrases they find most effective, explaining what each one means and why they like it. Have them discuss what qualities of the speech made it such a classic. *(Emotional appeal, parallel structure, catchy phrases)*

Access Strategy

Remind students of their discussion about whether they would remain in their state or leave it if it were to secede from the United States (Access Strategy in Lesson 1). Ask students what they would do if their state seceded and they had the option of fighting. Would you enlist? Why or why not? Would you feel pressured to join if some of your friends did? If you did join, what would you expect your role in the war to be? If you did not join, how would you feel if your side started losing?

Tell students that in this lesson they will read about how boys their age served in both the Union and Confederate armies as drummer boys and soldiers.

Draft Riots Rage

Riots against the draft were the most violent reactions to wartime limitations on civil rights. The Union Draft Law of March 3, 1863, made every male citizen between 20 and 45 subject to the draft. What enraged the working classes across the country was that a man could avoid serving in the army by paying $300. This discriminated against the laborers whose pay averaged about $500 a year.

Draft riots broke out across the country between the police and the poor in Chicago, Pennsylvania, and Vermont. The worst riots happened in New York City on July 13, 1863. The rioters were mostly Irish immigrants from the city's poorest neighborhoods. The violence began with the burning of a recruiting office and spread throughout the city. The rioters' rage over the draft was mixed with their distrust of black Americans, whom they said wanted to take their jobs. The rioters torched abolitionists' houses and burned a black orphanage. A dozen blacks were hanged at the hands of a such rioters.

Police and firefighters, many of whom were Irish, fought the rioters with great bravery but could not stop them. Army troops arrived from Gettysburg, including an all-Irish unit, to calm the large groups of rioters. In the four days of rioting, over one hundred people were killed and several thousand wounded—most of them rioters.

People felt horror at the brutality of the riots, but many agreed with the rioters that allowing the rich to pay the poor to fight was unfair. The government finally ended exemptions in exchange for money. (Read about another problem with the draft in Making Decisions on page 360.)

Wartime Life in the South

Tensions also mounted in the South, in response to wartime policies. The Confederate government also started a draft in which substitutes could be hired to fight. The writ of habeas corpus was suspended for about a year. An exemption that allowed slaveowners with more than 20 slaves exemption from the draft caused great resentment. Again, people accused the government of favoring the rich. Many Confederate soldiers chose to desert their fighting posts. Civilians living in the path of the enemy lost their animals. Union soldiers often burned Confederate homes and took personal property. Homeless women and children had little money or food. The war affected every level of life in the South.

◄ In this etching from 1863, fire sweeps the Coloured Orphan Asylum as angry crowds react to the provisions of the draft. The day before the riots began, names of those drafted had been listed in the Sunday newspaper.

SOCIAL SYSTEMS

Critical Thinking

Ask students to evaluate the $300 exemption to the Union Draft Law. Was the law fair? *(Students should analyze the justice of favoring the wealthy.)* If you were able to pay the money, would you take advantage of the law to avoid being drafted? Fight the law for the sake of those who were not exempt? What would you do if you could not afford to pay the $300 and did not want to be drafted?

Political Context

In 1863, Lincoln said he feared "the fire in the rear—more than our military chances." The antiwar faction of the Democratic party was the "fire" to which he referred. The leader of the Peace Democrats, Clement Vallandigham, wanted to stop fighting, make an armistice, and withdraw the Union Army from the seceded states. Newspaper articles called the antislavery war illegal and the newly elected legislatures of Indiana and Illinois passed resolutions calling for an armistice and a retraction of the Emancipation Proclamation. Vallandigham, hoping to get arrested and gain publicity while running for governor of Ohio, made a deliberately inflammatory speech against the "war for the freedom of the blacks and the enslavement of the whites." He was arrested and sentenced to imprisonment, a sentence Lincoln changed to banishment to the Confederacy. Vallandigham ran his campaign for governor in exile, but lost the election.

Critical Thinking

Remind students that people were arrested for resisting the draft during the Civil War. Point out that during the Vietnam War, some college students burned their draft cards because they were opposed to the war. Were either actions justified? Why or why not? *(Students should weigh patriotism against personal convictions.)*

■ *Both resented the government for favoring the rich, allowing them to be exempt from the draft. Northerners rioted because of the draft and distrust of black Americans; Southerners rioted because of food shortages.*

HISTORY

Critical Thinking

Help students analyze why young boys wanted to join the Northern and the Southern armies and why they were accepted. How might the shattered Southern economy have spurred some youths to enlist? *(As soldiers they would earn money to help their families.)* How might the large number of casualties have affected enlistment of youths? *(Armies were desperate for soldiers.)*

■ *The young became drummer boys, carried gunpowder to men firing the cannon, and faced enemy fire.*

■ *Why did both Northern and Southern citizens resent the terms of the draft? What caused citizens to riot?*

Food shortages caused rioting in cities throughout the eastern Confederacy. In 1863, bread riots rocked the capital of Richmond. Most of the rioters were women who were desperate to feed their families. They looted stores and even hijacked goods from trains. In addition, gangs of deserters raided trains and attacked supply depots.

In the last year of the war, desertions increased alarmingly. Soldiers were barefoot, hungry, and discouraged by their military losses. In ever-increasing numbers, soldiers deserted in order to go home to save their families from starvation and from being forced off their farms. ■

Draft Sends Youth to War

➤ *About 5 percent of those fighting for the Confederacy were under 18 years of age.*

The Civil War was fought by the young: 60 percent of the soldiers and sailors on both sides were 25 years of age or younger. The ranks also included many boys under the legal enlistment age of 18.

Drummer boys of 10 or 12 served in both armies. Young boys in both navies carried gunpowder to the men firing the cannon. Nicknamed "powder monkeys," they could scramble quickly down the narrow ship ladders to where the powder was stored.

In addition, young soldiers held dangerous and exhausting jobs. Boys of 13 and 14 often marched all day, slept on the ground, and faced enemy fire along with the men. Once a boy entered the armed forces, regardless of his age, he received no special treatment.

Some teenagers became high-ranking officers, commanding men twice their age. Arthur MacArthur entered the Union army at 18 as a color-bearer, carrying the flag into battle, and rose to the high rank of lieutenant general.

Fifteen-year-old Union Private Nathaniel Gwynne lost an arm in battle and received the Medal of Honor for his bravery. David O. Dodd was 17 when the Union Army arrested him on Christmas 1863. He admitted that he was a Confederate spy but refused to earn a pardon in exchange for giving information. He was tried and sentenced to be hanged on January 8, 1864. On the morning of the hanging, he wrote to his parents and sisters: "I was sentenced to be hung [hanged] today at 3 o'clock. The time is fast approaching, but, thank God: I am prepared to die." Dodd was hanged on a tree on the lawn of the same school where he had been a student. ■

■ *What kinds of jobs were held by the young in the Civil War?*

Visual Learning

Have students examine the pictures of the young soldiers on this page. Ask them to imagine themselves in the pictures. How would they feel as they posed in uniform? How would they feel about fighting and perhaps dying at such a young age? *(Proud, afraid, confused, angry)*

Health Connection

Clara Barton established the American Red Cross in 1882 and became its first president (Lesson 4). Realizing the Red Cross could help civilians as well as soldiers, she added a clause to its constitution providing for relief in disasters other than war. Have students contact the local Red Cross and interview officials about their relief and aid programs.

Writing an Editorial

Students can write a one-page newspaper editorial attacking or defending one of the following: the suspension of the writ of habeas corpus; the Union Draft Law; the exemption of slaveowners from the Confederacy draft; the draft riots. Students should use details from the lesson to support their case.

War Creates New Roles for Women

While men fought the Civil War, women's traditional roles as wives, homemakers, and mothers were expanded to include new social, political, and economic duties. Over the course of the war, thousands of homemakers were forced to support and protect themselves and their families while their husbands were in military service. A very heavy burden fell on those whose husbands were killed or wounded.

Many jobs that had been for men only before the war were opened to women. They worked as printers, blacksmiths, and farmers. Hundreds filled previously all-male government jobs, including important executive positions. Frances Spinner became Treasurer of the United States. Sally Tomkins was made a captain in the Confederate army. Women also directly helped the war effort by working in munitions factories where they made weapons and ammunition. Mary Livermore formed the U.S. Sanitary Commission, which aided sick Union soldiers and their families.

Women were employed by both armies as cooks and laundresses. Three thousand women became Army and Navy nurses—jobs previously restricted to men. Mary Bickerdyke, known as "Mother Bickerdyke," ran one of the more successful Union hospitals. In the South, Phoebe Yates Pember ran a hospital for Confederate soldiers.

More than 400 women, disguised as men, served as soldiers. Ellen Goodridge chose to join the army with her Union fiancé. Sarah Edmonds served as a nurse with the Second Michigan Calvary under the name Franklin Thompson. Amy Clark continued to fight after her Confederate soldier husband was killed at Shiloh. Most of these women were discovered when they were wounded in battle. Southern women, like women in the North, most often posed as men so they could be with their husbands.

During the Civil War, women filled factory jobs that were previously held by men.

Women also served as spies. Dr. Mary Walker served the Union as a doctor but was also captured for spying. Rose O'Neal Greenhow, a Southern society hostess, became a famous Confederate figure in 1864 when she drowned while returning from a mission to Europe. Union spy Pauline Cushman, an actress, passed information to Union officers during theatrical tours and was put in jail as a spy. ■

■ *How did many women, who were not allowed to fight in the Civil War, find a way to help the war effort?*

REVIEW

1. **FOCUS** What major changes took place in American society as a result of the Civil War?
2. **CONNECT** How did the response of angry Northerners forced to pay high taxes during the Civil War differ from the response of colonists forced to pay a tax on British tea?
3. **HISTORY** In what way did the Civil War provide an opportunity for women to participate in the work force?
4. **CRITICAL THINKING** Was President Lincoln justified in suspending the writ of habeas corpus to maintain order during wartime? Offer support for your opinion.
5. **WRITING ACTIVITY** Write a short essay on the employment of the very young in the military, stating why you think this should or should not be allowed. Use one of the descriptions of a boy soldier in this chapter as an example in your argument.

SOCIAL SYSTEMS

Critical Thinking

Point out to students that women took on new roles during the Civil War and also during other wars in our nation's history. Why are such role changes likely to occur in wartime? *Many jobs are left open as men enlist. During the chaos of war, social patterns often break down quickly. Women often welcome the opportunity to assume greater responsibility.)*

■ *Women worked in munitions factories, in the U.S. Sanitary Commission, and as army and navy cooks, laundresses, and nurses. Some women served as spies; others, disguised as men, became soldiers.*

CLOSE

Tell students to answer the Thinking Focus and to evaluate the predictions that they made before reading the lesson. Copy on the board the structure and main heads of the Graphic Overview from page 355. Ask students to complete a cause-and-effect chart together, using the lists they made while reading the lesson. As an extension of the lesson, students can do the Writing an Editorial activity on page 358.

Answers to Review Questions

1. The Civil War brought dissent over war taxes, caused conflict over threatened civil liberties, spurred the emancipation of slaves in Confederate states, sent youth into battle, and created new roles for women.
2. Although Northerners were resentful of the high taxes, they did not rebel against them as the colonists had.
3. Because the war removed men from the work force, women gained jobs traditionally held by men, including working as printers, blacksmiths, farmers, and government officials.
4. Sample answer: Lincoln's action was justified by the need to keep the Union force strong; draft evaders and spies had to be punished. Allow for personal opinion.
5. Students representing different points of view may read their essays aloud in class.

Homework Options

Have students bring to class newspaper or magazine articles about people in war-torn countries, such as El Salvador, and compare their situation with that of the Civil War civilians.

Study Guide: page 52.

DECISION-MAKING PROCESS

1. Recognize the need for a decision.
2. Define the goals and values involved.
3. Acquire and evaluate necessary information.
4. Identify and analyze possible alternatives.
5. Choose the best alternative.

This Making Decisions lesson on the Shakers and the Civil War will focus on steps 4 and 5 of the decision-making process.

CITIZENSHIP

Critical Thinking

Discuss the alternatives President Lincoln could have considered in dealing with the pacifism of the Shakers. Ask students what they think they would have done if they had been Abraham Lincoln, and why. *(Sample answer: Might have forced them to fight or to serve in other ways or to pay extra taxes)*

MAKING DECISIONS

The Shakers and the Civil War

As we have received the grace of God in Christ, by the gospel, and are called to follow peace with all men, we cannot, consistent with our faith and conscience, bear the arms of war, for the purpose of shedding the blood of any, or do anything to justify or encourage it in others.

Joseph Meacham, Shaker elder

You [the Shakers] ought to be made to fight. We need regiments of just such men as you.

President Abraham Lincoln

Background

When George Ingels, a member of the Shaker society in North Union, Ohio, was drafted in 1862, he and his fellow community members faced a crisis. During the Civil War, nearly 6,000 Shakers lived scattered across the country in approximately 20 settlements from Maine to Ohio, supporting pacifism (opposition to war). In accordance with their beliefs, Shaker communities had withdrawn from the outside world; they shunned contact with those outside their faith and devoted themselves to seeking spiritual perfection. When the country went to war and the government started a military draft, Shakers who were summoned to military service had to choose between the dictates of their conscience and obedience to the law. All Shakers opposed slavery. But their opposition to war was stronger. Shaker elders (church leaders and policy makers) had taken a firm stand against participation in the military from the era of the Revolution well into the 1800s. Indeed, Shaker elders repeatedly petitioned state legislatures to repeal any taxes levied for military purposes.

Shakers wanted to avoid even indirect support of bloodshed. The Union government, however, was fighting the Civil War to abolish slavery and to preserve the Union. It needed every able-bodied man it could enlist, and it needed more funds to support the war effort.

Shakers valued well-crafted items such as the basket below.

Objectives

1. Identify the alternatives that Lincoln had in the issues involving the Shakers and pacifism. (Critical Thinking 1)
2. Define the goals and values of both sides in a debate over pacifism. (Citizenship 5)

Activities

Divide the class into two groups. Ask one group to imagine that they are Shakers. Have them write letters to President Lincoln, detailing their belief that no cause justifies killing other human beings and asking that they be excused from military service. The other group will imagine that they are President Lincoln and will write letters replying to the Shakers. The students will then read their letters aloud.

Have students research conscientious objection during World War II and the Vietnam War including the constitutional arguments raised by both sides of the issue (First Amendment rights regarding freedom of religion). Then divide students into groups to debate the issue.

Conflict Between Conscience and Country

When several young Shakers were threatened with being drafted, elders responded by sending representatives to Washington to appeal directly to the President. They presented Lincoln with a petition that clearly outlined their philosophical reasons for refusing to participate in the war effort. The Shakers were not content with ordinary status as conscientious objectors (those who refuse military service on religious or moral grounds). They wanted a total exemption from any support of the war, even indirect financial aid.

Secretary of War Stanton believed that although the Union might respect Shaker beliefs and not make them fight, the government could hardly let the Shakers avoid financial obligations in support of the war. To resolve this conflict, Elder Frederick Evans made the following proposal. The U.S. government still owed pension payments to veterans who had become Shakers after fighting in the War of 1812. If the federal government would agree not to draft Shaker men, the Shakers would forgive the debt. The government agreed to this proposal.

Later, when more Shakers were drafted, Secretary of War Stanton exempted them from service and ordered that other conscientious objectors also be exempted. Throughout the rest of the Civil War, Shakers neither bore arms nor paid fees for others to fight in their place.

Shakers avoided military service, but those who lived in the border states could not entirely escape the war. They lost money and property. The community at South Union, Kentucky, alone lost over $100,000 worth of property and had to feed 50,000 meals to invading soldiers—from both sides. Shakers considered this a small price to pay for the knowledge that they had upheld their principles and had not betrayed their country.

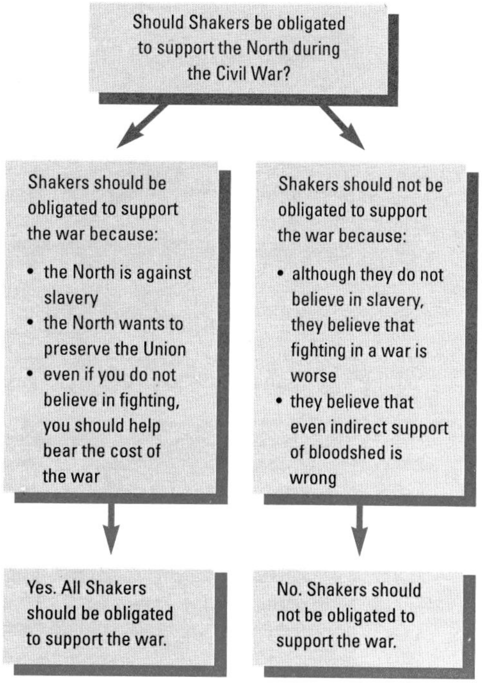

Should Shakers be obligated to support the North during the Civil War?
Shakers should be obligated to support the war because:
• the North is against slavery
• the North wants to preserve the Union
• even if you do not believe in fighting, you should help bear the cost of the war
Shakers should not be obligated to support the war because:
• although they do not believe in slavery, they believe that fighting in a war is worse
• they believe that even indirect support of bloodshed is wrong
Yes. All Shakers should be obligated to support the war.
No. Shakers should not be obligated to support the war.

Decision Point

1. Why did the Shakers refuse to pay for substitutes to fight in their place during the war?
2. Why did Lincoln let Shakers avoid the draft when the country needed soldiers so badly?
3. What alternatives did Lincoln have?
4. What else could the Shakers have done? What would another compromise position have been?
5. Can you think of any contemporary situations in which there has been opposition to fighting a war? How was that conflict resolved?

BELIEF SYSTEMS

Critical Thinking

How did the religious beliefs of the Shakers differ from those of many other Americans regarding war? *(They believed that there is no good reason to kill others. Many Americans believed that there were reasons why war was sometimes necessary.)*

CITIZENSHIP

Visual Learning

Have students analyze in the decision-making chart the reasons given to support the two alternatives to the Shaker issue. Can students use the reasons given to choose one alternative over the other? Why or why not? *(There is not a clear-cut case for a best answer.)*

Answers to Decision Point

1. They believed that no one should kill another human being.
2. Lincoln understood and respected the Shakers' beliefs, so he worked out a compromise with them.
3. He could have forced them to fight, taxed them, or put them in prison.
4. Shakers might have served as medics, treating the wounded on both sides.
5. Encourage students to read about the Vietnam War, especially the feelings about anti-war protests of those who served in the army, as well as the beliefs of those who refused to serve.

Collaborative Strategy

A recommended strategy for this lesson is pair-debate. For more details about collaborative learning strategies, see pages T34–35.

INTRODUCE

Have a student read aloud the lesson title and Thinking Focus. Ask students to recall why the war was turning out to be longer than either side anticipated. *(Both sides were determined to win.)* Remind them that the South was clearly losing the war and suffering greatly. Tell students to read to find out how developments in the war affected the South's will and ability to prolong the fighting.

1860 1861 1862 1863 1864 1865

LESSON 4

The Long March to Surrender

THINKING FOCUS

What events led to General Lee's surrender at Appomattox?

Before the invention of photography, war was often shown as a series of heroic fights between handsome, elegantly dressed soldiers riding sleek, prancing horses.

This romantic image was changed forever by thousands of Civil War photographs of battlefields. Gory depictions of the bodies of dead soldiers and the carcasses of skinny horses showed the reality.

Photographers, such as Matthew Brady, moved their heavy cameras and equipment in specially designed wagons that also served as darkrooms. The cameras of the time were too slow to take action shots, so photographers focused instead on post-battle pictures. Often, bodies were arranged to show more shocking images.

Techniques for copying photographs in newspapers did not exist. However, weekly magazines printed woodcuts and engravings copied from war photographs. Hand-held viewers, called stereoscopes, turned single images into three-dimensional views. Thousands of people nationwide gathered to view exhibits of war photographs depicting death and the ruined lands and buildings.

➤ *Wartime photography showing the military in various states: at ease and guarding their commands. Photography changed the romantic images of war.*

Objectives

1. Summarize the toll of the Civil War in terms of deaths, destruction of land, and loss of morale.
2. Evaluate how the lack of medical advantages and the gains in weapon technology contributed to the high death tolls.
3. Describe the concluding battles and the "total war" that finally forced the South's surrender.

Graphic Overview

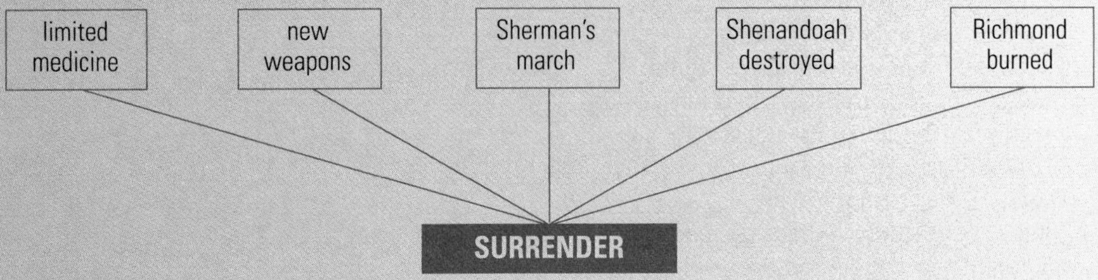

The Final Tally

The horrors of three years of fighting, so clearly illustrated in battle photographs, increased a great deal in the last months of the war. Throughout the war, the North tried to hurt the South economically, politically, and morally. Yet in the third year of war, it was clear that a new instrument of war was necessary to end the conflict. The new approach, "psychological warfare," involved destroying the hopes of the entire South. General Sherman said, "We cannot change the hearts of those people of the South, but we can make war so terrible . . . that generations would pass away before they would again appeal to it."

In March 1864, Lincoln appointed Ulysses S. Grant head of all Union forces. With Grant's strong support, General Sherman in the west and General Sheridan in the east planned new tactics of destruction to bring the war to a close. No one would be spared the effects of "total war." The army burned houses and fields; people starved to death—all in the name of forcing the South to surrender.

Shocking Losses

Even without these harsh military tactics, the war was taking a tremendous toll in human suffering. Although doctors and nurses provided medical and social services to wounded soldiers, the science of medicine had advanced little since the Revolutionary War. Doctors came to the battlefield without much formal training. The importance of clean medical tools was unknown to them, and many patients survived surgery only to die later of infection. Amputation was seen as the only treatment for injury to the bone and was a common procedure. Seventy-five percent of soldiers suffering chest and stomach wounds died from their injuries.

However, some medical breakthroughs did take place during the Civil War. These included the discovery of the importance of providing a room with fresh air for the patient and the invention of a disinfectant that reduced the rate of death from gangrene. Despite such improvements, a staggering number of Americans—1 out of every 50—died in the Civil War.

One important figure in medical care was Clara Barton. During the war, Barton risked her life to carry supplies to Union soldiers and to nurse the wounded on the battlefield. She was known as "the Angel of the Battlefield."

New weapon technology also added to the shocking death tolls of Northern and Southern soldiers. The next two pages show you a Closer Look at Civil War technology.

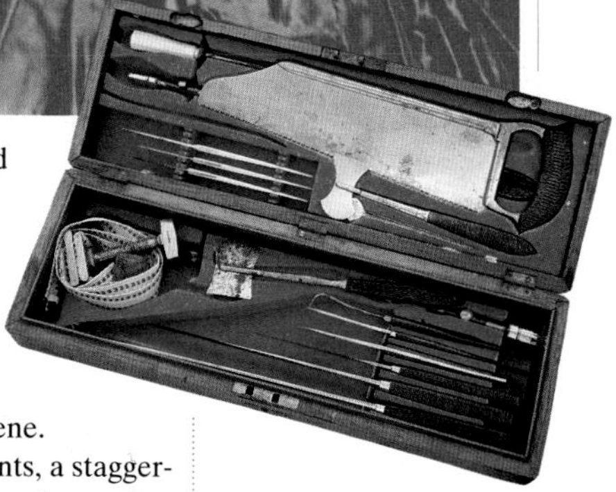

Nurse Clara Barton introduced battlefield emergency care and later founded the American Red Cross. Doctors performed surgery with instruments such as the ones featured in the medic's kit.

DEVELOP

Tell students that they will learn about what caused the South to surrender. Copy on the board the structure and the main head (Surrender) of the Graphic Overview on page 362. Have students copy it in their notes and, as they read the lesson, fill in the causes of the Southern surrender.

HISTORY

Critical Thinking

Point out to students that it was not until 1928 that Fleming discovered penicillin, the drug commonly used today to fight infections caused by bacteria. What medical procedures contributed to the death toll during the Civil War? *(Using unclean tools, performing amputations frequently)* What conclusion can be drawn about advances in weapon technology compared to those in medicine? *(Learned earlier about how to destroy than about how to heal)*

Access Strategy

Have students consider the lives of civilians who live in a war zone. Some students may be able to recall descriptions from current news reports. How might civilians' lives be affected? *(They could lose their way of life, supplies, homes; they could be displaced temporarily or permanently; some could even lose their lives.)* What happens when an entire region becomes a war site? *(The scale of destruction increases and the entire region's economy suffers.)* Tell students they will read in this lesson about how the Union forces treated the entire Southern region as a war zone in order to force the South to surrender.

Access Activity

Read the Lesson Opener aloud and then have students look at the photographs in this lesson and in Lesson 2. How might this new medium—photography—have affected people living during the Civil War? *(Might have changed their ideas about war)* What do these pictures say about war? *(It is ugly and destructive.)*

HISTORY

Visual Learning

Point out how unusual the perspective from a hot air balloon must have been to people at that time, who did not experience air travel as we do today. Ask students how a Union soldier might have felt when up in a hot air balloon compared to when on a battlefield. *(Excited, less vulnerable, more detatched)* Why? *(New perspective, less chance of being hurt, the enemy distant)*

More About the Hot Air Balloon
From a height of 1,000 feet, soldiers could observe 20 miles. They communicated valuable information by using the telegraph in the basket or by sending down the guide cables a message that was weighted with a bullet.

A CLOSER LOOK

Civil War Technology

Rifles cracked. Cannons roared. Observation balloons hung over fields; and silent, ironclad ships floated on the waterways. Technology introduced in the Civil War would change the way war was waged. It was called the first modern war.

Just bad aim? Hot air balloons were used by the Union during the war to drop messages, sketch maps, and watch enemy maneuvers. Not one was ever shot down.

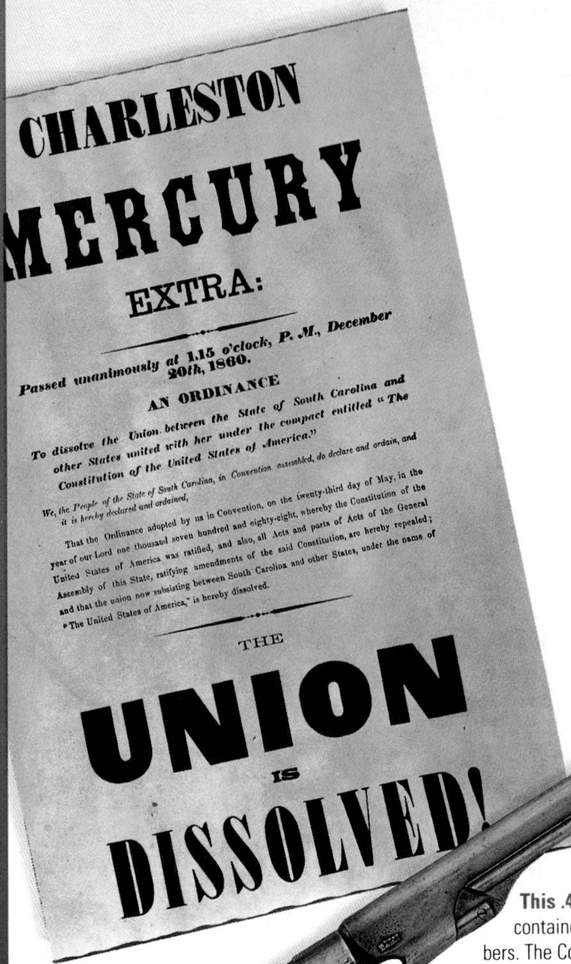

CHARLESTON

MERCURY

EXTRA:

Passed unanimously at 1.15 o'clock, P. M., December 20th, 1860.

AN ORDINANCE

To dissolve the Union between the State of South Carolina and other States united with her under the compact entitled "The Constitution of the United States of America."

We, the People of the State of South Carolina, in Convention assembled, do declare and ordain, and it is hereby declared and ordained,

That the Ordinance adopted by us in Convention, on the twenty-third day of May, in the year of our Lord one thousand seven hundred and eighty-eight, whereby the Constitution of the United States of America was ratified, and also, all Acts and parts of Acts of the General Assembly of this State, ratifying amendments of the said Constitution, are hereby repealed; and that the union now subsisting between South Carolina and other States, under the name of "The United States of America," is hereby dissolved.

THE

UNION

IS

DISSOLVED!

Bring out the big guns! The largest cannons ever made up to the Civil War were produced by the North. They rotated on huge circular tracks.

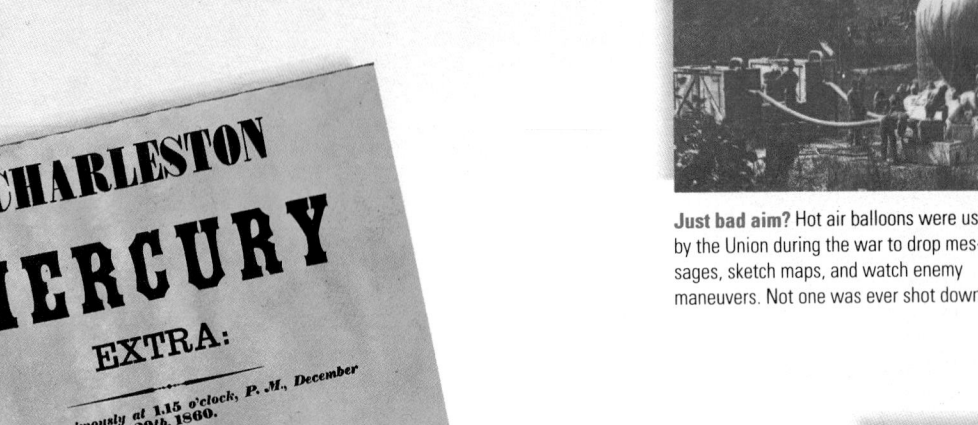

This .44 caliber Colt revolver contained six ammunition chambers. The Colt was famous for rapid fire in close combat. Confederate soldiers often used Colts they had stolen from Union cavalry.

Visual Learning

Refer students to the timeline on page 257. Point out the picture and caption of the Colt revolver. When was it first invented? *(1833)* Why was it so effective? *(Could be used on horseback)*

Historical Context

As the heavy fighting of 1864 continued, many prisoners were taken to camps where they suffered disease, starvation, and brutality. The camp at Andersonville in southwest Georgia was generally considered the worst Southern camp. Andersonville was a stockade camp of 16 acres, designed for 10,000 prisoners. It was enlarged to 26 acres, and by August 1864 it held 33,000 men (an average of 34 square feet per man). The men had no shade from the strong summer sun and no shelter except whatever they could rig from sticks, blankets, and odd bits of cloth. During some weeks in the summer of 1864, more than 100 prisoners died a day. Altogether, 13,000 of the 45,000 men imprisoned there died of disease, exposure, or malnutrition. In comparison, the worst Northern prison camp, in Elmira, New York, had a 40-acre enclosure for 9,600 captives (an average of 180 square feet per man).

If it floats, it's in the navy. Both pleasure boats and merchant ships were converted into official transport vehicles for the North. This ferry could penetrate narrow rivers and channels.

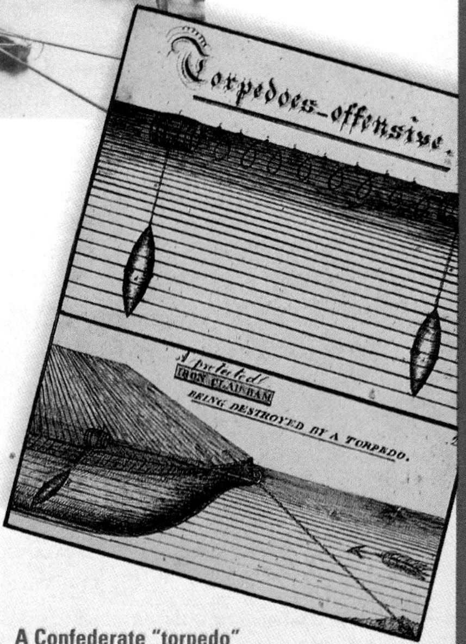

A Confederate "torpedo" blew up the U.S.S. *Cairo* in 1862. It was the first time an underwater mine ever sank a warship. Some "torpedoes" with trigger mechanisms floated underwater. The bottom of a boat would brush the trigger and Kaboom!

HISTORY

Visual Learning

Request that students use the pictures and captions on page 364 and on this page to determine which weapons were used by the North and which were used by the South. *(The North—hot air balloons, cannons, Colt revolvers, ships; the South— "torpedoes," Colt revolvers)*

More About the Cannons These large 20-inch guns were used not only in forts, but also on navy ships. The ships patrolled harbors and rivers and used heavy fire to protect troops' movement on land.

Mathematics Connection

When General Sherman and his army marched 285 miles from Atlanta to Savannah, they destroyed a strip of land 50 miles wide. To help students grasp the extent of the destruction, have them locate on a copy of a map of their state or region a town that is 50 miles from their town. Then have them extend that 50-mile-wide area for 285 miles. Ask students to mark the section in black on the map.Also have students compare casualty figures (page 350) from one of the major Civil War battles to the population figures of a city in their state with approximately the same population, a crowd at a football game, or the total population of a number of schools.

Critical Thinking

Have students read the caption on "torpedoes" on this page. Why would the explosion of the *U.S.S. Cairo* have been shocking to an observer on land? *(An observer could see no visible attack.)* How did the floating "torpedoes" differ from torpedoes used today? *(Torpedoes were not aimed and launched then.)*

HISTORY

Critical Thinking

Have students evaluate the strategy of "total war." In what way can its use in the Civil War be viewed as successful? *(It ended the war.)* How did this strategy force the South to surrender? *(Spared no one; destroyed morale, homes, jobs, lives)* Ask students to explain why they do or do not approve of this approach. *(Students should weigh its "success" with the vast destruction it caused.)*

■ *They thought total war was necessary to force surrender and end the war.*

HISTORY

Critical Thinking

Tell students to analyze the toll taken by the Civil War. *(Students should consider loss of life, destruction of land, and the psychological effect of a long, bitter war.)*

The repeater rifle allowed for shooting from longer distances and firing without stopping to reload. The machine gun was also introduced in the Civil War, along with water mines, flame throwers, and gas shells. Although these weapons can be viewed as technological advances, such devices also brought about tremendous loss of human life.

Sherman Marches to the Sea

Throughout the summer of 1864, the Union army of 60,000 men led by General William Tecumseh Sherman made its way east through Georgia. In September, Sherman's men captured Atlanta, an important city in the Southern railroad network. Union forces destroyed or took anything of use to the Confederates. Sherman and his troops then forced all the people to leave Atlanta and burned the city to the ground. Sherman's army, with almost no opposition, marched through Georgia toward Savannah on the Atlantic coast. The troops lived off the countryside, eating whatever they could take from citizens' homes. They also destroyed and then burned a 50-mile-wide strip of land along their way. After the destruction of Atlanta, and Sherman's march across the Georgia countryside, the citizens of Savannah were so frightened they quickly surrendered. Following the Union army was a large group of slaves who freed themselves from their Confederate owners. The sight of free black men and women marching through the streets frightened many Southerners. They feared the ex-slaves would seek a bloody revenge for their treatment by slave owners.

Savannah fell to Sherman in December 1864. He then turned north to South Carolina. In February, his men took the state capital of Columbia. Sherman then moved on into North Carolina on his drive toward Richmond, Virginia. However, before he reached the Confederate capital, the war was over.

The North Empties the Breadbasket

While Sherman was cutting his path of destruction through the Deep South, Union General Philip Henry Sheridan was destroying the Shenandoah Valley in Virginia. Farms in this area provided most of the food for Lee's hungry army. Grant instructed Sheridan to lay waste to the valley so that even a crow crossing it would have to bring its food supply from elsewhere. Sheridan also destroyed the Confederate army of the Shenandoah despite its brave efforts to resist. ■

■ *Why did Grant and his generals believe that "total war" was necessary?*

➤ *Cities and towns across the South suffered destruction by Union troops.*

Critical Thinking

Refer students to Sherman's explanation for choosing "total war" (page 363). In what way do his words resemble the rationale of some people for the existence of the nuclear bomb today? *(Supposedly, both prevent future war.)* Ask students to explain why they do or do not believe that such methods deter war.

Writing a News Account

Ask students to imagine they are journalists for a Southern newspaper. Have them write eyewitness accounts of General Sherman's army marching through Georgia. Students should use details from the lesson and from research in the library to bring their accounts to life.

Writing a Script

Divide students into small groups to research the conversation between General Robert E. Lee and General Ulysses S. Grant at Appomattox. Have each group of students write a script of this conversation, basing it on the actual words spoken, but also adding words to make the dialogue flow and to make the encounter as vivid as possible. Students may perform their scripts.

Surrender at Appomattox

By the spring of 1865, the South was broken and discouraged. General Lee's army of Virginia, reduced to 35,000 men, retreated from troops led by General George G. Meade, who commanded the army of the Potomac. Meade's troops numbered 80,000 strong. Sherman's army would soon arrive to separate Lee from the rest of the South.

On April 3, President Davis fled Richmond. As Lee's retreating troops departed, they set fire to army installations and warehouses. The fire spread quickly, leaving the Confederate capital in ashes.

Lee's men, ragged and barefoot, had been surviving on dried corn. They were about to run out of ammunition. Yet even at this desperate hour they held on. Seldom in history has a general enjoyed such respect from his men.

He said to his officers, "There is nothing left for me to do but go and see General Grant, and I would rather die a thousand deaths." Lee then wrote to Grant, requesting a meeting to discuss terms of the South's surrender. Lee's only choice was to save what was left of the South by surrendering immediately.

That meeting took place on April 9, 1865, at the town of Appomattox Court House, Virginia, where General Robert E. Lee surrendered to General Ulysses S. Grant. Lee was wearing his dress uniform and gold-mounted sword. Grant's personal belongings had not been sent ahead to him. He wore a faded shirt and his mud-caked battlefield boots.

Grant's appearance was shabby, but his terms were generous. He set free Lee's troops, provided them with food, and allowed them to take home their horses and mules, which they themselves had provided (most of the South's farm animals had been slaughtered for food). "The war is over," Grant reminded his troops, as he forbade them to fire their guns in celebration of the victory.

Grant wrote in his memoirs how sad he had felt at Lee's surrender. He hated to see "the downfall of a foe who had fought so long and valiantly, and had suffered so much for a cause though that cause was . . . one of the worst for which a people ever fought." ■

At the home of William McLean, in the village of Appomattox Court House, Virginia, Robert E. Lee and Ulysses S. Grant brought four years of bloody war to an end.

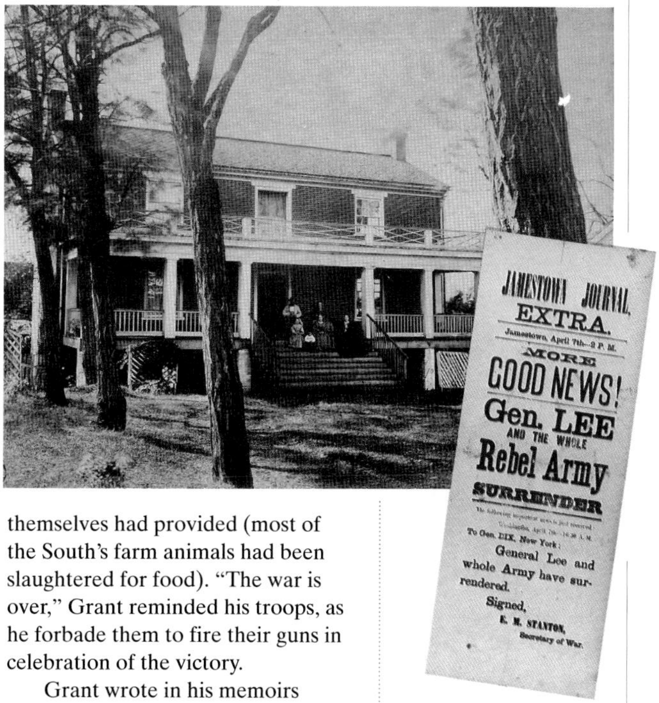
JAMESTOWN JOURNAL.
EXTRA.
Jamestown, April 7th—2 P. M.
MORE
GOOD NEWS!
Gen. LEE
AND THE WHOLE
Rebel Army
SURRENDER
To Gen. DIX, New York:
General Lee and whole Army have surrendered.
Signed,
E. M. STANTON,
Secretary of War.

■ *What terms did Grant set for Lee's surrender?*

REVIEW

1. **FOCUS** What events led to General Lee's surrender at Appomattox?
2. **CONNECT** How did advances in weapon technology make the fighting of the Civil War different from previous wars?
3. **ECONOMICS** How did Sherman's march make it economically impossible for the South to remain at war?
4. **CRITICAL THINKING** Do you think that General Grant should have offered additional aid to the South after the war? Offer support for your answer.
5. **WRITING ACTIVITY** Write a short essay describing all the aspects of a war that you think need to be represented in photographs to fully illustrate the impact of war on soldiers and civilians. Explain your choices.

■ *Grant freed Lee's troops, provided them with food, and allowed them to take home their horses and mules.*

CLOSE

After students have read the lesson, ask them to answer the Thinking Focus. Copy on the board again the structure and main head of the Graphic Overview from page 362. Have students complete it together, using the notes they made as they read the lesson. To help students see the final events of the war in relation to earlier events, have them study page 670 and 671 in the Minipedia.

Answers to Review Questions

1. Events included Sherman's march through Georgia and Sheridan's destruction of the Shenandoah Valley.
2. The new, efficient weapons caused a great death toll in the Civil War.
3. The Southern people were unable to support themselves because of the thorough destruction—crops were ruined, animals were killed, and vital supplies were cut off by the North.
4. Sample answer: Rebuilding of some kind should be offered to the losing side in a war. Allow for personal opinion.
5. Students may also bring in photographs from newspapers and magazines to show how war is represented today.

Homework Options

Ask students to research and write a one- to two-page report on the life and work of Clara Barton.

Study Guide: page 53.

UNDERSTANDING WRITTEN REPORTS

This skill lesson will show students how to write a report using reference materials, note-cards, and outlines.

HISTORY

Study Skills

Ask students how they could research who won the battle of Antietam as a collaborative activity. *(Different groups of students could research specific topics: geography, casualty figures, field reports, territory gained or lost, aftermath.)* You may want to divide up the class and have different groups of students research specific topics.

UNDERSTANDING WRITTEN REPORTS

Reporting on Antietam

Here's Why

In our society, reports are the main way people gather and distribute important information in school and in business. Reports can answer questions, give a point of view on a subject, or identify a problem. Knowing how to prepare a report is a skill you will use in many different ways throughout your life.

Reports from the battlefront were the only way President Lincoln was able to determine the outcome of the Battle of Antietam, one of the bloodiest battles of the Civil War. Lincoln claimed that it was a victory for the North. However, most historians believe that evidence shows neither side won the battle decisively.

Suppose you wanted to decide for yourself which side actually won, or show that there was, in fact, no clear winner. Suppose also that you wanted to convince your class that your findings were valid. Combining the skills you learned in previous chapters—use of primary and specialized sources, note and bibliography cards, and outline development—will help you to prepare a written report.

Here's How

Follow these steps:

1. **Identify your purpose.** Is your report meant to inform, to convince, or does it have some other purpose? All of the information you present should support your purpose. In this case your report is meant to convince the reader that your research on the Battle of Antietam shows who did or did not win the battle.

368

Objective

Use reference materials, note-cards, and outlines to create a written report. (Study Skills 3)

Science Connection

This method of preparing a report will help the students in their other subjects. Ask volunteers to suggest topics from science class. Go through the eleven steps, pointing out how each applies.

2. **Identify your audience.**
Who will read your report? If you are writing a report that will be read by someone who knows the subject well, you may be able to concentrate only on your specific topic. If it will be read by someone who does not know the subject well, you might need to provide more background information. Decide how much information you need to provide in order to convince your classmates that your decision on the outcome of the Battle of Antietam is correct.

3. **Choose a topic.**
Make your topic clear and specific, and put it in the form of a question you will answer. For this report your topic may be: Who won the Battle of Antietam?

4. **Locate sources.**
Use reference systems such as the library card catalogue or a computerized reference system to locate books. Use *The Readers' Guide to Periodical Literature* to find magazine articles. Refer to pages 274–275 in Chapter 9 on how to use computerized resources.

5. **Use index cards.**
Take notes, create bibliography cards, and record exact quotations from primary sources (noting the book and page number).

6. **Determine point of view in any quotations.**
Refer to the pages 88 and 89 to determine which of your sources are primary sources. For any primary sources, you should review pages 336 and 337 to determine the point of view.

7. **Organize the information into an outline.**
You may want to re-read pages 228 and 229 to review outlines.

8. **Prepare a bibliography.**
Alphabetize the bibliography cards that you created while taking notes, and use them to create a bibliography page.

9. **Write the report.**
Expand your outline into paragraphs. Each paragraph should have a topic sentence that states one main idea, followed by sentences that add details to develop the main idea.

10. **Write an introduction.**
Your introduction should interest your readers in your topic and explain what the report is about.

11. **Write a conclusion.**
Your conclusion should restate the main ideas you have presented and should complete the report.

Try It

Choose a major Civil War battle described in this chapter, and research it for a two-page written report. Follow the steps listed above to prepare the report.

Apply It

Choose a current topic that is heavily debated, such as gun control. Research both sides of the issue, and then write a topic question that your report will answer. Locate sources in your library, prepare bibliography cards, and develop an outline.

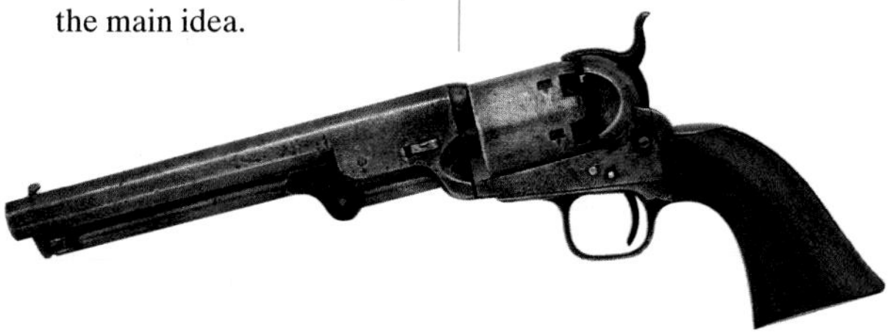

HISTORY

Study Skills

Students may need additional help in turning their outlines into written reports. Suggest that, as they write their outlines, they think of the A, B, and C heads as paragraph topics. These can be expanded into topic sentences in the final report. Details under the 1, 2, and 3 heads in the outline can be expanded into detail sentences within each paragraph.

Answers to Try It

Students may write their reports on the attack on Ft. Sumter; the battles of Bull Run, Fredericksburg, Chancellorsville, Vicksburg, and Gettysburg; the campaigns of Shiloh and the Shenandoah Valley; Sherman's march to the sea; and Grant's pursuit of Lee's army in Virginia. Check their use of the eleven-step process. Students may work on their reports either individually or in small groups.

Answers to Apply It

Discuss possible topics with the class before students begin their individual research. You may wish to review the skills lessons in Chapters 3, 5, 8, 9, and 11 (pages 88–89, 152, 228–229, 274–275, and 336–337) with the students. Set aside time to check each student's progress through the eleven steps as they prepare their reports.

Study Skills

Students may work in groups of four to apply the eleven-step process to a topic. One member will perform the first four steps; a second will do the next two steps; a third will do the next two steps; a fourth will write the report, and then the group can collaborate on the last two steps.

INTRODUCE

Have students recall what they learned about the Battle of Gettysburg in Lesson 2. Point out that this selection is part of a historical novel about the Battle of Gettysburg. Explain that an author of historical fiction must be a researcher as well as a writer. An author who wants to describe an actual battle must collect and read the reports from both sides, as well as many personal accounts of those who took part in the battle.

READ AND RESPOND

Read the selection aloud to the students and tell them to listen for the details the author uses to make the story vivid and convincing. When you finish reading, ask students what they heard and what they saw. As students answer the purpose-setting question, make sure they give reasons for their answers.

In this chapter, you read about the important Northern victory at the Battle of Gettysburg and about the battle's terrible death toll for both sides. In this fictional account, the events of that battle are told from General Lee's perspective.

LITERATURE

The Slopes of War

Norah A. Perez

N.A. Perez is the author of The Slopes of War (1984), *from which this selection is taken, as well as several other historical novels. On a trip to Gettysburg, Perez was moved to write about the human suffering endured by the townspeople of Gettysburg and the soldiers who fought there. Many authors who have written about war never set foot on a battlefield. What do you think such authors need to do in order to create a vivid and convincing account of war?*

At Chambersburg General Lee tried to make sense out of the reports coming in to him. On Tuesday Pettigrew's men had headed into Gettysburg to find some desperately needed shoes; they had seen a few enemy uniforms and had reported back to General Heth. Convinced that what they had seen was probably the local militia, Heth had agreed to let Pettigrew return for the shoes the next morning. That was how it had started. Now a little skirmish had developed into something bigger.

militia citizen army
skirmish a minor encounter in war

As he pressed Traveller to reach Gettysburg quickly, Lee hoped that the Old Soldier's Disease, which was draining his energy, wouldn't be a nuisance to him much longer. He was feeling his age these days. It was as if his body, once fit and healthy and uncomplaining, nagged him for attention. First the heart and the troubling shortness of breath, and then this annoying dysentery. It worried him not to be in peak condition. A victory here and it was possible the war might end.

dysentery a stomach disorder

A. P. Hill, the commander of the Third Corps, was waiting, his bearded face blotched with red, twitching nervously above the collar of the crimson shirt he liked to wear into battle. He admitted that the brigades had met some surprising resistance on their shopping trip to town that morning. "But I have another division ready to go in and back up Heth. Dorsey Pender's men . . . good fellows." Hill was usually unsettled during military operations, but on this bright July morning Lee thought the man really looked quite ill as he repeated that he had men ready to go in. "With your permission, sir."

"Wait. Wait. . . ." Lee would not be rushed into this. He moved to and fro on his horse, listening to the familiar crack of muskets and the steady rumble of artillery, straining to understand what lay behind it. Heavy casualty reports were coming in now, and word had arrived that General Archer had been taken prisoner. In spite of his composure a hot cone of anger against his cavalry burned in his chest. No, he was not angry with them, but with his favorite, Jeb Stuart, the officer who had let him down. He had known that the marvelous man had flaws, that he

artillery large firing weapons

Thematic Connections

Social Studies: Civil War

Houghton Mifflin Literary Readers: Responding to Challenge

Background

The Battle of Gettysburg is regarded as the most important battle of the Civil War. Fresh from victory over the Union army at Shenandoah, General Lee moved his army into the North. Blocking his march through Pennsylvania was the Army of the Potomac under General George Meade. If Lee had defeated Meade's forces, he could have cut Washington, D.C., off from the rest of the North. Very likely, President Lincoln would have been forced to seek peace terms.

Meade's forces held, however, and the Union won the battle. Two days later, Lee pulled his army back, retreating southward. Never again would the South threaten Northern territory.

was sometimes too buoyant and reckless, but this time he was unforgivably late, and Lee felt like a blinded man. He did not know what the danger was or where it was located. For all he knew, the soldiers scrambling through the woods and fields northwest of town might be involved with the whole Army of the Potomac. A spy had reported columns of the enemy in the area, but he knew he wasn't ready yet for a major encounter, not until all of his troops had arrived.

Hill said, "Just give me the word, sir. Pender will clear the road for us in no time."

"Not yet." The general never minded taking risks when he had to, but he refused to be stupid. "Let's wait and see just what it is we're up against."

And so a lull occurred, a little yawn in time, even as the snap of musketry went on and shells continued to burst and blossom white against the innocent blue sky. Time for parched soldiers to swallow tepid water and exhausted gun crews to reposition batteries and replenish ammunition, as a long slow scarf of yellow smoke drifted across the damaged ground.

Then, abruptly, things began to happen again. The murky puzzle that was baffling Lee came together sharply with a sudden shape and clear design. Five brigades of Rodes's division appeared north of the pike on Oak Hill in exactly the right position to swoop down on the tired blue troops that faced the west. If Pender drove in now with his fresh supports, and Rodes's men slammed down hard from the hill, the Union line would have to give. Integral parts clicked smoothly into place as if they had been planned. General Lee, his instincts for opportunity humming, gave the orders.

Yet Federal gears were whirring, too. The Eleventh Corps had just arrived, men fresh for battle hurrying double-quick along the pike and fanning out north of town. It was a hard luck unit, the scapegoat of the army because of its large number of immigrant recruits, but this time it was fortunate. The Confederates rushing down from Oak Hill came too fast, too eagerly, and the Eleventh hurled them back and forced them to regroup. Now the war machine boomed heavily across the landscape, knocking down fence rails, blasting wildflowers, smashing thousands of men under as it rumbled through the sultry summer afternoon.

Further Reading

Thunder at Gettysburg. Patricia L. Gauch. The Battle of Gettysburg is seen through the eyes of 14-year-old Tillie, who becomes involved in the tragic battle that takes place near her town.

buoyant enthusiastic
reckless without regard to outcome

tepid slightly warm

integral needed for functioning

scapegoat a person or group bearing the blame for others

What is the chief piece of information Lee needed to know before giving orders? *(Where the main Army of the Potomac was, and how strong it was)*

What prevented Lee's strategy from succeeding? *(The Union Eleventh Corps arrived in time to hurl back the Confederate forces.)*

EXTEND

Have students reread page 354 about the Battle of Gettysburg. Then have them write a news account of the battle for an 1863 newspaper.

Further Reading

You may want to ask students to go to the school or local library to find more books about the Battle of Gettysburg or about military leaders of the Civil War.

Answers to Reviewing Key Terms

A. Sample answers:
1. The Emancipation Proclamation freed the slaves.
2. The Confederacy was a group of Southern states that withdrew from the United States.
3. Both Abraham Lincoln and Jefferson Davis were moderates because both disagreed with the most extreme political views in their own parties.
4. In an effort to win the war, Lincoln and the Congress changed people's civil rights by allowing people to be arrested and held without trial.
5. By September 1862, President Lincoln declared that anyone who resisted the draft could be arrested.

B. Answers:
1. False. A confederacy is a group of states.
2. True. Maryland, Delaware, Kentucky and Missouri did not secede.
3. False. Moderates take a middle-of-the-road position.
4. False. Emancipation made it possible for black men to serve in the army.
5. True. Lincoln suspended some civil rights in order to enforce the draft.
6. True. All United States citizens are protected by the civil rights defined in the Constitution.

Answers to Exploring Concepts

A. Answers:

South—Economic: none / agricultural economy; fewer manufacturing plants; held less of nation's money

Geographic: fighting on their own ground; familiar with land and climate / had few railroads, less developed transportation system

Military: had many of best U.S. Army officers / no navy; less production of firearms

North—Economic: produced most of nation's goods; controlled most of nation's money / none

Geographic: had 70 percent of railroads / fought far from home; unfamiliar with area; far from supply sources

Military: owned fleet of ships and had more shipyards / needed more troops, better officers at beginning of war

Chapter Review

Reviewing Key Terms

civil rights (p. 356)
Confederacy (p. 342)
draft (p. 356)
emancipation (p. 352)
moderate (p. 348)
secede (p. 343)

A. The sentences below have been started for you. Complete each sentence so that the meaning of the key term is clear.
1. The Emancipation Proclamation . . .
2. The Confederacy was a group of states that . . .
3. Both Abraham Lincoln and Jefferson Davis were moderates because . . .
4. In the effort to win the war, Lincoln and the Congress changed people's civil rights by . . .
5. By September 1862, President Lincoln declared that anyone who resisted the draft . . .

B. Based on what you have read in the chapter, decide whether each of the following statements is accurate. Write an explanation of each decision.
1. Each Southern state in favor of slavery became a confederacy.
2. Several slave states refused to secede, and stayed within the Union.
3. The moderates in Lincoln's party took the most extreme positions on slavery.
4. Emancipation made it possible for women to serve in the army.
5. During the Civil War, President Lincoln ordered the Union military to arrest anyone who resisted the draft.
6. All United States citizens are protected by civil rights.

Exploring Concepts

A. On a separate sheet of paper, make two tables modeled on the ones shown below. Complete the tables by filling in the advantages and disadvantages that the North and South faced in waging war against each other.

South	Advantages	Disadvantages
Economic		
Geographic		
Military		

North	Advantages	Disadvantages
Economic		
Geographic		
Military		

B. Support each of the following statements with facts and details from the chapter.
1. The South's economy was its greatest weakness.
2. President Davis faced many challenges in holding the Confederacy together.
3. President Lincoln also faced problems in carrying the war to a successful conclusion.
4. The Emancipation Proclamation benefited the North in several ways.
5. Lincoln restricted civil rights in the North during the war.
6. The many hardships of war drove people to riot in both the North and South.
7. The war gave women new opportunities in many fields.
8. Several factors contributed to the high casualty rate among soldiers who fought in the war.
9. Military leaders in the North used psychological warfare to wear down the South.

B. Sample answers:
1. The South depended on the North and on Europe for its trade.
2. President Davis had to gather troops, form battle plans and raise taxes to run the war.
3. President Lincoln had to appoint good military leaders and keep the support of the border states.
4. The Proclamation reduced the South's labor source and increased Union troops.
5. Lincoln allowed the military to arrest journalists, draft resisters, and Southern sympathizers.
6. Northerners rioted against the fact that people could buy their way out of the army. Southerners rioted for food to feed their families.
7. Women worked as printers, blacksmiths, farmers, military nurses, and spies.
8. Many soldiers died because there was poor medical equipment, and many doctors had little training.
9. Military leaders in the North ordered troops to destroy Confederate homes, fields, and anything of value.

Reviewing Skills

1. Read the section about the battle of Gettysburg in this chapter, and make note cards on the information.
2. Based on the notes you have taken, write a topic question for a report on the battle of Gettysburg.
3. Use your note cards to create an outline for a report that will clearly answer your topic question. Be sure to include subtopics and supporting details.
4. Create a timeline for the major events that were presented in this chapter.
5. Suppose you wanted to write a report on different types of weapons used during the Civil War. What process would you follow to put the report together?

Using Critical Thinking

1. General Sherman wrote, "I say with the press unfettered [unchained; free to publish all news], we are defeated to the end of time. 'Tis folly to say the people must have news." Do you agree that some rights must be suspended in times of war or other dangers? For example, do you think that the government has the right to prohibit the publication of school newspapers during times of conflict?
2. Lincoln said, "If I could save the Union without freeing any slave, I would do it; and if I could do it by freeing all the slaves, I would do it; and if I could save it by freeing some and leaving others alone, I would also do that." What did he mean by that statement? Do you think the Emancipation Proclamation was consistent with that statement?
3. Some historians have said that given the South's lack of industries and its smaller population, it could never have won the war. Do you agree or disagree? Give reasons for your answer.

Preparing for Citizenship

1. **WRITING ACTIVITY** The Civil War was a war that affected every single household in both the North and the South. Part of the recovery process for a society that survives such horrors is to create art from history. Novels, plays, and paintings depicting a war usually become very popular in the years afterward. Identify movies or novels that are based on more recent wars. View one of these movies or read one of these novels, and write a short report about it.
2. **WRITING ACTIVITY** The Gettysburg Address is considered one of the most beautiful, moving speeches ever written. Lincoln wrote the speech to dedicate a cemetery. It is thus a eulogy, or formal praise, for those who died in the battle at Gettysburg. Read the account of Sherman's March to the Sea on page 366 and write a short eulogy for those who fell in his path.
3. **ART ACTIVITY** Clara Barton was the founder of the American division of the International Red Cross. She began her career during the Civil War by advertising in newspapers and urging officials to make sure that soldiers received necessary medical supplies. Look up information on the Red Cross today. Create a poster that identifies current medical needs.
4. **COLLABORATIVE LEARNING** One way a nation can come to terms with a painful past is to create movies and novels based on the disruptive periods of its history, such as the Civil War. *Gone With the Wind*, a movie about the effects of the Civil War on the Southern way of life, has become a classic. During its production the public was fascinated by the two-year search for exactly the right actor to play each role in the movie. As a class, create a list of major Civil War characters to be cast in a documentary about the North and South during the war. Read through previous chapters to include people such as Harriet Beecher Stowe and Harriet Tubman who played important parts in the events leading up to the war. Cast the characters from among current actors, explaining why each actor fits the part chosen for him or her.
5. **COLLABORATIVE LEARNING** "Dixie," "Battle Hymn of the Republic," "Tenting Tonight," and "Tramp! Tramp! Tramp!" were some of the songs that became popular during the Civil War. In small groups, look up the background of these songs, and give a presentation to the class.

Answers to Reviewing Skills

1. Notecards should include book title and page numbers.
2. Topic question should be well-defined, and answerable within the textbook.
3. Refer students to Understanding Information Organization on page 228.
4. Refer students to Understanding Timelines on page 60. Ask students to compare their timelines to see if they have included the same events, or if they have ordered events differently.
5. You may want to ask students to pay particular attention to identifying purpose and audience. Students should consider different kinds of primary sources when they are locating information.

Answers to Using Critical Thinking

1. Encourage students to consider how freedom of the press affects them in the classroom. Possible topics for discussion: the school's right to search lockers, drug-testing for athletes, and censorship of school newspapers.
2. Students may answer that Lincoln wanted to save the Union any way that he could. Encourage students to compare the popular view of history with the facts. For example, many people believe that Lincoln fought the Civil War solely to free the slaves, whereas this quotation shows that preserving the Union was actually more important.
3. Encourage students to consider how important believing in a cause may be to winning a war. Point out that the colonies were in a similarly weak position when the American Revolution began. Be sure students give specific reasons for their responses.

Answers to Preparing for Citizenship

1. **WRITING ACTIVITY** Begin activity by having the class create a list of current movies, novels, and television shows about a recent war. Alternatively, view posters and art with World War II or Vietnam themes.
2. **WRITING ACTIVITY** Discuss the fact that Lincoln wrote his short eulogy on the train to Gettysburg. Encourage students to write short, anonymous responses to the passage on page 366, then pass the pieces around and have them read aloud in class.
3. **ART ACTIVITY** Students may want to contact the Red Cross and ask for information. The class may offer their posters for use by the local Red Cross chapter.
4. **COLLABORATIVE LEARNING** Students should be careful to give specific reasons for each choice. The choice should reflect knowledge of the character's role in history.
5. **COLLABORATIVE LEARNING** Encourage students to perform the songs with their own instruments, or to make tapes of the performance.

CHAPTER 13

Planning at a Glance

Reconstruction

	Objectives	Reading Support *and* Other Resources	Diverse Learning Strategies
Lesson 1 A Time for Reconciliation *pp. 376–384* 2–3 days	• Assess the South's economic hardships after the Civil War. • Contrast President Lincoln's plans for Reconstruction with the approach favored by Congress. • Explain why President Johnson's Reconstruction policies caused conflict with Congress. • Examine the impact of the Black Codes on freed slaves.	• **Workbook** or **Reading Support:** pp. 182–185 Review p. 43 Extra Support/Transition p. 43 Multi-lang. Sum. pp. 85–86 • **Other Resources:** Geography Kit, Poster 5, Study Guide p. 55, Study Print 9	Access Strat. **(Extra Support)** TE p. 377 Visual Learning **(Visual)** TE pp. 380, 381 Role Playing **(Auditory)** TE p. 382 Research **(GATE)** TE p. 383 Audiotapes of Multi-language Lesson Summaries **(Auditory)**
Lesson 2 Radical Reconstruction *pp. 385–390* 1–2 days	• Explain how conflicts over Reconstruction policy led to a resolution of impeachment. • Consider the significance of the black vote in the South during Reconstruction. • Examine why Northerners went to the South after the Civil War. • State the provison and impact of the Fifteenth Amendment and the reasons for its passage.	• **Workbook** or **Reading Support:** pp. 186–189 Review p. 44 Extra Support/Transition p. 44 Multi-lang. Sum. pp. 87–88 • **Other Resources:** Geography Kit, Study Guide p. 56	Access Act. **(SDAIE)** TE p. 386 Art Connection **(Visual)** TE p. 388 Making a Chart **(Visual)** TE p. 389 Audiotapes of Multi-language Lesson Summaries **(Auditory)**
Lesson 3 Southern Life Under Reconstruction *pp. 391–397* 2–3 days **Literature** **"The Lincoln Poems" and "It Was A Glorious Day!"** *pp. 400–403*	• Explain why emancipation did not guarantee black southerners economic opportunities. • Examine how white Southerners resisted granting black Americans equality. • State how the bargain to elect Rutherford B. Hayes ended Reconstruction. • Examine the legacy of the Reconstruction Era.	• **Workbook** or **Reading Support:** pp. 190–193 Review p. 45 Extra Support/Transition p. 45 Multi-lang. Sum. pp. 89–90 • **Other Resources:** Study Guide p. 57	Access Strategy **(Extra Support)** TE p. 392 Visual Learning **(Visual)** TE pp. 393, 394, 395 Making a Mural **(Visual)** TE p. 396 Homework Options **(GATE)** TE p. 397 Audiotapes of Multi-language Lesson Summaries **(Auditory)**
Skill: **Analyzing the Civil War** *pp. 398–399*	• Use Civil War events to compare cause-and-effect relationships.	• **Other Resources:** Study Guide p. 58	
Chapter Review *pp. 404–405* 1 day		Chapter 13 Test pp. 49–52 *(See facsimiles on TE p. 761.)*	Assessment Multiple-Use Masters pp. 81–88

Reading Support Resources *for Every Lesson*

Reading and Review

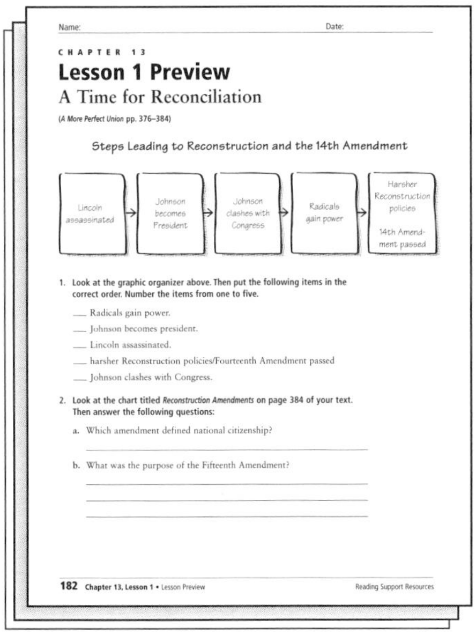
Name: Date:

CHAPTER 13

Lesson 1 Preview

A Time for Reconciliation

(*A More Perfect Union* pp. 376–384)

1. Look at the graphic organizer above. Then put the following items in the correct order. Number the items from one to five.
   - ___ Radicals gain power.
   - ___ Johnson becomes president.
   - ___ Lincoln assassinated.
   - ___ harsher Reconstruction policies/Fourteenth Amendment passed
   - ___ Johnson clashes with Congress.
2. Look at the chart titled *Reconstruction Amendments* on page 384 of your text. Then answer the following questions:
   a. Which amendment defined national citizenship?
   b. What was the purpose of the Fifteenth Amendment?

182 Chapter 13, Lesson 1 • Lesson Preview   Reading Support Resources

- **Chapter Overview*** p. 181
- **Lesson Previews*** using graphic organizers from the Teacher's Edition pp. 182, 186, 190
- **Reading Strategies*** pp. 183, 187, 191
- **Lesson Summaries*** pp. 184–185, 188–189, 192–193
- **Lesson Reviews** pp. 43, 44, 45

* **Workbook** includes starred items.

Multi-language Summaries

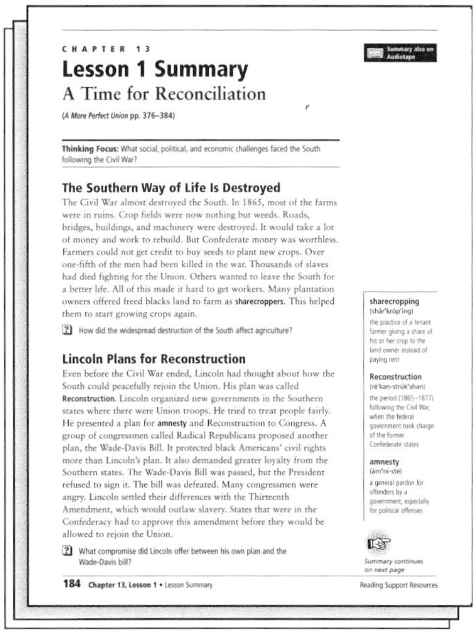
CHAPTER 13

Summary also on Audiotape

Lesson 1 Summary

A Time for Reconciliation

(*A More Perfect Union* pp. 376–384)

Thinking Focus: What social, political, and economic challenges faced the South following the Civil War?

The Southern Way of Life Is Destroyed

The Civil War almost destroyed the South. In 1865, most of the farms were in ruins. Crop fields were now nothing but weeds. Roads, bridges, buildings, and machinery were destroyed. It would take a lot of money and work to rebuild. But Confederate money was worthless. Farmers could not get credit to buy seeds to plant new crops. Over one-fifth of the men had been killed in the war. Thousands of slaves had died fighting for the Union. Others wanted to leave the South for a better life. All of this made it hard to get workers. Many plantation owners offered freed blacks land to farm as **sharecroppers**. This helped them to start growing crops again.

? How did the widespread destruction of the South affect agriculture?

Lincoln Plans for Reconstruction

Even before the Civil War ended, Lincoln had thought about how the South could peacefully rejoin the Union. His plan was called **Reconstruction**. Lincoln organized new governments in the Southern states where there were Union troops. He tried to treat people fairly. He presented a plan for **amnesty** and Reconstruction to Congress. A group of congressmen called Radical Republicans proposed another plan, the Wade-Davis Bill. It protected black Americans' civil rights more than Lincoln's plan. It also demanded greater loyalty from the Southern states. The Wade-Davis Bill was passed, but the President refused to sign it. The bill was defeated. Many congressmen were angry. Lincoln settled their differences with the Thirteenth Amendment, which would outlaw slavery. States that were in the Confederacy had to approve this amendment before they would be allowed to rejoin the Union.

? What compromise did Lincoln offer between his own plan and the Wade-Davis bill?

sharecropping (shâr'krŏp'ĭng) the practice of a tenant farmer giving a share of his or her crop to the land owner instead of paying rent

Reconstruction (rē'kən-strŭk'shən) the period (1865–1877) following the Civil War, when the federal government took charge of the former Confederate states

amnesty (ăm'nĭ-stē) a general pardon for offenders by a government, especially for political offenses

Summary continues on next page

184 Chapter 13, Lesson 1 • Lesson Summary   Reading Support Resources

Lesson Summaries in:

- English (See Reading and Review.)
- Spanish pp. 184–185, 188–189, 192–193
- Chinese pp. 85–90
- Hmong pp. 85–90
- Khmer pp. 85–90
- Vietnamese pp. 85–90

Summaries available on audiotapes

Lesson Support / Transition

S D A I E

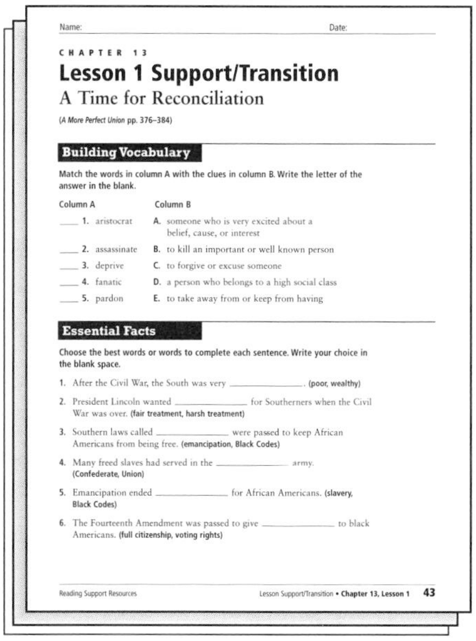
Name: Date:

CHAPTER 13

Lesson 1 Support/Transition

A Time for Reconciliation

(*A More Perfect Union* pp. 376–384)

Building Vocabulary

Match the words in column A with the clues in column B. Write the letter of the answer in the blank.

Column A	Column B
___ 1. aristocrat	A. someone who is very excited about a belief, cause, or interest
___ 2. assassinate	B. to kill an important or well known person
___ 3. deprive	C. to forgive or excuse someone
___ 4. fanatic	D. a person who belongs to a high social class
___ 5. pardon	E. to take away from or keep from having

Essential Facts

Choose the best words or words to complete each sentence. Write your choice in the blank space.

1. After the Civil War, the South was very ________. (poor, wealthy)
2. President Lincoln wanted ________ for Southerners when the Civil War was over. (fair treatment, harsh treatment)
3. Southern laws called ________ were passed to keep African Americans from being free. (emancipation, Black Codes)
4. Many freed slaves had served in the ________ army. (Confederate, Union)
5. Emancipation ended ________ for African Americans. (slavery, Black Codes)
6. The Fourteenth Amendment was passed to give ________ to black Americans. (full citizenship, voting rights)

Reading Support Resources   Lesson Support/Transition • Chapter 13, Lesson 1 43

Activities for SDAIE

Specially **D**esigned **A**cademic **I**nstruction in **E**nglish

- **Lesson Support/Transition** pp. 43, 44, 45

Technology Options

Internet Support

http://www.eduplace.com

Social Studies Center at Education Place

Internet support for Chapter 13:

- ***Lesson at a Glance***
- ***The Rebuilding of Richmond***

Software

Student Writing Center® (CD-ROM) (Macintosh® or Windows®)

School to Career

Reconstruction of the South was not only a rebuilding of a way of life and political influence but also of cities and farms destroyed in the Civil War. Have students select a profession involved in construction, and create a word web including terminology and tools used by these individuals.

Character Education

Trust is essential if individuals are to live together peacefully. What characteristics do students feel an individual should have to be considered trustworthy? Have them find examples in the local community as well as in the international arena of people or countries that do or do not "trust" one another.

CHAPTER PREVIEW

Have students read the chapter title and the narrative underneath it. Ask students to use the visuals on this page and page 375 to predict what changes would occur in the South during Reconstruction. *(Cities would be rebuilt; black Americans would be given new opportunities.)*

Looking Back

Have students recall what they learned about Southern economy and culture in Chapter 10. What effects might the lack of slave labor and the amount of destruction in the South's few urban centers have on the region? *(The South will face terrible financial difficulties. The cotton economy will suffer.)*

Looking Forward

Tell students that the next three lessons explain the events and issues that shaped the postwar policy of the North toward the South and how Reconstruction affected life in the South: A Time for Reconciliation, Radical Reconstruction, and Southern Life under Reconstruction.

Chapter 13
Reconstruction

Houses, streets, railroads, even entire cities lay in ruins. The war was over. It was a time to rebuild. New laws would help to rebuild peoples' lives. New schools would bring education and increased opportunities to all.

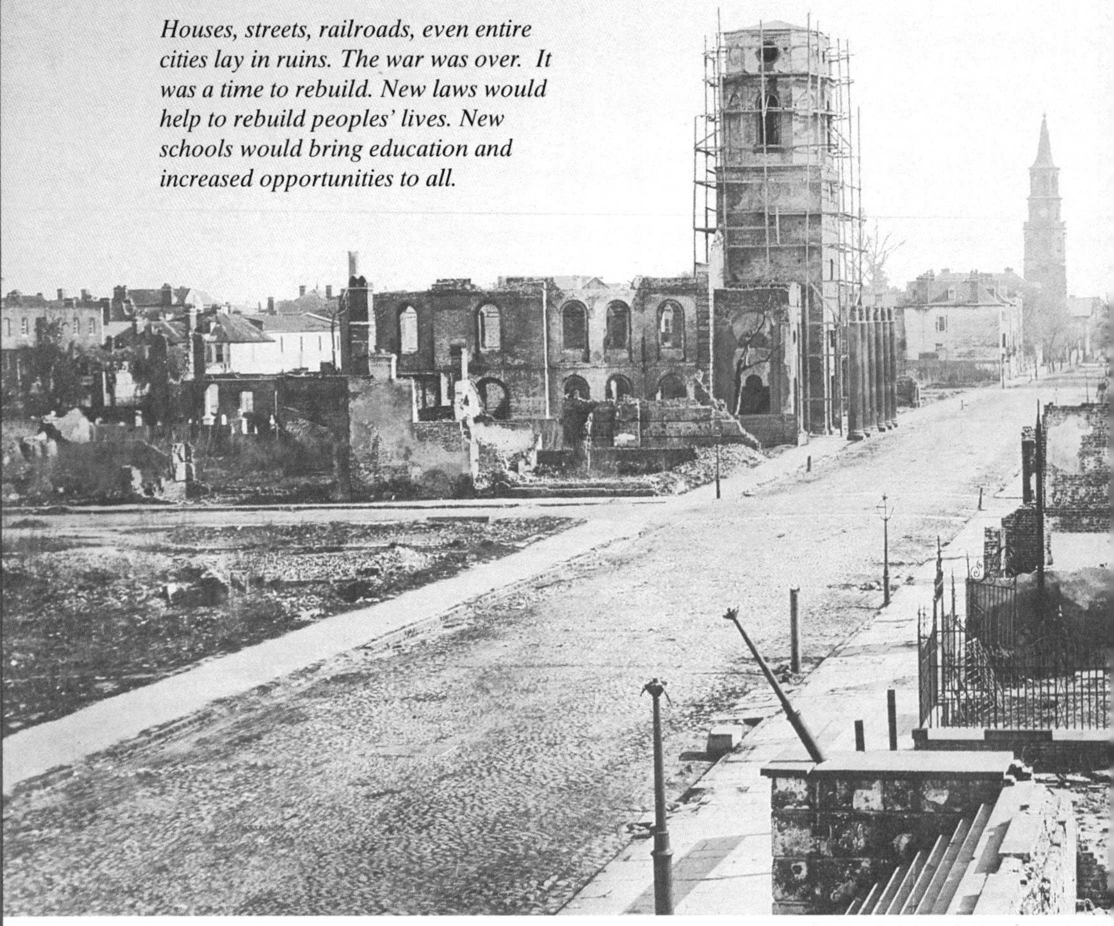

1865 The rebuilding of Richmond, Virginia, symbolizes the country's desire to heal its war wounds and move forward.

1865 | 1869

Presidents

1865-1869 A. Johnson

1869-1877 Grant

374

1865

BACKGROUND

The Civil War ended in 1865, leaving the North and the South with the challenging task of reconciliation. The Reconstruction years of 1865–1877 brought about serious social, economic, and political changes in the South.

The South Is Destroyed

The destruction of the South during the Civil War was nearly complete. Farmland, livestock, and homes were lost. In addition, commerce and industry suffered. Excluding the loss of slaves as property, the general wealth of the region declined by 43 percent from 1860 to 1865. Even greater financial losses came as a result of emancipation through the loss of slave labor.

The financial destruction of the South was brought about, in part, by the Confederacy's need for paper money to finance the war. By printing excessive quantities, however, the Confederate government created runaway inflation and ruined the banking system. The value of a one-dollar treasury note declined to 1.7 cents by early 1865. People who invested heavily in Confederate bonds to support the war effort suffered terrible losses.

The bankruptcy of Southern financial institutions, the damage to commercial ties with Europe and the North, and the loss of a productive labor force caused by emancipation and wartime casualties all made it very difficult to rebuild the South.

Adults and children alike learned in newly established freedmen's schools.

Documents called family records helped black families reconstruct their past.

1873

1877

1877

Understanding the Visuals

Point out the photograph of Richmond, Virginia, in ruins. Students will learn more about why the city was ruined and how it was rebuilt in A Closer Look at Rebuilding the South.

The photo of the freedmen's school was taken in North Carolina. By 1866, the Freedmen's Bureau was operating 965 schools for 90,778 students.

The family record was a document given out by Northern reformers to freed slaves because slave families had often been broken up as members were sold to different plantations. Point out the phrases "Before the War" and "After the War" and the scenes underneath them.

Understanding Chronology

Draw students' attention to the chapter timeline. Tell students to note who the Presidents were during this time period. What factors might have helped Grant win the Presidency after the Civil War? *(He was a popular war hero; he had people's confidence because he led a winning war effort.)*

375

Equality Before the Law

The Thirteenth Amendment outlawed slavery in 1865. By guaranteeing the equality of black Americans before the law, supporters of abolitionism hoped to end further discrimination. Northern ideals clashed with Southern values, however, and the strong resentment between the two regions continued throughout the Reconstruction period.

Many Southerners refused to accept the idea of freeing the slaves. Some plantation owners did not tell their slaves that they were free. Even white Southerners who accepted emancipation found it difficult to believe black Americans could perform any work besides slave labor. Although there were varying degrees of resistance to emancipation, most white Southerners did not want to include former slaves in their social, economic, and political order.

INTRODUCE

Refer students to the lesson title. Ask them to define *reconcile. (To bring back into harmony)* Have students read the Thinking Focus and recall the conflicts that had produced the war. Tell them to read the lesson to find out why reconciliation would be difficult.

Key Terms

Vocabulary strategies: T36–37

sharecropping—a system in which a tenant farmer gives a share of the crop to the farmer instead of paying rent

Reconstruction—the period (1865–1877) following the Civil War in which the former Confederate states were controlled by the federal government

amnesty—a general pardon by a government, especially for political offenders

segregated—the maintenance of separate facilities for members of different races

■ *Southern agriculture was crippled by the widespread destruction of farmland, crops, livestock, and the loss of slave labor.*

1864 1865 1877 1878

LESSON 1

A Time for Reconciliation

THINKING FOCUS

What social, political, and economic challenges faced the South following the Civil War?

Key Terms

- sharecropping
- Reconstruction
- amnesty
- segregated

Today your father, a Confederate soldier, is coming home. The war is over. General Robert E. Lee has surrendered to General Ulysses S. Grant. You are relieved to know that your father is not among the thousands of men killed in the war. As you wait and watch, you wonder what your father will say when he sees your home and the empty fields. Before the war, your father was a cotton farmer —just like his father—but now all that remains is one cow and an apple tree.

Your mother's sister from Atlanta lives with you now. Her husband was killed in the war and her son was captured by the enemy. Her home was burned during Sherman's March, and she had nowhere else to go. She arrived without money or possessions.

Your own home was spared, but you've seen your crops destroyed. Northerners drove the livestock off your land. For months you have survived on what little you could grow in a small garden patch. Supper often meant squirrels or rabbits or rats. Once a neighbor shared some mule meat he had stolen.

The war is over. Your father, once a proud farmer and soldier, will return to find only destruction and an uncertain future.

The Southern Way of Life Is Destroyed

The South in 1865 faced extreme poverty. The Civil War crippled Southern agriculture, which was the foundation of its economy. Burned-out plantations, weed-filled fields, and plundered homes left many Southerners without shelter, crops, or money.

The widespread destruction of roads, bridges, farm buildings, and machinery meant that the process of rebuilding the South would be slow and difficult. Confederate money issued during the war was worthless. White planters were ruined financially. Farmers could not get credit to buy seeds and plant new crops. Without money, many Southerners resorted to a barter system, or trading of one kind of goods for another.

The loss of human life would also affect the effort to rebuild the South. Nearly 290,000 men—over one-fifth of the adult male population in the South—died for the Confederate cause. Some 37,000 blacks, most of whom were from the South, died serving in the Union army.

Nearly four million freed blacks, called freedmen, fled the plantations in search of a better life. To attract workers back to the fields, many plantation owners offered freedmen land to farm in return for a portion of the crop. This practice was called **sharecropping**. ■

■ *How did the widespread destruction of the South affect agriculture?*

Objectives

1. Assess the South's economic hardships after the Civil War.
2. Contrast President Lincoln's plans for Reconstruction with the approach favored by Congress.
3. Explain why President Johnson's Reconstruction policies caused conflict with Congress.
4. Examine the impact of the Black Codes on freed slaves.

Graphic Overview

Lincoln assassinated ➤ Johnson becomes President ➤ Johnson clashes with Congress ➤ Radicals gain power ➤ Harsher Reconstruction policies; 14th Amendment passed

Lincoln Plans for Reconstruction

President Lincoln had led the nation through the Civil War, the nation's bloodiest conflict. He eagerly sought a plan to reunite the nation in a peaceful way. This plan to bring the 11 Confederate states back into the Union was called **Reconstruction.** The Reconstruction period lasted from 1865 to 1877. The whole process would raise enormous questions about the nation's political, economic, and social future.

Proclamation of Amnesty

During the war, Lincoln worried about the conditions under which the South would rejoin the Union. "I do not want to hurt the hair of a single man in the South if it can possibly be avoided," he said. He wanted to help the South rebuild its cities and homes. Richmond, Virginia, once the Confederate capital, now lay in ruins. See A Closer Look on pages 380–381 about efforts to rebuild this city.

In those Southern states policed by Union troops, Lincoln organized new state governments. Fair treatment of Southerners in occupied areas, he felt, would discourage the remaining Confederate states from resisting. He also hoped it would bring about a more comfortable peace when the war finally ended.

On December 8, 1863, Lincoln presented to Congress his Proclamation of Amnesty and Reconstruction. **Amnesty** meant that every Southerner who then took an oath of loyalty to the United States would be pardoned. Any Confederate state could form a new government and adopt a new constitution. Ten percent of those who had voted in the presidential election of 1860 simply had to take the oath of loyalty to the United States. While the proclamation prohibited slavery, it did nothing about civil rights for blacks. Their right to vote and to have rights in society were not ensured. Several states took advantage of the plan. By 1864, they had reorganized new civilian governments.

The Wade-Davis Bill

When the war ended, Lincoln's party, the Republicans, had two main branches: the Radicals and the Moderates. Radical Republicans thought that Lincoln's plan should be more forceful. They believed that the federal government should take an active role in protecting the rights of blacks and loyal whites in the South.

In July 1864, the Radicals in Congress passed their own plan, the

In this 1865 cartoon by Thomas Nast, a woman symbolizes the Union. She considers whether to pardon the Confederates as Robert E. Lee kneels before her.

DEVELOP

Explain that after the Civil War, a series of events led to harsher policies toward the South. As students read, have them list events that had an effect on Reconstruction.

ECONOMICS

Critical Thinking

Ask students to think about the white Southern families whose homes, fields, and crops were destroyed; whose currency was worthless; and whose workforce disappeared with the freeing of the slaves. How would lack of money and labor affect the efforts of white Southerners to rebuild? *(Without money to buy seed, replant land, repair buildings, and hire workers, Southerners wouldn't be able to rebuild.)*

Access Strategy

Have students think of an argument they had with a friend or relative. Ask them to focus on the time period before they made up. How did they feel? Were they thinking about revenge? Or were they trying to find a way to end the quarrel by compromise? Ask students to think about the way the winner of an argument should treat the loser. How does the winner's attitude affect their future relationship? What about the loser's attitude?

Remind students that the North and the South had disagreed bitterly for many years because of their different belief systems. Ask students to brainstorm a list of the differences and conflicts between the North and the South before the war. Have one student write the list on the board. These differences, plus four years of war, would make reconciling their differences extremely difficult. Tell students that this lesson begins to explain the North's treatment of the South after the Civil War.

Access Activity

Have students study the political cartoon on this page. Ask students to discuss what the woman and the throne symbolize. *(The victorious Union)* Then ask students to analyze what the kneeling position might mean. *(Robert E. Lee and the Confederacy must bow before the Union and ask for mercy.)*

POLITICAL SYSTEMS

Critical Thinking

Ask students to characterize Lincoln's plans for Reconstruction. *(Kind, forgiving)* How did Lincoln's Proclamation of Amnesty and Reconstruction differ from the Wade-Davis Bill? *(Proclamation—10 per cent of a state's voters had to swear allegiance to the United States before forming a government. Wade-Davis—majority of a state's voters had to swear allegiance and the new state had to declare its debts unpayable.)*

■ *He compromised by proposing the Thirteenth Amendment. Former Confederate states were required to ratify it before rejoining the Union.*

How Do We Know?

HISTORY *Diaries provide personal accounts of the past. Susan Dabney Smedes wrote about her father, Thomas Dabney, a rich Mississippi planter. After the war, "when he was seventy years of age, he determined to learn to cultivate a garden. He had never before performed manual labor."*

■ *What compromise did Lincoln offer between his own plan and the Wade-Davis bill?*

Wade-Davis bill. The bill required that the majority (instead of 10 percent) of a state's 1860 voters in each Southern state swear allegiance to the United States and take part in drafting a new constitution. Only then could that state be readmitted to the Union. The bill demanded that Confederates swear past and present loyalty.

The Wade-Davis bill also required the new state constitutions to outlaw slavery and declare the Confederate debt unpayable. Confederate bonds and money thus became worthless.

Republican Moderates in Congress agreed with Lincoln's easier terms for Reconstruction. However, the bill gained support because it gave Congress a strong role in forming Reconstruction policy. Members of Congress were unwilling to let the President single-handedly determine the course of Reconstruction.

With the support of Moderates, Congress passed the Wade-Davis bill. Congress then adjourned, however, and Lincoln refused to sign the bill. This defeated the Wade-Davis bill and angered many congressmen. In January 1865, Lincoln compromised by proposing the Thirteenth Amendment to outlaw slavery. Former Confederate states were required to ratify, or formally approve, the amendment before rejoining the Union.

The struggles between Lincoln and Congress reflected different views, even among Republicans, about what Reconstruction should mean. Radical Republicans hoped to reshape the South in the image of the North and to weaken the plantation system. Moderates, on the other hand, wanted to establish the power of the federal government and equality before the law for blacks and whites. ■

▼ *At a performance of the play advertised in this poster, President Lincoln was assassinated.*

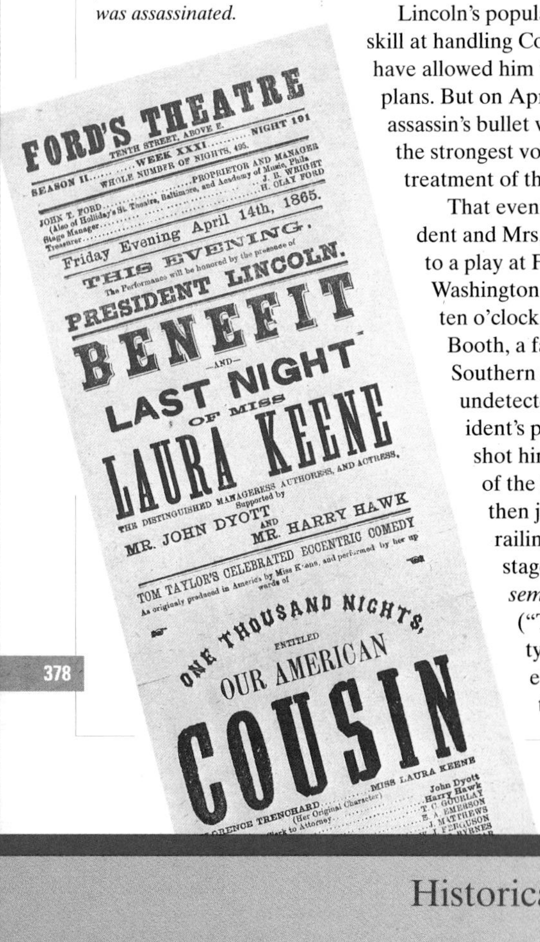

Lincoln Assassinated

Lincoln's popularity and his skill at handling Congress might have allowed him to carry out his plans. But on April 14, 1865, an assassin's bullet would silence the strongest voice for generous treatment of the South.

That evening, the President and Mrs. Lincoln went to a play at Ford's Theatre in Washington. Shortly after ten o'clock, John Wilkes Booth, a fanatically pro-Southern actor, slipped undetected into the President's private box and shot him in the back of the head. Booth then jumped over the railing onto the stage, crying, *"Sic semper tyrannis"* ("Thus always to tyrants"). Booth escaped from the theater on horseback. Later, federal troops cornered and killed the President's assassin in a Virginia barn.

President Lincoln was carried to a nearby house. Doctors could only wash his wounds and try to make him comfortable. Secretary of War Edwin Stanton arrived and sent an officer to notify the Vice President, Andrew Johnson.

When word spread, crowds of people gathered around the house. The people waited for hours, remaining even when rain began to fall. Lincoln never regained consciousness and died the next morning. "Now he belongs to the ages," Stanton said.

News of Lincoln's death, just six days after Lee's surrender, stunned the North. For two days his body lay in state in the Capitol where thousands of people filed past his coffin. Then a special train carried his body back to Illinois for burial. Seven million people lined the route, waiting for hours to pay their final respects.

378

Critical Thinking

Ask students to analyze the causes of Lincoln's assassination. *(Southern anger, Booth's agitated mental state, lack of security in the theater)* Ask them to predict the long-term consequences of Lincoln's death. *(Lincoln's support of emancipation would be lost, and it would be more difficult for former slaves to achieve equality.)*

Historical Context

In the spring and summer of 1865, the black South celebrated. Felix Haywood, a witness to the great outpouring of joy, said nothing like it had ever been seen before. "Hallelujah broke out," he said. "Soldiers, all of a sudden, was everywhere—coming in bunches, crossing and walking and riding. Everyone was a-singing. We was all walking on golden clouds. Hallelujah!"

The golden clouds of freedom meant different things to different freedmen and freedwomen. To some it meant getting married before a preacher, signing papers, and knowing no one could sell them to separate masters. For others, it was the right to come and go as they pleased. For still others, it was identity. Freed slaves selected names, and if they didn't like them, they could change them. Some freed slaves chose the names of their former masters.

Many white Southerners saw freed slaves as a threat. "What will we do with all of

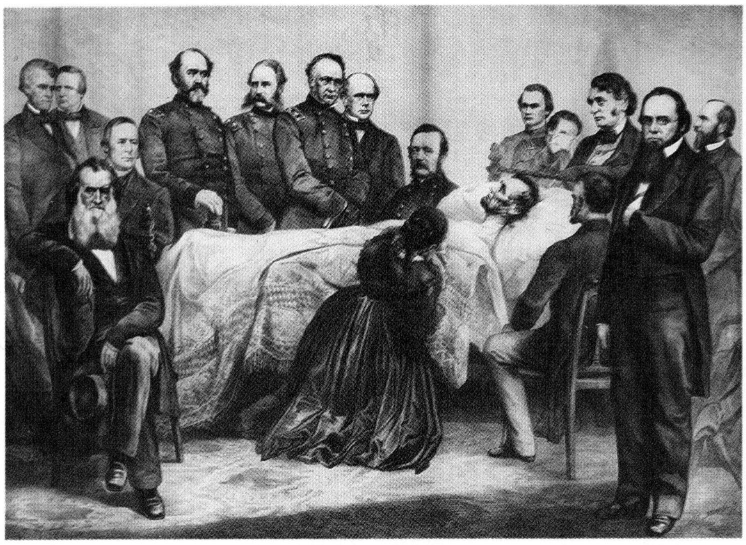

On his deathbed, President Lincoln was surrounded by leaders from his Cabinet and administration.

Johnson Takes the Reins

Hours after Lincoln's death, Chief Justice Salmon P. Chase went to Vice President Andrew Johnson's hotel to administer the oath of office. Johnson was a Southern Democrat who had remained loyal to the Union after his state, Tennessee, had seceded. He was well known for hating Southern aristocrats and wishing to punish those in the South who were guilty of treason. White Southerners naturally feared what Johnson's Reconstruction policy might bring.

Yet Johnson was once a slave owner. He strongly believed in states' rights. He did not believe the federal government had a right to control the society of the South, as long as its people accepted the abolition of slavery. However, Johnson came up short on political and diplomatic skills. He did not share Lincoln's ability to negotiate. Unfortunately, he found compromise impossible.

Johnson made public his plan for Reconstruction in May 1865. Its goal was to encourage the white South to renew its loyalty voluntarily. The plan disappointed the Radicals because it looked like Lincoln's 10 percent plan. Johnson set easy terms for the states to form new governments and send representatives to Congress. Johnson gave back voting rights to most whites, but he only encouraged new states to allow freedmen to vote.

Black Codes Keep Slavery Alive

The Southern states followed Johnson's policies, but not happily. None gave blacks the right to vote. Instead, the new state governments tried to bring back slavery in all but name. They used laws known as the Black Codes.

Enacted from 1865 to 1866, the Black Codes varied from state to state. But everywhere the laws were meant to keep blacks from being free. In Mississippi, black orphans or children whose parents could not raise them could be forced to work as apprentices, often for their former owners.

In Louisiana, freedmen had to sign yearly labor contracts that bound them to their place of work. South Carolina forbade blacks to hold any job except that of farmer or servant, unless they paid from $10 to $100 for a license. Plantation workers could only leave the grounds with permission from their "masters." ■

President Andrew Johnson, a Southern Democrat from Tennessee, angered both white Southerners and Radical Republicans with his moderate Reconstruction policies.

■ *How did the Black Codes keep freed blacks in virtual slavery?*

HISTORY

Critical Thinking

Ask students to explain why President Johnson's determination to set the course of Reconstruction policies caused such conflict with Radical Republicans in Congress. *(Radicals wanted more far-reaching policies, while Johnson wanted to allow white Southerners to renew their loyalty voluntarily. Congress disagreed with Johnson's approach and became engaged in a power struggle over who should control Reconstruction policy)*

■ *The Black Codes restricted the basic freedom to live and work freely by limiting opportunities for black Americans.*

them?" they asked. Frederick Douglass, a prominent black abolitionist, had an answer. "Do nothing with [them]. Your doing is the greatest misfortune . . . the Negro should have been let alone in Africa . . . let alone when the pirates offered him for sale . . . let alone by courts, judges, politicians, legislators and slave drivers.

"If you see [the black man] plowing in the open field, leveling the forest, at work with a spade, a rake, a hoe, a pick-axe . . . let him alone; he has a right to work. If you see him on his way to school . . . let him alone . . . If he has a ballot in his hand, and is on his way to the ballot-box to deposit his vote for the man whom he thinks will most justly and wisely administer the Government which has the power of life and death over him, as well as others—let him alone."

Critical Thinking

In discussing why white Southerners created the Black Codes, have students suggest psychological as well as economic reasons. *(To retain control over their former slaves; also needed a productive labor force to work in the fields)*

Note: You may want to use A Closer Look at Rebuilding the South to introduce the lesson.

HISTORY

Visual Learning

Have students consider how Richmond looked before and after the Civil War. Tell them to make a list of what needed to be rebuilt. *(Homes, businesses, city-run services, and parks)* Ask students how this effort might have changed the character of the city. *(New buildings would change how the city looks; people might feel differently about a new city.)*

A CLOSER LOOK

The Rebuilding of Richmond

In the dead of the night, on April 2, 1865, Confederate soldiers, upon hearing that Union troops were approaching, torched their capital of Richmond, Virginia. As arsenals exploded, red-hot embers rained on the city. People stood on their rooftops, coughing from the black smoke, fanning away sparks to protect their homes.

Why torch your own capital? The Confederates wanted to prevent Northerners from taking valuable military supplies and equipment.

Hammering and chipping could be heard all over Richmond in the days that followed the fire. Chain gangs of convicts helped clear the rubble from streets and vacant lots. Rebuilding began as soon as the fire was under control.

Critical Thinking

Ask students if any parts of their community or a neighboring community have been destroyed or rebuilt. Was the destruction deliberate or accidental? Have them identify different aspects of the project. *(Funding, planning, construction)* Have the people who previously lived or worked in the area returned to it?

Language Arts Connection

Remind students that Lincoln was assassinated while attending a performance of *Our American Cousin* and that his assassin, John Wilkes Booth, was a well-known actor. Ask students to research and write a two-page report on the American theater and other actors of the time, such as Edwin Booth (John Wilkes's brother).

Art Connection

During the second half of the 1800s, artists such as John Frederick Kensett, Richard Caton Woodville, and Daniel Huntington were popular. Many painters were at work during this time, and most large towns supported at least one portrait painter. With the introduction of the camera, many people turned away from painting and toward photography. Have students write a one-page report on the advantages and disadvantages of using photography to record history.

The Confederates left timed charges to explode after the Union soldiers arrived. Explosions around 2:00 A.M. shattered most of the city's mirrors and windows and killed more than a dozen people. Riots broke out. Union prisoners escaped, and panic-stricken dogs and thousands of squealing rats dashed through the streets.

Rebuilding transformed Main Street into a modern downtown area. This time around, builders used bricks and mortar instead of wood. The building boom provided many Richmonders with jobs, as new structures rose four or five stories high.

ECONOMICS

Visual Learning

Refer students to the picture of the demolished locomotive. Ask them to consider why the people of Richmond would destroy their own railway system and bridges. *(They did not want the enemy to gain valuable military supplies and equipment.)*

More About Richmond The Confederate capital's access to iron and coal supplies meant that war materials, especially cannons, were built there.

Language Arts Connection

Slaves were denied their African names when they were brought to the United States and given names by their masters. In recent years, many black people have acknowledged their African roots by adopting African names. Have students write a one-page paper listing some of the reasons people change their names and supporting these reasons with several examples.

Critical Thinking

Have students make a list of the professions of people who must have worked to rebuild Richmond. *(Sample answers: masons, architects, city planners, laborers of all kinds)*

Freed People Struggle for Rights

Despite the Black Codes, former slaves rejoiced in their new freedom. Many had served in the Union army and were determined to have the rights they had fought to gain. Emancipation would not rid the opposition of Southern whites to ending slavery. But it did offer African Americans the chance to travel, worship, and earn a living as their own masters. Under slavery, blacks were required to carry passes. Emancipation ended the pass system. Soon, freedmen were leaving plantations and searching for better opportunities.

Cities and towns across the South experienced a great influx of blacks during and just after the Civil War. Between 1865 and 1870, the black population of the South's 10 largest cities doubled. Black institutions such as schools, churches, and social organizations were available to the newcomers. The Union army's presence in the cities also gave a measure of protection against the violence that African Americans had suffered in the rural areas of the South.

Blacks were also now free to look for family members who had been sold to other masters. In 1865, a Northern reporter met a black man who had walked nearly 600 miles from Georgia to North Carolina to look for his wife and children. Some could not find missing relatives and faced crushing disappointment. Still others were able to reestablish their family ties that had been broken by the cruelties of slavery. A Union officer wrote to his wife: "I wish you could see [these] people as they step from slavery into

In this engraving, African Americans in Washington, D.C. turn out to celebrate their freedom.

HISTORY

Visual Learning

Have students look closely at the engraving on this page. Ask them to identify the participants in the celebration. Also ask why the military would be present at such an event. *(They are possibly black soldiers still in uniform.)*

Critical Thinking

Just as the Freedmen's Bureau lacked adequate funding (page 383), Congressional funding for similar programs helping disadvantaged people today—such as the Legal Aid Society—is still controversial. Ask students why they think people might oppose such public funding. *(Tax caps; opposed to government involvement)*

Role Playing

Divide the class into two groups, representing Northern congressmen debating Reconstruction policy. One group should play Radical Republicans, who sought far-reaching reforms in the South, while the other group should play Moderates, who wanted to make it easier for Southern states to be readmitted to the Union.

Speaking and Listening

Ask four students to imagine being one of the following: a plantation owner just coming home after the war to discover his home in ruins, a family member who witnessed the destruction, a freed slave who remains with the family, and a Northern soldier passing through. In one-minute extemporaneous speeches, have each person describe his or her initial feelings and thoughts at this moment.

Critical Thinking

Ask students to discuss the difficulties blacks faced as they struggled for jobs, education, and social equality. What was the purpose of the Freedmen's Bureau and how well did it succeed? *(The Freedmen's Bureau helped freed slaves find work, drew up employment contracts, and aided in the establishment of schools. The organization's success was mixed, however, because it lacked funding from Congress for its projects.)*

Located in Washington, D.C., Howard University (left) *is one of the largest chiefly black universities in the United States. It is supported by both federal and private funds. The university was named in honor of the Freedmen's Bureau's white administrator, General Oliver O. Howard* (above).

freedom. Men are taking their wives and children, families which had been for a long time broken up are reunited and oh! such happiness. I am glad I am here."

Freedmen's Bureau Provides Aid

Just before the war's end, Congress established the Freedmen's Bureau to give aid and support to newly freed blacks. For emergency relief, the Bureau distributed food to the needy of both races. Finding jobs for former slaves was one of the Bureau's first tasks. To help those returning to plantations, it drew up contracts that guaranteed rights and payment. In addition, the Bureau performed thousands of marriages for freed blacks. Unfortunately, Congress failed to set aside money for the Freedmen's Bureau. Its programs were often short-lived, lasting only a year or two.

Equality Through Education

Blacks set out to get better jobs and an education. They also sought the right to own property and the right to vote. Before the war ended, blacks had been kept by law from learning to read and write. They had long seen education as their ticket to independence. Northern charitable and church groups and the Freedmen's Bureau helped in the effort to educate blacks. The American Missionary Association founded seven colleges, including Fisk and Atlanta universities, between 1866 and 1869. The Freedmen's Bureau helped to establish Howard University in 1867. The chief function of Howard is to train black students, but it is open to all students, regardless of race, sex, or color.

While advanced education was considered important, it was also necessary to provide very basic education to both freed blacks and poor whites. The Freedmen's Bureau set up more than 4,000 schools. Charlotte Forten, a free black woman from Philadelphia, taught in one of them. She wrote, "I never before saw children so eager to learn. . . . They come here as other children go to play. . . . Many of the grown people are [also] desirous of learning to read."

After 1868, state governments assumed responsibility for education and set up the first public school systems in the South. Though the schools were **segregated**, or separated by race, blacks and many poor whites were able to get an education.

Research

Remind students that when money was in short supply during and after the Civil War, people often bartered to get the goods and services they needed. The barter system is an old one, predating money. Have students research the barter system and write a two-page paper on it. When was it first used? Who used it? Who uses the barter system today? For example, the students may know of someone getting room and board in exchange for work.

Critical Thinking

Remind students that Chapter 11 discussed the prohibitions against educating slaves. After the war, freed slaves could receive the education that they had long been denied. Have students discuss why freed men and women of all ages were eager to embrace this opportunity. *(Chance for independence and better jobs)*

CONSTITUTIONAL HERITAGE

Critical Thinking

Refer students to the table on this page and to page 390 in Lesson 2. Ask them why Lincoln supported the Thirteenth Amendment. *(Because he wanted to work out a compromise with Congress)* Ask what provision in the Fourteenth Amendment was meant to protect the rights of freed slaves. *(Defining* citizen *as anyone born or naturalized in the United States)* Ask why the Fifteenth Amendment was written. *(To benefit the Radicals, who needed the black vote to maintain power in the South)*

■ *Congress feared that the Supreme Court might overturn the law.*

CLOSE

Have students answer the Thinking Focus. Ask students to use the lists that they made while reading the lesson to make a chart of the chronology of the Reconstruction period. Have students compare their charts. Then copy on the board the Graphic Overview from page 376 and have students add any missing information to their charts.

➤ Guaranteeing civil rights for black Americans has proved difficult. Each of these amendments solved some problems, but it was over 100 years later, in the 1960s, that true equal rights were guaranteed by the United States government.

Reconstruction Amendments

Thirteenth Amendment
Date passed by Congress: 1865
Prohibited slavery in the United States

Fourteenth Amendment
Date passed by Congress: 1866
1) Defined national citizenship.
2) Permitted representation in Congress to be reduced if a state interfered with a citizen's right to vote.
3) Denied former Confederate officials the right to hold office.
4) Declared Confederate debts invalid.

Fifteenth Amendment
Date passed by Congress: 1869
Prohibited denial of the right to vote because of race or previous servitude.

Fourteenth Amendment Passes

After the Southern states reorganized under President Johnson's plan, they elected representatives to Congress. Northerners were outraged to find that many representatives had been former Confederate leaders. Congress refused to admit them. The stage was set for a battle between Congress and the President.

In December 1865, Congress set up a Joint Committee on Reconstruction to form its own program, which would grant full citizenship to blacks. The Republican Moderates were less interested in black rights. They cooperated with the Radicals only because they wanted to maintain a Republican majority in Congress.

In April 1866, Congress passed a bill that guaranteed federal citizenship to blacks. Johnson vetoed it, but Congress overrode him. However, fearing that the Supreme Court might overturn the law, the Republicans passed a Constitutional amendment. The Fourteenth Amendment forbade states to deny political rights to any citizen. It gave for the first time a definition of "citizen": anyone born or naturalized in the United States. The amendment also declared that no state shall deprive any person of the rights of life, liberty, or property, without due process of law.

The amendment did not directly give blacks the right to vote. It did provide a penalty for states that denied the right to vote to male citizens. The Fourteenth Amendment also excluded from federal or state office any high-ranking Confederate who had taken an oath of loyalty to the United States before the war.

In providing federal protection of individual and property rights, the Fourteenth Amendment is a cornerstone of American political freedom. Although it was at first intended to protect black rights in particular, the amendment has become a lasting and important legacy from the Reconstruction. ■

■ What led to the passing of an amendment to the Constitution, rather than a bill, to guarantee federal citizenship to black Americans?

REVIEW

1. **FOCUS** What social, political, and economic changes faced the South following the Civil War?
2. **CONNECT** What were the terms of surrender for the South after the Civil War? How did the surrender affect the South?
3. **BELIEF SYSTEMS** Why was it so difficult for white Southerners to accept the idea of free labor?
4. **CRITICAL THINKING** What caused President Johnson's unpopularity with both Southerners and Radical Republicans? How do you think he could have gained more support for his programs?
5. **CRITICAL THINKING** Why was education such an important goal of the Freedmen's Bureau? Why did they also aim to educate poor whites?
6. **ACTIVITY** Read the text of the Fourteenth Amendment on page 649. With several classmates, list situations in which citizens' rights would change if this amendment were no longer in place.

Homework Options

Ask students to write a one-page plan to rebuild a country after a war. Students may focus on the economy, government, or education of the country.

Study Guide: page 55.

Answers to Review Questions

1. Changes included a crippled agricultural economy, political conflict over Reconstruction plans, and black Americans' struggle for rights.
2. Although Grant provided Lee's troops with food and allowed them to keep their horses and mules, they returned to a land that could not support their way of life.
3. Southern economy had been dependent on slave labor.
4. Sample answer: White Southerners feared the effects of his hatred of Southern aristocrats; Radical Republicans thought his plan resembled Lincoln's ten percent plan. He could have gained support by diplomacy. Allow for personal opinion.
5. Sample answer: Education would provide freed black Americans and poor whites with better employment opportunities. Allow for personal opinion.
6. Be sure each student contributes ideas.

1864 1865 1877 1878

L E S S O N 2

Radical Reconstruction

Mr. Senator Ross, how say you? Is the respondent Andrew Johnson guilty or not guilty of a high misdemeanor as charged in this article?" asked the Chief Justice of the Supreme Court Salmon P. Chase. The setting was a trial to remove President Andrew Johnson from office. All eyes fastened on the Republican senator from Kansas, Edmund G. Ross. His vote would determine the outcome of Johnson's presidency.

Ross had refused to state his decision earlier during a preliminary poll. For this he was branded a traitor to the Republican cause. By the time of the actual vote in May 1868, not one person in the Senate chamber knew how the young senator from Kansas would vote. He later remarked, "I almost literally looked down into my open grave. Friendships, position, fortune, everything that makes life desirable to an ambitious man were about to be swept away by the breath of my mouth, perhaps forever."

"Not guilty," he replied. The President was saved, and the conviction lost, by just one vote. But Johnson's effectiveness as President was over.

Reflecting on his role in the trial of the President, Ross later told his wife, "Millions of men cursing me today will bless me tomorrow for having saved the country from the greatest peril through which it has ever passed, though none but God can ever know the struggle it has cost me."

THINKING FOCUS

What were the effects of Radical Reconstruction on the South, and how did Southerners respond to the changes?

Key Terms

- martial law
- impeachment
- carpetbagger
- scalawag

This print shows Edmund G. Ross, fourth from the left, announcing his vote, at the impeachment trial of President Andrew Johnson.

INTRODUCE

After students have read the title and Thinking Focus, have them recall what they learned about the Radical Republicans in Lesson 1. *(Destruction suffered by the South and differing beliefs will make reuniting the nation a difficult task.)* Ask them to predict how the Radicals might approach Reconstruction policies and how white and black Southerners would respond to these policies. Have them read the lesson to verify or reject their predictions.

Key Terms

Vocabulary strategies: T36–37

martial law—temporary rule by military authorities imposed upon a civilian population

impeachment—the procedure of charging an office-holding official with misconduct

carpetbagger—a Northerner who went to the South after the Civil War for political or financial advantage

scalawag—a white Republican Southerner who supported Reconstruction

Graphic Overview

Cause
Radical Republicans win 1866 election.

→

Dominated Politics

Overrode Johnson's Vetoes

→

Effects
- Radical Reconstruction
- resolution of impeachment
- Fifteenth Amendment

Objectives

1. Explain how conflicts over Reconstruction policy led to a resolution of impeachment.
2. Consider the significance of the black vote in the South during Reconstruction.
3. Examine why Northerners went to the South after the Civil War.
4. State the provisions and impact of the Fifteenth Amendment and the reasons for its passage.

DEVELOP

Copy on the board the structure and main heads of the Graphic Overview from page 385. Have students copy it in their notes and complete it as they read the lesson.

POLITICAL SYSTEMS
Critical Thinking

Compare the provisions of the Military Reconstruction acts with Johnson's Reconstruction plan. *(The acts divided the South into five districts ruled by the military, while Johnson's plan limited the power of the military governors; the acts ordered Southern state constitutional conventions to ratify the Fourteenth Amendment, while Johnson opposed the amendment.)*

Congress Challenges Johnson

Across Time & Space

In 1974, the Judiciary Committee of the House of Representatives met to consider charges against President Richard M. Nixon. Nixon was accused of having misused his office and of obstructing justice by covering up the Watergate affair. A majority of the committee voted to recommend impeachment. Before the House could vote, Nixon resigned.

Before his trial, Johnson constantly opposed a congressional role in Reconstruction policy. This led to a long battle with the Radicals. The President urged former Confederate states to reject the Fourteenth Amendment. During the 1866 congressional campaign, Johnson asked voters to defeat the Radicals and to elect candidates who backed his Reconstruction plan. But Johnson's quick temper made him unpopular on the campaign trail. Race riots in New Orleans and Memphis convinced many in the North that Johnson's moderate policies had not worked. On election day, the Radicals won a huge victory.

Military Reconstruction Acts

The Radicals now had enough votes in both houses of Congress to override the President's vetoes and to take control of Reconstruction policy. They threw out Johnson's Reconstruction plan and put in one of their own—Radical Reconstruction.

In 1867, Congress passed a series of Military Reconstruction acts. These acts dissolved the governments of all the Confederate states except Tennessee, which had ratified the Fourteenth Amendment. The rest of the South was divided into five military districts. These states would be subject to **martial law**, or rule by the military.

Martial law would end only after the states met certain conditions set by Congress. The Southern states had to call constitutional conventions to set up state governments. These conventions had to ratify the Fourteenth Amendment and guarantee blacks the right to vote. Former Confederate officials and army officers—about one out of ten people in the South's population—were not allowed to vote, however.

Republican Party Sweeps the South

Federal military officials began to register voters in the South and helped to set up state conventions. Radical Republicans ruled these conventions

States' Readmission to the Union, 1870

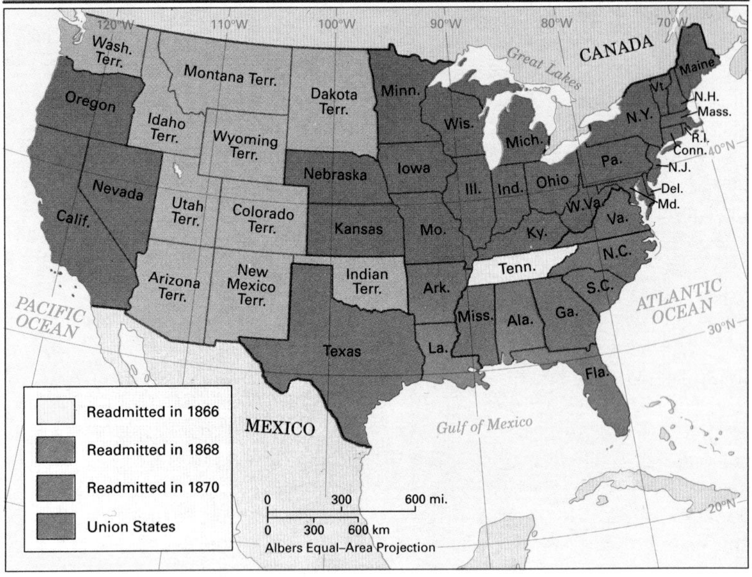

As this map shows, all Southern states were readmitted to the Union by 1870.

Access Activity

Refer students to the map on this page. Which Southern state was the first to rejoin the Union? *(Tenn.)* Which states were next? *(Ark., La., Ala., Fla., N.C., S.C.)* Last? *(Tex., Miss., Ga., Va.)* Why were all the Confederate states not admitted at once? *(Didn't fulfill requirements of Reconstruction)*

Access Strategy

Ask students to recall from Chapter 10 how slaves and their owners depended on one another before the Civil War. *(Slaves depended on owners for food, shelter, clothing; owners depended on slaves for labor.)* Have students compare the relationship between slave and owner before the Civil War with their relationship afterward, when the power balance was changed. *(Before, owners had complete control over slaves; after, slaves were no longer the personal property of owners.)* How would it be difficult for both slave and master to adjust to emancipation? *(Former slaves would have to assume new responsibilities as freed men and women, and owners would have to find a new source of productive labor.)* Tell students that this lesson explains some of the consequences of the changing roles in the South, including the struggles of freed slaves to gain political representation and the passage of the Fifteenth Amendment.

This November 16, 1867, cover of Harper's Weekly shows black men casting their votes for political representation.

and blacks responded with enthusiasm. Nearly all eligible black voters registered. Of course, most gave their votes to the Republican Party. Political groups such as the Union League joined both freedmen and white unionists in a strong Republican voting force. A British visitor noted that the conventions reflected "the mighty revolution that had taken place in America."

Republicans swept into power, gaining control of all the governorships and state legislatures. The new state constitutions had to be approved by a majority of registered voters. Many white Southerners decided to stay away from the polls in protest. By refusing to vote, they hoped to defeat Reconstruction policies. ■

■ How did Congress respond to Johnson's attempts to take control of Reconstruction policy?

■ *Congress overrode Johnson's vetoes, rejected his plan, and substituted its own plan, Radical Reconstruction.*

Johnson Stands Trial

President Johnson challenged the authority of Congress to decide and to enforce Reconstruction policy. He gave orders that limited the powers of military governors and supported officials who allowed disqualified Confederates to vote. He further angered Congress by trying to fire Secretary of War Edwin Stanton. He did so in direct opposition to the Tenure of Office Act. This bill took from the President the power to fire officials the Senate had approved.

Johnson's resistance to Congress caused great hostility. On February 24, 1868, the House of Representatives passed a resolution of **impeachment**. This formal charge of misconduct or wrongdoing was meant to remove Johnson from office.

Two other attempts to impeach Johnson had failed. The President was clearly in danger. Republicans were committed to granting blacks full political rights. Johnson's moderate policies, however, had restored the power of white Southerners who could not stand the idea of black rights.

Now, Johnson's presidency rested with the Senate, which served as a jury for his impeachment trial. All the elements of high courtroom drama were present, except Johnson himself, who did not attend the trial. Some one thousand tickets were sold to people who came to watch the trial.

With 54 members in the Senate, a two-thirds majority, (36 votes) was needed to convict Johnson. The 42 Republicans knew they could afford to lose only six votes if Johnson was to be removed from office. Six Republicans had already said that the facts presented were not enough to convict Johnson. Nineteen votes were needed to acquit Johnson. Then Senator Edmund G. Ross of Kansas cast his vote. He had refused to announce his verdict during the preliminary poll. Tension mounted. When Ross gave his vote of "Not guilty," Johnson's presidency was saved. ■

Like most political scandals, Johnson's impeachment created great curiosity. People came from all over the country to get a seat at the trial.

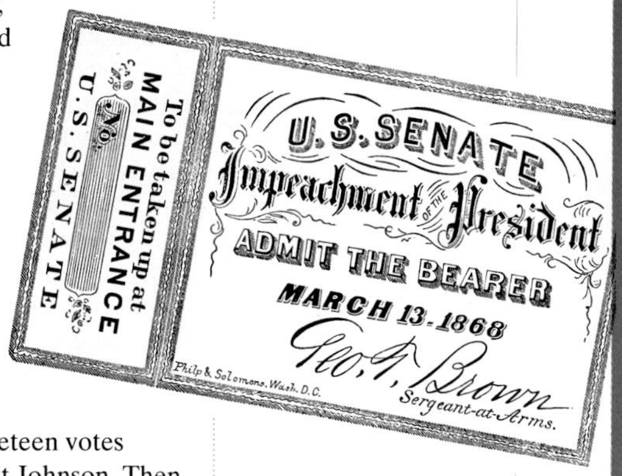

■ How did President Johnson's resistance to Congressional authority lead to his impeachment?

■ *He challenged the authority of Congress by limiting the powers of military governors, supporting officials who allowed disqualified Confederates to vote, and violating the Tenure of Office Act.*

HISTORY

Critical Thinking

Considering the events that led to the impeachment trial of President Johnson, why do you suppose that Republican Ross cast the vote that kept Johnson in office? *(Senator Ross did not believe that Johnson's continued defiance of congressional authority constituted a crime, and he may have expected serious consequences from removing a President from office.)*

Political Context

Most of the elected black officials were young men in their twenties and thirties. Some were self-educated and others were illiterate; a few held degrees from Northern colleges. Before the war, a number of these black officeholders had belonged to the Southern free black class made up of ministers, teachers, artisans, and farmers. Other officeholders had lived in the North.

Still other black officials had been slaves. As slaves, they had been unable to acquire the skills needed to run a government, but many learned new skills quickly. For example, Oscar Dunne, a former Louisiana slave, was elected lieutenant governor of Louisiana and served so competently that even his strongest Democratic opponents found little to criticize. Another former slave, John Roy Lynch, who served as justice of the peace in Mississippi, was elected to the legislature and then to Congress.

Critical Thinking

Remind students that freed blacks were voting for the first time. Have them discuss what might have influenced them to vote for one person rather than another. *(Probably voted for someone who promised fair and equal treatment)*

POLITICAL SYSTEMS

Critical Thinking

Remind students that nearly 300 black delegates served in the constitutional conventions during 1867–1868. What was the potential impact of that representation? *(Black Americans had the potential of serving in government as true equals of white Americans.)* What were the long-term effects? *(Black delegates initially served in large numbers in Southern legislatures and governments. As white Southerners regained power, they were able to keep most black Americans out of office until the 1960s.)*

■ *Sample answer: Many white Southerners probably viewed them with distrust. Allow for personal opinion.*

Black carpetbagger Robert B. Elliot, standing left, served as a Congressman from Mississippi.

■ *How do you think white Southerners regarded black officeholders?*

African Americans Enter Politics

With the federal army protecting voters, nearly three hundred black delegates (elected or appointed officials in the House of Representatives) served in the constitutional conventions during the winter of 1867–1868. In Louisiana and South Carolina, they formed a majority of the delegates, and in Florida about 40 percent.

Blacks were able to elect many of their own candidates to office. They served as lieutenant governors, treasurers, secretaries of state, and superintendents of public education. In South Carolina, the cradle of the Confederacy, blacks gained the majority of legislative offices.

In many plantation counties, freedmen formed the majority of the population. They took control of local governments, helping to ensure the rights of rural blacks.

Blacks also won election to the U.S. Congress, with 16 serving in the House of Representatives, and two in the Senate. Hiram Revels, a college graduate, became the first black senator in 1870, when the Mississippi legislature named him to finish the term begun by Jefferson Davis before the Civil War. Blanche K. Bruce of Mississippi was the first black to serve a full term as senator. But white leaders still dominated the Republican Party in the South, and no black governors were elected to office. ■

Reshaping the South

During Reconstruction, many Northerners went to the South for political or financial opportunities. Southern whites called them **carpetbaggers** because of their carpetbags, which were a type of suitcase. Southerners believed that the carpetbaggers came "to fatten on our misfortunes," and fill their deep bags with stolen Southern loot. It is true that some Northerners used their positions in Reconstruction governments to their own advantage.

However, carpetbaggers included teachers, ministers, and officials of the Freedmen's Bureau. They and others went to the South to help gain full rights for blacks. Many had long fought against slavery. Now they sought to build a freer and more equal society in the South. For the most part, carpetbaggers probably combined the desire for personal gain with a commitment to modernizing the South. In short, they wanted to take part in the effort "to substitute the civilization of freedom for that of slavery."

Many other carpetbaggers were Union veterans who were drawn by economic opportunities in the South. Many bought cotton land or opened businesses in the cities. More than 60 won election to Congress, and nine served as governors.

Albion Tourgée, a carpetbagger from Ohio who settled in North Carolina, was dedicated to the antislavery cause. He published a novel after his return to the North in 1879. The

Visual Learning

Have students study the picture on this page. Ask them to consider the impact of blacks entering state and national politics from the points of view of a white Southern Democrat, a white Northern Republican, and a black constituent of Elliot. How would each view the situation?

Art Connection

Tell students that the drama and tragedy of the Civil War made it a popular subject for Hollywood. The film *Gone With the Wind*, based on the best-selling novel by Margaret Mitchell, portrays the life of a rich Southern plantation family before, during, and after the Civil War.

Obtain a videotape of the film and show students a scene after the war, such as the one when Scarlett returns to her devastated home Tara and vows, "I'll never go hungry again." Have students explain in a one-page paper the Southern attitude toward Reconstruction that is portrayed in the scene and what elements of the scene—words, tone of voice, body posture, visual surroundings—make it so powerful.

novel's main character, Comfort Servosse, shared the early optimism of other Northerners. They felt that the South could be changed to be more like the North.

> Oh, he replied, there must be great changes of course! Slavery has been broken up, and things must turn into new grooves; but I think the country will settle rapidly, now that slavery is out of the way. Manufactures will spring up, immigration will pour in, and it will be just the pleasantest part of the country.
>
> Albion Tourgée, *A Fool's Errand*

Southern white conservatives also used the term **scalawags** to describe native white Southerners who had opposed secession and who had cooperated with the Republicans. Most scalawags were poor whites who lived in small towns and on farms. They supported Reconstruction. Some gave their loyalty to the North for political favors. They also resented the plantation owners who had dominated the economy and politics of the South before the war. Scalawags looked to the new state governments to provide educational and job opportunities. Many of those who remained loyal to the Confederate cause thought of scalawags as traitors to the South.

A number of other scalawags, however, were powerful, well-educated whites. Some had been judges, Congressmen, and local officials before the war. Confederate veteran Charles Hays came from one of the wealthiest plantation families in Alabama. He joined the Republicans in 1867 and later served in Congress. Scalawags helped blacks get the vote. But their main interest was in the benefits they would get by guiding the South away from its past. ■

▲ *The cartoon* (above) *shows "The Solid South" carrying General Ulysses S. Grant in a giant carpetbag.*

■ *Why were some Southerners angry at carpetbaggers and scalawags?*

Rebuilding the South

White Southerners used charges of political corruption to discredit Republican policies. They insisted that corruption was caused by greedy carpetbaggers and by allowing blacks to hold office.

To be sure, corruption in many forms did exist. Some government officials got bribes from people who wanted contracts for public projects. Officials in charge of railroad building, for example, received stock in new railroad lines for their help. Money for schools and public services was also stolen. State budgets grew, and the demands placed on them increased as well. Officials were handling large amounts of money, corporations were competing for business, and communities were seeking prosperity. These

HISTORY

Visual Learning

Refer students to the cartoon on this page and read the labels on Grant, the carpetbag, and the South. Ask students why the South is portrayed as walking barefoot on stones. *(It is so poor it does not even have shoes.)* Have students analyze the message in the cartoon. *(Carpetbaggers and other Northerners are crushing the South)*

HISTORY

Critical Thinking

What does the quote on this page from the novel by Albion Tourgée reveal about the character's state of mind? *(Optimistic)* What did the character hope to accomplish? *(To make the South similar to the North, with manufacturing and immigration)*

■ *They resented carpetbaggers for capitalizing on Southerners' economic hardships; they blamed scalawags for contributing to the Northern victory.*

Making a Chart

Have students compose a class letter to one of the political party's headquarters in their state, asking for a demographic breakdown of voters registered for that party. Have them make a chart showing the proportion of white citizens to black citizens and to citizens of other ethnic groups.

Research

Have students research and write a two-page paper on martial law. Was it applied for the first time in the United States during Reconstruction? Has it been applied by the U.S. Government since? Have students find newspaper or magazine accounts describing countries under martial law today.

Critical Thinking

Contrast the white Southern attitude toward carpetbaggers and toward scalawags. *(Carpetbaggers were thought to be outside agitators who sought personal gain from Southern misfortune; scalawags were thought of as traitors to their own people.)*

CONSTITUTIONAL HERITAGE

Critical Thinking

Have students evaluate the significance of the provisions of the Fifteenth Amendment. Students might want to refer to the print of the celebration parade on this page in their discussion. *(Because it guaranteed all citizens the right to vote, it made the U.S. Government more accountable to all its people, regardless of race or background.)*

■ *Because laws often were not enforced, Republicans believed an amendment was necessary to ensure black Americans' voting rights.*

CLOSE

Copy on the board the Graphic Overview from page 385. Have volunteers complete it, using the lists that they made while reading the lesson. Have students evaluate the predictions that they made at the beginning of the lesson and answer the Thinking Focus. As an extension activity, have students do the research activity described on page 389.

➤ *This print shows a parade held in celebration of the Fifteenth Amendment, which gave blacks the right to vote.*

conditions encouraged a "get rich quick" spirit. Many officials saw nothing wrong with looking out for their own interests in the process.

In the postwar years, corruption was taking over in Northern as well as Southern state and local governments. Democrats and Republicans alike were deep in their plans to gain money through fraud.

Amendment Passed amid Turmoil

The Radicals knew the right of blacks to vote was important to keep Republicans in office in the South. To make sure blacks could vote, they pushed for passage of the Fifteenth Amendment.

In 1869, Congress approved the new amendment. It declared that neither the federal government nor any state could deny a citizen the right to vote "on account of race, color, or previous condition of servitude." The following year, the states ratified the amendment.

Many Southerners were horrified. Democrats argued that this new amendment made blacks a favored race. Yet some Radicals believed the Fifteenth Amendment had not gone far enough. It did not set up standard voting requirements for all states. Some states would later take advantage of this omission to restrict the voting rights of blacks and others on grounds other than race. ■

■ *Review the arguments for and against the Fifteenth Amendment. Why did Republicans think an amendment was necessary?*

REVIEW

1. **FOCUS** What were the effects of Radical Reconstruction on the South, and how did Southerners respond to the changes?
2. **CONNECT** How did the black freedmen experience change following the passage of the Fourteenth and Fifteenth Amendments?
3. **POLITICAL SYSTEMS** Explain how the Republicans' need for a strong party in the South led the Radicals to support voting rights for blacks.
4. **CRITICAL THINKING** What differences of opinion led to the bitter hostility between President Johnson and Republican members of Congress?
5. **CRITICAL THINKING** What was the purpose of martial law under the Military Reconstruction acts? Under what conditions would martial law be lifted?
6. **ACTIVITY** Imagine you are a carpetbagger who has just arrived in the postwar South. Write a diary entry that describes your expectations.

Homework Options

Have students write a two-page report on the events leading up to the House Judiciary committee's consideration of an impeachment resolution against President Richard Nixon in 1974.

Study Guide: page 56.

Answers to Review Questions

1. Radical Reconstruction introduced martial law, increased rights for black Americans, strengthened the Republican party, and created opportunities for carpetbaggers. Southerners, feeling angry and fearful, resisted change whenever possible.
2. Black men were able to vote and hold government offices.
3. Since the Republicans had freed the blacks, they would probably get most of the black vote.
4. Sample answer: They differed on Reconstruction policy, especially on martial law. Allow for personal opinion.
5. Sample answer: Martial law was used to limit opposition forces; it would end only after the states met conditions set by Congress. Allow for personal opinion.
6. Encourage students to reflect in their diary entries the various motives of carpetbaggers.

1864 1865 1877 1878

LESSON 3

Southern Life Under Reconstruction

Mary Virginia Montgomery was a slave for the first 14 years of her life, but after the war, the Montgomery family took on a different role at her home, Davis Bend. Mary Virginia's parents, Benjamin and Mary, had been slaves on a plantation of Joseph Davis, older brother of Confederate President Jefferson Davis and owner of Hurricane and Brierfield plantations just south of Vicksburg, Mississippi. After the war, the Montgomery family returned to Davis Bend from Cincinnati, Ohio, where they had lived during the war.

Benjamin Montgomery and his family established a community of black tenant farmers at Davis Bend. This extraordinary community was successful in raising cotton and food crops. On February 3, 1872, Mary noted in her diary, "The sun shines beautifully today. I am so proud of the prospect of a flower yard and the orchard improvement that I feel like one just embracing the threshold of a new life. I feel now the study of agriculture most necessary."

Freedmen at Davis Bend formed a self-governing colony with elected sheriffs and justices of the peace. As an all-black community, Davis Bend was an exceptional example of how much blacks could achieve when freed from slavery and prejudice.

Mary Virginia was a talented and well-educated woman who eventually taught school at Davis Bend. But white conservatives regained control of Mississippi. After floods, then droughts, the Montgomery family's fortunes declined. After Benjamin and Mary Montgomery died, the land went back to Jefferson Davis and the grandchildren of Joseph Davis.

THINKING FOCUS

How did Reconstruction policies end in mixed results?

Key Terms

- redeem
- vigilante

Davis Bend, Mississippi, July 4, 1865. The Union Army had just freed these blacks. They stayed on to farm the land themselves.

INTRODUCE

Point out the lesson title and ask students to recall what they have learned so far about the situation for black and white Southerners under Reconstruction. *(Life was changing for all Southerners.)* Ask students if they think that black Southerners will be able to maintain their gains. Have students read the Thinking Focus and then read the lesson to find out what the "mixed results" of Reconstruction policies were.

Key Terms

Vocabulary strategies: T36–37

redeem—to recover or reclaim

vigilante—a group of citizens who, without authority, takes on powers such as pursuing and punishing those suspected of being criminals

Graphic Overview

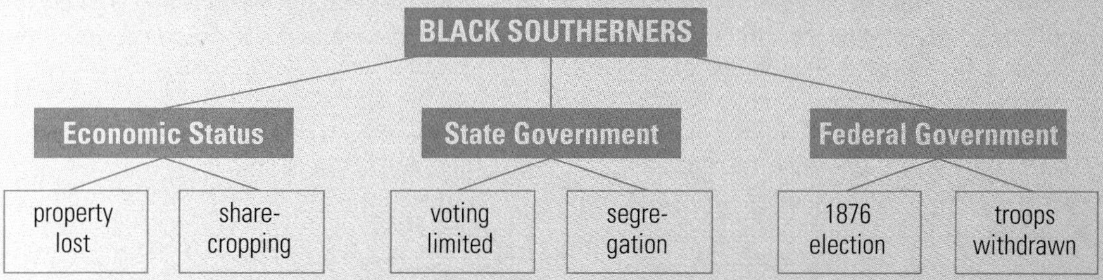

Objectives

1. Explain why emancipation did not guarantee black Southerners economic opportunities.
2. Examine how white Southerners resisted granting black Americans equality.
3. State how the bargain to elect Rutherford B. Hayes ended Reconstruction.
4. Examine the legacy of the Reconstruction era.

DEVELOP

Suggest that as students read this lesson, they think about what the end of Reconstruction meant for the South, especially for black Southerners. Copy on the board the structure and main heads of the Graphic Overview from page 391. Ask students to copy it in their notes and complete it as they read the lesson.

ECONOMICS

Critical Thinking

Why did black people want "40 acres and a mule"? *(They wanted to farm their own land.)* What did the words symbolize for freed slaves? *(Economic opportunity)*

Forty Acres and a Mule

In January 1865, Secretary of War Stanton went to Savannah, Georgia, which was then in Union hands. Stanton met with leaders of the blacks who had followed General Sherman's army on its march through Georgia. Stanton asked the blacks how the government could support their families in freedom. "The way we can best take care of ourselves," they said, "is to have land, and . . . till it by our labor." Blacks dreamed that with "forty acres and a mule" they could become economically independent.

General Sherman responded by setting aside for blacks large areas of the land under his control. Every head of a family received 40 acres of land. Freed blacks quickly resettled on these lands and by mid-1865, forty thousand freed people were living in new locations. One former slaveowner visited his old plantation in Beaufort, South Carolina, and received friendly and polite treatment. But his former slaves "firmly and respectfully" told him that "we own this land now. Put it out of your head that it will ever be yours again."

Later, Congress gave the Freedmen's Bureau control of "abandoned" land in the South. The Bureau was to rent this land to freedmen for a period of three years. After that time, they could buy it.

Congress did not actually hold legal title to much of this land. Therefore, when President Johnson restored the legal rights of white Southerners, they reoccupied their land, which meant blacks lost what little property they had gained.

Truly "abandoned" land was likely to be too dry, underwater, or hard to get to. The Freedmen's Bureau gave blacks seeds to plant for crops. But in most cases black farmers were not able to survive on such small farms. Davis Bend, while it lasted, was an exception. But even that farm failed and eventually went back to the original white owners.

Black Codes Backlash

Cotton plantations had depended entirely on slave labor. Plantation owners therefore tried to take away other chances for employment for blacks. The Black Codes were passed in an effort to make African Americans accept the same conditions under which they had labored before the war. People who were now supposed to be free were made to carry passes, keep to a curfew, live in housing supplied by landowners, and give up the right to live on an equal basis with whites.

In fact, white Southerners agreed to do away with slavery only in order to get back into the Union. But they

Sharecropping changed the pattern and rhythm of life for many freed black families. This plow and the pitchfork on the facing page are typical farm tools of the time.

Access Activity

Remind students that during Reconstruction, black Americans gained rights and opportunities that were later taken away. How do they think Southern blacks felt at the loss of the rights that they had so recently won? What would the students have done in the same situation?

Access Strategy

Ask students to suggest some advantages enjoyed by white Americans that freed slaves lacked as they faced the challenge of becoming citizens. *(Economic and educational opportunities, comfortable housing, political power)* Why was it so difficult for black Southerners to achieve their goals? *(Discrimination, prejudice)* Point out that midway through the Reconstruction period, the future looked bright for black Americans. Have students recall what they read in Lessons 1 and 2 about freed slaves. *(Land was being given away; black universities were founded and local schools set up; and blacks held many elective positions.)* Tell students that they will read in this lesson how blacks lost these gains during the final years of Reconstruction.

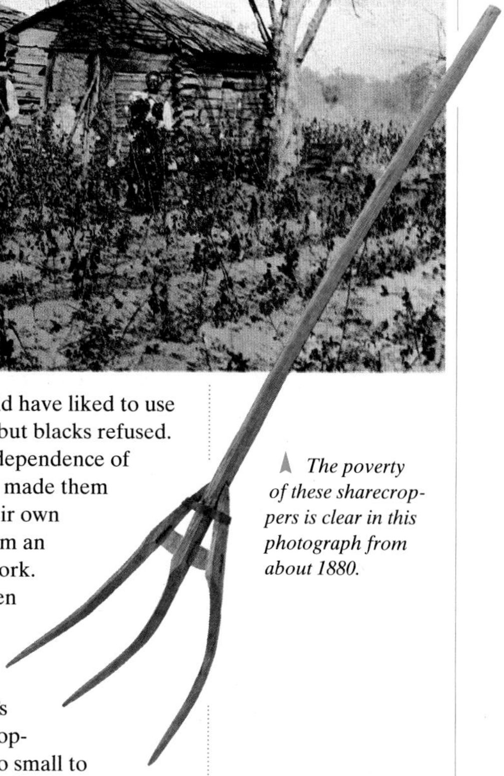

also wanted to keep a forced labor system. They fought long and hard to keep blacks from gaining any new freedoms. Reconstruction policy was fighting against the same social, political, and economic forces that had led the South into war. No amount of political idealism from the North would convince white Southerners that freeing blacks would ever work to their advantage.

Sharecropping

Some plantation owners paid their black workers a small wage. But the new plantation system that took shape in the South was the practice known as sharecropping. The white landowner broke up his estate into small units and set up a freed black family on each unit. In addition to the land, the black family was sometimes provided with housing, seeds, tools, and animals. The sharecroppers (black families) could keep part of what they grew as their pay. This share ranged between one-tenth and one-half of the crop.

Landowners would have liked to use the wage system, but blacks refused. They liked the independence of share cropping. It made them the masters of their own time and gave them an interest in their work.

However, when drought or other natural causes cut down on the year's harvest, a sharecropper's share was too small to feed a family. Businessmen got rich by giving credit to sharecroppers in return for part of next year's crop. Many sharecroppers found they could not get out of debt. Despite its financial drawbacks, this new labor system offered blacks an escape from constant supervision by whites.

Poorer whites—including some of the Confederate soldiers—sometimes became sharecroppers too. But whites, unlike blacks, could find many other ways to earn a living. ■

▲ *The poverty of these sharecroppers is clear in this photograph from about 1880.*

■ *Why did many blacks become sharecroppers?*

ECONOMICS

Critical Thinking

How did the Black Codes and sharecropping prevent blacks from earning a living? *(Black Codes limited blacks' job options by forcing them to carry passes, observe a curfew, and live in housing supplied by landowners. Sharecropping meant that their portion of the crops was often not enough to live on.)*

■ *Many black Americans turned to sharecropping because they did not own land or were unable to survive on their own through small-scale farming. Few other opportunities were available to them.*

Political Context

As Reconstruction drew to a close, Southern Democrats went to great lengths to discourage black voters. "We shall carry the next election if we have to ride saddle-deep in blood to do it," said General John McEnery of Louisiana. Polling places were hidden on islands and in barns, and only white voters were told how to reach the sites. In one Louisiana parish, the polls opened in the very early morning, and white citizens voted by candlelight. When black voters arrived, they were told that the polls were closed.

A U.S. Senate committee noted that on election day in Mississippi, armed men came to voting places and intimidated black voters. At one place, four or five cannoneers, supported by ten or twelve men, trained a cannon on the voting place. At the same time, armed men on horseback patrolled the street. Clearly, white Southerners were not willing to share voting rights with blacks.

Visual Learning

Have students compare the picture of the model community at Davis Bend on page 391 with the picture of the sharecropper family on this page. What mood does each picture convey? *(Optimism at initial freedom versus the bleak reality of the average sharecropper)* What elements—faces, structures, activities—create those impressions?

HISTORY

Critical Thinking

Have students examine how Redeemers used the Home Rule concept and the poll tax to deprive black Southerners of their rights. *(Home Rule, which held that states had the right to resist or ignore federal laws, provided the rationale for disobeying federal laws and allowed them to exclude blacks from the voting process. The poll tax kept most poor black Americans from voting.)*

■ *They elected Democratic majorities to state legislatures, adopted the poll tax, rearranged voting districts, and used violence through groups such as the KKK.*

The Reaction of White Southerners

Across Time & Space

In 1871, Congress passed the Ku Klux Klan Act, making it a crime to use force, threat, or intimidation to deny citizens their rights. In later years, the Klan attacked Jews and Catholics as well as blacks. Today, organizations such as the National Association for the Advancement of Colored People (NAACP) and the Anti-Defamation League (ADL) fight the Klan.

Though Southerners had lost the war, they refused to accept the position of a conquered people. They bitterly resisted the efforts of the North to change the political and social life of their region.

Fighting Back with States' Rights

White Southerners who had resisted surrender to the North gradually regained the right to vote. Some took the oaths of loyalty; others reached voting age in the years after the war. They began to exercise their political power by electing Democratic majorities to state legislatures.

Democrats in the South had a strong message: they promised to **redeem,** or recover, the region and restore "Home Rule." Redeemers revived the argument that the states had the right to resist or ignore federal laws. Democrats claimed that the states were not "morally bound" by postwar constitutional amendments.

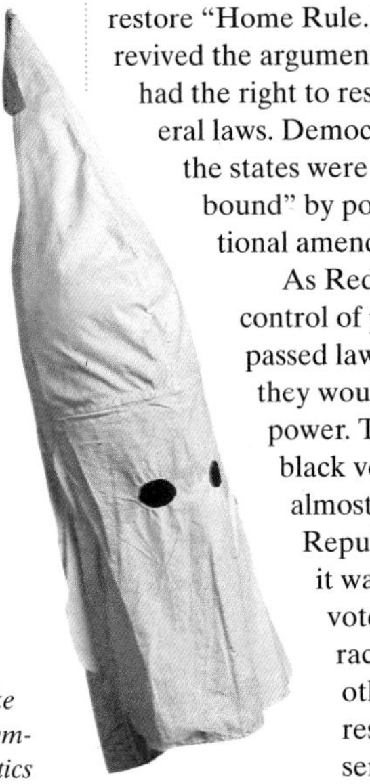

➤ *White hoods like this have come to symbolize the terror tactics of the KKK.*

As Redeemers took control of politics, they passed laws to make sure they would remain in power. They targeted black voters, who were almost exclusively Republican. Although it was illegal to bar voters because of race, they found other kinds of restrictions that served equally well.

In the early 1870s, Tennessee and Georgia adopted the poll tax—a tax that a citizen had to pay in order to vote. Many blacks (and poor whites) could not afford to pay the poll tax, and thus they were denied the right to vote. Other states gerrymandered, or rearranged, voting districts to reduce the political power of blacks.

Outside the Law: Secret Societies

Some Southerners resorted to violence. Secret societies such as the Knights of the White Camelia, the White Brotherhood, and the Ku Klux Klan spread fear throughout the South. The Klan, or KKK, begun in 1866, claimed to be an organization of "chivalry, humanity, mercy, and patriotism." But it was clearly designed to maintain white supremacy in the Southern states. By 1870, KKK groups had formed in every Southern state. The white robes and hoods they wore were meant to frighten blacks into thinking they were ghosts of Confederate soldiers. The hoods also hid the faces of the Klansmen during raids.

The Klan launched a reign of terror against Republican office-holders, both black and white. Klan mobs killed an Arkansas congressman and three members of the South Carolina legislature. Black Republican leaders were dragged from their homes, beaten, whipped, even lynched. The KKK burned black schools and churches, terrorizing or killing white and black teachers. A black teacher's library was burned. The Klan threatened to strike out against any black person who tried to obtain books.

Blacks faced Klan violence simply because they were prosperous. Freedmen saw the rewards of their hard work destroyed before their eyes.

As Southern white resistance to Reconstruction grew, the KKK—begun as a Confederate veterans organization—became a **vigilante** group. It took the law into its own hands. Upper-class Southern whites rarely opposed the Klan's activities. Either they were afraid or they supported the Klan's lawless efforts to interfere with Reconstruction. Republican state officials declared that Klan violence was a local matter. They avoided dealing directly with the vigilante groups. ■

■ *How did Southern whites seek to counter the effects of the Fifteenth Amendment?*

Visual Learning

Have students study the photograph of the Ku Klux Klan hood on this page. Why was the hood chosen as a means to intimidate people? *(They meant to frighten blacks into thinking they were ghosts of Confederate soldiers.)* How did it also protect the identity of KKK members? *(By hiding their faces)*

Cultural Context

The name Dixie or Dixieland is often given to the South. One explanation of the word's origin is that a Louisiana bank once printed $10 bills bearing the French word *dix*, which means "ten." People called Louisiana "Dix's Land" and that became Dixie. In time it came to mean the entire South. According to another story, a slave owner named Dixie lived in New York City. He had to send some of his slaves south because they were homesick for "Dixie's Land."

Music Connection

"Dixie" is the name of a famous song written by Daniel D. Emmett in 1859 that was, and still is, very popular in the South. Have students find and read the lyrics to this song. Ask them to write a one-page paper on why the song remains a powerful symbol of the South and what its continuing popularity reveals.

The End of Reconstruction

The South's refusal to accept Reconstruction finally wore down the North. Southern intimidation of blacks weakened the voting strength of the Republicans. The North was unwilling to send enough federal troops to enforce the rights of black voters. With the deaths of Congressmen Thaddeus Stevens and Charles Sumner, the cause of black rights lost two of its most powerful supporters.

Many Northerners, sick of the long, drawn-out struggle, wanted national harmony in order to promote economic growth. One businessman expressed the feeling: "What the South needs now is capital to develop her resources. . . . We have tried this long enough. Now let the South alone."

In the 1876 presidential election, Republican Rutherford B. Hayes ran against the Democrat Samuel J. Tilden. Tilden won more popular votes than Hayes but was one electoral vote short of a majority. Disputed election returns in three Southern states—Florida, South Carolina, and Louisiana—held the key to victory.

Congress named a special electoral commission to decide which claims were valid. Democrats and Republicans had an equal number of seats on the commission. In order to win the election, Hayes had to receive all the disputed electoral votes.

As inauguration day drew near, the commission members struck a bargain. The Democrats agreed to give the disputed votes to the Republican Hayes in return for the Republicans' promise to remove all federal troops from the South.

This so-called Compromise of 1877 left blacks with no federal protection. A former South Carolina governor exclaimed: "[The agreement] consists in the abandonment of the Southern Republicans, and especially the colored race." The bargain to elect Hayes in return for the withdrawal of federal troops assured the victory of Home Rule in the South. Reconstruction was over. ■

■ *How and why did Reconstruction end?*

Reconstruction absorbed much of the nation's attention for nearly twelve years.

Reconstruction, 1865–1877

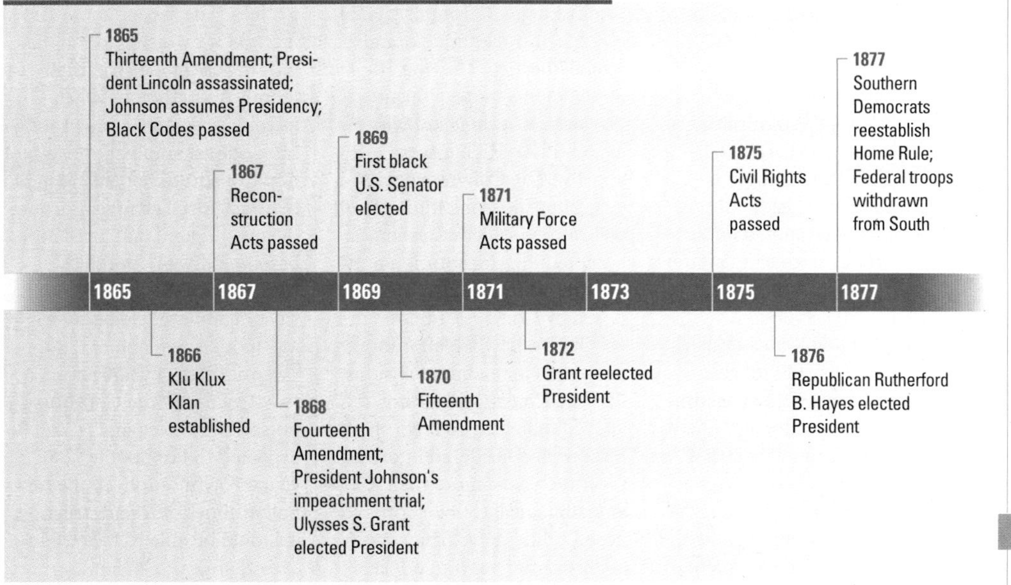

BELIEF SYSTEMS

Critical Thinking

Ask students to discuss why Republicans agreed to withdraw federal troops from the South. *(Democrats agreed to give disputed electoral votes to the Republicans in return.)* Have students evaluate this decision in terms of its ethical implications. How might history have been different if the Democrat Tilden had won but the troops had remained in the South? *(Sample answer: Southern Democrats supported Home Rule, so the outcome might not have been significantly different.)*

■ *Reconstruction ended with a bargain between Republicans and Democrats—disputed electoral votes in the presidential election were given to Republicans in return for the withdrawal of federal troops.*

Language Arts Connection

Have students read aloud the Fourteenth and Fifteenth amendments from the annotated Constitution beginning on page 636. Have students look up words that they find difficult to understand in the dictionary—for example, *jurisdiction, abridge, immunities, apportioned.* Then ask them to explain the meaning of each amendment in their own words.

Visual Learning

Refer students to the timeline on this page. How much time elapsed between the end of the war and the establishment of the Ku Klux Klan? *(One year)* Have students study the timeline and note the progression of Reconstruction from military rule to the reestablishment of Home Rule in the South.

CONSTITUTIONAL HERITAGE

Critical Thinking

The proposed Equal Rights Amendment would have guaranteed women more rights, such as equal pay for equal work. Is the proposed amendment necessary, or are its provisions already covered in previous amendments? *(Students should weigh the injustices women still face against the protections guaranteed in the Bill of Rights and the Nineteenth Amendment.)*

UNDERSTANDING CONSTITUTIONAL AMENDMENTS

That the Civil War occurred at all has been called the greatest failure of the Constitution. Despite checks and balances between federal and states' rights, and between majority rule and minority rights, the Constitution was unable to prevent the attempt at secession from the Union.

Yet the Constitution, its strength and its flexibility, played an important role in the preservation of the Union and in the reconstruction following the war. Together, the Thirteenth, Fourteenth, and Fifteenth Amendments redefined the protective powers of the federal government toward the individual citizen.

Rights of Individuals

During the writing of the Constitution, the protection of the rights of the individual from the potential tyranny of a centralized government provoked much discussion. With the passing of these three amendments, the government became the guardian of individual rights, rather than a threat to them. Basic civil rights were guaranteed under the law for everyone, no matter what their race,color, or past conditions of slavery.

The United States Constitution is the world's longest such surviving written constitution. No other nation has a written document to guide it that has been used without suspension for more than 200 years. A key to the Constitution's success is its capacity for amendment.

The Process of Change

During the writing of the Constitution, careful thought was given to the process of amendment. A major problem with the Articles of Confederation was that it required the approval of every state legislature before any alterations could be made. Thus James Madison suggested to the Constitutional convention a process of amending that could be initiated by a two-thirds majority of Congress. An amendment must then be ratified by a three-fourths majority of the states. Once ratified, the amendment is law and cannot be overturned by any branch of government. It can only be replaced or revoked by another amendment.

The importance of Article V defining the amendment process became immediately evident during the period of ratification of the Constitution. Initial opposition to the Constitution stemmed from its lack of any specific guarantee of individual liberties. The first 10 amendments to the Constitution, which became known as the Bill of Rights, were approved by Congress only a year after the Constitution itself was ratified. North Carolina accepted the Constitution only after the Bill of Rights was proposed by Congress, in 1789.

The somewhat laborious process of amendment ensures that the Constitution is not altered too easily to meet short-term or ill-considered interests. Over the years, more than 2,000 amendments have been proposed, while only 26 have been accepted and put into effect.

Change Without Amendment

The Constitution is not a rigid document. Because of imprecise language in some sections, it is open to interpretation. Most historians feel that this is more of a strength than a weakness. A level of interpretation is ensured, while another level can be reinterpreted by successive generations. One observer noted that there are two official ways to change the Constitution and two unofficial ways.

The two official ways are by the two-thirds and three-fourths process of amendment discussed above, or by a Constitutional Convention called for by two-thirds of the state legislatures. The second method has never been used.

By unofficial methods is meant, first, the Supreme Court's interpretation of the Constitution, which differs sometimes from court to court, depending on the views of new justices. The second unofficial method is by disregard on the part of the public. The Eighteenth Amendment, which introduced nation wide prohibition, is an example of the failure of a Constitutional amendment to effect social change. Because the amendment and legislation based on it was ignored by many people, Congress finally gave in and repealed it by passing another amendment, the Twenty-first, 14 years later.

Because of the Constitution's ability to change, it can be expected to last another 200 years. Having survived the turbulent times of Reconstruction, it should be able to face whatever changes lie ahead.

396

Social Participation

Ask students to imagine that they are Northern and Southern senators after the Civil War. Have them role play a debate on the ratification of the Thirteenth, Fourteenth, and Fifteenth amendments.

Writing a Report

Have students write a two-page report on one of two white Northerners who fought hard for black Americans' rights: Congressman Thaddeus Stevens, from Pennsylvania, or Senator Charles Sumner, from Massachusetts. The report should include specific actions these men took for black Americans' rights.

Making a Mural

Have students draw a mural showing a plantation in the South before and after the war. Have them include the manor house, the slave quarters, and the fields. Tell them to indicate the differences that the war made in the lives of slave owners and slaves by portraying them in different types of work and recreation in the two periods. Remind students to incorporate into their mural information about the cotton plantation system that they learned in Chapter 10.

Legacies of Reconstruction

The Reconstruction period brought great changes in the nation. With the defeat of the Confederacy, slavery vanished forever. The federal government had established its authority. The Fourteenth and Fifteenth Amendments set a constitutional basis for many civil and political rights. In the South, many black citizens received education and some measure of economic and social rights.

This poster celebrates the height of black participation in the government of the Reconstruction Era.

Yet enormous challenges remained for blacks in taking on citizenship. When federal troops pulled out from the South, blacks lost much of their freedom. White legislatures passed laws that replaced slavery with segregation, a legally enforced separation of the races. Radical Republicans had supported black voting rights for many reasons, including strengthening the Republican party. After Reconstruction, the South would remain solidly Democratic for nearly a century.

To escape poverty and racism, Southern blacks began moving elsewhere. Some went west, homesteading on the new frontier. In the early 1900s, thousands of blacks migrated to Northern cities such as Chicago and New York. There too they faced prejudice, but many found new opportunities in urban areas.

The ideals behind Radical Reconstruction—such as the attempt to enforce black suffrage—would not die. Amendments passed during Reconstruction would be used to attack other forms of injustice. The civil rights movement of the 1950s and 1960s, sometimes called the Second Reconstruction, continued the work that Reconstruction had begun. ■

Across Time & Space

Interpretations of historical events often reflect the prejudices of historians or a particular time. For many years, textbook descriptions of the Reconstruction Era supported racist views, showing it as a time when African Americans had too much power and whites were victims of that power. Today, historians try to present a more accurate view of Reconstruction.

■ *How did Reconstruction change the United States?*

REVIEW

1. **FOCUS** How did Reconstruction policies end in mixed results?
2. **CONNECT** How did the new black freedom contribute to the dissatisfaction with sharecropping and the desire for "forty acres and a mule"?
3. **CITIZENSHIP** What was meant by Home Rule, and why did Southern Democrats promise to redeem the South?
4. **CULTURE** Who were the earliest members of the Ku Klux Klan, and what was the basis of their support? What tactics did they use to terrorize and intimidate their victims?
5. **CRITICAL THINKING** Attempts at enforcing Reconstruction ended in 1876 after the election of Rutherford B. Hayes. How might history have been different if Democrats had not reestablished Home Rule and if Republican governments had remained in the South after the election?
6. **ACTIVITY** Prepare and give a five-minute presentation on the goals and accomplishments of the Reconstruction Era. Conclude your presentation with mention of the work that was left to be done to ensure the rights of black Americans.

HISTORY

Critical Thinking

What challenges remained for black Americans in their struggle for equal rights after Reconstruction? *(Segregation, lack of opportunities in employment and housing, social inequality)*

■ *Sample answers: Slavery was abolished forever and civil and political rights were extended to black Americans; more black citizens received an education, but segregation kept the races apart.*

CLOSE

Have students answer the Thinking Focus. Have volunteers use the graphic overviews that they made while reading the lesson to complete one together on the board. Add any elements in the Graphic Overview from page 391 missing from the one on the board.

Answers to Review Questions

1. The Fourteenth and Fifteenth amendments provided black Americans with the means to attain many civil and political rights; the Black Codes, sharecropping, the KKK, and the withdrawal of federal troops kept many black Americans from experiencing true freedom.
2. Having been declared free, black Americans wanted complete independence, not a new form of enslavement.
3. Southern Democrats favored Home Rule, arguing that states had the right to resist federal laws. They wanted to regain the Southern way of life.
4. The Klan began as a Confederate veterans organization. Members threatened, beat, whipped, and lynched their victims.
5. Sample answer: Black Americans might have gained rights sooner and with less difficulty. Allow for personal opinion.
6. Several students may present their speeches to the class.

Homework Options

Have students write a diary entry of a freedman or a freedwoman living at Davis Bend as the land reverted to its original owners.

Study Guide: page 57.

UNDERSTANDING CAUSE AND EFFECT

In this skill lesson, students will learn to analyze cause-and-effect relationships by using charts.

HISTORY

Critical Thinking

Events usually have complex causes. It is far easier to analyze cause and effect afterward than to predict it. What was Lincoln's purpose in freeing the slaves? *(To unite the North and encourage slaves to rebel)* In terms of the chart at the bottom of page 398, what was an ultimate effect of Lincoln's freeing the slaves? *(The passage of the Black Codes by the South)* Could he have foreseen this? *(Unlikely)* What was another ultimate effect of his action, and why? *(Sample answer: Encouraged the Civil Rights movement because Lincoln had set a precedent)*

UNDERSTANDING CAUSE AND EFFECT

Analyzing the Civil War

Here's Why

Everything happened at once. The dog grabbed at your lunch, your mother called out "You'll miss your bus," while your sister picked up a pile of books and ran on ahead. When you got to class you discovered that you had left your report at home. What was the cause and what was the effect?

In this case, the dog, your sister, and running for the bus were all contributing causes. A lower grade on your report predictably is an immediate, or short-term effect. A lower semester grade is a possible long-term effect.

Knowing how to sort out multiple causes and effects, main causes and contributing causes, and short-term and long-term effects helps you understand why things happened as they did. This skill can be applied to forgotten school reports. The skills can also be applied to understanding the Civil War and the Reconstruction period following the war.

Here's How

You already know that if two events are related and if one happens before the other, the first may be the cause of the second. The diagram below shows that sometimes events result in a chain reaction. What was the effect of the first event becomes the cause of a second event, and so on.

The diagram below analyzes the effects of Lincoln's assassination on the post-war South. Lincoln's freeing the slaves was only one factor among the many complex events that led to his death. It could thus be called a contributing cause. The main cause of course was a bullet fired by John Wilkes Booth.

The diagram shows that Lincoln's death was in turn the cause of Andrew Johnson's succession as President. You will notice that the diagram labels this as a short-term effect because the change in presidency happened immediately after Lincoln's death. Johnson's moderate reconstruction plan resulted in the passage by Southern legislatures of the Black Codes. So the black Codes might be termed long-term effects of Lincoln's death.

Now look at the diagram on the next page. It analyzes the multiple causes--both main causes and contributing causes--of the Civil War. It also shows the multiple effects of the war. The firing on Fort Sumter is frequently given as the immediate cause of the war. But as you know from your reading of Chapter 13, Fort Sumter was not an isolated event. What would you consider to be the main cause? Or do you think one cause can be singled out as the main cause of the Civil War?

The immediate effect of the war was that about 638,000 northern and southern soldiers were killed. But certainly the main effect was the preservation of the Union. Are there any effects of the Civil War, short-term or long-term, that you think should be added to the diagram?

Try It

Re-read the section on "Freed People Struggle for Rights" on pages 382-383. Using emancipation as your theme, see how long a cause-and-effect chain reaction you can create.

Now create a multiple

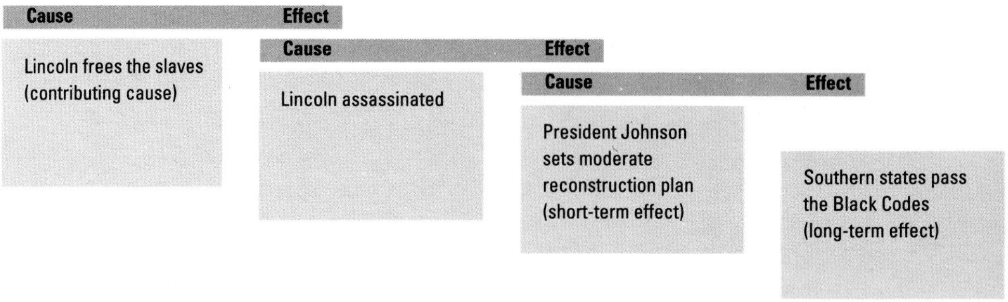

Objective

Use Civil War events to compare cause-and-effect relationships. (Critical Thinking 3)

Science Connection

The idea of cause and effect is also important in science. Tell students that causes are often much easier to see in science than they are in history. The reason for this is that scientists can carry out experiments to determine the exact cause of a particular effect. Ask the science teacher or a group of students to conduct an experiment that will show a scientific cause and effect. Have students discuss why historians can't do such experiments to test a theory.

cause-and-effect diagram placing the passing of the Fourteenth Amendment at the center of your diagram. Which of the causes would you label as main causes and which contributing causes? Which effects would you label immediate and which long-term?

Apply It

Think of a recent event, such as an earthquake, a military conflict, or a change of government. Write down the event as the center of a multiple cause-and-effect diagram. Then complete the diagram, labeling the main cause, contributing causes, immediate or short-term effects, and long-term effects.

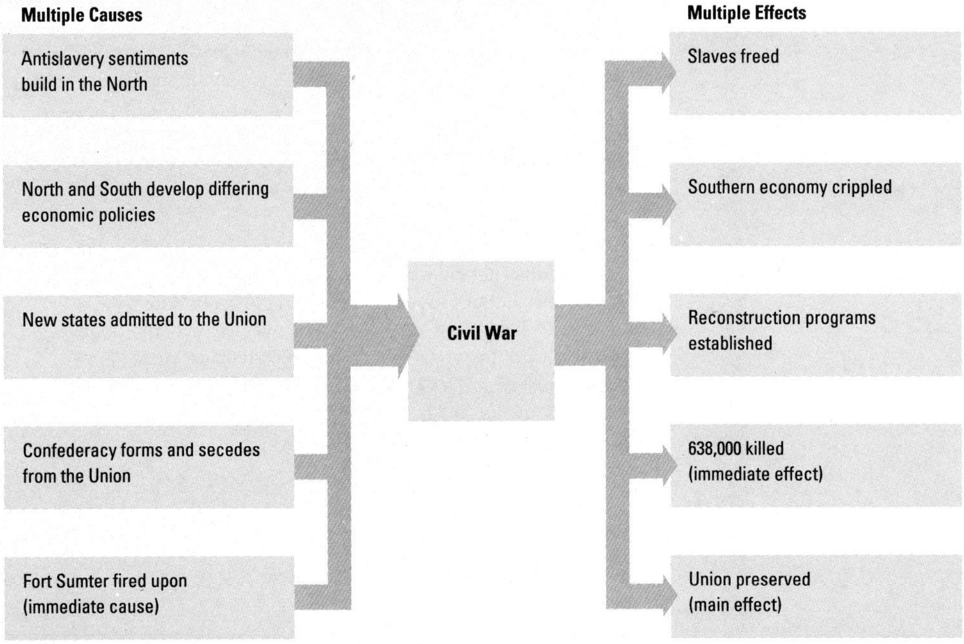

HISTORY

Critical Thinking

Compare the cause-and-effect chain on page 398 to the chart showing multiple causes and effects on this page. Discuss the last effect in the chain on page 398. Were there other causes besides Johnson's reconstruction plan? What were they? *(Sample answers: Southern agriculture's dependence on slave labor; Southerners' desire to restore slavery)* Which gives a better picture of events, a multiple cause-and-effect chart or a straight-line chain? Why? *(A multiple cause-and-effect chart, because any given event in history is likely to have many causes)*

Answers to Try It

Sample cause-and-effect chain: Blacks were freed / many left plantations / moved to cities / sought expanded opportunities.

Sample diagram: main cause—Congress wanted to grant full citizenship to blacks; contributing causes—South elected former Confederates to Congress, Johnson vetoed congressional bill guaranteeing citizenship to blacks, and Republicans feared Supreme Court would overrule law; immediate effects—defined citizenship for first time, forbade states to deny political rights to any citizens, and disqualified former Confederate officials from federal or state office; long-term effect—set a constitutional basis for many civil and political rights for citizens of all races and both sexes

Answers to Apply It

Make sure students follow the patterns provided in the text.

Social Participation

Divide students into groups of four. Have them compare and discuss in their groups their answers to Try It. Each student should have a chance to explain and defend the cause-and-effect choices that he or she made.

INTRODUCE

Explain that Walt Whitman wrote these three poems in response to the assassination of President Abraham Lincoln. Ask students to recall what they learned in Lesson 1 about the assassination and the public response to it. Remind students that Lincoln's death occurred only five days after Lee had surrendered, thus shattering the nation's happy, carefree mood.

READ AND RESPOND

Ask volunteers to perform choral readings of these three poems. Each student can read a different stanza. After the readers practice individually and together, have them perform for the class. As students answer the purpose-setting question, make sure they give reasons for their answers.

LITERATURE

The Lincoln Poems

Walt Whitman

In Lesson 1, you read about how President Lincoln was assassinated just days after the end of the Civil War. His death was devastating, because the nation had counted on him to guide it into peace.

Walt Whitman (1819-1892) published several editions of Leaves of Grass, *the collection of poems from which these selections are taken. During the Civil War, Whitman assisted in military hospitals and wrote poetry about his experiences of aiding wounded soldiers. After Lincoln's assassination, Whitman wrote several poems about his beloved President. As you read these poems, think about the three different ways Whitman portrayed Lincoln.*

rack storm condition
exulting celebrating
keel central structure of a ship
vessel boat

O Captain! My Captain!

O Captain! my Captain! our fearful trip is done,
The ship has weather'd every rack, the prize we sought is won,
The port is near, the bells I hear, the people all exulting,
While follow eyes the steady keel, the vessel grim and daring;
But O heart! heart! heart!
O the bleeding drops of red,
Where on the deck my Captain lies,
Fallen cold and dead.

O Captain! my Captain! rise up and hear the bells;
Rise—for you the flag is flung—for you the bugle trills,
For you bouquets and ribbon'd wreaths—for you the shores a-crowding,
For you they call, the swaying mass, their eager faces turning;
Hear Captain! dear father!
This arm beneath your head!
It is some dream that on the deck,
You've fallen cold and dead.

My Captain does not answer, his lips are pale and still,
My father does not feel my arm, he has no pulse nor will,
The ship is anchor'd safe and sound, its voyage closed and done,
From fearful trip the victor ship comes in with object won;
Exult O shores, and ring O bells!
But I with mournful tread,
Walk the deck my Captain lies,
Fallen cold and dead.

400

Thematic Connections

Social Studies: Lincoln's assassination

Houghton Mifflin Literary Readers: Freedom's Foundations

Background

Whitman published the first edition of *Leaves of Grass* in 1855. It sold poorly, although Ralph Waldo Emerson, one of the nation's leading literary figures, praised it highly in a letter to Whitman. During his lifetime, Whitman brought out eight more editions of the work, adding new poems and revising old ones each time.

Whitman's love poems, although rather tame by today's standards, caused some public condemnation of his work during his lifetime. After the Civil War, Whitman lost a job as a government clerk as a result of the controversy surrounding these love poems. A journalist friend defended him in print, however, and he soon was offered another government post.

Whitman's poems were typically rambling, free-verse celebrations of nature, himself, and those he loved and revered. The regular rhyme and meter of "O Captain! My Captain!" are not typical of his work.

Hush'd Be the Camps To-day

(May 4, 1865)

Hush'd be the camps to-day,
And soldiers let us drape our war-worn weapons,
And each with musing soul retire to celebrate,
Our dear commander's death.

musing deep in thought

No more for him life's stormy conflicts,
Nor victory, nor defeat—no more time's dark events,
Charging like ceaseless clouds across the sky.

ceaseless without stop

But sing poet in our name,
Sing of the love we bore him—because you, dweller in camps, know it truly.

As they invault the coffin there,
Sing—as they close the doors of earth upon him—one verse,
For the heavy hearts of soldiers.

invault bury

This Dust Was Once the Man

This dust was once the man,
Gentle, plain, just and resolute, under whose cautious hand,
Against the foulest crime in history known in any land or age,
Was saved the Union of these States.

resolute determined

Further Reading

Abraham Lincoln: The Prairie Years and the War Years. Carl Sandburg. This is one volume of Sandburg's classic six-volume study of Lincoln.

Abraham Lincoln and the First Shot. R. N. Current. This book recounts Lincoln's years at the beginning of the Civil War.

Who is the Captain to whom the poet is speaking in "O Captain! My Captain!"? *(Lincoln)*

What is "the prize we sought" in the second line of the first stanza? *(Victory in the war)*

In "This Dust Was Once the Man," what is "the foulest crime in history"? *(Lincoln's assassination)*

EXTEND

Have students find more of the poems of Walt Whitman in *Leaves of Grass.* Ask them to prepare to read aloud for the class one of the poems.

Further Reading

You may want to ask students to go to the school or local library to find more books about Lincoln's assassination.

INTRODUCE

Have students recall what they learned about Charlotte Forten in Lesson 1. Tell them that this selection is part of a journal in which she describes her experiences as a teacher of freed slaves. Remind them of what occasion Forten is describing. *(The reading of the Emancipation Proclamation to a group of former slaves in the South in 1863)*

READ AND RESPOND

Ask students to imagine how black Americans must have felt when they were told that they were finally free. Then have them read the selection independently. If you have LEP students, you may wish to read aloud the vocabulary words and their meanings noted in the margin. As students answer the purpose-setting question, make sure they give reasons for their answers.

In Lesson 1 you read about Charlotte Forten's involvement with the Freedmen's Bureau's efforts to provide a basic education to freed black slaves and poor whites.

LITERATURE

It Was a Glorious Day!

Charlotte Forten

Union ships captured Port Royal Harbor on the South Carolina coast late in 1861. The local slaveowners escaped, leaving behind their many slaves, who were now free. The U.S. government decided to send teachers south to educate these freedmen. The next spring 53 teachers arrived from the North, set themselves up on the plantations, and started to teach the former slaves how to read and write.

In the fall of 1862, young Charlotte Forten (1837-1914) from Philadelphia, the first black teacher, arrived just as the army had begun to raise an all-black regiment from the young freedmen. Forten was invited to the army camp to watch the celebration of Emancipation Day, January 1, 1863. She recorded the events in her diary. What seems to have impressed her the most?

New Year's Day, Emancipation Day, was a glorious one to us. General Saxton and Colonel Higginson had invited us to visit the camp of the First Regiment of South Carolina Volunteers on that day, "the greatest day in the nation's history." We enjoyed perfectly the exciting scene on board the steamboat *Flora*. There was an eager, wondering crowd of the freed people, in their holiday attire, with the gayest of headkerchiefs, the whitest of aprons, and the happiest of faces. The band was playing, the flags were streaming, and everybody was talking merrily and feeling happy. The sun shone brightly, and the very waves seemed to partake of the universal gayety, for they danced and sparkled more joyously than ever before. Long before we reached Camp Saxton, we could see the beautiful grove and the ruins of the old fort near it.

grove small wooded area

Some companies of the First Regiment were drawn up in line under the trees near the landing, ready to receive us. They were a fine, soldierly looking set of men, and their brilliant dress made a splendid appearance among the trees. It was my good fortune to find an old friend among the officers. He took us over the camp and showed us all the arrangements. Everything looked clean and comfortable; much neater, we were told, than in most of the white camps. . . .

The ceremony in honor of Emancipation took place in the beautiful grove of live-oaks adjoining the camp. I wish it were possible to describe fitly the scene which met our eyes, as we sat upon the stand, and looked down on the crowd before us. There were the black soldiers in their blue coats and scarlet pantaloons; the officers of the First Regiment, and of other regiments, in their handsome uniforms; and there were crowds of lookers-on, men, women, and children, of every complexion, grouped in various attitudes, under the moss-hung trees. The faces of all wore a

pantaloons pants

complexion skin tone

Thematic Connections

Social Studies: The Emancipation Proclamation

Houghton Mifflin Literary Readers: Freedom's Foundations

Background

The Emancipation Proclamation applied only to those slaves living in areas of the Confederacy that were under Union control. Slaves in states that remained within the Union, such as Kentucky and Missouri, were not freed by it.

Opposition to slavery was a tradition on both sides of Charlotte Forten's family. She was the granddaughter of James Forten, a free black who became a wealthy sailmaker. James Forten was active in the cause of abolition, as were many of his children and grandchildren. Charlotte Forten was also the niece of Robert Purvis, the son of a white Englishman and a black American woman. Purvis used his father's fortune in the anti-slavery cause. Charlotte Forten wrote a well-known autobiography, *A Free Negro in the Slave Era.*

happy, interested look.

The exercises commenced with a prayer by the chaplain of the regiment. An ode, written for the occasion, was then read and sung. President Lincoln's Proclamation of Emancipation was then read, and enthusiastically cheered. The Rev. Mr. French presented Colonel Higginson with two very elegant flags, a gift to the First Regiment, from the Church of the Puritans, in New York. He accompanied them by an appropriate and enthusiastic speech. As Colonel Higginson took the flags, before he had time to reply to the speech, some of the colored people, of their own accord, began to sing,—

"My country, 'tis of thee,
Sweet land of liberty,
Of thee we sing!"

It was a touching and beautiful incident, and sent a thrill through all our hearts. The Colonel was deeply moved by it. He said that reply was far more effective than any speech he could make. But he did make one of those stirring speeches which are "half battles." All hearts swelled with emotion as we listened to his glorious words, "stirring the soul like the sound of trumpet." His soldiers are warmly attached to him, and he evidently feels toward them all as if they were his children.

General Saxton spoke also, and was received with great enthusiasm. Throughout the morning, repeated cheers were given for him by the regiment, and joined in heartily by all the people. They knew him to be one of the best and noblest men in the world. His unfailing kindness and consideration for them, so different from the treatment they have sometimes received at the hands of United States officers, have caused them to have unbounded confidence in him.

At the close of Colonel Higginson's speech, he presented the flags to the color bearers, Sergeant Rivers and Sergeant Sutton, with an earnest charge, to which they made appropriate replies.

Mrs. Gage uttered some earnest words, and then the regiment sang John Brown's Hallelujah Song.

After the meeting was over, we saw the dress-parade, which was a brilliant and beautiful sight. An officer told us that the men went through the drill remarkably well, and learned the movements with wonderful ease and rapidity. To us it seemed strange as a miracle to see this regiment of blacks, the first mustered into the service of the United States, thus doing itself honor in the sight of officers of other regiments, many of whom doubtless came to scoff. The men afterward had a great feast, ten oxen having been roasted whole, for their especial benefit.

chaplain a clergyman

scoff mock

Further Reading

Journal. Charlotte Forten. The author describes more of her experiences in the Civil War era in this book of diary entries.

Lincoln: A Photobiography. Russell Friedman. A detailed account of the Emancipation Proclamation is put into perspective with a series of excellent pictures.

◄According to Forten, how did the black soldiers' camp compare to the white soldiers' camp? *(It was neater.)*

What did the officers of the white regiments think of the display? *(They were impressed, although they probably came to scoff.)*

EXTEND

Ask students to imagine that they are slaves living in a Confederate state. Have them write a journal entry in which they explain what they thought and felt on the day they were told of the Emancipation Proclamation. What are their hopes for the future?

Further Reading

You may want to ask students to go to the school or local library to find more books to read about the emancipation of slaves in the 1860s.

Answers to Reviewing Key Terms

A. Sample answers:

1. During Reconstruction, the United States tried to rebuild a country torn apart by war.
2. A vigilante takes the law into his or her own hands.
3. President Johnson was the first United States President to face impeachment because he tried to limit the power of Congress.
4. Carpetbaggers moved into the South to utilize political and economic opportunities.
5. Martial law was used to enforce Reconstruction policies.
6. A scalawag was a Southern white supporter of Reconstruction.

B. Answers:

1. False. Sharecroppers were forced to give part of their crops to the owners of the land.
2. True. Harsh Reconstruction policies angered the South.
3. False. *Martial law* is temporary military rule.
4. False. *Impeachment* is charging someone who holds office with misconduct.
5. False. Delegates, or elected representatives, would go to a state convention.
6. False. Plantation owners sometimes rented out their farmland to sharecroppers.
7. False. Vigilantes took the law into their own hands.

Answers to Exploring Concepts

A. Answers:

Lincoln Plan: 10% of voters in 1860 must take loyalty oath / no provisions for black rights

Wade-Davis Bill: Majority of voters must swear allegiance, past and present / outlawed slavery

Johnson Plan: Similar to 10% plan; easier for Southern states to form new governments with representatives to Congress / encouraged states to allow blacks to vote

Radical Reconstruction: Southern states had to set up new state governments to ratify the Fourteenth Amendment, and former Confederate officials and officers could not vote / states had to guarantee black voting rights

B. Answers:

1. It outlawed slavery and set conditions for former Confederate states rejoining the Union.
2. Southern states used these Codes to keep blacks in virtual slavery. Some didn't allow newly freed blacks to work without expensive licenses, and others said that workers could only leave the plantation grounds with permission from the owners.
3. They built their own homes, churches, and schools, and asked the government for land to start farms. They elected black candidates to office in many states.
4. It defined citizenship and prohibited states from choosing representatives to Congress if the state didn't allow people to vote.
5. Johnson opposed Radical Reconstruction. He urged Southern states to reject the Fourteenth Amendment and tried to fire the secretary of war.
6. The Radical Republicans wanted to win the black vote, since most Southern blacks would vote Republican. This gave Republicans control of the Congress.
7. White Southerners regained much of the land that had been given to the freed blacks. Blacks were sometimes left with swampy, infertile land.

Chapter Review

Reviewing Key Terms

amnesty (p. 377)
carpetbagger (p. 388)
impeachment (p. 387)
martial law (p. 386)
Reconstruction (p. 377)
redeem (p. 394)
scalawag (p. 389)
segregated (p. 383)
sharecropping (p. 376)
vigilante (p. 394)

A. The sentences below have been started for you. Complete each sentence so that the meaning of the key term is clear.

1. During Reconstruction, the United States tried to . . .
2. A vigilante . . .
3. President Johnson was the first United States president to face impeachment because . . .
4. Carpetbaggers moved into the South to . . .
5. Martial law was used to . . .
6. A scalawag . . .

B. Based on what you have read in the chapter, decide whether each of the following statements is accurate. Write an explanation of each decision.

1. A sharecropper generously offered to share his harvest with those who were in need of food.
2. The federal government's Reconstruction policies created bitter feelings among Southerners.
3. The Freedmen's Bureau asked for a martial law to legalize the marriages of slaves.
4. The impeachment process gave the South a new crop that gradually replaced cotton.
5. The vigilantes to a state convention voted to set up a new state constitution.
6. Wealthy landowners sometimes rented out their farmland to carpetbaggers.
7. A vigilante reported violations of laws to the local sheriff or police chief.

Exploring Concepts

A. On a separate sheet of paper, make a chart like the one shown below. In the second column, list the requirements for re-admission of states to the Union. In the third column, list the provisions for black citizens' rights.

B. Answer each of the following questions in one or two complete sentences.

1. What were the principal purposes of the Thirteenth Amendment?
2. Why were the Black Codes issued?
3. How did free blacks show that they were ready to take their place as full citizens of the United States?
4. What were the principal provisions of the Fourteenth Amendment?
5. Why did Congress try to force President Johnson from office?
6. What were the main reasons for the passage of the Fifteenth Amendment?
7. Why were free blacks generally unsuccessful in setting up their own farms?

Reconstruction Plans	Requirements for Re-admission of States	Provisions for Black Citizens' Rights
President Lincoln's Plan		
Wade-Davis Bill		
President Johnson's Plan		
Radical Reconstruction		

Reviewing Skills

1. Identify the different kinds of causes and effects, and explain how they are related.
2. How do you determine the difference between a contributing cause and a main cause?
3. If President Lincoln had not signed the Emancipation Proclamation, would that have made a significant change in the causes and effects of the Civil War? Explain.
4. Following the chart on page 399, create a cause-and-effect diagram for Reconstruction. Note the political, social, and economic causes and effects of Reconstruction.
5. Read the words of Albion Tourgee on page 389. Determine the point of view in the selection, and write a short paragraph outlining your findings.
6. Suppose you wanted to determine the causes and effects of the American Revolution What information would you need? What process would you follow?

Using Critical Thinking

1. Historians have said that when John Wilkes Booth assassinated Lincoln, he killed the South's most powerful friend. In what ways might Reconstruction have been different if Lincoln had lived? Why?
2. Just as it followed the American Civil War, a period of reconstruction for the defeated side follows every war. What should the goal of reconstruction be? Why might the victors want to follow a policy of revenge and punishment, as many Northerners did after the Civil War?
3. A Mississippi law written after the Civil War stated that "The negro is free, whether we like it or not. . . . To be free, however, does not make him a citizen or entitle him to social or political equality with the white man." Based on the wording of that law, what hardships do you think the newly freed blacks faced?
4. Frederick Douglass wrote that after the Civil War, African Americans were "free from the individual master but a slave to society." What did he mean by that statement? Do you agree or disagree with his conclusion? Explain your answer.

Preparing for Citizenship

1. **WRITING ACTIVITY** Imagine that you are a Northerner in 1866, and that the local newspaper has asked for a "man on the street" reaction to the following question: What should we (the Union) do with Robert E. Lee and other high-ranking Confederate soldiers? Write your response, making sure you cite specific reasons for your answer.
2. **WRITING ACTIVITY** Abraham Lincoln was a much-loved President. His death has been the subject of many books, paintings and poems. Read the Lincoln poems in this chapter and look up the following poems: *Abraham Lincoln Walks at Midnight* by Vachel Lindsay and *Lincoln, the Man of the People* by Edwin Markham. Write a short essay comparing how these poets present Lincoln.
3. **COLLECTING INFORMATION** In President John F. Kennedy's book *Profiles in Courage*, he described the courage of Senator Edmund G. Ross in voting not to impeach President Johnson. Find the book in your library and read the section on Ross. Write a short report on Ross's reasons for voting as he did.
4. **ART ACTIVITY** There have been a number of nations that have had to deal with the aftereffects of a civil war. Look up recent accounts of such situations, and prepare a bulletin board display on the process of Reconstruction. Use pictures, maps, newspaper articles, and songs to provide a visual overview of the recovery process for such a nation.
5. **COLLABORATIVE LEARNING** During Reconstruction, people with different goals argued over how to heal the nation's wounds. As a class, choose Reconstruction roles. For example, you may be a defeated Confederate soldier, a member of the Radical Republicans, an ex-slave, a carpetbagger, a scalawag, or a worker in the Freedmen's Bureau. Prepare a speech that describes how you view your role in the process of Reconstruction and that provides your opinion on how Reconstruction ought to proceed.

Answers to Reviewing Skills

1. Students should describe main, multiple and contributing causes and immediate, short-term and long-term effects.
2. The main cause is the single most significant cause of the event. There may be many contributing causes.
3. The South may have reached a compromise with the North to allow slavery. There may not have been a war.
4. Students may include the following causes: end of Civil War, economic collapse of the South, Emancipation Proclamation, and the following effects: Black Codes enacted, black migration to cities, Fourteenth Amendment, carpetbaggers migrate to South, Fifteenth Amendment, white supremacist organizations formed.
5. Students should refer to Tourgée's background as a carpetbagger and note that the excerpt is from a novel.
6. Students would need to review events just before and just after the war, and follow the diagram outlined on pages 398–399.

Answers to Using Critical Thinking

1. Students should compare Lincoln's policy of moderation with what actually occurred during Reconstruction. Refer to the "Lincoln Poems" (pages 400–401) and the Gettysburg Address (page 355) to determine what kind of person Lincoln was.
2. Encourage students to review the situation in the North and the South before the war. Point out that the conflict was very emotional on both sides.
3. Refer students to the Fourteenth and Fifteenth Amendments. Ask students to define social and political equality, and to identify how that could be denied to freed blacks.
4. Ask students to consider if it is easier to change laws than attitudes.

Answers to Preparing for Citizenship

1. **WRITING ACTIVITY** Ask students to consider the effects of their solution. If they choose punishment, how will that affect the nation? Would it be dangerous to let Lee and others become politically active again? Why?
2. **WRITING ACTIVITY** Discuss basic elements of poetry, such as metaphor and simile. Ask students to write a quick response to each poem, explaining what kind of a person they "see" when they read the poem. Then have them compare the images of Lincoln that each poem creates.
3. **COLLECTING INFORMATION** Ask volunteers to read their reports. Discuss the event, encouraging students to find contemporary situations in which political figures have taken unpopular stands.
4. **ART ACTIVITY** Refer students to Understanding Civil War on page 344. Students can be divided into media research teams.
5. **COLLABORATIVE LEARNING** Direct students to primary sources such as Frederick Douglass's autobiography (see pages 296–297). Speeches can be casual conversations between players.

UNIT
OVERVIEW

Draw students' attention to the unit title and the narrative underneath it. Ask them to name some of the technological advances that helped transform America. What impact might a period of revolutionary change have on a society? *(Create new areas of conflict)* Ask students how the lithograph illustrates the unit title and the narrative. *(Includes examples of new technology)*

Looking Back

Remind students that they learned in Chapter 9 about the growth of urban centers in the North. Ask them how the Civil War contributed to the growth of industry in the United States. *(Forced both sides to build factories and railroads)*

Looking Forward

Tell students that they will be studying how industrialization changed life in the United States after the Civil War in the next five chapters:

Chapter 14 *Reshaping the Great Plains*
Chapter 15 *Industry and Workers*
Chapter 16 *The Gilded Age*
Chapter 17 *The Reform Era*
Chapter 18 *America Emerges as a World Power*

Unit 6

A Time of Transformation

The changes that swept the United States in the decades following the Civil War were nothing short of revolutionary. Factories and cities experienced booming growth, immigrants poured in from Europe in record numbers, and technological advances in transportation and communication transformed the way Americans lived. The opening of the Brooklyn Bridge in 1883 symbolized America's movement from a rural agricultural nation to an urban, industrial power.

1850

Currier and Ives lithograph (detail). The Grand Opening of the Brooklyn Bridge on May 24, 1883. The Metropolitan Museum of Art, Bequest of Edward W. C. Arnold, 1954.

GEOGRAPHY PROJECT

American Slice of Life

Geography Skill **Reading Population and Election Maps**
Students use the skills of Acquiring and Analyzing geographic information.

Geography Theme Human/environment interaction

Geography Standard 17, applying geography to interpret the past, present, and future

Activity ***Create a Scrapbook***

Materials writing paper, construction paper, pencils, crayons

Management Whole Class/Small Group

Choose three years between 1870–1920 and create a scrapbook of text and images that tells about life in America during each of those years. The dates should be selected in a way that will show change over time.

Have students:

- write concise descriptions and/or create illustrations for a coffee-table book about life in each of the years selected.
- include maps to illustrate human movement, change in environment or resources.
- make facsimiles of the culture such as ticket stubs, menus.

Understanding the Lithograph

Currier and Ives was a firm of American lithographers that published more than 4,000 color pictures during the 1800s. The firm's prints illustrated both historic events and the manners and customs of the times. Nathaniel Currier (1813–1888), the founder of the firm, issued his first two prints in 1835. James Merritt Ives (1824–1895) served for many years as art director of the firm. After 1857, all the firm's lithographs carried the joint name.

Understanding Chronology

Explain that the historical period that Unit 6 covers had its roots in the 1850s, the decade before the Civil War, and ended with the conclusion of World War I and the U.S. Senate's rejection of the Treaty of Versailles in 1920.

For research support activities, see the *Research Handbook*.

For simulations correlated to this unit, see *Citizenship Simulations*, p. viii.

HOUGHTON MIFFLIN SOCIAL STUDIES

Bookshelf II

Kids At Work: Lewis Hine and the Crusade Against Child Labor

by Russell Freedman

The author uses Lewis Hines' photographs of young workers in many different settings to demonstrate dangerous and harsh child labor conditions in the early 1900s.

Motivate Read aloud pp. 47 to the break on p. 54 about boys who worked in coal mines during the early 1900s, sharing the photographs as you read. Ask students why they think adults allowed children to work under such poor conditions. Have students look at the painting on this page that shows one of the great engineering feats of the 1800s and predict what they think they will read about in this unit.

To connect this book with the unit content, use the planning guide and student activity blackline masters beginning on p. iv of the *Bookshelf II Teacher's Resources.*

For additional books that are Easy, Average, and Challenging, see the Unit Bibliography on p. T43. See bibliography updates at www.eduplace.com/ss/hmss.

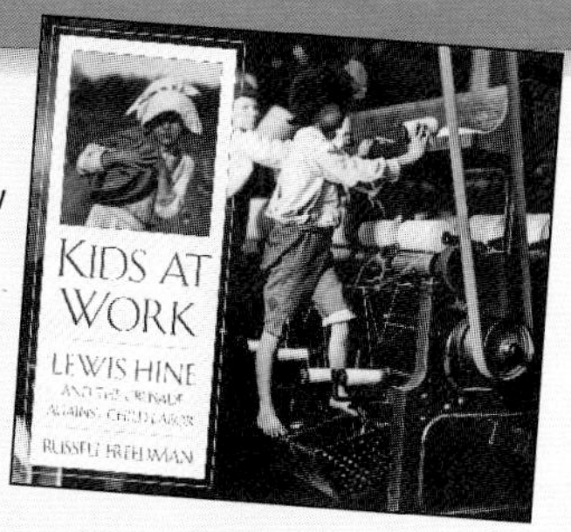

CHAPTER 14

Planning at a Glance

Reshaping the Great Plains

	Objectives	Reading Support and Other Resources	Diverse Learning Strategies
Lesson 1 A Time of Change *pp. 410–414* 1–2 days	• Identify how geography posed obstacles to Western settlement. • Describe the building of the transcontinental railroad. • Describe mining techniques and boom towns in California and Nevada.	• **Workbook** or **Reading Support:** pp. 195–198 Review p. 46 Extra Support/Transition p. 46 Multi-lang. Sum. pp. 91–92 • **Other Resources:** Geography Kit, Home Involvement 6, Poster 5, Study Guide p. 59	Access Act. **(SDAIE)** TE p. 411 Map and Globe Skills **(Visual)** TE p. 412 Making a Mural **(Visual)** TE p. 413 Audiotapes of Multi-language Lesson Summaries **(Auditory)**
Lesson 2 Culture of the Plains Indians *pp. 415–419* 2–3 days **Literature** **"How Indians Used Buffalo"** *pp. 420–421*	• Describe how the Plains Indians lived before the Europeans arrived. • Explain how the horse and the gun influenced the Plains Indians' lives. • Describe Plains Indian beliefs and practices, including counting coup and beliefs about land.	• **Workbook** or **Reading Support:** pp. 199–202 Review p. 47 Extra Support/Transition p. 47 Multi-lang. Sum. pp. 93–94 • **Other Resources:** Geography Kit, Study Guide p. 60	Access Act. **(SDAIE)** TE p. 416 Visual Learning **(Visual)** TE p. 417 Homework Options **(Visual)** TE p. 419 Audiotapes of Multi-language Lesson Summaries **(Auditory)**
Lesson 3 Indian Lands Lost *pp. 422–426* 1–2 days	• Explain why hostility between American Indians and white settlers increased after 1860. • Define *reservation* and *annuity* and explain their part in U.S. government policy. • Explain how programs to promote assimilation generally failed.	• **Workbook** or **Reading Support:** pp. 203–206 Review p. 48 Extra Support/Transition p. 48 Multi-lang. Sum. pp. 95–96 • **Other Resources:** Geography Kit, Study Guide p. 61	Language Arts Connection **(Kinesthetic)** TE p. 425 Collaborative Act. **(Multi Age)** TE p. 425 Homework Options **(GATE)** TE p. 426 Audiotapes of Multi-language Lesson Summaries **(Auditory)**
Lesson 4 Resettlement of the Land *pp. 427–432* 3–4 days **Literature** **"A New Home"** *pp. 434–435*	• List the provisions of the Homestead Act. • Explain how improved transportation affected the West. • Explain how farmers used technology on the Great Plains.	• **Workbook** or **Reading Support:** pp. 207–210 Review p. 49 Extra Support/Transition p. 49 Multi-lang. Sum. pp. 97–98 • **Other Resources:** Study Guide p. 62	Access Strat. **(Extra Support)** TE p. 428 Map and Globe Skills **(Visual)** TE p. 430 Research **(GATE)** TE p. 431 Homework Options **(Auditory)** TE p. 432 Audiotapes of Multi-language Lesson Summaries **(Auditory)**
Skill: **Tracing Routes West** *p. 433*	• Use a topographical map and a route map to determine the development of the West.	• **Other Resources:** Geography Kit, Study Guide p. 63	
Making Decisons: **Where the Buffalo Roam** *pp. 436–437*	• Clarify the issues regarding the protection of wildlife.	• **Other Resources:** Poster 8	
Chapter Review *pp. 438–439* 1 day		Chapter 14 Test pp. 53–56 *(See facsimiles on TE p. 762.)*	Assessment Multiple-Use Masters pp. 81–88

Reading Support Resources *for Every Lesson*

Reading and Review

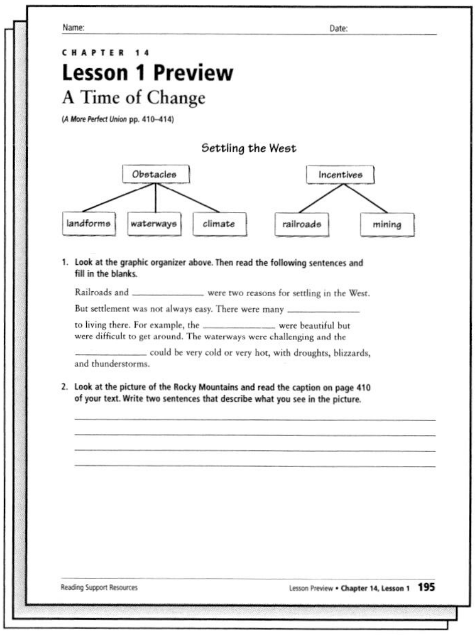
Name: Date:

CHAPTER 14

Lesson 1 Preview

A Time of Change

(*A More Perfect Union* pp. 410–414)

1. Look at the graphic organizer above. Then read the following sentences and fill in the blanks.

Railroads and ________ were two reasons for settling in the West. But settlement was not always easy. There were many ________ to living there. For example, the ________ were beautiful but were difficult to get around. The waterways were challenging and the ________ could be very cold or very hot, with droughts, blizzards, and thunderstorms.

2. Look at the picture of the Rocky Mountains and read the caption on page 410 of your text. Write two sentences that describe what you see in the picture.

Reading Support Resources — Lesson Preview • Chapter 14, Lesson 1 195

- **Chapter Overview*** p. 194
- **Lesson Previews*** using graphic organizers from the Teacher's Edition pp. 195, 199, 203, 207
- **Reading Strategies*** pp. 196, 200, 204, 208
- **Lesson Summaries*** pp. 197–198, 201–202, 205–206, 209–210
- **Lesson Reviews** pp. 46, 47, 48, 49

* **Workbook** includes starred items.

Multi-language Summaries

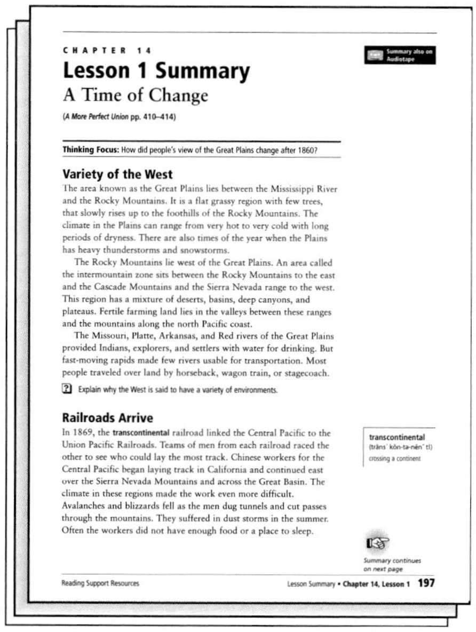
CHAPTER 14

Summary also on Audiotape

Lesson 1 Summary

A Time of Change

(*A More Perfect Union* pp. 410–414)

Thinking Focus: How did people's view of the Great Plains change after 1860?

Variety of the West

The area known as the Great Plains lies between the Mississippi River and the Rocky Mountains. It is a flat grassy region with few trees, that slowly rises up to the foothills of the Rocky Mountains. The climate in the Plains can range from very hot to very cold with long periods of dryness. There are also times of the year when the Plains has heavy thunderstorms and snowstorms.

The Rocky Mountains lie west of the Great Plains. An area called the intermountain zone sits between the Rocky Mountains to the east and the Cascade Mountains and the Sierra Nevada range to the west. This region has a mixture of deserts, basins, deep canyons, and plateaus. Fertile farming land lies in the valleys between these ranges and the mountains along the north Pacific coast.

The Missouri, Platte, Arkansas, and Red rivers of the Great Plains provided Indians, explorers, and settlers with water for drinking. But fast-moving rapids made few rivers usable for transportation. Most people traveled over land by horseback, wagon train, or stagecoach.

? Explain why the West is said to have a variety of environments.

Railroads Arrive

In 1869, the **transcontinental** railroad linked the Central Pacific to the Union Pacific Railroads. Teams of men from each railroad raced the other to see who could lay the most track. Chinese workers for the Central Pacific began laying track in California and continued east over the Sierra Nevada Mountains and across the Great Basin. The climate in these regions made the work even more difficult. Avalanches and blizzards fell as the men dug tunnels and cut passes through the mountains. They suffered in dust storms in the summer. Often the workers did not have enough food or a place to sleep.

transcontinental (trăns´ kŏn-tə-nĕn´ tl) crossing a continent

Summary continues on next page

Reading Support Resources — Lesson Summary • Chapter 14, Lesson 1 197

Lesson Summaries in:

- English (See Reading and Review.)
- Spanish pp. 197–198, 201–202, 205–206, 209–210
- Chinese pp. 91–98
- Hmong pp. 91–98
- Khmer pp. 91–98
- Vietnamese pp. 91–98

Summaries available on audiotapes

Lesson Support / Transition

S D A I E

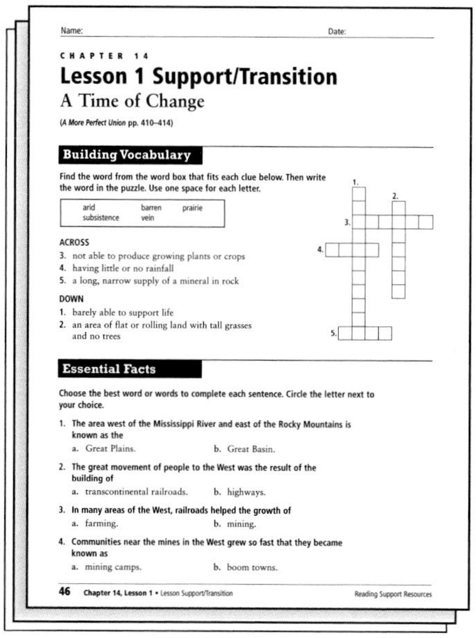
Name: Date:

CHAPTER 14

Lesson 1 Support/Transition

A Time of Change

(*A More Perfect Union* pp. 410–414)

Building Vocabulary

Find the word from the word box that fits each clue below. Then write the word in the puzzle. Use one space for each letter.

arid barren prairie subsistence vein

ACROSS
3. not able to produce growing plants or crops
4. having little or no rainfall
5. a long, narrow supply of a mineral in rock

DOWN
1. barely able to support life
2. an area of flat or rolling land with tall grasses and no trees

Essential Facts

Choose the best word or words to complete each sentence. Circle the letter next to your choice.

1. The area west of the Mississippi River and east of the Rocky Mountains is known as the
   a. Great Plains. b. Great Basin.
2. The great movement of people to the West was the result of the building of
   a. transcontinental railroads. b. highways.
3. In many areas of the West, railroads helped the growth of
   a. farming. b. mining.
4. Communities near the mines in the West grew so fast that they became known as
   a. mining camps. b. boom towns.

46 Chapter 14, Lesson 1 • Lesson Support/Transition — Reading Support Resources

Activities for SDAIE

Specially **D**esigned **A**cademic **I**nstruction in **E**nglish

- **Lesson Support/Transition** pp. 46, 47, 48, 49

Technology Options

Internet Support

http://www.eduplace.com

Social Studies Center at Education Place

Internet support for Chapter 14:

- ***Lesson at a Glance***
- ***Plains Indian Culture***

Videotape/Videodisc

We the People:

Supports and enhances major topics: **Themes: *Transportation; Native Americans; Cowboys***

Software

Student Writing Center® (CD-ROM) (Macintosh® or Windows®)

School to Career

Long after the transcontinental railroad opened up the West, cross-country rail travel continues. Have students create a chart comparing the railroad industry of yesterday and today. How have the responsibilities of workers changed? How have they remained the same?

Character Education

Despite signing treaties with the Indians promising to respect their rights to certain land, the government of the United States broke those promises and drove the Indians out. Have students write a brief essay on the importance of keeping one's word and taking responsibility for a promise.

CHAPTER
PREVIEW

Students should read the chapter title and the narrative underneath it. Draw attention to the visuals on the page, emphasizing the fact that the Great Plains was the homeland for many American Indian nations. Ask students to explain why the chapter is called Reshaping the Great Plains. *(The Great Plains were already "shaped" by the American Indians. The Plains were "reshaped" by American settlers.)* Ask students to predict what kinds of changes will occur on the Plains.

Looking Back

Ask students to recall Chapter 7 and the United States's forced removal of the American Indians from the southeastern United States (for example, the Cherokee people).

Looking Forward

Tell students that in the next four lessons they will be studying the changes that took place in the American West: A Time of Change, Culture of the Plains Indians, Indian Lands Lost, and Resettlement of the Land.

Chapter 14

Reshaping the Great Plains

Between 1848 and 1900, change swept across the Great Plains, completely transforming the region. The railroad, barbed wire, ranching, and farming radically altered the landscape. But the people and animals who lived on these plains for thousands of years experienced the most shattering changes of all.

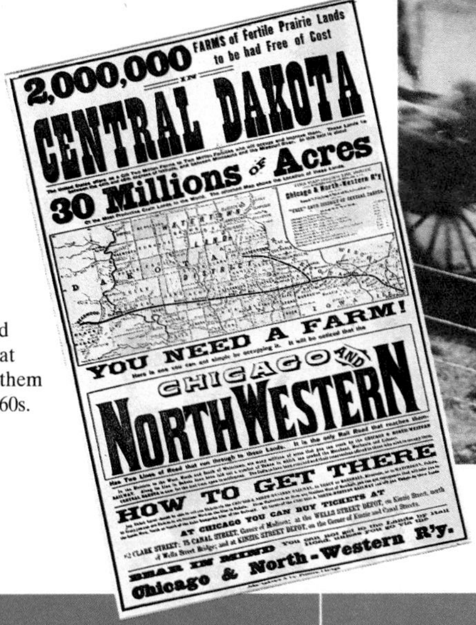

Railroads attracted settlers to the Great Plains by offering them free land in the 1860s.

1850 | 1860 | 1870

Presidents
1850-1853 Fillmore
1853-1857 Pierce
1857-1861 Buchanan
1861-1865 Lincoln
1865-1869 A. Johnson
1869-1877 Grant

408

1850

BACKGROUND

The Great Plains experienced dramatic demographic, economic, and cultural changes in the 1800s. The migration of white people (1860–1890) had a profound effect on the Plains Indians. The open plains became fenced ranches and farms connected to the rest of the country by transcontinental railroad lines.

Chinese Immigrants

Chinese immigrants played an important role in mining in the West, as well as in railroad construction. News of the California gold rush attracted Chinese immigrants to America in large numbers. By the time most of them arrived, however, the rich gold mines had been exhausted. Some immigrants traveled inland to new mining areas, where their willingness to serve as strikebreakers and to work long hours for low wages angered many Americans. Chinatown was burned and 28 Chinese miners were killed during a riot at Rock Springs, Wyoming.

With the decline in railroad construction and mining, most Chinese laborers returned to California, where manufacturers and farmers eagerly employed them. Some traveled to the East where they worked in factories—often, in fact, functioning as strikebreakers.

Anti-Chinese sentiment increased during the depression of the 1870s. Unemployed whites blamed their joblessness on the willingness of the Chinese to work for less money. A San Francisco teamster, Dennis Kearney, used the slogan, "The Chinese must

Under the Homestead Act, freed blacks like this family were able to move to the West and begin new lives.

1889 People rush to claim land when the U.S. government opens former American Indian territory to white settlement.

1890 Plains Indians settle on lands set aside for them by treaties with the U.S. government.

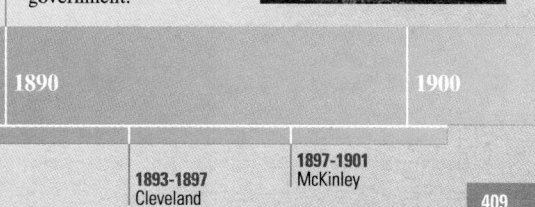

1880 1890 1900

1877-1881 Hayes
1881 Garfield
1881-1885 Arthur
1885-1889 Cleveland
1889-1893 B. Harrison
1893-1897 Cleveland
1897-1901 McKinley

1900

409

Understanding the Visuals

Point out the phrase "You Need a Farm" on the Central Dakota poster. This poster is from the Chicago and Northwestern Railroad, 1870. The posters were especially appealing to immigrants.

The center photograph was taken on April 22, 1889. It shows the land rush in Oklahoma at the moment of its official opening. Those who sneaked in ahead of time to stake claims were known as "Sooners."

The photograph at the top was taken by Solomon Butcher in the 1880s. The other photograph is of Red Cloud, leader of the Oglala (a band of Sioux Indians), and paleontologist Othniel Marsh at Yale University. Marsh befriended the Oglala and fought U.S. government corruption in Indian relations.

Understanding Chronology

Draw students' attention to the chapter timeline. What other major events occurred in the United States during this time period? *(The Civil War and Reconstruction)*

go," to organize The Workingman's Party in California. In 1882 Congress passed the Chinese Exclusion Act, which suspended Chinese immigration for a period of 10 years and forbade the naturalization of Chinese citizens already in this country.

Little Big Horn

George Armstrong Custer, a Civil War hero, became a temporary Brigadier General of the Union Army at age 24. Like other soldiers released from the Civil War, Custer transferred his fighting talents to clashes with American Indians.

When railroad surveying and the discovery of gold brought whites to the Dakotas, the Sioux resisted the encroachments. In the spring of 1876, Chief Sitting Bull warned the Indians to change their fighting tactics. Only by fighting to kill, he insisted, could they avoid losing all their land to the whites.

In June 1876, General Sheridan, commander of the United States Army in the West, planned an attack at Little Big Horn River, the chief encampment of the Sioux and their Cheyenne allies. Custer, then a colonel in the Seventh Cavalry, reached the encampment first and disobeyed orders. Instead of waiting for reinforcements, he led his men into an enemy camp of more than 2,000 well-armed Indians. Led by chiefs Crazy Horse and Sitting Bull, the Indian warriors quickly killed Custer and all his men.

INTRODUCE

Have one student read the lesson title and Thinking Focus aloud. Remind students that people began to travel to California and Oregon for gold and land prior to the Civil War. Ask them to recall from Chapter 8 what preconceptions these settlers had of the Great Plains. *(A place to get across, rough area)* What could cause people to change their view of the Great Plains? Ask students to predict the causes and then have them read to confirm or reject their predictions.

Key Terms

Vocabulary strategies: T36–37
transcontinental—crossing a continent
bonanza—rich, valuable (ore-bearing) rock
boom town—a town that comes into existence suddenly

1850
1900

LESSON 1

A Time of Change

THINKING FOCUS

How did people's view of the Great Plains change after 1860?

Key Terms

- transcontinental
- bonanza
- boom town

Two miles beyond South Pass City we saw for the first time that mysterious marvel which all Western untraveled boys have heard of and fully believe in, but are sure to be astounded at when they see it with their own eyes, nevertheless—banks of snow in dead summertime. We were now far up toward the sky, and knew all the time that we must presently encounter lofty summits clad in the "eternal snow"...yet when I did see it glittering in the sun on stately domes in the distance and knew the month was August and that my coat was hanging up because it was too warm to wear it, I was full as much amazed as if I never had heard of snow in August before. . . .

We were perched upon the extreme summit of the great range of the Rocky Mountains, toward which we had been climbing, for days and nights together—and about us was gathered a convention of Nature's kings that stood ten, twelve, and even thirteen thousand feet high. . . . It seemed that we could look around and abroad and contemplate the whole great globe, with its dissolving views of mountains, seas, and continents stretching away through the mystery of the summer haze. . . .

Monstrous rags of cloud hung low and swept along right over the spectator's head, swinging their tatters so nearly in his face that his impulse was to shrink when they came closest. In the one place I speak of, one could look below him upon a world of diminishing crags and canyons leading down, down, and away to a vague plain with a thread in it which was a road, and bunches of feathers in it which were trees.

Mark Twain, *Roughing It*

Travelers today, just as in Mark Twain's time, marvel to see snow capping the Rocky Mountains in summer. This condition shows the effect of altitude—height above sea level—on temperature. The higher a person climbs, the lower the temperature becomes.

Objectives

1. Identify ways in which geography posed obstacles to the settlement of the West.
2. Describe the hardships faced in the building of the transcontinental railroad.
3. Explain why mining techniques different from surface mining were necessary in California and Nevada.
4. Describe a boom town.

Graphic Overview

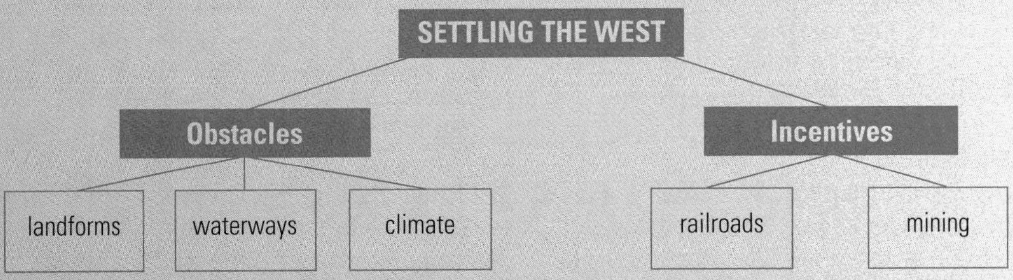

SETTLING THE WEST
Obstacles
Incentives
landforms
waterways
climate
railroads
mining

Variety of the West

Mark Twain wrote the preceding description of the Rocky Mountains while traveling west by stagecoach in 1861. On his journey Twain passed through several regions.

Varied Landforms

West of the Mississippi River stretch gently rolling grasslands called prairie. In this region of endless horizons, painter John Noble wrote, "You look on, on, on, out into space, out almost beyond time itself. You see nothing but the rise and swell of land and grass—the monotonous endless prairie!" Often compared to the sea, the grassland rises so gradually from east to west that it seems flat. From North Dakota to the foothills of the Rockies, this region is known as the Great Plains.

West of the Rockies lies a broad intermountain zone, a mixture of desert, basins, canyons, and plateaus. This region is mostly arid, or very dry. Mountains between this area and the Pacific coast cut off the moist air from the ocean. Here, strikingly beautiful natural formations such as the Grand Canyon alternate with barren desert.

Beyond the intermountain zone and running parallel to the Rockies are the Cascade Mountains and the Sierra Nevada, their steep slopes covered with forests and dotted with mountain lakes. Fertile valleys lie between these ranges and the mountains along the north Pacific Coast.

Climates of the West

The Great Plains are a region of climatic extremes—sweltering heat, frigid cold, severe drought when water supplies are exhausted, raging blizzards, and spectacular thunderstorms. Early white settlers looked on the treeless, windswept prairie as a hostile environment and called it the "Great American Desert." Land that did not support trees, people reasoned, must

Geographical Regions of the West

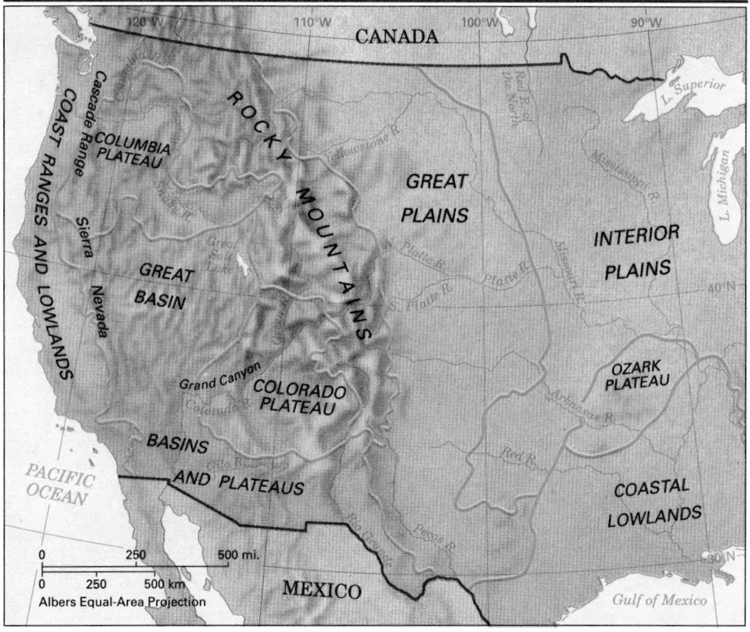

This map shows the major landforms west of the Mississippi River. What are the major rivers? What mountains divide the Great Plains from the Great Basin?

DEVELOP

Students can look through the pictures in the lesson to find examples of things that made settlement in the West difficult. *(Mountains, canyons, bad weather)* Have them look again to find something that made settlement and travel easier. *(Trains)* As they read the lesson, they can keep a list of both the obstacles and incentives to settling the West.

Major rivers: Missouri, Arkansas, Red, Pecos, Rio Grande, Columbia, and Colorado; Rocky Mountains

GEOGRAPHY

Map and Globe Skills

Using the precipitation and climatological maps on pages 706–707 of the Atlas, students can explain how the Cascade and Sierra Nevada ranges affect the climate to their east. *(The mountains cut the area off from the moist Pacific air, creating an arid climate.)*

Access Strategy

Explain that this lesson focuses on the geography of the West and how it affected the development of the region. Direct students to the map on this page and ask them to describe the kinds of landforms and climate they would meet if they traveled from the mouth of the Mississippi to the Pacific Coast. *(Plains, mountains, dry climate, moist climate)* Have students point out the areas that have these landforms and climatic conditions. If your students live in the West, have them describe their own area and compare it with what they know about other parts of the West. Otherwise, ask students to recall what they remember about the geography of the West from Chapter 8. Have them explain how mountains might get in people's way and yet how they might attract people. *(Made travel difficult; natural resources, such as mineral deposits, timber, and furs)*

Access Activity

Have students compare the map on this page with the modern political map of the United States on pages 700-701 in the Atlas. What states are in the Great Plains? *(Iowa, Minn., N.D., S. D., Neb., Kan., Okla., Texas, N.M., Colo., Wy., Mon.)* What states have borders defined by landforms? *(Iowa, Minn., Neb., Kan., Tex., Mon.)*

GEOGRAPHY

Critical Thinking

Many settlers thought the Great Plains was the "Great American Desert." Have students suggest reasons why the Great Plains got this other name. *(Seems very flat, no trees, extreme climatic conditions)* Point out that the Great Plains region has become known as America's "breadbasket." What does that phrase mean? *(Area where much grain is produced and then milled into flour to make bread)*

■ *The West includes prairies, deserts, mountains, and canyons. It also has climatic extremes, including frigid cold, severe heat, drought, blizzards, and thunderstorms.*

➤*Southern Pacific and Great Northern*

GEOGRAPHY

Map and Globe Skills

Have students use the maps on this page and on page 411 to explain why the rivers could not provide transcontinental transportation. *(None flow east–west or west–east over long enough distances to be "transcontinental.")*

be unfit for agriculture. In 1820, explorer Stephen H. Long wrote: "I do not hesitate in giving the opinion that [the prairie] is almost wholly unfit for cultivation, and of course uninhabitable by a people depending upon agriculture for their subsistence."

Impact of the Rivers

When Europeans first reached North America, most Indians of the Great Plains lived along the river systems—the Missouri, Platte, Arkansas, and Red rivers. These rivers all flow from the Rockies toward the Mississippi. They furnished water and transportation routes used by Indians, early explorers, and settlers.

Much of the West, however, lacked waterways that could be used for transportation. Although the Colorado River and Rio Grande provided water in a dry region, roaring rapids made them largely unusable and dangerous for travel. In the Great Basin—an area of 210,000 square miles—the rivers flow inland toward sinks or low places such as the Great Salt Lake instead of toward the sea. Often the water of these rivers is unfit to drink.

Because of the lack of water transportation, early pioneers traveled on horseback or by wagon train or stagecoach (Chapter 8). The building of railroads brought major changes to this region. ■

■ *Explain why the West is said to have a variety of environments.*

Railroads Arrive

In May 1869, with an echoing ring, railroad officials hammered a golden spike into the railroad ties at Promontory (*PROM uhn tawr ee*) Point, near Ogden, Utah. The ceremony marked the linking of the Central Pacific and Union Pacific railroads. It also marked the completion of the first **transcontinental** rail link in the world—the first railroad to cross an entire continent (see map).

In 1863, workers for the Central Pacific Railroad had begun laying tracks east from Sacramento, California. Two years later Union Pacific workers started to move west from

Railroad Network, 1893

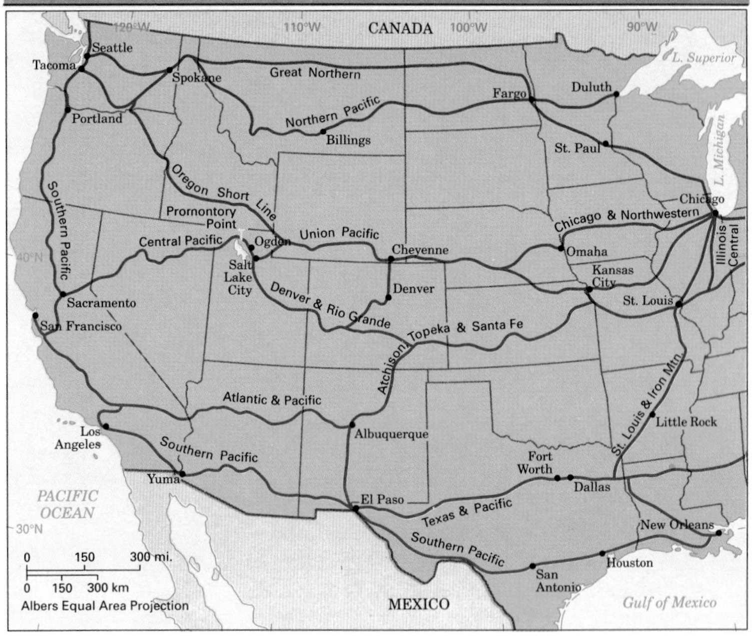

➤ *The map shows the major railroad lines in 1893. Locate the first transcontinental line. What other lines connect it with other parts of the West?*

Map and Globe Skills

Using the map on this page, have students find a railway route from St. Louis to San Francisco. Tell them to identify each of the lines that they would have to use on their route between these two cities. *(Sample answer: St. Louis and Iron Mtn., Texas and Pacific, and Southern Pacific)* Have students compare the routes they chose.

Historical Context

Because the far western edge of the continent was the first part of the American West to be extensively settled, it became increasingly important to form good transportation and communication links between the West and East coasts. Before the transcontinental railroad was completed in 1869, express companies such as Wells Fargo & Co. developed transcontinental freight lines via stagecoaches. By 1861, when Mark Twain made the journey described in *Roughing It*, travelers on the overland stage could make the entire trip from Missouri to California in three weeks. Even more remarkable was the Pony Express. Horseback riders carrying lightweight mail pouches raced across the continent in relays, covering 1,800 miles in 8 to 10 days. The Pony Express began in April 1860 and ended when the transcontinental telegraph system was completed in October 1861.

Omaha, Nebraska. By 1868, the two crews were racing to see who would lay the most track.

The Central Pacific hired thousands of young Chinese men. They faced the task of building the stretch over the Sierra Nevada and across the Great Basin. Braving avalanches and blizzards and often lacking food and shelter, the Chinese laid 689 miles of track. In the swirling red dust of summer it took 10 days for a crew of 300 to cut a pass through the mountain and lay a single mile of track. Lowered in a basket, a worker chipped holes in the sheer face of a cliff, inserted dynamite, and was pulled up before the explosion went off.

The workers also dug tunnels through the mountains. Working through one of the coldest winters in western history, the Chinese struggled to tunnel as much as a foot a day. Nevertheless, they managed to complete their part of the railroad on time.

Working westward on the Union Pacific Railroad were hundreds of European immigrants, many of them Irish. Their part of the mammoth project involved laying tracks across the Great Plains and over the Rockies. In addition to extremes in temperature, they faced attacks by American Indians. Nevertheless, these workers laid an incredible 1,086 miles of track westward from Omaha, Nebraska.

By 1900, four other railroad lines linked the Atlantic and Pacific coasts. ■

▲ *The train trestle at Georgetown, Colorado, built in 1881–1882, rises 85 feet above the canyon floor. It gives a vivid idea of some of the obstacles overcome by the railroad workers.*

■ *Describe some of the problems faced by the men who built the transcontinental railroad.*

Mining Develops

The railroads opened the West to settlement on a massive scale. They also made it possible to move western minerals to cities where the ore was used in industry. In California and Nevada, mining developed before the railroads were built. In other areas, railroads promoted the development of mines. The combination of natural resources and railways to move them changed the face of the West.

The Silver Boom

Following the gold rush in California (described in Chapter 8), prospectors roamed the West looking for gold. In Nevada in 1859, they found an immensely rich vein of silver that became known as the Comstock Lode. (A lode is a vein of valuable ore within common rock such as granite.)

Most of the Comstock silver was deeply embedded in hard quartz rock. Heavy equipment was needed to cut shafts through rock, carry minerals to the surface, and crush the ore-bearing stone. Such machinery was too expensive for individual prospectors, so large companies took over mining. They brought in heavy equipment and hired experienced hard rock miners—Cornish and Welsh from Britain and Germans from the German States.

The miners had to cut through layers of *borrasca* (Spanish for "barren rock") to reach the **bonanza**, or rich rock. The Big Bonanza, encountered at a depth of more than 1,000 feet, yielded $26 million in 1876. The Comstock Lode paid over $292

▲ *This silver bar from the Comstock Lode is marked 999.5, indicating that it is nearly pure silver.*

HISTORY

Critical Thinking

Why were immigrants hired to work on the railroad? *(Willing to work long hard hours for low wages; had mobility because few ties to one town)* Have students compare the hardships of the mainly Chinese crews who built the Central Pacific Railroad with those of the mainly Irish crews who built the Union Pacific Railroad. *(Chinese had to deal with Sierra Nevada and the Great Basin.)*

■ *They had to contend with avalanches, attacks by Indians, lack of food and shelter, and extremes in temperature.*

ECONOMICS

Critical Thinking

Compare the hardrock method of mining at Comstock Lode with the surface mining techniques discussed in Chapter 8. *(Surface mining required intensive labor but little equipment. The hardrock mining required heavy machinery.)* Ask students to name the skills a miner would need for each type of mining. *(Surface miners needed little training. Hardrock miners had to be trained to use equipment.)*

Science Connection

The wildlife of the American West was as astonishing to travelers as its landforms. Enormous herds of buffalo, vast prairie dog "towns," herds of antelope and elk, mountain goats, eagles, bears, and mountain lions populated the region. Have students research the wildlife of the Great Plains and the western mountains. Ask them to find out how these native animals were affected by settlement.

Making a Mural

What were the trains of the late 1880s like? Have a group of students do research on trains and then draw a mural showing various models of engines and the kinds of cars they pulled. Other students might want to find out which western towns grew up because of the railroads. Have them add important railroad towns to an enlarged copy of the map of railroad lines on page 412.

Critical Thinking

How did railroads make mining easier? *(Railroads could bring equipment and supplies to the mines and carry mining products to markets.)* How did mining contribute to the development of railroads? *(Mining gave railroads an economic incentive to build more lines.)*

HISTORY

Visual Learning

Have students use the photograph on this page to describe a boom town. How could you get to this town? *(By train, wagon)* How were these transportation routes both good and bad for the town? *(People and equipment could come to the town, but they could also leave quickly.)* What does the picture reveal about the changes in the land around a boom town? *(Cutting of trees)*

➤ *Building houses, firewood*

■ *The machinery was too expensive for individual prospectors.*

CLOSE

Students should summarize the lesson by answering the Thinking Focus. Put the heads and skeleton of the Graphic Overview from page 410 on the board, and have them use their list of obstacles and incentives to fill in the chart. Have them review their predictions from the beginning of this lesson to see how accurate they were.

▲ *This photograph shows Anaconda, Montana, famous for its rich copper ore. The bare hills were once covered with trees. What uses would miners have for lumber?*

million between 1859 and 1882, making it one of the richest in the West.

Boom Town to Ghost Town

Miners rushed to the Comstock Lode. Their shelters, writes J. Ross Browne, included the following:

> *Frame shanties, pitched together as if by accident; tents of canvas, of blankets, of brush, of potato-sacks and old shirts; ... smokey hovels of mud and stone; coyote holes in the mountain side forcibly seized and held by men; pits and shafts with smoke issuing from every crevice.*

Communities such as Cripple Creek, Goldfield, Poverty Gulch, Tombstone, and Last Chance Gulch appeared so rapidly they were known as **boom towns**. Some boom towns grew into cities. Last Chance Gulch, for example, became Montana's capital city of Helena.

■ *Why was mining after 1850 often undertaken by large companies rather than by individual prospectors?*

The most remarkable boom town, Virginia City, Nevada, sprang to life next to the Comstock Lode in 1859. By 1876, over 20,000 people, mostly single men who worked in the mines, lived in Virginia City and neighboring Gold Hill.

Mining equipment, together with most of the food, clothing, building materials, and even drinking water, had to be hauled from San Francisco to Virginia City. Yet the minerals extracted were so valuable that the city prospered.

Large mansions, decorated with the finest furniture, china, and paintings, lined the steep streets. People dined on expensive food; theaters drew leading performers from Europe and the East.

After 1882, however, the Virginia City bonanza gave out. Government demand for silver decreased, and silver prices fell. It was no longer profitable to mine ore that was not of the highest grade. By 1898, the miners had deserted Virginia City. The once-lively city was a virtual ghost town, with most of its buildings abandoned. Dust covered the goods in the stores, and mice ran through the rooms of once-elegant homes.

The presence of the miners hinted at the white settlement that would take place in the Western lands. In 1860, however, those lands were mainly occupied by many different American Indian peoples. ■

REVIEW

1. **FOCUS** How did people's view of the Great Plains change after 1860?
2. **CONNECT** In what parts of the West did people from the United States settle before 1860? What attracted them to each place?
3. **GEOGRAPHY** Name and briefly describe the major geographical regions of the West. Include major mountain ranges and river systems.
4. **ECONOMICS** Why is an efficient transportation system, such as the network of railroad lines, important to both farmers and factory owners?
5. **CRITICAL THINKING** What caused some boom towns to turn into ghost towns while others grew into cities? Consider geographical factors as well as economic reasons.
6. **WRITING ACTIVITY** Prepare to interview participants at the ceremony marking the completion of the first transcontinental railroad. Draw up a list of questions to ask. Be sure to include workers as well as officials.

Homework Options

Each student can research and report on a geological feature of the West, such as the Grand Canyon, the Great Salt Lake, the Black Hills, or Mount Rainier.

Study Guide: page 59.

Answers to Review Questions

1. Before 1860, many people viewed the Great Plains as a hostile desert area. People's views changed as the transcontinental railroad and the silver boom showed the area's potential for profit.
2. People went to California for gold and to Oregon for farmland. Mormons settled in Utah to escape religious persecution.
3. The major regions are the Great Plains, the Rockies, the intermountain zone, the Cascades and the Sierra Nevada, and the coastal mountains and plains.
4. A good transportation system allows farmers and factory owners to receive needed supplies and to have a larger market for their products.
5. Sample answer: As the demand for silver decreased, some boom towns became ghost towns because people could no longer pay for supplies. Allow for personal opinion.
6. Several students may role play the scene.

1850 1900

L E S S O N 2

Culture of the Plains Indians

"What is life?" asked the Blackfoot hunter Crowfoot as he lay dying in 1890. "It is the flash of a firefly in the night. It is the breath of a buffalo in the winter time." Crowfoot's reference suggests that the buffalo played an important part in the life of the Plains Indians.

White settlers moving westward across the Great Plains in the 1840s told of immense herds of buffalo that stretched as far as they could see. For the Indians who lived on the Plains, the buffalo were much more than an awe-inspiring spectacle. The great shaggy beasts provided them with food, clothing, weapons, tools, and shelter. Season after season the Indians followed the herds from one grazing ground to another.

Each part of the buffalo had its use. Hair and hide, hoofs, horns, bones—nothing was wasted. Buffalo meat that was not eaten right away was dried for later use. Bones were carved into weapons, tools, and ornaments; horns were used to make cups, ladles, and spoons. From the hides came clothing, bedding, moccasins, shields, and covers for tepees (also spelled *tipis*). "The tipi," said Chief Flying Hawk of the Oglala Lakota (Sioux), "is much better to live in [than a house]; always clean, warm in winter, cool in summer; easy to move."

THINKING FOCUS

What are four characteristics of the Plains Indians' lives?

Hunters of the Buffalo

The Indians' dependence on the buffalo, however, did not become typical of the Great Plains until after Europeans arrived in North America. When the Indians began to obtain guns and horses from the white people, their way of life changed radically.

Settled Farmers

Before the Europeans arrived, many of the Plains Indians farmed the fertile land along the rivers, growing corn, beans, and squash. They varied their diet with game they hunted on foot. These Plains people included the Mandan whom Lewis and Clark had met on their expedition. They lived settled lives for much of the year. Their houses were rounded lodges built of earth and sturdy poles and were not meant to be moved. From

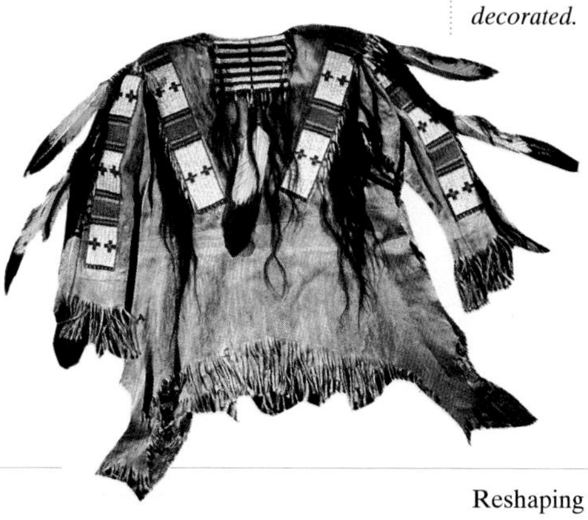

Plains Indian clothing, such as this shirt owned by Kicking Bear, was often beautifully decorated.

INTRODUCE

Point out the lesson title and ask what aspects of culture the students can expect to learn about in this lesson. *(Customs, religion, skills, art)* Have students read the Thinking Focus. As they read the lesson, they can look for information about how the Plains Indians lived.

Graphic Overview

	Before Eurpoeans	After Europeans
Homes	lodges	tepees
Economy	farming	hunting
Travel	foot, dog sledge	horse
Weapons	bow and arrows	guns

Objectives

1. Describe how the Plains Indians lived before the Europeans arrived.
2. Explain how the horse and the gun influenced the Plains Indians' lives.
3. Explain how a Plains Indian gained status in his tribe.
4. Identify the place of the Sun Dance in Plains Indians' beliefs.

DEVELOP

Tell the students that as they read the lesson, they should look for ways that the coming of white settlers changed lives of the Plains Indians. Copy on the board the structure and headings of the Graphic Overview from page 415. Tell the students that they can structure their reading of the lesson by filling in the Graphic Overview as they read.

Note: You may wish to use A Closer Look to stimulate interest in further research into the customs and lifestyle of the Plains Indians.

CULTURE

Visual Learning

Ask students to identify each of the artifacts in A Closer Look. Then ask if they can figure out which items would be used for special occasions and which would be used for practical everyday occasions. *(It's sometimes hard to tell because the Plains Indians decorated nearly everything they used.)*

their villages, small hunting parties went out on the Plains to hunt the buffalo as the herds migrated to new pasture.

The sedentary Indians traded their surplus food for skins and meat from hunting tribes such as the Comanche and Kiowa, who stalked game on foot. They usually traveled no more than a very short distance each day because the dogs they used could only pull a limited weight.

A Nomadic Way of Life

Toward the end of the 1600s, this sedentary way of life changed dramatically with the introduction of two critical items—the gun and the horse. European fur traders from what is now Canada gave guns to the Chippewa in exchange for furs. Once the Chippewa used these guns against the Sioux, the Indians quickly realized what an advantage guns provided.

About the same time, Indians in

A CLOSER LOOK

Plains Indian Culture

As they moved in search of buffalo, the Plains Indians carried along their art. They expressed their love of beauty by decorating nearly everything they used, from weapons to cookware.

Ceremonial headdresses such as this were worn by the most distinguished men of the tribe on special occasions. They included special feathers indicating brave deeds.

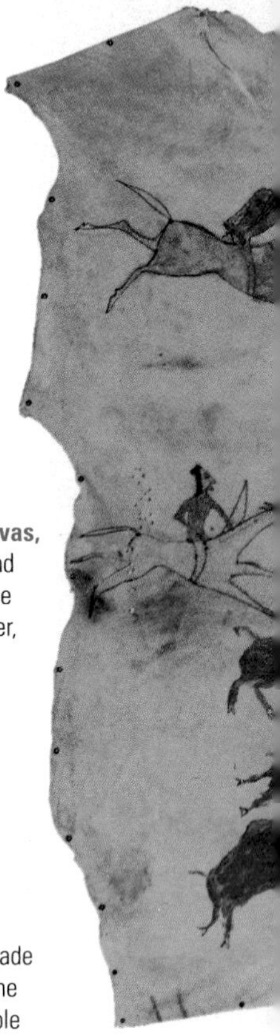

This hide is an artist's canvas, depicting warriors, tepees, and the all-important buffalo—the Indians' source of food, shelter, and clothing.

A horse's mask? This Cheyenne horse mask is made from thousands of porcupine quills colored with vegetable dyes, and sewn onto buckskin. Warriors decorated their horses for special occasions.

Access Activity

Have students suggest occasions when they might want to decorate a room. *(For a party or holiday, to surprise someone, to impress someone)* Then ask them to suggest other things that people decorate. *(Clothing, walls of a house, dishes)* Students can then refer to A Closer Look to find examples of the kinds of things that the Plains Indians decorated.

Access Strategy

Ask students to recall what they have heard or seen about the American Indians of the West. What kinds of houses do they associate with American Indians? What were their weapons like and how did they travel? After students have shared their ideas, remind them that there were many different groups of American Indians in the West and that some of our ideas about them may be unfair or inaccurate stereotypes formed by our familiarity with just one group of Indians.

Explain that at first the Plains Indians had neither horses nor guns. Have the students suggest ways that the Indians could get food without horses or guns. *(Hunting on foot, farming, trading)* Then have them consider how the arrival of guns and horses might have changed their lifestyle. *(Could hunt large animals, travel farther, have more to trade)*

New Mexico revolted against Spanish settlers. Horses that the fleeing Spaniards left behind in 1680 were quickly adopted by Indians such as the Apache and Comanche. Soon horses became the symbol of wealth.

Guns from the north and horses from the south spread rapidly across the Great Plains, altering the lives of Indian peoples. Tribes on the Plains and in nearby regions competed to obtain them, for they made travel faster and hunting easier. Many Plains Indians became nomads who followed the vast herds of buffalo. The Closer Look below shows some articles the Plains Indians created as part of their nomadic lifestyle.

The Kiowa and Blackfoot, who already lived on the Plains, were joined by other tribes (see map, page 419). The Cheyenne and the Arapaho moved south and west from what is now Minnesota. The Comanche, a

Hide moccasins such as these were decorated with beads. A woman might bead a leather shirt like this for her husband.

Even containers were decorated. Folded pieces of rawhide such as this were used to carry a variety of objects. Women decorated them with abstract geometrical designs.

CULTURE

Critical Thinking

Suggest ways that the lives of the Plains Indians would change once the buffalo were gone. *(Sample answer: Need to find other sources of food and housing and clothing material)*

More About the Moccasins Most Great Plains Indians wore moccasins made of a hard leather sole sewn to an upper piece of soft, beaded buckskin. To show their importance, wealthy tribe members wore moccasins with beaded soles on formal occasions. Frontiersmen claimed that you could determine which tribe had walked in an area by looking at the moccasin tracks. Features, such as toe form and heel fringes, varied from tribe to tribe, which made identification possible.

Religious Context

Spiritual beliefs and practices played an important role in the lives of the Plains Indians. They believed in the life of the spirit after the death of the body and in many ghosts, gods, and other entities. Many Plains Indians carried tokens, amulets, or talismans to protect themselves from harm.

Rituals and ceremonies were part of their life. There were prayers before hunting, fishing, planting, and harvesting. Rituals were held to mark such major events as pregnancy, childbirth, adolescence, and death.

Each community had its medicine men, or shamans, who interceded with supernatural spirits. They knew the tribe's oral literature, which was expressed in stories, songs, chants, prayers, and sometimes, in puns, proverbs, and riddles.

Visual Learning

Ask students to find buffalo symbols on the artifacts in A Closer Look. Then have students suggest reasons why the Plains Indians decorated many objects with images of the buffalo. *(The buffalo were very important to their livelihood.)* Students could then consider what symbols they would use if they wanted to decorate an item of clothing.

CULTURE

Visual Learning

Have students look at the examples of sign language on this page. Why do they think the different Indian peoples would need to use sign language? *(So that they could communicate without knowing each other's language)*

■ *Their sedentary way of life was changed into a nomadic one because horses and guns made travel and hunting easier.*

BELIEF SYSTEMS

Critical Thinking

Ask students to compare how men gained status in a Plains Indian tribe to how a student today achieves status in a school setting. *(Sample answer: Physical deeds versus mental work)*

▲ *The signs this Indian is making read (from left to right):* trade, friend, buffalo, and tepee.

■ *How did the horse and gun transform the life of the Plains Indians?*

branch of the Shoshone, traveled southeast from the Rockies to the plains of Texas, where horses were plentiful. From the Minnesota-Wisconsin area came the various Dakota tribes. The Crow—hostile to the Sioux, Cheyenne, and Arapaho alike— moved west from the Missouri.

The nomadic way of life followed by the Plains Indians lasted only a short time. However, it provided what became the familiar image of Indian life—the mounted warrior wearing a feathered headdress. ■

Tribal Status

To obtain the horses on which their way of life depended, Plains Indians raided one another's herds. They also raided isolated settlements of pioneers and sometimes attacked wagon trains moving westward. Success in raids and warfare increasingly defined a man's status, or standing in the tribe.

Steps in Achieving Status

Although customs varied from tribe to tribe, the Plains Indians looked on certain actions as determining tribal status. A boy attained status by accompanying the men on a hunt. One improved his rank by stealing horses, fighting as a warrior, and leading a hunt or war party. This type of behavior became more common after the introduction of guns and horses. After a young man proved his ability to endure hardship in a demanding ceremony, he was eligible to become a tribal leader or chief. A man's rank reflected his bravery in warfare and in counting coup [*koo*]. A coup is a daring deed accomplished against heavy odds. What counted as a coup varied from tribe to tribe, but it always involved a daring act.

The greater the danger, the greater the coup. A major coup was to steal a rival chief's special horses, which were usually carefully guarded. In some tribes, the greatest coup was to ride into an enemy camp, touch the chief, and return unharmed.

After counting coup, a man might paint his face and body and also his wife's as part of the celebration held when he returned to the tribe. One Crow woman boasted:

> *It was my face that he painted when he had gained that right by saving a Crow warrior's life in battle. And it was I who rode his warhorse and carried his shield. Ahh, I felt proud when my man painted my face.*

Governing by Advice

Most Indians of the Plains were governed by a council of elders. These leaders discussed problems facing the tribe and tried to reach agreement on what action to take. The title *chief*, which white people equated with head of government, simply referred to a man who was a daring fighter or an experienced leader. A tribe might thus have several chiefs. The person lead-

Map and Globe Skills

Have students study the map on the opposite page. What names do they recognize? Have them speculate on why some names are familiar and some are unfamiliar to us today. *(Sample answer: The names of the tribes that survived in larger numbers are familiar to us.)*

Language Arts Connection

Some words from the languages of the Plains Indians, such as *tepee*, are now commonly used in English. The influence of these languages is most pronounced, however, in the American place names. Have students look through maps and atlases to create a gazetteer of place names in the Great Plains region that come from Indian languages. Include names of states, towns, rivers, and other geographic features. Whenever possible, include the meanings of the words.

Making a Chart

In addition to using sign language (see the page above) to communicate with one another, Plains Indians used pictorial symbols to express ideas. Have students use library resources to find the meanings of some Indian symbols, such as the radiating sun. Have them make a chart of symbols and their meanings.

ing the tribe at any one time depended on what the tribe was doing. One chief might be the leader in time of war, another might be chief of the hunt.

Beliefs and Ceremonies

The Plains Indians shared certain beliefs. They believed that people were deeply connected to the land and the natural world. A tribe might claim land for hunting, farming, or living, but it was held and used in common, not owned as individual personal property. Indians considered certain natural locations to be sacred places where they could contact spirits or ancestors. In 1912, Curly, a Crow Indian chief, rejected a government offer to buy tribal lands with the following statement:

> *The soil you see is not ordinary soil—it is the dust of the blood, the flesh, and the bones of our ancestors. . . . You will have to dig down through the surface before you can find nature's earth, as the upper portion is Crow. The land as it is, is my blood and my dead; it is consecrated [holy]; and I do not want to give up any portion of it.*

The Plains Indians' lives were enriched with numerous ceremonies. One important ceremony for some nomadic tribes was the Sun Dance, performed as a solemn ritual to ensure spiritual growth and tribal renewal. For three or four days, participants went without food and water, dancing to the beat of drums and the shrill piping of eagle-bone whistles. A few achieved a trancelike state. If they had a vision, it was believed to give them mystical power that would bring them success during the buffalo hunt or on a raid.

Eventually the U.S. government prohibited the Sun Dance in an effort to make the Indians give up their traditional ways. After the Civil War, the native peoples lost their lands and became dependent on the government for food and shelter. ■

American Indian Lands in 1850

In 1850, American Indians were the only inhabitants of most of the land west of the Mississippi River. In what parts of the West had white American people settled by 1850?

■ *How did a man on the Plains acquire status in his tribe?*

R E V I E W

1. **FOCUS** What are four characteristics of the Plains Indians' lives?
2. **CONNECT** What contacts did most Plains Indians have with white people before 1850?
3. **ECONOMICS** What constituted wealth among the Plains Indians? How was it acquired?
4. **POLITICAL SYSTEM** Why did many white people misunderstand the function and status of Indian chiefs?
5. **CRITICAL THINKING** How might a Plains Indian tribe react if gold or silver were found near its favorite hunting grounds? Why?
6. **ACTIVITY** Plains Indians often decorated their tepee covers with scenes of their life or important deeds. Draw a tepee and illustrate it with scenes from this lesson. You may wish to include some of the designs shown in A Closer Look (pages 416–417).

CULTURE

Critical Thinking

Have students explain why the Sun Dance was an important ceremony to some Plains Indians. *(They believed that it would keep the tribe strong.)*

◄*California, Oregon, Utah, Texas*

■ *He could achieve status by stealing horses, going on a raid, leading a hunt, fighting, taking part in a demanding ceremony.*

C L O S E

Have students summarize the lesson by answering the Thinking Focus. Draw the structure of the Graphic Overview on the board and let the students fill it in.

If you used the Access Strategy to introduce the lesson, have students compare their earlier impressions with what they now know about the Plains Indians. How accurate were their beliefs about Plains Indians?

Answers to Review Questions

1. They depended on buffalo, had a nomadic way of life, got tribal status through heroic feats, and had a deep respect for the earth.
2. They had contact with explorers, such as Lewis and Clark, with mountain men and government expeditions, and with early pioneers and "forty-niners" who went through the Plains but did not settle there.
3. Horses, the symbol of wealth, were often acquired by raids on rival tribes or on white settlements.
4. White people thought the title "chief" was for the head of government, but most tribes had several leaders who were considered chiefs.
5. Sample answer: Because a tribe depended on hunting, it might feel threatened as prospectors moved into an area where there was a gold or silver strike. Allow for personal opinion.
6. Students' drawings may be displayed on a bulletin board.

Homework Options

Have students look for stereotypes of American Indians in cartoons, books, movies, and television shows. Ask them to provide examples and discuss why these stereotypes are often incorrect.

Study Guide: page 60.

INTRODUCE

Have students recall what they learned about the culture of the Plains Indians in Lesson 2. This particular American Indian legend focuses on one of the most important aspects of Plains Indian life: the buffalo. Remind students that legends can be used to preserve a people's culture.

READ AND RESPOND

Explain to students that American Indian legends and myths were not written down but were part of the oral tradition. While you read the story aloud, students should think about what this legend reveals about the beliefs and values of the Plains Indians. As students answer the purpose-setting question, make sure they give reasons for their answers.

Settlement of the Great Plains offered new, exciting opportunities to many people. In the process, though, an American Indian way of life was destroyed.

LITERATURE

The World of the Buffalo Comes to an End

An Indian Legend

The Plains Indian culture depended on the buffalo, and the extinction of this great animal brought an end to the Plains Indian way of life. In this legend, Old Lady Horse (Spear Woman), a Kiowa, describes the extinction of the buffalo. Her story is told in American Indian Mythology *by Alice Marriott and Carol K. Rachlin. As you read, ask yourself whether there is anything in your everday life that is as important to you as the buffalo was to the Indians.*

And now we come to the end of a world. The end of the buffalo was the end of Plains Indian life. And before the white man's superior technology, the buffalo succumbed. This is one story of why there are no more buffalo in the world.

Everything the Kiowas had came from the buffalo. Their tipis were made of buffalo hides, so were their clothes and moccasins. They ate buffalo meat. Their containers were made of hide, or of bladders or stomachs. The buffalo were the life of the Kiowas.

Most of all, the buffalo was part of the Kiowa religion. A white buffalo calf must be sacrificed in the Sun Dance. The priests used parts of the buffalo to make their prayers when they healed people or when they sang to the powers above.

420

Thematic Connections

Social Studies: American Indian legends

Houghton Mifflin Literary Readers: Oral Traditions

Background

It is estimated that in 1850 there were 75 million buffalo, or bison as they are properly known, on the plains of North America. By the end of the century only about 1,000 buffalo were left.

The building of the transcontinental railroads was the chief cause of the decline in the size of buffalo herds. Railroad builders began to kill the animals to provide food for the workers who laid the track. After trains began to travel along the rails, engineers would stop to allow passengers to get out and kill dozens of the animals at a time. In the early 1870s, professional hunters arrived, killing animals by the thousands for their pelts. These hunters would skin the animals on the spot, leaving the meat to rot. Later, farmers ground up the bones for fertilizer.

So, when the white men wanted to build railroads, or when they wanted to farm or raise cattle, the buffalo still protected the Kiowas. They tore up the railroad tracks and the gardens. They chased the cattle off the ranges. The buffalo loved their people as much as the Kiowas loved them.

There was war between the buffalo and the white men. The white men built forts in the Kiowa country, and . . . shot the buffalo as fast as they could, but the buffalo kept coming on, coming on, even into the post cemetery at Fort Sill. Soldiers were not enough to hold them back.

Then the white men hired hunters to do nothing but kill the buffalo. Up and down the plains those men ranged, shooting sometimes as many as a hundred buffalo a day. Behind them came the skinners with their wagons. They piled the hides and bones into the wagons until they were full, and then took their loads to the new railroad stations that were being built, to be shipped east to the market. Sometimes there would be a pile of bones as high as a man, stretching a mile along the railroad track.

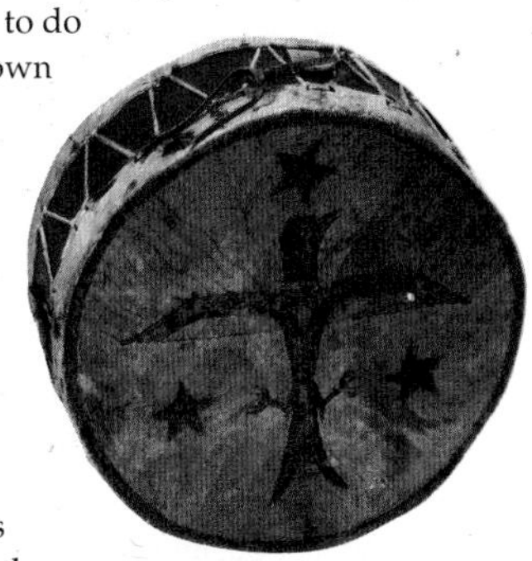

The buffalo saw that their day was over. They could protect their people no longer. Sadly, the last remnant of the great herd gathered in council, and decided what they would do.

The Kiowas were camped on the north side of Mount Scott, those of them who were still free to camp. One young woman got up very early in the morning. The dawn mist was still rising from Medicine Creek, and as she looked across the water, peering through the haze, she saw the last buffalo herd appear like a spirit dream.

Straight to Mount Scott the leader of the herd walked. Behind him came the cows and their calves, and the few young males who had survived. As the woman watched, the face of the mountain opened.

Inside Mount Scott the world was green and fresh, as it had been when she was a small girl. The rivers ran clear, not red. The wild plums were in blossom, chasing the red buds up the inside slopes. Into this world of beauty the buffalo walked never to be seen again.

Further Reading

The Mythology of North America. John Bierhorst. The author has prepared an invaluable guide to stories of the gods and heroes of Indian nations from the Arctic to the Southwest.

Anpao: An American Indian Odyssey. Jamake Highwater. The tale of the brave Anpao is taken from generations of Plains Indians' legends and includes revealing encounters with white men.

Indian Tales. Jaime de Angulo. This book is packed with Indian folklore, jokes, ceremonial rituals, games, and adventures.

◄ What role did the buffalo play in the Kiowa religion? *(A white buffalo calf was sacrificed in the Sun Dance. The priests used parts of the buffalo to make their prayers.)*

How did the buffalo protect the Kiowa from the whites? *(They tore up the railroad tracks and the gardens, and they chased the cattle off the ranges.)*

EXTEND

Divide students into groups to draw illustrations of various scenes in the legend. Combine the drawings to create a mural for the classroom.

Further Reading

You may want to ask students to go to the school or local library to find more books to read about the Plains Indians or the buffalo slaughter.

INTRODUCE

Students should consider what changes the Plains Indians would have to make if they wanted to live as the white settlers did. *(New language, food, religion)* Explain that giving up your old culture and adopting a new culture is called *assimilation*. Tell them that *assimilation* will be an important term in this lesson and in future chapters. Have students read the Thinking Focus. Suggest that students read the lesson to learn about some of the things that changed the Indians' way of life.

Key Terms

Vocabulary strategies: T36–37

annuity—a yearly provision to American Indians of food, clothing, and other necessary items (as part of an agreement with the U.S. Government)

reservation—land set aside for American Indians that was off-limits to white settlers

assimilate—to adopt the mainstream culture and give up one's own beliefs and culture

1850 — 1900

LESSON 3

Indian Lands Lost

THINKING FOCUS

What factors combined to end the Plains Indians' nomadic way of life?

Key Terms

- annuity
- reservation
- assimilate

It was July 4, 1876. All over the nation people were celebrating America's centennial, its hundredth birthday. In Philadelphia, where the Declaration of Independence had been adopted, thousands thronged to the grand opening of the Centennial Exposition. Throughout the nation flags flew, bands played patriotic marches, and fireworks delighted young and old alike.

The mood of jubilation, however, abruptly ended on the morning of July 6. At 3 A.M., telegraph messages from the West reached the Eastern newspapers. The content was brief but shocking. "Bismarck, Dakota Territory, July 5, 1876," they read. ". . . Custer attacked the Indians June 25, and he with every officer and man in five companies [was] killed."

Custer's defeat and the death of over 200 soldiers stunned people throughout the nation. They were aware that, for several years, clashes had taken place between the Indian peoples of the Plains and the U.S. army. However, they found it hard to believe troops representing a nation of 40 million had been destroyed.

In June 1876, the Sioux chiefs Sitting Bull and Crazy Horse led the Indians in the Battle of Little Big Horn, in which Colonel George A. Custer and his men were defeated. An unknown Indian artist painted this version of the battle.

Indians and White Settlers Clash

Before the gold rush of 1849, few clashes had occurred between the pioneers and the Plains Indians. In fact, several pioneers praised the Indians for the help that they had offered. In 1851, the northern Plains Indians—Assiniboine, Atsina, Arikara, Crow, Shoshone, Cheyenne, Arapaho, and Sioux—met U.S. government agents in a peace conference. They agreed to let pioneers pass through their lands unharmed. A similar agreement was made with southern tribes two years later.

Increasing Hostility

As more and more white settlers moved into the West, however, their oxen and horses ate the grass on which the buffalo depended. In addi-

Objectives

1. Explain why hostility between American Indians and white settlers increased after 1860.
2. Define *reservation* and *annuity* and explain their part in U.S. Government policy.
3. Explain how the Dawes Act and educational programs were used to promote assimilation and why assimilation of American Indians generally failed.

Graphic Overview

U.S. gives annuities in exchange for free passage across land. → • The number of white settlers increases. • White settlers kill buffalo. → Settlers, U.S. Army, and Indians clash. → • Indians are moved to reservations. • Dawes Act encourages assimilation.

tion, the settlers shot buffalo for food. Alarmed by the decreasing herds and attracted by the chance to gain horses, Indians attacked small groups of pioneers and isolated settlements.

Sometimes treaties between the U.S. government and the Indian peoples created problems. When U.S. officials made agreements with one or two chiefs in a tribe, they tended to think the agreement applied to the entire tribe. Some government officials failed to enforce the treaties that set aside areas for hunting. Revisions in the treaty with the Comanche, for example, gradually reduced their hunting grounds from 300 million acres to 3 million acres.

Dependent on Government Help

In exchange for Indian promises to allow pioneers to pass in peace, the U.S. government promised to supply the tribes with an **annuity**, a yearly provision of food, clothing, and other necessary items. The intention was to provide food only until the Indians learned to support themselves by farming or by a trade. The government agents who supplied the annuity, however, were often corrupt. They provided wormy flour, shoddy blankets, and defective guns—when they provided any supplies at all.

By the mid-1860s, white settlers from both East and West were closing on Indian lands. Once the transcontinental railroad was completed in 1869, the rush onto Indian lands became a stampede. At the same time hordes of hunters traveled west to shoot buffalo for hides or for sport. By 1880, only a few buffalo remained of the millions that had roamed the plains before 1850. Faced with starvation, Indians became dependent on annuities.

Sioux Uprising

The Santee Sioux in Minnesota, although not living on the Plains, were part of the annuity system. By 1862, they were on the verge of starvation because government agents had failed to deliver their annuity. Upset by white settlers who had moved onto their lands, the Sioux killed several hundred white settlers (the exact number is unknown). Thousands of settlers fled their homes and refused to return. Federal troops hanged 38 Sioux as punishment for the uprising, the biggest execution in U.S. history. Army troops finally drove many of the Sioux out of Minnesota.

Conflict on the Western Frontier, 1864–1890

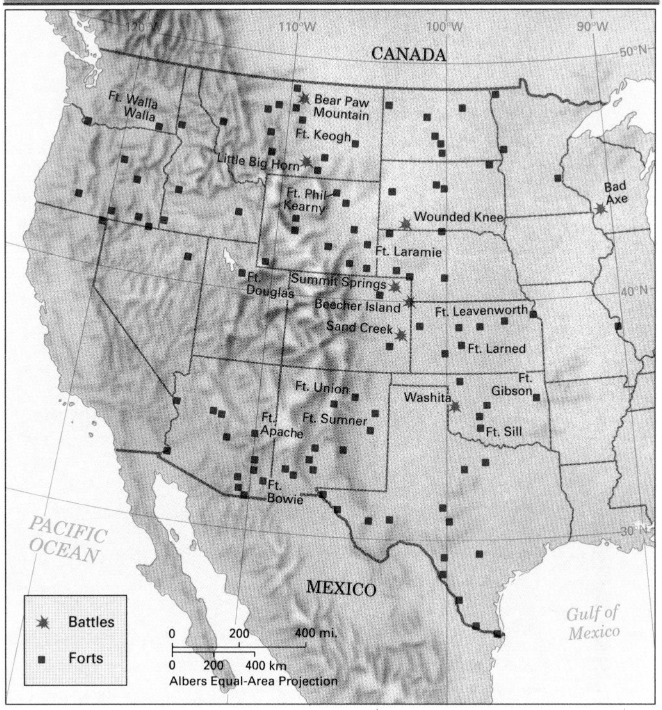

Battles between Indians and the U.S. army were often a series of skirmishes rather than formal warfare. Find three places on the map where battles were fought.

Sand Creek Massacre

The Sioux uprising was the beginning of the bloodiest period in the history of the West. The map above shows where some of the clashes took place. In 1864, the Cheyenne and their Arapaho allies left their lands at Sand Creek in Colorado because the tribe was starving. They began to raid ranches and attack travelers.

The Indians who opposed war

DEVELOP

Students should preview the lesson heads to find clues about what changed the way in which the Plains Indians lived. Explain that they are going to read about a sequence of events that ended the Plains Indians' nomadic way of life. Encourage them to keep a list of these events as they read.

Sample answers: Little Big Horn, Wounded Knee, and Sand Creek

HISTORY

Critical Thinking

What events in the 1860s, in addition to the building of the railroads, contributed to a large increase in the number of white settlers in the West? *(With the end of the Civil War, soldiers and former slaves were encouraged to homestead in the West.)*

Access Strategy

Have students recall from Lesson 1 the incentives to settlement in the West. *(Mineral riches, land)* What new development in transportation allowed more settlers to go west? *(Transcontinental railroad)* Ask students to recall from Lesson 2 details about the lives of the Plains Indians. *(Buffalo hunters, nomadic tribes)* Also have them recall the differences between the Indians' view of land and the white settlers' view (Chapter 7). *(Indians— land shared and viewed as sacred; white settlers—land viewed as private property)* How could this difference in attitude create difficulties? *(The two cultures would want to use the land differently.)* What were some of the other potential points of conflict between the Indians and the new settlers? *(Buffalo, fences, lifestyle, religious beliefs)* Have one student record class responses to these questions on the board. Tell students that they will read in the lesson about this conflict.

Access Activity

Read the lesson opener aloud and then ask students to look at the painting on page 422. Have them compare the Indian warriors with the Army soldiers. What is not in this painting? *(No background, everything shown from the side)* What aspect of the battle was important to this artist? *(How they fought)*

■ *The government wanted to make room for white settlers to claim land.*

HISTORY

Critical Thinking

Have students contrast Indian reservations with other kinds of land reservations such as those for protecting animals and other wildlife. *(Both consist of land set aside, but Indian reservations limit Indians' opportunities rather than preserving and protecting life, as wildlife preserves do.)* Why did Indians become dependent on annuities? *(They had lost their old ways of living.)*

BELIEF SYSTEMS

Critical Thinking

During the next few years, the idea that humans have the right to control nature to achieve whatever end they want may well change. What effects might such a change in thinking have on your daily life? *(Sample answers: Fewer, smaller, and more efficient automobiles; changes in diet; increased recycling of goods; closer, more interdependent communities)*

■ *Why did the U.S. government want to settle the Plains Indians on reservations?*

obeyed when they were ordered back to the reservation. In November, however, Colonel John Chivington led a surprise attack. His command was to "kill and scalp all." Between 200 and 450 Indian men, women, and children were massacred. (The total depends on who was reporting the incident.) ■

Policies That Changed Indian Life

Although the U.S. Commissioner of Indian Affairs denounced the Sand Creek massacre, the U.S. government continued its efforts to make the Plains Indians give up their nomadic lifestyle. As you learned in Chapter 7, resettlement of the Indian peoples dated back to the 1830s, when the southeastern tribes were moved to Indian Territory (in what is now the state of Oklahoma).

The Move to Reservations

After the Civil War, the government began to move the Plains tribes to **reservations**, land set aside for a particular tribe and off limits to white settlers. Many of these reservations were in Indian Territory. To make room for the new arrivals, tribes who were already there, such as the Cherokee and Creek, were forced to give up some of their lands.

UNDERSTANDING ECOLOGY

Between 1870 and 1900, American settlers took control of the lands of the West, and they were often irresponsible caretakers. They cut millions of acres of timberlands, choked streams with slag from mines, and crisscrossed great sweeps of plain with railroads. In short, humans permanently altered the relationship of living things to each other and to their environment. Biologists refer to this relationship as ecology.

American settlers believed that the resources of the West were limitless. Because these settlers believed that nature existed for their benefit, they molded the land to meet their short-term interests.

The Indian View

In contrast to settlers, American Indians respected the earth and all of nature. Since Indians believed that spirits could be found in all living things, they tried to live in harmony with nature, not to conquer it. Young Chief, a Cayuse Indian, expressed the relationship between nature and spirits this way.

"The Earth says, God has placed me here. The Earth says, that God tells me to take care of the Indians on this earth. . . . The water speaks the same way. . . the grass says the same thing. . . . God, on placing [men] on the Earth, desired them to take good care of the Earth and to do each other no harm."

Ecology Today

Today, people throughout the world are still upsetting ecological balances. In Brazil, for example, companies are cutting down the Amazon rain forests to clear land for cattle ranching to satisfy the world's huge appetite. Poor people desperate for land are also clearing forests, burning the remains to plant crops. Entire species of animals who only live in these special regions are losing their habitats and facing extinction. Even the world's climate is being altered by this huge loss of plant life.

The question of humankind's place in the environment is a difficult one. In the United States, we are blessed with a diversity of land and climate that matches the diversity of our people. We must not waste it. Perhaps we can learn from the American Indians who sought to live in harmony with nature. Like them, we must learn to see ourselves as part of a larger ecological system.

Study Skills

Have students research the religious beliefs about nature of two or three Indian tribes. What could we learn from the Indians' beliefs? Students can report orally to the class.

Cultural Context

The encounter between American Indians and white settlers in the late 19th century was a clash of cultural values. The cooperative living that characterized Indian culture was deplored by influential thinkers of the time. Senator Henry Dawes of Massachusetts had learned about the Indians' way of life during his visits to Indian Territory. In 1883, he told a group of Eastern humanitarians about a tribe in which no family was without a home of its own. "There was not a pauper in that [Indian] nation and the nation did not owe a dollar . . . it built its own schools and its hospitals. Yet the defect of the system was apparent. They have got as far as they can go, because they own their land in common . . . there is no enterprise to make your home any better than that of your neighbors. There is no selfishness, which is at the bottom of civilization."

Once the Indian peoples were on reservations (see map), government officials believed they would **assimilate**, or adapt to white culture and give up their traditional ways.

Futile Resistance

After 1870, all the Indians faced the choice of accepting peace on the U.S. government's terms or being exterminated. The U.S. Army had rapid-fire guns and many more soldiers, and took advantage of tribal rivalries to overcome the Indian peoples.

Nevertheless, some Indians still resisted being moved to a reservation. The Nez Perce were ordered to move onto a reservation in 1877. In the process, some angry young Nez Perce killed 13 settlers. Pursued by army troops, their leader, Chief Joseph led his people on a desperate retreat of more than 1,300 miles. Yellow Wolf, another Nez Perce, described Chief Joseph's final surrender.

> *The chiefs and officers crossed among themselves and shook hands all around. The Indians lifted their hands towards the sky, where the sun was then standing. This said: "No more battles! No more war!"*

Geronimo, a shaman and leader of the Chiricahua *(chihr ih KA wa)* Apache, was known for his daring raids. Several times, he fled the harsh conditions of an Arizona reservation to lead followers to the Sierra Madre mountains in Mexico. The U.S. Army had to use one-fourth of its troops to force the surrender in 1886 of his tiny band of Apaches—which included women and children

New Landholding Policies

In 1871, Congress ended the practice, in effect since 1789, of treating Indian tribes as separate nations. Indians could no longer make treaties, yet they were not U.S. citizens. They had to obey U.S. laws, but they had none of the rights of other Americans.

In 1887, the Dawes Acts divided reservation land into grants of 160 acres for individual Indian families to farm. Any surplus land was opened to settlement by white pioneers. Well-intentioned reformers hoped the act would encourage assimilation and improve Indians' lives.

But the results were disastrous. Few Plains Indians had experience farming or even wanted to farm. Many went into debt and lost their land, or sold it to white settlers for pitifully small sums. Indian land holdings shrunk by more than 60 percent because of this act.

Assimilation by Education

Another way the government tried to assimilate the Indians was to send Indian children to special day schools or boarding schools. Teachers

American Indian Lands in 1890

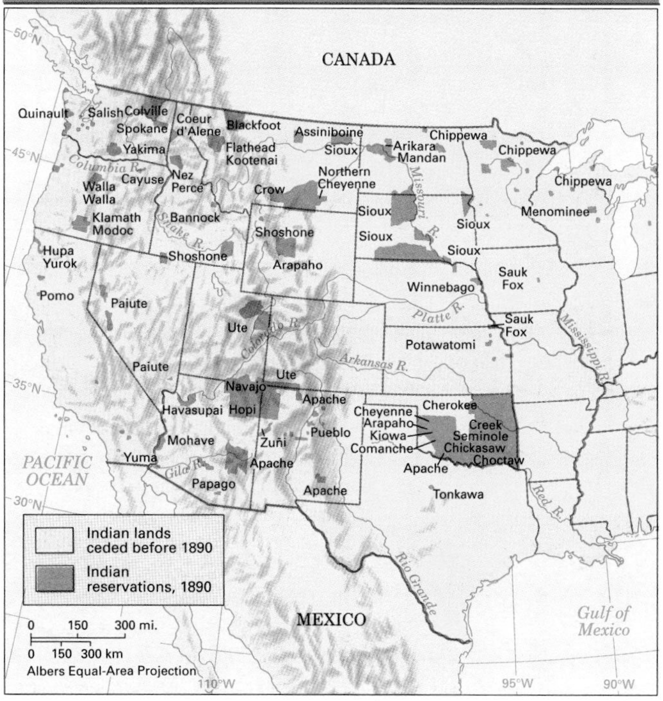

Compare this map with the one on page 419 showing Indian lands in 1850. What major change took place between 1850 and 1890?

BELIEF SYSTEMS

Critical Thinking

Why did reformers think that the Dawes Act would encourage assimilation? Why did it fail to have the desired effect? *(It was designed to give individual Indian families land for farming. But few Indians knew or cared about farming. They lost their land through debt or sold it to white settlers for little money.)* Share with students some of the material from the Cultural Context on page 424 to make clear that reformers were well-meaning and sincere but tended to think of white culture as superior to Indian culture.

All the Plains Indians, and other Indian peoples as well, were settled on reservations.

POLITICAL SYSTEMS

Critical Thinking

Before 1871, how was an Indian nation similar to a foreign nation in its relations with the U.S. Government? *(It made its own treaties with the United States.)* How were the Indian nations treated differently after 1871? *(They could no longer make their own treaties; they had to comply with U.S. laws.)*

Language Arts Connection

Encourage students to read some American Indian legends. Point out to them the Indians' oral tradition—the passing of such stories from generation to generation by reciting them and learning them by heart. Ask students to memorize favorite legends to share with the class. You might want to simulate a scene in which the group sits in a circle, as if around a campfire, listening to "tribal elders" passing on stories in the oral tradition.

Collaborative Learning

Have teams of students choose one tribe to research. Do not limit them to Plains Indian peoples, but include peoples of the Southwest and the Northwest as well. Have each student on a team research a particular aspect of the tribe: religious beliefs, housing, tribal organization, daily life. Ask each group to present its findings to the class. The team members should together decide if they will present their information through reports, models, dioramas, murals, or other means.

Map and Globe Skills

Have students make a rough estimate of the total amount of land in Indian hands in 1890 by tracing the Indian lands on the map on this page and then combining them. *(Roughly 65,000 square miles)* Have them compare this area of land with the amount of Indian land in 1850, as shown on the map on page 419. *(Roughly 2,500,000 square miles)*

BELIEF SYSTEMS

Critical Thinking

Ask students to suggest ways in which the Plains Indians were able to resist assimilation and keep their culture alive. *(They continued to practice old rituals, and they also adapted their rituals to changes in their lives.)*

■ *The Dawes Act divided the Indian reservation land into grants for individual families. The education program taught Indian children the language, culture, and religion of white society.*

CLOSE

Students should use the notes they made as they read the lesson to make a flow chart similar to the Graphic Overview on page 422. They can then answer the Thinking Focus by referring to this chart. As an extension activity, have them do the Language Arts Connection on page 425.

Indian students at Carlisle Indian School in Pennsylvania.

replaced the children's tribal clothing with modern dress, gave them new names, and forced them to speak English. The schools taught the Indians Christianity and the customs of white society. Lone Wolf, a Blackfoot Indian, remembered his school this way:

> *Once there our belongings were taken from us, even the little medicine bags our mothers had given us to protect us from harm. Everything was placed in a heap and set afire.*

The schools, and assimilation in general, were a failure. Taken from their families and forbidden from familiar activities, many unhappy students tried to run away. Even those who did well had trouble finding jobs in the vocations they were taught—printing, baking, drafting, and bricklaying. Those who adapted to white society often felt like misfits.

■ *Explain how the Dawes Act and government education programs were used as part of the assimilation policy.*

The Indian Response

As Plains Indians experienced this loss of power and freedom, many turned to a Paiute religious leader named Wovoka. Wovoka claimed that he had seen visions of all Indians, living and dead, reunited in a world without whites. To get to this world and bring their ancestors back to life, his followers performed a ritual known as the ghost dance. Wovoka's visions and message gave hope to his people, but also alarmed many whites.

The Sioux in Dakota, who were starving on their reservations, began following the ghost dance religion. Fearing an uprising, U.S. troops tried to round up the Sioux, which led to the killing of Sitting Bull. His followers went to Wounded Knee, South Dakota, in 1890. When fighting broke out, the soldiers turned their guns on the Sioux, killing or wounding 200, mostly women and children. Another hundred froze to death in the snow after they fled.

In spite of these deaths and the loss of their land, the Plains Indians never lost their pride. They continued to practice their old beliefs and rituals, but also proved to be adaptable to new conditions. For example, when the government approved a gathering on the Fourth of July, Indians set up tepees, dressed in ceremonial clothing, and performed traditional dances.

The massacre at Wounded Knee marked the end of Indian resistance. The land from which they had been removed could now be settled by white farmers and ranchers. ■

REVIEW

1. **FOCUS** What factors combined to end the Plains Indians' nomadic way of life?
2. **CONNECT** How did the attempt to assimilate the Indians reflect the concept of Manifest Destiny?
3. **HISTORY** Trace the policies the U.S. government followed in its attempts to remove the Indians from the Great Plains.
4. **CRITICAL THINKING** Why might some Indians choose to adopt some aspects of white society? How might they use an American education to help their people?
5. **ACTIVITY** With a classmate, prepare a dialogue between a Plains Indian leader and a U.S. army commander about moving the tribe to a reservation. Be sure to present both points of view in a convincing way.

Homework Options

Write an imaginary diary entry by a 12-year-old American Indian who has just returned home after a year at a government boarding school.

Study Guide: page 61.

Answers to Review Questions

1. Factors include the increased numbers of white settlers, the decreased number of buffalo, the government's failure to honor treaties, the annuities system, the placing of Indians on reservations, and the attempts at assimilation.
2. The belief in white superiority, one aspect of Manifest Destiny, is evident in the government's attempt to force Indians to give up their culture and adopt that of the white Americans.
3. The government used treaties, the annuities system, armed force, and, finally, reservations to remove the Indians from the Great Plains.
4. Sample answer: Through assimilation, a Plains Indian could learn U.S. law, gain political power, and represent the Indian people. Allow for personal opinion.
5. Several students may perform their dialogues for the class.

L E S S O N 4

Resettlement of the Land

When Charles Ingalls, the father of author Laura Ingalls Wilder, tried to file a claim for land in the Dakota Territory, he slept all night on the doorstep of the land office to be sure he got his claim. He told his family:

> It looks like the whole country's trying to file on land. When I showed up at the land office, I couldn't get anywheres near the door.
>
> I've bet Uncle Sam $14.00 against a 160 acres of land, that we can make out to live on the claim for five years. Going to help me win the bet?

After the Civil War, thousands of people like the Ingalls family eagerly took advantage of the opportunity offered by the Homestead Act of 1862. It allotted a settler 160 acres of government-owned land. The only cost for the land was the few dollars needed to record a claim. Anyone could **homestead**, that is, file a claim for land, build a house there, and work the land for five years. If these conditions were met, the homesteader became the owner of the property.

The Homestead Act seemed to offer opportunity to people who had never even dreamed they could own land. Thousands of people, including recently freed slaves and white settlers seeking a better life, moved West and filed homestead claims.

THINKING FOCUS

In what ways did ranching and farming transform the American West?

Key Terms

- homestead

The Sylvester Rawding family built their sod house in the 1880s. On the roof they kept tools such as scythes, which were used for cutting grass or hay or for harvesting grain.

INTRODUCE

Point out the lesson title and ask why the term *resettlement* rather than *settlement* is used. *(Indians had previously lived on the land.)* After one student reads the Thinking Focus aloud, have the class suggest ways in which the lives of ranchers or farmers would be different from that of the Plains Indians. *(Different use of the land, need for fences, stay in one place)* Tell students that in this lesson they will read how ranching and farming changed the West.

Key Term

Vocabulary strategies: T36–37

homestead—to file a claim for land, build a house, and work the land for five years

Graphic Overview

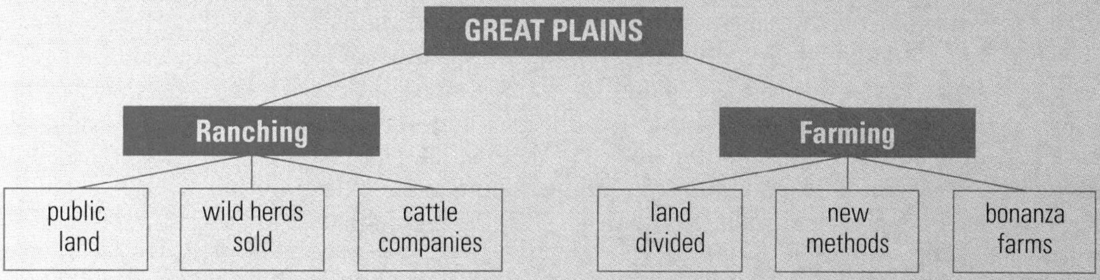

Objectives

1. List the provisions of the Homestead Act.
2. Explain how improved transportation helped farmers and ranchers settle the West.
3. Locate the Chisholm Trail and explain its significance.
4. Explain how technology was used in farming on the Great Plains.

DEVELOP

Suggest that students structure their reading of the lesson by focusing on the following questions: What role did the railroad play in the development of ranching and farming? What was the Homestead Act, and how did it affect ranching and farming?

CULTURE

Visual Learning

Refer students to the illustration of the Texas cowboy on this page. How did the clothing and rigging of Texas cowboys resemble that of the California vaqueros (Chapter 8)? *(Leather boots, western saddle, hackamore, rope)* How did the cowboys' clothing differ? *(Chaps, bandanna)*

Ranching on the Plains

Cowboys used branding irons (above) *to identify cattle. The brand was registered with local officials; this helped ranchers trace lost or stolen stock.*

Some homesteaders became farmers; others turned to ranching. Settlers who went to Texas and the Southwest found a long tradition of cattle ranching. About 1690, Mexican vaqueros brought cattle north to Texas. These cattle had little commercial value and were left to roam freely over the range. By the early 1800s, there were hundreds of thousands of wild longhorns.

The long-legged longhorns were tough animals that thrived on buffalo grass and did not need as much water as other breeds. Their meat, however, was lean, stringy, and tough. Gradually ranchers replaced them with purebred cattle imported from Britain. These cattle produced better meat and brought a higher price in the market.

Ranchers needed more than the 160 acres of a homestead for their herds. In the arid Plains each steer needed about 15 acres of grazing land. Ranchers used the public lands owned by the government for part of their cattle range. Several ranchers might use the same range. At roundup time their cowboys herded all the cattle together. Each owner's cattle were identified by a brand—a special symbol such as the owner's initials—burned into the animal's hide. Mounted on nimble-footed horses, the cowhands separated cattle bearing the same brand from the main herd.

On the Trail

After the roundup, cattle that were to be sold were driven to market. The trail boss hired 10–12 cowhands —usually single young men—to herd 2,000 or more cattle along the trail. The most experienced riders rode at the point or head of the herd. Riders farther back kept the herd moving and

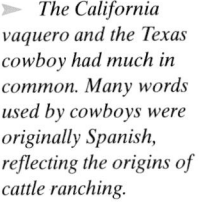

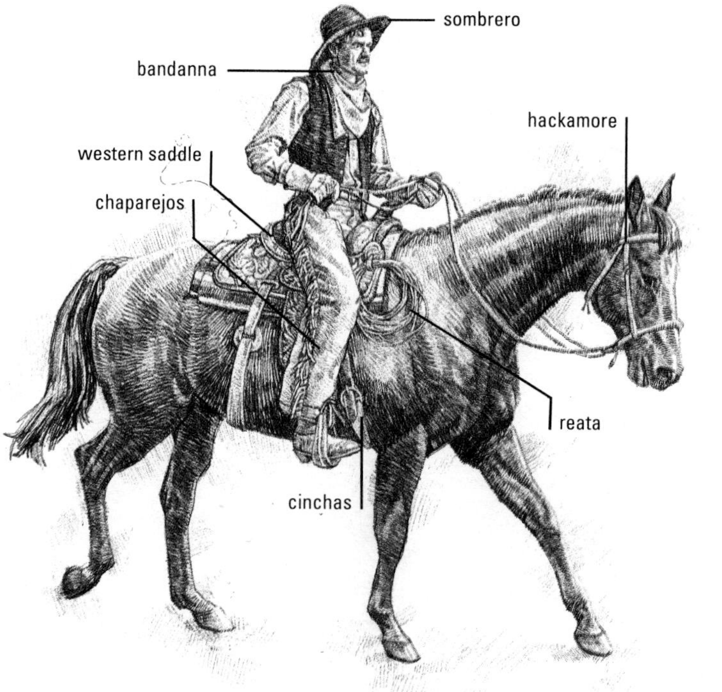

The California vaquero and the Texas cowboy had much in common. Many words used by cowboys were originally Spanish, reflecting the origins of cattle ranching.

Access Activity

Have students look at the picture of the sod house on page 427. What can they learn about the Rawding family from this picture? *(Probably farmers; don't have machinery; don't seem wealthy)* What question does this picture raise about farming in the West? *(Sample question: Did people use machinery?)*

Access Strategy

Write the words *ranch* and *farm* on the board and ask students to brainstorm a list of words that are found on or describe each word. As they suggest words, write them under the correct heading. Some words will probably fit in both categories. After students have contributed as many words as they can, have them make statements comparing and contrasting ranches and farms.

Then write the words *Great Plains* on the board and ask students to recall what they have learned in this chapter so far by making a list of words that describe the Great Plains—its geography, climate, and other features. Ask students to make a list of the problems and challenges that were involved in setting up the first ranches and first farms on the plains in the days before power machinery. Tell students that as they read this lesson they will learn more about how people developed ranches and farms in the Great Plains.

stopped cattle from straying. At the back of the herd, in the clouds of dust the cattle kicked up, rode the least experienced cowboys.

During the two-to three-month trail drive, cowboys rode for up to 18 hours a day. Their job was dirty, tiring, and dangerous. The slightest noise, like a clap of thunder, could panic a herd. Then cowboys would have to gallop up hills or through brush, racing to turn the terrified herd. If a cowboy fell, he could be dragged by his horse or run over by the cattle.

During the night, cowboys calmed the restless cattle by singing songs they made up about their lives. One such song, "Git Along, Little Dogies," appears below. (A dogie is a steer.)

Cowboys came from many different backgrounds. About one in seven was Mexican American, and many, like sharpshooter Nat Love, were African Americans. Other cowboys were Indians or the descendants of Indians. Few women rode the trails in what was mainly a man's world.

The Cattle Boom

Early ranchers raised cattle mainly for their hides and tallow. After the Civil War, however, the growing population in the East demanded more beef. Men returning from the Civil War saw the wild Texas herds as a way to earn money. Ranchers rounded up the wild herds, branded them as their own, and drove them to towns on the railroad lines. Cattle cars then carried them to markets farther east.

The first herds of Texas longhorns were driven north to cow towns in Missouri. As farmers moved west, however, they objected to herds of cattle trampling their crops and eating their grass. The state legislature passed laws that forced the cattlemen to use trails farther west.

As the map on page 430 shows, trails from southern and western Texas met at the Red River. They formed the Chisholm Trail, which was opened in 1867 to reach the newly built railroad in Abilene, Kansas.

In 1869, more than 350,000 cattle

This 1877 painting shows Mexican vaqueros. As early as 1690, vaqueros had brought cattle north from Mexico to Texas. A cowboy's spur is shown at the bottom of the page.

Across Time & Space

In 1872, newspaper publisher Julius Sterling Morton persuaded Nebraska homesteaders to plant young trees. When they matured, the trees served as windbreaks and helped conserve moisture in the soil. Today, most states in the United States have set aside Arbor Day, a special day for planting trees.

As I walked out one morning for pleasure,
I met a cowpuncher a-jogging along.
His hat was thrown back and his spurs was a-jingling,
And as he advanced he was singing this song.
Sing hooplio get along my little dogies,
For Wyoming shall be your new home.
Its hooping and yelling and cursing those dogies
To our misfortune but none of your own.

In the Springtime we round up the dogies,
Slap on the brands and bob off their tails.
Then we cut herd and herd is inspected,
And then we throw them on the trail.

John Avery Lomax, *Cowboy Songs and Other Frontier Ballads*, 1910

ECONOMICS

Critical Thinking

What did ranchers do to keep track of their cattle on shared public lands? *(They branded their own cattle.)* Have students suggest other things that people do to label or claim property as their own. *(Writing names in books, registering cars, engraving codes on bicycles)*

Historical Context

In the years following the Homestead Act of 1862, settlers rushed into the West. Most available land had been claimed by 1889, when President Harrison proclaimed that "unassigned" lands in Indian Territory (now Oklahoma) would be opened for public homesteading. A frantic land rush followed. By noon on April 22, more than 50,000 land-hungry people had gathered at the borders of the territory to claim land formerly set aside for the Indians. When the gun went off, they set off into the territory in every type of conveyance, from buggies and ox carts to bicycles, carrying stakes, rope, tents, and other belongings with them.

By sunset, all of the allotted 2 million acres had been claimed. The first Oklahoma land rush was followed by other ones until much of the land set aside for Indians had been settled by white people.

Critical Thinking

The life of a cowboy has often been portrayed as being exciting and glamorous. Have students discuss the realities of a cowboy's job. Which aspects of the cowboy's life seem glamorous? *(Sample answer: Riding the range)* Which aspects do not? *(Sample answer: The long hours)* What do the song lyrics on this page tell about a cowboy's life?

ECONOMICS

Critical Thinking

Ask students how ranchers in the West were able to meet the demand for beef in the East. *(Used railroads to ship steers to meat-packing plants; new methods of meat packing; refrigerated railroad cars)*

How did the demand for beef affect the quality of the stock raised? *(When ranching became more profitable, investors and ranchers were able to buy better breeds of cattle.)*

■ *Barbed wire divided up the open land, making it impossible for large herds to graze freely.*

GEOGRAPHY

Map and Globe Skills

Students can locate the Chisholm Trail on the map on this page. Have them use the map scale to determine how far a cowboy would travel from the most southern point in Texas to Abilene. *(Roughly 900 miles)*

▲ *In cattle towns, large corrals held cattle to be fattened.*

■ *How did barbed wire change ranching?*

▼ *Trace the route a shipment of beef might have taken from San Antonio to New York.*

were driven along the Chisholm Trail. Two years later, the number had doubled. After that year, however, the trail drives gradually shifted to the Western Trail, which ended at Dodge City, Kansas.

The growth of the railroad network and new methods of meat packing and refrigeration helped to meet the demand for Western beef. As raising cattle became more profitable, ranching spread from Texas to Montana, Wyoming, Colorado, and North and South Dakota. Within three years, the number of cattle in Montana increased from 250,000 to 600,000.

Once Eastern businessmen became aware that a steer worth $5 on the range could bring $45–60 on the market, cattle ranching became a big business. People in the East and in England and Scotland organized and financed cattle companies. By the mid-1880s, some of these companies had ranches, each of which covered an area larger than the entire New England states.

The rancher was king for only a short period, however. Unusually harsh winters in 1885–1886 and 1886–1887 took a terrible toll of livestock. Falling prices for beef made ranching unprofitable. The introduction of barbed wire fences limited the open range. Ranchers had to rent or buy the public lands they had used at little or no cost. By the 1890s, the ranches that remained were operated as large, fenced-in livestock farms, and cowboys were as likely to be mending fences as roping steers. ■

Moving Western Beef to Market

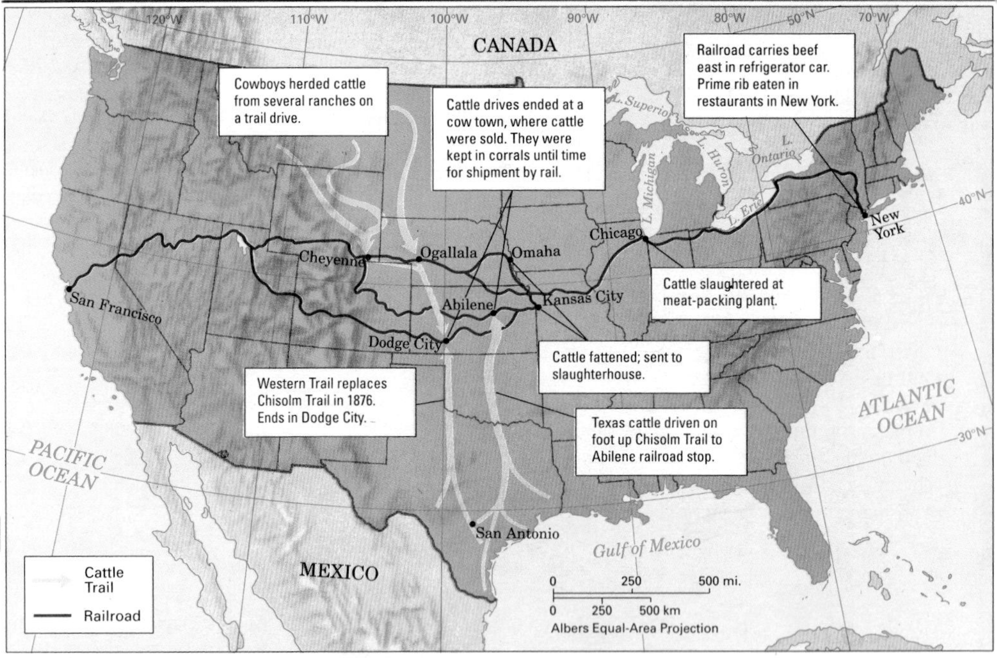

Critical Thinking

Ask students to analyze why, despite the many difficulties, homesteaders were still willing and anxious to obtain and farm a homestead. *(Sample answer: Desire to be independent, hope for a better life)*

Art Connection

Frederick Remington (1861–1909) was one of the great recorders of the American West. At the age of 20, as he sat on a bluff watching a train cross the prairie, he suddenly knew that "the wild riders and vacant land were about to vanish forever." He devoted the rest of his life to recording the legendary "Wild West" in 2,739 paintings, illustrations for 147 books, and 25 bronze sculptures.

An earlier recorder of life in the West, George Catlin (1796–1872), specialized in painting American Indian scenes. He produced more than 500 paintings depicting the lives of Indian peoples, especially the Plains Indians.

Locate examples of artwork of the West in books and magazines such as *American Heritage*. Students should describe the pictures and explain what they represent.

Farming on the Plains

The introduction of barbed wire in the 1860s created tensions between farmers and ranchers. Ranchers feared that farmers would try to fence in the water supplies, so ranchers tried to fence in the range, which included government land. After several violent clashes, the U.S. government ruled that ranchers could not fence in government lands. This opened the Plains so that farmers could come in and establish their claims.

Homesteaders Settle the Plains

Completion of the transcontinental railroad brought about 500,000 new families to the Plains by 1900. They were drawn by railroad and government advertisements, the Homestead Act's promise of free land, and access to the railroads. By 1875, newcomers had settled most of the available land in eastern Kansas and Nebraska. Settlers arriving later moved farther west, to areas where the climate was too dry for conventional farming.

The first tasks of a homesteading family were to build a shelter and obtain water. On the treeless plain, most settlers made dugouts or houses of sod—soil held together by the roots of grass—like that on page 427.

Homesteaders dug wells for their water, drawing it up by bucket or by a hand pump. For fuel they gathered dried buffalo droppings or cut grass and made twists of it when it dried.

The prairie farmers were often called sodbusters because they broke up the sod to plant crops. If they failed to get a crop the first fall, they risked starving during the winter. With hard work and good weather, a family could build up a successful farm in five years. Each year they would try to break more ground and plant more crops, using cash they earned from their harvest to buy machinery.

Exodusters

Among the settlers were many African Americans, recently freed from slavery. Benjamin "Pap" Singleton, from Tennessee, led a migration of African Americans out of the South in the "Exodus of 1879." Comparing themselves to the Jews Moses led out of Egypt, they were known as Exodusters.

Some Exodusters succeeded on farms in Kansas and Nebraska. Others settled in growing towns like Topeka and Kansas City. Unfortunately, blacks still faced discrimination in their new homes in the West.

Farming Methods

Homesteaders had to learn new techniques to be successful farmers. Irrigation was one solution to the arid climate, but it required a reliable source of water and money for building an irrigation system. Water on the Plains was rarely adequate.

Many homesteaders turned to dry farming techniques. Each year they left half the land unplanted to preserve the moisture in the soil. Other fields were plowed deeply, and fewer seeds were planted per acre than in a wetter climate. Wheat was especially suited for the dry climate. Over time, the Great Plains became one of the world's great wheat-producing areas.

Windmills were a necessity on the Plains because water sources were deep underground. The nearly constant wind turned the blades of these windmills, pumping up water for the home or a small garden or for watering livestock.

Problems of Homesteading

For many homesteaders, the dream of acquiring land turned into a nightmare. Many had started their claims without any extra money. Often they had to borrow funds to buy machinery, seed, and livestock. No

The hardships endured by homesteaders can be seen in the faces of this woman and her children.

HISTORY

Critical Thinking

Explain why a rancher would probably not have supported the Homestead Act. *(Ranchers needed open land; the purpose of the Homestead Act was to divide up the land.)* What other factors led to the end of the "cattle kingdom"? *(Severe weather, falling beef prices, and the invention of barbed wire)*

SOCIAL SYSTEMS

Critical Thinking

Ask students to define the term *homesteaders*. *(People who filed a claim for land, built a house, and worked the land for five years.)* Read aloud the quote by Charles Ingalls on page 427. What does it reveal about the attitude of homesteaders? *(They had an optimistic attitude.)* What kind of person would have been likely to succeed as a homesteader? *(Sample answer: Hardworking, daring person)*

Research

Many African Americans took part in settling the West. Most trail drives included black cowboys. Poet Paul Dunbar wrote for a Denver paper, and rodeo star Bill Pickett got his start as a cowhand in Oklahoma. Have students do research on the history of black Americans in the West. Paul Stewart's *Black Cowboys* (Broomfield, Co.: Phillip Publishers, 1986) is a good source of information.

Reader's Theater

Many works of fiction portray the lives of homesteaders in the West. Laura Ingalls Wilder's *By the Shores of Silver Lake* (New York: Harper & Row, 1939), Charlene Joy Talbot's *An Orphan for Nebraska* (New York: Antheneum Publishers, 1979), and Willa Cather's *My Ántonia* (Social Studies Bookshelf, page 407)—listed in order from easiest to most difficult—all provide excellent chapters to adapt for Reader's Theater.

Critical Thinking

Remind students that they learned in Lesson 1 that the Great Plains was once termed the "Great American Desert." Why was that term inaccurate? *(New techniques, such as planting a hardy strain of wheat, made it possible to farm the land. The railroads made cattle raising and farming in this area profitable.)*

ECONOMICS

Critical Thinking

Ask students to explain how railroads helped to make farming a profitable enterprise on the Great Plains. *(They brought farmers important supplies and provided a means to ship farm produce to Eastern markets.)* What kinds of things made it difficult for some small homesteaders to make farming profitable? *(Crop failure, not enough money to buy good equipment)*

■ *Irrigation systems, including windmills; dry farming techniques; new strains of wheat; new machinery*

CLOSE

Students should summarize the lesson by answering the Thinking Focus. Ask them to describe the role of the railroad in the development of ranching and farming. *(It made it possible for people and equipment to get to the West more easily and to sell meat and grain in the East.)* How did the Homestead Act affect ranching and farming? *(It encouraged farming but helped to bring an end to the ranchers' use of the open range.)*

Horse-drawn reaper-binders harvest wheat on the Great Plains. Reaper-binders cut the wheat, and bound it together to be collected later.

matter how hard they worked, they could not make enough to pay off their debts. Wealthy people who bought land to sell for a profit forced up the value of land.

As taxes rose, the small homesteader fell further into debt. Many had to sell some or all of their land to pay back loans. Others lost their land to the banks whose loans they could not repay.

Technology Transforms Farming

Some farmers who were able to invest in the new technology met with astounding success. In 1874, the Northern Pacific Railroad and a Minnesota wheat grower named Oliver Dalrymple cooperated on a farming project in the Dakotas. Dalrymple used a mechanical sower to plant seeds; self-binding reapers to cut, gather, and bind the stalks of wheat; and steam-powered threshers to separate the wheat kernels from the husks and straw. He made a profit of more than 100 percent in the first year.

Impressed by these results, Eastern bankers formed companies that bought nearly all the land in the fertile Red River Valley of North Dakota. Using expensive equipment, they created huge factory-style farms that were so profitable they were called bonanza farms. Their success attracted thousands of settlers, increasing North Dakota's population from 2,400 in 1870 to almost 191,000 in 1890.

As settlers poured into the Red River Valley, railroad lines were built to reach the northern part of the Great Plains. This railroad network linked Plains farmers to the rest of the country. It allowed farmers to ship their produce East. The transcontinental railroad lines made prairie farmers part of the nation's economy. Aided by the machines manufactured in the industrial cities, they produced much of the food on which people in those cities depended. Three great regions of the nation—West, Great Plains, and East—had been joined together. ■

■ *What methods did farmers use to grow crops successfully on the Great Plains?*

REVIEW

1. **FOCUS** In what ways did ranching and farming transform the American West?
2. **CONNECT** How did U.S. government policy toward the Indians benefit other Americans?
3. **GEOGRAPHY** What geographical problems did farmers and ranchers face on the Great Plains?
4. **ECONOMICS** Explain how Western farming and ranching became part of the national economy.
5. **CRITICAL THINKING** Did the Homestead Act achieve its aims? Explain.
6. **WRITING ACTIVITY** Write a review of a Western you have read or watched on TV or in the movies. How does it describe the cowboy's life? How does the information differ from what you have learned about the real West?

Homework Options

Have students compare the cowboy song on page 429 with modern Country and Western songs on the radio or television or with those in movie Westerns.

Study Guide: page 62.

Answers to Review Questions

1. Ranching and farming changed the West from open plains, sparsely inhabited by nomadic Indians, to large farms and ranches that were tied to the national economy.
2. It opened up land for many ranchers and farmers and encouraged railroad building and the development of mines.
3. The lack of a water supply and the extremes of climate presented problems.
4. Improved shipping methods allowed Western ranchers to sell beef in many parts of the country. New farming machinery, as well as the railroads, made Western farm products part of the national economy.
5. Sample answer: The Homestead Act provided an opportunity for some people to own land, but many homesteaders failed when they could not make enough profit from the land to pay off their loans. Allow for personal opinion.
6. Encourage students to use details from the lesson in their comparisons.

UNDERSTANDING TOPOGRAPHICAL MAPS

Tracing Routes West

Here's Why

Knowing how to relate transportation routes to the topography of the land and its resources can help you understand the development of an area.

As you have read, the completion of the transcontinental railroad changed our nation forever. The railroads were built to connect major cities and to reach new resources such as gold and silver. In addition, the routes had to accommodate vast changes in the landscape.

Suppose you wanted to understand how these ideas are presented on a map. Reading a topographic map is one way to relate what you have read with what you see on a map.

Here's How

Look at the map on this page that combines topographical information with the railroad routes. Follow the path of the Central Pacific Railroad from San Francisco to Ogden. You'll see that the route must go through many geographic regions—the Central Valley, the Sierra Nevada, and the Great Basin. It curves dramatically since it must allow for natural land formations like mountains, canyons, and rivers.

Now find the Denver & Rio Grande line. It winds as it crosses the Rockies, not just to cut through the mountain passes, but also to connect with the mining towns of Leadville and Cripple Creek. You can see here that the choice of routes depended as much upon the location of natural resources as it did on the lay of the land.

Try It

Trace the route of the Northern Pacific Railroad from Fargo to Seattle, and answer the following questions. What major geographic regions does this route cross? Between which two cities is it straightest? What might this tell you about the land there?

What section is the route crossing when it starts to curve noticeably? What does this tell you about the landscape there? What two major mines did this railway pass? Identify major cities along the route. How do you think the geographical features affected the way people settled this part of the country? How do you think the resources available affected the route of the railroads?

Apply It

Now go back to the map of the First Roads West in Chapter 7. What natural feature does the Nashville Road follow directly west of Richmond? Explain why the Wilderness Road does not go in a straight line from North Carolina to Boonesborough, Kentucky. What do these two maps tell you about the effect of topography on the development of the routes in the East and the West?

Western Regions and Railroad Routes

UNDERSTANDING TOPOGRAPHICAL MAPS

This skill lesson will help students use topographical and route maps.

GEOGRAPHY

Map and Globe Skills

Point out that in several places the railroad routes follow rivers. The Platte and Yellowstone rivers are two examples. Why would the railroad builders choose these routes? What advantages did river valleys offer? *(Sample answers: Source of water for the steam-powered trains; rivers had already cut through hills and mountains, making it easier to build railroad tracks along these paths through natural obstacles.)*

Answers to Try It

Great Plains, Rocky Mountains, Cascade Range; straightest between Fargo and Billings, suggesting that the land there is flat; crossing Rocky Mountains, suggesting that it is mountainous; mines at Virginia City, Montana and Coeur d'Alene, Idaho; Fargo, Billings, Butte, Spokane, Seattle; geographical features made it harder for people to settle this part of country; railroad routes probably were designed to pass as many resources as possible.

Answers to Apply It

Follows James River; Wilderness Road crosses Appalachian Mountains and turns to go through the Cumberland Gap. The maps both show the importance of topography in determining where roads and railroads were placed.

Objective

Use a topographical map and a route map to determine the development of the West. (Map and Globe Skills 3)

INTRODUCE

Explain to students that Willa Cather's family were homesteaders on the Great Plains in the 1880s. Have them recall what they read about homesteaders in Lesson 4. Tell students that Cather used her childhood experiences on the plains as material for the short stories and novels she wrote later, including the novel excerpted here.

READ AND RESPOND

After students read the selection independently, discuss their responses to it. Ask them what is most striking about the landscape the narrator describes. *(Its size, color, and openness)* As students answer the purpose-setting question, make sure they give reasons for their answers.

You have read about the hundreds of thousands of homesteaders who settled the Great Plains. This selection tells of how one young boy experienced his new home.

LITERATURE

A New Home

Willa Cather

Willa Cather (1873-1947) grew up in Nebraska among immigrant families. My Antonia *is the story of a Czech family is struggling to maintain its farm in hard economic times. In this excerpt Jim Burden, the novel's narrator, sees the land for the first time. As you read, consider the details Jim sees and how he describes his new home.*

Early the next morning I ran out-of-doors to look about me. I had been told that ours was the only wooden house west of Black Hawk—until you came to the Norwegian settlement, where there were several. Our neighbors lived in sod houses and dugouts—comfortable, but not very roomy. Our white frame house, with a storey and half-storey above the basement, stood at the east end of what I might call the farmyard, with the windmill close by the kitchen door. From the windmill the ground sloped westward, down to the barns and granaries and pig-yards. This slope was trampled hard and bare, and washed out in winding gullies by the rain. Beyond the corncribs, at the bottom of the shallow draw, was a muddy little pond, with rusty willow bushes growing about it. The road from the post-office came directly by our door, crossed the farmyard, and curved round this little pond, beyond which it began to climb the gentle swell of unbroken prairie to the west. There, along the western sky-line it skirted a great cornfield, much larger than any field I had ever seen. This cornfield, and the sorghum patch behind the barn, were the only broken land in sight. Everywhere, as far as the eye could reach, there was nothing but rough, shaggy, red grass, most of it as tall as I.

North of the house, inside the ploughed fire-breaks, grew a thick-set strip of box-elder trees, low and bushy, their leaves already turning yellow. This hedge was nearly a quarter of a mile long, but I had to look very hard to see it at all. The little trees were insignificant against the grass. It seemed as if the grass were about to run over them, and over the plum-patch behind the sod chicken-house.

As I looked about me I felt that the grass was the country, as the water is the sea. The red of the grass made all the great prairie the colour of wine-stains, or of certain seaweeds when they are first washed up. And there was so much motion in it; the whole country seemed, somehow, to be running.

I had almost forgotten that I had a grandmother, when she came out, her sunbonnet on her head, a grain-sack in her hand, and asked me if I did not want to go to the garden with her to dig potatoes for dinner.

The garden, curiously enough, was a quarter of a mile from the

434

Thematic Connections

Social Studies: Pioneer life

Houghton Mifflin Literary Readers: The Natural World

Background

Willa Cather was nine when her family moved from Virginia to Nebraska. She grew up among immigrants from Sweden, Russia, Germany, and Eastern Europe. She went to the University of Nebraska and was successful in journalism. She did not begin to publish novels until she was nearly 40.

Cather's novels celebrate the spirit of the pioneers, but they also describe the stifling effects of the loneliness and hardships on the frontier. *My Ántonia*, from which this selection is taken, is told from the viewpoint of a middle-aged New York lawyer, Jim Burden, recalling his childhood. The reader comes to understand that Jim is unhappy with his urban existence and yearns for the freedom of his boyhood home on the plains.

house, and the way to it led up a shallow draw past the cattle corral. Grandmother called my attention to a stout hickory cane, tipped with copper, which hung by a leather thong from her belt. This, she said, was her rattlesnake cane. I must never go to the garden without a heavy stick or a corn-knife; she had killed a good many rattlers on her way back and forth. A little girl who lived on the Black Hawk road was bitten on the ankle and had been sick all summer.

draw ditch

I can remember exactly how the country looked to me as I walked beside my grandmother along the faint wagon-tracks on that early September morning. Perhaps the glide of long railway travel was still with me, for more than anything else I felt motion in the landscape; in the fresh, easy-blowing morning wind, and in the earth itself, as if the shaggy grass were a sort of loose hide, and underneath it herds of wild buffalo were galloping, galloping . . .

Alone, I should never have found the garden—except, perhaps, for the big yellow pumpkins that lay about unprotected by their withering vines—and I felt very little interest in it when I got there. I wanted to walk straight on through the red grass and over the edge of the world, which could not be very far away. The light air about me told me that the world ended here: only the ground and sun and sky were left, and if one went a little farther there would be only sun and sky, and one would float off into them, like the tawny hawks which sailed over our heads making slow shadows on the grass. While grandmother took the pitch-fork we found standing in one of the rows and dug potatoes, while I picked them up out of the soft brown earth and put them into the bag, I kept looking up at the hawks that were doing what I might so easily do.

When grandmother was ready to go, I said I would like to stay up there in the garden awhile.

She peered down at me from under her sunbonnet. "Aren't you afraid of snakes?"

"A little," I admitted, "but I'd like to stay, anyhow."

"Well, if you see one, don't have anything to do with him. The big yellow and brown ones won't hurt you; they're bull-snakes and help to keep the gophers down. Don't be scared if you see anything look out of that hole in the bank over there. That's a badger hole. He's about as big as a big 'possum, and his face is striped, black and white. He takes a chicken once in a while, but I won't let the men harm him. In a new country a body feels friendly to the animals. I like to have him come out and watch me when I'm at work."

Grandmother swung the bag of potatoes over her shoulder and went down the path, leaning forward a little. The road followed the windings of the draw; when she came to the first bend, she waved at me and disappeared. I was left alone with this new feeling of lightness and content.

Further Reading

O, Pioneers. Willa Cather. This novel tells another tale of a hardy immigrant woman who matches her determination against the harsh, lonely life of the Nebraska prairie.

Why did Jim's grandmother carry a cane when she walked to the garden? *(To protect herself from rattlesnakes)*

How did the landscape make Jim feel? *(It made him feel light and content.)*

EXTEND

Have students write a letter to a friend in which they describe their house and neighborhood as if they were seeing it for the first time. Tell students to look at their home with fresh eyes and to see it as a newcomer would. Students should include many details.

Further Reading

You may want to ask students to go to the school or local library to find *My Ántonia* or other novels by Willa Cather.

DECISION-MAKING PROCESS

1. Recognize the need for a decision.
2. Define the goals and values involved.
3. Acquire and evaluate necessary information.
4. Identify and analyze possible alternatives.
5. Choose the best alternative.

This Making Decisions lesson about hunting the buffalo will focus on steps 3 and 4 of the decision-making process.

ETHICS

Critical Thinking

Discuss the points of view reflected in the two quotations at the beginning of the lesson. What point of view does each reflect? *(Sample answer: The jingle about "Buffalo Bill" is a glorification of the killing of buffalo. The second quotation by the hunter John Cook shows regret for reckless slaughter.)*

MAKING DECISIONS

Where the Buffalo Roam

Buffalo Bill, Buffalo Bill
Never missed and never will;
Always aims and shoots to kill
And the company pays his buffalo bill.

Popular jingle in the late 1800s about "Buffalo Bill" Cody

I moved up a dead buffalo and got in several good shots . . . I moved again, on through the dead ones, to the farthermost one, and fired three more shots and quit. As I walked back through where the carcasses lay the thickest, I could not help but think that I had done wrong to make such a slaughter for the hides alone.

John Cook, buffalo hunter

Background

During the early 1800s, enormous herds of buffalo roamed the Great Plains of America. Daniel Boone followed a buffalo trail through the Appalachian Mountains. This trail became the National Road, or so-called Cumberland Trail, which opened up the American West to settlement. As settlers moved slowly westward, they used buffalo meat as a source of food, buffalo hides for clothing and shelter, and buffalo droppings for heat and cooking fuel.

The buffalo helped in other ways as well. Guides and scouts used the trails of migratory buffalo to identify water holes as well as shallows in rivers where the settlers' heavy wagons could cross. Occasionally, a ribbon of greener, taller, grass fertilized by buffalo droppings marked the path to a water hole.

Western settlers were often amazed at the size of buffalo herds. One traveler in Kansas reported driving a wagon for 25 miles through one continuous herd. (Scientists estimate that the total number of buffalo in the early 1800s was between 50 and 70 million animals.) A great buffalo slaughter, however, began in 1871.

Between 50 and 70 million buffalo roamed the Great Plains during the early 1800s. By the early 1870s, only 7 million remained.

Objectives

1. Acquire and use information necessary to making decisions. (Critical Thinking 2)
2. Clarify the issues regarding the use of land and resources. (Geography 3)

Activities

Have groups of students do research about animals that have become extinct due to hunting. Have them make a list of these animals with the date on which the last one was observed and the reasons why the animal was hunted. Have students consider ways in which these animals might have been protected. Ask them to write a report about how people would have had to change their behavior to accommodate these now-extinct animals.

Have students gather information on animals that have recently been put on the endangered species list. Have them interview a conservationist or invite one to speak to the class about the factors that cause a species to become endangered. Then have students write about possible solutions to the problem of endangered species.

A Resource or a Nuisance?

There were so many buffalo the supply must have seemed endless. Often settlers would shoot several buffalo weighing 1,800 pounds and take only 50 or 75 pounds of meat from each animal. One hunter could kill over 100 buffalo in an hour while standing in one spot. The invention of the Sharp's rifle in 1871 made shooting buffalo even easier, since now the buffalo could be shot from a greater distance.

As the plains became more settled, farming and ranching brought further harm to the buffalo. In order to keep buffalo away from their cattle and crops, farmers used barbed wire. This also served to cut the buffalo off from their water supply.

Buffalo were no longer regarded as a resource, but as a nuisance. Migrating herds often blocked shipping on rivers for days as they swam across, or stopped railroads in their tracks. Angry buffalo bulls were capable of overturning a locomotive. Professional hunters were hired by the railroad companies to guard water holes, shooting the animals when they came to drink.

By 1865, there were only 15 million buffalo remaining, and by 1872 only 7 million. In 1883, a herd of 10,000 animals, the largest in Montana, was exterminated in just a few days. It was while working as such a professional buffalo hunter that William Cody earned his nickname, "Buffalo Bill."

Realizing that the buffalo were in danger of extinction, Walking Coyote, an Indian of the Pend d'Oreille tribe, captured, protected, and bred two pair of buffalo. They became the basis for two herds living in Montana today.

In 1905, Theodore Roosevelt and others founded the American Bison Society to create a buffalo sanctuary. Today, 35,000 buffalo live under government protection in the U.S. and Canada. Although this is a tiny fraction of their former number, they are no longer in danger of extinction.

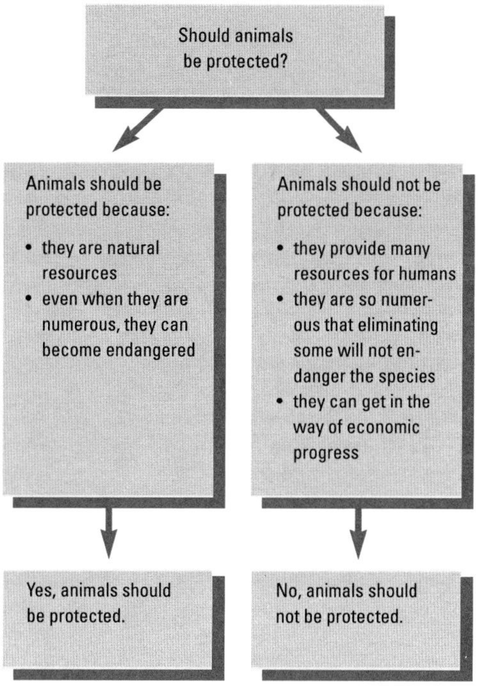

Decision Point

1. Compare the goals and values of those who wanted to protect the buffalo with those who hunted the buffalo.
2. Buffalo herds require enormous amounts of range land—land that could be used for farming or ranching. Which use is more important? Can you think of a compromise to allow for both?
3. Identify an issue in your state or region that involves a conflict between protecting wildlife and meeting peoples' needs. Collect news articles about the issue and discuss it in class.

HISTORY

Critical Thinking

Initially the buffalo was useful to the early settlers, but later, as the plains became more populated, the buffalo was considered a nuisance. Can you imagine a way in which the buffalo might have continued to be useful to ranchers who then would have had an interest in protecting it? *(The animals could have been domesticated. The meat could have been marketed and the hides used for leather.)*

CITIZENSHIP

Visual Learning

Have students identify the point or points in the decision-making chart where information should be acquired and evaluated. Then have them identify the range of possible alternatives.

Answers to Decision Point

1. The Indians did not believe that they owned the land and could do whatever they wanted to on it. The settlers, on the other hand, often felt that the land was theirs, and they could get rid of whatever stood in their way.
2. Point out to students that the answer to the first question depends on one's point of view and that the second question can only be answered if both points of view are considered.
3. Encourage students to talk to local conservationists and businesspeople who are on opposite sides of such an issue. Students should pay particular attention to possible alternatives.

Collaborative Strategy

A recommended strategy for this lesson is pair-debate. For more details about strategies for collaborative learning strategies, see pages T34–35.

Answers to Reviewing Key Terms

A. Sample answers:

1. A boom town would often spring up when miners discovered a bonanza.
2. The U.S. Government gave Indians annuities in return for safe passage through Indian territory, and then moved the Indians to reservations.
3. The government moved Indians to reservations, hoping that they would assimilate into white culture.
4. Often the transcontinental railroad promoted the development of boom towns.

B. Answers:

1. False. Prairies are great, treeless expanses.
2. True. It was the first railroad to cross an entire continent.
3. True. The bonanza was the richest layer of rock in the mine.
4. True. Settlers who took advantage of the Homestead Act of 1862 used the land for farming or ranching.
5. True. Even though these agreements later dissolved, the government promised annuities to Indians who would let the settlers pass in peace.
6. True. Life was difficult for the children in these schools, and they faced just as many hardships after they graduated.

Answers to Exploring Concepts

A. Answers:

Santee Sioux uprising—1862
Transcontinental railroad completed—1869
Custer defeated—1876
Nez Perce resistance—1877
Dawes Act passed—1887
Wounded Knee massacre—1890

Students should address how both the transcontinental railroad and the Homestead Act served to bring so many settlers into the western regions that the Plains Indians' way of life was threatened. This threat, in turn, resulted in the many battles, uprisings, and government acts on the timeline.

B. Sample answers:

1. Responses should include prairies, several mountain ranges, deserts, basins, canyons, plateaus, foothills, and valleys.
2. They did not think the land could support crops, and the climate was too extreme for settlement.
3. Indians used the meat of the buffalo for food, the hides for clothing and shelter, and the bones and horns for tools and weapons.
4. Indians lead nomadic existences and did not settle in one place as a nation; the tribes had different beliefs, languages, and cultures; and government policies often pitted one nation against another.
5. The government took their lands, killed the buffalo (their means of livelihood), forbade certain religious customs, and tried to assimilate them into white society.
6. Farmers needed to fence in their lands to keep the cattle from ruining the crops, while ranchers needed the water supplies on farmers' lands for their cattle.

Chapter Review

Reviewing Key Terms

annuity (p. 423)
assimilate (p. 425)
bonanza (p. 413)
boom town (p. 414)
homestead (p. 427)
reservation (p. 424)
transcontinental (p. 412)

A. In each of the following pairs, the two terms are related in some way. Write a sentence for each pair that clearly explains the relationship between the two terms.

1. bonanza, boom town
2. reservation, annuity
3. assimilate, reservation
4. transcontinental, boom town

B. Based on what you have read in the chapter, decide whether each of the following statements is accurate. Write an explanation of each decision.

1. Before homesteaders could settle on the prairie, they had to cut down the forests.
2. The transcontinental railroad connected the East Coast of North America with the West Coast.
3. Miners had to cut through layers of rock in order to reach the bonanza that contained silver or gold.
4. The opportunity to homestead enabled many people to start their own farms and ranches.
5. In order to allow people to pass safely through Indian territory, the government offered to supply tribes with food, clothing, and other necessities.
6. The government's efforts to assimilate the Indians by sending them to government schools was a failure.

Exploring Concepts

A. On a separate sheet of paper, copy the timeline below. Complete your timeline by using the events listed below (one event has been entered as a model for you to follow). How did the Homestead Act and the completion of the transcontinental railroad affect the other events listed on your timeline?

- Homestead Act passed
- Custer defeated
- Transcontinental railroad completed
- Dawes Act passed
- Wounded Knee massacre
- Nez Perce resistance
- Santee Sioux uprising

B. Support each of the following statements with facts and details from the chapter.

1. The American West has a variety of landforms.
2. When white settlers first crossed the Great Plains, they didn't settle there for a number of reasons.
3. The Plains Indians used the buffalo in many ways.
4. Many factors kept the Plains Indians from uniting into a single people.
5. The U.S. government sought to destroy the Indians' traditional way of life.
6. Farmers and ranchers had conflicting needs for the land.

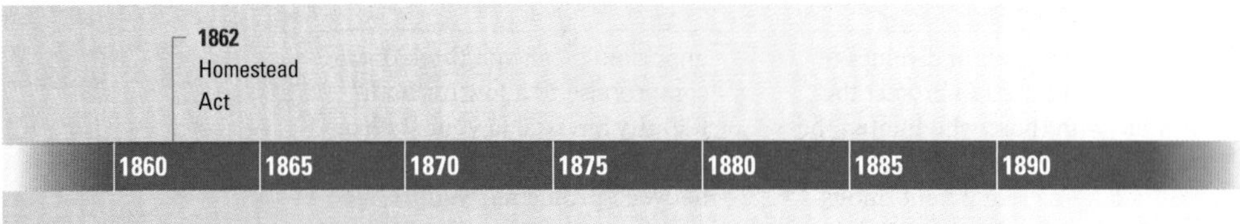

Reviewing Skills

1. Look at the map of Routes of Western Explorers on page 227, and trace the route of Lewis and Clark. Determine how their path followed the natural features of the land.
2. Follow the route of the Union Pacific Railroad in the map on page 433. What natural feature did it follow west of Omaha? What regions of the country did it cover? How does this information relate to what you already know about the difficulties faced by the men who built the railroad? Note the photo at right of the "loop" at Georgetown, Colorado where the railroad crosses Clear Creek, 85 feet above another set of tracks.
3. Based on what you have read in this chapter, determine the causes and effects of the Santee Sioux uprising. Write a paragraph explaining your determination.
4. Suppose you wanted to plan a hiking trip across the Cascade Mountains that would take you across in the straightest line with the least difficulty. What kind of map (or maps) would you need to consult before you made such a trip?

Using Critical Thinking

1. The U. S. government loaned the companies that built the transcontinental railroads between $16,000 and $48,000 for each mile of track they built. The government also gave them vast tracts of public land along the rails. Why do you think the government did this? What effects did it have?
2. Black Elk, a Sioux Indian, wrote in 1886: "Once we were happy in our own country and we were seldom hungry, for then the two-leggeds and the four-leggeds lived together like relatives, and there was plenty for them and for us." What do you think he meant by that statement? What do you think he would have said about the white settlers who took over his lands?
3. It has been said that the settlement of the Great Plains was made possible by the killing of the buffalo, the development of the transcontinental railroads, and the introduction of the windmill. Why was each of those actions important to the settlement of the plains? Would you add any items to that list? Explain your answer.

Preparing for Citizenship

1. **WRITING ACTIVITY** Just as many people who live in America today have very different lifestyles, the Plains Indians and the white settlers had very different ways of living. Make a table comparing the two cultures in the following areas: (a) forms of government, (b) beliefs about owning land, (c) types of shelter, (d) religious beliefs, and (e) ways of making a living. Write a short report explaining how the conflicts between these two cultures were resolved. Include your opinion on whether there could have been a better way for the Indians to have become a part of the United States society.
2. **ART ACTIVITY** Imagine you are working for the government or a railroad company in the late 1800s. Design a poster or video advertisement encouraging settlers to move West.
3. **COLLABORATIVE LEARNING** As a class, form committees that have the goal of attracting more people to your area. Each committee should design advertisements explaining different aspects of the benefits of life in your area. You might stress such things as climate, scenic landscape, good transportation, recreational and cultural opportunities, job opportunities, and the availability of schools.

Answers to Reviewing Skills

1. They followed several rivers, including the Missouri, the Snake, and the Colorado.
2. The Union Pacific Railroad followed the Platte River and crossed the Great Plains, the Rocky Mountains, and part of the Great Basin. By looking at the relief map, students can better see the great variety of regions that created difficulties for the workers.
3. Refer students to Understanding Cause and Effect on pages 398–399.
4. Students would need to look at a topographical map. Often hiking clubs provide regional maps with specific trails outlined.

Answers to Using Critical Thinking

1. Students should point out how the transcontinental railroad opened up new territory for the nation and revolutionized domestic trade.
2. Ask students to consider how differently the Indians and the government viewed natural resources. Could they ever have come to an agreement or compromise?
3. Students might also include in their answers how advancements in technology in white society affected relations with the first settlers of the land, the American Indians.

Answers to Preparing for Citizenship

1. **WRITING ACTIVITY** Tables should include information from the chapter. Allow for personal opinion in students' reports.
2. **ART ACTIVITY** Depending on available media equipment, ask students to expand on this activity by creating similar advertisements that might be used in the future to encourage people to settle on other planets.
3. **COLLABORATIVE LEARNING** Direct students to tourist bureaus and chambers of commerce for information on their area.

CHAPTER 15

Planning at a Glance

Industry and Workers

	Objectives	Reading Support *and* Other Resources	Diverse Learning Strategies
Lesson 1 Building the American Dream *pp. 442–446* 1–2 days	• Explain how inventions helped U.S. industry grow. • Evaluate the role of entrepreneurs in the United States' becoming an industrial power. • Describe what is meant by the American Dream.	• **Workbook** or **Reading Support:** pp. 212–215 Review p. 50 Extra Support/Transition p. 50 Multi-lang. Sum. pp. 99–100 • **Other Resources:** Geography Kit; Posters 5, 7; Study Guide p. 64	Access Act. **(SDAIE)** TE p. 443 Visual Learning **(Visual)** TE p. 444 Research **(GATE)** TE p. 445 Audiotapes of Multi-language Lesson Summaries **(Auditory)**
Lesson 2 Moving into Industrial Cities *pp. 447–453* 2–3 days	• Identify the main characteristics of an industrial city. • Explain why so many rural people migrated to cities. • List the factors that caused black Southerners to move to the North.	• **Workbook** or **Reading Support:** pp. 216–219 Review p. 51 Extra Support/Transition p. 51 Multi-lang. Sum. pp. 101–102 • **Other Resources:** Geography Kit, Study Guide p. 65	Access Strat. **(Extra Support)** TE p. 448 Art Connection **(Kinesthetic)** TE p. 449 Making Charts **(Visual)** TE p. 452 Audiotapes of Multi-language Lesson Summaries **(Auditory)**
Skill: Comparing Population Maps *p. 454*	• Use maps with graduated circles to determine population.	• **Other Resources:** Geography Kit, Study Guide p. 66	
Lesson 3 The Workers' Changing World *pp. 455–461* 1–2 days	• Describe production along an assembly line. • Describe ways in which workers were exploited. • Identify the role of early labor unions in organizing workers, including early strikes.	• **Workbook** or **Reading Support:** pp. 220–223 Review p. 52 Lesson Support/Transition p. 52 Multi-lang. Sum. pp. 103-104 • **Other Resources:** Study Guide p. 67	Access Strat. **(Extra Support)** TE p. 456 Visual Learning **(Visual)** TE p. 457 Role Playing **(Kinesthetic)** TE p. 460 Audiotapes of Multi-language Lesson Summaries **(Auditory)**
Lesson 4 Destination American *pp. 462–467* 1–2 days	• Contrast the immigrants to the United States after 1870 with earlier immigrants. • Compare immigrants' jobs and experiences in the late 1800s. • Explain how immigrants helped American industry.	• **Workbook** or **Reading Support:** pp. 224–227 Review p. 53 Lesson Support/Transition p. 53 Multi-lang. Sum. pp. 105–106 • **Other Resources:** Geography Kit, Study Guide p. 68, Study Print 10	Access Strat. **(SDAIE)** TE p. 463 Visual Learning **(Visual)** TE p. 466 Writing a Letter **(GATE)** TE p. 466 Audiotapes of Multi-language Lesson Summaries **(Auditory)**
Chapter Review *pp. 468–469* 1 day		Chapter 15 Test pp. 57–60 *(See facsimiles on TE p. 763.)*	Assessment Multiple-Use Masters pp. 81–88

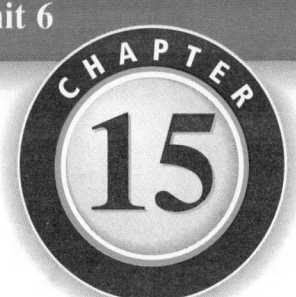

Reading Support Resources *for Every Lesson*

Reading and Review

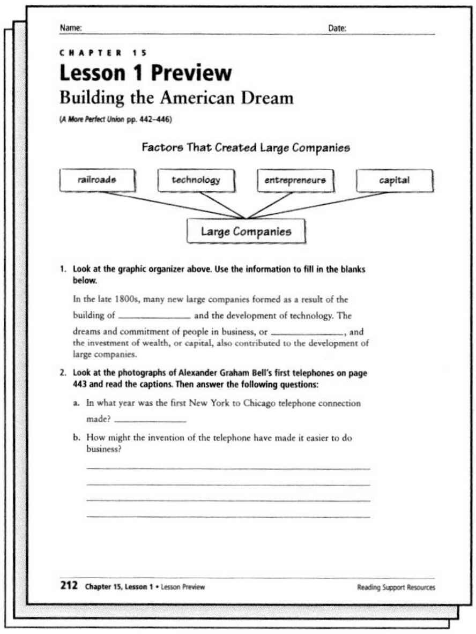
Name: Date:

CHAPTER 15

Lesson 1 Preview

Building the American Dream

(*A More Perfect Union* pp. 442–446)

Factors That Created Large Companies

railroads · technology · entrepreneurs · capital → Large Companies

1. **Look at the graphic organizer above. Use the information to fill in the blanks below.**

   In the late 1800s, many new large companies formed as a result of the building of ______ and the development of technology. The dreams and commitment of people in business, or ______, and the investment of wealth, or capital, also contributed to the development of large companies.

2. **Look at the photographs of Alexander Graham Bell's first telephones on page 443 and read the captions. Then answer the following questions:**

   a. In what year was the first New York to Chicago telephone connection made? ______

   b. How might the invention of the telephone have made it easier to do business?

212 Chapter 15, Lesson 1 • Lesson Preview — Reading Support Resources

- **Chapter Overview*** p. 211
- **Lesson Previews*** using graphic organizers from the Teacher's Edition pp. 212, 216, 220, 224
- **Reading Strategies*** pp. 213, 217, 221, 225
- **Lesson Summaries*** pp. 214–215, 218–219, 222–223, 226–227
- **Lesson Reviews** pp. 50, 51, 52, 53

* **Workbook** includes starred items.

Multi-language Summaries

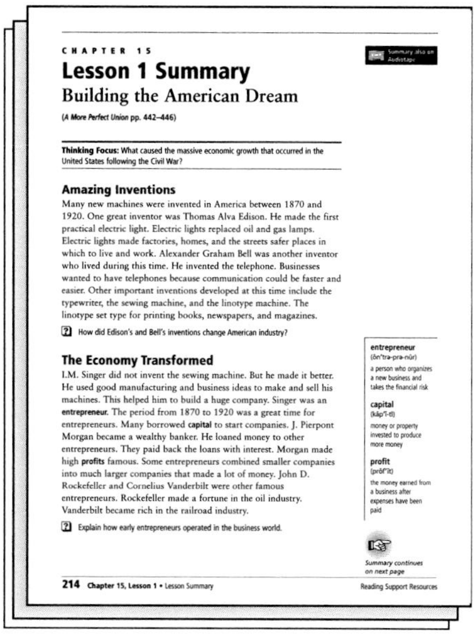
CHAPTER 15

Lesson 1 Summary

Building the American Dream

(*A More Perfect Union* pp. 442–446)

Summary also on Audiotape

Thinking Focus: What caused the massive economic growth that occurred in the United States following the Civil War?

Amazing Inventions

Many new machines were invented in America between 1870 and 1920. One great inventor was Thomas Alva Edison. He made the first practical electric light. Electric lights replaced oil and gas lamps. Electric lights made factories, homes, and the streets safer places in which to live and work. Alexander Graham Bell was another inventor who lived during this time. He invented the telephone. Businesses wanted to have telephones because communication could be faster and easier. Other important inventions developed at this time include the typewriter, the sewing machine, and the linotype machine. The linotype set type for printing books, newspapers, and magazines.

? How did Edison's and Bell's inventions change American industry?

The Economy Transformed

I.M. Singer did not invent the sewing machine. But he made it better. He used good manufacturing and business ideas to make and sell his machines. This helped him to build a huge company. Singer was an **entrepreneur.** The period from 1870 to 1920 was a great time for entrepreneurs. Many borrowed **capital** to start companies. J. Pierpont Morgan became a wealthy banker. He loaned money to other entrepreneurs. They paid back the loans with interest. Morgan made high **profits** famous. Some entrepreneurs combined smaller companies into much larger companies that made a lot of money. John D. Rockefeller and Cornelius Vanderbilt were other famous entrepreneurs. Rockefeller made a fortune in the oil industry. Vanderbilt became rich in the railroad industry.

? Explain how early entrepreneurs operated in the business world.

entrepreneur (ŏn'trə-prə-nûr) a person who organizes a new business and takes the financial risk

capital (kăp'ĭ-tl) money or property invested to produce more money

profit (prŏf'ĭt) the money earned from a business after expenses have been paid

Summary continues on next page

214 Chapter 15, Lesson 1 • Lesson Summary — Reading Support Resources

Lesson Summaries in:

- English (See Reading and Review.)
- Spanish pp. 214–215, 218–219, 222–223, 226–227
- Chinese pp. 99–106
- Hmong pp. 99–106
- Khmer pp. 99–106
- Vietnamese pp. 99–106

Summaries available on audiotapes

Lesson Support /Transition

S D A I E

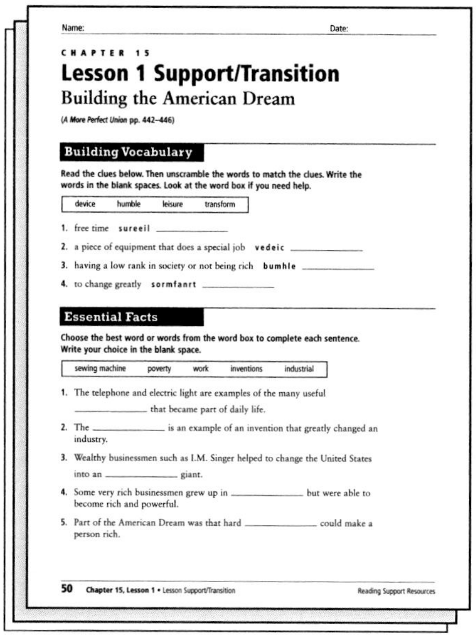
Name: Date:

CHAPTER 15

Lesson 1 Support/Transition

Building the American Dream

(*A More Perfect Union* pp. 442–446)

Building Vocabulary

Read the clues below. Then unscramble the words to match the clues. Write the words in the blank spaces. Look at the word box if you need help.

device · humble · leisure · transform

1. free time **sureeil** ______
2. a piece of equipment that does a special job **vedeic** ______
3. having a low rank in society or not being rich **bumhle** ______
4. to change greatly **sormfanrt** ______

Essential Facts

Choose the best word or words from the word box to complete each sentence. Write your choice in the blank space.

sewing machine · poverty · work · inventions · industrial

1. The telephone and electric light are examples of the many useful ______ that became part of daily life.
2. The ______ is an example of an invention that greatly changed an industry.
3. Wealthy businessmen such as I.M. Singer helped to change the United States into an ______ giant.
4. Some very rich businessmen grew up in ______ but were able to become rich and powerful.
5. Part of the American Dream was that hard ______ could make a person rich.

50 Chapter 15, Lesson 1 • Lesson Support/Transition — Reading Support Resources

Activities for SDAIE

Specially **D**esigned **A**cademic **I**nstruction in **E**nglish

- **Lesson Support/Transition** pp. 50, 51, 52, 53

Technology Options

Internet Support

http://www.eduplace.com

Social Studies Center at Education Place

Internet support for Chapter 15:

- ***Lesson at a Glance***
- ***Ellis Island Immigrants***

Videotape/Videodisc

We the People:

Supports and enhances major topics: **Themes:** ***The Immigrants; The Rise of the City***

American Discovery: Stories of Invention and Ingenuity, Vol. I, II

Software

Student Writing Center® (CD-ROM) (Macintosh® or Windows®)

School to Career

The world is full of inventions that meet very practical needs. Have students each design and construct their own inventions. What need does the invention meet? Hold a classroom inventors' fair where each student could demonstrate his or her invention, how it was built, and the materials used in its construction.

Character Education

Philanthropists such as Carnegie believe in using their wealth to help others. Divide students into small groups, and have each group research a philanthropist of their choice. Then, have them write a biographical sketch of that individual, similar to those done on public television, to present to the class.

CHAPTER
PREVIEW

After students have read the chapter title and the narrative underneath it, point out that between 1850 and 1920 the United States made great technological advances. Refer students to the visuals on these pages to find evidence that this period marked a transition to a modern way of living. *(Introduction of modern transportation: the car; modern means of production: the assembly line; development of modern city around industry; modern entertainment and advertising)*

Looking Back

Ask students to recall from Chapter 14 developments in mining, farming, and transportation. *(Hard rock mining, dry farming, transcontinental railroad)*

Looking Forward

Industry grew rapidly following the completion of the transcontinental railroad. The major changes in people's lives will be described in the next four lessons: Building the American Dream, Moving into Industrial Cities, The Workers' Changing World, and Destination: America.

Chapter 15
Industry and Workers

After the Civil War, a new America was in the making. New building techniques transformed the nation's cities. Immigrants expanded the nation's workforce. Together with new inventions, new methods of manufacturing, and new ways to sell products, the United States became an industrial leader.

Use of the assembly line cut the price of the Model T in half. Millions of people could now buy cars.

Workers at the Ford factory assembly line could put together a Model T Ford in an hour and a half.

1850 | 1860 | 1870 | 1880

Presidents

- 1850-1853 Fillmore
- 1853-1857 Pierce
- 1857-1861 Buchanan
- 1861-1865 Lincoln
- 1865-1869 A. Johnson
- 1869-1877 Grant
- 1877-1881 Hayes
- 1881 Garfield
- 188 Arth

1850

BACKGROUND

By the mid-1800s, electric trolleys were a popular form of city transportation. They were twice as fast and carried three times more people than horse-drawn cars. Public transportation rearranged the physical form of American cities, dividing them into an inner center of commerce and outer region of commuter suburbs.

New Ways of Marketing

Two developments in business led to a change in how Americans purchased consumer goods: the department store and the mail order catalog. Introduced in Philadelphia in 1861 by John Wanamaker, department stores were found in all major cities by the end of the decade. People liked the displays and the fixed price for each item in the store. In 1872, Aaron Montgomery Ward introduced mail order catalogs and modern goods became available to people in rural areas. Catalogs from Montgomery Ward and from Sears, Roebuck and Company were even used as textbooks to teach students reading, geography, and mathematics.

Early Labor Unions

The Noble Order of the Knights of Labor was founded as a secret society in 1869 and became national in 1879. The Knights "sought to secure to the workers the full enjoyment of the wealth they create" by establishing cooperative systems of production and starting the eight-hour workday. In 1884 and 1885, the Knights began a political

Immigrants throng to factories in industrial cities such as Cleveland, seeking new jobs and a new life in America.

1888 The lantern slide projector is one of the many inventions that provide Americans with new kinds of entertainment.

Advertisers used pictures of stylishly dressed women and children to promote labor-saving devices for the home.

1890 | 1900 | 1910 | 1920

-1889 eland

1889-1893 B. Harrison

1893-1897 Cleveland

1897-1901 McKinley

1901-1909 T. Roosevelt

1909-1913 Taft

1913-1921 Wilson

1920

Understanding the Visuals

Draw students' attention to the visuals on these pages. How did these advances change the way people lived and worked? *(Cars allowed people to commute faster and easier; assembly lines might have created worker boredom; sewing machines and lawn mowers eased chores; and industrial towns created jobs.)*

Understanding Chronology

Point out the timeline and explain that this chapter covers the transition from the 19th to the 20th century.

effort to secure labor laws and to create a federal Department of Labor. Leaders of the Knights disagreed with using strikes as a labor weapon, but members found them effective. The American Federation of Labor, founded in 1886, supported workers' interests and did not object to using strikes.

INTRODUCE

Point out the lesson title and ask students to describe what the term *American Dream* means to them. Have students read the Thinking Focus and discuss the phrase "massive economic growth." What kinds of changes does this phrase imply? Ask students to predict the factors that might have contributed to economic growth after the Civil War. Have them read to confirm or reject their predictions.

Key Terms

Vocabulary strategies: T36–37

entrepreneur—a person who organizes and assumes the risk for a business venture

capital—material wealth, such as money or property, invested to produce more wealth

profit—the gain from a business undertaking after expenses have been paid

philanthropist—a person who often funds beneficial public institutions

1850 1920

LESSON 1

Building the American Dream

THINKING FOCUS

What caused the massive economic growth that occurred in the United States following the Civil War?

Key Terms

- entrepreneur
- capital
- profit
- philanthropist

As the sun reached noon that May day in 1876, a chorus broke into the soaring music of Handel's "Hallelujah Chorus," a hundred guns boomed, steam whistles blew, bells rang, and swarms of people cheered. The occasion? It was the Centennial Exhibition in Philadelphia, a gigantic fair celebrating 100 years of American independence.

Over the next six months, eight million people jammed the exhibition grounds, jostling to see the exhibits. They marveled at animated wax figures, an automated baby feeder, and a gas-heated iron. They sampled bread made with a new kind of yeast, the products from a cheese factory, and foods from many countries. What impressed them most, however, were the wondrous new machines.

These machines were put into motion when President Ulysses S. Grant started the gigantic Corliss steam engine. Forty feet high, the Corliss engine operated 13 acres of machinery. Humming textile machines combed wool, spun cotton, and sewed cloth. Clattering presses printed newspapers and stamped wallpaper. Other machines sawed logs, pumped water, and carved wood.

Commented Western poet Joaquin Miller, "How the American's heart thrills with pride and love of his land as he contemplates the vast exhibition of art and prowess here." He then predicted, "Great as it seems today, it is but the acorn from which shall grow the wide-spreading oak of a century's progress."

The Centennial did indeed herald the world of the future. It announced America's coming of age as one of the great industrial nations of the world.

➤ *The 1876 Centennial Exposition in Philadelphia attracted eight million people. Visitors gathered to see America's latest technological advances.*

Objectives

1. Explain how inventions helped make the United States an industrial power.
2. Evaluate the role entrepreneurs played in making the United States an industrial power.
3. Describe what is meant by the American Dream.

Graphic Overview

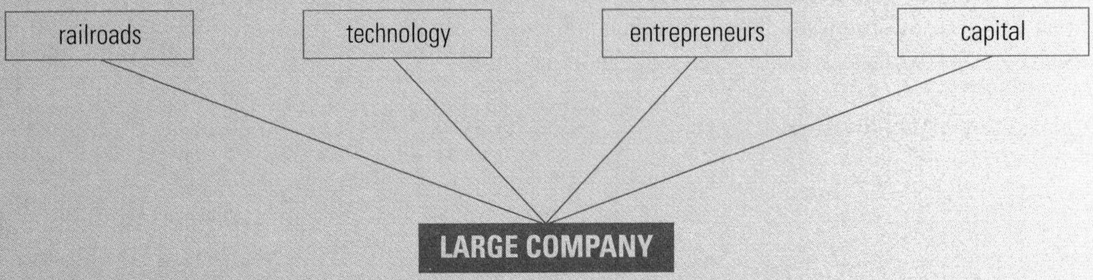

Amazing Inventions

Between 1870 and 1920, U.S. inventors came up with many mechanical and scientific innovations. Ranging from impractical gadgets to major innovations, their inventions poured into the U.S. Patent Office, where new inventions are registered. Between 1860 and 1900 alone, some 676,000 patents were filed. Many of these inventions became part of daily life everywhere.

One of the most influential inventions, a practical electric light, radically changed the face of cities. Lighted streets discouraged crime and invited people to stroll through the city after dark. Blinking lights on theater entrances caught public attention. By replacing oil and gas lamps, electric lights eliminated the danger of fires in theaters, factories, and homes.

The Electric Spark

Thomas Alva Edison, one of the greatest inventors in history, developed the first practical electric light. He also developed the generating system needed to produce electricity as well as hundreds of other useful inventions.

Edison is an outstanding example of a person whose curiosity and imagination brought him great success. Educated largely by his schoolteacher mother and motivated by boundless curiosity, Edison at the age of nine was busy conducting chemistry experiments. In later life, he performed as many as 10,000 experiments for a single project.

Impatient to try out new ideas, he often worked around the clock, stopping only for brief naps in a corner of his workroom. "Genius," Edison said, "is one percent inspiration and ninety-nine percent perspiration." In addition to the electric light, Edison's phonograph and improved motion pictures helped change the way people spent their leisure time.

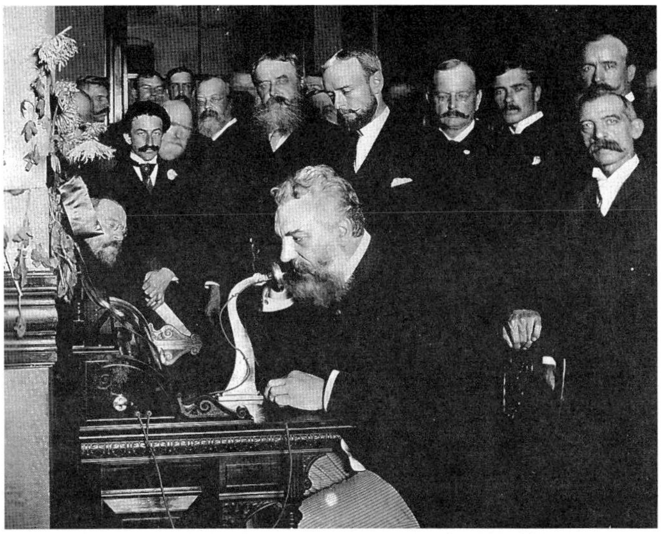

Alexander Graham Bell is seated at the New York end of the first New York-Chicago telephone connection in 1892.

Faster Communications

Almost equaling the electric light in importance was the telephone invented by Alexander Graham Bell. Like his father, who taught the hearing-impaired to speak, Scottish-born Bell was fascinated by the mechanics of speech. Bell developed the idea of transmitting speech by electric waves and worked 10 years to devise the necessary machinery.

In March 1876, Bell patented the telephone, and within a year the first telephone company was founded. Businesses everywhere wanted this new invention. By 1900, about 1.5 million telephones were in use in the United States. The age of modern communications had begun.

Bell's first model of his 1875 telephone was exhibited at the Centennial Exhibition in 1876.

Two other innovations that made business operations easier were the typewriter and the linotype machine. In 1872, the first commercially produced keyboard typewriter was developed by Christopher Latham Sholes in Milwaukee, Wisconsin. Businesses enthusiastically welcomed the new machine, which

DEVELOP

Before students read the lesson, have them work in small groups to brainstorm a list of inventions created prior to this century that have made our way of life today different from life in America before the Civil War. Point out the heading *Amazing Inventions* on this page. Tell students to circle inventions on their list as they read about them in the lesson, adding any that are not already on their list.

ECONOMICS

Critical Thinking

Which of Edison's inventions made it possible for his electric light to be used in homes and factories? *(A power generating system to produce electricity)* What were some of the effects of his inventions on urban life? *(Lighted streets discouraged crime; electric lights helped prevent fires; movies and the phonograph provided new forms of entertainment.)*

Access Strategy

Ask students to think about an invention that would make their lives easier or more fun. Ask volunteers to share their ideas, and then have the class vote for their favorite invention idea. Have students name all the things they would need in order to manufacture and sell the new invention. Have a volunteer write their responses on the board. *(A patent, a manufacturing site, workers, a way to transport raw materials and finished products, money to buy raw materials and pay workers)* Have them discuss how they might go about obtaining these things.

Tell students that they will be reading in this lesson about a time when there were many new inventions and new ideas about manufacturing. In this lesson they will learn about the creation of big business—a new force in American life and politics.

Access Activity

Refer students to the photographs on this page of Alexander Graham Bell and the 1875 telephone. What might their lives be like without the telephone? How might it change the way people do business? Students can also consider what life might be like without these inventions: the light bulb, the typewriter, and the adding machine.

ECONOMICS

Critical Thinking

Remind students that I.M. Singer was the first person to spend $1 million a year advertising his product. How do they think his success affected other American businesses? *(They began advertising heavily.)* In what ways did the growth of Singer's company reflect the growth of American industry? *(Quick adoption of technological improvements and organizational efficiencies)*

■ *Factories used Edison's electric lights, which were safer than oil or gas; Bell's telephone revolutionized communications.*

➤ *In 1845, Elias Howe built this sewing machine—the first of its kind—but I. M. Singer developed the modern machine we know today.*

helped productivity. Author Mark Twain commented, "One may lean back in his chair and work it. It piles up an awful stack of words on one page. It don't muss things or scatter ink blots around."

The introduction of the linotype machine in 1884 by German-born Ottmar Mergenthaler revolutionized the publishing industry. Instead of positioning each line of type manually letter by letter, an operator used a typewriter-like keyboard to set a whole line of type automatically. A full page of type was then inked and run through the rotary press (in use since 1846). This invention greatly speeded the production of newspapers, magazines, and books.

In addition to the telephone, typewriter, and linotype machine, adding machines and cash registers increased the speed of business transactions. All these machines helped to transform communications and production in American business.

How Do We Know?

HISTORY *Catalogs, such as the Sears and Roebuck catalog, were filled with pictures of mass-produced products. As industry grew, advertising became important. Newspapers from the late 1800s carried advertisements with detailed drawings of the latest inventions.*

From Invention to Industry

Another invention that revolutionized an industry was the sewing machine. Since the 1700s, inventors had experimented with crude mechanical sewing devices. But the first practical sewing machine was not patented until 1846.

While working in a factory that made machinery for the cotton industry, Elias Howe realized that sewing was the only part of the process still done by hand. For the next five years he labored to invent a sewing machine. Howe demonstrated the new machine's speed by competing with five girls sewing by hand. Although Howe held the patent on the sewing machine, the marvelous device came to be associated with a machinist named I. M. Singer.

In 1851, Singer was given a sewing machine to fix. He immediately saw how it could be improved, and within a short time he set up a company that used a unique system to manufacture sewing machines. An organizational genius and innovator, Singer was the first person to spend one million dollars a year on advertising.

By 1880, the Singer Manufacturing Company was manufacturing over 500,000 sewing machines each year and shipping them to homes and factories all over the world. By continually adopting new technological developments and using energetic promotion, the company grew into the world's largest manufacturer of a single product. ■

■ *How did Edison's and Bell's inventions change American industry?*

➤ *Advertisements for the Singer sewing machine such as the one shown here boasted about the convenience of the cabinet table where the machine could be stored.*

Visual Learning

Encourage students to look carefully at the advertisement on this page of the Singer sewing machine. What is the message of this advertisement? *(Convenience for mothers)* How has advertising changed over the years? In what ways has it stayed the same?

Economic Context

The growth of big business resulted in many new office jobs. Up to this time, male clerks had handled paperwork in business offices. As paperwork increased and as office machines such as telephones, typewriters, and addressographs came into use, the number of office jobs expanded rapidly. For the first time, women entered the business world in large numbers. Businesses were glad to hire women for these new jobs. Women's wages were lower than men's for the same job; and by 1890 a majority of high school graduates were women.

New jobs for men included many middle management positions. Companies began to employ scientific management practices. Employers conducted time and motion studies to increase the speed and productivity of workers, and they kept track of employee work hours with time clocks.

The Economy Transformed

Singer started his business with very little money. Through innovative manufacturing and efficient business methods he built a huge industry. He is an example of the **entrepreneur** *(ahn truh pruh NUR)*, a farsighted, ambitious person who organizes and assumes the risk of a business venture. Between 1870 and 1920, entrepreneurs built companies that helped to transform the United States into an industrial giant.

Building Bigger Businesses

Efficient, large-scale production like Singer's depended on large amounts of **capital** or wealth—money or property used in a business. Capital is used to build factories, then to buy raw materials and to hire employees. Some money came from the government. For example, to promote the building of railroads, the government granted the railroad companies huge tracts of free land for the tracks. The companies could then sell the adjoining property to raise money. Other funds came from banks and individual investors. Banker J. Pierpont Morgan, for example, loaned money to companies manufacturing steel, farm equipment, telephones, and electricity. Each loan was repaid with interest. The amount left over after all expenses had been paid was **profit**.

Often entrepreneurs combined several small businesses to form larger companies. Well organized and efficiently operated, these huge companies repaid investors several times over.

Because large companies often made high profits, banks did not hesitate to lend them money. In this way big companies tended to get bigger. Soon men like John D. Rockefeller, one of the founders of the U.S. oil industry, banker J. Pierpont Morgan, and railroad entrepreneur Cornelius Vanderbilt became fabulously wealthy and earned the nickname "Captains of Industry." ■

■ *Explain how early entrepreneurs operated in the business world.*

Realizing the American Dream

Many successful entrepreneurs rose to their positions of power from great poverty. These wealthy people represented "the American Dream." Young people were taught to believe that they could be financially wealthy, no matter how humble their beginnings, if only they would work hard enough. The popular writer Horatio Alger promoted this idea in his many novels with the theme of rags-to-riches. The heroes in his novels were poor boys who achieved wealth, a high social position, and power through hard work, virtuous living, and an unusual amount of luck.

The American Dream Achieved

Perhaps there is no better example of someone achieving the American Dream than Andrew Carnegie. The son of a Scottish weaver, Carnegie came to America at the age of 12 and began working for low wages at a cotton mill near Pittsburgh. By age 17, he was private secretary to the president of the Pennsylvania Railroad.

Carnegie became rich from an oil well he bought in his mid-twenties. He moved into steel production and introduced the newly invented blast furnace. It used a process in which a blast of air was introduced as iron ore melted. The oxygen in the air

For thousands of readers, Horatio Alger's heroes represented the American Dream.

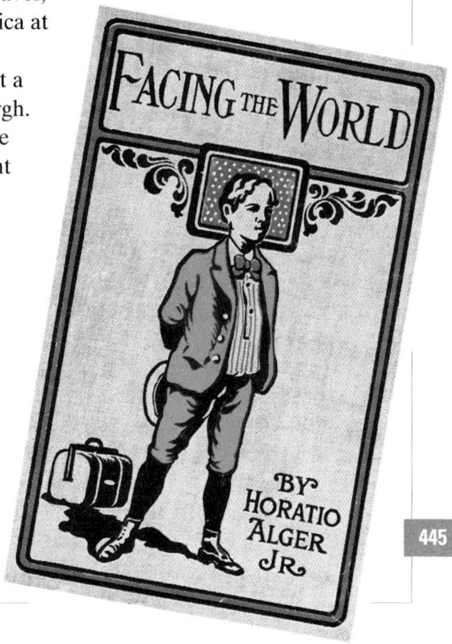

SOCIAL SYSTEMS

Critical Thinking

Ask students to explain why libraries were especially important to Carnegie. How did his philanthropy relate to the idea of the American Dream—wealth achieved through hard work and virtuous living? *(He saw educational opportunities as the key to success.)*

■ *They developed an idea for a business; raised money from investors to begin their operations; and used innovative, efficient manufacturing and business methods to build an industry.*

Language Arts Connection

Select appropriate passages from one of Horatio Alger's books to read aloud to the class. Encourage students to discuss the ideals expressed in the book. Be sure students understand the meaning of the word *realize* in the heading *Realizing the American Dream* on page 445. To what extent is this type of rags-to-riches dream still alive today?

Research

The period from the 1870s to 1920 was a very exciting period for inventors. Ask students to research one of the following and report their findings to the class:

- the life story of an inventor, such as George Westinghouse, Nikola Tesla, George Eastman, or Lewis Edson Waterman
- an invention, such as the automobile, the internal combustion engine, or the air brake (railroads)

Study Skills

After students have read the lesson, ask them to organize the information into an outline with the following three headings: Inventors, Entrepreneurs, Captains of Industry. Under each heading, have students list the people named in the lesson who fit the category, as well as the inventions or industries associated with each person.

■ *The term* rags to riches *is used to describe people like Andrew Carnegie, who began poor and achieved wealth, usually through hard work.*

CLOSE

Have students answer the Thinking Focus and evaluate the predictions they made before reading the lesson. Ask students to return to the lists of inventions they made earlier and explain how these inventions changed peoples' lives. Then copy on the board the Graphic Overview from page 442 with only the final theme labeled and have students complete it. Have them name the ways in which large companies might have used the inventions on their lists.

▲ *The Carnegie Library in Pittsburgh is one of many libraries established by philanthropist Andrew Carnegie.*

■ *What does the term "rags to riches" mean? Give an example of someone who "realized" the American Dream.*

combined with the carbon in the iron, leaving the steel nearly pure. The new process was so efficient that Carnegie's factory produced more steel than all the other U.S. mills combined. The cost of a ton of steel dropped from $100 to $12.

Despite this lower price, demand and Carnegie's profits soared because of the many new ways in which steel was being used. These uses included rails for railroads, frames for buildings and bridges, and everyday wire, nails, and bolts. Soon Carnegie owned not only steel mills and the pig iron and coal used to make steel but also the railroads and ships that carried the finished product to market. By 1900, the company's yearly profits had reached $40 million. Carnegie had become one of the world's richest men.

Carnegie was quick to defend the accumulation of great wealth. He believed that business benefited when a few industrialists controlled the wealth, because such leaders were interested in promoting efficiency and good organization.

The Gospel of Wealth

In later life, Carnegie became a famous **philanthropist**—a person who promotes human welfare by funding beneficial public institutions. Though he himself had almost no formal education, Carnegie believed that access to books was a key to success. He therefore established libraries in towns throughout the United States. He also gave large sums to set up many scholarships, to construct public buildings, and to found the Endowment for International Peace.

Carnegie's great generosity sprang from his belief that those who acquired great wealth had a responsibility to give a portion of it back to society. In 1889, he wrote a series of essays expressing this idea. Known as the "Gospel of Wealth," Carnegie's ideas reflected his belief that hard work brought success. ■

REVIEW

1. **FOCUS** What caused the massive economic growth that occurred in the United States following the Civil War?
2. **CONNECT** How do you think the railroad contributed to the development of American cities?
3. **CULTURE** How did inventions change the way Americans lived and worked?
4. **ECONOMICS** How did new developments in transportation, communications, and production affect business?
5. **CRITICAL THINKING** What does the term *American Dream* mean?
6. **WRITING ACTIVITY** Imagine how different your life would be without a telephone. Write a short essay describing how an average day would be different if you couldn't use a phone.

Homework Options

Ask students to list all the ways in which electricity is used in their homes.

Study Guide: page 64.

Answers to Review Questions

1. Many inventions and the rise of entrepreneurs caused economic growth.
2. The railroad brought increased mobility and opened new markets across the nation.
3. Inventions helped people work more efficiently and spend more time on leisure activities.
4. These developments made businesses more efficient and thus more profitable.
5. Sample answer: The American Dream reflects the belief that anyone can achieve wealth and success through hard work. Allow for personal opinion.
6. Encourage students to focus on three or four main differences.

1850 1860 1870 1920

L E S S O N 2

Moving into Industrial Cities

A popular legend says that a cow kicked over a lantern and started the great fire that burned down much of Chicago in October 1871.

Whether the cow actually ignited the blaze is unknown. Historians are sure, however, that the flames first appeared in the O'Leary barn. High winds fanned the fire through block after block of wooden buildings. The blaze, an eyewitness later wrote, devoured "the most stately and massive buildings as though they had been the cardboard playthings of a child."

Fleeing before the flames, terrified crowds plunged into the icy waters of Lake Michigan. The fire raged for over 24 hours, destroying 18,000 buildings. Firefighters had to dynamite entire city blocks in order to deprive the fire of fuel and bring it under control.

The fire's toll was staggering: 300 people died, and 90,000 people—nearly a third of the city's population—lost their homes. Property damage amounted to $200 million.

Yet the disaster did not destroy the spirit of the people, who immediately began to rebuild the city. The massive reconstruction attracted some of the nation's best architects as well as thousands of laborers, many of them immigrants. Within a year Chicago was well on its way to becoming the second largest city in the United States and revolutionizing American architecture in the process.

THINKING FOCUS

How did industrial development and the growth of cities change American life during the late 1800s and early 1900s?

Key Terms

- urban society

This lithograph by Currier and Ives shows Chicago's great fire of October 1871.

INTRODUCE

Point out that the growth of American cities up until the last decades of the 1800s had been based on trade, while the growth of the new industrial cities was based on manufacturing. Have students read the Thinking Focus and then read the lesson to find out how American life changed in the late 1800s and early 1900s.

Key Term

Vocabulary strategies: T36–37

urban society—a social structure that is based on city life

Graphic Overview

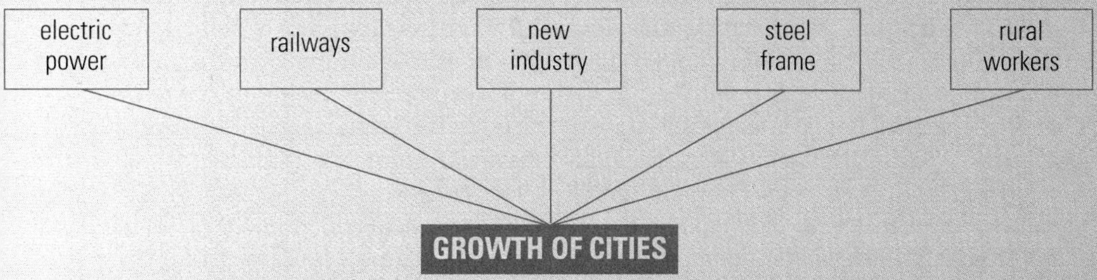

Objectives

1. Identify the main characteristics of an industrial city.
2. Explain why so many rural people migrated to cities.
3. List the factors that caused black Southerners to move to the North.

DEVELOP

Copy on the board the Graphic Overview from page 447 and point out that it highlights five major factors that contributed to the growth of industrial cities. Have students read to find out why each of these factors was important. Have students use these factors as headings in a chart in which they will list specific ways in which each factor contributed to the growth of cities as they read the lesson.

ECONOMICS

Critical Thinking

Encourage students to consider the advantages and disadvantages of living in late-nineteenth-century American cities such as Cleveland. *(Advantage—people could find work in industry; disadvantage—workers lived in inadequate housing, there was no management of sewage and industrial wastes, and the air was polluted.)*

Industrial Cities Develop

The rebirth of Chicago was part of a dramatic industrial expansion that caused incredible growth in the nation's cities. Between 1850 and 1900, the population of many American cities doubled and then doubled again. As the map on page 452 shows, many of today's large cities grew from towns to cities during this period. Such growth heralded the birth of a new **urban society**, a society based on city life.

Industry Creates Cities

Before the Civil War, most factories were built along lakes or rivers in order to harness water power and to take advantage of the low cost of water transportation. As oil and electricity began to power the machines of industry, these factory towns experienced tremendous growth. Cities that were centrally located became junctions for many railroad lines.

Cleveland, Ohio, was one of the cities that made the dramatic change from a commercial to an industrial center. Located on Lake Erie, Cleveland was a busy town of 6,000 people in the early 1800s. In 1851, when the railroad connected it with Columbus, the state capital, Cleveland was transformed into a thriving city. By 1900, nearly 290,000 people lived there.

Railroad connections brought iron ore from Minnesota and coal from Pennsylvania, helping Cleveland become a major producer of locomotives and other iron products. During this period the city also became the chief refining center for Pennsylvania oil. In 1870, John D. Rockefeller organized the Standard Oil Company in Cleveland.

A traveler entering Cleveland passed bustling steel factories and oil refineries on the outskirts. The poor part of the city housed thousands of immigrants—Hungarians, Poles, Lithuanians, and Russians—who worked in the mills. Most lived in shabby houses where several families were crowded together. Few houses had any plumbing, and the stench of wastes

Cleveland's rapid growth as an industrial center led to a population in 1900 that was nearly 50 times greater than that in the early 1800s.

Access Activity

Read the lesson opener aloud and ask students to discuss why the Chicago fire spread so rapidly. *(Buildings were wooden.)* Have them list possible reasons why a fire in a large city today would not be as destructive as the Chicago fire. *(Fewer wooden buildings, more smoke alarms, better fire-fighters)*

Access Strategy

Ask students why they think people choose to live in cities or rural areas today. Tell them that in the late 1800s many people moved from rural areas to cities primarily because of the availability of jobs. Ask students to think about what a city must provide for people in addition to jobs. Have students list things that people who move to cities need. *(Housing, a place to buy food, a water supply, streets, public transportation)* After they have listed as many things as they can think of, ask them what is likely to happen if a city grows very quickly. What kinds of problems might rapid growth cause in a city's ability to provide the things that people need? *(Too many people too quickly, not enough resources, not enough money to provide services)*

Tell students that this lesson will tell about why cities grew, who came to cities, how people adjusted to cities, and how cities adjusted to the new populations.

and garbage mixed with factory smoke, choking the air. Sludge from industries and sewage from homes were dumped into Lake Erie, contributing to widespread disease.

Yet a traveler could also feel a sense of excitement in Cleveland. On every side new buildings were going up; horse-drawn wagons, trolley cars (vehicles powered by an overhead wire), and pedestrians crowded the streets. Vendors sold vegetables, coal, ice, and fish. Newspaperboys such as the one shown on page 450 yelled the day's headlines. In the city's center, shoppers thronged to the new department stores, where they could buy everything from shoes to china.

Cities That Specialized

Cleveland's main industry was building locomotives for the nation's busy railroads. Other cities that specialized in one regional product were Pittsburgh, Pennsylvania (steel); Minneapolis, Minnesota (flour from midwestern wheat); Schenectady, New York (electrical goods); Corning, New York (glass); Memphis, Tennessee (cottonseed oil); Birmingham, Alabama (iron and steel); Denver, Colorado (mining); and Portland, Oregon (metal processing).

Chicago, with the largest manufacturing base of all, also enjoyed a strategic location. Located between the East and the Great Plains, Chicago was linked to the Atlantic Ocean by the Great Lakes and the St. Lawrence River. A canal joining it to the Illinois and Mississippi rivers connected it with New Orleans and the Gulf of Mexico. Chicago's superior transportation system linked it to resources and markets all over the country. The city quickly became the hub, or center, of U.S. railroad traffic.

New Uses for Steel

In the growing industrial cities, space became increasingly valuable. For decades, architects had dreamed of lofty buildings that would tower into the sky, but such buildings had been impossible to build with wood, brick, and stone. Those materials could not support the enormous weight of many stories. The use of steel frames as interior skeletons solved this problem. In Chicago, William LeBaron Jenney designed the Home Insurance building, the first skyscraper constructed with a metal frame, in 1884.

Steel frames also made the suspension bridge possible. The bridge's roadway is suspended by thick cables, and is strong enough to support trains and other traffic.

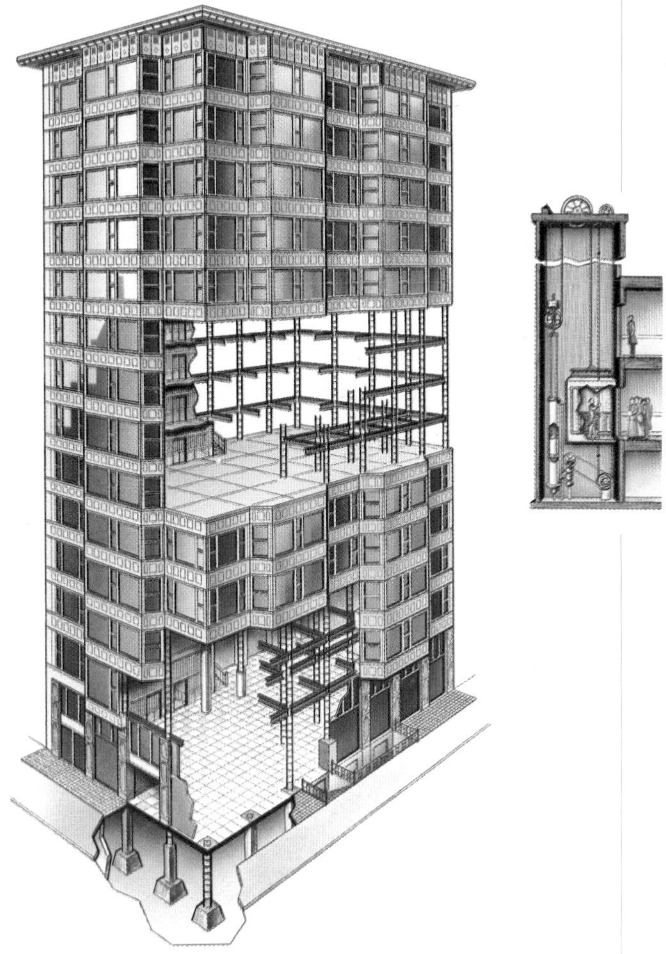

The Reliance building, constructed in 1895 in Chicago, is an example of steel frame construction. Electric elevators moved people to the upper stories. Multistory buildings changed the American cityscape forever.

GEOGRAPHY

Critical Thinking

What factors made Chicago's location ideal for industrial growth? *(Its proximity to railroad and water transportation routes; its location between the East and the Great Plains on Lake Michigan)*

Art Connection

The rebuilding of Chicago gave birth to an exciting period in American architecture. Have students do research on famous Chicago architects of the time, such as William Le Baron Jenney, Daniel Burnham, and Louis Sullivan. If possible, display pictures of some of their buildings. Have interested students work in small groups to create a scale model of an early skyscraper.

Language Arts Connection

The urban landscape of America's industrial cities has inspired many poets. Read aloud from Carl Sandburg's *Chicago Poems* first published in 1914. You may want to choose one of his poems for choral reading by the entire group or by a few interested students. If your students live in a city, have them write city poems of their own.

Visual Learning

What technological developments made the building of skyscrapers possible? *(Steel-frame construction and elevators)* What else can be learned about the Reliance Building from the illustration on this page? *(Number of floors, shape and design of building)* What cannot be learned? *(Interior layout, exterior building materials)*

Note: You may wish to use this Moment in Time after students read the section under the heading The Job-Seekers.

VISUAL LEARNING

Critical Thinking

Have students look at the picture of the Chicago newsboy. Ask them to think about why a boy of his age might do this kind of work. *(Chance to earn money for the family)* What other kinds of work were available at the time for children? *(Factories, small businesses)*

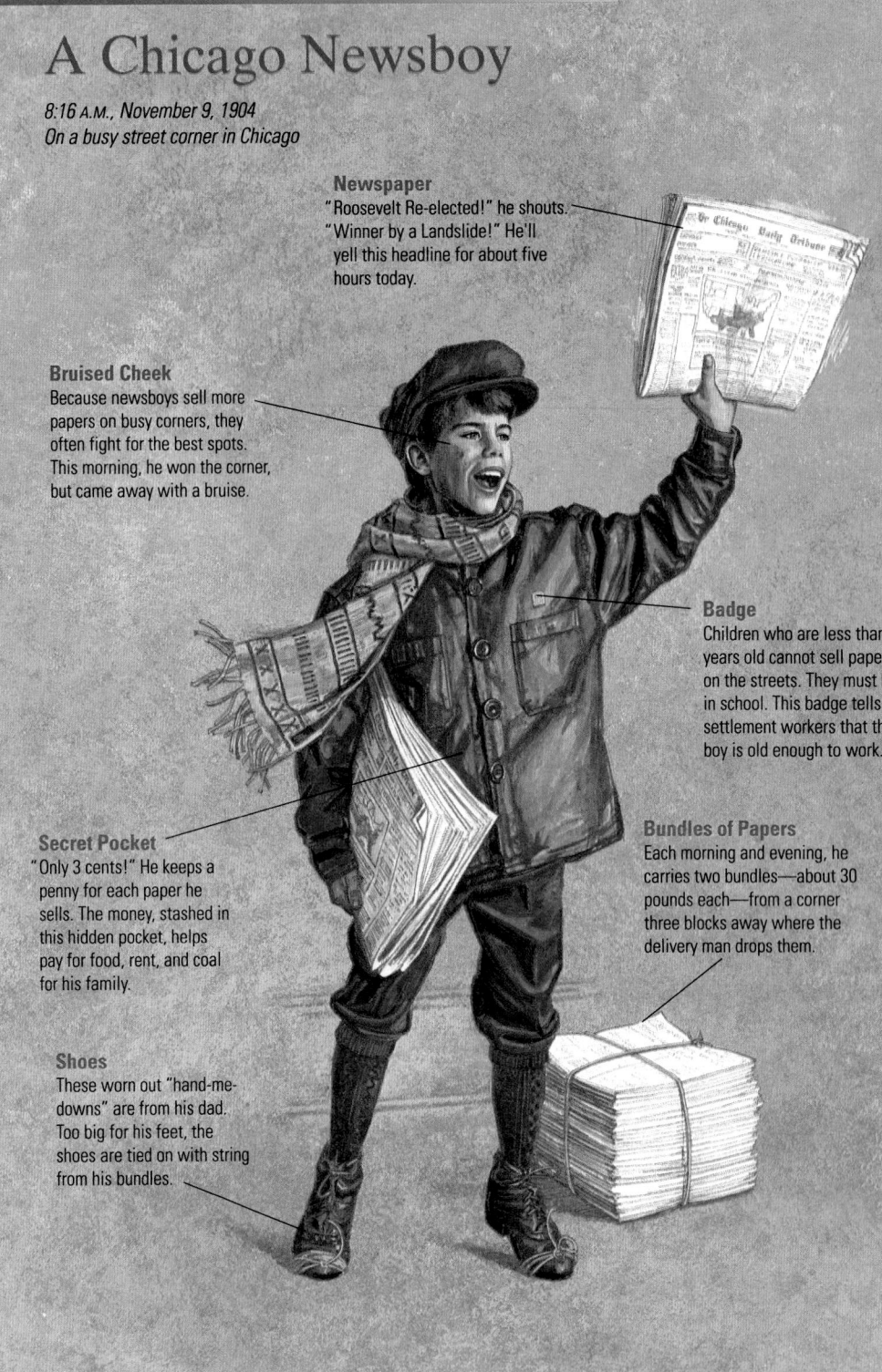

A MOMENT IN TIME

A Chicago Newsboy

8:16 A.M., November 9, 1904
On a busy street corner in Chicago

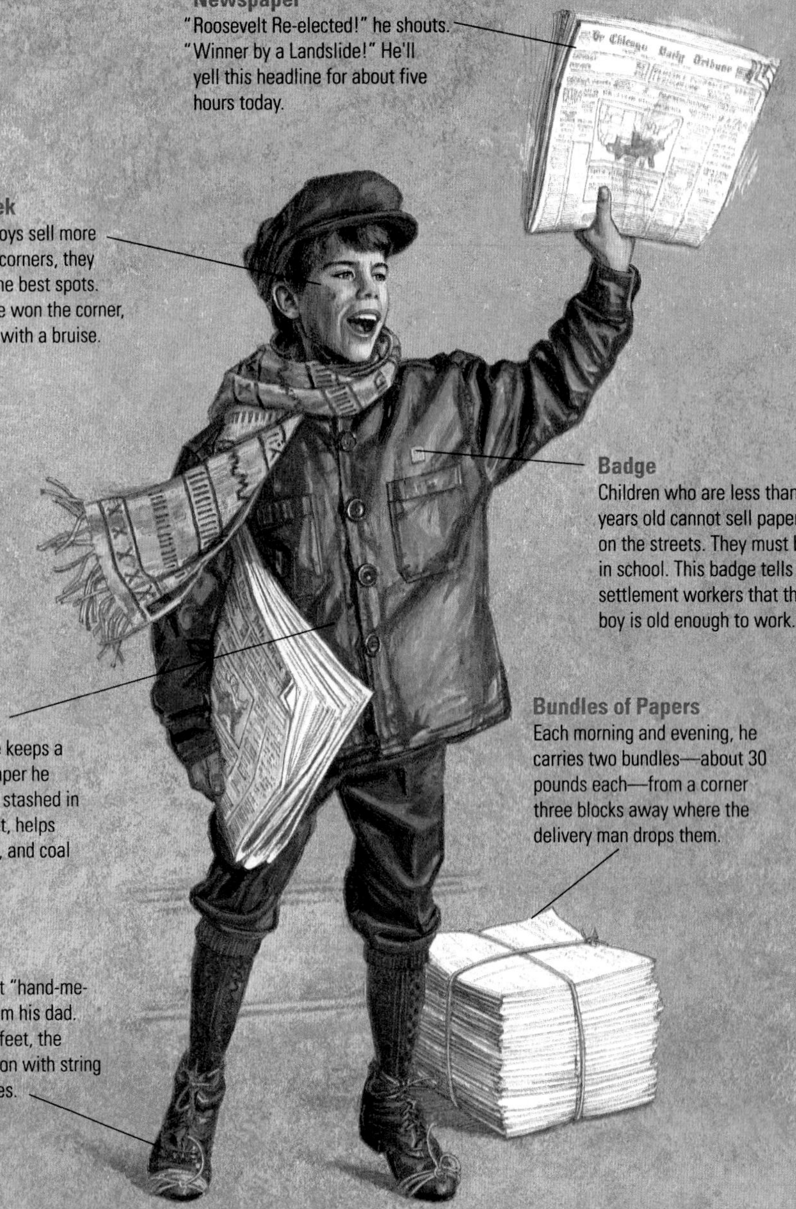

Newspaper
"Roosevelt Re-elected!" he shouts. "Winner by a Landslide!" He'll yell this headline for about five hours today.
Bruised Cheek
Because newsboys sell more papers on busy corners, they often fight for the best spots. This morning, he won the corner, but came away with a bruise.
Badge
Children who are less than 10 years old cannot sell papers on the streets. They must be in school. This badge tells settlement workers that this boy is old enough to work.
Secret Pocket
"Only 3 cents!" He keeps a penny for each paper he sells. The money, stashed in this hidden pocket, helps pay for food, rent, and coal for his family.
Bundles of Papers
Each morning and evening, he carries two bundles—about 30 pounds each—from a corner three blocks away where the delivery man drops them.
Shoes
These worn out "hand-me-downs" are from his dad. Too big for his feet, the shoes are tied on with string from his bundles.

Critical Thinking

Tell students to make a list of the types of work young people do today. Then have them compare their list with what they know young people did in the 1800s and early 1900s.

Geographic Context

The Chicago fire of 1871 left the city in such ruin that some people thought it would never recover. The effort to rebuild the city, however, began overnight. The first new building, a real estate office, was begun two days after the fire. Within a month, 5,000 new homes had been built. The fact that most of the city's lumber mills, stockyards, and grain bins had survived the fire was an important factor in the city's phenomenal recovery.

Investors organized companies to finance the construction of new office buildings in Chicago's downtown. These companies had two main concerns: They wanted their buildings to be fireproof so that the disaster of 1871 would not be repeated; and they wanted them to be as big as possible, since the companies' profits depended on the amount of floor space they could rent.

Land in Chicago's downtown area was severely restricted by Lake Michigan to the east, rivers to the north and west, and a vast

■ *Steel frames made skyscrapers possible, as well as suspension bridges strong enough to support trains and other industrial traffic.*

German immigrant John A. Roebling, a pioneer in the field, employed a steel framework in his design for the Brooklyn Bridge. The bridge was completed in 1883, and spanned the East River, connecting Brooklyn, New York to the island of Manhattan. With a span of 1,595 feet, the bridge was the longest of its kind in the world at that time. ■

■ *How did the new uses of steel change ways of constructing buildings? How did such changes aid transportation?*

Rural People Migrate to Cities

Just as the gold fields had lured settlers westward, the promise of a glowing future drew millions of rural Americans into the cities. In 1860, only one person in five lived in a city. By 1915, urban centers contained fully one-half the population of the United States.

▲ *This scene of Chicago in the early 1900s shows a busy State Street, where trolley cars, shoppers, visitors, and workers crowd the city's shopping district.*

Cheap Transportation

In 1850, cross-country travel had been a major undertaking lasting months. The railroads drastically reduced travel time. For far less money, and in relative comfort and safety, a family could travel to a distant state in only a few days. By 1900, cheap, practical transportation had created a more mobile society in which people could pack up and follow the trail of opportunity. This trail most often led to the cities, where people hoped they would find employment.

The Job-Seekers

Chicago's industrial boom changed many lives. In his novel, *Sister Carrie*, author Theodore Dreiser described how the great promise of opportunity and excitement attracted people to the city of Chicago. A passage from the novel appears below.

Some rural people moved to the cities in search of a new life. Many, however, were forced to move because they had lost their jobs when new inventions mechanized farming. With a single machine capable of doing the work formerly done by a dozen people using horse-drawn implements, the need for farm workers declined. Other rural workers lost their jobs when large businesses drove foundries, sawmills, and other small rural industries out of business. By 1910, a third of those living in cities had come from farms and small towns in the countryside. ■

> Chicago had the peculiar qualifications of growth which made . . . adventuresome pilgrimages even on the part of young girls plausible. Its many and growing commercial opportunities gave it widespread fame, which made of it a giant magnet, drawing to itself, from all quarters, the hopeful and the hopeless—those who had their fortune yet to make and those whose fortunes and affairs had reached a disastrous climax elsewhere. It was a city of over 500,000, with the ambition, the daring, the activity of a metropolis of a million.

■ *What led people living on farms and in small towns to move to cities?*

ECONOMICS

Critical Thinking

How were cities in the late 1800s becoming like the gold fields of California? *(The cities promised opportunity and hope and drew people from all over the country.)*

■ *Aided by cheap transportation and often spurred on by joblessness, millions of rural Americans moved to cities to find employment.*

expanse of railroads and freight yards to the south. To construct large buildings, they had to build them taller, not wider. However, Chicago was located on marshy, soft soil, that could not support the weight of tall stone and brick buildings. This combination of factors led Chicago's architects to experiment with new methods of construction.

Architect and engineer William Le Baron Jenney came up with the solution of using metal-frame construction. His Home Insurance Company Building, completed in 1885, consisted of two stories of thick granite, on top of which rose an eight-story frame of iron and steel. A brick facing was bolted to the outside of the frame with brackets. Although these buildings were not tall by today's standards, they began a trend that has forever changed the urban skyline.

Critical Thinking

As students read the literature excerpt on this page, have them pay special attention to the ways in which Dreiser describes the city's growth. Why does he compare the city to a magnet? *(Opportunities draw people.)* What evidence does he give to support the idea that the city anticipated enormous growth? *(It acted as if it were a "metropolis of a million.")*

Southern Blacks Move North

Northern cities also attracted many Southern blacks. They sought not only economic opportunity but also an escape from the unfair and often brutal treatment they received at the hands of Southern whites.

Although African Americans had been freed from slavery, many whites still considered them inferior. Persecuted by violent racist organizations such as the Ku Klux Klan, tens of thousands of blacks left the South after 1877.

Despite this wave of migration, in 1880, nine out of ten of America's 6.6 million blacks still worked on Southern farms or as domestic servants. Some of them enrolled in the abandoned Alabama church where Booker T. Washington had established Tuskegee Institute in 1881. At Tuskegee, blacks learned vocational, or trade-related, skills and took courses in teaching. Washington was convinced that blacks could improve their lives by learning practical skills or by becoming teachers. Instead of demanding that blacks seek social

Maps Comparing Major Cities in the United States

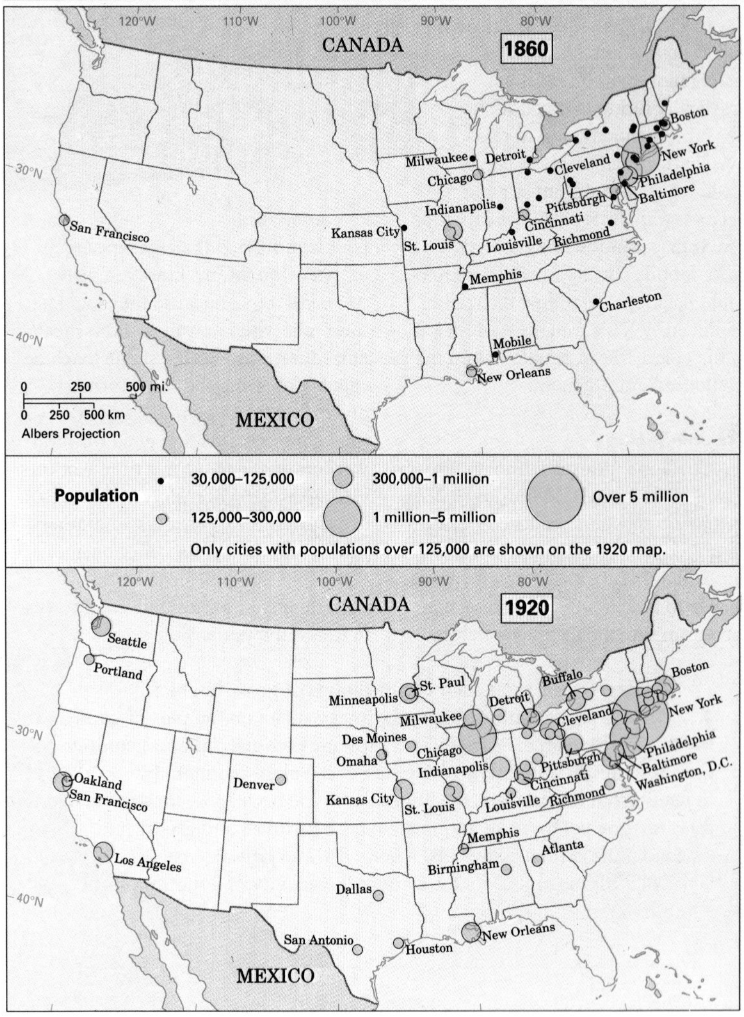

➤ *Before the Civil War, fewer than one in five Americans lived in cities. By 1920, industrial centers across the country drew increasing numbers of people seeking better opportunities. America's population became almost equally divided between urban and rural areas.*

Across Time & Space

In contrast to 19th-century cities, modern cities are beginning to run out of space. Consequently, architects like Paolo Soleri design cities for the future that will occupy very small areas. Apartments, stores, robot-run factories, businesses, schools, and theaters will be grouped around parks and walkways in order to provide land for crops, woodland, and environmental preservation.

GEOGRAPHY

Map and Globe Skills

After students study the maps on this page, ask them to compare and contrast cities and populations in 1860 and 1920. *(Number of cities and urban populations expanded as industrial centers attracted more people.)*

Map and Globe Skills

Ask students to compare and contrast the maps on this page to the modern political map of the United States on pages 698–699 in the Atlas. Ask which present-day cities do not appear on the maps of 1860 or 1920.

Making Charts

Have students graph the population growth of a major American city between the years 1870 and 1920. Each student should choose one city, use an almanac to find out the population statistics for the years 1870–1920, and choose a method for representing the population growth in graphic form. If they wish, students may extend their graphs to include decades before and after the target years.

Research

Students can use almanacs or state history books to find answers to questions such as these for each major city in their state or region:

- When was the city founded?
- What was its population in 1870? In 1900? In 1920?
- What industry or industries contributed most to its growth?

Have them report their findings in oral or written form.

equality. Washington focused on economic opportunity rather than political status. This was a view that most blacks, especially those in the South, accepted reluctantly.

Washington's views helped African Americans make some gains, but poverty and intolerance remained. Many white mobs killed blacks, without a trial, for crimes they had not committed. This practice was known as lynching. In the 1890s, with lynching at an all-time high, a new wave of blacks migrated to Northern cities.

The largest black migration to cities in this period occurred during World War I. About 330,000 Southern blacks moved to the North and West from 1910 to 1920. Crop failures and economic hardship in the South forced many to move. A growing need for factory workers also offered blacks opportunities in industrial cities.

Help for Black Migrants

The move north gave many African Americans opportunities they had never known before. But adjusting to a completely different way of life proved difficult. Several groups stepped in to help rural blacks adjust to urban life. Black churches, which had provided aid during the long years of slavery, supplied information about jobs and housing.

The largest organization offering assistance to blacks was the National Urban League. Founded in 1911, it provided blacks with temporary housing, information about work, and training for industrial jobs.

As an industrial center, the city of Chicago attracted thousands of Southern blacks in search of jobs and better lives. This Southern family is shown arriving in Chicago.

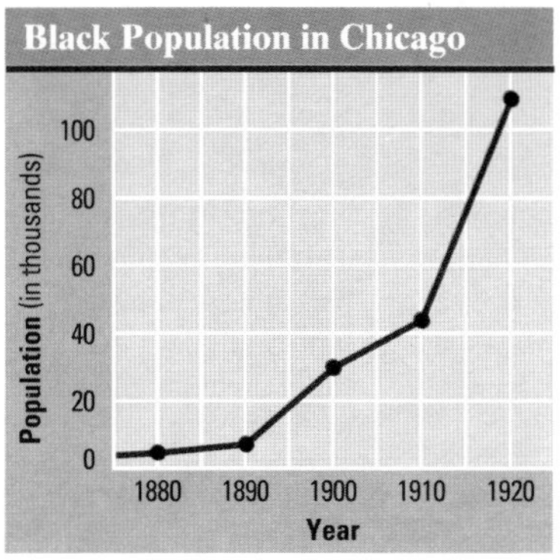

This graph shows the dramatic increase in the migration of Southern black people to urban areas.

With the help of such organizations, blacks were able to make a place for themselves in Northern cities. There they, like other American workers, found themselves competing for jobs with newly arrived immigrants from Europe and Asia. ■

■ *How did black communities help people adjust to city life?*

REVIEW

1. **FOCUS** How did industrial development and the growth of cities change American life during the late 1800s and early 1900s?
2. **CONNECT** Why did black Americans leave the South and migrate north and west after Reconstruction? What new challenges did they face?
3. **HISTORY** How did industrialization affect rural workers? Why would a farmer have moved to a large city?
4. **ECONOMICS** What effect did cheap transportation have on American business?
5. **CRITICAL THINKING** How did technological improvements change the lives of Americans?
6. **WRITING ACTIVITY** You are a farmer who has moved to the city to work in a factory. Write two or three diary entries that describe the sights and sounds of city and factory.

SOCIAL SYSTEMS

Critical Thinking

Ask students why the social and economic situation for African Americans moving to urban centers across the nation was especially difficult. *(Even though African Americans had been freed from slavery, many whites considered them inferior. In addition, African Americans found urban life difficult to adjust to; housing was hard to find and there was competition for jobs.)*

■ *Social and political institutions such as schools, churches, and fraternal organizations helped black Americans adjust to their new surroundings.*

CLOSE

Students should return to the Thinking Focus and answer it. Then have students compare the charts they made using the headings from the Graphic Overview on page 447. As an extension activity, students can do the research activity on page 452.

Answers to Review Questions

1. American life now included increasing mobility, the development of urban society, and factory employment.
2. They migrated to escape mistreatment by Southern whites and to gain economic opportunities. They continued to suffer from discrimination and poverty; they faced the new challenges of finding housing and competing for jobs.
3. Farmers moved to cities to find new opportunities after losing their jobs to mechanized farming or big business.
4. American business grew because of the increased mobility of people and products.
5. Sample answer: Technological advances, such as electric lights, telephones, and sewing machines brought conveniences to everyday life. Allow for personal opinion.
6. Encourage students to use concrete details as they write their entries.

Homework Options

Have students write two positive things and two negative things about living in a city such as Chicago or Cleveland in the years 1870–1900.

Study Guide: page 65.

UNDERSTANDING THEMATIC MAPS

This skill lesson will show students how to use thematic maps.

ECONOMICS

Map and Globe Skills

Remind students that they read on page 382 about a migration of the former slaves. How would this movement have been reflected on a population map of Southern cities? *(Growth of cities would make them look bigger.)* On page 397, students read about another migration of black Americans in the early 1900s. How might that migration have affected a map of the South? *(There would have been a thinning of Southern population.)* How is this population shift reflected in the history of the South? *(Black Americans moved away from the South to seek opportunity and to escape the effects of post-Reconstruction policies.)*

UNDERSTANDING THEMATIC MAPS

Comparing Population Maps

Here's Why

A thematic map presents a specific kind of information about the area it shows. Comparing thematic maps from different time periods will help you understand historical trends.

One such trend that has played an important role throughout American history is the movement of people from one area to another. From 1900 to 1920 the United States experienced rapid change as the economy shifted from agriculture to industry. This shift was reflected in the rapid growth of cities.

Suppose you wanted to see the changes in both population and industry of an area over a particular period of time. Comparing thematic maps is one way to do that.

Here's How

Look at the maps below of the midwestern United States. Note the key for population size and industrial areas. In 1900, Chicago was the largest city on the map, having a population of over one million. St. Louis and Pittsburgh were the only other cities over 500,000. Now look at the 1920 map. Chicago is still the largest city, but notice how many other cities—Detroit, Cleveland, and Buffalo—are now as large as St. Louis and Pittsburgh. Such comparisons show that Americans moved into these cities quite rapidly in only 20 years.

Look at the two maps again. This time compare the shaded parts that represent major industrial areas. Notice how those areas changed from 1900 to 1920.

Try It

Look at the maps again. How does the number of cities on the 1920 map compare with the number on the 1900 map? How does the change in industrial areas compare with the change in the number of cities? What relationship can you see between the change in the number and size of cities and the change in the industrial areas?

Apply It

Look at the U. S. population maps on pages 704 and 705. Compare the population density of the West Coast in 1870 to that of 1910. Which areas grew to have over 45 people per square mile? Which areas on the 1980 map now have more than 90 people per square mile? How has West Coast population changed in this century?

Development of Industrial Cities, 1900-1920

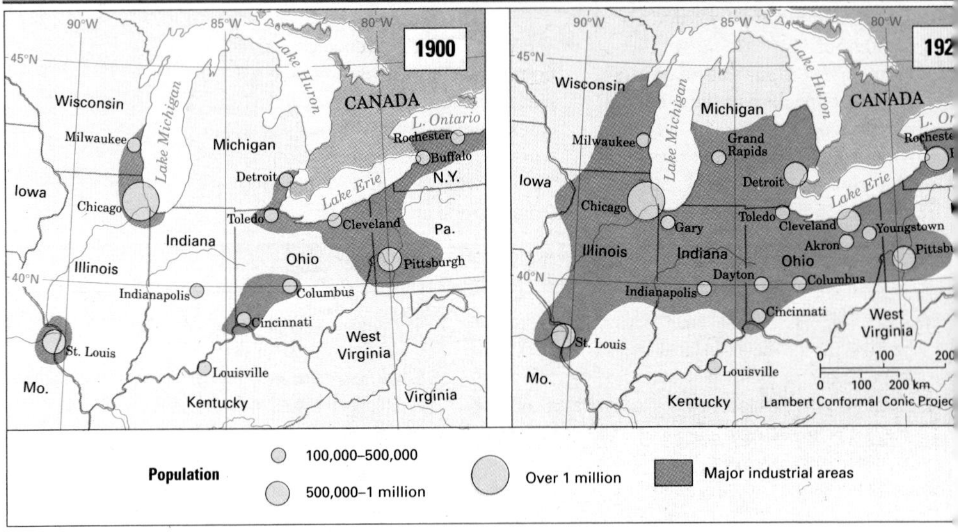

Objective

Use maps with graduated circles to determine population growth. (Map and Globe Skills 4)

Answers to Try It

There are 13 cities on the 1900 map, 18 on the 1920 map. The industrial areas grew much larger between 1900 and 1920. As industry grew, so did the cities within the industrial areas.

Answers to Apply It

In 1870, no West Coast area had more than 45 people per square mile. By 1910, the San Francisco–Sacramento area, Los Angeles, Portland, and the Seattle–Tacoma area had reached this population density. By 1980, the California coast between San Diego and Santa Barbara, San Jose–San Francisco–Oakland–Sacramento, Portland–Salem–Eugene, and Seattle–Tacoma all had more than 90 people per square mile. West Coast population has risen greatly in this century.

1850 1860 1870 1920

LESSON 3

The Workers' Changing World

"Our machines were on long tables in large rooms, and we operators sat on both sides of the tables. At last I was where I wanted to be, and here I worked for ten years." Thus Agnes Nestor begins her account of life in a glove-making shop. Five feet tall, blue eyed, and delicate because of her poor health, Agnes started work when she was 17. "To drown the monotony of work," she continued, "we used to sing. This was allowed because the foreman could see that the rhythm kept us going at high speed. We sang 'A Bicycle Built for Two' and other popular songs.

"Before we began to sing we used to talk very loudly so as to be heard above the roar of the machines. We knew we must not stop our work just to hear what someone was saying; to stop work even for a minute meant a reduction in pay."

The women did piecework—that is, they were paid not by the hour but according to the number of pieces that they completed. The more gloves they sewed, the more they earned. They therefore had to work as fast as they could. However, Agnes pointed out, "There were always pace makers, a few girls who could work faster than the rest. . . . Their rate of work had to be the rate for all of us, if we were to earn a decent wage. It kept us tensed to continual hurry." This was known as "the sweating system," and the shops were known as "sweatshops."

Although their wages were pitifully small, Agnes noted that the women had to pay for some of the equipment they used. "We were charged fifty cents a week for the power furnished our machines. . . . We were obliged, besides, to buy our own needles. If you broke one, you were charged for a new one to replace it. We had, also, to buy our own machine oil."

THINKING FOCUS

How did changes in production affect the way in which Americans lived and worked during the late 1800s and early 1900s?

Key Terms

- assembly line
- strike
- labor union

Henry Bergman photographed these German immigrant seamstresses in a Wisconsin clothing factory around 1890.

INTRODUCE

Point out the Thinking Focus. Tell students that the treatment of industrial workers was motivated by the desire of owners for high profits. Many businessmen had little regard for the welfare of their workers. Ask students to predict how workers might have reacted to this treatment. Have them read the lesson to confirm or reject their predictions.

Key Terms

Vocabulary strategies: T36–37

assembly line—method of production in which each specific task in the assembly process is achieved on a continuously moving belt that carries parts past workers

strike—a temporary work stoppage in support of demands made on employers by workers

labor union—organization of workers formed to serve workers' interests with respect to wages and working conditions

Graphic Overview

Cause owners' desire for high profits → **Low Wages Long Hours Dangerous Conditions** → **Effect** labor unions

Objectives

1. Describe division of labor and mass production along an assembly line.
2. Describe the ways in which workers were exploited.
3. Identify the role of early labor unions in organizing workers.
4. Explain why strikes at Homestead and Pullman failed.

DEVELOP

Point out to students that this lesson has a cause-and-effect structure. Tell them to look for answers to the following questions. Why did the nature of work change? How did this change affect the workers? Why were industrialists able to exploit their workers? What were the results of exploitation? What were the effects of labor union activities?

ECONOMICS

Critical Thinking

Ask students to describe division of labor. *(Workers each have a different task in production.)* Have them explain why an assembly line was considered an advantage by the owners and a disadvantage by the workers. *(Made mass production fast and cheap and increased profits for owners; made work monotonous, low-paying, and sometimes dangerous for workers)*

Production Speeds Up

Women did not work under such conditions by choice. Like many rural migrants, they lacked job training and could only work as unskilled laborers. As factories became more mechanized, however, the need for unskilled labor grew.

Assembly Line

In 1913–1914 Henry Ford introduced the first moving **assembly line** in his automobile plant in Detroit, Michigan. A continuously moving belt carried parts past workers, each of whom performed one specific task in the assembly process. Wrote Ford, "The idea came . . . from the overhead trolley that the Chicago packers used in dressing—that is, cutting up—beef."

Ford envisioned an automobile that almost anyone could afford. The assembly line helped him meet his goal. Before Ford's innovation, a car body took twelve and a half hours to assemble. The cost of this labor helped make cars expensive. By reducing the time to a mere hour and a half, the assembly line process allowed Ford to sell cars for less money.

Assembly-line techniques were quickly applied to other industries. Floor space in manufacturing plants was arranged so that one step followed another in a logical sequence, eliminating wasted movements.

Mass Production

The assembly line permitted mass production—that is, the manufacture of large quantities of the same item. Mass production allowed manufacturers to turn out products more quickly, more cheaply, and in larger amounts than ever before.

Mass production not only speeded up manufacturing; it also increased the investor's profit. The new system allowed factory managers to order raw materials in large quantities. As a result, costs were reduced. Producing many of the same items meant that machines could be used over and over for the same job. Such use of machines also reduced costs.

Improved communications and transportation networks also contributed to faster production. Between 1870 and 1920, railroads and steamships provided a cheap means of transporting goods. The telephone and telegraph helped manufacturers keep

Across Time & Space

When Americans and Canadians take the first Monday in September as a holiday, they are celebrating Labor Day, the day that honors all working people. The Australian version is called Eight-Hour Day, which honors workers' success in gaining a shorter working day. Appropriately, Labor Day was first suggested by two American workers—machinist Matthew Maguire and carpenter Peter McGuire.

Workers leave the Ford Motor Company factory in Detroit, Michigan. The plant covers more than 47 acres of floor space. Each worker specializes in one part of assembling an automobile.

Access Activity

To keep profits high, entrepreneurs often reduced workers' pay and increased their hours. Ask students why it might be more in the entrepreneurs' interest to provide favorable working conditions and pay. *(It would increase productivity: more workers would probably become consumers.)*

Access Strategy

Encourage students to imagine what it might have been like working ten to twelve hours a day in uncomfortable and sometimes dangerous surroundings for very little money. Ask what might have kept workers at such jobs. *(The need for money; inability to do other kinds of work)* How could they improve their working conditions? *(Form a union)* What would be the risks involved? *(They could lose their job and perhaps be unable to get another.)* Explain that this lesson will tell about the life of the men, women, and children who worked in the industries that developed after the Civil War. Have them read the lesson to learn how people dealt with their harsh work situations.

in touch with current trends in industry. Electric lighting made it possible to operate factories for a full 24-hour period, thus increasing production.

Machine-tending workers provided the labor for much of the work done in factories. As more efficient machines were invented, fewer skills were needed to run them. Previously, one person might have been involved in several stages of production. Under the system known as division of labor, the different stages were divided among several workers. Each worker performed a single operation. For example, every 20 seconds the worker might pull down a lever so a machine could punch a hole in a steel plate. The punched plate then slid along a moving belt and a new one replaced it. The worker pulled the lever again, repeating the process, over and over, for 10 hours a day. Besides being repetitious, such jobs paid very low wages, causing workers to change jobs frequently. This turnover contributed to the increasing call for unskilled labor. ■

■ Explain how the assembly line changed production.

■ *Dividing assembly into specific tasks arranged in a logical sequence decreased production time and cost, which led to mass production.*

The Workers Struggle

Workers shared few of the increased profits of mechanized production. The fear of losing their jobs made workers endure abuses and made it easy for managers to take advantage of them.

Working Conditions

Young, inexperienced workers or those who could not speak English suffered most, but nearly all industrial laborers felt the effects of harsh working conditions. Andrew Carnegie described how he himself was exploited when he was a boy working in the cotton mills. He worked in "the dark cellar running a steam engine at two dollars a week, begrimed with coal dirt, without a trace of the elevating influences of life" (such as books, music, art, and recreation).

Factories often paid low wages; unskilled workers in the 1880s might earn an average daily wage of $1.50. They worked six days a week, earning $9 a week, $36 a month with no vacation time. Since rent for a single room might cost $10 a month, such a worker had only $26 left each month to buy food and clothing for the family and fuel for heat and cooking. Nothing was left over for medical emergencies. The need for more income made it necessary for as many members of the family to work as much as possible.

This photograph, taken by Lewis Hine in the early 1900s, shows young workers in a Georgia cotton mill.

Workers could not afford to refuse when employers demanded they work 10 to 12 hours each day.

The piecework system forced people to work as quickly as possible, sometimes to the point of exhaustion, in order to earn decent wages. When business was good, employers expected their employees to take extra work home. When business dropped off, however, the same boss laid off workers without pay.

Workers also faced many hazards in the workplace. They were often exposed to high temperatures and poisonous gases; many lost fingers and other limbs in machines that lacked

SOCIAL SYSTEMS

Critical Thinking

As a boy, Andrew Carnegie was one of the exploited, yet he later accumulated great wealth through the labor of his own workers. Ask students to discuss what this tells them about the prevailing attitudes of the day. *(Sample answer: Each person was responsible for his or her own success.)*

Social Context

One of the best known union organizers in America was Mary Harris Jones, better known as Mother Jones. She was born in Ireland in 1830 and came to America in 1841. Yellow fever killed Mary's husband and her four children in 1867. She moved to Chicago to work as a seamstress but then lost everything she owned in the fire of 1871. She turned to the Knights of Labor for help, was drawn to their campaign for improved working conditions, and soon became a highly visible figure in the union movement. She never had a home again, but she traveled across the country for more than 50 years, speaking out against injustice, organizing for the United Mine Workers, campaigning to prohibit child labor, and supporting strikes. One reporter said she was "probably the most patriotic citizen this country has ever known." An attorney in West Virginia called her "the most dangerous woman in America."

Visual Learning

Ask students to use the picture on this page of the young mill workers to make inferences about the work conditions for people who worked at jobs like these for ten or more hours a day, six days a week. *(The jobs were probably dangerous and monotonous. These children were not attending schools or out playing.)*

SOCIAL SYSTEMS

Critical Thinking

Have students compare the life of industrial workers who lived in towns owned by their companies—Pullman, Illinois, is an example—with the lives of slaves before the Civil War. In what ways were their lives similar? *(Workers depended on their employer's good will.)* In what ways were they different? *(Workers earned money and were free to leave their jobs for something better elsewhere.)*

■ *Contributing factors included low pay, long hours, no benefits, physical hazards, and high pressure for quick performance.*

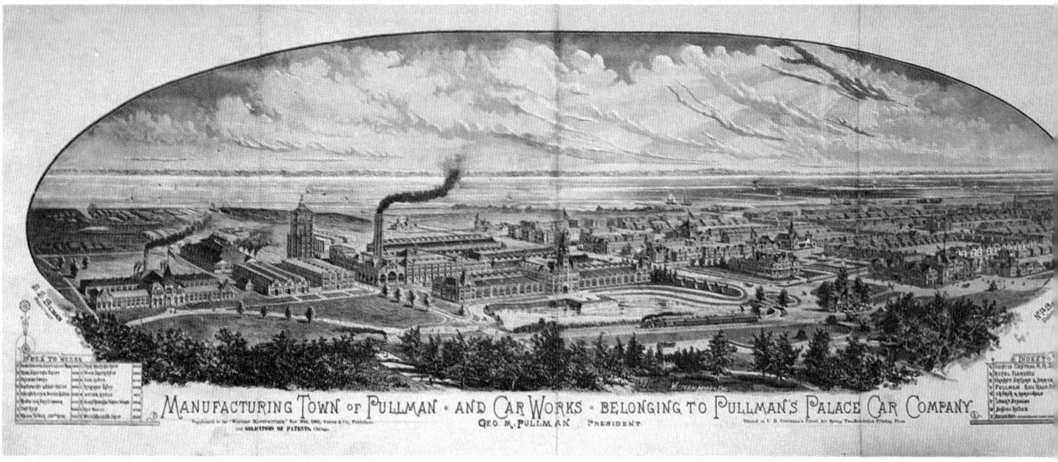

MANUFACTURING TOWN OF PULLMAN · AND CAR WORKS · BELONGING TO PULLMAN'S PALACE CAR COMPANY
GEO. M. PULLMAN PRESIDENT

This 1881 view of the Pullman community appeared in a supplement to the Western Manufacturer. *George Pullman hoped his company town would help workers live happier, healthier, and more productive lives.*

■ *What factors contributed to the poor working conditions in most industries?*

safety devices. No programs existed to help the unemployed, the sick, the injured, or the families of those killed in industrial accidents.

Life in Company Towns

Some businesses set up company towns. The Pullman Palace Car Company in Chicago, which manufactured sleeping and dining cars for railroads, built a company town (named Pullman) in Illinois. George Pullman approved of the neat rows of brick houses, each with a flower garden, because he believed keeping his workers happy and healthy would make them work harder. At the time, Pullman workers were the best housed workers in the country, and the town was regarded as a landmark in city planning. It contained a church, a school, a bank, a hotel, a theater, and a shopping area.

To Pullman's surprise, the workers were not pleased. One worker complained that the company had too much control over their lives. He commented, "We are born in a Pullman house, fed from the Pullman shop, taught in the Pullman school, catechized in the Pullman church, and when we die we shall be buried in the Pullman cemetery."

Often workers fell in debt because their wages were not enough to cover their expenses. The pastor of the church noted, "After deducting rent the men invariably had only from one to six dollars or so on which to live for two weeks. One man has a pay check in his possession of two cents [left] after paying rent." ■

Unions Develop

As abuses continued year after year, workers grew increasingly bitter. The growing discontent of millions of people could not be contained for long. But workers found their individual complaints were ignored. They began to organize so that they would be heard. Agnes Nestor, for example, persuaded the women sewing gloves to go on **strike**—to stop working—in order to get better wages. They not only succeeded but also gained the right to join together in a **labor union,** a workers' organization that would try to obtain better wages and better working conditions.

Early Unions

Small, isolated attempts to organize trade unions dated back to the 1700s. The formation of the short-lived Philadelphia Mechanics Union in

Critical Thinking

Ask students what the purpose of a strike is. Why is it sometimes an effective way to make management pay attention to workers' concerns? *(Companies need workers.)* Why does it also pose risks to workers? *(Loss of pay; reduced hours; profits fall; strikers may be fired; company may go out of business)*

History Context

Workers living in American cities in the mid-to-late 1800s were plagued by many problems—one of which was the souring and contamination of milk. This continued until the discoveries of the French chemist and biologist Louis Pasteur became available to the world. Pasteur had been working on the problem of soured wine and beer, a major economic problem in France. Pasteur discovered that the souring was caused by the presence of bacteria. He found that these bacteria could be killed by heating the solutions to high temperatures. He applied these studies to the problem of sour milk, and the process, termed pasteurization, is still in use today. After the development of pasteurization equipment in the 1890s, fresh milk became available even to city residents.

the 1820s, however, marked the beginning of the modern labor movement. The first influential union in the United States was the Knights of Labor, founded in 1869. The Knights had the idealistic goal of organizing all workers in society. They supported equal pay for men and women who did the same job and did not discriminate on the basis of race or religion. The group's motto was "An injury to one is the concern of all."

Although the Knights of Labor included 700,000 members by 1886, the union was troubled with internal disagreements and weak leadership. More successful was the American Federation of Labor (AFL), founded in 1886. Its first president was a Dutch-Jewish immigrant named Samuel Gompers.

A cigar maker since the age of 13, Gompers knew about working conditions from his own experience. He took a practical approach to unionization, seeking gradual improvement in the workers' welfare. The focus was on shorter hours, better wages, and improved working conditions. He avoided involvement in politics. Gompers created a lasting organization. The AFL did not try to enlist unskilled workers. It concentrated on organizing skilled workers into thousands of local unions separated according to specific skills or occupations.

Gompers believed that organized workers had the right to strike. He also felt that strikes could be avoided if union leaders and employers met to work out agreements on such matters as wages and hours. If an agreement could not be reached, Gompers supported the use of boycotts—the refusal of union members to buy or use a company's products—as a form of protest. ■

▲ *Women picket a New York factory during the Ladies' Tailors strike in 1910.*

■ *How did workers use strikes and boycotts to change their working conditions?*

Unions Meet Opposition

The AFL succeeded in gaining higher wages for its members. More and more workers, however, belonged to the unskilled labor force, and they saw little improvement in their pay or working conditions. As discontent grew, major strikes occurred. Management's reactions to these strikes revealed their fear of organized labor.

On May 3, 1886, strikers at Chicago's McCormick Harvester Company fought with strikebreakers trying to enter the plant. Strikebreakers were people hired to work in place of those on strike. The police rushed in, and in the confusion four strikers were killed. The next day crowds gathered at Haymarket Square to protest the incident. Ordered by the police to end the meeting, the speaker began to step down. Suddenly a bomb went off, killing 7 officers and injuring 67 others. The frightened police fired into the crowd, wounding over 50 people and killing 10. No one ever found out who had tossed the bomb, but the unions, particularly the Knights of Labor, were blamed.

Despite this setback, unions continued to work for better conditions. In 1892, the AFL steelworkers at Carnegie's plant in Homestead, Pennsylvania, asked for a raise. In response, the manager locked out the workers.

▼ *Samuel Gompers was AFL president almost continuously from 1886 until 1924. The chief weapon of the AFL was the strike.*

ECONOMICS

Critical Thinking

Ask students to explain why workers needed labor unions. Why couldn't workers deal with managers on their own? *("Strength in numbers"; alone, each worker could be dismissed or discounted, but if they were organized, workers had the power to stop production for a while—thus cutting profits.)*

■ *These techniques caused their employers to lose money and productivity. Employers found they were better off granting the workers' demands.*

Music Connection

Singer and songwriter Woody Guthrie, born in 1912, was very much inspired by the struggles of the common worker. He wrote the song "Union Maid" to convey the spirit of the union organizers who fought against the privileged class that held economic power. Play a recording of the song for students, or have several interested students learn it and perform it for the class. Discuss the courage it took to stand up to a company's powerful owners.

Language Arts Connection

Tell students to create a glossary of terms associated with labor and unions. Some of these words, such as *strike, lockout, injunction,* and *boycott* are included in this lesson. You may want to offer other words and phrases such as *arbitration, union shop, picket, shop steward, mediation*, and *wildcat strike*. Slang words such as *goon* and *fink* refer to hired strikebreakers. You may also suggest that students find more examples by talking to adults involved in unions.

Critical Thinking

Have students compare what the Knights of Labor and the American Federation of Labor wanted to accomplish. *(Both wanted better working conditions for laborers.)* In what major way did the two unions differ? *(Knights—more idealistic goals, wanted to organize all workers; AFL—practical goals and only represented skilled workers)*

ECONOMICS

Critical Thinking

When more than 9,000 pilots employed by American Airlines went on strike in 1997, they were concerned over who should fly new jets. The jets were to be operated by a subsidiary commuter airline, whose pilots were lower-paid and belonged to a different union than American Airlines' pilots. President Clinton, invoking his powers under the 1926 Railway Labor Act, ordered the union to halt the strike and set up a Presidential Emergency Board to settle the dispute. If you had been President, how would you have handled this situation? *(Encourage student discussion of the rights of workers versus the interests of the country or government.)*

Understanding Labor Unions

Before labor unions were formed, wage earners were at the mercy of their employer. They had no voice in determining their wages, work hours, or working conditions. Nor did they have anyone to represent them. Because work was a necessity to clothe, feed, and house themselves, workers were forced to accept the conditions of their employment.

Until the early 1800s, workers in the United States tended to act as individuals rather than as a group when dealing with their employers. During these years, factory management held most of the power. Bosses could ask workers to put in long hours for six days a week. They could offer low wages, few benefits, and little job security. Conditions in the factories and foundries were often dismal, even dangerous. Management was often in complete control.

The establishment of labor unions enabled workers to gain some control over their working conditions. A labor union is an organization of employees whose purpose is to obtain, through bargaining with an employer, better working conditions, pay, and benefits. The idea behind unions is that banding together gives workers power that they do not have as individuals.

Over the years, unions have achieved many gains for workers, including the outlawing of child labor, the adoption of health and safety regulations for the workplace, and the establishment of federal minimum hourly wage rates. Other important union achievements include a work day of eight hours (or fewer), a five-day work week, overtime pay, and paid vacations and holidays.

Kinds of Labor Unions

Since the start of the labor movement in the 1800s, workers in the United States have formed three main kinds of unions. These types of unions are craft unions, industrial unions, and public employee unions.

Membership in a craft union is limited to workers skilled in a particular craft or trade, such as carpenters or brick layers. The American Federation of Labor (AFL), organized in 1886, was made up of craft unions consolidated into a single group. Within the AFL, however, each craft union continued to govern itself—that is, each had a constitution, rules, and steps for dealing with employers.

Membership in industrial unions is open to skilled, semiskilled, and unskilled workers in mass-producing industries, such as the automobile and steel industries. Industrial unions started in the late nineteenth century when machinery and mechanical power began to drive the production process. The Knights of Labor, organized in 1869, and the Industrial Workers of the World (IWW), begun in 1905, were the first two unions to make a serious attempt to organize unskilled industrial workers. Since its founding in 1935, the Congress of Industrial Organizations (CIO) has numbered among its members auto, electric, mine, steel, and textile workers.

Membership in public employee unions consists of municipal employees, such as firefighters and police officers. Unlike unions dealing with private industries, public employee unions do not have the right to strike. They sometimes do strike, however, as the Professional Air Traffic Controllers did in 1981. As a result, President Reagan fired 11,500 controllers and broke up the union.

Unions Today

In 1955, the AFL and the CIO merged into the AFL-CIO, which today is the nation's major labor organization. For the last 40 years, the percentage of U.S. workers who belong to a union has been slowly declining. From a peak of about 25 percent around 1950, union membership has fallen to about 15 percent today. Despite this decline in the number of union members, the unions remain an important force in the nation's economy. And millions of nonunion workers also benefit from the higher wages and improved working conditions won through union efforts.

Study Skills

Have students research and write a one- to two-page report on the early history of a union such as the Teamsters or the International Ladies' Garment Workers Union. Why did they organize? What difficulties did they face?

Role Playing

Have students simulate a common type of nineteenth-century work, that of a bobbin worker in a spinning mill. You will need a peg board with 36 pegs (spindles) and 36 spools that fit over the pegs (bobbins). Have students take turns being the laborer, while someone times the activity. The bobbin worker must put all the bobbins on the spindles and take them off again in one minute; then do it again; then again. This is the kind of job that some mill workers did for ten hours every day.

Interviewing

Contact a local labor union to invite a representative to speak to the class. Students could interview the representative to learn about such things as when the union was formed and who may join; what significant improvements in working conditions it has won over the years; and the role of unions today. Remind students to prepare specific questions in advance and to take careful notes as they listen.

One steelworker commented that the union had only 800 members but that the lockout caused 3,000 unskilled workers to join them. The plant manager then sent for Pinkerton detectives to act as strikebreakers. A steelworker described how the Pinkerton guards arrived on barges at dawn and how shooting began when they tried to step ashore. The fighting continued for hours before the guards retreated. The Pinkertons were replaced by the National Guard, who protected the plant and the men hired to take the strikers' jobs. The union finally had to admit defeat.

Another union defeat occurred in 1892 when miners in Coeur d'Alene, Idaho rejected a wage reduction. The striking miners were locked out and replacements were brought in under armed guard. Soon violence erupted between the miners and company gunmen. State militia and federal troops were called in and the violence was ended. Although the miners at Coeur d'Alene experienced defeat, a new militant organization, the Western Federation of Miners, was established in 1893.

Strike at Pullman

In 1894, a strike at the Pullman plant led to bloodshed. When orders for new rail cars fell off and then stopped altogether, Pullman cut wages by about a third without lowering rent or prices in the company stores. To protest, the workers went on strike. Pullman then shut down the plant. Acting in sympathy with the strikers, railroad workers refused to handle Pullman cars. This action halted most rail traffic.

Claiming that this action interfered with trade and with the U.S. mails, which were carried on the railroad, the courts issued an order to end the strike. Federal troops were sent to Pullman to enforce the court's ruling. Although the strikers at first fought the militia, they soon realized they could not go on, and the Pullman strike ended. However, the order and use of federal troops had set an example. In the years to come, such court orders would be used again and again as a means of halting strikes, but it would always be bitterly resented and opposed by the unions. ■

▲ *Troops were called in to settle a labor dispute at Andrew Carnegie's steel plant in Homestead, Pennsylvania. What started as a strike of 800 workers ended with 3,000 people locked out of their jobs.*

■ *What methods were used in the Pullman and Homestead strikes to stop unions from influencing workers?*

REVIEW

1. **FOCUS** How did changes in production affect the way in which Americans lived and worked during the late 1800s and early 1900s?
2. **CONNECT** What types of new work became available with the growth of industry?
3. **ECONOMICS** What effect did mass production have on the cost of business in the United States?
4. **ECONOMICS** Why did workers unionize? How did employers react to unions?
5. **CRITICAL THINKING** Do you think that unions can help or hurt the cause of workers? Do you believe all workers should belong to unions? Be sure to explain your reasons in detail.
6. **ACTIVITY** Imagine you are a union member in the early 1900s. Draw a creative poster or political cartoon that protests poor working conditions, such as long hours.

SOCIAL SYSTEMS

Critical Thinking

Ask students to explain why lockouts can undermine the efforts of labor unions. *(Workers can be replaced with non-union employees; leverage of union is lost)*

■ *Both plants locked out the workers and used an armed guard; in addition, the Pullman plant had the court issue an order to end the strike.*

CLOSE

You may wish to copy on the board the Graphic Overview on page 455 to begin the review. Ask students to recall their answers to the Thinking Focus at the beginning of the lesson. How accurate were they? As a reteaching activity, have students name four factors that caused the dissatisfaction of industrial workers and then describe the tactics used by management to break strikes.

Answers to Review Questions

1. For many Americans, assembly lines and mass production led to long hours of repetitive, tedious work in poor working conditions. The low wages, barely covering the cost of living expenses, made life hard.
2. The new work included tending machines and performing single, repetitive tasks in factories.
3. Cheaper, faster production led to financial gain for employers and investors.
4. Because workers believed their individual complaints were being ignored, they organized to be heard. Employers feared the power of unions and tried to thwart their techniques.
5. Students should consider unions at the turn of the century as well as unions today. Allow for personal opinion.
6. Remind students that their drawings should be as descriptive as possible.

Homework Options

Ask students to collect newspaper or magazine articles on present-day union activities. *(Strikes, appeals to the NLRB, work slowdowns, gaining union recognition)*

Study Guide: page 67.

INTRODUCE

Encourage students to recall what they learned about immigrants earlier in this book, for example in Chapter 7. *(German and Irish immigrants)* Tell them that this lesson is about immigrants from Southern and Eastern Europe and from Asia. Have students read the Thinking Focus and consider what the word *influx* means in this question. *(To flow in)* Tell students to read the lesson to find out the kinds of jobs and living conditions these immigrants would find in America.

CULTURE
Critical Thinking

What does *quarantine* mean in the excerpt quoted on this page? *(Enforced isolation to prevent the spread of disease)* Why would the Germans have insisted on isolating Mary Antin's family on their journey to America? *(To prevent the spread of cholera)*

1850 1860 1870 1920

L E S S O N 4

Destination: America

THINKING FOCUS

How did the influx of immigrants during the late 1800s affect American society?

"Happy journey!" "God help you!" "Good-bye!" These were the shouts that echoed in Mary Antin's ears in 1894 as she and her family joined the thousands of Russian Jews fleeing religious persecution.

Mary's father had immigrated to Boston, Massachusetts, several years earlier. Now 12-year-old Mary, her mother, her brother, and her sisters were on their way to join him.

At the Russian border, their passports were taken from them. A friendly German helped them cross the border. They then journeyed in crowded railroad cars to Hamburg, Germany. There they were locked up for two weeks because the Germans feared they might be carrying cholera, the deadly disease then raging in Russia. (See column 2 for Mary's recollection of the quarantine.)

Finally, the Antin family boarded a steamship bound for Boston. For 16 days they sailed westward.

> *Quarantine, they called it, and there was a great deal of it—two weeks of it. Two weeks within high brick walls, several hundred of us herded in half a dozen compartments, . . . sleeping in rows, like sick people in a hospital; with roll-call morning and night, and short rations three times a day; with never a sign of the free world beyond our barred windows; with anxiety and longing and homesickness in our hearts, and in our ears the unfamiliar voice of the invisible ocean, which drew and repelled us at the same time.*

"And so suffering, fearing, brooding, rejoicing," wrote Mary, "we crept nearer and nearer to the coveted shore until, on a glorious May morning, . . . our eyes beheld the Promised Land, and my father received us in his arms."

Promise of America

Mary and her family were but a few of the thousands of immigrants who poured into the United States after the Civil War. Between 1860 and 1900, 14 million people arrived. Eight million more came between 1901 and 1910.

New Immigrants from Europe

Until 1880, three-fourths of the Europeans who immigrated to the United States had come from Britain, Ireland, Germany, and Scandinavia. By 1890, the majority were from southern and eastern Europe. Most numerous were the Jews, who emigrated to escape poverty and religious persecution. Other immigrants fled from political turmoil. The vast majority, however, were escaping the ravages of poverty. They came from Italy, Poland, and Russia. They arrived from Austria-Hungary, Greece, Turkey, and Serbia. Most of these immigrants landed at Ellis Island in New York harbor. There, as many as

Objectives

1. Contrast the immigrants who came to the United States after 1870 with earlier immigrants.
2. Describe the work available to immigrants in the second half of the 19th century.
3. Compare the immigrants' ideals with their experiences.
4. Explain how immigrants helped American industry.

Graphic Overview

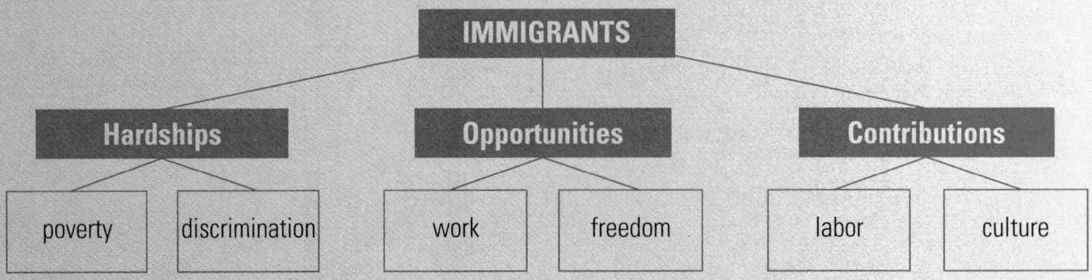

5,000 newcomers were processed in a single day. As the Closer Look on pages 464–465 shows, the country had to find a way to process all these people. Ellis Island in New York harbor became the East Coast reception center for immigrants.

Immigrants from Europe who had friends and relatives already in the United States were encouraged to join them. Many of the young, single men, however, did not expect to stay. They planned to make as much money as they could and then return to their homelands to start a business or raise a family. A large percentage of these return migrants were farmers. Organizations such as the Sons of Italy and the Polish Women's Alliance helped newcomers to find housing and jobs.

Advertisements from steamship companies and low fares helped to lure immigrants to the United States. Further encouragement came from the governments of some states and from industries seeking cheap labor. Some companies even sent recruiters abroad to urge people to come to the United States.

Asian Immigrants

At the same time that Europeans were arriving on the East Coast, thousands of Asians were arriving on the West Coast of the United States. The majority of these Asian immigrants were Chinese.

Between 1865 and 1882, 320,000 Chinese immigrated to the United States. They fled from southern China, which had struggled with warfare, overpopulation, and economic problems.

The first major wave of Chinese came after the discovery of gold in California in 1849. By 1852, visions of Gam Saan, the Mountain of Gold, had lured 20,000 Chinese to San Francisco. As you learned in Chapter 14, the demand for workers on the Union Pacific railroad later brought many Chinese to the Pacific coast.

In addition, the Japanese and the Filipinos immigrated to the United States. Like southern China, Japan was overpopulated and was suffering from economic hardships. Starting in 1885, the Japanese government permitted its people to emigrate.

From 1870 to 1920, thousands of immigrants from European and Asian countries joined the American workforce.

Immigration to the United States, 1870–1920

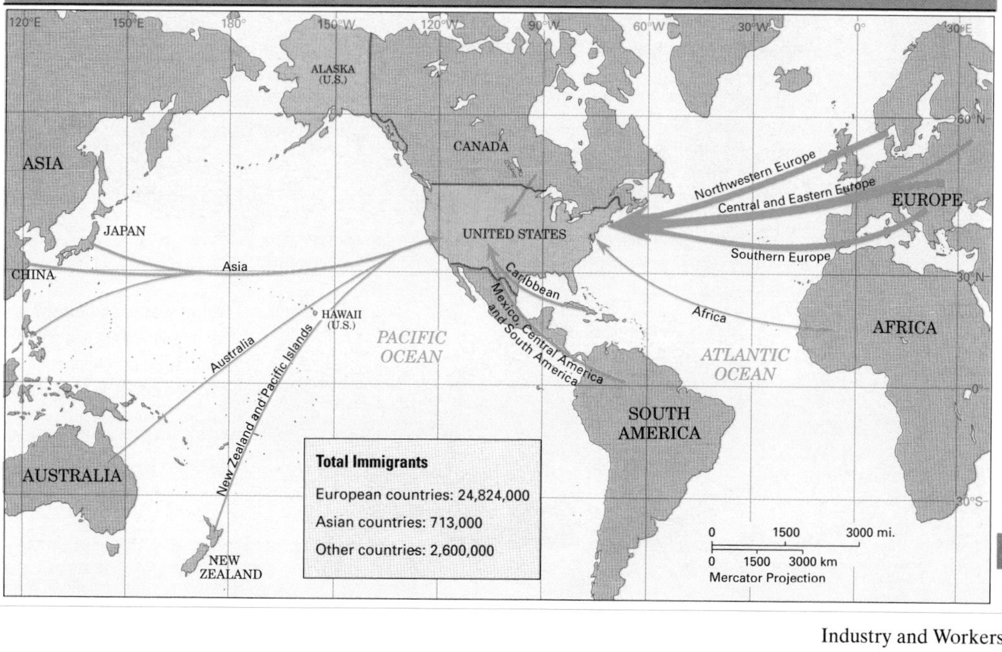

DEVELOP

Copy on the board the main headings of the Graphic Overview from page 462—*Hardships, Opportunities,* and *Contributions*—to show the basic structure of the lesson. Have students read the lesson and take notes on these three areas of the immigrants' experience.

CULTURE

Critical Thinking

Encourage students to compare the immigrant groups that came to the United States after 1880 to immigrant groups that had come earlier. Why did the groups that came after 1880 immigrate? *(Sample answer: Earlier groups came from Britain, Ireland, Germany, and Scandinavia. After 1880 most groups came from Asia and from Southern and Eastern Europe; they came to escape war, poverty, and cruelty in their native lands.)*

Access Strategy

The day before starting Lesson 4, have students ask their parents what country their ancestors came from and if they know when they came to America. Write the countries and the years of arrival on the board. Point out that the ancestors of almost all Americans were immigrants, whether they came in 1620 or 1980, and whether they came freely or as slaves. Tell them that they will read in this lesson about the period from 1870 to 1920, during which hundreds of thousands of immigrants came to America. Ask students if they can trace their ancestry to immigrants of this period.

Access Activity

Have students use the width of the arrows in the map on this page to find out which countries sent the most people to the United States between 1870 and 1920. Where did immigrants from different parts of the world go? *(Asians, the West; Europeans, East Coast; Canadians, Midwest; Central and South Americans, Southwest)*

Note: You may wish to use A Closer Look to review this lesson.

CULTURE

Visual Learning

Ellis Island served as a processing center for as many as 5,000 immigrants a day during the late 1800s and early 1900s. When the great influx stopped, however, Ellis Island stood unused for years. Why did Americans decide to restore this site? *(To preserve cultural heritage)*

A CLOSER LOOK

Ellis Island Immigrants

Welcome to the United States—get in line! The Statue of Liberty towered over a big waiting room for thousands of immigrants who arrived in the early 1900s. In fact, the waiting could even begin offshore. Even ships lined up in New York Harbor for days until space was available on Ellis Island.

What would you bring?
Many immigrants had only one small suitcase. Children brought toys and books. People like this Italian family brought bedding, a few dishes, maybe a violin, or a favorite photograph.

Critical Thinking

Have students consider the expectations and hopes that many arriving immigrants had for their new lives in the United States. Ask them to make a list of these expectations and hopes.

Historical Context

The Statue of Liberty was the inspiration of a French sculptor, Frederic Auguste Bartholdi, who believed very strongly in the ideals represented by the American Revolution. He decided to build a great monument to liberty that would be financed by voluntary donations from the French people and given to the people of the United States. His original hope was that it would be presented to the United States during the centennial celebrations of 1876. That goal became impossible because it took far too long to raise money to build the colossal structure.

In June 1886, Lady Liberty (packed in 214 crates) arrived at Bedloe's Island in New York Harbor. Americans had raised money to pay for a pedestal on which the steel skeleton was erected. The copper skin was attached with more than 600,000 rivets. The Statue of Liberty was officially unveiled on October 28, 1886.

You've passed inspection! Immigrants had to pass inspections and answer dozens of questions. A story goes that when one flustered German was asked his name, he answered, "Ich hab's vergessen" ("I forgot!"). The official wrote down his name as "Ferguson" and it stuck.

After weeks of seasickness, these Russian Jews smile with relief. More than 1 million Jews came to Ellis Island in the early 1900s. Men usually traveled ahead of their families, to secure housing and work.

All Aboard! 75% of those leaving Ellis Island headed for New York City, but others bought tickets for Chicago, Cleveland, and St. Louis. Railroad agents pinned numbered tags to the immigrants' clothing if they couldn't speak English. The numbers told other agents where the families were destined.

ECONOMICS

Visual Learning

Immigrants who experienced poverty in their native lands came to America in search of a better life. How was their experience different, do you think, from that of the immigrants who come to our country today?

More About Immigrants Of the 26 million people who arrived at immigration stations in New York City between 1870 and 1920, only two percent were turned away.

Language Arts Connection

Immigrants brought their languages with them. Students might look for names of streets and towns that reflect the backgrounds of immigrants. Students can contribute words to a class list and use an etymological dictionary to check the history of these words.

Science Connection

Two Chinese immigrants are cited on page 467 in this lesson for their contributions to fruit cultivation. Have students do research to find out more about how new strains of fruits, vegetables, and grains are developed, including the techniques of hybridization and selective breeding.

Critical Thinking

Ask students to identify the immigrant groups that have settled in their own communities throughout American history and to consider how that has changed over time.

■ *Groups included Asians and Eastern and Southern Europeans.*

CULTURE

Critical Thinking

Ask students why, considering the kinds of jobs that were available in the United States, people continued to immigrate to this country. *(There were often no better jobs at home; in America, they had a chance to better themselves and improve their children's opportunities; and some wanted to escape religious and ethnic strife.)*

CULTURE

Critical Thinking

How did the treatment of immigrants—ridicule, hostility, violence, job and housing discrimination—compare with the ideals of the Declaration of Independence and the Constitution? *(Sample answer: These ideals hold that all people are equal and have rights to life, liberty, and freedom of religion and speech.)*

■ *What groups immigrated to America during the mid- to late 1800s?*

As a result, thousands of Japanese migrated to Hawaii, where they worked on American sugar plantations. When the islands of Hawaii became a United States territory in 1898, many Japanese moved on to the U.S. mainland. By 1900, more than 10,000 Japanese were living in the United States, mostly on the Pacific coast. ■

Immigrants Become Americans

Although welcomed by employers as cheap labor, the hard-working European and Asian immigrants often encountered fear and prejudice. Most had to learn a new language as well as to adjust to a new culture. Their dress and accents were often ridiculed; in many instances their religious beliefs met with intolerance. Most of the new immigrants were poor, uneducated, and untrained in any skilled labor. They could find only backbreaking, poorly paid jobs and had little choice but to live in dirty, crowded slums where disease and crime were common.

Facing Discrimination

Most immigrants dreamed of becoming true Americans—of adopting American dress and customs, as well as speaking the English language. However, some—particularly the older immigrants—clung to the traditions of their past, to the customs they had cherished all their lives. Their cultural differences were often viewed with suspicion by native-born Americans. Because immigrants would work for lower wages than the native-born, they were resented by the workers who were trying so hard to raise their own wages and standard of living.

As more and more immigrants arrived, the tide of nativism—a policy of favoring native-born inhabitants over immigrants—gained wide support. Nativists claimed that immigrants would exhaust American resources and endanger American culture with their foreign beliefs and "exotic" customs.

Foremost among these groups was the American Protective Association. Shouting "America for Americans," APA members tried to bar Catholics from entering the United States and opposed immigration generally.

In addition to facing discrimination in finding jobs and housing, immigrants sometimes encountered violence. Despite the problems they faced, the immigrants' new lives were

➤ *Asians, such as this Chinese family in California, faced discrimination in finding jobs and housing during the late 1800s and early 1900s.*

Visual Learning

Point out that the items in the photograph of Chinese immigrants on this page were props; the photograph was probably taken to send back to China. Why would they want to send a picture back home that used as props a bicycle and a sewing machine, items they did not currently own? *(Sample answer: To try to impress friends and relatives at home)*

Writing a Letter

Have students imagine that they are recent immigrants to the United States in 1890. Have each choose a particular role—for example, a twelve-year-old boy from Italy—and imagine how their character feels about life in the United States. Have them write an imaginary letter from the immigrant to relatives at home, either encouraging them to come or warning them not to come to this country, depending on their character's experiences.

Oral Report

Tell students to find out about the life of an immigrant who arrived in the United States between 1870 and 1920 by reading an account of an immigrant's life. What were the reasons for immigrating? What were the immigrant's early experiences in America? Students could choose an immigrant who became famous—Mayo, Carnegie, or Pulitzer, for example (page 467)—or one who did not. Have them report their findings to the class.

Immigrant Populations, 1920

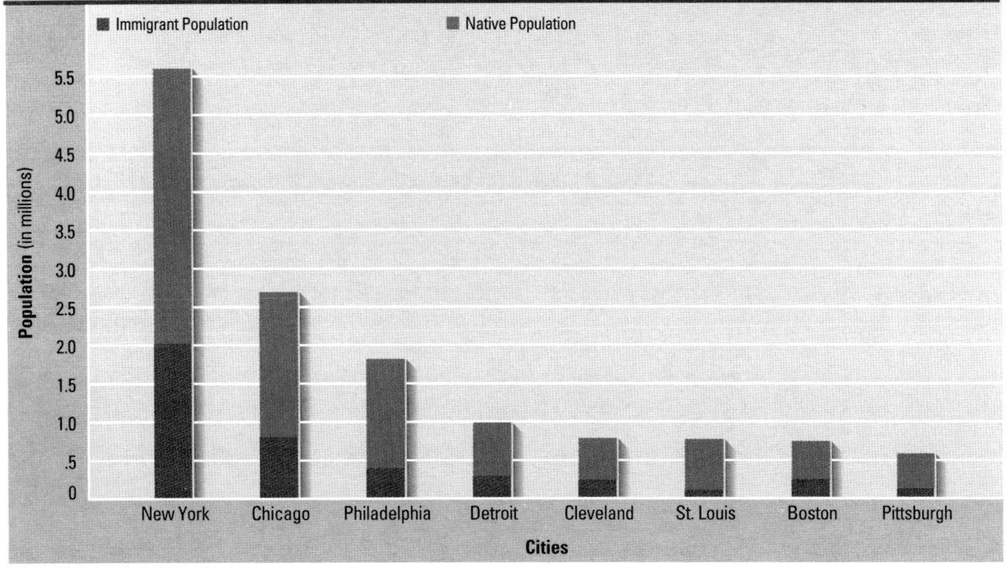

Despite hardships, immigrants continued to settle in major urban centers. Which cities had the largest immigrant populations in 1920? Why do you think so many immigrants lived in New York City?

usually better than the ones they had left behind. Few other countries offered the freedom and opportunities that were available to Americans.

Contributions of Immigrants

Immigrants like Carnegie, Gompers, and Bell changed American industry and labor forever. Other immigrants also made outstanding contributions in these years. English-born William Mayo set up an emergency hospital that became the world-famous Mayo Clinic. Hungarian-born Joseph Pulitzer, a newspaper editor, used his fortune to establish the Pulitzer Prizes that are awarded annually in journalism and the arts. Two Chinese men developed popular fruits—the Bing cherry, named for Ah Bing, and the Lue Gim Gon Mediterranean Valencia orange.

In spite of their success, many immigrants felt pressure to become "American" and to give up the customs of their old countries. Jews, who faced more discrimination than many other European groups, often felt torn about holding onto their religious identity. Rabbi Solomon Schindler expressed his fear of losing his culture, saying: "I believed in making the Jew like the Gentile [Christian]. . . . The more he became near to . . . being like his Gentile fellowmen, the more I believed success would crown my work. It was a great mistake."

While immigrants gave up many of their traditions, they also managed to hold onto some of them. These traditions, which include beliefs, music, art, and food, have enriched American culture. In the same way, the hard work and talent of these immigrants helped to make the United States an industrial giant by 1920. ■

■ *What problems did immigrants face in becoming Americans?*

REVIEW

1. **FOCUS** How did the influx of immigrants during the late 1800s affect American society?
2. **CONNECT** Why did companies send recruiters abroad to encourage people to come to America?
3. **CULTURE** How did American workers react to competition from immigrants?
4. **CRITICAL THINKING** Why did the promise of America lead so many people to immigrate to this country?
5. **ACTIVITY** Prepare a short presentation on what opportunities were available to immigrants when they arrived in the United States.

ECONOMICS

Critical Thinking

Students may answer this question from the point of view of an immigrant: How do you feel about giving up some or all of your cultural traditions to become "American"? *(Sample answer: I want to learn new ways but also keep family traditions.)*

■ *Job and housing discrimination, racism and bigotry, low wages, and poor working conditions all made it difficult for immigrants to gain a good position in American society.*

CLOSE

Have students answer the Thinking Focus. Students can complete a Graphic Overview on the board, like the one on page 462, using the details they noted while reading the lesson. As a reteaching activity, have students do the Writing a Letter activity on page 466.

Answers to Review Questions

1. Earlier immigrants competed with and discriminated against new immigrants. The economy flourished because of the abundant labor supply.
2. Unskilled workers were needed to tend machines and do repetitive tasks.
3. Some American workers discriminated against the new immigrants.
4. Sample answer: Dreams of success and great opportunities in America led many immigrants to leave behind poverty in their homelands. Allow for personal opinions.
5. Students may role play recruiters making oral presentations to lure immigrants to the United States.

Homework Options

Have students list favorite foods brought here by immigrants from Southern or Eastern Europe or from Asia, either foods they eat at home or in restaurants.

Study Guide: page 68.

Chapter Review

Reviewing Key Terms

assembly line (p. 456)
capital (p. 445)
entrepreneur (p. 445)
labor union (p. 458)
philanthropist (p. 446)
profit (p. 445)
strike (p. 458)
urban society (p. 448)

A. In each of the following pairs, the two terms are related in some way. Write a sentence for each pair that clearly explains the relationship between the two terms.

1. capital, profit
2. assembly line, mass production
3. labor union, strike
4. profit, entrepreneur
5. philanthropist, urban society

B. Based on what you have read in the chapter, decide whether each of the following statements is true or false. If a sentence is false, rewrite it so that it is true.

1. An entrepreneur was careful not to take risks.
2. Only a wealthy person could be an important philanthropist.
3. As more people took up farming, they moved from cities to rural areas, and the United States became an urban society.
4. Employers used children on assembly lines because they worked for lower wages.
5. Washington D.C. is the capital of the United States.

Exploring Concepts

A. On a separate sheet of paper, copy the chart below. In the second column, list the inventor of each invention. In the third column, briefly describe the impact that each invention had on society.

Invention	Inventor	Impact on society
Lightbulb		
Sewing machine		
Phonograph		
Telephone		
Linotype		
Generator		

B. Support each of the following statements with facts and details from the chapter.

1. Immigrants added much to American society during the late nineteenth century.
2. New inventions revolutionized American life between 1870 and 1920.
3. Efficient methods of manufacturing helped to create new businesses.
4. Improved transportation helped cities to grow.
5. There were many reasons why people moved from farms to the cities during this time.
6. Workers did not benefit from mass production methods.
7. Workers' discontent with job conditions had several effects.
8. In the cities, several groups helped newcomers such as Southern black people and immigrants.
9. The rising tide of immigrants caused resentment among native-born Americans.
10. The American Dream was an idea that appealed to all Americans, no matter what their income level.
11. Steel changed the way cities were designed and built in the nineteenth century.
12. Andrew Carnegie was an excellent example of the new American philanthropist.

Answers to Reviewing Key Terms

A. Sample answers:

1. Investors put capital into a business in hopes of making a profit.
2. The technique of the assembly line permitted mass production of many items that used to be made by hand.
3. Workers who organized into labor unions could effectively use strikes to obtain their goals.
4. By taking risks in business, entrepreneurs often make large profits.
5. The generosity of philanthropists at the turn of the century greatly benefited urban society in the United States.

B. Answers:

1. False. Entrepreneurs took great risks in order to be successful.
2. True.
3. False. The United States became an urban society because more people moved to the cities for jobs with large industries.
4. True.
5. True.

Answers to Exploring Concepts

A. Answers:

Light bulb: Edison / reduced the threat of fire, changed working hours and home life

Sewing Machine: Howe / clothing could be mass-produced

Phonograph: Edison / made music more accessible to general public

Telephone: Bell / changed business and personal communication

Linotype: Mergenthaler / speeded up publishing process

Generator: Edison / produced electricity to run other machines

B. Sample answers:

1. Students should cite the achievements of individual immigrants as well as general immigrant contributions to industry and culture.
2. Students should mention inventions other than those on the chart.
3. The assembly line led to mass production. New methods of communication and steel production led to new industries.
4. Better transportation increased the population and the movement of goods within cities.
5. Many people moved to cities for job opportunities; others moved to escape discrimination.
6. Answers should show how mass production resulted in loss of jobs, boredom, injury, lower wages, and poorer working conditions.
7. Laborers formed unions, and strikes resulted in both violence and improved working conditions.
8. The National Urban League helped blacks. Groups such as the Sons of Italy and the Polish Woman's Alliance helped immigrants.
9. Workers resented the fact that immigrants worked for lower wages, and nativists feared that immigrants would endanger American culture.
10. The American Dream proposed that anyone could get ahead with hard work and perseverance.
11. Buildings could now support more stories, so steel-framed skyscrapers changed the American skylines.
12. He believed that his wealth should also benefit society, so he donated great sums of money for public education and cultural institutions.

Reviewing Skills

1. Look at the map of the Development of Industrial Cities, 1900–1920, on page 454. What was the population of Detroit in 1900? In 1920? Name three cities that were not on the 1900 map but had populations of at least 100,000 by 1920.
2. Turn to the thematic maps of U.S. climate and precipitation on pages 706 and 707. Look at the southeastern states. How do the climate and precipitation of this area relate to one another? Now look at the southern part of Florida. How do the climate and precipitation of this area differ from the rest of the Southeast?
3. Find a road map and a topographic map of your state. Trace a route from your town to the state capital or another large city. What type of terrain does the road cover? Write a short paragraph explaining what this tells you about how transportation routes developed in your area.
4. Suppose you wanted to use a computerized reference system to research the background of a particular invention, such as the telephone shown on this page. Write down three topics you could use to begin your search.

Using Critical Thinking

1. Thomas Edison said "Genius is 1 percent inspiration and 99 percent perspiration." What did he mean by this? How does his statement reflect the values of many Americans, both in the late 1800s and today?
2. Do you think black Americans have faced obstacles other ethnic groups—including the immigrants discussed in this chapter—did not have to face? Explain your answer.
3. Many immigrants coming to the United States today face forms of discrimination. Based on what you know about the hardships earlier immigrants faced, why do you think some Americans still respond negatively to immigrants?
4. The right of entrepreneurs to make a profit by investing in new businesses is part of the economic system called capitalism. Do you think the new businesses described in this chapter could have developed if they had depended only on the government for support? Explain your answer.

Preparing for Citizenship

1. **WRITING ACTIVITY** Today, unions represent professional groups as well as labor groups. Interview someone who is a member of a union. Find out in what ways belonging to a union has been of benefit to them. Write a short report on your findings.
2. **WRITING ACTIVITY** Research the growth of your city or of a nearby large city. Find out when it was founded and how fast its population increased. When did it grow most rapidly? What accounted for this growth? What were, and are, its principal industries? Write a newspaper profile of the town or city, based on your research.
3. **ART ACTIVITY** Create a poster display on the evolution of one of the inventions mentioned in this chapter. Find as many pictures of different versions of the invention as you can. Use advertisements from old newspapers and magazines to find out how much examples of the invention cost long ago. Compare those advertisements and prices with current advertisements and prices for modern versions of the invention.
4. **COLLABORATIVE LEARNING** Assume that the class is a textile company. Divide into two groups, one representing management and one representing the union. Draw up a list of demands for each side, based on nineteenth-century working conditions. As a group, work out a compromise to keep the company running.

Answers to Reviewing Skills

1. Between 100,000 and 500,000; between 500,000 and 1 million; Students should choose three from Grand Rapids, Akron, Youngstown, Dayton, and Gary.
2. In general, the southeastern states are humid and subtropical with 40–60 inches of annual precipitation. The southern tip of Florida is more extreme; it is tropical wet and dry with more than 60 inches of annual precipitation in some areas.
3. Refer students to Understanding Topographical Maps on page 433.
4. Refer students to Understanding Reference Materials on pages 274–275.

Answers to Using Critical Thinking

1. Students should note that even a genius such as Edison needed to work hard to bring his inventions to fruition. Discuss the relationship between the American Dream and the work ethic.
2. If necessary, remind students that African Americans were brought to this country as slaves.
3. Students should note how several immigrant groups were discriminated against, and, in turn, discriminated against newly arrived immigrants from other countries.
4. Ask students to consider how willing they would be to take the risks entrepreneurs take. While the government promoted the building of railroads, most new businesses required entrepreneurs to be willing to risk losing their investments in exchange for the possibility of great profit.

Answers to Preparing for Citizenship

1. **WRITING ACTIVITY** Point out that various unions exist, including teachers' unions.
2. **WRITING ACTIVITY** Direct students to the chamber of commerce for information.
3. **ART ACTIVITY** Point out that many of the machines and appliances we use daily, such as computers, are relatively new.
4. **COLLABORATIVE LEARNING** Refer students to material within the book, such as the list of rules and regulations for factory workers on page 271 and the interior of a mill on page 259.

Chapter 16 Planning at a Glance

The Gilded Age

	Objectives	Reading Support and Other Resources	Diverse Learning Strategies
Lesson 1 The Politics of Corruption *pp. 472–476* 1–2 days	• Identify the ways in which big business attempted to manipulate the political system during the Gilded Age. • Describe the corruption and scandals that took place during Grant's presidency. • Explain the connection between urban problems and the rise of political bosses and machine politics.	• **Workbook** or **Reading Support:** pp. 229–232 Review p. 54 Lesson Support/Transition p. 54 Multi-lang. Sum. pp. 107–108 • **Other Resources:** Geography Kit, Poster 5, Study Guide p. 69	Access Strat. **(Extra Support)** TE p. 473 Access Act. **(SDAIE)** TE p. 473 Drawing a Cartoon **(Visual)** TE p. 475 Homework Options **(Visual)** TE p. 476 Audiotapes of Multi-language Lesson Summaries **(Auditory)**
Lesson 2 The Reforming Impulse *pp. 477–485* 2–3 days	• Identify the Mugwumps and what they sought to change. • State why reformers wanted to institute a civil service. • Describe the abuses and unfair business practices that led to regulation of the big railroad companies. • Analyze the effect monopolies and trusts had on the nation's economy.	• **Workbook** or **Reading Support:** pp. 233–236 Review p. 55 Lesson Support/Transition p. 55 Multi-lang. Sum. pp. 109–110 • **Other Resources:** Geography Kit, Study Guide p. 70	Access Act. **(SDAIE)** TE p. 478 Access Strat. **(Extra Support)** TE p. 478 Art Connection **(Visual)** TE p. 482 Science Connection **(GATE)** TE p. 482 Audiotapes of Multi-language Lesson Summaries **(Auditory)**
Lesson 3 The Populist Revolt *pp. 486–491* 2–3 days	• Summarize the economic and political factors that led to the rise of the Populist movement. • Describe the steps farmers took to try to improve their economic situation. • Explain why the Populist movement declined rapidly following the 1896 presidential election.	• **Workbook** or **Reading Support:** pp. 237–240 Review p. 56 Lesson Support/Transition p. 56 Multi-lang. Sum. pp. 111–112 • **Other Resources:** Study Guide p. 71, Study Print 11	Science Connection **(GATE)** TE p. 489 Map and Globe Skills **(Visual)** TE p. 490 Collaborative Act. **(Visual)** TE p. 490 Audiotapes of Multi-language Lesson Summaries **(Auditory)**
Skill: Reading Mark Twain *pp. 492–493* 1 day	• Use an excerpt from *Innocents Abroad* to evaluate contemporary views of historical time periods.	• **Other Resources:** Study Guide p. 72	Role Playing **(Auditory)** TE p. 492
Chapter Review *pp. 494–495* 1 day		Chapter 16 Test pp. 61–64 *(See facsimiles on TE p. 764.)*	Assessment Multiple-Use Masters pp. 81–88

Reading Support Resources *for Every Lesson*

Reading and Review

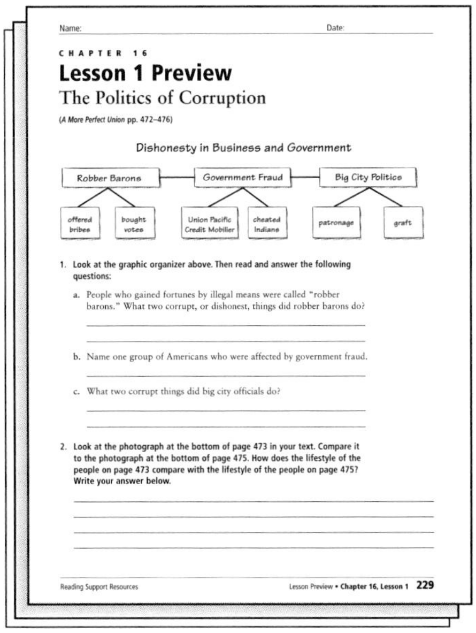
Name: Date:

CHAPTER 16

Lesson 1 Preview

The Politics of Corruption

(A More Perfect Union pp. 472–476)

1. Look at the graphic organizer above. Then read and answer the following questions:
   a. People who gained fortunes by illegal means were called "robber barons." What two corrupt, or dishonest, things did robber barons do?
   b. Name one group of Americans who were affected by government fraud.
   c. What two corrupt things did big city officials do?
2. Look at the photograph at the bottom of page 473 in your text. Compare it to the photograph at the bottom of page 475. How does the lifestyle of the people on page 473 compare with the lifestyle of the people on page 475? Write your answer below.

Reading Support Resources — Lesson Preview • Chapter 16, Lesson 1 229

- **Chapter Overview*** p. 228
- **Lesson Previews*** using graphic organizers from the Teacher's Edition pp. 229, 233, 237
- **Reading Strategies*** pp. 230, 234, 238
- **Lesson Summaries*** pp. 231–232, 235–236, 239–240
- **Lesson Reviews** pp. 54, 55, 56

* **Workbook** includes starred items.

Multi-language Summaries

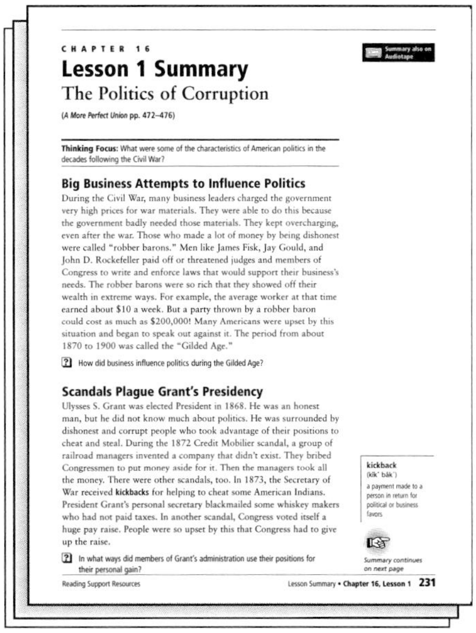
CHAPTER 16

Summary also on Audiotape

Lesson 1 Summary

The Politics of Corruption

(A More Perfect Union pp. 472–476)

Thinking Focus: What were some of the characteristics of American politics in the decades following the Civil War?

Big Business Attempts to Influence Politics

During the Civil War, many business leaders charged the government very high prices for war materials. They were able to do this because the government badly needed those materials. They kept overcharging, even after the war. Those who made a lot of money by being dishonest were called "robber barons." Men like James Fisk, Jay Gould, and John D. Rockefeller paid off or threatened judges and members of Congress to write and enforce laws that would support their business's needs. The robber barons were so rich that they showed off their wealth in extreme ways. For example, the average worker at that time earned about $10 a week. But a party thrown by a robber baron could cost as much as $200,000! Many Americans were upset by this situation and began to speak out against it. The period from about 1870 to 1900 was called the "Gilded Age."

? How did business influence politics during the Gilded Age?

Scandals Plague Grant's Presidency

Ulysses S. Grant was elected President in 1868. He was an honest man, but he did not know much about politics. He was surrounded by dishonest and corrupt people who took advantage of their positions to cheat and steal. During the 1872 Credit Mobilier scandal, a group of railroad managers invented a company that didn't exist. They bribed Congressmen to put money aside for it. Then the managers took all the money. There were other scandals, too. In 1873, the Secretary of War received **kickbacks** for helping to cheat some American Indians. President Grant's personal secretary blackmailed some whiskey makers who had not paid taxes. In another scandal, Congress voted itself a huge pay raise. People were so upset by this that Congress had to give up the raise.

kickback (kik' bak') a payment made to a person in return for political or business favors

? In what ways did members of Grant's administration use their positions for their personal gain?

Summary continues on next page

Reading Support Resources — Lesson Summary • Chapter 16, Lesson 1 231

Lesson Summaries in:

- English (See Reading and Review.)
- Spanish pp. 231–232, 235–236, 239–240
- Chinese pp. 107–112
- Hmong pp. 107–112
- Khmer pp. 107–112
- Vietnamese pp. 107–112

Summaries available on audiotapes

Lesson Support / Transition

S D A I E

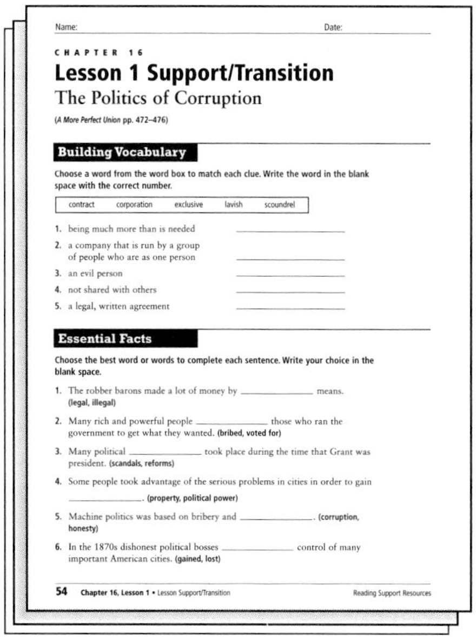
Name: Date:

CHAPTER 16

Lesson 1 Support/Transition

The Politics of Corruption

(A More Perfect Union pp. 472–476)

Building Vocabulary

Choose a word from the word box to match each clue. Write the word in the blank space with the correct number.

contract — corporation — exclusive — lavish — scoundrel

1. being much more than is needed
2. a company that is run by a group of people who are as one person
3. an evil person
4. not shared with others
5. a legal, written agreement

Essential Facts

Choose the best word or words to complete each sentence. Write your choice in the blank space.

1. The robber barons made a lot of money by ______ means. (legal, illegal)
2. Many rich and powerful people ______ those who ran the government to get what they wanted. (bribed, voted for)
3. Many political ______ took place during the time that Grant was president. (scandals, reforms)
4. Some people took advantage of the serious problems in cities in order to gain ______. (property, political power)
5. Machine politics was based on bribery and ______. (corruption, honesty)
6. In the 1870s dishonest political bosses ______ control of many important American cities. (gained, lost)

54 Chapter 16, Lesson 1 • Lesson Support/Transition — Reading Support Resources

Activities for SDAIE
Specially **D**esigned **A**cademic **I**nstruction in **E**nglish

- **Lesson Support/Transition** pp. 54, 55, 56

Technology Options

Internet Support

http://www.eduplace.com

Social Studies Center at Education Place

Internet support for Chapter 16:

- ***Lesson at a Glance***
- ***Gilded Age Elections***

Software

Student Writing Center® (CD-ROM) (Macintosh® or Windows®)

School to Career

Farming grew rapidly during the 1800s. Today, however, farmers are a very small percentage of the national population, yet there are thousands of individuals involved in the field of agriculture. Have students research and write a brief report on an agricultural occupation such as farmer, soil technician, or agricultural journalist.

Character Education

Today, conglomerates and other big businesses have great power over people. What is it about big business/monopolies that is a problem? How do monopolies and conglomerates conflict with our basic economic system?

CHAPTER
PREVIEW

Read aloud the chapter title and the narrative underneath it. Have students explain the meaning of the word *gilded*. *(When something is gilded, it is made to appear brighter and more attractive than it actually is.)*

Have students examine the visuals and read the captions. Ask what these pictures tell them about the Gilded Age.

Looking Back

Ask students to discuss what they learned about the tensions between the rich and the poor in Chapter 15. What tactics did the owners of companies use to keep their profits high? How did this affect the working poor? *(Low wages, piecework, and strikebreaking contributed to poor working conditions and high profits.)*

Looking Forward

Tell students that the greed that dominated business practices also dominated the politics of the time. In the next three lessons students will be learning about dishonest politicians and the people who fought for reform: The Politics of Corruption, The Reforming Impulse, and The Populist Revolt.

Chapter 16

The Gilded Age

gild: *to cover in a thin layer of either fake or real gold, usually done to make things look better than they really are*

The years following the Civil War offered many business opportunities. Plentiful resources, cheap labor, and government connections helped some Americans become wealthy on a truly grand scale. Business people became some of the nation's new heroes. Not everyone, though, was blinded to the problems beneath the gilded surface of power and money.

1880 Many wealthy Americans want to have the social standing of royal families in Europe. In this 1880 family portrait, the beautiful clothes and the fine furnishings make a royal impression. This carved rocking horse would make a fine toy for these children.

1868 | 1874 | 1880

Presidents

1869-1877 Grant

1877-1881 Hayes

1881 Garfield

1881- Arthu

1868

BACKGROUND

Widespread political corruption and business abuse characterized the decades following the Civil War. This era became known as the Gilded Age. Political revolt in response to this corruption led eventually to a series of government reforms.

Land Grants

Because the area between the Mississippi Valley and California was sparsely populated, the Union Pacific and Central Pacific railroad companies could expect few customers and little quick return on private investment. To encourage construction of a transcontinental railroad, the federal government provided generous subsidies to the railroad companies.

As amended in 1864, the Pacific Railway Act provided low-interest loans and donated land from the public domain. For each mile of track the companies built, they received 20 square miles of land and loans of $16,000, $32,000, or $48,000, depending on the terrain. Located in alternating sections on each side of the tracks, land grants created a 40-mile-wide checkerboard belt of railroad company land from Omaha to Sacramento. Since the total number of miles that each company built determined the size of its subsidy, the companies raced to lay track.

In all, the federal government donated 131 million acres of the public domain, and state governments granted 45 million acres, making the total area larger than the area of

Opera glasses gave audiences a better view of the stage and each other.

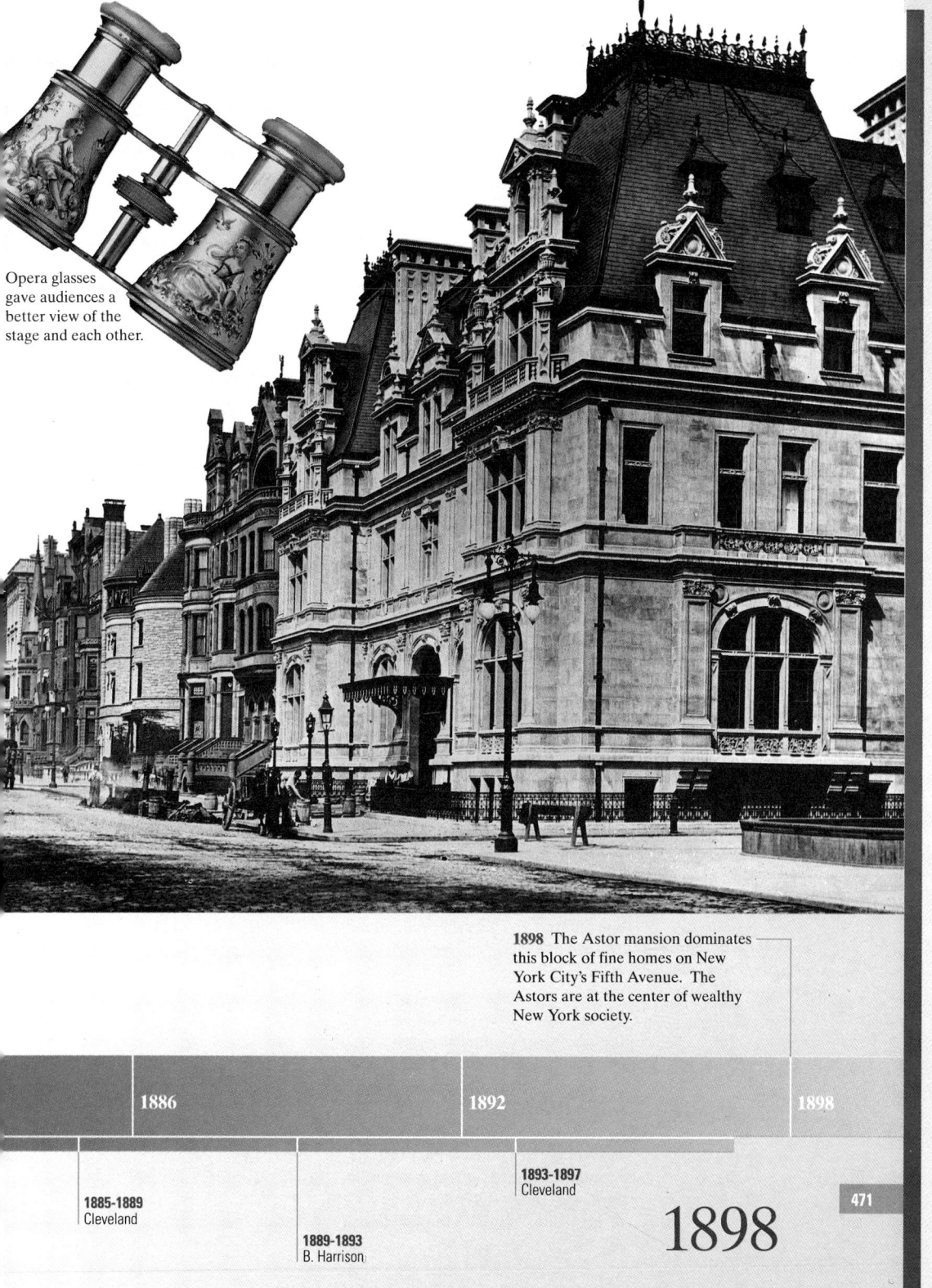

1898 The Astor mansion dominates this block of fine homes on New York City's Fifth Avenue. The Astors are at the center of wealthy New York society.

1886 | 1892 | 1898

1885-1889
Cleveland

1889-1893
B. Harrison

1893-1897
Cleveland

1898

Understanding the Visuals

Direct student attention to the family portrait: *Mrs. John Hudson Hall and her children John Hudson, Charles Ward, Cornelia Katherine, and Martha Jane* by Michael Gordiani, 1880. What about this painting tells them that this family is extremely wealthy? *(The rich colors; the fine clothing; the portrait itself is evidence of the family's wealth, since an artist's services are expensive)*

Point out the artifacts on these pages: the toy horse is hand carved from valuable black walnut and the opera glasses are mother-of-pearl.

New York's Fifth Avenue continues to be a center of wealthy American society.

Understanding Chronology

Refer to the timeline and point out that great corruption and wealth only for the few, coupled with reaction and with reform measures, developed during the thirty-year period from 1870 to 1900.

France and Belgium. By selling the land, companies raised money to finance construction and created customers who would depend on the railroad in the future. Railroad companies used unsold land as collateral for bank loans.

Philanthropy in the Gilded Age

During the Gilded Age, some rich businessmen turned to philanthropy. According to some critics, philanthropists wanted to offset their negative reputations. John D. Rockefeller and other millionaires gave huge sums to churches, universities, libraries, and hospitals. Leland Stanford, president of the Southern Pacific Railroad, founded Stanford University in 1885.

In "The Gospel of Wealth," an essay published in 1889, Andrew Carnegie presented a theory which justified the accumulation of wealth on the basis of stewardship. As Carnegie explained, the duty of a wealthy person was "to set an example of modest, unostentatious living, . . . and after doing so to consider all surplus funds which come to him simply as trust funds, which he is called upon to administer, . . . the man of wealth thus becoming the mere agent and trustee for his poorer brethren." In short, those who had acquired vast fortunes should distribute them for the public good.

Carnegie followed this practice in his own life. He retired in 1901 and devoted the rest of his life to granting money to public libraries, educational institutions, and the cause of world peace.

INTRODUCE

Read aloud the lesson title and ask students to give examples of corruption in politics or business. *(Taking bribes, giving jobs to friends)* Have students read the Thinking Focus and predict the answer based on the lesson title. Tell them to read the lesson to learn specific examples of corruption in politics after the Civil War.

Key Terms

Vocabulary strategies: T36–37

kickback—a payment made to a person in return for political or business favors

patronage—the practice of giving out government jobs in exchange for political support

political machine—a powerful, tightly run political organization that controlled many American cities in the late 1800s and early 1900s

graft—money gained by elected or appointed officials through dishonest or illegal means

1850
1860
1865
1896
1900

LESSON 1

The Politics of Corruption

THINKING FOCUS

What were some of the characteristics of American politics in the decades following the Civil War?

Key Terms

- kickback
- patronage
- political machine
- graft

James ("Big Jim") Fisk died of a gunshot wound when he was only 37 years old, but he made a lot of mischief during his short life. He smuggled cotton from the South to the North in the Civil War. He printed and sold phony bonds to get control of the profitable Erie Railroad. He bribed government officials to interfere with justice on his behalf. And in the most sensational financial scandal in U.S. history, he helped take control of the gold market in 1869.

Fisk's personal life was as shady as his business dealings. Fisk's New York City office, on the top floors of his Opera House, was the scene of wild parties. "Some people are born to be good, other people are born to be bad. I was born to be bad," the huge and jovial Fisk said. Fisk loved to make a splash in everything he did. For example, he had the boats of his shipping line painted lavender and yellow, and dressed in a fancy, custom-made uniform to see them off. He was well liked, despite public knowledge of his corrupt ways. Thousands of Fisk's friends, enemies, and employees attended his lavish funeral. One newspaper even compared Fisk's funeral with that of Abraham Lincoln.

Big Jim's delight in being caught in scandals was unusual among business leaders, who generally sought to avoid bad publicity. However, Fisk's disregard for law and ethics was not unusual among the men who dominated American business and politics from about 1870 to 1900.

The writer Mark Twain called this period the "Gilded Age." It was a time when the glamorous lives of the rich and powerful hid the dishonest ways in which many of them made their money.

➤ *The millions James Fisk made in dishonest deals paid for expensive clothes, a mansion, and lavish parties.*

Objectives

1. Identify the ways in which big business attempted to manipulate the political system during the Gilded Age.
2. Describe the corruption and scandals that took place during Grant's presidency.
3. Explain the connection between urban problems and the rise of political bosses and machine politics.

Graphic Overview

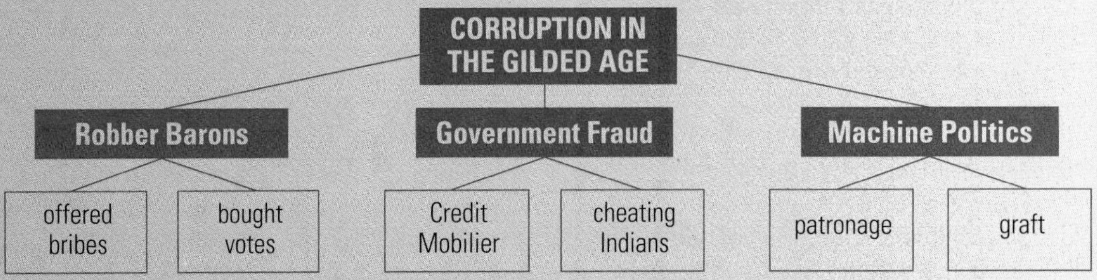
CORRUPTION IN THE GILDED AGE
Robber Barons
Government Fraud
Machine Politics
offered bribes
bought votes
Credit Mobilier
cheating Indians
patronage
graft

Big Business Attempts to Influence Politics

The Civil War had created many profitable opportunities for business leaders who had government contracts for war materials. Very often, businesses took advantage of the government's need for supplies to charge very high prices. Businesses also bribed congressmen and government officials to get contracts. These shady relationships didn't stop after the war. At the same time, as corporations became larger and more complex, it became harder to find out about such dishonest practices.

People who gained fortunes by illegal means were popularly known as "robber barons." Rich and powerful men like James Fisk, Jay Gould, and John D. Rockefeller often bribed or threatened congressional representatives and judges to write and interpret the law to suit their business needs. They bought votes and helped elect politicians whose decisions they could control. In this atmosphere of corruption, government officials used their positions to make money rather than to serve the public good.

The robber barons represented a new social class that became famous for showing off wealth in public. Even men from humble backgrounds like railroad giant Cornelius Vanderbilt found that, with enough money, they could buy their way into exclusive social circles.

Vanderbilt started the trend of building huge castle-like houses on New York's Fifth Avenue. Many of the wealthy also built mansions they called "summer cottages" in Newport, Rhode Island, and in other resort communities.To impress society further, they threw outrageously expensive parties. Some cost as much as $200,000. (The average worker earned $10 a week.) A small replica of the Palace of Versailles was built for one party. At another, thousands of orchids decorated the walls, and a layer of rose petals covered the floor. At a party in Newport, guests used silver shovels to dig for diamonds, sapphires, and rubies in a sandbox.

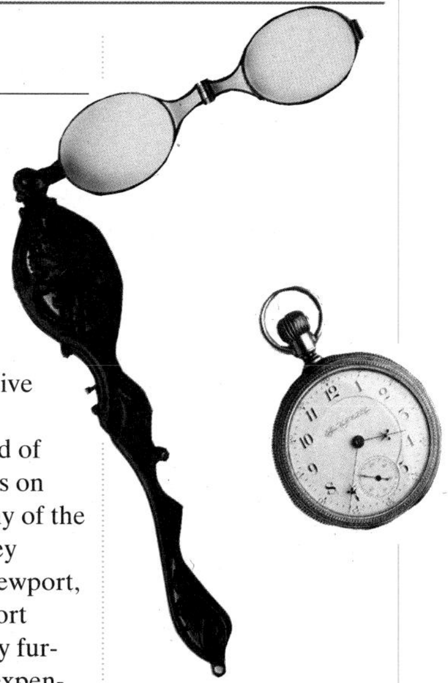

One way to upgrade one's social standing was to be seen at cultural events. At the opera, one could draw attention by the use of fold-out glasses (above). *Children of the rich were indulged in many ways. Here* (below) *a group of girls attend a dog show.*

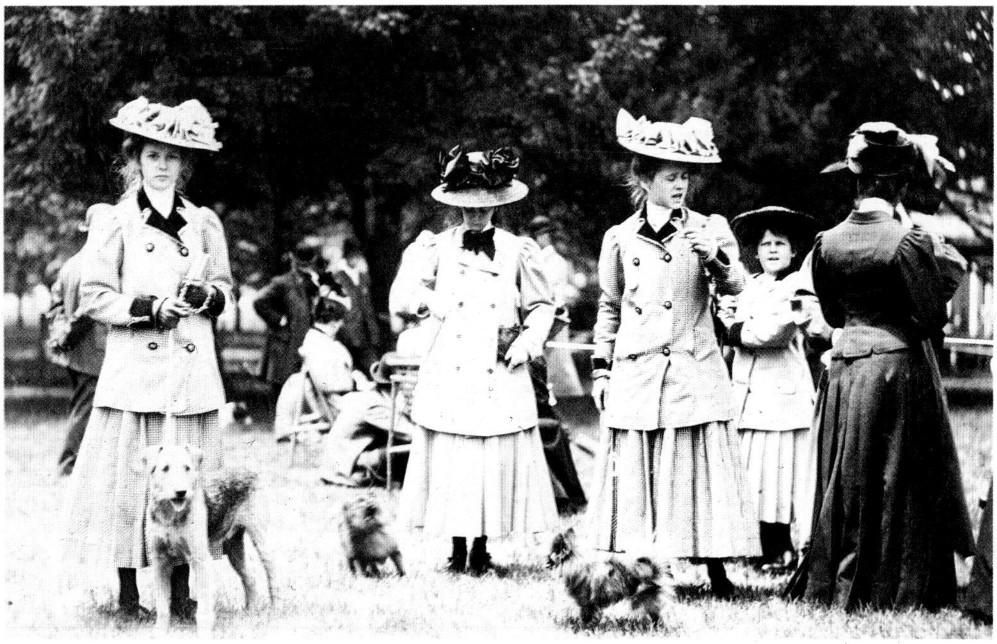

DEVELOP

Have students preview the boldfaced headings in the lesson and look for clues about corruption in the Gilded Age. Then copy on the board the main heads of the Graphic Overview from page 472 and have students copy it in their notes. As they read the lesson, they can add specific examples of each type of corruption.

POLITICAL SYSTEMS

Critical Thinking

Ask students to name two dishonest practices used by robber barons to manipulate politics in the late 1800s. *(Bribery of government officials to get government contracts, vote buying to elect officials whom they could manipulate)* Why do you think these tactics worked? *(Sample answer: Officials at the time were more interested in personal gain than in serving the public.)*

Access Strategy

To help students understand how a dishonest person might gain a position of power, ask them what they might do in the following situation. You just arrived in a new school and you feel confused because you don't know anyone. Someone offers to show you around, saying that you can repay the favor later. What would your response be? If the person later ran for class president, would you feel obliged to vote for him or her?

Many students will probably say that they would accept the stranger's help, especially if the offer seemed to be sincere. Point out that dishonest people can often gain the confidence of others who are in need of help. Tell them that they will read in this lesson about such situations in the second half of the 1800s.

Access Activity

Refer students to the cartoon on page 474 and have them identify the buildings. *(White House and Capitol)* How does the cartoonist show the close relationship between the government and the oil industry? *(Washington filled with oil barrels and stacks; name of oil company on Capitol, Rockefeller holds White House)*

POLITICAL SYSTEMS

Critical Thinking

Have students explain what Walt Whitman meant by "hollowness at heart" in the excerpt on this page *(Sample answer: People have no sense of honesty, decency, or interest in the public good.)* How do the scandals that took place during Grant's presidency reflect Whitman's view? *(Government officials showed their "hollowness at heart" by stealing federal money, by cheating American Indians out of rights, and by using blackmail.)* What did Whitman advise people to do? *(People should look at the situation closely, like a physician diagnosing a disease.)*

■ *Businessmen elected officials whose decisions they could control. They also used bribes and threats.*

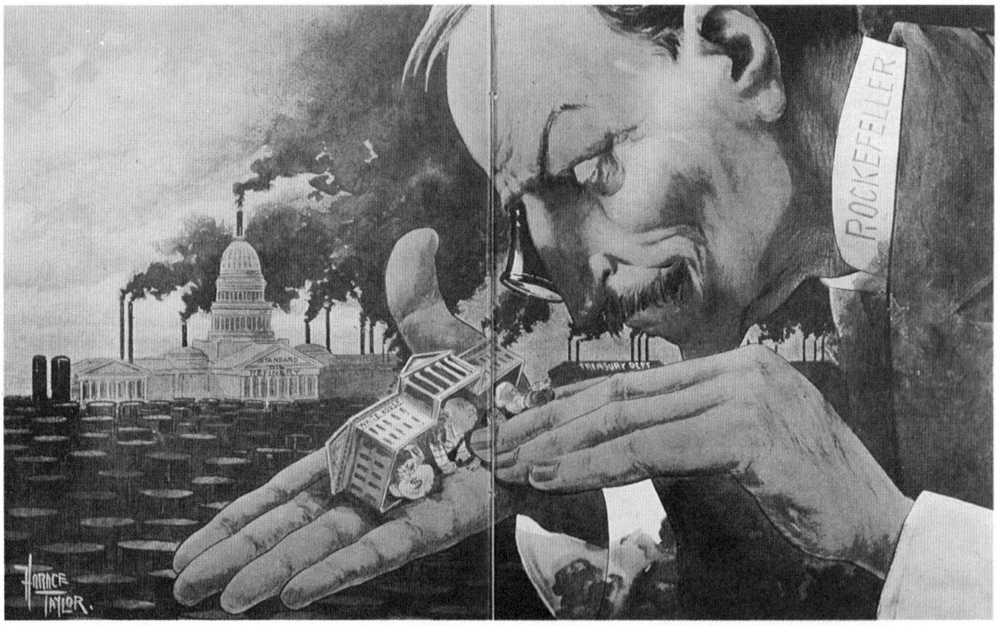

▲ *This famous cartoon suggested that oil baron John D. Rockefeller was the real power behind the United States government.*

■ How did business influence politics during the Gilded Age?

Many Americans were upset and spoke out against the widespread corruption and public display of wealth. Among those speaking out against corruption was Walt Whitman—poet, essayist, and journalist.

> *I say we had best look our times and lands searchingly in the face, like a physician diagnosing some deep disease. Never was there, perhaps, more hollowness at heart than at present here in the United States. . . . We live in an atmosphere of hypocrisy throughout. An acute and candid person in the revenue department in Washington, who regularly visits the cities to investigate frauds, had talked much with me about his discoveries. The depravity of the business classes of our country is not less than has been supposed, but infinitely greater. The official services of America, national, state, and municipal, in all their branches and departments are deep in corruption, bribery, and falsehood.*
>
> Walt Whitman, 1871.

Scandals Plague Grant's Presidency

Ulysses S. Grant had no political experience before he ran for President. However, his friends felt that he would win in 1868 because of his popularity as a Civil War hero.

As President, Grant remained loyal to his friends. As it turned out, they were mostly dishonest and corrupt. Although Grant himself was an honest man, he was easily influenced by scoundrels in his political party. Many took advantage of their political positions.

The Credit Mobilier Scandal

In 1872, during Grant's campaign for reelection, a New York newspaper reported that leaders of the Union Pacific Railroad had persuaded a number of government leaders to cooperate in a multimillion-dollar fraud. At the time, the Union Pacific

Critical Thinking

Ask students to identify the aspects of President Grant's personality that allowed corruption to thrive in his administration. *(Loyalty to friends and blindness to their faults)* To what extent was Grant to blame for the scandals? *(Students should give reasons for their answers.)*

Political Context

The growth of cities after the Civil War was rapid and unplanned. With no tradition of big-city government, unprincipled individuals attained powerful positions.

William "Boss" Tweed began his career as a bookkeeper in New York City. He was elected alderman in 1851, and the next year he was elected to a single term in Congress. He was not re-elected, but he gained power in the Democratic organization known as Tammany Hall. By 1860 he headed a committee that controlled nominations to all city positions, giving him the power to put his own henchmen into city and state offices. In 1870 he was a state senator and held several city posts, including that of president of the Board of Supervisors. Tweed increased his opportunities for embezzling from New York City by forcing passage of a new city charter that created a Board of Audit that allowed him and his associates to control—and raid—the city treasury.

was receiving millions of dollars in government money to build a transcontinental railroad. To steal some of this money, the Union Pacific's managers formed a railroad construction company called the Credit Mobilier *(cray DEE mo bee YAY)*. To cut off any political opposition, Massachusetts Congressman Oakes bribed selected congressmen with stock in this phony company.

No railroad track was ever laid with the public money that Congress set aside for Credit Mobilier. The money went instead into the pockets of the Union Pacific's managers and the Congressional representatives they had bribed. Grant's Vice President, Schuyler ("Smiler") Colfax, and Congressman James A. Garfield, later President, took part in the fraud.

More Corruption

The Credit Mobilier scandal was only the beginning of a string of embarrassing exposés about the Grant administration. In 1873, it was revealed that Secretary of War William Belknap had received **kickbacks**, or payoffs, for helping to cheat American Indian people out of rights to their trading posts. That same year, Grant's personal secretary, Orville Babcock, used blackmail to get more than $25,000 from whiskey makers who had not been paying excise taxes to the federal government. Among the favors received by Babcock was a $2,400 diamond shirt stud.The chief clerk of the Treasury also received money in the Whiskey Ring scandal.

Congress Tarnishes Its Reputation

Shortly after the Credit Mobilier scandal broke, Congress voted itself a 50 percent pay raise, including two years of back pay at the higher rate. This act raised salaries from $5,000 to $7,500, and gave each Congressman a gift of $5,000. Public outcry over this "back-pay steal" forced the legislators to back down. ■

■ *In what ways did members of Grant's administration use their positions for their personal gain?*

Machine Politics Develop

During Grant's presidency, serious urban problems arose that many city governments could not fix. Overwhelmed by immigrants from both rural areas and foreign countries, cities were overcrowded, dirty, and riddled with poverty and violence.

Expanding at the rapid pace set by industrial growth and immigration, cities required water, sewer, fire, police, and social services. But most city governments lacked the money, leadership, staff, and organization to meet these needs. Some people took

◄ *This photograph was taken in New York in 1885. Corrupt political machines did little to solve the serious urban problems of the period.*

ECONIMICS

Critical Thinking

Ask students to explain what the Credit Mobilier was supposed to do and what it actually did. *(It was supposed to build rail lines, but it actually did nothing.)* What might the company officials have done to hide their fraud? *(Bribe officials, make phony bills and work reports)* Whose money did the Credit Mobilier steal? *(The public's money)*

■ *They committed fraud, used blackmail, received kickbacks, and voted to raise their own salaries substantially.*

SOCIAL SYSTEMS

Critical Thinking

Ask students what could have been done to slow the rapid growth of cities at this time. *(Sample answer: restrictions on immigration; improving working conditions in the countryside)* Why do you think little was done to slow the growth of cities? *(More immigrants meant industrial growth which, in turn, meant money for some people.)*

Science Connection

Mark Twain gave the last decades of the 1800s their nickname, "The Gilded Age." Ask students to explain what he meant. Then have them research in encyclopedias to find out more about the process of gilding. What techniques have been developed for applying a thin layer of gold to objects made of other materials? Are metals other than gold ever used for gilding?

Drawing a Cartoon

Refer students to Across Time and Space on page 476. Ask them to examine the cartoons in the lesson and to draw their own cartoon of one of the people discussed in this lesson. Remind them that the cartoon does not need to look exactly like the person but should express one of that person's main characteristics. A brave person, for example, might be shown with the head of a lion or an eagle.

Study Skills

Students can create an outline of the information in the lesson. Tell them to use two main headings: *Corruption in Federal Government* and *Corruption in City Politics*. Have them organize the main points of the lesson under these headings.

POLITICAL SYSTEMS

Critical Thinking

Remind students that political bosses gave gifts to new immigrants. Ask students how these bosses also took money from the very same people. *(Sample answer: They found ways to take city money that had been paid by taxpayers.)*

■ *Machine politics took advantage of the poor conditions in cities by helping people in return for political support.*

CLOSE

Begin drawing the structure of the Graphic Overview from page 472 on the board and have students complete it by using their notes on the examples of corruption. They should then answer the Thinking Focus. As a reteaching activity, have them do the Study Skills activity on page 475.

➤ *This Thomas Nast cartoon clearly shows what the artist felt was on the mind of William "Boss" Tweed.*

advantage of this situation to gain political power.

Big City Political Bosses

Political bosses were usually men who had grown up in the neighborhoods they served. Bosses gained power by supplying basic needs to poor workers and immigrant families. Food baskets, loans, and job opportunities gave these people hope and a sense of belonging. In return, the bosses expected votes and other political support. Bosses also exchanged political favors, such as city jobs or work contracts, for money or votes. This system was called **patronage**.

A political organization known as the **political machine** grew out of the patronage system. Eventually, because of the personal loyalty the bosses commanded, their machines gained more control of the city. Bosses controlled jobs in the public schools, public works projects, and virtually every other aspect of city government. Often bosses did not even hold office themselves, but directed a city's government from a political club.

Once in power, bosses and their machines rewarded themselves with **graft**, money stolen from the city treasury. They also demanded kickbacks from contractors and companies who wanted the city's business. As a result, the cost of running the city skyrocketed.

Across Time & Space

HISTORY *Political cartoons like this one often help historians understand more about a political period. For instance, Thomas Nast helped dethrone William "Boss" Tweed of Tammany Hall with cartoons that pictured Tweed and his associates as vultures or smiling tricksters. "I don't care so much what the papers write about me," Tweed said, "My constituents can't read. But… they can see pictures."*

The Tweed Ring

The most famous and possibly the most corrupt political boss of the Gilded Age was William Marcy Tweed. Although he had little formal education, Tweed established and controlled New York's Democratic political machine. His political operation was called the Tammany Society. Its home was Tammany Hall. Tweed and his friends in the Tweed Ring stole about $200 million from New York City between 1868 and 1871. One of Tweed's friends named Garvey, who received $3 million for plastering, came to be known as the "Prince of Plasterers." Tweed was arrested, tried, convicted and imprisoned. But his political machine carried on.

Many reformers tried to rid their cities of machine politics—of bribery and corruption. Their efforts were not really effective, however, until the Progressive era in the early 1900s. ■

■ *In what sense were machine politics a direct response to conditions in American cities during the Gilded Age?*

REVIEW

1. **FOCUS** What were some of the characteristics of American politics in the decades following the Civil War?
2. **CONNECT** How did the Civil War encourage corruption in the federal government?
3. **HISTORY** Summarize the scandals that arose during Grant's presidency.
4. **CRITICAL THINKING** In what ways did machine politics ease some problems and aggravate others in American cities during the Gilded Age?
5. **WRITING ACTIVITY** Make a list of the basic facilities and services the local government provides in your city or hometown.

Homework Options

Have students look in magazines and newspapers for cartoons that expose political corruption.

Study Guide: page 69.

Answers to Review Questions

1. At this time politics were characterized by corruption in the form of bribes, blackmail, patronage, graft, political machines, and kickbacks.
2. During the Civil War, businesses bribed Congressmen and government officials to get contracts for war materials.
3. The Credit Mobilier scandal was the first of a series of disgraces. Other scandals included the Secretary of War and the chief clerk of the Treasury receiving kickbacks, Grant's personal secretary using blackmail, and the Congress voting itself a 50 percent raise.
4. Sample answer: Machine politics provided people with short-term relief by supplying their basic needs; however, it also led to higher taxes and increased corruption. Allow for personal opinion.
5. Students can use a telephone directory to find information on local government services.

LESSON 2

The Reforming Impulse

Charles Guiteau waited nervously for President James Garfield at the train station in Washington, D.C., on July 2, 1881. He held a gun in his hand. As the President strolled into the station, Guiteau stepped forward and fired. Garfield fell to the ground, wounded. For another two months, he clung to life.

"I did it and will go to jail for it!" Guiteau screamed, "I am a Stalwart and [Vice President] Arthur will be President!"

At the time of the shooting, President Garfield was in a bitter fight with the Stalwarts, a group of people in his own Republican party. Stalwarts like Guiteau claimed that Garfield had not rewarded them enough for their hard work in his campaign. The Stalwarts wanted to control key political offices. The President, however, was weary of the "spoils system," in which the people with the best political connections got the best government jobs.

Even before President Garfield was shot, people were dissatisfied with the spoils system. Critics pointed out that the government was filled with unqualified people who had gotten their jobs in return for political support. Critics also claimed that the system barred the best workers from public service. Honest and capable people couldn't get government jobs unless they were also known as loyal party members.

When the President was assassinated by a Stalwart who had not received his "spoils," Americans demanded a change in the way government offices were filled. The corruption of the Gilded Age had finally inspired a call for reform.

THINKING FOCUS

What political and business practices did reformers in the 1870s and 1880s want to change? Why?

Key Terms

- Mugwumps
- civil service
- regulate
- monopoly
- trust

◄ This engraving of the assassination of President Garfield accompanied newspaper accounts of his death. The technology to print photographs was not available to newspapers until the late 1890s.

INTRODUCE

Have students recall from Lesson 1 examples of corruption. *(Credit Mobilier, Tweed ring)* Then point out the lesson title and ask students what a reform is. *(Something that corrects a problem)* Ask one student to read the Thinking Focus aloud and have other students predict practices that might become a focus of reform at this time. Have them read to confirm or reject their predictions.

Key Terms

Vocabulary strategies: T36–37
Mugwumps— reformers in the Republican party who sought to eliminate corruption during the Gilded Age
civil service—jobs in federal, state, or local governments that are awarded on the basis of merit
regulate—to control or manage based on established rules
monopoly—a company that completely controls the market for a particular commodity or service
trust—a combination of business firms formed by legal agreement especially to reduce competition

Graphic Overview

Problems		Solutions		Results
• spoils system • railroads using unfair practices • trusts controlling markets	→	• Civil Service Act of 1883 • Interstate Commerce Act of 1887 • Sherman Antitrust Act of 1890	→	• got rid of unqualified employees • government regulation of business • later break-up of monopolies

Objectives

1. Identify the Mugwumps and what they sought to change.
2. State why reformers wanted to institute a civil service.
3. Describe the abuses and unfair business practices that led to regulation of the big railroad companies.
4. Analyze the effect monopolies and trusts had on the nation's economy.

DEVELOP

Have students preview the lesson heads to look for clues about the activities of the reform movement. Copy on the board the first box of the Graphic Organizer from page 477. As students read, they can look for the reform proposed as the solution for each of these problems and the result of the reform in addressing corruption.

POLITICAL SYSTEMS

Visual Learning

Refer students to the cartoon of donkeys and elephants on this page. Ask them to read the words in the cartoon and suggest why the elephant and donkey are stamping on these words. *(The cartoonist wanted to show that the political parties were not paying attention to these issues.)*

More About Thomas Nast Nast's cartoons were so influential in several presidential elections that Democrats imported cartoonist Matt Morgan from England to counteract Nast's influence.

The Mugwumps Seek Reform

From the end of Reconstruction in 1877 to the turn of the century, American politics suffered from a stalemated condition. The two major parties largely agreed on economic, political, and social issues. They differed only in their constituencies, the people they represented. The Republicans were mostly Northern white Protestants. The Democrats were most often Southerners, Catholics, and immigrants. Since the two parties were balanced in the number of their supporters, presidential elections—as shown in A Closer Look below—were won by only a few thousand votes.

A Closer Look

Gilded Age Elections

After the Reconstruction Era, neither the Republicans nor the Democrats enjoyed a clear majority. The result: the four presidential elections of the Gilded Age were "fifty-fifty" races. Unfortunately for the voters, the campaigns were often reduced to little more than name-calling matches.

Elections were "gilded,"—ornate, but lacking substance. In the election of 1884, which pitted Republican James Blaine *(left)* against Democrat Grover Cleveland *(right)*, rumors and false accusations flew.

Donkeys and elephants became the popular symbols of the two parties. Cartoonist Thomas Nast sent Democrats hee-hawing and Republicans stampeding through the editorial pages at the turn of the century. The symbols have lasted to the present day.

478

Access Activity

Read aloud the lesson opener on page 477. Have students look at the engraving on the same page and ask them what Guiteau was trying to acomplish, and whether he succeeded. *(He wanted a government job. He went to jail instead.)* How would they feel toward an assassin? *(Angry, confused, afraid)*

Access Strategy

To help students understand the spoils system, have them imagine the following situation. You have just been elected class president. As president, you must organize the class dance at the end of the year. One of the people who worked hardest in your campaign wants his or her band to play at the dance. You appreciate how much that person did for your campaign, but you do not think the band plays very well. The student who leads a better band worked very hard for your opponent in the campaign. Which person do you choose?

Point out to students that if they give the job of providing dance music to the first person, they are operating according to the spoils system. Tell them that they will read more about the spoils system in this lesson.

The President and the federal government did not use the powers or take the responsibilities that they do today. The main goal of each party was to control offices and jobs, not to create new policies. The most time-consuming duty of the President was to make the political appointments—nearly one hundred thousand—required by the spoils system. This period of corruption and stalemate eventually inspired public pressure for reform.

One of the strongest forces for change following the Civil War were the **Mugwumps**, a group of Republicans who supported reform. Taking their name from an American Indian word meaning "big chiefs," the Mugwumps condemned the spoils system.

Four years later, in 1892, Harrison and Cleveland ran against each other again. This time Cleveland won. In this painting titled *The Lost Bet,* a Harrison supporter pulls a Cleveland supporter on a float, in order to settle their bet.

The people's choice? In 1888, Democrat Grover Cleveland gained 90,000 more popular votes than Republican Benjamin Harrison. But Harrison won the electoral vote and the presidency. Key states such as New York swung the election away from Cleveland.

POLITICAL SYSTEMS

Critical Thinking

Ask students to compare the role of Presidents in the Gilded Age and now. *(Sample answer: In the Gilded Age, Presidents were expected largely to make political appointments; now a President is expected to set new policies to handle the country's problems.)*

POLITICAL SYSTEMS

Visual Learning

Refer students to the painting *The Lost Bet* on this page. What does the picture reveal about the attitude of people towards elections? *(Sample answer: It seems more like a sporting event; people don't seem very serious.)*

Economic Context

In 1885, Chief Sitting Bull of the defeated Sioux was touring with Buffalo Bill's Wild West show. He gave away most of his money to the crowd of hungry boys who followed the show. "The white man knows how to make everything," he said, "but he does not know how to distribute it."

Data from the 1890 census confirm that the distribution of wealth in the United States was very uneven. The richest one percent of the population received more income than the poorest fifty percent of the population. Half of the nation's wealth was enjoyed by one-eighth of its families. By 1901, according to Frank Parsons, a writer of the time, one-eighth of the population owned seven-eighths of the wealth, and two hundredths of one percent—4,000 millionaires—had 20 percent of the wealth, or 4,000 times more than the national average.

Study Skills

Have students find the image on page 478 of James Blaine and the year in which he ran for the presidency. Have students use several library resources—the card catalog, encyclopedias, indices of history books—to find information on Blaine's life before and after the 1884 election.

POLITICAL SYSTEMS

Critical Thinking

Point out that the cartoonist Thomas Nast was a Mugwump leader. Have students explain how the Mugwumps and the reform movement probably benefited from Nast's membership. *(He could use his cartoons to focus attention on reform.)*

POLITICAL SYSTEMS

Critical Thinking

Remind students that they first read about German immigrant Carl Schurz in Chapter 7. Refer them to the excerpt from Schurz's speech on this page and ask them to explain Lincoln's attitude toward the spoils system. *(Political appointments are not based on a person's qualifications.)* Why did the spoils system last so long? *(Politicians and wealthy businessmen stood to gain from it; it took a while for the public to get angry enough to insist on reforms.)*

■ *The Mugwumps were a group representing the reform wing of the Republican Party; they sought to reform the spoils system and reduce the protective tariff.*

They favored a fair and honest relationship between the North and South. They also wanted to reduce the protective tariff. (A tax on imports, the tariff was meant to encourage Americans to buy U.S. goods.)

Mugwumps were a powerful and well-educated group. Their leaders included cartoonist Thomas Nast, magazine editors E. L. Godkin and George W. Curtis, and Carl Schurz, the German-American senator from Missouri. Senator Schurz was a longtime advocate of reform. He often spoke out against the spoils system in Congress as well as in the press.

Must it not be clear to every observing mind, that our present mode of making appointments is a blindfold game, a mere haphazard proceeding? Was Mr. Lincoln very wrong when once, in a moment of despair, he said with grim humor: "I have discovered a good way of providing officers for the government: put all the names of the applicants into one pepper-box and all the offices into another, and then shake the two, and make appointments just as the names and the offices happen to drop out together."

Carl Schurz, in a Senate speech, 1871

■ *Who were the Mugwumps and what features of the American political system did they seek to reform?*

Attacking the Spoils System

Mugwumps and other political reformers wanted a **civil service** system to replace the spoils system. Under their plan, government jobs would no longer be given out in exchange for party loyalty. Instead, people who wanted to work for the government had to prove their abilities by taking a test. This civil service examination would weed out unskilled people.

Reformers also had some selfish reasons for making a change in the way that government jobs were filled. Most of them were white middle-class Protestants. Just as much as they disliked the spoils system, they resented the immigrants and party boosters

Job-seekers wait to see the President. It was with dread that Presidents faced the endless lines of applicants. Few job-seekers were qualified for the jobs they obtained.

Study Skills

Have students use the information in this lesson, including A Closer Look, to create their own charts showing what was happening during the administration of each President elected during the Gilded Age. Tell them to focus especially on government abuses and reforms.

Social Context

The great personal fortunes that were built up after the Civil War affected not only the economic climate, but also the social, political, and ethical climate of America. Money became the measure of social success, and people who achieved wealth were admired, regardless of their methods for achieving it. As an etiquette book of the time explained, "To be happy, we strive for the acquisition of wealth, for position and place, for social and political distinction."

Rich and poor alike tended to believe that what was good for business was good for the country and, conversely, what was bad for business was bad for the country. Thus, opposition to the labor movement was not confined to the wealthy few. Bills to eliminate child labor and to shorten working hours were viewed as unpatriotic by some, who argued that such laws would increase the labor costs in most factories and cause American industry to lose its competitive edge.

who shared in the spoils.

Nevertheless, reformers had strong evidence to support their case. The spoils system had deep roots in American government. Since Andrew Jackson's day, people who could not read or write had held clerical jobs. Some officials put their family members and pets on the government payroll. American diplomats were often untrained and poorly educated.

Hayes Investigates the Customs House

The New York Customs House represented the spoils system at its worst. The customs house collected taxes levied on foreign goods that entered the United States through the port of New York. One of the most corrupt centers of patronage in the nation in the 1870s, it was run by New York Senator Roscoe Conkling. He was known as an arrogant man who sported dazzling, expensive clothes. Conkling used the customs house to run and finance his political machine. Fiercely opposed to reform, Conkling called the civil service the "snivel service."

Conkling met his match in President Rutherford B. Hayes, who was elected President in 1876. Hayes wanted no part of the scandal and corruption that had run wild in the Grant administration. In 1878, Hayes launched an investigation of the New York Customs House. The investigation found that more than 200 people who did no work for the customs house were on its payroll. Over Conkling's loud objections, President Hayes fired two senior customs house officials.

The Civil Service Act of 1883

In the wake of President Garfield's assassination and the Customs House investigation, Congress passed the Civil Service Act of 1883. President Chester Arthur signed this act into law just two years after Garfield's death. An important step toward reform, the new law set aside about 15,000 federal jobs to be filled through a competitive test. Only persons who proved their abilities on the civil service test could be hired. The act also forbade elected officials to fire civil service workers because of their political views. ■

Owners of the Railroads, 1904

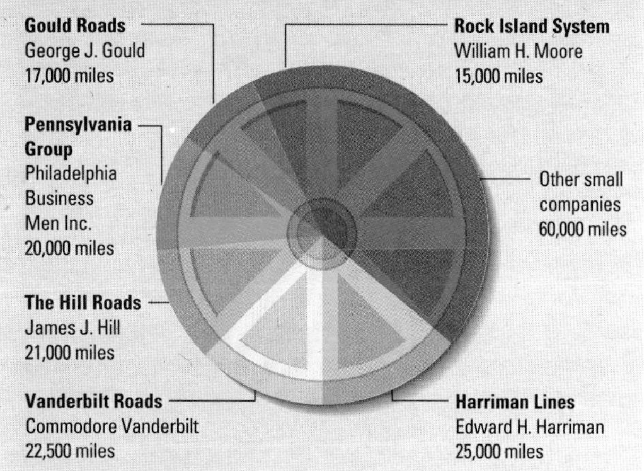

▲ *This graph shows the ownership of the leading railroads in 1904. Because transportation was an important factor in the industrial growth of the nation, the owners of the large railroads became powerful national leaders in this period.*

■ *Why did reformers want to replace the spoils system with a civil service?*

Regulating the Railroads

Following the Civil War the federal government gave millions of acres of land and millions of dollars to the railroad companies to lay new track. It made political and economic sense to connect the huge country with railroads. But after misusing these privileges for many years, the big railroad companies became the next targets of reform.

Railroad Abuses Cause Outrage

"What do I care about the law? Hain't I got the power?" growled Cornelius Vanderbilt, the most powerful of the railroad owners. Vanderbilt meant what he said. He and several other railroad owners with enormous holdings conspired to squeeze out smaller competitors. They charged more for short hauls, which farmers

ECONIMICS

Visual Learning

After students have read page 482, have them examine the pie graph on this page. Based on the information in the graph, why might they expect healthy competition among rail lines? *(The railroad lines were divided fairly equally among owners.)* How does this contradict the information in the lesson? *(The information in the chart is deceptive; there was actually little competition.)*

■ *They wanted qualified people to fill government jobs rather than unqualified people who had merely demonstrated party loyalty or given financial contributions.*

Little was done during the period to improve working conditions and safety standards. Investors, who made their fortunes buying and selling stock, were more concerned about profits than about workers' lives. About 500,000 workers were either killed or badly maimed each year, yet inventors found no market for safety devices. When managers made improvements in working conditions, they excused themselves by saying that it was done simply to augment output. Commodore Vanderbilt, Jim Fisk, and Jay Gould bought and sold shares in railroad stock at a frantic pace while letting the lines deteriorate. The press was generally pro-business and rarely criticized such attitudes and practices. In this climate, it was difficult to rally support for reform.

Critical Thinking

After students have read the section in the lesson on the spoils system, ask them to explain why Conkling was opposed to reform in the customs house. *(Sample answer: If the customs house were reformed, Conkling would no longer be able to use it for his own purposes.)*

ECONOMICS

Critical Thinking

Have one student read aloud the quotation at the top of the right column of this page. Refer students to Article I, Section 8, Clause 3 of the Constitution on pages 636–655. Have students explain what this clause allows Congress to do. *(It can regulate commerce between states.)* Then have students explain why Congress can make laws about the railroads but not about a person's homestead. *(Because the railroads move goods from one state to another)*

■ *Railroads became targets for reform because of their abuse of government grants, their unfair practices against smaller competitors, and their bribing of politicians.*

William Henry Vanderbilt, son of Cornelius Vanderbilt, took over his father's railroads. He is shown here towering over two other railroad men, Jay Gould on his left, and Jim Fisk on his right.

■ *For what reasons did the big railroad companies become targets of reform?*

required for their produce, than for the long hauls that manufacturers needed. Large shippers also received secret discounts for giving their business to the railroads.

For many years, railroad owners used bribes and threats to keep politicians from interfering with their shady business dealings. However, in the 1870s, some state governments passed laws against the unfair business practices of railroad companies. Many conservatives did not want government to **regulate**, or set rules for, the railroads. They argued that regulation was a violation of the Fifth Amendment protection of private property.

"Who owns the locomotives and the cars. . .?" asked a Republican delegate to the 1878 California Constitutional Convention. "Are they not private property?. . . And yet you propose to hand over that property. . . to [government regulators] just as if you proposed to take from the gentleman his homestead and give it to me."

In firm agreement, the railroad owners took the regulators to court. Their lawyers intended to prove that regulation was unconstitutional. However, in the 1877 case of *Munn* v. *Illinois*, the Supreme Court ruled in favor of state regulation. Reformers were pleased, but their victory was short-lived. The Court reversed itself nine years later. Then it ruled that only Congress, and not state commissions, had the power to regulate interstate commerce, or the movement of goods across state lines.

The Interstate Commerce Act of 1887

The Supreme Court's ruling against state regulation of railroads forced the federal government to address mounting public demands for regulation. In 1887, Congress passed the Interstate Commerce Act. This act outlawed many of the unfair practices that railroad companies had used. It also set up an Interstate Commerce Commission (ICC) to enforce the new regulations.

The Interstate Commerce Act, however, had little power in regulating railroads in the years after its passage. Between 1887 and 1906, the Supreme Court ruled in favor of the railroad companies in almost every case raised by the ICC. Railroads found they could also count on long and expensive court proceedings to discourage their opponents. Nonetheless, the Interstate Commerce Act was an important achievement. It established the government's right to regulate business and paved the way for more effective regulation in later years. ■

Visual Learning

Refer students to the cartoon on this page. Write on the board the cartoon title: "The Modern Colossus of (Rail) Roads." Show them a picture of the Colossus of Rhodes in an encyclopedia. Ask students to explain the title of the cartoon. *(Vanderbilt compared to the sun god to show his power and control over the railroads; play on words* roads *and* Rhodes*)*

Art Connection

Although many of the new rich Americans had little interest in the arts, they did not want to appear ignorant. Instead of developing an American style of art, they copied European architecture and fashion. Have students research in guide books and architecture books the houses rich people built during the Gilded Age. Some students may also want to create a mural showing the homes, hair styles, and clothing that were fashionable in the 1870s and 1880s.

Science Connection

In colonial days, bottled petroleum was sold as a medicine. It was not until the 1850s that interest in the value of petroleum for industrial uses grew. By 1870, when John D. Rockefeller seized control of the oil industry, oil was an extremely valuable commodity. Have students research petroleum. What is petroleum and how do we get it? What was it used for in the 1870s and 1880s? What are some of its many uses today?

Restraining the Trusts

In the same way that reformers wanted to control the power of the railroads, they also wanted to curb the power of monopolies. A **monopoly** is a company that completely controls the market for one product or service. A **trust** is a combination of companies that work together to control the market. In the years after the Civil War, monopolies and trusts threatened to take control of the American economy.

The Power of the Monopolies

The story of oil baron John D. Rockefeller shows why reformers wanted to fight monopolies. A financial genius, Rockefeller began his career as a bookkeeper but soon built a great fortune in oil. He saw early in his career that the person who controlled the oil refineries—the places where "crude oil" from the ground was made into fuel—could control the entire oil industry. Rockefeller started buying oil companies as fast as he could.

Rockefeller was almost always able to force other owners to sell their companies to him. When he met resistance to his offer, he often resorted to bribery and intimidation. In one case, Standard Oil officials bribed the mechanic at another refinery to arrange for a small explosion there.

Rockefeller didn't need to buy every oil company in the country in order to control the industry. The trust, devised by his lawyer Samuel Dodd, enabled Rockefeller to control companies that he did not own. Through the Standard Oil trust, nine "trustees," led by Rockefeller, controlled 77 companies. Stockholders in those companies traded their stock for "trust certificates." They kept their share of the profits but lost their say in how their company was run.

From the beginning, reformers feared the power of the trusts. Journalist Ida Tarbell once described the Standard Oil trust as "an organization having no legal existence, independent of all authority, able to do anything it wanted anywhere....You could no more grasp it than you could an eel."

Oil fields, such as this one in Los Cerritos, California, helped John D. Rockefeller gain complete control over the oil business (bottom left). *Ida Tarbell* (below) *wrote a book exposing the unfair practices of the Standard Oil Company.*

ECONOMICS

Critical Thinking

Have students explain in their own words the strategy and methods that John D. Rockefeller used to control the oil industry. Then ask them to suggest reasons why he was so successful in controlling the industry. *(Sample answers: He used unfair tactics to put people out of business. He was a good problem solver.)*

483

Mathematics Connection

Use the population information presented in the Economic Context (page 479) to make other calculations. For example, if 4,000 millionaires represented two hundredths of one percent of the population in 1901, what was the population of the country? *(Approximately 80 million)* If one-eighth of the people held seven-eighths of the wealth, how many people shared the remaining one-eighth? *(Approximately 70 million)*

Critical Thinking

The attitude is sometimes expressed that although corruption is harmful, "it really doesn't affect me, and, anyway, there's nothing I can do about it." Have students discuss the implications of such an attitude in a democracy.

ECONOMICS

Critical Thinking

A monopoly on information can have devastating effects on Wall Street, the heart of the United States financial world. Some stock brokers, through "insider trading," find information about stocks and businesses that is not available to the public and then make investments for themselves. How is the outcome of such a monopoly on information similar to what happened as a result of industrial monopolies? *(Power and wealth can be concentrated in a few hands.)*

Understanding Monopolies

You may have played the board game Monopoly. The object of the game is to buy as much property as possible and to drive your opponents to bankruptcy—that is, to take all of their money. In the late 1800s and early 1900s, during the reign of such industrial giants as the United States Steel Corporation, this wasn't a game—it was a business.

A monopoly exists when one company or group controls the means of producing or selling a particular product or service. For example, John D. Rockefeller's Standard Oil Trust controlled over 90 percent of the oil business in the United States in the late 1800s.

Forming a Monopoly

A monopoly can control the price of a good or service by withholding or increasing supplies. At first, a monopoly may lower prices to drive its competitors out of business. Because of its vast resources, the monopoly can afford to charge less for a while. Smaller competitors, however, cannot afford the losses caused by lower prices.

Once a company has eliminated its competition, it is free to raise prices. In this way, a company with a monopoly can earn huge profits by selling the product or service at a high price. Such monopoly control not only raises costs for consumers but also limits their choice of a product or service.

The opposite of monopoly is competition, in which many sellers (often small companies) compete to produce and sell a certain kind of good or service. In a competitive market, so many sellers are competing that no one company can control the selling price.

You can tell how competitive a certain industry is by finding out how many separate companies supply similar products. If there is only one provider of a good or service, that company probably has a monopoly in that particular market. If there are that many suppliers, chances are that a high degree of competition exists in that industry.

Regulating Monopolies

In 1890, Congress passed the Sherman Antitrust Act to limit the negative effects of monopolies and to encourage competition. Although the act was not very effective at first, it did establish the precedent for government regulation of monopolies and trusts. These powers were later extended by the Clayton Antitrust Act and the Federal Trade Commission Act, both passed in 1914. Throughout most of the twentieth century, these laws have been strictly enforced to prohibit mergers that would create companies with a monopoly in a particular industry.

In regulating monopolies, governments must always balance the interests of competitors and consumers against the efficiency with which the economy operates. In some extreme cases, it would be highly inefficient for more than one firm to provide a good or service. Economists refer to this situation as a natural monopoly. A good example is local telephone service. It would be very costly and inefficient for more than one company to wire all the homes and businesses in a community. In the past, utility companies like those that provide electricity and natural gas have had monopolies, but they are now beginning to face competition. To protect the interests of consumers and to oversee the operation of these monopolies, state and local governments establish utility commissions.

Recent Trends

During the administration of President Ronald Reagan in the 1980s, the U.S. government modified its approach to the enforcement of antitrust laws. Basically, the government chose not to oppose most mergers because it felt they did not pose a threat to fair competition or to the interests of consumers. As a result, the 1980s and 1990s saw a new wave of huge mergers, particularly in banking and financial service industries.

Although they have not created monopolies, many of these mergers have resulted in a large concentration of economic power in certain corporations. Today, as in the late 1800s, the debate continues over whether this concentration of economic power is good or bad for the nation.

484

Critical Thinking

Ask students to explain how monopolies and trusts helped to concentrate money and power in the hands of just a few individuals. *(Trusts could force smaller companies out of business; when the competitors were gone, the trusts could raise prices.)*

Reader's Theater

Have students perform selections from *The Gilded Age* by Mark Twain and Charles Dudley Warner. (New York: Doubleday, 1873) Sections of the dialogue in Chapters 15, 28, 42, and 51 can be used to create humorous scenes that illustrate the corrupt practices of the day. Chapter 33 offers a humorous look at society customs. Note that the text may require some adaptation because students may find the book challenging to read.

Trusts based on the Standard Oil model soon arose in other industries. By 1900, trusts controlled the sugar, liquor, cattle, tobacco, nail, salt, leather, and bicycle industries.

The Sherman Antitrust Act of 1890

The extraordinary profits made by trusts were available only to a handful of owners. As trusts took over in more sections of the economy, they nearly wiped out their competitors. No governmental regulations restricted their behavior. As a result, prices rose, but the quality of goods and services often declined. Also, resources were wasted, and working conditions worsened. Many people became disgusted by the excesses of the trusts. Across the nation, both states and individuals looked to Congress to bring about a change.

"Congress alone can deal with the trusts," Ohio Senator John Sherman said, "and if we are unwilling or unable, there will soon be a trust for every production and a master to fix the price for every necessity of life." Sherman's speech as well as years of effort by reformers finally brought about the passage of the Sherman Antitrust Act in 1890. Its purpose was to limit the power of the trusts.

The language of the act suggested that monopolies would be banished from the American economy. "Every contract, combination in the form of trust or otherwise," it read, "or conspiracy in restraint of trade or commerce . . . is hereby declared to be illegal." Enforcing the law, however, proved another matter altogether. The bill failed to define its terms clearly. Loopholes prevented the law from fulfilling its purpose.

Rockefeller's lawyers immediately devised a legal substitute for the trust called the holding company. A holding company didn't actually make or sell anything. Its purpose was to gain control of other companies by buying their stock. Twenty-five holding companies were created in the first five years after the Sherman law was passed. In addition, the Supreme Court gave a narrow interpretation of the act in the 1895 case of *United States* v. *E. C. Knight Company.* The Court's ruling further weakened the law's effectiveness. Even so, the Sherman Antitrust Act laid an important legal foundation. This law enabled a willing president, Theodore Roosevelt, to break up many monopolies in the early 1900s. ■

This chart shows the percentage of the markets that six powerful monopolies controlled in 1904.

U.S. Monopolies, 1870–1900

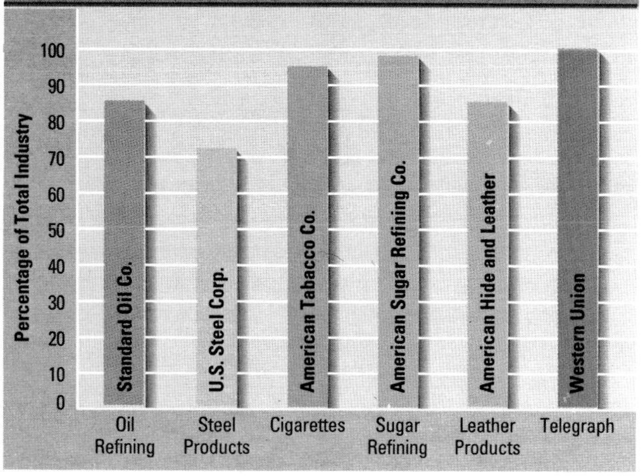

■ *In what way did monopolies and trusts act against the best interests of the people?*

R E V I E W

1. **FOCUS** What political and business practices did reformers in the 1870s and 1880s want to change? Why?
2. **CONNECT** Explain how political bribery might have affected government efforts to regulate business.
3. **POLITICAL SYSTEMS** How did the civil service method of filling government jobs differ from the spoils system method?
4. **CRITICAL THINKING** Could the actions of monopolies and trusts during the Gilded Age be described as undemocratic? Why or why not?
5. **ACTIVITY** Make a cartoon about one of the political or economic problems of the Gilded Age, such as the spoils system, the railroads, or the trusts. Choose a specific issue, and use real characters if possible.

ECONOMICS

Visual Learning

Refer students to the graph on this page. Approximately what percentage of the steel industry was controlled by a monopoly? *(Roughly 70 percent)* Were the smaller companies, which made up the remaining part of the steel industry, able to offer competitive prices? *(It is unlikely, but it is possible.)*

■ *They caused the price of goods to rise and the quality of goods and services to decline.*

C L O S E

To summarize the lesson, have students answer the Thinking Focus and evaluate their predictions. Copy again on the board the first box of the Graphic Overview from page 477 and ask students to use their notes to fill in the remaining two boxes. As a reteaching activity, have them do the Study Skills activity on page 480.

Answers to Review Questions

1. Reformers wanted to change the spoils system, monopolies, and trusts to give equal opportunity to everyone.
2. Businesses could use bribery to sway government officials to rule in their favor.
3. The civil service method hired people because of their qualifications rather than their political connections, as had been the case in the spoils system.
4. Sample answer: Because the monopolies and trusts favored the few at the expense of the many, their actions were not democratic. Allow for personal opinion.
5. For examples, refer students to cartoons in the lesson.

Homework Options

Ask students to research modern monopolies and the actions taken against them in recent decades by the U.S. Government under the Sherman Antitrust Act.

Study Guide: page 70.

INTRODUCE

After one student reads the lesson title aloud, explain that *Populist* refers to a political party formed by people who were dissatisfied with the policies of the other political parties. Point out that *revolt* in this context means peaceful, not violent, change.

Have students read the Thinking Focus and suggest reasons why farmers might want to form a political party. Tell them that they will read about some of the problems of farmers and how they tried to solve those problems.

Key Terms

Vocabulary strategies: T36–37

Populism—a political movement that represented the interests of farmers in the 1890s

cooperative—an organization or association that is owned jointly by those who use its facilities or services

L E S S O N 3

The Populist Revolt

THINKING FOCUS

Why did American farmers decide to form their own political party in the 1890s?

Key Terms

- Populism
- cooperative

➤ *William Jennings Bryan is shown here on the presidential campaign trail in 1896. Bryan lost to William McKinley in the election.*

The Democrats were sharply divided over the issue of money when they gathered in Chicago for their 1896 convention. Some felt that the value of American money should be based on the gold held by the government. Others supported American farmers in the belief that only an unlimited money supply would solve the country's economic woes.

None of the delegates knew what to expect when a young congressman from Nebraska stepped up to the platform on the evening of July 7. Only 36 years old at the time, William Jennings Bryan was often called the "Great Commoner" because he championed the cause of the common people. In particular, Bryan supported many of the goals of America's discontented farmers, who in the 1890s were demanding sweeping political changes. In his speech at the 1896 Democratic convention, Bryan—an unknown figure to many—electrified the delegates.

Illinois poet Edgar Lee Masters heard Bryan's speech and described its effects: "The delegates arose and marched for an hour, shouting, weeping, rejoicing. They lifted this orator upon their shoulders and carried him as if he had been a god." The next day the Democrats nominated Bryan for President.

The sympathies of the Democratic party, as shown by the platform, are on the side of the struggling masses who have ever been the foundation of the Democratic party. . . . You come to us and tell us that the great cities are in favor of the gold standard. We reply that the great cities rest upon our broad and fertile prairies. Burn down your cities and leave our farms, and your cities will spring up again as if by magic. But destroy our farms, and the grass will grow in the streets of every city in the country.

If the gold delegates dare to defend the gold standard as a good thing, we will fight them to the uttermost. Having behind us the producing masses of this nation and the world, supported by the commercial interests, the laboring interests, and the toilers everywhere, we will answer their demand for a gold standard by saying to them: You shall not press down upon the brow of labor this crown of thorns, you shall not crucify mankind upon a cross of gold!

William Jennings Bryan, July 7, 1896

Objectives

1. Summarize the economic and political factors that led to the rise of the Populist movement.
2. Describe the steps farmers took to try to improve their economic situation.
3. Explain why the Populist movement declined rapidly following the 1896 presidential election.

Graphic Overview

Problems	→	Solutions	→	Results
• rising farm costs • falling farm income		• Grange • cooperatives • Populism		• Democrats stealing Populist issues • Bryan losing election • eventual reforms

The Roots of Populism

Bryan's 1896 presidential campaign marked the high point of a farmers' movement known as **Populism**. Although Populism did not emerge until the early 1890s, the movement had its roots in the economic and social conditions that developed following the Civil War.

Hard Times for Farmers

In the 1870s and 1880s, American farmers were caught in a trap. They faced increasing costs for growing and shipping grain at a time when grain prices were falling sharply. High interest rates, property taxes, and shipping charges drained their profits. Because farmers depended on the nearest railroad to get their grain to market, they had no way to protect themselves from increases in shipping charges. Railroad companies took advantage of the farmers by raising rates higher and higher for the short hauls they used. Frank Norris's novel *The Octopus* shows just how angry farmers were about railroads:

> We're cinched already. It all amounts to just this: You can't buck against the railroad. We've tried it and tried it, and we are stuck every time . . . Shelgrim [railroad owner] owns the courts. . . . He's got the Governor of the State in his pocket. He keeps a million-dollar lobby at Sacramento every minute of the time the legislature is in session; he's got his own men on the floor of the United States Senate. He has the whole thing organized like an army corps. What are you going to do?

Another major reason for the increased cost of farming was industrialization. Mechanical reapers, planters, and combines had become available by the 1880s. Farmers had to buy the new farm machinery if they wanted to grow more grain. Since these machines were expensive, farmers had to borrow large amounts of money

Farmers like these suffered from many social and political problems created by the economics of the Gilded Age.

This photograph of a farm family harvesting red clover was taken in September of 1895 in Medford, Wisconsin.

DEVELOP

Tell students that in this lesson they will read about the problems that farmers faced, how they organized to solve the problems, and what the results of their actions were. Copy on the board the boxes and headings of the Graphic Overview from page 486. Have students fill in the boxes as they read the lesson.

ECONOMICS

Critical Thinking

Ask students to read the excerpt from Frank Norris's novel on this page and tell what they think "We're cinched already" means. *(The railroads have us tied up.)* Then ask them to explain how the activities of the railroad robber barons affected farmers. *(The railroad owners gave breaks and kickbacks to big industries while charging higher prices for the short hauls needed by farmers, thus increasing farming costs.)*

Access Strategy

Remind students that the majority of Americans in the 1870s and 1880s lived on farms or in rural areas. Have them recall from Chapter 14 some of the difficulties in farming on Western lands. *(Scarce water and timber)* Then have them recall how the railroad and new technology affected farming. *(Farmers could farm larger areas. Railroads could bring them supplies and take their products to faraway markets.)*

Ask students to suggest reasons why farmers sometimes got in debt. *(Sample answer: They had to borrow money to buy machinery and to pay shipping expenses.)* Explain that in this lesson they will read about some of the economic problems of farmers and what farmers did to try to solve these problems.

Access Activity

Ask students to recall from Chapter 15 some of the problems between big business and factory workers. What did farmers and factory workers have in common at this time? *(They worked under difficult conditions and had little control over economic factors affecting their livelihood.)*

SOCIAL SYSTEMS

Critical Thinking

After students read about the Grange movement, refer them to the poster at the top of this page. What are some of the ideals of the Grangers? *(Sample answer: Importance of community and family life)* Ask students to compare the Grange with labor unions. *(In both, working people united so they could be heard. Grangers pooled money and resources to control costs and prices; union members elected representatives to negotiate with management.)*

ECONOMICS

Critical Thinking

How would increasing the number of "greenbacks" in circulation help farmers? *(Increasing the money supply would lower the value of money. This would in turn bring higher prices for goods, including crops, and would lower the value of the loans farmers owed the banks.)*

▲ *This poster from the 1870s summarizes some of the goals and ideals of the Grangers.*

from banks in order to buy them. Because the banks saw farming as a risky business, they charged high interest rates.

As the cost of farming increased, the prices that farmers could get for their crops fell. Ironically, the ability to produce more food by machines was largely to blame. The price that people would pay for crops fell as the supply of corn, wheat, potatoes, and other agricultural products on the market increased. This economic principle is called the law of supply and demand.

The Grange Movement

A single farmer could do little to raise the price of crops or to reduce the cost of farming. But there was much that farmers could do together. In 1867, Oliver Kelley—described by his friends as "an engine with too much steam"—founded an organization of farmers know as the Grange. The Grange gave farmers the opportunity to discuss the large economic and political issues that affected their lives. It also encouraged them to work together to reduce costs and raise prices. In some places, Grangers pooled their money and bought farm machinery directly from manufacturers to avoid the extra retail costs. Grangers also pooled their crops. Such pooling allowed them to set their own prices, to sell directly to large merchants, and to avoid paying a commission to "middlemen."

Greenback-Labor Party

The value of paper money is a complex issue. Nowadays, the worth of paper currency is largely a measure of the confidence people have in the government and in the economy. In the 1870s, however, laws were passed guaranteeing that the value of paper money should depend on the amount of gold in the government's reserves.

People have always debated over what the worth of money should be. During and after the Civil War, the government issued paper money, called "greenbacks" because of their color, that could not be redeemed for gold. Farmers disagreed with bankers about how much money should be circulated and about whether its value should continue to be based on the price of gold.

Increasing the quantity of any item on the market, including money, lowers its value. Farmers believed that the government should put more dollars into circulation. This step would decrease the value of the money they owed the banks, making their loans easier to repay. They wanted the government to increase the money supply by printing more "greenbacks" and by introducing the unlimited, or "free," coinage of silver.

Bankers liked "hard" money, that

Critical Thinking

Have a student read aloud the excerpt of William Jennings Bryan's speech on page 486. What is Bryan's opinion of the relationship between cities and farms? *(Cities depend on farms.)* Was this idea more valid a century ago than it is today? *(Sample answer: Cities still depend on farms for food.)*

Economic Context

The Panic of 1893 was one of the worst depressions in U.S. history. Fearing a weak American economy, British investors had been unloading American securities for several years. In February 1893, the Philadelphia and Reading Railroad went bankrupt with debts of $125 million. Stocks fell, trusts collapsed, and thousands of farm mortgages were foreclosed. By April, U.S. gold reserves, already drained by the Sherman Silver Purchase Act, fell below the $100 million mark, and on June 27 there was a decisive stock market crash.

President Cleveland called a special session of Congress for August 7 and forced repeal of the Silver Purchase Act. The government, aided by J.P. Morgan, was able to borrow money and a slow economic recovery began. The Klondike gold strike in 1897 increased the supply of gold and helped restore prosperity in the country.

is, money based on the gold standard. The gold standard was an assurance that money would keep its value. Bankers feared that a sharp rise in prices would occur if there were more dollars in circulation than there was gold in the U.S. Treasury. They wanted to keep the dollars in circulation equal to the value of the government's gold. This "hard money" policy became law in 1875.

The Greenback-Labor Party was formed in 1878 to support an increased money supply and "free silver." Its members were farmers, laborers, and a few businessmen. With the help of farmers, the "Greenbacks" elected 14 members to Congress in 1878. Participating in the Greenback-Labor Party helped farmers realize the power they had to shape state law and influence national affairs. ■

■ *What economic and political factors led to the rise of the Populist movement?*

■ *Factors include falling grain prices, increasing costs for producing and shipping grain, and the success of organized efforts by farmers to work for change.*

Farmers Establish the Populist Party

> *This is a nation of inconsistencies. The Puritans fleeing from oppression became oppressors. We fought England for our liberty and put chains on four million blacks. We wiped out slavery and by our tariff laws and national banks began a system of white wage slavery worse than the first. . . .*
>
> *We were told . . . to go to work and raise a big crop . . . and we raised the big crop that they told us to; and what came of it? Eight-cent corn . . . two-cent beef, and no price at all for butter and eggs—that's what came of it.*

With statements like these, Kansas orator and reformer Mary Elizabeth Lease persuaded many farmers to join a Farmers' Alliance. The alliances of the 1880s were similar to, but more radical than, the Grange. As the wealth of robber barons and men like "Big Jim" Fisk increased, so did the discontent of the farmers. Led by the well-organized Southern Farmers' Alliance, the goal of these organizations was to fight for lower farming costs and higher crop prices. They tried out several kinds of farming cooperatives. In these **cooperatives**, farmers pooled their resources to save money on farm machinery and shipping costs. Although farming was their biggest concern, the farmers' alliances supported other causes. They wanted regulation of railroads and monopolies, improved public schools, and greater rights for women. The alliances also published newspapers and sent out speakers like Lease to spread their message.

Ocala sets Agenda

In 1889, the two biggest alliances, the Northwestern Farmers' Alliance and the Southern Farmers' Alliance, merged. The next year the new National Farmers' Alliance held a meeting at Ocala, Florida. There they developed a platform for sweeping political reform. To lower the cost of farming, the Ocala Platform urged government loans for farmers and called for strict railroad regulation. To raise the price of farm crops, the plat-

▲ *A fiery orator, Mary E. Lease was an effective spokesperson for the Populists.*

◄ *This cartoon expresses the view that the Populist party was a patchwork of special interest groups.*

ECONOMICS

Critical Thinking

Ask students to contrast the attitudes of bankers and of Farmers' Alliance members toward "free silver." *(Farmers Alliance members wanted "free silver" to decrease the value of the money they owed; bankers did not want money devalued because they held, and were owed, a lot of money.)*

Language Arts Connection

This chapter includes many words that refer to money and economics. Have students make a glossary of economics terms. Include terms from the chapter, such as *stocks, stock market, gold standard, free silver, greenbacks, hard money policy, monopoly, trust, graft, kickbacks, protective tariff, duties, depression, subsidies, rebates, holding company.* Have them add terms they have encountered in the news, such as *inflation, recession, mortgage,* and *foreclosure.*

Science Connection

During the last part of the 1800s, science and technology affected many aspects of people's lives. Have students research new inventions, such as the phonograph, the microphone, the Kodak box camera, and the motion picture projector. Ask them to imagine how these inventions changed entertainment.

Critical Thinking

Read aloud Lease's words quoted on this page. What inconsistencies does she mention? *(Sample answer: We fought for freedom and then took freedom from black people.)* Ask students to name other inconsistencies in America's past or present.

■ *Farmers formed alliances and experimented with cooperatives, pooling their resources to save money on farm machinery and shipping. They supported regulation of railroads and monopolies and called for government loans and inflating the money supply by minting silver coins.*

POLITICAL SYSTEMS

Critical Thinking

Ask students why they think many Democrats began to support Populist ideas after the financial collapse of 1893. *(Democrats questioned their old economic strategies.)* How did the Democrats' nomination of Bryan for President in 1896 affect the Populist Party? *(The Populists lost their momentum.)*

form called for a larger money supply through the minting of silver coins.

Farmers Support Populists

In the 1890 election, National Farmers' Alliance members supported candidates in both major parties who expressed support for agricultural reform. Once elected, however, most of these "reformers" broke the promises they had made to farmers. In some states, farmers responded by organizing their own political party.

In 1892, farmers held another national convention, this time in Omaha, Nebraska. The convention officially established the Populist Party. The delegates, Populist leaders in their local communities, had colorful nicknames like "Sockless Jerry" Simpson and "Pitchfork Ben" Tillman.

At their 1892 convention, the Populists nominated James B. Weaver for President. Although Weaver lost the election badly, he received a record number of popular votes for a national third-party candidate. The Populists also won 2 governorships and 14 seats in the Congress.

Farmers Favor "Free Silver"

As you read earlier, farmers supported the Greenback-Labor Party in the 1870s. They believed that a larger money supply would lower the value of the money they owed and improve their chances of paying off their debts. Although the Greenback Party declined after 1879, farmers in the Populist Party continued to argue for "free silver," the unrestricted production of silver coins. Bankers and business people repeated their opposition. They argued that the amount of money in circulation must never exceed the nation's reserves of gold. ■

■ *What measures did farmers take to lessen some of their economic hardships?*

Populism Peaks and Fades

After 1892, Populists continued to call for an end to the abuse of wealth and power and for economic justice. From their founding convention in 1892 to the presidential election of 1896, Populists quickly made significant gains.

▼ *These campaign materials are from the election of 1896. Notice the gold bug which undoubtedly adorned the clothes of gold standard supporters.*

The Depression of 1893

A financial collapse in 1893 gave Populism a big boost. With about 2.5 million people out of work and many others unable to buy basic necessities, Americans lost confidence in Democratic President Grover Cleveland. Some Democrats began to wonder whether the prescriptions of the Populists for the economy might work after all.

Further, President Cleveland showed little caring for unemployed people during the depression. In 1894, businessman Jacob Coxey led a march of 500 unemployed people from Massillon, Ohio, to Washington, D.C., to protest Cleveland's economic policy. Police, acting on the President's orders, welcomed Coxey's "army" with clubbings and arrests.

The Election of 1896

In 1896, the Democrats abandoned Cleveland and nominated William Jennings Bryan, who supported "free silver," for President. By nominating Bryan, a "silverite," the Democrats stole an important issue from the Populists and made their party more attractive to farmers. After bitter infighting, the Populists decided to throw their support to Bryan as well.

The Populists did not fare well with Bryan. In the national campaign against the Republican candidate, William McKinley, Bryan distanced

Map and Globe Skills

Refer students to the map at the top of page 491 to make generalizations about where the strongest support for Populist ideas could be found. *(In the South and the West)* Then have them look at the 1910 population density map on page 705 in the Atlas. What conclusions can they draw? *(The Populist states were not heavily populated.)*

Collaborative Learning

Once students have read the lesson, have them brainstorm a list of differences between the Democrats and Republicans in the election of 1896. Then assign pairs of students to illustrate one difference between the two parties. For example, students could draw a bar of gold (representing the Republicans) and greenbacks and silver coins (representing the Democrats). Have students combine their illustrations to make a mural.

Research

Students should use an atlas and other reference books to learn about farmers today. What percentage of the U.S. population is made up by farmers? In your state? Do the Grange, the Farmers' Alliance, and farm cooperatives still exist? If so, what role do they play in farmers' lives and in politics? If possible, have students interview farmers or state government officials to discover farmers' concerns today.

Election of 1896

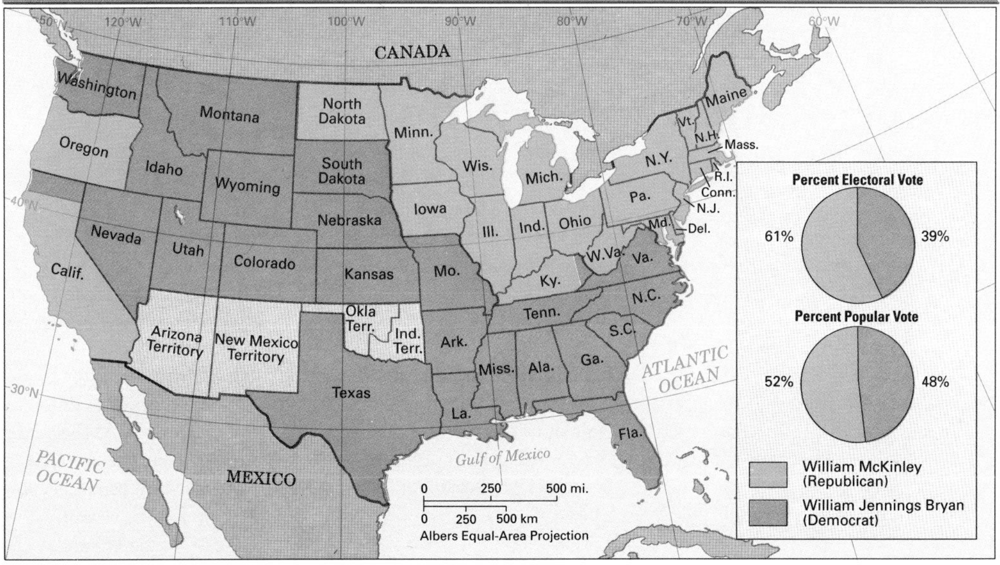

himself from the Populists. Many Americans thought that the Populists were too radical. And even though he had the support of two major parties, Bryan failed to earn the votes of workers. Workers were afraid that free silver would decrease the value of their wages.

Bryan campaigned at a frantic pace. He traveled a total of 18,000 miles and gave as many as 20 speeches a day. Meanwhile, McKinley sat on his front porch and read speeches to key political supporters, who did the traveling for him. The Republican campaign chest was full of contributions from the trusts, large banks, and railroads. A gift of $250,000 from Standard Oil nearly equaled the whole Democratic campaign chest. On election day, McKinley defeated Bryan by a comfortable margin.

The Decline of Populism

Bryan's defeat marked the end of the Populist Party. Several events guaranteed its fall. First, the economy began to boom after McKinley's election. The Republicans took the credit for the change. Second, the discovery of gold in Alaska in 1898 increased the nation's gold reserves. This brought about the inflation of currency that the Populists had been calling for. Finally, the Populists had not gained any support outside of the farming community.

The collapse of the Populist Party did not mark the end of their ideals. These were taken up by the major parties, and later, by Progressive reformers. The income tax and government regulation of transportation and utilities are all Populist goals that we take for granted today. ■

The popular vote in the 1896 presidential election was close, but McKinley clearly triumphed in the electoral vote—271 to Bryan's 176. What regions of the country did McKinley carry? What regions did Bryan carry?

■ *What factors contributed to the decline of the Populist Party?*

R E V I E W

1. **FOCUS** Why did American farmers decide to form their own political party in the 1890s?
2. **CONNECT** How did the rise of railroad monopolies hurt farmers?
3. **ECONOMICS** Why did farmers want the government to increase the money supply?
4. **CRITICAL THINKING** Why do you think it is difficult for a "third" party such as the Populist party to compete against established political parties?
5. **WRITING ACTIVITY** Imagine that you are the editor of a Populist newspaper. Write an editorial encouraging farmers to form cooperatives. Or as a private citizen, write a letter to the editor urging farmers to come together on an issue that is dividing them.

McKinley carried the North and Oregon and California. Bryan carried the South and many states in the West.

POLITICAL SYSTEMS

Critical Thinking

With the end of the Populist Party, how could farmers maintain their political influence? *(By working with labor groups, forming a political party with a broader base, getting support from outside the farming community)*

■ *Factors include Bryan's defeat, the period of prosperity following McKinley's election, the discovery of gold in Alaska, and the lack of Populist support outside the farming community.*

C L O S E

Have students answer the Thinking Focus. Copy on the board the structure and heads of the Graphic Overview from page 486 and have students use their notes to complete it.

Answers to Review Questions

1. Frustration with the two major parties caused farmers to form their own political party.
2. The railroad monopolies hurt farmers by making increases in shipping charges.
3. An increased money supply would devalue their bank loans, making them easier to repay.
4. Sample answer: Some people do not trust new, unproven ideas and will not vote for a new party. Allow for personal opinion.
5. Encourage students to use details from the lesson as support in the editorial or letter.

Homework Options

Have students look in magazines and newspapers for articles about the farm economy or other farm issues today.

Study Guide: page 71.

UNDERSTANDING PERIOD LITERATURE

This skill lesson will show students how to place literature in a historical context.

HISTORY

Critical Thinking

Have students reread the second paragraph of the selection. What is the "great popular movement" that Twain is particularly happy to be part of? *(Everybody is going to Europe and to the Paris Exposition.)* Did this "great popular movement" really include everybody? What conclusion can be drawn about the class of people Twain describes? *(He is describing upper-class society, those people who can afford such luxuries as an ocean voyage to Europe.)*

UNDERSTANDING PERIOD LITERATURE

Reading Mark Twain

Here's Why

Some pieces of literature are called "period pieces" because they are such clear reflections of the time period in which they were written. Historians read novels, short stories, and essays written during a certain period in order to learn how writers of the time viewed their society.

Knowing how to make inferences, or draw conclusions, about a society from what you read in the literature of that society, can provide you with a fuller view of history.

Mark Twain (the pen name for Samuel Langhorne Clemens) is best known for his novel *The Adventures of Huckleberry Finn.* However, Twain was also known for his humorous stories and novels about the society of his time.

Suppose you wanted to learn more about the Gilded Age from the perspective of someone who wrote about it. Reading "between the lines" of Twain's humor is an amusing way to do that.

Here's How

Twain's book *Innocents Abroad* pokes fun at Americans traveling through Europe in the late 1800s. At that time many wealthy people assumed that a year abroad was a necessary part of one's education.

In this passage from his book, Twain relates how he waited for and finally boarded his exclusive ship.

Read the passage from Twain's novel, and follow these steps to draw conclusions about American society during the Gilded Age.

1. **Identify the style of writing.** Is the work you are reading an autobiography, a novel, or another kind of literature? The excerpt below is from one of Twain's humorous novels.
2. **Identify how the style affects the subject matter.** In humor, you can assume that the writer may be exaggerating in order to entertain the reader. At the same time, you can assume that his or her exaggerations are

Occasionally, during the following month, I dropped in at 117 Wall Street to inquire how the repairing and refurnishing of the vessel was coming on, how additions to the passenger list were averaging, how many people the committee were decreeing not "select" every day and banishing in sorrow and tribulation. I was glad to know that we were to have a little printing press on board and issue a daily newspaper of our own. I was glad to learn that our piano, our parlor organ, and our melodeon were to be the best instruments of the kind that could be had in the market. I was proud to observe that among our excursionists were three ministers of gospel, eight doctors, sixteen or eighteen ladies, several military and naval chieftains with sounding titles, an ample crop of "Professors" of various kinds and a gentleman who had "COMMISSIONER OF THE UNITED STATES OF AMERICA TO EUROPE, ASIA, AND AFRICA" thundering after his name in one awful blast! . . .

During that memorable month I basked in the happiness of being for once in my life drifting with the tide of a great popular movement. Everybody was going to Europe—I, too, was going to Europe. Everybody was going to the famous Paris Exposition—I, too, was going to the Paris Exposition. The steamship lines were carrying Americans out of the various ports of the country at the rate of four or five thousand a week in the aggregate. If I met a dozen individuals during that month who were not going to Europe shortly, I have no distinct remembrance of it now . . .

In the fullness of time the ship was ready to receive her passengers. I was introduced to the young gentleman who was to be my roommate, and found him to be intelligent, cheerful of spirit, unselfish, full of generous impulses, patient, considerate, and wonderfully good-natured. Not any passenger that sailed in the Quaker City [ship's name] will withhold his endorsement of what I have just said. We selected a stateroom forward of the wheel, on the

Objective

Use an excerpt from *Innocents Abroad* to evaluate contemporary views of historical time periods. (Critical Thinking 2)

Language Arts Connection

Most students will enjoy Twain's humor and writing style. Some students may wish to read further in *Innocents Abroad* and report on the eventful trip that Twain took to Europe. Help other students find additional examples of his travel writing, such as *A Tramp Abroad* or *Following the Equator.*

Role Playing

Divide the class into groups of five. Assign each group one of the literature selections in the book. They should prepare a short skit in which each student role plays someone who lives in the period described. Encourage students to express the thoughts that their characters might have had.

based on activities or events that the audience would accept as rather common.

3. **Look for specific details that support general ideas.** When Twain makes general statements such as "steamship lines were carrying Americans out of the country at the rate of four or five thousand a week," look for details that illustrate his statement. He says, "If I met a dozen individuals during that month who were not going to Europe shortly, I have no distinct remembrance of it now. . ." It seemed to him as if everyone he met was going to Europe.

starboard side, "below decks." It had two berths in it, a dismal deadlight, a sink with a washbowl in it, and a long, sumptuously cushioned locker, which was to do service as a sofa—partly—and partly as a hiding place for our things. Notwithstanding all this furniture, there was still room to turn around in, but not to swing a cat in, at least with entire security to the cat. However, the room was large, for a ship's stateroom, and was in every way satisfactory.

The vessel was appointed to sail on a certain Saturday early in June . . .

Finally, above the banging, and rumbling, and shouting, and hissing of steam rang the order to "cast off!"—a sudden rush to the gangways—a scampering ashore of visitors—a revolution of the wheels, and we were off—the picnic was begun! Two very mild cheers went up from the dripping crowd on the pier; we answered them gently from the slippery decks; the flag made an effort to wave, and failed; the "battery of guns" spake not—the ammunition was out.

We steamed down to the foot of the harbor and came to anchor. It was still raining. And not only raining, but storming. "Outside" we could see, ourselves, that there was a tremendous sea on. We must lie still, in the calm harbor, till the storm should abate. Our passengers hailed from fifteen states; only a few of them had ever been to sea before; manifestly it would not do to pit them against a full-blown tempest until they had got their sea legs on. Toward evening the two steam tugs that had accompanied us with a rollicking champagne party of young New Yorkers on board who wished to bid farewell to one of our number in due and ancient form departed, and we were alone on the deep. On deep five fathoms, and anchored fast to the bottom. And out in the solemn rain at that. This was pleasuring with a vengeance . . .

Mark Twain, *Innocents Abroad*

4. **Look for general ideas that can be drawn from specific details.** Note Twain's list of passengers: "three ministers of gospel, eight doctors, sixteen or eighteen ladies, several military and naval chieftains with sounding titles, an ample crop of 'Professors' of various kinds. . . . " In his amusing way he gives you a good idea of the kind of people who were traveling abroad at that time: professional, upper class people.

5. **Draw a conclusion.** In this passage from his novel, Twain exaggerates general ideas but gives specific information about a way of life. This piece of literature presents an amusingly close look at how one level of society lived during the Gilded Age.

Try It

Read the passage from *East River* on page 522. Use the steps above to make inferences about the life the writer describes.

Apply It

Choose one of the literature excerpts presented in this book, such as the excerpt from *My Antonia*. Read through the passage, and write a brief paragraph explaining how the literature enhances the history discussed in the chapter.

HISTORY

Critical Thinking

Have students reread the last paragraph of the selection. What has happened to the ship? *(It moved only to the foot of the harbor and anchored there because of the storm.)* How does Twain create humor out of the situation? *(With irony, saying, "This was pleasuring with a vengeance," when most passengers were driven indoors by the rain)* Is Twain really as determined as the other passengers to think he's having a good time, no matter what happens? *(He is poking fun at the other passengers, and himself, by parodying their attitudes.)*

Answers to Try It

Step 1. Style is mock-serious, descriptive.

Step 2. Details make the reader feel the oppressiveness of the situation.

Step 3. Sample generalization—"The evening brought no relief . . . "; sample specific—"Walls, ceilings, floors sweated."

Step 4. Sample general idea—Tammany Hall helped its supporters; sample details—took over real-estate lot, gave tickets of admission to supporters

Step 5. Conclusion—The lives of most nineteenth-century immigrants were hard.

Answers to Apply It

Make sure that students apply the five-step process to their reading. They should be able to draw general ideas from specific details and draw at least one conclusion to enhance their reading of the chapter.

Study Skill

Refer students to page 442—the 1876 Centennial Exposition in Philadelphia—and then have them use library sources to research the history of expositions and world fairs.

Answers to Reviewing Key Terms

A. Sample answers:

1. The graft that took place in some cities included paying kickback money to politicians for favors.
2. Political machines built their power by giving jobs and contracts as patronage to their supporters.
3. If a business has a monopoly on a certain market, it does not want anyone to regulate, or control, its business practices.
4. Mugwumps were political reformers who wanted to establish the civil service system.
5. The civil service system was designed to eliminate graft.

B. Answers:

1. True. William Belknap and Orville Babcock were among those officials receiving kickbacks.
2. False. Mugwumps were Republicans who supported reform.
3. False. Farmers formed cooperatives to save on farm machinery and shipping costs.
4. True. Populism was primarily a farmer's movement.

Answers to Exploring Concepts

A. Answers:

A: 2. lower grain prices

B: 1. Grange, 2. Greenback-Labor Party, 3. Populist Party, 4. Farmers' Alliance

C: 1. Mary E. Lease, 2. William Jennings Bryan

D: 1. Economic prosperity helps Republicans, 2. Discovery of gold produces inflation, 3. Populism remained a farm-based movement

Chapter Review

Reviewing Key Terms

civil service (p. 480)
cooperative (p. 489)
graft (p. 476)
kickback (p. 475)
monopoly (p. 483)
Mugwump (p. 479)
patronage (p. 476)
political machine (p. 476)
Populism (p. 487)
regulate (p. 482)
trust (p. 483)

A. In each of the following pairs, the two terms are related in some way. Write a sentence for each pair that clearly explains the meaning of the two terms.

1. kickback, graft
2. patronage, political machine
3. monopoly, regulate
4. Mugwumps, civil service
5. graft, civil service

B. Based on what you have read in the chapter, decide whether each of the following statements is accurate. Write an explanation of each decision.

1. Some officials received kickbacks for helping to cheat people out of their means of earning money.
2. Mugwumps were immigrants who came to America to work on the railroad.
3. In a cooperative, railroads and large shippers teamed up to keep the prices of farm products low.
4. Populism never gained much support outside farming areas.

Exploring Concepts

A. Copy the outline below onto a separate sheet of paper. Complete the outline with details from the chapter.

I. The Rise of Populism

A. Reasons for Farmer's Discontent

1. Increased Costs
2.

B. Farmer's Movements

1.
2.
3.
4.

C. Leaders of the Populist Movement

1.
2.

D. Reasons for Decline of Populism

1.
2.
3.

B. On a separate sheet of paper, write the answer to the following questions. Support your answers with facts and details from the chapter.

1. How did the robber barons influence government officials?
2. Which of President Grant's personal qualities encouraged corruption in his administration?
3. What was the main difference between the two major political parties in the period from 1877 to 1900?
4. How did the owners of trusts get around the restrictions of the Sherman Anti-Trust Act?
5. How did the introduction of new farm machinery hurt the farmers?
6. What was the main reason why farmers wanted a larger money supply?
7. Why was this period in the history of the United States called the Gilded Age?
8. Why was the Interstate Commerce Act important despite the fact that it was ineffective in regulating the railroads?
9. Why did bankers and business people oppose the idea of unrestricted production of silver coins?

B. Sample answers:

1. They manipulated congressional representatives and judges by buying votes and bribery.
2. Grant showed poor judgment in trusting friends who were dishonest. He was also gullible and easily influenced.
3. Republicans were mainly Northern white Protestants whereas Democrats were mostly Southern Catholics and immigrants.
4. Their holding companies were legal substitutes for trusts.
5. Farmers took out large loans to pay for equipment, but larger crops brought lower prices.
6. To lower the real value of money they owed to banks, and to pay off loans more rapidly.
7. The "golden" (gilded) lives of many rich people covered up dishonest business practices.
8. It established the government's right to regulate business and made further regulations possible.
9. They believed that adding silver coins to the money supply would cause inflation.

Reviewing Skills

1. O. Henry was a short story writer who used the slang of his day in his writing. Find a copy of his classic short story "The Gift of the Magi," which first appeared in the *New York Sunday World* on December 10, 1905. Read the story, paying particular attention to the dialogue and the details. What does this story tell you about the way some people lived in the early twentieth century?
2. Read the passage from Frank Norris's novel *The Octopus* on page 487. Write a short paragraph explaining how that passage relates to the events in this chapter.
3. Create a timeline of the important events you have read about in this chapter. Write a short paragraph explaining what conclusions you can draw from the timeline.
4. Suppose you wanted to find out how people today view teenagers. Can you identify a particular piece of writing that you would consider a "period piece"? Explain your choice: what kind of writing is it, and why do you think it presents a contemporary view of teenagers?

Using Critical Thinking

1. Corruption in government did not end with the Grant administration. How do wealthy people and groups attempt to influence elected officials today? What can ordinary citizens do about it?
2. The debate over how much money to put into circulation still goes on today. Though the value of U.S. money no longer depends on gold or silver, the Federal Reserve Board decides how much money to put into circulation. What are the dangers of having too little money in circulation? What are the dangers of having too much money in circulation?
3. Farmers, unlike the members of labor unions, have never successfully used a strike to win higher prices for their labor. However, during the Depression they destroyed animals and crops to protest the low prices of their products. How do you think that affected the nation?

Preparing for Citizenship

1. **WRITING ACTIVITY** The two major parties, Republican and Democratic, still control American politics. Interview an adult who votes Republican and another who votes Democratic. Ask them to explain the reasons for their choice. Compare the results of your interviews, and decide if there are major differences between the parties today. Write a brief report on your findings.
2. **ART ACTIVITY** The Mugwump cartoonist Thomas Nast was the first one to use the elephant to represent the Republicans and the donkey to represent the Democrats (Note the cartoon at right.) Those symbols are still used today. Look through newspapers and magazines for cartoons or drawings that use those symbols. Create a "Republican" collage or a "Democrat" collage of your findings.
3. **COLLABORATIVE LEARNING** Advertising has always been an important part of politics. It is one way people have gained public attention and support of their beliefs. Divide the class into two groups, one representing big business and one representing independent farmers. Have each group develop a strategy for promoting its cause. Each group may create posters, write editorials, develop videos, or use other forms of contemporary communication. Present the advertising campaigns to another class, and ask the viewers to evaluate how well each campaign succeeds in presenting its group's beliefs.

Answers to Reviewing Skills

1. Students should identify how the dialogue reveals the financial and social status of the characters.
2. Students should cite specific examples in the text that relate to the passage.
3. Have students compare timelines and discuss any differences in them.
4. Encourage students to prepare a short report on their choice, and to compare choices within the class.

Answers to Using Critical Thinking

1. Students should consider tax laws and lobbyists as well as public watchdog groups.
2. Encourage students to set up a system of "play-money" within the classroom to illustrate what could happen.
3. Ask students to consider how the public views people who provide essential goods. Refer to the fact that police and other essential services are not allowed to strike.

495

Answers to Preparing for Citizenship

1. **WRITING ACTIVITY** Refer students to Understanding Interviewing on page 577. Have students present their reports and compare findings. Students may also contact the local newspaper and ask the political writers to speak to the class about the current differences between the two parties.
2. **ART ACTIVITY** This can be used as a bulletin board activity. Students can find Nast's cartoons in histories of the period, particularly those relating to the scandals of the time.
3. **COLLABORATIVE LEARNING** Encourage students to contact advertising agencies, farm cooperatives, and businesses for information.

CHAPTER 17

Planning at a Glance

The Reform Era

	Objectives	Reading Support *and* Other Resources	Diverse Learning Strategies
Lesson 1 The Shame of the Cities *pp. 498–506* 2–3 days	• Describe the origins and basic characteristics of the Progressive movement. • Summarize the Progressives' position on education. • Evaluate the Progressives' approach to city planning. • Explain why and how the Progressives went about reforming the nation's city governments.	• **Workbook** or **Reading Support:** pp. 242–245 Review p. 57 Lesson Support/Transition p. 57 Multi-lang. Sum. pp. 113–114 • **Other Resources:** Posters 5, 7; Study Guide p. 73; Study Prints 12, 13	Access Act. **(SDAIE)** TE p. 499 Social Participation **(Kinesthetic)** TE p. 503 Art Connection **(Visual)** TE p. 504 Collaborative Act. **(Visual)** TE p. 505 Audiotapes of Multi-language Lesson Summaries **(Auditory)**
Lesson 2 Progressive Reform *pp. 507–512* 1–2 days	• List the major Progressive reforms in state government. • Describe the federal government's role in advancing Progressivism. • Analyze the impact of the Bull Moose Party on the 1912 presidential election. • Evaluate the contributions of Woodrow Wilson's administration to the Progressives' cause.	• **Workbook** or **Reading Support:** pp. 246–249 Review p. 58 Lesson Support/Transition p. 58 Multi-lang. Sum. pp. 115–116 • **Other Resources:** Geography Kit, Study Guide p. 74	Access Strat. **(Extra Support)** TE p. 508 Research **(GATE)** TE p. 511 Map and Globe Skills **(Visual)** TE p. 511 Audiotapes of Multi-language Lesson Summaries **(Auditory)**
Lesson 3 Competing Crusades *pp. 513–519* 2–3 days **Literature** **"East River"** *pp. 522–523*	• Identify the common features of the movements for prohibition and against child labor. • Compare the goals of Progressives with the goals of radical political movements. • Explain how women's organizations won women's suffrage. • Describe the impact that the Progressive movement had on the lives of black Americans.	• **Workbook** or **Reading Support:** pp. 250–253 Review p. 59 Lesson Support/Transition p. 59 Multi-lang. Sum. pp. 117–118 • **Other Resources:** Study Guide p. 75	Writing a Report **(GATE)** TE p. 518 Music Connection **(Auditory)** TE p. 517 Visual Learning **(Visual)** TE pp. 516–517 Collaborative Act. **(Auditory)** TE p. 518 Audiotapes of Multi-language Lesson Summaries **(Auditory)**
Skill: Analyzing Historical Photographs *pp. 520–521*	• Use early nineteenth-century photographs to determine what the living conditions were like during that time.	• **Other Resources:** Study Guide p. 76	Visual Learning **(Visual)** TE p. 521
Chapter Review *pp. 524–252* 1 day		Chapter 17 Test pp. 65–68 *(See facsimiles on TE p. 765.)*	Assessment Multiple-Use Masters pp. 81–88

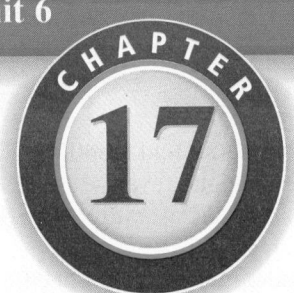

Reading Support Resources *for Every Lesson*

Reading and Review

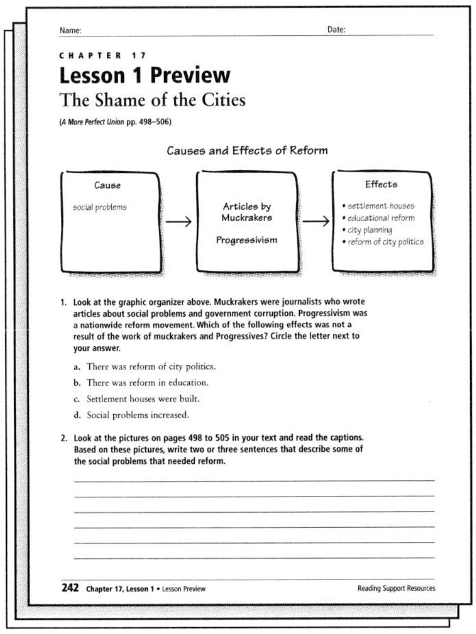
Name: Date:

CHAPTER 17

Lesson 1 Preview

The Shame of the Cities

(A More Perfect Union pp. 498–506)

Causes and Effects of Reform

Cause: social problems → Articles by Muckrakers; Progressivism → Effects: • settlement houses • educational reform • city planning • reform of city politics

1. Look at the graphic organizer above. Muckrakers were journalists who wrote articles about social problems and government corruption. Progressivism was a nationwide reform movement. Which of the following effects was not a result of the work of muckrakers and Progressives? Circle the letter next to your answer.
   a. There was reform of city politics.
   b. There was reform in education.
   c. Settlement houses were built.
   d. Social problems increased.
2. Look at the pictures on pages 498 to 505 in your text and read the captions. Based on these pictures, write two or three sentences that describe some of the social problems that needed reform.

242 Chapter 17, Lesson 1 • Lesson Preview — Reading Support Resources

- **Chapter Overview*** p. 241
- **Lesson Previews*** using graphic organizers from the Teacher's Edition pp. 242, 246, 250
- **Reading Strategies*** pp. 243, 247, 251
- **Lesson Summaries*** pp. 244–245, 248–249, 252–253
- **Lesson Reviews** pp. 57, 58, 59

* **Workbook** includes starred items.

Multi-language Summaries

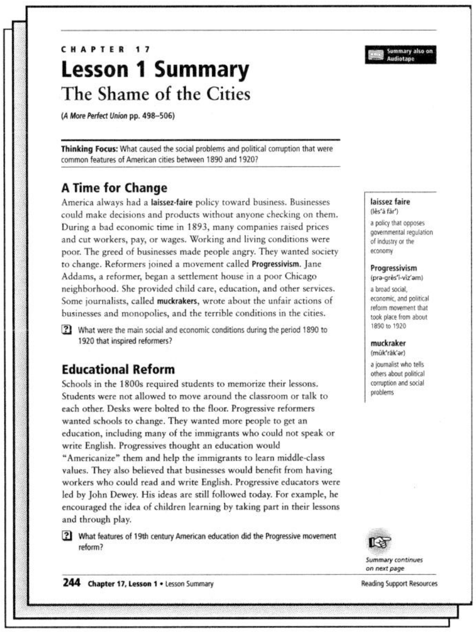
CHAPTER 17

Lesson 1 Summary

The Shame of the Cities

(A More Perfect Union pp. 498–506)

Summary also on Audiotape

Thinking Focus: What caused the social problems and political corruption that were common features of American cities between 1890 and 1920?

A Time for Change

America always had a **laissez-faire** policy toward business. Businesses could make decisions and products without anyone checking on them. During a bad economic time in 1893, many companies raised prices and cut workers, pay, or wages. Working and living conditions were poor. The greed of businesses made people angry. They wanted society to change. Reformers joined a movement called **Progressivism.** Jane Addams, a reformer, began a settlement house in a poor Chicago neighborhood. She provided child care, education, and other services. Some journalists, called **muckrakers,** wrote about the unfair actions of businesses and monopolies, and the terrible conditions in the cities.

What were the main social and economic conditions during the period 1890 to 1920 that inspired reformers?

Educational Reform

Schools in the 1800s required students to memorize their lessons. Students were not allowed to move around the classroom or talk to each other. Desks were bolted to the floor. Progressive reformers wanted schools to change. They wanted more people to get an education, including many of the immigrants who could not speak or write English. Progressives thought an education would "Americanize" them and help the immigrants to learn middle-class values. They also believed that businesses would benefit from having workers who could read and write English. Progressive educators were led by John Dewey. His ideas are still followed today. For example, he encouraged the idea of children learning by taking part in their lessons and through play.

What features of 19th century American education did the Progressive movement reform?

laissez faire a policy that opposes governmental regulation of industry or the economy

Progressivism a broad social, economic, and political reform movement that took place from about 1890 to 1920

muckraker a journalist who tells others about political corruption and social problems

Summary continues on next page

244 Chapter 17, Lesson 1 • Lesson Summary — Reading Support Resources

Lesson Summaries in:

- English (See Reading and Review.)
- Spanish pp. 244–245, 248–249, 252–253
- Chinese pp. 113–118
- Hmong pp. 113–118
- Khmer pp. 113–118
- Vietnamese pp. 113–118

Summaries available on audiotapes

Lesson Support / Transition

SDAIE

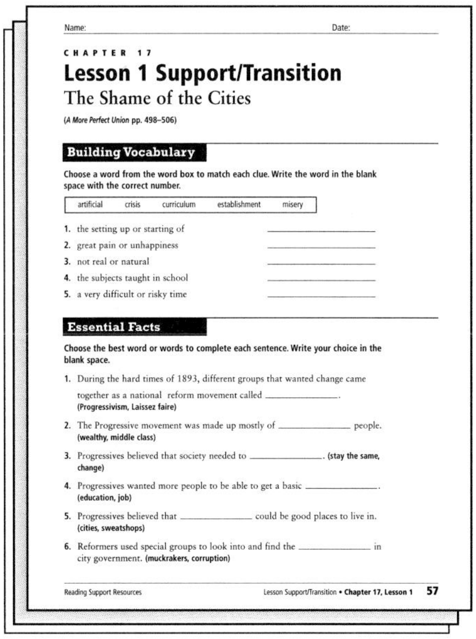
Name: Date:

CHAPTER 17

Lesson 1 Support/Transition

The Shame of the Cities

(A More Perfect Union pp. 498–506)

Building Vocabulary

Choose a word from the word box to match each clue. Write the word in the blank space with the correct number.

artificial crisis curriculum establishment misery

1. the setting up or starting of
2. great pain or unhappiness
3. not real or natural
4. the subjects taught in school
5. a very difficult or risky time

Essential Facts

Choose the best word or words to complete each sentence. Write your choice in the blank space.

1. During the hard times of 1893, different groups that wanted change came together as a national reform movement called ______. (Progressivism, Laissez faire)
2. The Progressive movement was made up mostly of ______ people. (wealthy, middle class)
3. Progressives believed that society needed to ______. (stay the same, change)
4. Progressives wanted more people to be able to get a basic ______. (education, job)
5. Progressives believed that ______ could be good places to live in. (cities, sweatshops)
6. Reformers used special groups to look into and find the ______ in city government. (muckrakers, corruption)

Reading Support Resources — Lesson Support/Transition • Chapter 17, Lesson 1 57

Activities for SDAIE
Specially **D**esigned **A**cademic **I**nstruction in **E**nglish

- **Lesson Support/Transition** pp. 57, 58, 59

Technology Options

Internet Support

http://www.eduplace.com

Social Studies Center at Education Place

Internet support for Chapter 17:

- ***Lesson at a Glance***
- ***Sweatshops***

Videotape/Videodisc

We the People:
Supports and enhances major topics: **Themes: *Rise of the City; Moving West***

Software

Student Writing Center® (CD-ROM) (Macintosh® or Windows®)

School to Career

People have always lobbied behind causes and interests they wanted to see represented in state and federal policy. Today, government officials rely upon professional lobbyists to gather and present information that affects government policy. Have students contact groups to learn what role, if any, lobbyists play in their organizations.

Character Education

Service Learning: Theodore Roosevelt made conservation of the nation's resources federal policy. Today, the National Park Service and state park systems help protect millions of acres of land. Many of these rely upon volunteers or paid summer interns. Have students look into opportunities to volunteer at a city, state, or national park or monument in your area.

CHAPTER
PREVIEW

After students have read the chapter title and the narrative underneath it, have them use the photographs on this page to name the types of problems people faced and the solutions to these problems that reformers sought in the late 1800s and early 1900s. *(Problems—overcrowding, illiteracy; solutions—shelters, community programs)* What might the popularity of the boardgame about Nellie Bly, a journalist famous for writing articles that inspired social change, reveal about reform during this time? *(Many Americans supported reform movements.)*

Looking Back

This chapter continues the discussion on the reform movement begun in Chapter 16. You may also want to remind students of the reform movements in the North that they learned about in Chapter 9.

Looking Forward

Tell students that they will be reading about a wide variety of reform movements in the next three lessons: The Shame of the Cities, Progressive Reform, and Competing Crusades.

Chapter 17
The Reform Era

Overcrowding. Hunger. Dangerous working conditions. By 1900, social problems fueled by immigration and industrial growth troubled America's cities. These problems inspired a new generation of reformers to fight to improve the quality of American life.

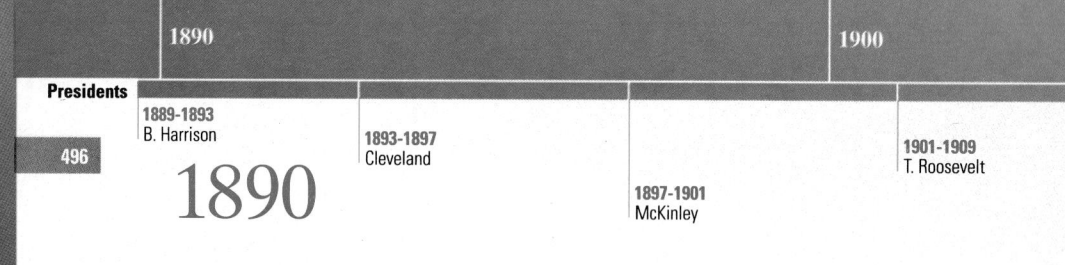

Immigrants and the poor find hope and help in social and educational centers set up by reformers.

1890	1900

Presidents

1889-1893 B. Harrison	1893-1897 Cleveland	1897-1901 McKinley	1901-1909 T. Roosevelt

1890

BACKGROUND

A variety of social problems—resulting from rapid urbanization, industrialization, and immigration—sparked numerous movements for political, social, and moral reform, beginning in the 1890s and continuing through the first two decades of the 20th century.

Jane Addams

Born to a middle-class Illinois family in 1860, Jane Addams belonged to the first generation of women to graduate from colleges in America. She put her principles and privileges into action as a crusader for social justice and as a pioneer in the field of social work. Besides the activities associated with Hull House, her strong ideals led her into pacifist and civil liberties work. Addams formed the Women's International League for Peace and Freedom in 1915 and became its first president, using the position to argue against the United States's entry into World War I. In 1920 she helped found the American Civil Liberties Union.

Addams's concern for humanity is reflected in her writing: *Democracy and Social Ethics* (1902), *Newer Ideals of Peace* (1907), *Twenty Years at Hull House* (1910), *The Second Twenty Years at Hull House* (1930), and *The Excellent Becomes the Permanent* (1932). A co-winner of the Nobel Peace Prize in 1931, Addams characteristically donated the prize money to the Women's Peace Party. She died in 1935.

Understanding the Visuals

Point out that the photos of the Hull House settlement, by Lewis Hine, and the tenement house, by Jacob Riis, were both taken in 1910. These photographers exposed the social problems of American cities at the turn of the century. Riis is sometimes called America's first photojournalist because his pictures accompanied the books he wrote, such as *How the Other Half Lives.*

1910 The cities are overwhelmed with new residents. The photograph above shows an immigrant family in New York City. The small room serves as their living room, kitchen, and bedroom.

Journalist Nellie Bly, who earned fame for her shocking stories about jails and mental institutions, turned to travel. In this boardgame, Americans recreated her record-setting journey around the world .

1910

1920

1909-1913 Taft

1913-1921 Wilson

1920

Understanding Chronology

Ask students to compare the chapter timeline to the timeline in Chapter 16 (pages 470-471). Which presidential terms are found on both timelines? *(That of B. Harrison and Cleveland's second term)*

The Federal Reserve Act of 1913

President Woodrow Wilson's Federal Reserve Act of 1913 was the first reorganization of the nation's banking system in almost sixty years. The bill put the control of banks and of the nation's money supply into the hands of the public by creating the Federal Reserve System. Previously, the "money trust," a group of private banks and trust companies led by J.P. Morgan, had effectively controlled the money supply and directed the concentration of resources and power into the hands of a few New York bankers.

The Federal Reserve Act created a flexible currency based on federal reserve notes—dollars—and gave the Federal Reserve Board the power to expand or contract the amount of currency as a way to stabilize prices. Federal Reserve Banks were set up as "bankers' banks." They only provided services for member banks, not for businesses or private citizens. In times of financial crises, the banks could transfer money reserves between Federal Reserve districts to prevent bank failures and loss of people's savings.

INTRODUCE

Read the lesson title and ask students what the "shame" might be. Ask them to recall from Chapters 9 and 16 some of the problems that cities were having. Have students read the Thinking Focus and then predict what effect social problems and political corruption had on each other. Have them read to confirm or reject their predictions.

Key Terms

Vocabulary strategies: T36–37

laissez faire—a policy that opposes governmental regulation of industry or the economy

Progressivism—a broad social and political reform movement that took place from about 1890 to 1920

muckraker—a journalist who exposes political corruption and social problems

tenement—an apartment building whose facilities fail to meet minimum standards of sanitation, safety, and comfort

zoning law—a law restricting areas of a city to a certain use, such as residential, commercial, or industrial

1880 1890 1920 1930

LESSON 1

The Shame of the Cities

THINKING FOCUS

What caused the social problems and political corruption that were common features of American cities between 1890 and 1920?

Key Terms

- laissez faire
- Progressivism
- muckraker
- tenement
- zoning law

When smoke and flames started to pour out of the eighth-floor windows of the Triangle Shirtwaist Factory in New York City on March 26, 1911, a passerby quickly contacted the fire department. The events that followed shocked and horrified the nation.

Out of the windows of the upper floors and off the roof of the 10-story building, workers—mostly young women—began leaping to their deaths on the sidewalks below. As the flames shot higher and higher, more workers jumped. Some held hands with friends as they plummeted to the ground. When the blaze ended only half an hour later, 146 of the 500 workers in the building had died in the fire or had leapt to their deaths. Only one outside fire escape, required by law, provided a way out of the building. An investigation revealed that the factory owners had locked the doors to the fire escape to prevent the workers from "loafing" on the stairs.

The tragedy of the Triangle Shirtwaist fire caused an uproar against health- and life-threatening conditions in American factories and sweatshops. One observer blamed the Triangle tragedy on "the greed of man." The observer mourned that "we might have foreseen it, and some of us did; we might have controlled it, but we chose not to do so."

Ironically, those who died in the fire had replaced women who had joined unions and struck for better working conditions. When the owners of the factory came to trial for the deaths of their workers, however, they were sentenced only to pay a small fine. The Triangle fire soon came to symbolize the indifference of business and government to the lives of ordinary workers.

The Triangle Shirtwaist factory was typical of overcrowded, unsafe workplaces at the turn of the century. Newspaper reports helped create pressure for reform.

Objectives

1. Describe the origins and the basic characteristics of the Progressive movement.
2. Summarize the Progressives' position on education.
3. Evaluate the Progressives' approach to city planning.
4. Explain why and how the Progressives went about reforming the nation's city governments.

Graphic Overview

Cause
social problems

→ **Exposés by Muckrakers** **Progressivism** →

Effects
- settlement houses
- educational reform
- city planning
- reform of city politics

A Time for Change

The United States has always had a capitalistic economy in which people are free to make or sell goods and services for a profit. The French term **laissez faire** *(LESS ay fair)* means "let it be." It refers to the economic policy that advocates no government interference in business. Its theory is that free trade and open competition stimulate production. America had a laissez-faire policy before the 1893 depression.

During the depression, monopolies raised prices even though there was less demand for their goods. At the same time, they cut the pay of their workers despite the fact that they were making more money than ever. The monopolies were placing their own greed above the public good. Many people became angry.

A popular movement arose in the late nineteenth and early twentieth centuries that called for the reform of unfair business practices. Reform movements were already under way in other areas of U.S. society. The "good government" movement had begun in the 1870s while Grant was President. It aimed to get rid of government corruption and inefficiency through civil service reform. The social welfare movement had begun before the Civil War. It fought for better education and safe housing. It also aimed to stop both the sale of alcohol and the use of child labor. Labor unions fought the conditions in sweatshops such as the sweatshop shown in A Closer Look on pages 500–501.

The depression of 1893 was severe. Many people feared that the economy and the government might collapse. In this time of uncertainty, reformers were able to bring together the separate reform movements. A broadly based nationwide reform movement emerged. Named **Progressivism** around 1905, the movement sought basic social, economic, and governmental reforms. It favored regulation by the government of big business, women's right to vote, and the establishment of child labor laws.

Members of the Ash Can School were famous for their realistic paintings of urban life. George Bellows completed this painting of a city slum in 1913.

The Progressive movement was made up mainly of people from the middle class. They were well educated, and eager to change society to fit their values. On some issues, Progressives also came from the working class, the upper class, and all political parties.

Progressives often did not agree about how to achieve reform. Some did not trust government and felt that volunteer groups would be enough to solve social problems. Some wanted government to watch over business. A few wanted public ownership of monopolies. Progressives were united, however, in believing that society needed to change. They tried to find a vision or direction to guide society away from the unfairness they saw in laissez-faire capitalism.

DEVELOP

Copy on the board the structure and main heads of the Graphic Overview from page 498 to show students the cause-and-effect structure of the lesson. Fill in the key developments in the middle box. Have students copy this much of the Overview in their notes and add the social conditions (causes) that the reforms (effects) addressed as they read the lesson.

ECONOMICS

Critical Thinking

Have students work in small groups to prepare charts that contrast Progressive-movement values with laissez-faire policy values. *(The Progressive movement valued human rights and intervention in business for the good of society. The laissez-faire policy valued nonintervention, individualism, and profits.)*

Access Strategy

Bring clippings of two or three investigative articles to class to share and discuss with students. Do the articles present important information? To whom is it important? Why? Who writes these reports, and how do they get the information? Point out that journalists expose issues to increase awareness. Ask students whether a news story has ever made them want to change things. Explain that the nation's serious social and political problems became more evident after the depression of 1893. Tell students that they will read in this lesson how investigative journalists, who came to be known as muckrakers, helped to inspire reform by exposing those problems.

Access Activity

Give students time to study and react to the painting by George Bellows on this page. What is happening in the painting? What is the setting, and who are the people? What are their lives like? Ask students why a painting such as this might move people to push for reforms.

Note: Have students examine A Closer Look after they have read the section City Planning, pages 504–505.

SOCIAL SYSTEMS

Visual Learning

Ask students to recall the reasons why Italians and Jews came to America in the late 1800s. *(Crop failures, political and religious persecution)* Ask them to evaluate the quality of life of an immigrant family working in a sweatshop. Were they better off than they were in their homeland?

More About the Children As soon as children were strong enough to work, at about six years old, they began adding to the family income. Those children who were able to go to school worked for two hours in the morning before school and another two to four hours when they got home in the evening.

A CLOSER LOOK

Sweatshops

Their name says it all. Men, women, and children worked 14-hour days in hot, stuffy upper-story apartments. The more pieces you made, the more you were paid. But the pay for each piece was low. So you had to work fast—and sweat.

Children worked in the sweatshops with their families. An entire family such as this might work 70 hours a week and earn only $3.00. The goal of the owners was to produce as much as possible, as cheaply as possible.

Making artificial flowers w strenuous task. Sharp wires c cause cuts and punctures. Clo detail work caused eyestrain.

Italian and Jewish immigrants made up most of the sweatshop workforce. The more skilled work, such as operating sewing machines, required an apprenticeship period in which workers would not even be paid while they trained.

Ready-made clothing was the most common sweatshop product. A family might make 12 dozen pairs of pants in one week.

Critical Thinking

Ask students how sweatshop labor affected the family in terms of health. *(Poorly, due to lack of ventilation, heat, light, and time for relaxation)* In terms of social life? *(The family would have a lot of contact with one another, but little with the outside world.)*

Social Context

Life for children in the 1800s centered on work, duty, and obedience. Children were expected to be "seen and not heard." Corporal punishment was common. Poor children were sometimes treated brutally at work and at home. Orphans received little, if any, care. Many grew up sleeping in doorways, surviving by selling newspapers, or begging. The Children's Aid Society and the Society for the Prevention of Cruelty to Children worked to eliminate these conditions.

By the turn of the century, there was a shift in middle-class attitudes toward children. Despite the large number of children toiling in mines, factories, and on farms, people began to view childhood as a time of carefree exploration. Children were encouraged to use imagination in creative play. Kindergarten, with its emphasis on the educational value of play, had begun in the 1840s in Germany. Its influence began to spread throughout America in the 1890s.

This family assembles jackets in a windowless attic.
Sweatshop rooms had no heat in the winter and only two small gas lights.
Families could rent rooms for a nickel a night.
Often, six to twenty workers crowded into tight spaces.
Finished dry goods go straight to market. The sweatshop owner owns the whole building.
501

POLITICAL SYSTEMS

Visual Learning

Ask students to recall the purposes of a trade or labor union. *(To protect the workers from unfair practices by employers)* Explain that unions for garment workers were established during the Progressive Era. Ask the students to list some of the obstacles blocking sweatshop workers from organizing or joining unions. *(Little time, did not speak English, opposition from employers who may be friends or relatives)*

This new attitude about childhood also fueled an explosion of children's toys and books. *Peter Rabbit,* by British writer Beatrix Potter, and *The Wizard of Oz,* by American writer L. Frank Baum, became popular. John Dewey, a leader of Progressive education, believed in knowledge as a tool for changing the environment in order to improve the quality of human life. He proposed that children be taught in skill-related environments such as laboratories, kitchens, and gymnasiums. He wanted education to be relevant to, and supportive of, the students' everyday lives. Proponents of a child-centered approach to education argued that the school should fit the needs of the child, not vice versa. Francis W. Parker, whom Dewey called the "father of progressive education," introduced child-centered education in Quincy, Massachusetts, and Chicago, Illinois, in the 1870s and 1880s.

Study Skills

Have students research in an encyclopedia or library the current laws governing child labor, the minimum wage, and maximum working hours. Have students present their findings in a chart or a written report.

POLITICAL SYSTEMS

Critical Thinking

Ask students to name the ways in which Progressives tried to change society. *(They planned and worked for reforms in business, government, education, and cities.)* Remind students that the Progressive movement was led mainly by people of the middle class who tried to change society to fit their values (page 499). Then ask them to discuss whether they agree that all of American society should be changed to fit the values of one group. How might it be possible for such a change to happen? *(The group would have to have political power.)*

■ *Conditions included political corruption, business abuses, and human misery.*

Jane Addams (above) *not only sought to improve conditions in urban slums, she also urged women to find new social outlets for their energies and talents. In the shop* (top), *boys are learning skills that will help them find jobs later.*

■ *What were the main social and economic conditions during the period 1890 to 1920 that inspired reformers?*

Muckrakers Inspire Reform

Around 1900, a new generation of journalists began investigating and writing about the corruption, business abuses, and human misery in the nation's cities. Reporter Nellie Bly, for example, had herself committed to a mental institution. She later wrote a shocking account of the conditions there. Lincoln Steffens exposed bribery in the city government of St. Louis in his 1904 book *The Shame of the Cities*. Ida M. Tarbell wrote the *History of the Standard Oil Company* the same year. Other writers followed the example of these pioneers.

Theodore Roosevelt called these journalists **muckrakers** because they wrote about evil and corruption. Muckrakers found that monopolies were exploiting the public and keeping prices artificially high. Monopolies often sold poor and even harmful products. Muckrakers also exposed businesses that made their employees work in dangerous and unhealthful workplaces. These stories not only shocked the nation but also won strong support for many important reforms.

Settlement Houses Nourish the Poor

The misery of the cities and the cause of feminist liberation changed Jane Addams, a polite young woman from a well-to-do family, into a tough social reformer. Addams introduced the settlement house to America in 1889. A settlement house was a community center in an urban neighborhood. It provided childcare, education, and other services to immigrants and the poor.

Addams began Hull House in Chicago's poverty-stricken 19th ward. It became the model for the 50 settlement houses that were established by 1895. Hull House grew to take up a full city block. It offered a nursery, boys' clubs, a theater, a playground, a gym, classes in English, health, and nutrition, a pottery workshop, and a book bindery.

On the whole, Progressives were well educated. They recognized that scientifically gathered facts would strengthen their arguments for reform. They were also interested in finding scientific, efficient ways to distribute the services they offered.

Addams and her friends made scientific studies of American cities. They used the studies to fight child labor and workplace abuses. Addams also helped to put in place the nation's first factory inspection law and its first juvenile court.

Despite the major contributions of the settlement houses to the lives of the immigrants and the poor, Addams remained unsatisfied. She believed that private gifts and volunteer work were "totally inadequate to deal with the vast numbers of the city's [poor]." Like many other Progressives, she felt that the help of the government was needed to solve the nation's serious social problems. ■

Critical Thinking

Remind students that Hull House provided services and programs for the urban poor. Ask students which services then offered by Hull House are still needed now. What new services might be offered at a Hull House of today? *(Nursery, gym, playground, classes, health education, and perhaps addiction rehabilitation)*

Art Connection

George Bellows, who painted the picture on page 499, belonged to a 20th century group of painters known as the Ash Can School. These artists portrayed slum living conditions, back alleys, garbage cans, and other realistic aspects of poverty. You may want to have students find some other paintings of this genre (in illustrated art books or art encyclopedias) by artists such as Robert Henri, John French Sloan, or George Benjamin Luks.

Science Connection

In the early 20th century, the scientific method became important for gathering information. Jane Addams and other social reformers used this method to insure the effectiveness and efficiency of reforms and their administration. Ask students to use an encyclopedia or other reference books to define *scientific method.* Then ask them to think of ways in which this method can be used in social research. *(To determine population and health statistics to predict trends)*

Understanding Reform

What does the photograph on this page tell you about life in a New York City tenement at the turn of the century? Can you understand why many people who were concerned about the welfare of the city poor became Progressive reformers in the early 1900s? The reformers attacked not only the problems of the poor but also a wide range of problems at the city, state, and national levels.

In the two decades of the Progressive Era, American citizens participated in and witnessed some of the most important and creative reforms in U.S. history. But what exactly does reform mean? Basically, reform is a movement that tries to improve social, political, or other conditions without revolutionary changes. As you will read later in this chapter, there were others during this period who sought to make radical political changes. But the Progressive reformers wanted to improve the system, not overthrow it. Most of the reform leaders were from the middle class and college-educated, and so they had strong interests in preserving but improving the social and political system.

Varieties of Reform

Reform efforts can take a variety of approaches. In some cases, reformers are seeking to eliminate corruption, or the abuse of power. This is the type of reform that Progressives brought to city and state governments. In other cases, reformers simply seek improved ways of doing things. For example, Progressives sought to change educational methods to make schools more effective. Finally, reform may take the form of remedying problems by providing services and resources that no one else has supplied. Jane Addams's work through Hull House is a good example of this third kind of reform.

Reform Today

Of course, the Progressive movement did not solve all the nation's ills. Today, many people are working to bring about reforms similar to those carried out at the beginning of the century. For example, educational reform is once again a major goal at both the state and national levels. In addition, other reformers seek to enact ethics ordinances and other measures to curb corruption in government. People across the nation are also concerned with issues such as the lack of affordable housing, alcohol and drug abuse, pollution, and reducing crime in the nation's urban centers.

CITIZENSHIP

Critical Thinking

Today people disagree on how to solve the problem of homelessness. Have students name the benefits and problems of using governmental regulation for real estate and housing construction to provide more affordable housing. *(Encourage discussion of reform as opposed to laissez faire policies.)*

Mathematics Connection

Statistics, the science of collecting and analyzing data, is very important in the social sciences, government, and business. Statistics involves four basic steps: defining the problem, collecting data, analyzing the data, and reporting the results. Have students research the statistical methods used by pollsters today.

Language Arts Connection

Books of fantasy and adventure for children were extremely rare prior to the last decades of the 1800s. Have students read and report on books in this genre written between 1870 to 1920. Examples include books by the French author Jules Verne; British authors E. Nesbit, Frances Hodgson Burnett, J. M. Barrie; and American writer L. Frank Baum.

Social Participation

Ask students to imagine that they are union organizers in the early 1900s. Have them role play a scene in which they confront the owner of the Triangle Shirtwaist Factory about its dangerous conditions.

SOCIAL SYSTEMS

Critical Thinking

Ask students to make a list of things that illiterate people cannot do because of their handicap. *(Read signs, books, newspaper reports; write job applications)* Then ask why they think it was important to the Progressives that more people be able to read and write. *(Literate people can take better care of themselves in society and can be well-informed voters.)*

■ *They stressed moving away from rote learning, promoting literacy, and introducing subject matter relevant to students' lives, including vocational training and health education.*

Educational Reform

Traditional classrooms of the 1800s would never have allowed the students to study together or to leave their seats.

Progressives did not think highly of the traditional American school of the 1800s, which emphasized rote learning. Under this system, teachers dictated a lesson that the class then wrote down and memorized. Not allowed to talk or move, students also sat in desks that were bolted to the floor.

Many Americans at this time did not know how to read or write English. Progressive reformers wanted more people to be able to get a basic education. Middle-class Progressives also wanted schools to have an "Americanizing" function. They thought immigrants would pick up middle-class values as they learned to read, write, and speak English.

Following the lead of the Progressives, many businesses found that they benefited from having workers who could read. These businesses helped "Americanize" their employees by sending them for English lessons and job training. This business-sponsored educational is known as "industrial education."

Led by John Dewey, a Columbia University philosopher, Progressive educators began teaching students through participation. The Progressive curriculum also brought in subject matter important to students' lives. Job training and health education helped the poor get better jobs. School desks were unbolted from the floor to allow flexible use of the classroom. Nurseries, kindergartens, and playgrounds in which children learn through play became a new standard. Many of these reforms have become familiar traditions today. ■

■ *What features of 19th century American education did the Progressive movement reform?*

City Planning

The state of American cities in the late 1800s and early 1900s could be seen in Chicago. There pigs roamed the streets, and open sewers ran down the alleyways. In one section, six out of ten babies died in their first year. In some cities, elevated railroads coughed ashes, fouled the air with smoke, and shook buildings as they rumbled by. People in **tenements**—cheaply made apartments—lived as many as ten to each windowless room. The journalist Jacob Riis reported on the squalor and the terrible conditions of New York City slums in his 1890 book, *How the Other Half Lives*:

Swine roamed the streets and gutters as their principal scavengers. The death of a child in a tenement was registered at the Bureau of Vital Statistics as "plainly due to suffocation in the foul air of an unventilated apartment," and the Senators, who had come down from Albany to find out what was the matter with New York, reported that "there are annually cut off from the population by disease and death enough human beings to people a city...."

Critical Thinking

Ask students to read the excerpt on this page from Jacob Riis's book, *How the Other Half Lives.* Ask them to use the images in the description to write a paragraph in their own words about the number of people who died in the city during that time and the causes of their deaths.

Art Connection

Many of the nation's oldest and most beautiful city parks— Central Park in New York, the series of parks in Boston known as the Emerald Necklace, and Belle Isle Park in Detroit—were designed late in the 1800s by landscape artist Frederick Law Olmsted. He also designed the landscapes of several colleges and universities, as well as the grounds around the Capitol building in Washington, D.C. You may want to share with students some photos of the area around the Capitol. You can find these in an encyclopedia or in a landscape book. Point out the thoughtful, artistic planning that went into such a design. Then ask students to work alone or in pairs to plan an ideal park for their town or city.

American cities had grown wildly, many without planning. Many politicians either did not care about or could not deal with the problems that resulted.

Urban Progressives believed that cities could be pleasant, livable, even beautiful places. They called for zoning laws and city planning. **Zoning laws** restricted the kinds of buildings and businesses that could be developed in a given place. Smoke-belching factories could then be separated from houses and markets. Traffic jams and crowding could also be prevented.

The Progressives' plans for the cities included safe apartment buildings to replace cheaply built tenements. In many cities Progressives also won tough housing laws. These laws required landlords to build safe buildings with fire escapes and a window in each room for light and air.

Hull House built the first public playground in 1892. In 1906, Progressives founded the National Playground Association of America. Its goal was to encourage cities to build public parks and playgrounds for children.

The grandest goal of the urban-planning movement was to improve cities with beautiful architecture. The "city beautiful" movement counted steel millionaire Andrew Carnegie among its members. With his support, the movement helped to build new libraries, museums, and government buildings. Many of these grand buildings were modeled after the most beautiful buildings in Europe. They became monuments to the "city beautiful" campaign to improve American urban life. ■

◀ *Progressives wanted to rid cities of overcrowded, unsafe living conditions. These kinds of conditions existed everywhere, including in this San Francisco neighborhood.*

How Do We Know?

HISTORY *Historians interested in the living and working conditions in the United States at the turn of the century study the photographs of Jacob Riis and Lewis Hine. Their pictures vividly convey the stark poverty and appalling working conditions that were widespread in America at the beginning of the Progressive Era.*

■ *In what ways did the Progressives believe that urban planning and zoning laws would help solve the "shame of the cities"?*

Reforming City Politics

The squalor of a city's darkest slum was often reflected in the corruption of the city's politics. Many cities across the country were still run by the "boss" system described in Chapter 16. Reports by muckrakers revealed the dishonesty and greed at the heart of this system. Businesses bribed city officials for government contracts; the railroads "bought" favorable legislation; and machine politicians stuffed the ballot boxes with illegal votes.

GEOGRAPHY

Critical Thinking

Have students discuss the Progressives' approach to city planning. To what extent do cities today reflect the ideas promoted by Progressives? *(Zoning for residential, commercial, and industrial areas, city parks, and playgrounds are examples of their success.)*

■ *Progressives believed that they could improve American life by designing beautiful architecture and by keeping residential and commercial areas separate from industrial areas.*

Collaborative Learning

Divide the students into groups to research the government of their own city or town. They may refer to the chart on page 506 to determine which form of government their city or town uses. Have them contact their city or town hall to gather information about the elected and appointed officials now in office. Assign each group to a different level or department of the government. Have them find out the names of the important officials. What are their duties? How long have they been in office? Then have the groups work together to draw a diagram of the government, showing the relationship of the various departments to one another. They can also show the structure of responsibility within each department and fill in the names of the officers in their appropriate positions.

Critical Thinking

Rent in the tenements in New York City's Lower East Side was often higher than in much better apartments in other areas of the city. Ask students how this might have happened. *(Ethnic prejudice in better areas, language barriers, building codes, the profit motive, the need to be near one's job, and the law of supply and demand)*

POLITICAL SYSTEMS

Critical Thinking

Have students form small groups to discuss what both the bosses and the Progressives expected to accomplish. *(The bosses wanted votes; Progressives wanted to "Americanize" immigrants.)* How did each group "take care of" urban immigrants? *(The bosses gave favors; Progressives promoted education and better city services.)*

■ *Their greed and their patronage system put incompetent people in important offices. These people could not or would not deliver the services that were needed.*

CLOSE

Ask students to answer the Thinking Focus and evaluate the predictions that they made before reading the lesson. Copy on the board the structure of the Graphic Overview from page 498. Have students complete it together, using the notes that they made while reading the lesson.

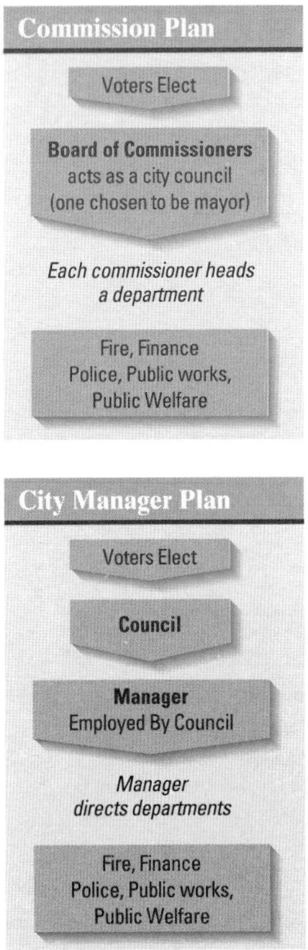

▲ *These charts show the structure of the commission and the city manager forms of government.*

■ *How did corrupt politicians increase the social and economic problems of the cities?*

Life in the cities depended upon efficient police, sanitation, and human services provided by city governments. Political corruption often put unqualified and incompetent people in jobs of great importance. As a result, these people could not deliver important services. Poor sanitation in Pittsburgh, for instance, endangered citizens when the city's water became contaminated with dysentery, cholera, and typhoid germs.

The Mechanics of Corruption

Before Progressive reform, most city governments organized elections by wards, or districts. In each district, each political party hired a ward heeler. This person told the people in that district whom to vote for and saw to it that they got to the polls on voting day. Political parties earned the loyalty of the voters by finding jobs, food, and housing, and by granting other favors for them. The efficiency of this political system is recognized in the term *party machine*.

Many immigrants were unskilled and could not speak English very well. They were willing to trade their votes for the practical rewards that the party machines offered them. On the larger scale, however, the machines bred unfair political practices and deep-seated corruption.

Forms of Government

Reformers used commissions and investigations to expose the corruption in city government and to take control of city hall. Reform politicians then changed the way the city did its business. Except in the biggest cities, they did away with the ward system and the political machines based in the neighborhoods. Instead, they had city-wide elections. These were easier to supervise and cut down on cheating.

Progressive reformers were ready to capture and reform city government whenever they had a chance. Their boldest success in city government blew in on the winds of a hurricane in September 1900.

That year, a powerful storm charged off the Gulf of Mexico and smashed Galveston, Texas. The city government could not manage the severe crisis that followed. Leading citizens threw the city government out. They replaced it with a small elected commission consisting of five members who were given executive and legislative power.

The commission form of government proved to be very effective. In this government, each of the commissioners took charge of one department of the city, such as roads, utilities, schools, and police. The system was soon adopted in Houston, Des Moines, and many other cities around the country.

The city manager form of government was a refinement of the commission. It was first used in Staunton, Virginia, in 1908. In this model, elected city officials hire a professional city manager, who has no political connections, to run the city. Hundreds of other American cities also adopted this efficient model. ■

REVIEW

1. **FOCUS** What caused the social problems and political corruption that were common features of American cities between 1890 and 1920?
2. **CONNECT** What were some of the reform movements that began before the Civil War?
3. **HISTORY** What steps did the Progressives take in the early 1900s to reform city government? Were their reform efforts successful?
4. **CRITICAL THINKING** Why do you think that Jane Addams and many other Progressives believed that private charity was not enough to solve the serious social problems in American cities at the turn of the century?
5. **ACTIVITY** Plan a neighborhood. Draw a map of a neighborhood where you would like to live. Show where you would locate apartments, factories, stores, parks, and roads.

Homework Options

Have students watch a television program that exposes social ills or political misconduct. Have them give an oral report to the class about the case.

Study Guide: page 73.

Answers to Review Questions

1. Rapid urban growth and the rise of powerful businesses together created an environment that encouraged these problems.
2. The reforms that began before the Civil War include the temperance movement, labor reform, utopian societies, and women's education.
3. They used commissions and investigations. They had success in instituting city-wide elections and the commission and city manager forms of city government.
4. Sample answer: The problems were so deep and widespread that government intervention was needed as well. Allow for personal opinion.
5. Remind students to consider the size of the neighborhood and its population as they begin their plans.

1880 1890 1920 1930

LESSON 2

Progressive Reform

There was never the least attention paid to what was cut up for sausage. . . . There would be meat that had tumbled out on the floor, in the dirt and sawdust, where the workers had tramped and spit uncounted billions of consumption [tuberculosis] germs. There would be meat stored in great piles in rooms; and the water from leaky roofs would drip over it, and thousands of rats would race about on it. . . . These rats were nuisances, and the packers would put poisoned bread out for them; they would die, and then rats, bread, and meat would go into the [sausage] together. This is no fairy story and no joke; the meat would be shoveled into carts, and the man who did the shoveling would not trouble to lift out a rat even when he saw one—there were things that went into the sausage in comparison with which a poisoned rat was a tidbit. . . .

Upton Sinclair, The Jungle

THINKING FOCUS

What kinds of changes in state and federal government resulted from Progressive reform?

Key Terms

- initiative
- referendum
- recall
- conservation

Muckraking journalist Upton Sinclair wrote this account of the Chicago meatpacking industry for his novel *The Jungle*, published in 1906. Sinclair had worked his way through City College in New York writing cheap novels. An urge to expose the exploitation of workers led Sinclair to the stockyards of Chicago. There he talked to workers and took notes on what he saw. Sinclair intended his book to inspire labor reform.

When *The Jungle* was published, however, readers were more shocked by the descriptions of meatpacking than by the difficult life of workers. After President Theodore Roosevelt read *The Jungle*, he shoved his breakfast sausages away and ordered a study of the meat industry. The study was used to support the Meat Inspection Act of 1906, which provided for government inspection of all meat shipped from one state to another.

State Government Reform

Progressives found that changes at the city level were often blocked by state governments. They set out to win control of state government to carry out their programs. Many Progressive reforms were intended to make state governments more responsive to the citizens who elected them. The most remarkable instance of this reform process was carried out in the state of Wisconsin.

Robert La Follette's Wisconsin Idea

Robert M. La Follette of Wisconsin was the first and most radical reformer of state politics and one of the most extraordinary figures of the early 1900s. "Now his face was calm; now a thundercloud; now full of sorrow," one journalist wrote of this energetic politician. A lawyer and former congressman, La Follette led an alliance of Wisconsin farmers, labor-

INTRODUCE

Have students read the lesson title and ask them to name some of the reforms that they learned about in Lesson 1. *(Settlement houses, city governments)* Have students read the Thinking Focus and then read the lesson to find out how government functioned before and after these reforms were instituted.

Key Terms

Vocabulary strategies: T36–37

initiative—a procedure that allows citizens to propose a bill by collecting a specific number of signatures from registered voters on a petition

referendum—the process by which people can vote directly for or against the passage of a bill

recall—a special election that allows voters to remove an elected official from office before his or her term has expired

conservation—the act or process of protecting and preserving natural resources and wilderness areas

Graphic Overview

Government Reform → City → State → Federal

Objectives

1. List the major Progressive reforms in state government.
2. Describe the federal government's role in advancing Progressivism.
3. Analyze the impact of the Bull Moose Party on the 1912 presidential election.
4. Evaluate the contributions of Woodrow Wilson's administration to the Progressives' cause.

DEVELOP

Explain that reforms were needed at the state and national levels as well as the local (city) level. Copy on the board the Graphic Overview from page 507 and explain that the reform movement made changes first at the city, then the state, and finally the federal level. Have students copy the Overview in their notes and, as they read the lesson, write details of the reforms at each level.

POLITICAL SYSTEMS

Critical Thinking

Have students explain in their own words why the initiative, referendum, and recall are considered instruments of "direct democracy." *(Voters have direct power to start legislation and to get rid of bad laws and bad government officials.)*

■ *Other states based their reforms on his program, which included direct primary elections, government appointment by merit, public commissions, and a law that prohibited contributions to political parties from businesses.*

▲ *Wisconsin Governor "Battling Bob" La Follette was a powerful speaker as well as an effective reformer.*

■ *How did Robert La Follette's "Wisconsin Idea" spur reform of state governments?*

ers, and immigrants who had been hurt by the depression of 1893.

La Follette was elected governor in 1900. He stormed into office, promising to take the government away from the bosses and give it "back to the people."

He quickly won passage of a law that provided direct primary elections. This change allowed voters, instead of political bosses, to choose candidates for political office. He reformed civil service so that appointments were based on ability, not patronage. He pushed through a law that prohibited business contributions to political parties. And he persuaded the state legislature to set up public commissions to watch over the utilities and the powerful railroads. The new program gained fame across the country as the "Wisconsin idea."

The Revolt Spreads

Beginning in 1905, a wave of scandals in state governments led to reforms based on those in Wisconsin. Of all the states to reform themselves, California made the most significant changes. Governor Hiram Johnson introduced constitutional reforms that wiped out the political machines. The once-powerful Southern Pacific Railroad withdrew from politics and accepted state regulation. Reformers in most states brought in several new instruments of "direct" democracy.

The secret ballot replaced the old colored ballots. Sometimes called the Australian ballot, secret ballots reduced fraud and violence at voting places. The **initiative** gave voters in each state the power to start a bill with a simple petition. The **referendum** allowed a direct vote on a bill or law already passed by the legislature. The **recall** gave voters the power to remove an elected official from office at any time.

Not all the reforms were so democratic. Many white middle-class Progressives thought it was dangerous to give political power to the poor and minorities. In many Southern states, Progressives passed laws that took voting power away from blacks. In Louisiana, for instance, the number of registered black voters dropped from 130,000 in 1896 to 1,000 in 1904. ■

The Federal Government Responds

When President McKinley was assassinated in Buffalo, New York, on September 6, 1901, 42-year-old Theodore Roosevelt became President. Progressivism soon became a strong, widespread movement. Roosevelt was drawn to Progressive ideas. He encouraged many reforms at the federal level. In order to get the reforms he wanted, Roosevelt dramatically expanded the power of the presidency and of the federal government.

Roosevelt promised Americans "a square deal" from the government. By "square deal" he meant protection from unfair business practices.

Access Activity

Read to students the passage from Upton Sinclair's *The Jungle* on page 507. Whom was Sinclair targeting as his reading audience? *(Consumers and government)* Ask what effects this exposé might have brought about. *(Investigation and regulation of the specific company and of the meat-packing industry in general)*

Access Strategy

Ask students if they believe that the medicines and foods that are used in their homes today are generally safe and uncontaminated. Why or why not? Point out that regulation of the food and drug industries today is more thorough and that food processing is safer, cleaner, and more scientific than it was in the 1800s. Ask students what might happen if the government were not able to regulate business at all. Would businesses voluntarily provide pure and safe products? Would companies voluntarily protect the natural environment from pollution even if it cost them extra money to do so?

Tell students that during the Progressive Era people realized that government would have to take on a new regulatory role in order to protect people and the environment from the consequences of uncontrolled business practices. This lesson describes the process by which government took on this new role.

The Meat Inspection Act of 1906 shows how Roosevelt won passage of laws to regulate irresponsible businesses. The Pure Food and Drug Act of the same year followed a like pattern.

A series of articles by muckraker Samuel Hopkins Adams uncovered the fraud in ordinary medicines. Most medicines on the market until 1906 were mixtures of alcohol, addictive drugs like opium, and other harmful additives. Even medicine for crying babies contained opium.

Adams's articles inspired the Pure Food and Drug Act. This law banned the use of harmful additives in food and medicine and the use of false advertising. The federal government was taking on a new role as the regulator of American businesses.

Busting the Trusts

At the turn of the century, powerful corporations often joined together to form giant trusts. Then they ran their competitors out of business. President Roosevelt was not opposed to all monopolies, but he would not allow one that took unfair advantage of the public. "We do not wish to destroy corporations," he said, "but we do wish to make them subserve the public good."

One of Roosevelt's earliest acts as President was to file suit against the Northern Securities Company. This company had been created to control railroads in the Northwest. The suit shocked the business world but pleased Progressives. Roosevelt won the case after two years in court, and the monopoly was dissolved. Government became a power for business to reckon with.

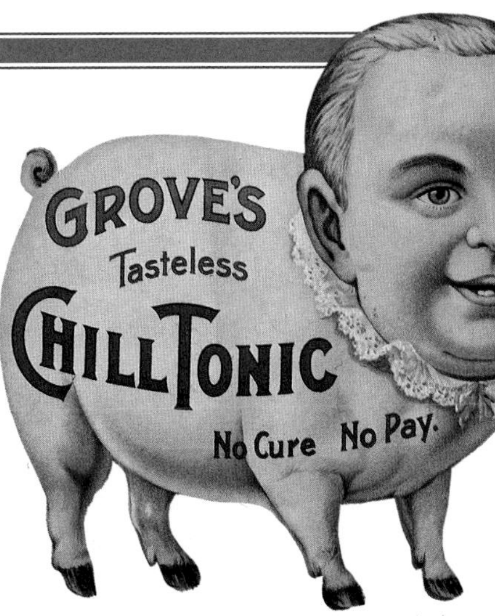

▲ *Before the passage of the Pure Food and Drug Act in 1906, Americans spent millions of dollars on quack remedies.*

▼ *In this political cartoon, the giant king represents the monopolies. The long line of various types of working people bring tributes, or gifts, to King Monopoly. What point do you think the cartoonist was trying to make?*

POLITICAL SYSTEMS

Critical Thinking

What group was meant to gain power as a result of the state governmental reforms proposed by the Progressives? *(Individual citizens)* Who was intended to lose power as a result of these reforms? *(Political bosses, big businesses and corporations, and corrupt governmental groups)*

➤ *The cartoon implies that monopolies had control over the nation's economy.*

509

Social Context

It took great determination for women to become doctors in the 19th century. Two women who did become doctors made great contributions in the area of public health. Dr. Alice Hamilton worked at Hull House in Chicago. Alarmed by the dangers of toxic substances in workplaces, she became a pioneer in the field of industrial medicine. Her work contributed to the passage of workmen's compensation laws and to safer working conditions.

After working in New York's slums, where 1,500 babies died every week in the summer of 1902, Dr. Josephine Baker worked in the field of preventive medicine. Her work inspired the creation of the Division of Child Hygiene in 1908, which she headed. By 1913, the death rate among the city's babies had been reduced by a third. Still, Dr. Baker observed, "It's six times safer to be a soldier in the trenches of France than to be born a baby in the United States."

Visual Learning

Have students read the labels in the cartoon on this page. *(Sample answers: King Monopoly, War Tariff, American Industries, Booty, Tribute from the Farm)* What kind of role does King Monopoly play in this cartoon? *(A rich, greedy king who takes the profit from the people's labor)*

ECONOMICS

Critical Thinking

Ask students how the federal government was funded after the passage of the Sixteenth Amendment. *(By taxes on citizens' and corporations' incomes)* How did the passage of the Sixteenth Amendment support Progressive goals? *(The federal income tax made the government more powerful and better able to carry out Progressive reforms.)*

■ *His reforms include the Meat Inspection Act, the Pure Food and Drug Act, the conservation program, and the dismantling of the Northern Securities Company monopoly.*

President Theodore Roosevelt (at right) *rides with his friend, conservationist John Muir, at Yosemite National Park in California.*

Conservation

Roosevelt had a lifelong love for America's wilderness. By the time he became President, it was clear that the natural resources of the United States, once thought to be inexhaustible, had actually been wastefully reduced. Influenced by his friends John Muir, the naturalist, and Gifford Pinchot, the head of the U.S. Forest Service, Roosevelt instituted a program of **conservation,** or protection and efficient use of natural resources. The program included reform of public land use. In all, he set aside 148 million acres of land for forests, parks, and national monuments, including Pinnacles National Monument and Muir Woods in California.

Giving the Senate to the People

Amendments were added to the Constitution in 1913. They aided Progressive reform at the national level. These were the Sixteenth Amendment and the Seventeenth Amendment.

The Sixteenth Amendment provided for a federal income tax. This changed the way the government was funded and allowed for a more powerful federal government. A government with greater capabilities was needed to carry out Progressive reforms.

Before the Seventeenth Amendment, Americans did not directly elect U.S. Senators. Instead, state legislatures chose them. As a result, Senate seats were often handed over to the friends of political bosses and business leaders. Such senators were more loyal to those who put them in power than they were to the voters. The Senate seemed to be a political club whose members sold their votes.

David Graham Phillips, a muckraking journalist, exposed the buying and selling of Senate appointments in his 1906 article "The Treason of the Senate." A reform movement grew up around the issue. State after state passed provisions for an amendment to the Constitution to require the direct election of senators. The Senate itself refused to consider such an amendment. Finally, when even more scandals erupted, the Senate lost its credibility. It offered no more opposition to election reform. The Seventeenth Amendment required that U.S. Senators be elected directly by the voters of each state. ■

■ *What government reforms did Theodore Roosevelt institute at the federal level?*

Critical Thinking

Ask students to recall that the election of senators had been entrusted to state governments to protect the nation from uninformed voters. Ask if the framers of the Constitution could have anticipated the problems that grew out of this method of electing senators. *(Unlikely—businesses fewer and smaller; cities not politically powerful)*

Health Connection

Have students research the impact of advances in medicine around the turn of the century—for example, how a growing understanding of germ theory led to the prevention of many deadly diseases and to safer water supplies, public sewers, and surgical procedures. How were vaccines developed? What was the impact of improved sanitation on the numbers of deaths from diseases such as cholera and tuberculosis?

The Bull Moose Party

Roosevelt had promised to limit himself to two terms as President. Accordingly, he announced in 1908 that he would not run again.

Roosevelt chose Secretary of War William Howard Taft to take his place as the Republican nominee. Taft easily won the presidency.

A former federal judge from Cincinnati and a friend of Roosevelt, Taft was quiet and politically unsure of himself. He did not have Roosevelt's energy and leadership ability. Taft preferred his courtroom to the White House. He believed that government should not be too active in the nation's affairs.

Taft did, however, make some strong reform moves. He established the Children's Bureau and became an even more active trustbuster than Roosevelt. But he became more conservative as his presidency wore on. He turned more and more to the "Old Guard" faction of the Republican Party. After a while, he lost the support and friendship of Roosevelt.

By the time of the 1912 elections, Roosevelt had decided to try to reclaim the presidency. Roosevelt's bid split the Republican Party into two angry, warring factions: conservatives who supported Taft and Progressives who supported Roosevelt. Although Roosevelt beat Taft in the primaries, the powerful conservatives who controlled the party still gave Taft the nomination.

Roosevelt and his supporters stormed out of the convention and started a third party. They called it the "Bull Moose Party," because Roosevelt had said, "I'm as strong as a bull moose."

The new Bull Moose Party split the Republican vote. This division gave the election to the Democratic nominee, a scholarly, inspiring man named Woodrow Wilson.

Although Roosevelt lost, the election was still a clear victory for the Progressives. Both Wilson and Roosevelt had campaigned on Progressive platforms. Woodrow Wilson took office in March 1913. ■

▲ *Democratic candidate Woodrow Wilson benefited from the split in the Republican Party in the election of 1912.*

■ *How did Roosevelt's "Bull Moose Party" contribute to a Progressive victory in the 1912 election?*

▼ *Although Roosevelt easily outdistanced Taft in the 1912 election, he still lost the presidency to Woodrow Wilson by a wide margin.*

Election of 1912

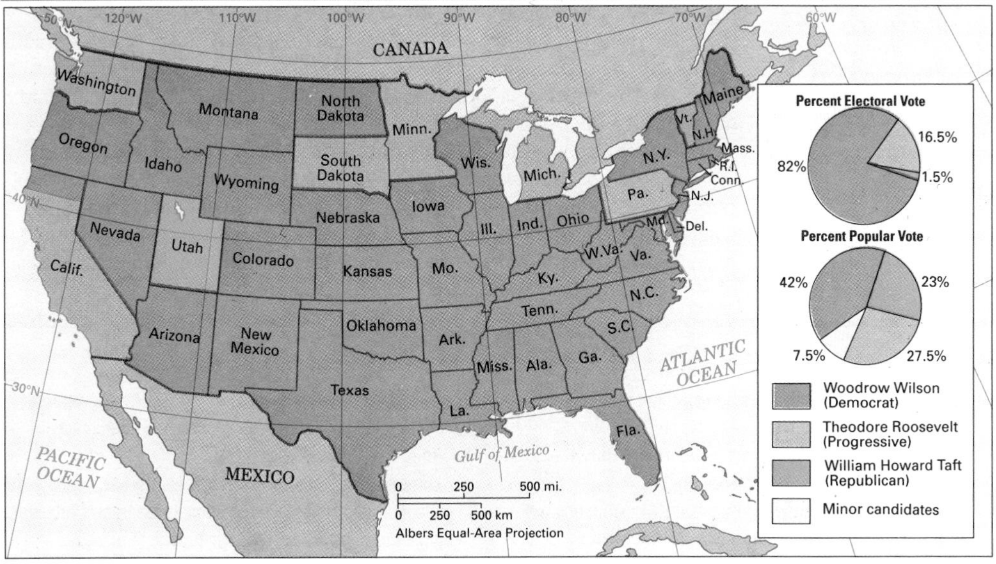

HISTORY

Critical Thinking

Ask students whether Roosevelt's loss of the 1912 presidential election under the Bull Moose Party was, in fact, a loss for the Progressive cause. Have them explain their answers. *(Sample answer: No, Woodrow Wilson, who won, was a Progressive.)*

■ *It split the Republican vote, leading to the victory of Woodrow Wilson, who was a Democrat and a Progressive.*

◄ *Students can read more about third political parties on page 681 in the Minipedia.*

Research

During the Progressive Era, the government became involved in protecting consumers and the natural environment. Many private organizations today put pressure on the government, or work alongside the government, to promote even stronger protections. Provide a list of some of these organizations, such as the Consumers' Union, Public Interest Research Groups, the National Wildlife Federation, the Sierra Club, the Audubon Society, and the Center for Science in the Public Interest. Then have students choose an organization to research, either individually or in small groups. Have them use various research methods to find out about the goals and activities of the organization that they have chosen. For example, they might write a letter to the organization requesting information, they might interview someone from a local chapter, or they might read the organization's publications.

Map and Globe Skills

Ask students why there is a difference between the electoral and popular votes as shown in the two pie charts on this page. Remind students of the elections of 1828 and 1876. *(Because all of a state's electoral votes go to the most popular candidate, the opposition votes go unrecognized in the electoral vote count.)*

HISTORY

Critical Thinking

Ask students to recall from Chapter 6 what President Jackson had tried to do with the banking system, and why. *(Shift power and resources from the national bank to state banks, benefiting his Western supporters)* Ask them to contrast Wilson's reforms in 1913 to Jackson's approach. *(Wilson set up a successful federal bank system.)*

■ *His successes include a tariff reduction, the Federal Reserve Act, the Clayton Antitrust Act, and the Federal Trade Commission. His failures include allowing racial segregation in the federal government and withholding support for women's suffrage.*

CLOSE

Have students answer the Thinking Focus. Copy on the board the Graphic Overview from page 507 and have students add any notes about the reforms at each level of government that they made.

As a reteaching activity, ask students to discuss what each of the following leaders contributed to Progressive reform in the United States: Robert La Follette, Theodore Roosevelt, William Howard Taft, Woodrow Wilson.

Wilson Continues Reform Efforts

Woodrow Wilson was an unlikely politician. An intellectual, he had been the president of Princeton University. Born and raised in Virginia, he was also the first Southerner to serve in the White House since 1846. As governor of New Jersey (1910–1912), Wilson had gained a reputation as a Progressive politician. He supported many reforms that increased "direct democracy" in that state.

▲ *Few U.S. Presidents have had such strong academic credentials as Woodrow Wilson, formerly president of Princeton University.*

■ *What were President Woodrow Wilson's successes and failures in advancing Progressive causes?*

As President, Wilson launched one of the most ambitious programs of legislation in American history. He spoke eloquently in support of a reform program he called the "New Freedom." It was aimed at protecting the rights of individuals from economically powerful companies and banks.

Wilson's first target was tariff reform. Tariffs kept prices on foreign goods high and protected American manufacturers. But farmers and consumers in this country wanted lower tariffs so that prices would go down. Wilson won the first meaningful tariff reduction since the Civil War when Congress passed the Underwood Tariff Act in 1913.

Wilson turned next to banking reform. The banking system then in place was entirely private and was not very stable. Nearly everyone agreed that it did not meet the nation's need for a stable supply of money and credit. Wilson's answer was the Federal Reserve Act, which established the first national banking system since Andrew Jackson's presidency.

The 1913 act set up 12 Federal Reserve Banks and a Federal Reserve Board appointed by the President. The new banks regulated credit and the amount of money in circulation and provided services for banks.

The Federal Reserve Act was followed by the Clayton Antitrust Act of 1914. Like the Sherman Antitrust Act of 1890, the Clayton Act put restraints on monopolies. The Clayton bill prohibited a list of business practices used by monopolies. In 1914, Wilson also prodded Congress into creating the Federal Trade Commission. This agency had the power to investigate and prevent "unfair trade practices" by American businesses.

As a reformer, Wilson had blind spots. He allowed segregation by race in the federal government. He also withheld support for the women's suffrage amendment until passage seemed certain. But, on the whole, Wilson's contribution to Progressivism was impressive. ■

REVIEW

1. **FOCUS** What kinds of changes in state and federal government resulted from Progressive reform?
2. **ECONOMICS** List and explain the importance of two economic reforms of the Progressive Era.
3. **CONNECT** In what sense did Roosevelt's trustbusting activities continue the reform efforts of an earlier era?
4. **CRITICAL THINKING** Do you think the new state reforms championed by Progressives improved democracy in America? Why or why not?
5. **ACTIVITY** Read your local newspaper for several days and choose the article that most closely resembles muckraking journalism. Share this article with your class.

Homework Options

Have students find current news stories about the government regulation of businesses in the areas of pollution control or product safety.

Study Guide: page 74.

Answers to Review Questions

1. Reforms resulted in the weakening or elimination of political machines, three new forms of state government, and new state regulations on business; the direct election of senators and a new role for the federal government as regulator of business and finance.
2. Sample answer: The Federal Reserve Act established a national banking system. The Clayton Antitrust Act put restraints on monopolies.
3. Roosevelt revived the Sherman Antitrust Act, which had been an unsuccessful tool when it was first passed.
4. Sample answer: Many of the reforms improved democracy because they increased the degree to which people were represented in government. Allow for personal opinion.
5. Encourage several students to read their articles aloud dramatically.

1880
1890
1920
1930

LESSON 3

Competing Crusades

She must have looked like the angel of death swooping down for a visit: The saloon door swings open, and she shoves through it, almost six feet tall, a hatchet hanging from her waist, her long black dress nearly dragging on the floor as she walks. She plants herself squarely in the middle of the saloon, challenging anyone to try to stop her.

Then she attacks. Raising her hatchet, she destroys row after row of liquor bottles. Broken glass and liquor spray across the bar. Spinning around, she delivers a crashing blow to a bar chair, splintering the back. She then storms from one end of the saloon to the other, leaving a broad path of devastation behind her.

This was Carry Amelia Moore Nation on another mission to close down a saloon, or "joint," as they were then called. Nothing short of arrest or physical force would stop her. More than once she was beaten up and thrown into the street. She even spent time in jail. She soon became a national figure and helped to rally an army of supporters for the outlawing of alcohol.

Carry Nation began her famous mission after her first husband died of alcoholism. She was, no doubt, the most radical—and the most dramatic—anti-saloon crusader in a land full of fiery supporters of temperance.

Nation spent three years attacking saloons. She was widely admired but publicly criticized by the Women's Christian Temperance Union (WCTU) for her unusual tactics. Replicas of her hatchet were sold in the thousands. The words on each hatchet seemed to sum up her story: "Carry Nation, Joint Smasher."

THINKING FOCUS

What other social movements attempted to change American society during the Progressive Era, and what were their goals?

Key Terms

- prohibition
- socialist
- anarchist
- enfranchise

◄ *Although many prohibitionists disagreed with her tactics, Carry Nation was one of the best known and most colorful figures in the temperance movement.*

INTRODUCE

Have students read the lesson title and define *crusade. (A focused effort for a cause or against an abuse)* Have students read the Thinking Focus and tell them to notice as they read how social reform movements were sometimes in competition with each other.

Key Terms

Vocabulary strategies: T36–37

prohibition—the forbidding by law of the manufacture, transportation, sale, and possession of alcoholic beverages

socialist—a person who supports an economic system in which the workers possess both political power and the means of producing and distributing goods

anarchist—a person who opposes all organized forms of government

enfranchise—to give the rights of citizenship, especially the right to vote

Graphic Overview

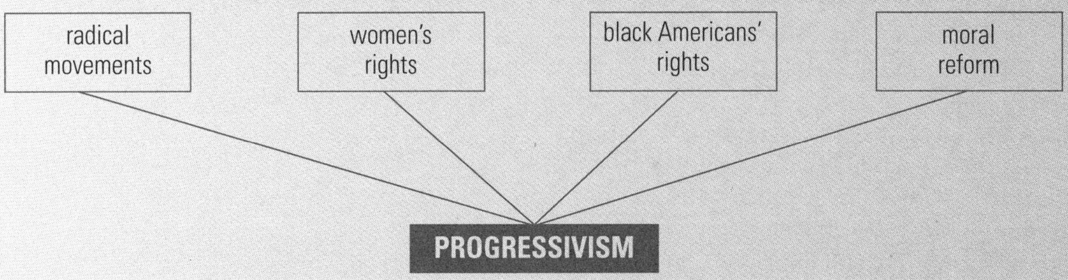
radical movements
women's rights
black Americans' rights
moral reform
PROGRESSIVISM

Objectives

1. Identify the common features of the movements for prohibition and against child labor.
2. Compare the goals of the Progressives with the goals of radical political movements.
3. Explain how women's organizations won women's suffrage.
4. Describe the impact that the Progressive movement had on the lives of black Americans.

DEVELOP

Point out that during the Progressive Era many movements seeking different social reforms arose. Copy on the board the Graphic Overview from page 513 to introduce the four primary movements discussed in the lesson. Tell students to write the four heads in their notes and, as they read, record the organizations associated with each movement and the names of the people associated with each organization.

Moral Reform

Across Time & Space

Child labor is still practiced in the United States. In 1997, an estimated 800,000 children had jobs as migrant farm workers in this country. In developing countries around the world, more than 250 million children are working. About half of them will either drop out of school or have never gone to school.

Carry Nation was not a lonely crusader. The country was full of women battling for change in American life. Throughout the 1800s and into the 1900s, women were a major force in almost every leading movement for moral reform. The temperance movement was also headed by women.

The Call for Prohibition

Born in the 1830s as the "temperance movement," the crusade against alcohol achieved some early successes. **Prohibition** laws in more than a dozen states made it illegal to buy alcohol.

The Anti-Saloon League was founded in 1895. The ASL grew into one of the strongest reform groups in American history. Joining with the Women's Christian Temperance Union, it publicized the link between alcohol and health problems, family problems, and poverty.

Marching in the streets, armies of women protested the sale and manufacture of alcohol. Success for the prohibitionists finally came. In 1917, the Eighteenth Amendment, prohibiting the manufacture or sale of alcohol, was passed by Congress. It was ratified by the necessary three-fourths of the states in 1919.

The Fight Against Child Labor

Nothing made Progressives angrier than the sight of children working in front of dangerous machinery. Children worked for long hours, their bodies limp with fatigue and their faces grim with pain. Children as young as 6 years old breathed the dust of coal mines and sweated in textile mills. In Southern cotton mills, 6-year-olds worked 12-hour days. They made 10 cents a day. Farther north, some went to work at 5 P.M. and sweated for 12 hours in front of the glass blowers' furnaces. These children earned less than a dollar a day.

Child laborers suffered more industrial accidents than adults. Thou-

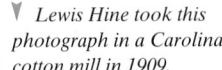

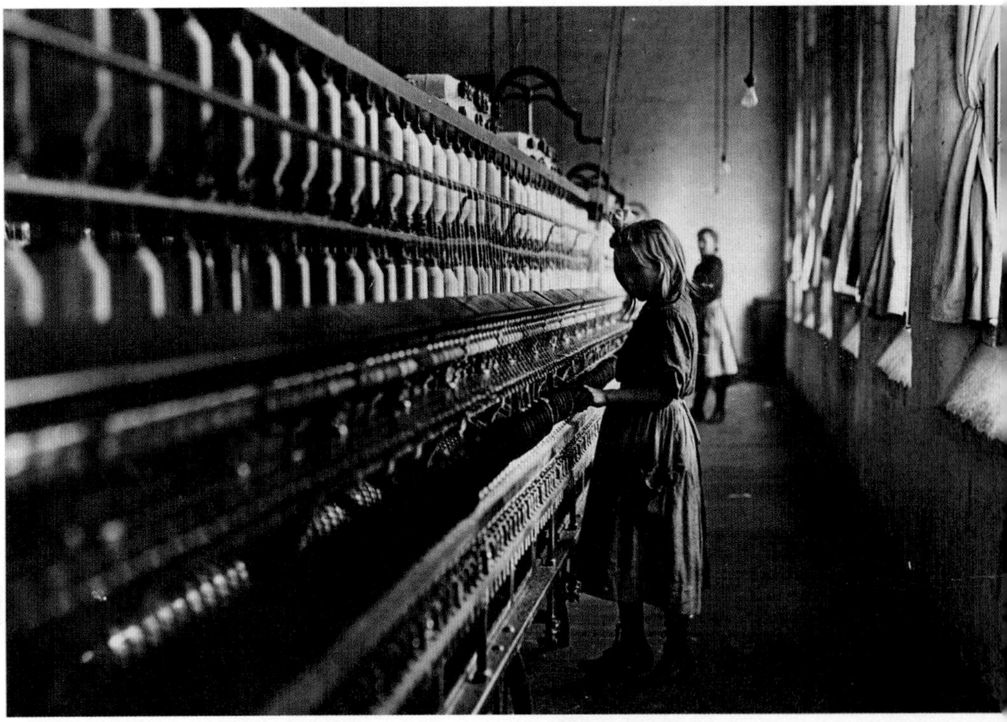

Lewis Hine took this photograph in a Carolina cotton mill in 1909.

Access Activity

Read the lesson opener aloud and have students look at the picture of Carry Nation on page 513. Point out the Bible and the hatchet that she is holding. Ask students how they would have responded to this woman's actions and point of view.

Access Strategy

Review with students the origins of the women's suffrage movement, the temperance movement, and the labor union movement from Chapters 9 and 15. Ask students to refer to these chapters to review the approximate dates each of these movements began. *(Suffrage—1848; temperance—1830s; labor—1840s)* Which changes started by these groups are still in place today? *(Women's suffrage; most of the changes in labor rights)* Would reforms in voting rights and labor rights have come about eventually had there not been crusading groups? Tell students that they will read in this lesson about the efforts of several crusading groups.

sands of working children were killed or maimed each year. Throughout most of the 1800s, hard work was considered good for children. Poor families always needed the extra money their children earned.

Progressives like Florence Kelley set out to restrict child labor. Kelley came from a well-to-do Philadelphia family. She went to Hull House in the early 1890s, where she found her life's work in the fight against child labor. When no attorney would argue a child labor case for her, she earned a law degree and argued the case herself. Kelley and other child labor reformers took many cases to court. They were responsible for the enactment of state laws in Illinois that prohibited child labor and limited working hours for women. In 1904, Kelley helped to form the National Child Labor Committee to begin a campaign for state child labor laws. Between 1905 and 1907, nearly two-thirds of the states enacted some child labor reforms. But few states prohibited child labor outright, and many had no labor restrictions at all.

Aware of the limitations of state laws, child labor reformers first persuaded Congress to establish a Children's Bureau in the Department of Labor in 1912. The Child Labor Act, passed in 1916, banned interstate trade in goods made with child labor. Two years later, the Supreme Court struck this law down because it took from children the right to "sell" their labor.

Because of legal loopholes and court decisions, the Progressives' fight against child labor was largely ineffective. In the end, school attendance laws and changes in technology drained the profit out of child labor. The Supreme Court did not uphold laws against child labor until 1938. ■

■ *Why didn't the Child Labor Act work?*

Radical Political Movements

Many social activists believed that the liberal reforms of the Progressives were not enough. These people didn't want to reform the American political and economic system. They wanted to replace it with something entirely different.

Eugene V. Debs and the Socialists

"The issue is Socialism versus Capitalism," pronounced Eugene V. Debs. "I am for Socialism because I am for humanity."

Debs, who had helped start a union for railroad workers in the 1890s, joined with other reformers in 1901 to establish the Socialist Party of America. The **Socialists** believed that capitalism was destroying small-scale businesses, that it denied workers the chance to earn fair wages and caused depressions and unemployment. The Socialists wanted workers or government to control the "means of production," that is, the factories and other facilities of America's industries. Their final goal was that all the people should enjoy equally the wealth produced by the nation.

In his run for the presidency in 1904, Eugene V. Debs received

▼ *A strong supporter of equality and social justice, Eugene V. Debs ran five times as the Socialist candidate for President.*

SOCIAL SYSTEMS

Critical Thinking

Ask students to compare Florence Kelly and Carry Nation. How were their goals similar? *(Both were seeking reforms that they thought would improve the lives of poor families and children.)* How did their methods differ? *(Nation took a very dramatic, direct approach. Kelly earned a law degree and fought child labor through the courts.)*

■ *The Supreme Court ruled that the Child Labor Act denied children the right to sell their labor.*

Political Context

The Socialist Party in the United States was formed in 1901 with a membership of about 10,000. Under the leadership of Eugene Debs, its membership grew to 150,000 by 1912. The Socialist Party included many European immigrants, but it also had American roots in utopian communities, the abolitionist movement, labor unions, and agrarian reform movements.

The Socialist Party under Debs always included a variety of members—reformers, Christian ministers, populists, laborers, Marxists, and revolutionaries. Debs himself is best understood as a part of the Progressive movement. He advocated relief for workers through practical solutions, such as municipal ownership of public utilities.

Critical Thinking

Have students analyze the statement, "Children are the wealth of a nation." What might it have meant to an early 20th-century industrialist? To a business person today? (*Child labor contributed to the industrialist's wealth. Today, children's minds and abilities are considered important resources for the future.*)

400,000 votes. The Socialist Party continued to gain power through the election of 1912. Debs earned almost a million votes that year, and Americans elected 79 Socialist mayors in 24 states.

During World War I, the federal government used patriotic feelings to hush public criticism of the war. Debs was thrown in jail for making an antiwar speech. Nonetheless, he won nearly a million votes from his prison cell in the 1920 presidential election. After the war, the government harassed radicals even more. Many were arrested. Socialist party membership declined. The party never recovered its former size or influence.

Anarchists and Radical Unionists

Among the most feared political radicals of their time were **anarchists**, because of their belief that all social structures, such as governments, are unnecessary and should be abolished. Some anarchists advocated violence to reach their goals. Emma Goldman, a famous anarchist, was thrown in jail because she told workers to steal bread if they were starving. Goldman eventually stopped believing in violence, but went on supporting anarchy. There were never very many anarchists, however, and anarchism died out as a movement by the 1940s.

A similar end was in store for the radical wing of the American labor movement. In 1905, workers unhappy with the traditional trade unions formed the Industrial Workers of the World (IWW). Its aim was "to abolish the wage system." The IWW often used threatening language, but it never started a fight. It tried to unionize both skilled and unskilled workers. It welcomed immigrants, women, and blacks. Most other unions, such as the American Federation of Labor (AFL), built their membership only among skilled white males.

The IWW's leader, William "Big Bill" Haywood, showed its aggressive spirit. Cowboy, miner, prospector, Haywood had lost an eye and mangled a hand as a young worker. He was a big, forceful man who impressed workers and businessmen alike. Haywood led the IWW in a successful strike for higher pay in the textile mills of Lawrence, Massachusetts, in 1912.

During World War I, the federal government attacked the IWW by imprisoning its leaders or deporting them to Russia. The union was no longer a force in the labor movement after the 1920s. ■

➤ *The Industrial Workers of the World used posters, songs, and poems to spread its message of radical unionism.*

■ *How did the goals of radical political movements differ from those of the Progressives?*

Women's Rights

As you learned in Chapter 9, in 1848 in Seneca, New York, Elizabeth Cady Stanton and Lucretia Mott organized a convention at which they called for women's suffrage, claiming that women had a right to vote. But by the beginning of the Progressive Era, the women's suffrage movement was split and badly demoralized. And though the Fifteenth Amendment had **enfranchised,** or given the vote to, black men in 1870, women were still not allowed to participate in the democratic system.

ECONOMICS

Visual Learning

Refer students to the IWW poster on this page. Who does the man represent? What is he doing? *(Probably represents the IWW. He is climbing up from the city behind him.)* What is the tone of the poster? *(Dramatic, bold, perhaps even threatening)* How does the style of this poster compare with the styles of the cartoon and the advertisement on page 509? *(This one is more forceful, modern)* Tell students that they will be analyzing more posters in the next chapter.

■ *The Progressives wanted to reform the American political and economic systems. The new activists wanted to replace the existing system.*

Critical Thinking

Given the extreme difference between the goals of mainstream Progressives and radicals, what conclusion can students draw about their relative positions in society? *(Sample answer: Mainstream reformers had a more solid position in society. The radicals had little to lose.)*

Language Arts Connection

Paul Dunbar was one of the first black writers in the United States to attain national attention. Born in 1872, Dunbar was the son of former slaves. His father had escaped to freedom in Canada and then returned to fight in the Civil War. After reading the excerpt on page 518, from the poem "Sympathy" by Paul Dunbar, have a group of students rehearse and perform a choral reading of it for the class. Encourage students to read other poems by this writer, such as "We Wear the Mask." Ask students to explain how Dunbar's poetry can help them understand the experience of black Americans at the turn of the century.

▲ *Women marched for suffrage in this parade in New York City in 1912. Several Western states had already given women the vote.*

The idea of women voting seemed outrageous to many men and women in the 1800s. Strong opposition came from all over. The Catholic Church argued that a woman's place was in the home. The liquor industry feared women would vote in favor of prohibition. Political bosses were afraid women would vote to remove them from power. Stiff opposition also came from more conservative women's groups. Many of their members believed that their interests would be best protected by leaving politics to men.

Progress came rather slowly. Women presented a more united front when both the National and the American Suffrage Associations merged in 1890. Under the presidency of Carry Chapman Catt, the National American Women's Suffrage Association (NAWSA) testified at legislative hearings and carried on state-by-state campaigns. Eleven states had given women the right to vote by the year 1910.

Over time, more women began to see that the vote was the only way they could fully participate in American society. Even conservative women's organizations were converted. By 1914, the last of the major women's organizations had joined the suffrage campaign.

About a year earlier, Alice Paul, a Quaker with strong convictions and little patience with NAWSA's conservative methods, left NAWSA and started the militant Congressional Union. In the election of 1916, it became the National Women's Party (NWP). In 1917, the National Women's Party posted members around Woodrow Wilson's White House, holding a round-the-clock watch. Wilson's reaction was extreme. He had the protesters arrested. When some of them began a hunger strike, prison authorities let them be force-fed. Reports of the event in national newspapers helped the women's cause.

Wilson was driven by this confrontation to give his support to NAWSA, which had rejected the radical ways of the NWP. But still Congress would not budge.

Then two developments boosted the cause of women's suffrage. First, states began to pass suffrage legisla-

SOCIAL SYSTEMS

Critical Thinking

Women's suffrage was opposed by the Catholic Church, the liquor industry, and political bosses. Ask students to analyze why each group opposed women's rights. Ask them to support their responses. *(Sample answers: The Catholic Church probably preferred women to stay in their traditional roles as mothers. Perhaps the liquor industry was afraid women, the mainstay of the temperance movement, would ruin its profits. The bosses were probably afraid that women would vote them out of power. Allow for personal opinion.)*

Music Connection

What kind of music was popular in the early 1900s? Students may enjoy listening to the ragtime music of Scott Joplin and the marches of John Philip Sousa to get a feel for the music of the times. Popular songs included "In the Shade of the Old Apple Tree" and "Bicycle Built for Two." Also popular were sentimental songs sung by "barbershop quartets."

Science Connection

George Washington Carver was one of the most famous and influential scientists of his time. He devoted much of his life's work to improving the agricultural methods of black farmers in the South. His work resulted in the development of more than 300 food and industrial products from peanuts, as well as 100 products from sweet potatoes. Have students research how Carver's work helped inspire an agricultural revolution in the South.

Visual Learning

Have students examine the photograph on this page. What differences and similarities does it reveal between women's lives in 1912 and women's lives today? *(Sample answer: Women's clothes today are much less restrictive than they were in 1912; women are still active in political demonstrations.)*

■ *NAWSA testified at legislative hearings and concentrated on state-by-state campaigns. NWD picketed and engaged in a hunger strike.*

■ *How did the women's rights movement go about winning the right to vote for women?*

tion, putting pressure on the Congress. Second, the country went to war. Women very successfully took over the home front during the war. Their performance may have done more than anything else to convince the public and Congress that women deserved the right to vote.

Finally, in 1919, Congress passed a constitutional amendment that gave women nationwide the right to vote. In 1920, the Nineteenth Amendment became law when Tennessee became the thirty-sixth state to ratify it. ■

Progressivism for Whites Only

Even before the end of Reconstruction in 1877, violence against black Americans was taking place. Racist organizations such as the Ku Klux Klan attacked and killed blacks and were never brought to justice.

Blacks also suffered legal oppression. Most Southern states passed laws meant to keep blacks from using their right to vote. These laws set up qualifications that applied to most blacks but to few whites. Often the states would not allow anyone to vote who could not read and write. In addition, voters had to pay an annual poll tax of $1 or $2. Many poor blacks could not afford to pay the tax.

"Jim Crow" laws required "separate but equal" treatment for blacks. (They were named for an obedient, uncomplaining black character from a minstrel show.) These laws led to separate schools, restrooms, restaurants, and trains for white and black Americans.

A black man named Homer Plessy boarded a train in Louisiana on June 7, 1892, and sat in a "whites only" coach to challenge these laws. He was arrested and tried. His case went all the way to the Supreme Court. The court declared that "separate but equal" was a reasonable use of state powers. The 1896 case, *Plessy* v. *Ferguson,* approved a system of segregation that lasted for years. A few years later, the black poet Paul Laurence Dunbar wrote about the effects of discrimination in his poem, "Sympathy," two stanzas of which appear below.

The rise of Jim Crow laws contributed to a time of terrible racial hatred and violence. From 1895 to 1912, lynchings averaged nearly one every three days.

NEGRO EXPULSION FROM RAILWAY CAR, PHILADELPHIA.

▲ *This illustration shows one of the effects of "Jim Crow" laws: a white man orders a black man out of the "white" section of the train.*

I know what the caged bird feels, alas!
When the sun is bright on the upland slopes;
When the wind stirs soft through the springing grass,
And the river flows like a stream of glass;
When the first bird sings and the first bud opes,
And the faint perfume from its chalice steals—
I know what the caged bird feels!
. . . .
I know why the caged bird sings, ah me,
When his wing is bruised and his bosom sore,—
When he beats his bars and he would be free;
It is not a carol of joy or glee,
But a prayer that he sends from his heart's deep core,
But a plea, that upward to Heaven he flings—
I know why the caged bird sings!

Paul Laurence Dunbar *Sympathy*

SOCIAL SYSTEMS

Critical Thinking

Have students analyze why discrimination against blacks worsened during the Progressive Era. *(Many Progressives believed that minorities should not have political power.)* Why did some Progressives eventually ally themselves with blacks to establish the NAACP? *(They were disturbed by the lynchings of black Americans.)*

Social Participation

After students have read the excerpt from the poem "Sympathy" on this page, ask: who is the "the caged bird"? *(The poet, black people)* Where will the caged bird find help? *(From Heaven)* What do these images tell you about the situation of black people in the early 1900s? *(They felt imprisoned and in need of help.)*

Writing a Report

Both W.E.B. DuBois and Booker T. Washington were black leaders dedicated to working for the rights of black people. The two leaders disagreed with each other, however, on the role of blacks in society. Have students research both men in encyclopedias or other reference books and write a report on each man, stating his goals, views, and life accomplishments. Student reports should make clear the different views of the two leaders.

Collaborative Learning

Ask students to work in pairs to role play an interview with one of the reformers discussed in this lesson. The pairs should work together to write a script for the interview. (Sample questions: What would you most like to see happen in the next year? What are the greatest obstacles blocking the reforms you want?) The reformer should answer in accordance with information presented in this lesson.

Ida B. Wells, the daughter of a slave, began to write against lynchings in her newspaper, the *Memphis Free Speech.* Her outspoken attitude led to death threats and to the bombing of her newspaper's office while she was away speaking in the North. Wells did not return to the South. She set herself up in Chicago where she went on writing and speaking against lynching.

Lynching was not only a Southern crime, however. In Springfield, Illinois, the home of President Lincoln, whites rioted in 1908. They were bent on driving blacks out of their town. The mob lynched a black man.

This terrible act seared the consciences of a number of Northern Progressives including Jane Addams and John Dewey. They helped organize a protest on the centennial of the birth of Abraham Lincoln in 1909. In 1910, a group of black leaders and white Northern Progressives joined together to found the National Association for the Advancement of Colored People (NAACP), which has fought to defend African Americans against discrimination ever since.

W.E.B. Du Bois helped to found the NAACP. He was a Fisk- and Harvard-educated writer who went on to become the moral and intellectual leader of the black movement. Unlike one of his contemporaries, Booker T. Washington, Du Bois urged African Americans to demand their civil rights. ■

▲ *W.E.B. Du Bois* (left) *felt that black Americans should speak out constantly against discrimination. Writer and educator Ida B. Wells* (right) *worked much of her life to end the vicious practice of lynching.*

■ *What impact did the Progressive movement have on the lives of black Americans?*

REVIEW

1. **FOCUS** What other social movements attempted to change American society during the Progressive Era, and what were their goals?
2. **CONNECT** Black men won the right to vote during Reconstruction. How was this right restricted by the 1890s?
3. **CITIZENSHIP** Name three events that contributed to the passage of the women's suffrage amendment.
4. **CRITICAL THINKING** Why do you think American businesses fought so hard to defeat child labor laws during the Progressive Era?
5. **WRITING ACTIVITY** Imagine that you are a prohibitionist, a socialist, a member of the IWW, a supporter of anti-lynching laws, or a supporter of the women's right to vote. Write a one-page statement in which you try to persuade others to join your cause.

■ *People such as Ida B. Wells and John Dewey spoke out against violence and hatred of black Americans. Then, in 1910, NAACP founder Du Bois urged black Americans to demand their civil rights.*

CLOSE

Have students answer the Thinking Focus. Then have them compare the lists that they made under the heads from the Graphic Overview on page 513. As an extension activity, have students do the Collaborative Learning exercise on page 518.

Answers to Review Questions

1. Other social movements included the prohibition, child labor, Socialist, anarchist, women's rights, and civil rights movements.
2. It was restricted by poll taxes, literacy tests, and other laws establishing voting qualifications that many black Americans could not meet.
3. The 1848 Seneca Falls convention, the states' passage of suffrage legislation, and the country's going to war contributed to the passage of the women's suffrage amendment.
4. Sample answer: Businesses could profit from the cheap labor children provided. Allow for personal opinion.
5. Have volunteers make speeches based on their statements.

Homework Options

Have students find current news stories about women's rights and civil rights.

Study Guide: page 75.

UNDERSTANDING VISUAL INFORMATION

In this skill lesson, students will analyze historical photographs as a source of information.

CULTURE

Visual Learning

Why is it important to know both the date and the location of a historical photograph? Point out that if either of these facts is not known, it is harder to place the photograph in historical context. However, photographs often give clues that will help determine these facts. If one didn't know the time period of the photo on page 520, what clues could help? *(Sample answer: The automobiles and the clothing styles, which come from the early 1900s)*

UNDERSTANDING VISUAL INFORMATION

Analyzing Historical Photographs

Here's Why

Photography is a powerful art. People say "the camera doesn't lie." Therefore people often believe that what they see is accurate. However, photographers always make choices about how to use the camera in order to create the kind of image they want.

A painter interprets the world around him or her by selecting certain colors, brushes and even style to convey a particular viewpoint. In the same way, a photographer decides what to photograph and how to present it.

Lighting can be used to highlight an object or person, or to create a certain mood or feeling. Sometimes a photographer will pose people or objects in a scene in order to communicate an idea. In addition the photographer can change the image in the process of developing it. By using such techniques, a photographer can sometimes create an image on paper that looks very different from the actual scene that was photographed.

As you have learned in this chapter, Jacob Riis and Lewis W. Hine used photography to inform the public of the terrible working and living conditions that many people faced in the late 1900s. Riis and Hine chose their subjects very carefully, highlighting the depressing surroundings and the emotions of hopelessness and despair in the people. They were able to use their art to influence how the camera reflected what they saw. In that way they were able to get their viewpoints across to the public. The public reacted to the grim scenes in their photos by pushing for reforms.

Knowing how to recognize the different ways in which the photographer can interpret an image will help you to analyze historical photographs.

Objective

Use early nineteenth century photographs to determine the living conditions during that time. (Visual Learning 3)

Research

Encourage students to bring in books that have other photographs of American life in the early 1900s. In most public libraries, students can find collections of the work of Lewis W. Hine or Jacob Riis. *This Fabulous Century, Vol. 1, 1900–1910* (New York: Time-Life Books, 1969) contains a variety of interesting photos. Display the results of the students' research in the classroom.

Art Connection

In the early 1900s, other American photographers were using their cameras to create art. You can find examples of the work of photographers such as Edward Steichen and Alfred Stieglitz in the library. Display them for the class, and discuss how they are different from the photographs on these pages. Discuss how artistic photographers achieved new effects through lighting, camera angle, or selection of details.

Here's How

There are four steps that will help you analyze historical photographs:

1. If possible, identify the date when the photograph was taken and the location where it was shot.
2. Identify the subject of the photograph.
3. Identify any special photographic techniques the photographer may have used, such as a flash or a fake background.
4. Determine what the photographer was trying to show in the photograph.

Study the photograph on page 520. It was taken in Cleveland, Ohio, in 1908. The date tells you that this photograph was taken at a time when photographic equipment was rather simple. Therefore you can assume that the photographer was limited in the number of techniques available. There was no color photography at that time, and cameras were not equipped with zoom lenses.

The photographer has taken this photo from a point above the scene, from which the viewer can look across the beach at many people and activities. It is a daytime scene that uses normal light, and does not focus on one particular object. The people do not appear posed. Rather, the photographer seems to have wanted to show people enjoying a leisurely day at the beach.

Try It

Now study the photograph on this page of Hester Street, New York City, in 1905. Identify the subject and possible photographic techniques. What information does the photograph provide? Based on your analysis of the photograph, write a short paragraph outlining what you think the photographer was trying to show by taking the photograph.

Apply It

Look through a contemporary news magazine, and choose two photographs of people your age. They can be of people at home, at school, or at play. Approach these photographs as if you were a historian and you wanted to find out about our culture. Following the steps listed above, compare and contrast the two photographs. Write a paragraph describing how these images depict everyday life and what they say about today's culture.

CULTURE

Visual Learning

Contrast the photos on these pages with those of the tenement and textile mill depicted on pages 505 and 514. Do any of the photos show a complete picture of American life? *(No, any photograph can show only a small part of a society.)* What would be needed to make more accurate generalizations about American society as a whole? *(Sample answer: Many different photographs reflecting the way of life of different classes of people in different places)*

Answers to Try It

The photographer was trying to show how crowded and busy the streets of New York were at the turn of the century. The camera scans the length of the street to underscore his point. Most people's faces are serious, perhaps reflecting their struggle to make a living.

Answers to Apply It

Encourage students to choose two photographs that are as different from each other as possible. Students should follow the three steps by labeling their photographs with time and place. They should list the details that are apparent and draw appropriate conclusions about the way of life of the people shown.

Visual Learning

Ask students to choose one of the photographs in this lesson, in the previous chapter, or any other that they have gathered during their research. Have them pretend that they are one of the people in the photograph and write a brief narrative about what is happening in the photo and their feelings about it.

INTRODUCE

Tell students that Sholem Asch, born in Poland, became an American citizen in 1920. Have them recall what they learned about urban life and political machines in Lesson 1. Point out that the 1946 novel *East River* is based on the experiences of many people who lived in the poor immigrant neighborhoods of New York.

READ AND RESPOND

As students read this excerpt independently, they should keep in mind that the immigrants in the story had no fans, no air conditioning, and no swimming pools. As students answer the purpose-setting question, make sure they give reasons for their answers.

In Chapter 16 you read about Tammany Hall. This excerpt shows how political bosses did favors for their immigrant voters.

LITERATURE

Summer in New York

Sholem Asch

In his book East River, *Sholem Asch describes life in an immigrant neighborhood on 48th Street in New York City. As you read this excerpt think about how Asch uses details to create a picture of what life was like in a big city in the late 1800s.*

The evening brought no relief from the oppressive heat. On the contrary, the walls of the buildings, having absorbed the heat all day, now began to throw it back into the street. The air was so humid that the people of the neighborhood had the feeling they were wrapped in a damp sheet which hampered their movements and from which they were unable to free themselves. It was impossible to stay indoors. The walls, the ceilings, the floors sweated with heat; the dampness filled the rooms and made it impossible to breathe. The heavy smells of food, sweat, and clothing, and the stale smell of mattresses and bedclothes added to the oppressiveness. The heat seemed to make bodies enormous and cumbersome. It sapped the energy and tortured the limbs.

The block dwellers swarmed out of their rooms, searching for a relieving gust of air. They crowded the fire escapes, the steps in front of doors, and the sidewalks.

Most of all they sought relief in the cool winds that came once in a while over the East River. But direct approach to the river shore was blocked to them. The streets ended in "dead ends" hemmed in by fences erected by the owners of the feed storehouses and stables. In a couple of places, however, there was an old unused dock, the planks water-soaked and rotted. From these docks one could hear the splashing of children swimming close to the shore, driven to find relief from the overpowering heat, disregarding the perils of the holes and falling timbers of the dock.

Other entrances to the waterfront were provided by the stables on the river shore. By climbing over fences and scrambling over the stable roofs it was possible to get down to the water's edge.

But 48th Street had two yards that opened on the river, and of these the people of the adjoining blocks were properly jealous. One of them was Harry's, to which, naturally, only his intimate friends, the people of his own block, who were interested in his pigeons, had admission. The other belonged to a private real-estate firm. Tammany had taken over the use of it so that the legitimate dwellers on 48th Street could come there to take their ease on the hot summer nights. With Judge Greenberg's help Uncle Maloney had managed to get permission to keep the property open to the Tammany members in the block. There was a lot of competition for the privilege among the inhabitants of the street. The yard

522

Thematic Connections

Social Studies: Immigrant neighborhoods

Houghton Mifflin Literary Readers: Finding Ways to Cope

Background

Sholem Asch (1880–1957) was born in a small Polish city where he received his education at a Hebrew school. Writing in Hebrew, he soon won a reputation as a skilled author of fiction. In his twenties, he began to compose his work in Yiddish, the popular language of European Jews. *East River* has a plot similar to *Romeo and Juliet*, but in this story the lovers are a Jew and a Catholic.

Asch's plays and novels made him well known in the United States by the time he made his first visit in 1909. Soon after that visit, he settled permanently here. In 1920, he became a United States citizen.

stretched to the river shore, and the general belief was that cool winds blew there. Everyone in the neighborhood besieged the office of the Tammany captain for tickets of admission. The first tickets, naturally enough, went to the members in good standing of the local Tammany club; Maloney knew all of them. But in time everyone on the block came to feel that he or she had special rights to the place, even Heimowitz, the socialist, who had little enough to do with Tammany in other matters.

The yard was full of people; men, women, and children of the neighborhood. They had brought with them mattresses, blankets, pillows, cans of cold tea or beer or ice water, ready to spend half the night there, until the tenement rooms got cool enough to return to.

The river lay motionless in its broad bed, its dark patches of oily scum reflecting the star-studded sky. Now and then a light blinked from a slowly moving coal barge. A heavy silence lay over the river.

From time to time the hoarse blast of a freight boat cut through the air. The morbid prison shadows of Blackwell's Island in the middle of the river pressed on the water's surface. The dimly lighted mist that hung over the island seemed to oppress the spirit and burden the heart more than it served to lighten the darkness. Involuntarily, everyone who saw the lights gleaming through the island's mist would think of the poor devils sent "across the river." The melancholy which the sight of the island brought to every one of Manhattan's dwellers fell like a pall on the group gathered in the Tammany yard to escape the unbearable heat. How could anyone of them know what the morrow might bring? Poverty ruled their lives and—who could know?—might drive them relentlessly to a similar fate. The same melancholy drove them to find escape in sleep, to find a rest from all the cares and worries of the day.

morbid somber

Some of them sprawled out on blankets they had brought with them from their homes. Others, the Slavs, for instance, talked with animation about the old country, about the boats that floated down its rivers; the nearness of the East River had brought it to their minds. Yes, along the Vistula, the Bug, and the Volga enormous rafts of logs floated; people would live on them all summer. They talked about horses being led in the night to graze on the green plains.

animation excitement

"Another year's work in the slaughterhouse, and I'll save enough, and then back home, back to Czezov. I'll buy my brother's share and take over my father's farm, eight acres and ten head of cattle." Choleva let his fantasy roam. His speech was a mixture of Polish, Russian, and English.

"It'll be no good. You'll use up your few dollars in the old country and then you'll come back to America. Everybody comes back. One smell of the American air , and it draws you back. There's some kind of magic in it," someone said.

Further Reading

The New Immigrants. Carol Olsen Day and Edmond Day. This book describes the conditions of immigrants in the United States today.

A Tree Grows in Brooklyn. Betty Smith. The story of Francie Nolan, a young girl growing up in an immigrant neighborhood in the early 1900s.

Why couldn't the people simply walk to the river and swim in it? *(The streets ended in dead ends blocked by fences.)*

What was on Blackwell's Island? *(A prison)* Why did the sight of it cause the people to feel melancholy? *(It reminded them that poverty might drive them to a life of crime.)*

EXTEND

Have students imagine that they are immigrants living in the New York described by Sholem Asch. Ask them to write a brief description of their lives in America, including their jobs and housing situations. Read these descriptions aloud for the class.

Further Reading

You may want to ask students to go to the school or local library to find more books by Sholem Asch or other books about life in immigrant neighborhoods during the Progressive era.

Answers to Reviewing Key Terms

A. Sample answers:

1. Muckrakers wrote articles and books to support the causes of Progressivism.
2. Both the referendum and the recall were part of the movement to reform the state governments.
3. A socialist wanted to change the American political and economic systems, while an anarchist believed in abolishing all government.

B. Answers:

1. True. *Laissez faire* means noninterference.
2. False. Jane Addams introduced the settlement house.
3. False. A zoning law restricted the kinds of buildings and businesses that could be developed in a certain area.
4. True. An initiative allowed voters to petition for a vote on proposed bills.
5. False. Conservation was the government's program to preserve natural resources.
6. False. Anarchists proposed radical changes that would abolish government.
7. False. To be enfranchised is to be able to vote.
8. False. Supporters of prohibition wanted to outlaw all alcoholic beverages.

Chapter Review

Reviewing Key Terms

anarchist (p. 516)
conservation (p. 510)
enfranchise (p. 516)
initiative (p. 508)
laissez faire (p. 499)
muckraker (p. 502)
Progressivism (p. 499)
prohibition (p. 514)
recall (p. 508)
referendum (p. 508)
socialist (p. 515)
tenement (p. 504)
zoning law (p. 505)

A. In each of the following pairs, the two terms are related in some way. Write a sentence for each pair that clearly explains the meaning of the two terms.

1. Progressivism, muckraker
2. recall, referendum
3. socialist, anarchist

B. Based on what you have read in the chapter, decide whether each of the following statements is accurate. Write an explanation of each decision.

1. Laissez-faire policies allowed businesses to operate without government restriction.
2. The tenement house was one of the reforms introduced by Jane Addams.
3. A zoning law allowed poor people to live in any area of the city they could afford.
4. Through the initiative, voters could propose laws that they felt were necessary.
5. Conservation programs were part of the government's effort to control railroad monopolies.
6. Anarchists proposed change through gradual social reforms.
7. The purpose of the Nineteenth Amendment was to enfranchise women by prohibiting them from voting.
8. Supporters of prohibition felt that giving women the right to vote would give them too much freedom.

Exploring Concepts

A. On a separate sheet of paper, copy the timeline below. Place each of the following items in the correct time position on the timeline.

- *The Shame of the Cities*
- *How the Other Half Lives*
- *The Jungle*
- Meat Inspection Act
- Pure Food and Drug Act
- Sixteenth Amendment ratified
- Seventeenth Amendment ratified
- Federal Reserve Act
- Eighteenth Amendment ratified
- Nineteenth Amendment ratified

B. Support each of the following statements with facts and details from the chapter.

1. Muckrakers identified three serious abuses of power by business monopolies.
2. The Progressive movement resulted in many improvements in children's lives.
3. The public supported women's right to vote.
4. Under Robert La Follette, Wisconsin provided many new ideas for state governments.
5. Progressive reforms at the state level gave voters more influence.
6. Theodore Roosevelt expanded the power of the presidency and the federal government.

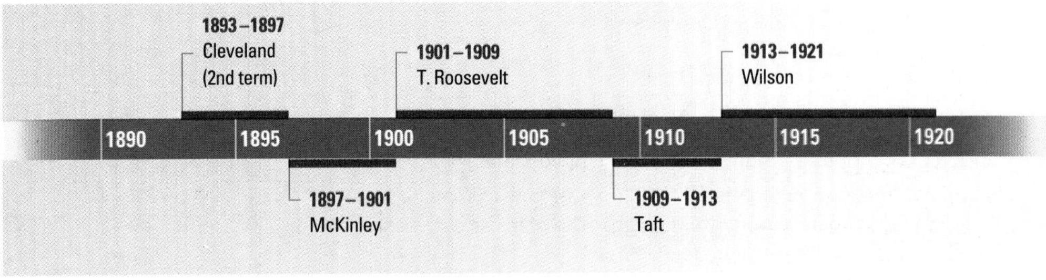

524

Chapter 17

Answers to Exploring Concepts

A. Answers:

How the Other Half Lives—1890
The Shame of the Cities—1904
The Jungle—1906
Meat Inspection Act—1906
Pure Food and Drug Act—1906
Sixteenth Amendment—1913
Seventeenth Amendment—1913
Federal Reserve Act—1913
Eighteenth Amendment—1919
Nineteenth Amendment—1920

B. Sample answers:

1. Monopolies kept prices high, sold poor and harmful products, and made their employees work in dangerous workplaces.
2. The Progressive movement worked to restrict child labor, provide services to poor children, and improve the educational system.
3. Women's right to vote was strongly opposed until women proved they could support the war effort during World War I.
4. La Follette's reforms included direct primary elections, civil service reform, prohibition of corporate contributions to political parties, and creation of public commissions to regulate utilities and powerful railroads.
5. Progressive reforms included the initiative, referendum, and recall.
6. Roosevelt used government to regulate irresponsible monopolies and to expand the conservation of natural resources.

Reviewing Skills

1. What are four steps that will help you analyze historical photographs?
2. What are some choices that a photographer makes before actually taking a photograph?
3. As you learned in Chapter 6, political cartoons are pictures that communicate a strong message. Photographers like Jacob Riis and Lewis Hine also communicated strong political messages in their photographs. In what way are political cartoons different from photographs?
4. Look at the photograph at the right taken by Jacob Riis. Using the four steps you already know, analyze this photograph. What do you think Riis was trying to say about living conditions in New York tenements?
5. Read the literature selection in this chapter on pages 522-523. Identify the style of writing, and explain how that style affects the subject of the selection.

6. Suppose you wanted to study the Progressive Era by examining photographs from that time period. What would you need to know about photography to be able to use it as a research tool for this project?

Using Critical Thinking

1. Theodore Roosevelt called the presidency a "bully pulpit." (*Bully* was slang for *very good.*) He meant that the president, like a national preacher, can make his views widely known to influence opinion. Identify methods that presidents use today to gain support for their policies. Do you think any of those methods have been successful? Explain.
2. Thomas Jefferson once said that a free press was the most important right Americans had. How did this right contribute to the Progressive movement's success? Does the media today carry on the tradition of exposing problems in business and government? Explain your answer.
3. Progressive reforms in education have been criticized by people who believe they made the schools too easy and did not require students to memorize facts or to learn things that were important but "boring." How do you feel about today's Progressive-influenced school system? Does it help you to learn things that are relevant to your life? Do you think the system could be improved? If so, how?

Preparing for Citizenship

1. **WRITING ACTIVITY** Be a muckraker! Identify a problem that you think exists in business, society, or government today. Write an article in which you try to convince others that this problem is serious. Describe what action you think should be taken to correct the problem.
2. **WRITING ACTIVITY** Find out if your state allows the initiative, referendum, and recall. If so, find out when they have been used recently, and write a report on how they were used and whether they were successful. If not, write a letter to a state official asking why those methods are not used.
3. **COLLABORATIVE LEARNING** Make a classroom display of the benefits of the Progressive movement. Choose one of the major areas from the chapter in which Progressives worked to improve their nation and communities. You could choose, for example, the area of government, food, conservation, labor, schools, or banking. Work with others who chose the same subject. Your display may include photographs, drawings, clay models, or any other means of displaying the results of Progressivism in today's world.

Answers to Reviewing Skills

1. 1. Identify the date and location; 2. identify the subject; 3. identify any special photographic techniques; 4. determine the photographer's intention.
2. Students may suggest: lighting, posing of people or objects, and changing the image in the developing process.
3. Political cartoons often make an exaggerated point, usually with humor and irony. Photographs are usually more subtle, more serious in tone.
4. Ask students to compare this photo with the one shown in Understanding Reform on page 503.
5. Students should identify the writing as a novel, and note that although the selection gives a vivid picture of the immigrant experience, it is a work of imagination.
6. Students would need to know what the state of photography as an art form was at that time.

Answers to Using Critical Thinking

1. Today, Presidents can speak to the nation on TV and in press conferences to explain their policies. Students might note how well some leaders come across on television as compared to others.
2. In books and articles, the muckrakers exposed evils in society and created public support for government action. Ask students if the news media today still serve as "watchdogs" for the public interest. Point out that the news media have become a big business themselves.
3. Encourage students to research the educational process in other countries.

Answers to Preparing for Citizenship

1. **WRITING ACTIVITY** Direct students to read newspapers and magazines to find a problem that they think needs correction and then to follow the coverage of that problem over a specific period of time.
2. **WRITING ACTIVITY** Members of state legislatures will have local offices that students can visit or call to obtain this information.
3. **COLLABORATIVE LEARNING** Possible examples are: food or medicine packages that include labeling of the contents, photographs of national forests, a list of work safety rules from a parent's workplace, models of playgrounds and libraries built during the Progressive era, zoning laws, old photos showing slum conditions, and anything else suggested by the chapter.

CHAPTER 18

Planning at a Glance

America Emerges as a World Power

	Objectives	Reading Support *and* Other Resources	Diverse Learning Strategies
Lesson 1 International Expansion *pp. 528–532* 1–2 days	• Describe the impact of social Darwinism on America. • Explain why the United States began to look abroad for new markets and territories. • Explain United States relations with Japan, Korea, China, Samoa and Hawaii.	• **Workbook** or **Reading Support:** pp. 255–258 Review p. 60 Lesson Support/Transition p. 60 Multi-language Summaries pp. 119–120 • **Other Resources:** Poster 5, Study Guide p. 77	Access Strat. **(SDAIE)** TE p. 529 Collaborative Act. **(Kinesthetic)** TE p. 531 Study Skills **(Visual)** TE p. 531 Audiotapes of Multi-language Lesson Summaries **(Auditory)**
Lesson 2 Conflict and Conquest *pp. 533–540* 2–3 days	• Explain why the United States strictly enforced the Monroe Doctrine. • Describe the causes and events of the war with Spain. • State why the United States built the Panama Canal. • Describe the tension between the United States and Mexico during the 1910s.	• **Workbook** or **Reading Support:** pp. 259–262 Review p. 61 Lesson Support/Transition p. 61 Multi-language Summaries pp. 121–122 • **Other Resources:** Geography Kit, Poster 7, Study Guide p. 78	Access Act. **(SDAIE)** TE p. 534 Language Arts Connection **(Visual)** TE p. 537 Building a Model **(Kinesthetic)** TE p. 538 Audiotapes of Multi-language Lesson Summaries **(Auditory)**
Lesson 3 America at War *pp. 541–546* 1–2 days	• Summarize the factors that led to World War I. • Describe how the United States was eventually drawn into the conflict in Europe. • Evaluate the U.S. role in World War I and the role of modern warfare.	• **Workbook** or **Reading Support:** pp. 263–266 Review p. 62 Lesson Support/Transition p. 62 Multi-language Summaries pp. 123–124 • **Other Resources:** Geography Kit, Study Guide p. 79	Access Strat. **(Extra Support)** TE p. 542 Art Connection **(Visual)** TE p. 544 Writing a News Account **(GATE)** TE p. 545 Audiotapes of Multi-language Lesson Summaries **(Auditory)**
Lesson 4 Impact of the War *pp. 547–553* 3–4 days **Literature** "War Songs" *pp. 554–555*	• Summarize the impact of the war on dissenters, foreigners, women, and black Americans. • Describe the Treaty of Versailles and the U.S. response to it. • Analyze why the war was followed by a period of unrest and conflict.	• **Workbook** or **Reading Support:** pp. 267–270 Review p. 63 Lesson Support/Transition p. 63 Multi-language Summaries pp. 125–126 • **Other Resources:** Geography Kit, Study Guide p. 80, Study Print 14	Access Act. **(SDAIE)** TE p. 548 Access Strat. **(Extra Support)** TE p. 548 Map and Globe Skills **(Visual)** TE p. 550 Audiotapes of Multi-language Lesson Summaries **(Auditory)**
Skill: Understanding Propaganda *pp. 556–557*	• Use government pamphlets from World War I to evaluate and judge propaganda.	• **Other Resources:** Study Guide p. 81	Visual Learning **(Visual)** TE p. 557
Chapter Review *pp. 558–559* 1 day		Chapter 18 Test pp. 69–72 *(See facsimiles on TE p. 766)*	Assessment Multiple-Use Masters pp. 81–88

Reading Support Resources *for Every Lesson*

Reading and Review

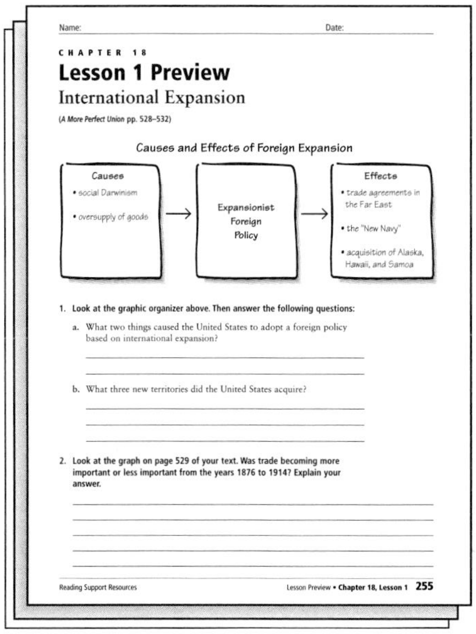
Name: Date:

CHAPTER 18

Lesson 1 Preview

International Expansion

(*A More Perfect Union* pp. 528–532)

Causes and Effects of Foreign Expansion

Causes		Effects
• social Darwinism • oversupply of goods	→ Expansionist Foreign Policy →	• trade agreements in the Far East • the "New Navy" • acquisition of Alaska, Hawaii, and Samoa

1. Look at the graphic organizer above. Then answer the following questions:
   a. What two things caused the United States to adopt a foreign policy based on international expansion?
   b. What three new territories did the United States acquire?
2. Look at the graph on page 529 of your text. Was trade becoming more important or less important from the years 1876 to 1914? Explain your answer.

Reading Support Resources — Lesson Preview • Chapter 18, Lesson 1 255

- **Chapter Overview*** p. 254
- **Lesson Previews*** using graphic organizers from the Teacher's Edition pp. 255, 259, 263, 267
- **Reading Strategies*** pp. 256, 260, 264, 268
- **Lesson Summaries*** pp. 257–258, 261–262, 265–266, 269–270
- **Lesson Reviews** pp. 60, 61, 62, 63

* **Workbook** includes starred items.

Multi-language Summaries

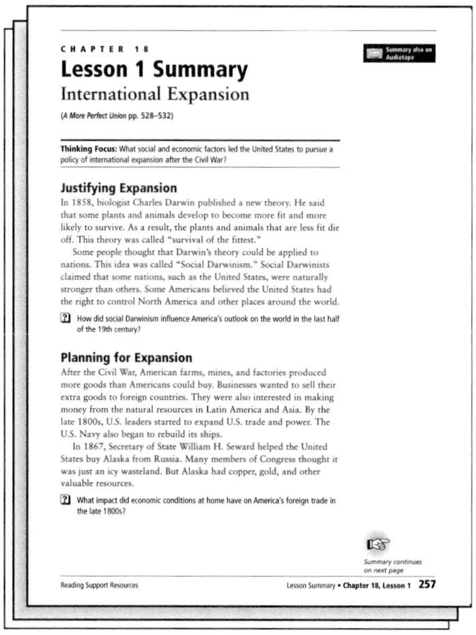
CHAPTER 18

Summary also on Audiotape

Lesson 1 Summary

International Expansion

(*A More Perfect Union* pp. 528–532)

Thinking Focus: What social and economic factors led the United States to pursue a policy of international expansion after the Civil War?

Justifying Expansion

In 1858, biologist Charles Darwin published a new theory. He said that some plants and animals develop to become more fit and more likely to survive. As a result, the plants and animals that are less fit die off. This theory was called "survival of the fittest."

Some people thought that Darwin's theory could be applied to nations. This idea was called "Social Darwinism." Social Darwinists claimed that some nations, such as the United States, were naturally stronger than others. Some Americans believed the United States had the right to control North America and other places around the world.

? How did social Darwinism influence America's outlook on the world in the last half of the 19th century?

Planning for Expansion

After the Civil War, American farms, mines, and factories produced more goods than Americans could buy. Businesses wanted to sell their extra goods to foreign countries. They were also interested in making money from the natural resources in Latin America and Asia. By the late 1800s, U.S. leaders started to expand U.S. trade and power. The U.S. Navy also began to rebuild its ships.

In 1867, Secretary of State William H. Seward helped the United States buy Alaska from Russia. Many members of Congress thought it was just an icy wasteland. But Alaska had copper, gold, and other valuable resources.

? What impact did economic conditions at home have on America's foreign trade in the late 1800s?

Summary continues on next page

Reading Support Resources — Lesson Summary • Chapter 18, Lesson 1 257

Lesson Summaries in:

- English (See Reading and Review.)
- Spanish pp. 257–258, 261–262, 265–266, 269–270
- Chinese pp. 119–126
- Hmong pp. 119–126
- Khmer pp. 119–126
- Vietnamese pp. 119–126

Summaries available on audiotapes

Lesson Support / Transition

S D A I E

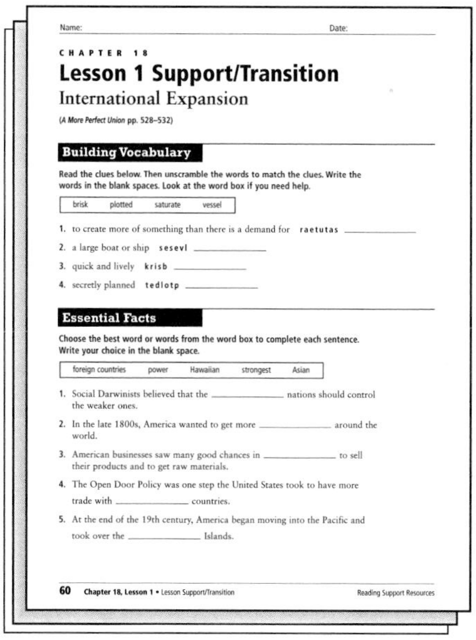
Name: Date:

CHAPTER 18

Lesson 1 Support/Transition

International Expansion

(*A More Perfect Union* pp. 528–532)

Building Vocabulary

Read the clues below. Then unscramble the words to match the clues. Write the words in the blank spaces. Look at the word box if you need help.

brisk plotted saturate vessel

1. to create more of something than there is a demand for **raetutas** ______
2. a large boat or ship **sesevl** ______
3. quick and lively **krisb** ______
4. secretly planned **tedlotp** ______

Essential Facts

Choose the best word or words from the word box to complete each sentence. Write your choice in the blank space.

foreign countries power Hawaiian strongest Asian

1. Social Darwinists believed that the ______ nations should control the weaker ones.
2. In the late 1800s, America wanted to get more ______ around the world.
3. American businesses saw many good chances in ______ to sell their products and to get raw materials.
4. The Open Door Policy was one step the United States took to have more trade with ______ countries.
5. At the end of the 19th century, America began moving into the Pacific and took over the ______ Islands.

60 Chapter 18, Lesson 1 • Lesson Support/Transition — Reading Support Resources

Activities for SDAIE
Specially **D**esigned **A**cademic **I**nstruction in **E**nglish

- **Lesson Support/Transition** pp. 60, 61, 62, 63

Technology Options

Internet Support

http://www.eduplace.com

Social Studies Center at Education Place

Internet support for Chapter 18:

- ***Lesson at a Glance***
- ***Building the Panama Canal***

Software

Student Writing Center® (CD-ROM) (Macintosh® or Windows®)

School to Career

Trade is big business. Have students brainstorm a product they would like to market and sell. Then help them set up a model work environment with each student taking a specific position. Students should draw up a mission statement for their company as well as operating policies. They should also consider finances and costs.

Character Education

Service Learning: If possible, arrange for the class to visit an elderly care facility or community to meet with and interview residents who were in America during World War II. Afterward, have students share what they learned. How may the experiences of these individuals be similar to those of people living in the United States during WWI?

CHAPTER PREVIEW

Have students read the chapter title and the narrative underneath it. Remind students that in previous chapters in this unit they have studied U.S. internal affairs. In this chapter, they will read about the United States's role in international affairs. Using the world map on pages 694–695 in the Atlas, point out some of the areas referred to in this chapter—for example, Europe, the Carribbean Islands, and the Philippines.

Looking Back

Ask students to recall from the earlier chapters in this unit some developments that might have helped the United States achieve world power status. *(The rise of industry; the development of American cities; the settlement of the Great Plains)*

Looking Forward

Tell students that they will learn as they read the next four lessons how a belief in the superiority of the white American culture also affected the nation's foreign policy: International Expansion, Conflict and Conquest, America at War, and Impact of the War.

Chapter 18

America Emerges as a World Power

By the late 1800s, the United States had pushed its boundaries westward and settled the nation. U.S. farms and factories produced more than enough food and goods for the country. Americans looked to foreign shores for new markets and resources. This activity brought the nation into competition with other countries, and conflicts resulted.

Lieutenant Colonel Theodore Roosevelt leads the "Rough Riders" during the Battle of San Juan Hill. Later, as President, Roosevelt continues to involve the United States in international affairs.

1850 | 1860 | 1870 | 1880

1850

1850-1853 Fillmore

1853-1857 Pierce

1857-1861 Buchanan

1861-1865 Lincoln

1865-1869 A. Johnson

1869-1877 Grant

1877-1881 Hayes

1881 Garfield

188 Arth

BACKGROUND

During the late 1800s, the desire for economic expansion led the United States into the imperialist scramble for new territories. During the Spanish-American War and World War I, the United States established its worldwide sphere of influence.

Airplanes in World War I

Airplanes were first used for military purposes in World War I. At first they only observed enemy troops and chased enemy planes away. Later they were also used in bombing missions. Industrial sites, transportation depots, and supply lines were the chief targets of the planes. Planes did not attack enemy troops on the ground until near the end of the war.

The exploits of American flyers captured the popular imagination of the country. One of the United States's best known aces was former race car driver Eddie Rickenbacker, who was credited with shooting down 26 enemy aircraft.

Jeannette Rankin

Jeannette Rankin, the first woman elected to the House of Representatives, was one of the most influential pacifists in the United States. In April 1917, she led the campaign against the United States's involvement in World War I. "I want to stand by my country, but I cannot vote for war," she declared. Rankin and 56 other members of Congress

This map from the Spanish-American War shows the Caribbean islands that were a source of international conflict.

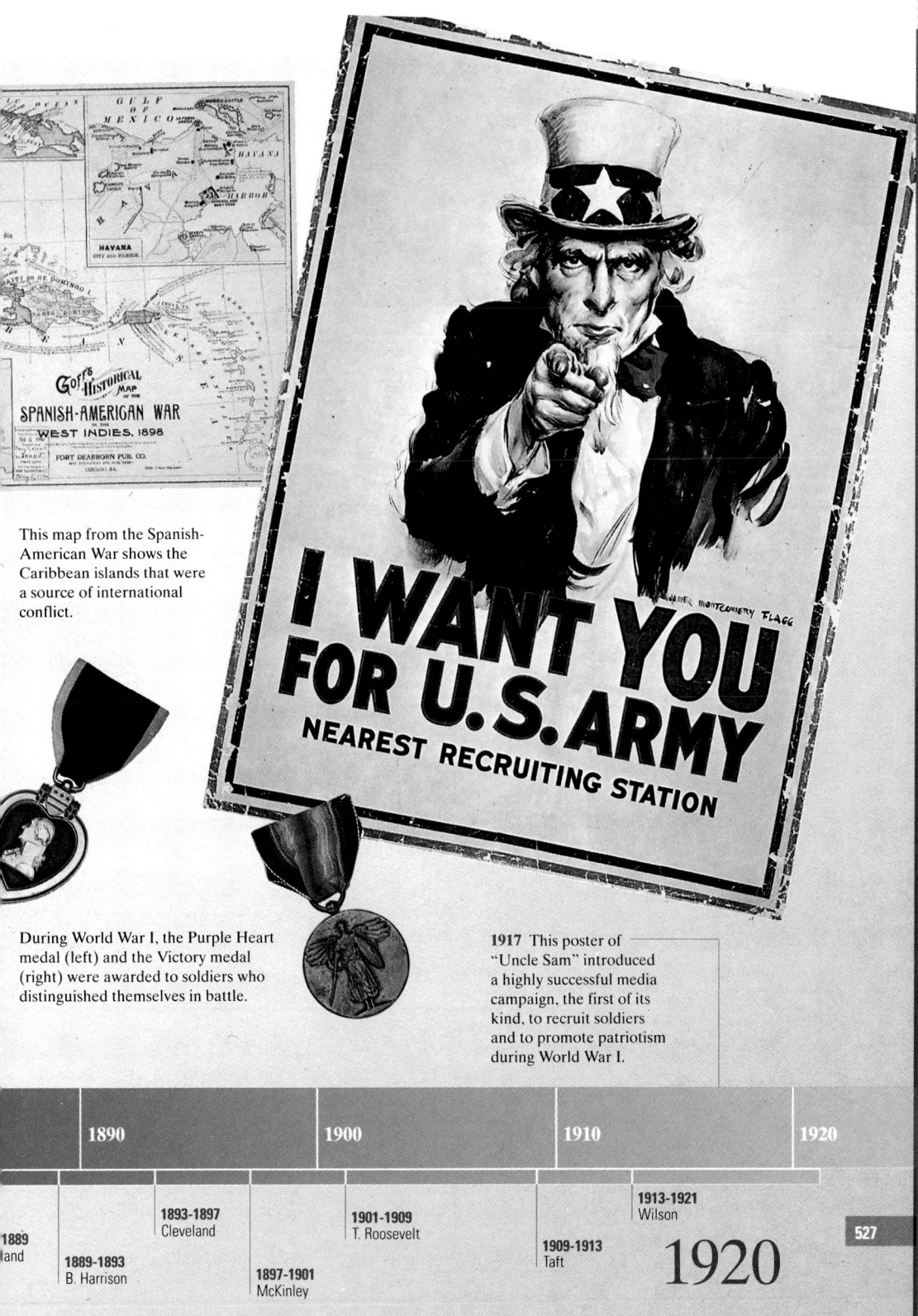

During World War I, the Purple Heart medal (left) and the Victory medal (right) were awarded to soldiers who distinguished themselves in battle.

1917 This poster of "Uncle Sam" introduced a highly successful media campaign, the first of its kind, to recruit soldiers and to promote patriotism during World War I.

1890	1900	1910	1920

1889 ...and

1889-1893 B. Harrison

1893-1897 Cleveland

1897-1901 McKinley

1901-1909 T. Roosevelt

1909-1913 Taft

1913-1921 Wilson

527

1920

Understanding the Visuals

Draw students' attention to the painting *The Battle of San Juan Hill*, a National Guard Heritage painting by Mort Kunstler. Point out that Roosevelt's Rough Riders were volunteer businessmen, cowboys, and outdoorsmen.

Refer students to the Uncle Sam poster painted by James Montgomery Flagg in 1917. Ask students to explain why this poster might have been especially effective during the war. *(Uncle Sam is staring straight at the viewer and pointing his finger, making the viewer feel obligated to help.)*

Understanding Chronology

Draw students' attention to the timeline. Explain that the United States was gaining influence in international affairs even before the Civil War.

voted against U.S. entry into World War I.

She was the only member of Congress to oppose both world wars. On December 8, 1941, the day after the attack on Pearl Harbor, she cast the only vote against U.S. entry into World War II.

World War I Propaganda

The Committee on Public Information, founded in 1917, headed a major government effort to stir up support for World War I among the reluctant American public. The Committee sponsored 75,000 speakers who gave a total of 750,000 speeches in 5,000 American cities and towns. It churned out 75 million pieces of literature designed to evoke feelings of American patriotism and to convey exaggerated images of German militarism.

As a result of the Committee's campaign, pro-war feelings and the fear of Germans, "radicals," and dissidents increased. Some Americans took it upon themselves to purge the country of German culture. German books were burned and German china was smashed. Many U.S. citizens of German descent Anglicized their names to avoid the stigma of being associated with Germany.

INTRODUCE

After students have read the lesson title and Thinking Focus, ask them to suggest a difference between international expansion and the expansion that the United States had been carrying out since its founding. Remind them that up until this time, territories of the United States had eventually become states. Have students suggest reasons why the United States might want to pursue international expansion in the last half of the 1800s. Explain that the United States was now interested in colonizing other parts of the world for economic, not territorial, gain.

Key Terms

Vocabulary strategies: T36–37

protectorate—a country or region that is protected and partially controlled by a more powerful country

abdicate—to formally give up power, such as a throne or a high office

1850 1898 1910 1920

L E S S O N 1

International Expansion

THINKING FOCUS

What social and economic factors led the United States to pursue a policy of international expansion after the Civil War?

Key Terms

- protectorate
- abdicate

Writing in 1885, minister Josiah Strong captured the new mood that was sweeping the United States in the 1880s and 1890s when he made the following prediction:

> *This Anglo-Saxon [Western European] race of unequaled energy, with all the majesty of numbers and the might of wealth behind it, will spread itself . . . down upon Mexico, down upon Central and South America, out upon the islands of the sea, over upon Africa and beyond."*

Strong believed that Americans had a special responsibility to bring progress to people on other continents who, in his view, were primitive and uncivilized. In an 1899 campaign speech, Senator Albert Beveridge of Indiana echoed Strong's sentiments when he claimed that Americans would become:

> *The master organizers of the world . . . American factories are making more than the American people can use; American soil is producing more than they can consume. Fate has written our policy for us; the trade of the world must and shall be ours.*

Reverend Strong and Senator Beveridge were among many people who envisioned a new role for the United States in world affairs. Before the Civil War, the United States had spent much of its energy expanding across North America. During the decades following the war, however, more Americans became interested in the world beyond their own borders. Many of these people—including foreign policy makers, bankers, ministers, and people in business—believed that the United States had a "divine" or God-given right to dominate the continent and the world.

Justifying Expansion

People like Strong and Beveridge drew support for their views from the world of science. In 1858, British biologist Charles Darwin published a new idea. Through his extensive travels and studies, Darwin had collected evidence that all species of living things have gradually evolved, or changed, over time. According to the theory Darwin developed, some plants and animals are more fit to survive than other members of their species. They have physical features that help them to live longer and healthier lives. These plants and animals are more likely to survive and reproduce, while the less fit tend to die off.

For some people, the "survival of

Objectives

1. Describe the impact of social Darwinism on America.
2. Identify the factors that led the United States to look abroad for new markets and territories.
3. Explain why the United States wanted to establish relations with Japan, Korea, and China.
4. State why Samoa and Hawaii became important to the United States.

Graphic Overview

Causes
- social Darwinism
- supplies of goods

→ **Expansionist Foreign Policy** →

Effects
- trade agreements in the Far East
- the "New Navy"
- acquisition of Alaska, Hawaii, and Samoa

the fittest" seemed to be the law of nations as well as the law of nature. They claimed that, just as the best-adapted animals dominate in the natural world, the strongest nations will and should dominate nations that are weaker. This idea became known as social Darwinism.

Social Darwinists believed that people with power and wealth had certain obligations, including the "improvement" of the "lower classes." Since most social Darwinists were white, this obligation became known as the "White Man's Burden." Some people said this view was not scientific and was racist. Social Darwinists countered that these critics were being misguided by their feelings. William Graham Sumner, a professor at Yale University and an enthusiastic advocate of the social Darwinist theory, proclaimed: "If we do not like the survival of the fittest, we have only one possible alternative, and that is survival of the unfittest." ■

■ *How did social Darwinism influence America's outlook on the world in the last half of the 19th century?*

Planning for Expansion

As you learned in chapter 8, in the 1840s Americans believed that it was the manifest destiny, or God-given right, of the United States to expand to the Pacific Ocean. In the late 1800s, Americans used the philosophy of social Darwinism to justify international expansion. Through trade, diplomacy, and conquest, America was determined to gain power around the world.

Businesses Seek New Opportunities

After the Civil War, American farmers produced more milk, cheese, corn, and wheat than Americans could eat. Miners dug out more copper and iron than the nation's businesses could use. And factories made more goods than Americans could buy.

The market in the United States had become saturated. That is, the supply of goods was greater than the demand for them. American businesses had to find somewhere to trade their goods. They began to look to foreign markets.

The desire to sell goods was not the only interest American businesses and banks had in other lands. Americans were also attracted by the raw materials of other countries. For example, they saw huge profits waiting for them in the sugar, fruits, oil, minerals, and rubber found in parts of Latin America and in Asia.

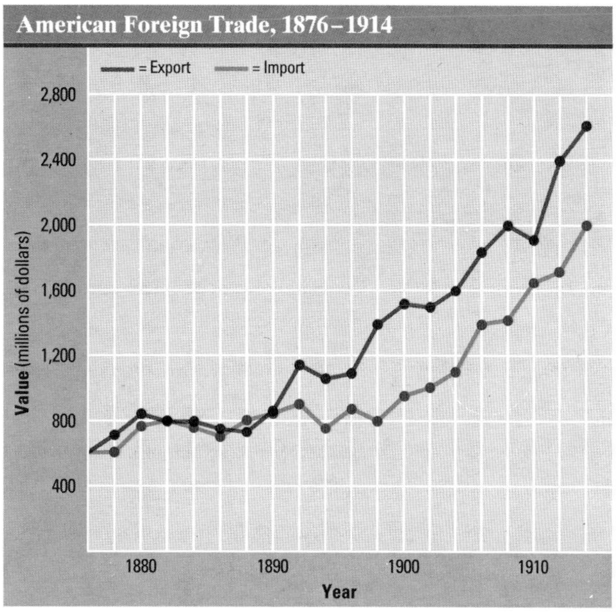

▲ *During the period of economic expansion following the Civil War, U.S. imports and exports grew at a rapid rate.*

Seward Envisions Vast Empire

William H. Seward, secretary of state under President Abraham Lincoln, was a well-known and respected Republican. After the Civil War, Seward dreamed of establishing a huge American empire that would include Canada, the Caribbean, Cuba, Central America, Mexico, Hawaii, and Iceland. In Seward's vision, a canal across Central America would connect this vast empire geographically. A telegraph system

DEVELOP

Explain that this lesson focuses on the reasons why international expansion was attractive to people in the United States at the end of the 1800s (the *causes* in the Graphic Overview on page 528) and on the results of expansionist policies (the *effects* in the Graphic Overview). Copy on the board the structure of the Graphic Overview and have students complete it as they read the lesson.

SOCIAL SYSTEMS

Critical Thinking

In order to clarify the philosophy of social Darwinism, ask students how social Darwinism compares with Manifest Destiny. *(They are very similar.)* With the philosophy of the Declaration of Independence? *(They are basically opposites.)*

■ *Social Darwinism influenced some Americans to see their nation as being superior to non-European nations and as having a God-given right to expand and dominate weaker countries.*

Access Strategy

In order to help students understand the law of supply and demand, explain that tomatoes cost more when the weather is bad because fewer are available. Farmers and, subsequently, stores can then ask a higher price. Ask students to suppose what would happen to the price of tomatoes if tomatoes suddenly started growing like weeds beside the road. *(The price would drop.)* Explain that in the last part of the 1800s, America was producing more of certain products than Americans could use. Ask students why this might have been a problem for businesses. *(Prices dropped so low that they couldn't make any money on their goods.)*

Tell students that many Americans in the late 1800s wanted to create new markets for their goods and to gain control of foreign resources. Explain that they will be reading more about the China trade, first introduced in Chapter 3.

Access Activity

After students examine a wall map or a globe, have them guess two or three places that the United States might try to colonize in the late 1800s. Encourage them to use any information that they may already know to help them with their guesses. Ask for reasons why the United States would expand to these places.

The construction of the Great White Fleet in the 1890s transformed the United States into a naval power.

would allow people in all parts of the empire to communicate with each other.

Although Seward did not succeed in building an empire, he did expand America's territory. His most famous achievement as secretary of state was the 1867 purchase of Alaska from Russia for $7.2 million. Some representatives in Congress thought Alaska was nothing but an ice-covered wasteland. They ridiculed the purchase as "Seward's Folly," and they called the land itself "the Polar Bear Garden" or "Walrussia."

But Seward had the last laugh. As it turned out, Alaska contained rich deposits of copper, gold, and other minerals. Sea otters, seals, and whales filled its coastal waters, and its vast interior was a land of unique beauty.

■ *What impact did economic conditions at home have on America's foreign trade in the late 1800s?*

Mahan's Powerful Navy

During the 1870s, the U.S. Navy was badly equipped. It was not able to support American plans for international expansion. Civil War veteran and naval historian Captain Alfred T. Mahan was a social Darwinist. He claimed that stronger nations like the United States had a duty to dominate weaker ones. In his 1890 book, *The Influence of Sea Power upon History, 1660-1783,* Mahan called for the United States to obtain defensive overseas bases and later to establish foreign colonies. He also argued that a strong navy would be needed to protect these distant American territories.

Even before Mahan wrote his book, Congress had taken steps to build a "New Navy" in the 1880s. Presidents Chester A. Arthur, Grover Cleveland, and Benjamin Harrison had all given their support. One by one, wooden sailing ships were replaced with steam-powered vessels made of steel. Congress also authorized the construction of a fleet of big, modern battleships during this period. By 1895, the "Great White Fleet" was nearly finished. ■

HISTORY

Critical Thinking

What connection might have existed between the needs of American businesses and Congress's willingness to fund the "New Navy"? *(Businesses were very eager to gain access to overseas markets.)* How did the new ships differ from the old ones? *(New ships were made of steel and driven by steam engines. The old ones were wooden sailing ships.)*

■ *The saturated market at home led American businesses to look to foreign markets to trade their goods.*

Critical Thinking

Have students examine the graph on page 529. When did trade increase most rapidly? *(After 1900, especially after 1910)* Least rapidly? *(1880–1890)* How much greater were imports in 1914 than in 1890? *(2.5 times)* Exports? *(3.25 times)* Have students refer to the graph as they read the chapter to see how events affected exports and imports.

Geographical Context

The importance of the Pacific islands to the United States was due in part to the fact that the ships of the 1890s were fueled by coal. Vessels could not travel to the Far East without refueling. Secure coaling stations were a strategic necessity that led to the establishment of a chain of U.S. bases across the Pacific: the Midway Islands in 1867; Hawaii, Guam, and the Philippines in 1898; and Wake Island and Samoa in 1899.

American opinion was by no means united in regard to these takeovers. Many people expressed concern that the principles upon which the United States was founded could not survive when the machinery for governing an empire was set up. People also feared that the commitment to defend an empire would draw the United States into Europe's quarrels and result in war.

Expanding Trade with Asia

America's desire for economic expansion first became clear in the nation's relations with Asia. Long before the Civil War, the United States had tried to establish good trade relations with the countries of East Asia. As America's economy became more industrial, its interest in Asian markets grew steadily.

The China Trade

By the early 19th century, American trade with China was already brisk and profitable. American merchants made huge fortunes trading cloth, iron products, and fur for Chinese porcelain, tea, silk, jade, and other goods.

In 1842, the British forced China to give them extensive trading rights. Afraid Britain might keep China for itself, the United States demanded and received similar rights two years later. Trade between America and China continued to grow in the following decades.

When China lost a war with Japan in 1895, European nations saw a chance for even more economic gain. Right away France, Great Britain, Germany, and Russia divided China into trading areas, or "spheres of influence." But the plan removed the United States, not yet a world power, from the China trade.

The U.S. government would not let China be carved up into European colonies. Consequently, in 1898, the United States persuaded the Europeans to accept an Open Door Policy. This policy allowed China to remain independent while trading with all nations on an equal basis.

Opening Japan and Korea

On July 8, 1853, residents of Edo (now Tokyo) who looked out at the ocean stopped and rubbed their eyes in disbelief. Four black warships were sailing into the bay—against the prevailing winds.

Commodore Matthew C. Perry commanded these steam-powered vessels. Perry was faced with the difficult task of persuading the rulers of Japan to agree to open its ports to trade. The Japanese government had steadily refused almost all communications with other nations for more than two hundred years.

Impressed by Perry's ships, Japanese authorities accepted a letter from President Franklin Pierce asking Japan for friendship and trading privileges. Upon his return in early 1854, Perry negotiated for the United States the first trading agreement that Japan had ever signed with a Western nation. Japan's ports were opened to the commerce of the Western world.

Nearly 30 years later the United States signed a similar trading agreement with the nearby nation of Korea. Compared with Japan, Korea had been at least as cut off from the world.

How Do We Know?

HISTORY *Historians know many of the details of the first meeting between Matthew Perry and the Japanese thanks to Perry's 1856 book on his experiences in East Asia,* Narrative of the Expedition of an American Squadron to the China Seas and Japan.

An unknown Japanese artist painted this watercolor of Admiral Perry's 1853 landing in Japan.

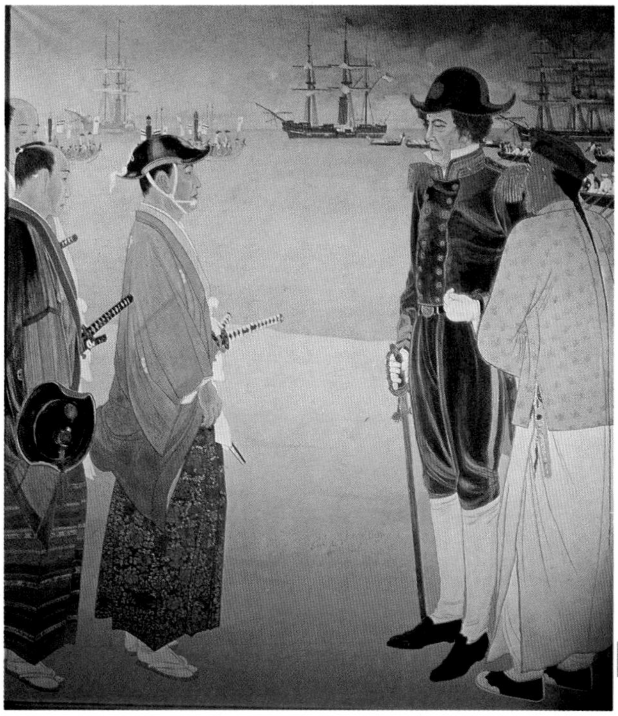

ECONOMICS

Critical Thinking

Ask students what the economic and political developments in Asia meant to the United States. *(Americans felt that their freedom to trade in China was not secure.)*

CULTURE

Visual Learning

If students have not noticed that Perry "looks" Japanese in the Japanese painting of Admiral Perry's landing in Japan, point this out. Have students discuss this, as well as the differences in dress. How is the meeting portrayed—friendly, hostile, cool, warm? *(Sample answer: Stiff and uncomfortable)*

Art Connection

When trade relations opened with Japan in the mid-1800s, the art of Japanese printmaking first became known in the West. The abstract handling of color and design in Japanese prints had a profound influence on artists in Europe and America. This can be seen in color prints created by the American painters Mary Cassatt and James Whistler. Provide slides and prints of their work and of Japanese prints and have students look for similarities.

Collaborative Learning

Divide students into three groups—one each for Japan, Korea, and China—and have them work within the groups to draw up questions about life in each country in the late 1800s. Topics might include the culture, the belief systems, the government, and the geography of each nation. Each group can choose an oral report, mural or dramatization. Then have each student pick a topic to research or a task that will support their group's presentation.

Study Skills

Have students identify institutions or individuals in their city or state who are authorities on China, Japan, or Korea. Have them make a chart listing the authorities and identifying each one's area of expertise. *(For example: Director of the Japan Society; chairman of Chinese Language Studies at a state university; Korean consul)*

■ *The United States saw the opportunity for major economic gain through trade with Asian countries.*

GEOGRAPHY

Critical Thinking

Ask students to locate China, Korea, and Japan on the world political map in the Atlas on pages 694–695. Ask students to identify the shortest water route from these nations to Europe and to America."

■ *The smaller nations in the Pacific were important as "stepping stones" to China and Japan.*

CLOSE

Have students answer the Thinking Focus. Ask them to analyze how social and economic factors affected U.S. relationships with Pacific and Far Eastern countries. As a reteaching activity, you may also wish to have the students put their completed cause-and-effect diagrams on the board.

■ *Why did the United States seek to establish trade relations with Asian countries?*

It was known for much of the 19th century as the "Hermit Kingdom." But in 1876, Japan—by then an imperialist nation—forced Korea into a trade relationship. By this time, American businesses were aggressively seeking out new markets for their extra goods. As a result, the United States established a trading agreement with Korea in 1882. ■

Moving into the Pacific

▲ *Queen Liliuokalani, the last monarch of Hawaii, lost control of her country to the United States.*

■ *In what way were smaller nations in the Pacific important to American expansionist plans?*

As the end of the 19th century approached, U.S. foreign policy officials decided that America needed some "stepping stones" to China and Japan. To achieve this goal, the United States claimed the Midway Islands in 1867 and acquired a naval station in the Samoan Islands in 1878. But the stepping stone the American government most wanted to get hold of was Hawaii.

By the end of the 1800s, the population of Hawaii included large numbers of wealthy American sugar planters. They owned much of the land in the islands. Native Hawaiians objected to the growing wealth and power of the Americans.

In 1891, Queen Liliuokalani (*lee lee oo oh kah LAH nee*) ascended the throne in Hawaii. A strong nationalist, she was determined to cut down foreign influence in the islands. "Hawaii for the Hawaiians" was her slogan.

At about the same time, the U.S. Congress placed a tariff on sugar imported from Hawaii to the United States. This policy made Hawaiian sugar more expensive than American sugar. That hurt the fortunes of American planters in Hawaii. The planters knew, however, that if Hawaii became part of the United States, the tariff would no longer apply. Consequently, they plotted to overthrow Queen Liliuokalani. They would then declare Hawaii an American **protectorate,** a country or territory controlled by another nation.

John L. Stevens, the American minister to Hawaii, supported the planters. Stevens had U.S. marines surround the Hawaiian royal palace in January 1893. The queen and her army were not able to resist the marines. The planters forced the queen to **abdicate,** or give up, her throne. A treaty calling for the annexation of Hawaii was drafted.

In 1893, newly-elected President Grover Cleveland became upset over the matter and called for an investigation. He then rejected the planters' revolution and offered to reinstate Queen Liliuokalani. Cleveland abandoned the matter, however, when the angry queen said that she would cut off the heads of the revolutionists. Five years later, in 1898, Congress annexed the Hawaiian Islands through a joint resolution. ■

REVIEW

1. **FOCUS** What social and economic factors led the United States to pursue a policy of international expansion after the Civil War?
2. **CONNECT** In what ways was the philosophy of social Darwinism similar to the earlier concept of Manifest Destiny?
3. **ECONOMICS** After the Civil War, "supply exceeded demand" in the United States. Why did this overproduction lead to the desire to create a worldwide American empire?
4. **CRITICAL THINKING** What assumptions did many Americans have about the peoples of Asia and Latin America in the late 1800s?
5. **ACTIVITY** Using the world map on pages 694–695, locate Hawaii, Samoa, and the Midway Islands.

Homework Options

Ask students to find newspaper and magazine articles that explain the current U.S. relationships with Japan, Korea, China, and the Philippines.

Study Guide: page 77.

Answers to Review Questions

1. A saturated market at home and the philosophy of social Darwinism led the United States to expand internationally.
2. Both concepts provided a justification for expansion based on a belief in cultural superiority.
3. Businesses wanted to have more places to sell their goods, as well as access to more raw materials and cheap labor.
4. Sample answer: Many Americans saw themselves as "fitter" than the peoples of Asia and Latin America. Allow for personal opinion.
5. Hawaii is directly south of Alaska and west of Los Angeles; Samoa is south and west of Hawaii; and the Midway Islands are northwest of Hawaii.

1850 1860 1870 1880 1890 1917 1920

L E S S O N 2

Conflict and Conquest

When French Emperor Napoleon III saw a chance to expand his empire at the United States' expense, he didn't hesitate. With the Union and the Confederacy bogged down in a bloody Civil War, he decided to extend his country's influence into the Americas.

The Monroe Doctrine clearly warned against European colonization in North and South America. But Napoleon III took advantage of the American Civil War to occupy Mexico in 1863. He wanted to set up a "puppet" government—one that would appêar to be independent but would follow Napoleon III's orders. The emperor chose Archduke Maximilian of Austria to be the head of this government. Maximilian went to Mexico. With the help of Mexicans who supported Napoleon III, he took the throne offered him.

Secretary of State Seward immediately protested the move. He took no further action, however, because he did not want to bring France into open alliance with the Confederacy. But when the Civil War ended, Seward quickly sent an army of 50,000 Union troops to the Mexican border. Preoccupied with tensions in Europe, Napoleon III did not want war with America. He immediately abandoned his puppet empire. The Mexicans quickly overthrew the government and executed the ill-fated Maximilian.

THINKING FOCUS

What steps did U.S. Presidents take in the late 19th and early 20th centuries to keep European nations away from Latin America and to extend U.S. control over the region?

Key Terms

- yellow journalism
- imperialism

Policing the Hemisphere

Latin America was not only a source of profitable trade for the United States. It also acted as a defense against invasion by foreign countries. Through the use of diplomacy and military force, the United States maintained its leading role in the region during the last half of the 19th century. The American government used the Monroe Doctrine to explain its position.

In spite of the Monroe Doctrine, European nations went on trying to establish claims in Latin America. In 1878, for example, the French made plans to build a canal through Panama. "A canal under American control, or no canal," President Rutherford B. Hayes declared. He sent two warships into Panamanian waters to enforce his resolve.

Similarly, in 1895, Venezuela

This 1889 political cartoon shows Uncle Sam invoking the Monroe Doctrine against European governments that wanted to participate in the building of a canal through Panama.

INTRODUCE

Read the lesson title and the Thinking Focus aloud. Ask students why the expansionist outlook of the United States might lead to conflict. Ask what the word *conquest* probably refers to in this context. *(Conquering other nations in battle)* Have students scan the lesson to find out which part of the world will be the lesson's main focus. *(Latin America)*

Key Terms

Vocabulary strategies: T36–37

yellow journalism—a style of newspaper reporting popular in the 1890s that featured exaggerated writing and sensational headlines

imperialism—the attempt to create an empire by controlling other countries through either economic or political means

Graphic Overview

Cause
Monroe Doctrine

→ **U.S. Interests in Western Hemisphere** →

Effects
- Panama Canal
- Spanish-American War
- interference in Mexican affairs

Objectives

1. Explain why the United States decided to enforce the Monroe Doctrine strictly.
2. Summarize the factors that led to war with Spain and describe the course of the war.
3. State why the United States built the Panama Canal.
4. Identify the reasons for the tension between the United States and Mexico during the 1910s.

DEVELOP

Have students preview the main heads of the lesson to note the major conflicts covered in this lesson. Tell them to read the lesson to find out the effects of each conflict.

■ *The United States invoked the Monroe Doctrine when Venezuela asked the United States to take its side in a boundary dispute with Great Britain.*

POLITICAL SYSTEMS

Critical Thinking

The sort of imperialism practiced by powerful nations in the nineteenth century is less common today. Ask students to consider how world powers such as the United States and the Soviet Union exert control over other countries. *(Sample answer: They make certain that friendly leaders are elected or installed; they use economic aid as a tool of control; and they maintain armies to prop up unpopular governments.)*

■ *Under what circumstances did the United States invoke the Monroe Doctrine in the late 1800s?*

asked the United States to take its side in a dispute with Great Britain over the boundary between British Guiana (now Guyana) and Venezuela. Secretary of State Richard Olney urged Britain to choose a neutral nation to resolve the dispute. The British refused. They said that the United States had no right to step in. In the end, however, Britain backed down and agreed to arbitration. Once again, the United States had shown it was determined to enforce the Monroe Doctrine. ■

Conflict with Spain

America's desire for Cuba was the main factor that led to armed conflict between the United States and Spain. With its profitable sugar cane crops and well-situated harbors, Cuba was a prize worth winning. During the 1800s, the United States tried several times to take the island away from Spain. Although the attempts failed, they reflected a widely held desire by Americans for expansion.

The Pressure for War Builds

The Cuban people eventually tried to cast off Spanish rule in 1895. To punish the Cubans, Spanish General Valerano Weyler—called the "Butcher" in Cuba—sent hundreds of thousands of Cuban civilians to "concentration" camps. Nearly one quarter of Cuba's population died of starvation or disease in those deadly camps.

Most Americans sympathized with the Cubans' fight for independence. When reports of the horrible suffering in Weyler's camps began to reach the United States, the public's sympathy turned to outrage. American newspapers kept this sense of outrage alive with exaggerated stories of Spanish cruelty. "The old, the young, the weak, the crippled—all are

UNDERSTANDING IMPERIALISM

In the late 1800s and early 1900s, a handful of countries took control of less powerful nations all over the globe. France, Germany, and Great Britain established colonies in Asia and Africa. Following their lead, the United States set up colonies in Latin America and the Pacific. By 1930, the United States and European nations controlled about 84 percent of the land surface of the world. The term *imperialism* is the name we give this policy of extending a nation's power by gaining economic and political control of other nations.

Why Expand?

The chief motivation behind imperialism is usually economic gain. Powerful nations can establish new markets for their manufactured goods. In addition, less developed nations often provide huge sources of inexpensive labor and raw materials.

Despite the importance of economics, Americans usually cited other reasons to justify their imperialism. Many Americans believed that they had a right and obligation to extend what they considered their superior culture to people less fortunate than themselves. In some cases, religious and humanitarian goals lead to imperialistic action. Many imperialists believed that they had a God-given mission to spread Christianity. In the process, they often brought schools, modern medicine, and advanced technologies to the countries they controlled.

What Happened to Colonies?

Colonies all over the globe sought independence from imperialist powers in the 1900s. After World War II, the United States and Europe let go of colonies as their peoples demanded freedom.

Access Activity

Refer students to the cartoon on page 533. What does it show? *(America is a lion blocking the way of comical European figures.)* Was the cartoonist in favor of or opposed to U.S. policy? *(In favor)* How is that apparent? *(The lion is a positive symbol.)* What message do the relative sizes of the figures convey? *(That America is more powerful than the Europeans)*

Access Strategy

Use a globe to review with students the continents in the Western Hemisphere. Remind students that in Chapter 5 they learned about an 1823 declaration known as the Monroe Doctrine. Ask them who wrote it. *(Secretary of State John Quincy Adams and President James Monroe)* What did it concern? *(Further expansion of European power into North and South America)* What did it forbid European countries from doing? *(Colonizing the Americas or interfering with newly created countries in the Americas)* What did the United States promise in return? *(Not to interfere in the internal concerns of European countries)*

Explain that this lesson explores the actions that the United States took at the turn of the twentieth century to establish and maintain power in the Western Hemisphere. Point out that Americans claimed that the Monroe Doctrine gave them the right to take these actions.

butchered without mercy," reported the New York *World*.

Newspapers such as Joseph Pulitzer's *World* and William Randolph Hearst's New York *Journal* developed a new kind of reporting called **yellow journalism**. Featuring huge headlines and melodramatic stories, the yellow press twisted facts in order to influence public opinion and to attract readers.

In February 1898, an American warship named the *Maine* blew up in Havana harbor. Two hundred sixty-two officers and sailors were killed. The official investigation proved inconclusive. Still, the yellow press blamed Spain for the tragedy. Newspapers stirred up the public with the cry, "Remember the *Maine*!" Over the next two months the calls for war grew steadily louder. Finally, on April 19, 1898, Congress declared Cuba's independence and authorized President McKinley to use force to drive Spain from the island.

The Spanish-American War

The dispute over Cuba directly set off the Spanish-American War. The first battles of the war, however, took place on the other side of the world in the Spanish-controlled Philippine Islands. Two months before the war began, Assistant Secretary of the Navy Theodore Roosevelt had alerted Commodore George Dewey, who was stationed near the Philippines, to be ready for war.

As soon as the war began, Dewey set off from Hong Kong for the Philippines. On April 30, less than a week after the United States' official declaration of war, Dewey arrived at Manila Bay. The next morning at dawn he opened fire and sank Spain's entire Pacific fleet in the battle of Manila. He then requested additional troops from President McKinley. With the help of Filipino rebels, he took complete control of the Philippines by early August.

Dewey's great naval victory in the Philippines increased the American public's excitement about what Secretary of State John Hay called a "splendid little war." Future U.S. President Theodore Roosevelt viewed war as an adventure and a challenge. When the conflict with Spain began, he quickly resigned as Assistant Secretary of the Navy. He became second in command of a ragtag group of volunteers called the Rough Riders.

Made up of cowboys, miners, college students, and society men, the Rough Riders embodied the frontier spirit and "joy in battle" that Roosevelt so dearly loved. Roosevelt became a national hero when he led the Rough Riders to victory in a charge up San Juan Hill.

The fighting in Cuba proved to be as one-sided as the fighting in the Philippines had been. On July 3, two days after the Rough Riders took San Juan Hill, the U.S. Navy destroyed the Spanish Caribbean fleet in Santiago Harbor. Spain could hardly keep fighting after that. On August 12, 1898, the defeated Spanish government signed a truce.

But while victory came quickly and only 379 Americans died in actual combat, the Spanish-American War was far from splendid. Because of the army's bad management and poor planning, many American

The yellow press was quick to blame Spain for the sinking of the Maine. *William Randolph Hearst's* New York Journal *offered a $50,000 reward for evidence explaining the disaster.*

$50,000 REWARD.—WHO DESTROYED THE MAINE?—$50,000 REWARD.

NEW YORK JOURNAL AND ADVERTISER.

DESTRUCTION OF THE WAR SHIP MAINE WAS THE WORK OF AN ENEMY

$50,000! $50,000 REWARD! For the Detection of the Perpetrator of the Maine Outrage!

Assistant Secretary Roosevelt Convinced the Explosion of the War Ship Was Not an Accident.

The Journal Offers $50,000 Reward for the Conviction of the Criminals Who Sent 258 American Sailors to Their Death. Naval Officers Unanimous That the Ship Was Destroyed on Purpose.

$50,000! $50,000 REWARD! For the Detection of the Perpetrator of the Maine Outrage!

HISTORY

Critical Thinking

Ask students why the United States was determined to maintain its exclusive interest in the affairs of Latin America. *(Latin America provided profitable trade as well as a defense against potential invasion.)* Ask whether they think these reasons could justify U.S. military actions in the region. Why or why not?

SOCIAL SYSTEMS

Critical Thinking

Ask students to describe the intended effect of "yellow journalism" stories on readers. *(To influence public opinion and attract readers)* Ask them whether distorting the facts to achieve these goals was justified. Why or why not?

Historical Context

Theodore Roosevelt was a man of great complexity. A well-regarded historian and an accomplished writer, he inspired poet Robert Frost to say, "He was our kind." He was also a tough reformer. As governor of New York, he angered corporations and political bosses with new tax and regulatory programs and pro-labor laws. He also had a boyish enthusiasm for adventure, especially for war. "No triumph of peace is quite so great as the supreme triumph of war," he said.

Roosevelt's vibrant personality attracted reporters and enabled him to gain most of the press on the Rough Riders, though he was only the second in command. His war record with the Rough Riders helped him to win the governorship of New York. Anxious to get rid of this reformer, Boss Platt of New York talked him into running for the vice-presidency. A year after his election, McKinley was assassinated, and Roosevelt, at 42, became America's youngest President.

Critical Thinking

Ask students to contrast the purpose of the Monroe Doctrine when it was first formulated with its later application as a rationale for imperialist policies. *(The American attitude changed from protectionism to domination of Latin America.)* Ask students whether they think the United States needed the Monroe Doctrine to accomplish its goals.

GEOGRAPHY

Map and Globe Skills

Have students use the maps on this page to answer the following questions. What strategy did U.S. ships use to win the battle in Cuba? *(A blockade)* Where was the blockade set up? *(Around Santiago Bay)* How far is Havana from Key West, Florida? *(Less than 100 miles)* From what direction did Dewey sail into Manila Bay? *(Northwest)*

HISTORY

Critical Thinking

Ask students why the United States was so eager for the war with Spain. *(National pride and desire for expansion)* Why did the war with Spain lead to an even longer war with the Philippines? *(For American military and economic reasons)*

Spanish–American War in Cuba

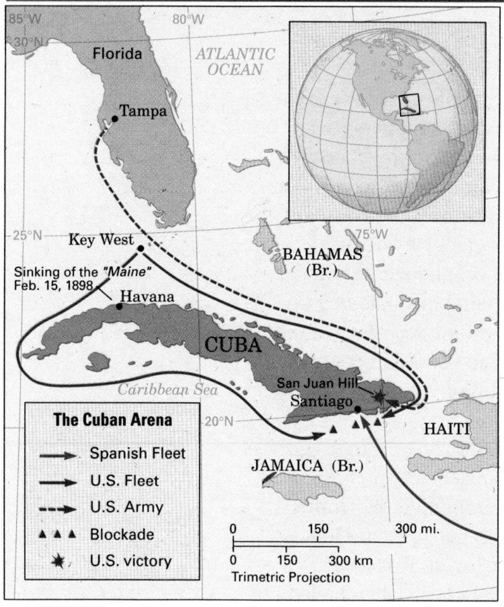

Spanish–American War in Philippines

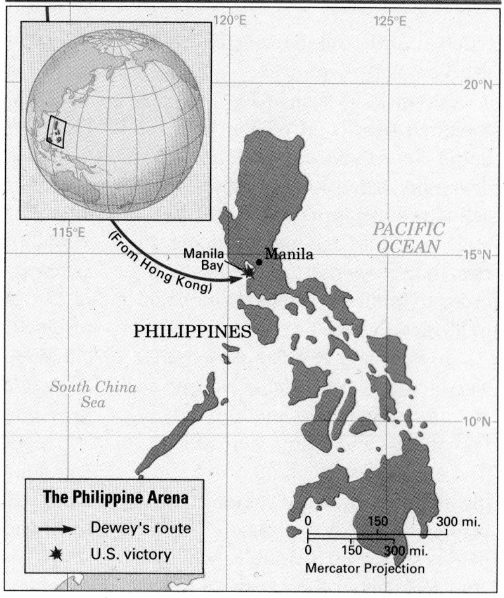

The Spanish-American War was fought on two fronts on opposite sides of the world; nevertheless, the United States defeated Spain in just three months.

soldiers did not have guns, tents, or blankets. Food was often in short supply. Much worse, more than 5,400 Americans died of food poisoning, malaria, dysentery, and yellow fever.

Under the provisions of the peace treaty signed on December 10, 1898, Spain gave up Puerto Rico, Guam, and the Philippines to the United States. Although Cuba received its independence, the United States refused to withdraw its army. The United States wanted the Cubans to incorporate the Platt Amendment of 1901 into their new constitution. This amendment gave the United States the right to ensure "a government adequate for the protection of life, property, and individual liberty." Between 1901 and 1934, when the U.S. Congress finally repealed the Platt Amendment, the United States sent troops into Cuba several times to protect American business interests on the island.

Filipinos Fight for Independence

Filipino rebels helped the United States to defeat Spain in the summer of 1898. These Filipinos, who were fighting to secure their own independence, thought that once the war was over, the Americans would pack up and go home. When Spain had been defeated, however, the American government decided it wanted to keep control of the islands for military and economic reasons.

A small but outspoken group of Americans, calling themselves the Anti-Imperialist League, argued against the takeover of the Philippines. The League's members included such well-known and influential people as Mark Twain, William Jennings Bryan, Jane Addams, Samuel Gompers, and Andrew Carnegie. They were against all forms of **imperialism,** the attempt to control other nations by economic or political means. They also believed that seizing the Philippines went against the political ideals on which America had been founded:

> *We hold that the policy known as imperialism is hostile to liberty and tends toward militarism, an evil from which it has been our glory to be free. . . . We insist that the subjugation of any people is "criminal aggression" and open disloyalty to the distinctive principles of our government.*

Critical Thinking

Have students read the quotation on this page from the Anti-Imperialist League. Do they agree or disagree with its sentiments? Why? What is meant by "the distinctive principles of our government"? *(Democracy, individual liberty, self-determination)*

Cultural Context

In 1896, Joseph Pulitzer initiated in the *New York World* the first colored Sunday comics. In the comic strip "The Yellow Kid" by Richard C. Outcault, captions were written on "the Kid's" baggy yellow shirt. Pulitzer's competitor William Randolph Hearst quickly enticed the creator of this popular cartoon over to the *New York Journal.* Pulitzer bought him back. There were bids and counterbids and competitive sensations, creating the term *yellow journalism.*

Economic Context

Americans made great advances in transportation between 1860 and 1920. Steamships were an important improvement in the United States's new merchant and naval fleets. George B. Selden achieved the first working gasoline auto engine in 1879. Charles and Frank Duryea perfected the first American automobile in 1893. Henry Ford built his first automobile in 1896 and an improved version in 1899. Orville and Wilbur Wright made their first successful flight in 1903.

To the imperialists, the idea that the United States might do something wrong was inconceivable. Convinced by social Darwinism of America's superiority, they swept aside all opposing arguments and annexed the Philippines in 1899. President McKinley declared it was America's duty to "educate the Filipinos, and uplift and civilize and Christianize them."

The resulting war against the Philippines (1899–1902) proved to be longer and more difficult than the war against Spain. In a total about-face, the United States became the unwelcome oppressor of an unwilling colony. About 70,000 American troops spent two years fighting in the jungles of the Philippines, and 5,000 of them died there. Eight thousand Filipinos—men, women, and children—died in the first year of the war alone. After a bitter struggle, the Filipinos finally surrendered in early 1902. They did not gain their independence until July 4, 1946. ■

■ *What events led the United States to declare war on Spain?*

Building the Panama Canal

Victory over the Spanish fueled American desire to rule the Western Hemisphere. To advance this goal and to improve their access to markets in Asia and Latin America, American businesses planned to build a canal through Central America. Theodore Roosevelt, who had become President after McKinley's assassination in 1901, quickly acted on this plan.

In 1903, Panama was still a province of Colombia. That year the Colombian government refused to sell the strip of land in Panama that the United States needed to build a canal. President Roosevelt was furious.

In Panama, however, many people were eager for the money that would pour into their region if the canal were built. They staged a revolution with unofficial encouragement from the United States government. No one died in the revolt, which soon ended with a Panamanian victory and a declaration of independence. Fifteen days later, on November 18, 1903, the United States secured the right to build and operate a canal through Panama. The Closer Look on the following two pages examines the difficulties involved in building the canal.

In 1904, the President added the "Roosevelt Corollary" to the Monroe Doctrine. He claimed the right to intervene in the internal affairs of Latin American nations to ensure that the United States had "stable, orderly, and prosperous neighbors."

◄ *This political cartoon portrays Teddy Roosevelt as the police officer of the world. The "big stick" came to symbolize Roosevelt's foreign policy.*

BELIEF SYSTEMS

Critical Thinking

Refer students to the statement on this page by President McKinley that it was America's duty to "educate the Filipinos, and uplift and civilize and Christianize them." Explain that many Filipinos were then and still are Catholic. What does McKinley's statement reveal about his attitude toward the Filipinos? *(Attitude of superiority)* Can "uplifting" a country ever be a good reason for taking it over? Why or why not?

■ *The actions of Valeriano Weyler and the attack on the Maine led the United States to declare war on Spain.*

537

Language Arts Connection

Supply students with copies of a couple of major city newspapers such as the *New York Times* or the *Los Angeles Times*, as well as copies of more sensational papers such as those at grocery store checkout counters. Help them analyze the extent to which each paper uses sensationalism to attract readers. How does journalism today compare with the "yellow journalism" of the early 1900s?

Science Connection

Have students do research to find out how steamships, early automobile engines, and early airplanes worked. Have them write short reports tracing the improvements that were made between 1900 and 1920. Encourage them to make drawings or models of the period's ships, cars, and airplanes. Display their reports on the board or have students combine them in a class publication.

Visual Learning

Ask students to interpret the cartoon on this page. Why is President Roosevelt wearing a police uniform? *(To show that he is acting as police officer of the world)* How do the other figures in the cartoon seem to feel about Roosevelt? *(Afraid and respectful)* What do the contrasting sizes of the figures indicate? *(Roosevelt is the most powerful.)*

GEOGRAPHY

Visual Learning

Explain that the drawing extending across both pages shows a horizontal cross section of the Isthmus, the location of the canal. Have the students identify the locations of the Gatun, Pedro Miguel, and Miraflores locks on the map on this page. Ask them to refer to the cross-sectional drawing to identify the approximate elevations of the locks. Ask them to locate on the map the mountain range shown on the cross-sectional drawing.

More About the Mosquitoes The deadly diseases yellow fever and malaria are each carried by a different kind of mosquito. The *Anopheles* mosquito carries malaria, and the *Stegomyia* mosquito carries yellow fever.

A CLOSER LOOK

Building the Panama Canal

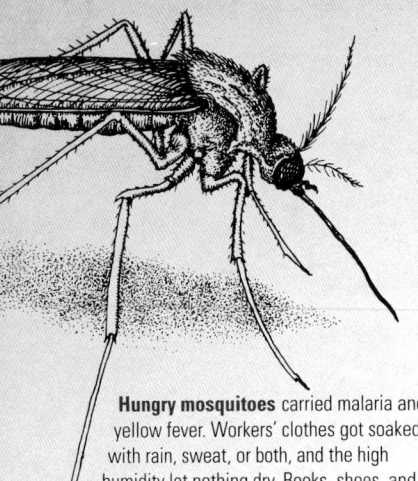

The French had tried to build a canal across Panama in the 1880s, but bad planning and widespread disease forced them to give up. After the United States secured the rights to build a canal through Panama, Americans arrived in droves. They brought dreams of hefty wages and high adventure. But for them too, the challenges of living and working in a hot, wet jungle soon set in.

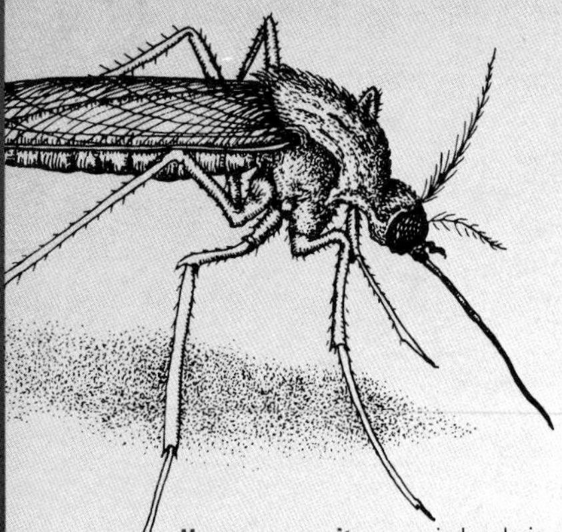

Hungry mosquitoes carried malaria and yellow fever. Workers' clothes got soaked with rain, sweat, or both, and the high humidity let nothing dry. Books, shoes, and knapsacks grew mold overnight.

From north to south, ships journey through an elaborate system of locks that raise and lower the water level. As the map and drawing below show, they also travel through various channels and lakes on the 50-mile journey that connects the Atlantic and Pacific Oceans.

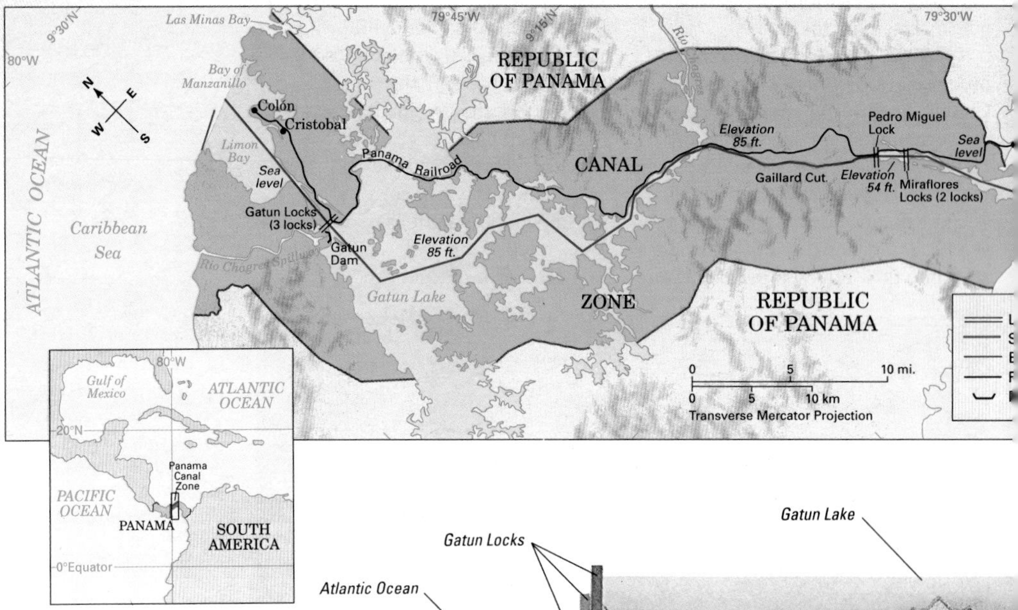

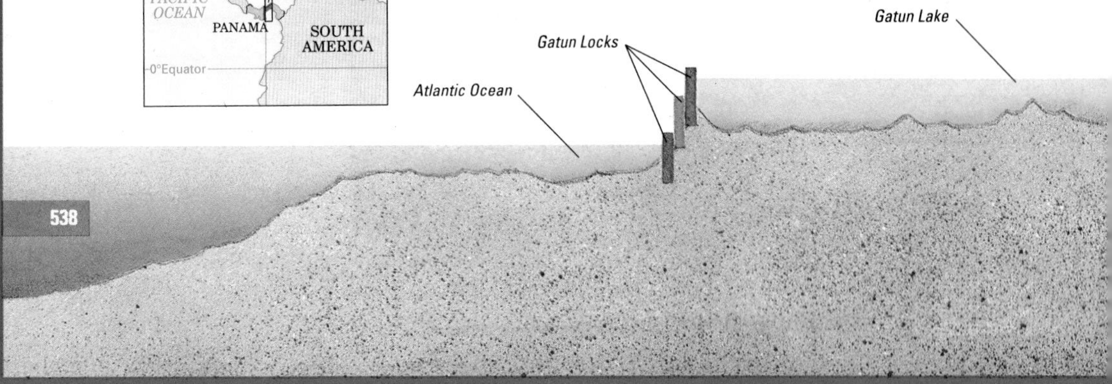

Critical Thinking

After students have examined A Closer Look at the Panama Canal, ask them to imagine that they have signed on to work on the canal. How do they feel about the threat of yellow fever and malaria? What would make facing these dangers worthwhile?

Building a Model

To accommodate changes in the elevation of the land, the Panama Canal uses locks, huge chambers of water, to raise and lower ships as they cross the Isthmus of Panama. Have students research to find out how locks work. Encourage students to construct a model of a Panama Canal lock.

Debate

Have students role play a debate in 1898 between the Philippines and the United States over the issue of Philippine independence. Have both teams research the issue to find out the political and economic needs of each country. The American team should focus on the technological and economic benefits of annexing the Philippines. The Philippine team can focus on their desire to solve their own problems in their own way.

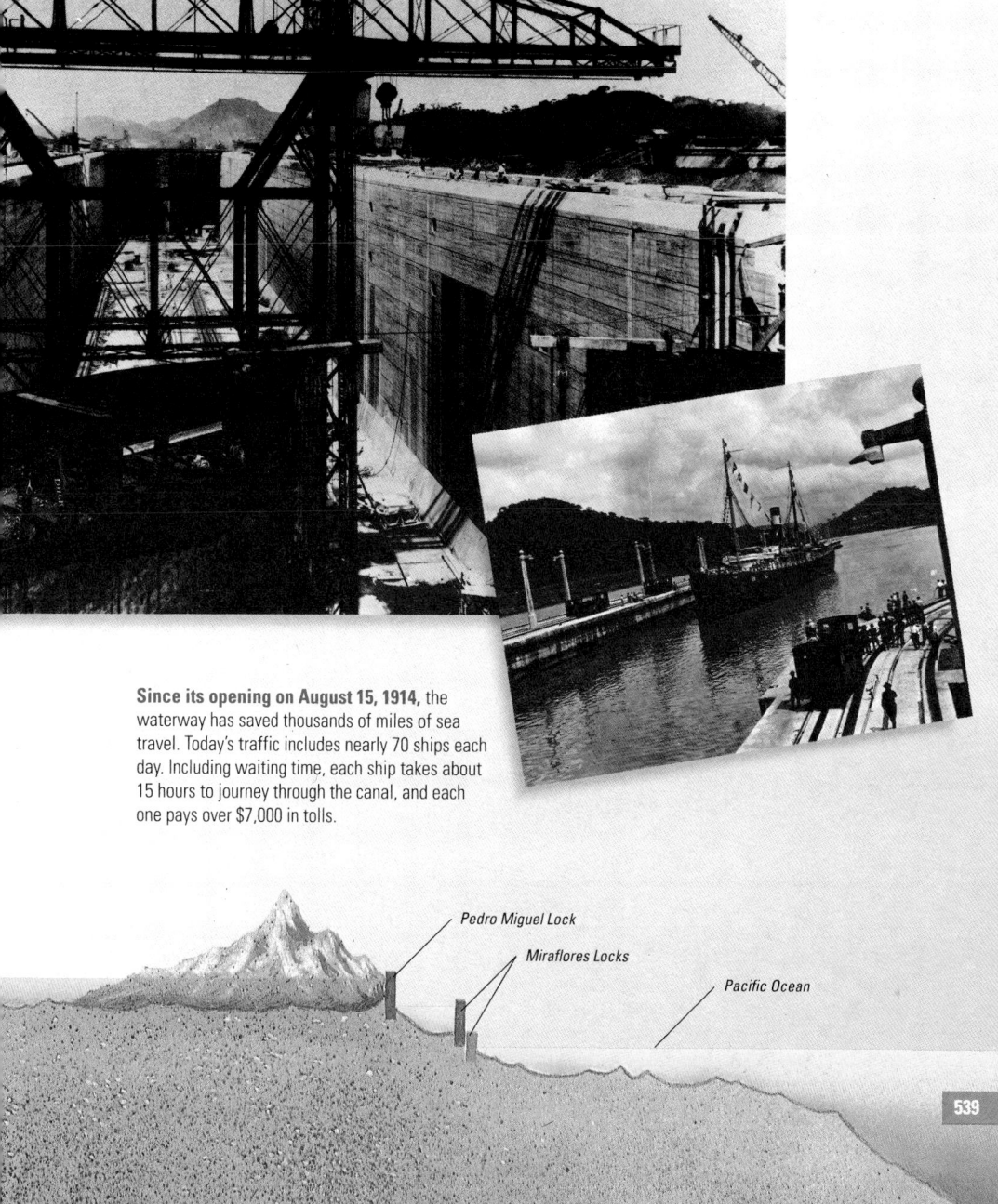

"They are eating steadily into the ground." This was President Roosevelt's comment when he saw the construction work. Engineers studied and sketched, but during the rainy season, whole sides of mountains collapsed into the newly formed ditches. Construction took ten years, and costs were astronomical: $352 million and 5,609 lives.

Since its opening on August 15, 1914, the waterway has saved thousands of miles of sea travel. Today's traffic includes nearly 70 ships each day. Including waiting time, each ship takes about 15 hours to journey through the canal, and each one pays over $7,000 in tolls.

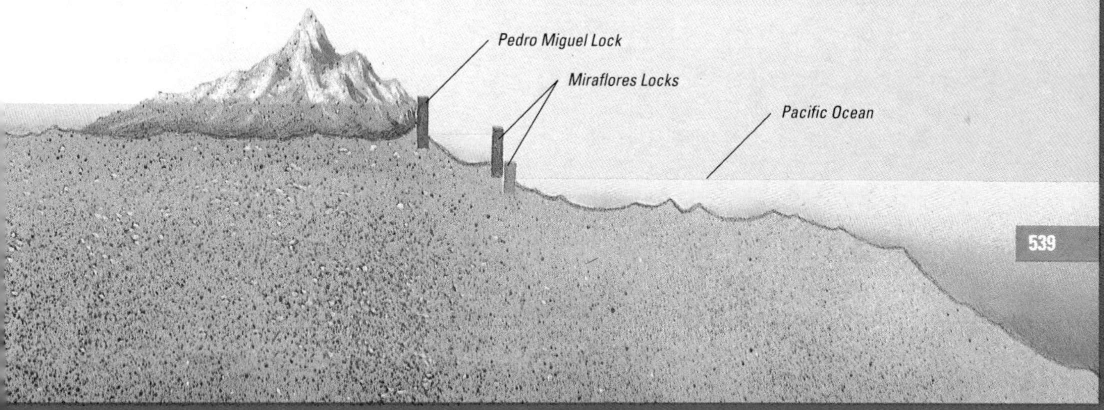

ECONOMICS

Visual Learning

Point out that although the engineering technology that made the canal possible was well known at the turn of the century, the sheer size of the task put its successful completion into doubt. Have students list some of the practical problems that might plague a large project in a distant location.

More About the Cost of Lives

The digging of the Panama canal took a tremendous toll on human life. Of the 5,609 people who died on the American project, 4,500 were black, mostly Jamaicans. Only 350 Americans died. Estimates of deaths that took place during the French canal attempt ran to nearly 20,000.

Writing a Diary Entry

Have students imagine that they are a Filipino leader in 1898 who has fought to remove Spanish rule from the Philippines and who has just learned that the Americans now plan to stay. Write an entry for that person's diary, describing his or her reaction and predicting what the American decision will mean for the future of the Philippines.

Visual Learning

Each lock of the Panama Canal is 1,000 feet long and 110 feet wide. Point out to students that, as large as the canal is, some ships cannot navigate it. Ask students whether a new canal should be dug to accommodate those ships. Might a new canal cause political problems? Why or why not?

■ *The Panama Canal gave American businesses better access to markets in Asia and Latin America.*

BELIEF SYSTEMS

Critical Thinking

Have students identify the ways in which U.S. military intervention in Mexico could be justified and the ways in which it could be criticized. *(Students should give reasons for their answers.)*

■ *When Mexican officials arrested members of the* USS Dolphin *in 1914, President Wilson had an excuse for trying to topple Huerta's regime. Wilson also sent troops to Mexico in 1916 in response to Pancho Villa's raids.*

CLOSE

After students answer the Thinking Focus, copy on the board the Graphic Overview from page 533 and have students complete it together. As a reteaching activity, ask students to define *imperialism* and clarify how it related to America's expansionist goals.

■ *What was the importance of the Panama Canal to the United States?*

As a result of this corollary, Roosevelt was known to "speak softly and carry a big stick" in foreign affairs.

Between 1904 and 1917, American Presidents invoked the Roosevelt Corollary on numerous occasions. The United States sent troops at one time or another to Haiti, Panama, Cuba, Nicaragua, Mexico, and the Dominican Republic, both to put down political revolts and to protect U.S. citizens and businesses. ■

Tension with Mexico

➤ *Mexican revolutionary leader "Pancho" Villa eluded the American troops that President Woodrow Wilson sent to capture him in 1916.*

A revolution in Mexico in 1911 overthrew dictator Porfirio Diaz and established a democratic government. Two years later, however, General Victoriano Huerta, head of the Mexican army, murdered the new President and seized power. President Woodrow Wilson refused to recognize Huerta's regime and vowed to remove the "government of butchers."

On April 9, 1914, Mexican officials arrested members of the USS *Dolphin* in Tampico for landing their boat without authorization. This incident gave Wilson the excuse he wanted to intervene in Mexican affairs. The President ordered the U.S. Navy to take the Mexican port of Veracruz. Nineteen Americans and 126 Mexicans died in the battle that followed. Huerta's government fell soon afterwards, but the Mexican people were outraged by America's intervention.

■ *Why did the United States intervene in Mexican affairs on several occasions between 1914 and 1917?*

In August 1914, the American-supported candidate, Venustiano Carranza, became President of Mexico. However, many Mexicans continued to resent American interference in their nation's affairs. One of these Mexicans, a rebel general named Francisco "Pancho" Villa, held up a train in Chihuahua, took 16 American passengers hostage, and killed them. In a separate raid, he killed 19 Americans in New Mexico.

Furious, President Wilson sent troops under the command of General John J. Pershing into Mexico in 1916, but they failed to capture Villa. The Carranza government immediately protested this intervention. Tension between the two nations was nearing the breaking point when the United States abruptly withdrew its troops in January 1917. Wilson had more pressing concerns: German submarine attacks on U.S. ships were triggering American involvement in World War I. ■

REVIEW

1. **FOCUS** What steps did U.S. Presidents take in the late 19th and early 20th centuries to keep European nations away from Latin America and to extend U.S. control over the region?
2. **CONNECT** In what way did the 1823 Monroe Doctrine play an important role in American foreign affairs in the late 1800s?
3. **HISTORY** Why did the United States want a canal through Panama? What challenges did the United States have to overcome to build the canal?
4. **CRITICAL THINKING** Why did President Theodore Roosevelt claim for the United States the right to intervene in the internal affairs of Latin American countries?
5. **ACTIVITY** Read the Monroe Doctrine on pages 668–669. Think about how this document influenced events in the late 1800s.

Homework Options

Have students gather and share newspaper articles on the United States's current policies in Mexico, Central or South America, or the Philippines.

Study Guide: page 78.

Answers to Review Questions

1. U.S. Presidents engaged the nation in wars with Spain and the Philippines, interfered in Mexican affairs, and secured the right to build and operate the Panama Canal.
2. The United States used the Monroe Doctrine to maintain its exclusive interest in Latin America.
3. The Colombian government would not sell the necessary strip of land in Panama. After the Panamanians successfully revolted against Colombia, the United States secured the right to build and operate the canal.
4. Sample answer: Roosevelt claimed that intervention was necessary to ensure that the United States had "stable, orderly, and prosperous neighbors." Allow for personal opinion.
5. The Monroe Doctrine allowed the United States to explain its expansionist policy as a long-held traditional right.

1850 1860 1870 1880 1890 1900 1910 1914 1918 1920

L E S S O N 3

America at War

"It is a fearful thing to lead this great peaceful people into war, into the most terrible and disastrous of all wars," said President Woodrow Wilson on April 2, 1917. His audience of Congressional representatives, Supreme Court justices, Cabinet officers, and diplomats rose to its feet in a long round of cheering and handclapping.

President Wilson thought it strange that America had received his message—which spelled certain death for many of its young men—with applause. Late that night, the President laid his head on the long table in the Cabinet room and cried.

Ironically, Wilson had won reelection just a few months earlier as the peace candidate. In fact, his slogan during the 1916 campaign was, "He kept us out of war!" The message was one that Americans wanted to hear in the fall of 1916.

However, within months of Wilson's victory, German submarines sank five American ships. With a heavy heart, the "peace candidate" declared that America would enter the First World War.

THINKING FOCUS

What kept the United States out of World War I initially, and what prompted it to enter the war in 1917 on the side of the Allies?

Key Terms

- mobilize
- armistice

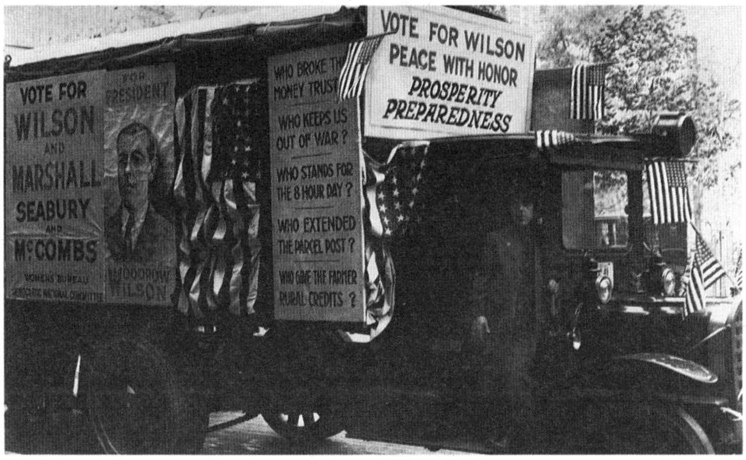

This photograph shows one of President Woodrow Wilson's campaign trucks in the 1916 election. Although Wilson won reelection as the "peace" candidate, he led the United States into World War I a few months later.

War Sweeps Europe

By the time the United States became involved in 1917, the war in Europe had been going on for three years. Powerful European countries were always aware that their colonized people could start a war in order to gain independence. In addition, the competition for colonies had created intense rivalries that could spark war between European powers.

The nations of Europe tried to create some security for themselves by

INTRODUCE

Compare the lesson title with the title of the previous lesson. Point out that the military conflicts described in the last lesson were far more limited in scope than those in World War I—the war they will read about in this lesson. Have students read the Thinking Focus and recall how Americans had felt about the war with Spain. Explain that war raged in Europe for almost three years before the United States became actively involved. Suggest that students read the lesson to find out why U.S. policy toward the European war changed in 1917.

Key Terms

Vocabulary strategies: T36–37

mobilize—to prepare or put into operation for war

armistice—a truce or temporary pause, agreed to by both sides, in a war or battle

Graphic Overview

U.S. neutrality ➤ • Zimmermann Telegram • Lusitania ➤ U.S. declaration of war on Germany ➤ • mobilization • Selective Service Act ➤ new kind of war

Objectives

1. Summarize the factors that led to World War I.
2. Describe the process by which the United States was eventually drawn into the conflict in Europe.
3. Evaluate the role that the United States played in World War I and describe the nature of modern warfare.

DEVELOP

Tell students to look for answers to the following questions as they read. What key events occurred before United States's entry in the war? What was warfare like in this first major war of the modern industrial age? What effect did modern technology have on the course of World War I?

HISTORY

Critical Thinking

Ask students whether the European nations were wise to form a network of alliances. *(It probably looked like a neccessity at the time because there was such strong competition for territory.)* What problems did the alliances create? *(A nation could be drawn into other nations' squabbles.)*

■ *Austria's annexation of Bosnia, the assassination of Archduke Ferdinand, and the formation of alliances among European countries were factors that led to war.*

■ *What factors and events led to the outbreak of World War I?*

building up huge military forces and making agreements called alliances. The members of an alliance agreed to fight on the side of any other member that was attacked. In 1914, before the outbreak of war, there were two major European alliances: the Triple Alliance, made up of Germany, Austria-Hungary, and Italy, and the Triple Entente, made up of Britain, France, and Russia.

On June 28, 1914, Archduke Francis Ferdinand, heir to the Austro-Hungarian throne, and his wife Sophie led a parade through the streets of Sarajevo, capital of Bosnia. Many Bosnians resented Austria for taking their province from the kingdom of Serbia in 1908. As the Archduke's open car drew up beside a barber shop, an 18-year-old student who belonged to a Serbian nationalist society called "Union or Death" fired into the cab. The Archduke and his wife were instantly killed.

Austria immediately declared war on Serbia, whom it blamed for the assassination. Germany, in accordance with its promise, supported Austria; Russia came to the aid of Serbia. Within weeks, all the powers of Europe were at war. ■

Entering the War

President Wilson at first succeeded in keeping the nation out of World War I. Eventually, however, the United States was forced to choose sides.

American Neutrality

When war broke out in Europe in 1914, President Wilson promoted neutrality, the policy of not taking sides in a war. Although Wilson also discouraged American citizens from taking sides in the war, most Americans were sympathetic toward the Allied Powers: chiefly Britain, France, and Russia. Many Americans had English ancestors, and the French had helped in the American Revolution.

▲ *World War I was the first war in which airplanes played an important role in the fighting.*

Other Americans, many of German descent, sided with the Central Powers: chiefly Germany and Austria-Hungary (Italy had withdrawn its support.) Regardless of their sympathies, most Americans did not want to enter the war on either side.

The End of Neutrality

Throughout the war, President Wilson made efforts to establish a peace agreement. Neither side would agree to negotiate. Each side thought it would soon win the war and be able to name its own terms.

Eventually, Americans got caught in the crossfire of British and German ocean warfare. In 1916, Britain tried to starve the Germans into surrender by preventing ships of any nation from delivering food and raw materials to Germany. The Germans fought Britain's naval blockade with a new weapon: the U-boat, or submarine. German submarines attacked both passenger ships and warships in their attempt to break the British blockade.

Germany had warned early in 1915 that it would attack any ship that entered a war zone around Britain. Americans protested that the policy was brutal and unfair. Germany countered that many "neutral" vessels were in fact carrying American-made weapons to the British.

On May 7, 1915, while sailing

Access Activity

Use the following questions to stimulate discussion of the concept of war. What are the goals of combatants in war? Does a war actually secure these goals? Who loses in a war? What positive results of war might be obtained in a peaceful manner?

Access Strategy

Explain that an alliance consists of people bonding together for a common purpose. Ask them to name alliances that Americans had formed earlier in their history for a political or social cause. Have one student write the class responses on the board. *(The colonies formed the United States under the Articles of Confederation; the United States allied itself with France against England; and the Southern states formed the Confederate States of America.)*

Tell students that in this lesson they will learn about European alliances that were primarily promises between nations to help each other in war. Tell them that these alliances brought many nations into World War I in spite of the fact that those countries had little to do with the issues that started the war.

from New York to Liverpool, the British passenger ship *Lusitania* was attacked and sunk by a German submarine. The death toll of more than 1,200 people included 128 Americans. Although the United States did not enter the war as a result of this incident, pressure mounted on President Wilson to change his policy from one of neutrality to one of military preparation.

America finally decided to enter the war in February 1917. That month Britain intercepted and conveyed to American officials a secret message from the German foreign secretary, Arthur Zimmermann, to the German minister in Mexico. The "Zimmermann Telegram" asked Mexico to fight with Germany against the United States if the United States abandoned its policy of neutrality and entered the war. In exchange for its support, Germany promised to win for Mexico the territory it had lost to the United States in 1848 in Texas, New Mexico, and Arizona.

Faced with such concrete evidence of Germany's hostile attitude toward the United States, President Wilson could hold out no longer. On April 2, 1917, he delivered the speech that you read about at the beginning of this lesson. On April 6, the Congress of the United States officially declared war on Germany. ■

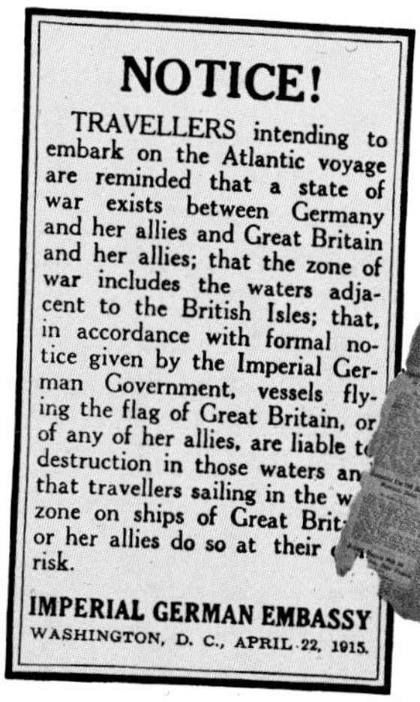
NOTICE!

TRAVELLERS intending to embark on the Atlantic voyage are reminded that a state of war exists between Germany and her allies and Great Britain and her allies; that the zone of war includes the waters adjacent to the British Isles; that, in accordance with formal notice given by the Imperial German Government, vessels flying the flag of Great Britain, or of any of her allies, are liable t destruction in those waters an that travellers sailing in the w zone on ships of Great Brit or her allies do so at their risk.

IMPERIAL GERMAN EMBASSY
WASHINGTON, D. C., APRIL 22, 1915.

LOS ANGELES TRIBUNE
37 AMERICANS IN 1214 LUSITANIA LOSS

▲ *Before sinking the* Lusitania, *the German government published a warning in American newspapers to people considering an Atlantic crossing.*

■ *What caused President Wilson to turn his back on neutrality and declare war on Germany?*

Fighting the War

Now the American government faced the problem of how to **mobilize,** or assemble, an army that could help the Allies. President Wilson had started to strengthen the nation's army in 1916. He also had a powerful navy ready for battle. But when America entered the war, rifles, machine guns, and artillery pieces were in short supply. Clearly a large army would have to be recruited and trained at short notice, and industry would have to start producing war materials. By the end of 1917, every part of American society was focused on the war effort.

Mobilizing an Army

Shortly after the United States entered the war, Congress passed a Selective Service Act, which required all men between 21 and 30 years of

THE NAVY
NEEDS YOU!
DON'T READ
AMERICAN HISTORY—
MAKE IT!
U·S·NAVY RECRUITING STATION
34 EAST 23rd ST., NEW YORK

◄ *The government used dramatic posters like this one to encourage the public to purchase war bonds, to do volunteer service, and to enlist in the military.*

HISTORY

Critical Thinking

Ask students to consider why the British wanted the United States to know about the intercepted Zimmermann Telegram. *(They wanted the United States's support in the war.)* Why did Germans assume that the United States would fight against Germany if it abandoned its policy of neutrality? *(Public opinion in the United States had always favored the Allies, and the sinking of the Lusitania had reinforced that position.)*

■ *The German attack on the Lusitania and the Zimmermann Telegram led to the United States's officially entering the war.*

Historical Context

Despite its late entry into World War I, the United States paid a high price for its participation. Of the approximately two million American soldiers who landed in Europe, some 49,000 were killed in action and another 230,000 were wounded. Disease took an even greater toll than military action, claiming the lives of 57,000 American soldiers. By the end of the war, the cost to the United States was almost $42 billion.

The impact of the war was, of course, far greater in Europe. In all, at least two million people died and another 20 million were wounded. The economies of the European countries were left in ruins, and war casualties were compounded by the deaths caused by starvation and epidemics in the immediate postwar years.

Critical Thinking

Remind students that the United States had long been neutral regarding European conflicts (as first discussed in Chapter 5). Ask students to discuss whether United States neutrality was a realistic goal at the outbreak of World War I. What were the benefits and costs of the neutrality policy? Could the United States have avoided war?

How do you think African Americans felt about being mostly assigned to non-combat duties or to a few fighting regiments,which were all black? *(Sample answers: They were proud to serve their country both on the field and off the field; many African Americans, however, wanted to show that they could fight as well as white regiments; they did not like being segregated.)*

HISTORY

Critical Thinking

What was the purpose of the Selective Service Act, and why was it necessary? *(The United States did not have enough soldiers. By requiring men to register for military service, the country could be sure of getting enough recruits for the war effort.)*

Back our girls over there
Y.W.C.A.
United War Work Campaign

Posters encouraged women and men alike to aid in the war effort.

age to register for military service. Some people feared that the draft would produce riots. But the response of young men eligible for the draft was very positive. Urged on by government posters and popular songs, they stood in long lines to enlist. The Literature Selection on page 554 contains several of the patriotic songs that supported the war. By June 1917, nearly 10 million men had registered for the draft. By the end of the war, close to 5 million men were serving in the armed forces.

Some people hoped that the draft would increase tolerance by bringing together soldiers from different backgrounds. This was not the case. Most of the African Americans, Mexican Americans, and Native Americans who fought in the war faced harsh discrimination.

About 370,000 African Americans enlisted or were drafted in the war. Most of these troops were separated from white troops and assigned to noncombat duties, such as working on the docks or in kitchens. Several all-black regiments that did see combat fought closely with French troops. Three of these regiments received a French medal, the Croix (*krwah*) de Guerre.

Women were not required to register for the draft, but several thousand served voluntarily in the armed forces. Many other women volunteered as nurses or ambulance drivers overseas, serving in such organizations as the Red Cross, Salvation Army, and U.S. Army Signal Corps.

A New Kind of War

The use of deadly new weapons—machine guns, poison gas, submarines, torpedoes, tanks, and airplanes—made World War I the bloodiest confrontation in human history. Submarines destroyed huge ships with one or two torpedoes. Machine guns mowed down whole companies of soldiers. And mustard gas, the deadliest of chemical weapons used in the war, burned its victims' lungs and blistered their exposed flesh. Those soldiers who lived through heavy artillery attacks often suffered from shell shock, which left them unable to speak or

These soldiers, from the all-black 369th Infantry Regiment, are returning home at the end of the war. They fought beside French combat units and are all wearing the Croix de Guerre, a French medal awarded to their regiment.

544

Visual Learning

Ask students to contrast the recruitment poster on this page and page 543 with the pictures of trench warfare on page 545. How was war portrayed in recruitment posters? *(As glorious)* What was the reality in Europe? *(Dirty and deadly)*

Art Connection

A new medium for communicating was developed during World War I—the illustrated poster. Have students draw posters to recruit soldiers, raise relief funds, or in some other way to support World War I. Students can also draw posters in support of a current cause.

Music Connection

In 1940 Congress awarded songwriter George M. Cohan a special medal for his famous World War I song "Over There" (see page 554). "Over There" epitomizes the enthusiastic spirit behind America's participation in the war. Provide a recording of this song so that students can listen to it.

move for hours, days, or weeks.

The war was fought from rat-infested trenches 8 to 12 feet deep. From 1914 to 1917, neither the Allies nor the Central Powers were able to gain control of the Western Front, where thousands of men died to secure only a few yards of territory. At the 1916 Battle of the Somme, 60,000 men died in the first day of fighting. Altogether, more than a million British, French, and German sol-

Suddenly the nearer explosions cease. The shelling continues but it has lifted and falls behind us, our trench is free. We seize the hand-grenades, pitch them out in front of the dug-out and jump after them. The bombardment has stopped and a heavy barrage now falls behind us. The attack has come.

No one would believe that in this howling waste there could still be men; but steel helmets now appear on all sides out of the trench, and fifty yards from us a machine-gun is already in position and barking.

The wire entanglements are torn to pieces. Yet they offer some obstacle. We see the storm-troops coming. Our artillery opens fire. Machine-guns rattle, rifles crack. The charge works its way across. Haie and Kropp begin with the hand-grenades. They throw as fast as they can, others pass them, the handles with the strings already pulled. Haie throws seventy-five yards, Kropp sixty, it has been measured, the distance is important. The enemy as they run cannot do much before they are within forty yards.

We recognize the smooth distorted faces, the helmets: they are French. They have already suffered heavily when they reach the remnants of the barbed wire entanglements. . . . The forward trenches have been abandoned. Are they still trenches? They are blown to pieces, annihilated—there are only broken bits of trenches, holes linked by cracks, nests of craters, that is all.

Erich Maria Remarque, from *All Quiet on the Western Front*, 1929

▲ *Trench warfare and poison gas were two of the chief horrors of World War I. Soldiers lived, ate and slept in trenches. With shells exploding around them, soldiers rarely left the trench, except to retreat or attack. At left, soldiers who have been temporarily blinded by mustard gas await medical treatment.*

How Do We Know?

HISTORY *Many participants in World War I wrote diaries, letters, histories, biographies, poetry, and novels about their experiences. Chroniclers of World War I have used these records to describe daily life in the trenches.*

HISTORY

Critical Thinking

Ask students what effect modern technology had on the progress and outcome of World War I. Do they think the war would have been longer or shorter without tanks, machine guns, and mustard gas? *(Students should give reasons for their answers.)*

CULTURE

Critical Thinking

After students have read the excerpt on this page from *All Quiet on the Western Front*, have them discuss the role of literature in forming or reinforcing people's values. Politicians often rally patriotism and support by making war seem glorious. Ask whether they think Remarque would support nationalistic sentiments. Why or why not?

Reader's Theater

Locate World War I poems in poetry anthologies and have students do a dramatic reading of the poems to the class. The class can also discuss what they learned from the poems and what feelings the poems conveyed. The poems might include "In Flanders Fields" by John McCrae, a Canadian, or poems by Englishman Wilfred Owen.

Writing a News Account

Have students imagine that they are working for a newspaper in 1917 and they have just gotten the news of the intercepted Zimmermann Telegram. Have them write a headline and a news story about the incident. Display their work on a bulletin board.

Map and Globe Skills

Have students compare the map on page 546 with the modern political world map on pages 694–695 in the Atlas. What are the differences? *(Germany is smaller.)* Did the war result in any permanent changes in national boundaries? *(Yes)*

The Western Front, 1918

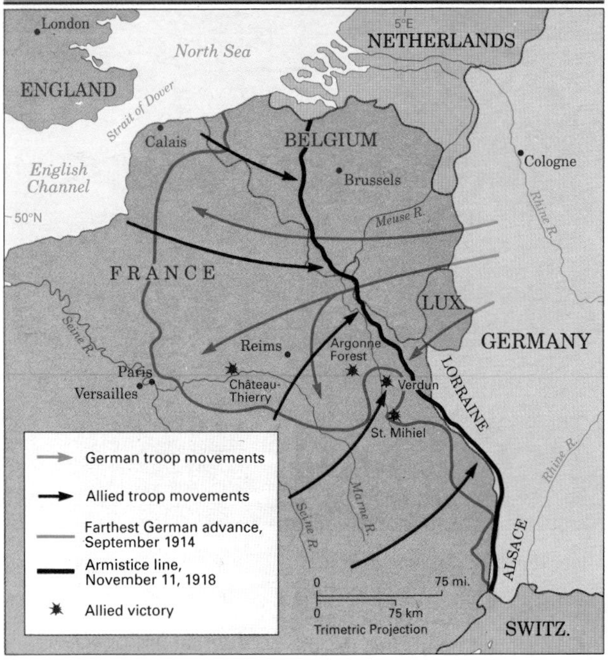

▲ *Although World War I lasted for four years, neither side gained much territory during that time, as the map above shows.*

diers lost their lives in this one battle.

Troops that ventured from their trenches were cut down by machine gun fire. Those who remained in the trenches did not fare much better. Many soldiers died from drowning in the water-logged trenches or from diseases spread by mosquitoes and other insects in the polluted trench waters.

Two antiwar novels related the horrors of trench warfare and the pointlessness of war. *Under Fire* was published in 1916 by French novelist Henri Barbusse. *All Quiet on the Western Front* was published in 1929 by German author Erich Maria Remarque. (See page 545 for an extract from Remarque's work.)

■ *What impact did the United States' entry into the war have on the fighting in Europe?*

An Allied Victory

When American soldiers reached the scenes of battle in 1917, three years of fighting had drained the Allies of men and war supplies. The arrival of fresh American troops and supplies made the difference that enabled the Allies to win.

The first American contribution to the war took place on the seas. The German U-boat blockade hurt Britain badly. The U.S. Navy foiled the U-boats by guarding large convoys of supply ships with American destroyers and cruisers. The U.S. Navy also placed mines in the sea lanes around German ports, creating danger for U-boats entering or leaving Germany.

American soldiers were inexperienced but enthusiastic. The typical American soldier was a young white draftee, about 22 years old, who had never attended high school. Because of short training periods and early shortages of guns, many soldiers had never handled their weapons before they went to the front.

Nevertheless, Americans distinguished themselves in the fighting. Sergeant Alvin York earned fame and the Medal of Honor for his single-handed defeat of 160 German troops. In the fall of 1918, over one million Americans took part in the final Allied offense that broke the German army and ended the war. A temporary peace agreement called an **armistice** was signed by both sides on November 11, 1918. ■

REVIEW

1. **FOCUS** What kept the United States out of World War I initially and what prompted it to enter the war in 1917 on the side of the Allies?
2. **CONNECT** In what earlier American wars did naval blockades play an important role?
3. **HISTORY** How did World War I differ from all wars that had preceded it?
4. **CRITICAL THINKING** How were both the Spanish-American War and World War I the result of imperialist rivalries?
5. **ACTIVITY** Look at the map of Europe in the Atlas and locate the nations in the Triple Alliance and the Triple Entente. Then, with a classmate, debate which group of nations was in a better geographical position from which to fight the war.

HISTORY

Critical Thinking

Have students analyze whether a war such as World War I could happen today. Why or why not?

■ *The fresh American troops and supplies enabled the Allies to win the war.*

CLOSE

Students should summarize what they have learned by answering the Thinking Focus. Then have them answer the questions raised on page 542. You may also wish to copy on the board the Graphic Overview from page 541 so that students can review the steps leading to U.S. participation in the war.

Homework Options

Have students write a letter from an imaginary World War I American soldier to his family contrasting his expectations with the reality of the trenches.

Study Guide: page 79.

Answers to Review Questions

1. The policy of neutrality initially kept the United States out of World War I. Before long, however, the nation got caught in the crossfire between Great Britain and Germany. It entered on the side of the Allies because of the Zimmermann Telegram, the sinking of the Lusitania, and pro-Allies sentiment.
2. Naval blockades played an important role in the Revolutionary War; during Jefferson's presidency; in the Civil War; and in the Spanish-American War.
3. World War I was bloodier than earlier wars because of new weapons, including machine guns, poison gas, submarines, torpedoes, tanks, and airplanes.
4. Sample answer: Both wars were caused by conflicts that resulted from expansion. Allow for personal opinion.
5. After debating in pairs, the class as a whole may compare their conclusions.

1850 1860 1870 1880 1890 1900 1910 1917 1920

L E S S O N 4

Impact of the War

During the depression of 1893, a young Russian-born woman named Emma Goldman spoke to a huge gathering of unemployed workers in New York City. "If your children need food," the 24-year-old woman told the crowd, "go into the grocery stores and take it!"

When the United States entered the war in 1917, Goldman spoke out against the draft. She had earlier given up her support of violence. She was now opposed to the use of military or police force for any reason. Because Goldman expressed her antiwar views publicly, government agents arrested her for violating the Sedition Act, a law that restricted free speech during the war.

As an admitted radical and critic of the wartime government, Emma Goldman—and thousands of others like her—faced harsh punishment. After the war was over, the U.S. government deported Goldman and many other radicals to Russia.

During World War I, the United States would not tolerate criticism. Anyone who did not fully support the war was considered "anti-American" for speaking his or her views. Many brave and patriotic people served jail or prison sentences for not agreeing with the U.S. government's position on the war.

President Wilson claimed the war would make the world "safe for democracy." Emma Goldman replied, "Poor as we are in democracy, how can we give of it to the world?"

◄ *During World War I, the U.S. government imprisoned antiwar activists such as Emma Goldman.*

THINKING FOCUS

What impact did World War I have on American society during and after the war?

Key Terms

- dissent
- reparations
- isolationism

War at Home

In contrast to outspoken critics of the war such as Goldman, most Americans got behind the war effort. At the government's request, they grew their own food in backyard "victory gardens." They also responded to newspaper editorials and government pamphlets encouraging them to scrimp and save. At the urging of popular songs and posters, they bought large numbers of Liberty Bonds. Such purchases gave the government billions of dollars in loans for arms and military supplies. Patriotic Americans

INTRODUCE

Point out the lesson title and have students read the Thinking Focus. Tell students that although the war was fought in Europe, it greatly affected life in the United States as well. Have them predict which groups were affected. Ask them also to predict what life in the United States was like after the war. Have them read the lesson to confirm or reject their predictions.

Key Terms

Vocabulary strategies: T36–37

dissent—disagreement or difference of opinion with established authority

reparations—payments made by defeated nations as compensation for the damages and injuries they caused in war

isolationism—the belief or policy that a nation should avoid alliances and minimize its involvement in the affairs of other nations

Graphic Overview

During the War
- changes in jobs
- civil liberties restricted
- anti-German feelings

→

End of the War
- isolationism
- League of Nations rejected

→

After the War
- "Red Scare"
- labor strikes
- race riots
- KKK

Objectives

1. Summarize the impact of the war on dissenters, foreigners, women, and black Americans.
2. Compare Wilson's vision for a peace treaty with the Treaty of Versailles.
3. Describe the U.S. response to the Treaty of Versailles.
4. Analyze why the war was followed by a period of social unrest and conflict.

DEVELOP

Copy on the board the main heads of the Graphic Overview on page 547 as an aid for students in preparing for reading. Explain that the lesson is structured chronologically, showing the impact of World War I on the United States during the war, at the end of the war, and after the war. Suggest that students take notes as they read the lesson about how different groups of people were affected by the war at each of these points in time.

CONSTITUTIONAL HERITAGE

Critical Thinking

Have students discuss the purpose of the Espionage and Sedition acts. What constitutional rights did these laws limit? *(First Amendment freedoms of speech and press)*

Government posters like this one urged Americans who stayed at home to buy Liberty Bonds. The government used the money for the war effort.

Across Time & Space

The suspicion and hostility that white Americans of English-speaking ancestry demonstrated toward other Americans during World War I reemerged in World War II. In February 1942, President Franklin D. Roosevelt authorized the arrest of all Japanese-Americans on the West Coast. The U.S. Army sent 110,000 Japanese-Americans into camps, where they were imprisoned for three years.

gladly did without certain foods and products, but critics of the government and foreign-born Americans lost many of their civil liberties because of wartime legislation.

Attacking the Critics

In the summer of 1918, Eugene V. Debs gave an antiwar speech in Canton, Ohio. Debs, who won 12% of the vote as the Socialist Party candidate for President in 1912, spoke against American involvement in the war and for free speech. He was arrested and convicted under the Espionage Act, which Congress had passed in 1917. This act made it illegal to say anything that could discourage men from registering for the draft. During World War I, even the courts, which were designed to safeguard Americans' freedom from the excesses of Congress and of the President, bowed to the public pressure for conformity. The Supreme Court upheld the conviction of Debs.

In 1918, Congress passed another law, called the Sedition Act, which was also meant to put down **dissent,** or criticism. The Sedition Act made it a crime to speak disrespectfully of either the government or its symbols, including the flag, the Constitution, and the military uniform. Like the Espionage Act, the Sedition Act was most often enforced against Americans whose political views did not go along with the patriotic spirit of the day. Members of the Socialist party and the Industrial Workers of the World, a radical labor union, were singled out for prosecution.

Suspicion of Foreigners

During the war, Americans who did not have family roots in an English-speaking nation, especially those of German background, were often suspected and accused of being traitors. The attempt to eliminate all things German from American society symbolized this suspicion and fear of foreigners. Sauerkraut was renamed "liberty cabbage," and hamburger became "liberty sausage." High schools in various parts of the country even stopped teaching the German language.

Sometimes German-Americans were physically attacked. In the worst such incident, a mob caught a German-American named Robert Prager. The mob wrapped Prager in an American flag, marched him through the streets of St. Louis, and then lynched him. The Prager affair was an extreme case, but abuse of foreigners was a common occurrence during the war.

Expanding Opportunities

Some Americans indirectly benefited because of the war. With two million white men fighting in Europe and no new immigrants entering the country, many jobs in the United

Access Activity

Ask students whether they would give up the right to free speech and a free press in order to support a war effort. Remind students that some civil rights were suspended during the Civil War. Should these rights be suspended during wartime? Is it dangerous to allow dissent? Can someone who is against war be a patriot? Why or why not?

Access Strategy

Ask students to imagine the following situation. It is 1917. Your father has gone to Europe to fight against Germany. You have a classmate whose parents are immigrants from Germany. They speak with a German accent. Are your feelings about this classmate affected by the fact that your father is fighting Germans? Why or why not?

Now take your classmate's place. How would you feel if people called you names because of a war in a country you had never even been to? What would it be like to be afraid for your safety?

Explain to students that all prejudice is based on false assumptions, yet it hurts many innocent people. Explain that people's suspicions are heightened during wartime. Have students suggest reasons for this. Tell them that they will read in this lesson how suspicion and fear affected society and politics in the United States.

States became available to blacks and women for the first time.

Both groups proved their ability to do any kind of job. Women became railroad conductors, brick layers, and factory workers. Their presence in traditionally male workplaces produced many problems. Men were annoyed by women's higher productivity and willingness to work for lower pay. Working mothers were often criticized for leaving their families. But many women welcomed the responsibilities. "It was not until our men were called overseas," said one woman bank executive, "that we made any real onslaught on the realm of finance, and became tellers, managers of departments, and junior and senior officers."

Women who did not take jobs helped in the war effort in other ways. They made uniforms, rolled bandages, and campaigned for the sale of Liberty Bonds to help finance the war.

American manufacturers offered jobs to large numbers of black Americans for the first time as a result of the war. Most factories were located in the North. To take advantage of these new job opportunities, many black families moved from their homes in the South to Northern cities such as Pittsburgh, Cleveland, Buffalo, Chicago, and Detroit.

White Americans were of two minds about the role of black Americans in the war effort. On the one hand, black workers' ability to learn new jobs quickly and do them well strengthened the home front, and their fighting ability helped the Allies win the war. However, many whites did not want to acknowledge that blacks were capable, effective workers. White soldiers returning from the war had no desire to compete for jobs with blacks on equal terms. At the same time, many blacks were not willing to return to a lesser role once the war had ended. ■

■ *What was life like for different groups of Americans who stayed at home during the war?*

▼ *World War I gave many American women the opportunity to work in jobs traditionally held by men. The woman in the photograph at left is welding a bomb casing in a munitions factory. The women below are assembling wings for airplanes.*

SOCIAL SYSTEMS

Critical Thinking

Why did some women during World War I take jobs traditionally held by men? *(Men not available; needed income; job provided personal and professional challenges)* What pressures might keep women from taking such jobs *(Low pay; women not allowed to join unions; faced criticism)* Ask students to analyze why societal roles change so much in wartime and during other traumatic times, such as economic depressions and natural disasters. Why is there often conflict afterwards?

■ *Government critics and foreign-born Americans lost many of their civil liberties; women and black Americans gained new job opportunities.*

Political Context

The vaguely worded Espionage and Sedition acts of 1917 and 1918 were similar to the Alien and Sedition acts of 1796. Both sets of acts were broadly interpreted to punish anyone who expressed an opinion against the government. In the case of the acts of 1917 and 1918, the attitude that they reflected continued after the acts expired. Fears were fueled by the success of the Bolshevik revolution in Russia. In 1920, thousands of innocent people were arrested without warrants because Attorney General Palmer perceived a "Red Menace." Five legitimately elected members of the New York legislature were expelled for being members of the Socialist Party and were refused seats when their constituents re-elected them. In the "return to normalcy," President Harding signed an order releasing Eugene Debs, the Socialist Party leader, from prison.

Critical Thinking

Ask students to explain how wartime job opportunities and opportunities in the military helped black Americans in their struggle for equality. *(They had a chance to prove their value.)* Was there a negative side to wartime progress? *(After the war, black Americans faced increased hostility and violence from white workers who feared them as competitors for jobs.)*

HISTORY

Critical Thinking

What did President Wilson hope to accomplish by presenting his Fourteen Points at the Paris Peace Conference? *(He hoped his plan would bring about a lasting worldwide peace.)* Why did he support the League of Nations? *(He thought that disputes between nations could be settled peacefully, especially if there was a place for negotiations to take place.)*

The Treaty of Versailles

World War I had a major impact on the lives of Americans who remained at home. The war also shaped the peacetime world that soldiers and civilians would eventually inhabit.

Wilson's 14 Points

One of the reasons President Wilson made the painful decision to lead the United States into war was his desire to influence the peace terms. The President called his plan for peace the Fourteen Points. In the postwar world that Wilson envisioned, nations would settle their disputes by negotiations—never by war. President Wilson proposed an international body called the League of Nations, whose members would promise to respect the "territorial integrity," or boundaries, of all other members.

The President was sure that only he could persuade the other Allies to look past their desire for revenge against Germany to shape a just and lasting peace. He announced in November 1918 that he would head the American delegation to the Paris Peace Conference.

The Final Treaty

Because France and England had fought longer and lost more during the war, they played a larger role than the United States in shaping the peace settlement. They also had a different vision. Instead of a peace of equals, the European Allies wanted to reward themselves and punish Germany by

Europe after World War I

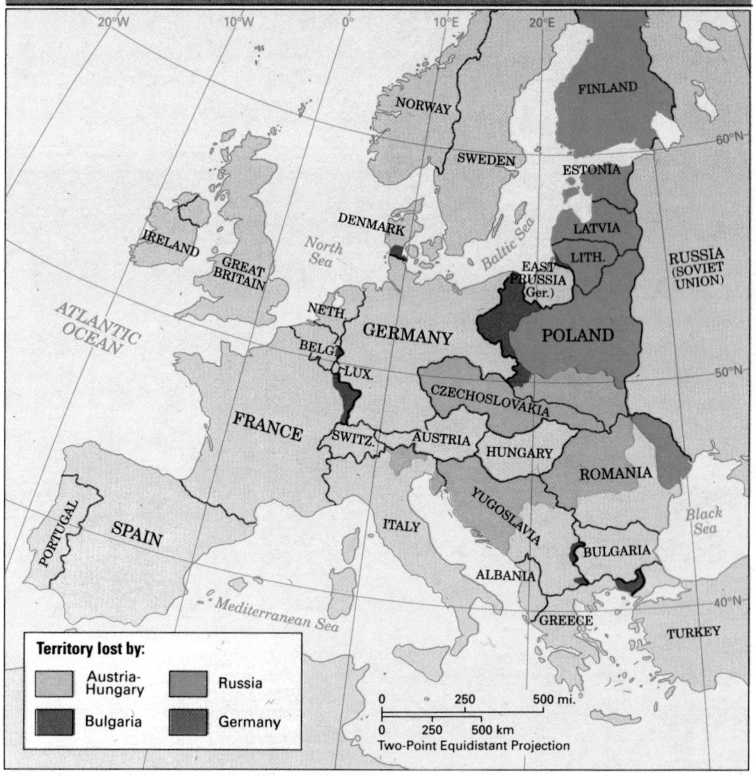

➤ *The Treaty of Versailles changed the map of Europe. Austria-Hungary and Russia lost the most territory as a result of the war.*

Map and Globe Skills

Have students examine the map on this page. What does it show about the outcome of the war? *(Many national boundaries changed.)* Which countries lost territory and which countries gained territory? *(Germany, Austria-Hungary, and Russia lost territory; France and several new countries gained territory.)*

Economic Context

The Zimmermann Telegram was sent in code over the wireless transmission system that President Wilson had allowed both warring sides to use. Wireless (radio) telegraphy was developed at the end of the 1800s by an Italian physicist and inventor, Guglielmo Marconi. By 1916 it was widely used for communications with ships. During World War I, Marconi continued to experiment with wireless communication, eventually developing the short-wave wireless system that is the basis for nearly all modern long-distance radio communication.

The first successful demonstration of speech transmitted by radio was made in 1915. After the war, military restrictions on the use of radios were relaxed, and experimental radio stations sprang up. Soon there was a boom in the sale of radio receiving sets for in-home use.

taking German territory and large sums of money called **reparations.**

The Treaty of Versailles fulfilled their hopes. Under the terms of the treaty, Germany was forced to accept total blame for the war, to give up 13 percent of its territory, and to pay $15 billion for damage to Allied property. The German government signed the treaty because it had no choice, but the German people never accepted it. Most Germans felt the terms were unfair and humiliating. Economically, they suffered terribly as a result of the conditions imposed by the treaty. The bitterness and resentment that the treaty inspired indirectly paved the way for World War II. ■

■ *In what way did President Wilson attempt to shape peace terms after the war?*

The Allied Powers met in the Hall of Mirrors at the Palace of Versailles to sign the 1919 peace treaty. President Woodrow Wilson is shown in the center of this painting holding the treaty.

Retreating from World Affairs

President Wilson believed that the new League of Nations, whose charter was part of the peace treaty, would somehow make up for the harsh terms that Germany had received. Wilson also believed that the League of Nations would cut down on the risk of war. He hoped it would change the basis of international relations from competition to cooperation.

Rejecting the League

The Senate had other ideas. Most Democratic Senators voted to ratify the treaty. Senate Republicans, however, led by Henry Cabot Lodge, refused to give their support. Senator Lodge believed that the League of Nations would draw the United States into foreign wars. As proof he pointed to the provision that called for members of the League to regard a threat to any one of them as a threat to all. The Republicans' position had come to be known as **isolationism.**

When President Wilson saw that he could not get the votes he needed in the Senate, he took his case directly to the American people. He traveled across the country, explaining at each stop why he believed the treaty was so important. The American public responded to the President's words with enthusiasm. However, it was not the general public Wilson needed to convince but the Senators who had the power to ratify or kill the treaty.

Wilson's refusal to compromise with the Republican majority in the Senate and his high-handed methods

HISTORY

Critical Thinking

Remind students of England and France's long participation in World War I. France especially suffered great destruction. Ask students if the Germans would have been less angry and resentful about the Treaty of Versailles if the terms had been less harsh. Could a more even-handed treaty have produced a better result? Why is it often difficult for nations to be generous after winning a military victory?

■ *His Fourteen Points envisioned a state of peace among equals, in which members of the League of Nations would respect each other's boundaries.*

Science Connection

To help students understand more about the technology of the war, have them research either short-wave radio or mustard gas. If they research radio technology, they may include diagrams showing how radio receivers work. If they research mustard gas, they can also report about modern chemical warfare.

Art Connection

Have students research the history and architecture of the Palace of Versailles. Students may then either draw a floor plan of the building and sketches of the grounds or make a model out of paper or cardboard.

Visual Learning

Have students analyze the views that the artist conveys in the portrait on this page. How is the signing of the Treaty of Versailles presented? *(As a serious, important event)* Is President Wilson shown as a major or minor figure? *(Major, because he is placed at the center)*

POLITICAL SYSTEMS

Critical Thinking

Ask students to explain why the Treaty of Versailles was never ratified in the United States. *(Republicans in the Senate refused to ratify the treaty because they did not want to involve the United States in world affairs through a League of Nations.)* Have them analyze how the refusal of the Senate to ratify it affected President Wilson. *(For Wilson, it was the collapse of his lifetime hope for international peace. He had spent all his energy fighting for this issue but was unable to get the votes he needed.)*

■ *The United States adopted a policy of isolationism because it feared future entanglements in foreign wars.*

▲ *Edith Galt, President Wilson's second wife.*

led to defeat. After many votes on several versions, the Senate conclusively rejected the Treaty of Versailles in March 1920.

Wilson: A Broken Man

In 1919, on his cross-country trip to persuade Americans to preserve their hard-won peace through the League of Nations, Wilson collapsed from exhaustion. Shortly afterwards, he suffered a stroke that paralyzed his entire left side. He never fully regained his health, and for the rest of his presidency remained tired and depressed—a broken man.

Wilson's weakness symbolized the collapse of his dream for a world order based on lasting peace and justice. In his last months in office, President Wilson was greatly helped by his second wife, Edith Galt. An intelligent and strong-minded woman, she held the White House together during Wilson's long illness.

The League of Nations had to sink or swim without the United States. Promises of mutual defense, which members of the League had to make, had led many nations into the First World War.

Americans had had enough of "foreign" wars. In 1920, they looked inward once again. Isolationism, it was thought, would keep the United States safe. ■

■ *Why did the United States adopt a policy of isolationism after the war?*

The Aftermath of War

Having turned their backs on the world, Americans proceeded to fight bitterly against each other. From 1919 to 1920, people whose race, religion, or political views differed from those of the majority became the targets of violence and arrest.

A strong revival of the Ku Klux Klan sparked much violence. Based in the South, the Klan called for violence against anyone who was not white, Anglo-Saxon, and Protestant. It expanded rapidly into new areas, including the Midwest. At its postwar peak, it boasted five million members.

In addition, factory workers struck against low wages, long hours, and unsafe conditions. And both government officials and private citizens threatened the property and lives of political radicals.

Labor Unrest and Race Riots

In 1919, the year after the war, American silk workers, cigar makers, steel workers, carpenters, bakers,

➤ *The United States experienced a wave of strikes and protests at the end of World War I. This photograph shows striking steel workers in 1919.*

Critical Thinking

Have students analyze the connection that factory owners made between labor unions and political radicals. Why did they think that labor strikes were unpatriotic? What was the connection that the government saw between the "Red Scare," "political radicals," and the Russian Revolution?

Collaborative Learning

Messages during wartime are usually sent in secret codes. Intelligence divisions of the armies involved often try to intercept and decode these messages to find out the enemy's plans. Have students work in pairs to create their own codes. Have each pair write a message in code. Then pairs should exchange their messages to see whether they can decipher each other's codes.

Research

Although the United States never joined the League of Nations, it actually did exist. It was the forerunner of our present-day United Nations. Have students research the original League of Nations and today's United Nations. Students should write a two-page paper that compares the membership and goals of each.

barbers, and police went out on strike. Over four million workers were involved. Many of them were working 12 hours a day, 6 days a week for pay that had not gone up as fast as the cost of living. Factory owners didn't believe that patriotic Americans would ever strike against their employers. They thought that radicals were stirring up labor unrest.

Meanwhile, in the summer of 1919, more than 25 race riots broke out across the nation. These riots resulted largely from the determination of white Americans to prevent blacks from keeping the economic gains they had made during the war. Mobs of whites lynched more than 70 African Americans. Stabbings, burning, and shootings took the lives of hundreds of Americans.

The Red Scare

On April 28, 1919, a package arrived at the home of Georgia Senator Thomas Hartwick. The bomb it contained badly injured the senator's maid. Two months later, another bomb exploded at the home of U.S. Attorney General A. Mitchell Palmer.

The bombings set off a year-long "Red Scare." During that time the Justice Department arrested over 6,000 Americans—many of them foreigners—on charges of plotting to overthrow the government. Almost none of those arrested were found guilty of the crimes with which they were charged.

The Bolshevik Revolution, which had established a Communist government in Russia in 1917, intensified Americans' fears of political radicals. During the war, Americans whose ancestors did not speak English were suspected of working with the enemy. After the war, anyone whose political views were different from those of the mainstream could earn himself or herself the label "radical." Immigrants from Russia or Eastern Europe were often suspected of being Communist spies.

In his 1920 campaign for the presidency, Republican Senator Warren G. Harding promised Americans a "return to normalcy."

The Return to "Normalcy"

By the presidential election of 1920, Americans were tired of both war and the fearful events of the postwar period. After eight years of Democratic rule, they were also ready for a change.

When the Republicans nominated a handsome and amiable Ohio Senator named Warren Harding, the public liked what it saw. Americans felt that the Republicans could return the nation to a time of, as Harding put it, "normalcy." The longing for peace and the desire to avoid foreign wars helped Harding to win a landslide victory in the 1920 election. His victory signaled the beginning of a new era of American history. ■

■ *What internal problems disrupted American society in the postwar period?*

REVIEW

1. **FOCUS** What impact did World War I have on American society during and after the war?
2. **CONNECT** How was the impact of World War I similar to and different from the impact of the American Revolution on women and black Americans?
3. **HISTORY** Why did America's European Allies reject President Wilson's Fourteen Points as a basis for peace?
4. **CRITICAL THINKING** Was the U.S. Congress justified in passing the Espionage and Sedition acts because of the threat of war? Why or why not?
5. **WRITING ACTIVITY** Make a chart that lists the pros and cons of the League of Nations. Then write a short statement for or against the plan.

SOCIAL SYSTEMS

Critical Thinking

Have students consider the social conflict in the United States after World War I. Ask them to state what the United States "won" in the war. *(A role as a leading world power)* What did it "lose" in the war? *(Many lives, much money, and the trust of Americans in one another)*

■ *Internal problems included labor unrest, race riots, and the Red Scare.*

CLOSE

Ask students to answer the Thinking Focus. Have them evaluate the predictions that they made before reading the lesson. As a reteaching activity, copy on the board again the main heads from the Graphic Overview on page 547 and have volunteers add details from the notes that they made while reading the lesson.

Answers to Review Questions

1. During the war, critics of the government and foreign-born Americans experienced discrimination, while women and black Americans gained new job opportunities. After the war, Americans experienced great internal conflict, including labor unrest, race riots, and the Red Scare.
2. Women and black Americans gained new job opportunities during both wars. In World War I, women faced criticism for taking jobs and many black American families moved to Northern cities.
3. England and France wanted to reward themselves and punish Germany.
4. Sample answer: Congress had the right to pass these laws, but there is no proof that the laws aided the war effort. Allow for personal opinion.
5. Encourage students to discuss with each other their conclusions.

Homework Options

Have students draw up their own "Fourteen Points," listing fourteen things that people could do to promote peace.

Study Guide: page 80.

INTRODUCE

Ask students to recall what they read about World War I in Lesson 3. Point out that patriotic songs, such as the ones reprinted here, were meant to raise people's spirits. Soldiers sang them in training camps and on the ships going to Europe. At home, the songs were often sung at rallies that were held to sell liberty bonds to support the war effort.

READ AND RESPOND

If you can find a recording of these two songs, play it for the class. Have students sing the songs or read the lyrics aloud. Ask students to analyze the mood of the songs. As students answer the purpose-setting question, make sure they give reasons for their answers.

In Lesson 3 you read about how popular songs encouraged Americans to support the war effort during World War I. Keep this information in mind as you read the two songs reprinted here.

LITERATURE

American War Songs

Wars are fought not only by soldiers on the battlefields, but also in the hearts and minds of the civilian population. Songs like the ones reprinted below became very popular in World War I. Their rousing words and short verses were easy to remember, and their patriotic tone was encouraging and enthusiastic. For a population engaged in a world struggle, the songs promoted involvement and participation in the war effort. As you read these songs, ask yourself what kinds of images are used to arouse your patriotic impulses.

OVER THERE
George M. Cohan

Johnnie get your gun, get your gun, get your gun,
Take it on the run, on the run, on the run,
Hear them calling you and me,
Ev'ry son of liberty.
Hurry right away, no delay, go today,
Make your daddy glad to have had such a lad,
Tell your sweetheart not to pine,
To be proud her boy's in line.

pine suffer

CHORUS
Over there, over there,
Send the word over there
That the Yanks are coming,
The drums rum tumming ev'rywhere,
So prepare, say a prayer,
Send the word to beware,
We'll be over, we're coming over
And we won't come back till it's over,
Over there, over there.

Johnnie get your gun, get your gun, get your gun,
Johnnie, show the Hun you're a son of a gun,
Hoist the flag and let her fly,
Yankee Doodle do or die.
Pack your kit, show your grit, do your bit,
Yankees to the ranks from the towns and the tanks,
Make your mother proud of you
And the Red, White and Blue.

Hun negative term for German

Thematic Connections

Social Studies: World War I

Houghton Mifflin Literary Readers: Freedom's Foundations

Background

George M. Cohan (1878–1942) was an immensely popular performer, songwriter, and playwright. Among his songs were "Give My Regards to Broadway" and "I'm a Yankee Doodle Dandy." His song "Over There" was the favorite marching song of American soldiers in World War I. In 1940, Congress awarded Cohan a special medal for writing the song. It was almost as popular during World War II as it had been during World War I.

UNCLE SAM
Edward Bushnell

So you've drawn your sword again, Uncle Sam!
You're lined up with fighting men, Uncle Sam!
For when freedom is at stake,
You will fight for honor's sake,
And you'll fight till tyrants quake, Uncle Sam!

We know war is not your game, Uncle Sam!
'Twas at peace you made your fame, Uncle Sam!
And 'tis always with regret
That you make a war-like threat;
But they've never whipped you yet, Uncle Sam!

We will sail on all the seas, Uncle Sam!
Without saying "if" or "please," Uncle Sam!
We'll not wear the Kaiser's tag,
And we'll fly no checkered rag,
For Old Glory is our flag, Uncle Sam!

Let the Eagle flap his wings, Uncle Sam!
These are sorry days for kings, Uncle Sam!
And the Kaiser and his crew
Will be missing when they're through
With the old Red, White and Blue, Uncle Sam!

Kaiser German emperor

Further Reading

Songs America Voted By. Irwin Silber. The author presents a collection of presidential compaign songs which, like the war songs, were designed to influence the course of current events.

Songs That Made America. James A. Warner. This book presents a broad regional, racial, and ethnic overview of the makers of America with folk-songs from all across the country.

Songs of Independence. Irwin Silber. This selection of ballads captures the spirit of the great battles and political struggles of the Colonial Era.

Who is "Johnnie" in the song "Over There"? *(Young American men)* What do the last four lines of the first stanza of "Over There" encourage young men to do? *(Enlist in the armed forces; fight in the war)*

What reasons does "Uncle Sam" give for going to war? *(To preserve freedom; for honor's sake)*

EXTEND

The posters created to promote America's involvement in World War I are another example of popular art applied to patriotic purposes. Have students find examples of such posters in their textbooks and in the school or local library. Display them and discuss the visual images used to stir patriotic fervor. Compare these images to and contrast them with the images used in the songs.

Further Reading

You may want to ask students to go to the school or local library to find books with other World War I songs.

UNDERSTANDING WRITTEN PROPAGANDA

In this skills lesson, students will learn how to evaluate and judge samples of propaganda.

HISTORY

Critical Thinking

Ask students to explain why propaganda might be used more often in times of war than during other periods. *(Sample answers: A nation at war is in special danger; it must devote most of its energies and resources to winning war; and it must unify people by appealing to their emotions, such as patriotism.)*

UNDERSTANDING WRITTEN PROPAGANDA

Supporting the War Effort

Here's Why

Knowing how to recognize and analyze propaganda is a useful way to learn about public opinion during a particular period. Propaganda is the use of words or familiar symbols to persuade a great number of readers to accept a certain point of view or to take a certain action.

Public interest groups use propaganda to promote their causes. The pamphlets you may see in a dentist's office urging you to brush your teeth daily are a form of propaganda.

During the first World War, the United States believed that Americans needed to think in new ways. In order to supply money for military goods, the people at home needed to be persuaded to buy bonds—a form of loaning their money to the government. The poster on the facing page was designed to make people want to buy bonds "For Home and Country." At the same time the government published numerous pamphlets in order to convince people of the need to support the war effort by making changes in their way of life.

Suppose you wanted to learn more about how the American government tried to influence people's opinions about World War I. Recognizing and analyzing written propaganda from that period would give you a great deal of information about how governments can use propaganda to affect people's lives.

Here's How

Look at the pamphlet below, which was published in the United States during the first World War. Ask the following questions to determine if it is propaganda:

1. Does it appeal to emotion or to reason? If it appeals to both, is the appeal to reason presented in emotional terms?
2. Does it include unsupported statements of opinion?
3. Does it call for a specific action on the part of the reader?
4. Does it make use of colorful language?

If the answer to some or all of these questions is "yes," you are probably reading propaganda. Specific answers to each question will tell you why. In this example, the answer to all four questions is "yes."

The man you love is fighting for your security and happiness. He is helping to bring this war to an early end—and to make another war like this impossible. He is doing something that HAS to be done for your sake. The more hopefully you write, the easier for him—and the quicker he comes back.

Of course his life is no bed of roses. Yet his discomforts are the discomforts of a red-blooded life in the open—the sort of life enjoyed by the cowboy of Arizona, by the mounted police of Canada, and by the adventurous spirits of all the world and of all times. . .

His fighting equipment, his bayonet, gas mask and ammunition embody every known advantage and improvement—American ingenuity has profited by all the past experience of our allies and the enemy as well. . . In all the history of the world no soldier has been so well equipped, so well taken care of as the American soldier. . .

The great majority of American soldiers will return stronger and more vigorous in body and in mind than when they joined the army.

Every conceivable condition contributes to his safety, comfort, and happiness EXCEPT ONE—The strong arm of Uncle Sam can do everything in the world for him—except control his thoughts of you. That one condition is entirely within your control.

His fighting power, his health, his chance of winning and living depend in the end upon WHAT YOU WRITE TO HIM. . .

So write him newsy, cheerful letters. Tell him the pleasant, treasured bits of gossip from home. . .

Do your part to maintain this spirit, this courage!

United States Gov't Comm. on Public Information

556

Objective

Use government pamphlets from World War I to evaluate and judge examples of propaganda. (Critical Thinking 2)

Writing Propaganda

After students have read the selections, have them each write a sample of propaganda. Each student may choose some personal goal, such as asking all of the teachers in the school never to give homework on weekends. Remind them that they should be able to answer "yes" to most of the questions from Here's How when applied to the sample of propaganda they have written.

Reader's Theater

Popular entertainers helped the propaganda campaigns in both World Wars I and II by appearing in public for bond drives. Students will find that reading a propaganda piece aloud adds to its effect. Have groups of five students prepare a reading of one of the selections on these pages. Students should take turns reading paragraphs from the selections.

Back of every war activity lies—coal. Ships, shells, guns, transportation. For all these we must have—coal. The more coal, the more shells with which to destroy the machine-gun nests of our enemies—and thereby save the lives of our own boys.

The larger the supply of coal—the shorter the war and fewer casualties....

Save coal....

If you feel that one shovel-ful of coal won't make any difference—think of it as a shell for the boys over there.

If you find yourself burning two lights when one will do—turn one out.

You, who have bought bonds and thrift stamps, you who have given of your money for war charities, given until you have felt the pinch, you whose sons and neighbors' sons are over there, will you not give up, too, just a bit of lazy, enervating comfort to help hurry along the job those brave boys have tackled?

Save light and heat, save coal.

United States Gov't Comm. on Public Information

Notice the appeal to emotion: Americans are assured that the soldiers are well taken care of. The pamphlet likens them to the cowboys of the West and describes their adventurous spirit. The appeals to reason are written to get an emotional reaction from the reader: "Every conceivable condition contributes to his safety, comfort, and happiness EXCEPT ONE . . . except control [of] his thoughts of you. That one condition is entirely within your control."

Notice the unsupported statements of opinion: "He is helping to bring this war to an early end—and to make another war like this impossible. He is doing something that HAS to be done for your sake." The piece presents no facts to back up these statements.

Notice the call for action: American citizens are directed to write cheerful, uplifting letters to soldiers overseas in order to keep them happy and ready to fight for an early end to the war.

Notice the use of emotional language: the frequent use of italics, capital letters, and exclamation points adds a sense of urgency and excitement to the piece.

Try It

Now read the excerpt above, and use the four questions from the previous page to decide whether the excerpt is qualifies as propaganda. Write a short paragraph explaining your answer.

Apply It

Choose a current issue and find out if there is a public interest group that has published pamphlets or posters about it. Analyze the writing of the group's documents to see if propaganda is used. Use the four-question format to decide whether or not it is propaganda.

For Home and Country
VICTORY LIBERTY LOAN

HISTORY

Critical Thinking

Point out that propaganda is not always bad. What was the primary purpose of the propaganda excerpts on these pages? *(To urge people to support the war effort)* Was World War I considered a "good" cause? *(Students should consider reasons why the United States entered war.)* How would a person judge whether propaganda is "good" or "bad"? *(If it serves a "good" or "bad" cause)*

Answers to Try It

The explanation of what coal is needed for is reasonable, but the appeal is presented in the emotional terms, such as of thinking of coal as "a shell for the boys." The statement "The larger the supply of coal—the shorter the war and fewer casualties" is an unsupported opinion. The excerpt calls for the specific action of turning out lights. It makes use of colorful language, such as "lazy, enervating comfort" and "job those brave boys have tackled."

Answers to Apply It

Students can use direct mail solicitations as a source of public interest groups' positions. They can also use newspapers or military recruiting pamphlets as sources of official government statements. Have them try to select a phrase or sentence from their example of propaganda that illustrates their answer to each of the four questions.

Visual Learning

Have students study the poster above. How does it appeal to emotion or reason? *(Emotion: Soldier protecting his wife and child, showing love and courage)* How would this poster make people want to help the war effort? *(Makes them feel that the war is being fought to protect their own families)*

Chapter Review

Reviewing Key Terms

abdicate (p. 532)
armistice (p. 546)
dissent (p. 548)
imperialism (p. 536)
isolationism (p. 551)
mobilize (p. 543)
protectorate (p. 532)
reparations (p. 551)
yellow journalism (p. 535)

A. Use each of the following terms in a complete sentence that clearly shows the meaning of the term.

1. dissent
2. yellow journalism
3. protectorate
4. imperialism
5. armistice
6. reparations

B. Based on what you have read in the chapter, decide whether each of the following statements is accurate. Write an explanation of each decision.

1. One way for a stronger nation to control a weaker nation is to declare the weaker nation a protectorate.
2. After the king abdicates, he is no longer the ruler of his nation.
3. Newspapers that practiced yellow journalism could be relied on to tell the truth.
4. After the armistice, nations built large supplies of arms and ammunition for war.
5. All the nations of Europe wanted to pay reparations to repair the war damage.
6. Those Americans who supported a policy of isolationism following World War I were generally strong supporters of the League of Nations.
7. After the United States declared war on Germany, President Woodrow Wilson decided not to mobilize American troops.
8. Imperialism was a policy large nations adopted in order to help small nations.

Exploring Concepts

A. On a separate sheet of paper, create two columns. In one column, list the terms shown below. In the other column, list the consequences of each item in the first column.

- Social Darwinism
- Roosevelt Corollary
- European Alliance System
- Zimmermann Telegram
- Sedition Act

B. Support each of the following statements with facts and details from the chapter.

1. Many Americans in the late 1800s used social Darwinism to justify the nation's economic and political expansion.
2. Americans sought new opportunities abroad because they wanted to both sell and buy goods.
3. The United States was determined that it alone should control a canal across Central America, and the American government took steps to protect its interests there.
4. Trade with Asian nations was important to the United States in the 1800s.
5. The United States was determined not to allow an unfriendly government to take power in Mexico.
6. American imperialist ambitions were among the causes of the Spanish-American War and were further fueled by the war's results.
7. Germany's actions overcame the desire most Americans had to remain neutral during World War I.
8. During and after World War I, the United States became increasingly intolerant of minorities and dissenters.
9. President Wilson failed to achieve his goal of constructing a fair and lasting peace after World War I.
10. The two-year period following World War I was a time of great social unrest in the United States.

Answers to Reviewing Key Terms

A. Sample answers:

1. During World War II, the Sedition Act allowed the government to presecute its critics, or dissenters.
2. Yellow journalism distorts the facts to increase public interest.
3. Hawaii became a protectorate when it came under the control of the United States.
4. Social Darwinism was a factor in U.S. imperialism.
5. Germany and the Allied powers declared an armistice, a temporary peace agreement.
6. The European Allies demanded reparations from Germany in the form of money and land.

B. Answers:

1. True. A protectorate is a country or territory controlled by another, stronger country.
2. True. To abdicate is to give up the throne.
3. False. Yellow journalism often exaggerated the truth.
4. False. An armistice is a peace treaty.
5. False. The European Allies wanted only Germany to pay war damages.
6. False. American isolationists feared that membership in the League of Nations would lead the U.S. into another war.
7. False. President Wilson needed to assemble troops in order to prepare them for war.
8. False. Imperialist nations wanted economic and political control of smaller nations.

Answers to Exploring Concepts

A. Answers:

Social Darwinism: U.S. increased international trade and adopted an imperialist policy

Roosevelt Corollary: allowed U.S. intervention in Latin America

European Alliance System: divided European countries into two camps and led to World War I

Zimmermann Telegram: led to U.S. involvement in World War I

Sedition Act: made it possible to prosecute Americans who disagreed politically with the U.S. government

B. Sample Answers:

1. Students can use the following examples: Strong, Beveridge, Mahan, Roosevelt, McKinley.
2. Students should mention trade with Asia as well as Latin America.
3. Hayes sent warships to stop the French, U.S businesses planned the canal with Roosevelt's support, and the U.S. unofficially encouraged revolution in Panama.
4. Answers should show how the U.S. expanded trade with China, Japan, Korea.
5. The U.S. sent troops to the border to oust the empire of Napolean III and went to war over the Zimmermann Telegram.
6. America wanted control of Cuba and the Philippines, and victory encouraged the U.S. to secure the Panama Canal.
7. The attack on the *Lusitania* and the German threat in Mexico changed U.S. sentiment.
8. Students should distinguish between actions against dissenters and those against minorities.
9. Answers should include European reparations, the failure of the League of Nations, and the policy of isolationism.
10. Students should mention the racial and cultural intolerance, violence, and labor strikes.

Reviewing Skills

> *Look well at the loaf on your breakfast table and treat it as if it were real gold, because the British loaf is going to beat the German. . . . Women have done nobly in the war, but they must do still more. . . . Today the kitchen is the key to victory and is in the fighting line alongside our undying heroes of the trenches and our brave men of the sea,*
>
> Kennedy Jones, Director General of Food Economy

1. What are the four questions you should ask in order to determine if a piece of writing qualifies as propaganda?
2. Read the passage at left written in London by the Director General of Food Economy, Kennedy Jones, during World War I. Do you think it is propaganda? Explain your answer.
3. Use the library to find a photograph from the World War I period. What information does the photograph you found provide about how people lived during that period? Write a short paragraph summarizing the information provided by the photograph.
4. Suppose you wanted to find out more about how the Vietnam War affected citizens of the United States. What source of information could you use?

Using Critical Thinking

1. Arthur Zimmermann insisted that Germany never sent the famous telegram bearing his name. If he was speaking the truth, what forces do you think might have been responsible for starting this rumor? What do you think their motives might have been?
2. Social Darwinism appealed to Americans who wanted their country to expand into an empire. To what extent did their dreams come true? Explain your answer.
3. According to Wilson, the most important of his Fourteen Points was the creation of a League of Nations. Do you believe such an organization could work? Explain your answer.
4. The 1918 Sedition Act made it a crime to speak disrespectfully of the government or its symbols. Do you think the government should restrict what people say during wartime? Explain your answer.

Preparing for Citizenship

1. **WRITING ACTIVITY** Look for examples of yellow journalism in a contemporary newspaper. Choose an article you think uses wild headlines and distorts the facts, and write a short report on the article, pointing out its use of facts and opinions.
2. **WRITING ACTIVITY** One of the great mysteries in American history is the question of who sank the battleship *Maine*. Investigate this subject and determine all of the possible forces behind the incident. Write a short article explaining what the incident might indicate about the role of public opinion in American foreign policy.
3. **ART ACTIVITY** Look at the sheet music cover at right. It is from the World War I song "Over There," which appears on page 554. Read the words to the song "Uncle Sam" on page 555, and then design a sheet music cover for that song.
4. **COLLABORATIVE LEARNING** Set up a class debate on this question: "Should the United States become involved in World War I?" Research both sides of the question, and conduct the debate according to Robert's Rules of Order. At the end of the debate, hold a vote on the issue.

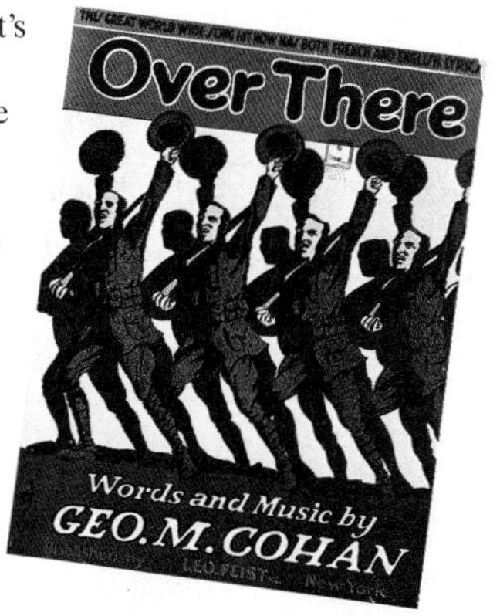

Answers to Reviewing Skills

1. Refer to Understanding Written Propaganda on pages 556–557.
2. Students should cite specific passages in their responses.
3. Refer to Understanding Visual Information on pages 520–521.
4. Encourage students to look at propaganda of the time (recruitment posters, government brochures), as well as magazine and newspaper articles, to explore the differences between how the war was presented and how it was perceived.

Answers to Using Critical Thinking

1. Answers can include: Europeans who wanted U.S. military help; U.S. pro-Allied forces; U.S. imperialists who feared a German takeover of Mexico.
2. Students should consider American world influence today as well as the success of imperialist policies prior to World War I.
3. Encourage students to research the United Nations. How does this organization differ from the League of Nations? Is it successful?
4. Allow for personal opinion. Students should consider the First Amendment in their response.

Answers to Preparing for Citizenship

1. **WRITING ACTIVITY** Direct students to the tabloid-type of newspapers at their local supermarket.
2. **WRITING ACTIVITY** Discuss how a project such as this is similar to investigative reporting.
3. **ART ACTIVITY** Encourage students to seek information about patriotic art and songs from art and music classes.
4. **COLLABORATIVE LEARNING** An allied activity would be to role play key leaders on both sides of this question.

UNIT
OVERVIEW

After students have read the unit title and the narrative underneath it, ask them to name some of the groups of Americans who have not always enjoyed their full rights as U.S. citizens. Explain that the nation has not always lived up to the ideals of liberty and equality set forth in the Constitution.

Ask students to explain how the photograph relates to the unit title and the narrative. *(Shows immigrants drawn to the U.S. by promise of a better life)*

Looking Back

Remind students that they learned in Unit 6 about America's transformation from an isolated agricultural nation to an industrial world power. Ask them what groups of Americans did not always enjoy the rights promised in the Constitution.

Looking Forward

Tell students that in the following chapters they will be reading about the history of immigration in the 20th century and about the extension of rights to a much wider segment of the population.

Chapter 19 *Pluralism*
Chapter 20 *Modern American Democracy*

Unit 7

The Promise Continues

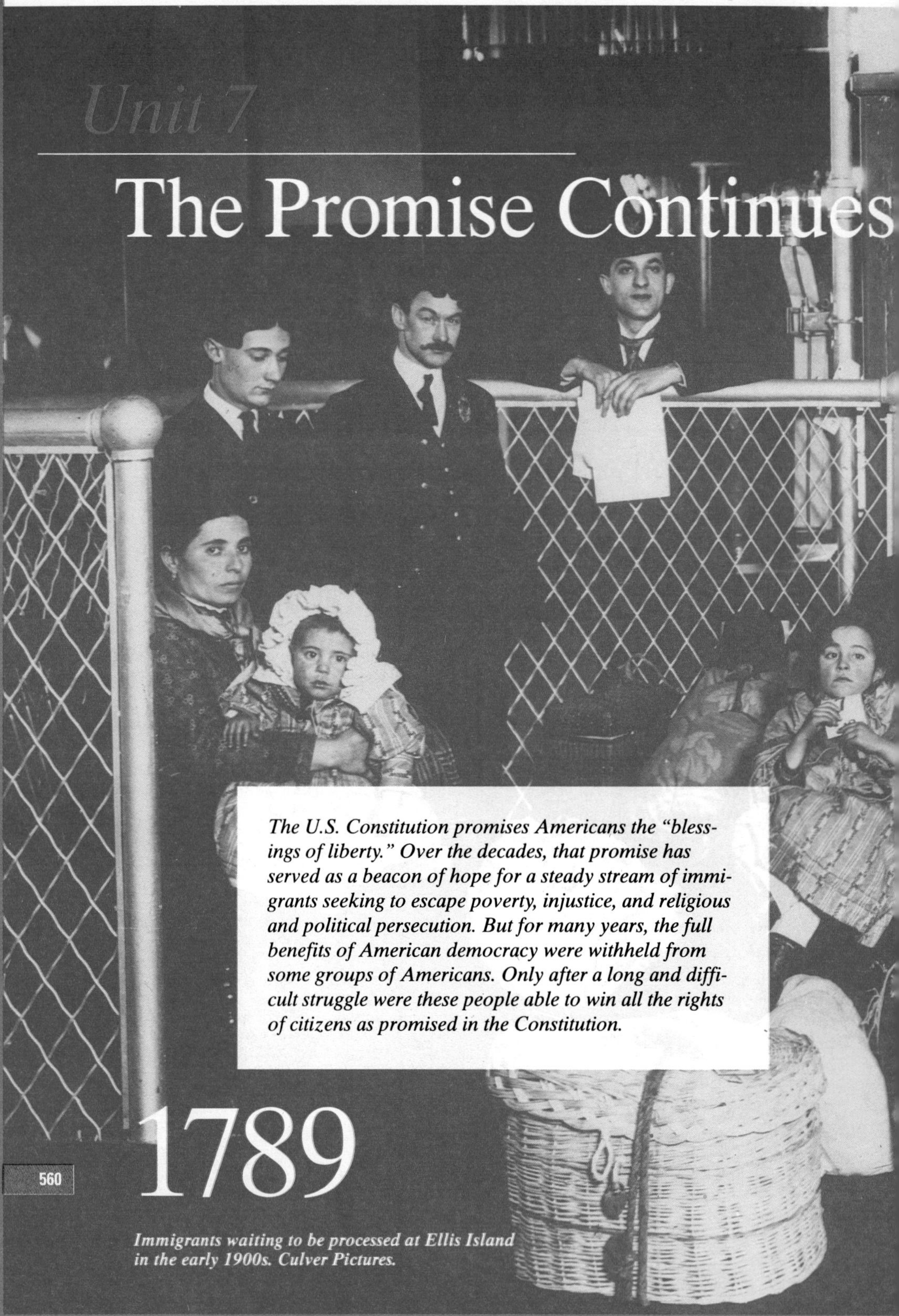

The U.S. Constitution promises Americans the "blessings of liberty." Over the decades, that promise has served as a beacon of hope for a steady stream of immigrants seeking to escape poverty, injustice, and religious and political persecution. But for many years, the full benefits of American democracy were withheld from some groups of Americans. Only after a long and difficult struggle were these people able to win all the rights of citizens as promised in the Constitution.

1789

Immigrants waiting to be processed at Ellis Island in the early 1900s. Culver Pictures.

GEOGRAPHY PROJECT

A Cultural Mosaic

Geography Skill **Interpreting Geographic Information**
Students use the skills of Asking, Analyzing, and Answering geographic questions.

Geography Theme Movement

Geography Standard 10, characteristics, and complexity of earth's cultures.

Activity ***Create an Exhibit Catalog***

Materials cardboard or oaktag, construction paper, scissors, markers, found items for the museum exhibits

Management Small Group

Choose one of the cultures represented in the United States and create a museum exhibit that demonstrates the cultural elements of that group.

Have students:

- write descriptive text for a museum exhibit catalog and/or create an audio tape tour of the exhibit.
- make or collect cultural exhibit items such as traditional clothing, art, music, and artifacts.
- create a historical map that shows where immigrants came from and where they first settled.

Understanding the Photograph

Taken by an unknown photographer of immigrants at Ellis Island in the early years of the 1900s, this photograph vividly captures a moment experienced by many immigrants of that era. U.S. immigration officials at Ellis Island processed thousands of newcomers to the United States every week in the late nineteenth and early twentieth centuries.

Understanding Chronology

Point out that Unit 7 begins in 1789, the year that the Constitution was ratified, and continues up to the present and beyond. Ask students why they think this unit covers such a long period of time. *(The struggle to fulfill the promise of the Constitution began the moment it was ratified and is an ongoing effort.)*

For research support activities, see the *Research Handbook.*

For simulations correlated to this unit, see *Citizenship Simulations,* p. viii.

HOUGHTON MIFFLIN SOCIAL STUDIES

Bookshelf II

Tae's Sonata

by Haemi Balgassi

A Korean American girl tells of her confusion and final acceptance of her dual cultural background.

Motivate Read aloud pp. 18–21 of *Tae's Sonata* in which Taeyoung talks about the things that she likes about her Korean heritage and the things that annoy her. Ask students why the United States is sometimes called a land of immigrants. Have them look at the old photograph on this page and predict what this final unit is about.

To connect this book with the unit content, use the planning guide and student activity blackline masters beginning on p. iv of the *Bookshelf II Teacher's Resources.*

For additional books that are Easy, Average, and Challenging, see the Unit Bibliography on p. T43. See bibliography updates at www.eduplace.com/ss/hmss.

Chapter 19 Planning at a Glance

Pluralism

	Objectives	Reading Support and Other Resources	Diverse Learning Strategies
Lesson 1 A Land of Immigrants *pp. 564–570* 1–2 days	• Identify the different "waves" of immigrants that came to the United States. • Describe the restrictions that the U.S. Government placed on immigration. • Explain why the U.S. Government limited immigration. • Explain why exceptions were made to the U.S. immigration policy.	• **Workbook** or **Reading Support:** pp. 272–275 Review p. 64 Lesson Support/Transition p. 64 Multi-lang. Sum. pp. 127–128 • **Other Resources:** Posters 1, 3, 5, 7; Study Guide p. 82	Access Act. **(SDAIE)** TE p. 565 Language Arts Connection **(Auditory)** TE p. 567 Interviewing **(Auditory)** TE p. 568 Making a Collage **(Visual)** TE p. 569 Audiotapes of Multi-language Lesson Summaries **(Auditory)**
Lesson 2 America's Many Cultures *pp. 571–576* 1–2 days	• Describe how immigrants have become a part of U.S. society. • Explain why the United States is more accurately called a "salad bowl" than a "melting pot". • Identify the role of education in the success of immigrants. • Give examples of ways immigrants have enriched the culture of the United States.	• **Workbook** or **Reading Support:** pp. 276–279 Review p. 65 Lesson Support/Transition p. 65 Multi-lang. Sum. pp. 129–130 • **Other Resources:** Poster 9, Study Guide p. 83	Access Act. **(SDAIE)** TE p. 572 Map and Globe Skills **(Visual)** TE p. 574 Writing a Biography **(GATE)** TE p. 575 Debate **(Auditory)** TE p. 575 Audiotapes of Multi-language Lesson Summaries **(Auditory)**
Skill: Conducting an Interview *p. 577*	• Use the background information about Jesse de la Cruz to develop interviewing strategies.	• **Other Resources:** Study Guide p. 84	
Lesson 3 The Gates Reopened *pp. 578–583* 2–3 days **Literature** "Immigrant Poetry" *pp. 584–587*	• Explain the purposes of the immigration laws of 1965 and 1986. • Contrast the status of a refugee to that of an immigrant. • Explain why some people enter the United States illegally. • Identify the issues surrounding bilingual education. • Compare newer patterns of immigration to past patterns.	• **Workbook** or **Reading Support:** pp. 280–283 Review p. 66 Lesson Support/Transition p. 66 Multi-lang. Sum. pp. 131–132 • **Other Resources:** Geography Kit, Study Guide p. 85	Access Strat. **(Extra Support)** TE p. 579 Mathematics Connection **(GATE)** TE p. 581 Visual Learning **(Visual)** TE p. 581 Making a Chart **(Visual)** TE p. 582 Audiotapes of Multi-language Lesson Summaries **(Auditory)**
Chapter Review *pp. 588–589* 1 day		Chapter 19 Test pp. 73–76 *(See facsimiles on TE p. 767.)*	Assessment Multiple-Use Masters pp. 81–88

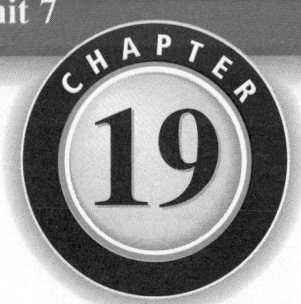

Reading Support Resources *for Every Lesson*

Reading and Review

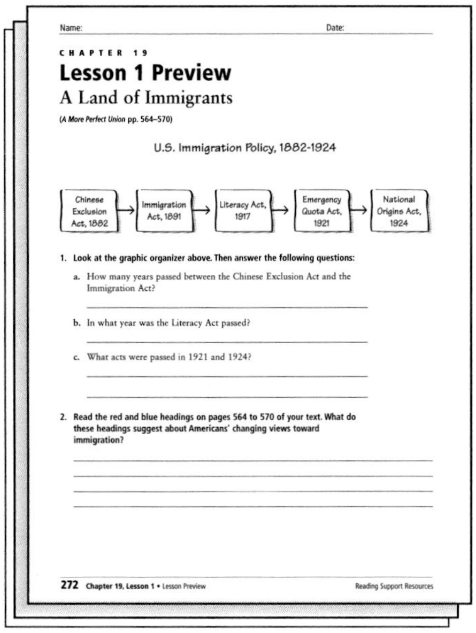
Name: Date:

CHAPTER 19

Lesson 1 Preview

A Land of Immigrants

(*A More Perfect Union* pp. 564–570)

U.S. Immigration Policy, 1882-1924

Chinese Exclusion Act, 1882 → Immigration Act, 1891 → Literacy Act, 1917 → Emergency Quota Act, 1921 → National Origins Act, 1924

1. Look at the graphic organizer above. Then answer the following questions:

a. How many years passed between the Chinese Exclusion Act and the Immigration Act?

b. In what year was the Literacy Act passed?

c. What acts were passed in 1921 and 1924?

2. Read the red and blue headings on pages 564 to 570 of your text. What do these headings suggest about Americans' changing views toward immigration?

272 **Chapter 19, Lesson 1** • Lesson Preview — Reading Support Resources

- **Chapter Overview*** p. 271
- **Lesson Previews*** using graphic organizers from the Teacher's Edition pp. 272, 276, 280
- **Reading Strategies*** pp. 273, 277, 281
- **Lesson Summaries*** pp. 274–275, 278–279, 282–283
- **Lesson Reviews** pp. 64, 65, 66

* **Workbook** includes starred items.

Multi-language Summaries

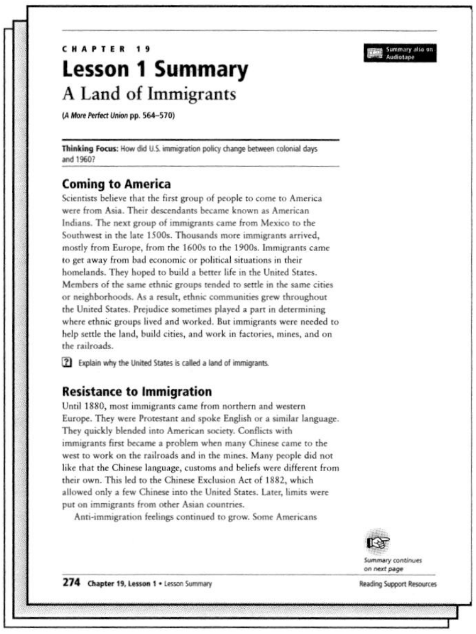
CHAPTER 19

Summary also on Audiotape

Lesson 1 Summary

A Land of Immigrants

(*A More Perfect Union* pp. 564–570)

Thinking Focus: How did U.S. immigration policy change between colonial days and 1960?

Coming to America

Scientists believe that the first group of people to come to America were from Asia. Their descendants became known as American Indians. The next group of immigrants came from Mexico to the Southwest in the late 1500s. Thousands more immigrants arrived, mostly from Europe, from the 1600s to the 1900s. Immigrants came to get away from bad economic or political situations in their homelands. They hoped to build a better life in the United States. Members of the same ethnic groups tended to settle in the same cities or neighborhoods. As a result, ethnic communities grew throughout the United States. Prejudice sometimes played a part in determining where ethnic groups lived and worked. But immigrants were needed to help settle the land, build cities, and work in factories, mines, and on the railroads.

? Explain why the United States is called a land of immigrants.

Resistance to Immigration

Until 1880, most immigrants came from northern and western Europe. They were Protestant and spoke English or a similar language. They quickly blended into American society. Conflicts with immigrants first became a problem when many Chinese came to the west to work on the railroads and in the mines. Many people did not like that the Chinese language, customs and beliefs were different from their own. This led to the Chinese Exclusion Act of 1882, which allowed only a few Chinese into the United States. Later, limits were put on immigrants from other Asian countries.

Anti-immigration feelings continued to grow. Some Americans

Summary continues on next page

274 **Chapter 19, Lesson 1** • Lesson Summary — Reading Support Resources

Lesson Summaries in:

- English (See Reading and Review.)
- Spanish pp. 274–275, 278–279, 282–283
- Chinese pp. 127–132
- Hmong pp. 127–132
- Khmer pp. 127–132
- Vietnamese pp. 127–132

Summaries available on audiotapes

Lesson Support / Transition

S D A I E

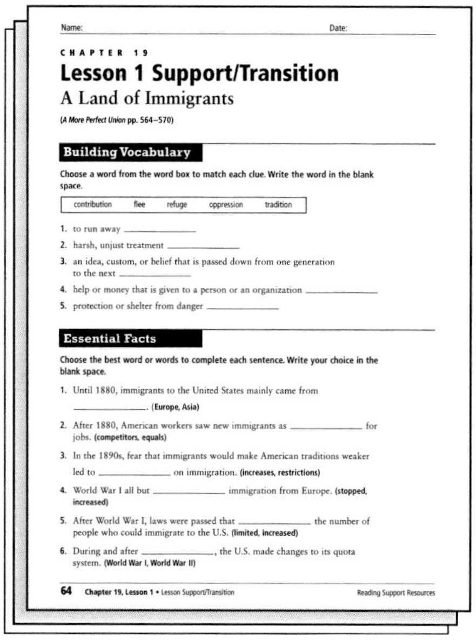
Name: Date:

CHAPTER 19

Lesson 1 Support/Transition

A Land of Immigrants

(*A More Perfect Union* pp. 564–570)

Building Vocabulary

Choose a word from the word box to match each clue. Write the word in the blank space.

contribution flee refuge oppression tradition

1. to run away ______
2. harsh, unjust treatment ______
3. an idea, custom, or belief that is passed down from one generation to the next ______
4. help or money that is given to a person or an organization ______
5. protection or shelter from danger ______

Essential Facts

Choose the best word or words to complete each sentence. Write your choice in the blank space.

1. Until 1880, immigrants to the United States mainly came from ______. **(Europe, Asia)**
2. After 1880, American workers saw new immigrants as ______ for jobs. **(competitors, equals)**
3. In the 1890s, fear that immigrants would make American traditions weaker led to ______ on immigration. **(increases, restrictions)**
4. World War I all but ______ immigration from Europe. **(stopped, increased)**
5. After World War I, laws were passed that ______ the number of people who could immigrate to the U.S. **(limited, increased)**
6. During and after ______, the U.S. made changes to its quota system. **(World War I, World War II)**

64 **Chapter 19, Lesson 1** • Lesson Support/Transition — Reading Support Resources

Activities for SDAIE
Specially **D**esigned **A**cademic **I**nstruction in **E**nglish

- **Lesson Support/Transition** pp. 64, 65, 66

Technology Options

Internet Support

http://www.eduplace.com

Social Studies Center at Education Place

Internet support for Chapter 19:

- ***Lesson at a Glance***
- ***A Hmong Woman***

Videotape/Videodisc

We the People:
Supports and enhances major topics: **Theme:** ***The Immigrants***

Software

Student Writing Center® (CD-ROM) (Macintosh® or Windows®)

School to Career

Divide the class into several small groups. Have each group select and research a type of government position. Students could contact the various agencies and departments for information, such as training required and job responsibilities. Afterward, students can share what they learned with the class.

Character Education

Immigrants to the U.S. can have difficulty adjusting to the language and way of life in this country. What can individuals do to make the transition to a new place easier? Divide students into several small groups. Have each group create a brief skit that deals with a scenario of showing acceptance to someone new, whether it be a new student or new neighbor.

CHAPTER
PREVIEW

After students have read the chapter title and the narrative underneath it, ask them to recall what they learned about pluralism in Chapter 2. How do the images on these pages reflect the concept of pluralism? *(The images represent the many different types of people who live in the United States.)*

Looking Back

Remind students of immigration throughout American history: immigration to the colonies (Chapter 2); Irish and German immigration (Chapter 7); Chinese immigration (Chapter 14); and East European immigration (Chapter 15).

Looking Forward

Tell students that in the next three lessons, they will be learning about the waves of immigration to the United States: A Land of Immigrants, America's Many Cultures, and The Gates Reopened.

Chapter 19
Pluralism

Just as the New World drew the earliest explorers and settlers to its shores in search of a new life, the United States continues to attract people from all over the globe. Some have come seeking better jobs. Others have fled war-torn countries. All bring hopes and dreams of a better life. Their contributions have helped create a rich and vibrant society.

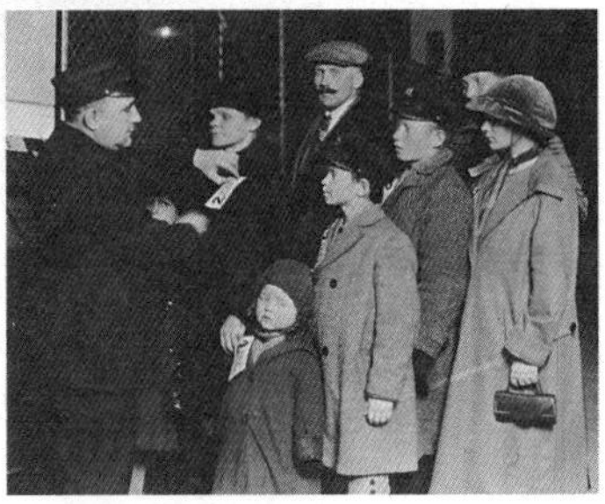

In the late 1800s and early 1900s, Ellis Island was the main reception center for immigrants.

These Chinese immigrants photographed in San Francisco's Chinatown around 1900, maintain their distinct "high class" dress. Colorful masks such as the one at the left are also a part of the Chinese tradition.

1775 | 1825 | 1875

1789

BACKGROUND

The multicultural aspects of American society were created by the different waves of immigration. The groups of people who have immigrated to the United States since 1880 have especially contributed towards enriching American culture in recent years.

Southeast Asia

From the late 1880s to 1954, French Indochina consisted of Cambodia, Laos, and Vietnam, though the French called North Vietnam Tonkin and South Vietnam Annam. Unable to resist the Vietnamese movement for independence, the French withdrew in 1954. An international agreement, the Geneva Accords, divided the country in half, and North Vietnam became a communist country. The United States tried to check the spread of communism by supplying South Vietnam with economic and military assistance. This involvement grew into a large-scale war in the 1960s. Hostilities ended in 1975 when the United States withdrew and communist regimes were established in Vietnam, Laos, and Cambodia (renamed Kampuchea by the new government).

In 1975 the Vietnamese government began to expel Vietnamese of Chinese extraction, as well as capitalists, intellectuals, and those who opposed the new regime. The result was a massive exodus of over a million people. The main routes used by the "boat people" took them to Singapore, Malaysia, Indonesia

A small boat filled with Vietnamese refugees arrives in Hong Kong. Many Vietnamese people, fleeing war and its aftermath in their own land, try to seek refuge in the United States.

Japanese Americans honor their sons by flying banners shaped like carp, a fish noted for its strength.

Hispanic Americans, some of the nation's earliest immigrants, still celebrate customs that have their origins in Spain.

1925 | 1975 | 2025

2000

Understanding the Visuals

Have students identify the different cultures represented in the images on page 562 and this page. *(European, Chinese, Japanese, Vietnamese, and Hispanic)*

Draw student attention to the picture of Ellis Island. The immigrants in this photo were being tagged for a railroad trip to an American city such as Pittsburgh or Chicago. Because the immigrants did not speak English, the tags helped the railroad conductors guide the immigrants to their destination.

Understanding Chronology

Draw students' attention to the timeline. Point out that this timeline covers a 211-year span, reviewing past immigration and covering present-day immigration to the United States.

Korea, Japan, Hong Kong, and as far away as the Philippines and Australia. Others traveled on foot through Cambodia to Thailand or through North Vietnam to China. Many came to the United States to live.

Central America

The seven tiny states of Central America—Guatemala, Belize, Honduras, El Salvador, Nicaragua, Costa Rica, and Panama—have been the site of political turmoil since the 1960s. Authoritarian governments have used violence to repress those who try to change economic and political structures.

More than two million people, particularly Salvadorians and Guatemalans, have left their countries to seek safety in other countries. Many have taken great financial and physical risks to reach the United States and enter it illegally, hoping to be classified as political refugees.

Puerto Rican Migration

Because Puerto Ricans have been citizens of the United States since the end of the Spanish-American War in 1898, there has been a continual movement of citizens from the island to the mainland. However, because Puerto Ricans have a language and cultural background different from the mainland, they are perceived as newcomers and as a minority in the country of their citizenship.

INTRODUCE

After students have read the Thinking Focus, ask them to recall why the United States encouraged immigration during colonial days. *(Needed workers)* Why might the United States have wanted to restrict later immigration? *(Cities crowded, too much competition for jobs)* Tell students to read the lesson to find out how the United States both encouraged and discouraged immigration.

Key Terms

Vocabulary Strategies: T36–T37

quota—the number of people of a nationality allowed to enter the United States in one year

asylum—political protection

refugee—a person who has fled his or her country after facing persecution or severe hardship

➤ *They might feel a sense of freedom; a feeling of hope for a better life.*

1775 1789 1965 1975 2000

LESSON 1

A Land of Immigrants

THINKING FOCUS

How did U.S. immigration policy change between colonial days and 1960?

Key Terms

- quota
- asylum
- refugee

School, soccer practice, chorus practice, homework. These are typical activities for many elementary or middle school students. And Imaan Issa, who is ten years old, does all of these things just about every day.

She also does something else. Either with her family, with other students, or on her own, Imaan prays five times a day. Imaan is one of about 6 million Muslims in the United States. According to Islamic teaching, all Muslims must stop what they are doing five times a day and pray. Daily prayer is one of the "Five Pillars of Islam," the duties that all Muslims practice.

Imaan is an American citizen who lives in Los Angeles. Her parents are both immigrants to the United States. Imaan's mother came from Tanzania when she was eight years old. Her father emigrated from Kuwait to attend college in the United States.

The Issas each practiced their Muslim faith before they moved to the United States. Before Mrs. Issa's family emigrated, "It [religion] was sort of taken for granted because our culture was predominant." Once they moved to the United States, they "realized that religion played more of a role in our lives. It held us [Muslims] together, no matter what country we came from," explains Mrs. Issa.

About 40 percent of the Muslims in the United States are African Americans who were born here. But many other Muslims, like the Issas, are immigrants or the children of recent immigrants. Throughout history, immigrants have brought their religions to the United States. Today, almost all world religions are practiced here. This multitude of religions is only one result of the millions of people who have immigrated to the United States. These immigrants have helped to create a pluralistic society that benefits all Americans.

Imaan Issa, whose parents immigrated to the United States, is seen here in her soccer uniform and at home praying with her brother and sister. How do these two photographs reflect Imaan's two cultures?

564

Objectives

1. Identify the different "waves" of immigrants that came to the United States.
2. Describe the restrictions that the U.S. Government placed on immigration.
3. Explain why the U.S. Government limited immigration.
4. Explain why exceptions were made to the U.S. immigration policy.

Graphic Overview

Chinese Exclusion Act, 1882 ➤ Immigration Act, 1891 ➤ Literacy Act, 1917 ➤ Emergency Quota Act, 1921 ➤ National Origins Act, 1924

Coming to America

Scientists believe that the first Americans arrived thousands of years ago, by crossing a narrow strip of land that joined Asia and North America. Their descendants have become known as American Indians.

As you learned in Chapter 1, the next group of immigrants came from Spanish-held Mexico and arrived in what is now the southwestern United States in the late 1500s. In the early 1600s, men such as Champlain and Hudson explored parts of eastern North America, and eager European settlers soon followed.

Thousands more immigrants followed—decades, even centuries later. Many conditions drove people to leave their homes and to seek a new life in America. Some people fled starvation brought on by crop failures. Others were escaping revolutions or the power struggles among nations that caused unrest throughout their homelands. For still others, the United States offered the opportunity for economic success and social advancement—something that could not be found in Europe, where distinct lines were often drawn between different social classes.

This drawing shows Germans boarding a ship to go to America. What does it suggest about the mood of the people?

Immigrant Communities Grow

While each immigrant had a unique experience in the United States, those experiences were often shaped by an immigrant's ethnicity and country of origin. Once they arrived in America, members of the same ethnic group tended to settle in the same cities or neighborhoods. Often, an immigrant who worked at a certain job would help someone from the same country find a job where that person worked. In this way, ethnic communities grew throughout the United States.

In the late 1800s, for example, Eastern European Jews settled overwhelmingly in New York City and in other cities in the Northeast and Midwest. One occupation held by many Jews was making clothes. In the early 1900s in New York, almost three-fourths of the people who worked in the clothing industry were Eastern European Jews.

Fresno, California became known for its sizable population of Armenians, who emigrated from Turkey. One Armenian named Hagop Seriopan visited Fresno in 1881 and wrote home describing the numerous fruits and vegetables that could be grown in Fresno's warm climate. Within months, more Armenians began arriving in Fresno, where they became successful farmers.

Immigrant groups didn't always live in ethnic communities by choice. Prejudiced, native-born Americans often prevented immigrants from living in certain areas or working in some jobs. Immigrants had to face this racial, ethnic, and religious prejudice in their new homes.

A Welcome Mat in the Early Years

Despite some mixed feelings about immigration, newcomers were generally welcomed into the United States. After all, the nation had vast lands to settle, lands that expanded

DEVELOP

To give students a frame of reference for this lesson, have them preview the graph on page 569. Ask students to take notes on the dates of the passage of acts that changed U.S. immigration policy and to relate these dates to the information in the chart.

The people seem eager to start their voyage.

HISTORY

Visual Learning

As students look at the drawing on this page, have them first describe what is happening and then infer what the next few weeks will bring to these German immigrants. *(Carrying their few possessions and bidding farewell to family; sea voyage on a crowded ship; much uncertainty)*

Access Strategy

Remind students that all Americans are immigrants or descendents of immigrants. If students did not discuss when and from where their ancestors emigrated while reading Chapter 15, have them do so now. Suggest that students unsure of their family origins talk to family members to get more information. Tell students that immigration from 1880 to 1920 alone added over 23 million people to the population.

Continue the discussion by exploring with students what it is like to be a newcomer in a community or school. Divide the class into groups of four to discuss their experiences as newcomers. Then encourage students to share their experiences with the class, especially if any of them have come from other countries. Tell students that they will read in the lesson about the immigration experiences of many groups of people.

Access Activity

Allow students a day or two to find out more about their heritage. Then, on a wall map of the world, have students mark the country or countries of their families' origins. The marking may be done with stickers, tape, or flags.

■ *Everyone who has settled in the United States, from the American Indians to the most recent immigrants, has come from somewhere else.*

BELIEF SYSTEMS

Critical Thinking

Have students recall the principles of social Darwinism from Chapter 18. *(Survival of the fittest; stronger nations dominating weaker nations)* Then ask what effect this system of beliefs might have had on the attitude of Americans toward immigrants. *(Sample answer: Native-born Americans would tend to feel superior to the newcomers.)*

■ *Explain why the United States is called a land of immigrants.*

greatly after the Louisiana Purchase and the Mexican War, as you learned in Chapter 8.

To become a strong nation, the United States needed people to develop its resources, clear the land, grow crops and raise livestock, and build cities and ports. After the Civil War, when industry began to boom, thousands of people were needed to run the machines in factories, mine the ores needed in industry, and build the railroads to carry goods and people. Thousands more people were needed to produce the food for city workers and the materials used in industry. Immigrants, mainly from Europe, supplied this need. ■

Resistance to Immigration

Until 1880, most of the immigrants came from northern and western Europe. They spoke English or languages closely related to English, were mainly Protestant, and shared many of the ideals of the original colonists. Most of these immigrants quickly assimilated, or blended their cultures, into American society.

After 1880, however, increasing numbers of immigrants came from southern and eastern Europe. Many spoke Italian or one of the Slavic languages. Most were Roman Catholics, but significant numbers were Jews or Eastern Orthodox Christians, for example, Greeks and Russians. They came from countries governed by absolute rulers that granted few, if any, rights to their subjects. Many of these immigrants were fleeing oppression that restricted their freedom and threatened their lives.

These new immigrants came to a United States that had changed since the early 1800s. By this time, much of the frontier had been cleared and settled. The railroads had been built, and fewer jobs were available in industry. U.S. laborers saw the new immigrants as competitors because immigrants would work long hours and accept far lower wages than Americans.

Many immigrants from eastern Europe were Slavic people from countries such as Poland and Russia.

Restrictions Begin

A sharp change in the attitude toward immigrants first became apparent in California. Chinese immigrants, who had come to work in the mines and later on the railroad (see Chapter 14), increased in number from 6,000 in 1880 to 30,000 in 1882.

Chinese people were brought in as contract workers who had pledged to work a certain period of time for Chinese labor contractors who sold the immigrants' labor to railroad or other projects. Most worked very hard for low wages, saved their money, and then returned to China.

The few Chinese who stayed often

Social Participation

Ask students to design a program that would help students from foreign countries to feel comfortable in their school. Have them first consider the difficulties a foreign student would have and then suggest things that they as individuals could do to help.

Social Context

One common notion in industrialized nations in the late nineteenth and early twentieth centuries was that racial or ethnic background affected a person's abilities. This idea formed the unconscious basis of many of the restrictions on immigration, particularly on those immigrants from China and Japan.

Popularizers of Darwin's theories claimed that life was a struggle in which only the fittest could survive. Many of them interpreted "fittest" to mean those Americans whose ancestors came from Western and Northern Europe. Some anthropologists also contributed to the problem by claiming that "desirable" and "undesirable" traits were clustered in particular racial and ethnic groups. Because many of the "undesirable" groups also were illiterate (through nothing more than lack of education or opportunity), a literacy test became a convenient means of implementing racial and ethnic restrictions on immigration.

faced scorn. Chinese customs, language, and beliefs were different from those of many Americans. One difference was that many Chinese practiced Buddhism, or Daoism, beliefs that were unfamiliar to most Americans.

Up to this time the United States had done little to encourage or restrict immigration. Growing friction between American and Chinese workers, however, led to government restrictions on Asian immigration. In 1882, Congress passed the Chinese Exclusion Act, which banned most Chinese from the United States. In 1907, a Gentlemen's Agreement with Japan placed similar limits on Japanese immigrants, then excluded them beginning in 1924. Restrictions were also enacted against Asian Indians in 1917, Koreans in 1924, and Filipinos in 1934. Except for a few students and educated people, these measures effectively halted immigration from Asia until 1965.

After 1910, the Chinese who immigrated to the United States came through Angel Island, an immigration station in San Francisco harbor. Only a few groups of Chinese people, such as government officials, teachers, and children of Americans, were allowed to enter the United States. So those who arrived at Angel Island, a much worse facility than Ellis Island, were kept there and questioned to be sure they were legal immigrants. Conditions were poor, families were separated, and people often stayed there for weeks or even months before being allowed to enter the United States or forced to return to China.

Fear of Foreigners Grows

The exclusion of most Asian immigrants reflected the strength of the anti-immigration or nativist movement of the late 1800s. At this time, immigration to the United States was reaching record levels. In fact, 60 percent of the world's immigrants in the 19th century came to the United States. Some Americans insisted on "America for Americans." Fears that "new immigrants" would change American culture and traditions led to even more restrictions.

The Immigration Act of 1891 ordered all new arrivals to pass a physical examination before entering the United States. At both Angel Island and Ellis Island, doctors checked newcomers for diseases such as smallpox, tuberculosis, and cholera. A number of people at Ellis Island were sent back to their home countries, but it was a much smaller number than those who were sent back from Angel Island, because of the Exclusion Act. Most Europeans were admitted to the United States

Besides working in the mines and on the railroad, many Chinese people set up small businesses. Here some Chinese merchants are selling fish.

ETHICS

Critical Thinking

Ask students to speculate on why the facility at Angel Island was in worse condition than the facility at Ellis Island. *(Sample answers: Many fewer immigrants arrived at Angel Island than at Ellis Island so the facility may have been smaller and not as well organized; there was discrimination against Chinese immigrants and Asian immigrants generally; the Angel Island facility may not have been kept in good condition.)*

SOCIAL SYSTEMS

Critical Thinking

Have students classify the reasons for favoring or not favoring the arrival of immigrants in the past into the following categories—economic, political, and cultural. *(Economic—workers were needed; political—fear that people who had lives under absolute rule would threaten democratic principles; cultural—resentment of newcomers' strange language and customs)* Encourage students to keep these categories in mind as they continue reading the lesson.

Health Connection

The doctors at Ellis Island and Angel Island checked for contagious diseases that could cause an epidemic. Have students choose one of those diseases to investigate (smallpox, tuberculosis, cholera, typhoid). Ask them to describe it and to tell how it is spread. If possible, have them find information about specific epidemics or how the diseases were treated around 1900. Have them find out how the diseases are combated today.

Language Arts Connection

To help students understand the challenge of learning a new language, devote class time to listening to another language. Have students listen to a foreign language broadcast on a short wave radio or watch an excerpt from a foreign film. After listening to the language, students can write a short paragraph describing what they think was happening. Have students compare ideas. What clues helped them to identify what was happening? What was it impossible for them to know?

Study Skills

Have students look in an almanac for statistics on population and immigration. Ask them to find answers to the following questions: *How has the country of origin of immigrants changed over the past hundred years? During what periods was immigration the greatest or the least?*

HISTORY

Study Skills

Have students scan the lesson for the names and dates of legislation and other government actions that attempted to reduce or control immigration. *(1882, Chinese Exclusion Act; 1907, Gentlemen's Agreement; 1891, Immigration Act of 1891; 1906, Dillingham Commission; 1917, literacy test; 1921, Emergency Quota Act; 1924, National Origins Act)*

➤ *It was frightening because they might not be allowed into the country. It was exciting because it was the first step toward a new life in America.*

CULTURE

Critical Thinking

Ask students what they think people hoped to gain by "Americanization" in the early 20th century. What was there to lose? *(Sample answer: Americanization would force newcomers to become loyal to their adopted country. America would lose a potentially rich cultural heritage.)*

■ *The threat of war in Europe and the willingness of immigrants to work for low wages caused some people to fear immigrants during this period.*

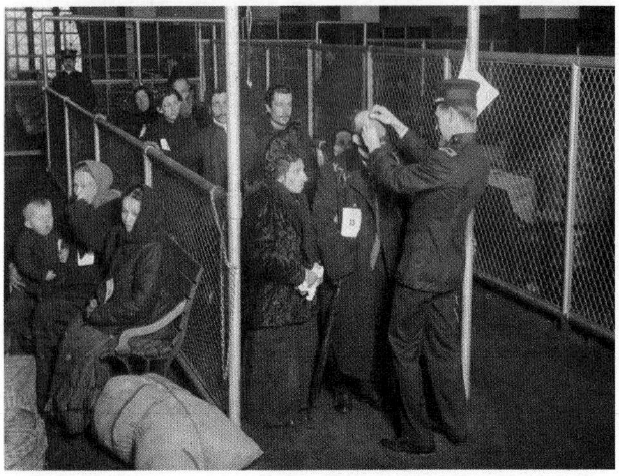

▲ *Over 12 million immigrants passed through the immigration center at Ellis Island between 1892 and 1922. Why was the experience both frightening and exciting?*

and faced the challenge of finding jobs and housing and learning a new language and new customs. As you learned in Chapter 17, reformers worked to improve conditions for these immigrants, but many still had to overcome great hardships.

As the movement to organize labor grew, new fears arose. Business people welcomed the cheap labor immigrants provided, but feared the radical social ideas of some of them, especially the idea of labor unions. American business leaders were afraid that the immigrants would stir up trouble among American workers. These business owners wanted no more strikes like those at Homestead Steel Plant or Pullman Car Works (Chapter 15).

For their part, U.S. workers argued that cheap immigrant labor drove down wages and lowered the standard of living for the average American worker. Their resentment increased when immigrants were hired as strikebreakers.

Congress Passes Literacy Bill

During the early 1900s, the threat of war in Europe grew steadily and added to antiforeign feelings in the United States. In 1907, President Theodore Roosevelt set up the Dillingham Commission to study immigration. The commission's 42-volume report took four years to complete.

The report concluded that immigrants from southern and eastern Europe were less likely to become a part of American life than had the older groups from northern and western Europe. Immigration, the commission implied, should be restricted according to the nation of origin. In other words, the United States should decide how many immigrants it would accept from each foreign nation. The door to America was slowly beginning to close.

In 1914, just before the beginning of World War I in Europe, a number of American groups called for the immediate assimilation of immigrants. These groups joined President Woodrow Wilson in promoting the idea of "Americanization." They questioned the loyalties of immigrants, especially those from countries that did not have democratic governments. Across the nation, they encouraged immigrants to abandon their cultural heritage and embrace "100 percent Americanism."

Because of German attacks on France and Great Britain, German Americans faced particular hostility. They avoided speaking German in public places. Some changed their names to English-sounding names. For example, a person named Grünwald might change the name to Greenwood.

World War I all but halted immigration from Europe. Then, in 1917, Congress added a literacy test to its growing list of restrictions on immigrants. The test required an immigrant to be able to read his or her language in order to enter the United States. The restriction was aimed at newer immigrant groups such as Slavs, Italians, and Russians, who were coming to America in increasing numbers. Since illiteracy was generally declining, however, the literacy test had a limited effect. ■

■ *Why did people in the United States tend to fear immigrants in the early 1900s?*

Social Participation

Have students contribute to a list of things that they would not be able to enjoy under a plan of "100 percent Americanism." *(Sample answers: Many interesting "ethnic" foods, certain clothing styles, most classical music, British-based rock music, many sports)*

Interviewing

Suggest to students that they interview a person who has immigrated to the United States and become a citizen. You may want to have them develop a list of questions for at least part of their interviews. They could ask about the person's reasons for coming to the United States, what problems he or she encountered, and what the citizenship process was. Encourage students to write down or tape-record exact words of the interviewed person.

When they have completed their interviews, have students share what they found out—first in discussion and then by writing up their interviews and putting them in a folder for others to read. If any students have used tape recorders, encourage them to play their recordings for the rest of the class.

The Closing Door

After World War I ended in 1918, Europe was in a shambles. Hundreds of thousands of people had been uprooted by the war and by boundary changes after the war.

The Number of Immigrants Is Limited

Alarmed that new waves of immigrants would flood into the United States, Congress passed the Emergency Quota Act of 1921 (also called the Johnson Act). This law established a **quota**. It meant that only a certain number of people were allowed to immigrate to the United States. The quota limited each nationality to 3 percent of that group's foreign-born population living in the United States in 1910. For example, if 100,000 Italians lived in the United States in 1910, only 3,000 Italians would be allowed to immigrate in 1922. The number of visas—official authorizations to live in a country—was restricted to a total of 350,000 immigrants.

In 1924, Congress replaced the Johnson Act with the National Origins Act, which reduced the quota from 3 percent to 2 percent of those present in 1890. By changing the base year from 1910 to 1890, the law favored the national groups that had arrived in the United States before 1890. It sharply reduced immigration by eastern and southern Europeans, most of whom had immigrated after 1890. It also reduced the number of visas to about 150,000. Most of them went to northern and western Europeans.

The law did not apply to immigrants from the Western Hemisphere, primarily because of pressure from employers in the Southwest who depended on Mexican workers. Filipinos, too, were unaffected. They were considered American nationals, because the United States had annexed the Philippines in 1899.

When an economic depression began in 1929, U.S. immigration dropped severely. Thousands of Americans lost their jobs and foreigners ceased to view America as the land of opportunity. Immigration dropped from over 800,000 in 1921 to less than 150,000 by 1929.

World War II Brings Exceptions

By the late 1930s, economic conditions slowly began to improve in the United States. Growing numbers of people in other nations applied for visas. During this period, widespread unrest was sweeping Europe and Asia. Some national groups feared for their lives because they were being blamed

U.S. Foreign-Born Population, 1860–1996

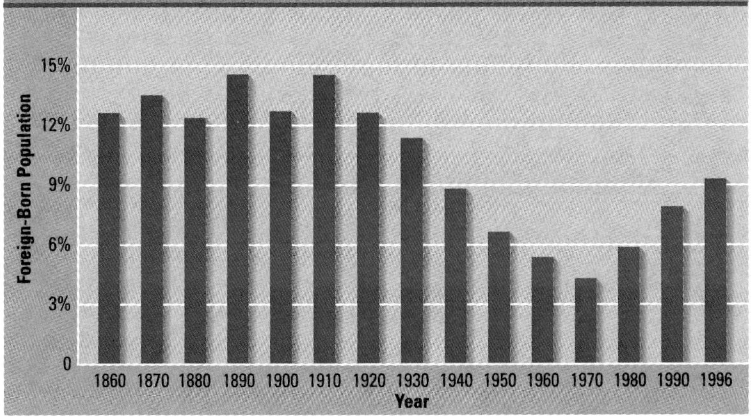

In what two years did the U.S. population have the highest percentage of foreign born? In what year was the foreign-born population the lowest percentage of the total U.S. population?

POLITICAL SYSTEMS

Critical Thinking

Ask students to evaluate the fairness and objectivity of the 1921 and 1924 quotas and then compare them to the idea of basing immigration on literacy. *(Sample answer: The 1921 law unfairly favored some groups; literacy requirements also favor more privileged groups.)* What other plan might be fairer? *(Students should give reasons for their answers.)*

The highest percentage of foreign-born Americans lived in the United States in the period between 1890 and 1910. The percentage of foreign-born Americans was the lowest in 1970.

Role Playing

Have pairs of students work together to write and perform a dialogue or a skit illustrating a difficult situation of a newly arrived immigrant. Examples might be the person's first day at work or shopping for food. Encourage students to show not just the negative side of such an encounter but also the generosity that some Americans are capable of showing.

Making a Collage

Have students each make a collage of images showing the cultural diversity of the United States as a result of the immigrants from many lands. Supply magazines for cutting or have students draw images. When the collages are complete, have each student explain his or her choice of images and their placement within the collage.

Visual Learning

Have students use the percentages in the chart on this page, plus the following statistics on the total U.S. population, to calculate the approximate number of foreign-born residents of the United States: 1900—76,212,168 *(9,907,582)*; 1940—132,164,199 *(11,894,778)*; 1980—226,542,580 *(13,592,550)*; 1990—248,718,301 *(19,648,746)*; 1996—265,557,000 *(24,696,801)*.

POLITICAL SYSTEMS

Critical Thinking

Have students consider some of the pros and cons to each of these positions: quota rules should be bent based on a person's potential contribution; anyone who wants to move to this country should be allowed to do so; a lottery system should determine who may immigrate to this country. Students should choose a position and name reasons that support it.

■ *Fewer people emigrated from Southern and Eastern Europe; Northern and Western Europeans were entitled to three-fourths of the available visas.*

CLOSE

Have students list the sequence of changes in U.S. immigration policy, as in the Graphic Overview on page 564, and then use this information to answer the Thinking Focus. As a reteaching activity, ask students to identify the attitudes in the early 1900s that led to the tightening of immigration restrictions.

On October 1, 1940, Albert Einstein, his daughter Margot (right), *and his secretary Helene Dukas were sworn in as citizens of the United States.*

■ *What effect did the quota system have on immigration?*

for problems that beset their homelands. Most threatened were the Jews, who faced imprisonment and often death in Germany.

Recognizing the contributions that well-educated people, especially scientists, might make, the United States bent its quota rules. It offered **asylum**, or political protection, to highly educated Europeans, many of whom were Jewish writers and scholars. Several of these people made brilliant contributions to science and helped the United States become a leading power in the world.

One such scholar was a German Jew named Albert Einstein, winner of the Nobel Prize in Physics in 1921 and author of *The Meaning of Relativity* (1921). Einstein revolutionized modern science with his new theories about time, space, mass, and motion. Einstein, along with scientists Edward Teller from Hungary and Enrico Fermi from Italy, helped make the United States the first nation with nuclear weapons.

Unfortunately, in order to maintain the immigration quotas during this time, the United States turned away many immigrants who were not distinguished people. Among them were Jews, millions of whom were brutally executed in the lands ruled by Germany during World War II.

Other Exceptions to the Quota System

The United States also made exceptions to its quota system after World War II ended in 1945. The country took in thousands of **refugees**, people who faced persecution because of their political beliefs. Many of these people came from eastern Europe, which had fallen under communist control. Since the United States opposed communism, it allowed many people from those countries to seek refuge in America.

When communist leader Fidel Castro took power in Cuba in 1959, thousands of Cubans sought refuge in the United States. Most of these immigrants were educated professionals who brought their skills and knowledge to the United States. Cuban immigrants became very successful in the United States.

In general, despite the restrictions, immigrants from many nations reached the United States between 1820 and 1960. Most became American citizens. Yet each group held on to some of its own customs and beliefs. In this way immigrants gave new meaning to the phrase *e pluribus unum*, which means, "Out of many, one." ■

REVIEW

1. **FOCUS** How did U.S. immigration policy change between colonial days and 1960?
2. **CONNECT** Compare and contrast the patterns of immigration from 1840 to 1860 and after 1880.
3. **ECONOMICS** Explain how the quota system worked.
4. **CULTURE** Describe the reasons for some of the exceptions to U.S. immigration laws.
5. **CRITICAL THINKING** In a nation developed by immigrants, why are immigrants often unwelcome?
6. **WRITING ACTIVITY** Make a chart showing the different attitudes people have had toward immigrants. In one column, list the reasons in favor of immigration. List the reasons against immigration in a second column. You may wish to include years to indicate changing attitudes.

Homework Options

Ask students to find out the requirements for United States citizenship by naturalization.

Study Guide: page 82.

Answers to Review Questions

1. Colonial America had few restrictions: in the early 1800s, the United States encouraged immigration; and by the late 1880s, it made laws to restrict immigration.
2. 1840–1860: Most immigrants were Protestants, spoke English, and came from Northern and Western Europe. After 1880: Many were Catholic, Eastern Orthodox, Jewish, didn't speak English, and were from Southern and Eastern Europe.
3. In 1910, the quota limited the number of people coming to the United States each year to a given percentage of the foreign-born population for each nationality.
4. The United States bent its quota rules for well-educated people and for those who were persecuted.
5. Sample answer: People may fear competition from immigrants who will work for lower wages. Allow for personal opinion.
6. Charts should include economic, social, and cultural reasons.

1775 1789 2000

LESSON 2

America's Many Cultures

Early in the morning, grocers bustle about, arranging boxes of vegetables and fruits or displays of toys and curios from Asia. As they work, they chat with their neighbors and customers, talking about the weather and neighborhood events, wishing one another a good day. As the fog lifts from San Francisco Bay, tourists will be pouring through the dragon gates that mark the entrance to Chinatown.

Most of the residents here work in or close to their homes. The traditional good luck colors of gold and scarlet and the Chinese paper lanterns give the shops a festive air. Each shop identifies itself and tells of its goods in large Chinese characters. In the windows are T-shirts with fanciful dragons, hand-embroidered linens, delicate laces, silk clothing, hand-painted porcelain, lacquerware, enamelware, carvings of wood, stone, and ivory, and jewelry of jade, rose quartz, and many other semiprecious stones.

One shop follows another, interrupted occasionally by restaurants serving barbecued chicken, dim sum, and other dishes from various regions in China. Along the side streets are small family-run groceries selling dried shrimp, pressed duck, fresh vegetables, dried or preserved fruit, spices, teas, and ginger.

San Francisco's Chinatown, one of the largest Chinese communities outside Asia, is only one example of the kind of ethnic neighborhood that can be found in the United States today. Miami has its Little Havana, populated mainly by Cubans. Chicago's Pilsen neighborhood houses a huge Mexican population. Los Angeles has Koreatown. In playgrounds across the nation, many children speak a wide range of languages—Chinese, Spanish, Italian, Arabic, Hindu, and dozens more—often with a mixture of English.

THINKING FOCUS

What are some of the benefits and challenges of being an immigrant in the United States?

◄ *Why do many immigrant groups come together in communities like this one in San Francisco?*

INTRODUCE

After students read the Thinking Focus, have them suggest answers based on what they read in Lesson 1. Tell them to read the lesson to learn more about the benefits and challenges of being an immigrant in the United States.

CULTURE

Visual Learning

As students examine the photograph on this page, have them identify elements of Chinese culture. *(Architecture, Chinese characters on signs)* Ask them also to name clues that reveal that this picture was taken in the United States. *(American cars, signs in English)*

◄ *Gathering in communities such as this one allows immigrant groups to share their cultural background and to help one another socially and economically.*

Graphic Overview

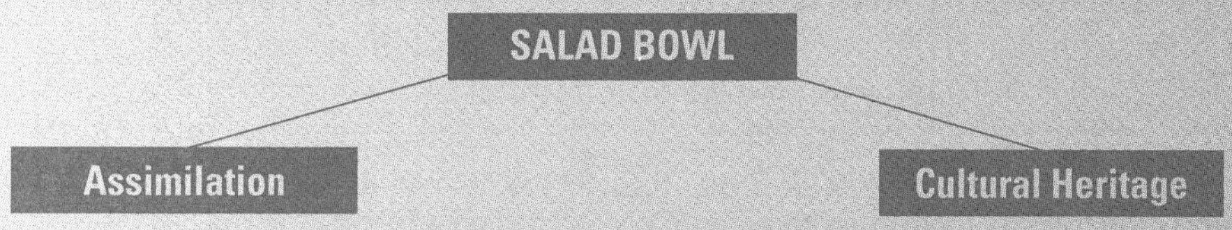

Objectives

1. Describe how immigrants have become a part of U.S. society.
2. Explain why the United States is more accurately called a "salad bowl" than a "melting pot."
3. Identify the role of education in the success of immigrants.
4. Give examples of ways immigrants have enriched the culture of the United States.

DEVELOP

Explain that this lesson deals with some of the issues facing immigrants in the United States. As they read, students can look for examples of the different ways immigrants have adapted to the culture of the United States and ways that they can keep ties to their culture of birth.

➤ *North America and Asia*

CULTURE

Social Participation

Encourage students to interview neighbors and family members to learn about the ancestry of people in their town. Is there a diversity of cultural backgrounds, or do most people have the same background? Have them compare their findings with the information on the map on this page.

From Melting Pot to Salad Bowl

How Do We Know?

HISTORY *One way to discover what life was like in ethnic neighborhoods of the past is to collect oral histories—that is, to talk to elderly people who have vivid memories of olden times. Their personal photographs, letters, diaries, and mementos can also provide a lively picture of the past. Stories, reports, and historical photos also help reconstruct the past.*

For many years, America was called a "melting pot," a country where the customs of new arrivals melted down and blended into one American culture. Many people now believe this view is outdated. The United States does not have one culture. It is made up of many interconnected cultures.

Today, many people compare the United States to a salad bowl. Like a salad, the United States is made up of various "ingredients" or cultures. Although they are mixed together, these ingredients remain separate. Just as each component in a salad bowl gives a separate taste, each cultural contribution adds to the variety and diversity of American life.

How Groups Assimilate

When an immigrant culture and a local culture meet, each adapts to the customs of the other. Assimilation, the process of taking on the language, customs, and viewpoints of another culture, takes time. Some people do it easily, while others resist it altogether. Most immigrants choose to blend into American culture, but also to hold onto parts of their ethnic identity.

One ethnic group that arrived in the United States within the past 30 years is the Hmong people, from the Asian country of Laos. The Hmong were mainly farmers in the mountains of Laos. They began emigrating in the 1970s after the Vietnamese War.

The Hmong brought many of their cultural traditions to America. Many Hmong in the United States practice their traditional religion, eat Hmong foods, and know as much about politics in Laos as American politics. Yet many Hmong have learned English in order to drive. Some have also begun selling their traditional stitchery to earn a living.

Unlike the Hmong, Mexican Americans have long been in the United States. In fact, many Mexican Americans are not immigrants. They are descendants of Mexicans who lived in places that once were part of Mexico, but became part of the United States after the Mexican War.

Mexicans also continue to immigrate to the United States and to hold onto their culture. This may be because they live so close to Mexico, or because they are such a large group here (over 12 million people). Mexican Americans tend to live in very concentrated areas, and most speak some Spanish, or both Spanish and English. About three-fourths of Mexican Americans practice the Catholic religion. Many are members of social and political organizations that help strengthen their ethnic ties.

As shown by both Hmong and Mexican Americans, immigrants do not need to give up their cultures once they arrive in the United States. Whether they have been here for a few years or for many generations, most immigrants choose to keep some of their cultural traditions.

▼ *This graph shows the ten countries that the most U.S. immigrants came from in 1995. Countries from which continents appear on this graph?*

Immigration to the United States

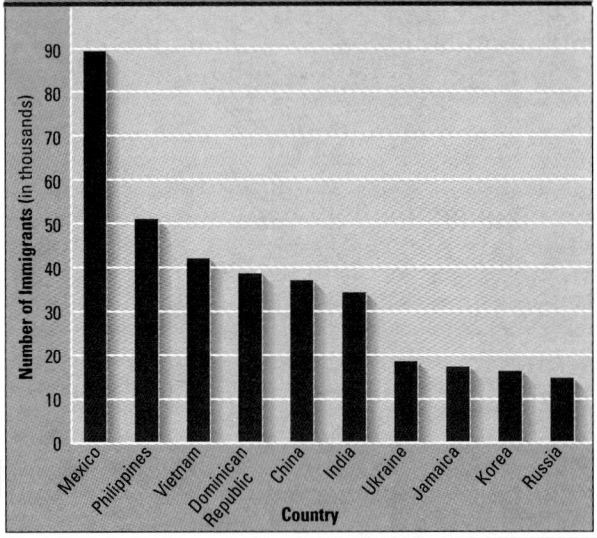

Access Activity

Have students use the chart on this page to tell which country had the highest number of immigrants to the United States in 1995; and, therefore, which language was spoken by the highest number of immigrants in 1995? *(Mexico; Spanish)*

Access Strategy

Ask students to identify some of the problems that a newcomer to the United States would have. *(New language, no friends, unfamiliar customs, homesickness)* In what ways would it help to be near an established community of people from their native country? *(These people could give them information about jobs, places to live, U.S. laws, and English lessons.)* Explain that students will read in this lesson about the different strategies new Americans have followed to assimilate and to retain aspects of their native cultures.

A MOMENT IN TIME

A Hmong Woman

3:07 p.m., May 16, 1985
In a small apartment in Fresno, California

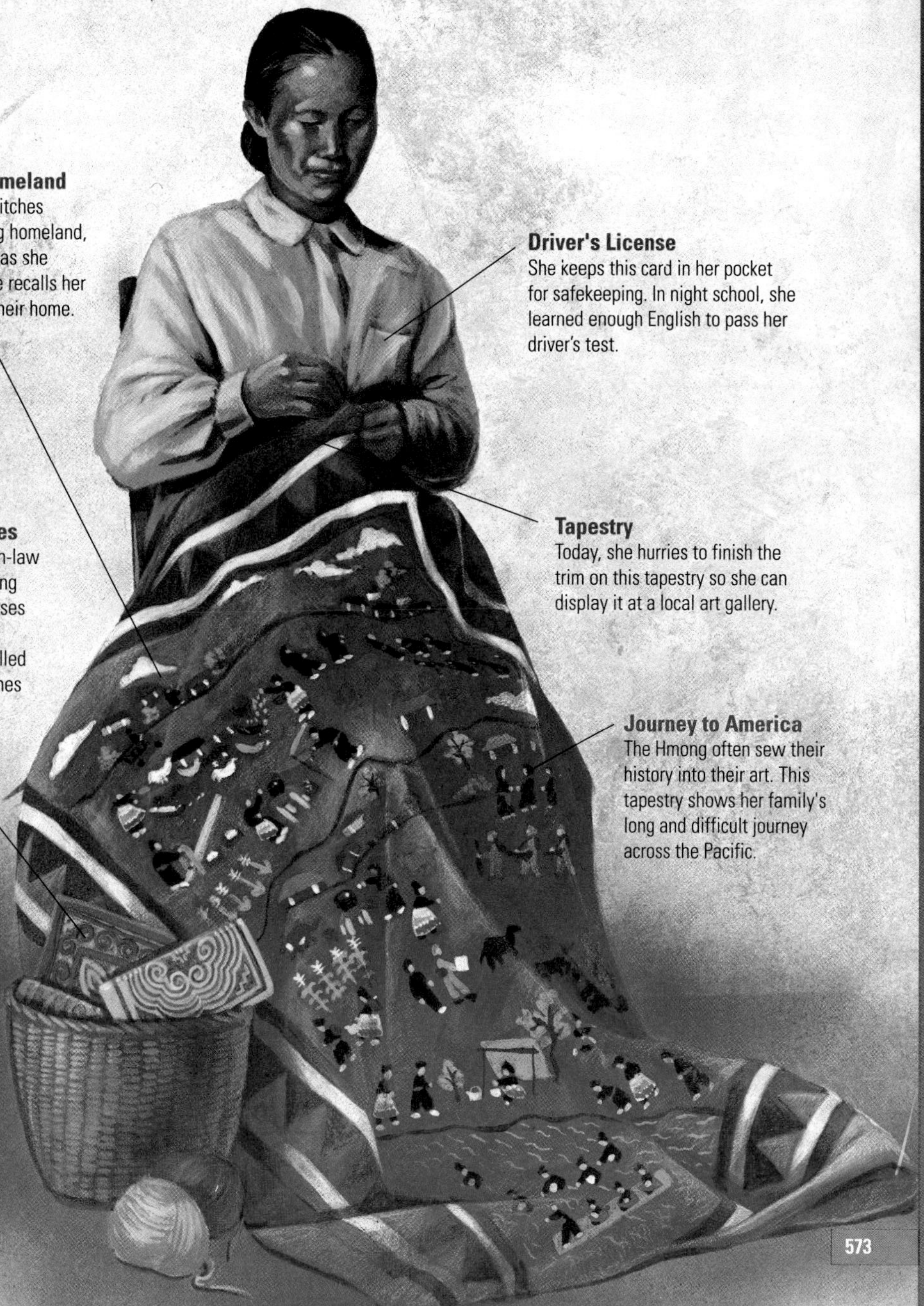

Scenes of Her Homeland
For long hours, she stitches pictures of the Hmong homeland, Laos. This afternoon, as she finishes her work, she recalls her family's garden and their home.

Driver's License
She keeps this card in her pocket for safekeeping. In night school, she learned enough English to pass her driver's test.

Hand-Sewn Purses
She and her mother-in-law spend mornings sewing these small fancy purses to sell to a handicraft store. The designs called *pa ndau*, use 20 stitches per inch.

Tapestry
Today, she hurries to finish the trim on this tapestry so she can display it at a local art gallery.

Journey to America
The Hmong often sew their history into their art. This tapestry shows her family's long and difficult journey across the Pacific.

Note: After students have read on page 572 about the Hmong people, use A Moment in Time as an example of an immigrant woman using specialized skills to earn a living in the United States.

More About Hand-Sewn Purses
The art of pa ndau is produced without the use of sewing machines, pins, or patterns.

CULTURE

Visual Learning

After students read the information about the tapestry in A Moment in Time, ask them to identify some of the images on the tapestry. *(Crops, people on a raft, water)* What can they learn from the tapestry about this woman's journey to the United States? *(Sample answer: She had to walk a long distance and cross a wide river on a simple raft.)*

Cultural Context

Immigrant contributions to American culture are so pervasive that they have become commonplace and easy to overlook. The influence of a diverse population is probably most evident in the American diet. Aside from exotic foods such as Chinese dim sum, Americans enjoy frankfurters and hamburgers (German and Russian origin respectively), chocolate and tacos (Mexico), pizza (Italian), noodles (Chinese), coffee and yogurt (Middle East), peanuts and peanut butter (Africa), sugar (Southeast Asia), and potatoes (South America).

Many holidays, songs, and sports were brought into this country from other cultural traditions. The use of Christmas trees, for instance, was brought to the colonies by German immigrants.

Critical Thinking

Have students study the pictures and captions in A Moment in Time to find examples of the way the Hmong woman's life has changed since she came to America. *(She can no longer work in her family garden; she drives; and she speaks English.)* In what ways is her life the same? *(She is here with family members; she still sews in a traditional way.)*

CULTURE

Critical Thinking

After students have read the Jade Snow Wong quotation on this page, ask them to explain what she means in the last sentence. What are some of the benefits she probably had to do without? *(Sample answer: Any special treatment, hand-outs, or assistance)*

■ *Many immigrants believed that education would help them succeed and improve their standard of living. They were willing to make sacrifices so that their children would have an education.*

To support the family in America, Daddy tried various occupations—candy making, the ministry to which he was later ordained—but finally settled upon manufacturing men's and children's denim garments. He leased sewing equipment, installed machines in a basement where rent was cheapest, and there he and his family lived and worked. There was no thought that dim and airless quarters were terrible conditions for living and working, or that child labor was unhealthful. The only goal was for all in the family to work, to save, and to become educated. It was possible, so it would be done. . . .

I observed from birth that living and working were inseparable. My mother . . . was at her machine the minute housework was done, and she was the hardest working seamstress, seldom pausing, working after I went to bed. The hum of sewing machines continued day and night, seven days a week. . . . We knew that to overcome poverty, there were only two methods: working and education. It was our personal responsibility. Being poor did not entitle us to benefits.

Jade Snow Wong, Chinese American

Japanese Americans package fruit to ship to other parts of the United States.

For Many, Hard Work Brings Success

In the passage above, Jade Snow Wong, who immigrated to the United States from China with her parents, describes her father's determination to succeed in his new homeland.

Work and education helped many immigrants to blend easily into American society. Older immigrants often accepted the fact that they themselves might never achieve the golden future they believed America promised. Yet they did not lose faith in the future. They were determined that their children would fulfill their dream.

To achieve that goal, they were willing to make enormous sacrifices—to work long hours at low-paying jobs, to spend little on themselves, and to save as much money as they could so that their children would have the opportunity to learn. Many immigrants believed that education served as the road to success in the United States.

Immigrants often struggled for years before they established themselves. Many achieved great personal and financial success. Their determination and achievements are all the more noteworthy in light of the hardships they had to overcome.

I.M. Pei is a Chinese-born American architect whose works include the John F. Kennedy Library in Boston, Massachusetts and the East Building of the National Gallery of Art in Washington, D.C. Pei said of his design for the National Gallery, "To make the visit a pleasant one . . . we built a circus." The design has a large central core of ramps, balconies and escalators covered by monumental skylights. The "big top", as it has been called, adds a sense of fun to the traditional idea of a museum, and is an example of one of the many ways American culture has benefited from the unique perspective immigrants can provide. ■

■ *What attitudes did many immigrants have toward education?*

Map and Globe Skills

Refer students to the world map on pages 694–695 of the Atlas. Ask them to find the countries mentioned in this lesson: China, Cuba, Mexico, Korea, Italy, Laos, Vietnam, Philippines, Ireland. Point out that these countries are only a small sampling of the many places from which U.S. citizens have come.

Language Arts Connection

The study of word origins, or etymology, reveals that English has borrowed words and expressions from many languages. Not only did immigrants learn English, but certain words and expressions from their native languages also found their way into English. Have students look up these words to find their origins and meanings: *lasso, mesquite, hoosegow, pueblo* (Mexican Spanish); *fondue, Mardi Gras* (French); *gumbo, goober* (African); *tycoon, tsunami* (Japanese); *bagel, schtick, schmaltz* (Yiddish); *jeans* (Italian); *kitsch, kindergarten, kaput* (German).

Adjusting to America

Adjusting to life in the United States is usually easier for children than for parents or grandparents. Adults often have more vivid memories of the people and places they left behind and can frequently be homesick. Children, on the other hand, have few memories of the old country. In school they quickly learn the language and customs of the new country and adapt quickly. In immigrant neighborhoods children often act as translators and interpreters for their parents when English is required.

Coping in a New Country

Just as children can help parents adjust to American life, certain organizations can also help new immigrants. Korean immigrants, for example, benefit from many community groups. Korean churches and schools give classes in Korean culture and language, which helps immigrants keep their ethnic identity. The family is central to Korean culture and relatives in America can help Korean immigrants to assimilate.

Korean organizations can also help new immigrants financially. Some Korean immigrants use the gye (*geh*) loan system, where several small business owners each lend money to an immigrant who is starting a business. That person uses the money for one year and keeps the profits. The next year, that person also contributes to the gye, which goes to another new business owner.

Understanding Assimilation

Melting pot or salad bowl? How best to describe the United States? Should new immigrants discard their ethnic identities to become 100 percent Americans? Or should they retain some features of their old culture, which then become part of the American "mix"?

How Assimilation Occurs

Assimilation means to be absorbed into the dominant culture. Assimilation is not the same as naturalization. If an immigrant fulfills all the requirements and takes an oath of allegiance, then he or she may become an American citizen. The action of the naturalization judge in conferring citizenship does not also include assimilation. That process may be immediate, or it may last a lifetime.

Factors that influence assimilation include the age of the newcomer, the motives that brought the person to America, and the degree of contact with people outside the new citizen's ethnic group. Also important are the criteria the dominant group—the Americans already here—use to judge assimilation.

Some examples clarify this. Suppose a Filipino child comes to this country with his parents and his widowed grandmother. The boy will probably learn a new language and new customs much faster than his parents or grandmother. He has many more opportunities for learning—in the classroom, on the playground, around the neighborhood.

His parents, who came here because they wanted better jobs, also learn quickly. They know that a good knowledge of English will help them move ahead.

His grandmother, on the other hand, may have fewer opportunities for meeting new people. Her English may be poor or she may be uncomfortable speaking to anyone other than Filipinos. She has come to America to be with her family. Because she is retired and has less outside contact, it may be harder for her to learn the English language and American ways.

CULTURE

Critical Thinking

Ask students to list some of the advantages Korean immigrants in the United States may have. *(Strong sense of community and family; Korean organizations often help out financially; Korean schools and churches help preserve Korean heritage.)*

CULTURE

Critical Thinking

Have students imagine a fictional immigrant family in this country. Have students consider what problems each person in the family will have, based on the information on this page in Understanding Assimilation. How will each person cope with the problems of immigration?

Writing a Biography

Tell each student to select a notable person who immigrated to the United States in the twentieth century. Ask students to write a one-page biography of the person, telling where the person was born, when he or she arrived in the United States, what the early years in the United States were like, and what the person's accomplishments were. Combine the reports to form a "book" entitled *Notable Immigrants* and distribute copies to the class.

Debate

Suggest that students debate the "salad bowl" versus the "melting pot" images of American assimilation. Has the melting pot really given way to the salad bowl? What evidence can students cite from their own lives? Is there another metaphor which better describes the situation?

Critical Thinking

Remind students that they encountered the word *assimilation* in Chapter 14. Ask them to identify the benefits and drawbacks of rapid and total assimilation. *(It might help one get a job and fit into the community, but it might also make one feel disconnected and confused.)*

CULTURE

Critical Thinking

Encourage students to name one or more ways in which their own lives have been enriched by the contributions of immigrants and their cultures.

■ *Some immigrants did not want to give up their own culture; they associated mainly with people who shared their native culture.*

CLOSE

Students should summarize the lesson by answering the Thinking Focus. Copy on the board the Graphic Overview from page 571 and have students suggest ways that foreign-born Americans have both assimilated American culture and preserved their own cultural heritage.

➤ *This newspaper is written in Korean for people who live around San Francisco. Newspapers like this one can help immigrants to keep their language and culture as they adapt to their new home.*

Unlike Koreans, many Jamaican immigrants have immigrated to the United States alone, or have few family members here. Because of immigration restrictions and economic hardships in Jamaica, entire families cannot always immigrate at the same time. So one parent may move to the United States to earn enough money so the rest of the family can come several years later. This separation of parents and children can be painful for both.

You've read that immigrants who are close to family members in their home country, like Mexican Americans, are often less likely to assimilate in a new country. Once a family reunites, assimilating can become easier. But because of racial prejudice in the United States, some Jamaicans still find American life difficult. So many Jamaicans choose to live and work in the United States for only a few years and then return home.

■ *Why did some immigrants find it difficult to become assimilated?*

The United States Enriched

Immigrants have helped to broaden and deepen Americans' view of their world. Their presence in the United States helps Americans to appreciate different points of view. It also helps Americans realize how differently they themselves may appear to others. Immigrants have helped to shape the meaning of the word *American*. They have contributed to the varied foods Americans eat, the beliefs Americans hold, and to almost all aspects of American life: politics, science, theater, art, music, literature, sports, medicine, and education.

Numerous immigrant groups have made their way to the United States with hope, faith, and determination. Although it is impossible to describe the contributions all of these groups have made, the richness and diversity of American life proudly tells their stories. ■

REVIEW

1. **FOCUS** What are some of the benefits and challenges of being an immigrant in the United States?
2. **CONNECT** How did basing immigration quotas on national origins make it easier for immigrants to become assimilated after 1920?
3. **ECONOMICS** Why were immigrants willing to work at low-paying jobs?
4. **CRITICAL THINKING** What are some ways that community groups can help new immigrants adjust to the United States?
5. **ACTIVITY** Look through a large city's newspaper or a national magazine for evidence of immigrants in the United States. Look for announcements of ethnic festivals, recipes for ethnic food, reports on famous immigrants, and books or movies about the immigrant experience. Share your findings with the class.

Homework Options

Tell students to imagine immigrating to a foreign country. Ask them to write a paragraph telling what parts of American culture they would want to keep.

Study Guide: page 83.

Answers to Review Questions

1. Benefits include becoming part of a multicultural society, sharing in democratic practices, and having the chance to succeed through hard work and education. Challenges include learning a new language and traditions.
2. The quota system favored immigrants from Northern and Western Europe who found it easier to adapt.
3. Immigrants were sure that hard work would help them succeed. They believed that taking low-paying jobs would eventually help them achieve a better living.
4. Sample answer: Community groups often help new immigrants secure loans for starting businesses; they also help immigrants feel welcome in America and yet hold on to their culture.
5. Students should try to present a variety of cultural items.

UNDERSTANDING INFORMATION COLLECTION

Conducting an Interview

Here's Why

Interviewing people who lived during a certain period is a good way to gather firsthand information about that time. Such oral histories are important primary sources for future historians.

In this chapter you have read about the experiences of different immigrant groups who came to the United States. Suppose you wanted to find out what life was like for the children of Mexican-American immigrants. One way to get that information firsthand would be to interview a child of Mexican-American immigrants.

Here's How

Before you interview someone, it is a good idea to find out as much about the person as you can. In addition, when you contact the person to set up the interview, you should tell them why you want to interview them, what you want to know, and how you plan to use the information.

Growing up, I could see all the injustices and I would think, "If only I could do something about it! If only there was somebody who could do something about it!" That was always in the back of my mind. And after I was married, I cared about what was going on, but I felt I couldn't do anything. So I went to work, and I came home to clean the house, and I fixed the food for the next day, took care of the children and the next day went back to work. The whole thing over and over again. Politics to me was something foreign, something I didn't know about.

Jessie de la Cruz

Jessie de la Cruz (pictured at left) is the daughter of Mexican-American immigrants. Read the profile below to find out more about her:

> Jessie de la Cruz grew up in a family that had immigrated from Mexico to California before World War II. After her father and grandfather died, the family became migrant farm workers. During her 30 years of migrant work, de la Cruz became active in changing the poor working conditions for migrant farmers. She was a union organizer, a delegate to the Democratic Party national convention, and the developer of a cooperative ranch. Today she is a living witness to the exploitation of immigrant families as farm laborers and has often been interviewed by historians.

Based on the information above, you can now make a list of 10 questions to ask de la Cruz if you were interviewing her about her experiences. The interview should begin with general questions and work toward specific questions that include the "five W's and an H" (who, what, when, where, why, and how) to make sure it covers all areas of information. Possible questions are:

1. What was it like growing up in an immigrant family?
2. When did your family first move to the United States?
3. Where did you live when you were growing up?
4. How did you get involved in union activities?

Try It

Above is a passage from an interview with de la Cruz. Read it, and make a list of five questions you would ask in order to gather more information.

Apply It

Each family has its own history. Decide which member of your family you would like to interview for an oral history project. Make a list of basic questions to ask. Write or call the person to set up an interview, and take notes or tape-record the interview.

UNDERSTANDING INFORMATION COLLECTION

This skill lesson will give students practice in the research and critical thinking skills required to conduct an effective interview.

SOCIAL SYSTEMS

Study Skills

Ask the students why it is important to learn as much as they can about the person before an interview. *(Sample answers: So that they will not waste time during the interview; so that they will be able to ask specific questions about the person's life)* Why is it important to prepare some questions before the interview? *(So that the interview can begin smoothly)* Should students rely only on prepared questions? *(No, they should listen carefully to the person being interviewed. If that person says something that interests them, question him or her further about the topic.)*

Answers to Try It

Suggested questions: Why did your life begin to change? When did you first learn about politics? Who was the most important influence on your life? What did your husband and children think about your decision to get involved in politics? What was your biggest success?

Answers to Apply It

Remind students to use the "five W's and an H" as a guide to preparing their questions. Ask them to prepare at least ten questions in advance. Check to see that they worked from general to more specific questions.

Objective

Use the background information about Jessie de la Cruz to develop interviewing strategies. (Study Skills 1)

INTRODUCE

Ask students to recall some of the restrictions put on immigration between the 1880s and 1920s. *(Health, literacy, country of origin)* Have students read the Thinking Focus and name countries from which a number of people have come in recent years. *(Sample answers: Vietnam, Cambodia, Cuba)* Tell them that they will read about changes in U.S. immigration policy since the 1960s.

Key Terms

Vocabulary strategies: T36–37

undocumented immigrant—an immigrant who enters the United States without permission and lacks a passport or visa

migrant worker—a person who travels across the United States planting and harvesting crops as jobs are available

bilingual education—education presented in two languages

1775 1800 1825 1850 1875 1900 1925 1950 1965 2000

L E S S O N 3

The Gates Reopened

THINKING FOCUS

How did the pattern of immigration to the United States change after the 1960s?

Key Terms

- undocumented immigrant
- migrant worker
- bilingual education

So we got a private ship . . . not for money. The owner left Saigon already and everybody—maybe three thousand people, oh my!—just got on the ship. A lot of soldiers force themselves on. One of the people on the ship was a ship captain so he took the ship on the ocean. Others helped. Many times engine stopped. Stop. Stop. Stop. On the sea we run out of food and water. . . .

We see a lot of small ships but they cannot help. We send message. Nobody answer. The engine was finished and ship almost sinking. Then we pretty lucky a Denmark ship see us and take us to Hong Kong. . . .

Americans come to Hong Kong to interview. Everybody fill out a form and everybody happy, think that next day we go to the United States. But after that United States embassy don't come anymore to camp. A week later, a month later, nobody come. Everybody very depressed. We lucky, but we not very lucky. Then they change to let more people in and again they [the American embassy officials] interview.

A Vietnamese Refugee, *Today's Immigrants, Their Stories*

This refugee's story reflects a growing problem in the world today. As nations around the globe have been torn by war, the number of refugees has increased. Although finding asylum may be difficult, the United States has struggled to offer fleeing people refuge. Yet, at the same time, the U.S. government must ensure that the needs of its own citizens are not neglected. How many people can the United States realistically accept? This issue remains as pressing today as it was in the early 1960s, when Congress introduced the laws reopening immigration to the United States.

Expanding Opportunities for Immigrants

On October 3, 1965, at the base of the Statue of Liberty, President Lyndon B. Johnson signed a new immigration law. He was carrying out a wish of his predecessor, President John F. Kennedy. A strong supporter of immigration, Kennedy had proposed a new immigration law. He was assassinated before his proposal could be passed.

The new law ended the quota system. It allowed each nation to send as many as 20,000 people to the United States in a single year, up to a total worldwide of 270,000 immigrants. The law was particularly concerned with reuniting families. Often families had been separated when the male head of the household immigrated to the United States in search of work. Moreover, many immigrants entered the United States illegally and could not send for their families.

Under the 1965 law, 74 percent of the available visas were allotted to the foreign relatives of American citizens and legal immigrants already

Objectives

1. Explain the purpose of the immigration laws of 1965 and 1986.
2. Contrast the status of a refugee to that of an immigrant.
3. Explain why some people enter the United States illegally.
4. Identify the problems that bilingual education may create.
5. Compare newer patterns of immigration to past patterns.

Graphic Overview

U.S. IMMIGRATION POLICIES

- 1960s
- 1970s
- 1980s

in the country. President Johnson spoke of the new law in the following words:

> *This bill . . . does repair a very deep and painful flaw in the fabric of American justice. It corrects a cruel and enduring wrong in the conduct of the American nation. . . . From this day forth those wishing to immigrate to America shall be admitted on the basis of their skills and their close relationship to those already here. This is a simple test and it is a fair test.*

Although the new law treated foreigners more fairly than did the old, it still tended to prevent people from some nations from immigrating to the United States. Since it favored immigrants with relatives already in the United States, it discriminated against people from Asia, Africa, and Latin America. Most immigration from Asia had been banned altogether since the early 1900s, and only limited numbers of Latin Americans had been allowed under the old quota system.

Under the 1965 law, people from these regions could enter the United States only if they were professionals, technicians, or workers with other needed skills. By 1975, however, enough emigrants from Latin America and Asia had come to the United States that they were attracting large numbers of family members who wished to join them.

Admitting Soviet Jews

In 1974, the United States began to grant more visas when it was "in the interests of foreign policy." In other words, the United States increased the number of visas it allowed from a country in order to maintain good relations with that country or to get that country to make a desired change. For example, the United States offered to increase trade with the Soviet Union, provided the Soviet government allowed more Jews to leave that country.

These policies also changed the immigration balance. Increasing the number of visas for people in one country required reducing visas for people in other countries. When the Soviet Union allowed more Jews to leave in the 1980s, the United States increased the number of visas for Soviet Jews. However, the total number of immigrants to the United States did not change. The increase in visas for Soviet Jews resulted in a decrease in visas for Asians.

Admission of Refugees

After 1960, U.S. immigration policies were affected by growing numbers of refugees. Congress defined a refugee as "any person outside his country, victimized by persecution on racial, religious, political, or social grounds."

In the 1970s and 1980s, thousands of Vietnamese, Cambodians, and Laotians fled their native countries during the Vietnam War and the later upheaval in Southeast Asia. They were known as "boat people" because they escaped in leaky, overcrowded boats, seeking asylum in a safer region. Up to 4,000 refugees fled each week.

President Jimmy Carter expressed

Vietnamese boat people use northward-blowing trade winds to reach Hong Kong. In 1989, the government there refused to admit more Vietnamese. Claiming they were looking for a better way of life rather than political asylum, the Hong Kong government threatened to send all the refugees who were then in Hong Kong back to Vietnam.

DEVELOP

Students should preview the lesson heads to find indications of the changes in immigration since the 1960s. Copy on the board the Graphic Overview from page 578 and have students copy it in their notes. Ask students to look for examples of U.S. immigration policy in the three time periods as they read the lesson. Have them note this information in their own charts.

POLITICAL SYSTEMS

Critical Thinking

How did the immigration law of 1965 have both a restricting effect and a liberalizing effect on America's population? *(Restricting—fewer immigrants from countries without significant existing American communities; liberalizing—allowed families to reunite)*

Access Strategy

Ask students to brainstorm the provisions for a new immigration law that would be fair to all immigrants and to the people already living in the United States. You may wish to divide the class into heterogeneous groups. Have them consider the following questions to help them get started: Should immigration be limited at all? What might happen if we allowed unlimited immigration? If immigration is to be limited, what would be a fair way to do it? Should any group have special privileges—for instance, people with relatives already in the United States, refugees who might be killed if they cannot escape their native countries, or people with special skills that might benefit the United States? Tell the students that they will read in this lesson about some recent developments in U.S. immigration policy.

Access Activity

Read aloud the refugee's story in the lesson opener on page 578. Ask students to describe some of the problems this refugee had on the boat. *(No food, water, bad engine, no help)* When were the refugees happy? *(When they got to Hong Kong)* What made them depressed? *(They were stuck in a camp.)*

SOCIAL SYSTEMS

Critical Thinking

What do you think will happen to the thousands of refugees who remain in temporary camps? What choices do they have? *(They can return to their own country or wait until a country accepts them.)* Why do you think some countries do not welcome refugees? *(Sample answer: Economic problems, prejudice)*

■ *It reunited families, but discriminated against people from Asia and Latin America, because most of them did not already have relatives in the United States.*

➤ *From 1901–1920; from Asia.*

▲ *Vietnamese boat people arrive in Manila, the capital of the Philippines.*

the following view about American acceptance of refugees:

> *Refugees are the living homeless casualties of our world's failure to live by the principles of peace and human rights. To help them is a simple human duty. As Americans, as a people made up largely of the descendants of refugees, we feel that duty with a special keenness.*

■ *How did the immigration law of 1965 affect the people who immigrated to the United States?*

Numbers of Refugees Increase

In 1980, about 130,000 Cubans sailed from Mariel, Cuba, to Florida. The United States was reluctant to welcome such a large group of foreigners, many of whom were suspected of being criminals or mentally or physically unfit. President Carter, however, called for "an open heart and open arms" for the Cubans, although most did not qualify as legal refugees.

Each year 10 million to 13 million people become refugees. The number has tripled since the 1970s. Most are innocent men, women, and children who are caught in regional wars— Southeast Asians such as the Cambodians and Vietnamese and Central Americans such as the Salvadorians.

The United States, with its tradition of welcoming the persecuted, has accepted many refugees—up to 94,000 a year. Thousands of refugees, however, remain in temporary camps around the world. Many other nations are not as welcoming as the United States in admitting refugees. ■

Undocumented Immigration

The line between refugee and immigrant is often blurred. An immigrant may come to the United States looking for a better life. A refugee, by definition, is a person who flees a country because his or her life is threatened. The United States does not always agree that people who say they are seeking protection in the United States are refugees.

▼ *When did most immigrants from southern and eastern Europe come to the United States? Where did most immigrants come from after 1981?*

Temporary Workers

During World War II, when U.S. soldiers were fighting in Europe and

The Changing Tide of U.S. Immigration

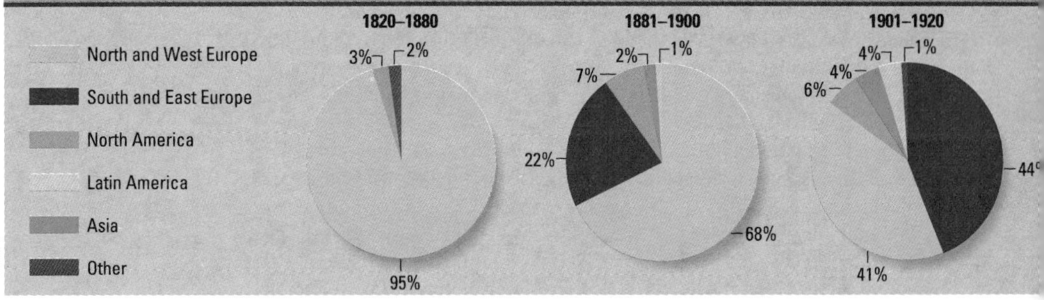

Critical Thinking

Compare President Carter's quotation on this page with President Johnson's on page 579. To what group does each refer? *(Johnson was talking about all immigrants while Carter referred to refugees.)* Do you think refugees should be treated differently than other immigrants? Why or why not?

Political Context

Today, the immigration system in the United States is more flexible than it was in the 1920s. Beginning in the year 1995, for example, there was an overall flexible cap of 675,000 immigrants of which 480,000 are to be family-sponsored; 140,000 employment-based; and 55,000 "diversity immigrants." "Diversity immigrants" are citizens of nations allotted few immigrants in past years.

In 1996, a total of 915,900 immigrants entered the United States legally from a total of eight countries.

There is no current limit on immigrants who are immediate relatives of U.S. citizens. There are also certain categories of immigrants that are accepted for one year, which depend on the number accepted in the previous year.

Asia, the United States needed workers. It admitted many Mexicans as *braceros*—workers with temporary permits—to grow and harvest crops. The braceros had to return to Mexico when their permits expired.

About four million braceros entered the United States before 1964, when the program ended. Some returned to Mexico, but many stayed in the long-established Mexican-American communities. They became part of a growing underground community known as **undocumented immigrants** because they have no passports or visas to indicate their origins.

"Being illegal is nonexistence" said an Irish-born secretary who entered the United States illegally. "You've got no job security, no medical insurance, no right to open a bank account, and are an open target for landlords and employers."

Growing Number of Undocumented

Each year thousands of people enter the United States as undocumented immigrants. Living outside the law, they often work at seasonal jobs, such as growing and harvesting crops. Because they fear being caught and deported, they move frequently. In 1984, U.S. Customs agents found over one million undocumented immigrants; probably thousands more were not caught.

Many of these immigrants are desperately poor Mexicans seeking to survive. No one knows how many Mexicans cross the 1,936-mile border between the two countries each year. The comments of one Mexican man reflect the thoughts of many of these undocumented immigrants:

> *Even when there is work available back home, you're only making $2.25 for nine hours of work. You're working six days a week just to buy a pair of shoes. Compare that to the stupendous money you can make working in the United States, and you'll know why I'm here.*

In recent years, increasing numbers of undocumented immigrants have been arriving from Central America, Ireland, Korea, the Philippines, and the Caribbean nations as

These migrant workers are picking celery in California.

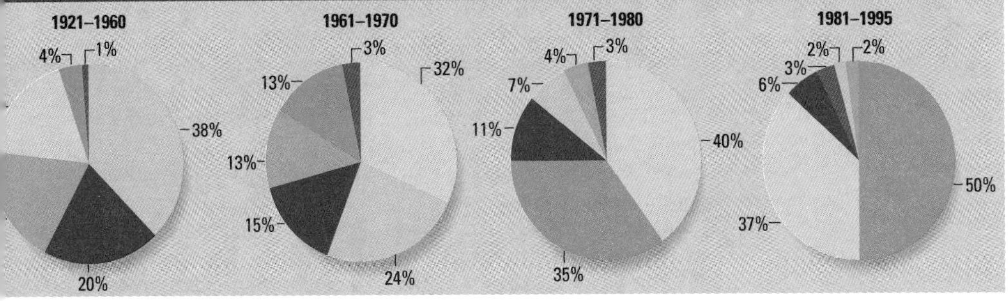

581

GEOGRAPHY

Visual Learning

Have each student choose an ethnic group from the key on the left of the graph on page 580 and trace the history of that group's immigration. You may want to ask questions about each ethnic group, such as: When did immigration begin? When did immigration reach its peak? When did immigration begin to decline?

Mathematics Connection

Have the students use the figures on pages 582–583 (37% and 77%) to calculate the current number of Hispanic and Asian immigrants per year, based on a total quota of 270,000. *(37% x 270,000 = 99,900, 77% − 37% = 40% and 40% x 270,000 = 108,000)* How many Asians and Hispanics will have immigrated to the United States in the decade from 1990 to 2000? *(10 times the above figures: 999,000 Hispanics and 1,080,000 Asians)* Explain to students that these kinds of projections are often made by scientists, government agencies, and advocacy groups in observing population patterns.

Study Skills

Immigrants often work for the minimum wage or less. Almost all undocumented immigrants work for less than the minimum wage. Have students use an almanac to compare the current federal minimum wage with the average U.S. income. Students may have to convert hourly wage rates to annual rates.

SOCIAL SYSTEMS

Critical Thinking

What are some of the problems that an undocumented immigrant faces, both at home and in the United States? *(Home—few opportunities, financial problems; In the United States—no stability or security, possible exploitation and deportation)* Why do you think people would be willing to put up with these problems? *(Sample answer: These problems are less serious than the problems they had in their native country.)*

■ *They proved they had been living and working in the United States since January 1, 1982.*

POLITICAL SYSTEMS

Critical Thinking

Ask students why they think the United States Government offered amnesty to undocumented immigrants in 1986. *(Sample answer: Because prosecuting and deporting them would have been impossible or too costly)*

Cesar Chávez founded the United Farm Workers, a union for migrant workers. He also organized sit-ins and national consumer boycotts of grapes and lettuce.

well as from Mexico. On an April day in 1989, for example, a young Korean tearfully greeted his wife. The Korean couple had been separated for eight years, ever since he became an undocumented immigrant to the United States. He did whatever work he could get, working for 70 hours each week. He sent as much money as he could to his family in Korea.

The Korean Association arranged the visit with his wife. He expected, however, that he would have to work at least three or four more years before he could send for his family permanently.

The Undocumented Create Tensions

Many Americans argue that undocumented immigrants take jobs away from U.S. citizens. Using undocumented immigrants, they say, allows U.S. employers to pay less and offer poor working conditions. They also claim that these immigrants are often supported by the welfare programs that are paid for by U.S. citizens.

Others argue that the undocumented take only those jobs that legal residents do not want. They point to statistics that seem to indicate that less than 20 percent of the undocumented immigrants depend on welfare money.

■ *How did some undocumented workers gain the right to stay in the United States?*

A Chance for a Pardon

In 1986, Congress passed the Immigration Reform and Control Act. The new law had three parts. It called for increasing the size of the United States Border Patrol. People who knowingly hired undocumented workers faced fines and criminal penalties. Most important, the law granted amnesty, a general pardon, to all immigrants who had been in the United States illegally since 1982. Those who could prove they had been living in the United States continuously since January 1, 1982 were allowed to remain as legal immigrants.

Many undocumented workers, however, had purposely kept no records. Some found clever ways to prove they had been in the United States—a letter from a business, school records of their children, or magazine subscriptions. Other undocumented immigrants had arrived after the cut-off date and did not qualify for amnesty. They faced the loss of their jobs. Employers would no longer hire workers without papers because of the threat of fines.

Changes for Migrant Workers

Special measures were taken in 1986 for **migrant workers,** who traveled across the United States growing and harvesting crops as jobs became available. Farm workers who could prove they had spent at least 90 days in the United States between May 1, 1985, and May 1, 1986, could apply for permanent status. They had to pay $185, a large amount for people who often earned less than the minimum wage. Nevertheless, thousands of migrant workers applied for legal immigration. ■

Across Time & Space

The on-going process of American immigration can be seen in the recently opened immigration center in San Antonio, Texas. Those immigrants who pass through its doors today, like their counterparts who went through Ellis Island in generations past, believe in the promise of a better life in the United States.

Other Challenges of Immigration

The 1986 law did not decrease the flood of immigrants from Mexico and Central America. Although U.S. Customs agents caught many and sent them back to their own countries, most undocumented immigrants simply waited a while, and then tried to cross the border again. Unemployment and poverty in the nations of Latin America, as well as political unrest in Central America, made these people desperate for a new life in the United States.

Changing Tide of Immigration

Today, about 37 percent of the legal immigrants to the United States are Hispanics. The exact number of Hispanics who enter the country ille-

Critical Thinking

How could an employer hire workers at decent wages and still make a reasonable profit? Divide students into groups to brainstorm a list of suggestions. *(Sample answers: Raise prices of finished goods, provide training and machines to increase workers' efficiency, reduce profits somewhat)*

Writing a Biography

Have students do research on Cesar Chavez—his early life, his work on American farms, his founding of the United Farm Workers, and his achievements. (see page 591). Ask students to prepare a two-page biography of Chavez and his role in improving the situation of migrant workers in the United States. Encourage students to explain the basic motivations behind his life work.

Making a Chart

Using an almanac, students can find information on the population of several ethnic groups in New York City or in another major city. Have them compare this information to the population of the capital city of each ethnic group's country of origin. Students should make a chart that shows the total figures as well as the proportion of total population of the group in each city.

gally is not known. By the year 2000, experts estimate, the U.S. population will include between 30 million and 35 million Hispanic Americans, making them the largest minority in the United States.

The number of Asian immigrants to the United States continues to increase also, particularly from Southeast Asia. Experts predict that the largest number will come from the Philippines, China, Korea, Vietnam, and India.

Together, Asian and Latin American immigrants make up about 77 percent of the legal immigrants to the United States. In other words, the United States is undergoing a population shift similar to that caused by the immigration from southern and eastern Europe in the early 1900s.

The Hispanic population, in particular, seems more inclined to keep its native language than do most other immigrant groups in the United States. This reluctance to use English poses a problem for many U.S. institutions, including schools and governments.

The Language Question

An organization that wants English to be declared the official language of the country states: "Language is one of the few things we have in common in the U.S." The movement to make English the official U.S. language is in part a reaction to education presented in two languages, or **bilingual education**. In 1968, Congress passed the Bilingual Education Act. It called for teaching subject matter in the student's native language in addition to English. The bill's sponsors hoped that this process would help foreign-born students make an easy transition to using English.

Some people in the United States, however, feel that bilingual education is not really helping students learn English. They argue that students should learn only English, claiming that bilingualism encourages a person to remain outside U.S. society. They have called for laws to make English the official U.S. language and to teach classes only in English in public schools. Those who support bilingual education, on the other hand, say that people can be U.S. citizens and still keep their cultural roots.

Although the United States continues to pride itself as a nation of immigrants, immigration patterns today continue to challenge U.S. public policy makers. Bilingual education and the problems of illegal immigration remain issues for Americans to resolve in the coming years. ■

In this second-grade classroom in Austin, Texas, the Pledge of Allegiance is written in Spanish as well as in English so that Hispanic students will have a better understanding of it.

■ *What different views do people have on bilingual education?*

REVIEW

1. **FOCUS** How did the pattern of immigration to the United States change after the 1960s?
2. **CONNECT** Compare the immigration law of 1965 with that of 1924.
3. **SOCIAL AND ECONOMICS** Why do people risk entering a country illegally?
4. **CRITICAL THINKING** What issues do growing numbers of immigrants create for public services such as education, housing, fire and police protecion, and health care?
5. **WRITING ACTIVITY** Imagine your family has moved to a country where English is not spoken. What problems might your family encounter? Describe those problems.

SOCIAL SYSTEMS

Critical Thinking

What would it be like to go to a school in another country where all the classes were taught in a language other than English? Have students suggest some of the things they would be unable to do in class. *(Ask and answer questions, follow directions, understand discussions)* If the teacher could speak English, how might the situation be better or worse? *(Could learn other subjects better, but have less need to learn the country's language)*

■ *Some people think that it enables students to learn English without falling behind a grade level. Others believe that the English language unifies people in the United States and that it should be the only language used in schools.*

CLOSE

Copy on the board the Graphic Overview from page 578 and have students use the notes they made while reading the lesson to add examples to it. Have them use this chart to answer the Thinking Focus. As an extension, have students do the Making a Chart activity on page 582.

Answers to Review Questions

1. American policy changes allowed increased numbers of some foreigners, including refugees, to immigrate. Immigration restrictions have resulted in large numbers of undocumented immigrants.
2. The 1924 law limited immigrants to 2 percent of their group's population living in the United States in 1890. The 1965 law allowed up to 20,000 people a year to come from each nation.
3. Many people leave their homes to escape poverty or persecution for their political or religious beliefs.
4. Sample answer: Immigrants add to the population and increase the need for public services. Because many immigrants are poor or work illegally, they do not pay a lot in taxes, which pay for public services. Allow for personal opinion.
5. Student could focus on the first month in the new country.

Homework Options

Language is one of the things Americans have in common. Have students write a paragraph suggesting additional things that U.S. citizens have in common.

Study Guide: page 85.

INTRODUCE

Ask students to recall what they learned about the immigrant experience in Lesson 3. Point out that the poetry reprinted on this page and pages 585–587 reveals the unique and personal feelings of being a new immigrant in America.

READ AND RESPOND

Ask whether any students have relatives who are recent immigrants to the United States, or who came through Angel Island or Ellis Island as immigrants. What stories or memories did they pass on? How did they feel when they first arrived?

As students read the poems independently, ask them to keep in mind the mood of each poem. Then, have volunteers reread the poems aloud. Encourage class discussion of the differences in mood between the first poem and the last three poems.

In this chapter, you have read how immigrant groups have helped to create a pluralistic United States. These poems, by immigrants and their descendants, reveal different aspects of the immigrant experience.

dispelled driven away

LITERATURE

Immigrant Poetry

Many immigrants to the United States have had mixed feelings about their new home, and some have written poetry to express those feelings. The poem below was written in Chinese by a Chinese immigrant who was detained on Angel Island, in San Francisco Bay. It was later translated into English. The other three poems were written in recent years by immigrants or their descendants. How would you compare the feelings expressed in the first poem with the feelings in the last three poems?

Imprisoned in the wooden building day after day,
My freedom withheld; how can I bear to talk about it?
I look to see who is happy but they only sit quietly.
I am anxious and depressed and cannot fall asleep.
The days are long and the bottle constantly empty; my sad mood,
even so, is not dispelled.
Nights are long and the pillows cold; who can pity my loneliness?
After experiencing such loneliness and sorrow,
Why not just return home and learn to plow the fields?

囚困木屋天復天，
自由束縛豈堪言？
舉目誰歡惟靜坐，
關心自悶不成眠。
日永樽空愁莫解，
夜長枕冷倩誰憐？
參透箇中孤苦味，
何如歸去學耕田？

584

Thematic Connections

Social Studies: Immigrant experiences

Background

Modeled after Ellis Island, Angel Island in San Francisco Bay served as a detention center from 1910 to 1940 almost exclusively for Chinese who had failed to convince officials that they had legitimate claims of eligibility for entry into the United States, under U.S. exclusion laws. Those who failed were quickly deported, unless they appealed the decision, which often prolonged their stay for months, even years. While waiting, many painted or carved poems on the walls to express their fears, anger, hopes, and loneliness. Many poems, such as the one on this page, survive and have been translated into English.

Two Pictures of My Grandparents: 1914
by Joseph Bruchac

I.

Her feet stitch the sidewalks
of the Garment District.
It is as grey
in those distant stories
as the shawls
of Middle European women.

Her fingers are thin,
polished bone spools.

II.

The sun peers down on him
through coal-smoke clouds.
It squints like the Asian eye
of a Slovak steelworker.

His breath is hesitant
from burned lungs.
It whitens the throat
of the winter sky.

III.

My Uncles do not recognize
their parents in these words.
The images are as strange to them
as that language they still remember
is to me, a tongue
which never gathered money
though it warmed them
as they shared it, the one fire
they could always afford.

◄ In the poem on page 584, what do you think the poet means by the words "the bottle was constantly empty"? *(These words might mean that the immigrant was hungry and thirsty; there was not enough to drink or eat; or, that the future seemed uncertain; nothing was happening.)* How would you describe the immigrant's mood? *(Sad and lonely; worried about whether the decision to come to America was the right one; the immigrant has not given up hope, however. The immigrant awaits a hint or clue that the long journey and detainment is worth it.)*

◄ In the poem on page 585, how would you describe the poet's grandmother? *(hard-working, tired, frail)* Which words does the poet use to tell you this? *(Her fingers are thin/polished bone spools.)*

Background

Joseph Bruchac is an award-winning short-story writer, poet, novelist, and storyteller. Born in Saratoga Springs, New York, he worked as a laborer, surveyor, and tree surgeon during his school years. He taught English and literature in West Africa from 1966 to 1969. His works for children are numerous and include *The First Strawberries: A Cherokee Story, The Great Ball Game,* and *The Boy Who Lived with the Bears: and Other Iroquois Stories.* Many of Bruchac's stories have been recorded on audio cassette, including *The Boy Who Lived with Bears, Iroquois Stories,* and *Dawn Land.* Mr. Bruchac, who is of Abenaki Indian and European origin, lives in New York.

➤ How does the daughter feel, watching her mother and her grandmother sing a song from a country she knows nothing of? *(The daughter feels happy that, just by listening to her mother and grandmother sing, she can imagine what life must have been like, growing up in China.)*

➤ Why are the two women crying? *(The song reminds them of their homeland, China, and the land and places they miss.)*

I Ask My Mother to Sing
by Li-Young Lee

She begins, and my grandmother joins her.
Mother and daughter sing like young girls.
If my father were alive, he would play
his accordion and sway like a boat.

I've never been in Peking, or the Summer Palace,
nor stood on the great Stone Boat to watch
the rain begin on Kuen Ming Lake, the picnickers
running away in the grass.

But I love to hear it sung;
how the waterlilies fill with rain until
they overturn, spilling water into water,
then rock back, and fill with more.

Both women have begun to cry.
But neither stops her song.

586

Thematic Connections

Social Studies: Immigrant experiences

Hay un naranjo ahí
by Alfonso Quijada Urías

Hay un naranjo enfrente, tras de ese viejo tapial
abandonado,
pero no es el mismo naranjo que sembramos,
y es un bello naranjo
tan bello que nos hace recordar
aquel naranjo que sembramos
—en nuestra tierra—
antes de venir a esta casa
tan distante y lejana de aquélla
donde sembramos un naranjo
y hasta lo vimos—como éste—florecer.

There's an Orange Tree Out There
Translated by Darwin J. Flakoll

There's an orange tree out there, behind that old,
abandoned garden wall,
but it's not the same orange tree we planted,
and it's a beautiful orange tree
so beautiful it makes us remember
that orange tree we planted
—in our earth—
before coming to this house
so distant and remote from that one
where we planted an orange tree
and even saw it—like this one—in flower.

Further Reading

Destination America. Maldwyn A. Jones. A study of immigrants who came to the United States between the years 1814 and 1914.

The New Immigrants. Carol Olsen Day and Edmond Day. Describes the problems immigrants face and examines the controversies surrounding immigration today.

◄ What does the orange tree symbolize in the poem? *(Answers may include that the orange tree symbolizes people, places, events, and traditions in America that, although they are to be respected and perhaps learned, are not the same as those in the immigrant's homeland.)*

EXTEND

Have students imagine that they are a recent immigrant in America today. Ask them to write five brief journal entries (one for each day in a week) to describe their feelings during their first week in America.

Further Reading

You may want to ask students to go to the school or local library to find more books to read about immigrants' experiences.

Answers to Reviewing Key Terms

A. Sample answers:
1. A person who cannot obtain a visa under the quota system sometimes comes into the country as an undocumented immigrant.
2. The United States grants asylum to refugees who leave their country because of religious or political persecution.
3. Some undocumented immigrants move about the country as migrant workers.

B. Answers:
1. bilingual education
2. quotas; undocumented immigrants
3. refugees
4. asylum

C. Sample answers:
1. True. These people often work at seasonal jobs, such as harvesting crops.
2. False. A quota restricts immigration.
3. False. The U.S. government gives refugee status only to a person coming in search of safety.
4. False. Bilingual classes offer English as well as the students' native language.
5. False. They often receive wages far lower than the average American's.

Answers to Exploring Concepts

A. Answers:
1. Chinese Exclusion Act: Banned contract laborers from China
2. Gentlemen's Agreement: Limited Japanese immigration
3. Immigration Act: All new arrivals were physically examined before entry into the United States.
4. Emergency Quota Act: Limited the number of immigrants allowed into the United States from certain countries
5. National Origins Act: Further limited immigrants from Southern and Eastern Europe
6. Immigration Act of 1965: Ended quota system based on national origin

In the paragraph students should give specific examples of changing immigration laws.

Chapter Review

Reviewing Key Terms

asylum (p. 570)
bilingual education (p. 583)
migrant worker (p. 582)
quota (p. 569)
refugee (p. 570)
undocumented immigrant (p. 581)

A. In each of the following pairs, the two terms are related in some way. Write a sentence for each pair that clearly explains the meaning of the two terms.
1. quota, undocumented immigrant
2. asylum, refugee
3. undocumented immigrant, migrant worker

B. Choose the key term that best completes each of the following sentences.
1. In order to assist new immigrants in their assimilation process to American culture, many schools offer ________ programs.
2. Because of ________ , which limit the number of immigrants allowed in the United States, many people live here as ________ .
3. The U.S. government allows many ________ to come to America because they are unsafe in their own countries.
4. The Vietnamese boat people sought ________ when they escaped from their native country.

C. Based on what you have read in the chapter, decide whether each of the following statements is accurate. Write an explanation of each decision.
1. Many undocumented immigrants find jobs as migrant workers, and work on farms across the United States.
2. Quotas allow for unrestricted immigration into the United States.
3. Refugees come to the United States because they cannot find employment in their home countries.
4. Classes taught only in English are part of this country's bilingual education program.
5. Undocumented immigrants often receive wages that are greater than the average American worker's wages.

Exploring Concepts

A. On a separate sheet of paper, copy the chart of immigration laws shown below. In the right-hand column, list the provisions of each law. Then write a paragraph explaining how immigration laws have changed in the past century, from 1882 to 1965.

Immigration Laws

Law and Year Enacted	Provisions
Chinese Exclusion Act–1882	
Gentlemen's Agreement–1907	
Immigration Act of 1891	
Emergency Quota Act of 1921	
National Origins Act–1924	
Immigration Act of 1965	

B. Support each of the following statements with facts and details from the chapter.
1. Between 1882 and 1924, Congress passed a series of laws aimed at restricting immigration.
2. There were many reasons why Americans resisted the new immigrants of the late nineteenth and early twentieth centuries.
3. Since 1960 the United States government has tried to make its immigration policy fairer.
4. Assimilation affected immigrants and American culture in many ways.
5. Opposition to immigrants has often resulted from the fear that they will take jobs away from other Americans.
6. Many immigrants come to the U.S. today because of economic and political desperation.

B. Sample answers:
1. The Chinese Exclusion Act and the Gentleman's Agreement limited Asian immigration. The Emergency Quota Act and the National Origins Act tried to limit immigration of people from Southern and Eastern Europe.
2. The immigrants coming to the U.S. after 1880 had unfamiliar languages and customs. Americans feared that they would lost jobs to immigrants.
3. A 1965 law lifted quotas based on national origin.
4. Immigrants, particularly children, learned the English language and American culture in schools. Immigrants have enriched American culture in many areas such as science, theater, and cuisine.
5. Immigrants often accepted very low wages, which angered Americans.
6. Many immigrants come to the United States because they can earn better wages here, while others, such as the Vietnamese boat people, are seeking safety from political persecution.

Reviewing Skills

1. List the "five W's and an H" questions that interviews should cover.
2. What kind of preparations should you make before contacting a person to interview? What information should you give the person you wish to interview?
3. Read a newspaper or magazine interview with a person of interest to you, such as an actor, a sports figure, or a politician. Make a list identifying which information given in the interview answers the "five W's and an H" questions.
4. What could you learn from interviewing an immigrant or a child of immigrants that you could not learn from reading a history textbook?
5. Go back to the charts on United States Immigration on pages 580 and 581. What was the change in the percentage of immigrants from northern and western Europe from 1820–1860 to 1981–1995?
6. Suppose you wanted to interview your state representative. Make a list of guidelines you would follow in order to set up and conduct the interview. Then, if possible, arrange and conduct the interview.

Using Critical Thinking

"Keep, ancient lands, your storied pomp!" cries she
With silent lips. "Give me your tired, your poor,
Your huddled masses yearning to breathe free,
The wretched refuse of your teeming shore.
Send these, the homeless, tempest-tost to me,
I lift my lamp beside the golden door!"

Emma Lazarus, 1883

1. The preceding verse is written on the base of the Statue of Liberty. According to this verse, what type of people does America welcome? In your opinion, has the American immigration policy been true to the words written on the Statue of Liberty?
2. Because earlier immigrants assimilated into American life by learning English, many people think that today's policy of bilingual education is unwise. Do you think that bilingual education helps or hurts new immigrants in their attempt to become a part of the American culture? Explain your response.
3. President Franklin Roosevelt once said, "All of our people—except full-blooded Indians—are immigrants, or descendents of immigrants." Assuming that this statement is true, why do you think Americans have so often treated immigrants badly?

Preparing for Citizenship

1. **WRITING ACTIVITY** Most of today's immigrants are from Asia or Latin America. Choose an Asian or Latin American country that interests you and write a report using the following questions as guidelines: (a) What conditions are people from this country trying to escape from? and (b) What kind of treatment are new immigrants from this country receiving in the United States?
2. **WRITING ACTIVITY** As you have read throughout this book, the history of the United States is a history of immigration. Imagine you are an immigrant, either today or at some point in history, and imagine that you are the first person in your family to arrive in the U.S. Write a letter to your family describing your new life and how it differs from life in your native land.
3. **ART ACTIVITY** Create a poster or a collage that illustrates the contributions the immigrant groups that arrived in the United States after 1880 have made to American culture. You may focus your collage on one area of contribution or on one country.
4. **COLLABORATIVE LEARNING** Divide into small groups. Write down as many ethnic foods offered in American restaurants and supermarkets as you can think of. Be sure to note each food's culture of origin. As a class, write on the board all of the foods you came up with. Which parts of the world are most represented?

Answers to Reviewing Skills

1. Who, what, where, when, why, and how
2. Before interviewing a person, students should try to learn as much about the person as possible. Students should explain the reason for the interview, what they want to know, and how they plan to use the information.
3. Students should cite specific quotes for each question.
4. Oral histories provide personal perspectives and emotional details.
5. The change in percentage of immigrants from Northern and Western Europe for the period 1820–1860 to 1981–1995 was from 95 percent to 2 percent.
6. Students' guidelines should include the five W's and the H questions, as well as specific questions based on what they know about the person whom they plan to interview.

Answers to Critical Thinking

1. Alert students to the fact that terms such as "wretched refuse" and "huddled masses" are not derogatory but are meant to reflect how immigrants may have been treated in their homeland.
2. Ask students to imagine what it would be like to move to another country and go to a school where English was not spoken.
3. Point out how difficult it is for people to accept change.

Answers to Preparing for Citizenship

1. **WRITING ACTIVITY** If possible, encourage students to interview a recent immigrant.
2. **WRITING ACTIVITY** Students will need to research the country they "choose" to be from.
3. **ART ACTIVITY** Discuss different areas of cultural influence, such as art, politics, science, and cuisine.
4. **COLLABORATIVE LEARNING** If possible, extend this activity into the development of a class cookbook based on students' family recipes, or prepare a class meal using these recipes.

CHAPTER 20

Planning at a Glance

Modern American Democracy

	Objectives	Reading Support and Other Resources	Diverse Learning Strategies
Lesson 1 A Government of Citizens *pp. 592–597* 2–3 days	• Define citizenship and describe how a person becomes a U.S. citizen. • Explain how citizenship was extended to groups previously denied this status. • Describe how groups of Americans won the right to vote. • Explain why a gap between constitution ideals and reality has often existed in America.	• **Workbook** or **Reading Support:** pp. 285–288 Review p. 67 Lesson Support/Transition p. 67 Multi-lang. Sum. pp. 133–134 • **Other Resources:** Posters 1, 3, 5, 7; Study Guide p. 86	Access Strat. **(Extra Support)** TE p. 593 Access Act. **(SDAIE)** TE p. 593 Visual Learning **(Visual)** TE p. 596 Making a Mural **(Visual)** TE p. 596 Audiotapes of Multi-language Lesson Summaries **(Auditory)**
Skill: Analyzing an Editorial *pp. 598–599*		• **Other Resources:** Study Guide p. 87	
Lesson 2 Putting the Constitution to Work *pp. 600–608* 2–3 days	• Summarize the constitutional rights of U.S. citizens. • Describe the rise and impact of the civil rights movement. • Identify some of the gains made by American Indians. • Describe opportunities created by the women's movement. • Explain why the struggle for equality in American society is an ongoing process.	• **Workbook** or **Reading Support:** pp. 289–292 Review p. 68 Lesson Support/Transition p. 68 Multi-lang. Sum. pp. 135–136 • **Other Resources:** Geography Kit, Study Guide p. 88	Access Strat. **(Extra Support)** TE p. 601 Access Act. **(SDAIE)** TE p. 601 Visual Learning **(Visual)** TE pp. 603, 604, 605 Oral Report **(GATE)** TE p. 606 Audiotapes of Multi-language Lesson Summaries **(Auditory)**
Lesson 3 Making a Difference *pp. 609–613* 3–4 days **Literature** "A Call for Civil Rights" and "Dreams of Freedom" *pp. 616–618*	• Identify some citizens in U.S. history who have made significant contributions to American society. • Explain why American citizens have responsibilities as well as rights. • Describe how citizens can participate in the political process.	• **Workbook** or **Reading Support:** pp. 293–296 Review p. 69 Lesson Support/Transition p. 69 Multi-lang. Sum. pp. 137–138 • **Other Resources:** Geography Kit, Study Guide p. 89	Access Act. **(SDAIE)** TE p. 610 Access Strat. **(Extra Support)** TE p. 610 Visual Learning **(Visual)** TE p. 612 Art Connection **(Visual)** TE p. 612 Audiotapes of Multi-language Lesson Summaries **(Auditory)**
Exploring Work-Past and Present *pp. 614–615*	• Identify how jobs and the work process have changed. • Obtain historical information from family and acquaintances.		
Chapter Review *pp. 619–620* 1 day		Chapter 20 Test pp. 77–80 *(See facsimiles on TE p. 768.)*	Assessment Multiple-Use Masters pp. 81–88

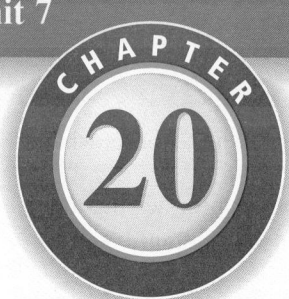

Reading Support Resources *for Every Lesson*

Reading and Review

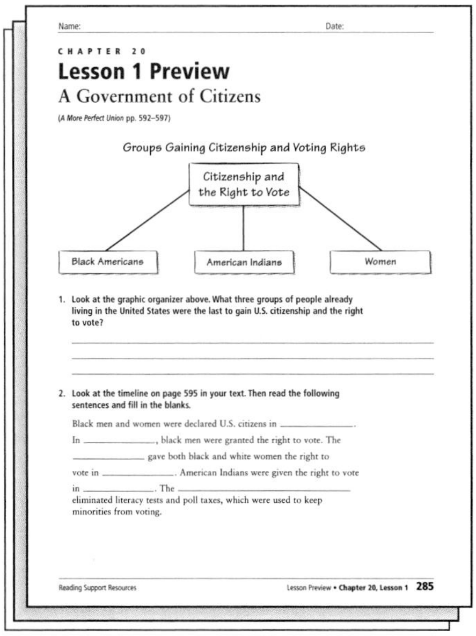

Name: Date:

CHAPTER 20

Lesson 1 Preview

A Government of Citizens

(*A More Perfect Union* pp. 592–597)

1. Look at the graphic organizer above. What three groups of people already living in the United States were the last to gain U.S. citizenship and the right to vote?

2. Look at the timeline on page 595 in your text. Then read the following sentences and fill in the blanks.

Black men and women were declared U.S. citizens in ______. In ______, black men were granted the right to vote. The ______ gave both black and white women the right to vote in ______. American Indians were given the right to vote in ______. The ______ eliminated literacy tests and poll taxes, which were used to keep minorities from voting.

Reading Support Resources — Lesson Preview • Chapter 20, Lesson 1 285

- **Chapter Overview*** p. 284
- **Lesson Previews*** using graphic organizers from the Teacher's Edition pp. 285, 289, 293
- **Reading Strategies*** pp. 286, 290, 294
- **Lesson Summaries*** pp. 287–288, 291–292, 295–296
- **Lesson Reviews** pp. 67, 68, 69

* **Workbook** includes starred items.

Multi-language Summaries

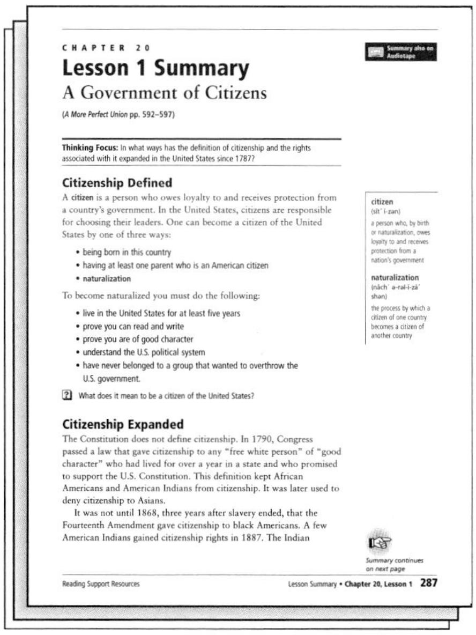

CHAPTER 20

Lesson 1 Summary

A Government of Citizens

(*A More Perfect Union* pp. 592–597)

Summary also on Audiotape

Thinking Focus: In what ways has the definition of citizenship and the rights associated with it expanded in the United States since 1787?

Citizenship Defined

A **citizen** is a person who owes loyalty to and receives protection from a country's government. In the United States, citizens are responsible for choosing their leaders. One can become a citizen of the United States by one of three ways:

- being born in this country
- having at least one parent who is an American citizen
- **naturalization**

To become naturalized you must do the following:

- live in the United States for at least five years
- prove you can read and write
- prove you are of good character
- understand the U.S. political system
- have never belonged to a group that wanted to overthrow the U.S. government.

? What does it mean to be a citizen of the United States?

citizen (sĭt' ĭ-zən) a person who, by birth or naturalization, owes loyalty to and receives protection from a nation's government

naturalization (năch' ə-ral-ĭ-zā' shən) the process by which a citizen of one country becomes a citizen of another country

Citizenship Expanded

The Constitution does not define citizenship. In 1790, Congress passed a law that gave citizenship to any "free white person" of "good character" who had lived for over a year in a state and who promised to support the U.S. Constitution. This definition kept African Americans and American Indians from citizenship. It was later used to deny citizenship to Asians.

It was not until 1868, three years after slavery ended, that the Fourteenth Amendment gave citizenship to black Americans. A few American Indians gained citizenship rights in 1887. The Indian

Summary continues on next page

Reading Support Resources — Lesson Summary • Chapter 20, Lesson 1 287

Lesson Summaries in:

- English (See Reading and Review.)
- Spanish pp. 287–288, 291–292, 295–296
- Chinese pp. 133–138
- Hmong pp. 133–138
- Khmer pp. 133–138
- Vietnamese pp. 133–138

Summaries available on audiotapes

Lesson Support / Transition

S D A I E

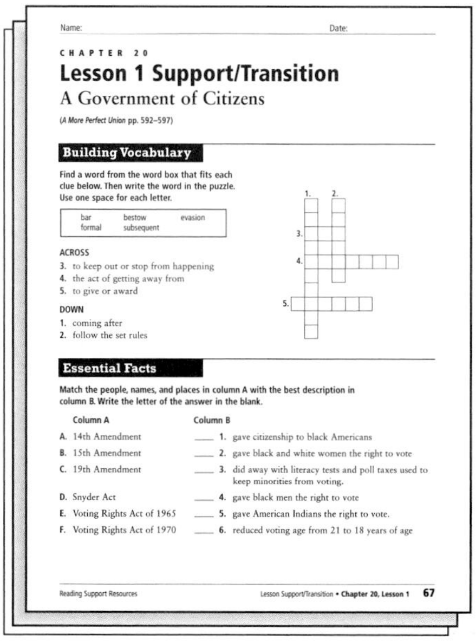

Name: Date:

CHAPTER 20

Lesson 1 Support/Transition

A Government of Citizens

(*A More Perfect Union* pp. 592–597)

Building Vocabulary

Find a word from the word box that fits each clue below. Then write the word in the puzzle. Use one space for each letter.

bar, bestow, evasion, formal, subsequent

ACROSS
3. to keep out or stop from happening
4. the act of getting away from
5. to give or award

DOWN
1. coming after
2. follow the set rules

Essential Facts

Match the people, names, and places in column A with the best description in column B. Write the letter of the answer in the blank.

Column A	Column B
A. 14th Amendment	____ 1. gave citizenship to black Americans
B. 15th Amendment	____ 2. gave black and white women the right to vote
C. 19th Amendment	____ 3. did away with literacy tests and poll taxes used to keep minorities from voting.
D. Snyder Act	____ 4. gave black men the right to vote
E. Voting Rights Act of 1965	____ 5. gave American Indians the right to vote.
F. Voting Rights Act of 1970	____ 6. reduced voting age from 21 to 18 years of age

Reading Support Resources — Lesson Support/Transition • Chapter 20, Lesson 1 67

Activities for SDAIE
Specially **D**esigned **A**cademic **I**nstruction in **E**nglish

- **Lesson Support/Transition** pp. 67, 68, 69

Technology Options

Internet Support

http://www.eduplace.com

Social Studies Center at Education Place

Internet support for Chapter 20:

- ***Lesson at a Glance***
- ***The March on Washington***

Software

Student Writing Center® (CD-ROM) (Macintosh® or Windows®)

School to Career

Sometimes individuals face discrimination in the working world. Have students create a chart showing fair business practices on one side and unfair practices on the other. Do students think these unfair practices still happen? If so, what should be done to improve the working environment?

Character Education

People often practice their civic responsibility by speaking out for a cause they believe in. Have students brainstorm issues in their school and communities that they feel are currently in need of change and ways they could bring these issues to the forefront in their school or communities. They can use the individuals from the text as examples.

CHAPTER PREVIEW

Have students read the chapter title and the narrative underneath it. How have the American citizens depicted in the portraits on these pages fulfilled the basic ideals of the American democratic government? *(The American government is a democracy, a government run by the people. It depends on active citizens.)*

Looking Back

Ask students if they can recall from previous chapters some groups that fought to be included in the United States democracy. *(Both black Americans and women fought for and won the right to vote.)*

Looking Forward

Tell students that they will read about citizens' rights and responsibilities in government in the next three lessons: A Government of Citizens, Putting the Constitution to Work, and Making a Difference.

Chapter 20

Modern American Democracy

The work and dedication of many people have helped to shape the social and political landscape of modern America. Unwilling to accept injustice and suffering, these women and men have spoken and acted on their dreams and beliefs. Their lives are proof that active, informed citizens are necessary to maintain a healthy democracy.

Frederick Douglass escaped slavery and began a lifelong fight against slavery, segregation, and racism.

A student of religion and government, James Madison proposed the system of checks and balances in our federal government.

1775 | 1825 | 1875

1789

BACKGROUND

The United States Constitution guarantees all American citizens certain basic rights. For much of the nation's history, however, many groups of Americans have struggled to secure these rights. To achieve the ideals stated in the Constitution, America needs active, informed citizens.

In November 1969, Indian activists who called themselves "Indians of all tribes" seized the deserted federal prison on Alcatraz Island in San Francisco Bay and symbolically claimed the island for the Indian people. They occupied Alcatraz until the summer of 1971, offering the government $24 worth of trinkets to pay for it (the amount paid by settlers to the Indians for Manhattan in 1626.) Later, these activists became leaders in the American Indian Movement (AIM).

In February of 1973, members of AIM participated in the occupation of Wounded Knee to protest the light sentences given to white men convicted of killing a Sioux in 1972. The siege collapsed when a gun battle left one protester dead and another wounded.

Since militant actions do not always win public support, some American Indians used other methods to advance their cause. Vine Deloria, Jr., a Sioux, for example, increased awareness of empathy for Indian concerns in his novel *Custer Died for Your Sins.*

Ida B. Wells, born a slave, began a crusade against lynchings of blacks. She spoke for women's suffrage and helped found the National Association for the Advancement of Colored People.

Cesar Chávez led the United Farm Workers union as it fought for reasonable pay and safe working conditions. He organized nationwide consumer boycotts of lettuce and grapes to attain these goals.

Social worker and reformer Jane Addams led in the development of research into social problems. An expert organizer and leader, she established social and educational services for the urban poor.

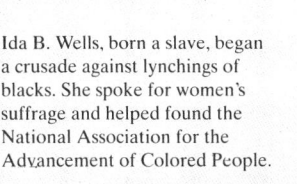

Rosa Parks, called by some the mother of the modern civil rights movement, challenged the system of racial segregation.

1925 1975 2025

2000

Understanding the Visuals

Students will be familiar with most of the people shown on these pages. Ask them if they can recall the time period in which they made their major contributions. *(Madison—late 1700s when the Constitution was established; Douglass—mid-1800s at the time of the Civil War; Jane Addams, Ida B. Wells—early 1900s during the reform era; Cesar Chavez—1960s–today)*

Understanding Chronology

Draw students' attention to the timeline. Point out that the chapter includes the present day. Why would a chapter on American Democracy begin in 1789? *(The Constitution was ratified in 1789.)*

Cesar Chavez

In 1962 Cesar Chavez founded the United Farm Workers, the first successful union to represent immigrant workers. Chavez's childhood experiences were instrumental in his effort to make a difference in the lives of migrant workers. During the 1930s, members of Cesar Chavez's Mexican American family were migrant farm workers in California's Imperial Valley, where they experienced racial discrimination, poor wages, and unsteady employment. His father's involvement in the unsuccessful labor strikes of the Imperial Valley gave young Chavez a heritage of labor organizing.

Supported by the Mexican American community, the Filipino community, and white liberals, the United Farm Workers' 1966 grape-pickers' strike and a nation-wide boycott of table grapes and lettuce brought Chavez and his union national publicity and increased political support.

Women's Studies

The rise of the women's movement in the 1960s led to increased scholarship on the subject of women in all academic disciplines. In the 1970s, federal and private agencies gave colleges funds to balance curricula by introducing research on women into the study of liberal arts or by eliminating sex bias from courses. Many colleges started women's studies programs. In 1985, over 30,000 women's studies courses, 500 degree-granting women's studies programs, and 50 centers for research on women were available in the nation's colleges and universities.

INTRODUCE

Have students read the lesson title and explain what they think the relationship is between the U.S. Government and its citizens. Then ask students to read the Thinking Focus and try to answer the question based on the first 19 chapters in this book. Suggest that they read the lesson to find out how well they have understood citizenship throughout U.S. history.

Key Terms

Vocabulary strategies: T36–37

citizen—a person who, by birth or by naturalization, owes loyalty to and receives protection from a nation's government

naturalization—the process by which a citizen of one country becomes a citizen of another country

1775 1789 1924 1950 1975 2000

LESSON 1

A Government of Citizens

THINKING FOCUS

In what ways has the definition of citizenship and the rights associated with it expanded in the United States since 1787?

Key Terms

- citizen
- naturalization

Nobody has to tell new Americans what it means to be a citizen. They have spent long hours studying the history and principles of the American democratic system. Many of them have had to learn a new language in the process. And all of them have had to wait years for the opportunity to stand before a judge and swear allegiance to their new country:

"I solemnly swear that I will support and defend the Constitution of the United States of America against all enemies, foreign and domestic, and that I will bear true faith and allegiance to the same, and that I take this obligation freely without any mental reservation or purpose of evasion; so help me God."

The entire ceremony lasts only five or ten minutes, but for many new citizens it is a moment they will never forget. After all, they have emigrated from their home countries, often leaving behind family, friends, and personal belongings. They have lived as strangers in a strange land, carrying a green card to prove their legal status as resident aliens. They have worked hard to learn the customs of a new country and waited patiently for the day when they could raise their right hands and take the oath of citizenship.

Most of us don't have to make such dramatic moves and sacrifices to become Americans. For us, citizenship is something we are born with, something we take for granted. But for those people who have struggled to become Americans, citizenship is a treasure worth the great effort they have made to attain it:

"Here, you have your rights," a new citizen of Palestinian origin named Rima Butros told the *New York Times*. "You finally belong some place. You're an American citizen."

At mass swearing-in ceremonies, such as the one pictured here, hundreds of immigrants take the oath of American citizenship at the same time.

Objectives

1. Define citizenship and explain how a person becomes a U.S. citizen.
2. Explain how citizenship was extended to groups previously denied this status.
3. Describe how groups of Americans won the right to vote.
4. Explain why a gap between constitutional ideals and reality has often existed in America.

Graphic Overview

CITIZENSHIP AND THE RIGHT TO VOTE

- Black Americans
- American Indians
- Women

Citizenship Defined

"But what exactly does it mean to be a citizen?" you may be asking yourself. Technically, a **citizen** is a person who, by birth or naturalization, owes loyalty to and receives protection from a nation's government. As Rima Butros realized, however, being a citizen involves more than just loyalty and protection. Citizenship implies that a person has certain rights and privileges, which carry with them certain obligations and responsibilities. Citizenship also helps to bestow upon a person a sense of belonging.

A Government of the People

In 1776, the colonists declared their independence from England. Those who supported the Declaration of Independence chose to be united under a single government—to become the citizens of a new nation. Before this moment they had been subjects of the English king, owing their loyalty to him. Now they supported the idea that governments receive "their just powers from the consent of the governed."

The framers of the U.S. Constitution realized that a government must have the trust and loyalty of its citizens in order to be effective. They also understood that if people felt their government belonged to them, they would be more likely to develop that trust and loyalty. The framers captured their vision in the Preamble to the Constitution:

> *We the people of the United States, in order to form a more perfect union, establish justice, insure domestic tranquility, provide for the common defense, promote the general welfare, and secure the blessings of liberty to ourselves and our posterity, do ordain and establish this Constitution for the United States of America.*

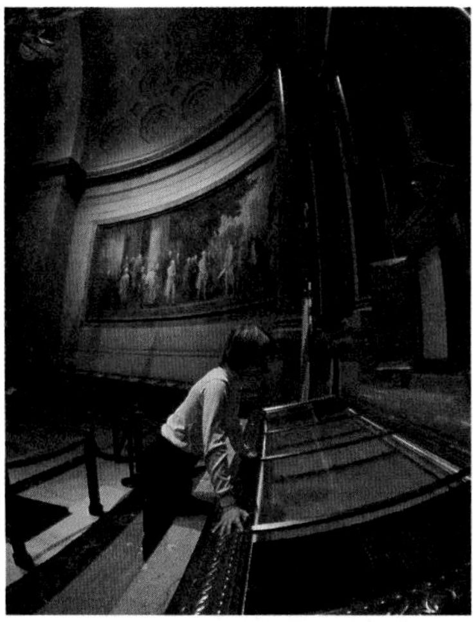

On a visit to the National Archives in Washington, D.C., this student examines the original copy of the U.S. Constitution.

"We the people. . . ." With those three words, the framers signaled the kind of government they proposed to create. Theirs would be a government *of the people*. In other words, the power of the American government would come from the citizens of the United States. As citizens, they would be responsible for shaping and maintaining the kind of government they wanted. The new republic, as the framers envisioned it, was to be built on a foundation of its citizenry.

The 18th-century philosopher Jean Jacques Rousseau said it clearly:

> *There can be no patriotism without liberty; no liberty without virtue; no virtue without citizens; create citizens and you will have everything you need. . . .*

Becoming a Citizen

You can become a citizen of the United States in one of three different ways: by birth, by blood, or by naturalization. To become a citizen by birth you must be born either in the United States or in an American embassy, ship, or airplane. If you are born to at least one parent who is an American citizen, on the other hand, you

DEVELOP

Copy on the board the Graphic Overview from page 592. Ask students to copy it in their notes and list the achievements of each group under the proper heads as they read the lesson.

CONSTITUTIONAL HERITAGE

Critical Thinking

Read aloud to students the Preamble to the Constitution found on this page. Ask students to name any unfamiliar words or phrases, such as *perfect union* or *domestic tranquility*. Use these words in familiar contexts so that students can define them on their own. Then have students paraphrase the Preamble to show that they understand it.

Access Strategy

To help students build background for the lesson, have them share with each other their knowledge of voting. Who can vote in this country? *(Citizens)* How old must someone be to vote for the first time? *(At least 18)* When are elections for state and federal offices? *(Tuesday after the first Monday in November)* Ask students to recall important elections from the lessons they have read. *(For example, 1800 election of Jefferson; 1828 election of Jackson)* Remind students that in U.S. history some Americans were not considered citizens and did not have the right to vote. Tell students that they will learn in this lesson how various groups of Americans gained their citizenship and the right to vote.

Access Activity

Have students study the picture and caption on page 592. How might the people in the photograph feel? *(Excited, proud)* Why? *(They have new opportunities, such as the right to vote.)* Ask if anyone in the class has been sworn in as a new citizen or if anyone knows someone who has been. Read aloud the lesson opener to the class.

■ *A citizen of the United States is a person who, by birth or naturalization, owes loyalty to and is protected by this country.*

CITIZENSHIP

Critical Thinking

Ask students to name a similarity in the political situation of women, black Americans, and American Indians in the early 1800s. *(All three groups, with a few exceptions, were unable to vote.)* How was the situation different for women? *(Women were citizens; black Americans and American Indians were not.)*

■ *What does it mean to be a citizen of the United States?*

become a citizen by blood.

Or you can become a citizen by **naturalization**, the process by which a citizen of one nation becomes a citizen of another. To become a naturalized citizen, you must have lived in the United States for at least five years. If you can also prove you are literate and of "good moral character," understand the U.S. political system, and have never been a member of an organization advocating the overthrow of the U.S. government, you can apply for U.S. citizenship.

Today any person who meets the above qualifications can become an American citizen. Such was not always the case, however. For a long period of America's history, certain groups were excluded from citizenship. ■

Citizenship Expanded

Partly to avoid the thorny issue of slavery, the framers did not include a definition of citizenship in the Constitution. As a result, it was not clear whether states or the national government had the right to determine who qualified as a citizen.

➤ *The American flag has come to symbolize the basic freedoms of democracy promised by the Constitution.*

In 1790, Congress passed the first law concerning citizenship. It granted citizenship to any "free white person" who lived for over a year in a state, proved "good character," and took an oath to support the Constitution. The law, however, barred African Americans and American Indians from becoming U.S. citizens. In the early 1800s, many states also passed laws that effectively excluded black and native peoples from American citizenship. The 1790 law was used in later court decisions to deny U.S. citizenship also to Asian immigrants.

Even the U.S. Supreme Court supported the notion that certain groups could be barred from citizenship. In the 1857 Dred Scott decision, the Supreme Court declared that slaves were property, not American citizens. Chief Justice Roger Taney wrote that the framers of the Constitution did not intend slaves or blacks to be included in the term *sovereign people* (See Chapter 11). Similarly, in the 1884 case *Elk* v. *Wilkins*, the Court ruled that a well-educated American Indian named John Elk did not have the right to vote because Indians were not American citizens.

In 1865, the Thirteenth Amendment to the Constitution finally abolished slavery. A subsequent campaign for black civil rights in the Congress resulted in both the 1866 Civil Rights Act and the Fourteenth Amendment.

Ratified in 1868, the Fourteenth Amendment concretely defined U.S. citizenship for the first time, using the following nonracial terms:

> *All persons born or naturalized in the United States and subject to the jurisdiction thereof are citizens of the United States and of the state wherein they reside. No state shall make or enforce any law which shall abridge the privileges or immunities of citizens of the United States. . . .*

As a result of the Fourteenth Amendment, black Americans won the right to be U.S. citizens just three

Critical Thinking

Have a student read aloud the excerpt from the Fourteenth Amendment on this page. How did this amendment make it possible for black Americans to secure, at least on paper, their rights as citizens? *(It protected them from having state laws take away their rights as citizens.)*

Historical Context

Even after the Civil Rights Act of 1866, discrimination against black Americans continued, especially in the South. Some of the most widespread abuses of blacks' civil rights came about because of state-authorized "Jim Crow" laws that allowed for segregated facilities, such as transportation. The Supreme Court supported this kind of discriminatory procedure in its ruling in *Plessy* v. *Ferguson* in 1896. In this landmark case, the Court supported a Louisiana statute requiring segregation on railroad facilities. The Court said that as long as "separate but equal" accommodations were provided for blacks, there was no denial of equal protection of rights. This "separate but equal" concept became the basis for segregating blacks and whites on land and water vehicles for over fifty years.

years after winning their freedom.

Despite the broad language of the Fourteenth Amendment, American Indians were denied citizenship for another half century. Federal laws such as the Dawes Act of 1887 did give a few Indians the right to be citizens. However, it was not until the Indian Citizenship, or Snyder, Act of 1924, that all American Indians born in the United States were finally admitted to full citizenship. ■

■ *What groups of Americans have won their citizenship since 1787?*

■ ***Black Americans and American Indians have won their citizenship since 1787.***

Voting Rights Expanded

Today most Americans think of the right to vote as one of the most basic rights of a U.S. citizen. However, citizenship and voting have not always been so closely associated. During the first century of the nation's existence, for example, a large number of people who were American citizens could not vote.

Restricting Voting Rights

As you read in Chapter 4, many of the framers of the Constitution feared giving too much power to the people and encouraging mob rule. They felt that voting should be limited to white men who were landowners. Owning property, they believed, gave men a stake in society and made them more responsible citizens.

To check the power of the people, the framers created indirect methods of electing senators and Presidents. But they gave the states the power to decide which of their citizens should have the right to vote. As the framers hoped, most states did enact laws requiring some kind of property requirement—usually a certain amount of land—before allowing men to vote.

Fighting for the Vote

During the early 1800s, an increasing number of people began to see property requirements as unfair. Beginning with Ohio in 1802, state after state passed laws giving the vote to all white men, whether they owned property or not. By the late 1820s, most states had eliminated all property qualifications, though Virginia retained its requirement until 1851.

Although most white men had

▼ *The percentage of Americans who can become citizens and vote has expanded considerably since 1790.*

Citizenship and Voting Rights, 1790–1970

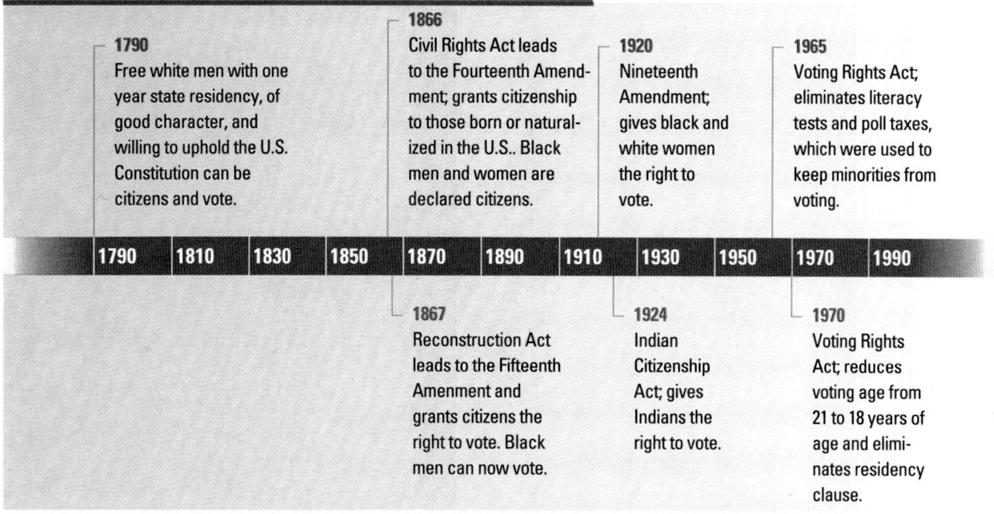

1790
Free white men with one year state residency, of good character, and willing to uphold the U.S. Constitution can be citizens and vote.
1866
Civil Rights Act leads to the Fourteenth Amendment; grants citizenship to those born or naturalized in the U.S.. Black men and women are declared citizens.
1920
Nineteenth Amendment; gives black and white women the right to vote.
1965
Voting Rights Act; eliminates literacy tests and poll taxes, which were used to keep minorities from voting.
1790
1810
1830
1850
1870
1890
1910
1930
1950
1970
1990
1867
Reconstruction Act leads to the Fifteenth Amenment and grants citizens the right to vote. Black men can now vote.
1924
Indian Citizenship Act; gives Indians the right to vote.
1970
Voting Rights Act; reduces voting age from 21 to 18 years of age and eliminates residency clause.

HISTORY

Critical Thinking

Have students evaluate how democratic the framers of the Constitution were in allowing only white male landowners to vote. *(Students should weigh the framers' fear of mob rule against the need for representation of all population groups.)*

Language Arts Connection

Phillis Wheatley was purchased directly off a slave ship by John Wheatley in 1761 to be the personal servant of his wife. Recognizing Phillis's intelligence and eagerness to learn, Mrs. Wheatley and her children taught Phillis to read and write in English. In 1773 Phillis published *Poems on Various Subjects, Religious and Moral*, the first book published by a black American woman. Abolitionists referred to her work as proof that American blacks were not intellectually inferior to white Americans. Have students read aloud some of Phillis Wheatley's poems and compare their style and subject matter to the poetry of other talented black poets, such as Paul Laurence Dunbar, Langston Hughes, and Maya Angelou.

Critical Thinking

Refer students to the timeline on this page and have them note the time intervals between major events. What key events not shown on the timeline may have influenced some of the events on it? *(Civil War, World War I)*

■ *People who owned no property, women, black Americans, American Indians, and people aged 18 to 20 have gained the right to vote since 1787.*

CITIZENSHIP

Critical Thinking

Have students contrast the lengths of time between when each of the following groups became citizens and when they attained the right to vote—white women, black American women, black American men, American Indian women, American Indian men. *(White women—144 years; black American women—54 years; black American men—one year; American Indians—occurred simultaneously)*

Students should keep in mind that not all states agreed right away with giving certain groups the right to vote, even though the right had been granted.

How Do We Know?

HISTORY *Historians know that many of the framers supported property requirements for voting by studying James Madison's notes on the Constitutional Convention and by reading many of the framers' personal letters.*

■ What groups of Americans have won the right to vote since 1787?

▼ *Many women marched to win the right to vote* (below right) *in the early 1900s. In the 1960s and 1970s, women participated in marches again*(below)*—this time for peace and equal rights.*

won the right to vote by 1830, women had to wait another 90 years to achieve that right at the national level. As early as 1848, the women at the Seneca Falls Convention were demanding "immediate admission to all the rights and privileges which belong to them as citizens of the United States." Despite the gains they achieved in some areas, however, these women did not make much progress in winning the right to vote. And when Virginia Minor directly challenged the denial of the vote to women, the Supreme Court ruled in *Minor* v. *Happersatt* (1874) that voting was not a right protected by the U.S. Constitution.

In the late 1800s, many Western states began granting women the right to vote in state and local elections. A revived women's suffrage movement won this same right in many other states during the first two decades of the twentieth century. Finally, in 1920, the Nineteenth Amendment granted national suffrage: "The right of citizens of the United States to vote shall not be abridged by the United States or by any state on account of sex."

The right to vote was officially granted to both African Americans and American Indians by the federal government many years before all states allowed these groups to vote. In 1870, two years after the Fourteenth Amendment granted African Americans citizenship, the Fifteenth Amendment formally gave them the right to vote. It was not until the civil rights movement of the 1960s, however, that blacks in many states could actually vote.

The Snyder Act, passed in 1924, made American Indians U.S. citizens and officially granted them suffrage. In reality, they were denied the right to vote in some states until the late 1950s.

The most recent group of Americans to gain the right to vote were young men and women aged 18 to 20. If these young people were old enough to pay taxes and old enough to be sent to war, many argued, they should also be able to vote. With the ratification of the Twenty-Sixth Amendment in 1971, all American citizens aged 18 and older could vote. ■

Visual Learning

Ask students to compare the more recent picture on this page of women striking for peace and equality with the picture of a march for voting rights 60 years earlier. What do the photographs reveal about how the women felt about their goals? *(The photographs show their determination to achieve these goals.)*

Making a Mural

Divide students into three groups. Have each group research one of the groups in this lesson that fought for civil rights— women, black Americans, and American Indians. Suggest that they use encyclopedias and other library reference books to find out about important court cases, group demonstrations or marches, public responses, dynamic leaders, and notable speeches or books about their group's fight for civil rights. Then ask each group to draw illustrations and write captions to depict the major events in the cause. Combine the work of the three groups as a bulletin board display.

Ideal Versus Reality

Unfortunately, legal rights are not always the same as actual rights. According to the law of the land, no American was denied citizenship or the right to vote on account of race, sex, religion, or country of origin by the year 1925. In reality, many Americans were denied their most basic rights as citizens as a result of prejudice and discrimination.

For example, in the years following Reconstruction, whites in the South devised several ways to strip black Americans of their suffrage. Poll taxes were imposed to sift the poor out of the voting population. The result was that most black citizens were unable to "pay" for their right to vote. In 1890, Mississippi became the first state to establish literacy tests as a further barrier against black people. Even educated blacks fell victim to these tests, since they were given questions that were purposely impossible to answer. In addition, a series of formal and informal laws called Jim Crow laws segregated Southern blacks from whites and denied them an equal opportunity to good schools and decent-paying jobs.

In practice, many American Indians lost the right to vote as the result of such barriers as education, transportation, and the prejudice of white election officials. Most American Indians lived on reservations that were miles from the nearest polling booth. When they did manage to get to town, white officials often made it difficult for them to register or to vote.

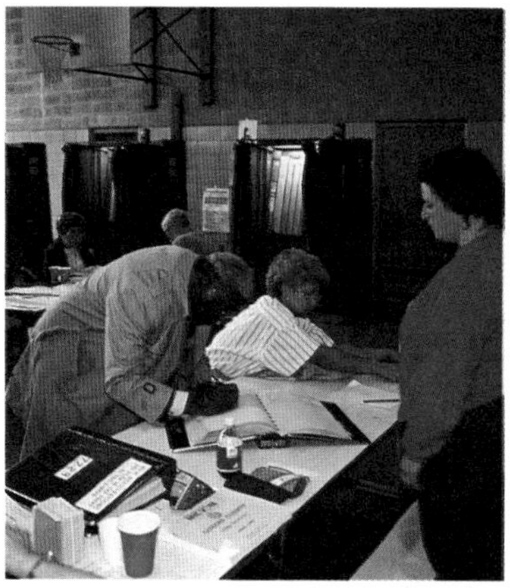

The process of registering to vote, shown here, is a simple one, but for many decades discriminatory laws and practices prevented black Americans and American Indians from registering.

Although no one prevented them from voting, women also discovered that gaining the right to vote did not end their treatment as second-class citizens. During the decades following 1920, women experienced discrimination in countless ways. They were denied entrance to certain professions, paid less than men for equal work, and prevented from advancing professionally to positions of leadership because of their sex.

Black Americans, American Indians, and women discovered that winning citizenship and the right to vote were only the first steps in their struggle for equal rights. In order to win that struggle, these and other groups of Americans who experienced discrimination needed a powerful ally. They found that ally in the United States Constitution. ■

■ *How have Americans sometimes been denied the rights legally guaranteed to them by the Constitution?*

REVIEW

1. **FOCUS** In what ways has the definition of citizenship and the rights associated with it expanded in the United States since 1787?
2. **CONNECT** How did their lack of citizenship put American Indians in a weaker position during the decades following the Civil War?
3. **HISTORY** How did being a citizen of the United States differ from being a subject of the king of England?
4. **CRITICAL THINKING** What does it reveal about the attitudes of many Americans before 1920 that women were one of the last major groups to win the right to vote?
5. **ACTIVITY** Construct a timeline on which you would indicate when different groups in American society won their citizenship and when they won the right to vote.

CONSTITUTIONAL HERITAGE

Critical Thinking

Women, black Americans, and American Indians all sought "equal treatment under the law." Ask students to explain what that phrase means. *(All should have the same rights, protected by the law)* What did groups do when they were deprived of their legal rights? For example, what did black Americans do when they were forced to pay poll taxes in order to vote? *(They appealed to the Constitution to make their legal rights a reality.)*

■ *Some Americans have been denied their legal rights through such forms of discrimination as poll taxes, literacy tests, Jim Crow laws, and unequal pay.*

CLOSE

Copy on the board the Graphic Overview from page 592. Have students name the achievements that they noted as they read the lesson. Ask them to evaluate how well they answered the Thinking Focus before they had read the lesson. How would they now change their answers?

Answers to Review Questions

1. Since 1787, the definition of citizenship has expanded to include black Americans and American Indians. Voting rights have expanded for people who do not own land, people aged 18 to 20, women, black Americans, and American Indians.
2. The American Indians' lack of citizenship prevented them from receiving protection from the U.S. Government.
3. Both subjects and citizens owed loyalty to the governing power. The power of a king or queen of England was not dependent on the subjects, but the United States government belonged to the people, who consented to give it power.
4. Sample answer: Before 1920, many people viewed women as "second-class citizens" or extensions of their husbands. Allow for personal opinion.
5. Students may use the timeline on page 595 as a basis, adding information as appropriate.

Homework Options

Have students write an essay explaining why they look forward to voting or why they think they would not bother to vote.

Study Guide: page 86.

UNDERSTANDING WRITTEN ARGUMENTS

This skill lesson will teach students to analyze and evaluate arguments that appear in written editorials.

CITIZENSHIP

Critical Thinking

You may wish to guide the students through the first editorial. Point out that the goal of the McCain-Feingold bill is stated in the fourth paragraph. *(To ban soft-money contributions to political candidates, which have increased tremendously since 1996.)* Opponents of the bill say that it violates free speech. The writer does not agree with opponents but suggests a solution. What is it? *(Pass the McCain-Feingold bill, which would ban certain kinds of contributions to political campaigns)*

UNDERSTANDING WRITTEN ARGUMENTS

Analyzing Editorials

Here's Why

As a citizen of the United States, your beliefs about public affairs are important. Any democratic government relies on the judgment and participation of its citizens. If you simply believe whatever you read or hear about an issue, you have no power to make a reasoned judgment about it. If voters cannot make reasoned judgments of their own, the democratic process is weakened.

A free press is also necessary to democracy. Newspapers report important public occurrences. Newspapers also express their opinions in editorials, which are meant to persuade the reader to think or act in certain ways. No matter what position it takes, an editorial should be supported by facts and sound reasoning.

Today, as throughout our history, Americans are asked to vote on important issues. Suppose you want to decide how to vote on a certain issue. Reading newspaper editorials and determining the strength of their arguments would give you a closer understanding of the issue and the possible solutions. Then you could make up your own mind.

Here's How

Read the following editorial from *The Boston Globe*, of February 22, 1998, entitled "The Free-Speech Fallacy."

Analyze the strength of the argument using these steps:

1. **Identify the issue.**
The issue is the McCain-Feingold bill, a proposal in Congress to ban certain kinds of contributions people can make to political campaigns.

When campaign finance reform reaches the floor of the Senate, probably tomorrow afternoon, opponents will likely continue to wrap their very murky [unclear] purpose—preserving the scandal-plagued system that elected them—in the sparkling, red-white-and-blue package of the First Amendment.

Money is speech, they say—relying on Supreme Court rulings that limit the regulation of campaign contributions—and free speech is one of our most treasured constitutional protections. While this argument has been repeated endlessly by . . . proponents [supporters] of unfettered [unrestrained] campaigns, it is fundamentally wrong.

With few exceptions, the First Amendment protects what we say so the broadest range of opinion can enter the marketplace of ideas. But the amendment does not always protect how we say it. A political candidate, or a carnival barker, cannot run a sound truck through a residential neighborhood at 3 A.M. blaring his or her message.

The McCain-Feingold bill that is now the central focus of reformers says very little about the content of political debate; its main goal—banning the soft-money contributions that mushroomed poisonously in 1996 and have continued since—would essentially turn down the volume knob now held by the monied few. In doing so, it would promote fair elections, a goal that is cherished by Americans as much as free speech and that is in more trouble.

The Supreme Court has allowed some narrowly defined restrictions on political contributions. For instance, individual donations to a candidate are capped at [limited to] $1,000 because larger amounts could be corrupting. But the entire system has been corrupted—and many individuals driven away from politics—by the multimillion-dollar scourge [evil] of soft money, which does far more to smother debate than promote it.

A vote for McCain-Feingold is a vote for free speech and democracy.

The Boston Globe, February 22, 1998

Objective

Use two editorials to determine the strength of an argument. (Critical Thinking 2)

Writing an Editorial

Have students choose a topic of current interest and write their own editorials on the subject. They should apply the five-step process to their writing. Each student can critique another student's editorial. The editorials will then be read and discussed.

2. **Determine the writer's argument.**
   The argument is that the bill should be passed.

3. **Determine whether the information presented is relevant to the argument.**
   The information presented has a direct relationship to the issue. The editorial explains why the bill is necessary and why arguments that the bill is unconstitutional are not valid.

4. **See if the argument is supported by facts.**
   Does the information come from reliable, up-to-date sources? Is opinion presented as fact?
   The article does not cite any sources. It refers in general to Supreme Court rulings, but it does not identify specific court cases. It also mentions contributions made in 1996 without giving many details. More information may be needed.

5. **Decide, based on the above steps, if the argument as a whole makes sense.** Does the conclusion match the evidence presented?

McCain-Feingold is an inadequate, misguided and probably unconstitutional measure that won't fix the problems it addresses. By focusing reformist energy on the flawed proposal, the Senate has surely abandoned any opportunity for genuine reform this year.

McCain-Feingold's declared intention is worthy enough: to stop the flow of unlimited, essentially unregulated "soft money" contributions that have become the centerpiece of the money chase. But since spending money to influence elections is a constitutionally protected exercise in free speech, bills such as McCain-Feingold can only tinker with parts of the system—forcing money away from the political parties, for example, but by no means prohibiting its use by even less accountable entities [groups or people]. . . .

The reformist instinct is honorable, and necessary. Giving candidates with access to bigger checkbooks and deeper pockets unfair advantage hurts democracy. Left unaddressed, such advantages can compound [build] into a crisis for elected government. . . .

Far better would be adoption of reform designed to create not ceilings on campaign spending, but floors. That would mean ensuring that candidates who show they are viable have access to enough money and media to make an effective pitch to voters. Repeated studies show that once a certain level of spending is ensured, additional spending isn't as pernicious [harmful]. That means that giving everybody a fair opportunity to be heard can mitigate [lessen] the financial advantage that may unavoidably accrue [be gained] by others.

How can that happen? Some form of public financing is an essential component. We could also mandate that television broadcasters make the public airwaves they use available free, or at reduced cost, for campaigns. A constitutional amendment to shorten the length of campaigns—something nearly every other democracy in the world already does—would reduce the need for piles of cash and ought to be considered. National or regional primaries could make campaigning for national office less expensive. . . .

The Sacramento Bee, February 26, 1998

Try It

Read the excerpt above from an editorial in *The Sacramento Bee*. Decide which of these two editorials you think presents the stronger argument.

Apply It

Find an editorial in your local newspaper that takes a stand on an issue that interests you. Analyze the strength of the editorial's argument and its relevance to the issue as a whole. Write a short paragraph outlining your findings. Do you agree with the editorial's view?

CITIZENSHIP

Critical Thinking

Editorials do not contain the only opinions found in a newspaper. Point out the signed opinion columns in the local newspaper. These columns are often written by syndicated columnists whose work appears in many newspapers. While an editorial usually represents the judgment of the editors and the newspaper publisher, opinion columns are the views of the columnists. Have students apply the five-step process to an opinion column. Would an opinion column be more or less reliable than an editorial?

Answers to Try It

Students' answers may vary on which editorial presents a stronger argument. Answers may include that the *Sacramento Bee* article suggests practical solutions such as shorter campaigns and some form of public financing.

Answers to Apply It

Make sure that the students' paragraphs use each of the five steps to analyze the editorial that they have chosen.

Critical Thinking

Remind students that they studied political cartoons in Chapter 6 (pages 184–185). Such cartoons often appear on the editorial page of a newspaper. How are political cartoons similar to and different from editorials? *(Similarity: Both express opinions about events and people, but cartoons often look at the light side of an issue.)*

INTRODUCE

Have students read the lesson title and Thinking Focus. Ask them to recall from Lesson 1 groups that wanted to secure rights and freedoms previously denied them. *(Black Americans, American Indians, women)* Have students read the lesson to find out how groups of Americans have used the Constitution for this purpose.

Key Term

Vocabulary strategies: T36–37

sit-in—a form of protest in which participants occupy a room, building, or outdoor space to pressure their opponents into meeting their demands

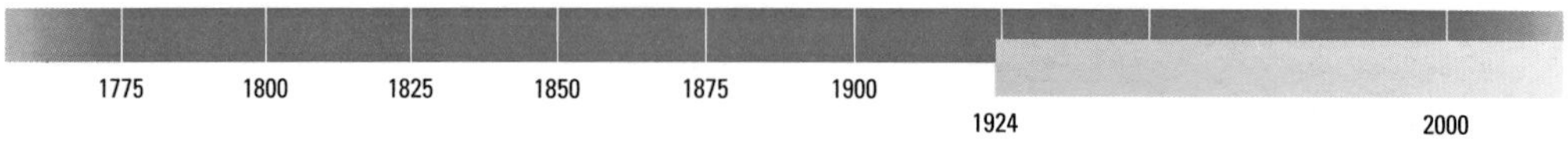

LESSON 2

Putting the Constitution to Work

THINKING FOCUS

How have some groups of Americans used the Constitution to obtain the rights and freedoms previously denied them?

Key Term

- sit-in

When a 42-year-old black seamstress named Rosa Parks boarded a bus in Montgomery, Alabama, in December 1955, she had no idea that she was about to make history. Tired after a hard day of work, Parks took a seat in the front of the bus, a section reserved according to Jim Crow laws for whites.

Moments later, Parks was asked to give up her seat to a white passenger and to move to the back of the bus. Although she had not intended to challenge the law that day, Parks suddenly decided she had had enough of being treated like a second-class citizen and refused to give up her seat. After warning her several times to move, local police arrested Parks and charged her with violating segregation laws.

Parks's action sparked a year-long boycott by blacks of Montgomery's bus system. Organized by such groups as the Alabama NAACP and the Women's Poitical Council, this boycott also witnessed the rise to prominence of a 27-year-old black minister of the Baptist church named Martin Luther King, Jr. Well educated and an inspiring speaker, King advocated nonviolent protest against unjust laws.

For 381 days, the black citizens of Montgomery refused to ride local buses. Instead, they organized car pools, accepted rides from sympathetic whites, or simply walked to their jobs—sometimes over long distances. Their actions cut the income of the bus company by 65 percent and hurt the business of downtown stores.

Finally, almost a year after the protest began, the U.S. Supreme Court ruled that segregation in public transportation was unconstitutional and therefore illegal. With the help of the Court, the black people of Montgomery had won a great victory against segregation. By a single act of courage, Rosa Parks had inspired the modern civil rights movement.

The Rights of Citizens

The U.S. Constitution guarantees American citizens certain basic freedoms. The Constitution also gives citizens—no matter what their age, race, income, sex, or religion—the right to seek enforcement of the law and to challenge unjust laws. Rosa Parks's effort to win the right to sit where she pleased is a good example of how citizens can use the Constitution to secure the fundamental rights it promises.

As you read in Chapter 4, critics of the newly drafted U.S. Constitution feared the powerful central government it established. They demanded that a bill of rights be added to the document to prevent this government

Objectives

1. Summarize the constitutional rights of U.S. citizens.
2. Describe the rise and impact of the civil rights movement.
3. Identify some of the gains made by American Indians.
4. Describe opportunities created by the women's movement.
5. Explain why the struggle for equality in American society is an ongoing process.

Graphic Overview

from abusing individual liberties. Thus, one of the first acts of the new Congress in 1789 was to pass ten amendments to the Constitution that came to be known as the Bill of Rights.

The Bill of Rights spells out the basic freedoms guaranteed to every American citizen. It promises freedom of speech, religion, assembly, and the press. It protects citizens against "unreasonable" searches and seizures of property by government officials or the police. It assures citizens that they will receive a jury trial in criminal cases and a lawyer to defend them. And it guarantees due process of law — that is, the government must follow a set of fair, specific rules when a person is accused of and tried for a crime.

The original purpose of the Bill of Rights was to protect America's citizens from a tyrannical central government. But the Constitution said nothing about the states having to obey these amendments. The passing of the Fourteenth Amendment in 1868 completely changed this situation.

The Fourteenth Amendment declared that states could not "deprive any person of life, liberty, or property, without due process of law; nor deny to any person within its jurisdiction the equal protection of the law." What the amendment did, in effect, was to federalize the Bill of Rights. In other words, it affirmed that no government—federal, state, or local—could deny a citizen freedoms guaranteed in the Bill of Rights.

The Fourteenth Amendment was originally intended to protect the rights of America's black citizens. In the twentieth century, however, the Supreme Court has interpreted the amendment's language more broadly. Over the years, many other minority groups have turned to the Fourteenth Amendment to obtain or protect their basic liberties. ■

■ *In what ways does the Constitution guarantee American citizens certain basic rights?*

The Civil Rights Movement

The Montgomery bus boycott provided the civil rights movement with a set of tactics. However, the movement had its beginnings in a crucial Supreme Court case.

In its landmark 1954 decision, *Brown* v. *Board of Education of Topeka*, the Supreme Court completely reversed its ruling in the 1896 *Plessy* v. *Ferguson* case and rejected the idea of segregated public schools. "Separate educational facilities," the Court declared, "are inherently unequal" and have "no place in public education." In addition to rejecting the concept of "separate but equal" schools, the Court also ordered school integration to proceed immediately.

Challenging Segregation

The 1954 *Brown* decision shook the Southern institution of segregation to its foundation. It also provided civil rights leaders with a firm constitutional basis for future action.

Increasingly, the most important of these leaders was the Rev. Martin Luther King, Jr. With a deep, resonant voice and a charismatic presence, King spoke movingly from the pulpit about

Until the civil rights movement began to challenge segregation laws, black Americans often had to use separate and unequal facilities.

DEVELOP

Copy on the board the Graphic Overview from page 600. Suggest that students write down the three headings and add details about each group's fight for civil rights as they read the lesson.

CONSTITUTIONAL HERITAGE

Study Skills

Have students recall how the Bill of Rights is related to the Constitution. *(The Constitution, as it was first written, defines and describes the government and its functions; the Bill of Rights consists of the first ten amendments to the Constitution and names guaranteed civil rights.)*

■ *The Constitution guarantees citizens certain rights by allowing them to seek enforcement of the law and to challenge unjust laws.*

601

Access Strategy

Lead into the lesson by reading aloud the lesson opener and discussing it with the class. Why might Rosa Parks have chosen to act as she did? *(Perhaps she was tired of accepting discrimination in many areas of her life.)* How might she have felt at the moment when she refused to give up her seat? How might the other black people on the bus have felt? The bus driver? The white passengers? Ask students if they think anyone on the bus might have realized that this act was the beginning of a movement that would dramatically change history. Tell students that they will find out about three movements that helped groups of people gain their constitutional rights.

Access Activity

Refer students to the picture and caption on this page. How might the people in the picture feel about having to wait in a separate room because of the color of their skin? *(Encourage a range of responses.)* In what way might some of the facilities be "separate and unequal"? *(Might be poorly built, dirty, too small)*

CONSTITUTIONAL HERITAGE

Critical Thinking

Ask students to analyze what the 1954 *Brown* decision showed about the change in the Court's attitude toward black Americans. *(Perhaps when the Court previously allowed for segregated facilities, it actually viewed black Americans as being inferior. The* Brown *decision shows the Court affirming equal rights for black citizens.)* How did the Court continue to affirm black rights? *(Repeatedly ruled against segregation)*

HISTORY

Critical Thinking

Have students evaluate the concept of nonviolent civil disobedience promoted by Martin Luther King, Jr. Ask students to explain why they believe it was right or wrong for black Americans to break segregation laws purposefully. *(Students should weigh obeying governmental laws against challenging injustice.)*

Across Time & Space

The attorney who made the argument against segregation in Brown v. Board of Education of Topeka *was a black lawyer named Thurgood Marshall. Thirteen years later, in 1967, Marshall became the first black American to be appointed to the U.S. Supreme Court.*

the economic and social discrimination suffered by blacks. But King was also dedicated to nonviolence. "We must use the weapon of love," he told his followers. "We must have compassion and understanding for those who hate us."

In the late 1950s and early 1960s, many blacks and whites began to break segregation laws purposefully in order to challenge those laws in court. They swam in segregated swimming pools, worshiped in segregated churches, and rode on segregated buses. They participated in **sit-ins** at restaurants and lunch counters, refusing to leave until they were served.

Citing the Fourteenth Amendment, the Supreme Court ruled that segregation was illegal in case after case. But many Southerners did not accept those rulings quietly. Volunteers working on behalf of civil rights for blacks were jailed, beaten, and murdered across the South.

Throughout the civil rights movement, the relatively new medium of television kept Americans aware of unfolding events in the South. Many Americans were startled and upset by the images that began to appear on the nightly news. As the nation looked on, young civil rights workers were dragged away from lunch counters and arrested, federal troops escorted black children to school past angry mobs, and law enforcement authorities turned police dogs and fire hoses on peaceful demonstrators. The brutality of the authorities and the courage of the protesters soon won the sympathy of much of the nation.

The March on Washington

In 1963, King and other civil rights leaders organized a demonstration in Washington, D.C., to protest the increasing violence in the South. The response was overwhelming. People from all over the nation, both black and white, poured into the capital to take part in the March on Washington.

On August 28, 1963, Martin Luther King, Jr., stood on the steps of the Lincoln Memorial, facing a crowd of 250,000 people. As millions more watched on television, King shared his dream with the American people:

So I say to you, my friends, that even though we must face the difficulties of today and tomorrow, I still have a dream. It is a dream deeply rooted in the American dream that one day this nation will rise up and live out the true meaning of its creed—we hold these truths to be self-evident, that all men are created equal.

I have a dream that one day on the red hills of Georgia, sons of former slaves and sons of former slave-owners will be able to sit down together at the table of brotherhood. . . .

I have a dream my four little children will one day live in a nation where they will not be judged by the color of their skin but by the content of their character. . . .

This will be the day when all of God's children will be able to sing with new meaning—"my country 'tis of thee; sweet land of liberty; of thee I sing; land where my father died, land of the pilgrim's pride; from every mountain side, let freedom ring"—and if America is to be a great nation, this must become true. . . .

And when we allow freedom to ring, when we let it ring from every village and hamlet, from every state and city, we will be able to speed up that day when all of God's children—black men and white men, Jews and Gentiles, Catholics and Protestants— will be able to join hands and to sing in the words of the old Negro spiritual, "Free at last, free at last; thank God Almighty, we are free at last."

Social Participation

Have students discuss how Martin Luther King, Jr., might have used his voice, facial expressions, and body movements to convey emotion when he gave the speech excerpted on this page. Then ask volunteers to read aloud paragraphs from the excerpt, giving their interpretations of King's delivery.

Historical Context

When the Supreme Court rejected the "separate but equal" doctrine in the *Brown* v. *Board of Education of Topeka* case in 1954, it ordered the integration of schools, with "a prompt and reasonable start toward full compliance." The pace of school desegregation in many Southern towns, however, was slow and violent.

In Little Rock, Arkansas, for example, nine black students were refused admittance to the previously all-white Central High School in 1957. Arkansas Governor Orval Faubus had ordered the National Guard to keep the black students out. When the Guard was withdrawn by Court order, mob protest and violence followed. In response, President Eisenhower sent federal troops to escort the black students to school.

Violent reactions to segregation occurred at the college level also. Mississippi Governor Ross Barnett, along with many supporters, angrily protested a federal court

A CLOSER LOOK

The March on Washington

The Civil Rights movement of the early 1960s reached its peak with the March on Washington. On August 28, 1963, a quarter of a million Americans arrived in the nation's capital from almost every state in the union to make their demands known: "Jobs and Freedom!"

"I have a dream that one day my four little children will live in a nation where they will not be judged by the color of their skin but by the content of their character." Dr. King's inspiring speech stirred the nation.

Black, white, young, and old marched together. They came from every religion, every race, every profession, and every political party. The Washington Monument towers over their cause.

Note: Encourage students to refer to A Closer Look as they read the speech excerpt on page 602.

HISTORY

Critical Thinking

Have students study the picture and caption of Martin Luther King, Jr., on this page, as well as the excerpt of his speech on page 602. How does he connect his "dream" with previous American history? *(Refers to the American dream and Jefferson's words in the Declaration of Independence)* What effect might King's dream have on the people listening to his speech? *(Might give them hope for a future in which they would have equal rights and freedom)*

order and blocked the admission of James Meredith, a black student, into the University of Mississippi in the fall of 1962. Approximately 16,000 federal troops tried to quell the violence in Mississippi that resulted in two murders and numerous injuries.

To provide students with additional background on the civil rights struggle, you may wish to show the videotapes "Eyes on the Prize," a six-part series. (See page 561 under Visual Media.)

Visual Learning

Have students study the pictures and captions of the March on Washington on this page. Ask students to analyze why this particular gathering led to the Civil Rights Act. *(Massive number of people, representing black, white, young, and old people; persuasive speech of Martin Luther King, Jr.)*

■ *Basing their actions on the Constitution, black Americans and other Americans broke segregation laws, used boycotts and sit-ins, and marched on Washington to win their civil rights.*

SOCIAL SYSTEMS

Critical Thinking

Both black Americans and American Indians fought for their civil rights in the 1960s and 1970s. Have students form small groups and discuss the similarities and differences of these groups' goals. *(American Indians wanted to protect their historical lands and way of life; black Americans sought greater access to "mainstream" American society.)*

■ *What strategies did black Americans use to win their civil rights?*

Demonstators in Washington demanded passage of the Civil Rights Act, which President John Kennedy had recently proposed. When Kennedy was assassinated three months later, President Lyndon Johnson hurried the Civil Rights Act of 1964 through Congress as a memorial to the nation's slain leader. That same year the states abolished poll taxes by ratifying the Twenty-fourth Amendment to the Constitution. Just one year later, Congress passed the Voting Rights Act of 1965, which abolished state laws designed to prevent black Americans from exercising the right to vote.

Discrimination against blacks did not end in 1964. But through a series of Supreme Court decisions and major pieces of legislation, black Americans—basing their efforts on the Constitution—were able to obtain many rights long denied them. Their tactics and their successes inspired other groups of Americans to look to the Constitution for help. ■

American Indians Make Gains

Though recognized as citizens and granted suffrage in 1924, American Indians had little control over their lives in the 1950s. The Bureau of Indian Affairs determined their education, livelihood, access to justice, and most aspects of their daily lives. Like African Americans, they still suffered racial prejudice and discrimination. Life on the reservations in the 1950s was bleak. Because of poor land, poor schools, and few economic opportunities, American Indians lived in appalling poverty and squalor. Alcoholism and infant mortality rates were high. Their average life expectancy was only half that of whites.

Angered at these conditions and inspired by the black civil rights movement, American Indians took bold action for political and social change in the 1960s and 1970s. Indian peoples across the nation formed political organizations, staged protest demonstrations, and pressured Congress and state legislatures for more Indian involvement in government programs affecting them.

American Indians benefited from the broad civil rights antipoverty programs in the 1960s. But in the late 1960s, Indian activists began to push for new laws aimed specifically at the problems of Indian peoples. Calling Indian citizens the "forgotten Americans," President Lyndon B. Johnson supported Congress in the passage of the Indian Civil Rights Act in 1968. This act guaranteed American Indians their basic rights and protection against the taking of their property without compensation.

In the early 1970s, American Indians made important gains. Under President Richard M. Nixon, they won 20 top appointments in the Bureau of Indian Affairs. In addition, the Indian Self-Determination and Education Assistance Act of 1975 gave Indian peoples more control of their reservations, their education, and the programs that affected them.

Like black Americans of the same period, American Indians turned to the courts to have their grievances heard and their claims resolved. For instance, in the mid-1970s, the Pas-

During the first half of the 20th century, Bureau of Indian Affairs schools, such as the one pictured below, attempted to assimilate American Indian students into the dominant white culture.

Visual Learning

Ask students to recall what they have learned about assimilation (Chapter 14). What evidence of assimilation can be seen in the picture on this page? *(Students are not wearing traditional Indian clothing.)* What are the students probably studying? *(Aspects of white culture)*

Cultural Context

The civil rights movement spurred many black writers to reflect their culture and individual experiences through literature. Ralph Ellison's novel *The Invisible Man,* winner of the 1953 National Book Award, was partly autobiographical, telling of the frustration and humiliation suffered by Ellison at the hands of Northern and Southern racists. Ellison also published a collection of interviews and essays, *Shadow and Act,* expressing his belief that black Americans could find freedom from stereotypes through a celebration of their own rich culture.

Gwendolyn Brooks considered poetry to be a weapon against social evils such as poverty and racism. In *Selected Poems*, published in 1963, she reflected the hopes and dreams of the early civil rights movement, telling how black and white people worked together for justice. Brooks focused on black pride and unity in her collection of poems entitled *Riot*, published in 1969.

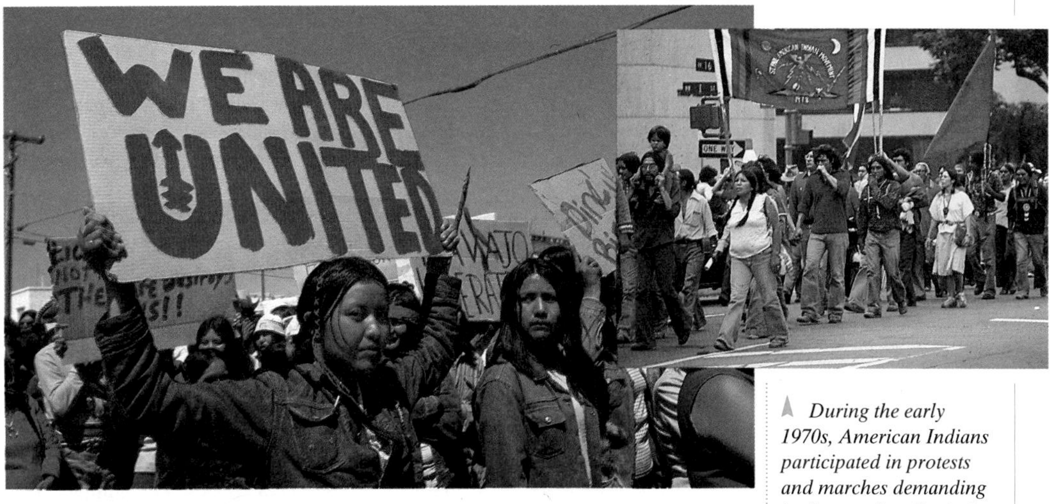

During the early 1970s, American Indians participated in protests and marches demanding both an end to discrimination and respect for Indian cultures.

samaquoddy and Penobscot tribes of Maine went to court claiming that a huge area of land in Maine had been taken away from them by an illegal treaty in the 1800s. In the 1977 case of *Passamaquoddy Tribe* v. *Morton,* a federal judge ruled in favor of the state's Indians. Eventually the federal government negotiated a settlement in the form of the Maine Indian Claims Settlement Act of 1980. By the terms of this act, Maine's Indians received more than 300,000 acres of land and nearly $30 million in compensation.

Asserting their constitutional rights through appeal to the courts, American Indians won their land claims in case after case in the 1970s and 1980s. In 1971, for instance, after a long legal battle, President Nixon signed a bill returning to the Taos Pueblo their sacred Blue Lake in New Mexico. A 1980 Supreme Court decision ordered the federal government to pay $117 million plus interest to the Sioux Indian Nation to compensate them for the loss of the Black Hills of South Dakota.

Despite these gains, life remains difficult on many American Indian reservations. Levels of unemployment, alcoholism, and suicide are still much higher than the national average. However, by skillful use of the American political and legal systems, American Indians have asserted their constitutional rights and corrected past injustices. Indian tribes have also invested money received from the federal government and provided new economic and educational opportunities for many of their people. ■

■ How did American Indians win greater control over their lives and regain territory lost in the 18th and 19th centuries?

The Fight for Women's Rights

Although American women won suffrage in 1920, their struggle for equal rights continued. Shut out of many jobs, paid less than men for equal work, and portrayed as the "weaker sex" whose place was in the kitchen, women endured discrimination on a scale similar to that of minority groups for many decades.

The Rebirth of a Movement

In the 1960s, women joined the ranks of those Americans fighting to secure their equal rights. Many historians attribute the rebirth of the women's movement to a book published in 1963. In *The Feminine Mystique*, Betty Friedan claimed that women were as capable as men of

605

HISTORY

Study Skills

After students have read about the specific victories won by American Indians in the 1960s and 1970s to regain, or be compensated for, some of the land they had lost to white settlers centuries before, have them recall from previous chapters why Indians had not been able to protect their lands originally. *("White settler diseases" killed many Indians; settlers had superior weapons at first; white people broke many treaties and promises; settlers did not believe Indians owned the land they lived on.)*

■ *American Indians formed political organizations, staged protest demonstrations, and pressured Congress and state legislatures.*

Language Arts Connection

Many people consider the speech Martin Luther King, Jr., gave on the steps of the Lincoln Memorial in 1963 to be one of the finest speeches ever given. Provide students with a copy of the full speech and show them a videotape of it (see page 561 under Visual Media). Have students analyze the literary devices that King used to make his speech powerful. How did he use metaphors effectively? Repetition of key phrases? Parallel structure? Pauses?

Reader's Theater

Have students devise a Reader's Theater presentation from an excerpt of a novel or poem by a contemporary black writer. Possible selections include Gwendolyn Brooks's *Selected Poems* (New York: Harper and Row, 1963); James Baldwin's *Go Tell It on the Mountain* (New York: Grosset and Dunlap, 1953); Maya Angelou's *I Know Why the Caged Bird Sings* (New York: Random House, 1969); Lorraine Hansberry's *A Raisin in the Sun* (New York: Random House, 1959).

Visual Learning

Ask students to compare the pictures of American Indian demonstrations on this page with the pictures of the March on Washington on page 603. Have students cite evidence that shows that, to some degree, the success of the black civil rights movement inspired American Indians. *(Used peaceful demonstrations to try to gain constitutional rights)*

CULTURE

Visual Learning

Ask students to look at the pictures on this page of women in the early 1900s and of women today. What changes in women's clothing do the photographs reveal? *(Early 1900s—distinct difference in clothing of men and women; today—women wearing same clothing men would wear for these jobs)* What inference can be drawn from these pictures about women's roles? *(Less distinction today between men's and women's roles)*

In the early 1900s, women were expected to dress in certain ways and to perform narrowly defined roles.

doing any job and should be given the opportunity to fulfill "their unique possibilities as separate human beings."

Three years later, Friedan helped to found the National Organization for Women. "There is no civil rights movement to speak for women," the NOW organizers claimed, "as there has been for Negroes and other victims of discrimination." NOW's goal—and the goal of other women's organizations that sprang up in the late 1960s—was to fight for equal rights by lobbying for legislation and testing unjust laws in the courts.

The first major victory for the women's rights movement was accidental. In 1964, Southern Democrats offered an amendment to the proposed Civil Rights Act to prohibit discrimination on the basis of sex as well as race. They assumed this amendment would persuade more legislators to vote against the Civil Rights Act and thus help to defeat it. However, the amendment passed and became the basis for later attacks on sex discrimination.

Citing the Civil Rights Act and the Fourteenth Amendment, women won a series of judicial and legislative victories in the 1960s and 1970s. In one very important case, the Supreme Court ruled in 1971 that unequal treatment based only on gender violated the Fourteenth Amendment. Women used this ruling again and again to fight discriminatory laws and practices. In *Cleveland Board of Education* v. *Le Fleur* (1974), for example, the Supreme Court ruled that Jo Carol Le Fleur did not have to take leave without pay after a certain period of pregnancy and could return to work as soon as she wanted. Women won important legislative battles as well. The Educational Amendments of 1972 provided that college athletic programs for women receive financial support equal to those for men. That same year Congress passed the Equal Employment Opportunity Act, requiring equal pay to men and women for equal work. Other new

Today women work in a variety of fields once reserved for men. The woman on the left is a biologist. The woman on the right is a telephone repair person.

Critical Thinking

Ask students to explain how the Southern Democrats' strategy in opposing the Civil Rights Act backfired, granting all women, as well as black Americans, more rights. *(They thought that adding an amendment that made gender discrimination illegal would cause the proposed Civil Rights Act to fail.)*

Oral Report

Have students research and give an oral report on one or two leaders of the civil rights movement, such as W. E. B. DuBois, Rosa Parks, Stokeley Carmichael, Medgar Evars, James Meredith, Ralph David Abernathy, Clarence Mitchell, Roy Wilkins, Whitney Young, Andrew Young, Malcolm X, Huey Newton, Bobby Seale, Eldridge Cleaver, and Jesse Jackson. Students may use encyclopedias, magazines, and history books from the library. One good resource is the videotape series "Eyes on the Prize" (See page 561 under Visual Media). Students should focus on the leaders' contributions to the civil rights movement rather than mere biographical information about them. What were the leaders' visions? What techniques did they advocate to secure civil rights for black Americans? In what ways did their lives influence their work? How successful were they in achieving their goals?

laws—both state and federal—ended many discriminatory practices and opened new career opportunities for women.

Despite an impressive list of achievements, the women's movement did experience one important defeat. In 1972, Congress passed an Equal Rights Amendment (ERA). More than 30 states quickly ratified this amendment, but then it ran into serious opposition from conservatives, who feared it would disrupt traditional family patterns and eliminate certain protections for women, such as exemption from military service. The amendment died in 1982.

The appointment of Madeline Albright to Secretary of State in 1996 symbolized the gains women have made in recent decades.

New Roles for Women

Since the mid-1960s, the role of women in American society has changed immensely. More women now work in such traditional male occupations as computer scientists, business executives, truck drivers, engineers, pilots, car mechanics, architects, politicians, and psychiatrists. The two-career family, in which both husband and wife work, has increasingly become the norm.

The number of women entering the professions has skyrocketed during the past two decades. In the early 1970s, only 7 percent of the nation's physicians and 3 percent of its lawyers were women. By the mid-1990s, women accounted for 26 percent of all doctors and 30 percent of all lawyers in the United States.

Since 1980, twelve women have won seats in the United States Senate, and an increasing number have served in presidential cabinets. Sandra Day O'Connor was named the first woman Supreme Court Justice in 1981, and two years later, Sally Ride became the first woman astronaut to fly in outer space. The Democratic Party broke new ground in 1984 when it chose a woman, Representative Geraldine Ferraro, to serve as its vice-presidential candidate. Although some barriers and discrimination remain, women have clearly achieved a great deal in a very brief time. ■

■ *What gains did women make as a result of the revival of the women's movement?*

■ *Through this movement women have gained new opportunities in jobs and education.*

The Ongoing Struggle for Justice

Black Americans, American Indians, and women are not the only people who have turned to the Constitution when faced with injustice. Since World War I, Asian Americans, Hispanic Americans, Jews, and a variety of religious groups have also fought, with the help of the Constitution and the courts, to obtain and protect their basic rights. More often than not, these groups have been successful in their charges of discrimination and prejudice. But occasionally they have lost important battles.

During World War II, for example, Japanese Americans became the targets of hostility and suspicion. Many Americans, including defense officials, thought that these Japanese Americans might try to betray the United States to Japan. As a result, President Franklin Roosevelt granted the War Department the authority to put more than 110,000 in detention camps.

With little warning, the govern-

HISTORY

Critical Thinking

Have students analyze Sandra Day O'Connor's role as the first female Supreme Court justice. Ask them whether they think she is a living symbol of the success of the women's movement or merely a "token figure" in a society still dominated by males.

Writing a Report

Have students research American Indian reservation life today in newspapers and magazines. How do the tribal councils work? What is their relationship with the U.S. Government? With corporations? How do they decide between developing land and preserving it for traditional Indian use, such as for burial grounds? How successful have reservations been in fairly dividing the proceeds gained from mineral discoveries?

Study Skills

Have students use microfilm or microfiche library resources to find news articles on the appointment of Madeline Albright, the first flight of Sally Ride, and the nomination of Geraldine Ferraro. How did each woman feel about her role as a pioneer? How did the public react? Have students share their findings with the class.

➤ *The 442nd Infantry Combat Team, composed entirely of Japanese American citizens, became the most decorated unit in all the armed forces, proving the loyalty of Japanese Americans during the war.*

CITIZENSHIP

Visual Learning

Ask students to explain how the picture of Japanese Americans on this page highlights the difference between ideals and reality in American democracy. *(Responsibilities as citizens reflected in their being drafted; lack of rights shown in their living in relocation camps)*

■ *Because prejudice still exists and people in authority can make mistakes, the effort to ensure constitutional rights for all must continue.*

CLOSE

Copy on the board the Graphic Overview from page 600. Ask volunteers to write details under each heading, using the notes they made while reading the lesson. Have students summarize the lesson by answering the Thinking Focus.

➤ *Many Japanese Americans were selected out of relocation camps and drafted to serve in the U.S. Army in Europe. The men shown here are being sworn into service.*

ment moved Japanese Americans, two-thirds of whom were American citizens, into prison-like relocation camps. Most had to sell their houses, businesses, and personal possessions at great losses. But one of these Japanese Americans, Fred Korematsu, refused to obey the order to move. When he was arrested, tried, and convicted, he appealed his case to the U.S. Supreme Court.

In 1944, the Supreme Court upheld Korematsu's conviction in a 6-3 decision. The Court ruled that the relocation program was a "justifiable wartime measure."

Today, most Americans believe that the Supreme Court was wrong in 1944 and that the order to relocate Japanese Americans denied them their most basic constitutional rights. In fact, Congress passed a law in 1988 admitting to and apologizing for the injustice that had been done. It also gave symbolic financial compensation to those Japanese Americans who were interned.

■ *In what sense is the effort to guarantee all Americans their constitutional rights a never-ending process?*

In the United States—as in all countries—there is sometimes a gap between the nation's political ideals and the reality of certain political and legal decisions. What the *Korematsu* case shows—as the *Plessy* v. *Ferguson* case did earlier—is that the system can sometimes fail the very people it is designed to protect. And because prejudice and discrimination still exist and people in positions of authority make mistakes, the struggle for equality and liberty is never-ending. For these reasons, it is important that American citizens know the Constitution, understand their rights, and get involved in the political process. ■

REVIEW

1. **FOCUS** How have some groups of Americans used the Constitution to obtain the rights and freedoms previously denied them?
2. **CONNECT** In what sense did the civil rights movement of the 1950s and 1960s complete the work started during the period of Reconstruction?
3. **HISTORY** How did the Fourteenth Amendment make the rights of all Americans more secure?
4. **CRITICAL THINKING** Do you think the spread of television ownership helped or hurt the civil rights movement? Explain.
5. **ACTIVITY** Make a list of at least three ways in which prejudice and discrimination have kept people from enjoying their full rights as American citizens.

Homework Options

Have students bring to class newspaper and magazine articles on South Africa today. What comparisons can be drawn with American history?

Study Guide: page 88.

Answers to Review Questions

1. Groups of Americans have used court cases to ensure that they receive the rights guaranteed by the Constitution, especially by the Fourteenth Amendment.
2. During the period of Reconstruction, black Americans gained some constitutional rights; the civil rights movement of the 1950s and 1960s continued this process.
3. The Fourteenth Amendment affirmed that no government could deny citizens the freedoms guaranteed in the Bill of Rights.
4. Sample answers: Television helped the civil rights movement by exposing the reality of discrimination. Allow for personal opinion.
5. Have students combine their lists on the board. Answers should be based on what students have read in this lesson.

1775 1789 2000

LESSON 3

Making a Difference

In October, 1992, a group of Los Angeles high school students and their biology teacher decided to restore an abandoned, weed-infested garden near their school. They planned to grow vegetables and give the food to needy families in South-Central Los Angeles. That was just the beginning of the project, which they named Food From the 'Hood.

The following year, the group began selling some of its produce at local farmers' markets, although they still gave away part of their crop. They realized that they could give something to their community, and still make a profit.

They also realized that they could expand their business with other products. So they contacted local business leaders about starting a salad dressing business. "We wanted to work with other companies which were in the economically disadvantaged area of Los Angeles," said founding student-owner Mark Sarria.

Community groups and business leaders donated time and money to help. Soon, Food From the 'Hood had created a recipe, designed a label, and begun selling their own salad dressing. It now sells in more than 2,000 stores around the country.

The group uses half of their salad dressing earnings for college scholarships for the student-owners. Food From the 'Hood still donates 25 percent of their produce to the needy in Los Angeles. They also provide after-school tutoring, college counseling, and an SAT prep course.

The students who run Food From the 'Hood want to run a successful business, prepare for their futures, and provide jobs for young people. They also want to show that young people can be socially responsible. As Carlos Lopez, one of the student-owners of the company says, "It doesn't matter what you look like or where you live, if you see it, you can achieve it—and as you can see, we are achieving it."

THINKING FOCUS

Why is it important to be a responsible, active citizen?

Key Term

- civic responsibility

The students who work for Food From the 'Hood have shown that they can run a successful business and also give something back to their community.

INTRODUCE

Have students read the lesson title and Thinking Focus. Ask them to explain what they think it means for citizens to be "responsible" and "active." *(For example, reading or watching the news, voting, participating in campaigns)* Suggest that students read to find out how individuals can make a difference in our country.

Key Term

Vocabulary Strategies: T36–T37

civic responsibility—a sense of duty and pride in one's local neighborhood or community; a willingness to contribute to society

Graphic Overview

Objectives

1. Identify some citizens in U.S. history who have made significant contributions to American society.
2. Explain wny American citizens have responsibilities as well as rights.
3. Describe how citizens can participate in the political process.

DEVELOP

Suggest that as students read the lesson they list situations in which the actions of individual citizens have made a difference in American society.

Citizens Who Made a Difference

In his 1961 inaugural address, President John F. Kennedy urged his fellow citizens to "ask not what your country can do for you; ask what you can do for your country." Kennedy knew that ordinary people can have a dramatic impact on society when they are inspired by a cause or an idea and become active in public affairs. As you have seen throughout this book, it was individuals—people like you—who made a difference in the history of America.

In addition to helping the poor, Jane Addams (bottom right) *was involved in the effort to keep the United States out of World War I.*

A Sense of Duty

Deborah Sampson, for example, was a heroic figure. A former teacher, she was determined to help in the fight for American independence. Disguising herself as a man, she joined the Continental Army and fought bravely for the cause of freedom in several battles.

A black slave, Frederick Douglass escaped to the North in 1838. Many people would have simply settled down and enjoyed their newly won freedom at this point. However, Douglass immediately threw himself into the abolition movement, lecturing and writing against slavery. In addition to describing the worst features of slavery in his eloquent autobiography (see pages 296–297), Douglass also helped to enlist black troops for the Union cause during the Civil War and spoke on behalf of women's rights.

One of the earliest and most important advocates of women's rights was a mother and homemaker named Elizabeth Cady Stanton. Although she cared deeply for her husband and children, Stanton also felt a responsibility to right social wrongs and improve the society in which she lived.

Originally involved in the abolition and temperance movements, Stanton helped organize the historic Seneca Falls Convention in 1848. She also drafted a Declaration of Sentiments—a variation on the Declaration of Independence—demanding that women "have immediate admission to all the rights and privileges which belong to them as citizens of the United States." Stanton remained active in the fight for women's rights until her death in 1902.

A well-educated but frail young woman named Jane Addams became one of the most important reformers of her time. Like Stanton, Addams considered it her duty to help those suffering from poverty and discrimination. In 1889, at the age of 29, she

Access Activity

Ask students to recall from previous lessons ordinary citizens who made a difference in our country. *(Rosa Parks, Susan B. Anthony)* Have students name small things they as individuals could do to help our country protect the environment. What could they do to help preserve an endangered species? To eliminate toxic waste dumps? To fight global warming?

Access Strategy

To help students understand that being a citizen includes having certain responsibilities as well as rights, have them analyze the phrase Lincoln used to describe the U.S. Government in the Gettysburg Address—"of the people, by the people, and for the people." What does "of the people" mean? *(The government is composed of its citizens.)* What does "by the people" mean? *(People created it.)* What does "for the people" mean? *(It exists to benefit the people.)* What happens if most Americans do not concern themselves with politics? Why? *(Because our government depends directly on the involvement of its citizens, it would be ineffective, causing us to receive fewer benefits from it.)* Tell students that they will read in this lesson about how they can be involved in the government of our nation.

founded Hull House in one of the poorest slums of Chicago. Called a "settlement house," Hull House served as a school, a club, a counseling center, a political organization, a doctor's office, and a refuge from the small, crowded homes of many of Chicago's poor immigrants. It became the model for settlement houses all across the United States.

Students Getting Involved

Like Jane Addams, people today are still working to improve their communities. Students, not just adults, are also making a difference. Thousands of middle school students across the country participate in a special program called CityYouth: Education and Community in Action. Through this program, students work together in many different ways to make positive changes in the world around them.

In Providence, Rhode Island, about 400 CityYouth students and over 30 police officers joined together for a conference on crime and safety. Students and officers at the conference role-played scenes of police responding to citizens' calls. It gave the students a chance to see how the police do their jobs, and gave the officers a chance to understand some of the students' fears and concerns. After the conference, the students and officers continued to meet to plan ways to improve community safety.

At the Imperial Middle School in La Habra, California, and the Bret Hart Middle School in Los Angeles, several hundred students also met with police to discuss crime and safety issues in their communities. Then the students made posters to help people understand the importance of working with police to reduce crime. They put the posters up in stores and other public places around their communities.

Through CityYouth programs, students in other schools have collected warm clothing to donate to elementary schools, cleaned up parks and riverbanks, and adopted a senior center. All of these projects help the students develop a sense of **civic responsibility,** which means they realize that they can and should contribute to society. ■

▲ *As part of a CityYouth program, police officers visited these students at the Imperial Middle School in La Habra, California, to discuss ways to improve community safety.*

■ *How have ordinary American citizens made the nation a better place in which to live?*

Rights Involve Responsibilities

At the end of the Constitutional Convention in 1787, someone asked the oldest delegate, Benjamin Franklin, "What have you created here?" Franklin answered sharply, "A republic, if we can keep it."

Franklin knew that a government whose power came from the people was only as good as its citizens. He also understood that, in order to survive, a democracy had to depend on its citizens to understand their government and know their rights, to participate in the political process, and to keep informed about the public issues of the day. Along with rights and freedoms, Franklin might have said, a citizen also has certain responsibilities.

CONSTITUTIONAL HERITAGE

Critical Thinking

Have students examine the Bill of Rights and other amendments to the Constitution on pages 636–655. Which constitutional rights were exercised by activists such as Jane Addams, Frederick Douglass, Deborah Sampson, and Elizabeth Cady Stanton? *(First, Fifth, Fourteenth, and Fifteenth amendments)*

■ *Ordinary American citizens, such as CityYouth groups, have started campaigns to protect the environment, to increase civil rights, to establish reform in areas such as poverty, and to improve foreign relations.*

Research

Divide students into small groups to research and present an oral report on what volunteer programs, agencies, or organizations are available in their local area. What kind of volunteer help do they think is especially needed? What would they be willing do as a class, or as individuals?

Mention that in California, for example, in addition to many CityYouth programs, a nonprofit organization in San Francisco called CHALK (Communities in Harmony Advocating for Learning and Kids) has a unique way of getting communities more involved in the lives of youths—through technology. One of CHALK's purposes is to help minority youths learn online Internet skills, and help teachers and students in underserved school systems use the Internet in their classroom.

Study Skills

Ask students to bring to class newspaper and magazine articles on current relations between the United States and the former Soviet Union. Divide the class into pairs to work on paraphrasing different articles. Ask volunteers to explain the information in their articles in their own words to the class.

CITIZENSHIP
Social Participation

Have students share what they know about citizen action groups such as Students Against Drunk Driving (SADD), Amnesty International, the Audubon Society, the National Wildlife Association, the Sierra Club, and the American Civil Liberties Union (ACLU). In what recent campaigns or actions have these groups been involved? Have any legislative actions been taken recently to support the groups' goals? How can students get involved in such social and political forums? *(Encourage students to make specific suggestions.)*

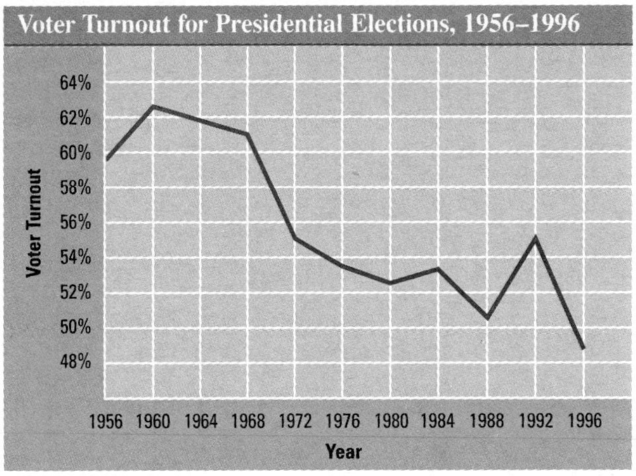

Voter turnout in Presidential elections has declined steadily since a post-World War II high point in 1960.

Today, however, many Americans are neither active nor informed. In recent surveys, for example, some American citizens have not been able to identify the Declaration of Independence or the United States Constitution. And in the presidential election of 1996, more than half of the eligible voters chose to remain at home.

Getting Involved

Either because they aren't interested or don't believe they can make a difference, some Americans have chosen not to take part in the democratic process. But as the students of West Milford, New Jersey, have proved, what Americans think—and what they do about what they think—can have a measurable impact on society.

Even though you may not be old enough to vote, you can still be active in politics and public affairs. Participating in your school's student government is one good way to learn about the nuts and bolts of the political process. You may also choose to take part in the model United Nations program at your school, if it has one, or start one if it doesn't.

In addition, students between the ages of 13 and 19 can join the youth organizations of various political parties, such as the Teen Age Republicans or the Young Democrats of America. Working through these organizations in local, state, and national elections, young people can learn how the political system works at the grass roots level. For example, club members might assist people in registering to vote, might pass out campaign flyers at shopping malls and on street corners, or might make phone calls to prospective voters.

Young people can have a voice in important issues of the day by joining organizations devoted to particular issues as well. Students Against Drunk Driving (SADD) offers programs to educate fellow teenagers about the dangers of drinking and driving. Amnesty International, on the other hand, works to support human rights. Its members write letters to oppressive governments around the world on behalf of political prisoners. The Audubon Society and the Sierra Club are dedicated to cleaning up and protecting the environment. For every important issue there usually exist several organizations with varying points of view about that issue.

Students can also become active in local affairs. They might volunteer to tutor in an illiteracy program or read for the blind. They could also organize a community effort to clean up a park or beach. They might write letters to city officials about the need for better public transportation or take part in petition campaigns to prohibit smoking in public places. They could also participate in walk-a-thons or read-a-thons to help raise money for the homeless.

Promises to Keep

Throughout American history, dedicated citizens have struggled to realize and expand the ideals set forth in the Constitution. They have fought to abolish slavery and segregation. They have worked to extend the right to vote to women and minorities, to

Visual Learning

Refer students to the graph on this page. How much did voter turnout in presidential elections decline between 1960 and 1996? *(14 percent)* What can be inferred about Americans' participation in other aspects of politics? *(Probably decreased also)* What will happen if this trend continues? *(The government will become less and less representative.)*

Art Connection

Photographs have played an important role in battles for citizens' rights. Divide the class into groups of four or five students to gather pictures from newspapers and magazines covering different national or international civil rights issues. Each group should pool its pictures to create an "issue exposé" to share with the class. After all the groups have made their presentations, have the class evaluate the power of pictures to increase public awareness.

Conducting a Survey

Remind students that surveys often suggest appropriate courses of action, as well as revealing people's views on an issue. Have students create together a list of questions for a survey on a wildlife conservation or preservation issue, such as sea otters, whales, dolphins, eagles, or rain forests. Ask each student to conduct a survey of 25 people outside of class by questioning friends, relatives, or even strangers. Then have students compile their results in a chart.

In September, 1987, Americans gathered in front of the U.S. Capitol to celebrate the 200th anniversary of the Constitution. American democracy inspired the students who demonstrated in Tiananmen Square, Beijing, China, in the spring of 1989 (inset).

■ What responsibilities does being a good American citizen include?

provide legal assistance to the poor, and to root out corruption in public office. They have called their government to account in the name of the people.

What has united them in these varying struggles is a simple but powerful idea: that the United States is a nation "of the people, by the people, and for the people." This idea has inspired people fighting for freedom in every part of the globe.

Throughout its history, the United States has held out a promise to all its citizens—the promise of a nation with "liberty and justice for all." During the 20th century, Americans have worked hard to fulfill that promise and have achieved many of their goals. But to provide liberty and justice for all, a nation needs informed and dedicated citizens. Keeping the promise of America will depend ultimately on you—the people. ■

REVIEW

1. **FOCUS** Why is it important to be a responsible, active citizen?
2. **CONNECT** Name at least one reform or event in American history that was partly the result of a piece of writing by a concerned citizen.
3. **CITIZENSHIP** What are some ways that young people can make a difference in their communities?
4. **CRITICAL THINKING** Why do you think it is dangerous for a democracy when a large number of citizens are neither active nor informed?
5. **ACTIVITY** Choose an important issue or event and follow how it is reported in two different newspapers, on two different television stations, and on two different radio stations. Report your findings to the class.

POLITICAL SYSTEMS

Visual Learning

After students examine the picture and read the caption on this page, ask them why gatherings such as this one might inspire people in other countries, such as China. *(Large groups of Americans are gathered to celebrate the freedoms guaranteed in the Constitution; Americans are also free to gather peacefully in protest demonstrations.)*

■ *Responsibilities include being informed and being actively involved in politics.*

CLOSE

Have students answer the Thinking Focus. Ask them to use the lists that they made while reading the lesson to name individuals who have made a difference in American society. As a reteaching activity, copy on the board the Graphic Overview from page 609 and ask students to explain why "responsibilities" are as much a part of citizenship as are "rights."

Answers to Review Questions

1. Because the United States is a democracy, dependent on the people, it is important for Americans to be informed, active citizens.
2. Sample answer: Upton Sinclair's *The Jungle* inspired reform in meat packing.
3. Sample answers: Volunteer as a tutor; raise money for the homeless; participate in student government.
4. Sample answer: Citizens who are uninformed and inactive may allow leaders to make bad choices for the country. Allow for personal opinion.
5. You may wish to divide the class into groups to focus on various issues.

Homework Options

Ask students to use current events to evaluate whether we are "keeping it," as Benjamin Franklin referred to the republic on page 611.

Study Guide: page 89.

DISCOVERY PROCESS

Students will use the following steps in the discovery process to complete the activity:
Get Ready Think about different kinds of work.
Find Out Talk to your grandparents or other older members of your family.
Move Ahead Invite a personnel director of a local company to speak to your class.
Explore Some More Find out how work has changed over the past century. Find out about possible jobs of the future.

Materials needed: Yellow Pages of the telephone book, newspapers and magazines, notebook, pen or pencil

ECONOMICS

Critical Thinking

Imagine that you are a mechanic living in the 1890s. You have just started experimenting with making an automobile. Your friends may not take your idea seriously, but you want to decide whether there is a future in it. What questions would you ask yourself? *(Are there roads that a car can travel on? Will people be willing to give up horses and carriages and invest in a new form of transportation?)*

EXPLORING

Work Past and Present

How long has it been since you visited the shop of a slater, coach maker, tinner, teazle maker, razor strop maker, or bell founder? Probably not recently. These occupations and many others, once the work of thousands of Americans, disappeared long ago.

The Stock Exchange on Wall Street attracts people who are interested in business and finance.

Get Ready

Changing times create new jobs and make others outdated. It will happen—it's happening right now—in your lifetime. To explore the ways in which work has changed over the years, you'll need to think about the kinds of work people used to do and what they do today. Then you can begin to ask questions about how and why work changes. You will also want to think about what types of work interest you.

Some of your exploring will be done at the local public library or at the school library. Some research can be done at home with your family or at school with your classmates. You may want to visit businesses in your community to learn firsthand about the work people do. You will need a notebook, and a pen or a pencil.

Find Out

Start your research by thinking about what types of work people have done in the past. Think about the types of work you have read about so far in this book. Make a list of the work people did in the 1800s and a separate list of the work people did in the past that is still done today.

Next, ask older members of your family—your parents, aunts, uncles, grandparents—what adults did to earn a living when they were young. Write their answers in your notebook, and note which types of work are still done today. Also note the kinds of work that interest you.

Now you are ready to make a list of the work that is done today by looking at the Yellow Pages of the telephone book. Make a list of present-day work by using the index or by looking at advertisements. Choose from your present-day inventory an occupation that interests you. Call a company or a person listed in the Yellow Pages under that occupa-

Objectives

1. Identify how jobs and the work process have changed. (Economics 3)
2. Obtain historical information from family and acquaintances. (Social Participation 3)

Activities

Jobs such as bookbinding by hand were once much more common than they are now. Today these skills are mainly kept alive by dedicated craftspeople who make their living doing fine custom work. These people sometimes have a wealth of historical information about their craft.

Have the students invite a craftsperson, such as a bookbinder or wood carver, to speak to the class about his or her craft and its history.

Have students talk to doctors or other professionals who perform a service about changes they would like to see in their professions. Are some of these changes already being made? How have or will these changes affect the public's access to those services?

tion. Arrange to visit their workplace to talk with them about their work. Ask them about the educational requirements for their work, how they were trained, and what opportunities there are for young people today in that field. Prepare a report on your interview describing the work being done there and the products or services the company provides.

Move Ahead

Would you like to know something about the future of the occupation you've chosen? Arrange for a vocational counselor or the personnel director of a local company to visit your class. Find out from this person how young people can best prepare themselves for an occupation that interests them.

Explore Some More

The following list shows just a few of the hundreds of occupations listed in the Boston Directory for the year 1882. Look at the list and think about what each occupation might have been like. Also consider how work has changed throughout American history.

bill poster	ship bread baker
blacksmith	shipwright
carver	chimney sweep
troche maker	glass blower
washer woman	horse shoer
lamp wick maker	wharfinger
marble worker	wig maker
wood carver	lace weaver

Now turn your attention to the present and future by collecting articles from newspapers and magazines about occupations, professions, training programs, and schools, Look for predictions on jobs in the future, especially occupations that interest you. If one particular occupation interests you more than all the others, collect information for your notebook.

Increasing numbers of women have joined the American work force in fields such as science (left) and business.

Here is a list of occupations that are common in today's job market. Do any of these appear in your present-day inventory? Compare this list with your inventory, and make notes relating to such factors as regions, natural resources, types of industry, and education.

accountant
plumber
teacher
cabinet maker
chef
photogragher
computer programmer
physician

Industry provides employment for people with a variety of skills and backgrounds.

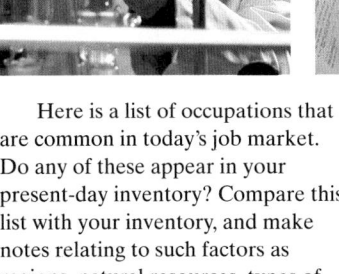

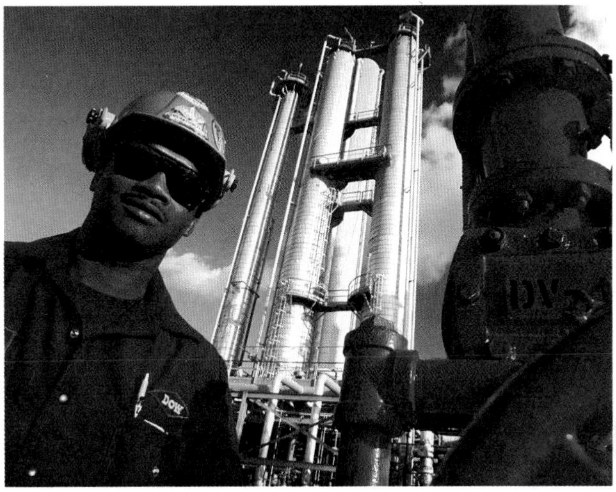

ECONOMICS

Critical Thinking

Many skilled jobs that are no longer common, such as wrought ironworking, or chimney sweeping, are nonetheless very interesting and necessary. Would you be interested in such work? How would you go about deciding whether a job would interest you? *(Talk to people who are doing the work and decide whether you like to work independently)*

Collaborative Strategy

A recommended strategy for this lesson is the jigsaw approach. For more details about collaborative learning strategies, see pages T34–35.

INTRODUCE

Have students recall what they learned about the civil rights movement in Lesson 2. Explain that at the time Kennedy delivered this speech, the nation had seen on television police in Birmingham, Alabama, attack civil rights marchers with clubs, dogs, and cattle prods. Seeing these attacks led people to demand that the federal government take action to support the movement for the rights of black Americans.

READ AND RESPOND

Write on the board the following purpose-setting question, "Which of Kennedy's reasons for supporting the cause of civil rights seems most important to you?" Ask students to keep this question in mind as they read the selection independently. If you have LEP students, you may wish to read aloud the vocabulary words and their definitions noted in the margin.

LITERATURE

A Call for Civil Rights

John F. Kennedy

President Kennedy delivered this speech to the nation in June 1963, a time when violence in the South over civil rights issues was growing worse.

As you read this selection, keep in mind what you learned in Lesson 2 about the civil rights movement and the response in the South to civil rights protests and sit-ins.

It ought to be possible for American consumers of any color to receive equal service in places of public accommodation, such as hotels and restaurants and theaters and retail stores, without being forced to resort to demonstrations in the street, and it ought to be possible for American citizens of any color to register and to vote in a free election without interference or fear of reprisal.

reprisal retaliation or revenge

It ought to be possible, in short, for every American to enjoy the privileges of being American without regard to his race or his color. In short, every American ought to have the right to be treated as he would wish to be treated, as one would wish his children to be treated. But this is not the case.

The Negro baby born in America today, regardless of the section of the Nation in which he is born, has about one-half as much chance of completing a high school as a white baby born in the same place on the same day, one-third as much chance of completing college, one-third as much chance of becoming a professional man, twice as much chance of becoming unemployed, about one-seventh as much chance of earning $10,000 a year, a life expectancy which is seven years shorter, and the prospects of earning only half as much.

This is not a sectional issue. Difficulties over segregation and discrimination exist in every city, in every State of the Union, producing in many cities a rising tide of discontent that threatens the public safety. Nor is this a partisan issue. In a time of domestic crisis men of good will and generosity should be able to unite regardless of party or politics. This is not even a legal or legislative issue alone. It is better to settle these matters in the courts than on the streets, and new laws are needed at every level, but law alone cannot make men see right.

partisan devoted to a single political party or cause

We are confronted primarily with a moral issue. It is as old as the scriptures and is as clear as the American Constitution.

The heart of the question is whether all Americans are to be afforded equal rights and equal opportunities, whether we are going to treat our fellow Americans as we want to be treated. If an American, because his skin is dark, cannot eat lunch in a restaurant open to the public, if he cannot send his children to the best public school available, if he cannot vote for the public officials who represent him, if, in short, he cannot enjoy the full and free life which all of us want, then who among us would be content to have the color of his skin changed and stand in his

Thematic Connections

Social Studies: Civil rights movement

Houghton Mifflin Literary Readers: Freedom's Foundations

Background

The nonviolent protests led by Dr. Martin Luther King, Jr., and the Southern Christian Leadership Conference attracted wide attention in the early years of the Kennedy administration. President John Kennedy's brother, Attorney General Robert Kennedy, ordered the Justice Department to make sure the civil rights marchers were protected. Even so, civil rights workers often met with violence from Southern law enforcement officers.

Fearing nationwide violence, President Kennedy gave this speech to signify the federal government's support of civil rights for black Americans. Later that summer, hundreds of thousands of people gathered in Washington, D.C., to hear Dr. King give his famous "I Have a Dream" speech (see page 602–603).

place? Who among us would then be content with the counsels of patience and delay?

One hundred years of delay have passed since President Lincoln freed the slaves, yet their heirs, their grandsons, are not fully free. They are not yet freed from the bonds of injustice. They are not yet freed from social and economic oppression. And this Nation, for all its hopes and all its boasts, will not be fully free until all its citizens are free.

We preach freedom around the world, and we mean it, and we cherish our freedom here at home, but are we to say to the world, and much more importantly, to each other that this is a land of the free except for the Negroes; that we have no second-class citizens except Negroes; that we have no class or caste system, no ghettoes, no master race except with respect to the Negroes?

Now the time has come for this Nation to fulfill its promise. The events in Birmingham and elsewhere have so increased the cries for equality that no city or State or legislative body can prudently choose to ignore them.

prudently wisely

The fires of frustration and discord are burning in every city, North and South, where legal remedies are not at hand. Redress is sought in the streets, in demonstrations, parades, and protests which create tensions and threaten lives.

redress satisfaction for wrong done

We face, therefore, a moral crisis as a country and as a people. It cannot be met by repressive police action. It cannot be left to increased demonstrations in the streets. It cannot be quieted by token moves or talk. It is a time to act in the Congress, in your State and local legislative body and, above all, in all of our daily lives.

It is not enough to pin the blame on others, to say this is a problem of one section of the country or another, or deplore the fact that we face. A great change is at hand, and our task, our obligation, is to make that revolution, that change, peaceful and constructive for all.

Those who do nothing are inviting shame as well as violence. Those who act boldly are recognizing right as well as equality.

Next week I shall ask the Congress of the United States to act, to make a commitment it has not fully made in this century to the proposition that race has no place in American life or law. The Federal judiciary has upheld that proposition in a series of forthright cases. The executive branch has adopted that proposition in the conduct of its affairs, including the employment of Federal personnel, the use of Federal facilities, and the sale of federally financed housing.

But there are other necessary measures which only the Congress can provide, and they must be provided at this session. The old code of equity law under which we live commands for every wrong a remedy, but in too many communities, in too many parts of the country, wrongs are inflicted on Negro citizens and there are no remedies at law. Unless the Congress acts, their only remedy is in the street.

Further Reading

Why We Can't Wait. Martin Luther King. A collection of essays in which King explains why black Americans can no longer wait for their rights.

◄ Why did President Kennedy describe discrimination as a national problem? *(Because it was found not only in the South, but throughout the nation)*

According to Kennedy, in what sense did discrimination affect the world's perception of the United States? *(We could not tell the world that America was a land of the free as long as black Americans were second-class citizens.)*

EXTEND

Give students the complete text of Martin Luther King's "I Have a Dream" speech. Ask them to write a brief essay comparing and contrasting King's and Kennedy's speeches.

Further Reading

You may want to ask students to go to the school or local library to find more books to read about the civil rights movement.

INTRODUCE

Have students recall what they learned in Lessons 1 and 2 about some of the effects of discrimination and prejudice on black Americans throughout U.S. history. Remind them that in the 1920s, when Langston Hughes began to write, black Americans lacked many civil rights. The Hughes poems reprinted here illustrate the discrimination that Hughes and other black Americans experienced.

READ AND RESPOND

As a purpose-setting question, write on the board, "What is the tone of each of these poems?" Ask students to keep this question in mind as they read the poems aloud and discuss them.

EXTEND

Have students go to the school or local library and find other poems by Langston Hughes. Have volunteers read these poems aloud in class and identify recurring themes in Hughes's work.

In Lesson 2 you read about the rise and impact of the modern civil rights movement. Think about what you learned in that lesson as you read these two poems by Langston Hughes.

LITERATURE

Dreams of Freedom

Langston Hughes

The most famous writer to emerge from the Harlem Renaissance of the 1920s, Langston Hughes published many volumes of poetry, fiction, and drama during his life. Much of his work captures the longing of black Americans for freedom and acceptance. The following poems are from Selected Poems of Langston Hughes.

I, Too

I, too, sing America.
I am the darker brother.
They send me to eat in the kitchen
When company comes,
But I laugh,
And eat well,
And grow strong.

Tomorrow,
I'll be at the table
When company comes.
Nobody'll dare
Say to me,
"Eat in the kitchen,"
Then.

Besides,
They'll see how beautiful I am
And be ashamed—

I, too, am America.

Refugee in America

There are words like *Freedom*
Sweet and wonderful to say.
On my heart-strings freedom sings
All day everyday.

There are words like *Liberty*
That almost make me cry.
If you had known what I knew
You would know why.

Thematic Connections

Social Studies: Discrimination

Houghton Mifflin Literary Readers: Finding Ways to Cope

Background

Born in Joplin, Missouri, Langston Hughes attended high school in Cleveland, Ohio. As a young man, he traveled extensively in Mexico, Europe, Africa, and the United States, finding jobs as a waiter or servant to support himself. Working at a Washington, D.C. hotel, Hughes met the poet Vachel Lindsay. Lindsay praised Hughes's work and encouraged him to publish it. Soon Hughes became one of the leaders of a black literary movement called the Harlem Renaissance. Although he is best known for his poems, Hughes also wrote plays and short stories. In 1960, he received the Spingarn Medal as "poet laureate of the Negro race."

Chapter Review

Reviewing Key Terms

civic responsibility (p. 611)
sit-in (p. 602)
citizen (p. 593)
naturalization (p. 594)

A. Use a dictionary to look up the derivation of each of the key terms listed above.

B. Use each of the terms above in a complete sentence that clearly explains the meaning of the term.

C. Based on what you have read in the chapter, determine if the following statements are true or false. If a statement is false, rewrite it to make it true.

1. If you feel a sense of civic responsibility, you think the people in your community should do whatever they can to improve your life.
2. A person who is born in the United States is a naturalized citizen.
3. Civil rights workers organized sit-ins as part of their nonviolent protest against the policy of segregation.
4. Citizens in a democratic society have an obligation to participate in the government.

Exploring Concepts

A. On a separate sheet of paper, copy the chart below. In the right-hand columns, list the groups that benefited from each amendment or Supreme Court action, as well as the important features of each amendment or action.

B. Support the following statements with facts and details from the chapter.

1. Many groups used the Fourteenth Amendment as a way to gain greater rights.
2. Property qualifications for voting were gradually removed.
3. Segregation was challenged in many different ways.
4. American Indians slowly gained rights using the courts and the Constitution.
5. Women have made many political and economic advances since the 1960s.
6. There are many ways that Americans can get involved in the Democratic process.
7. There are three ways to become a citizen of the United States.
8. Several of the constitutional amendments served to expand voting rights.

Action/Date	Groups Affected by Action	Important Features
14th Amendment–1868		
15th Amendment–1870		
19th Amendment–1920		
26th Amendment–1971		
Brown v. Board of Education–1954		
Indian Civil Rights Act–1968		

Answers to Reviewing Key Terms

A. This activity can be extended to key terms throughout the book.

B. Sample answers:

1. If you feel a sense of civic responsibility, you think you should help people in your community live a better life.
2. Civil rights activists staged a sit-in, refusing to leave the lunch counter until they had been served.
3. A citizen of the United States is guaranteed personal freedoms in the Constitution.
4. After having lived in the United States for five years, a person may become a United States citizen through naturalization.

C. Sample answers:

1. False. Because of the Soviet Union's recent policy of *glasnost*, citizens of that country have more freedoms than they had before.
2. False. A citizen who is born in the United States is a citizen by birth.
3. False. Civil rights workers organized sit-ins as part of their nonviolent protest against the policy of segregation.
4. True

Answers to Exploring Concepts

A. Answers:

1. 14th amendment: All Americans, but especially black Americans / defined citizenship
2. 15th amendment: Black Americans / guaranteed voting rights in all states
3. 19th amendment: Women / extended the vote
4. 26th amendment: Citizens 18 and older / extended the vote
5. *Brown* v. *Board:* Schoolchildren / rejected segregation in public schools
6. Indian Civil Rights Act: American Indians / guaranteed American Indians their basic rights and protected them against the taking of their property without compensation

B. Sample answers:

1. Black Americans gained the right to vote. Women used the amendment to fight unfair labor policies. American Indians, Asians, Hispanics, and Jews have used it in defense of their civil rights.
2. In 1789 only white males who were over 21 and owned land could vote. Ohio removed the property requirement in 1802. After 1851, no state had one.
3. Rosa Parks and others disobeyed segregation laws, boycotted segregated facilities, and sued for equal rights.
4. After they gained citizenship in 1924, Indians began seeking fair treatment through the court system and through laws such as the Indian Civil Rights Act of 1968.
5. Some of the advances have been the Civil Rights Act, the Equal Opportunity Act, and women in space, politics, and law.
6. Americans can vote, join political parties, and form groups to support causes.
7. Citizenship is granted through birth, blood relationship, and naturalization.
8. The Fifteenth, Nineteenth, and Twenty-Sixth amendments expanded voting rights.

Answers to Reviewing Skills

1. Refer to Understanding Editorials on pages 598–599.
2. Newspapers publish editorials to support ideas or actions.
3. Editorials can help you make a decision about an issue by presenting an argument for approaching or solving the issue a certain way. The reader can then analyze the argument, and, based on its strengths and weaknesses, make a decision or seek more information.
4. It's an opinion. The Supreme Court decides whether a law is constitutional.
5. Students should support their answers, which may vary, and may include: The alternatives to the McCain-Feingold bill are relevant to the issue because they give practical solutions to the fact that political campaigns are indeed expensive and need a venue for funding.
6. Students should identify the fact that one editorial is written by two individuals while the other provides the newspaper's point of view.
7. Editorials might appear in magazines and on news-related television programs.

Answers to Using Critical Thinking

1. Discuss why those born outside the country are excluded.
2. King was referring to the power of compassion and understanding.
3. Choose a current event as a focus for discussing this issue.
4. Ask students to compare the Athenian idea of civic duty with the idea of sharing family chores.
5. Students should give specific examples to support their responses.
6. Encourage students to consider whether men and women should be expected to do the exact same work, such as serving in combat.

Reviewing Skills

1. What steps would you follow to evaluate the strength of a newspaper editorial or other argument?
2. For what reasons does a newspaper publish editorials?
3. How can a newspaper editorial help you make up your mind about an issue?
4. In the editorial on page 598, the writer says that the McCain-Feingold bill is constitutional. Is that statement a fact or an opinion? Explain your answer. (Hint: Who determines whether a law is constitutional or not?)
5. In the editorial on page 599, the writer lists several alternatives to the McCain-Feingold bill. Is that information relevant to the issue of whether the bill should be supported or not? Explain your answer.
6. Reread "Understanding Point of View" on pages 336-337. Using what you know about point of view, analyze the editorials in this chapter.
7. Suppose electronic voting by telephone became a national issue. Where else might you find editorials on this subject other than in newspapers?

Using Critical Thinking

1. The U.S. Constitution states that no one but natural-born citizens, those born in the United States or to American parents, may be President. Which American citizens does this exclude from the Presidency? Do you think the law should be changed? Why or why not?
2. What was "the weapon of love" Martin Luther King, Jr. urged his followers to use in their protest against unjust laws? What effect do you think King's tactics had on public opinion? Explain your answer.
3. "In a democratic society, the citizens are responsible for the actions of their government." Do you agree or disagree with this statement? Why or why not?
4. In the democracy of ancient Athens, all eligible voters devoted some part of the year to civic duties. Do Americans have the same attitudes toward democratic responsibility?
5. President Johnson called Indian citizens the "forgotten Americans." What did he mean by that statement? Do you think it still holds true today? Explain your answer.
6. In 1848 the Seneca Falls Declaration said, "The history of mankind is a history of repeated injuries and usurpations [illegal authority over a person] on the part of man toward woman, having in direct object the establishment of an absolute tyranny over her. . . ." Compare those words with Abigail Adams's letter to her husband John on page 88. Based on those two writings, and on what you have read in this chapter, do you think women are now equal to men in the eyes of the law?

Preparing for Citizenship

1. **WRITING ACTIVITY** Rosa Parks is an example of an ordinary person who did extraordinary things. Do some research to find out what motivated her to make the stand she did in 1955. Then write a short report on who she was and how her actions have affected life in the United States today.
2. **WRITING ACTIVITY** Write a short newspaper article for each of the following headlines:
   - Brown Decision Declares Segregation Unconstitutional
   - Rosa Parks Arrested for Violating Segregation Laws
   - Indians Take Over Alcatraz
3. **ART ACTIVITY** People say that fashion follows politics. Look through the photos in this book to see how dress styles have changed throughout American history. Design outfits that you think may appear in the future.
4. **COLLABORATIVE LEARNING** Divide into groups, and choose an issue in society that you believe the government has not handled effectively. Form an imaginary organization, and write a statement of your beliefs, your organization's goals, and the tactics you will use to enact change. Did each group come up with the same tactics? Could you use these tactics in a non-democratic society?

620

Answers to Preparing for Citizenship

1. **WRITING ACTIVITY** This activity can be extended by asking students to select other people throughout history who have taken personal stands that created social action.
2. **WRITING ACTIVITY** Provide a number of different newspapers for the class to review in preparation for this activity.
3. **ART ACTIVITY** Review the concept of physical and human geography with students. Ask them to consider how much impact climate and workplace situations have on fashion.
4. **COLLABORATIVE LEARNING** Students should show an understanding of the difference between violent and nonviolent forms of protest.

Time/Space Databank

OUR CONSTITUTION TODAY

It took just under seventeen weeks for the delegates to the Convention to complete the Constitution. But in this short period of time, the delegates were able to establish the framework of a government that functions as well today as it did 200 years ago.

How could the framers of the Constitution—men from a rural, agricultural society—devise a system of government that could handle the problems of an industrial, technological society? How could this group of white male property owners foresee the vastly different political, economic, and social problems that the government would have to deal with 200 years later? Clearly they were men of vision. They knew that the nation would grow and change. The government that they created had to be able to respond to these changes. And it had to be designed so that no one person or group could gain total power. Their solution was a flexible constitution that could respond to a variety of problems.

The person who delivers your mail is an employee of the federal government.

PRINCIPLES OF LIMITED SELF-GOVERNMENT

The framers of the Constitution were very distrustful of power. They had seen how the King and Parliament tried to control local matters in the colonies. The colonists had protested against this control and had fought a war to gain local self-government. Now the framers had the task of creating a new government. If they gave this new government too much power, a few people might take control. The framers also worried about taking powers away from the states. Each state jealously guarded its independence and individuality and feared the creation of a strong national government.

Yet the framers of the Constitution knew that the national government had to have certain powers. The United States could not defend itself and regulate its commercial activities without the authority to raise money and enforce laws.

Federalism Divides Powers

Part of the solution lay in the idea of a federal system of government. Under a federal system, the national government would be given the power to do certain things. But it would be carefully limited from having other powers. These other powers would either belong to the states or be shared between the states and the national government.

Article I, Section 8, of the Constitution explains what powers belong to the national government. For example, only the national government may declare war or make treaties. You can imagine what might happen if any state could declare war. A state at war with another country could draw the rest of the nation into war or cause a war between states.

The Constitution also delegates, or authorizes, the national government to print or coin money and to run the post office. Think of the confusion if every state had its own money system and post office. People doing business in more than one state would never be able to keep up with the local rates and laws.

Another very important power given to the national government is the power to regulate commerce among the states. In order to understand the importance of this power, you have to understand how the government defines commerce. Commerce is much more than the buying and selling of goods. The courts have decided that commerce refers to all things that cross state borders—goods, persons, and even communications. It also includes the means used to move these goods across state borders such as trains, trucks, or airplanes. And commerce even includes the corporations and labor used to carry out these activities.

You can see that commerce has a very broad meaning for the government. This has given Congress the power to make laws covering a wide range of activities. As examples, Congress has made laws to regulate railroads and to improve harbors and transportation routes. It has made laws to regulate wages and work hours and to make air travel safe.

What about the states? What powers do they have? The Constitution tells more about what the states cannot do than what they can do. States cannot make treaties with other countries. They cannot print money or tax goods coming into or leaving the state. So what powers do the states have? The answer lies in the Tenth Amendment to the Constitution. It reads:

> *The powers not delegated to the United States by the Constitution, nor prohibited by it to the states, are reserved to the states respectively, or to the people.*

This amendment was added to the Constitution to prevent the federal government from taking powers away from the states. The Constitution reserves these powers to the states.

State governments use these reserved powers to make laws and regulations about all sorts of things. For example, your state runs its public school system. It sets the safety and

The Federal System

Powers Delegated to National Government

- Regulate interstate and foreign commerce
- Set standard weights and measures
- Coin money
- Regulate copyrights and patents
- Establish lower federal courts
- Declare war
- Create and maintain armed forces
- Make foreign policy
- Make laws governing citizenship

Powers Reserved to States

- Regulate commerce within states
- Establish local governments
- Maintain system of public schools
- Make laws about marriage and divorce
- Conduct elections
- Make laws for traffic
- Make laws governing corporations

Powers Shared by National Government and States

- Collect taxes
- Borrow money
- Charter banks
- Provide for general welfare
- Punish criminal offenses

◄ *This chart shows how the Constitution divides the powers between the national and state governments. Which one has the power to make foreign policy?*

➤ *It is the duty of the states to protect and promote public safety. This police officer works for the state government.*

educational standards for your school. It decides what courses you will study, and it certifies your teachers and principal. Each state has its own code of criminal laws to protect people and their property within the state. The police officers that you see on the highway are state police. They make sure that people obey the state laws and regulations. State programs give assistance to people who are unemployed, handicapped, or elderly. These are just a few of the many activities of state governments.

Separate Powers Given to the Three Branches

A national government must be able to make laws, carry out the laws, and interpret the laws. The framers of the Constitution did not want any one group to have all three of these powers. They wanted to prevent any group from becoming too powerful.

The Constitution does this by dividing the powers among three separate branches of government. The legislative branch makes the laws. This is our Senate and House of Representatives. The executive branch carries out the laws and runs the government on a day-to-day basis. The President, Cabinet, and federal agencies make up the executive branch. The judicial branch interprets the laws, usually by ruling on civil and criminal cases from lower courts.

This system is clearly different from a parliamentary system. In a parliamentary system, the powers are not divided among branches of government. In Great Britain, for example, Parliament is the central governing body. This body holds both the legisla-

➤ *The three branches of government meet together in the House chamber to hear President Clinton's State of the Union Address.*

Checks and Balances

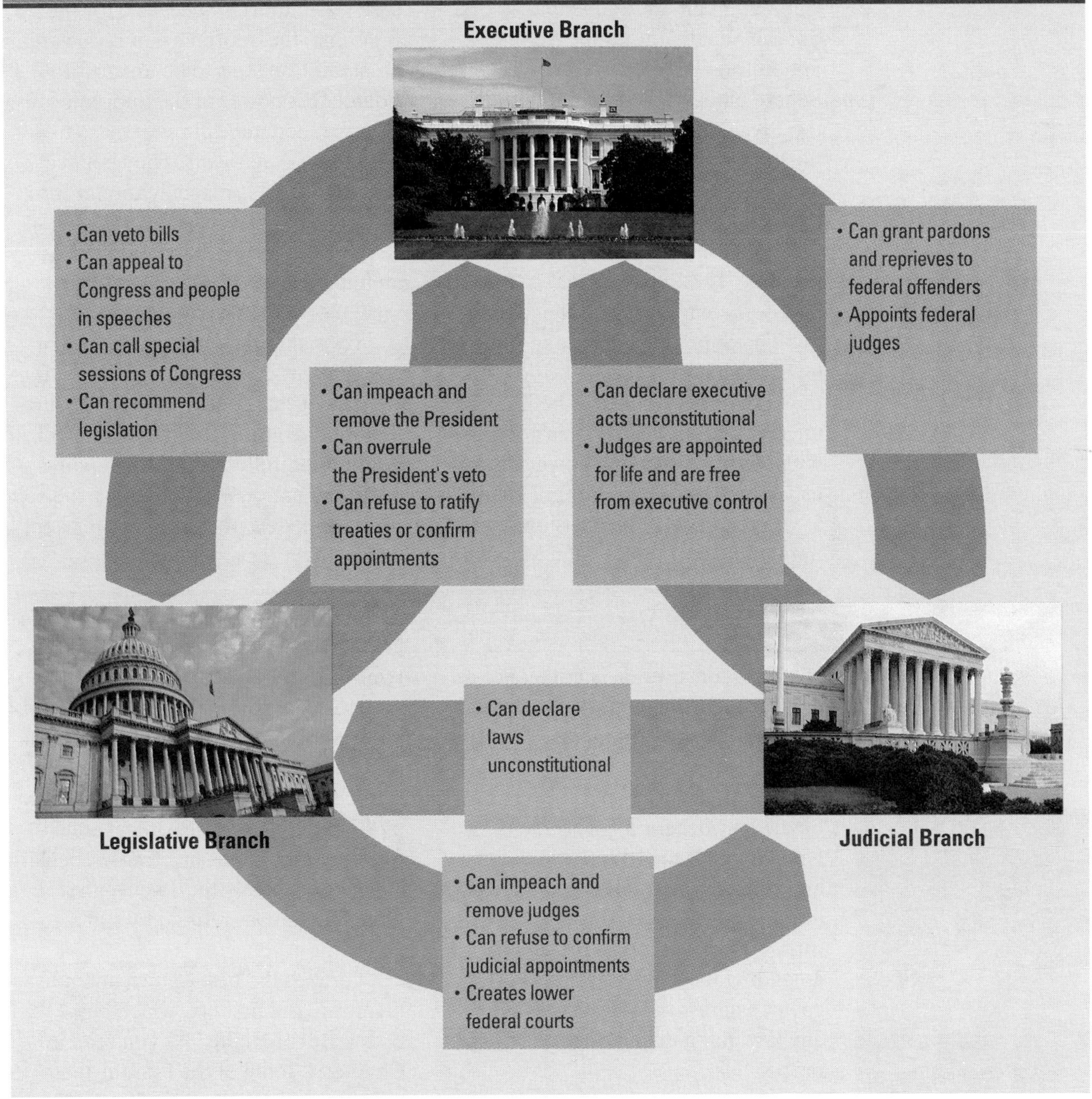
Executive Branch
• Can veto bills
• Can appeal to Congress and people in speeches
• Can call special sessions of Congress
• Can recommend legislation
• Can grant pardons and reprieves to federal offenders
• Appoints federal judges
• Can impeach and remove the President
• Can overrule the President's veto
• Can refuse to ratify treaties or confirm appointments
• Can declare executive acts unconstitutional
• Judges are appointed for life and are free from executive control
• Can declare laws unconstitutional
Legislative Branch
Judicial Branch
• Can impeach and remove judges
• Can refuse to confirm judicial appointments
• Creates lower federal courts

This diagram shows how each branch of government checks the activities of the other two branches.

tive and the executive powers of the country. The executive—the British Prime Minister—is a member of the legislative branch. He or she is chosen by Parliament and is responsible to it.

Checks and Balances Provide Controls

The other way the Constitution prevents any one group from having total power is by making the three branches depend on each other for their authority. The legislative branch—the House of Representatives and the Senate—has the power to pass bills, that is, proposed laws. However, a bill must go to the President before it can become law. The President can veto, or reject, a bill that he or she believes is unwise. In turn, the House and Senate can reconsider the bill. If two-thirds of each house approve the vetoed law, it becomes law without the President's signature.

The President nominates judges, Cabinet members, and ambassadors, but the Senate must approve the appointments. In one recent case, the Senate blocked the appointment of the President's nominee for a Cabinet position. The Senate investigated the candidate's qualifications and performance in previous jobs, and it decided that he wasn't the right person for the position. The President had to nominate someone else to fill the job.

The Supreme Court cannot make laws. It can, however, strike down laws that a majority of justices believe are unconstitutional—that is, in conflict with the principles and powers established by the Constitution. In Chapter 5, you read about the decision of the Supreme Court under John Marshall in the case *Marbury* v. *Madison*. This case was important because, for the first time, the Supreme Court declared an act of Congress to be unconstitutional. This power of the Supreme Court, called judicial review, has troubled some Americans. They believe that the Court is reaching too far into the lawmaking process. Most Americans, however, see judicial review as an important part of the American system of checks and balances.

By making the three branches of government depend on each other, the framers of the Constitution made sure that no one group could take control. And by carefully restricting the powers of the national government, the framers made sure that the states kept control over local matters.

A Living Document

The Constitution is not a once-and-for-all listing of everything Americans need to govern themselves. The framers knew better than to do that. Instead, they designed a strong, flexible framework for a government. Knowing that the country would grow and change, the framers provided two important ways to add to the Constitution. They outlined a process for amending the Constitution, and they gave Congress the power to make any law that it deems "necessary and proper."

The First Amendment protects the right of these people to assemble peacefully.

Amendments Allow Formal Changes

Realizing that people might want to make changes in the Constitution, the framers provided a way to amend it, or make formal changes. Then they made sure that these procedures had their own system of checks and balances.

A constitutional amendment can be proposed by a two-thirds vote of the Senate and the House of Representatives. It can also be proposed if two-thirds of the state legislatures vote to call a national convention (this has never happened). After Congress proposes an amendment, it must be ratified, or approved, by three-fourths of the state legislatures or by three-fourths of the states meeting in special conventions. Only the Twenty-first Amendment was ratified by state conventions.

Perhaps the best-known amendments are the first ten, which make up the Bill of Rights. As you read in Chapter 4, some of the first thirteen states were reluctant to ratify the Constitution. The first Congress proposed the Bill of Rights in response to the concerns of these states. The first three amendments secure rights that had been denied or threatened by the British. These include freedom of religion and speech and the right to assemble peacefully. Half of the Bill of Rights, in Amendments Four through Eight, deal with how trials and criminal investigations are to be carried out. The last two amendments in the

These people are demonstrating their position on a public issue. Public assemblies such as this one must not disturb the peace or cause harm to anyone.

Bill of Rights assure that individual and state rights will be preserved even if the Constitution does not mention them.

Approximately 9,000 resolutions for amending the Constitution have been proposed in Congress, but only 33 have been sent to the states for ratification. Just 26 amendments have been passed and made part of the Constitution.

Beyond the Bill of Rights, how has the amendment process been used? Here are some examples.

The framers did not see a need to raise money through an income tax. By the early years of this century, however, it was clear that the government had to find a way to raise more money. Income taxes were authorized by the Sixteenth Amendment, which was ratified in 1913.

Sometimes an amendment is needed to make something official that had been a custom before. George Washington, the first President, chose not to seek a third four-year term. The next thirty Presidents followed the custom. Franklin Roosevelt, however, was elected to a third and then a fourth term. A few years after he died, the Twenty-second Amendment set the maximum number of presidential terms at two.

On one occasion, Congress made an attempt to control social behavior. The Eighteenth Amendment outlawed the making, selling, or transporting of alcoholic beverages. This prohibition, as it was called, lasted from 1920 to 1933, when the Twenty-first Amendment repealed the Eighteenth Amendment. Why was the Eighteenth Amendment repealed? Primarily because it didn't work. Many people ignored the law by making their own alcoholic beverages or by buying it from "bootleggers" who made or imported the beverages illegally.

Laws Meet New Needs

You might wonder how a document as simple as the Constitution can be used to run a large country today. You might imagine that the limits placed on the federal government would have prevented it from responding to new issues.

One clause—just a few words—has been the source of almost all governmental growth. It is Article I,

Section 8, Clause 18, which gives Congress the power:

> *To make all laws which shall be necessary and proper for carrying into execution the foregoing powers, and all other powers vested by this Constitution in the government of the United States, or in any department or officer thereof.*

Read the clause again, slowly. It does not say exactly what Congress can do. Instead, this clause gives Congress implied powers, that is powers suggested indirectly. This means that, in addition to the clearly expressed powers given to it in the Constitution, Congress can pass laws that help it run the nation. Clause 18 allows Congress to stretch its powers as the needs of the country change. This is why it is sometimes called the "elastic clause."

The lawmaking powers of Congress affect a wide range of activities. These air traffic controllers are subject to federal legislation.

The first use of implied powers under the elastic clause occurred in 1791. According to the Constitution, Congress has the power to tax, borrow money, and regulate commerce. Some members of Congress thought the government had to have a national bank in order to use these powers. Congress used the elastic clause to justify setting up a national bank. It said that a national bank would help Congress to run the country.

Since 1791, Congress has used the elastic clause to pass laws in many different areas. One example is federal legislation in education. You might wonder why the federal government is involved in education. After all, the Constitution gives the states the authority to establish and maintain public schools. But the Constitution also gives Congress the power to "provide for the general welfare of the United States." Congress has stretched this power to include dealing with educational issues that affect large numbers of Americans. For example, many students in the United States have a native language other than English. Because this issue affects many Americans, the federal government has gotten involved in bilingual education. The Bilingual Education Act of 1968 provided federal aid for non-native speakers to receive instruction in both English and their native language.

A more recent example of the use of the elastic clause is the Federal Election Campaign Act passed in 1971. The purpose of this act is to control the use of money in federal elections. It requires detailed reporting of campaign contributions and spending by all candidates. The passage of the Federal Election Campaign Act reflects people's growing disgust with the "dirty tricks" used by political parties to get their candidates elected. The "last straw" in dirty tricks was the break-in of Democratic Party offices in the Watergate Hotel by Republican Party spies in the 1972 presidential election. President Richard Nixon's attempts to cover up the break-in forced him to resign the presidency. In response to the Watergate scandal, Congress also established the Federal Election Commission in 1974. This

Race for the White House

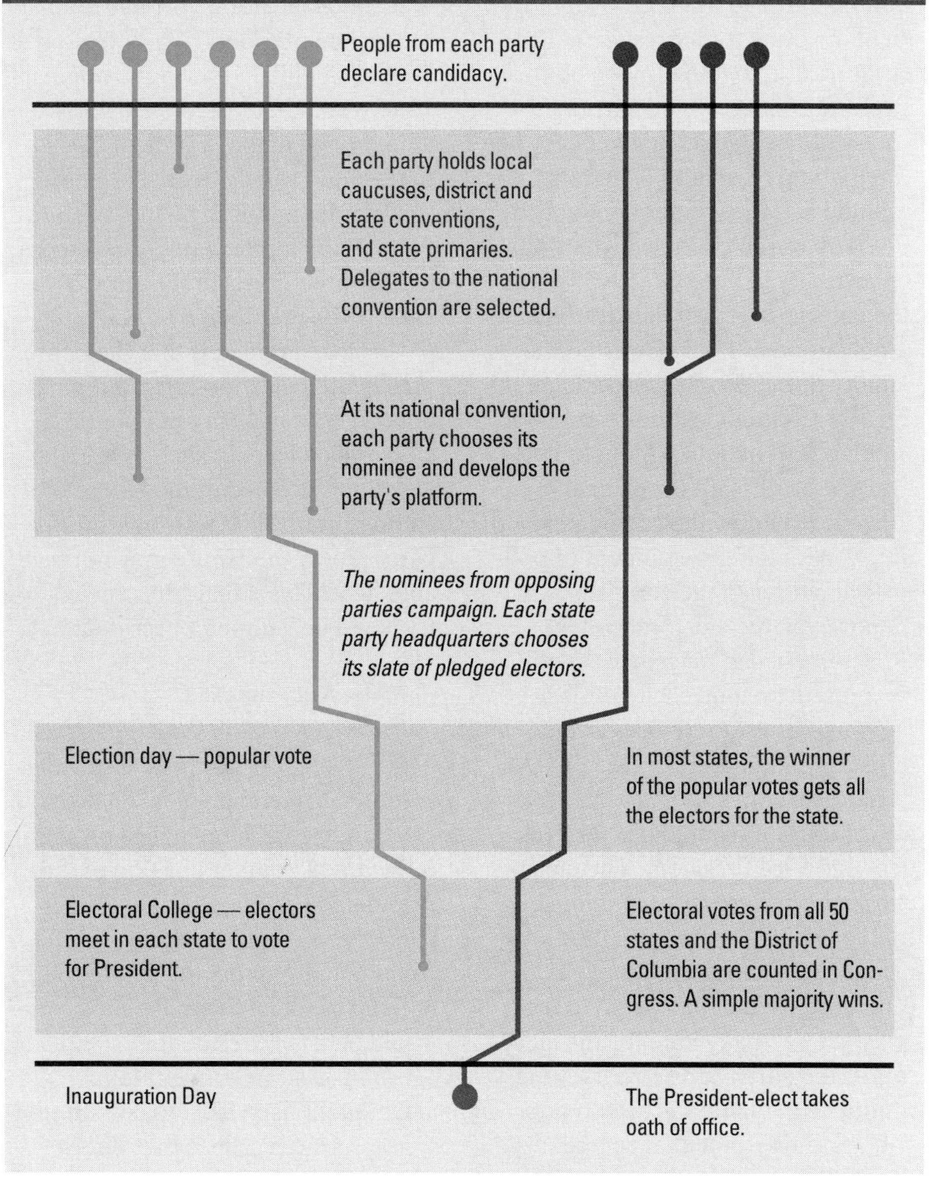

People from each party declare candidacy.
Each party holds local caucuses, district and state conventions, and state primaries. Delegates to the national convention are selected.
At its national convention, each party chooses its nominee and develops the party's platform.
The nominees from opposing parties campaign. Each state party headquarters chooses its slate of pledged electors.
Election day — popular vote
In most states, the winner of the popular votes gets all the electors for the state.
Electoral College — electors meet in each state to vote for President.
Electoral votes from all 50 states and the District of Columbia are counted in Congress. A simple majority wins.
Inauguration Day
The President-elect takes oath of office.

The race to the White House begins when people from each political party declare their candidacy.

independent agency in the executive branch makes sure that candidates and their supporters obey the law.

The Election System Evolves

Constitutional change, however, can take place by means other than formal amendment or congressional legislation. In some cases, custom and the actions of the political parties have also played a part in constitutional change. One example is the way in which the President and the Vice President are elected.

The framers of the Constitution disagreed about how the President should be elected. Some delegates thought that Congress should choose the President. Others thought that this would give Congress too much control over the President. Some of the delegates suggested that the states choose the President but others thought this would make the states too powerful. Then an idea was presented which the delegates agreed was the best solution. Each state would choose a special group of people called electors. The number of electors for each state would be equal in number to its repre-

Benjamin Harrison, *the Republican presidential candidate in 1888, supported high tariffs to protect American industry. John F. Kennedy ran against Richard M. Nixon in the 1960 race to the White House.*

sentatives in Congress. These electors would be free to use their own judgment in voting for a President. The electors, who together make up the electoral college, would cast their votes at their state capitals. Then their votes would be sent to Congress to be counted and the winner announced.

Why weren't people given the opportunity to vote directly? Because the delegates at the Constitutional Convention in 1787 distrusted the ability of the people to decide intelligently. Communications were poor at the time, and they thought it would be difficult for ordinary people to know the candidates.

With the development of political parties in the early 1800s, however, the electoral college system began to change. In our present system, each political party in each state chooses a slate, or list, of candidates for electors. At its national convention, each party also chooses its candidates for President and Vice President. The electors chosen by each party are no longer free to choose a President; they are pledged to vote for their party's candidates. When people go to the polls, they actually vote for the electors of the party whose presidential candidate they prefer; they do not vote for the presidential candidates themselves. In fact, at one time the names of the electors actually appeared on the ballot. But today most states list only the names of the presidential and vice-presidential candidates.

The electoral college system has its defects. In every state except Maine, the presidential election is a winner-take-all contest. Whichever slate of electors wins the popular vote—the majority of votes by the people—wins all of that state's electoral votes. It is possible for the presidential and vice-presidential candidate to win the popular vote overall but lose the electoral vote. For example, a slate of candidates could win by huge margins in small states and lose by just a few votes in the larger states. This has happened three times, in the elections of 1824, 1876, and 1888.

Another defect is that the entire presidential election can fail if no candidate gets a majority of votes in the electoral college. In such a case, the election is decided in the House of Representatives. If a strong third party grows, the House may not be able to achieve a majority. The country could be without a President.

Reforms Are Proposed

In every session since 1789, members of Congress have proposed constitutional amendments to change the election system. One logical proposal is the direct popular election of the President and Vice President. Each person's vote in the country would count equally across the whole country. The candidate with the most votes would become President.

Why hasn't a constitutional amendment been used to change the system? One reason is that three-fourths of the state legislatures would have to ratify the proposed amendment. Small states, which enjoy greater power than large states in the electoral college, would be reluctant to ratify an amendment that would take away their power.

The flexibility of the Constitution has permitted the government to cope with a wide variety of issues and problems. Because necessary changes can be made in the Constitution, it has survived more than 200 years as a workable framework of government.

Our National Government at Work Today

Today, the federal government functions very much as its designers intended more than 200 years ago. Each of the branches of the federal government has its specific duties and responsibilities. Together the three branches provide a system of checks and balances.

The President Acts As Chief Executive

Just as in any large company, the President's job is that of a chief, or leader. As chief executive, the President issues rules and directives for running the executive branch of the government. He or she can also grant reprieves or pardons to criminals or those accused of crimes.

The President is the chief of state, negotiating treaties and other international agreements (as President Jimmy Carter did in the Camp David accords between Israel and Egypt in 1978). As chief diplomat, the President appoints ambassadors to other countries and receives the ambassadors and ministers of other countries.

As chief administrator, the President chooses the heads of fourteen executive departments and many

The Executive Branch

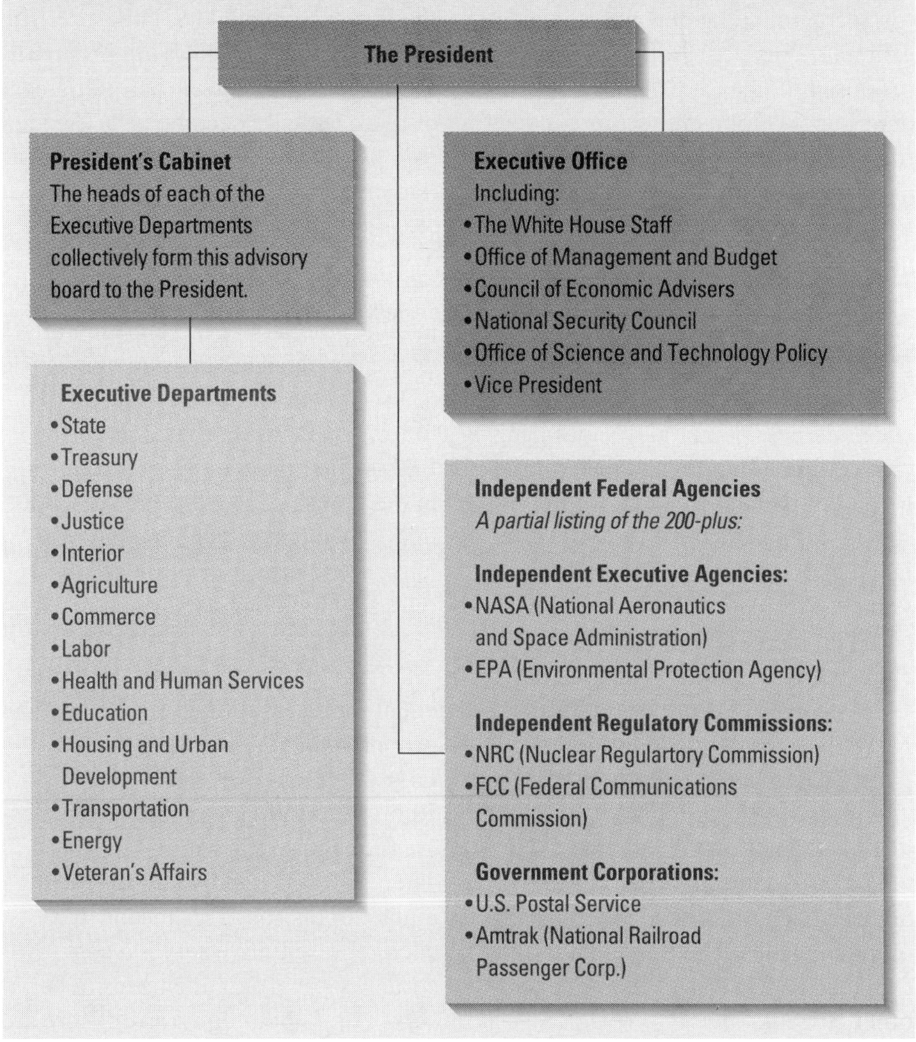

This chart shows the many agencies and departments in the Executive branch. Who makes up the President's Cabinet?

Illinois Senator Carol Moseley-Braun takes part in the confirmation hearings of Supreme Court Justice Ruth Bader Ginsburg. The Senate has the job of confirming or rejecting the President's nominations to the Supreme Court and other high-level government offices.

other agencies. If the Vice President dies or is otherwise removed from office, the President may choose a replacement.

The President is the chief legislator, recommending new programs. For example, President John F. Kennedy proposed the Peace Corps and President Lyndon Johnson recommended the War on Poverty. A President may also veto laws that he or she feels are against the national interest or his or her own beliefs.

The President is commander in chief of the armed forces. In times of war, he or she has the final authority. The President may also try to influence military spending by supporting or recommending certain programs. President Ronald Reagan, for instance, campaigned for the Strategic Defense Initiatives (S.D.I., or "Star Wars"). President Bill Clinton proposed an increase in the defense budget to raise military salaries.

As chief of his or her political party, the President can influence party policies and help other party members get elected. Finally, the President is the nation's chief citizen. He or she represents all other United States citizens at official meetings in other countries. The President is also expected to serve as an example to other citizens.

Congress Passes Laws

Congress—the House of Representatives and the Senate—is the legislative or lawmaking branch of the government. It is the only branch with the power to make U.S. laws.

Many ideas for laws are proposed to Congress, but fewer than 10 percent of these actually become law. The idea for a law may come from the executive branch, a congressional committee, or even from private individuals who see a need for a new law. These proposed laws are introduced as bills in either the House of Representatives or the Senate. The diagram on page 633 shows the basic steps that a bill follows on its route to becoming law. In this diagram, the bill is introduced in the House of Representatives, but bills may begin in the Senate too. A more complete description of how a bill becomes a law begins on page 690 of the Minipedia.

The Constitution gives each state equal representation in the Senate and proportional representation in the House. Members of the House of Representatives are elected from Congressional districts within the states. These districts are, by law, of roughly equal population. This means that each representative serves a constituency—a group of citizens to be served—of about equal size. There are

435 representatives in the House. The Constitution sets the minimum age of representatives at 25.

The Senate is much smaller than the House with just two senators from each state. Both senators are elected at large. In other words, their constituency consists of the entire population of their state. Senators must be at least 30 years old.

Because of its larger size, the House of Representatives imposes stricter rules on debate than does the Senate. Much of the House's work is done in committees, far from the House "floor," the chamber where actual laws are debated. In the Senate, debate can be much freer and can treat broader national issues. The Senate also depends heavily on committee work, but not as much as the House.

Senators were selected by state legislatures until 1913 when the Seventeenth Amendment was ratified. The only directly elected national officials had been members of the House.

A Bill Becomes Law

House of Representatives

- A new law is needed.
  A bill is drafted and sent to the House.
- The Clerk of the House sends the bill to a committee.
- The House committee studies the bill and makes revisions. The committee approves the bill and puts it on the House calendar.
- The Rules Committee decides to send the bill to the floor of the House.
- The bill is debated on the floor of the House. The House approves the bill and sends it to the Senate.

The Senate

- The clerk of the Senate sends the bill to the "presiding officer" who assigns the bill to a committee.
- The Senate committee studies the bill, makes several revisions, and approves it. The bill goes on the Senate calendar.
- The Senate majority leader chooses to send the bill to the Senate floor.
- The Senators debate the amended bill and approve it. The amended bill goes to a conference committee.

The Conference Committee

The conference committee, made up of members from both houses, works out differences between House and Senate versions. The revised bill goes back to both houses and is approved.

The President

- The bill goes to the President. If he does not act on the bill in 10 days, it becomes law.
- The President can approve the bill by signing it.
- The President can veto the bill.
  Congress can override the veto by a two-thirds vote.

A bill must go through many stages before it can become law. Follow the route of this bill as it moves through the legislative process.

Today, senators are also elected by the people.

Both houses of Congress are involved in policing the ethics of government officials, including themselves. The Senate and House have the power to investigate wrongdoing among government officials. They can also censure, or publicly condemn, any member for serious misdeeds.

Much of the actual work of Congress is done in committees such as this Senate subcommittee.

The Supreme Court Guards Our Rights

The framers of the Constitution agreed on the need for a federal court system that would include a Supreme Court. They were clear about the types of cases that federal courts could hear. Beyond that, they didn't give many details. The task of organizing the court system was left to Congress.

What kinds of cases can the Supreme Court and lower federal courts hear? The answer is in Article III, Section 2, Clause 1, of the Constitution. For the most part, federal jurisdiction, or the authority to hear and decide a case, is limited to those cases in which the United States government has a direct interest. These include cases in which states are in dispute or citizens from different states have sued each other. Any matter that is not mentioned in the Constitution is left to the various state court systems to decide.

A case usually ends up at the Supreme Court after it has traveled through at least one lower court. As you can see in the illustration on page 635, a case can go from a District Court through a Court of Appeals to the Supreme Court. The Supreme Court can also hear cases on appeal from the highest state courts. It can review the decisions of any of the state supreme courts if that decision has something to do with a question of federal law.

When the Supreme Court hears an appeal, it reviews the decisions of the lower court. It decides if the lower court's previous decision was based soundly on the principles of law and did not violate the Constitution. In these cases, the Supreme Court is said to have appellate jurisdiction, or authority to hear appeals. In a few special circumstances, the Supreme Court has original jurisdiction. This means that it can hear a case firsthand. This can happen in cases where two states disagree with each other or one state disagrees with the federal government.

About 5,000 cases are appealed to the Supreme Court each year. However, the Supreme Court agrees to hear only a small fraction of them. In many cases, the justices agree with the lower court's decision, and often the justices see no important point of law to be decided.

About 120 cases are actually reviewed by the Court every year. Most decisions are made and announced without giving reasons. For some cases, however, the justices may write long or short opinions explaining their decisions.

Only the most important cases from state and lower federal courts reach the Supreme Court. Sometimes the justices are called upon to interpret or defend important concepts of the Constitution. In this way, the Supreme Court guards our constitutional rights against laws or law enforcement methods that would ignore those rights or take them away.

The Supreme Court has made important decisions on many different issues. Here are a few significant cases. *NAACP* v. *Alabama* (1958) affirmed the First Amendment's guarantee of freedom of assembly by deciding that the state of Alabama could not force the National Association for the Advancement of Colored People to publish its membership list. In *Mapp* v. *Ohio* (1961), the Court upheld the Fourth Amendment prohibition against unreasonable search and seizure, saying that materials illegally seized in a raid could not be used as evidence. In 1963, the Court extended to everyone the right to legal counsel for those accused of serious crimes (*Gideon* v. *Wainwright*). The Fifth Amendment right against self-incrimination (testifying against oneself) was extended to suspects who had not yet been charged. In *Escobedo* v. *Illinois* and *Miranda* v. *Alabama*, the Court set guidelines for police questioning.

The Constitution Serves the People

Through interpretation by the Supreme Court, amendments, and legislation, the Constitution is a living piece of American history. Far more than just a yellowing piece of parchment, the Constitution is a daily guide for the U.S. government. It provides for a strong central government, assuring that national tasks such as defense will be carried out. It then limits the central government to just those essential tasks. The Constitution preserves the rights of individuals to determine their own destinies and to be treated fairly by their government. For more than 200 years, the Constitution has provided guidance and protection, yet is as fresh and vital today as it was when it was new.

The Federal Judiciary

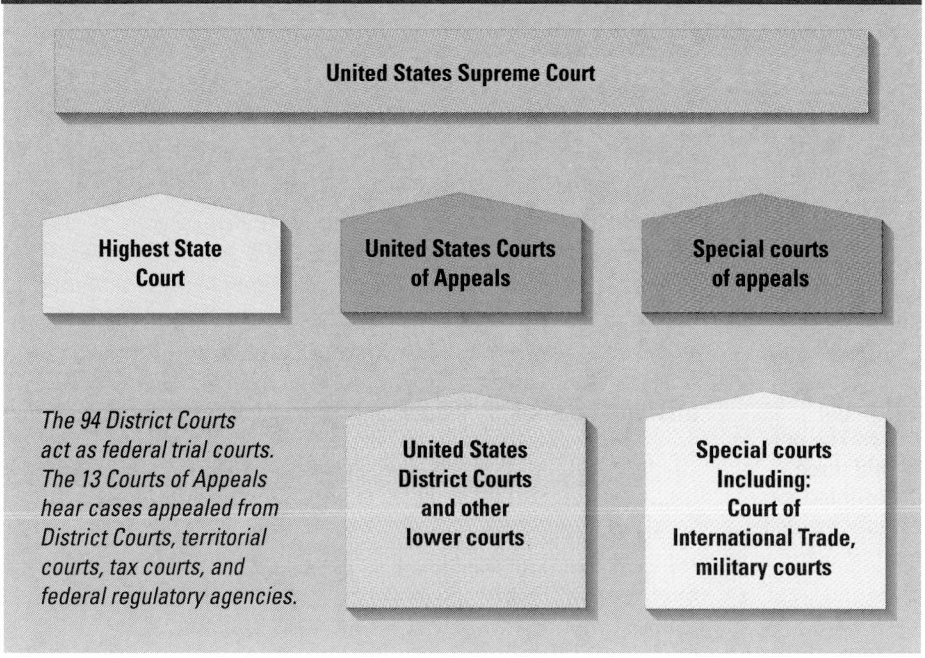

The Supreme Court hears cases on appeal from the highest state courts, the U.S. Courts of Appeals, and from the special courts of appeal. In only a few special circumstances does a court case begin in the Supreme Court.

★ ★ ★ ★ ★ ★ ★ ★ ★

The Constitution of the United States

PREAMBLE*

The Preamble states the purposes of the Constitution. The writers wanted to strengthen the national government and to secure peace for the United States. The Preamble makes it clear that the government's power comes from the people.

We the people of the United States, in order to form a more perfect union, establish justice, insure domestic tranquility, provide for the common defense, promote the general welfare, and secure the blessings of liberty to ourselves and our posterity, do ordain and establish this Constitution for the United States of America.

ARTICLE 1
LEGISLATIVE BRANCH

Section 1 gives Congress the power to make laws. Congress has two parts, the House of Representatives and the Senate. These two parts form the federal government's legislative branch.

SECTION 1. CONGRESS

All legislative powers herein granted shall be vested in a Congress of the United States, which shall consist of a Senate and House of Representatives.

Clause 1 Citizens elect the members of the House of Representatives every two years.

Clause 2 Representatives must be at least 25 years old. They must have been United States citizens for at least seven years. They must also live in the state they represent, but are not required to live in their district.

Clause 3 The number of representatives each state has is based on its population. The biggest states have the most representatives. Each state must have at least one representative. Congress has fixed the number of representatives in the House at 435 by a legislative act. The portion of the clause that states only three fifths of the slaves were to be counted for purposes of representation was overruled by the Thirteenth Amendment, which freed the slaves.

SECTION 2. HOUSE OF REPRESENTATIVES

1. ***Election and Term of Members*** *The House of Representatives shall be composed of members chosen every second year by the people of the several States, and the electors in each State shall have the qualifications requisite for electors of the most numerous branch of the State legislature.*

2. ***Qualifications*** *No person shall be a representative who shall not have attained to the age of twenty-five years, and been seven years a citizen of the United States, and who shall not, when elected, be an inhabitant of that State in which he shall be chosen.*

3. ***Number of Representatives per State*** *Representatives* ~~and direct taxes~~ *shall be apportioned among the several States which may be included within this Union, according to their respective numbers,* ~~which shall be determined by adding to the whole number of free persons, including those bound to service for a term of years, and excluding Indians not taxed, three-fifths of all other persons.~~** *The actual enumeration shall be made within*

* The titles of the Preamble, and of each article, section, clause, and amendment have been added to make the Constitution easier to read. These titles are not in the original document.

** Parts of the Constitution have been crossed out to show that they are not in force any more. They have been changed by amendments or they no longer apply.

★ ★ ★ ★ ★ ★ ★ ★ ★

three years after the first meeting of the Congress of the United States, and within every subsequent term of ten years, in such manner as they shall by law direct. The number of representatives shall not exceed one for every thirty thousand, but each State shall have at least one representative; ~~and until such enumeration shall be made, the State of New Hampshire shall be entitled to choose three, Massachusetts eight, Rhode Island and Providence Plantations one, Connecticut five, New York six, New Jersey Four, Pennsylvania eight, Delaware one, Maryland six, Virginia ten, North Carolina five, South Carolina five, and Georgia three.~~

4. ***Vacancies*** *When vacancies happen in the representation from any State, the executive authority thereof shall issue writs of election to fill such vacancies.*

5. ***Special Powers*** *The House of Representatives shall choose their speaker and other officers, and shall have the sole power of impeachment.*

Clause 4 *Executive authority* refers to the governor of a state.

Clause 5 The speaker of the House is chosen by the party that has a majority in the House.

SECTION 3. SENATE

1. ***Number, Term, and Selection of Members*** *The Senate of the United States shall be composed of two senators from each State,* ~~chosen by the legislature thereof,~~ *for six years; and each senator shall have one vote.*

2. ***Overlapping Terms and Filling Vacancies*** *Immediately after they shall be assembled in consequence of the first election, they shall be divided as equally as may be into three classes.* ~~The seats of the senators of the first class shall be vacated at the expiration of the second year, of the second class at the expiration of the fourth year, and of the third class at the expiration of the sixth year, so~~ *that one-third may be chosen every second year;* ~~and if vacancies happen by resignation, or otherwise, during the recess of the legislature of any State, the executive thereof may make temporary appointments until the next meeting of the legislature, which shall then fill such vacancies.~~

3. ***Qualifications*** *No person shall be a senator who shall not have attained to the age of thirty years, and been nine years a citizen of the United States, and who shall not, when elected, be an inhabitant of that State for which he shall be chosen.*

4. ***President of the Senate*** *The Vice President of the United States shall be President of the Senate, but shall have no vote, unless they be equally divided.*

5. ***Other Officers*** *The Senate shall choose their other officers, and also a President pro tempore, in the absence of the Vice President, or when he shall exercise the office of President of the United States.*

6. ***Impeachment Trials*** *The Senate shall have the sole power to try all impeachments. When sitting for that purpose, they shall be on oath or affirmation. When the President of the United States is tried, the Chief Justice shall preside: and no person shall be*

Clause 1 In each state, citizens elect two members of the Senate. This gives all states, whether big or small, equal power in the Senate. Senators serve six-year terms. The original Constitution specified that state legislatures choose the senators for their states. Today, however, people elect their senators directly. The Seventeenth Amendment made this change in 1913.

Clause 3 Senators must be at least 30 years old and United States citizens for at least nine years. Like representatives, they must live in the state they represent.

Clause 4 The Vice President of the United States acts as the President, or chief officer, of the Senate. The Vice President votes only in cases of a tie.

Clause 6 If the House of Representatives impeaches an official for a crime, the Senate conducts the trial. If two-thirds of the senators find the official guilty, then the person is removed from office. The only President ever impeached was Andrew Johnson in 1868. He was found not guilty.

★ ★ ★ ★ ★ ★ ★ ★ ★

convicted without the concurrence of two-thirds of the members present.

Clause 7 The term judgment in this clause means conviction by the Senate.

7. ***Penalties*** *Judgment in cases of impeachment shall not extend further than to removal from office, and disqualification to hold and enjoy any office of honor, trust or profit under the United States: but the party convicted shall nevertheless be liable and subject to indictment, trial, judgment and punishment, according to law.*

SECTION 4. ELECTIONS AND MEETINGS

Clause 1 Unless Congress acts, each state may decide where and when to hold elections. Today, as a result of an 1872 act of Congress, congressional elections are held in even-numbered years, on the Tuesday after the first Monday in November.

1. ***Election of Congress*** *The times, places and manner of holding elections for senators and representatives shall be prescribed in each State by the legislature thereof; but the Congress may at any time by law make or alter such regulations, except as to the places of choosing senators.*

Clause 2 The Constitution requires Congress to meet at least once a year. In 1933, the Twentieth Amendment moved the required meeting date of Congress to January 3.

2. ***Annual Sessions*** *The Congress shall assemble at least once in every year,* ~~and such meeting shall be on the first Monday in December, unless they shall by law appoint a different day.~~

SECTION 5. RULES OF PROCEDURE

Clause 1 A quorum is the smallest number of members that must be present for an organization to hold a meeting. For each house of Congress, this number is the majority, or more than one-half, of its members.

1. ***Organization*** *Each house shall be the judge of the elections, returns and qualifications of its own members, and a majority of each shall constitute a quorum to do business; but a smaller number may adjourn from day to day, and may be authorized to compel the attendance of absent members, in such manner, and under such penalties as each house may provide.*

Clause 2 Both Houses of Congress have developed detailed rules of procedure.

2. ***Rules*** *Each house may determine the rules of its proceedings, punish its members for disorderly behavior, and, with the concurrence of two-thirds, expel a member.*

Clause 3 The Constitution requires each house to keep a record of its proceedings. *The Congressional Record* is published every day. It allows any person to look up the votes of his or her representative.

3. ***Journal*** *Each house shall keep a journal of its proceedings, and from time to time publish the same, excepting such parts as may in their judgment require secrecy; and the yeas and nays of the members of either house on any question shall, at the desire of one-fifth of those present, be entered on the journal.*

Clause 4 Both Houses of Congress must meet in the same place and remain in session for the same period of time.

4. ***Adjournment*** *Neither house, during the session of Congress, shall, without the consent of the other, adjourn for more than three days, nor to any other place than that in which the two houses shall be sitting.*

SECTION 6. PRIVILEGES AND RESTRICTIONS

Clause 1 Congress sets the salaries of its members, and they are paid by the federal government. No member can be arrested for anything he or she says while in office. This protection allows members to speak freely in Congress.

1. ***Pay and Protection*** *The senators and representatives shall receive a compensation for their services, to be ascertained by law, and paid out of the treasury of the United States. They shall in all cases, except treason, felony and breach of the peace, be privileged from arrest during their attendance at the session of their respective houses, and in going to and returning from the same; and for any speech or debate in either house, they shall not be questioned in any other place.*

Clause 2 Emolument means salary. Members of Congress cannot hold other federal offices during their terms. This rule protects the checks and balances system set up by the Constitution.

2. ***Restrictions*** *No senator or representative shall, during the time for which he was elected, be appointed to any civil office under the authority of the United States, which shall have been created, or the emoluments thereof shall have been increased during such time; and*

★ ★ ★ ★ ★ ★ ★ ★ ★

no person holding any office under the United States shall be a member of either house during his continuance in office.

SECTION 7. MAKING LAWS

1. ***Tax Bills*** *All bills for raising revenue shall originate in the House of Representatives; but the Senate may propose or concur with amendments as on other bills.*

2. ***Passing a Law*** *Every bill which shall have passed the House of Representatives and the Senate, shall, before it becomes a law, be presented to the President of the United States; if he approve he shall sign it, but if not he shall return it, with his objections to that house in which it shall have originated, who shall enter the objections at large on their journal, and proceed to reconsider it. If after such reconsideration two-thirds of that house shall agree to pass the bill, it shall be sent, together with the objections, to the other house, by which it shall likewise be reconsidered, and if approved by two-thirds of that house, it shall become a law. But in all such cases the votes of both houses shall be determined by yeas and nays, and the names of the persons voting for and against the bill shall be entered on the journal of each house respectively. If any bill shall not be returned by the President within ten days (Sundays excepted) after it shall have been presented to him, the same shall be a law, in like manner as if he had signed it, unless the Congress by their adjournment prevent its return, in which case it shall not be a law.*

3. ***Orders and Resolutions*** *Every order, resolution, or vote to which the concurrence of the Senate and House of Representatives may be necessary (except on a question of adjournment) shall be presented to the President of the United States; and before the same shall take effect, shall be approved by him, or being disapproved by him, shall be repassed by two-thirds of the Senate and House of Representatives, according to the rules and limitations prescribed in the case of a bill.*

Clause 1 *Revenue* is money raised by the government through taxes. Only the House of Representatives can introduce bills that tax the people.

Clause 2 A bill, or proposed law, must be passed by the majority of members in each house of Congress. Then it is sent to the President. If the President signs it, the bill becomes a law. If the President refuses to sign it and Congress is in session, the bill becomes law 10 days after the President receives it.

The President can also *veto,* or reject, a bill by sending it back to the house where it was introduced. However, if each house of Congress repasses the bill by a two-thirds vote, it becomes a law. Passing a law after the President has vetoed it is called overriding a veto. This process is an important part of the checks and balances system set up by the Constitution.

Clause 3 Congress can also pass orders and resolutions that have the same power as laws. Such acts are also subject to the President's veto. This clause prevents Congress from bypassing the President by calling bills by other names.

SECTION 8. POWERS DELEGATED TO CONGRESS

1. ***Taxation*** *The Congress shall have power to lay and collect taxes, duties, imposts, and excises, to pay the debts and provide for the common defense and general welfare of the United States; but all duties, imposts and excises shall be uniform throughout the United States;*

2. ***Borrowing*** *To borrow money on the credit of the United States;*

3. ***Commerce*** *To regulate commerce with foreign nations, and among the several States, and with the Indian tribes;*

4. ***Naturalization and Bankruptcy*** *To establish a uniform rule of naturalization, and uniform laws on the subject of bankruptcies through the United States;*

5. ***Coins and Measures*** *To coin money, regulate the value thereof, and of foreign coin, and fix the standard of weights and measures;*

6. ***Counterfeiting*** *To provide for the punishment of counterfeiting the securities and current coin of the United States;*

7. ***Post Offices*** *To establish post offices and post roads;*

Clause 1 *Duties* are tariffs, *excises* are taxes on the production or sale of certain goods, and *imposts* are taxes in general. Only Congress has the power to collect taxes and spend tax money.

Clause 3 Congress controls trade with foreign countries and interstate trade.

Clause 4 *Naturalization* is the process by which a person from another country becomes a United States citizen. *Bankruptcy* is the condition in which an individual or business is unable to pay its debts. Congress has the power to pass laws on these two procedures.

★ ★ ★ ★ ★ ★ ★ ★ ★

Clause 8 A *copyright* protects an author's words. *Patents* allow inventors to profit from their work by keeping control over it for a certain number of years. Congress grants patents to encourage scientific research.

Clause 11 Only Congress can declare war on another country.
Clauses 12, 13, 14 Congress controls the army and navy. It has the power to decide the size of the armed forces and to write the laws that govern them.

Clause 15 Today the militia is called the National Guard. The National Guard often helps people after floods, tornadoes, and other disasters. Governors usually have control over the National Guard, though it can be placed under the command of the President.

Clause 17 Congress makes the laws for Washington, D.C., the nation's capital. In 1973, Congress gave residents of the District of Columbia the right to elect local officials.

Clause 18 This clause allows Congress to make laws on issues, such as television or radio, that are not mentioned in the Constitution. This clause is often called the *elastic clause* because it allows Congress to stretch its powers.

Clause 1 This clause was another compromise between the North and the South. It prevented Congress from regulating the slave trade for 20 years. Congress outlawed the slave trade in 1808.
Clause 2 A writ of habeas corpus requires the government to either charge a person in jail with a particular crime, or else let the person go free. Except in emergencies, Congress cannot deny the right of a person to a writ.

Clause 4 The Sixteenth Amendment gave Congress the power to tax income without regard to state populations.

8. ***Copyrights and Patents*** *To promote the progress of science and useful arts by securing for limited times to authors and inventors the exclusive right to their respective writings and discoveries;*

9. ***Courts*** *To constitute tribunals inferior to the Supreme Court;*

10. ***Piracy*** *To define and punish piracies and felonies committed on the high seas, and offenses against the law of nations;*

11. ***Declaring War*** *To declare war,* ~~grant letters of marque and reprisal~~, *and make rules concerning captures on land and water;*

12. ***Army*** *To raise and support armies, but no appropriation of money to that use shall be for a longer term than two years;*

13. ***Navy*** *To provide and maintain a navy;*

14. ***Military Regulations*** *To make rules for the government and regulation of the land and naval forces;*

15. ***Militia*** *To provide for calling forth the militia to execute the laws of the Union, suppress insurrections and repel invasions;*

16. ***Militia Regulations*** *To provide for organizing, arming, and disciplining the militia, and for governing such part of them as may be employed in the service of the United States, reserving to the States respectively the appointment of the officers, and the authority of training the militia according to the discipline prescribed by Congress;*

17. ***National Capital*** *To exercise exclusive legislation in all cases whatsoever, over such district (not exceeding ten miles square) as may, by cession of particular States and the acceptance of Congress, become the seat of the government of the United States, and to exercise like authority over all places purchased by the consent of the legislature of the State in which the same shall be, for the erection of forts, magazines, arsenals, dockyards, and other needful buildings; and*

18. ***Necessary Laws*** *To make all laws which shall be necessary and proper for carrying into execution the foregoing powers, and all other powers vested by this Constitution in the government of the United States, or in any department or officer thereof.*

SECTION 9. POWERS DENIED TO CONGRESS

1. ***Slave Trade*** ~~The migration or importation of such persons as any of the States now existing shall think proper to admit, shall not be prohibited by the Congress prior to the year one thousand eight hundred and eight, but a tax or duty may be imposed on such importation, not exceeding ten dollars for each person.~~

2. ***Habeas Corpus*** *The privilege of the writ of habeas corpus shall not be suspended, unless when in cases of rebellion or invasion the public safety may require it.*

3. ***Special Laws*** *No bill of attainder or ex post facto law shall be passed.*

4. ***Direct Taxes*** ~~No capitation, or other direct, tax shall be laid, unless in proportion to the census or enumeration herein before directed to be taken.~~

★ ★ ★ ★ ★ ★ ★ ★ ★

5. ***Export Taxes*** *No tax or duty shall be laid on articles exported from any State.*

Clause 5 Congress cannot tax exports.

6. ***Ports*** *No preference shall be given by any regulation of commerce or revenue to the ports of one State over those of another; nor shall vessels bound to, or from, one State be obliged to enter, clear, or pay duties in another.*

Clause 6 When regulating trade, Congress must treat all states equally. Also, states cannot tax goods traveling between the states.

7. ***Regulations on Spending*** *No money shall be drawn from the treasury, but in consequence of appropriations made by law; and a regular statement and account of the receipts and expenditures of all public money shall be published from time to time.*

Clause 7 Congress controls the spending of public money. This clause checks the President's power.

8. ***Titles of Nobility and Gifts*** *No title of nobility shall be granted by the United States: and no person holding any office of profit or trust under them, shall, without the consent of the Congress, accept of any present, emolument, office, or title, of any kind whatever, from any king, prince, or foreign State.*

Clause 8 Congress cannot award titles of nobility. Americans cannot accept titles of nobility unless Congress gives its consent.

SECTION 10. POWERS DENIED TO THE STATES

1. ***Complete Restrictions*** *No State shall enter into any treaty, alliance, or confederation; grant letters of marque and reprisal; coin money; emit bills of credit; make anything but gold and silver coin a tender in payment of debts; pass any bill of attainder, ex post facto law, or law impairing the obligation of contracts, or grant any title of nobility.*

Clause 1 The Constitution prevents the states from acting like individual countries. States cannot make treaties with foreign nations. They cannot issue their own money.

2. ***Partial Restrictions*** *No State shall, without the consent of the Congress, lay any imposts or duties on imports or exports, except what may be absolutely necessary for executing its inspection laws: and the net produce of all duties and imposts laid by any State on imports or exports, shall be for the use of the treasury of the United States; and all such laws shall be subject to the revision and control of the Congress.*

Clause 2 States cannot tax imports and exports without approval from Congress.

3. ***Other Restrictions*** *No State shall, without the consent of Congress, lay any duty of tonnage, keep troops, or ships of war in time of peace, enter into any agreement or compact with another State, or with a foreign power, or engage in war, unless actually invaded, or in such imminent danger as will not admit of delay.*

Clause 3 States cannot declare war. They cannot keep their own armies or navies.

ARTICLE II
EXECUTIVE BRANCH

SECTION 1. PRESIDENT AND VICE PRESIDENT

1. ***Term of Office*** *The executive power shall be vested in a President of the United States of America. He shall hold his office during the term of four years, and, together with the Vice President, chosen for the same term, be elected as follows:*

Clause 1 The President has the power to carry out the laws passed by Congress. The President and the Vice President serve four-year terms.

2. ***Electoral College*** *Each State shall appoint, in such manner as the legislature thereof may direct, a number of electors, equal to the whole number of senators and representatives to which the State may be entitled in the Congress; but no senator or representative, or person holding an office of trust or profit under the United States, shall be appointed an elector.*

Clause 2 A group of people called the Electoral College actually elect the President. Each state chooses electors, or delegates, to serve in the Electoral College. The number of electors each state receives equals the total number of its representatives and senators.

★ ★ ★ ★ ★ ★ ★ ★ ★

Clause 3 The Twelfth Amendment overruled this clause and changed the way the election process worked. Today, electors almost always vote for the candidate who won the popular vote in their states. In other words, the candidate who wins the popular vote in a state also wins its electoral votes.

3. ***Election Process*** ~~The electors shall meet in their respective States, and vote by ballot for two persons, of whom one at least shall not be an inhabitant of the same State with themselves. And they shall make a list of all the persons voted for, and of the number of votes for each; which list they shall sign and certify, and transmit sealed to the seat of the government of the United States, directed to the President of the Senate. The President of the Senate shall, in the presence of the Senate and House of Representatives, open all the certificates, and the votes shall then be counted. The person having the greatest number of votes shall be the President, if such number be a majority of the whole number of electors appointed, and if there be more than one who have such majority, and have an equal number of votes, then the House of Representatives shall immediately choose by ballot one of them for President; and if no person have a majority, then from the five highest on the list the said house shall in like manner choose the President. But in choosing the President, the votes shall be taken by States, the representation from each State having one vote; a quorum for this purpose shall consist of a member or members from two-thirds of the States, and a majority of all the States shall be necessary to a choice. In every case, after the choice of the President, the person having the greatest number of votes of the electors shall be the Vice President. But if there should remain two or more who have equal votes, the Senate shall choose from them by ballot the Vice President.~~

Clause 4 Today, we elect our President on the Tuesday after the first Monday in November.

4. ***Time of Elections.*** *The Congress may determine the time of choosing the electors, and the day on which they shall give their votes; which day shall be the same throughout the United States.*

Clause 5 A President must be at least 35 years old, a United States citizen by birth, and a resident of the United States for at least 14 years.

5. ***Qualifications*** *No person except a natural-born citizen,* ~~or a citizen of the United States at the time of the adoption of this Constitution~~, *shall be eligible to the office of President; neither shall any person be eligible to that office who shall not have attained to the age of thirty-five years, and been fourteen years a resident within the United States.*

Clause 6 If the President resigns, dies, or is impeached and found guilty, the Vice President becomes President.

6. ***Vacancies*** *In case of the removal of the President from office, or of his death, resignation, or inability to discharge the powers and duties of the said office, the same shall devolve on the Vice President, and the Congress may by law provide for the case of removal, death, resignation, or inability, both of the President and Vice President, declaring what officer shall then act as President, and such officer shall act accordingly, until the disability be removed, or a President shall be elected.*

Clause 7 The President receives a yearly salary that cannot be increased or decreased during his or her term. The President cannot hold any other government positions while in office.

7. ***Salary*** *The President shall, at stated times, receive for his services a compensation, which shall neither be increased nor diminished during the period for which he shall have been elected, and he shall not receive within that period any other emolument from the United States, or any of them.*

Clause 8 Every President must promise to uphold the Constitution. The Chief Justice of the Supreme Court usually administers this oath.

8. ***Oath of Office*** *Before he enter on the execution of his office, he shall take the following oath or affirmation:—"I do solemnly swear*

★ ★ ★ ★ ★ ★ ★ ★ ★

(or affirm) that I will faithfully execute the office of President of the United States, and will to the best of my ability, preserve, protect and defend the Constitution of the United States."

SECTION 2. POWERS OF THE PRESIDENT

1. ***Military Powers*** *The President shall be commander in chief of the army and navy of the United States, and of the militia of the several States, when called into the actual service of the United States; he may require the opinion, in writing, of the principal officer in each of the executive departments, upon any subject relating to the duties of their respective offices, and he shall have power to grant reprieves and pardons for offenses against the United States, except in cases of impeachment.*

Clause 1 The President is the leader of the country's military forces. The President is also in charge of state militias when they are called into national service. The military forces are under civilian, or nonmilitary, control.

2. ***Treaties and Appointments*** *He shall have power, by and with the advice and consent of the Senate, to make treaties, provided two-thirds of the senators present concur; and he shall nominate, and by and with the advice and consent of the Senate, shall appoint ambassadors, other public ministers and consuls, judges of the Supreme Court, and all other officers of the United States, whose appointments are not herein otherwise provided for, and which shall be established by law: but the Congress may by law vest the appointment of such inferior officers, as they think proper, in the President alone, in the courts of law, or in the heads of departments.*

Clause 2 The President can make treaties with other nations. However, treaties must be approved by a two-thirds vote of the Senate. The President can also make executive agreements with foreign governments that have the same force as treaties but do not need Senate approval. The President appoints Supreme Court Justices and ambassadors to foreign countries. The Senate must approve these appointments.

3. ***Temporary Appointments*** *The President shall have power to fill up all vacancies that may happen during the recess of the Senate, by granting commissions which shall expire at the end of their next session.*

SECTION 3. DUTIES

He shall from time to time give to the Congress information of the State of the Union, and recommend to their consideration such measures as he shall judge necessary and expedient; he may on extraordinary occasions, convene both houses, or either of them, and in case of disagreement between them with respect to the time of adjournment, he may adjourn them to such time as he shall think proper; he shall receive ambassadors and other public ministers; he shall take care that the laws be faithfully executed, and shall commission all the officers of the United States.

The President has the power to recommend legislation. The President must report to Congress at least once a year and make recommendations for laws. This report is known as the State of the Union Address. The President delivers it each January. The President can call special sessions of Congress in times of emergency.

SECTION 4. IMPEACHMENT

The President, Vice President and all civil officers of the United States, shall be removed from office on impeachment for, and conviction of, treason, bribery, or other high crimes and misdemeanors.

The President can be forced out of office only if found guilty of particular crimes. This clause protects government officials from being impeached for unimportant reasons.

ARTICLE III
JUDICIAL BRANCH

SECTION 1. FEDERAL COURTS

The judicial power of the United States shall be vested in one Supreme Court, and in such inferior courts as the Congress may from time to time ordain and establish. The judges, both of the Supreme and inferior courts, shall hold their offices during good behavior, and

The Supreme Court is the highest court in the nation. It makes the final decisions in all of the cases it hears. Today nine judges sit on the Supreme Court. Congress also has the power to set up a system of lower federal courts. All federal judges may hold their offices for as long as they live.

★ ★ ★ ★ ★ ★ ★ ★ ★

shall, at stated times, receive for their services, a compensation which shall not be diminished during their continuance in office.

SECTION 2. AUTHORITY OF THE FEDERAL COURTS

Clause 1 Federal Courts have authority in cases that involve the Constitution, federal laws, treaties, and disagreements between states. The Supreme Court established the right to judge whether a law is constitutional in *Marbury* v. *Madison* (1803). This right is known as *judicial review.*

1. ***General Jurisdiction*** *The judicial power shall extend to all cases, in law and equity, arising under this Constitution, the laws of the United States, and treaties made, or which shall be made, under their authority;—to all cases affecting ambassadors, other public ministers and consuls;—to all cases of admiralty and maritime jurisdiction;—to controversies to which the United States shall be a party;—to controversies between two or more States;—* ~~between a State and citizens of another State~~; *between citizens of different States;—between citizens of the same State claiming lands under grants of different States, and between a State, or the citizens thereof, and foreign states, citizens or subjects.*

Clause 2 *Original jurisdiction* means the right to try a case before any other court hears it. *Appellate jurisdiction* means the right of a court to try cases appealed from lower federal and state courts.

2. ***The Supreme Court*** *In all cases affecting ambassadors, other public ministers and consuls, and those in which a State shall be party, the Supreme Court shall have original jurisdiction. In all the other cases before mentioned, the Supreme Court shall have appellate jurisdiction, both as to law and fact, with such exceptions, and under such regulations as the Congress shall make.*

Clause 3 The Constitution guarantees everyone the right to a trial by jury. The only exception is in impeachment cases, which are tried in the Senate.

3. ***Trial by Jury*** *The trial of all crimes, except in cases of impeachment, shall be by jury; and such trial shall be held in the State where the said crimes shall have been committed; but when not committed within any State, the trial shall be at such place or places as the Congress may by law have directed.*

SECTION 3. TREASON

Clause 1 People cannot be convicted of treason in the United States for what they think or say. To be guilty of treason, a person must rebel against the government by using violence or helping enemies of the country.

Clause 2 Congress has the power to decide the punishment for treason, but it may not punish the children of convicted traitors.

1. ***Definition*** *Treason against the United States shall consist only in levying war against them, or in adhering to their enemies, giving them aid and comfort. No person shall be convicted of treason unless on the testimony of two witnesses to the same overt act, or on confession in open court.*

2. ***Punishment*** *The Congress shall have power to declare the punishment of treason, but no attainder of treason shall work corruption of blood, or forfeiture except during the life of the person attainted.*

ARTICLE IV
RELATIONS AMONG THE STATES

SECTION 1. OFFICIAL RECORDS

Each state must accept the laws, acts, and legal decisions made by other states.

Full faith and credit shall be given in each State to the public acts, records, and judicial proceedings of every other State. And the Congress may by general laws prescribe the manner in which such acts, records, and proceedings shall be proved, and the effect thereof.

SECTION 2. PRIVILEGES OF THE CITIZENS

Clause 1 States must give the same rights to citizens from other states that they give to their own citizens.

1. ***Privileges*** *The citizens of each State shall be entitled to all privileges and immunities of citizens in the several States.*

★ ★ ★ ★ ★ ★ ★ ★ ★

2. ***Return of a Person Accused of a Crime*** *A person charged in any State with treason, felony, or other crime, who shall flee from justice, and be found in another State, shall on demand of the executive authority of the State from which he fled, be delivered up, to be removed to the State having jurisdiction of the crime.*

Clause 2 If a person charged with a crime escapes to another state, he or she must be returned to the original state to go on trial. This act of returning someone from one state to another is called *extradition.*

3. ***Return of Fugitive Slaves*** ~~No person held to service or labor in one State, under the laws thereof, escaping into another, shall, in consequence of any law or regulation therein, be discharged from such service or labor, but shall be delivered up on claim of the party to whom such service or labor may be due.~~

Clause 3 The Thirteenth Amendment eliminated this clause, which required states to return runaway slaves to their owners.

SECTION 3. NEW STATES AND TERRITORIES

1. ***New States*** *New States may be admitted by the Congress into this Union; but no new State shall be formed or erected within the jurisdiction of any other State; nor any State be formed by the junction of two or more States or parts of States, without the consent of the legislatures of the States concerned as well as of the Congress.*

Clause 1 Congress has the power to create new states out of the nation's territories. All new states have the same rights as the old states. This clause made it clear that the United States would not make colonies out of its new lands.

2. ***Federal Lands*** *The Congress shall have power to dispose of and make all needful rules and regulations respecting the territory or other property belonging to the United States; and nothing in this Constitution shall be so construed as to prejudice any claims of the United States, or of any particular State.*

Clause 2 Congress has the power to make rules for the management of land owned by the United States government.

SECTION 4. GUARANTEES TO THE STATES

The United States shall guarantee to every State in this Union a republican form of government, and shall protect each of them against invasion; and on application of the legislature, or of the executive (when the legislature cannot be convened) against domestic violence.

The federal government must defend the states from attacks by other countries and from rebellions.

ARTICLE V
AMENDING THE CONSTITUTION

The Congress, whenever two-thirds of both houses shall deem it necessary, shall propose amendments to this Constitution, or, on the application of the legislatures of two-thirds of the several States, shall call a convention for proposing amendments, which, in either case, shall be valid to all intents and purposes, as part of this Constitution, when ratified by the legislatures of three-fourths of the several States, or by conventions in three-fourths thereof, as the one or the other mode of ratification may be proposed by the Congress; provided ~~that no amendments which may be made prior to the year one thousand eight hundred and eight shall in any manner affect the first and fourth clauses in the ninth section of the first article, and~~ *that no State, without its consent, shall be deprived of its equal suffrage in the Senate.*

An amendment to the Constitution may be proposed either by a two-thirds vote of each house of Congress or at the request of two-thirds of the states. To be ratified, or approved, an amendment must be supported either by three-fourths of the state legislatures or by three-fourths of special conventions held in each state.

Once an amendment is ratified, it becomes a part of the Constitution. Only a new amendment can change it. Amendments have allowed people to alter the Constitution to meet the changing needs of the nation.

ARTICLE VI
GENERAL PROVISIONS

1. ***Public Debt*** *All debts contracted and engagements entered into, before the adoption of this Constitution, shall be as valid against the United States under this Constitution, as under the Confederation.*

Clause 1 The United States government agreed to pay all debts built up under the Articles of Confederation.

★ ★ ★ ★ ★ ★ ★ ★ ★

Clause 2 The Constitution is the highest law in the nation. Whenever a state law and a federal law conflict, the federal law must be obeyed.

2. ***Federal Supremacy*** *This Constitution, and the laws of the United States which shall be made in pursuance thereof; and all treaties made, or which shall be made, under the authority of the United States, shall be the supreme law of the land; and the judges in every State shall be bound thereby, anything in the constitution or laws of any State to the contrary notwithstanding.*

Clause 3 All state and federal officials must promise to obey the Constitution. The use of religious qualifications for office holders is prohibited.

3. ***Oaths of Office*** *The senators and representatives before mentioned, and the members of the several State legislatures, and all executive and judicial officers, both of the United States, and of the several States, shall be bound by oath or affirmation to support this Constitution; but no religious test shall ever be required as a qualification to any office or public trust under the United States.*

ARTICLE VII
RATIFICATION

The framers provided that the Constitution would be approved as soon as nine of the thirteen states voted to accept it.

Each state held a special convention to debate the Constitution. The ninth state to approve the Constitution, New Hampshire, voted for ratification on June 21, 1788. The Constitution went into effect in March 1789.

The ratification of the conventions of nine States shall be sufficient for the establishment of this Constitution between the States so ratifying the same.

Done in Convention by the unanimous consent of the States present the seventeenth day of September in the year of our Lord one thousand seven hundred and eighty-seven and of the independence of the United States of America the twelfth. In witness whereof we have hereunto subscribed our names.

George Washington, President and deputy from Virginia

DELAWARE
George Read
Gunning Bedford, Junior
John Dickinson
Richard Bassett
Jacob Broom

MARYLAND
James McHenry
Daniel of St. Thomas Jenifer
Daniel Carroll

VIRGINIA
John Blair
James Madison, Junior

NORTH CAROLINA
William Blount
Richard Dobbs Spaight
Hugh Williamson

SOUTH CAROLINA
John Rutledge
Charles Cotesworth Pinckney
Charles Pinckney
Pierce Butler

GEORGIA
William Few
Abraham Baldwin

NEW HAMPSHIRE
John Langdon
Nicholas Gilman

MASSACHUSETTS
Nathaniel Gorham
Rufus King

CONNECTICUT
William Samuel Johnson
Roger Sherman

NEW YORK
Alexander Hamilton

NEW JERSEY
William Livingston
David Brearley
William Paterson
Jonathan Dayton

PENNSYLVANIA
Benjamin Franklin
Thomas Mifflin
Robert Morris
George Clymer
Thomas FitzSimmons
Jared Ingersoll
James Wilson
Gouverneur Morris

★ ★ ★ ★ ★ ★ ★ ★ ★

AMENDMENT 1 (1791)*
BASIC FREEDOMS

Congress shall make no law respecting an establishment of religion, or prohibiting the free exercise thereof; or abridging the freedom of speech, or of the press; or the right of the people peaceably to assemble, and to petition the government for a redress of grievances.

The first 10 amendments to the Constitution are known as the Bill of Rights.

The First Amendment protects the five basic civil liberties: freedoms of religion, speech, press, assembly, and petition. The government cannot pass laws that favor one religion over another.

AMENDMENT 2 (1791)
WEAPONS AND THE MILITIA

A well-regulated militia being necessary to the security of a free State, the right of the people to keep and bear arms shall not be infringed.

This amendment was included to prevent the federal government from taking away guns used by members of state militias.

AMENDMENT 3 (1791)
HOUSING SOLDIERS

No soldier shall, in time of peace, be quartered in any house, without the consent of the owner, nor in time of war, but in a manner to be prescribed by law.

The army cannot use people's homes to house soldiers unless it is approved by law. This amendment grew out of the colonial period when the British housed soldiers in private homes without the owners' permission.

AMENDMENT 4 (1791)
SEARCH AND SEIZURE

The right of the people to be secure in their persons, houses, papers, and effects, against unreasonable searches and seizures, shall not be violated, and no warrants shall issue, but upon probable cause, supported by oath or affirmation, and particularly describing the place to be searched, and the persons or things to be seized.

This amendment protects people's privacy in their homes. The government cannot search or seize anyone's property without a warrant, or written order, from a court. A warrant must list the people and property to be searched and give reasons for the search.

AMENDMENT 5 (1791)
RIGHTS OF THE ACCUSED

No person shall be held to answer for a capital or otherwise infamous crime, unless on a presentment or indictment of a grand jury, except in cases arising in the land or naval forces, or in the militia, when in actual service in time of war or public danger; nor shall any person be subject for the same offense to be twice put in jeopardy of life or limb; nor shall be compelled in any criminal case to be a witness against himself, nor be deprived of life, liberty, or property, without due process of law; nor shall private property be taken for public use without just compensation.

No person may be tried for a capital crime (a crime punishable by death) or an *infamous crime* (a crime punishable by a prison term or other loss of rights) unless a *grand jury*, a panel of between 12 and 23 citizens, rules that there is enough evidence for a trial.

A person cannot be tried twice for the same crime. This amendment also protects a person from self-incrimination, or having to testify against himself or herself. In addition, a person accused of a crime is entitled to *due process of law*, meaning fair and equal treatment under the law.

AMENDMENT 6 (1791)
RIGHT TO A FAIR TRIAL

In all criminal prosecutions, the accused shall enjoy the right to a speedy and public trial, by an impartial jury of the State and district wherein the crime shall have been committed, which district shall have been previously ascertained by law, and to be informed of the nature and cause of the accusation; to be confronted with the witnesses against him; to have compulsory process for obtaining witnesses in his favor, and to have the assistance of counsel for his defense.

Anyone accused of a crime is entitled to a quick and fair trial by jury. This right protects people from being kept in jail without being convicted of a crime. Also, the government must provide a lawyer for anyone accused of a crime who cannot afford to hire a lawyer.

* The date beside each amendment is the year that the amendment was ratified.

★ ★ ★ ★ ★ ★ ★ ★ ★

AMENDMENT 7 (1791)
JURY TRIAL IN CIVIL CASES

Civil cases usually involve two or more people suing each other over money, property, or personal injury. A jury trial is guaranteed in lawsuits where the property in question is valued at more than $20.

In suits at common law, where the value in controversy shall exceed twenty dollars, the right of trial by jury shall be preserved, and no fact tried by a jury shall be otherwise reexamined in any court of the United States, than according to the rules of the common law.

AMENDMENT 8 (1791)
BAIL AND PUNISHMENT

Bail is money that the accused leaves with the court as a guarantee that he or she will appear for trial. Courts cannot treat people accused of crimes in ways that are unusually harsh.

Excessive bail shall not be required, nor excessive fines imposed, nor cruel and unusual punishments inflicted.

AMENDMENT 9 (1791)
POWERS RESERVED TO THE PEOPLE

The citizens keep all rights not listed in the Constitution.

The enumeration in the Constitution of certain rights shall not be construed to deny or disparage others retained by the people.

AMENDMENT 10 (1791)
POWERS RESERVED TO THE STATES

Any rights not clearly given to the federal government by the Constitution belong to the states or the people.

The powers not delegated to the United States by the Constitution, nor prohibited by it to the States are reserved to the States respectively, or to the people.

AMENDMENT 11 (1795)
SUITS AGAINST STATES

A citizen from one state cannot sue the government of another state in a federal court. Such cases are decided in state courts.

The judicial power of the United States shall not be construed to extend to any suit in law or equity, commenced or prosecuted against one of the United States by citizens of another State, or by citizens or subjects of any foreign State.

AMENDMENT 12 (1804)
ELECTION OF THE PRESIDENT AND VICE PRESIDENT

Under the original Constitution, each member of the Electoral College voted for two candidates for President. The candidate with the most votes became President. The one with the second highest total became Vice President.

The Twelfth Amendment changed this system. Members of the electoral college distinguish between their votes for President and Vice President. This change was an important step in the development of the two-party system. It allows each party to nominate its own team of candidates. Under this system, however, it is possible for a candidate to win the popular vote and lose in the Electoral College. This happened in 1824, 1876, and 1888.

The electors shall meet in their respective States, and vote by ballot for President and Vice President, one of whom, at least, shall not be an inhabitant of the same State with themselves; they shall name in their ballots the person voted for as President, and in distinct ballots the person voted for as Vice President, and they shall make distinct lists of all persons voted for as President, and of all persons voted for as Vice President, and of the number of votes for each, which lists they shall sign and certify, and transmit sealed to the seat of government of the United States, directed to the President of the Senate;—The President of the Senate shall, in the presence of the Senate and House of Representatives, open all the certificates and the votes shall then be counted;—The person having the greatest number of votes for President shall be the President, if such number be a majority of the whole number of electors appointed; and if no person have such majority, then from the persons having the highest numbers not exceeding three on the list of those voted for as President, the House of Representatives shall choose

★ ★ ★ ★ ★ ★ ★ ★ ★

immediately, by ballot, the President. But in choosing the President, the votes shall be taken by States, the representation from each State having one vote; a quorum for this purpose shall consist of a member or members from two-thirds of the States, and a majority of all the States shall be necessary to a choice. And if the House of Representatives shall not choose a President whenever the right of choice shall devolve upon them, ~~before the fourth day of March next following~~, *then the Vice President shall act as President, as in the case of the death or other constitutional disability of the President. The person having the greatest number of votes as Vice President shall be the Vice President, if such number be a majority of the whole number of electors appointed, and if no person have a majority, then from the two highest numbers on the list, the Senate shall choose the Vice President; a quorum for the purpose shall consist of two-thirds of the whole number of senators, and a majority of the whole number shall be necessary to a choice. But no person constitutionally ineligible to the office of President shall be eligible to that of Vice President of the United States.*

AMENDMENT 13 (1865)
END OF SLAVERY

SECTION 1. ABOLITION

Neither slavery nor involuntary servitude, except as a punishment for crime whereof the party shall have been duly convicted, shall exist within the United States, or any place subject to their jurisdiction.

Section 1 This amendment ended slavery in the United States. It was ratified right after the Civil War.

SECTION 2. ENFORCEMENT

Congress shall have power to enforce this article by appropriate legislation.

Section 2 Congress has the power to pass laws to carry out this amendment.

AMENDMENT 14 (1868)
RIGHTS OF CITIZENS

SECTION 1. CITIZENSHIP

All persons born or naturalized in the United States, and subject to the jurisdiction thereof, are citizens of the United States and of the State wherein they reside. No State shall make or enforce any law which shall abridge the privileges or immunities of citizens of the United States; nor shall any State deprive any person of life, liberty, or property, without due process of law; nor deny to any person within its jurisdiction the equal protection of the laws.

Section 1 This amendment defined citizenship for the first time in the Constitution. "Due process under law" means that no state may deny its citizens the rights and privileges they enjoy as United States citizens. The goal of this amendment was to protect the rights of the recently freed blacks.

SECTION 2. NUMBER OF REPRESENTATIVES

Representatives shall be apportioned among the several States according to their respective numbers, counting the whole number of persons in each State, excluding Indians not taxed. But when the right to vote at any election for the choice of electors for President and Vice President of the United States, representatives in Congress, the executive and judicial officers of a State, or the

Section 2 This clause replaced the Three-Fifths Compromise in Article 1. Each state's representation is based on its total population. Any state denying its male citizens over the age of 21 the right to vote will have its representation in Congress decreased.

★ ★ ★ ★ ★ ★ ★ ★ ★

members of the legislature thereof, is denied to any of the male inhabitants of such State, being twenty-one years of age, and citizens of the United States, or in any way abridged, except for participation in rebellion, or other crime, the basis of representation therein shall be reduced in the proportion which the number of such male citizens shall bear to the whole number of male citizens twenty-one years of age in such State.

SECTION 3. PENALTY FOR REBELLION

Section 3 Officials who fought against the Union in the Civil War could not hold public office in the United States after the the war. This clause tried to keep Confederate leaders out of power. In 1872, Congress removed this ban.

No person shall be a senator or representative in Congress, or elector of President and Vice President, or hold any office, civil or military, under the United States, or under any State, who, having previously taken an oath, as a member of Congress, or as an officer of the United States, or as a member of any State legislature, or as an executive or judicial officer of any State, to support the Constitution of the United States, shall have engaged in insurrection or rebellion against the same, or given aid or comfort to the enemies thereof. But Congress may by a vote of two-thirds of each house, remove such disability.

SECTION 4. GOVERNMENT DEBT

Section 4 The United States paid all of the Union's debts from the Civil War. However, it did not pay any of the Confederacy's debts. This clause prevented the Southern states from using public money to pay for the rebellion or to pay citizens who lost their slaves.

The validity of the public debt of the United States, authorized by law, including debts incurred for payment of pensions and bounties for services in suppressing insurrection or rebellion, shall not be questioned. But neither the United States nor any State shall assume or pay any debt or obligation incurred in aid of insurrection or rebellion against the United States, or any claim for the loss or emancipation of any slave; but all such debts, obligations, and claims shall be held illegal and void.

SECTION 5. ENFORCEMENT

Section 5 Congress has the power to pass laws to carry out this amendment. The Civil Rights Act of 1964 is an example of such a law.

The Congress shall have power to enforce, by appropriate legislation, the provisions of this article.

AMENDMENT 15 (1870)
VOTING RIGHTS

SECTION 1. RIGHT TO VOTE

Section 1 No state can deny its citizens the right to vote because of their race or previous condition of slavery. This amendment was designed to protect the voting rights of blacks.

The right of citizens of the United States to vote shall not be denied or abridged by the United States or by any State on account of race, color, or previous condition of servitude.

SECTION 2. ENFORCEMENT

Section 2 Congress has the power to pass laws to carry out this amendment. The Voting Rights Act of 1965 is an example of such a law.

The Congress shall have power to enforce this article by appropriate legislation.

AMENDMENT 16 (1913)
INCOME TAX

Income Tax Congress has the power to tax personal incomes.

The Congress shall have power to lay and collect taxes on incomes, from whatever source derived, without apportionment among the several States, and without regard to any census or enumeration.

★ ★ ★ ★ ★ ★ ★ ★ ★

AMENDMENT 17 (1913)
DIRECT ELECTION OF SENATORS

SECTION 1. METHOD OF ELECTION

The Senate of the United States shall be composed of two senators from each State, elected by the people thereof, for six years; and each senator shall have one vote. The electors in each State shall have the qualifications requisite for electors of the most numerous branch of the State legislatures.

Section 1 In the original Constitution, the state legislatures elected senators. This amendment gave citizens the power to elect their senators directly. It made senators more responsible to the people they represented.

SECTION 2. VACANCIES

When vacancies happen in the representation of any State in the Senate, the executive authority of such State shall issue writs of election to fill such vacancies: Provided, that the legislature of any State may empower the executive thereof to make temporary appointments until the people fill the vacancies by election as the legislature may direct.

Section 2 If a Senate seat should become vacant for any reason, the governor of that state has the power to order a new election to fill the vacancy. A governor may also temporarily fill the vacant seat until an election can be held.

SECTION 3. EXCEPTION

~~This amendment shall not be so construed as to affect the election or term of any Senator chosen before it becomes valid as part of the Constitution.~~

Senators who had already been chosen by state legislatures were not affected by this amendment.

AMENDMENT 18 (1919)
BAN ON ALCOHOLIC DRINKS

SECTION 1. PROHIBITION

~~After one year from the ratification of this article the manufacture, sale, or transportation of intoxicating liquors within, the importation thereof into, or the exportation thereof from the United States and all territory subject to the jurisdiction thereof for beverage purposes is hereby prohibited.~~

Section 1 This amendment made it against the law to make or sell alcoholic beverages in the United States. This law was called Prohibition. Fourteen years later, the Twenty-First Amendment ended Prohibition.

SECTION 2. ENFORCEMENT

~~The Congress and the several States shall have concurrent power to enforce this article by appropriate legislation.~~

Section 2 Both Congress and the states had the power to pass laws to carry out this amendment.

SECTION 3. RATIFICATION

~~This article shall be inoperative unless it shall have been ratified as an amendment to the Constitution by the legislatures of the several States, as provided in the Constitution, within seven years from the date of the submission hereof to the States by the Congress.~~

Section 3 This amendment was the first one to include a time limit for ratification. To go into effect, the amendment had to be approved by three-fourths of the states within seven years.

AMENDMENT 19 (1920)
WOMEN'S SUFFRAGE

SECTION 1. RIGHT TO VOTE

The right of citizens of the United States to vote shall not be denied or abridged by the United States or by any State on account of sex.

Section 1 This amendment gave the right to vote to all women 21 years of age and older.

★ ★ ★ ★ ★ ★ ★ ★ ★

Section 2 Congress has the power to pass laws to carry out this amendment.

SECTION 2. ENFORCEMENT

The Congress shall have power to enforce this article by appropriate legislation.

AMENDMENT 20 (1933)
TERMS OF OFFICE

Section 1 The President and Vice President's terms begin on January 20 after being elected. The terms for senators and representatives begin on January 3. Before this amendment, an official defeated in a November election stayed in office until March. Such officeholders are known as *lame ducks.*

SECTION 1. BEGINNING OF TERMS

The terms of the President and Vice President shall end at noon on the twentieth day of January, and the terms of senators and representatives at noon on the third day of January, of the years in which such terms would have ended if this article had not been ratified; and the terms of their successors shall then begin.

Section 2 Congress must meet at least once a year. The new session begins on January 3.

SECTION 2. SESSIONS OF CONGRESS

The Congress shall assemble at least once in every year, and such meeting shall begin at noon on the third day of January, unless they shall by law appoint a different day.

Section 3 A President who has been elected but has not yet taken office is called the President-elect. If the President-elect dies, the Vice President-elect becomes President. If neither the President-elect nor the Vice President-elect can take office, then Congress decides who will act as President.

SECTION 3. PRESIDENTIAL SUCCESSION

If, at the time fixed for the beginning of the term of the President, the President-elect shall have died, the Vice President-elect shall become President. If a President shall not have been chosen before the time fixed for the beginning of his term, or if the President-elect shall have failed to qualify, then the Vice President-elect shall act as President until a President shall have qualified; and the Congress may by law provide for the case wherein neither a President-elect nor a Vice President-elect shall have qualified, declaring who shall then act as President, or the manner in which one who is to act shall be selected, and such persons shall act accordingly until a President or Vice President shall have qualified.

Section 4 In the event that a candidate fails to win a majority in the Electoral College, and then dies while the election is being decided in the House of Representatives, Congress shall have the power to pass laws to resolve the problem. Congress has the same power in the event that a vice-presidential candidate dies while the election is in the Senate.

SECTION 4. ELECTIONS DECIDED BY CONGRESS

The Congress may by law provide for the case of the death of any of the persons from whom the House of Representatives may choose a President whenever the right of choice shall have devolved upon them, and for the case of the death of any of the persons from whom the Senate may choose a Vice President whenever the right of choice shall have devolved upon them.

SECTION 5. EFFECTIVE DATE

Sections 1 and 2 shall take effect on the fifteenth day of October following the ratification of this article.

SECTION 6. RATIFICATION

This article shall be inoperative unless it shall have been ratified as an amendment to the Constitution by the legislatures of three-fourths of the several States within seven years from the date of its submission.

★ ★ ★ ★ ★ ★ ★ ★ ★

AMENDMENT 21 (1933)
END OF PROHIBITION

SECTION 1. REPEAL OF EIGHTEENTH AMENDMENT

The eighteenth article of amendment to the Constitution of the United States is hereby repealed.

Section 1 This amendment repealed, or ended, the Eighteenth Amendment. It made alcoholic beverages legal once again in the United States. Prohibition ended December 5, 1933.

SECTION 2. STATE LAWS

The transportation or importation into any State, territory, or possession of the United States for delivery or use therein of intoxicating liquors, in violation of the laws thereof, is hereby prohibited.

Section 2 States can still control or stop the sale of alcohol within their borders.

SECTION 3. RATIFICATION

This article shall be inoperative unless it shall have been ratified as an amendment to the Constitution by conventions in the several States, as provided in the Constitution, within seven years from the date of submission hereof to the States by the Congress.

AMENDMENT 22 (1951)
LIMIT ON PRESIDENTIAL TERMS

SECTION 1. TWO-TERM LIMIT

No person shall be elected to the office of the President more than twice, and no person who has held the office of President, or acted as President, for more than two years of a term to which some other person was elected President shall be elected to the office of the President more than once. But this article shall not apply to any person holding the office of President when this article was proposed by the Congress, and shall not prevent any person who may be holding the office of President, or acting as President, during the term within which this article becomes operative from holding the office of President or acting as President during the remainder of such term.

Section 1 Article II is silent on the number of terms a President may serve. In spite of this silence, George Washington set a precedent that Presidents should not serve more than two terms in office. However, Franklin Roosevelt broke the precedent. He was elected President four times between 1932 and 1944. Some people feared that a President holding office for this long could become too powerful. This amendment limits Presidents to two terms in office.

SECTION 2. RATIFICATION

This article shall be inoperative unless it shall have been ratified as an amendment to the Constitution by the legislatures of three-fourths of the several States within seven years from the date of its submission to the States by Congress.

AMENDMENT 23 (1961)
PRESIDENTIAL VOTES FOR WASHINGTON, D.C.

SECTION 1. NUMBER OF ELECTORS

The District constituting the seat of government of the United States shall appoint in such manner as the Congress may direct:

A number of electors of President and Vice President equal to the whole number of senators and representatives in Congress to which the District would be entitled if it were a State, but in no event more than the least populous State; they shall be in addition

Section 1 This amendment gives people who live in the nation's capital a vote for President. Washington, D.C.'s electoral votes are based on its population. However, it cannot have more votes than the state with the smallest population. Today Washington, D.C. has three electoral votes.

★ ★ ★ ★ ★ ★ ★ ★ ★

to those appointed by the States, but they shall be considered, for the purposes of the election of President and Vice President, to be electors appointed by a State; and they shall meet in the District and perform such duties as provided by the twelfth article of amendment.

SECTION 2. ENFORCEMENT

The Congress shall have power to enforce this article by appropriate legislation.

Section 2 Congress has the power to pass laws to carry out this legislation.

AMENDMENT 24 (1964) BAN ON POLL TAXES

SECTION 1. POLL TAXES ILLEGAL

The right of citizens of the United States to vote in any primary or other election for President or Vice President, for electors for President or Vice President, or for senator or representative in Congress, shall not be denied or abridged by the United States or any State by reason of failure to pay any poll tax or other tax.

SECTION 2. ENFORCEMENT

The Congress shall have power to enforce this article by appropriate legislation.

Section 1 A poll tax requires a person to pay a certain amount of money to register to vote. These taxes were used to stop poor blacks from voting. This amendment made any such taxes illegal in federal elections. The Supreme Court later ruled, in 1966, that poll taxes were illegal in state elections as well.

AMENDMENT 25 (1967) PRESIDENTIAL SUCCESSION

SECTION 1. VACANCY IN THE PRESIDENCY

In case of the removal of the President from office or of his death or resignation, the Vice President shall become President.

SECTION 2. VACANCY IN THE VICE PRESIDENCY

Whenever there is a vacancy in the office of the Vice President, the President shall nominate a Vice President who shall take office upon confirmation by a majority vote of both houses of Congress.

SECTION 3. DISABILITY OF THE PRESIDENT

Whenever the President transmits to the President pro tempore of the Senate and the speaker of the House of Representatives his written declaration that he is unable to discharge the powers and duties of his office, and until he transmits to them a written declaration to the contrary, such powers and duties shall be discharged by the Vice President as Acting President.

SECTION 4. DETERMINING PRESIDENTIAL DISABILITY

Whenever the Vice President and a majority of either the principal officers of the executive departments or of such other body as Congress may by law provide, transmit to the President pro tempore of the Senate and the speaker of the House of Representatives their written declaration that the President is unable to discharge the powers and duties of his office, the Vice President shall immediately

Section 1 In the event that the President dies, resigns, or is removed from office, the Vice President becomes President.
Section 2 If the Vice President becomes President, he or she may nominate a new Vice President. This nomination must be approved by both houses of Congress.

Secton 3 This section tells what happens if the President suddenly becomes ill or is seriously injured. The Vice President takes over as Acting President. When the President is ready to take office again, he or she must tell Congress.
Section 4 If the President is unconscious or refuses to admit to a disabling illness, the Vice President and the Cabinet have the right to inform Congress that the President is disabled. The Vice President then becomes acting President until the President as able to resume the duties of office. If there is a disagreement between the President and the Vice President and Cabinet about the President's ability to perform the duties of office, Congress has

★ ★ ★ ★ ★ ★ ★ ★ ★

assume the powers and duties of the office as Acting President.

Thereafter, when the President transmits to the President pro tempore of the Senate and the speaker of the House of Representatives his written declaration that no inability exists, he shall resume the powers and duties of his office unless the Vice President and a majority of either the principal officers of the executive departments or of such other body as Congress may by law provide, transmit within four days to the President pro tempore of the Senate and the speaker of the House of Representatives their written declaration that the President is unable to discharge the powers and duties of his office. Thereupon Congress shall decide the issue, assembling within forty-eight hours for that purpose if not in session. If the Congress, within twenty-one days after receipt of the latter written declaration, or, if Congress is not in session, within twenty-one days after Congress is required to assemble, determines by two-thirds vote of both houses that the President is unable to discharge the powers and duties of his office, the Vice President shall continue to discharge the same as Acting President; otherwise, the President shall resume the powers and duties of his office.

the power to decide the issue. A two-thirds vote would be required to find the President unfit to perform his or her duties.

AMENDMENT 26 (1971) VOTING AGE

SECTION 1. RIGHT TO VOTE

The right of citizens of the United States, who are eighteen years of age or older, to vote shall not be denied or abridged by the United States or by any State on account of age.

Section 1 This amendment gave the vote to all American citizens 18 years of age and older.

SECTION 2. ENFORCEMENT

The Congress shall have power to enforce this article by appropriate legislation.

Section 2 Congress has the power to pass laws to carry out this amendment.

AMENDMENT 27 (1992) CONGRESSIONAL PAY RAISES

No law, varying the compensation for the services of the Senators and Representatives, shall take effect, until an election of Representatives shall have intervened.

Limits on Pay Raises This amendment prohibits a Congressional pay raise from taking effect during the current term of the Congress that voted for it.

★ ★ ★ ★ ★ ★ ★ ★ ★

The Declaration of Independence

In Congress, July 4, 1776

The unanimous declaration of the thirteen united States of America

INTRODUCTION*

When, in the course of human events, it becomes necessary for one people to dissolve the political bands which have connected them with another, and to assume, among the powers of the earth, the separate and equal station to which the laws of nature and of nature's God entitle them, a decent respect to the opinions of mankind requires that they should declare the causes which impel them to the separation.

In the Declaration of Independence, the colonists explained why they were breaking away from Great Britain. They believed they had the right to form their own country.

powers of the earth *other nations* ***station*** *place* ***impel*** *drive*

BASIC RIGHTS

We hold these truths to be self-evident: That all men are created equal, that they are endowed by their Creator with certain unalienable rights; that among these are life, liberty, and the pursuit of happiness; that, to secure these rights, governments are instituted among men, deriving their just powers from the consent of the governed; that whenever any form of government becomes destructive of these ends, it is the right of the people to alter or to abolish it, and to institute new government, laying its foundation on such principles, and organizing its powers in such form, as to them shall seem most likely to effect their safety and happiness. Prudence, indeed, will dictate that governments long established should not be changed for light and transient causes; and accordingly all experience hath shown that mankind are more disposed to suffer, while evils are sufferable, than to right themselves by abolishing the forms to which they are accustomed. But when a long train of abuses and usurpations, pursuing invariably the same object, evinces a design to reduce them under absolute despotism, it is their right, it is their duty, to throw off such government, and to provide new guards for their future security. Such has been the patient sufferance of these colonies; and such is now the necessity which constrains them to alter their former systems of government. The history of the present King of Great Britain is a history of repeated injuries and usurpations, all having in direct object the establishment of an absolute tyranny over these states. To prove this, let facts be submitted to a candid world.

The opening part of the Declaration is very famous. It says that all people are equal. Everyone has certain basic rights that are unalienable. That means that these rights are so basic that they cannot be taken away. Governments are formed to protect these basic rights. If a government does not do this, then the people have a right to begin a new one.

endowed *given* ***deriving*** *receiving* ***prudence*** *wisdom* ***transient*** *temporary* ***usurpations*** *seizing powers unjustly* ***absolute despotism*** *complete and unjust control* ***constrains*** *forces*

Forming a new government meant ending the colonial ties to the king. The writers listed the wrongs of King George III to prove the need for their actions.

*Titles have been added to the Declaration to make it easier to read. These titles are not in the original document.

★ ★ ★ ★ ★ ★ ★ ★ ★

CHARGES AGAINST THE KING

He has refused his assent to laws, the most wholesome and necessary for the public good.

He has forbidden his governors to pass laws of immediate and pressing importance, unless suspended in their operation till his assent should be obtained; and, when so suspended, he has utterly neglected to attend to them.

He has refused to pass other laws for the accommodation of large districts of people, unless those people would relinquish the right of representation in the legislature, a right inestimable to them, and formidable to tyrants only.

He has called together legislative bodies at places unusual, uncomfortable, and distant from the depository of their public records, for the sole purpose of fatiguing them into compliance with his measures.

He has dissolved representative houses repeatedly, for opposing, with manly firmness, his invasions on the rights of the people.

He has refused for a long time, after such dissolutions, to cause others to be elected; whereby the legislative powers, incapable of annihilation, have returned to the people at large for their exercise; the state remaining, in the mean time, exposed to all the dangers of invasions from without and convulsions within.

He has endeavored to prevent the population of these states; for that purpose obstructing the laws for the naturalization of foreigners; refusing to pass others to encourage their migration hither, and raising the conditions of new appropriations of lands.

He has obstructed the administration of justice, by refusing his assent to laws for establishing judiciary powers.

He has made judges dependent on his will alone, for the tenure of their offices, and the amount of payment of their salaries.

He has erected a multitude of new offices, and sent hither swarms of officers to harass our people and eat out their substance.

He has kept among us, in times of peace, standing armies, without the consent of our legislatures.

He has affected to render the military independent of, and superior to, the civil power.

He has combined with others to subject us to a jurisdiction foreign to our constitution and unacknowledged by our laws, giving his assent to their acts of pretended legislation:

For quartering large bodies of armed troops among us;

For protecting them, by a mock trial, from punishment for any murders which they should commit on the inhabitants of these states;

For cutting off our trade with all parts of the world;

For imposing taxes on us without our consent;

For depriving us, in many cases, of the benefits of trial by jury;

Colonists said the king had not let the colonies make their own laws. He had limited the people's representation in their assemblies.

assent *agreement* ***inestimable*** *immeasurable* ***formidable*** *causing fear* ***compliance*** *giving in to a request or a demand*

The king had made colonial assemblies meet at unusual times and places. This made going to assembly meetings hard for colonial representatives.

In some cases the king stopped the assembly from meeting at all.

annihilation *complete destruction* ***convulsions*** *disturbances* ***endeavored*** *tried*

The king stopped people from moving to the colonies and into new western lands.

hither *here* ***appropriations*** *grants* ***judiciary powers*** *system of law courts*

The king prevented the colonies from choosing their own judges. Instead, he sent over judges who depended on him for their jobs and salaries.

tenure *term* ***multitude*** *large number* ***harass*** *bother, cause trouble*

The king kept British soldiers in the colonies, even though the colonists had not asked for them.

render *make* ***jurisdiction*** *authority* ***quartering*** *providing housing for* ***mock*** *false* ***imposing*** *forcing* ***depriving*** *taking away*

The king and Parliament had taxed the colonists without their consent. This was one of the most important reasons the colonists were angry at Great Britain.

★ ★ ★ ★ ★ ★ ★ ★ ★ ★ ★ ★

For transporting us beyond seas, to be tried for pretended offenses;

abolishing *getting rid of* ***arbitrary*** *tyrannical* ***fit instrument*** *suitable tool* ***invested*** *having*

For abolishing the free system of English laws in a neighboring province, establishing therein an arbitrary government, and enlarging its boundaries, so as to render it at once an example and fit instrument for introducing the same absolute rule into these colonies;

For taking away our charters, abolishing our most valuable laws, and altering fundamentally the forms of our governments.

For suspending our own legislatures, and declaring themselves invested with power to legislate for us in all cases whatsoever.

The colonists felt that the king had waged war on them.

abdicated *given up* ***plundered*** *robbed*

He has abdicated government here, by declaring us out of his protection and waging war against us.

He has plundered our seas, ravaged our coasts, burned our towns, and destroyed the lives of our people.

The king had hired German soldiers and sent them to the colonies to keep order.

mercenaries *hired soldiers* ***desolation*** *misery* ***perfidy*** *treachery* ***barbarous*** *uncivilized* ***insurrection*** *revolt*

He is at this time transporting large armies of foreign mercenaries to complete the works of death, desolation, and tyranny already begun with circumstances of cruelty and perfidy scarcely paralleled in the most barbarous ages, and totally unworthy the head of a civilized nation.

He has constrained our fellow-citizens, taken captive on the high seas, to bear arms against their country, to become the executioners of their friends and brethren, or to fall themselves by their hands.

He has excited domestic insurrection among us, and has endeavored to bring on the inhabitants of our frontiers, the merciless Indian savages, whose known rule of warfare is an undistinguished destruction of all ages, sexes, and conditions.

RESPONSE TO THE KING

The colonists said that they had asked the king to change his policies, but he had not listened to them.

petitioned *requested* ***redress*** *relief* ***unwarrantable*** *unfair* ***magnanimity*** *generosity* ***conjured*** *requested earnestly* ***disavow*** *turn away from* ***consanguinity*** *kinship* ***acquiesce*** *agree* ***denounces*** *condemns*

In every stage of these oppressions we have petitioned for redress in the most humble terms; our repeated petitions have been answered only by repeated injury. A prince, whose character is thus marked by every act which may define a tyrant, is unfit to be the ruler of a free people.

Nor have we been wanting in our attentions to our British brethren. We have warned them, from time to time, of attempts by their legislature to extend an unwarrantable jurisdiction over us. We have reminded them of the circumstances of our emigration and settlement here. We have appealed to their native justice and magnanimity; and we have conjured them, by the ties of our common kindred, to disavow these usurpations, which would inevitably interrupt our connections and correspondence. They, too, have been deaf to the voice of justice and of consanguinity. We must, therefore, acquiesce in the necessity which denounces our separation, and hold them, as we hold the rest of mankind, enemies in war, in peace friends.

★ ★ ★ ★ ★ ★ ★ ★ ★ ★ ★ ★

INDEPENDENCE

We, therefore, the representatives of the United States of America, in General Congress assembled, appealing to the Supreme Judge of the world for the rectitude of our intentions, do, in the name and by the authority of the good people of these colonies, solemnly publish and declare, that these United Colonies are, and of right ought to be, FREE AND INDEPENDENT STATES; that they are absolved from all allegiance to the British crown, and that all political connection between them and the state of Great Britain is, and ought to be, totally dissolved; and that, as free and independent states, they have full power to levy war, conclude peace, contract alliances, establish commerce, and do all other acts and things which independent states may of right do. And for the support of this declaration, with a firm reliance on the protection of Divine Providence, we mutually pledge to each other our lives, our fortunes, and our sacred honor.

John Hancock

NEW HAMPSHIRE
Josiah Bartlett
William Whipple
Matthew Thornton

MASSACHUSETTS
John Adams
Samuel Adams
Robert Treat Paine
Elbridge Gerry

NEW YORK
William Floyd
Philip Livingston
Francis Lewis
Lewis Morris

RHODE ISLAND
Stephen Hopkins
William Ellery

NEW JERSEY
Richard Stockton
John Witherspoon
Francis Hopkinson
John Hart
Abraham Clark

PENNSYLVANIA
Robert Morris
Benjamin Rush
Benjamin Franklin
John Morton
George Clymer
James Smith
George Taylor
James Wilson
George Ross

DELAWARE
Caesar Rodney
George Read
Thomas McKean

MARYLAND
Samuel Chase
William Paca
Thomas Stone
Charles Carroll of Carrollton

NORTH CAROLINA
William Hooper
Joseph Hewes
John Penn

VIRGINIA
George Wythe
Richard Henry Lee
Thomas Jefferson
Benjamin Harrison
Thomas Nelson, Jr.
Francis Lightfoot Lee
Carter Braxton

SOUTH CAROLINA
Edward Rutledge
Thomas Heyward, Jr.
Thomas Lynch, Jr.
Arthur Middleton

CONNECTICUT
Roger Sherman
Samuel Huntington
William Williams
Oliver Wolcott

GEORGIA
Button Gwinnett
Lyman Hall
George Walton

The writers declared that the colonies were free and independent states, equal to the world's other states. They had the powers to make war and peace and to trade with other countries.

rectitude *moral rightness* ***absolved*** *freed* ***allegiance*** *loyalty* ***levy*** *declare* ***contract*** *make* ***mutually*** *together*

The signers pledged their lives to the support of this Declaration. The Continental Congress ordered the Declaration of Independence to be read in all the states and to the army.

★ ★ ★ ★ ★ ★ ★ ★ ★ ★ ★ ★ ★ ★ ★ ★ ★

The Federalist, No. 10

James Madison

After the Constitutional Convention had been held and the delegates had signed the Constitution in 1787, the states still needed to ratify the new plan for government. To gain support for the Constitution, Alexander Hamilton, James Madison, and John Jay wrote the *Federalist Papers,* a series of essays published by newspapers in 1787 and 1788. In this essay, Madison explains the benefits of the Constitution's plan for electing representatives to Congress.

---

delegation choosing someone to represent a group

discern detect, figure out

consonant in agreement

compass range

factious combinations divisive groups

The two great points of difference between a democracy and a republic are: first, the delegation of the government, in the latter, to a small number of citizens elected by the rest; secondly, the greater number of citizens and greater sphere of country over which the latter may be extended.

The effect of the first difference is, on the one hand, to refine and enlarge the public views, by passing them through the medium of a chosen body of citizens, whose wisdom may best discern the true interest of their country and whose patriotism and love of justice will be least likely to sacrifice it to temporary or partial considerations. Under such a regulation it may well happen that the public voice, pronounced by the representatives of the people, will be more consonant to the public good than if pronounced by the people themselves. . . .

The other point of difference is the greater number of citizens and extent of territory which may be brought within the compass of republican than of democratic government; and it is this circumstance principally which renders factious combinations less to be dreaded in the former than in the latter. The smaller the society, the fewer probably will be the distinct parties and interests composing it; the fewer the distinct parties and interests, the more frequently will a majority be found of the same party; and the smaller the number of individuals composing a majority, and the smaller the compass within which they are placed, the more easily will they concert and execute their plans of oppression. Extend the sphere and you take in a greater variety of parties and interests; you make it less probable that a majority of the whole will have a common motive to invade the rights of other citizens. . . .

★ ★ ★ ★ ★ ★ ★ ★ ★ ★ ★ ★ ★

Farewell Address

George Washington

In 1796, George Washington wrote the following speech to announce that he would not run for President again. In it, he offered three main pieces of advice to the American people: be more loyal to your nation than to your geographic region, do not form political parties, and do not become involved in permanent foreign alliances.

A solicitude for your welfare which cannot end with my life . . . urges me on an occasion like the present . . . to recommend to your frequent review some sentiments which are the result of much reflection, of no inconsiderable observation, and which appear to me all important to the permanency of your felicity as a people. . . .

The name of American, which belongs to you in your national capacity, must always exalt the just pride of patriotism more than any appellation derived from local discriminations. . . . You have in a common cause fought and triumphed together. The independence and liberty you possess are the work of joint councils and joint efforts, of common dangers, sufferings, and successes. . . . Every portion of our country finds the most commanding motives for carefully guarding and preserving the union of the whole. . . .

This government, the offspring of our own choice, . . . completely free in its principles, in the distribution of its powers, uniting security with energy, and containing within itself a provision for its own amendment, has a just claim to your confidence and your support. Respect for its authority, compliance with its laws, acquiescence in its measures, are duties enjoined by the fundamental maxims of liberty. . . .

Let me now take a more comprehensive view, and warn you in the most solemn manner against the baneful effects of the spirit of party generally. . . . It serves always to distract the public councils and enfeeble the public administration. It agitates the community with ill-founded jealousies and false alarms; kindles the animosity of one part against another. . . . it is a spirit not to be encouraged. . . .

Against the insidious wiles of foreign influence, . . . the jealousy of a free people ought to be constantly *awake, since history and experience prove that foreign influence is one of the most baneful foes of republican government. . . . The great rule of conduct for us in regard to foreign nations is in extending our commercial relations to have as little* political *connection as possible. . . . It is our true policy to steer clear of permanent alliances, with any portion of the foreign world. . . .*

felicity great happiness

appellation name or title

acquiescence quiet agreement

enjoined required

baneful harmful

insidious wiles dangerous tricks

The Treaty of Guadalupe Hidalgo

In 1848, the United States and Mexico signed this treaty, which ended the two-year-long Mexican War. Mexico gave up most of the land north of the Rio Grande, and the United States agreed to pay Mexico $15 million and pay up to $3.25 million in Mexican debts to Americans. In addition, the treaty promised that Mexicans who chose to stay in the new U.S. territories would automatically become American citizens and would keep all their property.

---

reside live

proceeds amount of money raised

exonerating freeing from responsibility

stipulation specific detail or condition

Article I. *There shall be firm and universal peace between the United States of America and the Mexican Republic, and between their respective countries, territories, cities, towns, and people, without exception of place or persons. . . .*

Article VIII. *Mexicans now established in territories previously belonging to Mexico, and which remain for the future within the limits of the United States, as defined by the present treaty, shall be free to continue where they now reside, or to remove at any time to the Mexican Republic, retaining the property which they possess in the said territories, or disposing thereof, and removing the proceeds wherever they please, without their being subjected, on this account, to any contribution, tax or charge whatever. . . .*

Article XII. *In consideration of the extension acquired by the boundaries of the United States, as defined in the fifth article of the present treaty, the Government of the United States engages to pay to that of the Mexican Republic the sum of fifteen millions of dollars. . . .*

Article XV. *The United States, exonerating Mexico from all demands on account of the claims of their citizens . . . and considering them entirely and forever canceled, whatever their amount may be, undertake to make satisfaction for the same, to an amount not exceeding three and one quarter millions of dollars. . . .*

Article XXI. *If unhappily any disagreement should hereafter arise between the governments of the two republics, whether with respect to the interpretation of any stipulation in this treaty, or with respect to any other particular concerning the political or commercial relations of the two nations, the said governments, in the name of those nations, do promise to each other that they will endeavor, in the most sincere and earnest manner, to settle the differences so arising, and to preserve the state of peace and friendship in which the two countries are now placing themselves. . . .*

★ ★ ★ ★ ★ ★ ★ ★ ★ ★ ★ ★ ★ ★ ★ ★ ★

The Emancipation Proclamation

Abraham Lincoln

On January 1, 1863, Abraham Lincoln issued this proclamation freeing all enslaved people in the states that were fighting against the United States. This proclamation changed the character of the war, giving Northerners a new ideal to fight for, and officially allowing African Americans to fight in the army.

I, Abraham Lincoln, President of the United States, by virtue of the power in me vested as Commander-in-Chief of the Army and Navy of the United States in time of actual armed rebellion against the authority and government of the United States, and as a fit and necessary war measure for suppressing said rebellion, do, on this 1st day of January, A.D. 1863, and in accordance with my purpose so to do, publicly proclaimed for the full period of one hundred days from the first day above mentioned, order and designate as the States and parts of States wherein the people thereof, respectively, are this day in rebellion against the United States the following, to wit:

Arkansas, Texas, [parts of] Louisiana, Mississippi, Alabama, Florida, Georgia, South Carolina, North Carolina, and [parts of] Virginia. . . .

And by virtue of the power and for the purpose aforesaid, I do order and declare that all person held as slaves within said designated States and parts of States are, and henceforward shall be, free; and that the Executive Government of the United States, including the military and naval authorities thereof, will recognize and maintain the freedom of said persons.

And I hereby enjoin upon the people so declared to be free to abstain from all violence, unless in necessary self-defense; and I recommend to them that, in all cases when allowed, they labor faithfully for reasonable wages.

And I further declare and make known that such persons of suitable condition will be received into the armed service of the United States to garrison forts, positions, stations, and other places, and to man vessels of all sorts in said service.

And upon this act, sincerely believed to be an act of justice, warranted by the Constitution upon military necessity, I invoke the considerate judgment of mankind and the gracious favor of Almighty God.

suppressing ending, crushing

enjoin call for, require

garrison station troops at a base

★ ★ ★ ★ ★ ★ ★ ★ ★ ★ ★ ★ ★ ★ ★ ★ ★ ★

"Give Me Liberty, or Give Me Death"

Patrick Henry

Patrick Henry, a distinguished lawyer and politician, was one of the first colonial leaders to take a strong public stand against the Stamp Act in 1765. Ten years later, on March 23, 1775, he delivered his most famous speech to the Virginia Provincial Convention. At a time when tensions between England and the colonies were reaching the breaking point, Henry advocated the use of the Virginia militia in defending the colony against England. A portion of the speech is reprinted below in the version reconstructed by Henry's first biographer, William Wirt.

Mr. President," said he, "it is natural to man to indulge in the illusions of hope. We are apt to shut our eyes against a painful truth and listen to the song of that siren, till she transforms us into beasts. Is this," he asked, "the part of wise men, engaged in a great and arduous struggle for liberty?. . ."

"Is it that insidious smile with which our petition has been lately received? Trust it not, sir; it will prove a snare to your feet. Suffer not yourselves to be betrayed with a kiss. Ask yourselves how this gracious reception of our petition comports with those warlike preparations which cover our waters and darken our land. Are fleets and armies necessary to a work of love and reconciliation? Have we shown ourselves so unwilling to be reconciled that force must be called in to win back our love? Let us not deceive ourselves, sir. These are the implements of war and subjugation—the last arguments to which kings resort. I ask gentlemen, sir, what means this martial array, if its purpose be not to force us to submission? Can gentlemen assign any other possible motive for it? Has Great Britain any enemy in this quarter of the world to call for all this accumulation of navies and armies? No, sir, she has none. They are meant for us; they can be meant for no other. They are sent over to bind and rivet upon us those chains which the British Ministry have been so long forging.

"And what have we oppose to them? Shall we try argument? Sir, we have been trying that for the last two years. Have we anything new to offer upon the subject? Nothing. We have held the subject up in every light of which it is capable; but it has been all in vain. Shall we resort to entreaty and humble supplication? What terms shall we find which have

arduous difficult
insidious wicked or treacherous

comports agrees or corresponds

martial military

supplication begging or pleading

not been already exhausted? Let us not, I beseech you, sir, deceive ourselves longer. Sir, we have done everything that could be done to avert the storm which is now coming on. We have petitioned; we have remonstrated; we have supplicated; we have prostrated ourselves before the throne and have implored its interposition to arrest the tyrannical hands of the Ministry and Parliament. Our petitions have been slighted; our remonstrances have produced additional violence and insult; our supplications have been disregarded; and we have been spurned, with contempt, from the foot of the throne. In vain, after these things, may we indulge the fond hope of peace and reconciliation.

"There is no longer any room for hope. If we wish to be free; if we mean to preserve inviolate those inestimable privileges for which we have been so long contending; if we mean not basely to abandon the noble struggle in which we have been so long engaged, and which we have pledged ourselves never to abandon, until the glorious object of our contest shall be obtained; we must fight! I repeat it, sir, we must fight!! An appeal to arms and to God of hosts is all that is left us!

"They tell us, sir,. . . that we are weak, unable to cope with so formidable an adversary. But when shall we be stronger? Will it be the next week or the next year? Will it be when we are totally disarmed, and when a British guard shall be stationed in every house? Shall we gather strength by irresolution and inaction? Shall we acquire the means of effectual resistance by lying supinely on our backs and hugging the delusive phantom of hope, until our enemies shall have bound us hand and foot? Sir, we are not weak if we make a proper use of those means which the God of nature has placed in our power. Three millions of people armed in the holy cause of liberty and in such a country as that which we possess are invincible by any force which our enemy can send against us. . . .

"Besides, sir, we have no election. If we were base enough to desire it, it is now too late to retire from the contest. There is no retreat but in submission and slavery! Our chains are forged. Their clanking may be heard on the plains of Boston! The war is inevitable —and let it come! ! I repeat it, sir, let it come! ! !

"It is vain, sir, to extenuate the matter. Gentlemen may cry, peace, peace; but there is no peace. The war is actually begun! The next gale that sweeps from the north will bring to our ears the clash of resounding arms! Our brethren are already in the field! Why stand we here idle? What is it that gentlemen wish? What would they have? Is life so dear or peace so sweet as to be purchased at the price of chains and slavery?

"Forbid it, Almighty God—I know not what course others may take; but as for me," cried he, with both his arms extended aloft, his brows knit, every feature marked with the resolute purpose of his soul, and his voice swelled to its boldest note of exclamation—"give me liberty, or give me death!"

He took his seat. No murmur of applause was heard. The effect was too deep. After the trance of a moment, several members started from their seats. The cry, "To arms!" seemed to quiver on every lip and gleam from every eye.

remonstrated argued
prostrated thrown down
interposition intervention

inviolate untouchable or unspoiled
inestimable immeasurable

adversary opponent

supinely passively or lethargically
delusive false

extenuate downplay

★ ★ ★ ★ ★ ★ ★ ★ ★ ★ ★ ★ ★ ★ ★ ★ ★ ★

Common Sense

Thomas Paine

After failing at various careers, Thomas Paine emigrated from England to America in 1774. Less than two years later he became one of the most important political writers of the revolutionary period. His pamphlet *Common Sense*, part of which is reprinted below, took the colonies by storm in the winter and spring of 1776. In clear, concise prose, Paine demanded a complete break from England and called for the establishment of an American republic. As Paine hoped, his pamphlet convinced thousands of colonists that a reconciliation with England was impossible. Paine's bold ideas also influenced such important figures as George Washington and Thomas Jefferson. During the American Revolution, Paine served in Washington's army and wrote a series of pamphlets entitled *The Crisis* that encouraged the Patriots in their fight for independence.

---

embarked entered

fallacious false

Volumes have been written on the subject of the struggle between England and America. Men of all ranks have embarked in the controversy, from different motives, and with various designs: but all have been ineffectual, and the period of debate is closed. Arms as a last resort decide the contest; the appeal was the choice of the king, and the continent has accepted the challenge. . . .

I have heard it asserted by some, that as America hath flourished under her former connection with Great Britain, the same connection is necessary towards her future happiness, and will always have the same effect. Nothing can be more fallacious than this kind of argument. We may as well assert that because a child has thriven upon milk, that it is never to have meat, or that the first twenty years of our lives is to become a precedent for the next twenty. But even this is admitting more than is true; for I answer roundly, that America would have flourished as much, and probably much more, had no European power taken any notice of her. The commerce by which she hath enriched herself are the necessaries of life, and will always have a market while eating is the custom of Europe. . . .

Alas! we have been long led away by ancient prejudices, and made large sacrifices to superstition. We have boasted the protection of Great Britain without considering that her motive was interest, *not* attachment; *and that she did not protect us from* our enemies *on* our account, *but from her enemies on her own account. . . .*

But Britain is the parent country, say some. Then the more shame upon her conduct. Even brutes do not devour their young, nor savages make war upon their families. . . . Europe, and not England, is the parent country of America. This new world hath been the asylum for the persecuted lovers of civil and religious liberty from every part of Europe. Hither have they fled, not from the tender embraces of a mother, but from the cruelty of the monster; and it is so far true of England, that the same tyranny which drove the first emigrants from home, pursues their descendants still. . . .

Europe is too thickly planted with kingdoms to be long at peace, and whenever a war breaks out between England and any foreign power, the trade of America goes to ruin, because of her connection with Britain. *The next war may not turn out like the last, and should it not, the advocates of reconciliation now will be wishing for separation then, because neutrality in that case would be a safer convoy than a man of war. Everything that is right or natural pleads for separation. The blood of the slain, the weeping voice of nature cries, 'TIS TIME TO PART. . . .*

But where, say some, is the king of America? I'll tell you, friend, he reigns above, and doth not make havoc of mankind like the Royal Brute of Great Britain. Yet that we may not appear to be defective even in earthly honors, let a day be solemnly set apart for proclaiming the charter; let it be brought forth placed on the divine law, the Word of God; let a crown be placed thereon, by which the world may know, that so far as we approve of monarchy, that in America THE LAW IS KING. For as in absolute governments the king is law, so in free countries the law ought *to be king, and there ought to be no other. But lest any ill use should afterwards arise, let the crown at the conclusion of the ceremony be demolished, and scattered among the people whose right it is.*

A government of our own is our natural right; and when a man seriously reflects on the precariousness of human affairs, he will become convinced, that it is infinitely wiser and safer to form a constitution of our own in a cool deliberate manner, while we have it in our power, than to trust such an interesting event to time and chance. . . .

O ye that love mankind! Ye that dare oppose not only the tyranny but the tyrant, stand forth! Every spot of the old world is overrun with oppression. Freedom hath been hunted round the globe. Asia and Africa have long expelled her. Europe regards her like a stranger, and England hath given her warning to depart. O receive the fugitive, and prepare in time an asylum for mankind.

asylum refuge

advocates supporters

convoy escort

absolute dictatorial

precariousness uncertainty

★ ★ ★ ★ ★ ★ ★ ★ ★ ★ ★ ★ ★ ★ ★ ★ ★

The Monroe Doctrine

James Monroe

During the first two decades of the 1800s, when many European nations were entangled in the Napoleonic Wars, a number of colonies in Latin America took advantage of the unrest in Europe to declare their independence. After these wars were over, it seemed that the mother countries intended to regain control of their former colonies, now such countries as Chile, Peru, Colombia, and Mexico. The United States supported the independence of these colonies and did not approve of Europe's intervention in the Americas. Consequently, in a message to Congress on December 2, 1823, President James Monroe warned the nations of Europe that the United States intended to protect all independent nations in the Western Hemisphere against European military intervention. The Monroe Doctrine, part of which is reprinted below, has remained an essential part of American foreign policy ever since.

A precise knowledge of our relations with foreign powers as respects our negotiations and transactions with each is thought to be particularly necessary. . . .

In the discussions to which this interest has given rise and in the arrangements by which they may terminate the occasion has been judged proper for asserting, as a principle in which the rights and interests of the United States are involved, that the American continents, by the free and independent condition which they have assumed and maintain, are henceforth not to be considered as subjects for future colonization by any European powers. . . .

It was stated at the commencement of the last session that great effort was then making in Spain and Portugal to improve the condition of the people of those countries and that it appeared to be conducted with extraordinary moderation. It need scarcely be remarked that the result has been so far very different from what was then anticipated. Of events in that quarter of the globe with which we derive our origin, we have always been anxious and interested spectators. The citizens of the United States cherish sentiments the most friendly in favor of the liberty and happiness of their fellow men on that side of the Atlantic. In the wars of

commencement
beginning

the European powers in matters relating to themselves we have never taken any part, nor does it comport with our policy so to do. It is only when our rights are invaded or seriously menaced that we resent injuries or make preparations for our defense.

With the movements in this hemisphere we are of necessity more immediately connected, and by causes which must be obvious to all enlightened and impartial observers. The political system of the allied powers is essentially different in this respect from that of America. This difference proceeds from that which exists in their respective governments; and to the defense of our own, which has been achieved by the loss of so much blood and treasure, and matured by the wisdom of their most enlightened citizens, and under which we have enjoyed unexampled felicity, this whole nation is devoted. We owe it, therefore, to candor and to the amicable relations existing between the United States and those powers to declare that we should consider any attempt on their part to extend their system to any portion of this hemisphere as dangerous to our peace and safety.

With the existing colonies or dependencies of any European power we have not interfered and shall not interfere. But with the governments who have declared their independence and maintained it, and whose independence we have, on great consideration and on just principles, acknowledged, we could not view any interposition for the purpose of oppressing them, or controlling in any other manner their destiny, by any European power in any other light than as the manifestation of an unfriendly disposition toward the United States. In the war between those new governments and Spain we declared our neutrality at the time of their recognition, and to this we have adhered, and shall continue to adhere, provided no change shall occur which, in the judgment of competent authorities of this government, shall make a corresponding change on the part of the United States indispensable to their security. . . .

Our policy with regard to Europe, which was adopted at an early stage of the wars which have so long agitated that quarter of the globe, nevertheless remains the same, which is not to interfere in the internal concerns of its powers; to consider the government de facto as the legitimate government for us; to cultivate friendly relations with it, and to preserve those relations by a frank, firm, and manly policy, meeting in all instances the just claims of every power, submitting to injuries from none. But in regard to those continents, circumstances are eminently and conspicuously different. It is impossible that the allied powers should extend their political system to any portion of either continent without endangering our peace and happiness; nor can anyone believe that our southern brethren, if left to themselves, would adopt it of their own accord.

It is equally impossible, therefore, that we should behold such interposition in any form with indifference. If we look to the comparative strength and resources of Spain and those new governments, and their distance from each other, it must be obvious that she can never subdue them. It is still the true policy of the United States to leave the parties to themselves, in the hope that other powers will pursue the same course.

comport agree

felicity happiness
candor straightforwardness of expression
amicable friendly

interposition intervention

adhered continued to follow

indispensable essential

eminently clearly

Civil War

Uniforms of the Civil War

At the start of the Civil War, the militia units that largely made up the Union and Confederate armies wore a variety of uniforms. Both sides soon established regulation uniforms, such as the Union blue and Confederate gray examples shown below.

WORLD BOOK illustration by H. Charles McBarron, Jr.

Important events during the Civil War

1861

April 12 Confederate troops attacked Fort Sumter.
April 15 Lincoln issued a call for troops.
April 19 Lincoln proclaimed a blockade of the South.
May 21 Richmond, Va., was chosen as the Confederate capital.
July 21 Northern troops retreated in disorder after the First Battle of Bull Run (Manassas).

1862

Feb. 6 Fort Henry fell to Union forces.
Feb. 16 Grant's troops captured Fort Donelson.
March 9 The ironclad ships *Monitor* and *Merrimack (Virginia)* battled to a draw.
April 6-7 Both sides suffered heavy losses in the Battle of Shiloh, won by the Union.
April 16 The Confederacy began to draft soldiers.
April 18-25 Farragut attacked and captured New Orleans.
May 4 McClellan's Union troops occupied Yorktown, Va., and advanced on Richmond.
May 30 Northern forces occupied Corinth, Miss.
June 6 Memphis fell to Union armies.
June 25-July 1 Confederate forces under Lee saved Richmond in the Battles of the Seven Days.
Aug. 27-30 Lee and Jackson led Southern troops to victory in the Second Battle of Bull Run.
Sept. 17 Confederate forces retreated in defeat after the bloody Battle of Antietam (Sharpsburg).
Sept. 22 Lincoln issued a preliminary Emancipation Proclamation.
Oct. 8 Buell's forces ended Bragg's invasion of Kentucky in the Battle of Perryville.
Dec. 13 Burnside's Union forces received a crushing blow in the Battle of Fredericksburg.
Dec. 31-Jan. 2, 1863 Union troops under Rosecrans forced the Confederates to retreat after the Battle of Stones River (Murfreesboro).

1863

Jan. 1 Lincoln issued the Emancipation Proclamation.
March 3 The North passed a draft law.
May 1-4 Northern troops under Hooker were defeated in the Battle of Chancellorsville.
May 1-19 Grant's army defeated the Confederates in Mississippi and began to besiege Vicksburg.
July 1-3 The Battle of Gettysburg ended in a Southern defeat and marked a turning point in the war.
July 4 Vicksburg fell to Northern troops.
July 8 Northern forces occupied Port Hudson, La.
Sept. 19-20 Southern troops under Bragg won the Battle of Chickamauga.
Nov. 19 Lincoln delivered the Gettysburg Address.
Nov. 23-25 Grant and Thomas led Union armies to victory in the Battle of Chattanooga.

1864

March 9 Grant became general in chief of the North.
May 5-6 Union and Confederate troops clashed in the Battle of the Wilderness.
May 8-19 Grant and Lee held their positions in the Battle of Spotsylvania Court House.
June 3 The Union suffered heavy losses on the final day of the Battle of Cold Harbor.
June 20 Grant's troops laid siege to Petersburg, Va.
July 11-12 Early's Confederate forces almost reached Washington but retreated after brief fighting.
Aug. 5 Farragut won the Battle of Mobile Bay.
Sept. 2 Northern troops under Sherman captured Atlanta.
Sept. 19-Oct. 19 Sheridan led his troops on a rampage of destruction in the Shenandoah Valley.
Nov. 8 Lincoln was reelected President.
Nov. 15 Sherman began his march through Georgia.
Nov. 23 Hood invaded Tennessee.
Nov. 30 Schofield's Union forces inflicted heavy losses on Hood in the Battle of Franklin.
Dec. 15-16 The Battle of Nashville smashed Hood's army.
Dec. 21 Sherman's troops occupied Savannah, Ga.

1865

Feb. 6 Lee became general in chief of the South.
April 2 Confederate troops gave up Petersburg and Richmond.
April 9 Lee surrendered to Grant at Appomattox.
April 14 Lincoln was assassinated.
April 26 Johnston surrendered to Sherman.
May 4 Confederate forces in Alabama and Mississippi surrendered.
May 11 Jefferson Davis was captured.
May 26 The last Confederate troops surrendered.

Leading Civil War generals

National Archives

Ulysses S. Grant (North)

Valentine Museum, Richmond, Va.

Robert E. Lee (South)

Bettmann Archive

William T. Sherman (North)

Bettmann Archive

Stonewall Jackson (South)

Battles and campaigns of the Civil War

World Book map

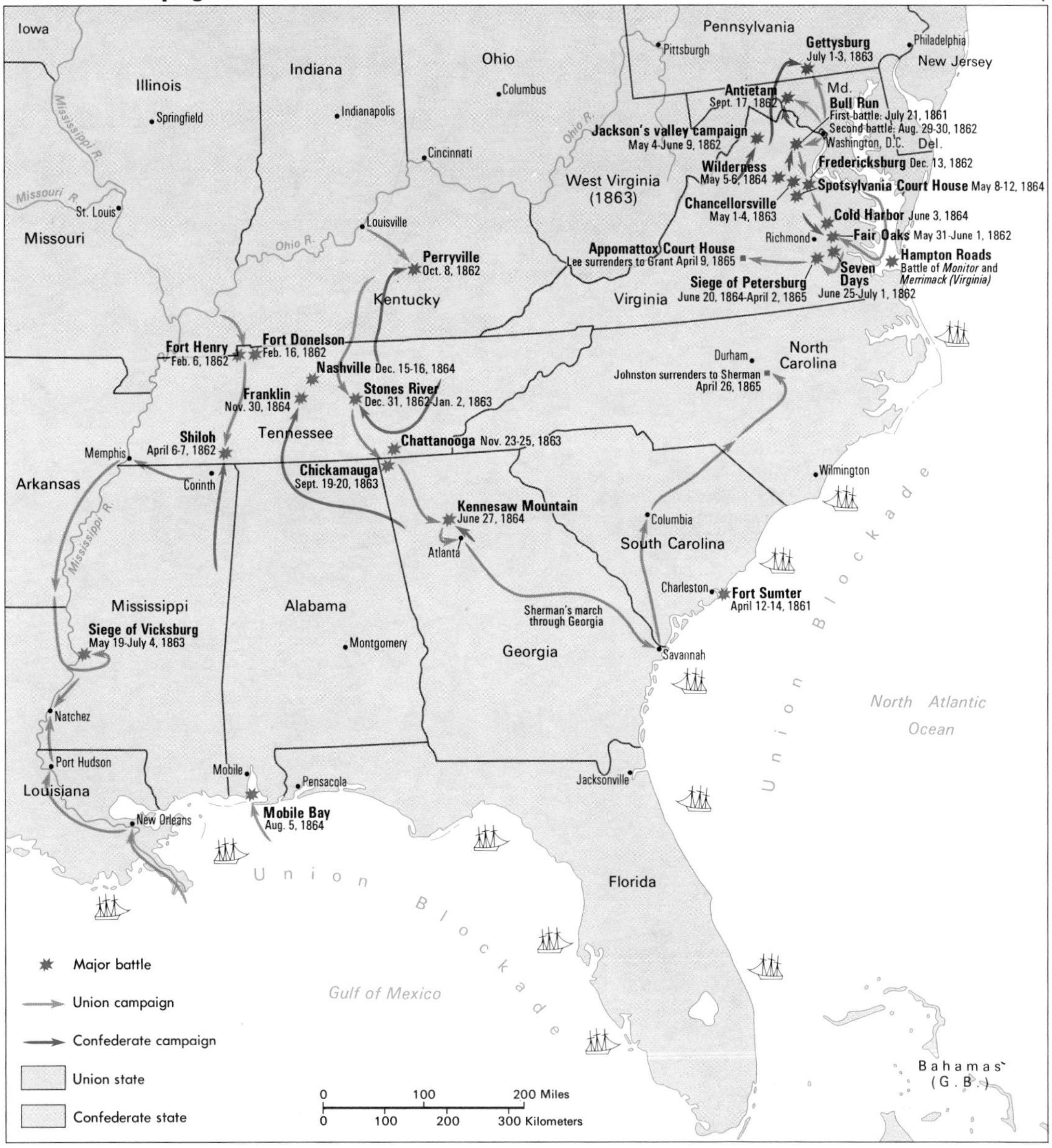

Indian, American

Where the Indians lived

The Indians of North and South America formed hundreds of tribes with many different ways of life. The location of many major tribes is shown below. Scholars divide the various tribes into groups of similar tribes that they call *culture areas.* Each culture area is shown in a different color.

WORLD BOOK maps

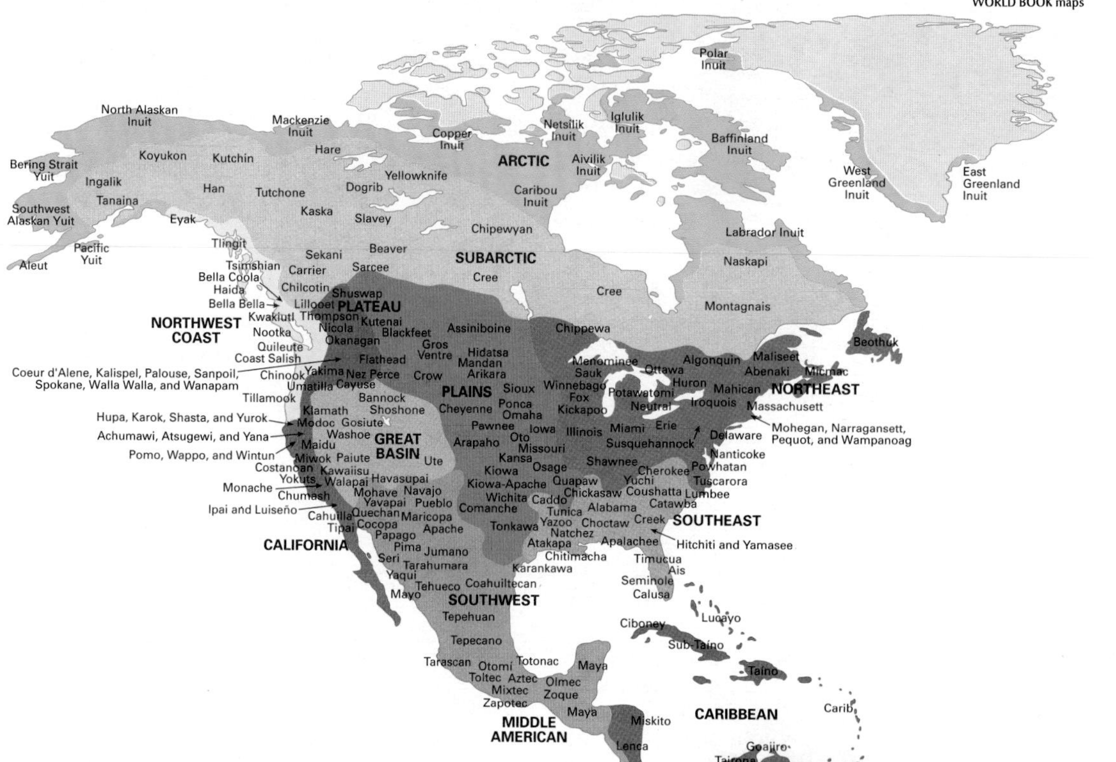

How the Indians obtained food

Most Indians hunted and fished for their food or gathered wild seeds, nuts, and roots. Farming was the main source of food only in the Southwest, Middle America, and the Andes. Many tribes of the Northeast and Tropical Forest areas also raised some crops.

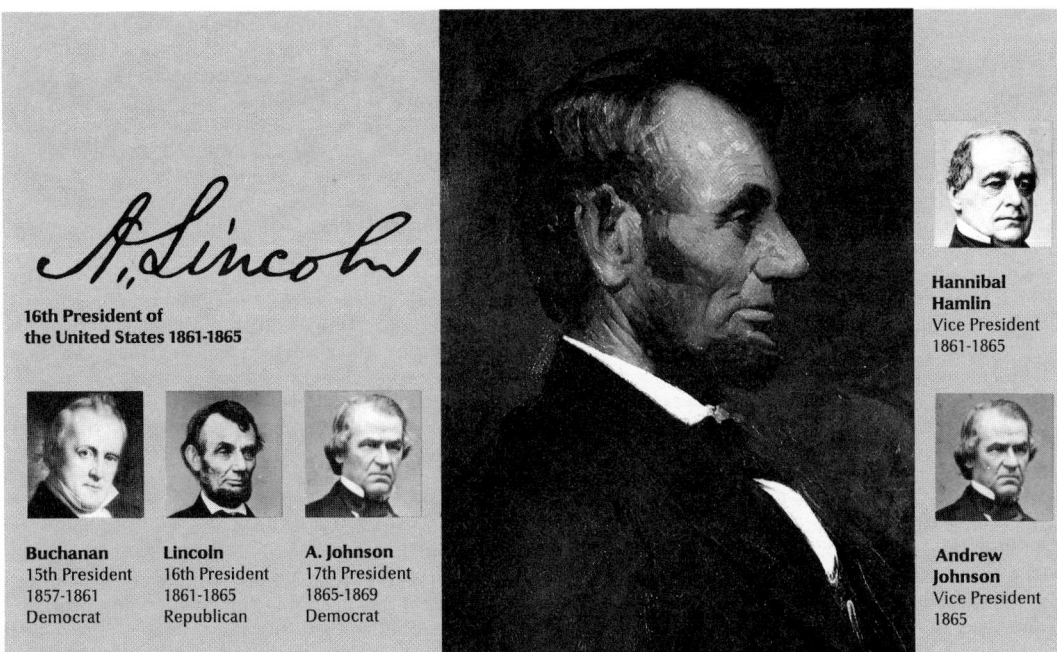

16th President of
the United States 1861-1865

Buchanan
15th President
1857-1861
Democrat

Lincoln
16th President
1861-1865
Republican

A. Johnson
17th President
1865-1869
Democrat

Hannibal Hamlin
Vice President
1861-1865

Andrew Johnson
Vice President
1865

Detail of an oil painting on canvas (1911) by Allen Tupper True; Henry E. Huntington Library and Art Gallery, San Marino, Calif.

Lincoln, Abraham (1809-1865), was one of the truly great men of all time. He led the United States during the Civil War (1861-1865), which was the greatest crisis in U.S. history. Lincoln helped end slavery in the nation and helped keep the American Union from splitting apart during the war. Lincoln thus believed that he proved to the world that democracy can be a lasting form of government. Lincoln's Gettysburg Address, second inaugural address, and many of his other speeches and writings are classic statements of democratic beliefs and goals. In conducting a bitter war, Lincoln never became bitter himself. He showed a nobility of character that has worldwide appeal. Lincoln, a Republican, was the first member of his party to become President. He was assassinated near the end of the Civil War and was succeeded by Vice President Andrew Johnson.

The American people knew little about Lincoln when he became President. Little in his past experience indicated that he could successfully deal with the deep differences between Northerners and Southerners over slavery. Lincoln received less than 40 per cent of the popular vote in winning the presidential election of 1860. But by 1865, he had become in the eyes of the world equal in importance to George Washington. Through the years, many people have regarded Lincoln as the greatest person in United States history.

During the Civil War, Lincoln's first task was to win the war. He had to view nearly all other matters in relation to the war. It was "the progress of our arms," he once said, "upon which all else depends." But Lincoln was a peace-loving man who had earlier described military glory as "that attractive rainbow, that rises in showers of blood—that serpent's eye that charms to destroy." The Civil War was by far the bloodiest war in U.S. history. In the Battle of Gettysburg, for example, the more than 45,000 total *casualties* (people killed, wounded, captured, or missing) exceeded the number of casualties in all previous American wars put together.

Lincoln became a remarkable war leader. Some historians believe he was the chief architect of the Union's victorious military strategy. This strategy called for Union armies to advance against the enemy on all fronts at the same time. Lincoln also insisted that the objective of the Union armies should be the destruction of opposing forces, not the conquest of territory. Lincoln changed generals several times because he could not find one who would fight the war the way he wanted it fought. When he finally found such a general, Ulysses S. Grant, Lincoln stood firmly behind him.

Lincoln's second great task was to keep up Northern morale through the horrible war in which many relatives in the North and South fought against one another. He understood that the Union's resources vastly exceeded those of the Confederacy, and that the Union would eventually triumph if it remained dedicated to victory. For this reason, Lincoln used his great writing and speechmaking abilities to spur on his people.

Important dates in Lincoln's life

1809	(Feb. 12) Born near present-day Hodgenville, Ky.
1834	Elected to the Illinois General Assembly.
1842	(Nov. 4) Married Mary Todd.
1846	Elected to the U.S. House of Representatives.
1858	Debated slavery with Stephen A. Douglas.
1860	(Nov. 6) Elected President of the United States.
1864	(Nov. 8) Reelected President.
1865	(April 14) Shot by John Wilkes Booth.
1865	(April 15) Died in Washington, D.C.

History of United States currency

In the American Colonies, money was scarce. England did not furnish coins and forbade the colonies to make them. The English hoped to force the colonies to trade almost entirely with England. One way of doing so was by limiting the money supply. Without money, the colonists could not do business with traders in other countries who demanded payment in cash. But the colonists could buy products from English traders with *bills of exchange.* They got these documents from other English traders in exchange for their own goods.

The American colonists used a variety of goods in place of money. These goods included beaver pelts, grain, musket balls, and nails. Some colonists, especially in the tobacco-growing colonies of Maryland and Virginia, circulated receipts for tobacco stored in warehouses. Indian wampum, which consisted of beads made from shells, was mainly used for keeping records. But Indians and colonists also accepted it as money.

The colonists also used any foreign coins they could get. English shillings, Spanish dollars, and French and Dutch coins all circulated in the colonies. Probably the most common coins were large silver Spanish dollars called *pieces of eight.* To make change, a person could chop the coin into eight pie-shaped pieces called *bits.* Two bits were worth a quarter of a dollar, four bits a half dollar, and so on. We still use the expression *two bits* to mean a quarter of a dollar.

In 1652, the Massachusetts Bay Colony became the first colony to make coins. It produced several kinds of silver coins, including a *pine-tree shilling* and an *oak-tree shilling,* which were stamped with a tree design. Massachusetts continued to issue coins for 30 years in defiance of an English law that said only the monarch could issue them. The colony dated all coins 1652, no matter when they were made, probably to get around the law. In 1652, there was no monarch in England. Thus, the colonists could claim the coins were minted at a time when royal authority did not exist.

Massachusetts also became the first colony to produce paper money. In 1690, the colonial government issued notes called *bills of credit.* The bills were receipts for loans made by citizens to the colonial government. Massachusetts used the bills to help finance the first French and Indian war, a war between English and French colonists for control of eastern North America.

The first United States currency. During the mid-1700's, Great Britain tried to tighten its control over the American Colonies with new taxes, stricter trade regulations, and other laws. Friction between the Americans and the British mounted. In 1775, the Revolutionary War

Money in the American Colonies

Money was scarce in the American Colonies. Paper currency was seldom used, and the British did not allow the colonies to mint coins. As a result, the colonists used any foreign coins they could get. Indian wampum and other goods also circulated as money.

Wampum, which consisted of beads made from shells, was used by the Indians to decorate garments and keep records. The colonists, who had few coins, used it as money. Most wampum was made into necklaces or belts.

The oak-tree shilling was one of the first coins made in Massachusetts. The colony began to issue coins like the one above in 1660.

The escudo was used throughout the Americas. The 8-escudo coin above was minted in the reign of King Ferdinand VI of Spain.

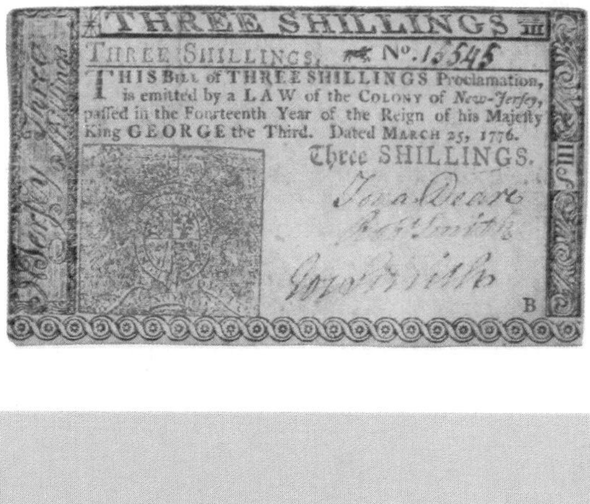

A 3-shilling note, *left,* was issued by the colony of New Jersey in 1776. A number of colonies issued their own paper currency.

broke out between the two sides. The next year, colonial leaders meeting as the Second Continental Congress declared independence and founded the United States of America. To help finance the war for independence, each state and the Continental Congress began to issue paper money.

As war expenses mounted, the states and Congress printed more and more money. Congress itself issued about $240 million in notes called *continentals.* So many continentals were printed that by 1780 they were almost worthless. Americans began to describe any useless thing as "not worth a continental." The experience with continentals was so bad that the U.S. government did not again issue paper currency for widespread use until the 1860's.

The United States won the Revolutionary War in 1783, but the struggle left the American monetary system in disorder. Most of the currencies circulated by the states had little value. The U.S. Constitution, adopted in 1789, corrected this problem by giving Congress the sole power to coin money and regulate its value. In 1792, an act of Congress set up the first national money system in the United States. The act made the dollar the basic unit of money. It also put the nation on a system called the *bimetallic standard,* which meant that both gold and silver were legal money. The value of each metal in relation to the other was fixed by law. For years, 16 ounces (448 grams) of silver equaled 1 ounce (28 grams) of gold.

The act also established a national mint in Philadelphia. The mint produced $10 gold coins called *eagles,* silver dollars, and other coins.

Americans continued to use many foreign coins in ad-

Money in the new nation

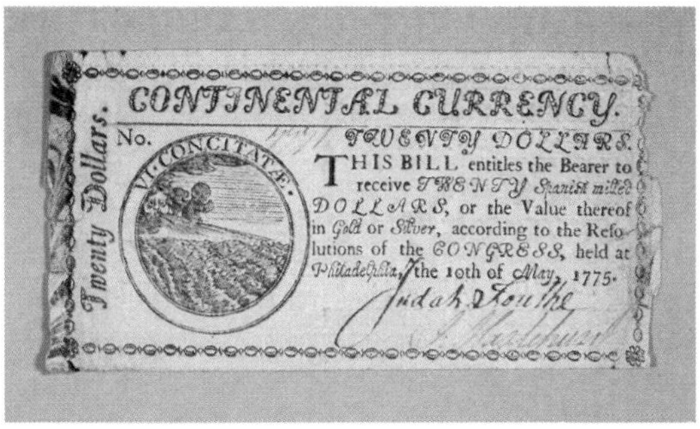

Continental currency was issued by the Continental Congress to help finance the Revolutionary War (1775-1783). So many of these notes were printed that they became almost worthless.

The écu, a French coin, was one of many foreign coins that circulated in the United States after the nation won independence. A 1793 law made these coins part of the U.S. monetary system.

The Spanish dollar, or piece of eight, was another foreign coin that circulated in the new nation. The coin shown at the far left and center was minted in Mexico in 1790. These dollars could be chopped into eight pieces, called *bits,* or into quarters, *near left,* called *two bits.*

A $10 gold piece called an *eagle* was issued by the U.S. Mint from 1795 to 1933. The eagle shown above dates from 1795. It has a liberty cap on the front and an eagle on the back.

Bank notes were the most common paper money in the United States until the 1860's. Banks vowed to exchange their notes for gold or silver. The State Bank of Illinois issued this note in 1840.

Later United States money

U.S. currency of the 1800's and early 1900's included silver coins, gold pieces, and various types of paper money. Many bills, including gold and silver certificates, could be exchanged for gold or silver coins on demand. The use of these two metals as money is called the *bimetallic standard.*

Silver dollar (1800)

U.S. Assay Office $50 gold piece (1851)

$20 gold double eagle (1865)

Confederate $10 bill (1861)

$5 legal tender note (about 1862)

$50 gold certificate (about 1882)

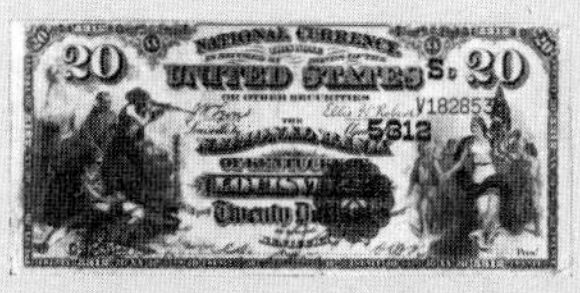

$20 national bank note (about 1882)

$50 silver certificate (about 1891)

Federal Reserve $10 bill (about 1914)

dition to their new currency. A law passed in 1793 made these coins part of the U.S. monetary system. The value of a foreign coin depended on how much gold or silver it had. In 1857, Congress passed a law removing foreign coins from circulation.

The rebirth of paper money. During the early 1800's, the only paper money in the United States consisted of hundreds of kinds of bank notes. Each bank promised to exchange its notes on demand for gold or silver coins. But numerous banks did not keep enough coins to redeem their notes. Many notes therefore were not worth their *face value*—that is, the value stated on them. As a result, people hesitated to accept bank notes.

The soundest bank notes of the early 1800's were issued by the two national banks chartered by the U.S. government. The First Bank of the United States was chartered by Congress from 1791 to 1811, and the Second Bank of the United States from 1816 to 1836. Both banks supported their notes with reserves of gold coins, and people considered the notes as good as gold.

Paper money as we know it today dates from the 1860's. To help pay the costs of the Civil War (1861-1865), the U.S. government issued about $430 million in paper money. The money could not be exchanged for gold or silver. The bills were called *legal tender notes* or *United States notes.* But most people called them *greenbacks* because the backs were printed in green. The government declared that greenbacks were *legal tender*—that is, money people must accept in payment of public and private debts. Nevertheless, the value of greenbacks depended on people's confidence in the government. That confidence rose and fell with the victories and defeats of the North in the Civil War. At one time, each greenback dollar was worth only 35 cents in gold coin. In the South, the Confederate States also issued paper money. It quickly became almost worthless.

In 1863 and 1864, Congress passed the National Bank Acts, which set up a system of privately owned banks chartered by the federal government. These national banks issued notes backed by U.S. government bonds.

Congress also taxed state bank notes to discourage banks from issuing them, and people from using them. As a result, national bank notes became the country's chief currency.

Some greenbacks also continued to circulate. The government announced that, beginning in 1879, it would pay gold coins for greenbacks. The U.S. Department of the Treasury gathered enough gold to redeem all the greenbacks likely to be brought in. But as soon as people knew they could exchange their greenbacks for gold, they were not anxious to do so. The fact that the Treasury paid out only gold coins meant the country was operating on an unofficial *gold standard,* rather than the bimetallic standard of the early 1800's. The gold standard is a system in which a nation defines its basic monetary unit as worth a certain quantity of gold and agrees to redeem its money in gold on demand.

The new national banks system eliminated the confusion that had existed when hundreds of different bank notes were in circulation. But the system did not provide for the federal government to increase the supply of money when needed. Shortages of money contributed to a series of economic slumps during the late 1800's. Many people called for the government to provide more money by coining unlimited amounts of silver. Such a policy was called *free silver,* and the argument over free silver became an important political issue.

The dispute reached a climax during the presidential election of 1896. The Republican candidate, William McKinley, favored the gold standard. McKinley defeated William Jennings Bryan, the Democratic candidate, who supported free silver. In 1900, Congress passed the Gold Standard Act, which officially put the nation on a gold standard. The United States went on and off the gold standard several times and finally abandoned it in 1971.

The United States suffered from repeated monetary difficulties until 1913, when Congress passed the Federal Reserve Act. This act created the Federal Reserve System, a central banking system that controls the nation's money supply.

United States currency today consists of coins and paper money. Under federal law, only the Department of the Treasury and the Federal Reserve System may issue U.S. currency. The Treasury issues all coins and a type of paper money known as *United States notes.* The Federal Reserve issues paper currency called *Federal Reserve notes.* All U.S. currency carries the nation's official motto, *In God We Trust.*

Coins come in six *denominations* (values): (1) penny, or 1 cent; (2) nickel, or 5 cents; (3) dime, or 10 cents; (4) quarter, or 25 cents; (5) half dollar, or 50 cents; and (6) $1. All coins are made of *alloys* (mixtures of metals). Pennies are copper-coated zinc. Nickels are a mixture of copper and nickel. Dimes, quarters, half dollars, and dollars are made of three layers of metal. The core is pure copper, and the outer layers are an alloy of copper and nickel.

Dimes, quarters, half dollars, and dollars have ridges called *reeding* or *milling* around the edge. Reeding helps blind people recognize certain denominations. For example, the reeding on a dime distinguishes it from a penny, which has a smooth edge.

Federal law requires that coins be dated with the year they were made. Coins also must bear the word *Liberty* and the Latin motto *E Pluribus Unum,* meaning *out of many, one.* This motto refers to the creation of the United States from the original Thirteen Colonies.

Mints in Denver and Philadelphia make most coins for general circulation. Mints in San Francisco and West Point, N.Y., make mostly commemorative coins to mark special occasions, and gold and silver bullion coins for investors. People buy bullion coins for the value of the metal. Coins made in Denver are marked with a small *D.* A *P* appears on most coins made in Philadelphia. Some coins made in San Francisco are marked with an *S* and some in West Point with a *W.*

Chief features of a Federal Reserve note

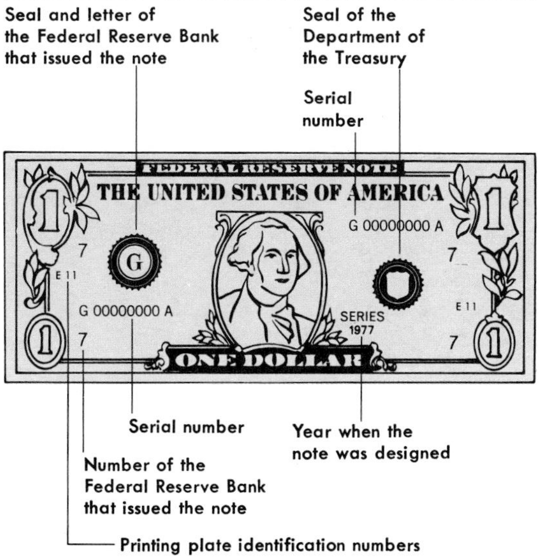

Paper money. Federal Reserve notes make up nearly all the paper money issued in the United States today. About $195 billion of these notes were in circulation during the mid-1980's. They come in seven denominations: $1, $2, $5, $10, $20, $50, and $100. The notes are issued by the 12 Federal Reserve Banks in the Federal Reserve System. Each note has a letter, number, and seal that identify the bank which issued it. In addition, each note bears the words *Federal Reserve note* and a green Treasury seal. Until 1969, Federal Reserve Banks also issued notes in four large denominations: $500, $1,000, $5,000, and $10,000.

The only other paper money issued in the United States today consists of United States notes. The Treasury issues them in the $100 denomination only. These notes, which are the descendants of Civil War greenbacks, carry the words *United States note* and a red Treasury seal. The Treasury keeps about $323 million in United States notes in circulation. All Federal Reserve and United States notes bear the printed signatures of the secretary of the treasury and the treasurer of the United States.

Parklands of the National Park System

This map shows the location of the parklands in the National Park System. Because of space limitations, the parklands within the East Coast area outlined in black are not named on the map. Their names can be found by matching their numbers with those in the tables on the right of the map.

WORLD BOOK map

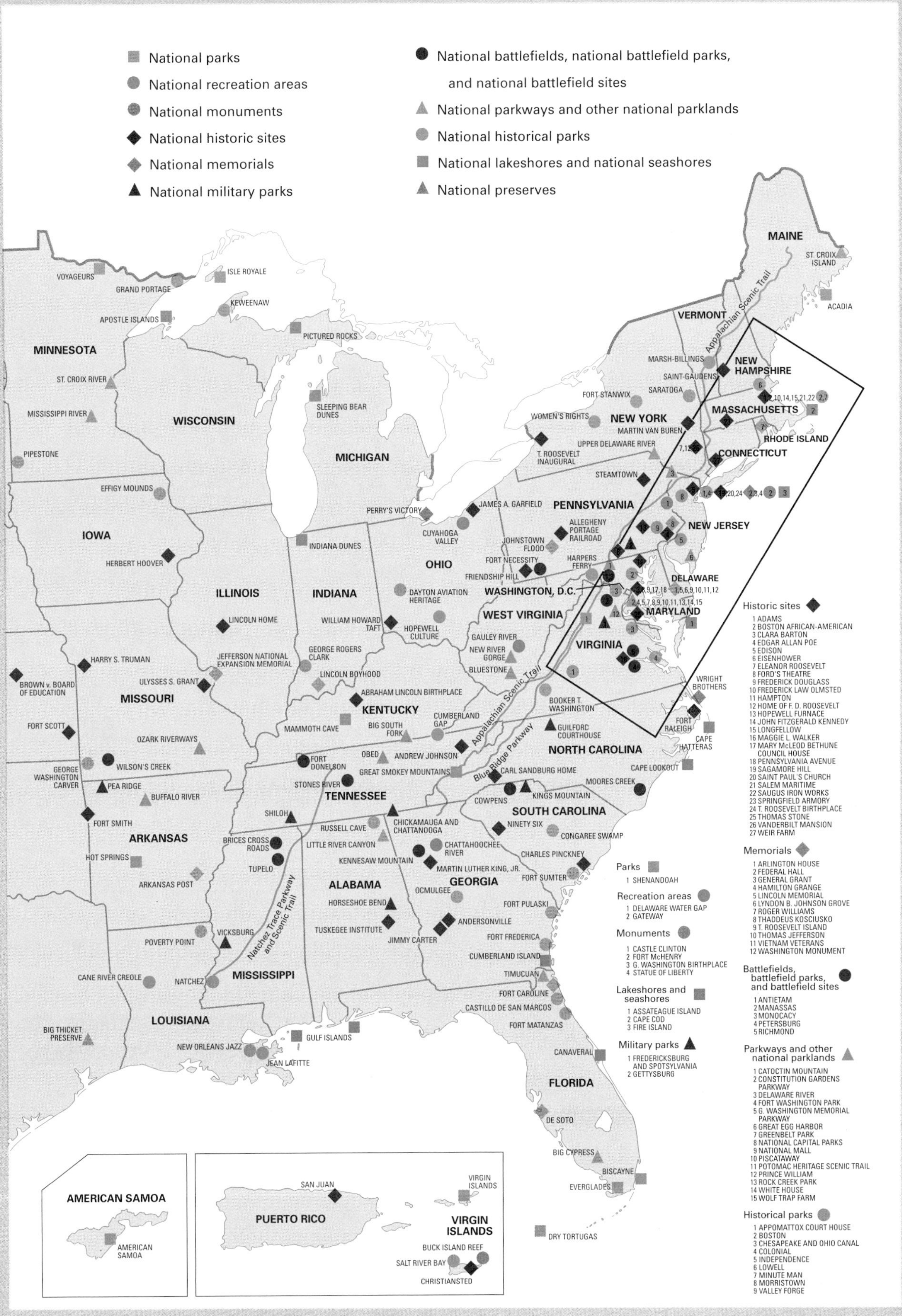
National parks
National recreation areas
National monuments
National historic sites
National memorials
National military parks
National battlefields, national battlefield parks, and national battlefield sites
National parkways and other national parklands
National historical parks
National lakeshores and national seashores
National preserves
MAINE
ST. CROIX ISLAND
ACADIA
VERMONT
Appalachian Scenic Trail
NEW HAMPSHIRE
MASSACHUSETTS
RHODE ISLAND
CONNECTICUT
NEW YORK
PENNSYLVANIA
NEW JERSEY
DELAWARE
MARYLAND
WASHINGTON, D.C.
WEST VIRGINIA
VIRGINIA
NORTH CAROLINA
SOUTH CAROLINA
GEORGIA
FLORIDA
ALABAMA
MISSISSIPPI
LOUISIANA
TENNESSEE
KENTUCKY
OHIO
INDIANA
ILLINOIS
MICHIGAN
WISCONSIN
MINNESOTA
IOWA
MISSOURI
ARKANSAS
VOYAGEURS
GRAND PORTAGE
ISLE ROYALE
KEWEENAW
APOSTLE ISLANDS
PICTURED ROCKS
ST. CROIX RIVER
MISSISSIPPI RIVER
PIPESTONE
SLEEPING BEAR DUNES
EFFIGY MOUNDS
HERBERT HOOVER
INDIANA DUNES
PERRY'S VICTORY
CUYAHOGA VALLEY
JAMES A. GARFIELD
MARSH-BILLINGS
SAINT-GAUDENS
SARATOGA
FORT STANWIX
WOMEN'S RIGHTS
MARTIN VAN BUREN
UPPER DELAWARE RIVER
T. ROOSEVELT INAUGURAL
STEAMTOWN
ALLEGHENY PORTAGE RAILROAD
JOHNSTOWN FLOOD
FORT NECESSITY
FRIENDSHIP HILL
HARPERS FERRY
DAYTON AVIATION HERITAGE
LINCOLN HOME
WILLIAM HOWARD TAFT
HOPEWELL CULTURE
GAULEY RIVER
NEW RIVER GORGE
BLUESTONE
JEFFERSON NATIONAL EXPANSION MEMORIAL
GEORGE ROGERS CLARK
LINCOLN BOYHOOD
HARRY S. TRUMAN
BROWN v. BOARD OF EDUCATION
ULYSSES S. GRANT
ABRAHAM LINCOLN BIRTHPLACE
MAMMOTH CAVE
BIG SOUTH FORK
CUMBERLAND GAP
BOOKER T. WASHINGTON
GUILFORD COURTHOUSE
WRIGHT BROTHERS
FORT RALEIGH
CAPE HATTERAS
CAPE LOOKOUT
FORT SCOTT
OZARK RIVERWAYS
GEORGE WASHINGTON CARVER
WILSON'S CREEK
PEA RIDGE
BUFFALO RIVER
FORT SMITH
HOT SPRINGS
ARKANSAS POST
FORT DONELSON
STONES RIVER
OBED
ANDREW JOHNSON
GREAT SMOKEY MOUNTAINS
Blue Ridge Parkway
CARL SANDBURG HOME
MOORES CREEK
KINGS MOUNTAIN
COWPENS
NINETY SIX
CONGAREE SWAMP
SHILOH
RUSSELL CAVE
CHICKAMAUGA AND CHATTANOOGA
LITTLE RIVER CANYON
CHATTAHOOCHEE RIVER
KENNESAW MOUNTAIN
MARTIN LUTHER KING, JR.
CHARLES PINCKNEY
FORT SUMTER
BRICES CROSS ROADS
TUPELO
Natchez Trace Parkway and Scenic Trail
HORSESHOE BEND
OCMULGEE
FORT PULASKI
TUSKEGEE INSTITUTE
ANDERSONVILLE
JIMMY CARTER
FORT FREDERICA
CUMBERLAND ISLAND
TIMUCUAN
FORT CAROLINE
CASTILLO DE SAN MARCOS
FORT MATANZAS
VICKSBURG
POVERTY POINT
CANE RIVER CREOLE
NATCHEZ
BIG THICKET PRESERVE
GULF ISLANDS
NEW ORLEANS JAZZ
JEAN LAFITTE
CANAVERAL
DE SOTO
BIG CYPRESS
BISCAYNE
EVERGLADES
DRY TORTUGAS
AMERICAN SAMOA
PUERTO RICO
SAN JUAN
VIRGIN ISLANDS
BUCK ISLAND REEF
SALT RIVER BAY
CHRISTIANSTED
Historic sites
1 ADAMS
2 BOSTON AFRICAN-AMERICAN
3 CLARA BARTON
4 EDGAR ALLAN POE
5 EDISON
6 EISENHOWER
7 ELEANOR ROOSEVELT
8 FORD'S THEATRE
9 FREDERICK DOUGLASS
10 FREDERICK LAW OLMSTED
11 HAMPTON
12 HOME OF F. D. ROOSEVELT
13 HOPEWELL FURNACE
14 JOHN FITZGERALD KENNEDY
15 LONGFELLOW
16 MAGGIE L. WALKER
17 MARY McLEOD BETHUNE COUNCIL HOUSE
18 PENNSYLVANIA AVENUE
19 SAGAMORE HILL
20 SAINT PAUL'S CHURCH
21 SALEM MARITIME
22 SAUGUS IRON WORKS
23 SPRINGFIELD ARMORY
24 T. ROOSEVELT BIRTHPLACE
25 THOMAS STONE
26 VANDERBILT MANSION
27 WEIR FARM
Memorials
1 ARLINGTON HOUSE
2 FEDERAL HALL
3 GENERAL GRANT
4 HAMILTON GRANGE
5 LINCOLN MEMORIAL
6 LYNDON B. JOHNSON GROVE
7 ROGER WILLIAMS
8 THADDEUS KOSCIUSKO
9 T. ROOSEVELT ISLAND
10 THOMAS JEFFERSON
11 VIETNAM VETERANS
12 WASHINGTON MONUMENT
Parks
1 SHENANDOAH
Recreation areas
1 DELAWARE WATER GAP
2 GATEWAY
Monuments
1 CASTLE CLINTON
2 FORT McHENRY
3 G. WASHINGTON BIRTHPLACE
4 STATUE OF LIBERTY
Lakeshores and seashores
1 ASSATEAGUE ISLAND
2 CAPE COD
3 FIRE ISLAND
Military parks
1 FREDERICKSBURG AND SPOTSYLVANIA
2 GETTYSBURG
Battlefields, battlefield parks, and battlefield sites
1 ANTIETAM
2 MANASSAS
3 MONOCACY
4 PETERSBURG
5 RICHMOND
Parkways and other national parklands
1 CATOCTIN MOUNTAIN
2 CONSTITUTION GARDENS PARKWAY
3 DELAWARE RIVER
4 FORT WASHINGTON PARK
5 G. WASHINGTON MEMORIAL PARKWAY
6 GREAT EGG HARBOR
7 GREENBELT PARK
8 NATIONAL CAPITAL PARKS
9 NATIONAL MALL
10 PISCATAWAY
11 POTOMAC HERITAGE SCENIC TRAIL
12 PRINCE WILLIAM
13 ROCK CREEK PARK
14 WHITE HOUSE
15 WOLF TRAP FARM
Historical parks
1 APPOMATTOX COURT HOUSE
2 BOSTON
3 CHESAPEAKE AND OHIO CANAL
4 COLONIAL
5 INDEPENDENCE
6 LOWELL
7 MINUTE MAN
8 MORRISTOWN
9 VALLEY FORGE

The Democratic Party is the oldest existing political party in the United States. Some historians believe it began in the 1790's as Jefferson's Democratic-Republican Party. Most historians trace the party's origin to the campaign organization that formed after the 1824 presidential election to win the presidency for Jackson in 1828.

From 1828 to 1860, the Democratic Party won all but two presidential elections—those of 1840 and 1848—even though its members often disagreed on several issues. They fought, for example, over banking policies, the slavery issue, and tariff rates. Democrats also met bitter opposition from outside the party. About 1832, several groups that opposed Jackson combined to form the Whig Party. But the Whigs never united sufficiently to propose a program with as much popular appeal as that of the Democrats.

During the 1850's, the Democrats split over whether to oppose or support the extension of slavery. In 1860, the party even had two nominees for President—John C. Breckinridge and Stephen A. Douglas. Both lost to the Republican candidate, Abraham Lincoln.

From 1860 to 1932, only two Democrats won the presidency—Grover Cleveland in 1884 and 1892 and Woodrow Wilson in 1912 and 1916. The Republican Party had gained so much strength during the Civil War that the Democrats had great difficulty winning control of the government. In addition, the Republicans repeatedly charged the Democrats with having caused the war and having been disloyal to the Union.

The situation changed after 1929. Just as the Republicans had blamed the Democrats for the Civil War, so the Democrats blamed the Republicans for the stock market crash of 1929 and the Great Depression of the 1930's. The Democrats held the presidency from 1933 to 1953. During most of this period, they also controlled both houses of Congress. The Democrats kept control of both houses from 1955 to 1981. In 1981, the Republicans took over the Senate, though the Democrats held the House. The Democrats regained control of both houses of Congress in the 1986 elections. But they lost both houses to the Republicans in the elections of 1994. Since 1948, the Democrats have won the presidency five times—in 1960, 1964, 1976, 1992, and 1996.

The Republican Party started as a series of antislavery political meetings in the Midwest in 1854. At that time, the Whig Party was breaking up. Many Whigs—as well as Northern Democrats—opposed the extension of slavery. The Republican Party represented this viewpoint and thus gained followers rapidly. The party's first presidential candidate, John C. Frémont, ran unsuccessfully in 1856, but he carried 11 Northern states.

From 1860, when Lincoln was elected, through 1928, the Republican Party won 14 of the nation's 18 presidential elections. Its policies appealed to many groups, including farmers, industrialists, and merchants. But financial scandals in Republican Ulysses S. Grant's presidency in the 1870's and economic unrest in the nation nearly cost the party the presidential election of 1876.

In 1912, President William Howard Taft was the leader of a divided Republican Party. Progressive Republicans wanted Theodore Roosevelt, who had been President from 1901 to 1909, to run again. But conservative Republicans renominated Taft at the party's 1912 national convention. Roosevelt then withdrew from the party and formed the Progressive, or "Bull Moose," Party. This split helped the Democratic candidate, Woodrow Wilson, win the election. The Republicans lost to Wilson again in 1916. They regained the presidency in 1920, and won in 1924 and 1928. But their popularity declined after the stock market crash of 1929.

During World War II (1939-1945), the Republicans began to show signs of recovery. In 1946, they won majorities in both houses of Congress for the first time since 1928. Then, in 1952, Dwight D. Eisenhower brought the Republicans their first presidential victory in 24 years. Eisenhower won again in 1956. But he had a Republican majority in both houses of Congress for only the first two of his eight years in office.

The Republicans lost to the Democrats in the 1960 and 1964 presidential elections. They regained the presidency in 1968 and held it in 1972, but the Democrats continued to control Congress. The Republicans lost the presidency to the Democrats in 1976 but regained it in 1980, when they also won control of the Senate. In the 1986 elections, the Democrats regained control of both houses. The Republicans held the presidency in 1984 and 1988 but lost to the Democrats in 1992 and 1996. In 1994, the Republicans took both houses of Congress from the Democrats.

Important political parties of the United States

This chart shows the time spans of some of the important political parties of the United States. A question mark means the date is disputed by political historians. For charts showing when each of the two major parties was in and out of office, see the articles on **Democratic Party** and **Republican Party**.

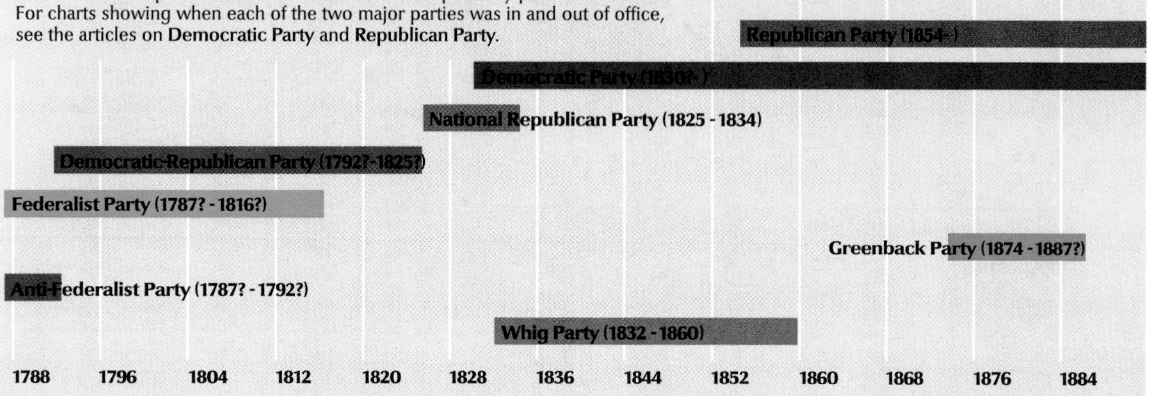

Administrations in office

WORLD BOOK graph

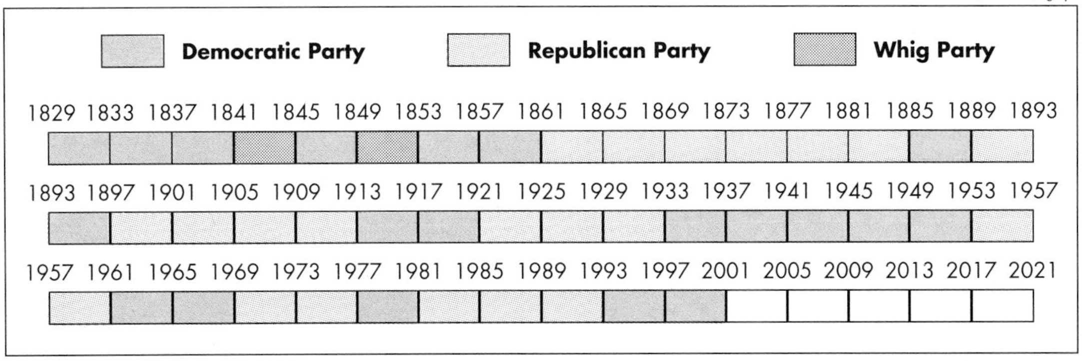

Third parties. There have been many third parties in the United States. None of them ever won the presidency. But many of their proposals gained such widespread public support that the two major parties were forced to adopt them. These proposals included the convention system of nominating presidential candidates and the direct election of U.S. senators.

Third parties in the United States can be divided into five types, according to their origins and goals. The first type consists of groups that broke away from the two major parties. For example, the Liberal Republicans in 1872 and the Roosevelt Progressives in 1912 left the Republican Party. The Gold Democrats in 1896, the Dixiecrats in 1948, and the American Independent Party in 1968 split from the Democratic Party.

The second type of third party consists of organizations formed chiefly to help a specific group of people. For example, debt-ridden farmers established the Greenback Party in the 1870's and the Populist Party in the 1890's.

The third type is made up of left wing protest groups. They include the Socialist Labor Party, formed in 1877; the Socialist Party, founded in 1901; the American Communist Party, organized in 1919; and the Socialist Workers Party, formed in 1938.

The fourth type consists of parties that have only one goal. These single-issue parties include the nation's oldest existing third party—the Prohibition Party, founded in 1869. This party seeks to prevent the manufacture and sale of alcoholic beverages in the United States.

The fifth type of third party consists of groups that have broad programs and attempt to gain national favor. Examples of this type of third party include the Progressive parties of 1924, 1948, and 1952.

WORLD BOOK chart

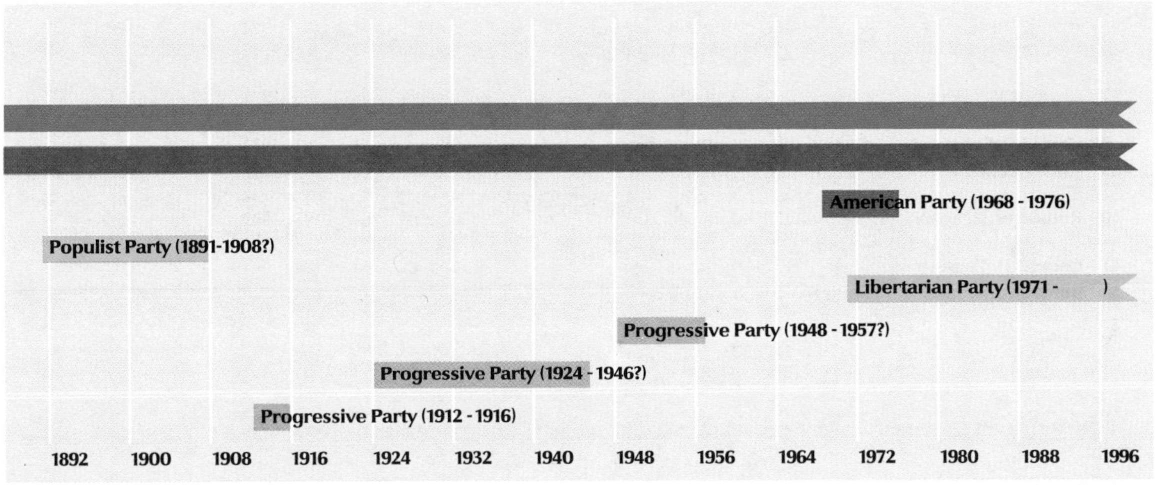

The Presidents of the United States

	President	Born	Birthplace	Political party	Age at inauguration	Served	Died	Age at death
1.	**George Washington**	Feb. 22, 1732	Westmoreland County, Va.	None	57	1789-1797	Dec. 14, 1799	67
2.	**John Adams**	Oct. 30, 1735	Braintree, Mass.	Federalist	61	1797-1801	July 4, 1826	90
3.	**Thomas Jefferson**	Apr. 13, 1743	Albemarle County, Va.	Dem.-Rep.*	57	1801-1809	July 4, 1826	83
4.	**James Madison**	Mar. 16, 1751	Port Conway, Va.	Dem.-Rep.*	57	1809-1817	June 28, 1836	85
5.	**James Monroe**	Apr. 28, 1758	Westmoreland County, Va.	Dem.-Rep.*	58	1817-1825	July 4, 1831	73
6.	**John Quincy Adams**	July 11, 1767	Braintree, Mass.	Dem.-Rep.*	57	1825-1829	Feb. 23, 1848	80
7.	**Andrew Jackson**	Mar. 15, 1767	Waxhaw settlement, S.C. (?)	Democratic	61	1829-1837	June 8, 1845	78
8.	**Martin Van Buren**	Dec. 5, 1782	Kinderhook, N.Y.	Democratic	54	1837-1841	July 24, 1862	79
9.	**William H. Harrison**	Feb. 9, 1773	Berkeley, Va.	Whig	68	1841	Apr. 4, 1841	68
10.	**John Tyler**	Mar. 29, 1790	Greenway, Va.	Whig	51	1841-1845	Jan. 18, 1862	71
11.	**James K. Polk**	Nov. 2, 1795	near Pineville, N.C.	Democratic	49	1845-1849	June 15, 1849	53
12.	**Zachary Taylor**	Nov. 24, 1784	Orange County, Va.	Whig	64	1849-1850	July 9, 1850	65
13.	**Millard Fillmore**	Jan. 7, 1800	Locke, N.Y.	Whig	50	1850-1853	Mar. 8, 1874	74
14.	**Franklin Pierce**	Nov. 23, 1804	Hillsboro, N.H.	Democratic	48	1853-1857	Oct. 8, 1869	64
15.	**James Buchanan**	Apr. 23, 1791	near Mercersburg, Pa.	Democratic	65	1857-1861	June 1, 1868	77
16.	**Abraham Lincoln**	Feb. 12, 1809	near Hodgenville, Ky.	Republican, Union†	52	1861-1865	Apr. 15, 1865	56
17.	**Andrew Johnson**	Dec. 29, 1808	Raleigh, N.C.	Union‡	56	1865-1869	July 31, 1875	66
18.	**Ulysses S. Grant**	Apr. 27, 1822	Point Pleasant, Ohio	Republican	46	1869-1877	July 23, 1885	63
19.	**Rutherford B. Hayes**	Oct. 4, 1822	Delaware, Ohio	Republican	54	1877-1881	Jan. 17, 1893	70
20.	**James A. Garfield**	Nov. 19, 1831	Orange, Ohio	Republican	49	1881	Sept. 19, 1881	49
21.	**Chester A. Arthur**	Oct. 5, 1829	Fairfield, Vt.	Republican	51	1881-1885	Nov. 18, 1886	57
22.	**Grover Cleveland**	Mar. 18, 1837	Caldwell, N.J.	Democratic	47	1885-1889	June 24, 1908	71
23.	**Benjamin Harrison**	Aug. 20, 1833	North Bend, Ohio	Republican	55	1889-1893	Mar. 13, 1901	67
24.	**Grover Cleveland**	Mar. 18, 1837	Caldwell, N.J.	Democratic	55	1893-1897	June 24, 1908	71
25.	**William McKinley**	Jan. 29, 1843	Niles, Ohio	Republican	54	1897-1901	Sept. 14, 1901	58
26.	**Theodore Roosevelt**	Oct. 27, 1858	New York, N.Y.	Republican	42	1901-1909	Jan. 6, 1919	60
27.	**William H. Taft**	Sept. 15, 1857	Cincinnati, Ohio	Republican	51	1909-1913	Mar. 8, 1930	72
28.	**Woodrow Wilson**	Dec. 29, 1856	Staunton, Va.	Democratic	56	1913-1921	Feb. 3, 1924	67
29.	**Warren G. Harding**	Nov. 2, 1865	near Blooming Grove, Ohio	Republican	55	1921-1923	Aug. 2, 1923	57
30.	**Calvin Coolidge**	July 4, 1872	Plymouth Notch, Vt.	Republican	51	1923-1929	Jan. 5, 1933	60
31.	**Herbert C. Hoover**	Aug. 10, 1874	West Branch, Iowa	Republican	54	1929-1933	Oct. 20, 1964	90
32.	**Franklin D. Roosevelt**	Jan. 30, 1882	Hyde Park, N.Y.	Democratic	51	1933-1945	Apr. 12, 1945	63
33.	**Harry S. Truman**	May 8, 1884	Lamar, Mo.	Democratic	60	1945-1953	Dec. 26, 1972	88
34.	**Dwight D. Eisenhower**	Oct. 14, 1890	Denison, Tex.	Republican	62	1953-1961	Mar. 28, 1969	78
35.	**John F. Kennedy**	May 29, 1917	Brookline, Mass.	Democratic	43	1961-1963	Nov. 22, 1963	46
36.	**Lyndon B. Johnson**	Aug. 27, 1908	near Stonewall, Tex.	Democratic	55	1963-1969	Jan. 22, 1973	64
37.	**Richard M. Nixon**	Jan. 9, 1913	Yorba Linda, Calif.	Republican	56	1969-1974	Apr. 22, 1994	81
38.	**Gerald R. Ford#**	July 14, 1913	Omaha, Nebr.	Republican	61	1974-1977		
39.	**Jimmy Carter**	Oct. 1, 1924	Plains, Ga.	Democratic	52	1977-1981		
40.	**Ronald W. Reagan**	Feb. 6, 1911	Tampico, Ill.	Republican	69	1981-1989		
41.	**George H. W. Bush**	June 12, 1924	Milton, Mass.	Republican	64	1989-1993		
42.	**Bill Clinton**	Aug. 19, 1946	Hope, Ark.	Democratic	46	1993-		

*Democratic- Republican. †The Union Party consisted of Republicans and War Democrats.
‡The Union Party consisted of Republicans and War Democrats; Johnson was a War Democrat.

#Inaugurated Aug. 9, 1974, to replace Nixon, who resigned that same day.
Each President has a separate biography and picture in *World Book*.

College or university	Religion	Occupation or profession	Runner-up		Vice President	
1.	Episcopalian	Planter	John Adams	(1789, 1792)	John Adams	(1789-1797)
2. Harvard	Unitarian	Lawyer	Thomas Jefferson	(1796)	Thomas Jefferson	(1797-1801)
3. William and Mary	Unitarian*	Planter, lawyer	Aaron Burr Charles C. Pinckney	(1800) (1804)	Aaron Burr George Clinton	(1801-1805) (1805-1809)
4. Princeton	Episcopalian	Lawyer	Charles C. Pinckney De Witt Clinton	(1808) (1812)	George Clinton Elbridge Gerry	(1809-1812) (1813-1814)
5. William and Mary	Episcopalian	Lawyer	Rufus King No opposition	(1816)	Daniel D. Tompkins	(1817-1825)
6. Harvard	Unitarian	Lawyer	Andrew Jackson	(1824)	John C. Calhoun	(1825-1829)
7.	Presbyterian	Lawyer	John Quincy Adams Henry Clay	(1828) (1832)	John C. Calhoun Martin Van Buren	(1829-1832) (1833-1837)
8.	Dutch Reformed	Lawyer	William H. Harrison	(1836)	Richard M. Johnson	(1837-1841)
9. Hampden-Sydney	Episcopalian	Soldier	Martin Van Buren	(1840)	John Tyler	(1841)
10. William and Mary	Episcopalian	Lawyer			None	
11. U. of N. Carolina	Methodist	Lawyer	Henry Clay	(1844)	George M. Dallas	(1845-1849)
12.	Episcopalian	Soldier	Lewis Cass	(1848)	Millard Fillmore	(1849-1850)
13.	Unitarian	Lawyer			None	
14. Bowdoin	Episcopalian	Lawyer	Winfield Scott	(1852)	William R. King	(1853)
15. Dickinson	Presbyterian	Lawyer	John C. Frémont	(1856)	John C. Breckinridge	(1857-1861)
16.	Presbyterian*	Lawyer	Stephen A. Douglas Geo. B. McClellan	(1860) (1864)	Hannibal Hamlin Andrew Johnson	(1861-1865) (1865)
17.	Methodist*	Tailor			None	
18. U.S. Mil. Academy	Methodist	Soldier	Horatio Seymour Horace Greeley	(1868) (1872)	Schuyler Colfax Henry Wilson	(1869-1873) (1873-1875)
19. Kenyon	Methodist*	Lawyer	Samuel J. Tilden	(1876)	William A. Wheeler	(1877-1881)
20. Williams	Disciples of Christ	Lawyer	Winfield S. Hancock	(1880)	Chester A. Arthur	(1881)
21. Union	Episcopalian	Lawyer			None	
22.	Presbyterian	Lawyer	James G. Blaine	(1884)	Thomas A. Hendricks	(1885)
23. Miami	Presbyterian	Lawyer	Grover Cleveland	(1888)	Levi P. Morton	(1889-1893)
24.	Presbyterian	Lawyer	Benjamin Harrison	(1892)	Adlai E. Stevenson	(1893-1897)
25. Allegheny College	Methodist	Lawyer	William J. Bryan	(1896, 1900)	Garret A. Hobart Theodore Roosevelt	(1897-1899) (1901)
26. Harvard	Dutch Reformed	Author	Alton B. Parker	(1904)	Charles W. Fairbanks	(1905-1909)
27. Yale	Unitarian	Lawyer	William J. Bryan	(1908)	James S. Sherman	(1909-1912)
28. Princeton	Presbyterian	Educator	Theodore Roosevelt Charles E. Hughes	(1912) (1916)	Thomas R. Marshall	(1913-1921)
29.	Baptist	Editor	James M. Cox	(1920)	Calvin Coolidge	(1921-1923)
30. Amherst	Congregationalist	Lawyer	John W. Davis	(1924)	Charles G. Dawes	(1925-1929)
31. Stanford	Friend (Quaker)	Engineer	Alfred E. Smith	(1928)	Charles Curtis	(1929-1933)
32. Harvard	Episcopalian	Lawyer	Herbert Hoover Alfred M. Landon Wendell L. Willkie Thomas E. Dewey	(1932) (1936) (1940) (1944)	John N. Garner Henry A. Wallace Harry S. Truman	(1933-1941) (1941-1945) (1945)
33.	Baptist	Businessman	Thomas E. Dewey	(1948)	Alben W. Barkley	(1949-1953)
34. U.S. Mil. Academy	Presbyterian	Soldier	Adlai E. Stevenson	(1952, 1956)	Richard M. Nixon	(1953-1961)
35. Harvard	Roman Catholic	Author	Richard M. Nixon	(1960)	Lyndon B. Johnson	(1961-1963)
36. Southwest Texas State	Disciples of Christ	Teacher	Barry M. Goldwater	(1964)	Hubert H. Humphrey	(1965-1969)
37. Whittier	Friend (Quaker)	Lawyer	Hubert H. Humphrey George S. McGovern	(1968) (1972)	Spiro T. Agnew Gerald R. Ford**	(1969-1973) (1973-1974)
38. Michigan	Episcopalian	Lawyer			Nelson A. Rockefeller§	(1974-1977)
39. U.S. Naval Academy	Baptist	Businessman	Gerald R. Ford	(1976)	Walter F. Mondale	(1977-1981)
40. Eureka	Disciples of Christ	Actor	Jimmy Carter Walter F. Mondale	(1980) (1984)	George H. W. Bush	(1981-1989)
41. Yale	Episcopalian	Businessman	Michael S. Dukakis	(1988)	Dan Quayle	(1989-1993)
42. Georgetown	Baptist	Lawyer	George H. W. Bush Robert J. Dole	(1992) (1996)	Al Gore	(1993-)

*Church preference; never joined any church.

**Inaugurated Dec. 6, 1973, to replace Agnew, who resigned Oct. 10, 1973.
§Inaugurated Dec. 19, 1974, to replace Ford, who became President Aug. 9, 1974.

Revolutionary War

Important dates in the Revolutionary War

1775

April 19 Minutemen and redcoats clashed at Lexington and Concord.
June 15 The Congress named George Washington commander in chief of the Continental Army.
June 17 The British drove the Americans from Breed's Hill in the Battle of Bunker Hill.

1776

Feb. 27 The patriots defeated the Loyalists at Moore's Creek Bridge.
March 17 The British evacuated Boston.
July 4 The Declaration of Independence was adopted.
Aug. 27 The redcoats defeated the patriots on Long Island.
Sept. 15 The British occupied New York City.
Dec. 26 Washington mounted a surprise attack on Hessian troops at Trenton.

1777

Jan. 3 Washington gained a victory at Princeton.
Aug. 6 Loyalists and Indians forced the patriots back at Oriskany, but then withdrew.
Aug. 16 The patriots crushed the Hessians near Bennington.
Sept. 11 The British won the Battle of Brandywine.
Sept. 19 Gates's forces checked Burgoyne's army in the First Battle of Freeman's Farm.
Sept. 26 The British occupied Philadelphia.
Oct. 4 Washington's forces met defeat in the Battle of Germantown.
Oct. 7 The patriots defeated the British in the Second Battle of Freeman's Farm.
Oct. 17 Burgoyne surrendered at Saratoga.
Dec. 19 Washington's army retired to winter quarters at Valley Forge.

1778

Feb. 6 The United States and France signed an alliance.
June 28 The Battle of Monmouth ended in a draw.
Dec. 29 The redcoats took Savannah.

1779

Feb. 25 British defenders of Vincennes surrendered to George Rogers Clark.
June 21 Spain declared war on Great Britain.
Sept. 23 John Paul Jones's ship, the *Bonhomme Richard,* captured the British ship *Serapis.*

1780

May 12 Charleston fell after a British siege.
Aug. 16 The British defeated the Americans at Camden.
Oct. 7 American frontiersmen stormed the Loyalist positions on Kings Mountain.

1781

Jan. 17 The patriots won a victory at Cowpens.
March 15 Cornwallis clashed with Greene at Guilford Courthouse.
Sept. 5 A French fleet inflicted great damage on a British naval force at Chesapeake Bay.
Oct. 19 Cornwallis' forces surrendered at Yorktown.

1782

March 20 King George's chief minister, Lord North, resigned.
Nov. 30 The Americans and British signed a preliminary peace treaty in Paris.

1783

April 15 Congress ratified the preliminary peace treaty.
Sept. 3 The United States and Great Britain signed the final peace treaty in Paris.

Major battles of the Revolutionary War

Name	Place	Date	Commander		Dead and wounded*		Results
			American	British	American	British	
Bennington	Vermont	Aug. 16, 1777	Stark	Baum, Breymann	80	200	British defeat encouraged the patriots in their campaign against Burgoyne.
Brandywine	Pennsylvania	Sept. 11, 1777	Washington	Howe	700	540	An American retreat enabled the British to occupy Philadelphia.
Bunker Hill	Massachusetts	June 17, 1775	Prescott	Howe	400	1,000	The patriots were driven from their positions overlooking Boston.
Camden	South Carolina	Aug. 16, 1780	Gates	Cornwallis	1,000	300	The British crushed an American army.
Cowpens	South Carolina	Jan. 17, 1781	Morgan	Tarleton	70	330	Patriot victory encouraged Southern militiamen to come out and fight.
Freeman's Farm (First Battle)	New York	Sept. 19, 1777	Gates	Burgoyne	300	600	The British advance from Canada was halted.
Freeman's Farm (Second Battle)	New York	Oct. 7, 1777	Gates	Burgoyne	150	600	The patriots turned back a second attack.
Germantown	Pennsylvania	Oct. 4, 1777	Washington	Howe	650	550	An American attack turned into a loss and a retreat.
Guilford Courthouse	North Carolina	March 15, 1781	Greene	Cornwallis	250	650	The British decided to give up most of North Carolina.
Kings Mountain	South Carolina	Oct. 7, 1780	Campbell	Ferguson	100	300	The British advance into North Carolina was delayed.
Lexington and Concord	Massachusetts	April 19, 1775	Parker and others	Smith	90	250	The Revolutionary War in America began.
Long Island	New York	Aug. 27, 1776	Washington	Howe	250	400	The British forced the Americans from Long Island.
Monmouth	New Jersey	June 28, 1778	Washington	Clinton	250	400	A patriot attack ended in a draw.
Princeton	New Jersey	Jan. 3, 1777	Washington	Cornwallis	50	100	The British withdrew from western New Jersey.
Quebec	Quebec	Dec. 31, 1775	Arnold, Montgomery	Carleton	100	18	The Americans failed to seize the city of Quebec.
Trenton	New Jersey	Dec. 26, 1776	Washington	Rall	10	100	The patriots crushed the Hessians in a surprise assault.
Yorktown	Virginia	Oct. 6-19, 1781	Washington	Cornwallis	100	600	The British surrendered in the war's last major battle.

*Approximate totals. The figures listed are a compromise between several conflicting estimates.

Revolutionary War battles and campaigns

British strategy at first called for crushing the American Revolution in the North. After 1778, the fighting shifted to the South. In 1781, an American and French force defeated the British at Yorktown in the last major battle of the war. This map locates important battles and campaigns.

WORLD BOOK map

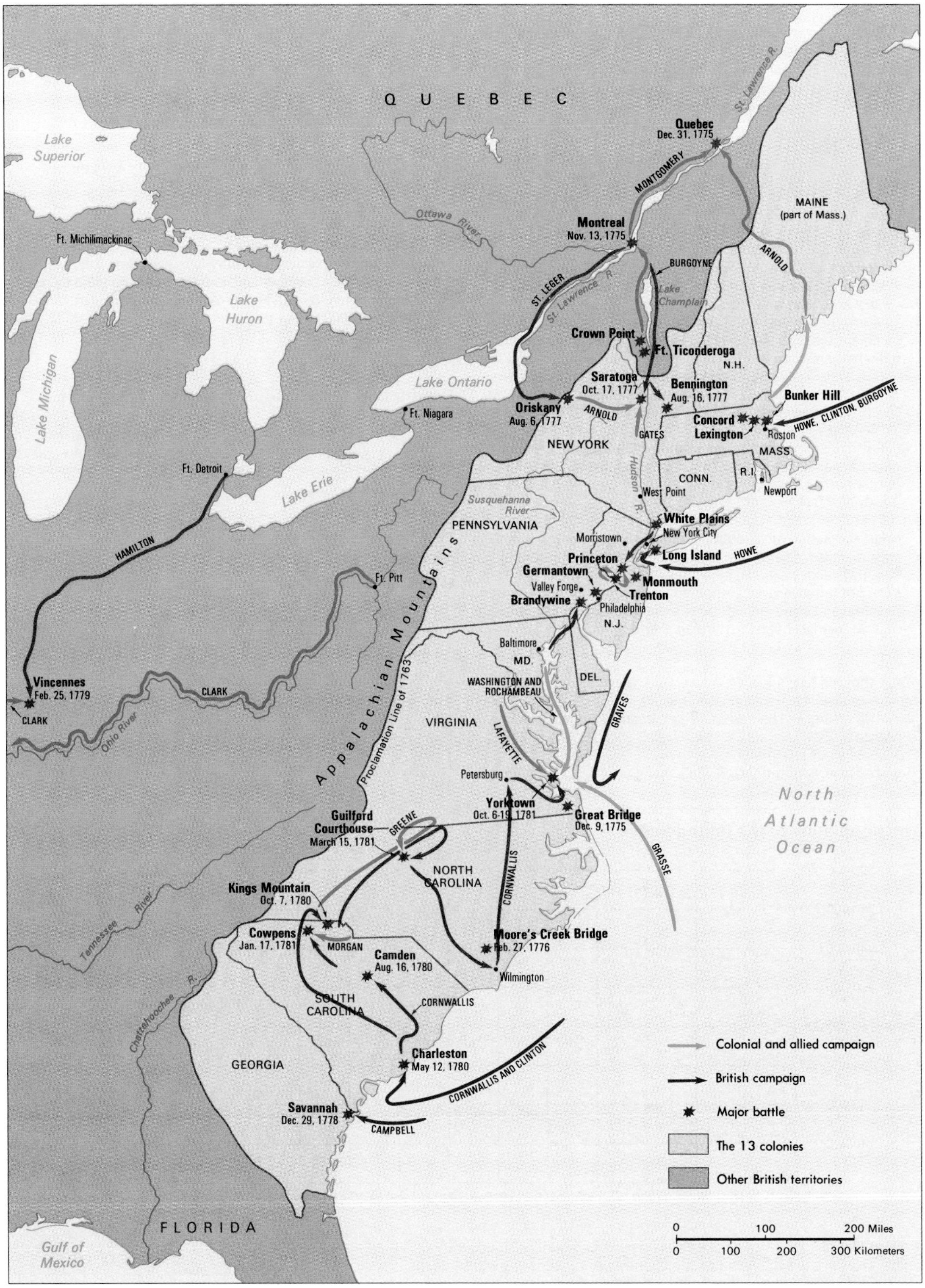

United States

Facts in brief

Capital: Washington, D.C.

Form of government: Republic. For details, see **United States, Government of the.**

Area: 3,615,292 sq. mi. (9,363,563 km²), including 78,937 sq. mi. (204,447 km²) of inland water but excluding 60,053 sq. mi. (155,535 km²) of Great Lakes and Lake Saint Clair and 42,529 sq. mi. (110,148 km²) of coastal water. *Greatest distances excluding Alaska and Hawaii*—east-west, 2,807 mi. (4,517 km); north-south, 1,598 mi. (2,572 km). *Greatest distances in Alaska*—north-south, about 1,200 mi. (1,930 km); east-west, about 2,200 mi. (3,540 km). *Greatest distance in Hawaii*—northwest-southeast, about 1,610 mi. (2,591 km). *Extreme points including Alaska and Hawaii*—northernmost, Point Barrow, Alaska; southernmost, Ka Lae, Hawaii; easternmost, West Quoddy Head, Maine; westernmost, Cape Wrangell, Attu Island, Alaska. *Coastline*—4,993 mi. (8,035 km), excluding Alaska and Hawaii; 12,383 mi. (19,929 km), including Alaska and Hawaii.

Elevation: *Highest*—Mount McKinley in Alaska, 20,320 ft. (6,194 m) above sea level. *Lowest*—In Death Valley in California, 282 ft. (86 m) below sea level.

Physical features: *Longest river*—Missouri, 2,540 mi. (4,090 km). *Largest lake within the United States*—Michigan, 22,300 sq. mi. (57,757 km²). *Largest island*—island of Hawaii, 4,038 sq. mi. (10,458 km²).

Population: *Estimated 1998 population*—270,002,000; density, 75 persons per sq. mi. (29 per km²). *Estimated distribution*—75 percent urban, 25 percent rural. *1990 census*—249,632,692. *Estimated 2003 population*—281,452,000.

Chief products: *Agriculture*—beef cattle, milk, corn, soybeans, hogs, chickens, wheat, cotton, eggs. *Fishing industry*—salmon, shrimp, crabs. *Manufacturing*—processed foods, motor vehicles and parts, industrial machinery, fabricated metal products, printed materials, computers and computer parts, paper, gasoline and other refined petroleum products, plastic products, industrial chemicals, airplanes and parts, textiles, clothing, steel, pharmaceuticals. *Mining*—petroleum, natural gas, coal.

Flag: Adopted June 14, 1777.

Motto: *In God We Trust*, adopted July 30, 1956.

National anthem: "The Star-Spangled Banner," adopted on March 3, 1931.

Bird: Bald eagle, adopted June 20, 1782.

Flower: Rose, adopted Oct. 7, 1986.

Money: *Basic unit*—dollar.

Gross domestic product of the United States

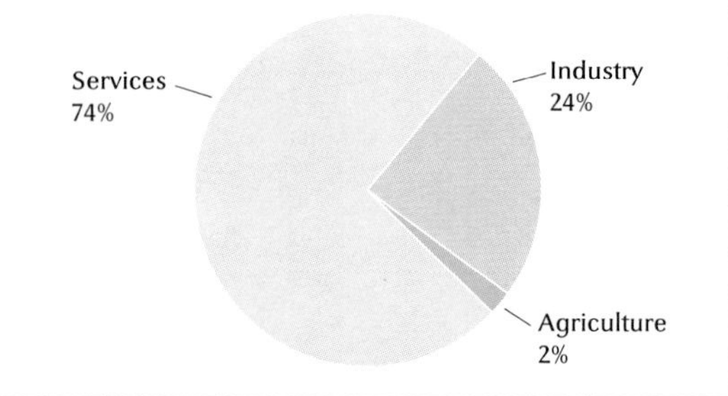

The gross domestic product (GDP) is the total value of goods and services produced within a country in a year. The GDP measures a nation's economic performance and can also be used to compare the economic output and growth of countries. The U.S. GDP was $7,254,000,000,000 in 1995.

Production and workers by economic activities

Economic activities	Percent of GDP produced	Employed workers: Number of persons	Employed workers: Percent of total
Community, business, & personal services	18	33,107,000	27
Finance, insurance, & real estate	18	6,830,000	6
Manufacturing	18	18,468,000	15
Wholesale & retail trade	17	27,585,000	23
Government	11	19,311,000	16
Transportation, communication, & utilities	10	6,165,000	5
Construction	4	5,158,000	4
Agriculture, forestry, & fishing	2	3,944,000	3
Mining	2	580,000	1
Total	100	6,830,000	100

Sources: U.S. Bureau of Economic Analysis; U.S. Bureau of Labor Statistics.

The population of the United States

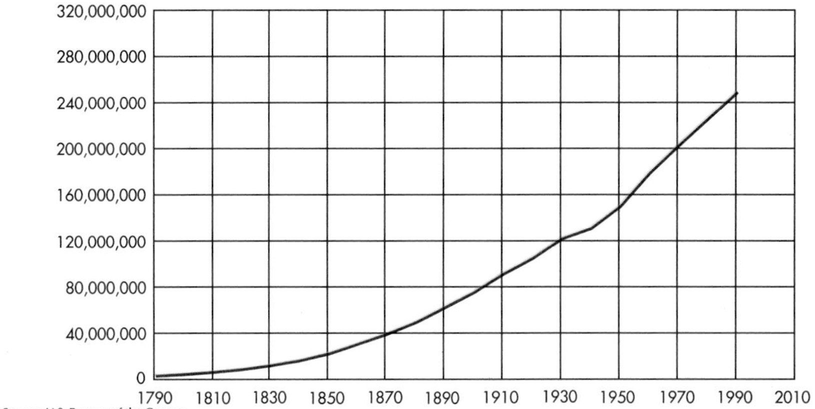

Source: U.S. Bureau of the Census.

Census year	Population
1790	3,929,214
1800	5,308,483
1810	7,239,881
1820	9,638,453
1830	12,866,020
1840	17,069,453
1850	23,191,876
1860	31,443,321
1870	39,818,449
1880	50,155,783
1890	62,974,714
1900	75,994,575
1910	91,972,266
1920	105,710,620
1930	122,775,046
1940	131,669,275
1950	150,697,361
1960	179,323,175
1970	203,235,298
1980	226,545,805
1990	249,632,692

The population of the United States has risen steadily since the country's first census was taken in 1790. The above graph illustrates the country's population growth since the first census. The table at the right lists the population figure for each census year.

Regions of the United States

The map below shows the location of the seven regions of the continental United States. The table below the map lists the states within each region.

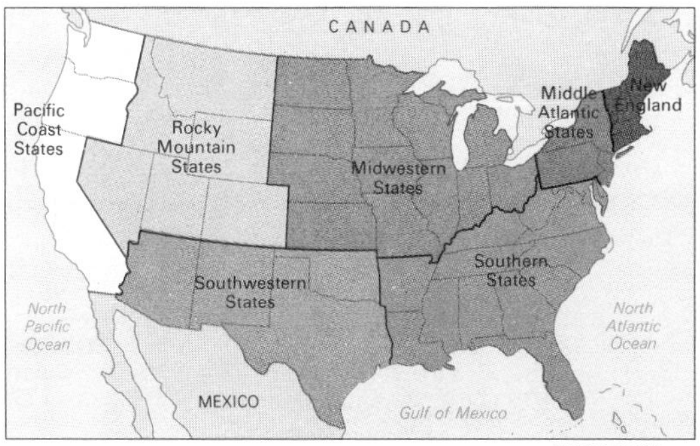

WORLD BOOK map

Symbols of the United States include the American flag and the Great Seal. The eagle holds an olive branch and arrows, symbolizing a desire for peace but the ability to wage war. The reverse side bears the Eye of Providence, representing God, and a pyramid dated 1776.

New England
Connecticut, Maine, Massachusetts, New Hampshire, Rhode Island, Vermont

Middle Atlantic States
New Jersey, New York, Pennsylvania

Southern States
Alabama, Arkansas, Delaware, Florida, Georgia, Kentucky, Louisiana, Maryland, Mississippi, North Carolina, South Carolina, Tennessee, Virginia, West Virginia

Midwestern States
Illinois, Indiana, Iowa, Kansas, Michigan, Minnesota, Missouri, Nebraska, North Dakota, Ohio, South Dakota, Wisconsin

Rocky Mountain States
Colorado, Idaho, Montana, Nevada, Utah, Wyoming

Southwestern States
*Arizona, *New Mexico, Oklahoma, Texas

Pacific Coast States
California, Oregon, Washington

*Arizona and New Mexico are often grouped with the Rocky Mountain States.

Main outlying areas of the United States

Name	Acquired	Status
American Samoa	*	Unorganized unincorporated territory
Baker Island and Jarvis Island	1856	Unincorporated territory
Guam	1898	Organized unincorporated territory
Howland Island	1856	Unincorporated possession
Johnston Island and Sand Island	1858	Unincorporated territory
Kingman Reef	1922	Unincorporated territory
Midway Island	1867	Unincorporated territory
Northern Mariana Islands	1947	Commonwealth
Palmyra Island	1898	Unincorporated possession
Puerto Rico	1898	Commonwealth
Trust Territory of the Pacific Islands	1947	UN trust territory (U.S. administration)
Virgin Islands of the United States	1917	Organized unincorporated territory
Wake Island	1898	Unincorporated possession

*Acquired in stages between 1900 and 1925.

The U.S. federal government dollar

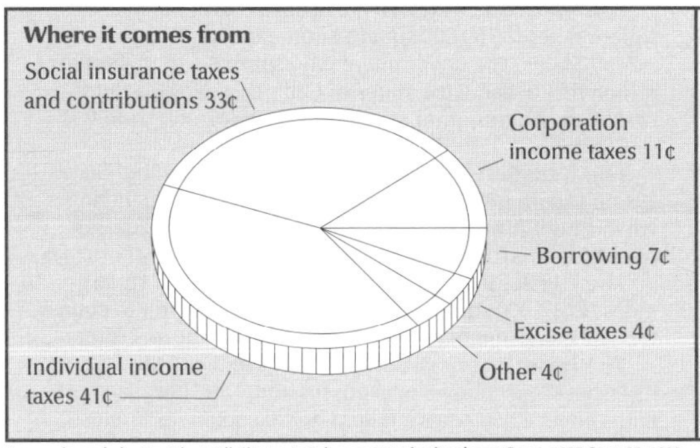

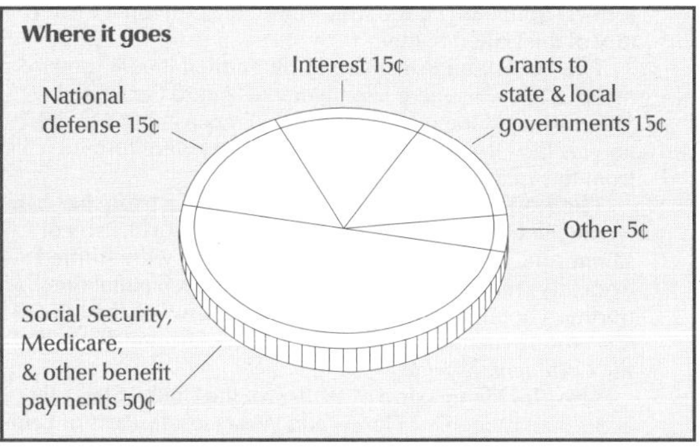

Proposals made by President Bill Clinton in February 1997 for fiscal year Oct. 1, 1997-Sept. 30, 1998.

Major territorial acquisitions of the United States

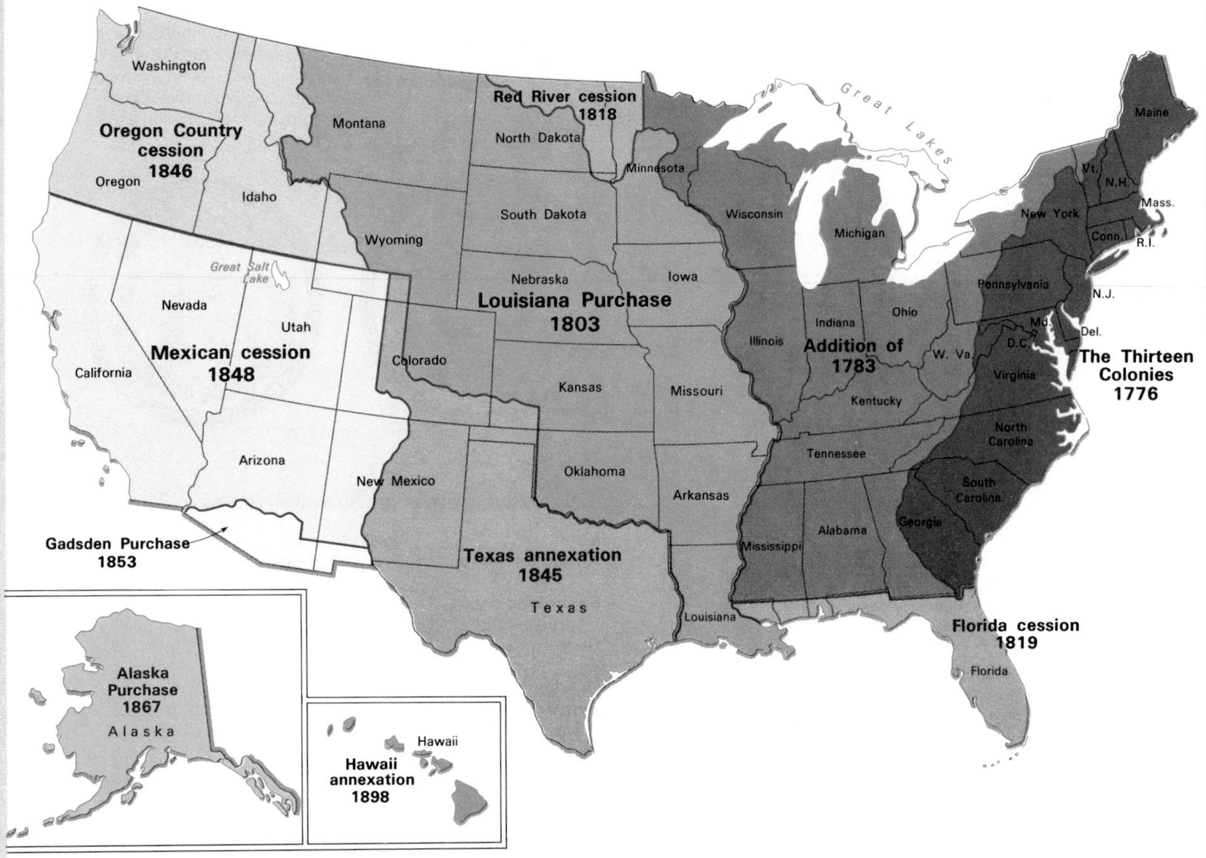

The United States added territory in a number of ways. It bought vast areas, gained others by treaty, and won much land through war. Following are brief descriptions of the major territorial acquisitions of the United States from 1776 to 1898.

The Thirteen Colonies occupied what became the original area of the United States. The 13 original states and parts of Maine, Vermont, and West Virginia were formed from this area.

The addition of 1783 extended the nation's boundaries north to the Great Lakes, south to the 31st parallel, and west to the Mississippi River. All or most of nine states were formed from this region, which more than doubled the territory of the United States.

The Louisiana Purchase of 1803 added 827,987 square miles (2,144,476 square kilometers) of land to the United States. The federal government paid France about $15 million for the territory. Part or all of 15 states were formed from the area.

The Red River cession was included in a treaty between the United States and Great Britain in 1818. Parts of Minnesota, North Dakota, and South Dakota were formed from this area. The treaty also made the 49th parallel the northern boundary of the United States between the Lake of the Woods and the high land in the Rocky Mountains called the *Continental Divide.*

The Florida cession of 1819 gave the United States the areas then called East Florida and West Florida. Parts of Louisiana, Mississippi, and Alabama and all of Florida were formed from this territory, which was ceded by Spain.

The Texas annexation of 1845 added what was then the nation's largest state. Most of the present boundaries of Texas were established in 1850, when the state gave up claims to western lands.

The Oregon Country cession extended the western border of the United States to the Pacific Ocean in 1846. This cession also established the 49th parallel as the nation's northern boundary in the area west of the Continental Divide. Idaho, Washington, and Oregon were formed from the Oregon region.

The Mexican cession of 1848 added over 525,000 square miles (1,360,000 square kilometers) of land to the United States. The government paid Mexico $15 million for a region that became the states of California, Nevada, and Utah. Parts of four other states were also formed from this region.

The Gadsden Purchase of 1853 gave the United States 29,640 square miles (76,770 square kilometers) of land in what is now Arizona and New Mexico. The United States paid Mexico $10 million for the land.

The Alaska Purchase of 1867 added 586,000 square miles (1,518,000 square kilometers) of territory to the country. The government paid Russia $7,200,000 for this region.

The Hawaii annexation of 1898 gave the United States its largest present overseas possession. The Hawaiian Islands cover 6,450 square miles (16,710 square kilometers).

How a bill becomes law in the United States

The drawings on this page and the next three pages show how federal laws are enacted in the United States. Thousands of bills are introduced during each Congress, which lasts two years, and hundreds become law. All bills not enacted by the end of the two-year period are killed.

WORLD BOOK illustrations by David Cunningham

Ideas for new laws come from many sources. The President, members of Congress, and other government officials may propose laws. Suggestions also come from individual citizens; special-interest groups, such as farmers, industry, and labor; newspaper editorials; and public protests. Congressional committees, in addition to lawyers who represent special-interest groups, actually write most bills and put them into proper legal form. Specialists called *legislative counsels* in both the Senate and House of Representatives also help prepare many bills for congressional action.

Individual citizens

Public protests

Newspaper editorials

Special-interest groups

The President

Members of Congress and other government officials

Each bill must be sponsored by a member of the House or Senate. Any number of senators or representatives may co-sponsor a bill. A bill may originate in either house of Congress unless it deals with taxes or spending. The Constitution provides that all such bills must be introduced in the House. The tradition that money bills must begin in the lower house came from England. There, the lower house—the House of Commons—is more likely to reflect the people's wishes because the people elect its members. They do not elect the upper house, the House of Lords. The rule has little meaning in the United States because voters elect both houses.

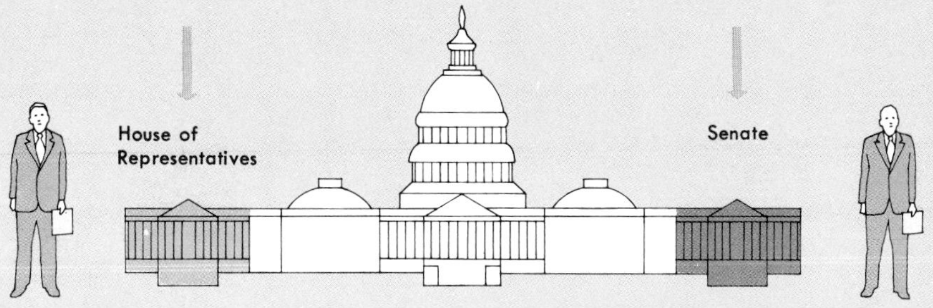

How a bill goes through Congress

The drawings on this page and the next show the normal path of a bill introduced in the House of Representatives. The process is the same for a bill introduced in the Senate, except that the House action comes after the Senate action. A bill may die at almost any stage of the process if no action is taken on it. A majority of the bills introduced in Congress fail and never become law.

Introduction in the House. A sponsor introduces a bill by giving it to the clerk of the House or placing it in a box called the *hopper.* The clerk reads the title of the bill into the *Congressional Record* in a procedure called the *first reading.* The Government Printing Office prints the bill and distributes copies.

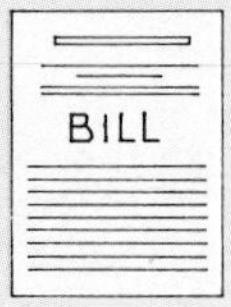

Assignment to committee. The speaker of the House assigns the bill to a committee for study. The House has about 20 *standing* (permanent) committees, each with jurisdiction over bills in a certain area.

Assignment to committee. The Vice President of the United States, who is the presiding officer of the Senate, assigns the proposed law to a committee for study. The Senate has about 15 standing committees.

Committee action. The committee or one of its subcommittees studies the bill and may hold hearings. The committee may approve the bill as it stands, revise the bill, or table it.

The bill goes to the Senate to await its turn. Bills normally reach the Senate floor in the order that they come from committee. But if a bill is urgent, the leaders of the majority party might push it ahead.

The Senate considers the bill. Senators can debate a bill indefinitely, unless they vote to limit discussion. When there is no further debate, the Senate votes. Most bills must have a simple majority to pass.

A conference committee made up of members of both houses works out any differences between the House and Senate versions of the bill. The revised bill is sent back to both houses for their final approval.

The committee studies the bill and hears testimony from experts and other interested persons. In some cases, a subcommittee conducts the study. The committee may release the bill with a recommendation to pass it, revise the bill and release it, or lay it aside so that the House cannot vote on it. Releasing the bill is called *reporting it out,* and laying it aside is called *tabling.*

The bill goes on a calendar, a list of bills awaiting action. The Rules Committee may call for quick action on the bill, limit debate, and limit or prohibit amendments. Otherwise, a bill might never reach the House floor.

Consideration by the House begins with a second reading of the bill, the only complete reading in most cases. A third reading, by title only, comes after any amendments have been added. If the bill passes by a *simple majority* (one more than half the votes), it goes to the Senate.

Introduction in the Senate. To introduce a bill, a senator must be recognized by the presiding officer and announce the introduction of the bill. A bill that has passed either house of Congress is sometimes called an *act,* but the term usually means legislation that has passed both houses and become law.

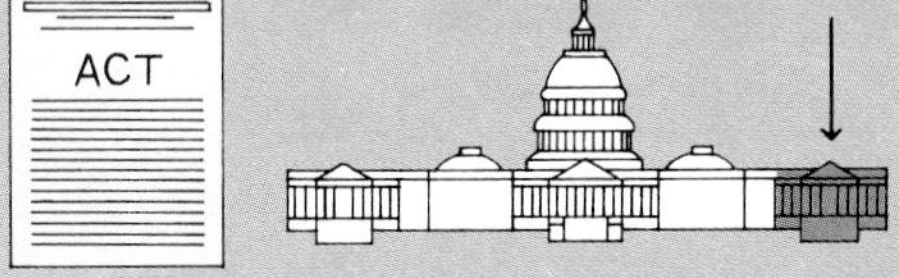

The bill is printed by the Government Printing Office in a process called *enrolling.* The clerk of the house of Congress that originated the bill certifies the final version.

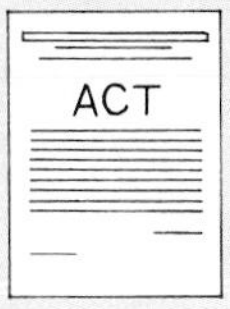

The Speaker of the House signs the enrolled bill, and then the Vice President signs it. Finally, Congress sends the proposed new legislation to the White House for consideration by the President.

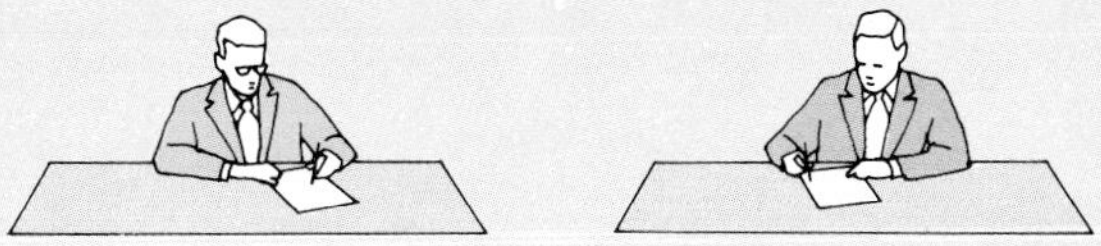

Action by the President

A bill passed by Congress goes to the President, who has 10 days—not including Sundays—to sign or veto it. The President may also let a bill become law by letting 10 days pass without acting.

Approval. After approving a bill, the President signs it, dates it, and often writes *approved* on it.

Veto. A vetoed bill must be returned to Congress with an explanation of the President's objections.

No action. The President might not veto the bill but may fail to sign it to show disapproval of some parts.

Reconsideration by Congress. If two-thirds of those members present approve the vetoed bill, it becomes law despite the veto.

Ten days pass. If the President holds the bill for 10 days—excluding Sundays—while Congress is in session, it becomes law without the signature of the chief executive. A bill that reaches the President fewer than 10 days—excluding Sundays—before Congress adjourns cannot become law without the President's signature. If the President fails to sign the proposed law, it dies. This procedure is called a *pocket veto.*

The bill becomes law and is given a number that indicates which Congress passed it. For example, a law enacted by the 95th Congress might be designated Public Law 95-250.

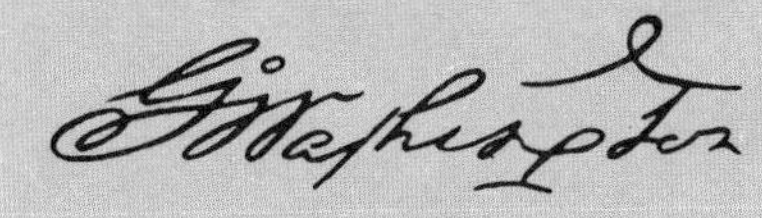

1st President of the United States 1789-1797

Washington
1st President
1789-1797
No political party

J. Adams
2nd President
1797-1801
Federalist

Oil painting on canvas (1796) by Gilbert Stuart; Jointly owned by the National Portrait Gallery, Smithsonian Institution, and the Museum of Fine Arts, Boston

John Adams
Vice President
1789-1797

Washington, George (1732-1799), won a lasting place in American history as the "Father of our Country." For nearly 20 years, he guided his country much as a father cares for a growing child.

In three important ways, Washington helped shape the beginning of the United States. First, he commanded the Continental Army that won American independence from Great Britain in the Revolutionary War. Second, Washington served as president of the convention that wrote the United States Constitution. Third, he was elected the first President of the United States.

The people of his day loved Washington. His army officers would have made him king if he had let them. From the Revolutionary War on, his birthday was celebrated each year throughout the country.

Washington lived an exciting life in exciting times. As a boy, he explored the wilderness. When he grew older, he helped the British fight the French and Indians. Many times he was nearly killed. As a general, he suffered hardships with his troops in the cold winters at Valley Forge, Pa., and Morristown, N.J. He lost many battles, but led the American army to final victory at Yorktown, Va. After he became President, he successfully solved many problems in turning the plans of the Constitution into a working government.

Washington went to school only until he was about 14 or 15. But he learned to make the most of all his abilities and opportunities. Washington's remarkable patience and his understanding of others helped him win people to his side in times of hardship and discouragement.

There are great differences between the United States of Washington's day and that of today. The new nation was small and weak. It stretched west only to the Mississippi River and had fewer than 4,000,000 people. Most people made their living by farming. Few children went to school. Few men or women could read or write. Transportation and communication were slow. It took Washington 3 days to travel about 90 miles (140 kilometers) from New York City to Philadelphia, longer than it now takes to fly around the world. There were only 11 states in the Union when Washington became President and 16 when he left office.

Important dates in Washington's life

1732 (Feb. 22) Born in Westmoreland County, Virginia.
1749 Became official surveyor for Culpeper County, Virginia.
1751 Went to Barbados Island, British West Indies.
1753 Carried British ultimatum to French in Ohio River Valley, as a major.
1754 Surrendered Fort Necessity in the French and Indian War, as a colonel.
1755 (July 9) With General Edward Braddock when ambushed by French and Indians.
1755-1758 Commanded Virginia's frontier troops, as a colonel.
1759 (Jan. 6) Married Mrs. Martha Dandridge Custis.
1774 Elected delegate to First Continental Congress.
1775 Elected delegate to Second Continental Congress.
1775 (June 15) Elected commander in chief of Continental Army.
1781 (Oct. 19) Victory at Yorktown.
1787 (May 25) Elected president of the Constitutional Convention.
1789 Elected first President of the United States.
1792 Reelected President of the United States.
1796 (Sept. 19) Published *Farewell Address,* refusing a third term.
1798 (July 4) Commissioned lieutenant general and commander in chief of new United States Army.
1799 (Dec. 14) Died at Mount Vernon at age 67.

WORLD: *Political*

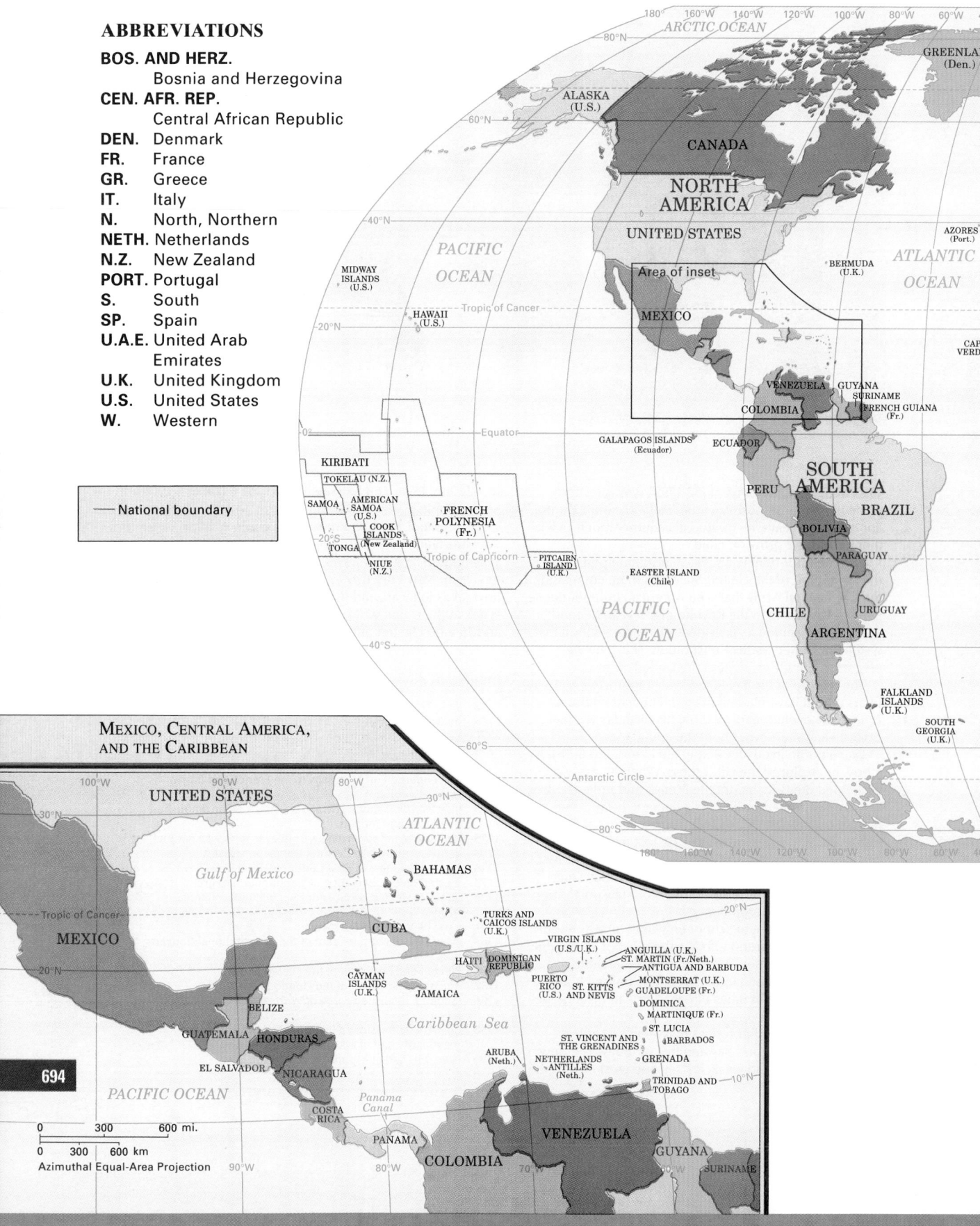

ABBREVIATIONS

BOS. AND HERZ. Bosnia and Herzegovina
CEN. AFR. REP. Central African Republic
DEN. Denmark
FR. France
GR. Greece
IT. Italy
N. North, Northern
NETH. Netherlands
N.Z. New Zealand
PORT. Portugal
S. South
SP. Spain
U.A.E. United Arab Emirates
U.K. United Kingdom
U.S. United States
W. Western

— National boundary

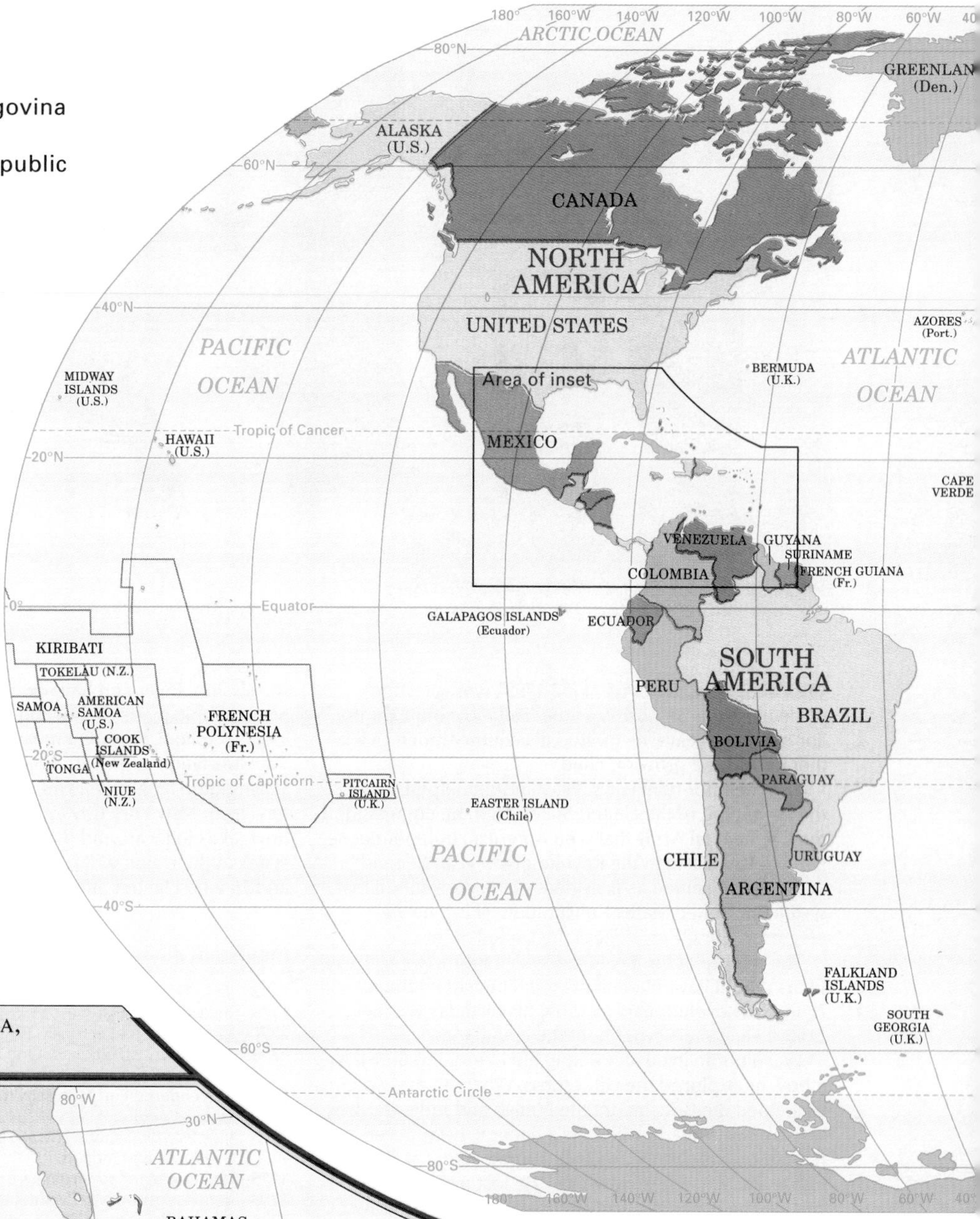

MEXICO, CENTRAL AMERICA, AND THE CARIBBEAN

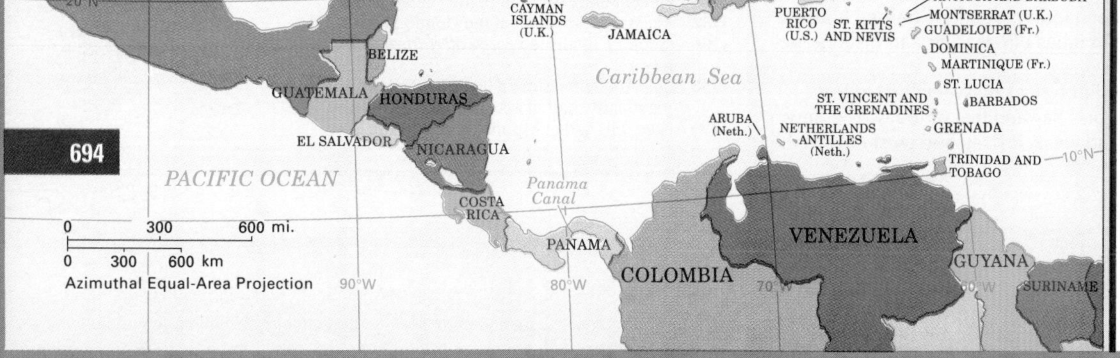

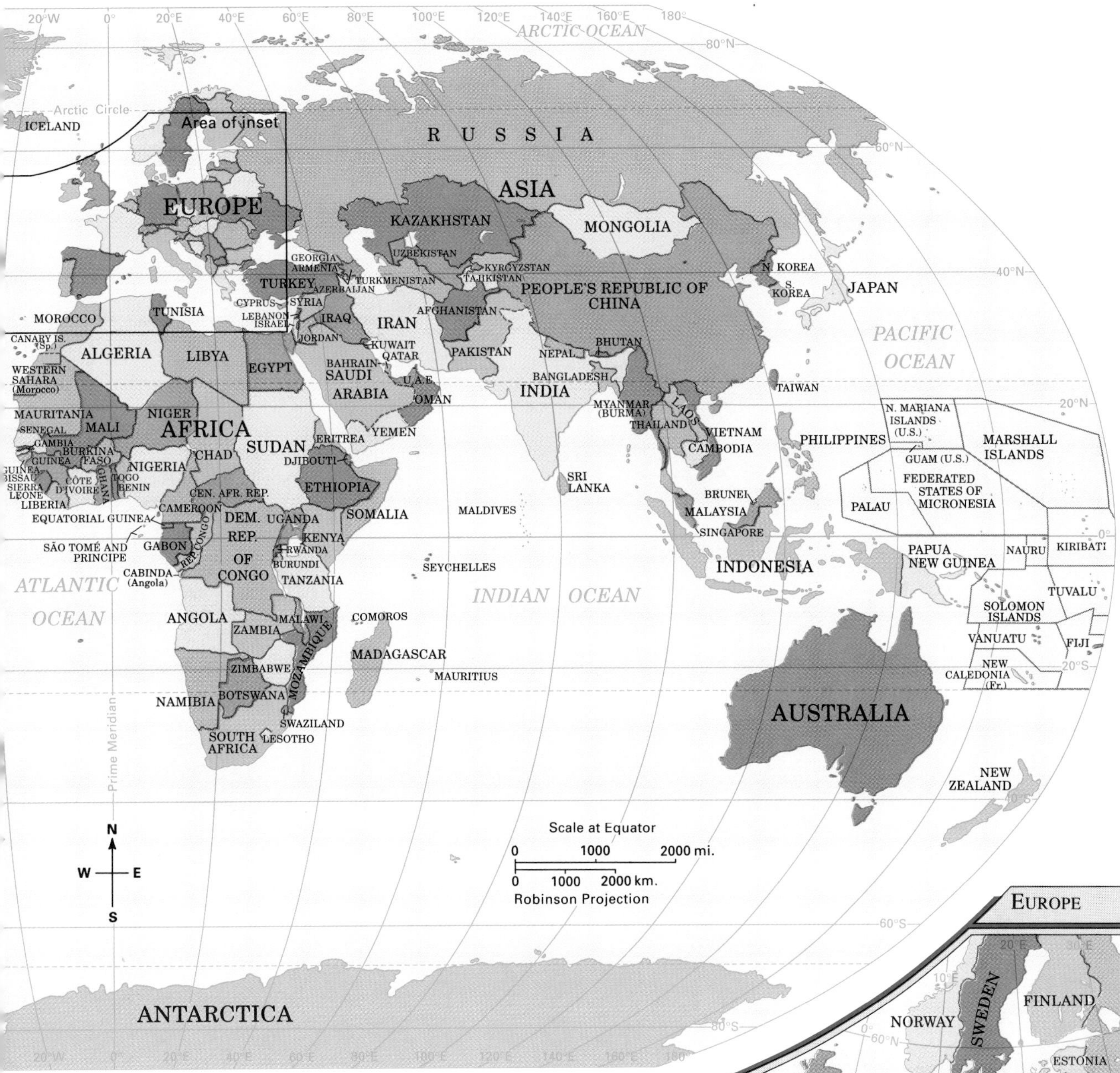
ARCTIC OCEAN
Arctic Circle
ICELAND
Area of inset
RUSSIA
EUROPE
ASIA
KAZAKHSTAN
MONGOLIA
UZBEKISTAN
KYRGYZSTAN
TAJIKISTAN
GEORGIA
ARMENIA
AZERBAIJAN
TURKMENISTAN
TURKEY
PEOPLE'S REPUBLIC OF CHINA
N. KOREA
S. KOREA
JAPAN
MOROCCO
TUNISIA
CYPRUS
SYRIA
LEBANON
ISRAEL
IRAQ
IRAN
AFGHANISTAN
JORDAN
KUWAIT
QATAR
BAHRAIN
SAUDI ARABIA
U.A.E.
OMAN
YEMEN
PAKISTAN
NEPAL
BHUTAN
BANGLADESH
INDIA
MYANMAR (BURMA)
LAOS
THAILAND
VIETNAM
CAMBODIA
TAIWAN
PHILIPPINES
PACIFIC OCEAN
N. MARIANA ISLANDS (U.S.)
GUAM (U.S.)
MARSHALL ISLANDS
FEDERATED STATES OF MICRONESIA
PALAU
CANARY IS. (Sp.)
ALGERIA
LIBYA
EGYPT
WESTERN SAHARA (Morocco)
MAURITANIA
MALI
NIGER
AFRICA
CHAD
SUDAN
ERITREA
DJIBOUTI
SENEGAL
GAMBIA
BURKINA FASO
GUINEA
GUINEA-BISSAU
SIERRA LEONE
LIBERIA
CÔTE D'IVOIRE
GHANA
TOGO
BENIN
NIGERIA
CEN. AFR. REP.
ETHIOPIA
SOMALIA
CAMEROON
EQUATORIAL GUINEA
SÃO TOMÉ AND PRINCIPE
GABON
REP. CONGO
DEM. REP. OF CONGO
UGANDA
KENYA
RWANDA
BURUNDI
TANZANIA
CABINDA (Angola)
SRI LANKA
MALDIVES
BRUNEI
MALAYSIA
SINGAPORE
INDONESIA
PAPUA NEW GUINEA
NAURU
KIRIBATI
SEYCHELLES
ATLANTIC OCEAN
INDIAN OCEAN
TUVALU
SOLOMON ISLANDS
ANGOLA
ZAMBIA
MALAWI
MOZAMBIQUE
COMOROS
VANUATU
FIJI
ZIMBABWE
MADAGASCAR
MAURITIUS
NEW CALEDONIA (Fr.)
NAMIBIA
BOTSWANA
SWAZILAND
AUSTRALIA
SOUTH AFRICA
LESOTHO
Prime Meridian
NEW ZEALAND
N
W
E
S
Scale at Equator
0 1000 2000 mi.
0 1000 2000 km.
Robinson Projection
ANTARCTICA

EUROPE

NORWAY
SWEDEN
FINLAND
RUSSIA
ESTONIA
North Sea
Baltic Sea
LATVIA
DENMARK
IRELAND
UNITED KINGDOM
LITHUANIA
(Russia)
BELARUS
0 300 600 mi.
0 300 600 km
Azimuthal Equal-Area Projection
NETHERLANDS
POLAND
BELGIUM
GERMANY
UKRAINE
LUXEMBOURG
CZECH REPUBLIC
SLOVAK REPUBLIC
FRANCE
LIECHTENSTEIN
AUSTRIA
MOLDOVA
ATLANTIC OCEAN
SWITZERLAND
HUNGARY
SLOVENIA
CROATIA
ROMANIA
BOS. AND HERZ.
YUGOSLAVIA
Black Sea
MONACO
SAN MARINO
ANDORRA
BULGARIA
PORTUGAL
SPAIN
CORSICA (Fr.)
ITALY
F.Y.R. MACE.
VATICAN CITY
ALBANIA
BALEARIC IS. (Sp.)
SARDINIA (It.)
TURKEY
GREECE
Mediterranean Sea
Adriatic Sea
GIBRALTAR (U.K.)
SICILY (It.)
MOROCCO
ALGERIA
MALTA
CRETE (Gr.)

WORLD: *Physical*

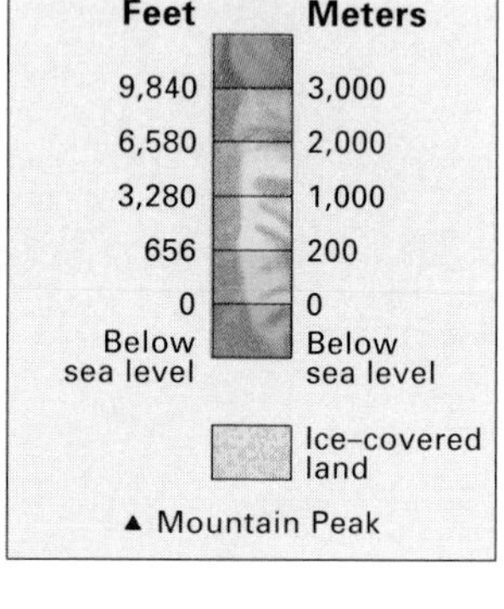

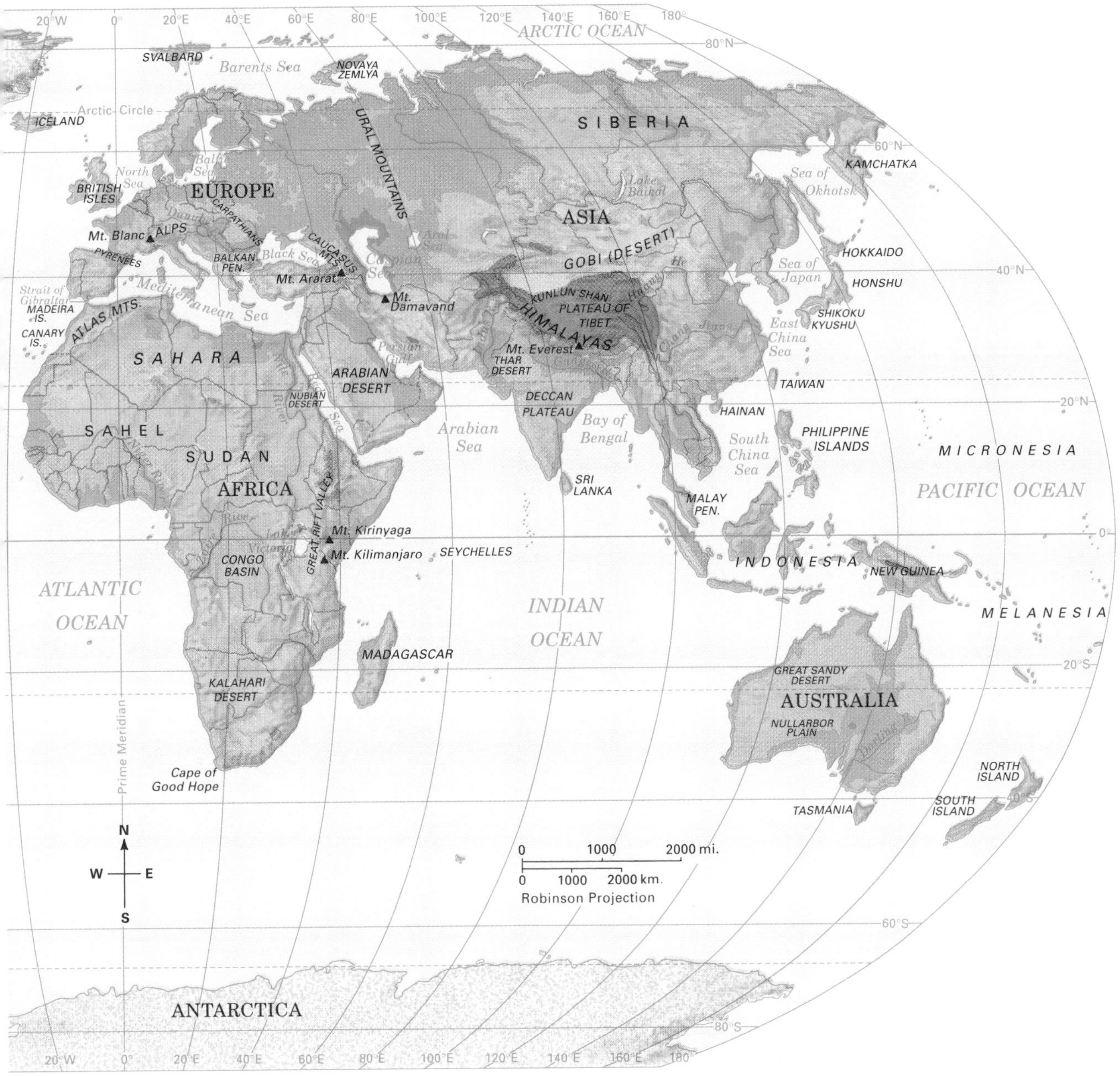
ARCTIC OCEAN
SVALBARD
Barents Sea
NOVAYA ZEMLYA
ICELAND
Arctic Circle
SIBERIA
URAL MOUNTAINS
KAMCHATKA
Sea of Okhotsk
Lake Baikal
North Sea
Baltic Sea
BRITISH ISLES
EUROPE
CARPATHIANS
Danube
Mt. Blanc
ALPS
PYRENEES
Aral Sea
ASIA
GOBI (DESERT)
HOKKAIDO
BALKAN PEN.
Black Sea
CAUCASUS MTS.
Caspian Sea
Mt. Ararat
Sea of Japan
HONSHU
Strait of Gibraltar
MADEIRA IS.
Mediterranean Sea
Mt. Damavand
KUNLUN SHAN
PLATEAU OF TIBET
HIMALAYAS
Huang He
Chang Jiang
SHIKOKU
KYUSHU
CANARY IS.
ATLAS MTS.
SAHARA
Nile River
Persian Gulf
Mt. Everest
THAR DESERT
Ganges
East China Sea
TAIWAN
ARABIAN DESERT
NUBIAN DESERT
Red Sea
DECCAN PLATEAU
HAINAN
SAHEL
Arabian Sea
Bay of Bengal
South China Sea
PHILIPPINE ISLANDS
MICRONESIA
SUDAN
Niger River
AFRICA
SRI LANKA
PACIFIC OCEAN
GREAT RIFT VALLEY
MALAY PEN.
Congo River
Mt. Kirinyaga
Lake Victoria
CONGO BASIN
Mt. Kilimanjaro
SEYCHELLES
INDONESIA
NEW GUINEA
ATLANTIC OCEAN
INDIAN OCEAN
MELANESIA
MADAGASCAR
GREAT SANDY DESERT
AUSTRALIA
KALAHARI DESERT
NULLARBOR PLAIN
Darling R.
Prime Meridian
Cape of Good Hope
NORTH ISLAND
SOUTH ISLAND
TASMANIA
N
W
E
S
0 1000 2000 mi.
0 1000 2000 km.
Robinson Projection
ANTARCTICA
20°W
0°
20°E
40°E
60°E
80°E
100°E
120°E
140°E
160°E
180°
80°N
60°N
40°N
20°N
0°
20°S
40°S
60°S
80°S

UNITED STATES: *Political*

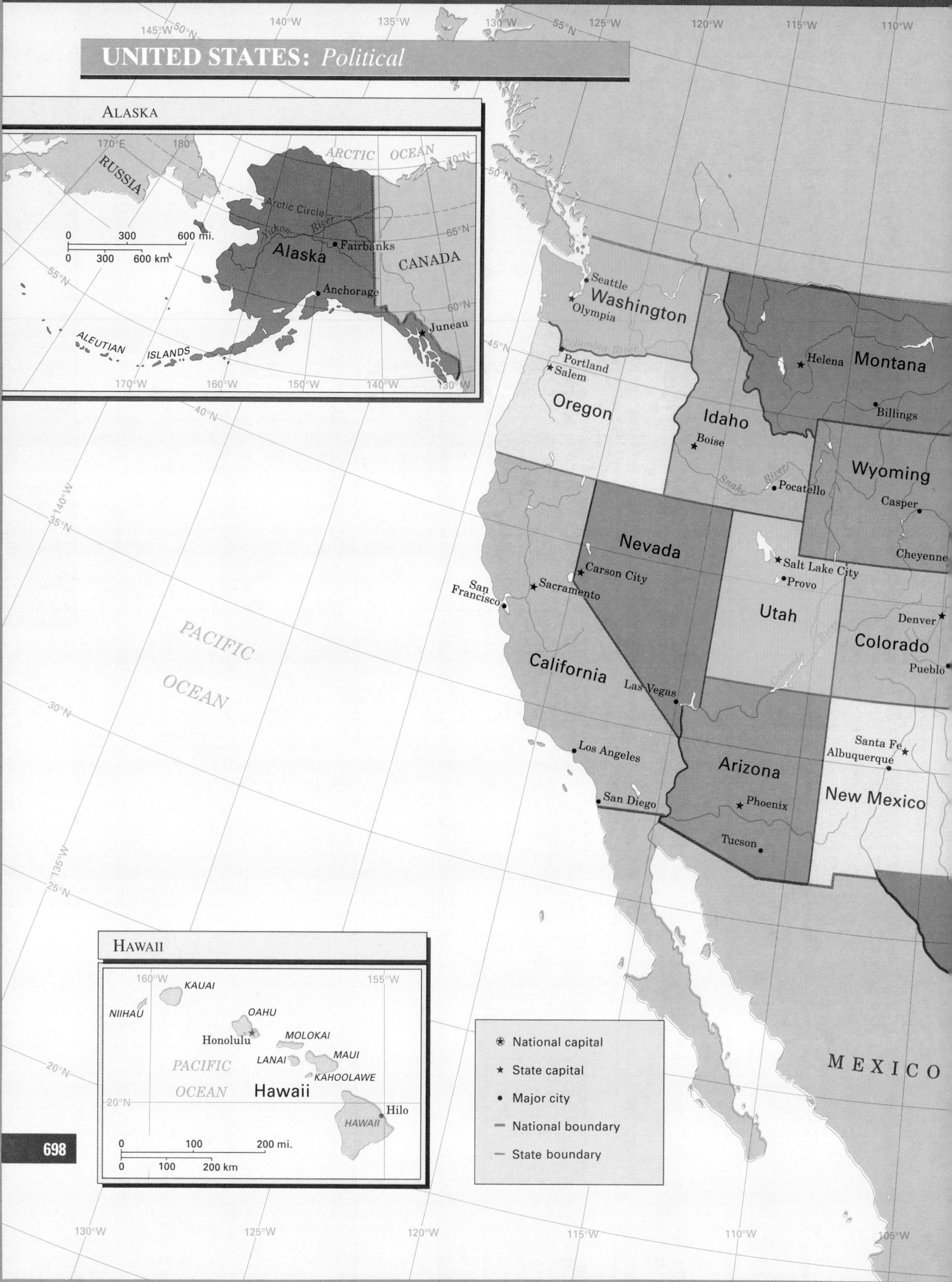

ALASKA
RUSSIA
ARCTIC OCEAN
Arctic Circle
Yukon River
Alaska
Fairbanks
Anchorage
Juneau
CANADA
ALEUTIAN ISLANDS
0 300 600 mi.
0 300 600 km
Seattle
Olympia
Washington
Columbia River
Portland
Salem
Oregon
Idaho
Boise
Snake River
Pocatello
Montana
Helena
Billings
Wyoming
Casper
Cheyenne
Nevada
Carson City
Sacramento
San Francisco
California
Las Vegas
Los Angeles
San Diego
Utah
Salt Lake City
Provo
Colorado River
Colorado
Denver
Pueblo
Arizona
Phoenix
Tucson
New Mexico
Santa Fe
Albuquerque
PACIFIC OCEAN
MEXICO
HAWAII
KAUAI
NIIHAU
OAHU
Honolulu
MOLOKAI
LANAI
MAUI
KAHOOLAWE
HAWAII
Hawaii
Hilo
PACIFIC OCEAN
0 100 200 mi.
0 100 200 km
National capital
State capital
Major city
National boundary
State boundary

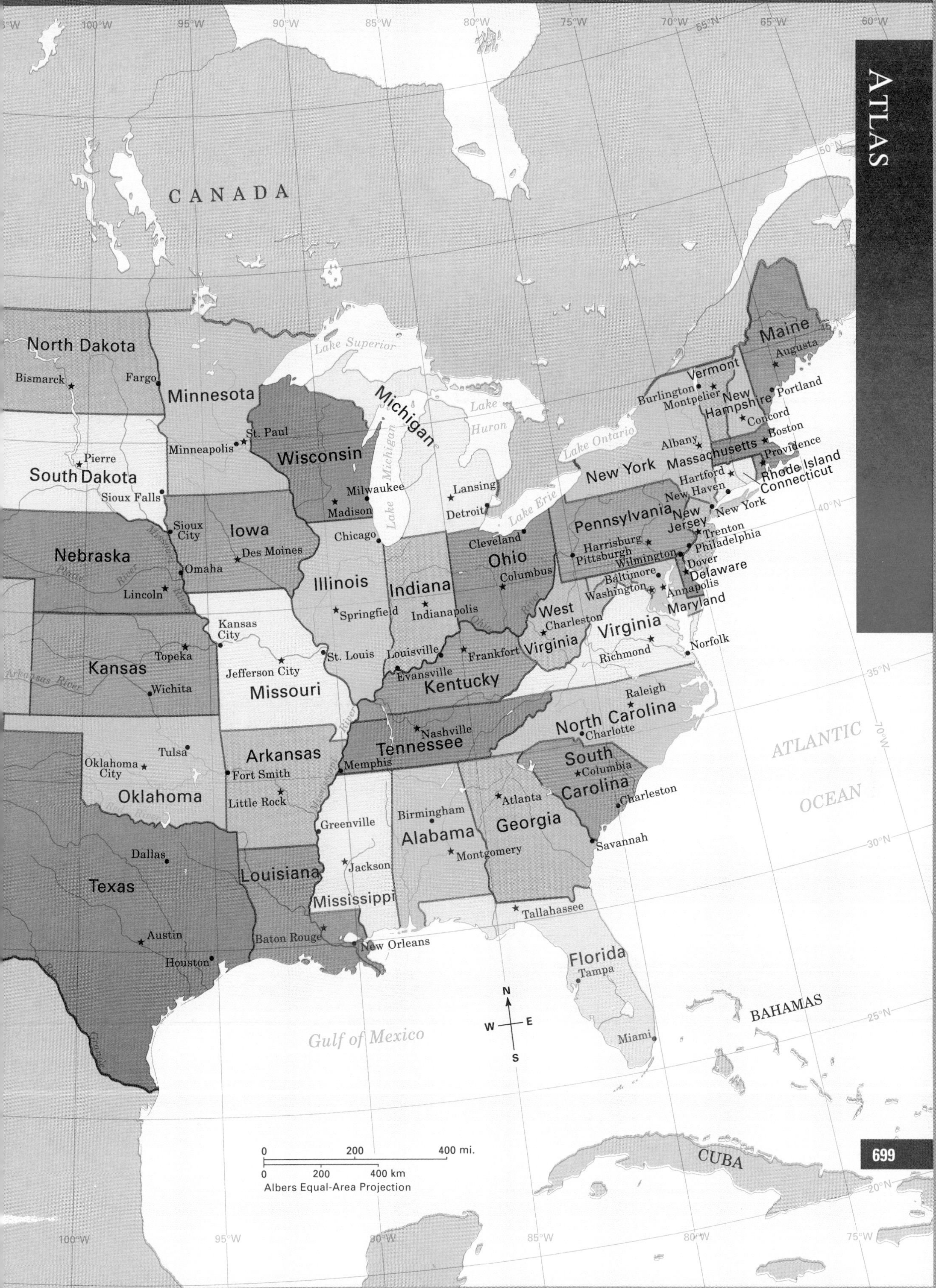
CANADA
North Dakota
Bismarck
Fargo
Minnesota
St. Paul
Minneapolis
South Dakota
Pierre
Sioux Falls
Wisconsin
Milwaukee
Madison
Michigan
Lansing
Detroit
Lake Superior
Lake Michigan
Lake Huron
Lake Ontario
Lake Erie
Iowa
Sioux City
Des Moines
Nebraska
Omaha
Lincoln
Platte River
Missouri River
Illinois
Chicago
Springfield
Indiana
Indianapolis
Ohio
Cleveland
Columbus
Ohio River
Kansas
Topeka
Wichita
Arkansas River
Kansas City
Jefferson City
Missouri
St. Louis
Louisville
Evansville
Frankfort
Kentucky
West Virginia
Charleston
Virginia
Richmond
Norfolk
Maryland
Baltimore
Washington
Annapolis
Delaware
Dover
Wilmington
Pennsylvania
Harrisburg
Pittsburgh
Philadelphia
New Jersey
Trenton
New York
Albany
New York
New Haven
Hartford
Connecticut
Rhode Island
Providence
Massachusetts
Boston
New Hampshire
Concord
Vermont
Montpelier
Burlington
Maine
Augusta
Portland
North Carolina
Raleigh
Charlotte
South Carolina
Columbia
Charleston
Tennessee
Nashville
Memphis
Oklahoma
Oklahoma City
Tulsa
Red River
Arkansas
Fort Smith
Little Rock
Mississippi River
Mississippi
Greenville
Jackson
Alabama
Birmingham
Montgomery
Georgia
Atlanta
Savannah
Texas
Dallas
Austin
Houston
Rio Grande
Louisiana
Baton Rouge
New Orleans
Florida
Tallahassee
Tampa
Miami
Gulf of Mexico
ATLANTIC OCEAN
BAHAMAS
CUBA
N
S
E
W
0 200 400 mi.
0 200 400 km
Albers Equal-Area Projection
100°W
95°W
90°W
85°W
80°W
75°W
70°W
65°W
60°W
55°N
50°N
40°N
35°N
30°N
25°N
20°N

UNITED STATES: *Physical*

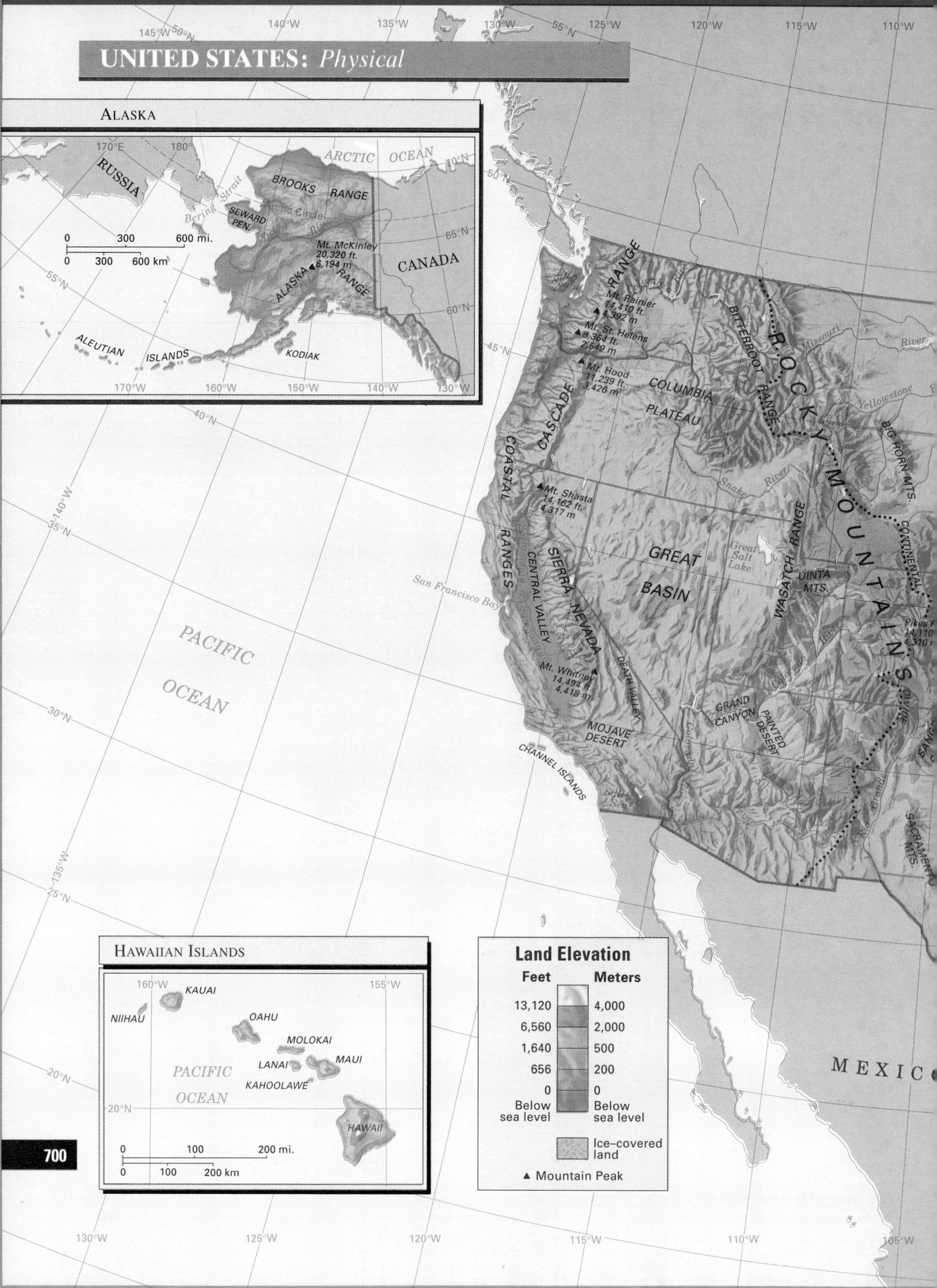
ALASKA
ARCTIC OCEAN
RUSSIA
BROOKS RANGE
Bering Strait
SEWARD PEN.
Arctic Circle
Mt. McKinley
20,320 ft.
6,194 m
ALASKA RANGE
CANADA
ALEUTIAN ISLANDS
KODIAK
0 300 600 mi.
0 300 600 km
HAWAIIAN ISLANDS
KAUAI
NIIHAU
OAHU
MOLOKAI
LANAI
MAUI
KAHOOLAWE
HAWAII
PACIFIC OCEAN
0 100 200 mi.
0 100 200 km
PACIFIC OCEAN
Mt. Rainier
14,410 ft.
4,392 m
Mt. St. Helens
8,364 ft.
2,549 m
Mt. Hood
11,239 ft.
3,426 m
Mt. Shasta
14,162 ft.
4,317 m
Mt. Whitney
14,494 ft.
4,418 m
CASCADE RANGE
COASTAL RANGES
COLUMBIA PLATEAU
BITTERROOT RANGE
ROCKY MOUNTAINS
BIG HORN MTS.
CONTINENTAL DIVIDE
GREAT BASIN
Great Salt Lake
WASATCH RANGE
UINTA MTS.
SIERRA NEVADA
CENTRAL VALLEY
San Francisco Bay
DEATH VALLEY
GRAND CANYON
PAINTED DESERT
MOJAVE DESERT
CHANNEL ISLANDS
Snake River
Missouri River
Yellowstone
SACRAMENTO MTS.
MEXICO
Land Elevation
Feet
Meters
13,120 4,000
6,560 2,000
1,640 500
656 200
0 0
Below sea level
Below sea level
Ice-covered land
▲ Mountain Peak

CANADA
Lake of the Woods
MESABI RANGE
Lake Superior
Lake Huron
Lake Michigan
Lake Ontario
Lake Erie
St. Lawrence River
WHITE MTS.
Mt. Washington 6,288 ft. 1,917 m
ADIRONDACK MTS.
CATSKILL MTS.
NANTUCKET
MARTHA'S VINEYARD
LONG ISLAND
GREAT PLAINS
BLACK HILLS
BADLANDS
SAND HILLS
Platte River
Missouri River
Des Moines River
Mississippi River
Red River
Susquehanna River
Arkansas River
CENTRAL PLAINS
OZARK PLATEAU
ALLEGHENY PLATEAU
APPALACHIAN MOUNTAINS
BLUE RIDGE MTS.
Mt. Mitchell 6,684 ft. 2,037 m
CUMBERLAND PLATEAU
FALL LINE
ATLANTIC COASTAL PLAIN
Delaware Bay
Chesapeake Bay
ATLANTIC OCEAN
OUACHITA MOUNTAINS
LLANO ESTACADO
EDWARDS PLATEAU
Colorado
GULF COASTAL PLAIN
Galveston Bay
Mobile Bay
Pensacola Bay
Tampa Bay
Lake Okeechobee
Gulf of Mexico
EVERGLADES
FLORIDA KEYS
BAHAMAS
CUBA
N
E
S
W
0 200 400 mi.
0 200 400 km
Albers Equal-Area Projection
100°W
95°W
90°W
85°W
80°W
75°W
70°W
65°W
60°W
55°N
50°N
40°N
35°N
30°N
25°N
20°N

NORTH AMERICA: *Political*

ASIA
EUROPE
ARCTIC OCEAN
Bering Sea
Bering Strait
Beaufort Sea
QUEEN ELIZABETH ISLANDS
ELLESMERE ISLAND
GREENLAND (Denmark)
BANKS ISLAND
VICTORIA ISLAND
BAFFIN ISLAND
Baffin Bay
Arctic Circle
Yukon River
Anchorage
KODIAK ISLAND
Gulf of Alaska
Mackenzie River
Labrador Sea
ALEXANDER ARCHIPELAGO
QUEEN CHARLOTTE ISLANDS
Peace River
Hudson Bay
VANCOUVER ISLAND
Edmonton
CANADA
NEWFOUNDLAND
Vancouver
Puget Sound
Seattle
Calgary
Columbia R.
PRINCE EDWARD ISLAND
CAPE BRETON ISLAND
Winnipeg
Portland
Quebec
St. Lawrence River
L. Superior
Montreal
Ottawa
Snake R.
Minneapolis
St. Paul
L. Michigan
L. Huron
L. Ontario
Toronto
Boston
Great Salt Lake
Missouri River
Milwaukee
Lake Erie
New York
ATLANTIC OCEAN
San Francisco
Sacramento
Oakland
San Jose
Salt Lake City
Omaha
Chicago
Detroit
Cleveland
Philadelphia
Platte R.
Denver
Columbus
Baltimore
Washington
Indianapolis
Kansas City
St. Louis
Ohio River
Louisville
Richmond
Norfolk
Colorado River
Wichita
Los Angeles
UNITED STATES
BERMUDA (U.K.)
San Diego
Nashville
Oklahoma City
Memphis
Phoenix
Atlanta
Red River
Birmingham
PACIFIC OCEAN
Fort Worth
Dallas
Mississippi River
Rio Grande
Ciudad Juárez
Austin
Mobile
Jacksonville
Tropic of Cancer
Chihuahua
Houston
New Orleans
San Antonio
Tampa
Miami
Nassau
BAHAMAS
Monterrey
Gulf of Mexico
MEXICO
Havana
CUBA
San Luis Potosí
Tampico
DOMINICAN REPUBLIC
San Juan
VIRGIN ISLANDS (U.S., U.K.)
ANGUILLA (U.K.)
ANTIGUA AND BARBUDA
Guadalajara
Santiago de Cuba
Port-au-Prince
HAITI
PUERTO RICO (U.S.)
ST. KITTS-NEVIS
GUADELOUPE (Fr.)
CAYMAN ISLANDS (U.K.)
JAMAICA
Kingston
Santo Domingo
DOMINICA
MARTINIQUE (Fr.)
ST. LUCIA
BARBADOS
Mexico City
Cuernavaca
Veracruz
Puebla
Belmopan
BELIZE
ST. VINCENT AND THE GRENADINES
GRENADA
TRINIDAD AND TOBAGO
Acapulco
Caribbean Sea
NETHERLANDS ANTILLES (Neth.)
ARUBA (Neth.)
GUATEMALA
HONDURAS
Tegucigalpa
Guatemala City
San Salvador
EL SALVADOR
NICARAGUA
Managua
San José
COSTA RICA
Panama City
PANAMA
SOUTH AMERICA
N
W
E
S
National capital
Major city
National boundary
0
400
800 mi.
0
400
800 km
Azimuthal Equal-Area Projection
Equator
170°E
180°
170°W
160°W
150°W
140°W
130°W
120°W
110°W
100°W
90°W
80°W
70°W
60°W
30°W
0°
70°N
80°N
60°N
50°N
40°N
30°N
20°N
10°N

NORTH AMERICA: *Physical*

ARCTIC OCEAN
ASIA
EUROPE
Bering Sea
Bering Strait
Beaufort Sea
QUEEN ELIZABETH ISLANDS
ELLESMERE ISLAND
GREENLAND
BANKS ISLAND
VICTORIA ISLAND
Baffin Bay
BAFFIN ISLAND
Davis Strait
BROOKS RANGE
Yukon River
Redoubt Volcano
ALASKA RANGE
Mt. McKinley
ALASKA PEN.
KODIAK ISLAND
Gulf of Alaska
Great Bear Lake
Mackenzie River
Foxe Basin
Hudson Strait
Labrador Sea
ALEXANDER ARCHIPELAGO
COAST MOUNTAINS
Great Slave Lake
LAURENTIAN SHIELD
UNGAVA PENINSULA
Hudson Bay
LABRADOR
QUEEN CHARLOTTE ISLANDS
Peace River
ROCKY MOUNTAINS
NEWFOUNDLAND
VANCOUVER ISLAND
Puget Sound
Mt. Rainier
Lake Winnipeg
GREAT PLAINS
Gulf of St. Lawrence
CAPE BRETON ISLAND
L. Superior
COLUMBIA PLATEAU
BLACK HILLS
Lake Huron
L. Michigan
Bay of Fundy
Niagara Falls
APPALACHIAN MTS.
Cape Cod
SIERRA NEVADA
COAST
GREAT BASIN
Great Salt Lake
Missouri River
Platte R.
L. Erie
CENTRAL PLAINS
Mt. Whitney
DEATH VALLEY
Colorado River
Ohio River
ATLANTIC COASTAL PLAIN
OZARK PLATEAU
Arkansas
Cape Hatteras
BERMUDA
PACIFIC OCEAN
RANGES
MOJAVE DESERT
GRAND CANYON
Red River
Mississippi River
ATLANTIC OCEAN
GULF COASTAL PLAIN
Gulf of California
Cape Canaveral
Tropic of Cancer
BAJA CALIFORNIA
SIERRA MADRE OCCIDENTAL
SIERRA MADRE ORIENTAL
Rio Grande
BAHAMAS
Gulf of Mexico
Straits of Florida
Cabo San Lucas
PLATEAU OF MEXICO
CUBA
LESSER ANTILLES
LEEWARD IS.
HISPANIOLA
PUERTO RICO
GREATER ANTILLES
YUCATÁN PENINSULA
JAMAICA
WINDWARD ISLANDS
Popocatépetl
ISTHMUS OF TEHUANTEPEC
Caribbean Sea
Tajumulco
MOSQUITO COAST
Lago de Nicaragua
Panama Canal
Irazú
ISTHMUS OF PANAMA
SOUTH AMERICA
Equator
Arctic Circle
Land Elevation
Feet
Meters
13,120
4,000
6,560
2,000
1,640
500
656
200
0
0
Below sea level
Below sea level
Ice–covered land
▲ Mountain Peak
N
W
E
S
0
400
800 mi.
0
400
800 km
Azimuthal Equal-Area Projection

UNITED STATES: *Population Density, 1790*

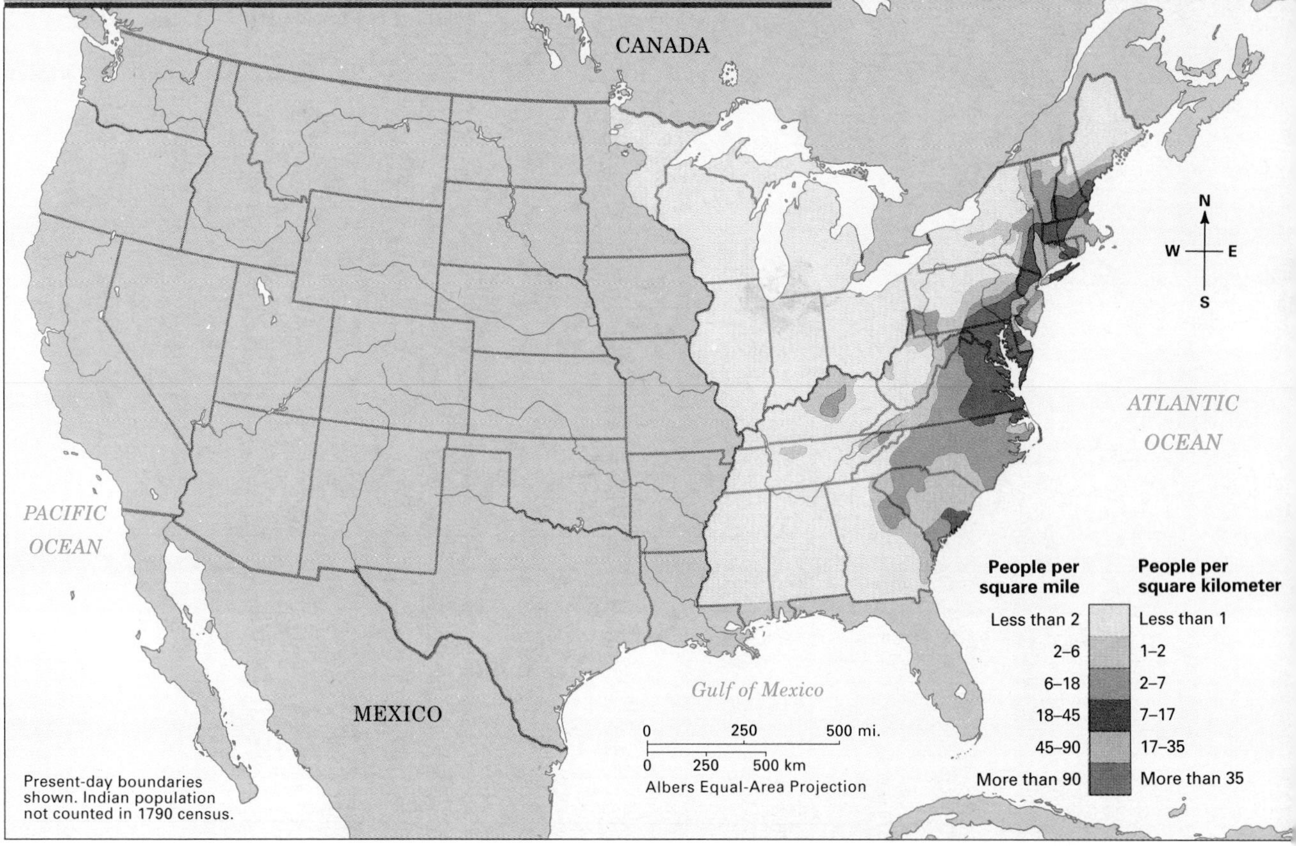

UNITED STATES: *Population Density, 1870*

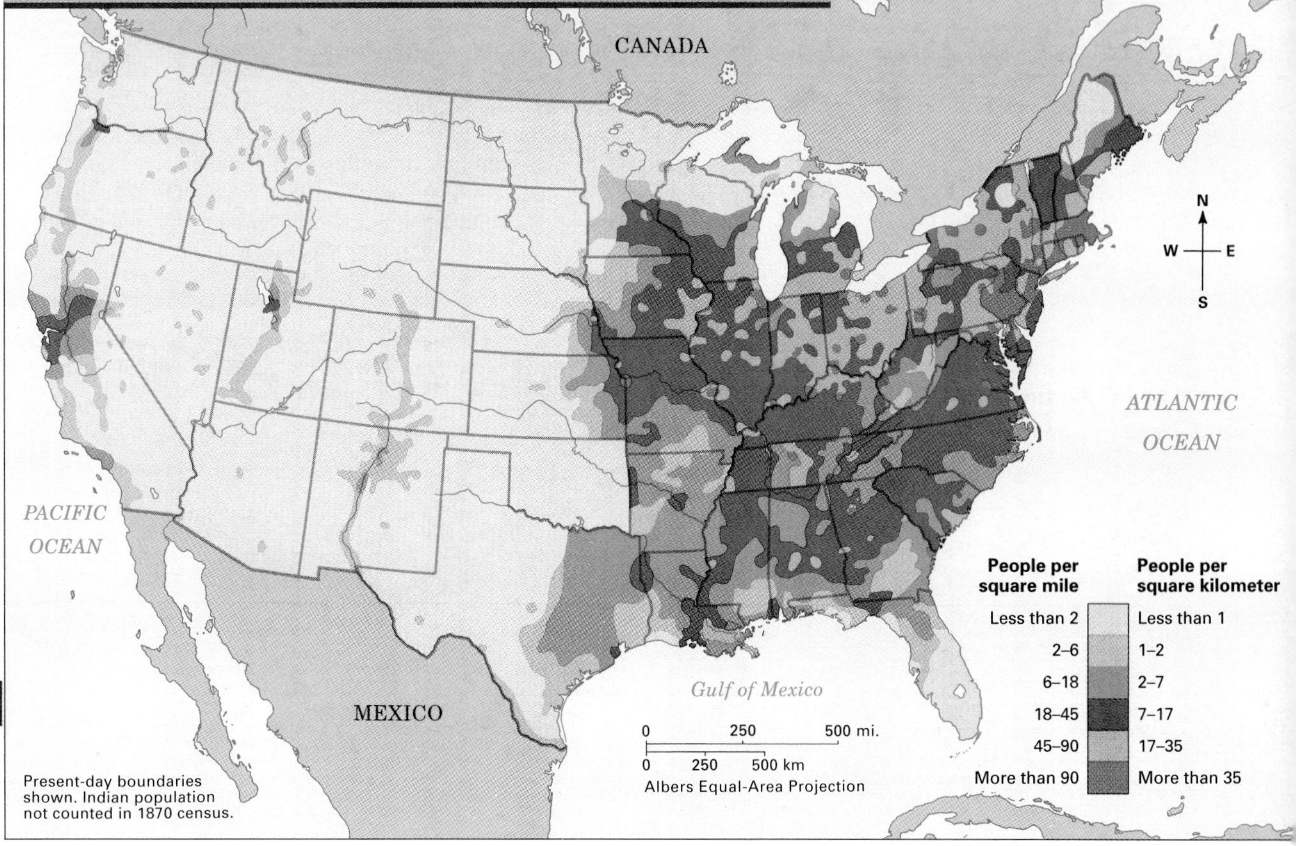

UNITED STATES: *Population Density, 1910*

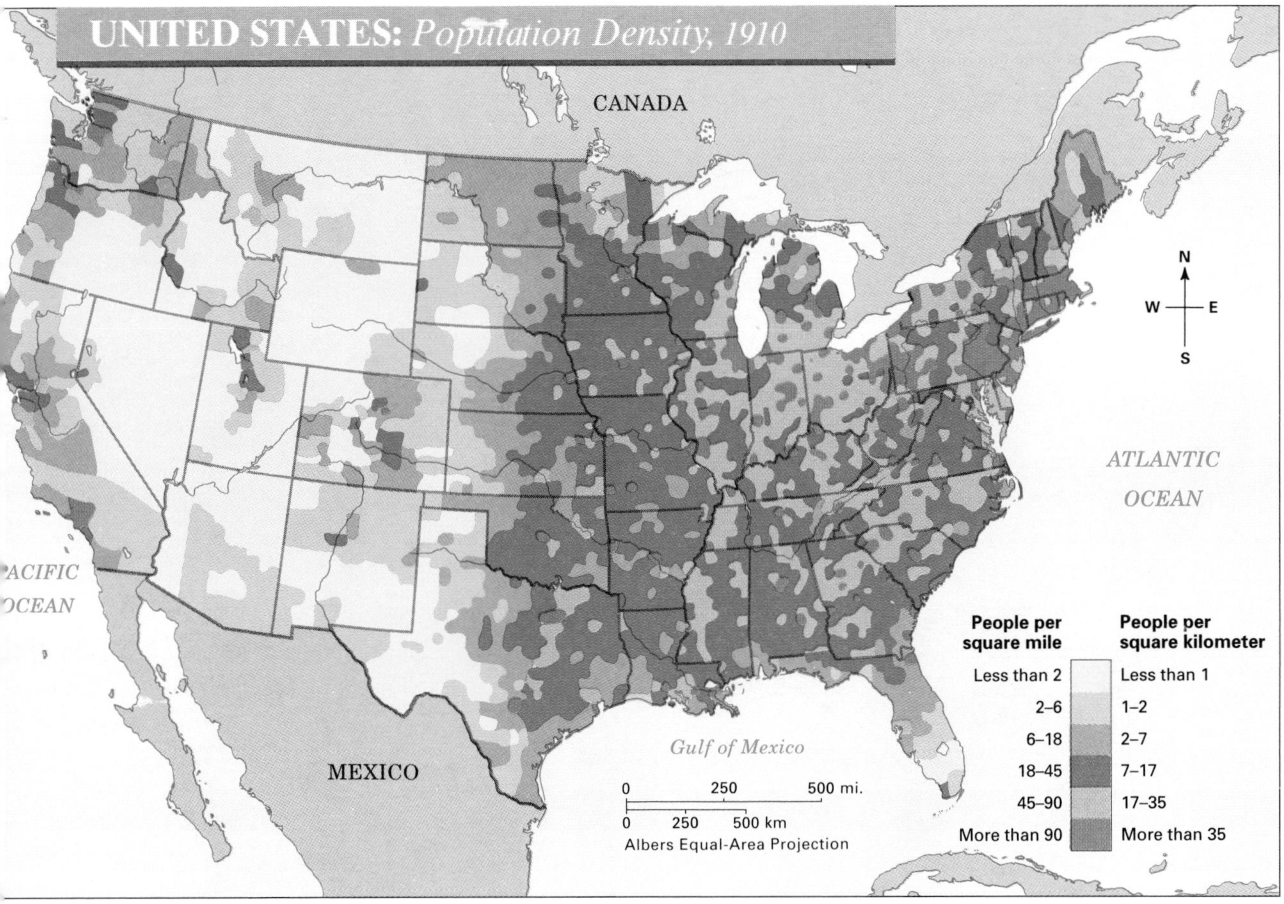

UNITED STATES: *Population Density, 1990*

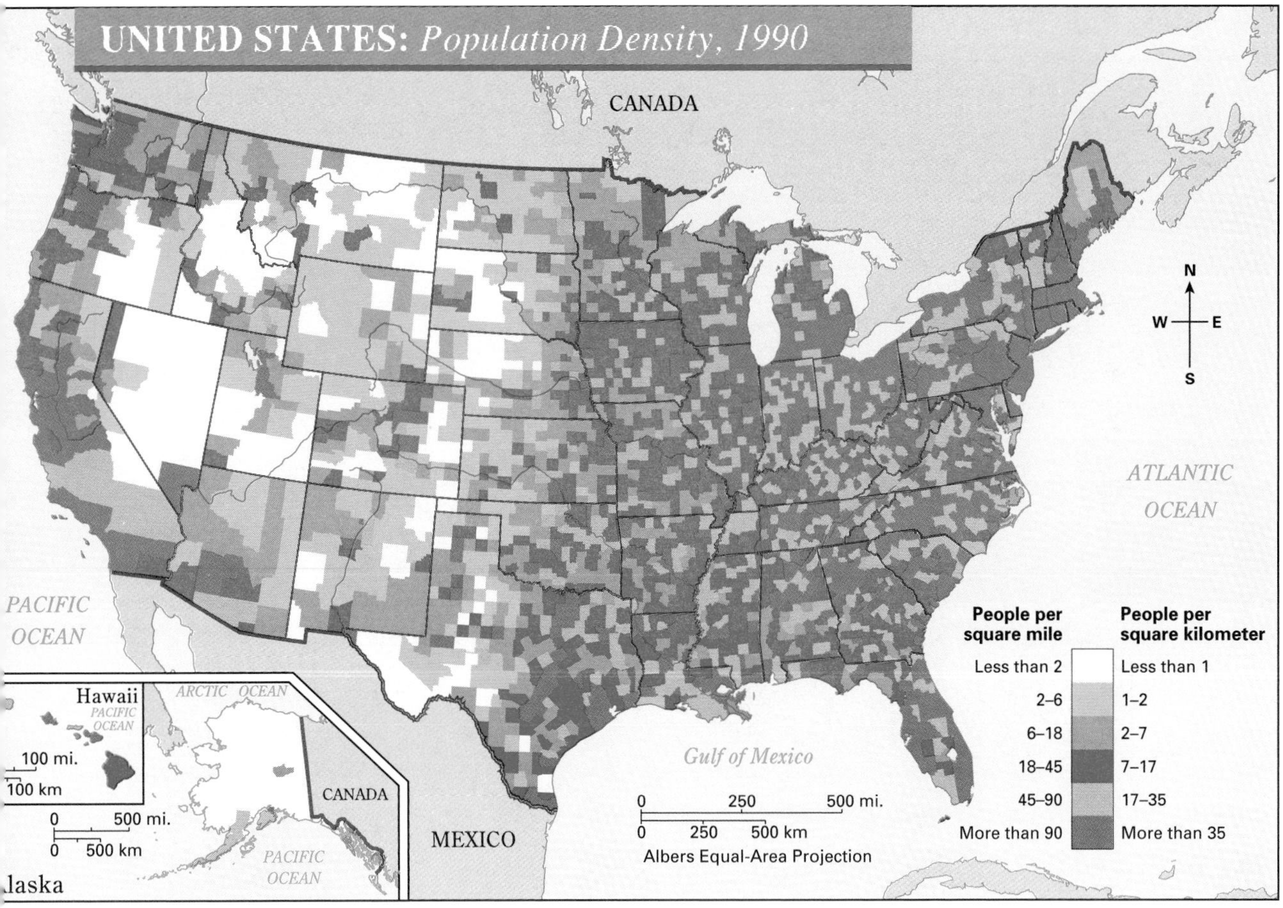

UNITED STATES: *Climate*

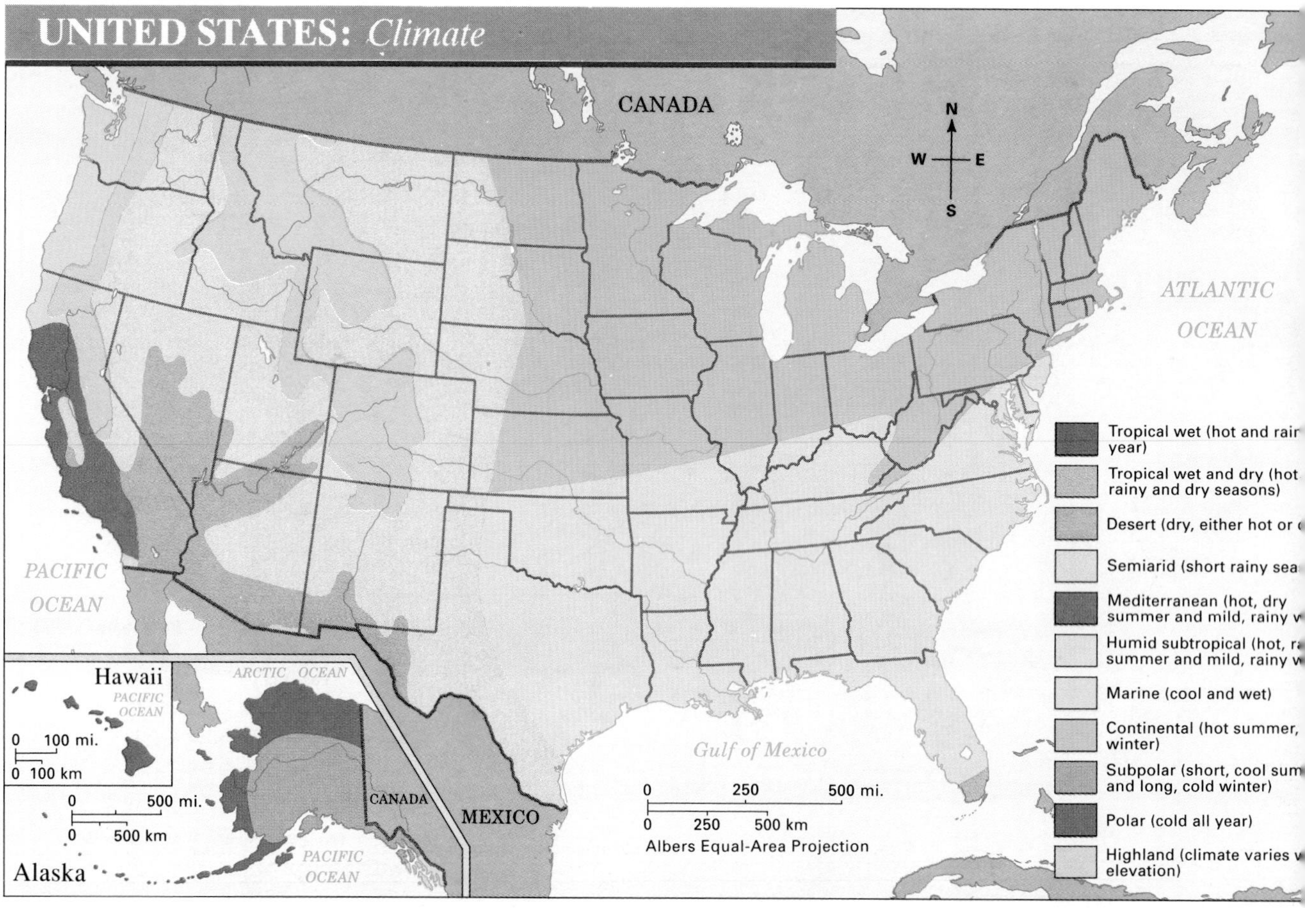

UNITED STATES: *Vegetation*

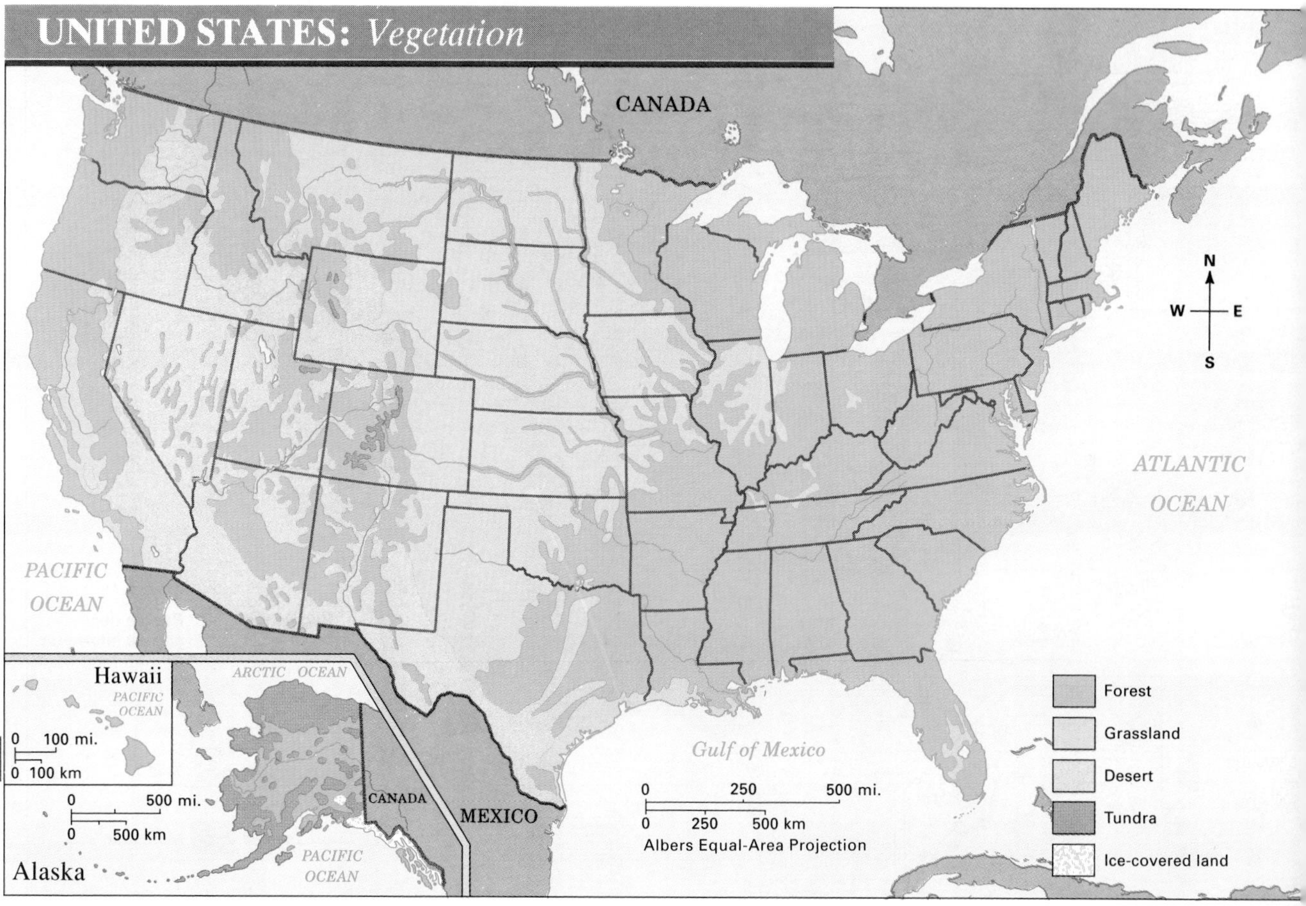

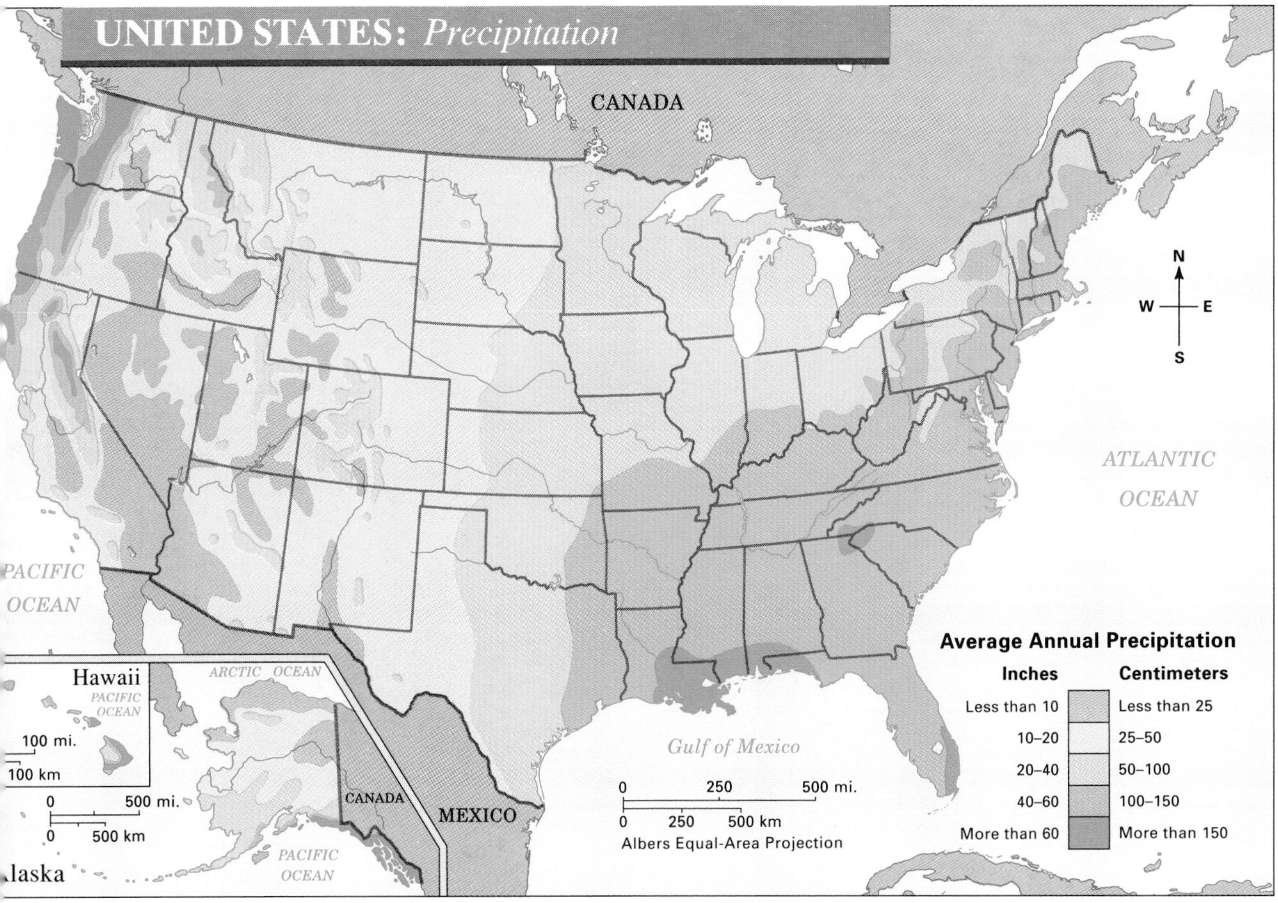
UNITED STATES: Precipitation
CANADA
N
W
E
S
ATLANTIC OCEAN
PACIFIC OCEAN
Hawaii
PACIFIC OCEAN
100 mi.
100 km
ARCTIC OCEAN
CANADA
MEXICO
PACIFIC OCEAN
Alaska
0
500 mi.
0
500 km
Gulf of Mexico
0
250
500 mi.
0
250
500 km
Albers Equal-Area Projection
Average Annual Precipitation
Inches
Centimeters
Less than 10
Less than 25
10–20
25–50
20–40
50–100
40–60
100–150
More than 60
More than 150

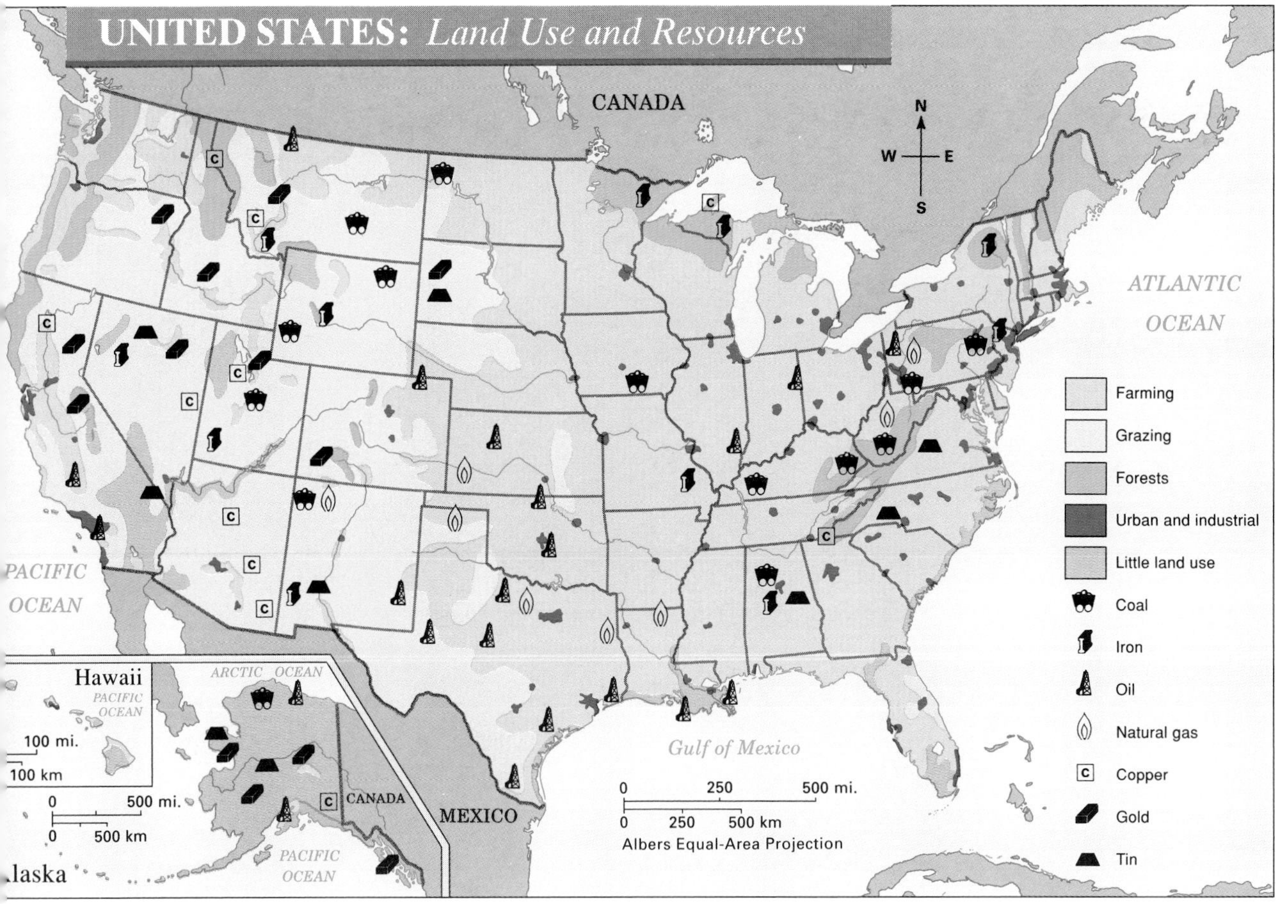
UNITED STATES: Land Use and Resources
CANADA
N
W
E
S
ATLANTIC OCEAN
PACIFIC OCEAN
Hawaii
PACIFIC OCEAN
100 mi.
100 km
ARCTIC OCEAN
CANADA
MEXICO
PACIFIC OCEAN
Alaska
0
500 mi.
0
500 km
Gulf of Mexico
0
250
500 mi.
0
250
500 km
Albers Equal-Area Projection
Farming
Grazing
Forests
Urban and industrial
Little land use
Coal
Iron
Oil
Natural gas
Copper
Gold
Tin

WORLD: *Gross National Product*

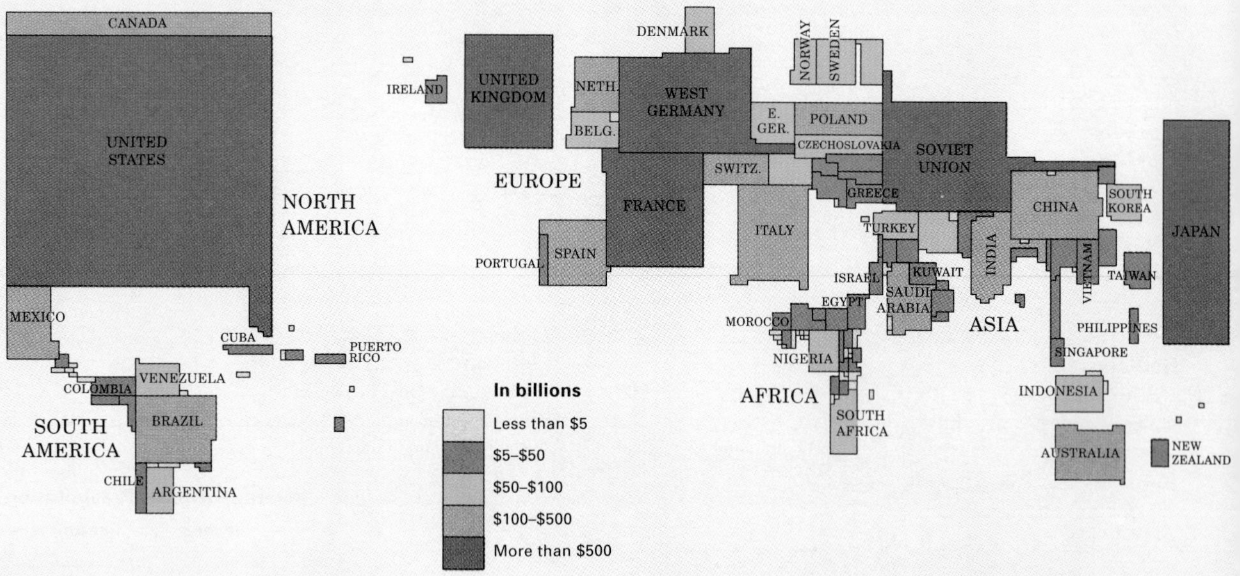

Each country's size in the cartogram represents the size of its GNP (Gross National Product) compared with those of other countries in the world. Based on information in the *1986 Britannica World Data* (1986) and *The World Factbook, 1987.*

UNITED STATES: *Time Zones*

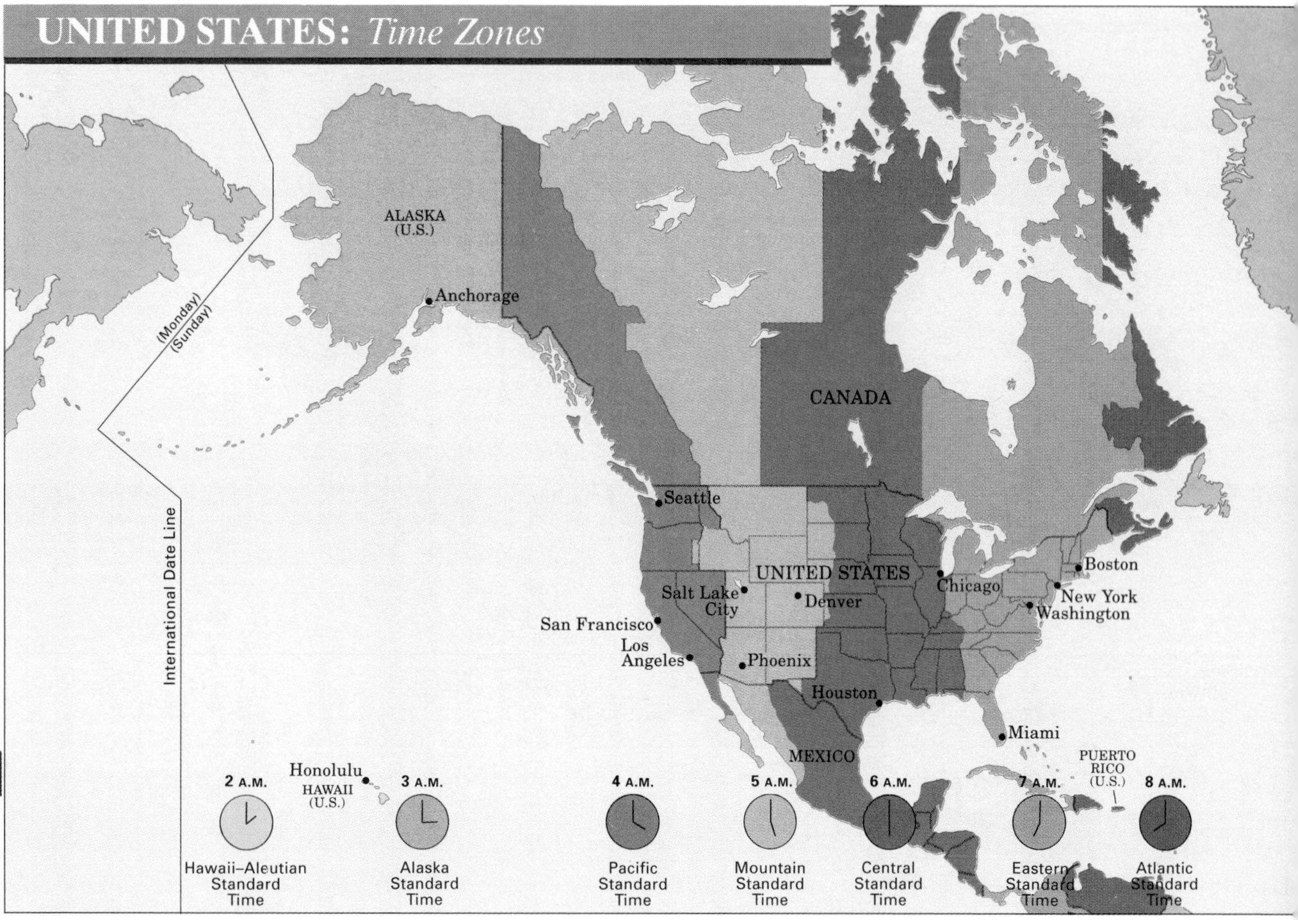

This gazetteer will help you locate many of the places discussed in this book. Latitude and longitude given for large areas of land and water refer to the centermost point of the area; latitude and longitude of rivers refer to the river mouth. The page number tells you where to find each place on a map.

PLACE	LAT.	LONG.	PAGE
A			
Abilene (city in Kansas)	32°N	99°W	**430**
Annapolis (capital of Maryland)	39°N	76°W	**699**
Antietam (civil war battle site in Maryland)	39°N	78°W	**350**
Appalachian Mts. (range in eastern U.S.)	37°N	82°W	**701**
Atlanta (capital of Georgia)	33°N	84°W	**699**
B			
Badlands (dry area of South Dakota)	43°N	102°W	**700**
Baltimore (port city in Maryland)	39°N	76°W	**699**
Baton Rouge (capital of Louisiana)	30°N	91°W	**699**
Bering Strait (joins Pacific and Arctic Oceans)	66°N	168°W	**702**
Boston (capital of Massachusetts)	42°N	71°W	**69**
Buffalo (city in New York)	42°N	78°W	**262**
Bull Run (Civil War battle site in Virginia)	39°N	78°W	**350**
Bunker Hill (Revolutionary War battle site in Massachusetts)	42°N	71°W	**69**
C			
Canada (country in North America)	50°N	100°W	**702**
Cape Horn (southern tip of South America)	56°S	67°W	**696**
Cape of Good Hope (southern tip of Africa)	34°S	18°E	**697**
Caribbean Sea (part of Atlantic Ocean)	14°N	122°W	**694**
Cascade Mts. (range in western U.S.)	42°N	122°W	**700**
Central America (southernmost part of North America)	10°N	87°W	**694**
Charleston (port city in South Carolina)	32°N	79°W	**699**
Chesapeake Bay (waterway bordering Maryland and Virginia)	38°N	76°W	**701**
Chicago (largest city in Illinois)	41°N	87°W	**699**
Chisholm Trail (cattle trail of old Southwest)	35°N	94°W	**430**
Cincinnati (city in Ohio)	39°N	84°W	**262**
Cleveland (city in Ohio)	41°N	81°W	**699**
Colorado R. (in southwestern U.S.)	36°N	112°W	**700**
Columbia R. (in northwestern U.S.)	46°N	123°W	**698**
Concord (Revolutionary War battle site in Massachusetts)	42°N	71°W	**69**
Cuba (island country in Caribbean sea)	22°N	79°W	**536**
Cumberland Gap (pass through Blue Ridge Mts. in Tennessee)	35°N	85°W	**198**
D			
Dallas (city in Texas)	32°N	96°W	**699**
Delaware Bay (inlet between Delaware and New Jersey)	39°N	75°W	**701**
Des Moines (capital of Iowa)	41°N	93°W	**699**
Detroit (largest city in Michigan)	42°N	83°W	**452**
District of Columbia (seat of U.S. government)	38°N	77°W	**699**
Dodge City (city in Kansas)	37°N	100°W	**430**
E			
England (part of United Kingdom)	51°N	1°W	**695**
F			
Fort Sumter (Civil War harbor battle site in South Carolina)	32°N	79°W	**343**
Fort Ticonderoga (Revolutionary War battle site in northern New York)	43°N	73°W	**69**
Fredericksburg (Civil War battle site in Virginia)	38°N	77°W	**350**
G			
Gadsen Purchase (land U.S. purchased from Mexico)	32°N	110°W	**235**
Gatun Lake (Panama)	9°N	79°W	**538**
Gettysburg (Civil War battle site in Pennsylvania)	39°N	77°W	**350**
Grand Canyon (Colorado River gorge in Arizona)	36°N	112°W	**700**
Great Lakes (freshwater lakes between U.S. and Canada)			**701**
Great Plains (farm and range region in central U.S.)	45°N	104°W	**411**
Great Salt Lake (large salty lake in Utah)	41°N	112°W	**700**
Greenland (largest island in the world)	74°N	40°W	**694**

PLACE	LAT.	LONG.	PAGE
Gulf of Mexico (part of Atlantic, south of U.S., east of Mexico)	25°N	93°W	**701**
Gulf of St. Lawrence (inlet in northeast Canada)	48°N	62°W	**703**

H

Harpers Ferry (Civil War battle site in West Virginia)	39°N	77°W	**333**
Havana (capital of Cuba)	23°N	82°W	**536**
Hispaniola (island in West Indies)	17°N	73°W	**55**
Hudson Bay (inland sea in Canada)	64°N	80°W	**55**
Hudson River (north-south waterway in New York)	41°N	73°W	**701**

I

Indian Ocean (Body of water south of India)	0°	70°E	**697**
Ireland (Island country in western Europe)	53°N	8°W	**550**
Isthmus of Panama (land separating Atlantic and Pacific Oceans)	9°N	81°W	**703**
Italy (country in southern Europe)	43°N	11°E	**550**

J

Jamaica (Caribbean island)	17°N	78°W	**55**
Jamestown (first English settlement in Virginia)	37°N	77°W	**21**
Japan (island country in East Asia)	36°N	133°E	**695**
Juneau (capital of Alaska)	58°N	134°W	**698**

K

Kansas City (City in Missouri)	39°N	94°W	**430**

L

Lake Champlain (borders Vermont and New York)	44°N	73°W	**69**
Lake Erie (Great Lake)	42°N	81°W	**699**
Lake Huron (Great Lake)	45°N	82°W	**699**
Lake Michigan (Great Lake)	43°N	87°W	**699**
Lake Ontario (Great Lake)	43°N	79°W	**699**
Lake Superior (Great Lake)	41°N	108°W	**699**
Lancaster (city in Pennsylvania)	40°N	76°W	**198**
Lexington (Revolutionary War battle site in Massachusetts)	42°N	71°W	**69**

PLACE	LAT.	LONG.	PAGE
Los Angeles (largest city in California)	34°N	118°W	**698**
Louisiana Purchase (land U.S. purchased from France)	35°N	92°W	**150**
Louisville (city in Kentucky)	38°N	85°W	**213**

M

Memphis (river port in Tennessee)	35°N	90°W	**452**
Mexican Cession (land ceded by Mexico to U.S.)	37°N	114°W	**235**
Mexico (North American country)	23°N	104°W	**702**
Milwaukee (city in Wisconsin)	43°N	87°W	**452**
Mississippi R. (one of longest rivers in central U.S.)	30°N	90°W	**150**
Missouri R. (tributary of Mississippi River)	40°N	96°W	**701**
Monterey (city in California)	36°N	123°W	**234**
Montgomery (capital of Alabama)	32°N	86°W	**699**
Montreal (largest city in Canada)	45°N	73°W	**702**

N

New Amsterdam (capital of New Netherlands, currently New York state)	41°N	74°W	**21**
New England (northeast section of U.S.)	42°N	71°W	**21**
Newark (city in New Jersey)	40°N	74°W	**262**
Newfoundland (Province of Canada)	48°N	56°W	**463**
New Orleans (port city in Louisiana)	30°N	90°W	**150**
Newport (port city in Rhode Island)	41°N	71°W	**262**
New Spain (North and Central American lands ruled by Spanish)	20°N	100°W	**21**
New York City (port city of New York)	40°N	73°W	**702**

O

Oakland (city in California)	37°N	122°W	**452**
Omaha (city in Nebraska)	41°N	95°W	**430**
Oregon Country (North American area claimed by U.S. and Canada)			**235**

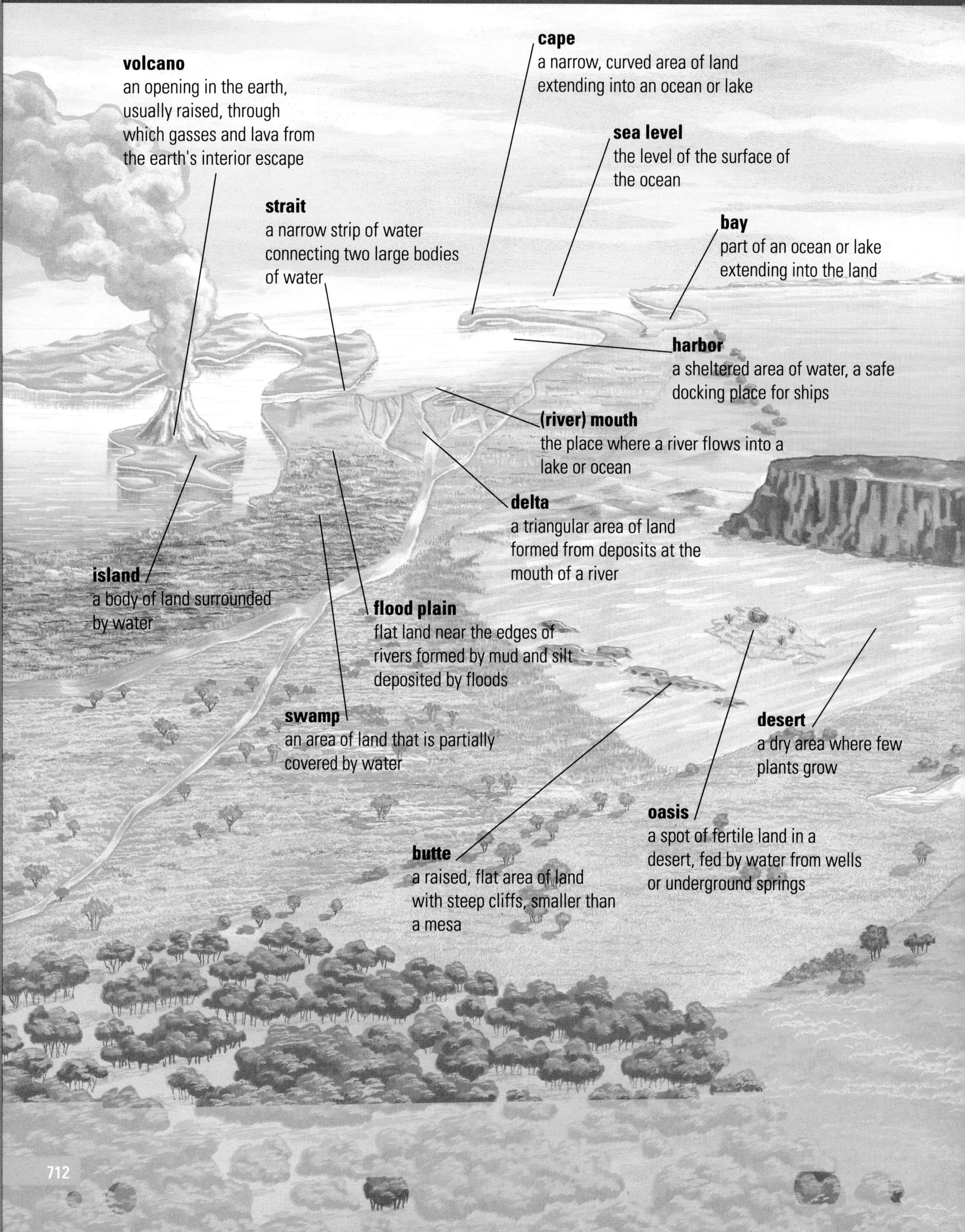
volcano
an opening in the earth, usually raised, through which gasses and lava from the earth's interior escape
cape
a narrow, curved area of land extending into an ocean or lake
sea level
the level of the surface of the ocean
strait
a narrow strip of water connecting two large bodies of water
bay
part of an ocean or lake extending into the land
harbor
a sheltered area of water, a safe docking place for ships
(river) mouth
the place where a river flows into a lake or ocean
delta
a triangular area of land formed from deposits at the mouth of a river
island
a body of land surrounded by water
flood plain
flat land near the edges of rivers formed by mud and silt deposited by floods
swamp
an area of land that is partially covered by water
desert
a dry area where few plants grow
oasis
a spot of fertile land in a desert, fed by water from wells or underground springs
butte
a raised, flat area of land with steep cliffs, smaller than a mesa

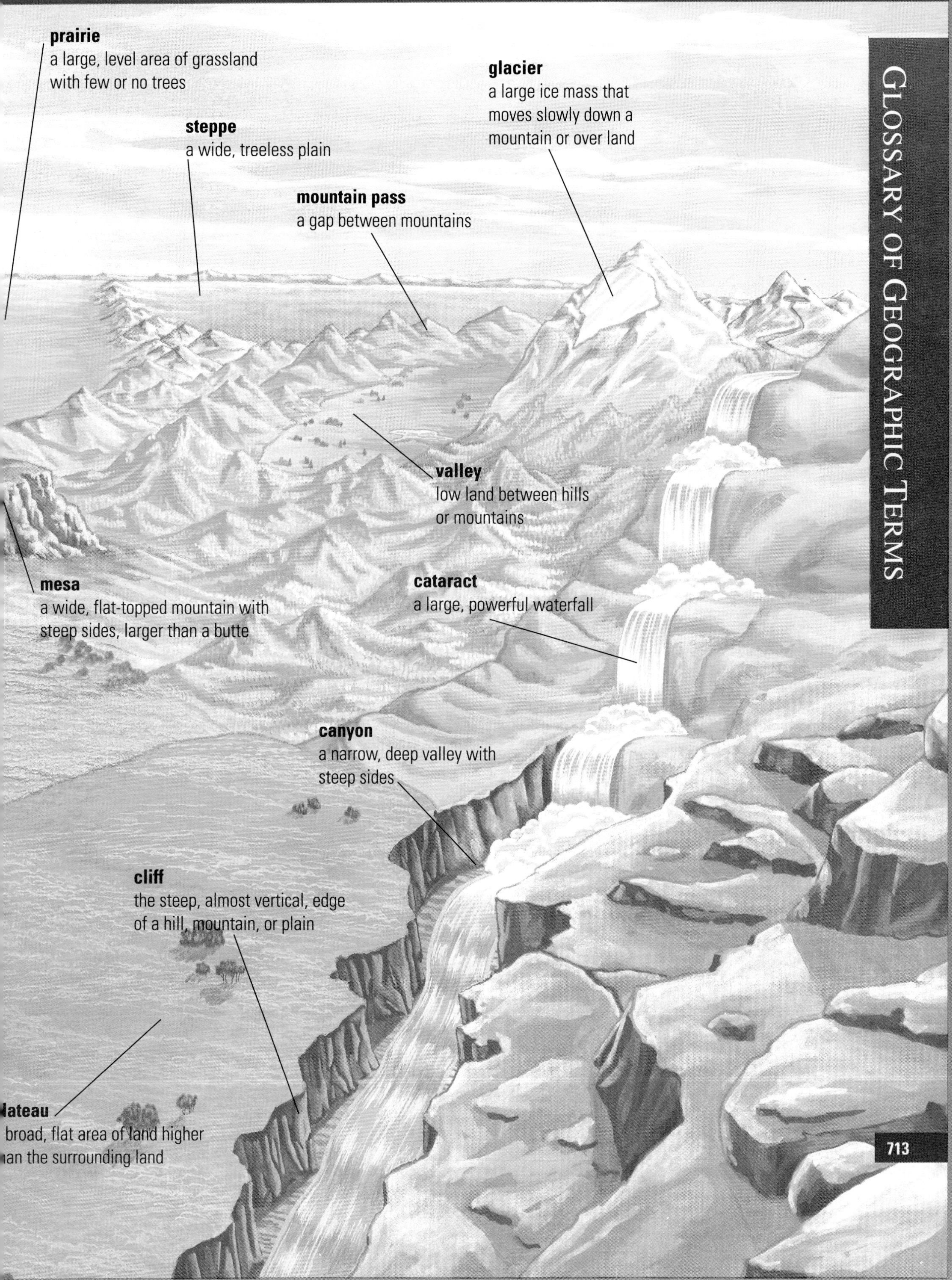
prairie
a large, level area of grassland with few or no trees
steppe
a wide, treeless plain
mountain pass
a gap between mountains
glacier
a large ice mass that moves slowly down a mountain or over land
valley
low land between hills or mountains
mesa
a wide, flat-topped mountain with steep sides, larger than a butte
cataract
a large, powerful waterfall
canyon
a narrow, deep valley with steep sides
cliff
the steep, almost vertical, edge of a hill, mountain, or plain
lateau
broad, flat area of land higher
an the surrounding land

Pronunciation Key

This chart presents the system of phonetic respellings used to indicate pronunciation in the Biographical Dictionary and in the chapters of this book.

Spellings	Symbol	Spellings	Symbol	Spellings	Symbol
pat	a	kick, cat, pique	k	thin, this	th
pay	ay	lid, needle	l	cut	uh
care	air	mum	m	urge, term, firm, word, heard	ur
father	ah	no, sudden	n	valve	v
bib	b	thing	ng	with	w
church	ch	pot, horrid	ah	yes	y
deed, milled	d	toe	oh	zebra, xylem	z
pet	eh	caught, paw, for	aw	vision, pleasure, garage	zh
bee	ee	noise	oy	about, item, edible, gallop, circus	uh
life, phase, rough	f	took	u	butter	ur
gag	g	boot	oo		
hat	h	out	ow		
which	hw	pop	p		
pit	ih	roar	r		
pie, by	eye, y	sauce	s		
pier	ihr	ship, dish	sh		
judge	j	tight, stopped	t		

Capital letters indicate stressed syllables.

A

Adams, John 1735–1826, 2nd U.S. President 1797–1801 (p. 84).

Adams, John Quincy 1767–1848, 6th U.S. President 1825–1829 (p. 183).

Addams, Jane 1860–1935, American social reformer (p. 502).

Allen, Ethan 1738–1789, Revolutionary leader at Fort Ticonderoga (p. 66).

Allen, Richard 1760–1831, African-American founder of an Episcopal Church (p. 195).

Anthony, Susan B. 1820–1906, American reformer (p. 268).

Attucks *(AT uhks),* **Crispus** 1723–1770, former slave killed in Boston Massacre (p. 58).

Austin, Stephen 1793–1836, political leader in Texas (p. 231).

B

Balboa, Vasco Nuñez de 1475–1517, Spanish discoverer of Pacific Ocean (p. 18).

Barton, Clara 1821–1912, founder of American Red Cross (p. 363).

Beecher, Catharine 1800–1878, American educator, antisuffragist (p. 192).

Beecher, Henry Ward 1813–1887, American clergyman, abolitionist (p. 190).

Bell, Alexander Graham 1847–1922, Scottish-born American inventor of telephone (p. 443).

Bonaparte, Napoleon 1769–1821, French emperor; sold Louisiana Territory to U.S. (p. 223).

Boone, Daniel 1734–1820, American frontiersman, helped settle Kentucky (p. 197).

Booth, John Wilkes 1838–1865, actor; assassinated Lincoln (p. 378).

Brady, Matthew 1823–1896, American Civil War photographer (p. 362).

Brown, John 1800–1859, American abolitionist; executed (p. 328).

Buchanan, James 1791–1868, 15th U.S. President 1857–1861 (p. 329).

Burgoyne *(bur GOYN),* **John** 1722–1792, English general, recaptured Fort Ticonderoga (p. 67).

Burr, Aaron 1756–1836, U.S. Vice President 1801–1805; killed Alexander Hamilton in duel (p. 147).

C

Cabot, John 1450–1498, Italian–born explorer (p. 20).

Carnegie, Andrew 1839–1919, Scottish-born American industrialist (p. 445).

Cartier *(kahr TYAY),* **Jacques** 1491–1557, French explorer (p. 20).

Catt, Carrie Chapman 1859–1947, American suffragist (p. 517).

Clark, George Rogers 1752–1818, American military leader (p. 68).

Clark, William 1770–1838, American explorer of the Northwest (p. 223).

Clay, Henry 1777–1852, American statesman (p. 315).

Cleveland, Grover 1837–1908, 22nd and 24th U.S. President 1885–1889; 1893–1897 (p. 532).

Columbus, Christopher 1451–1506, Italian explorer in the Americas (p. 18).
Cooper, James Fenimore 1789–1851, American writer of frontier novels (p. 197).
Cornwallis, Charles 1738–1805, British military leader in the Revolution (p. 68).
Cortés (*kawr TEHZ*), **Hernando** 1485–1547, Spanish explorer (p. 19).
Crèvecoeur (*kreh v KUR*), **Michel de** 1735–1813, French agriculturalist (p. 180).
Crockett, Davy 1786–1836, American frontiersman; Tennessee Congressman (p. 197).
Custer, George Armstrong 1839–1876, American general killed at Little Big Horn (p. 422).

D

Davis, Jefferson 1808–1889, President of the Confederacy (p. 348).
Deere, John 1804–1886, American inventor of steel-bladed plow (p. 191).
Dewey, John 1859–1952, American philosopher and educator (p. 504).
Dix, Dorothea 1802–1887, American reformer and educator (p. 266).
Douglas, Stephen A. 1813–1861, American legislator (p. 326).
Douglass, Frederick 1817?–1895, former slave, anti-slavery leader (p. 321).
Dreiser (*DRY zur*), **Theodore** 1871–1945, American author (p. 451).
Du Bois (*doo BOYS*), **W.E.B.** 1868–1963, American sociologist, founder of NAACP (p. 519).

E

Edison, Thomas Alva 1847–1931, American inventor (p. 443).
Edwards, Jonathan 1703–1758, American preacher of Great Awakening (p. 51).

F

Fillmore, Millard 1800–1874, 13th U.S. President 1850–1853 (p. 329).
Ford, Henry 1863–1947, American automobile manufacturer (p. 456).
Franklin, Benjamin 1706–1790, American statesman, scientist (p. 82).
Frémont, John C. 1813–1890, American explorer (p. 226).
Fulton, Robert 1765–1815, American inventor of steamboat (p. 257).

G

Gabriel 1775?–1800, planner of slave rebellion (p. 295).
Garfield, James A. 1831–1881, 20th U.S. President 1881 (p. 477).
Garrison, William Lloyd 1805–1879, American abolitionist (p. 321).
Geronimo 1829–1909, Chiricahua Apache leader (p. 425).
Gerry, Elbridge 1744–1814, Massachusetts governor; U.S. Vice President 1813–1814 (p. 113).
Gompers, Samuel 1850–1924, English-born American labor leader (p. 459).
Grant, Ulysses S. 1822–1885, 18th U.S. President 1869–1877; Union general (p. 442).
Greene, Nathanael 1742–1786, American Revolution general; defeated Cornwallis (p. 68).

H

Hamilton, Alexander 1757–1804, American statesman; killed by Aaron Burr in duel (p. 135).
Hancock, John 1737–1793, Signer of the Declaration of Independence (p. 66).
Harding, Warren 1865–1923, 29th U.S. President 1921–1923 (p. 553).
Harrison, William Henry 1773–1841, 9th U.S. President 1841 (p. 201).
Hayes, Rutherford B. 1822–1893, 19th U.S. President 1877–1881 (p. 481).
Hays, Mary Ludwig 1754–1832, known as Molly Pitcher; American Revolution heroine (p. 71).
Hearst, William Randolph 1863–1951, American newspaper publisher (p. 535).
Henry, Patrick 1736–1799, American Revolution leader; famous orator (p. 118).
Howe, Elias 1819–1867, American inventor of sewing machine (p. 444).
Howe, Sir William 1729–1814, British army commander-in-chief (p. 66).
Hudson, Henry d. 1611, English explorer (p. 20).

J

Jackson, Andrew 1767–1845, 7th U.S. President 1829–1837, called "Old Hickory" (p. 172).
Jackson, Thomas "Stonewall" 1824–1863, American Confederate general (p. 345).
Jay, John 1745–1829, American diplomat; signed treaty with England (p. 70).
Jefferson, Thomas 1743–1826, 3rd U.S. President 1801–1809; author of Declaration of Independence, scientist, architect, educator, diplomat (p. 147).
Johnson, Andrew 1808–1875, 17th U.S. President 1865–1869 (p. 379).
Joliet, Louis 1645–1700, French-Canadian explorer of America (p. 29).

K

Kelley, Florence 1859–1932, child labor activist (p. 515).

L

Lafayette, Marquis de 1757–1834, French leader in American Revolution (p. 70).
Lease, Mary E. 1850–1933, Populist leader (p. 489).
Lee, Ann 1736–1784, "Mother Ann"; English founder of American Shaker sect (p. 271).
Lee, Robert E. 1807–1870, American Confederate general; surrendered to Grant (p. 342).
Lewis, Meriwether 1774–1809, American Northwest explorer (p. 223).
Liliuokalani *(lee lee oo oh kah LAH nee)*, **Queen** 1838–1917, Hawaiian queen 1891–1893 (p. 532).
Lincoln, Abraham 1809–1865, 16th U.S. President 1861–1865; passed 13th Amendment; assassinated (p. 334).
Lincoln, Mary Todd 1818–1882, wife of Abraham Lincoln (p. 345).
Lowell, Francis 1775–1818, American textile producer (p. 259).

M

MacLeish, Archibald 1892–1982, American poet (p. 4).
Madison, Dolley 1768–1849, American First Lady, wife of James (p. 153).
Madison, James 1751–1836, 4th U.S. President 1809–1817 (p. 155).
Mann, Horace 1796–1859, American educator (p. 269).
Marion, Frances 1732?–1795, called "Swamp Fox"; American Revolution soldier (p. 68).
Marquette *(mahr KEHT)*, **Father Jacques** 1637–1675, French missionary and explorer (p. 29).
Marshall, James 1810–1885, American pioneer; started gold rush to California (p. 241).
Marshall, John 1755–1835, first Chief Justice of U.S. Supreme Court (p. 127).
Maximilian, Archduke 1832–1867, Austrian ruler and Emperor of Mexico 1864–1867 (p. 533).
McCormack, Cyrus 1809–1884, American inventor of reaper (p. 191).
McKinley, William 1843–1901, 25th U.S. President 1897–1901; assassinated (p. 491).
Monroe, James 1758–1831, 5th U.S. President 1817–1825 (p. 158).
Morgan, J. Pierpont 1867–1943, American financier (p. 445).
Morris, Robert 1734–1806, American Revolution financier (p. 91).
Mott, Lucretia Coffin 1793–1880, American social reformer (p. 322).

N

Nast, Thomas 1840–1902, German-born American cartoonist (p. 377).
Nation, Carry 1846–1911, American temperance reformer (p. 513).

O

Olmsted, Frederick Law 1822–1903, American landscape architect (p. 290).

P

Paine, Thomas 1737–1809, English-born American author of *Common Sense* (p. 65).
Paul, Alice 1885–1977, American social reformer (p. 517).
Penn, William 1644–1718, Quaker leader, settler of Pennsylvania (p. 30).
Perry, Matthew C. 1794–1858, American naval officer (p. 531).
Pierce, Franklin 1804–1869, 14th U.S. President 1853–1857 (p. 419).
Pike, Zebulon 1779–1813, American army officer and explorer (p. 226).
Polk, James K. 1795–1849, 11th U.S. President 1845–1849 (p. 234).
Pulitzer, Joseph 1847–1911, Hungarian-born American publisher (p. 467).
Pullman, George 1831–1897, American inventor of railroad sleeping cars (p. 458).

R

Raleigh *(RAW lee)*, **Sir Walter** 1552?–1618, English navigator, colonizer (p. 22).
Randolph, Edmund 1753–1813, American Revolutionary leader (p. 108).
Remarque *(ruh MAHRK)*, **Erich Maria** 1898–1970, German-born American novelist (p. 545).
Revels, Hiram 1827–1901, first African-American U.S. Senator (p. 388).
Revere, Paul 1735–1818, American Revolution patriot; silversmith (p. 58).
Riis *(rees)*, **Jacob A.** 1849–1914, Danish-born American reformer (p. 499).
Rockefeller, John D. 1839–1937, American industrialist and philanthropist (p. 474).
Roebling, John A. 1806–1869, German-born American engineer; built Brooklyn Bridge (p. 451).
Roosevelt, Theodore 1858–1919, 26th U.S. President 1901–1909; 1906 Nobel Peace Prize winner (p. 535).
Ross, John 1790–1866, Cherokee leader (p. 508).

S

Sacajawea (*sak uh juh WEE uh*) 1788?–1812, Shoshone Indian Guide, aided Lewis and Clark expedition (p. 222).

Santa Anna, Antonio de 1795?–1876, Mexican general and political leader during Mexican War (p. 232).

Schurz, Margaretha 1833–1876, German-born educator, started first U.S. kindergarten (p. 210).

Scott, Dred 1795?–1858, American slave involved in Supreme Court case (p. 331).

Sequoya (*se KWOI uh*) 1760?–1843, leader of Cherokee Indians (p. 205).

Serra, Padre Junípero (*hoo NEE peh roh*) 1713–1784, Spanish missionary in California (p. 22).

Shays, Daniel 1747?–1825, American soldier and leader of Shays's Rebellion (p. 95).

Sheridan, Philip Henry 1831–1888, American Union general (p. 366).

Sherman, William Tecumseh (*tih KUM suh*) 1820–1891, American Union general (p. 366).

Sinclair, Upton 1878–1968, American author; reformer (p. 507).

Singer, I.M. 1811–1875, American manufacturer of sewing machines (p. 444).

Slater, Samuel 1768–1835, English-born textile leader (p. 258).

Smith, Jedediah S. 1799?–1831, American fur trader, explorer (p. 226).

Smith, Joseph 1805–1844, American religious leader, founded Mormonism (p. 239).

Stanton, Elizabeth Cady 1815–1902, American feminist and social reformer (p. 322).

Stowe, Harriet Beecher 1811–1896, American novelist, author of *Uncle Tom's Cabin* (p. 322).

Stuart, Jeb 1833–1864, American Confederate general (p. 345).

Sumner, Charles 1811–1874, American politician; antislavery leader (p. 325).

Sutter, John Augustus 1803–1880, Swiss-born pioneer, found gold on his California land (p. 241).

T

Taney, Roger B. 1777–1864, American jurist involved in Dred Scott decision (p. 331).

Tarbell, Ida M. 1857–1944, American muckraking author (p. 502).

Taylor, Zachary 1784–1850, "Old Rough and Ready"; 12th U.S. President 1849–1850 (p. 234).

Tecumseh (*tih KUM suh*) 1768–1813, Shawnee Indian chief (p. 201).

Tenskwatawa *(ten skwa TA wa)* 1769–1834, called "the Prophet"; Shawnee leader (p. 204).

Tocqueville (*TOHK vihl*) **Alexis de** 1805–1859. French historian, author of *Democracy in America* (p. 181).

Trollope *(TRAHL uhp)*, **Frances** 1780–1863, English author on American manners (p. 179).

Truth, Sojourner 1797–1883, American abolitionist (p. 320).

Tubman, Harriet 1820–1913, American abolitionist (p. 333).

Turner, Nat 1800–1831, American leader of slave revolt (p. 295).

Twain, Mark (pen name of Samuel Clemens) 1835–1910, American author (p. 410).

V

Van Buren, Martin 1782–1862, 8th U.S. President 1837–1841 (p. 207).

Vanderbilt, Cornelius 1794–1877, American promoter of railroads (p. 407).

Verrazano, Giovanni *(joh VAH nee)* 1485?–1528? Italian explorer of Atlantic Coast (p. 20).

Vespucci *(vehs POOH chee)*, **Amerigo** 1454–1512, Italian navigator, explorer (p. 18).

W

Walker, David 1785–1830, American abolitionist (p. 320).

Walker, D. Mary 1832–1919, American physician and feminist (p. 359).

Warren, Mercy Otis 1728–1814, American author, historian (p. 74).

Washington, George 1732–99, 1st U.S. President 1789–1797; leader of Revolution (p. 134).

Webster, Daniel 1782–1852, American orator, Massachusetts politician (p. 178).

Webster, Noah 1758–1843, lexicographer; compiled first American dictionary (p. 164).

Weems, Mason 1759–1825, American clergyman; biographer of George Washington (p. 165).

Whitman, Marcus 1802–1847, American pioneer missionary in Oregon (p. 238).

Whitman, Walt 1819–1892, American poet (p. 474).

Whitney, Eli 1765–1825, American inventor of cotton gin (p. 284).

Wilder, Laura Ingalls 1867–1957, American author (p. 427).

Willard, Emma Hart 1787–1870, American author, favored women's education (p. 166).

Wilson, Woodrow 1856–1924, 28th U.S. President 1913–1921 (p. 541).

Y/Z

Young, Brigham 1801–1877, American Mormon leader in Utah (p. 239).

Zenger, John Peter 1697–1746, German-born colonial printer (p. 124).

Pronunciation Key
This chart presents the pronunciation key used in the Glossary. For a key to the phonetic respellings used to indicate pronunciation in the text of the chapters, see page 714.

Spellings	Symbol	Spellings	Symbol	Spellings	Symbol
pat	ă	**kick**, **c**at, pi**que**	k	**th**in	th
pay	ā	**l**id, need**le**	l	**th**is	*th*
care	âr	**mum**	m	**cut**	ŭ
father	ä	**n**o, sudd**en**	n	**ur**ge, t**er**m, f**ir**m, w**or**d, h**ear**d	ûr
bib	b	thi**ng**	ng	**v**al**v**e	v
chur**ch**	ch	p**o**t, h**o**rrid	ŏ	**w**ith	w
dee**d**, mill**ed**	d	t**oe**	ō	**y**es	y
p**e**t	ĕ	c**au**ght, p**aw**, f**o**r	ô	**z**ebra, **x**ylem	z
b**ee**	ē	n**oi**se	oi	vi**s**ion, plea**s**ure, gara**ge**	zh
li**f**e, **ph**ase, rou**gh**	f	t**oo**k	ŏŏ	**a**bout, it**e**m, ed**i**ble, gall**o**p, circ**u**s	ə
gag	g	b**oo**t	ōō	butt**er**	ər
hat	h	**ou**t	ou		
which	hw	**pop**	p		
p**i**t	ĭ	**r**oa**r**	r		
p**ie**, b**y**	ī	**s**au**ce**	s	Primary stress ´	
p**ier**	îr	**sh**ip, di**sh**	sh	Secondary stress ´	
ju**dge**	j	**t**igh**t**, stopp**ed**	t		

A

abdicate (ăb´ dĭ-kāt´) To formally give up power—such as a throne or a high office. (p. 532)

abolitionism (ăb´-ə-lĭsh´ ə-nĭz´ əm) Advocacy of the end of slavery in the United States. (p. 321)

administration (ăd-mĭn´ĭ-strā´shən) The executive branch of the United States government, consisting of the President, his Cabinet, and the Vice President. (p. 134)

agrarian (ə-grâr´ ē-ən) Having to do with the land, its ownership, and its cultivation. (p. 136)

alien (ā´ lē-ən) An unnaturalized foreign resident of a country. (p. 139)

alliance (ə-lī´ əns) An organization or an agreement to promote common interests among an organization's members. (p. 27)

amendment (ə-mĕnd´mənt) Addition or change to the Constitution, made into law through the process of ratification. (p. 125)

amnesty (ăm´ nĭ-stē) A general pardon for offenders by a government, especially for political offenses. (p. 377)

anarchist (ăn´ ər-kĭst) A person who opposes all organized forms of government. (p. 516)

annex (ə-nĕks´) To increase the area in a country by incorporating other territory into it. (p. 232)

annuity (ə-nōō´ĭ-tē) Yearly provision of food, clothing, and other necessary items (provided to American Indians as part of an agreement with the United States government). (p. 423)

antebellum (ăn´ tē-bĕl´ əm) The time period before the Civil War. (p. 286)

Antifederalist (ăn´tē-fĕd´ ər-ə-lĭst) One who opposed ratifying the Constitution. (p. 119)

armistice (är´ mĭ-stĭs) A truce or temporary pause, agreed to by both sides, in a war or battle. (p. 546)

artisan (är´ tĭ-zən) A worker trained in a skilled trade such as cabinetmaking or printing. (p. 302)

assembly line (ə-sĕm´ blē līn) A continuously moving belt that moves parts past workers who each have a specific task. (p. 456)

assimilate (ə-sĭm´ ə-lāt´) To adopt a country's dominant culture. (p. 425)

asylum (ə-sī´ ləm) Political protection. (p. 570)

B

bilingual education (bī-lĭng´ gwəl ĕj´ ə-kā´ shən) Education presented in two languages. (p. 583)

bill of rights (bĭl ŭv rīts) A list of the basic liberties of citizens. (p. 113)

bonanza (bə-năn´ zə) A rich, valuable (ore-bearing) rock. (p. 413)

boom town (bōōm toun) A town that comes into existence suddenly. (p. 414)

boycott (boi´ kŏt´) An organized refusal to buy or use a product to express protest or to force a government, company, or person to take some action. (p. 57)

buffer zone (bŭf´ ər zōn) A territory separating two opposing powers. (p. 231)

C

Cabinet (kăb´ ə-nĭt) The advisory group selected by

the President, made up of the heads of the executive departments. (p. 134)

capital (kăp´ ĭ-tl) Material wealth, such as money or property, invested to produce more wealth. (p. 445)

carpetbagger (kär´pĭt-băg´ər) A Northerner who went to the South after the Civil War for political or financial advantage. (p. 388)

cash crop (kăsh krŏp) A single crop grown in large quantities for sale, often as an important source of income. (p. 287)

caucus (kô´kəs) A closed meeting of political leaders to select candidates for office. (p. 175)

cede (sēd) To grant or surrender possession of something through a formal agreement. (p. 74)

checks and balances (chěks ənd băl´ən-səz) A system in which branches of government balance each other in order to protect against abuses of power. (p. 108)

citizen (sĭt´ ĭ-zən) A person who, by birth or naturalization, owes loyalty to and receives protection from a nation's government. (p. 593)

civic responsibility (sĭv´ ĭk rĭ-spŏn´sə-bĭl´ ĭ-tē) A duty to contribute to one's society or community. (p. 611)

civil rights (sĭv´əl rītz) The personal freedoms belonging to a person by virtue of his or her status as a citizen or as a member of society. (p. 356)

civil service (sĭv´əl sûr´vĭs) Jobs in federal, state, or local government that are awarded on the basis of merit rather than on political patronage. (p. 480)

commerce (kŏm´ərs) The buying and selling of goods on a large scale. (p. 96)

Confederacy (kən-fĕd´ər-ə-sē) The eleven Southern states that separated from the United States. (p. 342)

confederation (kən-fĕd´ə-rā´shən) A group of states joined loosely for a common purpose. (p. 84)

conquistador (kŏng-kē´stə-dôr´) A Spanish word meaning "conqueror." (p. 18)

conservation (kŏn´sûr-vā´shən) The act or process of protecting and preserving natural resources and wilderness areas. (p. 510)

constitution (kŏn´stĭ-tōō´shən) A document that defines the main principles and framework of a government. (p. 83)

constitutional (kŏn´stĭ-tōō´shə-nəl) In agreement with the principles established by the Constitution. (p. 151)

continental divide (kŏn´tə-nĕn´tl dĭ-vīd´) Line that divides the rivers that flow west from those that flow east. (p. 226)

cooperative (kō-ŏp´ər-ə-tĭv) An organization or association that is owned jointly by those who use its facilities or services. (p. 489)

cultural accommodation (kŭl´chər-əl ə-kŏm´ə-dā´shən) Reconciliation or compromise of opposing cultures. (p. 204)

cultural heritage (kŭl´chər-əl hĕr´ ĭ-tĭj) The customs, language, and beliefs of a people's culture. (p. 293)

currency (kŭr´ən-sē) Coins and paper bills that serve as money. (p. 73)

D

dissent (dĭ-sĕnt´) Disagreement or difference of opinion with established authority. (p. 548)

draft (drăft) A call to military service. (p. 356)

E

electoral vote (ĭ-lĕk´tər-əl vōt) The ballot cast by the persons chosen by each state to elect the President. (p. 146)

emancipation (ĭ-măn´sə-pā´shən) A condition of being freed from oppression, bondage, or restraint. (p. 352)

embargo (ĕm-bär´gō) A ban on trade with another nation. (p. 59)

emigrate (ĕm´ ĭ-grāt´) To leave one country to settle permanently in another. (p. 211)

enfranchise (ĕn-frăn´chīz´) To give the rights of citizenship, especially the right to vote. (p. 516)

entrepreneur (ŏn´trə-prə-nûr´) A person who organizes and assumes the risk for a business venture. (p. 445)

estuary (ĕs´chōō-ĕr´ē) An arm of the sea that extends inland to meet the mouth of a river. (p. 6)

executive (ĭg-zĕk´yə-tĭv) A person or group having administrative or managerial authority. (p. 85)

executive branch (ĭg-zĕk´yə-tĭv brănch) The division of government led by the President. (p. 110)

expansionist (ĭk-spăn´shən-ĭst) One who calls for increasing a nation's territory. (p. 230)

F

famine (făm´ ĭn) A drastic and wide-reaching shortage of food (p. 211)

federal (fĕd´ər-əl) Relating to a system of government that divides power between a central authority and a number of smaller states. (p. 84)

Federalist (fĕd´ər-ə-lĭst) One who supported ratifying the Constitution and believed in a strong central government. (p. 119)

free labor (frē lā´ bər) System of work in which employees have the right to leave their employer and their job for better opportunities. (p. 314)

free press (frē prĕs) The right to publish anything, including criticism of the government. (p. 124)

G

ghost town (gōst toun) A town that has been totally abandoned. (p. 243)

graft (grăft) Money gained by elected or appointed officials through dishonest or illegal means. (p. 476)
guerrilla (gə-rĭl′ ə) Irregular warfare by independent forces. (p. 328)

H

homestead (hōm′ stĕd′) Land claimed by a settler under the Homestead Act of 1862. (p. 424)
household economy (hous′ hōld′ĭ-kŏn′ ə-mē) Production of food and other necessary items by a family for use within the household or for exchange within the immediate community. (p. 164)
human geography (hyōō′ mən jē-ŏg′ rə-fē) The study of how human beings and places interact with and influence one another. (p. 5)

I

immigrant (ĭm′ ĭ-grənt) A person born in one country who moves into and takes up residence in another country. (p. 48)
impeachment (ĭm-pēch′ mənt) The procedure of charging an office-holding official with misconduct before a formal tribunal. (p. 387)
imperialism (ĭm-pîr′ ē-ə-lĭz′əm) The attempt to create an empire by controlling other countries through either economic or political means. (p. 536)
impressment (ĭm-prĕs′ mənt) The policy of forcing someone into military service. (p. 154)
indentured servant (ĭn-dĕn′ chərd sûr′ vənt) A person who agreed to work for a specified period of time in exchange for passage from Europe to the colonies. (p. 34)
Industrial Revolution (ĭn-dŭs′ trē-əl rĕv′ə-lōō′ shən) The social and economic changes that occurred when manufacturing shifted from people's homes and shops to factories. (p. 255)
inflation (ĭn-flā′ shən) A rapid rise in prices over a period of time. (p. 73)
initiative (ĭ-nĭsh′ ə-tĭv) A procedure that allows citizens to propose a new law or amendment for the approval of voters. (p. 508)
institution (ĭn′stĭ-tōō′ shən) An established organization dedicated to providing important social functions such as education. (p. 199)
isolationism (ī′sə-lā′ shə-nĭz′əm) The belief or policy that the United States should avoid alliance and minimize its involvement in the affairs of other nations. (p. 551)

J

judicial branch (jōō-dĭsh′ əl brănch) The division of government made up of the federal courts of law. (p. 110)
judicial review (jōō-dĭsh′ əl rĭ-vyōō′) The review of laws to determine whether or not they are constitutional. (p. 151)

K

kickback (kĭk′ băk′) A payment made to a person in return for political or business favors. (p. 475)

L

labor union (lā′ bər yōōn′yən) An organization of workers formed to serve workers' interests with respect to wages and working conditions. (p. 458)
laissez faire (lĕs′ā fâr′) A policy that opposes governmental interference in or regulation of industry and the economy. (p. 499)
landform (lănd′ fôrm) A natural feature of the earth's surface, such as a mountain, hill, plateau, or plain. (p. 5)
legislative branch (lĕj′ ĭ-slā′tiv brănch) Congress, the division of government that passes laws. (p. 110)
legislature (lĕj′ ĭ-slā′ chər) Officially selected body responsible for making the laws for a political unit. (p. 85)

M

Manifest Destiny (măn′ ə-fĕst′ dĕst′ tə-nē) The nineteenth-century belief that the United States had the right and duty to expand throughout North America to spread white American culture. (p. 227)
market economy (mär′ kĭt ĭ-kŏn′ ə-mē) Production of food and other goods and services for cash sale, often in distant markets. (p. 166)
martial law (mär′ shəl lô) Temporary rule imposed on a civilian population by military authorities. (p. 386)
middle class (mĭd′ l klăs) Members of society with better-than-average education and income. (p. 192)
migrant worker (mī′ grənt wûr′ kər) A person who travels from place to place planting and harvesting crops as jobs are available. (p. 582)
migrate (mī′ grāt′) To move from one region and settle in another. (p. 197)
militia (mə-lĭsh′ ə) A group of armed citizens who are prepared for military service if called to defend their town, state, or country. (p. 63)
minuteman (mĭn′ ĭt-măn′) A member of the colonial Massachusetts militia who was ready to fight the British at a minute's notice. (p. 63)
mobilize (mō′ bə-līz′) To prepare or put into operation for war. (p. 543)
moderate (mŏd′ ər-ĭt) An individual opposed to radical or extreme views or measures in politics or religion. (p. 348)

monopoly (mə-nŏp′ ə-lē) A company that completely controls the market for a particular commodity or service. (p. 483)
mountain man (moun′ tən măn) A fur trapper of the West during the early 1800s. (p. 226)
muckraker (mŭk′ rāk′ ər) A journalist who investigates and exposes political corruption and social problems in an effort to improve society. (p. 502)
Mugwumps (mŭg′ wŭmps′) A group of Republicans who sought to eliminate political corruption and business abuses during the Gilded Age. (p. 479)
municipal (myo͞o-nĭs′ ə-pəl) Of a city or urban political unit. (p. 263)

N

nativism (nā′ tĭ-vĭz′ əm) A policy favoring the interests of native-born inhabitants over those of immigrants. (p. 215)
naturalization (năch′ ə-rəl-ĭ-zā′ shən) The process by which the citizen of one country becomes the citizen of another country. (p. 594)
navigation (năv′ĭ-gā′ shən) The practice of plotting the course of a ship. (p. 17)
neoclassical (nē′ō-klăs′ ĭ-kəl) Pertaining to the revival of classical art forms. (p. 166)
neutrality (no͞o-trăl′ ĭ-tē) The state of being a nonparticipant in a war or other conflict. (p. 154)
nomad (nō′ măd′) One who moves from place to place rather than settling in one location. (p. 27)
nullify (nŭl′ ə-fī′) To refuse to recognize or enforce a law (a federal law within a state). (p. 178)

P

patronage (pā′ trə-nĭj) The practice of giving out government jobs in exchange for political support. (p. 476)
philanthropist (fĭ-lăn′ thrō-pĭst) A person who promotes human welfare through the funding of beneficial public institutions. (p. 446)
physical geography (fĭz′ ĭ-kəl jē-ŏg′ rə-fē) The study of the natural world, including the earth's climate, landforms, bodies of water, plants, animals, and resources. (p. 5)
plantation (plăn-tā′ shən) A large estate's farm on which crops are raised. (p. 285)
plateau (plă-tō′) An expanse of high, flat land. (p. 11)
pluralism (plo͝or′ ə-liz′əm) A condition of society in which numerous distinct ethnic, religious, or cultural groups coexist within one nation. (p. 49)
political machine (pə-lĭt′ ĭ-kəl mə-shēn′) A powerful, tightly run political organization that developed in many American cities in the late 1800s and early 1900s. (p. 476)
popular sovereignty (pŏp′ yə-lər sŏv′-ər-ĭn-tē) The idea that voters in a territory should decide for themselves if their territory should allow slavery. (p. 326)
popular vote (pŏp′ yə-lər vōt) The total number of votes by the people within each state. (p. 174)
Populism (pŏp′ yə-lĭz′ əm) A member or supporter of the Populist Party, a political party that represented the interests of farmers in the 1890s. (p. 487)
prairie (prâr′ ē) An area of rolling grasslands. (p. 8)
precipitation (prĭ-sĭp′ ĭ-tā′shən) Moisture, condensed in the atmosphere, that falls to the earth in the form of rain or snow. (p. 8)
profit (prŏf′ ĭt) The gain from a business undertaking after all expenses have been paid for. (p. 445)
Progressivism (prə-grĕs′ ĭ-vĭz′əm) A broad reform movement that worked to correct political abuses and social problems during the early decades of the 1900s. (p. 499)
Prohibition (prō′ə-bĭsh′ ən) The forbidding by law of the manufacture, transportation, sale, and possession of alcoholic beverages. (p. 514)
protectorate (prə-tĕk′ tər-ĭt) A country or region that is protected and partially controlled by a more powerful country. (p. 532)

Q

quota (kwō′ tə) The largest number of immigrants who may enter a country in one year. (p. 568)

R

ratify (răt′ ə-fī′) To approve formally. (p. 120)
raw materials (rô mə-tĭr′ ē-əl) Unprocessed natural products used in manufacturing. (p. 256)
recall (rĭ-kŏl′) A special election that allows voters to remove an elected official from office before his or her term has expired. (p. 508)
Reconstruction (rē′kən-strŭk′ shən) The period (1865–1877) during which the former Confederate states were controlled by the federal government before being readmitted into the Union. (p. 377)
redeem (rĭ-dēm′) To recover or reclaim. (p. 394)
referendum (rĕf′ə-rĕn′ dəm) The process by which people can vote directly on a bill. (p. 508)
refugee (rĕf′yo͞o-jē′) Person who flees his or her country because of persecution for political beliefs. (p. 570)
regionalism (rē′ jə-nəl-ĭz′əm) A sense of belonging to a distinct region. (p. 245)
regulate (rĕg′ yə-lāt′) To control or manage business or other activities by established rules. (p. 482)
rendezvous (rän′ dā-vo͞o′) French word meaning "meeting place." (p. 226)

reparations (rĕp´ə-rā´ shənz) Payments made by defeated nations as compensation for the damages they caused in war. (p. 551)

republic (rĭ-pŭb´ lĭk) A form of government in which the people exercise power through their chosen representatives. (p. 65)

reservation (rĕz´ ər-vā´ shən) Land that is set aside for American Indians. (p. 424)

revitalization (rē-vī´tl-ĭ-zā´ shən) The effort to bring new life and strength to a people or culture. (p. 204)

S

salutary neglect (săl´ yə-tĕr´ē nĭ-glĕkt´) The policy of weakly enforcing laws that England used in ruling the American colonies for much of the late 1600s and early 1700s. (p. 52)

satire (săt´ īr´) A literary work in which human faults are ridiculed through irony or wit. (p. 179)

scalawag (skăl´ ə-wăg´) A white Republican Southerner who had opposed secession and supported Radical Reconstruction. (p. 389)

secede (sĭ-sēd´) To withdraw formally from membership in an organization, association, or alliance. (p. 343)

sect (sĕkt) A small religious group that has formed a separate part of a larger denomination. (p. 21)

secularize (sĕk´ yə-lə-rīz´) To convert from religious use or ownership to civil use or ownership. (p. 237)

sedition (sĭ-dĭsh´ ən) Rebellion against the authority of the government. (p. 139)

segregated (sĕg´ rĭ-gāt´əd) The maintenance of separate facilities for members of different races or of facilities restricted to members of one race. (p. 383)

sharecropping (shâr´ krŏp´ĭng) A system of farming in which a tenant farmer gives a share of the crop to the farm owner instead of paying rent. (p. 376)

sit-in (sĭt=ĭn) A form of protest in which participants occupy a room or building until their demands are met. (p. 602)

social class (sō´ shəl klăs) A level of society characterized by certain cultural and economic traits. (p. 180)

socialist (sō´ shə-lĭst) A person who supports an economic system in which the workers have both political power and the means of producing and distributing goods. (p. 515)

sovereignty (sŏv´ ər-ĭn-tē) The supreme power or authority that an independent country or state has within its borders. (p. 91)

spoils system (spoilz sĭs´ təm) A system in which a winning candidate's supporters are rewarded with appointment to public office. (p. 175)

states' rights (stāts rīts) The idea that individual states could limit the power of the federal government. (p. 178)

strike (strīk) A temporary work stoppage in support of demands made on employers by workers. (p. 458)

subsistence farmer (səb-sĭs´ təns fär´ mər) A person who grows just enough food for his or her family's needs. (p. 35)

suffrage (sŭf´ rĭj) The right or privilege of voting. (p. 169)

T

tariff (tăr´ ĭf) A duty imposed by a government on imported or exported goods. (p. 175)

temperance (tĕm´ pər-əns) The resolution not to drink any alcoholic beverages. (p. 268)

tenement (tĕn´ ə-mənt) An apartment building whose facilities barely meet or fail to meet minimum standards of sanitation, safety, and comfort. (p. 504)

term of office (tûrm ŭv ô´ fĭs) A limited period of time during which an elected official serves the public. (p. 92)

territory (tĕr´ ĭ-tôr´ē) An area belonging to the United States that is not a part of any existing state. (p. 96)

transcontinental (trăns´kŏn-tə-nĕn´ tl) Crossing a continent. (p. 412)

trust (trŭst) A combination of business firms formed by legal agreement, especially to reduce competition. (p. 483)

U

Underground Railroad (ŭn´ dər-ground´ rāl´ rōd´) A secret network that helped slaves escape to freedom. (p. 333)

undocumented immigrant (ŭn-dŏk´ yə-mənt´əd ĭm´ ĭ-grənt) A person who enters the United States without documented permission. (p. 581)

urban society (ûr´ bən sə-sī´ ĭ-tē) A social structure that is based on city life. (p. 448)

Utopia (yōō-tō´ pē-ə) A community established to create social and political reform. (p. 271)

V

veto (vē´ tō) To prevent a legislative bill from becoming law by exercising executive authority. (p. 53)

vigilante (vĭj´ə-lăn´ tē) A group of citizens that, without authority, takes on itself powers such as pursuing and punishing those suspected of committing crimes. (p. 394)

W

working class (wûr´ kĭng klăs) Members of society who are employed for wages, usually in manual labor. (p. 192)

writs of assistance (rĭts ŭv ə-sĭs´ təns) Documents issued by the British government in the colonial period that allowed officials to conduct unrestricted searches. (p. 57)

Y

yellow journalism (yĕl′ ō jûr′ nə-lĭz′ əm) A style of newspaper reporting popular in the 1890s that featured exaggerated writing and sensational headlines. (p. 535)

yeoman farmer (yō′ mən fär′ mər) Owner of a small farm. (p. 299)

Z

zoning law (zōn′ ĭng lô) A law that restricts certain neighborhoods of a city to particular uses, such as residential, commercial, or industrial. (p. 505)

Italic numbers refer to pages on which illustrations appear; *quoted* refers to a quotation from a speech or writings of the person listed.

B

D

G

I

M

O

P

S

Y

Z

Text *(continued from page iv)*

16 Adapted excerpt from Fray Francisco Ximenez, *Historia de la Provincia de San Vicente de Chiapas y Guatemala de la Orden de Predicadores, Prolog del Lic. Antonio Villacorta, C.* 3 Vols., 1929 .
24 From *Indian Legends of the Pacific Northwest* by Ella E. Clark. Copyright ©1953 by The Regents of the University of California, renewed ©1981 by Ella E. Clark. Reprinted by permission of the University of California Press. **35** "The Slave Auction" by Frances E.W. Harper from *The Complete Poems of Frances E.W. Harper* edited by Maryemma Graham, New York: Oxford University Press, 1988.
40 Excerpts from *The Witch of Blackbird Pond* by Elizabeth George Speare. Copyright ©1958 by Elizabeth George Speare. Reprinted by permission of Houghton Mifflin Company. **166** From *Education and the Weaker Sex* by Emma Hart Willard, 1819. **183** Excerpts from *Democracy in America*, Vols I & II by Alexis De Tocqueville, translated by Henry Reeve, revised by Francis Bowen and edited by Phillips Bradley. Copyright 1945 and renewed 1973 by Alfred A. Knopf, Inc. Reprinted by permission of the publisher. **207** Quote by John G. Burnett from *The Cherokee* by Theda Perdue, New York: Chelsea House Publishers, 1989. **211** From *The Story of the Irish Race: A Popular History of Ireland* by Seumas MacManus, New York: The Devin-Adair Company, 1921. **212** Excerpt from *Famine* by Liam O'Flaherty. Copyright 1937, 1965 by Liam O'Flaherty. Reprinted by permission of Irish American Book Company, a division of Roberts Rinehart Publishers. **232** Quote by William Barret Travis from *The Texans* by David Nevin, New York: Time-Life Books, 1975. **241** Quote by James Marshall from *The World Rushed in: The California Gold Rush Experience* by J.S. Holiday, New York: Simon & Schuster, 1981.
243 Quotes by Elizabeth Goltra and anonymous woman from *The Other Civil War: American Women in the Nineteenth Century* by Catherine Clinton, New York: Hill & Wang, 1984. **244** Quotes by Charlotte Stearns Pengra and Elizabeth Smith Geer from *Women's Diaries of the Westward Journey* edited by Lillian Schlissel, New York: Schocken Books, 1982. **259** From *A New England Girlhood: Outlined from Memory* by Lucy Larcom, Boston: Houghton Mifflin Company, 1889. **276** From *Mother, Aunt Susan and Me* by William Jay Jacobs. Copyright ©1979 by William Jay Jacobs. Reprinted by permission of Coward-McCann, a division of Penguin Putnam Inc. **284** From "Correspondence of Eli Whitney" edited by M.B. Hammond, *The American Historical Review*, Vol. III, 1897–98. **370** Excerpts from *The Slopes of War* by Norah A. Perez. Copyright ©1984 by N. A. Perez. Reprinted by permission of Houghton Mifflin Company. **389** Excerpt from *A Fool's Errand* by Albion W. Tourgee. Copyright ©1961 by the President and Fellows of Harvard College, renewed 1989 by John Hope Franklin. Reprinted by permission of Harvard University Press.
411 Quote by John Noble from *The American Magazine*, August 1927.
414 Quote by J. Ross Browne from *Gold and Silver in the West: The Illustrated History of an American Dream* by T.H. Watkins, Palo Alto, California: American West Publishing Company, 1971. **415** Excerpt from *Canadian Portraits, Brant, Crowfoot, Oronhyatekha, Famous Indians* by Ethel Brant Monture, Ontario: Stoddart Publishing Company Ltd., 1960. **418** From *Red Mother* by Frank B. Linderman, New York: John Day Company, 1932. **420** From *American Indian Mythology* by Alice Marriott and Carol K. Rachlin. Copyright ©1968 by Alice Marriott and Carol K. Rachlin. Reprinted by permission of HarperCollins Children's Books. **427** Excerpts from *By the Shores of Silver Lake* by Laura Ingalls Wilder. Text copyright 1939 by Laura Ingalls Wilder. Copyright renewed 1967 by Roger L. MacBride. Reprinted by permission of HarperCollins Children's Books. **434** Excerpts from *My Antonia* by Willa Cather, Boston: Houghton Mifflin Company, 1918. **455** From "I Become a Striker" from *Woman's Labor Leader* by Agnes Nestor, Rockford, Illinois: Bellevue Books, 1954. **474** Quote by Walt Whitman from *Voices of Freedom: Sources in American History*, Englewood Cliffs, New Jersey: Prentice Hall Allyn & Bacon, 1987. **486** Quote by William J. Bryan from *The First Battle,* 1896. **487** Excerpt from *The Octopus: A Story of California* by Frank Norris, Boston: Houghton Mifflin Company, 1958. **498** Quote by Stephen Wise from *The Challenging Years,* New York: G. P. Putnam's Sons, 1949. **522** From *East River* by Sholem Asch, copyright 1946. **545** Excerpt from *All Quiet on the Western Front* by Erich Maria Remarque. Copyright 1928 by Ullstein A.G. Copyright renewed ©1956 by Erich Maria Remarque. Copyright 1929, 1930 by Little Brown and Company. Copyright renewed ©1957, 1958 by Erich Maria Remarque. Reprinted by permission of the Estate of Erich Maria Remarque. All rights reserved. **554** Song, "Over There" by George M. Cohan. Copyright ©1917 (Renewed 1945) *Leo Feist, Inc.* All Rights Assigned to *Emi Catalogue Partnership.* **555** Song, "Uncle Sam" by Edward Bushnell, copyright, 1917 by Edward Bushnell.
556–557 From *Holding Fast the Inner Lines: Democracy, Nationalism, and the Committee on Public Information* by Stephen Vaughn, Chapel Hill: The University of North Carolina Press, 1980. **564** From *Newsweek*, July 1986. **574** From "Puritans from the Orient: A Chinese Evolution" by Jade Snow Wong from *The Immigrant Experience* by Thomas C. Wheeler. Copyright ©1971 by Doubleday, a division of Bantam, Doubleday, Dell Publishing Group, Inc. Reprinted by permission of the publisher. **578, 580** From *Today's Immigrants, Their Stories: A New Look at the Newest Americans* by Thomas Kessner and Betty Boyd Caroli. Copyright ©1981 by Thomas Kessner and Betty Boyd Caroli. Reprinted by permission of Oxford University Press, Inc. **580** Quote by Jimmy Carter from *Today's Immigrants, Their Stories: A New Look at the Newest Americans* by Thomas Kessner and Betty Boyd Caroli, New York: Oxford University Press, 1981. **581** "Working to Help Irish Immigrants Stay, Legally" by Marvine Howe and "Immigration Law is Failing to Cut Flow From Mexico" by Larry Rother from *The New York Times*, November 27, and June 24, respectively. Copyright ©1988 by The New York Times Company. Reprinted by permission. **583** From *Time*, December 5, 1988. **584** Poem from *Island: Poetry and History of Chinese Immigrants on Angel Island 1910–1940* by Him Mark Lai, Genny Lim and Judy Yung. Copyright ©1980, 1986 by *Hoc Doi* Project. Reprinted by permission of the University of Washington Press. **585** "Two Pictures of My Grandparents: 1914" from *Near the Mountains* by Joseph Bruchac. Copyright ©1987 by Joseph Bruchac. Reprinted by permission of Barbara S. Kouts as agent for the author. **586** "I Ask My Mother to Sing" by Li-Young Lee from *Rose*. Copyright ©1986 by Li-Young Lee. Reprinted with the permission of BOA Editions, Ltd., 260 East Ave., Rochester, NY 14604. **587** "Hay un naranjo ahi/There's an Orange Tree Out There" by Alfonso Quijada Urías, translated by Darwin J. Flakoll. Copyright ©1991 by Curbstone Press. Reprinted by permission of Curbstone Press. **589** "The Free-Speech Fallacy" (editorial) from The Boston Globe, February 22, 1998. Copyright ©1998 The Boston Globe. Reprinted courtesy of The Boston Globe. **599** "Dance of Futility" from The Sacramento Bee, February 26, 1998. Copyright ©1998 by The Sacramento Bee. Reprinted by permission of McCatchy Newspapers, Inc. **602** Excerpt from the speech "I Have a Dream" by Martin Luther King, Jr. Copyright ©1963 by Martin Luther King, Jr. Reprinted by permission of Writers House Inc. **618** "I, Too" by Langston Hughes from *Selected Poems of Langston Hughes*. Copyright 1926 by Alfred A. Knopf, Inc., renewed 1954 by Langston Hughes. Reprinted by permission of Alfred A. Knopf, Inc. **618** "Refugee in America" by Langston Hughes from *Selected Poems of Langston Hughes*. Copyright 1943 by Curtis Publishing Co. Reprinted by permission of Alfred A. Knopf, Inc.
714 Pronunciation key copyright ©1985 by Houghton Mifflin Company. Adapted and reprinted by permission from *The American Heritage Dictionary*, Second College Edition. **iv** The material in the Minipedia is reprinted from *The World Book Encyclopedia* with the expressed permission of the publisher. Copyright ©1998 by World Book, Inc.

Illustrations

Literature border design by Peggy Skycraft.
Ligature 15, 50, 88, 89, 93, 109, 123, 161, 214, 228, 246, 274, 275, 281, 317, 361, 396, 398, 399, 437, 484, 598, 599. **Precision Graphics** 44, 49, 50, 61, 66, 67, 73, 76, 84, 92, 93, 102, 110, 122, 128, 136, 151, 160, 174, 186, 191, 209, 216, 217, 231, 250, 256, 257, 287, 306, 307, 309, 315, 326, 338, 346, 350, 372, 384, 395, 404, 438, 453, 467, 468, 481, 485, 494, 506,524, 529, 569, 580, 581, 588, 595, 612, 619, 623, 625, 629, 631, 633, 635. **Brian Battles** 64. **Jeani Brunick** 573. **Susan David** 284 **Ebet Dudley** 538. **Randall Fleck** 538. **Hank Iken** 259, 449. **Joe LeMonnier** 291. **Al Lorenz** 36, 37, 501. **Yoshi Miyake** 206. **Jim Needham** 211. **Frederick Porter** 428, 450. **Judy Reed** 127. **Joseph Scrofani** 418. **Richard Waldrep** 265. **Brent Watkinson** 323. **Paul Wenzel** 97.

Maps

© **GeoSystems Global Corporation** G15 (l), 694–707, 708(b). **GeoSystems Global Corporation** G2, G4, G5, G8, G13, G14, 708(t). **Mapping Specialists** G3, G9–10, G11, G12, 19, 21, 38, 55, 69, 83, 86, 112, 150, 159, 167, 175, 194, 198, 203, 207, 213, 223, 227, 234, 235, 244, 258, 262, 288, 316, 318, 327, 332, 333, 343, 350, 386, 411, 413, 419, 423, 425, 430, 433, 452, 454, 463, 491, 511, 536, 538, 546, 550. **Precision Graphics** G 6–7.

Photographs

Front Cover: The Planet, Side wheel paddle steamer, courtesy of the Chicago Maritime Society and Museum; photo by Peter Bosy; **Back Cover:** detail, New Jersey Historical Society, Newark; **ii** Smithsonian Institution (t); © PHOTRI/Marilyn Gartman Agency, Inc. (b); **iii** The Free Library of Philadelphia (l); The Shelburne Museum, Shelburne, VT (r); **vi** © FPG International (t); Private Collection (c); State Historical Society of North Dakota (b); **vii** Museum of American Political Life, University of Hartford, photo by Sally Andersen-Bruce; **viii** New Jersey Historical Society, Newark; **ix** The Oakland Museum History Dept.; **x** Southwest Museum, Los Angeles, CA; **G1** Earth Satellite Corporation / Science Photo Library / Photo Researchers; **xviii–1** © Grant Heilman Photography; **2** John Carter Brown Library, Brown University, Providence, RI (bl); © Fred Maroon (br); **2–3** National Maritime Museum; **3** Plimouth Plantation (b); **5** © Leonard Lee Rue III / Stock Boston; **6** © Jeff Gnass; **7** © Judy Canty / Stock Boston (t); © J. H. Carmichael Jr., The Image Bank (br); © Art Wolfe (cr); **8** © Nick Pavloff / The Image Bank (c); © James Tallon / Outdoor Exposures (tl); **9** © Art Wolfe (cr); © Grant Heilman / Grant Heilman Photography (b); **10** © Paul McCormick / The Image Bank; **11** © Alan Becker / The Image Bank (b); © Art Wolfe (cr); **12** © Dennis Stock / Magnum Photos, Inc. (t); © Jack Baker / The Image Bank (bl); **13** © Jeff Gnass (tr); © James Tallon / Outdoor Exposures (c); **14** © Art Wolfe; **15** © Jack Elness / Comstock; **17** The Granger Collection (tl); British Museum (br); **18** The Metropolitan Museum of Art (tl); British Museum / Newsweek Books (b); **20** The Granger Collection; **22** The Fine Arts Museum of San Francisco, gift of Eleanor Martin; **23** U.S. Dept. of the Interior, Colonial National Historical Park; **25** © Joern Gerdts / Photo Researchers, Inc.; **26** The Granger Collection; **27** New York Public Library / Newsweek Books; **29** Schlowsky Photography; **30** Laurie Platt Winfrey, Inc.; **31** © C. Vic Maris / Earthshine; **32** Old Sturbridge Village / photo by Henry E. Peach; **33** Yale University Art Gallery, New Haven, CT; **34** New York Public Library (b); The Granger Collection (cl); **35** National Gallery of Art; **36** Old Sturbridge Village / photo by Henry E. Peach (tr, cr); Ralph J. Brunke (br); **37** Old Sturbridge Village / photo by Henry E. Peach; **38** The Library Company of Philadelphia; **39** Private Collection; **46** National Gallery of Art, gift of Marian B. Maurice (cr); Colonial Williamsburg (cl); **47** The original painting hangs in the Selectmen's Meeting Room, Abbot Hall, Marblehead, MA (t); Smithsonian Institution (b); **49** The Free Library of Philadelphia, photo by Joan Broderick; **51** The Granger Collection; **52** American Antiquarian Society, Worcester, MA; **53** Concord Museum, Concord, MA; **54** Library of Congress; **56–57** Massachusetts Historical Society; **57** Library of Congress; **58** Library of Congress / Laurie Platt Winfrey, Inc.; **59** © Daughters of the American Revolution / Boston Tea Party Chapter; **60** Dover; **62** The Granger Collection; **63** Concord Antiquarian Society, Concord, MA; **65** The Granger Collection; **66** Dover (bc); Courtesy of The Bostonian Society / Old State House (bl); Smithsonian Institution (br); **67** Dover (t); Smithsonian Institution (b); **68** © FPG International; **70** Anne S. K. Brown Military Collection; **72** Connecticut Historical Society; **73** Smithsonian Institution; **74** The Museum of Fine Arts, Boston, bequest of Winslow Warren, 1931; **75** Historical Society of Pennsylvania / Newsweek Books; **78–79** The Shelburne Museum, Shelburne, VT.; **80** The Pennsylvania Academy of Fine Arts, Philadelphia (cr); The Free Library of Philadelphia, photo by Joan Broderick (cl); **81** The New Jersey Historical Society, Newark (tr); New York Public Library (l); **82** Yale University Art Gallery, New Haven, CT; **83** Her Majesty's Stationery Office / Newsweek Books; **85** The Granger Collection; **87** Virginia State Library and Archives; **88** New York State Historical Association, Cooperstown; **90** The Free Library of Philadelphia, photo by Joan Broderick; **91** Private Collection / Newsweek Books; **92** Steven A. Heassler; **94** The Granger Collection (l); Smithsonian Institution (c); **95** Corbis-Bettmann; **96** Historical Society of Pennsylvania (c); Percival David Foundation, London / Newsweek Books (cl); **98** Private Collection; **99** National Archives (tr); Smithsonian Institution Numismatics (cr); **100** The Pierpont Morgan Library / Art Resource, NY; **101** Jose L. Pelaez / The Stock Market; **104** Map Collection, The Free Library of Philadelphia / photo by Joan Broderick (c); **104–05** Independence National Historic Park Collection; **105** © Collection of The New-York Historical Society (tr); Independence National Historic Park Collection (br); **106** The Thomas Gilcrease Institute of American History and Art, Tulsa, OK; **107** Courtesy National Park Service, artist Lynn Gallagher; **108** Independence National Historic Park Collection (t); Library of Congress (bc); **111** Toledo Museum of Art; **113** The Board of Regents of Guntston Hall, VA; **118** Virginia Historical Society; **119** © Collection of The New-York Historical Society; **121** American Antiquarian Society, Worcester, MA (cr); Schlowsky Photography (cl); Ralph J. Brunke (tr); American Antiquarian Society, Worcester, MA (bl, bc); **124** Independence National Historic Park Collection; **125** The Granger Collection; **126** The Granger Collection; **130–31** Historical Society of Pennsylvania; **132** Museum of American Political Life, University of Hartford / photo by Sally Andersen-Bruce (tl, bl); © Collection of The New-York Historical Society (r); National Gallery of Art / Laurie Platt Winfrey, Inc. (c); **133** Courtesy National Geographic Society / photo by Pat Lanza Field; **135** Historical Society of Pennsylvania / Newsweek Books; **136** National Gallery of Art (b); Laurie Platt Winfrey, Inc. (t, c); **137** Henry Francis Dupont Winterthur Museum, Wilmington, DE; **139** Library of Congress; **141** The Shelburne Museum, Shelburne, VT; **143** © Collection of The New-York Historical Society / Laurie Platt Winfrey, Inc.; **146** The Historical Society of Pennsylvania / Newsweek Books; **147** Corbis-Bettmann; **148** Library of Congress (tr); Smithsonian Institution (bl); **149** Chicago Historical Society; **152** From *The True Aaron Burr*, by Charles Burr Todd, A.S. Barnes & Co., New York, 1902 (t, b); **153** The Granger Collection (bl); © Collection of The New-York Historical Society (br); **154** Essex Institute, Salem / MA (bl); The Granger Collection (cl); **155** © Eunice Harris, 1981 / Photo Researchers, Inc. (r); Henry Grosinski (b); **156** Maryland Historical Society (cl); The Granger Collection (tl); **157** New Orleans Museum of Art (tl); Ralph J. Brunke (r, br); The Granger Collection (cl); detail, New Orleans Museum of Art (cr); **158** Library of Congress; **162** © Donald Dietz / Stock Boston; **162–63** Shelburne Museum, Shelburne, VT.; **163** Photo by Tom Liddell (br); Abby Aldrich Rockefeller Folk Art Center, Colonial Williamsburg (tr); **164** The Granger Collection; **165** Henry Francis Dupont Winterthur Museum, Wilmington, DE; **166** The Granger Collection; **168** Image Copyright © 1998 PhotoDisc, Inc.; **169** Old Dartmouth Historical Society; **170** Private Collection (b); Laurie Platt Winfrey, Inc. (cl); **171** © Marvin Koner / Black Star (cl); Library of Congress (tr); © D. Staples, Black Star (bl); **172** New York Public Library; **173** © Collection of The New-York Historical Society (r); North Carolina Museum of Art (l); **176** Tennessee State Library & Archives (cl); Library of Congress (br); **177** © Collection of The New-York Historical Society; **178** Gibbes Museum of Art, Carolina Art Association; **179** The Granger Collection; **180** The Metropolitan Museum of Art; **181** Culver Pictures, Inc.; **182** Musée Jacquemart-André, Paris / Newsweek Books (br); Connecticut Historical Society (tr); Her Majesty's Stationery Office / Newsweek Books (bc); Cincinnati Historical Society (c); **183** Beinecke Library, Yale University, New Haven, CT; **184** © Collection of The New-York Historical Society; **185** Courtesy the Trustees of the Boston Public Library, Print Department; **188** Delaware Art Museum, Wilmington (cl); Shelburne Museum, Shelburne, VT (br); **189** National Collection of Fine Arts / Laurie Platt Winfrey, Inc.; **190** Ralph J. Brunke; **191** Smithsonian Institution; **192** From *Godey's Lady's Book*, 1859, courtesy Mark MacKay; **193** Metropolitan Museum of Art; **195** Free Library of Philadelphia; **196** The Granger Collection; **197** The Granger Collection (t); Private Collection (b); **199** National Archives; **200** Smithsonian Institution (tr); The Granger Collection (tl); **201** The Granger Collection; **202** © Kent & Donna Dannen 1980 / Photo Researchers, Inc.; **203** © Fort Malden National Historic Park, Amherstburg, Ontario; **204** Library of Congress; **205** New York Public Library; **210** New York Public Library; **211** Radio Times / Hulton Picture Library; **212** The Edward W.C. Arnold Collection lent by Metropolitan Museum of Art; **215** The Granger Collection; **218–19** Shelburne Museum, Shelburne, VT; **220** Library of Congress (br); Independence National Historic Park Collection (c); Smithsonian Institution (bl); **220–21** detail, Metropolitan Museum of Art / photo by Geoffrey Clements; **222** State Historical Society of North Dakota; **224** Missouri Historical Society (bl); New York Public Library (bc); **225** The Thomas Gilcrease Institute of American History and Art, Tulsa, OK (tl); American Museum of Natural History, New York (cr); **226** Colorado Historical Society, Denver; **229** The Granger Collection; **231** Courtesy of the San Antonio Museum Association, San Antonio, TX, on loan from Bexar County (tr); Barker Texas History Center (cr); **232** Courtesy of the Alamo / The Daughters of the Republic of Texas; **233** New York Public Library (cr); © Steve Elmore / Tom Stack and Associates (b); Texas State Library (cl); Courtesy the Alamo / The Daughters of the Republic of Texas (c);

© Jules Bucher / Photo Researchers, Inc. (tr); **236** Seaver Center for Western history Research, LA County Museum of Natural History; **237** Bancroft Library, University of California at Berkeley; **238** The Oakland Museum History Department; **239** The Oakland Museum History Dept.; **240** © David Muench 1990 (t); New York Public Library (c); **241** Courtesy, Colorado Historical Society. Negative # F20380; **242** Seaver Center for Western History Research, LA County Museum of Natural History (br); The Oakland Museum History Dept. (cl); **243** Church of Jesus Christ of Latter-Day Saints; **245** American Stanhope Collection; **247** National Park Service; **252** New York Public Library (b); Betty Willis Antiques, Marlborough, NH, photo by The Hansen Co. (c); **253** Cincinnati Historical Society (c); Betty Willis Antiques, Marlborough, NH, photo by The Hansen Co. (b); **254** Essex Institute, Salem, MA; **255** Wakefield Historical Society, Wakefield, MA; **256** New York Public Library (bl); © Collection of The New-York Historical Society (br); **257** Wide World (c); Smithsonian Institution (bl, bc); Private Collection (tr); The Granger Collection (br); **260** Museum of American Textile History, Andover, MA; **263** Brooklyn Museum, Brooklyn, NY; **264** © Collection of The New-York Historical Society; **266** U.S. Military History Institute / Corbis; **267** National Portrait Gallery / Smithsonian Institution, transfer from the National Museum of American History; gift of the National American Woman's Suffrage Association through Mrs. Harriet Stanton Blatch, 1924, Washington, D.C. / Art Resource, New York; **268** Private Collection (b); Sophia Smith Collection, Smith College (tl); **269** Massachusetts Historical Society; **270** © Murray Alcosser / The Image Bank; **271** Smithsonian Institution; **272** Brown Brothers; **273** State of Illinois; **278** Schlowsky Photography; **279** Schlowsky Photography; **282** Private Collection / Time-Life Books (c); **282–83** New York Public Library; **283** Courtesy Museum of Appalachia, Norris, TN / photo by Frank Hoffman (br); Courtesy National park Service / photo by William A. Bake (cr); **285** © Collection of The New-York Historical Society; **286** The Historic New Orleans Collection; **287** The Granger Collection; **289** William Gladstone Collection; **292** The Western Reserve Historical Society; **293** © Photography by Milt and Joan Mann / Cameramann International; **294** The Museum of Fine Arts, Boston / M. and M. Karolik Collection; **295** Culver Pictures (t); The Granger Collection (c); **298** Collection of Mr. & Mrs. Wilson Pile / photo by Clive Russ; **299** Great Smoky Mountain National Park; **300–01** Courtesy Museum of Appalachia, Norris, TN, photo by Frank Hoffman; **302** © Collection of The New-York Historical Society / Newsweek Books; **303** Private Collection; **305** The Charleston Museum, Charleston, South Carolina; **310–11** © Jerome Liebling; **312** Massachusetts Historical Society (cl); **312–13** Sophia Smith Collection, Smith College (tc); **313** Museum of American Political Life, University of Hartford, photo by Sally Andersen-Bruce; **315** © Collection of The New-York Historical Society; **319** Culver Pictures (t); New York Public Library (c); **320** © Collection of The New-York Historical Society; **321** Metropolitan Museum of Art (bc); New York Public Library (br); **322** The Granger Collection; **324** Schlesinger Library of Historic Women, Radcliffe College, Cambridge, MA (l); Metropolitan Museum of Art / Newsweek Books (t); **328** Kansas State Historical Society, Topeka (br); Boston Athenaeum (tl); **329** Private Collection; **330** Metropolitan Museum of Art; **331** Missouri Historical Society; **333** The Granger Collection; **334** New York Public Library; **335** Library of Congress; **336** National Portrait Gallery, Smithsonian Institution, gift of Mrs. Alan Valentine / Art Resource, New York; **340** Collection of Larry Williford (c); *The Civil War* series, *Decoying the Yanks,* photograph by Larry Sherer, © 1984, Time-Life Books, Inc. (bl); **341** Collection of Larry Williford (c); *The Civil War* series, *20 Million Yankees* photograph by Larry Sherer, © 1985, Time-Life Books, Inc. (br); **342** Library of Congress; **344** © Richard & Mary Magruder / The Image Bank; **345** West Point Museum; **347** © Collection of The New-York Historical Society; **348** Boston Atheneum; **348–49** Boston Atheneum; **349** Museum of the Confederacy © Larry Sherer; **351** Stock Montage, Inc. (t); U.T. Institute of Texan Cultures, San Antonio, Texas (b); **352** U.S. Army Military History Institute, Carlisle Barracks, PA; **353** © David Muench (bc) *The Civil War* series, *Spies, Scouts and Raiders* photograph by Larry Sherer, © 1985, Time-Life Books, Inc. (tr); **354** Boston Atheneum; **355** Lincoln Library, Fort Wayne, Indiana; **356** *The Civil War* series, *Tenting Tonight* photograph by Larry Sherer, © 1984, Time-Life Books, Inc.; **357** New York Public Library; **358** Cook Collection, Valentine Museum (cl); Library of Congress (cr); **359** The Granger Collection; **360** Schlowsky Photography; **362** Boston Atheneum; **363** National Archives (tr); *The Civil War* series, *Decoying the Yanks* photograph by Larry Sherer, © 1984, Time-Life Books, Inc. (cr); **364** Boston Atheneum (tr); *The Civil War* series, *20 Million Yankees* photograph by Larry Sherer, © 1985, Time-Life Books, Inc. (bl); The Granger Collection (cl); **365** Boston Atheneum (tc, b); Museum of the Confederacy / © Larry Sherer (cr); **366** Library of Congress; **367** National Archives (r); Boston Atheneum (l); **368** Boston Atheneum; **369** Boston Atheneum (t); *The Civil War* series, *20 Million Yankees* photograph by Larry Sherer, © 1985, Time-Life Books, Inc. (b); **374–75** National Archives; **375** Library of Congress (b); William Gladstone Collection (t); **377** The Granger Collection; **378** © Collection of The New-York Historical Society; **379** © Collection of The New-York Historical Society (tl); Library of Congress (cr); **380** Schlowsky Photography (cl); Library of Congress (cr); **380–81** Library of Congress (t, b); **381** Culver Pictures (cr); The Andover Historical Society, Andover, MA (tr); **382** Library of Congress; **383** Library of Congress (tr); © Bill Howe, PHOTRI / Maryilyn Gartman Agency, Inc. (tl); **385** Library of Congress; **387** *Harper's Weekly,* November 16, 1867 (tl); Library of Congress (br); **388** Chicago Historical Society; **389** © Dick Spahr, Time-Life Books (cr); Culver Pictures (tr); **390** Library of Congress; **391** Old Court House Museum, Eva W. Davis Memorial; **392** Old Sturbridge Village; **393** Brown Brothers (tc); John Deere Museum, photo by Boyd-Fitzgerald (cr); **394** Old Court House Museum, photo by Bob Pickett; **397** Library of Congress; **399** Collection of John Ridley; **406–07** Metropolitan Museum of Art, Bequest of Edward W.C. Arnold, 1954; **408** The Granger Collection; **408–09** Oklahoma Historical Society (c); **409** S.D. Butcher Collection, Nebraska State Historical Society, Negative # B983-1231 (tr); Peabody Museum of Natural History, Yale University, New Haven, CT. (br); **410** © Ann Duncan / Tom Stack & Associates; **413** Collection of John Ridley (tr) The Oakland Museum History Department (br); **414** Library of Congress; **415** The Granger Collection; **416** © Justin Kerr (cl); Museum of the American Indian, Heye Foundation (bc); **417** Southwest Museum, Los Angeles, CA (tl, tc); Museum of the American Indian, Heye Foundation (tr); Peabody Museum of Anthropology, Harvard University, photo by Carmelo Guadagno (bl); **420** Huntington Library and Art Gallery, San Marino, CA; **421** The Oakland Museum History Dept.; **422** The Granger Collection; **426** Library of Congress (tl); **427** Solomon D. Butcher Collection, Nebraska State Historical Society, Lincoln; **428** Jane Libby; **429** Walker, James (1819-1889) Am., Born England, *Vaqueros in a Horse Corral*, oil on canvas, 1877, 0126.1480, 24 1/4 x 40", From the Collection of Gilcrease Museum, Tulsa (tr); The Oakland Museum History Dept. (b); **430** Collection of John Ridley; **431** Library of Congress; **432** State Historical Society of Wisconsin; **436** The Granger Collection; **439** Collection of John Ridley; **440** © D. Lowe / FPG International (br); Brown Brothers (cl); **441** Collection of Susan W. and Stephen D. Paine, photo by Sally Fox (br); Collection of Sally Fox (b); The Oakland Museum History Dept. (bl); Corbis-Bettmann (t); **442** The Free Library of Philadelphia; **443** © American Telephone and Telegraph Co. (tr); Smithsonian Institution (br); **444** © Collection of The New-York Historical Society (br); Corbis-Bettmann (tl); **445** Culver Pictures, Inc.; **446** Corbis-Bettmann (t); Collection of John Ridley (cl); **447** The Granger Collection; **448** Corbis-Bettmann; **451** Collection of John Ridley; **453** © University of Chicago Press; **455** State Historical Society of Wisconsin; **456** Collection of John Ridley; **457** George Eastman House Collection / Laurie Platt Winfrey; **458** Chicago Historical Society; **459** AFL-CIO News (br); Corbis-Bettmann (tr); **460** National Archives; **461** Library of Congress; **464** The Granger Collection; **465** Library of Congress (tl); © Steve Elmore / Tom Stack and Associates (br); The Granger Collection (bc); George Eastman House Collection (tr); National Park Service (c); George Eastman House Collection / Laurie Platt Winfrey, Inc. (cl); **466** Holt-Atherton Center for Western Studies, University of the Pacific; **469** Smithsonian Institution; **470** The Oakland Museum History Dept. (cr); Museum of the City of New York (bl); **471** Museum of the City of New York (b); The Oakland Museum History Dept. (tl); **472** Brown Brothers; **473** The Oakland Museum History Dept. (tr); Brown Brothers (b); **474** New York Public Library; **475** Museum of the City of New York / Newsweek Books; **476** New York Public Library; **477** *Harper's Weekly,* July 8, 1881; **478** *Harper's Weekly*, Nov. 7, 1874 (b); Museum of American Political Life, University of Hartford, photo by Sally Andersen-Bruce (l, r); **479** The Granger Collection (tl); Museum of American Political Life, University of Hartford, photo by Sally Andersen-Bruce (b); Corbis-Bettmann (tr); **480** Library of

Congress; **482** The Granger Collection; **483** Security Pacific National Bank Historic Photograph Collection, Los Angeles Public Library (b); Culver Pictures (cr); **486** Library of Congress; **487** State Historical Society of Wisconsin; **488** The Granger Collection; **489** The Granger Collection; **490** Stanley King Collection (t, c); Private Collection (b); **495** *Harper's Weekly,* Nov. 7, 1874; **496** George Eastman House Collection; **497** Brown Brothers (t); Collection of John Ridley (br); **498** Brown Brothers (b); The Granger Collection (bl); **499** Los Angeles County Museum of Art; **500** The Jacob A. Riis Collection, Museum of the City of New York (tr, cl); Schlowsky Photography (bl); **502** Chicago Historical Society (tl); The Granger Collection (cl); **503** Library of Congress; **504** Culver Pictures; **505** Library of Congress/ Corbis; **508** Library of Congress; **509** The Granger Collection (tr); Culver Pictures (b); **510** Theodore Roosevelt Collection, Harvard College Library; **511** Stanley King Collection; **512** Collection of John Ridley; **513** Brown Brothers; **514** George Eastman House Collection; **515** Corbis-Bettmann; **516** National Archives; **517** Library of Congress; **518** Library of Congress; **519** New York Public Library (tr); © NAACP (tl); **520** Library of Congress; **521** The Granger Collection; **525** Museum of the City of New York; **526** © Mort Kunstler, National Guard Bureau; **527** Library of Congress (tl); The Granger Collection (r); Military Records, Commonwealth of MA, Natick (bl, bc); **530** The Granger Collection; **531** United States Naval Academy Museum; **532** Culver Pictures; **533** The Granger Collection; **535** The Granger Collection (br); Collection of John Ridley (cr); **537** The Granger Collection; **538** National Archives; **539** Panama Canal Company (cr); National Archives (c); **540** The Granger Collection; **541** Corbis-Bettmann; **542** © PHOTRI/Marilyn Gartman Agency, Inc.; **543** The Press Museum (tr); The Granger Collection (br); Brown Brothers (tc); **544** The Granger Collection (tl, b); **545** The Granger Collection (t); Imperial War Museum, London (tl); **547** Culver Pictures; **548** The Granger Collection; **549** The National Archives (t); Corbis-Bettmann (b); **551** Imperial War Museum / Newsweek Books; **552** Corbis-Bettmann (b); White House Collection (tl); **553** Private Collection; **557** New Jersey Historical Society, Newark; **559** Library of Congress; **560–61** Culver Pictures; **562** The Oakland Museum History Dept. (bc); California Historical Society, San Francisco (cr); George Eastman House Collection (cl); **563** © Eric Wheater / The Image Bank (tl); © Bob Daemmrich / Stock Boston (bc); Corbis-Bettmann (tc); **564** Photos courtesy of The Issa Family; **565** Corbis-Bettmann / Newsweek Books; **566** George Eastman House Collection, Newsweek Books; **567** California Historical Society; **568** Collection of John Ridley; **570** Corbis-Bettmann; **571** © David Weintraub, 1985 / Photo Researchers, Inc.; **574** Elihu Blotnick; **576** © Lawrence Migdale; **577** Wide World; **579** Corbis-Bettmann; **580** Corbis-Bettmann; **581** © Grant Heilman Photography; **582** Corbis-Bettmann; **583** © B. Daemmrich / Stock Boston; **590** Private Collection (c); The Thomas Gilcrease Institute of American history and Art, Tulsa, OK (cl); **591** © Andrew Sacks / Black Star (br); University of Illinois at Chicago, The University Library, Jane Addams Memorial Collection (tc); © Bob Riha / Gamma-Liaison (tr); New York Public Library (tc); **592** Wide World; **593** © David Marie / FOLIO; **594** © Grant Heilman Photography; **596** Wide World; **597** © R. Maiman / Sygma; **601** New York Public Library; **603** Corbis-Bettmann; **604** Library of Congress; **605** © Bob Fitch / Black Star (tl); © Frank Johnston / Black Star (tr); **606** © Gary Gladstone / The Image Bank (bl); Brown Brothers (tl); © Lawrence Fried, 1980 / The Image Bank (br); **607** Karin Cooper / AP / Wide World Photos; **608** Toyo Miyatake, courtesy Elihu Blotnick; **609** Lester Sloan / The Gamma-Liaison Network; **610** Wallace Kirkland, Hull House; **611** Courtesy CityYouth; **613** Corbis-Bettmann (t); © Eric Bouvet / Gamma-Liaison (tl); **614** © Marc Romanelli / The Image Bank; **615** © Michael Melford / The Image Bank (tc, br); © Alvis Upitis / The Image Bank (tr); **622** © Liane Enkelis, 1986 / Stock Boston; **624** © Markel / Liaison International (b); © Cary Wolinsky / Stock Boston (tl); **625** © Gary D. McMichael, 1987 / Photo Researchers (t); © Brian Parker / Tom Stack & Associates (cl); © Bill Gutmann / Marilyn Gartman Agency, Inc. (cr); **626** © Bob Daemmrich / Stock Boston; **627** © Gene Stein / Westlight; **628** © Susan Leavines, 1987 / Photo Researchers, Inc.; **630** Corbis-Bettmann; **632** Wide World Photo; **634** © Ellis Herwig / Stock Boston;; Photo research by Carousel Research, Inc., Meyers-Photo Art, and Pembroke Herbert / Picture Research Consultants

Chapter 1

PART ONE

page 1

(12 points)

A. 1. a
2. c
3. c
4. b

(21 points)

B. 5. a
6. b
7. c
8. b
9. c
10. a
11. c

page 2

(18 points)

C. 12. d
13. b
14. b
15. b
16. c
17. b

page 3

(15 points)

D. 18. a
19. b
20. a
21. a
22. b

(9 points)

E. 23. a
24. a
25. c

---

page 1 Date ________________

Chapter 1 — Test

Reviewing Exploration and Settlement

PART ONE

A. Write the letter of the best answer.

_____ 1. What landforms presented the greatest problems to settlers moving west?
a. mountain ranges
b. the Great Lakes
c. the Great Plains

_____ 2. The greatest problem for pioneers who tried farming on the Central Plains and Great Plains was created by the
a. climate.
b. quality of the soil.
c. root systems of the grass.

_____ 3. The Continental Divide is the ridge that
a. marks the highest point in North America.
b. divides the continent into two equal halves.
c. separates rivers that flow east from those that flow west.

_____ 4. The Pacific shoreline differs from the Atlantic shoreline in that the Pacific coast
a. has a wide coastal plain.
b. has fewer natural harbors.
c. is less rugged and dramatic in appearance.

B. Match each major physical region with the area of the United States in which it is located.

a. Eastern and Southern b. Central Heartland c. Western

_____ 5. Piedmont
_____ 6. Great Plains
_____ 7. Pacific Coast
_____ 8. Great Lakes
_____ 9. Rocky Mountains
_____ 10. Appalachian Highlands
_____ 11. Sierra Nevada

page 2 Date ________________

C. Write the letter of the best answer.

_____ 12. Which of the following did *not* exist in North America before the Europeans arrived?
a. beaver
b. buffalo
c. deer
d. horses

_____ 13. Which of the following men led a rebellion in Virginia?
a. King Philip
b. Nathaniel Bacon
c. Roger Williams
d. William Penn

_____ 14. Which of the following kinds of settlements were established in the New World primarily by the Spanish?
a. forts
b. missions
c. plantations
d. trading posts

_____ 15. Which of the following was England's first permanent settlement in the New World?
a. Plymouth
b. Jamestown
c. New Netherland
d. Roanoke Island

_____ 16. Which of the following was a Middle colony?
a. Virginia
b. Connecticut
c. Pennsylvania
d. Massachusetts

_____ 17. Which of the following was true of most New England farmers during colonial times?
a. They grew crops to sell.
b. They settled in small villages.
c. They bought slaves to work the land.
d. They came from a variety of countries.

page 3 Date ________________

D. Write the letter of the best answer.

_____ 18. The **conquistadors** were most interested in obtaining
a. gold.
b. land.
c. religious freedom.

_____ 19. A person who studies **human geography** studies chiefly
a. people and their cultures.
b. how people and places interact.
c. how people and animals are alike.

_____ 20. Advances in **navigation** assisted Europeans in
a. crossing the ocean.
b. surviving in the New World.
c. building trade with the Indians.

_____ 21. An example of an **alliance** is the
a. Iroquois League.
b. Puritans.
c. Quakers.

_____ 22. A **subsistance farmer** was one who
a. established a plantation.
b. raised just enough food to survive.
c. traded surplus crops in the port cities.

E. For each of the following types of reference books, write the letter of the information that could be found in that type of book.

_____ 23. REFERENCE: a historical atlas
a. a map of colonial Pennsylvania
b. a summary of important Quaker beliefs
c. the text of a speech given by William Penn

_____ 24. REFERENCE: a book of summary chronologies
a. the year that slaves first arrived in Georgia
b. a map of the Lower South during colonial times
c. the number of plantations in Virginia in 1790

_____ 25. REFERENCE: a statistical abstract
a. a summary of key events in the settlement of New England
b. a map showing that Rhode Island is in New England
c. the number of people living in Rhode Island in 1775

page 4 Date ________________

PART TWO

Answer the following questions.

1. What were two basic desires that motivated European explorers of the 1500s and 1600s?

2. How were Jamestown's early problems tied to its geographical location?

3. Newcomers to America in the 1600s were amazed by what seemed to be a limitless amount of land. Who suffered most from the fact that this was not true? Explain.

4. What were two developments or events that encouraged the growth of slavery in the colonies? Explain.

Answer the following question on the back or on another sheet of paper. Use complete sentences.

5. In what ways do you think America's geography has helped to bring Americans together as a nation? In what ways do you think it has helped to separate Americans from one another? Explain your answer.

PART TWO

(25 points)

page 4

1. Answers should include any two of the following desires (some of which are overlapping):
a. for wealth, exotic goods, and spices
b. for adventure, personal glory, and fame
c. for knowledge
d. to find a quicker route to Asia
e. to spread Christianity

2. Answers should recognize that its low, swampy land made farming difficult and contributed to disease. Some answers may include a reference to the proximity of Indians, with whom relations quickly deteriorated, mostly due to the actions of white settlers.

3. Answers should note that America's native peoples suffered most from this misconception. The land was certainly not limitless; there were serious conflicts over its division and use from the time of the first European settlements.

4. Answers should include two of the following:
a. England's involvement in the slave trade made it easier for colonists to get slaves.
b. The supply of indentured servants declined sharply as England's economy improved.
c. Bacon's Rebellion led wealthy planters to fear that bitter indentured servants would rise up against them.
d. Southern plantations were labor-intensive operations.

5. Answers will vary but may include:
a. The vastness of America's landscape and the challenges it provides have helped to create an American character that has been passed down from generation to generation. These shared character traits include self-reliance, optimism, and independence.
b. Americans have had to adapt their ways of life to the requirements of the land. As a result, in colonial times, different ways of life, including different values, customs, etc., developed along regional lines.

Chapter 2

PART ONE

page 5

(33 points)

A. 1. b
2. d
3. b
4. d
5. c
6. a

page 6

B. 7. c
8. d
9. b
10. d
11. c

(18 points)

C. 12. i
13. b
14. d
15. a
16. h
17. c

page 7

18. f
19. g
20. e

(12 points)

D. 21. h
22. a
23. f
24. e

(12 points)

E. 25. C
26. D
27. A
28. B

---

page 5 Date ____________

Chapter 2 — Test

Reviewing the American Revolution

PART ONE

A. Write the letter of the best answer.

_____ 1. During the mid-1700s, immigrants came to the United States for all of the following reasons *except*

a. to find religious freedom.
b. to join military campaigns.
c. to escape wars in their homelands.
d. to escape famine in their homelands.

_____ 2. African Americans in South Carolina made contributions in all of the following areas *except*

a. growing rice. c. herding cattle.
b. weaving baskets. d. building factories.

_____ 3. During the Great Awakening, ministers like George Whitefield tried to

a. close their congregations to new immigrants.
b. inspire people to dedicate themselves to God.
c. keep people who were not ministers from active participation in church services.
d. strengthen the ties between the church in America and the official church of England.

_____ 4. As a result of the Seven Years' War, England gained all of the following territory *except*

a. Canada. c. lands east of the Mississippi.
b. Florida. d. lands west of the Mississippi.

_____ 5. The Proclamation of 1763 stated that the territory west of the Appalachians would be

a. given to Spain.
b. sold back to France.
c. closed to colonial settlement.
d. divided into new colonies.

_____ 6. The colonists were required to provide housing and supplies for British troops by the

a. Quartering Act. c. Intolerable Acts.
b. Townshend Acts. d. Stamp Act.

page 6 Date ____________

_____ 7. When was the Declaration of Independence signed?

a. a few months before the war began
b. the day that the war began
c. about a year after the war began
d. several years after the war began

_____ 8. The American Revolution began in the colony of

a. New York. c. Pennsylvania.
b. Virginia. d. Massachusetts.

_____ 9. France was persuaded to support the American cause after which of the following battles?

a. Bunker Hill
b. Saratoga
c. Trenton
d. Yorktown

_____ 10. During the American Revolution, women did all of the following *except*

a. fight in battles. c. work in army camps.
b. operate businesses. d. elect representatives.

_____ 11. Which of the following never fought on the side of the Americans?

a. slaves c. Loyalists
b. Indians d. free blacks

B. Match each person with the description.

a. Ethan Allen f. Thomas Jefferson
b. William Howe g. Charles Cornwallis
c. Thomas Paine h. Benjamin Franklin
d. John Burgoyne i. George Washington
e. Paul Revere

_____ 12. led the Continental Army at Valley Forge.

_____ 13. led British troops that occupied Philadelphia.

_____ 14. lost a 50-pound bet on the outcome of the war.

_____ 15. led the Green Mountain Boys against the British.

_____ 16. worked out a treaty with Britain to end the war.

_____ 17. wrote *Common Sense*, a pamphlet urging revolution.

page 7 Date ____________

_____ 18. headed the committee to write the Declaration of Independence.

_____ 19. effectively ended the war by surrendering his troops at Yorktown.

_____ 20. warned the minutemen of the British march to Lexington and Concord.

C. In each blank, write the letter of the term that correctly completes the sentence. Not all of the terms will be used.

a. boycott e. pluralism
b. cede f. republic
c. inflation g. salutary neglect
d. militia h. writs of assistance

21. Americans today are protected from unreasonable searches, in part because of our historical experience with ____.

22. The colonists' joint refusal to buy taxed goods was a ____.

23. Free elections are necessary in a ____.

24. America's unique culture is due to the ____ that has existed here for hundreds of years.

D. For each listed event, write the correct letter from the timeline below.

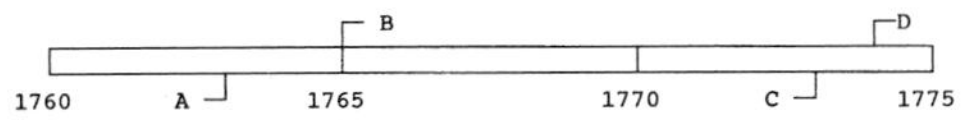

_____ 25. the Boston Tea Party

_____ 26. the meetings of the First Continental Congress

_____ 27. the end of the Seven Years' War

_____ 28. the passage of the Stamp Act

page 8 Date ____________

PART TWO

Answer the following questions.

1. What was one effect of the mix of cultures that existed together in the American colonies?

2. What is one freedom, or right, that members of minority religions did *not* have in the American colonies?

3. Give two effects of the Great Awakening.

4. How were free black men treated during the American Revolution? What, if anything, did they gain by the fact that many fought on the American side during the war?

Answer the following question on the back or on another sheet of paper. Use complete sentences.

5. The Declaration of Independence says that the government receives its just power from the consent of the governed. Does this mean that people are right to ignore laws they do not agree with? Explain your answer with possible effects or examples, from today's world or the world of the colonists.

PART TWO

(25 points)

page 8

1. Answers could name any of the following:
a. religious tolerance
b. a new form of English (or, mix of languages)
c. new American products and farming methods
Other answers are acceptable if they are based on an understanding of how pluralism has affected American life.

2. Answers should note either voting or holding public office.

3. Answers should include any two of the following:
a. Many people experienced conversion, or a deep commitment to the church.
b. Participants often felt a greater sense of self-worth.
c. Ties with the official English church were weakened.
d. Other religions in America were strengthened.
e. Lay people became more active in church services.
f. It made the colonists feel more independent.

4. Answers should include information similar to the following:
a. The Continental Army was forced to accept free blacks into its ranks after the British began enlisting slaves.
b. Once blacks joined the army, they fought in all major battles.
c. The participation of blacks in the war may have sparked anti-slavery sentiments after the war.
d. Free blacks gained few, if any, benefits in terms of their social status immediately following the war.

5. Answers will vary but should be judged on the basis of the logic and thoroughness with which a student considers the implications of his or her answer. Some answers will note that "the consent of the governed" does not mean "the consent of every individual."

Chapter 3

PART ONE

page 9

(32 points)

A. 1. b
2. a
3. c
4. a
5. c
6. b
7. a

page 10

8. c

(14 points)

B. 9. C
10. S
11. C
12. B
13. S
14. N
15. B

(15 points)

C. 16. a
17. b
18. a

page 11

19. a
20. b

(14 points)

D. 21. N
22. Y
23. Y
24. N
25. Y
26. N
27. Y

page 9

Date ____________

Chapter 3 Test

Pluralism

PART ONE

A. Write the letter of the best answer.

_____ 1. Which of the following was a completely new idea of government?
a. basing a government on the concept of republicanism
b. basing a government on the principles of the Enlightenment
c. defining a government's powers in a constitution

_____ 2. Under the Articles of Confederation, there was a national
a. legislature only.
b. legislature and executive.
c. legislature and court system.

_____ 3. Certain states had claims to western lands because they had
a. purchased these lands.
b. explored and claimed these lands.
c. been granted these lands in their colonial charters.

_____ 4. Under the Articles of Confederation, which of the following was the central government's *biggest* problem?
a. It lacked the power to tax citizens directly.
b. It could not enforce the treaties that it made.
c. Its elected representatives were inexperienced.

_____ 5. Daniel Shays led a rebellion for
a. the right to vote.
b. the right to hold public office.
c. relief from state property taxes.

_____ 6. Each of the following is a legacy of the Articles of Confederation *except*
a. the national postal system.
b. a strong national government.
c. expanded international trade.

_____ 7. The Northwest Ordinance provided a plan for
a. how territories could become states.
b. purchasing western lands from foreign nations.
c. the ceding of western lands to the central government.

page 10

Date ____________

_____ 8. A new convention was called to consider the defects of the Articles of Confederation because
a. other reforms of the Articles had been successful.
b. the national government had gained too much power.
c. the ineffectiveness of the government had become apparent.

B. Fill in the blanks below to make true statements about the government at the time of the Articles of Confederation. Use the following code:

C means "The central government"
S means "The state governments"
B means "Both the central and the state governments"
N means "Neither the central nor the state governments"

_____ 9. had the supreme power to make treaties with other countries

_____ 10. had the power to tax citizens directly

_____ 11. guaranteed sovereignty rights to American Indians

_____ 12. printed money

_____ 13. collected import taxes on foreign goods

_____ 14. protected American sailors from pirates

_____ 15. had an elected legislature

C. Write the letter of the best answer.

_____ 16. States that have formed a **confederation** have
a. joined together.
b. declared a civil war.
c. given up most of their rights.

_____ 17. In the phrase "**term of office**," the word *term* means
a. location.
b. time period.
c. duties and requirements.

_____ 18. An example of a **constitution** is
a. the Mayflower Compact.
b. the Declaration of Independence.
c. the Virginia House of Burgesses.

page 11

Date ____________

_____ 19. Settlers in the western **territories** were guaranteed
a. freedom of religion.
b. the right to own slaves.
c. the right to settle Indian lands.

_____ 20. A government that controls **commerce** controls
a. taxes.
b. trade.
c. factories.

D. Read the following excerpt from Abigail Adams's letter of March 31, 1776, about the "new code of laws."

> I long to hear that you have declared an independency—and, by the way, in the new code of laws, which I suppose it will be necessary for you to make, I desire you would remember the ladies . . . If particular care and attention is not paid to the ladies, we are determined to [instigate] a rebellion, and will not hold ourselves bound by any laws in which we have no voice or representation. . . . That your sex are naturally tyrannical is a truth so thoroughly established as to admit of no dispute. . . . Men of sense in all ages abhor those customs which treat us only as the vassals of your sex. Regard us then as beings, placed by providence under your protection . . .

Mark *Y* if the letter gives you some information about the topic. Write *N* if it does not.

_____ 21. whether Abigail loved John Adams

_____ 22. what Abigail's opinion of men's nature was

_____ 23. whether or not Abigail supported independence from Britain

_____ 24. when Abigail expected to hear back from her husband

_____ 25. the actions women would take if they were ignored

_____ 26. whether Abigail's opinions were popular

_____ 27. how Abigail believed men should treat women

page 12

Date ____________

PART TWO

Answer the following questions.

1. What was the basic philosophy of the Enlightenment?

2. Why were Americans of this period concerned about a strong central government?

3. Describe one of the problems related to currency that existed during the time of the Articles of Confederation.

4. Name one way that the central government's weakness under the Articles of Confederation affected the new nation's foreign affairs.

Answer the following question on the back or on another sheet of paper. Use complete sentences.

5. Why did the citizens of the new nation feel that government should be based on a constitution? Do these reasons still exist today? What problems did the new nation experience under the Articles of Confederation even though it had a constitutional government?

PART TWO

(25 points)

page 12

1. Answers should note the importance of reason to Enlightenment philosophy.

2. Answers should point out either that Americans feared the establishment of a monarchy or that they were unwilling to set up a government that might create the same problems they were attempting to escape.

3. Answers could include:
a. Simultaneous state and national currencies caused problems in trade.
b. Devalued state currencies caused problems for everyone using them.
c. Insecurities about any currency caused problems in trade, loans, and debt repayments.

4. Answers could include any one of the following:
a. Although the central government could make treaties, it could not enforce them.
b. It did not have the power to control foreign trade.
c. It could not tax imports.
d. It was too poor and too weak to protect American sailors from pirates.

5. Answers could include:
a. The idea of constitutional government was part of their heritage.
b. They wanted a single document that described their rights.
c. They wanted to avoid the kinds of disputes they had had with the British government.

Answers should note that these reasons still exist today.

Answers should also note two or more problems stemming from the weakness of the central government under the Articles.

Chapter 4

PART ONE

page 13

(14 points)

A. 1. A
2. F
3. A
4. A
5. A
6. F
7. F

(16 points)

B. 8. c
9. b
10. b

page 14

11. a

(18 points)

C. 12. f (or g)
13. g (or f)
14. a
15. l
16. j
17. i
18. b
19. d
20. e

(15 points)

D. 21. c
22. b

page 15

23. a
24. a
25. c

(12 points)

E. 26. c
27. b
28. c

page 13 ____________ Date ____________

Chapter 4 Test

The Constitutional Convention

PART ONE

A. Write *F* if the statement agrees with Federalist ideas. Write *A* if it agrees with Antifederalist ideas.

______ 1. A strong central government will overpower the individual states.

______ 2. A strong central government is the only hope for maintaining the union of states.

______ 3. The Constitution protects the interests of only a small group of people.

______ 4. The Constitutional Convention went far beyond its legal purpose.

______ 5. An elected government could be worse than a monarchy.

______ 6. A bill of rights is not a necessary part of the Constitution.

______ 7. The states' declarations of rights sufficiently protect individual liberties.

B. Write the letter of the best answer.

______ 8. The Constitutional Convention was originally called to
a. end slavery.
b. raise taxes.
c. strengthen the Articles of Confederation.

______ 9. Which of the following was *most* important in creating the Constitution?
a. the leadership of George Washington
b. a series of compromises on difficult issues
c. a group of essays by Hamilton, Jay, and Madison

______ 10. Before its adoption, the new Constitution had to be approved by
a. a majority (seven) of the thirteen states.
b. nine of the thirteen states.
c. all of the thirteen states.

page 14 ____________ Date ____________

______ 11. Which of these strategies was *not* used by the Federalists to win ratification of the Constitution?
a. preventing debate whenever possible
b. publishing their views in newspapers and books
c. acting quickly in states where they had a majority

C. In each blank, write the letter of the best word or phrase.

a. Senate	g. smaller states
b. slaves	h. Bill of Rights
c. one-half	i. Southern states
d. free citizens	j. Northern states
e. three-fifths	k. Antifederalists
f. larger states	l. House of Representatives

The delegates to the Constitutional Convention quickly agreed to a two-house legislature. However, the ___(12) and ___(13) split over how representatives would be elected. In the Connecticut Compromise, all agreed to equal representation of each state in the ___(14) and representation based on population in the ___(15).

The difficult question of how population would be counted for purposes of representation and taxation resulted in another compromise. The ___(16) wanted to count free citizens only, but the ___(17) wanted to increase their representation by including ___(18) in the count. The delegates compromised finally by deciding to count all ___(19) and ___(20) of all other persons.

D. Write the letter of the best answer.

______ 21. The system of **checks and balances** was designed to
a. make the Constitution flexible.
b. allow sufficient orderly debate of issues.
c. keep any branch of government from becoming too powerful.

______ 22. **Ratifying** the Constitution meant
a. changing it.
b. approving it.
c. rejecting it.

page 15 ____________ Date ____________

______ 23. In an important **free press** victory, the jury decided that John Peter Zenger should
a. not be punished for publishing the truth.
b. be allowed to print anything he wanted about anyone.
c. be jailed only if the criticisms he made were about the government.

______ 24. The procedure for allowing **amendments** to the Constitution was intended
a. to permit changes to be made.
b. to balance power between the House and Senate.
c. to make sure the Constitution would never change.

______ 25. Which of these statements about the government under the Constitution is *not* correct?
a. The **executive branch** is headed by the President.
b. The **judicial branch** is the system of federal courts.
c. The **legislative branch** is made up of the state legislatures.

E. Write the letter of the best answer.

______ 26. Which of the following best describes a compromise?
a. Everybody wins; nobody loses.
b. Everybody loses; nobody wins.
c. Everybody wins; everybody loses.

______ 27. In which of the following situations is one most likely to need to know how to compromise?
a. umpiring a baseball game
b. putting on a school dance
c. counting the votes in an election

______ 28. In order to participate in a compromise, you must be willing to give up
a. whatever is most important to you.
b. whatever the other person or people want.
c. something you want but can bear to lose.

page 16 ____________ Date ____________

PART TWO

Answer the following questions.

1. What did the Northern states gain by agreeing to postpone a vote on ending the slave trade?

2. How did the system of checks and balances protect against the possibility of the presidency becoming a monarchy?

3. Why did many people, even some who favored a strong national government, feel the Constitution needed a bill of rights?

4. The First Amendment protects the freedoms of religion, speech, press, assembly, and petition. Which of these or other right or freedom in the Bill of Rights do you think would have been most important to a newspaper publisher in 1787? Which would have been most important to someone accused of starting a riot?

Answer the following question on the back or on another sheet of paper. Use complete sentences.

5. The Bill of Rights lists only certain of the many rights Americans enjoy. Why do you think the rights that are named in the Bill of Rights were chosen to be listed? Choose one right guaranteed in the Bill of Rights and explain how it affects American life today.

PART TWO

(25 points)

page 16

1. Answers should note that the Northern states gained support for the Constitution, which was more important to the North at the time than a timely end to slavery.
2. Answers should note that this system provided a balance of power among branches so that both the legislative and judicial branches had some power over the executive.
3. Answers should note that it was necessary to balance the rights of the states and of the individual citizens against the powers of the central government. Answers may also consider the need to protect individual liberties.
4. Answers may vary, and any thoughtful response should be given credit. The most likely answers will note:
   a. newspaper publisher—freedom of the press
   b. someone accused of starting a riot—the right to a speedy trial by jury and/freedom of assembly or speech
5. Answers will vary but may note that the listed rights are those that had been most recently abused during colonial times. They were, therefore, the rights that were on people's minds at the time.

   Answers regarding the relevance of a certain right to modern life should involve an understanding of what the right is and a rational connection to contemporary life, including an explanation of what the right makes possible and/or what it prevents.

Chapter 5

PART ONE

page 17

(18 points)

A. 1. F
2. R
3. F
4. F
5. B
6. R

(36 points)

B. 7. a
8. a
9. c
10. b
11. b
12. a
13. c
14. c

page 18

15. b
16. b
17. b
18. b

page 19

(12 points)

C. 19. Farming
20. true
21. laws
22. presidency
23. true
24. true

(9 points)

D. 25. a
26. a
27. b

PART TWO

(25 points)

page 20

1. Answers should include the following:

a. The credit program seemed to favor Northerners over Southerners.

b. It appeared to favor speculators over original bond holders.

c. The credit program seemed to favor the federal government over individual states.

d. By paying off the states' debts, the federal government was creating a perception that it was more in control.

Hamilton responded by saying that the program would establish the nation's credit and give investors a good feeling about the new government.

2. Answers should include:

a. appointed Republican judges

b. adopted new liberal naturalization law

c. pardoned prisoners and paid back fines to those convicted under the Sedition Act

d. shortened residency requirement for naturalization

e. cut government costs

f. did away with taxes on U.S.-made goods

g. rid the government of its stiff formality

3. Answers could include:

a. need for control of the Mississippi River (for trade)

b. need for transportation routes for western crops

c. acquisition of a large land area for expansion

4. Foreign policy failures:

a. failure of neutrality policy

b. failure of the Embargo and Non-Intercourse Acts

c. inability to protect American soldiers from British impressment

d. troubles with Indians along the frontier

Foreign policy successes:

a. the Monroe Doctrine helps the United States earn the respect of Europe

b. negotiations with Spain expand U.S. territory

5. Farmers:

a. were the most vigorous

b. were the most independent

c. were the most virtuous

d. had the greatest stake in the continuation of liberty

Answers regarding today should reflect an understanding that good citizenship involves the qualities that Jefferson saw in farmers, regardless of what occupation the citizen might have.

---

page 17

_______________ Date _______________

Chapter 5 Test

The Creation of a Party System

PART ONE

A. Write *F* if the statement is true of the Federalist party. Write *R* if it is true of the Republican party. Write *B* if it is true of both.

_______ 1. Alexander Hamilton was influential in this party.

_______ 2. This party simplified protocol and eliminated stiff ceremony.

_______ 3. This party wanted a strong central government.

_______ 4. This party supported the Alien and Sedition Acts.

_______ 5. This party carried on an insulting campaign during the presidential election of 1800.

_______ 6. This party's candidate won the presidential election of 1800.

B. Write the letter of the best answer.

_______ 7. Who benefited most from Hamilton's credit program?
a. speculators
b. tax collectors
c. original bond holders

_______ 8. The group that most objected to the Whiskey Tax were
a. farmers. b. merchants. c. politicians.

_______ 9. The Sedition Act limited citizens' rights to
a. bear arms.
b. trial by jury.
c. freedom of speech.

_______ 10. Jefferson and the Federalists shared a dislike for
a. the National Bank.
b. political parties.
c. government by the elite.

page 18

_______________ Date _______________

_______ 11. Each of the following helped make the Republicans more popular *except*
a. Jay's treaty with Britain.
b. the actions of French revolutionaries.
c. Washington's actions during the Whiskey Rebellion.

_______ 12. Each of the following occurred during Jefferson's presidency *except*
a. the War of 1812.
b. the Louisiana Purchase.
c. the case of *Marbury* v. *Madison*.

_______ 13. Which of the following did the case of *Marbury* v. *Madison* do?
a. It limited the President's powers.
b. It set up a method for appointing judges.
c. It made the power of the Supreme Court clear.

_______ 14. Prior to the War of 1812, the United States wanted to
a. side with France against Britain.
b. side with Britain against France.
c. stay out of the conflict between France and Britain.

_______ 15. The people most opposed to the War of 1812 were
a. mid-Atlantic farmers.
b. New England merchants.
c. Southern plantation owners.

_______ 16. Which of the following best describes how the War of 1812 affected the Federalists?
a. It increased their power.
b. It destroyed their power at a national level.
c. It somewhat weakened their power in New England.

_______ 17. By 1821, what had happened to Spain's land claims in the New World?
a. Spain had gained considerable territory.
b. Spain had lost or ceded considerable territory.
c. The territory was about the same as in the 1700s.

_______ 18. The Monroe Doctrine was an effort to stop European nations from interfering in
a. each other's business.
b. the American continents.
c. neutral international trade.

page 19

_______________ Date _______________

C. If the statement is true, write *true* on the line below it. If it is false, change the term in dark type to make the statement true.

Example: The first U.S. Vice President was **John Adams.**

true

The first capital of the U.S. was **Washington, D.C.**

New York City

19. **Business** forms the base of an agrarian society.

____

20. Members of a Cabinet are appointed by the **President.**

____

21. Judicial review is the process by which **judges** are reviewed by the Supreme Court.

____

22. Electoral votes determine who is elected to the **Congress.**

____

23. The group most directly affected by impressment were **sailors.**

____

24. The policy of not taking sides in a disagreement is called **neutrality.**

____

D. Write the letter of the best answer.

_______ 25. In doing research, bibliography cards will remind you of
a. the sources you used.
b. the information you gathered.

_______ 26. When you have finished your research, it is most likely that you will have
a. more note cards than bibliography cards.
b. more bibliography cards than note cards.

_______ 27. The reason that you should write down the date of publication of a book is to
a. provide a clue for finding more sources.
b. let other people know which edition you used.

page 20

_______________ Date _______________

PART TWO

Answer the following questions.

1. Why did the opponents of Hamilton's credit program think it was unfair? What was Hamilton's response?

2. How did Jefferson reshape the government to fit Republican goals?

3. What were two reasons that Jefferson supported the Louisiana Purchase?

4. How did American foreign policy fail in the early 1800s? How did it succeed?

Answer the following question on the back or on another sheet of paper. Use complete sentences.

5. Why did Thomas Jefferson believe that farmers were the most valuable citizens? What do you think makes someone a valuable citizen today?

Chapter 6

PART ONE

page 21

(35 points)

A. 1. d
2. d
3. c
4. a
5. d
6. c

page 22

7. c

(16 points)

B. 8. b
9. h
10. a
11. c
12. d
13. e
14. f
15. g

(12 points)

C. 16. c
17. a

page 23

18. c
19. b

(12 points)

D. 20. b
21. c
22. b
23. a

---

page 21

Date ____________

Chapter 6 Test

The Maturing Republic

PART ONE

A. Write the letter of the best answer.

_____ 1. Which of the following was *not* one of the ideals in the value system of the new republic?
a. independence
b. virtue
c. the household economy
d. women's suffrage

_____ 2. The ideals of the new republic encouraged women to
a. vote.
b. hold public office.
c. work outside the home.
d. teach the proper values to their families.

_____ 3. The Second Great Awakening stressed the importance of a person's
a. material success.
b. individual rights.
c. usefulness to society.
d. intellectual approach to religion.

_____ 4. Which of the following groups would have been most likely to support President Jackson's policies?
a. western settlers
b. the ruling elite
c. New England bankers
d. supporters of nullification

_____ 5. Which policy did Jackson use in dealing with the Cherokee?
a. letting them keep their land
b. declaring an all-out war on them
c. negotiating a purchase of their land
d. brutally forcing them from their land

_____ 6. President Jackson complained that the Bank of the United States
a. printed too much money.
b. gave out too many loans.
c. treated the common people unfairly.
d. failed to pay the government's debts.

page 22

Date ____________

_____ 7. Which of the following struck both Crèvecouer and Tocqueville as a surprising and admirable characteristic of America?
a. the level of education
b. the quality of leadership
c. the lack of social class distinctions
d. the free and easy attitude on the frontier

B. Match each person with his or her description.

a. Henry Clay	e. Mason Weems
b. Noah Webster	f. John Marshall
c. John Calhoun	g. Frances Trollope
d. Andrew Jackson	h. John Quincy Adams

_____ 8. the writer of the first American dictionary

_____ 9. the President who stood for the values of the wealthy elite

_____ 10. an influential Congressional leader who supported the federal bank

_____ 11. the Vice President who resigned over the issue of states' rights

_____ 12. the President who represented the ideal of the self-made man

_____ 13. the writer who idealized George Washington in a popular biography

_____ 14. the Supreme Court judge whose ruling on Cherokee land rights was ignored by the president

_____ 15. the English writer who complained of Americans' poor manners

C. Write the letter of the best answer.

_____ 16. The **household economy** stressed ties to the
a. home.
b. nation.
c. community.

_____ 17. The people most likely to support high **tariffs** were
a. factory owners.
b. western settlers.
c. plantation owners.

page 23

Date ____________

_____ 18. Which statement of Andrew Jackson's defends his use of the **spoils system**?
a. "Our Union—it must be preserved."
b. "John Marshall has made his decision; now let him enforce it."
c. "No one man has any more . . . right to official station than another."

_____ 19. The idea of **nullification** was closely tied to the idea of
a. suffrage.
b. states' rights.
c. a market economy.

D. Use the cartoon on the right, captioned "The Rats Leaving a Falling House," to help you answer the questions.

_____ 20. In this cartoon, Jackson appears to be
a. angry.
b. depressed.
c. powerful.

_____ 21. When Jackson's Vice President resigned from office, his supporters in the Cabinet soon followed.In this cartoon, the rats symbolize
a. Jackson's entire Cabinet.
b. the Cabinet members who remained with Jackson.
c. the Cabinet members who left the administration.

_____ 22. The "falling house" in the caption refers to
a. the United States.
b. Jackson's administration.
c. the House of Representatives.

_____ 23. How did the cartoonist probably feel about Jackson?
a. scornful
b. supportive
c. undecided

page 24

Date ____________

PART TWO

Answer the following questions.

1. What was public opinion of George Washington in the early 1800s?

2. What was the Second Great Awakening?

3. What political changes were brought about by the Second Great Awakening?

4. Why was Andrew Jackson seen as the representative of the "common man"?

Answer the following question on the back or on another sheet of paper. Use complete sentences.

5. What characteristics, noted by visiting writers in the 1700s and early 1800s, are still part of what defines us as Americans today?

PART TWO

(25 points)

page 24

1. Answers should note that he was seen as the perfect citizen of the republic or that he was viewed as a hero.
2. Answers should note that it was a religious revival based on the desire to increase church membership and return to the values of virtue and sacrifice for the common good.
3. Answers should be similar to the following:
a. States no longer supported churches with tax money.
b. Laws discriminating against people because of their religion were changed, especially for Jews and Catholics.
c. Barriers to suffrage were brought down, especially for white males.
4. Answers should note that Jackson was not born into wealth or upper-class society, and that he built his reputation as a defender of the frontier. Answers may also note that he was the first President who was a self-made man.
5. Answers will vary but could include such characteristics as:
a. lack of class distinctions
b. the possibility of constant change
c. the quest for perfection
d. powerful influence of public opinion
e. the democratic climate

Chapter 7

PART ONE

page 25

(30 points)

A. 1. c
2. a
3. c
4. b
5. a
6. c

page 26

(18 points)

B. 7. c
8. a
9. b
10. c
11. b
12. a

(15 points)

C. 13. German
14. immigrant

page 27

15. true
16. true
17. food

(12 points)

D. 18. a
19. c
20. c
21. c

page 25

Date ______

Chapter 7 Test

People of the New Nation

PART ONE

A. Write the letter of the best answer.

_____ 1. How did wars in Europe affect American farmers in the mid-1700s?
a. Wheat prices dropped rapidly.
b. Farmers became less efficient.
c. The demand for wheat increased.

_____ 2. How did economic growth in the mid-1800s affect family life?
a. It created more job opportunities outside the home.
b. It caused middle-class women to neglect child-rearing.
c. It allowed women to earn large amounts of money working at home.

_____ 3. Around the turn of the 18th century, free blacks did each of the following *except*
a. start their own schools.
b. work in the merchant marine.
c. participate extensively in politics.

_____ 4. A major reason that people migrated west was because
a. eastern farmland had been given to Revolutionary War veterans.
b. population growth created competition for land.
c. eastern cities provided few economic opportunities.

_____ 5. How were Indians affected by trans-Appalachian migration?
a. They were pushed to less desirable land.
b. They coexisted peacefully as independent nations.
c. Their interests were protected by the government.

_____ 6. The new surveying system put into use by the Land Ordinance of 1785 was important because it
a. allowed Indians to keep their land.
b. used local landmarks to identify property lines.
c. allowed settlers to buy land with clearly defined boundaries.

page 26

Date ______

B. Below are three approaches used by the Indians to deal with the problems of white settlement. Match each numbered statement with the Indian approach that it describes.

a. resistance
b. accommodation
c. revitalization

_____ 7. This approach centered around bringing back traditional ways and beliefs.

_____ 8. This approach caused Tecumseh's warriors to fight on the side of the British in the War of 1812.

_____ 9. This approach involved a willingness to learn to read, write, and speak English.

_____ 10. This approach rejected white trading goods and cultural habits.

_____ 11. This approach often involved giving up hunting to become farmers or businessmen.

_____ 12. This approach could include forming an alliance to raid white settlements.

C. If the statement is true, write *true* on the line below it. If it is false, change the term in dark type to make the statement true.

Example: **Sequoyah** developed a written Cherokee language.

true

Daniel Boone led settlers into **Oregon.**

Kentucky

13. Most **Irish** immigrants quickly became part of the American middle class.

______

14. Americans who were part of the nativism movement feared the economic and political growth of **Indian** cultures.

______

page 27

Date ______

15. New settlers in the West created their own institutions, including **schools.**

______

16. A member of the working class might have had a job as a **factory worker.**

______

17. A famine is an overwhelming shortage of **clothing.**

______

D. Write the letter of the best answer.

_____ 18. In designing a map, the smaller the area shown,
a. the larger the scale.
b. the larger the country.
c. the shorter the distance.

_____ 19. Given a scale in which one-half inch equals one mile, how far apart are two churches shown three inches apart on the map?
a. one and one-half miles
b. three miles
c. six miles

_____ 20. Orientation of a map is usually indicated by
a. the section and township.
b. the angles of the streets and highways.
c. a compass or an arrow marked with directions.

_____ 21. A map needs a legend of symbols to
a. explain the history of a place.
b. show the longitude and latitude.
c. identify the kinds of information represented.

page 28

Date ______

PART TWO

Answer the following questions.

1. How did the mechanical reaper and steel-blade plow change American agriculture?

2. Why did master craftsmen become less important, even though people were buying more goods?

3. Give the reason or reasons why one of the following groups migrated to the West.

teachers
tradesmen
army veterans
African Americans

Answer the following questions on the back or on another sheet of paper. Use complete sentences.

4. Although European immigrants to America often suffered from severe poverty and discrimination, these newcomers suffered less than the original inhabitants of the land. Why? Which immigrants were most readily accepted? Why?

5. How did immigration benefit America in the past? Does it benefit America today? Explain your answer.

PART TWO

(25 points)

page 28

1. Answers should note that the reaper and plow made farming more efficient and profitable. Farmers planted more acres.
2. Answers should note that craftsmen couldn't keep up with demand and couldn't compete with factories that used less-skilled workers to produce goods more cheaply.
3. Answers should note the reason for one group:

a. Teachers were needed in the new township schools.
b. Tradesmen found economic opportunities in the settlers' needs for goods and services.
c. Army veterans were sometimes paid with western land instead of cash.
d. African American slaves were forced to work on cotton plantations; free black found work and safety in the West.

4. All answers should note that although European immigrants faced discrimination, they were still perceived as being more similar to white, native-born Americans than were the Indians. It was the Indians, not the immigrants, who inhabited the land white Americans wanted and forcibly took.

Answers should note that the most readily accepted immigrants were those who were most similar to established settlers and native-born Americans in terms of economic status, religion, and race.

5. Answers should note that immigration has provided many benefits to America in the past, such as enriching the cultural structure of the nation.

In terms of today's world, answers will vary. Answers should note that immigrantion still provides benefits, although some drawbacks may be noted. Opinions about the extent to which cultural accomodation should take place will vary, although all answers should give some thought to the benefits of diversity and the simultaneous need for a national identity.

Chapter 8

PART ONE

page 29

(18 points)

A. 1. a
2. d
3. b
4. a
5. a
6. b

page 30

(21 points)

B. 7. d
8. b
9. c
10. a
11. e
12. d
13. e

(24 points)

C. 14. f
15. d
16. g
17. a
18. c
19. b

page 31

(12 points)

D. 20. B and F
21. E
22. G

page 29

Date ____________

Chapter 8 Test

The West

PART ONE

A. Write the letter of the best answer.

_______ 1. Which of the following resulted from the Lewis and Clark expedition?
a. The Northwest was accurately mapped.
b. The Northwest Passage was discovered.
c. The United States bought the Louisiana Territory.
d. Mexico went to war with the United States.

_______ 2. Manifest Destiny *most* concerned the expansion of the United States'
a. northern border.
b. eastern border.
c. southern border.
d. western border.

_______ 3. Which of the following events occurred first?
a. The United States declared war on Mexico.
b. Stephen Austin settled in Texas.
c. Texas became a state.
d. Texas gained its independence from Mexico.

_______ 4. The Overland Trail was most used by
a. pioneers heading for California.
b. settlers heading for Stephen Austin's colony.
c. trappers heading for a rendezvous with traders.
d. priests traveling between missions in California.

_______ 5. Each of the following characterized pioneers going west *except*
a. laziness.
b. cooperation.
c. self-reliance.
d. resourcefulness.

_______ 6. John C. Fremont and Kit Carson
a. defended the Indians.
b. helped explore the West.
c. searched for the Northwest Passage.

page 30

Date ____________

B. Write the letter of the territory that best answers each question.

a. California
b. Louisiana
c. Oregon
d. Texas
e. Utah

_______ 7. Which was known as the Lone Star Republic?

_______ 8. Which was a part of the area purchased by President Jefferson?

_______ 9. Which was claimed by both Great Britain and the United States?

_______ 10. In which did the rancho system flourish?

_______ 11. In which did the Mormons establish Deseret?

_______ 12. In which did the Battle of the Alamo occur?

_______ 13. In which did settlers turn the desert known as the Great Basin into fertile farming land?

C. For each statement, write the letter of the term it describes.

a. annex
b. buffer zone
c. continental divide
d. expansionists
e. ghost towns
f. mountain men
g. secularize

_______ 14. They were important sources of information concerning overland trails to the West.

_______ 15. They applauded President Polk's efforts to provoke war with Mexico.

_______ 16. This is what Mexico did to California missions to decrease Californians' loyalty to Spain.

_______ 17. This is what the United States did to Texas in 1845 to fulfill the idea of Manifest Destiny.

_______ 18. This separates the rivers that flow west from those that flow east.

_______ 19. This is a territory that separates two opposing powers.

page 31

Date ____________

D. The following facts about Sam Houston are in the correct chronological order. Use them and your knowledge of chronological outlining to answer the questions below.

A. Went to Texas as government agent to work out Indian treaties.

B. Served Texas as military leader.

C. Chosen commander-in-chief of Texan army.

D. Led troops that fought Santa Anna at San Jacinto.

E. At San Jacinto, used battle cry, "Remember the Alamo!"

F. Served Texas as politician.

G. Elected first president of Lone Star Republic.

H. Elected senator from Texas when statehood granted.

I. After losing re-election to Congress, was elected governor of Texas.

_______ 20. Which *two* of the above facts should be marked with Roman numerals in an outline?

_______ 21. Which of the above facts is a supporting detail for fact D?

_______ 22. Suppose you wanted to add an additional fact about Houston, which was that he "Established Houston as capital of the Lone Star Republic." Which fact would this new fact *follow* in your outline?

page 32

Date ____________

PART TWO

Answer the following questions.

1. Briefly describe the mission system that flourished in California under Spanish control. How and why did this system come to an end?

2. Who took part in the gold rush? What was life like in the mining camps?

3. What were some of the hardships faced by pioneers on the trail and once they reached their destinations?

4. How were Western rancho owners and Indians affected by the arrival of large numbers of new settlers?

Answer the following question on the back or on another sheet of paper. Use complete sentences.

5. What did the popularity of the idea of Manifest Destiny reveal about the American character? What, if any, parts of this character seem positive? What, if any, seem negative? Explain your answers.

PART TWO

(25 points)

page 32

1. Answers should, in general, discuss the establishment of missions, each a day's walk from the next, that housed priests, laypeople, and Indians, each mission being self-sufficient and similar to a large farm.

   Regarding the end of the system, answers should note that, when Mexico became independent, it tried to decrease Californians' loyalty to Spain by secularizing the missions and assigning their lands to rancheros.

2. People came to California from all over the world, including Mexico, South America, China, and Europe. Whites, free blacks, slaves, and Indians all took part.

   Answers, in general, should note that life in the mining towns was disorderly and rough. Prices were outrageous and conditions were very uncomfortable.

3. Answers could note the following hardships:
   a. homesickness
   b. unending, hard physical labor
   c. new farming conditions
   d. no privacy
   e. poor sanitation
   f. sickness
   g. bad weather
   h. discarding personal possessions
   i. dehydration/poisonous water

4. Answers should reconigze that ranchero owners and Indians were adversely affected, due largely to racism. In addition, answers should include points similar to the following:
   a. Their land claims were not respected by pioneers.
   b. Their land rights were not upheld by U.S. courts.
   c. Many were reduced to working as hired hands on land they once owned.

5. Answers will vary. Possible character traits include:
   a. Negative: racist nationalism, self-righteousness, and arrogance
   b. Positive: patriotism, optimism, bravery, adventurousness

   The best answers will deal with both positive and negative traits.

Chapter 9

PART ONE

page 33

(30 points)

A. 1. d
2. c
3. b
4. d
5. c
6. d

page 34

(15 points)

B. 7. b
8. f
9. d
10. c
11. e

(20 points)

C. 12. d
13. c
14. a
15. d

page 35

(10 points)

D. 16. d
17. The key phrase matches the topic.
18. a
19. c
20. b

page 33

Date ______

Chapter 9 Test

The North

PART ONE

A. Write the letter of the best answer.

______ 1. By the mid-1800s, industry's transportation needs were *most* efficiently served by
a. horse power.
b. canal barges.
c. clipper ships.
d. steam power.

______ 2. The textile mills of the Northeast were powered by
a. oil.
b. coal.
c. water.
d. steam.

______ 3. Balloon frames were used in building
a. ships.
b. houses.
c. machinery.
d. multi-story factories.

______ 4. During the 1800s, most of the working poor
a. moved up into the middle class.
b. depended on government services.
c. commuted to work from rural areas.
d. were constantly threatened with unemployment.

______ 5. The main subject of the convention that met at Seneca Falls, New York, in 1848 was
a. slavery.
b. temperance.
c. women's rights.
d. workers' rights.

______ 6. Which reform movement was the *least* successful?
a. temperance
b. public education
c. education for women
d. utopian communities

page 34

Date ______

B. Match each person or group with the correct reform movement.

a. temperance
b. public education
c. education for women
d. utopian societies
e. equal rights for women
f. humane treatment of the mentally ill

______ 7. Horace Mann

______ 8. Dorothea Dix

______ 9. Ann Lee (Mother Lee)

______ 10. Emma Willard, Sara Josepha Hale, Mary Lyon

______ 11. Lucretia Mott, Elizabeth Cady Stanton, Susan B. Anthony

C. Write the letter of the answer that correctly fills in the blank.

______ 12. During the **Industrial Revolution**, the ______ did *not* increase.
a. problems with alcoholism
b. need for housing
c. size of urban populations
d. need for skilled craftspeople

______ 13. In the 1800s, **raw materials** such as ______ were shipped to industrial regions.
a. steel
b. cloth
c. cotton
d. glass

______ 14. **Municipal** services provided each of the following *except* ______.
a. cafeterias
b. police
c. sanitation systems
d. transportation

______ 15. **Utopians** believed in each of the following *except* ______.
a. equality
b. education
c. prosperity
d. competition

page 35

Date ______

D. Write the letter of the best answer.

______ 16. Which of the following terms or phrases would you type first in doing a computer search on the topic "Brook Farm"?
a. utopia
b. utopians
c. Shakers
d. Brook Farm

17. Briefly explain your answer to item 16 above.

Use the menu on the computer screen below to match the search option with the description of the reference material that would probably result from that search option. Your topic is "Brook Farm."

SET SEARCH OPTION

Options:
1. Search Titles
2. Search Topic Index
3. Search Text

a. Option 1 b. Option 2 c. Option 3

______ 18. a book entitled *Brook Farm: Success or Failure?* that answers the question that its title puts forth

______ 19. an article entitled "Modern American Utopianism" that briefly notes Brook Farm's influence on modern utopians

______ 20. a book entitled *Nathaniel Hawthorne: Nineteenth-Century Utopian* that concentrates on Hawthorne's Brook Farm experiences

page 36

Date ______

PART TWO

Answer the following questions.

1. Why is what happened in the early 1800s called the Industrial Revolution?

2. What were two changes experienced by women during the new industrial age?

3. What reforms improved the public education system in the 1800s?

4. Why do you think utopians objected to, and in many cases rejected, the lifestyle of the new industrial age?

Answer the following question on the back or on another sheet of paper. Use complete sentences.

5. Do you think that Horace Mann's statement, "Be ashamed to die until you have won some victory for humanity," is as meaningful to Americans today as it was in the 1800s? Why or why not?

PART TWO

(25 points)

page 36

1. Answers should reflect the knowledge that:
a. Production shifted from homes and small shops to factories.
b. The effects of this change were so far-reaching and widespread that they revolutionized society.

2. Answers should refer in some way to two of the following:
a. moved from the farm to work in facories
b. became actively involved in reform movements such as temperance and women's rights
c. were offered expanded educational opportunities

3. Answers could include:
a. Tax money was set aside for education.
b. Compulsory education laws were passed.
c. Normal schools for training teachers were established.

4. Answers will vary but could include points similar to the following:
a. Utopians blamed the new industrial age for the worsening of social problems.
b. Utopians disapproved of the separating effect of urbanization and industrialization on the social classes.

5. Answers will vary but should reflect the knowledge that:
a. Mann was speaking of the need to reform society.
b. Nineteenth-century America had a great need for reform.
c. Many of the problems of the 1800s remain problems today.
d. Many new social problems have developed since the 1800s.

Chapter 10

PART ONE

page 37

(36 points)

A. 1. a
2. b
3. b
4. c
5. a
6. c
7. a

page 38

8. b
9. a
10. b
11. c
12. c

(24 points)

B. 13. a
14. a
15. b

page 39

16. b
17. c

(10 points)

C. 18. c
19. a
20. b
21. c
22. b

(5 points)

D. 23. Sketch should be a line graph.

PART TWO

(25 points)

page 40

1. Answers, in general, should note that the economy of the North was based upon industry, while that of the South was based upon agriculture. Specific examples to support this statement may be given.
2. Answers should include two of the following:
a. They used songs to convey messages secretly.
b. They pretended to be sick.
c. They purposely broke tools.
d. They worked as slowly as possible.
e. They ran away.
3. Answers should include two of the following:
a. spirituals and work songs
b. natural cures and herbal medicines
c. having and using two names (African and English)
d. "jumping the broom"
e. church services that combined African rituals with Christian ceremonies
4. Answers should note that, while opportunities for free blacks were limited, they did exist. Some free blacks purchased land. Free black men worked as blacksmiths, carpenters, masons, barbers, and tailors. Women worked as laundresses, nurses, and domestic servants. Others ran small boarding houses.
Answers should note some of the following restrictions:
a. could not vote
b. wages unequal to those of whites
c. many jobs closed to them
d. laws restricted their travel
e. home searches without legal permits
f. could be sold into slavery if accused of a crime
g. could not socialize with slaves because of Southerners' suspicions
5. Answers will vary in the way the right to self-ownership is worded, but should recognize that basic civil right. Answers should note that, regardless of how well-treated a person is, slavery is counter to the most basic ideals of our democracy. These ideals contend that people are created equal and have unalienable rights including life, liberty, and the pursuit of happiness—all rights that could have been, or were, denied to slaves.

---

page 37

Date ________

Chapter 10 — Test

The South

PART ONE

A. Write the letter of the best answer.

_____ 1. The invention of the cotton gin
a. increased the need for slave labor.
b. caused plantation owners to diversify more.
c. encouraged mountain settlers to grow large cotton crops.

_____ 2. New machines in the textile industry
a. made factories safer.
b. increased cotton exports dramatically.
c. lessened the demand for slave labor.

_____ 3. Slaveowners defended slavery by saying that it
a. was their political right.
b. had existed for thousands of years.
c. allowed slaves many educational opportunities.

_____ 4. As Northern opposition to slavery increased,
a. Southern planters lost political power.
b. Southern slaves gained some legal rights.
c. Southerners defended slavery more firmly.

_____ 5. Abolitionists would see each of the following as a victory *except*
a. Florida joining the Union in 1845.
b. Congress's slave trade decision of 1808.
c. Great Britain's Atlantic slave trade decision.

_____ 6. White Southerners reacted to Nat Turner's slave rebellion by
a. expanding the slave trade.
b. treating slaves more fairly.
c. growing more fearful of slaves.

_____ 7. A planter's code of honor may demand he do each of the following *except*
a. allow his slaves to marry.
b. defend his family's name.
c. settle a dispute with a duel.

page 38

Date ________

_____ 8. In general, plantation mistresses
a. married late in life.
b. learned most of their duties from their slaves.
c. left the running of the plantation to their husbands.

_____ 9. One myth about slave life is that
a. house slaves had a better life than other slaves.
b. families often had little time for themselves.
c. slaves were punished cruelly for minor offenses.

_____ 10. Most white Southerners
a. relied upon slave labor.
b. had a strong oral tradition.
c. had little use for cooperative labor.

_____ 11. People of the Appalachians
a. grew cash crops.
b. preferred not to gather socially.
c. practiced a long musical tradition.

_____ 12. Public education in the South was
a. better than in the North.
b. the same as in the North.
c. worse than in the North.

B. Write the letter of the best answer.

_____ 13. The **antebellum** period in the South refers to the time
a. before the Civil War.
b. during the Civil War.
c. after the Civil War.

_____ 14. A crop is called a **cash crop** if it
a. is grown to be sold.
b. is expensive to plant and harvest.
c. meets so many of a farming family's needs that they have no need for actual cash.

_____ 15. A group's **cultural heritage** includes its
a. economic system.
b. language and art.
c. political system.

page 39

Date ________

_____ 16. A **yeoman farmer** was a farmer who
a. farmed rented land.
b. owned a small farm.
c. worked for pay on someone else's farm.

_____ 17. Southern **artisans** were
a. overseers.
b. slave laborers.
c. skilled workers.

C. Match each description with the type of graph that would best present that information.

a. bar graph b. line graph c. circle graph

_____ 18. a graph showing how much of the total land area of the South was used for cotton production

_____ 19. a graph showing how much Southern land between 1750 and 1850 was used for tobacco production compared to the amount used for cotton production

_____ 20. a graph showing how the population of New Orleans grew between 1850 and 1860

_____ 21. a graph showing how many Southern blacks in 1850 were slaves and how many were free

_____ 22. a graph showing the value of cotton exports between 1800 and 1850

D. In the space below, sketch the kind of graph that would best present the following information.

Information: In 1860, there were 4,441,830 blacks living in the United States. In 1900, there were 8,833,994. In 1930, there were 11,891,143. By 1960, there were 18,871,831.

page 40

Date ________

PART TWO

Answer the following questions.

1. How did the Northern and Southern economies differ?

2. How did slaves nonviolently resist the authority of their masters?

3. Give two examples of slave culture that were not part of the general Southern culture of the time.

4. What opportunities existed for free blacks in the South? What restrictions hindered their progress?

Answer the following question on the back or on another sheet of paper. Use complete sentences.

5. Why would slavery have been unjustifiable even if slaves had been kindly treated? What basic rights does slavery deny? How does it contradict our most basic democratic ideals?

Chapter 11

PART ONE

page 41

(28 points)

A. 1. b
2. a
3. b
4. b
5. a
6. c
7. a

page 42

(18 points)

B. 8. e
9. h and i
10. j
11. g
12. b
13. f
14. a
15. d
16. c

(20 points)

C. 17. b
18. a

page 43

19. a
20. c
21. a

(9 points)

D. 22. c
23. b
24. a

page 41

_______________ Date _______________

Chapter 11 Test

Causes of the Civil War

PART ONE

A. Write the letter of the best answer.

_____ 1. The South supported slavery in the territories and new states for each of the following reasons *except*

a. to increase its power in the U.S. Senate.
b. to reduce dependence on slavery in the South.
c. to expand its system of cotton-growing to these areas.

_____ 2. The North opposed slavery in the territories and new states for each of the following reasons *except*

a. to prevent Northern industries from moving west.
b. to protect or increase its power in the U.S. Congress.
c. to allow settlers from the North to compete with settlers from the South in these areas.

_____ 3. The Fugitive Slave Law required Northerners to

a. enslave free blacks.
b. aid in the return of runaway slaves.
c. support the international slave trade.

_____ 4. The idea of local control of slavery decisions was put to its harshest test in

a. Texas. b. Kansas. c. Missouri.

_____ 5. The part of the Dred Scott decision that *most* upset the Republicans was the

a. implication of opening all territories to slavery.
b. failure to establish the citizenship of slaves.
c. failure to end the controversy over slavery in the territories.

_____ 6. Which political party supported slavery?

a. Know-Nothing b. Republican c. Democratic

_____ 7. In what chronological order did these events occur? (I) The Missouri Compromise was reached. (II) The Compromise of 1850 was reached. (III) The Kansas-Nebraska Act was passed. (IV) The Battle of Fort Sumter took place.

a. I, II, III, IV
b. I, IV, III, II
c. II, III, I, IV

page 42

_______________ Date _______________

B. Write the letter of the best answer or answers.

a. John Brown
b. Stephen A. Douglas
c. Frederick Douglass
d. William Lloyd Garrison
e. Dred Scott
f. Harriet Beecher Stowe
g. Charles Sumner
h. Sojourner Truth
i. Harriet Tubman
j. David Walker

_____ 8. Which slave sued for freedom and lost?

_____ 9. Which former slave helped hundreds of slaves to freedom?

_____ 10. Which antislavery journalist died mysteriously?

_____ 11. Which politician was brutally beaten on the Senate floor?

_____ 12. Which Illinois politician debated Abraham Lincoln on the issue of slavery in the territories?

_____ 13. Which person wrote *Uncle Tom's Cabin*?

_____ 14. Which person was executed for the crimes of treason and murder?

_____ 15. Which person began the newspaper called the *Liberator* and started a new, unified antislavery movement?

_____ 16. Which former slave lectured, founded a newspaper, and wrote his autobiography?

C. Write the letter of the best answer.

_____ 17. The term **free labor** refers to

a. work, such as slave labor, for which no wages are paid.
b. a system of work in which paid employees have civil rights.
c. the idea that the government should not interfere in labor disputes.

_____ 18. **Abolitionism** called for

a. an immediate end to all slavery.
b. the return of free blacks to Africa.
c. a gradual decrease in the number of slaves.

page 43

_______________ Date _______________

_____ 19. The purpose of the **Underground Railroad** was to

a. get slaves out of the South to freedom.
b. get antislavery publications into the South.
c. get the antislavery viewpoint told in the North.

_____ 20. **Popular sovereignty** refers to the idea that

a. more populated states should have more power.
b. political leaders should be elected by popular vote.
c. the voters in a territory should decide the issue of slavery for themselves.

_____ 21. The **guerilla** warfare in Kansas was carried on by

a. civilians.
b. federal troops.
c. the state militia.

D. Read the passage below from a speech by Sojourner Truth and answer the questions that follow it.

"That man . . . says that women need to be helped into carriages, and lifted over ditches, and to have the best place everywhere . . . Nobody ever helps me into carriages, or over mud puddles, or gives me any best place, and ain't I a woman? . . . I have plowed, and planted, and gathered into barns, . . . and ain't I a woman? I could work as much and eat as much as a man (when I could get it), and bear the lash as well—and ain't I a woman? I have borne thirteen children and seen them most all sold off into slavery, and when I cried out with a mother's grief, none but Jesus heard—and ain't I a woman?"

Speech at the Woman's Rights Convention, 1851

_____ 22. The main subject of this passage is the

a. rights of women.
b. hardships of slaves.
c. capabilities of women.

_____ 23. Most of the members of the audience for this speech were probably

a. men.
b. women.
c. slaves.

_____ 24. The tone of this passage could best be described as

a. angry.
b. patient.
c. sympathetic.

page 44

_______________ Date _______________

PART TWO

Answer the following questions.

1. Why was it so important and so difficult to reach a lasting compromise on the issue of slavery in the western territories?

2. Describe the role that women played in the abolitionist movement. Why did their experiences lead them to seek their own rights?

3. What made Kansas's elections in 1854 and 1855 illegal? How did they result in the adoption of a proslavery constitution?

4. Why did white Southerners see the election of Abraham Lincoln as a threat to their way of life?

Answer the following question on the back or on another sheet of paper. Use complete sentences.

5. Are Americans ever justified in disobeying the laws of their nation? If so, under what conditions? In your answer, consider Northerners' reactions to the Fugitive Slave Law or Southerners' reactions to the election of President Lincoln.

PART TWO

(25 points)

page 44

1. Answers should indicate an understanding of the fact that the North and South, although very different, had to find ways to compromise in order for the nation to expand. This expansion, however, made it almost impossible to create or retain any balance of power between the regions.

2. Answers should recognize that women played an important role in the movement, including:
   a. organizing gatherings and recruiting new members
   b. circulating petitions
   c. hiding runaway slaves in their homes

   In addition, answers should reflect the knowledge that the discrimination women faced within the abolitionist movement led them to seek their own rights.

3. Answers should recognize that voting by "border ruffians," who were not residents of the territory, made the elections illegal. Although the majority of Kansans were opposed to slavery, the elections put people who were proslavery in power, and they were able to write slavery into the Constitution.

4. Answers should recognize that white Southerners feared Lincoln would make slavery illegal, thereby destroying their economy and way of life.

5. Answers will vary but justifications for breaking the law should deal with the issue of morality or "greater good" in some significant way. In addition, answers should reflect an understanding of either:
   a. many Northerners' refusal to obey the Fugitive Slave Law because it conflicted with their moral ideas of right and wrong
   b. many Southerners' refusal to be a part of the political process that elected a President whom they thought would destroy their way of life

Chapter 12

PART ONE

page 45

(16 points)

A. 1. N
2. S
3. N
4. S
5. S
6. N
7. N
8. N

(21 points)

B. 9. a
10. a
11. b

page 46

12. c
13. d
14. c
15. b

(20 points)

C. 16. the commemoration of the cemetary at Gettysburg
17. Union soldiers
18. through the use of total war tactics
19. Grant
20. Southern independence (or, the division of the Union)

page 47

(9 points)

D. 21. b
22. a
23. a

(9 points)

E. 24. b
25. b
26. b

---

page 45 Date ________

Chapter 12 Test

A Nation Divided

PART ONE

A. Write *S* if the item describes a Southern advantage at the time the Civil War broke out. Write *N* if it describes a Northern advantage.

_____ 1. larger population

_____ 2. closer to supply sources

_____ 3. healthier and stronger economy

_____ 4. greater motivation to fight

_____ 5. greater familiarity with the land and climate

_____ 6. larger fleet of ships and more shipyards

_____ 7. more manufacturing plants

_____ 8. more miles of railroad track

B. Write the letter of the best answer.

_____ 9. Which of the following is true of *both* Abraham Lincoln *and* Jefferson Davis?
a. political moderation
b. opposition to slavery
c. support for states' rights
d. poor frontier backgrounds

_____ 10. Lincoln issued the Emancipation Proclamation for each of the following reasons *except* to
a. free the slaves in the border states.
b. give Union forces a new source of troops.
c. increase, in the North, support for the war.
d. take away the South's major source of labor.

_____ 11. Each of the following was an important source of dissent in the Union during the war *except* the
a. use of the draft.
b. use of "total war" tactics.
c. adoption of income taxes.
d. restriction of civil liberties.

---

page 46 Date ________

_____ 12. Each of the following weapons were used in the Civil War *except*
a. cannons.
b. submarines.
c. machine guns.
d. hot air balloons.

_____ 13. Why did General Lee finally surrender?
a. He was trapped in Richmond.
b. His troops refused to continue fighting.
c. General Grant refused to meet with him.
d. His troops were running out of ammunition.

_____ 14. Grant gave the defeated Confederate troops all of the following *except*
a. food.
b. freedom.
c. new weapons.
d. their horses and mules.

_____ 15. How many years did the Civil War last?
a. two b. four c. six d. eight

C. For each quotation, answer the questions.

"The world will little note, nor long remember what we say here; but it can never forget what they did here. It is for us, the living, rather to be dedicated here to the unfinished work which they who fought here have thus far so nobly advanced."

16. On what occasion did Lincoln make the above statement? ________

17. Who is the *they* referred to? ________

"We cannot change the hearts of those people of the South, but we can make war so terrible . . . that generations would pass away before they would again appeal to it."

18. How did General Sherman make war terrible for the South?
____
____

"[I hated to see] the downfall of a foe who had fought so long and valiantly, and had suffered so much for a cause though that cause was . . . one of the worst for which a people ever fought."

19. Who said it? ________

20. What is the *cause* he speaks of? ________
____

---

page 47 Date ________

D. Write the letter of the best answer.

_____ 21. Although a confederacy is any group of states united for a common cause, the **Confederacy** was made up specifically of
a. the slave states.
b. the states that left the Union.
c. the seven cotton-growing states of the Deep South.

_____ 22. **Civil rights** are those rights that belong specifically to
a. citizens.
b. civilians.
c. minorities.

_____ 23. During the early years of the Civil War, anger about the **draft** was most intense among
a. the poor.
b. the young.
c. free blacks.

E. Suppose that you wanted to write a report about civilian suffering during the Battle of Vicksburg. Answer the following questions about the report you would write.

_____ 24. Before identifying your audience, you should
a. choose a topic.
b. identify your purpose.
c. locate your sources.

_____ 25. Which of the following documents would be the best primary source for your report, and why?
a. the papers of Jefferson Davis, because he was the president of the Confederacy
b. the journals of a woman living in Vicksburg, because she experienced the event
c. the journals of Ulysses S. Grant, because he led the attacking forces on the battlefield

_____ 26. The point of view of the document you chose in item 25 would *most* probably favor
a. the Union.
b. the Confederacy.
c. neither the Union nor the Confederacy.

---

page 48 Date ________

PART TWO

Answer the following questions.

1. Why did both the Union and Confederate governments feel that it was necessary to restrict civil liberties during wartime? What is one way in which they did this?
____
____
____

2. What are two ways in which the young aided the war efforts of both the Union and the Confederacy?
____
____

3. What are three non-traditional ways in which Union and Confederate women made contributions during the Civil War?
____
____
____

4. How did the invention of photography change people's perception of war?
____
____
____

Answer the following question on the back or on another sheet of paper. Use complete sentences.

5. In what ways did all Americans "win" the Civil War? In what ways did all Americans "lose"?

PART TWO

(25 points)

page 48

1. Answers should recognize that both governments believed that civil rights had to be restricted so that economic and social order could be maintained. In addition, answers should mention one of the following restrictions:
a. Lincoln suspended the writ of habeas corpus. (This term need not be used if this restriction is described.)
b. The Union gave the military the right to arrest civilians who did not cooperate with the war effort.
c. People could be arrested for draft resistance. Service was compulsory rather than voluntary.
d. People could be arrested on suspicion and sent to jail without being officially charged.

2. Answers should mention two of the following points. Young people served as:
a. regular soldiers
b. military drummer boys
c. gunpowder carriers
d. high-ranking officers
e. spies

3. Answers should mention any three of the following points. Women served by:
a. working at jobs traditionally held by men
b. working in munitions factories
c. working as military nurses
d. serving as soldiers
e. serving as spies
f. working as army cooks and laundresses

4. Before the invention of photography, war was glorified and romanticized. Photography brought the horrible realities of battle back to the homefront.

5. Answers will vary but may address the fact that with the end of the Civil War the United States was once again a unified nation.

Answers will vary but should reflect the knowledge that the suffering was so widespread and intense and the bitterness so sharp that the wound would take a long time to heal.

Chapter 13

PART ONE

page 49

(21 points)

A. 1. c
2. a
3. b
4. c
5. c
6. b
7. b

page 50

(6 points)

B. 8. c
9. a
10. b

(24 points)

C. 11. c
12. b
13. c
14. c
15. a
16. b
17. c
18. a

(12 points)

D. 19. b

page 51

20. a
21. a
22. a
23. c
24. b

(12 points, 2 points for each correctly placed event)

E. Cause boxes: a, c, f
Effect boxes: b, d, e

PART TWO

(25 points)

page 52

1. Answers could reflect the following view:

   Lincoln's and Johnson's views on Reconstruction were similar, but Lincoln was able to compromise when met with dissent. He was probably also better able to moderate between Radical Republicans and white Southerners.

2. Answers will vary but should reflect an understanding of the difference between having no legal rights and being a citizen. Possible answers:

   a. hope, optimism
   b. legal status as citizens
   c. the chance to travel, worship, and earn a living
   d. control of their family life and home life

3. Answers could include:

   a. Both Johnson and Congress wanted to control Reconstruction.
   b. Johnson undermined Congressional Reconstruction policies.
   c. Their attitudes and views were quite different.
   d. Johnson used his veto power to oppose Congressional goals.
   e. Johnson's inflexible personality caused conflict.

4. Possible similarities:

   a. Both involved white landowners and black laborers.
   b. Both exploited blacks.
   c. Both kept blacks poor and enriched whites.

   Possible differences:

   a. Sharecroppers were paid for their labor; slaves weren't.
   b. Sharecropping divided up the large plantation lands.
   c. Sharecropping gave blacks a degree of freedom and control over their lives.
   d. Sharecropping let blacks succeed and profit from that success.

5. Answers should note that white Southerners supported these societies, either actively or through noninterference. This encouraged their existence and did nothing to check their power. This shows that groups that work outside the law thrive under conditions of social acceptance, disinterest, or fear.

---

page 49

Date ____________

Chapter 13 Test

Reconstruction

PART ONE

A. Write the letter of the best answer.

____ 1. The foremost goal of Lincoln's Reconstruction plan was to
a. punish the South.
b. end the Civil War.
c. reunify the nation.

____ 2. Southern states passed laws known as "Black Codes" in an effort to
a. restrict the freedom of blacks.
b. encourage blacks to leave the South.
c. meet the conditions of readmission to the Union.

____ 3. The main purpose of the Freedmen's Bureau was to
a. help plantation owners find field laborers.
b. aid and support former slaves and poor whites.
c. elect black representatives to political office.

____ 4. Which of the following helped to elect Southern blacks during the early years of Reconstruction?
a. the growth of the Democratic party
b. the strength of Home Rule supporters
c. the protection of voters by the military

____ 5. Southern whites reduced the political power of blacks through each of the following *except* by
a. rearranging voting districts.
b. requiring voters to pay a tax.
c. refusing to vote on new state constitutions.

____ 6. What signaled the end of Reconstruction?
a. the passage of the Fifteenth Amendment
b. the removal of federal troops from the South
c. the readmission to the Union of the last Southern states

____ 7. At which of the following did Southern blacks have the best social conditions and exercise the most political power?
a. during the Civil War
b. right after the Civil War
c. twenty years after the Civil War

page 50

Date ____________

B. Match each description with the correct amendment.

a. Thirteenth Amendment   b. Fourteenth Amendment   c. Fifteenth Amendment

____ 8. It gave black men the right to vote.

____ 9. It prohibited slavery in the United States.

____ 10. It defined an American citizen as anyone born or naturalized in the United States.

C. For each question, write the letter of the correct person or group.

a. Abraham Lincoln
b. Andrew Johnson
c. Radical Republicans

____ 11. Who believed that the federal government should try to reshape the South in the image of the North?

____ 12. Who tried to gain control of Reconstruction efforts by opposing passage of the Fourteenth Amendment?

____ 13. Who believed that Congress should have the most important role in determining Reconstruction policy?

____ 14. Who was responsible for the Military Reconstruction acts that divided the South into military districts?

____ 15. Who proposed an amendment to outlaw slavery?

____ 16. Who supported officials who allowed disqualified Confederates to vote?

____ 17. Whose Reconstruction policies led to the Republicans' gaining control of all the governorships and state legislatures in the South?

____ 18. Whose Reconstruction policy was summed up in the statement, "I do not want to hurt the hair of a single man in the South if it can possibly be avoided"?

D. Write the letter of the best answer.

____ 19. **Sharecropping** was riskiest for the
a. landowners.
b. sharecroppers.
c. businessmen who gave credit to sharecroppers.

page 51

Date ____________

____ 20. **Segregation** policies in the South separated people on the basis of their
a. race.   b. wealth.   c. ability.

____ 21. The attitude of white Southerners to **carpetbaggers** was one of
a. anger.   b. sympathy.   c. gratitude.

____ 22. **Redeemers** were strong supporters of
a. Home Rule.
b. black suffrage.
c. Radical Reconstruction.

____ 23. A **vigilante** group is any group that
a. believes in white supremacy.
b. claims to be something it is not.
c. takes the law into its own hands.

____ 24. The **impeachment** of a President by the Congress is a
a. trial verdict.
b. formal accusation.
c. removal from office.

E. Complete the following cause-and-effect diagram by writing the letter of each statement in an appropriate box. A statement of cause may be placed in any box on the left. A statement of effect may be placed in any box on the right.

a. Congress passes Fourteenth and Fifteenth Amendments.
b. Election of Rutherford B. Hayes ends attempts to enforce Reconstruction.
c. Congress grants the Freedman's Bureau control of "abandoned land" in the South.
d. African Americans lose many civil and political rights gained during Reconstruction.
e. Southern whites fight back with Black Codes and other legislative attempts to replace slavery with segregation.
f. African Americans gain many civil and political rights.

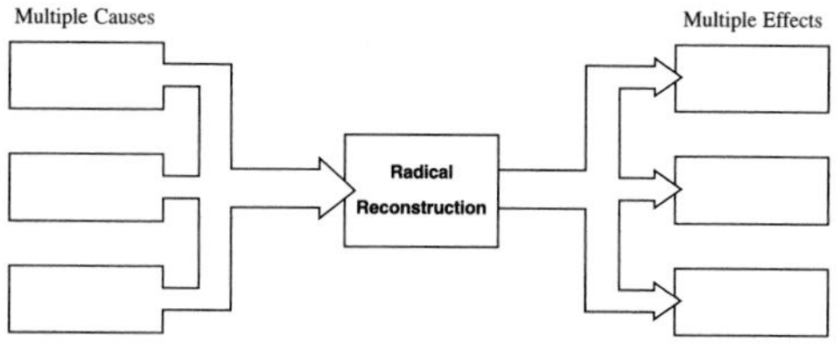

page 52

Date ____________

PART TWO

Answer the following questions.

1. How might Reconstruction have gone more smoothly if Lincoln had not been assassinated? Explain.

2. Name three things that emancipation gave former slaves that Black Codes and other forms of discrimination were not able to take away.

3. What caused the problems between Andrew Johnson and Congress over the issue of Reconstruction?

4. How was the system of sharecropping similar to the old plantation system? How was it different?

Answer the following question on the back or on another sheet of paper. Use complete sentences.

5. During and after Reconstruction, white supremist societies engaged in violent, illegal acts. How did the attitude of the general public in the South aid these societies? What lesson can be learned from this about individual and social responsibilities to protect human rights and oppose criminal acts?

Chapter 14

PART ONE

page 53

(15 points)

A. 1. c
2. b
3. c
4. b
5. a

page 54

(28 points)

B. 6. c
7. a
8. g
9. d
10. f
11. b
12. e

(16 points)

C. 13. b
14. a
15. c
16. a

page 55

(16 points)

D. 17. c
18. a
19. c
20. b

PART TWO

(25 points)

page 56

1. Answers should note that the railroad helped both industries by making it possible to move western minerals and cattle to the markets in the East.
2. Answers will vary but should include points similar to the following:
   - **a.** mostly lived as settled farmers before arrival of the Europeans
   - **b.** adopted a nomadic lifestyle once they got horses and guns from Europeans
   - **c.** buffalo filled almost every need
   - **d.** status defined by success in raids and warfare (counting coup)
   - **e.** most groups governed by a council of elders
   - **f.** lives enriched with numerous ceremonies
3. The Homestead Act allotted settlers 160 acres of government-owned land. Anyone could file a claim for the land, build a house there, and work the land for five years. The Act was more helpful to farmers than to ranchers because the amount of land allotted was insufficient for the ranchers' needs.
4. Answers should reflect the understanding that homesteading was difficult. Settlers had to stake a claim, dig a well, gather fuel, build a shelter, and break sod for farming. Many started their claims with no extra money and were forced to borrow money that they were never able to repay. Many ended up selling part or all of their land.
5. Answers will vary but should use the three terms correctly. Answers could include such topics as:
   - **a.** right to freedom of religion—Indians were forced to give up their traditional rituals and ceremonies.
   - **b.** right to own property—Indians' land was taken from them and given (or sold) to white settlers.
   - **c.** right to life—Indians were often massacred.
   - **d.** voting rights—Indians were not U.S. citizens and could not vote.
   - **e.** right to liberty—Indians were not allowed to move or travel freely but had to stay in assigned places.

   Answers need not refer only to rights listed in the Bill of Rights, but may include those (some of which are listed above) that are not enumerated but are part of the vast array of rights that are part of our political and cultural heritage.

---

page 53 Date ____________

Chapter 14 Test

Reshaping the Great Plains

PART ONE

A. Write the letter of the best answer.

______ 1. The area known as the intermountain zone contains
a. several mountain ranges.
b. many waterways good for transportation.
c. a mix of deserts, basins, canyons, and plateaus.

______ 2. The main reason that early white settlers were uninterested in settling on the Great Plains was because
a. so many Indians lived there.
b. they thought the land was unfit for farming.
c. travel on or across the plains was difficult.

______ 3. Ranching became unprofitable for each of the following reasons *except*
a. beef prices fell.
b. harsh winters killed livestock.
c. the railroad left Abilene, Kansas.

______ 4. The Comstock Lode near Virginia City, Nevada,
a. proved to be too dangerous to mine.
b. was a bonanza of silver worth millions of dollars.
c. was a rich source of clean water for miners.

______ 5. The Dawes Act of 1887 eventually resulted in Indians
a. losing more land.
b. embracing assimilation.
c. becoming successful farmers.

page 54 Date ____________

B. For each statment write the letter of the person or group it describes.

a. Santee Sioux
b. Wovoka
c. Sitting Bull
d. Geronimo
e. Cheyenne
f. Nat Love
g. Nez Percé

______ 6. His followers were massacred at Wounded Knee, South Dakota, in 1890.

______ 7. They led an uprising against white settlers in Minnesota.

______ 8. Chief Joseph led them on a 1,300-mile march in 1877.

______ 9. This shaman and Apache leader was known for his daring raids and survival skills.

______ 10. He was an African American sharpshooter and cowboy.

______ 11. Followers of this Paiute religious leader performed the ghost dance.

______ 12. In 1864, they and their allies left their lands at Sand Creek because they were starving.

C. Write the letter of the best answer.

______ 13. Which two companies met to complete the **transcontinental railroad** at Promontory Point, Utah?
a. the Grand Central and Comstock Rail
b. the Central Pacific and Union Pacific
c. the Southern Railroad and Grand Union

______ 14. Why did **boom towns** become ghost towns so quickly?
a. The ore ran out.
b. Water filled up the mines.
c. Miners refused to work for the big companies.

______ 15. The government promised Indians an **annuity** until
a. every chief surrendered.
b. the buffalo herds increased again.
c. they could support themselves by farming or a trade.

______ 16. **Assimilation** was intended to
a. help Indians adapt to white culture.
b. allow Indians to keep as much of their land as possible.
c. make Indians living on reservations U.S. citizens.

page 55 Date ____________

D. Use the map below to answer the questions that follow it.

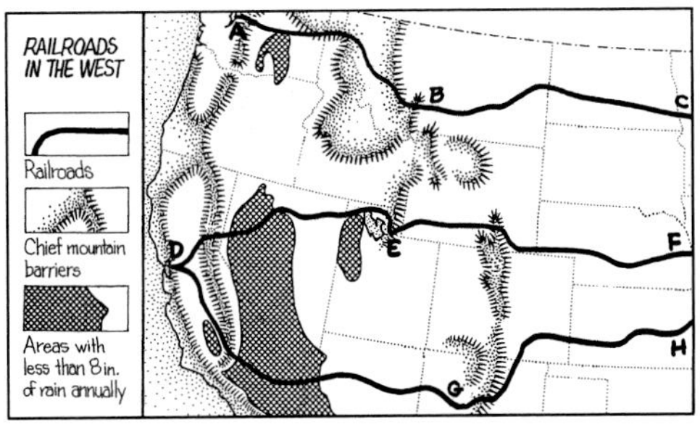

______ 17. Which section of railroad would have given the builders the *most* problems with heat and lack of water?
a. B-C b. E-F c. D-G

______ 18. Which section would have given the builders the *most* problems with snow and mountain passes?
a. A-B b. G-H c. E-F

______ 19. In which section would the builders have had the *most* contact with Plains Indians?
a. D-E b. A-B c. B-C

______ 20. Which section probably took the longest to build?
a. E-F b. A-B c. G-H

page 56 Date ____________

PART TWO

Answer the following questions.

1. How did construction of the transcontinental railroad affect the mining and cattle industries?

2. Describe the culture of the Plains Indians.

3. What were the conditions of the Homestead Act? Why was the Act more helpful for farmers than for ranchers?

4. Describe what life was like for homesteaders on the Plains.

Answer the following question on the back or on another sheet of paper. Use complete sentences.

5. What rights and freedoms that you take for granted were denied to American Indians by government policies in the 1800s? In your answer, discuss assimilation, annuities, and reservations.

Chapter 15

PART ONE

page 57

(20 points)

A. 1. b
2. b
3. c
4. a
5. a
6. c
7. b

page 58

8. b
9. a
10. a

(33 points)

B. 11. a
12. e
13. i
14. f
15. c
16. k
17. g
18. h
19. b
20. d
21. j

page 59

(14 points, 2 points each blank)

C. 22. f
23. a, c
24. e
25. d, g

(8 points)

D. 26. a
27. c

PART TWO

(25 points)

page 60

---

page 57

Date ____________

Chapter 15 Test

Building the American Dream

PART ONE

A. Write the letter of the best answer.

_____ 1. The Centennial Exhibition in Philadelphia was a strong indication of America's future as

a. a military power.
b. an industrial power.
c. a culturally diverse society.
d. a nation of equal opportunity.

_____ 2. "The American Dream" centered around the idea of obtaining

a. civil rights.
b. power and success.
c. political freedom.
d. religious freedom.

_____ 3. U.S. cities between 1850 and 1900 did *not*

a. experience tremendous growth.
b. become centers of industry and transportation.
c. offer well-paying jobs to unskilled workers.
d. suffer from problems of crime, poor sanitation, and disease.

_____ 4. Which of the following made it possible to build large multi-story buildings?

a. the use of steel frames
b. the use of brick and stone
c. the use of skilled laborers
d. the development of the electric lightbulb

_____ 5. Millions of rural Americans migrated to cities between 1850 and 1920 because

a. they had lost their jobs to new technology.
b. they could live more economically in the city.
c. they refused to work in the new, large businesses.
d. the city was much more interesting than the country.

_____ 6. It was *not* a primary goal of mass production to manufacture goods

a. more cheaply.
b. more quickly.
c. of higher quality.
d. in larger amounts.

_____ 7. The term "organized labor" means

a. well-planned work.
b. workers who unify to increase their power.
c. workers who specialize in one trade or skill.
d. the workers for any organization or company.

page 58

Date ____________

_____ 8. What was a company town, such as Pullman, Illinois?

a. a city that specialized in a regional product
b. a town, built by a company, where workers for that company lived
c. a town whose leaders sympathized with businesses rather than with workers
d. any city or town that had only one main industry

_____ 9. In the 1890s, the National Guard and federal troops were called out to

a. defeat strikes.
b. protect striking workers.
c. do the work left undone by strikers.
d. turn back strikebreakers hired by plant managers.

_____ 10. Between 1850 and 1900, most immigrants arriving on the West Coast came from

a. China.
b. Hawaii.
c. eastern Europe.
d. the British Isles.

B. For each description, write the letter of the correct person.

a. Alexander Graham Bell
b. Andrew Carnegie
c. Thomas Alva Edison
d. Henry Ford
e. Samuel Gompers
f. I. M. Singer
g. Booker T. Washington
h. Ottmar Mergenthaler
i. William Mayo
j. Joseph Pulitzer
k. Ah Bing

_____ 11. His work with the hearing impaired led to the development of a machine that transmits speech by electric waves.

_____ 12. He was the first president of the American Federation of Labor.

_____ 13. He set up an emergency clinic that became world famous.

_____ 14. He was an innovator both in the development of the sewing machine and in the promotion of it.

_____ 15. His light bulbs and generating systems changed the American way of life.

_____ 16. He developed a new type of agricultural product.

_____ 17. His institute in Tuskegee, Alabama, taught blacks trade and teaching skills.

_____ 18. He revolutionized the publishing industry.

_____ 19. He began his career as a twelve-year-old immigrant and became a "Captain of Industry" and one of the world's richest men.

_____ 20. He introduced the first moving assembly line.

_____ 21. He was a Hungarian-born newspaper editor.

page 59

Date ____________

C. In each blank, write the letter of the term that belongs. Each term may be used only once.

a. assembly line
b. capital
c. entrepreneurs
d. labor union
e. philanthropists
f. profit
g. strike

22. "You have to spend it to make it," could be stated as "You have to have ___ to make ___."

23. The use of the ___ in factories made workers' jobs more dangerous and made many ___ richer.

24. Many libraries and other institutions are named after industrialists because of these people's actions as ___.

25. If a ___ presented demands to company management and these demands were refused, the workers might call a ___.

D. The maps below show the growth of New York City as an urban area between 1881 and 1934. Use them to answer the questions that follow.

1881 1903 1934

_____ 26. The areas shaded black represent areas that have at least one house per acre. What is a reasonable assumption to make when you are looking at such a map?

a. that a spread in housing indicates a spread in population
b. that the housing density is equal in all of the shaded areas
c. that an average of three people live in each house and, therefore, on each acre of land

_____ 27. What happened to the urban area of New York City between the years 1881 and 1934?

a. It increased about 25 percent.
b. It became approximately twice as large.
c. It became at least three times as large.

page 60

Date ____________

PART TWO

Answer the following questions.

1. Describe the effect of the invention of the telephone, the electric light, and the typewriter on American business.

2. Why did African Americans migrate to the cities between 1850 and 1920?

3. What were the problems faced by the typical unskilled factory worker between 1850 and 1920? What were conditions like in their workplaces?

4. What hardships did newly arrived immigrants face upon coming to America?

Answer the following question on the back or on another sheet of paper. Use complete sentences.

5. Was the federal government justified in stopping the trainworkers' strike in 1894? Do you believe workers were justified in striking and forming unions? Explain your answers.

---

1. Answers should indicate the tremendous changes these inventions effected. Specifics could include:

a. The typewriter and telephone vastly increased the speed and accuracy of communications.

b. The electric lightbulb made it possible for factories to continue to produce products at night.

2. African Americans migrated to cities seeking economic opportunity and an escape from unfair and often brutal treatment by Southern whites. Answers should include support for this statement such as the occurrence of lynchings and the existence of racist organizations like the Ku Klux Klan.

3. Answers could include:

a. boring work
b. low pay
c. charges for necessary equipment
d. dangerous working conditions
e. long hours
f. lack of insurance

Working conditions were harsh, dirty, and often dangerous. There were high temperatures, poisonous gases, and machines lacking safety devices.

4. Answers could include:

a. fear and prejudice
b. ridicule
c. the need to learn a new language and culture
d. intolerance of their religious beliefs
e. poorly paying, backbreaking jobs
f. dirty, crowded living conditions where crime and disease were prevalent
g. violence

5. Any reasoned view, whichever side it takes, should be accepted. All answers should address the issue of balancing society's needs against individuals' needs.

Some answers may reflect the understanding that labor unions were not as socially and politically acceptable in 1894 as they are today and were dealt with much more harshly. Any answer presented with reasonable support should be accepted.

Chapter 16

PART ONE

page 61

(28 points)

A. 1. a
2. a
3. b
4. b
5. a
6. c
7. a

page 62

(16 points)

B. 8. B
9. B
10. F
11. B
12. M
13. F
14. M
15. F

(12 points)

C. 16. b
17. a
18. c
19. c

page 63

(18 points)

D. 20. e
21. c
22. b
23. b
24. e
25. c
26. a
27. d
28. a

(6 points)

E. 29. b
30. c
31. b

page 61 _____________ Date _____________

Chapter 16 Test

The Gilded Age

PART ONE

A. Write the letter of the best answer.

_______ 1. The term the "Gilded Age" was used in the late 1800s to refer to a period during which
a. glamor hid corruption.
b. the future seemed bright.
c. the government introduced the gold standard.

_______ 2. Credit Mobilier was the name of a
a. phony railroad company.
b. political machine in New York.
c. trust that controlled the oil industry.

_______ 3. Journalist Ida Tarbell wrote against the practices of the
a. Tammany Society.
b. Standard Oil Company.
c. New York Customs House.

_______ 4. "What do I care about the law? Hain't I got the power?" was spoken by a
a. Populist.
b. railroad owner.
c. U.S. President.

_______ 5. The Interstate Commerce Act was passed in an effort to control
a. railroads.
b. monopolies.
c. oil companies.

_______ 6. Following the Civil War, what threatened to take control of the American economy?
a. the spoils system
b. kickbacks and graft
c. monopolies and trusts

_______ 7. The Populist party finally collapsed, in part because
a. times got better anyway.
b. railroads reduced their fares.
c. the U.S. went off the gold standard.

page 62 _____________ Date _____________

B. Write *B* if the statement describes big business. Write *M* if it describes machine politicians. Write *F* if it describes farmers.

_______ 8. They fought anti-trust activities.

_______ 9. They bribed Congressmen.

_______ 10. They favored controls on the railroads.

_______ 11. They overcharged the government for war supplies.

_______ 12. They received graft and kickbacks.

_______ 13. They were angry with bankers.

_______ 14. They kept their power by trading jobs for money and votes.

_______ 15. They pooled their resources to save money.

C. Write the letter of the best answer.

_______ 16. **Patronage** was a system of controlling jobs in order to
a. make a city run efficiently.
b. get and keep control of a city.
c. increase the profits of a business.

_______ 17. The **Mugwumps** opposed
a. the spoils system.
b. the gold standard.
c. the Sherman Antitrust Act.

_______ 18. The main purpose of the **civil service** system was to
a. eliminate corruption in Congress.
b. decrease the power of big business.
c. increase the efficiency of government.

_______ 19. **Populists** supported each of the following *except*
a. lower rates for rail shipments.
b. higher prices for farm products.
c. increasing the value of the dollar.

page 63 _____________ Date _____________

D. For each statement, write the letter of the person it describes.

a. Ulysses S. Grant
b. William Marcy Tweed
c. John D. Rockefeller
d. Rutherford B. Hayes
e. William Jennings Bryan

_______ 20. He argued for "free silver."

_______ 21. He gained control of the oil industry.

_______ 22. His Tammany Hall machine controlled New York City.

_______ 23. One of his friends was the "Prince of Plasterers."

_______ 24. He championed the cause of the poor farmer.

_______ 25. He used legal maneuvers to get around the Sherman Antitrust Act.

_______ 26. He was an honest man easily influenced by dishonest politicians.

_______ 27. He used the power of the presidency to clean up the New York Customs House.

_______ 28. He was elected because he was a war hero, not because he was a good administrator.

E. Read the following quotation and then answer the questions below.

"We're cinched already. It all amounts to just this: You can't buck against the railroad. We've tried it and tried it, and we are stuck every time . . . Shelgrim [railroad owner] owns the courts. . . . He's got the Governor of the State in his pocket. He keeps a million-dollar lobby at Sacramento every minute of the time the legislature is in session; he's got his own men on the floor of the United States Senate. He has the whole thing organized like an army corps. What are you going to do?"

_______ 29. The person quoted above is upset about all of the following *except*
a. big business.
b. the military.
c. judicial corruption.
d. political corruption.

_______ 30. The main emotion that the quotation expresses is
a. jealousy.
b. admiration.
c. hopelessness.
d. determination.

_______ 31. The quotation gives several details about
a. why the speaker wants to "buck against" the railroad.
b. what makes it useless to "buck against" the railroad.
c. how to overcome the problems that the railroad has caused.
d. who is most affected by the problems that the railroad has caused.

page 64 _____________ Date _____________

PART TWO

Answer the following questions.

1. What made political machines so powerful during the late 1800s?

2. How did the spoils system operate? Why was it harmful to the nation?

3. Why did many poor farmers support the Populist party?

4. What were monopolies, and why were they bad for the country?

Answer the following question on the back or on another sheet of paper. Use complete sentences.

5. During the 1800s, the government often operated in a way that protected the rich and powerful against the poor and powerless. How did this work against the ideals of democracy?

PART TWO

(20 points)

page 64

1. Answers should deal in some way with the cyclical nature of the problem. For example: trading the promise of favors for votes put bosses in power; having power allowed bosses to trade jobs for votes; graft helped bosses become rich and spread the city's wealth among loyal supporters.
2. Answers should note that the spoils system operated by rewarding a President's supporters with government jobs. Regarding its harmful effects, answers could note:
   a. It awarded jobs to political supporters rather than to qualified people.
   b. It encouraged corruption.
   c. It discriminated against supporters of political parties not in power.
3. Answers could note that the Populists:
   a. supported an increase in the money supply, which would have eased farmers' debts
   b. believed in controlling the power of the railroads, which had been taking advantage of the farmers
   c. supported government loans for farmers
4. Answers should indicate an understanding that monopolies are companies that control the market for a good or service.
5. Harmful effects could include:
   a. prices are driven up
   b. competitors are destroyed
   c. quality of product or services often decreases
   d. unfair working conditions can be created.
6. Answers will vary but should note that the ideals of American democracy involve the idea that all people are created equal, have equal rights, and should be treated equally under the law. The best answers might note that, if people lose faith in a political system, it will inevitably fail.

Chapter 17

PART ONE

page 65

(32 points)

A. 1. c
2. a
3. c
4. a
5. c
6. c
7. a

page 66

8. b

(16 points)

B. 9. b
10. f
11. a
12. d
13. e
14. h
15. c
16. g

(18 points)

C. 17. c
18. b

page 67

19. b
20. a
21. b
22. a

(9 points)

D. 23. c
24. a
25. b

PART TWO

(25 points)

page 68

1. Answers could include:
a. laissez-faire economics
b. the greed of monopolies
c. the 1893 depression
d. political corruption
e. poor working conditions
f. poor housing
g. lack of city services
h. harmful consumer goods

2. Answers could include:
a. child labor laws
b. women's suffrage
c. government regulation of business
d. city planning
e. direct election of senators
f. educational reform
g. city-wide elections
h. consumer protection laws
i. conservation

Answers should be supported either by a statement of why each of the above was seen as an area in need of reform, or by a list of the actions Progressives were taking to achieve their reform goals.

Example:

a. Progressives were outraged to see young children working long hours in dangerous conditions.

b. Reformers like Florence Kelly formed committees such as the National Child Labor Committee to campaign for state child labor laws.

3. Answers should note that it was the party begun by Roosevelt and his supporters to allow him another chance at the presidency.

4. Events that helped to overcome objections:
a. the war—women's participation proved their capabilities
b. Wilson's harsh reactions to demonstrators—increased support for the demonstrators' cause
c. legislative support for suffrage at the state level—pressured Congress to accept women's suffrage at the national level

5. Answers should note that the Progressives wanted to make American life better. Answers should indicate either the understanding that Progressives had little to gain directly or personally, while society had much to gain.

Regarding citizenship, answers should recognize a citizen's duty to be concerned with society's issues.

---

page 65

Date ____________

Chapter 17 Test

The Reform Era

PART ONE

A. Write the letter of the best answer.

_____ 1. What made the Progressive movement different from earlier reform movements?
a. It wanted to change society.
b. It fought government corruption.
c. It was a broad-based, national movement.

_____ 2. A settlement house served mainly as a
a. community center.
b. legal assistance office.
c. shelter for the homeless.

_____ 3. Which of the following was *not* a primary goal of the urban-planning movement?
a. safe housing
b. beautiful architecture
c. increased urban growth

_____ 4. Cities run by political machines commonly had
a. deep-seated corruption.
b. adequate human services.
c. weak elected officials.

_____ 5. How did Progressivism affect the strength of the federal government?
a. It weakened it.
b. It left it basically unchanged.
c. It strengthened it.

_____ 6. In the 1912 presidential election, which candidate was supported by the Bull Moose Party?
a. Taft
b. Wilson
c. Roosevelt

_____ 7. The Progressive movement was *least* effective in its fight for
a. child labor laws.
b. women's suffrage.
c. consumer protection laws.

page 66

Date ____________

_____ 8. "Jim Crow" laws supported
a. tariff reforms.
b. racial segregation.
c. safe-housing codes.

B. Match each description with the correct person.

a. Jane Addams
b. Eugene V. Debs
c. Robert La Follette
d. Carry Nation
e. Theodore Roosevelt
f. William Howard Taft
g. Woodrow Wilson
h. Ida B. Wells

_____ 9. the socialist leader who ran for President from a prison cell
_____ 10. the President who became more conservative as his presidency wore on
_____ 11. the founder of Hull House, the first settlement house in America
_____ 12. the crusader who destroyed saloons with a hatchet
_____ 13. the "square deal" President who pushed away a square meal (of sausages)
_____ 14. the writer and speaker who worked to end lynching
_____ 15. the powerful supporter of government by the people and the person who came up with the "Wisconsin idea"
_____ 16. the President who supported reforms in banking, tariffs, and unfair business practices

C. Write the letter of the best answer.

_____ 17. What is limited by **laissez-faire** economic policies?
a. free trade
b. trusts and monopolies
c. government control of business

_____ 18. What were **muckrakers**?
a. social workers who tried to improve slum conditions
b. journalists who wrote about social issues and corruption
c. business leaders who placed personal gain over the public good

page 67

Date ____________

_____ 19. What would a **zoning law** have been used for during the Progressive movement?
a. to maintain "separate but equal" segregation
b. to keep a factory from being built in a residential neighborhood
c. to force a landlord to provide a fire escape in a tenement building

_____ 20. Roosevelt's **conservation** program dealt with
a. protecting natural resources.
b. conserving the power of trusts.
c. making the banking system stable.

_____ 21. The **anarchist** movement differed from other political movements of the early 1900s in that it was more
a. popular.
b. radical.
c. successful.

_____ 22. The **enfranchisement** guaranteed by an amendment to the Constitution during the Progressive era
a. gave women the right to vote.
b. provided for a federal income tax.
c. prohibited the sale of alcoholic beverages.

D. Write the letter of the best answer.

_____ 23. The photography of Jacob Riis
a. showed the prosperous side of America.
b. was taken mainly in photography studios.
c. was intended to influence the public.

_____ 24. The subject of a Riis photograph would most likely be
a. homeless children.
b. national parks.
c. people relaxing at the beach.

_____ 25. Which of the following gives an accurate reason that historical photographs can be helpful in the study of history?
a. They seldom communicate the emotions of their subjects.
b. They provide a good sense of what a time and its events were like.
c. They tell a historian everything he or she needs to know about a period in the past.

page 68

Date ____________

PART TWO

Answer the following questions.

1. What were two conditions, policies, events, or other causes that led (either directly or indirectly) to the Progressive movement?

2. What were three goals of the Progressive movement? Explain.

3. What was the Bull Moose Party and why was it formed?

4. What was one event that helped to overcome resistance to women's suffrage? Explain.

Answer the following question on the back or on another sheet of paper. Use complete sentences.

5. Why did the people who formed the Progressive movement work so long and hard for their goals? Did they stand to gain financially? Do their actions show a responsible approach to citizenship? Explain.

Chapter 18

PART ONE

page 69

(24 points)

A. 1. d
2. b
3. c
4. b
5. a
6. a
7. d
8. a

page 70

(21 points)

B. 9. b
10. g
11. h
12. e
13. d
14. f
15. c

(18 points)

C. 16. Alaska
17. true
18. true

page 71

19. Philippines
20. true
21. Panama

(12 points)

D. 22. a
23. b
24. b

page 69

Date ______________________

Chapter 18 — Test

America Emerges as a World Power

PART ONE

A. Write the letter of the best answer.

______ 1. Each of the following was used as a reason for America's international expansion in the late 1800s *except*
a. the benefits of trade.
b. the theory of social Darwinism.
c. the need to strengthen defenses.
d. the need to honor alliances with European nations.

______ 2. The motivation for imperialism is usually
a. fear. c. charity.
b. greed. d. curiosity.

______ 3. Which of the following was a cause of World War I?
a. normalcy c. imperialism
b. neutrality d. isolationism

______ 4. Which type of fighting is most closely associated with World War I?
a. air raids c. cavalry charges
b. trench warfare d. hand-to-hand combat

______ 5. How long did the United States fight in World War I?
a. less than two years c. about six years
b. about four years d. about eight years

______ 6. Each of the following was common in American society during America's involvement in World War I *except*
a. resistance to the draft.
b. the purchase of government bonds.
c. distrust of foreign-born Americans.
d. job opportunities for women and blacks.

______ 7. Each of the following increased soon after World War I *except*
a. isolationism. c. racial tensions.
b. labor unrest. d. social tolerance.

______ 8. The main goal of Wilson's Fourteen Points was to promote
a. peace. c. alliances.
b. trade. d. expansion.

page 70

Date ______________________

B. Match each statement with the term it describes.

a. abdicate e. mobilize
b. armistice f. protectorate
c. dissent g. reparations
d. imperialism h. yellow journalism

______ 9. This is what brought peace to Europe in 1918.

______ 10. This is what the Treaty of Versailles set at $15 billion.

______ 11. This was used to influence public opinion in favor of war with Spain.

______ 12. This is what the U. S. Army needed to do to get its soldiers ready for war.

______ 13. This was the reason for the Platt Amendment. It is also what led European nations to establish colonies in Asia and Africa.

______ 14. This is what Cuba became when Spain took control of it. It is also what Hawaii became when it came under the control of the United States.

______ 15. This is, today, considered every American's right. It is, however, something for which the Espionage and Sedition acts punished Emma Goldman and Eugene V. Debs.

C. If the statement is true, write *true* on the line below it. If it is false, change the word in dark type to make the statement true.

Example: The U.S. president during the Spanish-American War was **McKinley.**
true

The biggest killer of Americans in the Spanish-American War was **grenade explosions.**
disease

16. The purchase of **Hawaii** was ridiculed as "Seward's Folly."
____

17. The Monroe Doctrine affirmed the United States' exclusive interest in **North and South America.**
____

18. Social Darwinists' belief that the powerful had an obligation to "improve" the "lower classes" became known as the "White Man's Burden."
____

page 71

Date ______________________

19. Soon after the Spanish-American War, the people of the **Hawaiian Islands** went to war against the United States in order to obtain their complete independence.
____

20. The United States' desire to take control of **Cuba** was the main factor that led to the Spanish-American War.
____

21. The United States encouraged **Mexico** to win its independence largely because the U.S. wanted to build a canal there.
____

D. Read the passage below, which is from President Wilson's address to the American people on Flag Day, soon after the United States entered World War I. Then answer the questions that follow.

"The military masters under which Germany is bleeding see very clearly to what point Fate has brought them. If they fall back or are forced back an inch their power both abroad and at home will fall to pieces like a house of cards. It is their power at home they are thinking about now more than their power abroad. It is that power which is trembling under their very feet; and deep fear has entered their hearts.

"They have but one chance. . . . If they can secure peace now with the immense advantages still in their hands which they have up to this point apparently gained, they will have justified themselves before the German people; they will have gained by force what they promised to gain by it; an immense expansion of German power, an immense enlargement of German industrial and economical opportunities."

______ 22. The first paragraph of this passage appeals most to
a. emotion. b. reason.

______ 23. President Wilson's purpose in this passage is to persuade the American people that they should
a. accept any German offer of peace.
b. keep fighting until what Germany had gained had been recovered.

______ 24. Which of the following quotations is an example of colorful language?
a. "It is their power at home they are thinking about now more than their power abroad."
b. "The military masters under which Germany is bleeding see very clearly to what point Fate has brought them."

page 72

Date ______________________

PART TWO

Answer the following questions.

1. What methods did the United States use to expand its influence in the world in the late 1800s and early 1900s?

2. What two events convinced President Wilson that the United States had to abandon neutrality and declare war on Germany?

3. In what ways did the type of fighting used in World War I add to the horrors of the war?

4. How did the war expand opportunities for American women and blacks?

Answer the following question on the back or on another sheet of paper. Use complete sentences.

5. During World War I, steps were taken to protect the government and the war effort by limiting Americans' rights to free speech. Should criticism of a war effort be treated as a criminal act? Do you think that any limits should ever be put on free speech to protect national security or for other reasons? Which do you think is more dangerous to American society, exercising free speech or controlling criticism of the government? Explain your answers.

PART TWO

(25 points)

page 72

1. America used trade, diplomacy, and conquest to expand its influence and power worldwide. Specific examples should be used to support this statement, including the:
a. purchase of Alaska
b. annexation of Hawaii
c. Spanish-American War
d. America's "Great White Fleet"
e. establishment of trade with China, Japan, and Korea

2. Answers should note these two points:
a. the sinking of the *Lusitania*
b. the interception of the "Zimmerman Telegram"

3. Answers should include points similar to the following:
a. Machine guns cut soldiers down as soon as they left their trenches. As a result, both sides exchanged great numbers of deaths and casualties for insignificant territorial gains.
b. Within the trenches, drowning and disease were common causes of death.
c. New weapons, such as mustard gas, were used, with terrible effects.

4. Answers should recognize that the labor shortage brought about by mobilizing for the war allowed both groups to prove their abilities in jobs that had not been open to them before.

5. Answers will vary. Some answers may view criticism of war efforts as dangerous to national welfare; most will differentiate between criticism and active subversion.

Possible examples of limits to free speech that students might find acceptable include:
a. The safety of the public overrules an individual's right to free speech. No one has the right to yell "fire" in a crowded theater unless there is a fire.
b. No one has the right knowingly to tell lies to the public about another person.
c. Information that could negatively affect national security should not be divulged.

Regarding which is a greater danger, answers should reflect the understanding that American society as a whole is endangered when the government limits free speech to those people who agree with its policies.

Chapter 19

PART ONE

page 73

(45 points)

A. 1. d
2. a
3. d
4. d
5. c
6. b

page 74

7. a
8. a
9. a

(20 points)

B. 10. b
11. a
12. b

page 75

13. a
14. c

(10 points–2 points each for 15–17, 4 points for 18)

C. 15. a
16. b
17. c
18. c

PART TWO

(25 points)

page 76

1. Possible answers:

a. physical examinations (the Immigration Act of 1891)

b. literacy testing (ability to read and write native language)

Answers which give "exclusion acts" as an answer should also be accepted as being different from establishing quotas.

2. Ways immigrants retain their own cultures:

a. practice own religions

b. eat traditional foods

c. keep up with news from native country

d. celebrate native holidays

Some answers may also list ways in which immigrants adjust or assimilate to life in the United States.

3. Answers should include one point similar to the following:

a. Wars and social and political turmoil made refugees out of many Southeast Asians and Central Americans.

b. The U.S. foreign policy decision to increase trade with the Soviet Union in exchange for the Soviet Union's release of more Jews increased the number of Soviet Jews who were refugees.

4. In its early years, America needed people to develop its resources. There were mixed feelings about immigrants, but they were generally welcomed since there was so much to do. During these times, America essentially had an open-door immigration policy. Once the land was developed and the industry established, however, immigrants began to be seen as a threat. This is when restrictions on immigration began. Answers should also demonstrate an understanding that during prosperous times immigration was high because America was perceived as a land of opportunity. Economic depression beginning in 1929, however, changed this and immigration dropped sharply.

5. Answers will vary but should reflect an understanding of the melting pot theory (one blended culture) and of the salad bowl (many separate cultures making a whole).

Answers regarding the ideal American situation should be supported with references to either the benefits of pluralism or the challenges a pluralistic society faces.

---

page 73

Date ____________

Chapter 19 — Test

Pluralism

PART ONE

A. Write the letter of the best answer.

_____ 1. New arrivals to the United States tended to settle in
a. suburbs.
b. rural areas.
c. religious centers.
d. ethnic communities.

_____ 2. Exclusion acts were targeted most directly toward immigrants from
a. Asia.
b. Europe.
c. Mexico.
d. Russia.

_____ 3. Americans have had all of the following fears about immigrants *except* that they would
a. change American culture and traditions.
b. compete with native-born Americans for jobs.
c. influence the political structure of the United States.
d. stay only long enough to complete a job and then leave.

_____ 4. Between 1920 and 1960, American immigration policies made immigration easiest for people from
a. Asia.
b. Africa.
c. eastern and southern Europe.
d. northern and western Europe.

_____ 5. The U.S. refused to make an exception to its immigration limits for which of the following groups?
a. immigrants from the Western Hemisphere
b. highly educated Europeans and Cubans
c. Jews facing possible execution during World War II
d. refugees fleeing communist eastern Europe

_____ 6. The "salad bowl" definition of America says that
a. immigrants have blended into the dominant culture.
b. immigrants have created a diverse American culture.
c. different immigrant groups have never mixed together.
d. some immigrant groups have been more valuable to America than others.

page 74

Date ____________

_____ 7. For immigrants, assimilation into American culture is *most* encouraged by
a. attending American schools.
b. entering the United States late in life.
c. speaking a non-English language at home.
d. moving into ethnic neighborhoods.

_____ 8. In general, which age group has found it easiest, after immigrating, to adjust to American life?
a. children
b. the elderly
c. young adults
d. middle-aged adults

_____ 9. The 1965 immigration law proposed by President Kennedy was specifically designed to
a. reunite families.
b. reject illiterate immigrants.
c. ban immigration from certain nations.
d. tighten limits on numbers of immigrants.

B. Write the letter of the best answer.

_____ 10. Immigration **quotas** are designed to
a. stop immigration.
b. limit immigration.
c. encourage immigration.

_____ 11. Although all **refugees** are immigrants, a refugee is specifically someone who seeks
a. protection.
b. education.
c. employment.

_____ 12. **Undocumented immigrants** are those immigrants who do not have
a. jobs.
b. visas or passports.
c. families living in the United States.

page 75

Date ____________

_____ 13. Most **migrant workers** obtain jobs in the United States as
a. farm laborers.
b. factory workers.
c. household servants.

_____ 14. A Hispanic child who is receiving a **bilingual education** attends classes taught in
a. English only.
b. Spanish only.
c. both English and Spanish.

C. Write the letter of the best answer.

_____ 15. Which of the following would be, or would have been, the least likely subject for an interview on the immigrant experience?
a. Jimmy Carter
b. Jade Snow Wong
c. Albert Einstein

_____ 16. The purpose of interviewing someone is to
a. tell that person about yourself.
b. learn firsthand about the person's experiences.
c. give that person information that he or she should have.

_____ 17. An interview is most like a
a. debate.
b. lecture.
c. question-and-answer session.

Now, read the following information about someone who is to be interviewed about the immigrant experience. Then answer the question below.

Karl Aeppler entered the United States in 1922, at the age of 10, with his parents and eight brothers and sisters. The family lived in Chicago for six years and then moved to a small town in Michigan. After going to college in Detroit, Karl became the manager of a drugstore in the town. He married a woman he had known in Chicago, and they raised six children. Mr. Aeppler is now retired.

_____ 18. Which of the following would be the best question to ask in the interview?
a. What was it like to have so many brothers and sisters?
b. What policy do you think the United States should establish to solve the problem of illegal immigration?
c. How were Chicagoans' attitudes towards immigrants different from attitudes in the small town to which you moved?

page 76

Date ____________

PART TWO

Answer the following questions.

1. Besides quotas, how else has the United States restricted immigration?

2. What are some things immigrants do to keep their native cultures while adjusting to life in the U.S.?

3. What is one group of refugees that increased greatly in the 1970s? What was the main reason for this increase?

4. How has America's economic situation affected its immigration policies and immigration to the country?

Answer the following question on the back or on another sheet of paper. Use complete sentences.

5. Which view of America, the "melting pot" view or the "salad bowl" view, do you think is more true of what America is like today? Why? Which view do you think reflects the way that America should be? Why?

Chapter 20

PART ONE

page 77

(24 points)

A. 1. true
2. citizens
3. property
4. true
5. true
6. Western
7. vote

page 78

8. true

(33 points)

B. 9. c
10. d
11. a
12. b
13. a
14. b
15. d
16. c
17. a
18. b
19. c

page 79

(9 points)

C. 20. a
21. b
22. b

(9 points)

D. 23. a
24. b
25. c

PART TWO

(25 points)

page 80

1. Answers should note any three of these:
a. property ownership
b. sex
c. race and skin color
d. age
Opinions will vary but, except for age, the best answers will not try to justify the denial of voting rights based on the listed characteristics.
2. They were old enough to pay taxes and be sent to war, they should be allowed to vote.
3. Answers should refer to at least two items below:
a. African Americans—the Civil Rights Act of 1964; the Twenty-fourth Amendment (end of poll taxes); the Voting Rights Act of 1965 (abolishment of state laws designed to prevent African Americans from voting); *Brown* v. *Board of Education of Topeka* (end of school segregation)
b. American Indians—the Snyder Act (citizenship and suffrage); the Indian Civil Rights Act of 1968 (basic rights and protection against loss of property without compensation); increased involvement in political affairs; the Indian Self-Determination and Education Assistance Act of 1975 (increased control of reservations, education, and other programs); compensation for and return of native lands
c. Women—suffrage; the Equal Employment Opportunity Act (equal pay for women and men); other important legislative battles about gender discrimination; expansion of careers into traditionally male professions.
4. Answers will vary but specific support should be used to show an understanding that these students saw needs that weren't being met in their communities and took actions to change this.
5. Answers will vary but could include:
a. voting
b. knowing current issues
c. knowing the rights of citizens
d. understanding the way the U.S. government functions
e. becoming active in organizations seeking to improve life
Reasonable support should be given for any choice.

---

page 77

Date ______________

Chapter 20 — Test

Modern American Democracy

PART ONE

A. If the statement is true, write *true* on the line below it. If it is false, change the words or words in dark type to make the statement true.

Example: The Thirteenth Amendment abolished **slavery.**
true
The word *suffrage* refers to **employment** rights.
voting

1. The Preamble to the **Constitution** begins with the words "We the people."
2. The framers of the Constitution believed that the power of the American government would come mainly from its **president.**
3. In the 1857 Dred Scott decision, the Supreme Court held that slaves were **citizens.**
4. With the ratification of the Fourteenth Amendment, which defines citizens as "all persons born or naturalized in the United States," **African Americans** became citizens.
5. In the early 1800s, more white men had their right to vote recognized as states began to drop their **property** requirements for voting.
6. In the late 1800s, many **Southern** states began recognizing women's right to vote in state and local elections.
7. In 1920, the Nineteenth Amendment recognized the right of both black and white women to **own property.**

page 78

Date ______________

8. In 1971, the Twenty-Sixth Amendment recognized the right of Americans over the age of eighteen to **vote.**

B. Match each event with the correct movement.

a. civil rights for women
b. civil rights for black Americans
c. civil rights for American Indians
d. civil rights for Japanese Americans

_____ 9. President Lyndon Johnson recognized the need to guarantee the rights of the "forgotten Americans" and to protect them from the taking of their property without compensation.
_____ 10. Congress awarded symbolic financial compensation to those who lost their property as a result of the World War II relocation order.
_____ 11. *The Feminine Mystique* was published and read by millions.
_____ 12. Civil rights workers are jailed, beaten, and murdered across the South.
_____ 13. The Equal Employment Opportunity Act required equal pay for equal work.
_____ 14. *Brown* v. *Board of Education* rejected the idea of segregated public schools.
_____ 15. The Supreme Court upholds Fred Korematsu's conviction.
_____ 16. *Passamaquoddy Tribe* v. *Morton* returned more than 300,000 acres to the group that had originally owned the land.
_____ 17. Thirty states ratified the Equal Rights Amendment before it went down to defeat.
_____ 18. The Montgomery bus boycott cut the income of the bus company by 65 percent.
_____ 19. The federal government was forced to pay $117 million for unfairly taking the Black Hills area of South Dakota from its owners.

page 79

Date ______________

C. Write the letter of the best answer.

_____ 20. All people who become American **citizens** by **naturalization** are born
a. in a foreign country.
b. in the United States.
c. in an American embassy.

_____ 21. **Sit-ins** were a form of protest that took place primarily
a. in private homes.
b. in public places.
c. on reservation lands.

_____ 22. People with a strong sense of **civic responsibility** realize
a. America needs a tougher judicial system.
b. they can and should contribute to society.
c. immigration restrictions improve society.

D. Read the excerpt from an editorial, below, and then answer the questions that follow it.

We applaud the recent decision by the state legislature to require the use of automobile safety belts. Passage of this bill, however, cannot by itself reduce the shameful loss of life on America's roads. Voluntary compliance with the law is necessary to meet that goal.
There are many arguments against the use of safety belts, none of which can be supported by fact. "I can brace myself with my hands" is one of the most common. Yes, one can do this. But not successfully unless he or she can bench press 3000 pounds. For that is the effective weight of the human body when it is traveling at high speed.

_____ 23. What is the subject of this editorial?
a. the use of safety belts
b. the need to reduce highway speeds
c. the contributions of the state legislature

_____ 24. What action does the writer recommend?
a. the passage of highway safety laws
b. the use of safety belts by the public
c. the use of harsh penalties for people who do not obey the safety belt law

_____ 25. Which of the following is *not* a true statement about this editorial?
a. The writer uses fact to support opinion.
b. The writer makes his or her position clear.
c. It would be impossible to check the accuracy of the statements the writer makes.

page 80

Date ______________

PART TWO

Answer the following questions.

1. Name three characteristics which the United States government has used, at various times, to limit a citizen's right to vote. Choose one of these characteristics and tell whether it is important in a person's ability to make good voting decisions and why.
2. The Twenty-Sixth Amendment gave all Americans 18 and older the right to vote. What arguments were used in support of this amendment?
3. Describe the achievements made by African Americans, American Indians, and women since the turn of the century.
4. Think of the young people discussed in the text. How did they work to develop a sense of civic responsibility?

Answer the following question on the back or on another sheet of paper. Use complete sentences.

5. Name four responsibilities that American citizens have because they live in the United States. Which one of these responsibilities do you think is most important to the success of the United States as a nation? Why?

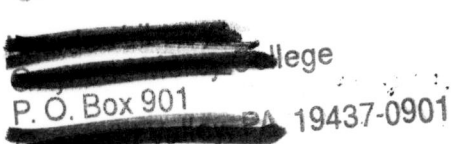